Windows
Configuration
Handbook

Windows Configuration Handbook

A Complete Guide to Optimizing Your System for Windows 3.1

John Woram

RANDOM HOUSE
ELECTRONIC PUBLISHING

To Christina Marie, my wife
before I started this.
I'm not sure why,
but she still is.

Contents

Preface xxiii

Acknowledgments xxvii

0 DOS 6.0 and Windows 1

What is Microsoft Windows? 1
What Is DOS? 2
Upgrading DOS and Windows (or vice versa) 3
DOS 6.0 Overview 3
Setup without Pain 3
Better Memory Management 4
No More Boot Diskettes? 4
DOS 6.0 File Summary 4
User's Guide 4
Microsoft Tools 6
VSafe 11
DoubleSpace 11
Setup Procedure for DOS 6.0 and Microsoft Tools 17
VSafe Installation 24
DOS 6.0 Supplemental Program Installation 25
Delete Old DOS Files and Directory 27
DOS 6.0 and Microsoft Tools Configuration 27
Minimum Configuration Considerations 27

Anti-Virus 28
    Anti-Virus Overview 28
    Anti-Virus Menus 31
    Anti-Virus Configuration 34
    Anti-Virus Support Files 36
Backup 37
    Backup Buttons and Menus 38
    Backup Configuration 42
    Automated Setup 45
    Backup Support Files 46
Undelete 51
    Undelete Buttons and Menus 51
    Undelete Configuration 56
    Undelete Support Files 64
VSafe 65
    VSafe Manager Menus 65
    VSafe Configuration 66
    DoubleSpace Configuration 70
    DoubleSpace Support Files 76
DOS 6.0 and Microsoft Tools Troubleshooting 77
    DOS 6.0 Troubleshooting 77
    Anti-Virus and VSafe Troubleshooting 79
    Backup Troubleshooting 82
    Undelete Troubleshooting 82
    DoubleSpace Troubleshooting 83
Error Messages 85
    DOS 6.0 Setup Error Messages 85
    Anti-Virus Messages 87
    Backup Error Messages 90
    Undelete Error Messages 91
    DoubleSpace Error Messages 92

1 Windows Setup Procedures 95

Definitions 96
    Applications and Applets 96
    Distribution Diskettes 96
    Expand Utility 96
    Microprocessors 96
    Operating Modes 97
    Setup 97
Hardware System Requirements 98
    Microprocessor 98

BIOS 98
Memory 100
Hard-Disk Space Requirements 100
Configuration Overview 100
Minimum Configuration 101
Intermediate Configuration 103
Full Configuration 103
Augmented Configuration 104
A Presetup Overview 104
Upgrade from Versions Predating Windows 3.0 104
Upgrade from Version 3.0 105
New Installation 106
Reinstallation of Version 3.1 106
Multimedia Installation 106
Windows-for-Workgroups Installation 106
Dual-Version (3.0 and 3.1) Operation 108
DOS 6.0 Considerations 108
Presetup Procedures 108
Running Setup 118
The Setup Switches 118
Begin Setup 119
Postsetup Review 149
Making Postsetup Modifications 152
The Windows 3.1 Setup Applet 153
Setup via Program Manager 156
Setup at the DOS Prompt 161
Set Up DOS 6.0 Microsoft Tools Applets 162
Two Setup Examples 162
Setup Troubleshooting 164
Troubleshooting an Upgrade Setup Procedure 164
Troubleshooting a New Setup Procedure 166
Setup Error Messages 167

2 Windows Startup and Exit Troubleshooting 177

Preliminary Troubleshooting Notes 178
Windows Essential Files 178
The BOOTLOG.TXT File 179
A READTHIS Error Message File 182
Windows Mode Test 182
Windows Memory Check 183

StartUp Troubleshooting 184
    Windows Does Not Run 184
    Troubleshooting Display Problems 185
    StartUp Group Problem 188
    WIN.INI Problems 188
Enhanced Mode Startup Troubleshooting 189
Windows Exit Troubleshooting 191
    System Locks Up 191
    PS/2 System Lock Up 192
    System Reboots 192
    Exit to DOS Prompt Takes Too Long 192
    Ctrl+Alt+Del Causes Post-Windows Lockup 193
    Startup Error Messages 194
    Real Mode Error Messages 201
    Standard Mode Error Messages 202
    Enhanced Mode Error Messages 203
Running Windows with Batch Files 209
    Windows Startup (WIN.BAT) 210
    Windows Mode Checking (WINMODE.BAT) 212
    Enhanced Mode Operations (WINSTART.BAT) 213
    Dual-System Operation (SWAP.BAT) 215

3 The Windows Desktop 217

A Windows Overview 217
The Program Manager 219
    Group Windows 220
    Window Components 221
The Windows Menu Structure 226
    Menus and Menu Options 232
The Task Manager 244
Configuring the Windows Desktop 248
    Window Configuration 248
    Program Manager Configuration 249
    Menu Configuration 250
    Properties Configuration 253
    Group Window Configuration 253
    Icon Configuration 255
    Shortcut Key Configuration 263
    Disable Window Configuration 265
    Desktop Troubleshooting 265
    Group Window Troubleshooting 265
    Shortcut Key Troubleshooting 269

Menu Troubleshooting 270
Icon Troubleshooting 271
Desktop Error Messages 273

4 General Troubleshooting Tips and Techniques 275

The Windows Help System 275
The Help Menu 277
The Help Button 281
Control Menu Help 281
Function Key (F1) Help 282
Help Screen Features 282
Using the WINHELP Applet 283
Help Screen Configuration 285
Jump Text (Solid Underline) 285
Popup Glossary (Dashed Underline) 286
The Windows Help Macro 287
Size and Position of Help Screens 287
Organizing the Windows Help Files 288
Editing a Help Screen 288
Routine Maintenance Techniques and Procedures 289
Editing Utilities 289
File Expansion Utilities 293
Backup and Restore Procedures 297
IRQ, I/O, and DMA Channel Assignments 297
General Windows Troubleshooting 301
Application Compatibility Check 302
Diagnostic Aids 304
Local Reboot Procedure 308
Help Screen Troubleshooting 311
Troubleshooting General Protection Faults 312
File Expansion Troubleshooting 316
Backup and Restore Troubleshooting 317
IRQ, I/O, and DMA Troubleshooting 317
Drive-Related Troubleshooting 317
Troubleshooting Other Problems 319
When-All-Else-Fails Troubleshooting 321
Error Messages 322
Help Screen Error Messages 322
File Expansion Error Messages 326
Backup and Restore Error Messages 327
IRQ, I/O Port, and DMA Channel Error Messages 328

Drive-Related Error Messages 328
A Few More Error Messages 329

5   The StartUp Group Window 337

StartUp Group Applet Selection 338
StartUp Group Window Configuration 340
   Run StartUp Applet As Minimized Icon 340
   Loading Sequence for StartUp Group Applets 340
   Use Any Group Window as StartUp Group 341
   Use Always-on-Top Option 341
   Disable StartUp Group 341
   Re-create StartUp Group 342
StartUp Group Troubleshooting 344
StartUp Group Error Messages 345

6   The File Manager 347

The File Manager Windows 348
   Application Window 349
   Directory Window 352
File Manager Icons 353
   Drivebar Icons 354
   Directory Tree Window Icons 354
   Current Directory Window Icons 355
   Minimized Directory Window Icon 356
File Manager Menus 356
   Menus and Menu Options 356
File Manager Configuration 381
   Assign File Manager As Windows Shell 381
   Reconfigure File Manager Access 383
   Configure Multiple Directory Windows 383
   Drag-and-Drop Configuration Procedures 386
   Select Multiple Files 388
   Disable Confirmation Messages 388
   Disable File Sharing 389
   Reconfigure File Associations 389
   Toolbar Configuration 391
   Status Bar Text Configuration 392
Network Configuration 392
   Network Definitions 393
   Software Configuration 394
   Registration Database Applet 399

File Manager Troubleshooting 406
Network Operations Troubleshooting 408
Error Messages 411
    General Error Messages 411
    Drag-and-Drop Error Messages 414
    Other Print-Related Error Messages 416
    Network-Related Error Messages 416

7 The DOS Window 427

    Definitions 427
    DOS Video Modes within Windows 428
    Executing a DOS Application within Windows 430
The DOS Window Menu 432
DOS Window Fonts 436
    Terminal (OEM) Font 436
    WOA Fonts 436
    Terminal Font Sources in Windows 3.0 436
    Terminal Font Sources in Windows 3.1 438
    Terminal Font Character Set 439
    Terminal Font List 440
PIF: The Program Information File 441
    The PIF Search Path 442
The PIF Editor Applet 442
    Enhanced Mode PIF Editor Dialog Box 444
    Enhanced Mode PIF Editor: Advanced Options Dialog Box 453
    Standard Mode PIF Editor Dialog Box 457
DOS Window Configuration 458
    Window Size Adjustments 459
    Character Set (Code Page) Configuration 463
    Use of WOA Terminal Fonts in Windows Applications 465
    DOS Session Configuration 467
    Limiting Access to Full-Screen or DOS Window Modes 467
    The Exclusive Mode Options 468
    Environment Size 469
    A Few Other Configuration Suggestions 470
    PIF Configuration 473
    PIF and Batch File Techniques 475
DOS Session Troubleshooting 476
    General DOS Application Problems 476
    Shortcut Key Problems 477
    DOS Window Problems 478
    DOS Font Troubleshooting 481

      Mouse Troubleshooting 483

      PIF Troubleshooting 484

   Error Messages 486

      Error Message when Trying to Start a DOS Application 486

      Error Messages during a DOS Session 492

      Error Messages when Exiting a DOS Application 495

8   The Clipboard and Clipbook Viewers 497

   Definitions 499

   The Bitmap File 507

      Color Depth 508

      The RGB Table (RGBQuad, Color Map) 510

      Bitmap Data Section 512

      Bitmap Comparisons 516

   The Windows 3.1 Clipboard Viewer 516

   The Workgroups Clipbook Viewer 517

      Application Window 517

   Clipboard and Clipbook Menus 523

   Clipboard and Clipbook Configuration 531

      Basic Copy/Paste Test Procedure 531

      Copy/Paste Text Configuration 533

      Determining Bitmap Color Depth 534

      Passwords and Clipbook Sharing 535

      Displayed Clipboard Formats 537

      CLP File Characteristics 538

      Clipboard File Restoration Techniques 543

      Status Bar Text Configuration 544

      Windows Video Driver Installation 545

   Troubleshooting 546

   Error Messages 552

9   Printer and Port Configuration 561

   Printer Management Group Configuration 561

      Definitions 565

   The Printers Applet 565

   The Print Manager 565

      Applet Window 567

      Print Manager Icons 570

      Print Manager Menus 571

Printers Applet Configuration 577
   The Printers Dialog Box 577
   Printer Configuration Considerations 585
Port Configuration 599
   Network Printer Port Selection (Workgroups) 599
   The Ports List 600
   Serial Port Configuration 602
Print Manager Configuration 603
   Enable or Disable Print Manager 604
   Load Print Manager at Startup 604
   Print Manager Window Configuration 604
   Other Configuration Options 606
   Print Queue Management 611
   Temporary Directory Location 613
   Print Manager Support Files 613
Print Setup Re-Configuration from within
      an Application 614
   Temporary Printer Reassignment 614
   Permanent Printer Reassignment 615
   Special Purpose Print Setup 616
Troubleshooting 616
   Printer Connection Problems 617
   Header Bar Troubleshooting (Workgroups) 618
   Other Print Management Problems 619
Error Messages 623

10 Fonts 633

   A Few Definitions 633
Font Categories 639
   Raster Fonts 639
   Vector Fonts 645
   TrueType Fonts 647
   Font File Extension Summary 651
Fonts on the Windows Desktop 651
   Location of Windows Fonts 654
   System Font Selection 654
   WIN.INI Font Selection 656
Font Installation Procedures 658
   Add New Fonts (General Information) 658
   Microsoft: TrueType Font Pack for Windows 662
   Agfa: Discovery TrueType Pack 662
   Bitstream: TrueType Font Pack for Windows 3.1 665

Hewlett-Packard: TrueType Screen Font Pack
(for LaserJet 4/4M) 667
Microsoft: Equation Editor TrueType Fonts 669
Microsoft: MS Line Draw Vector Font 672
Bitstream: Facelift for Windows 672
Agfa, Hewlett-Packard: Type Director 680
Windows: HP Font Installer 681
Font Configuration 687
The Character Map Applet 688
Font Leading Gauge 691
Font Relocation Procedures 693
INI File Font Configuration 696
Applet and Application Font Configuration 702
TrueType Font Configuration 704
Font Removal Procedures 706
Font Troubleshooting 707
General Font Troubleshooting 707
Character Map Troubleshooting 709
Screen Font Troubleshooting 711
Printer Font Troubleshooting 715
Combination Screen and Printer Font Troubleshooting 717
TrueType Font Troubleshooting 720
Equation Editor Font Troubleshooting 724
Font Download Batch File Troubleshooting 725
Error Messages 726
Character Map Error Messages 726
Font Installation Error Messages 726
Equation Editor Error Messages 727
A Colophon of Sorts 729

11 The Control Panel 731

Control Panel Menus 732
Control Menu 734
Settings Menu 734
Help Menu 734
Control Panel Configuration 734
The [MMCPL] Section of CONTROL.INI 735
Window Size and Position 735
Add Applets to Control Panel 735
Resequence Icons within the Control Panel 736
Remove Applets from Control Panel 739
Font Usage in the Control Panel 739

Applet Configuration within the Control Panel 740
Control Panel Record in CONTROL.INI File 741

386 Enhanced Applet 741
Device Contention 741
Scheduling 742
Virtual Memory Button 745
386 Enhanced Applet Record in SYSTEM.INI 745

After Dark Screen-Saver Applet 745
Control Menu 746
After Dark Configuration 746

Color Applet 749
The Color Dialog Box 752
Color-Change Section 752
The Custom Color Selector 759
Exiting the Color Dialog Box 763
Color Scheme Usage by Windows Applications 763
Color Applet Record in INI Files 763

Date/Time Applet 766
Date and Time Display Configuration 766
Date/Time Record in INI Files 767

Desktop Applet 767
Applications 767
Cursor Blink Rate 768
Icons 768
Pattern 769
Screen-Saver 771
Sizing Grid 778
Wallpaper 779

International Applet 781
The International Dialog Box 781
Custom International Format Configuration 786
International Record in INI Files 786

Joystick Applet 787
Joystick Record in SYSTEM.INI 789

Keyboard Applet 789
Keyboard Record in INI Files 789

Mouse Applet 791
Mouse Hardware Installation 791
Mouse Software Installation 791
Mouse Software Configuration 795
Custom Configuration Procedures
        for Microsoft Mouse Software 805
Mouse Record in INI Files 808

Network Applet 810
   Network Settings 810
   Logon Settings 813
   Network Record in SYSTEM.INI 814
   Ports Applet 814
   Communication Settings Configuration 815
   COM Port Address and IRQ Configuration 816
Troubleshooting 817
   Mouse and Mouse Applet Troubleshooting 824
Error Messages 828
   Mouse and Mouse Applet 829
   Network Applet 831

12 Control Panel: Part II 835

A Few Definitions 835
Drivers Applet 836
   The Drivers Dialog Box 837
   Driver Installation Record in SYSTEM.INI 840
Driver Configuration Procedures 841
   Driver File Review 841
CD Audio 841
   CD-ROM Discs and MSCDEX 843
   Internal PC Speaker 845
   MCI Sound 847
   Video for Windows 848
Media Player Applet 851
   Applet Versions 851
   Playback Control Buttons 853
   Media Player Menus 854
   OLE/Media Player Summary 857
MIDI Mapper Applet 858
   The MIDI File Format 859
   MIDI Mapper Overview 859
   MIDI Mapper Configuration 860
   The MIDI Mapper Dialog Boxes 863
   Revising the MIDI Mapper Configuration 869
   MIDI Mapper Configuration Test 871
   MIDI Mapper Record in SYSTEM.INI 872
The Sound Applet 873
   Sounds and System Events 873
   Sound Applet Record in WIN.INI 875
   Waveform Files Supported by Sound Applet 875

Sound Recorder and Pocket Recorder Applets 876
    Sound Recorder 876
    Pocket Recorder 877
A Multimedia System Overview 877
    Media Vision Pro Audio Spectrum 16 (PAS-16) System 878
    Audio System 879
    Video System 883
Troubleshooting 886
    Determining WAV File Parameters 886
    Enhanced-Mode Troubleshooting 887
    Startup Problems 888
    General CD-ROM Hardware and Software Problems 888
    Product-Specific CD-ROM Problems 891
    Driver Applet Troubleshooting 893
    Media Player 895
    MIDI Mapper 897
    Sound Applet 899
    Sound Recorder 899
Error Messages 901
    CD-ROM General and Application-Specific Messages 901
    Drivers Error Messages 904
    Media Player 905
    MIDI Mapper 908
    Sound and Sound Recorder Applets 910

 Memory 911

    Definitions 912
    System Resources 915
Memory-Management Utilities 918
    The DOS Memory Utility (MEM.EXE) 919
    The DOS 6.0 Memory Utility (MEM.EXE) 919
    The Microsoft Diagnostics Utility (*MSD.EXE*) 920
    System Meter (SYSMETER.EXE) in *Windows Resource Kit* 922
    PC-Kwik *WinMaster* 924
    hDC *Memory Viewer* 924
    Qualitas *ASQ* Utility (ASQ.EXE) 926
    Quarterdeck *Manifest* Utility (MANIFEST.EXE) 926
Microsoft Memory Managers 928
    Managing DOS Itself: The dos= Command Line 930
    Windows 3.1 Extended Memory Manager (HIMEM.SYS) 931
    Windows 3.1 Expanded Memory Emulator (EMM386.EXE) 934
    DOS 6.0 Memory Maker (MEMMAKER.EXE) 936
    Microsoft Memory Manager Summary 937

Third-Party Memory Managers 938
    Qualitas Memory Manager (386MAX.SYS) 938
    386MAX Installation 939
    Quarterdeck Expanded Memory Manager
            (QEMM386.SYS) 944
    Memory-Management Techniques 949
    System Memory 949
    Conventional Memory Management 951
    Upper Memory Management 954
    High Memory Area Management 956
    Additional Memory-Saving Techniques 957
Virtual Memory and the Swap File 960
    Virtual Memory 960
    The Swap File 960
    Smart Drive 964
    32-Bit Access (FastDisk) 970
    RAM Drives 971
Troubleshooting Memory-Related Problems 972
    Memory-Management Troubleshooting 972
    Bootup Problems with New Memory-Management Software 973
    Windows Startup Troubleshooting 982
    Windows Session Troubleshooting 983
    Swap File Troubleshooting 984
    Smart Drive Troubleshooting 985
    32-Bit Access Troubleshooting 988
    System Reboot Failure 988
Error Messages 988
    The Parity Error Message 989
    Error Messages during System Bootup 990
    Error Messages during a Windows Session 993
    Virtual Memory/Swap-File Error Messages 1001

14 The Windows INI Files 1005

    INI File Size Limitations 1006
    INI File Format 1006
INI File Reconstruction Techniques 1007
    A Setup Procedure Review 1007
    The Windows INI Source Template Files (filename.SRC) 1009
CONTROL.INI Reconstruction (CONTROL.SR_) 1010
    CONTROL.INI Default Sections 1010
    Other CONTROL.INI Sections 1013
SYSTEM.INI Reconstruction (SYSTEM.SR_) 1015

SYSTEM.INI Default Sections 1015
    Other SYSTEM.INI Sections 1022
    Restore Custom Configuration 1023
WIN.INI Reconstruction 1024
    WIN.INI Default Sections 1024
    Other WIN.INI Sections 1031
Reconstructing Other INI Files 1034
    MOUSE.INI 1034
    PROGMAN.INI 1035
    PROTOCOL.INI (Workgroups) 1036
    WINFILE.INI 1037
Third-Party INI File Editors 1038
    INI File Comparisons 1038
    INI File Housecleaning 1039

A Distribution Diskettes 104

B Windows Directory Listings 1061

C Error Message Finder 1067

D Getting More Help 1083

Call Tech Support 1083
Tech Support via Modem 1085
    CompuServe 1085
    The Forums 1086
    Libraries 1086
    Technical References 1094
WUGNET: The Windows User Group Network 1096
Local User Groups 1097

E Time Out 1099

Access 1100

AfterDark 1100
AMI Pro 1100
Excel 3.0 1101
Excel 4.0 1101
hDC Microapps 1101
Norton Desktop for Windows 1101
Object Vision 1102
PC-Kwik WinMaster 1102
Solitaire 1102
Windows 3.1, Windows-for-Workgroups 3.1 1103
Word-for-Windows 1104

Index 1105

Preface

This book is Steve Guty's fault. He's my editor at Random House, and some time ago we were sitting in his office, which was then part of the Bantam Doubleday Dell organization. He was pleased with the sales of my earlier *PC Configuration Handbook*, and I was practicing my "well-of-course, what-did-you-expect?" look. We tossed around some ideas for a new book, without much enthusiasm, until Steve had a brainstorm, as editors sometimes do. "What about a Windows configuration book?"

At the time, it seemed like a good idea, but that was a long time ago. No sooner had I adopted Steve's brain child than it turned into a little monster, as it became clear that using Windows may sometimes be easy, but explaining it never is. To describe just about any facet of Windows configuration, one must have already explained some other facet. Sometimes a little common sense helps, and sometimes it just gets in the way. For example, how do you turn on the *Print Manager*? Just double-click on the *Print Manager* icon, right? Wrong. Open the *Control Panel*, find the *Printers* icon, and double-click on that one instead. Click on the Use Print Manager check box, then close both the Printers dialog box and the *Control Panel*. Now you can open the *Print Manager*. Perhaps this makes perfect sense to a programmer, but others may have difficulty following (or even finding) the logic.

I began to suspect this monster was designed by a committee that did not meet very often. So I appointed my own one-member committee to reorganize it—if not Windows itself, then at least its explanation. The committee decided to organize each chapter into four separate sections which would offer an overview of the chapter topic, followed by sections on configuration, troubleshooting, and error messages. But Windows has a mind of its own, and sometimes it simply refused to accommodate itself to the committee's organization chart. Rather than create a scene, the committee therefore allowed some chapters to deviate slightly from standard configuration, at such times when the topic demanded special consideration. By mutual consent, those topics were gathered into chapters and appendixes as described in the next few paragraphs.

Like so many other computer publications, this opus has one of those "Before you begin" parts. With no explanation of how one might actually do something before one begins doing something, the book begins before it begins with a Chapter Zero. Such nomenclature may suggest an indexer who knows more about counting than about books, but there is a reason for it. If you read the chapter you'll know what it is.

And now to begin after the beginning, the next two chapters cover the initial Windows setup and the typical problems that might be encountered the first time Windows opens—or, *tries* to open. Once your system can make its way unscathed through the opening routine, your screen should display the Windows Desktop, which marks yet another beginning: the start of an actual Windows session. Chapter 3, therefore, covers the Windows Desktop, which serves as home base throughout much of the rest of the book, in which, fortunately, there are no more beginnings.

Much of Windows' configuration and troubleshooting can be localized to a specific application or applet, in which case one of the later chapters might be the best place to look for help. However, there are some general troubleshooting tips and techniques that might be useful in working out configuration problems wherever they occur; these are covered in Chapter 4. Here you'll find information about the Windows Help screen system, a look at a few editing and other utilities, and an introduction to the black art of IRQ and DMA.

The StartUp Group Window is unlike the others, in that any application installed within this window will run automatically whenever Windows is opened. It doesn't really need much explanation beyond the few topics described in Chapter 5.

A few Windows applets need a chapter of their own, which brings us to Chapters 6 through 8, which cover the *File Manager, DOS Window,* and the *Clipboard*—or, in Windows-for-Workgroups, the *Clipbook—Viewer.*

A coherent description of printer configuration is a chore to test any book's own configuration, including this one. The Windows print-related tasks are split between three—sometimes four—separate areas, which might logically be described in a single chapter. However, that would make for one *big* chapter, so here the printer itself is covered in Chapter 9, and its fonts are described separately in Chapter 10.

The innocent looking *Control Panel* applet is really not an applet at all, but a group window within a group window. A few of its own applets were described in the previous two chapters, but that still leaves a mixed bag of odds-and-ends to cover. Chapter 11 describes the *Control Panel* itself, plus those applets which support the general configuration of the Windows Desktop. With that out of the way, Chapter 12 is mostly a magical mystery tour of multimedia, as supported by various other applets in the *Control Panel* group. Since many of these applets depend on third-party hardware and software, the chapter offers a few typical examples in which such accessories contribute to configuration chaos.

We mustn't forget our memory (although it would be nice if we could). Accordingly, Chapter 13 covers memory configuration. Read it; you may not like it (I certainly didn't), but it'll be good for you.

The final chapter takes a separate look at the ubiquitous INI file. Although there's hardly a page throughout the book that doesn't refer to one or another line in one or another specific file, this chapter looks at INI file structure in general, with special emphasis on recovering from disaster if one of them gets wrecked. If you regularly back up your INI files, you'll never have to read Chapter 14. But if you don't, it's there for when you need it.

The appendixes may come in handy when trying to track down a missing Windows file (A) or to review the contents of the Windows or System directories (B). Appendix C is an index of error messages: Windows has lots of them and some are easier to understand than others. If the message context itself doesn't immediately suggest a chapter where help might be found, use this appendix as a guide for tracking down assistance. Appendix D offers some suggestions for finding additional help, and the final appendix (E) describes a few Windows features that don't exist. That is, officially.

Configuring a **Configuration** *Book*

The manuscript was written within Microsoft *Word-for-Windows* version 2.0, with all text typed on an ALR PowerVEISA 386/33 computer. All illustrations of Windows screens were captured via the *PrintScreen* key, on a Dell 486/50 EISA computer, and were then whipped into shape via that most underestimated utility, the Windows *Paintbrush* applet. In most cases, screen resolution was set at 800×600 pixels, and color depth at 16 colors.

For the Windows-for-Workgroups segments, the ALR and Dell computers were joined by an ancient IBM AT, all linked via Intel *EtherExpress 16* network adapter cards. Multimedia hardware included Media Vision's *Thunder&Lightning* and *Pro Audio Spectrum* 16 cards.

How to Read this Book

This seems to be a required section in any computer text, so here it is.

1. Sit down.

2. Pick up book.

3. Open it.

4. Read.

5. For further assistance, refer to Table of Contents or Index.

John Woram
Rockville Centre, New York
September 1993

Acknowledgments

I'd like to state here that I did it all by myself. But unfortunately, there are too many people out there who know very well that I didn't. And not a few of these folks can be found by just about anyone else looking for help—if not for writing a book (I hope), then perhaps for a little assistance resolving the latest configuration crisis. Some general information about all this is offered at the opposite end of the book, as Appendix D. But here at this end, I need to offer a special thanks to a few individuals who helped to make this book a very difficult project. I hope they'll take that as a compliment, for without them the task would not have been difficult at all—it would have been impossible.

On various Microsoft MS-DOS and Windows forums on CompuServe, Nat Bowman and Jordan Montgomery could always be depended upon to search for—and often enough, actually find—some obscure resource that would help fill in a bit of missing information. Now and then, I'd turn to the Microsoft Word forum, where Kate Edson usually set some kind of record for almost instant reply, as did Lisa Childers over in the Workgroups forum. Along the way I had the chance to participate in a few Microsoft beta forums, where Andy Thomas would ride herd on a pack of sometimes-snarling betazoids while simultaneously coordinating the I/O efforts of all participants. As this or that product release date drew near, even Microsoft VP Brad Silverberg would drop in to lend a helping hand (you'll find his picture here in the book somewhere, but you'll have to look for it—it's not listed in the index). My collective thanks to all these folks for lending a hand.

Of course, Windows is the sum of many parts, not all of which come from you-know-where. And since this book tries to cover (or at least, to step on) a few of these extra parts, it was often necessary to call for third-party help. Stefan Wennik at Bitstream and Steven Kreindler at the Agfa division of Miles,

Inc. were both very helpful in getting me through the Fonts' chapter. Thanks also to Allen Beebe at Computer Associates and Thomas Buckley at Truevision. Although there's not much about either company's products in this book, both were always willing to help resolve the obscure problem with bitmaps or figure out how this or that color system really works. Andy Fischer at Hercules Computer Technology also pitched in with some video-related assistance.

As a former sound recording engineer, I actually thought Windows multimedia would be a piece of cake—just as Jurassic Park is a petting zoo. Soon enough I discovered the former is but one letter removed from the DNA bugs that did in the latter, and it was time to call for reinforcements. On CompuServe (again) there was Courtney Harrington, who started out as just another Windows user. But he answered so many questions (not all from me) that someone really smart talked him into becoming Sysop on the Media Vision section on one of the forums (GO MEDIAV). Additional support came from Ryo Koyama at Media Vision. And a special thanks to Curtis Crowe, who called a time out in the middle of a busy PC Expo in Fun City to explain not only a few MIDI mysteries, but also how a Pennsylvania company came to be called Turtle Beach Systems.

To close on a hardware note, a Dell 450SE computer served as my hardware guinea pig for most of this little project. My thanks to this machine for putting up with many months of daily abuse. Although it was rarely necessary to call tech support, there were a few occasions when I did so anyway. It was always a pleasant experience, made even more so by a toll-free number. A special thanks to Dell's Matt Maupin for his assistance during the startup phase and again near the end. I enjoyed similar support from ALR when an experiment with a third-party hardware device did not turn out very well. My thanks to Dan Bell and his crew there for getting me back in business with a minimum of grief.

The ALR and Dell monitors were a Zenith ZCM-1790 and a Mag Innovision MX17F, respectively. Although the effects of neither show up here (except for the cover), I am grateful to both that after typing some 1000 manuscript pages, I can still see almost as well as I could when I started.

If you first judged this book by its cover, then I need to thank photographer Robert Wolsch for bringing it to your attention with his great shot of part of the Windows Desktop, as seen on the Mag Innovision monitor mentioned above. Or if a peek at the index persuaded you, then indexer Julie Kawabata gets the credit for her elegant delivery of this "we need it by yesterday at the latest" part of the book. If you must buy yet another book, make sure she did the index. And as for that thousand-page filler that separates the cover from the index, a special thanks to Michael Aquilante for overseeing all the logistics, which could easily be the subject of yet another book.

DOS 6.0 and Windows

Chapter *0*? Well, yes: Since this is a Windows configuration book, it's reasonable to expect that a Chapter 1 might introduce Windows itself. And so it does. But some readers might want a little background information about the newest generation of DOS, which is worth some consideration, especially for systems still working under anything prior to say, DOS 5.0. Other readers might *not* want to hear another word about DOS though. So, in an attempt to be all things to all readers, this opus puts the DOS stuff up front in a chapter that might not even be noticed by those who can't wait to get their hands on Windows itself and have therefore turned directly to Chapter 1.

For the interested reader, this chapter describes some of the properties of DOS 6.0 that have direct impact on the configuration of Windows and Windows-for-Workgroups. But first, a digression.

What Is Microsoft Windows?

"Windows is a graphical environment that introduces new, more stream-lined ways for you to work with your personal computer."

Microsoft Windows User's Guide
for the Windows Graphical Environment
version 3.0
for the MS-DOS or PC-DOS Operating System

"Welcome to the Microsoft Windows operating system, software that makes your computer easier and more fun to use."

Getting Started with Microsoft Windows
version 3.1
for the Microsoft Windows Operating System

1

So, first it was "more streamlined." Now it's "easier and more fun to use." Than *what?*

The above sources don't say, but it's a pretty safe bet that Windows is being compared to the operating system we all love to hate: the ubiquitous *Disk Operating System,* or just plain old DOS—MS-DOS, PC-DOS, or any other DOS you can think of. Or, as one new booklet puts it:

"Welcome to Microsoft MS-DOS, the most widely used operating system for personal computers."

> *User's Guide*
> *Microsoft MS-DOS 6*
> *for the MS-DOS Operating System*

Up to and including version 3.0 of Windows, it was reasonably clear that the software was offered as an enhancement to DOS. It was, in fact, a graphical *environment* that would protect the user from the vagaries of the operating system command line and its blinking evil eye—the user-unfriendly DOS prompt.

And now, we have version 3.1. Both Windows and Windows-for-Workgroups are billed as an operating system. Does that mean DOS is dead? In a word, "no." In fact, even Microsoft itself alternately describes MS-DOS as "a superior *platform* for Windows," which is perhaps a bit more realistic than calling it an operating system. If you doubt it, try pulling the Platform out from under the Environment and see what happens.

Although future-watching is always risky business, some observers swear they can see the three paths of Windows, Windows-for-Workgroups, and DOS merging into a single lane called—and here the crystal ball gets foggy—DOS 7.0, or maybe Windows 4.0, or maybe something else. For the moment, the sidewalk superintendents tell each other, and anyone else who will listen, that the whatever-it-is has a code name of "Chicago," to distinguish it from Microsoft's fast-lane NT product (or "Cairo" to those who must speak in code).

What Is DOS?

Back to the present. For those who feel that Windows by itself may be very nice, but that Windows by itself is no operating system, Microsoft has recently introduced a product that by itself *is* an operating system. There are no code names here: They call it the *MS-DOS Operating System, version 6.*

There are (or will be) many books explaining the intricacies of the new DOS, but this is not one of them. However, there are a few features of DOS 6.0 that are actually *Windows* features, and a few others that should be seriously considered by anyone concerned with keeping Windows and its memory-hungry family well fed. These features are briefly reviewed in this chapter for the benefit of the reader considering a DOS upgrade in addition to the Windows installation. If you are not one of those readers, then this chapter can be ignored. However, if you use anything that predates DOS 5.0, you might want to read on to find out what you're missing.

Upgrading DOS and Windows (or vice versa)

If you've bought your system recently, there's a very good chance that DOS (certainly) and Windows (probably) are already installed on the hard disk. So you may not have to answer the "Which comes first, the turkey or the egg?" question, or even know which is which. However, you may want to upgrade an early DOS to version 6.0, or an older Windows to version 3.1 (of Windows, or Windows-for-Workgroups). Or, you may be one of those few who have a brand new computer with nothing on it at all.

For whatever the reason, if you need to install both DOS 6.0 and Windows 3.1, this chapter may help with installation of the former. Refer to one of the other chapters in this book, as appropriate, if you need assistance with any of the Windows terminology found here.

DOS 6.0 Overview

For the reader who may wonder if an upgrade to DOS 6.0 should be considered, the quick answer is "yes." For the reader who may need a little more persuading, perhaps this section will do it.

Setup without Pain

As the platform gets more sophisticated, the installation kit gets simpler. Apparently word has reached Redmond that not all customers are power users. Some just want to get the damned system running, and don't really care which interrupt is serviced, or which service is interrupted, or whatever all that stuff means. Accordingly, you can pour yourself a cup of coffee before you start the DOS 6.0 setup procedure. You should have about half a cup left when the system reboots.

DISCLAIMER: You may need a bit more coffee—and perhaps a stronger brew—to get through the optional *DoubleSpace* and *MemMaker* routines.

Better Memory Management

Although you probably won't want to toss your Qualitas or Quarterdeck software, DOS 6.0 does offer its own suite of memory-management utilities, including MEMMAKER.EXE and MSD.EXE. Refer to Chapter 13 for more details.

No More Boot Diskettes?

Well, maybe. It's still a good idea to have a reliable boot diskette on hand, even if you just *know* you'll never, ever need it. However, DOS 6.0 introduces a handy *Configurable Startup* feature, which allows several startup configurations, as summarized here. For more details refer to the *DOS 6.0 Boot Failure* section of Chapter 13, since that's where the Windows user might find the need for additional help. For details about other startup options, refer to the *DOS 6.0 User's Guide,* or to *DOS 6.0 Power Tools* (Random House, 1993).

Clean Start. Just press function key F5 during bootup and your CONFIG.SYS and AUTOEXEC.BAT files are bypassed. When all else fails, it's one way to begin troubleshooting.

Interactive Start. As an alternative to the brute-force F5, press function key F8 instead to enable an interactive bootup. As each line in your CONFIG.SYS is read, you will be prompted to accept or bypass the command on that line.

DOS 6.0 File Summary

The PACKING.LST file on distribution diskette 1 lists the files included on the DOS 6.0 distribution diskettes (4,274,702 bytes in 161 files). For reference purposes, Table 0.1 lists 92 of these files that may be written into a typical new DOS directory. Your own directory listing may be slightly different, depending on which files are required for your specific configuration. Note that your previous DOS version is retained in an OLD_DOS.1 directory, so if you have any DOS-related files that you don't want to give up, you'll need to transfer them from that directory into the new DOS (6.0) directory.

User's Guide

This is not one of Microsoft's finer efforts, with a total page count (321) less than half that of its predecessor (668). One of its most spectacular omissions is a complete printed reference to the DOS commands, although

TABLE 0.1 Microsoft DOS 6.0 Files*

Filename	Ext.	Size	Filename	Ext.	Size
ANSI	SYS	9065	HELP	COM	413
APPEND	EXE	10774	HIMEM	SYS	14208
ATTRIB	EXE	11165	INTERLNK	EXE	17197
CHKSDK	EXE	12907	INTERSVR	EXE	37314
CHKSTATE	SYS	41600	KEYB	COM	14983
CHOICE	COM	1754	KEYBOARD	SYS	34694
COMMAND	COM	52925	LABEL	EXE	9390
COUNTRY	SYS	17066	LOADFIX	COM	1131
DBLSPACE	BIN	51214	MEM	EXE	32150
DBLSPACE	EXE	274484	MEMMAKER	HLP	17081
DBLSPACE	HLP	72169	MEMMAKER	INF	1652
DBLSPACE	INF	2178	MEMMAKER	EXE	118660
DBLSPACE	SYS	339	MODE	COM	23521
DBLWIN	HLP	8597	MONOUMB	386	8783
DEBUG	EXE	15715	MORE	COM	2546
DEFRAG	EXE	75033	MOUSE	COM	56408
DEFRAG	HLP	9227	MOUSE	INI	24[†]
DELOLDOS	EXE	17710	MOVE	EXE	17823
DELTREE	EXE	11113	MSCDEX	EXE	25377
DISKCOMP	COM	10620	MSD	EXE	158470
DISKCOPY	COM	11879	MSTOOLS	DLL	13424
DISPLAY	SYS	15789	NETWORKS	TXT	23444
DOSHELP	HLP	5667	NLSFUNC	EXE	7036
DOSKEY	COM	5883	OS2	TXT	6358
DOSSHELL	VID	9462	POWER	EXE	8052
DOSSHELL	INI	11882	PRINT	EXE	15640
DOSSHELL	GRB	4421	QBASIC	EXE	194309
DOSSHELL	COM	4620	QBASIC	HLP	130881
DOSSHELL	EXE	236378	RAMDRIVE	SYS	5873
DOSSHELL	HLP	161323	README	TXT	61857
DOSSWAP	EXE	18756	REPLACE	EXE	20226
DRIVER	SYS	5406	RESTORE	EXE	38294
EDIT	COM	413	SETVER	EXE	12015
EDIT	HLP	17898	SHARE	EXE	10912
EGA	CPI	58870	SIZER	EXE	7169
EGA	SYS	4885	SMARTDRV	EXE	42073
EMM386	EXE	115294	SMARTMON	EXE	28672

* Except as noted, all files dated 3-10-93.
† MOUSE.INI dated when installed.

TABLE 0.1 *(continued)*

Filename	Ext.	Size	Filename	Ext.	Size
EXPAND	EXE	16129	SMARTMON	HLP	10727
FASTHELP	EXE	11481	SORT	EXE	6922
FASTOPEN	EXE	12034	SUBST	EXE	18478
FC	EXE	18650	SYS	COM	9379
FDISK	EXE	29333	TREE	COM	6898
FIND	EXE	6770	UNFORMAT	COM	12738
FORMAT	COM	22717	VFINTD	386	5295
GRAPHICS	COM	19694	XCOPY	EXE	15820
GRAPHICS	PRO	21232	92 files		3,151,579
HELP	HLP	294741			

some (FORMAT, for example) are haphazardly scattered throughout the *User's Guide* (pp. 29, 128, 190, 215). The *Guide's* once-over-lightly treatment User's Guide may please the casual user (who will never see this little review), but anyone else will probably want the separately available *MS-DOS 6 Resource Kit,* which includes an *MS-DOS 6 Technical Reference.* This manual supplies the missing goodies, plus technical information about *DoubleSpace, MemMaker,* and other items. Use the coupon in the back of the *User's Guide* to order it.

Microsoft Tools

The three utilities known collectively as *Microsoft Tools* come in DOS and Windows versions, and both are included within the DOS 6.0 software package. If Windows (or Windows-for-Workgroups) was installed prior to installing DOS 6.0, then the tools described here may have been installed as part of that Setup procedure. The Tools may be installed later on, as described in the *Rerun Setup . . .* (SETUP /e) section below.

In any case, when you open Windows after the Tools are installed, a new *Microsoft Tools* Group Window should appear on the Desktop, as shown in Figure 0.1. The three applets shown in the Window are briefly described here. If you decide to consult the *MS-DOS 6 User's Guide* for additional information, you'll find most of it listed under the M word, as in *Microsoft Anti-Virus, Microsoft Backup, Microsoft Undelete,* and *Microsoft Just-about-Everything-Else.* For the purposes of this book, it will be assumed that the reader doesn't need the constant reminder about where the product came from.

Figure 0.1 The *Microsoft Tools* Group Window appears on the Windows Desktop when the Windows versions of the tools are installed. The *VSafe Manager* applet's icon is also shown in the figure.

Anti-Virus. Virus detection and removal (optional) is provided by *Anti-Virus for Windows*. Unlike the *VSafe* utility described later on, *Anti-Virus* does not operate automatically. Like the other applets in the *Microsoft Tools* group, you must open it, perform the desired detection and removal procedures, and close it when you are done.

Backup. The bad news first: The applet will not backup to tape. So if you don't have a Bernoulli (or other removable media) drive, you're stuck with diskette backups. You'll need lots of diskettes (to say nothing of patience). Therefore, for a major backup of your entire hard disk, you'll probably want to get a full-featured third-party backup utility. However, for a minor backup of a few files to a diskette, refer to the *Backup Configuration* section later in the chapter.

SYSTEM.INI Modification. If Windows or Windows-for-Workgroups is installed on your hard disk, the lines listed below are added to the indicated section of SYSTEM.INI under either of the following conditions:

1. You Install *Backup* for Windows during the initial DOS 6.0 Setup.
2. You install *Backup* at a later date, after the initial DOS 6.0 Setup.

```
[386Enh]
;========MS-DOS 6 Setup Modification—Begin========
device=C:\DOS\VFINTD.386
;========MS-DOS 6 Setup Modification—End========
```

The cited file is a virtual device driver required by the *Backup* applet. The lines above and below it (;===...) are for information only, and can be deleted.

Undelete. As the name suggests, *Undelete* is a file-recovery applet for restoring files that were previously erased, either by accident or because at that time you just knew you'd never need them, but now you suddenly know that you do. Unlike the previous (DOS 5.0) version, it is no longer necessary to exit Windows to undelete a file.

Microsoft Tools File Summary. Table 0.2a lists the files added to the DOS directory if any of the Microsoft Tools are installed, either during the initial Setup Procedure or later on. Note that in most cases, a separate set of files is required for the DOS and the Windows version of each tool. If one or more Windows Tools are installed, a Windows group file (WNTOOLS.GRP) will also be written into the DOS directory. The actual size of this file will depend on the currently installed video system.

In addition to the files cited in Table 0.2a, other files are written into the DOS directory when any Microsoft Tool is configured or actually used. Still other files are added if the Microsoft Mouse version 8.20 software is installed. These files are listed in Table 0.2b.

TABLE 0.2a   Microsoft Tools Included with DOS 6.0*

Microsoft Tool Filename	Ext.	File Size		
		Windows	DOS 6.0	Both
Anti-Virus				
MSAV	EXE		172,198	172,198
MSAV	HLP		23,891	23,891
MSAVHELP	OVL		29,828	29,828
MSAVIRUS	LST	35,520	35,520	35,520
MWAV	EXE	142,640		142,640
MWAV	HLP	24,619		24,619
MWAVABSI	DLL	54,576		54,576
MWAVDLG	DLL	36,368		36,368
MWAVDOSL	DLL	44,736		44,736
MWAVDRVL	DLL	7,744		7,744
MWAVMGR	DLL	21,712		21,712
MWAVSCAN	DLL	151,568		151,568
MWAVSOS	DLL	7,888		7,888
MWAVTSR	EXE	17,328		17,328
VSAFE	COM	62,576	62,576	62,576
		607,275	324,013	833,192

TABLE 0.2a *(continued)*

Microsoft Tool Filename	Ext.	File Size		
		Windows	DOS 6.0	Both
Undelete				
MWUNDEL	EXE	130,496		130,496
MWUNDEL	HLP	35,741		35,741
UNDELETE	EXE	26,420	26,420	26,420
		192,657	26,420	192,657
Windows Group File				
WNTOOLS	GRP†	3,741		3,741
Backup				
MSBACKDB	OVL		63,098	63,098
MSBACKDR	OVL		66,906	66,906
MSBACKFB	OVL		69,066	69,066
MSBACKFR	OVL		72,474	72,474
MSBACKUP	EXE		5,506	5,506
MSBACKUP	HLP		314,236	314,236
MSBACKUP	OVL		133,952	133,952
MSBCONFG	HLP		45,780	45,780
MSBCONFG	OVL		47,210	47,210
MWBACKF	DLL	14,560		14,560
MWBACKR	DLL	111,120		111,120
MWBACKUP	EXE	309,696		309,696
MWBACKUP	HLP	400,880		400,880
MWGRAFIC	DLL	36,944		36,944
		873,200	818,228	1,691,428
Summary‡				
DOS 6.0	92 92 92	3,151,579	3,151,579	3,151,579
Anti-Virus	12 5 15	607,275	324,013	833,192
Backup	5 9 14	873,200	818,228	1,691,428
Undelete	3 1 3	192,657	26,420	192,657
WIN Grp	1 0 1	3,741	0	3,741
Total	113 107 125	4,828,452	4,320,240	5,872,597

*File sizes taken from final DOS 6.0 beta release may vary in production version.

† Group file size at 800 × 600 pixel resolution.

‡ First three columns give file counts (Windows, DOS 6.0, both).

TABLE 0.2b Additional Files in DOS 6.0 Directories*

Microsoft Tool Filename	Microsoft Utility or Tool Filename	Microsoft Utility or Tool Filename	
Anti-Virus	**DoubleSpace**[†]	**Mouse (version 8.20)**[§]	
CHKLIST.MS	DBLSPACE.000	CPANEL.EXE	POINT.HLP
MSAV.INI	DBLSPACE.BIN	MOUSE.COM	POINTER.DLL
MWAV.INI	DBLSPACE.INI	MOUSE.DRV	POINTER.EXE
		MOUSE.GRP	POINTLIB.DLL
		MOUSE.INI	README.EXE
Backup	**MemMaker**[‡]	POINT.EXE	README.TXT
DEFAULT.CAT	AUTOEXEC.UMB		
DEFAULT.SET	CHKSTATE.SYS	**Undelete**	
MWBACKUP.INI	CONFIG.UMB	CONTROL.FIL	#A1B2C8X.MS
(number).FUL	MEMMAKER.STS	PCTRACKR.DEL	UNDELETE.INI

[*] Except as noted, files are added to DOS 6.0 directory when indicated *Microsoft Tool for Windows* or utility is configured or executed for first time. Additional DOS-mode files not listed here.

[†] DoubleSpace files added to root directory of Host drive.

[‡] UMB extensions indicate backups or original startup files.

[§] Files added if indicated *Microsoft Mouse* software is installed.

NOTE: The *Microsoft Tools* and a few other utilities in the DOS 6.0 package are limited-feature versions of more extensive software packages available from other sources, as listed here:

Anti-Virus	Central Point Software, Inc.
Backup	Symantec Corp. and Quest Development Corp.
Defragment	Symantec Corp. (DOS utility, not described here)
MemMaker	Helix Software Co., Inc.
Undelete	Central Point Software, Inc.
VSafe	Central Point Software, Inc.

In no case does the DOS 6.0 item replace full-feature software marketed by one of the companies listed above. If you are already using such software, there's not much point in downgrading to the *Microsoft Tool* or other utility listed here.

VSafe

The *VSafe* utility is a TSR system monitor that flashes various warning messages when some system activity suggests the presence of a virus. For example, a warning should appear if you attempt to copy a virus-infected file, or if the content of an executable file is about to be changed.

In its default setting, *VSafe* watches for formatting and other potentially lethal attempts. However, it can be reconfigured to a supersensitivity which interrupts just about any activity to warn that something bad may be about to happen. When *VSafe* is loaded, it works silently in the background and no user action is required unless it finds something to warn you about.

VSafe Manager for Windows. If *VSafe* is loaded into memory, then the *VSafe Manager for Windows* should be loaded as Windows opens. The applet performs two functions: It displays *VSafe* warning messages in the appropriate Windows format, and it provides access to *VSafe's* configuration options, in case you want to change them from within Windows.

> **NOTE:** Although the *VSafe* file (VSAFE.COM) is placed in the DOS directory if you install either the DOS or Windows *Anti-Virus* tool, and MWAVTSR.EXE is also transferred if you include the Windows tool (see Table 0.2a), neither is installed on your system as part of the Setup Procedure. To enable *VSafe* or *VSafe* and *VSafe Manager*, refer to the *VSafe Configuration* section later in the chapter.

DoubleSpace

Although Windows may have many virtues, slimness is not one of them; sooner or later you'll wish your hard drive was a lot bigger than it really is. To help make it so, this section offers a brief explanation of Microsoft's *DoubleSpace*, the data compression utility included with DOS 6.0. Using various encoding techniques, the utility compresses data in such a way that it may be reliably stored in a smaller-than-normal space. But does it live up to its name and double the amount of data that can be written to disk?

The answer is a firm "Yes and No." Depending on the actual file content, the compression ratio may vary from 1:1 (no compression at all) to 16:1, as shown by the examples in Table 0.3. Although the latter ratio is certainly impressive, note that the final part of the Table shows that the average compression ratio for an actual directory or drive is typically 2:1 or less.

TABLE 0.3   **Typical DoubleSpace File Compression Ratios***

File Type	Directory	Filename	Minimum Ratio	Filename	Maximum Ratio	Average Ratio[†]
386	SYSTEM	VREDIR.386	1.6:1	LANMAN10.386	16.0:1	2.1:1
BAT	BATFILES	*(a directory of batch files)*		*(all)*.BAT	16.0:1	16.0:1
BMP	WINDOWS	256COLOR.BMP	1.8:1	ZIGZAG.BMP	16.0:1	3.5:1
COM	DOS 6.0	FORMAT.COM	1.0:1	EDIT.COM	16.0:1	1.6:1
DLL	SYSTEM	VBRUN100.DLL	1.4:1	MMMIXER.DLL	3.4:1	1.6:1
DRV	SYSTEM	MMTLHI.DRV	1.0:1	SYSTEM.DRV	4.0:1	1.8:1
EXE	DOS	CHKDSK.EXE	1.0:1	README.EXE	4.0:1	1.4:1
FON	SYSTEM	CGA40WOA.FON	2.0:1	VGASB.FON	5.3:1	2.6:1
FOT	SYSTEM	ARIALNB.FOT	8.0:1	*(most)*.FOT	16.0:1	15.2:1
HLP	WINDOWS	CONTROL.HLP	1.2:1	CHARMAP.HLP	2.9:1	1.4:1
ICO	ICONS	*(some)*.ICO	8.0:1	*(others)*.ICO	16.0:1	11.6:1
INI	WINDOWS	WIN.INI	1.9:1	WINFILE.INI	16.0:1	7.7:1
MID	LUDWIG\MIDI	CRE001.MID	1.0:1	G12V.MID	16.0:1	9.1:1
TTF	SYSTEM	*(many)*.TTF	1.1:1	MTEXTRA.TTF	2.3:1	1.2:1
WMF	CLIPART	WM_BOOK.WMF	1.6:1	TRIANGLE.WMF	8.0:1	3.0:1
WRI	WINDOWS	NETWORKS.WRI	1.8:1	WININI.WRI	2.4:1	2.1:1
all[‡]	EXCEL\LIB	AUDIO.XLA	1.7:1	SWITCHTO.XLA	3.2:1	2.0:1
	WINDOWS	MSD.EXE	1.0:1	DOSPRMPT.PIF	16.0:1	1.8:1
	SYSTEM	MMTLHI.DRV	1.0:1	*(most)*.FOT	16.0:1	1.6:1
	Drive C	(87,531,517 bytes in 2223 files)				1.6:1
	Drive D	(52,041,986 bytes in 1218 files)				1.6:1
	DOS 6.0	ATTRIB.EXE	1.0:1	DBLSPACE.SYS	16.0:1	1.5:1

* Filename column lists typical file with indicated compression ratio.
[†] Average ratio for all files in indicated directory with extension listed in Column 1.
[‡] Average ratio for all files in indicated directory or drive.

As a further consideration, the reader may wonder how *DoubleSpace* can apply a 16:1 compression ratio to a tiny file—say, one containing nothing but the 26 characters of an alphabet plus carriage return and line feed. The reported ratio implies that this file is stored in a 1.75-byte space, or 14 bits—in other words, half a bit per character. If this is so, *DoubleSpace* is surely a wondrous machine indeed.

And so it is, but it's not quite *that* wondrous. On a 200 Mbyte hard disk, a single allocation unit is 8192 bytes, so that's what it takes to store any file of that many bytes or less. By contrast, *DoubleSpace* can write files to allocation units of 512 bytes, and of course a 28-byte file can fit quite comfortably in that smaller space, compressed or not. So, although an actual 8192:512 and an implied 28:1.75 are both ratios of 16:1, it is the former that is reported. *DoubleSpace* has indeed compressed the space required by the file. It may be high-tech, but it's not magic.

DoubleSpace is not installed as part of the regular DOS 6.0 Setup procedure. Instead, you must install it separately (if you want it) *after* concluding the DOS installation. But first, you might want to know a bit more about how it works. You also might want to know that once *DoubleSpace* is installed, you cannot uninstall DOS 6.0. Therefore, the contents of the OLD_DOS.1 directory, and the directory itself (both created during the DOS 6.0 Setup procedure), can be removed once *DoubleSpace* is in place.

Operational Summary. For the purposes of this explanation, the *DoubleSpace* utility is used to compress the contents of an active DOS 6.0 drive C. If drive C is one of two or more partitions on the same drive, the other partitions are not affected—unless of course you rerun *DoubleSpace* for each of the other partitions you wish to compress.

> **NOTE:** Actually, you *can* uninstall both *DoubleSpace* and then DOS 6.0, but it's no trivial pursuit; so, for the purposes of this chapter, Microsoft's semi-official "it can't be done" line is followed. For those who want to do it anyway, refer to Section 7.6: *Removing DoubleSpace from Your Computer* in the README.TXT file found in the new DOS 6.0 directory.

The Compressed Volume File (CVF). To begin, *DoubleSpace* reads a file on the hard disk, compresses and writes it sequentially into a *compressed volume file*, or CVF for short. Having done that, the original (uncompressed) file is erased and *DoubleSpace* moves on to the next file. Eventually—figure about 1 Mbyte per minute—all the files are compressed into a single CVF named DBLSPACE.000. However, the utility is smart enough to keep its hands off the few critical files needed to boot the system, such as COMMAND.COM and the system files (IO.SYS, MSDOS.SYS). *DoubleSpace* also adds a critical new system file (DBLSPACE.BIN) which remains uncompressed, and therefore accessible during startup.

In fact, DBLSPACE.BIN is the brains behind the brawn. It manages the disk space and compresses/expands files as required. Like MSDOS.SYS and IO.SYS, it goes to work automatically when the system is powered on, long before the bootup procedure gets around to looking for CONFIG.SYS and AUTO-EXEC.BAT (both of which are now compressed along with everything else).

DoubleSpace Allocation Units. As mentioned above, *DoubleSpace* can write compressed files into CVF allocation units of 512 bytes. Note, however, that this is an allocation unit internal to the CVF, *not* the allocation unit on the host drive itself. Use CHKDSK to verify the latter.

When the *DoubleSpace* compression routine is completed, there are but a handful of files on drive C. One is that very large DBLSPACE.000 which contains all the files that were compressed into it. The few others are the just-mentioned uncompressed files.

The Host Drive. To get all this to work (one hopes), *DoubleSpace* must do some fancy behind-the-scenes footwork as the system is powered on. The boot procedure begins as it always did, except that IO.SYS temporarily loads DBLSPACE.BIN at the top of conventional memory (so that it can be moved later on). Next, *DoubleSpace* sets up a *host drive,* so-called because it will contain the CVF (DBLSPACE.000) described above. By default, the host becomes drive H (or higher, if H is already assigned to something else). The drive H assignment allows a little "breathing space," so the host doesn't get in the way of network and other drives that may be installed. However, if no such drives are present, you may reassign the host as drive D (or whatever), as described in the *DoubleSpace Configuration* section later in the chapter.

With the host drive in place, *DoubleSpace* now swaps drive letters: Drive C becomes drive H, and the CVF on that drive becomes the new drive C. The CONFIG.SYS file is read in the usual manner and, if UMB space is made available, the DBLSPACE.SYS line in CONFIG.SYS moves DBLSPACE.BIN into it from its temporary roost at the top of conventional memory. Otherwise, it takes its place as the last device in the conventional memory area.

After executing the commands in your AUTOEXEC.BAT file, normal system operation can begin. As far as the outside world is concerned, drive C is no different than before, except bigger. For purposes of comparison, Figure 0.2 shows a File Manager Window in which an apparently conventional drive C window appears in the upper left-hand corner of the File Manager, with its host drive (J, in this example) immediately below. Note that the host contains the uncompressed COMMAND.COM, three startup system files, a small DBLSPACE.INI file, and the large CVF. The figure also shows a compressed drive A and its host drive K.

Drive Size Estimation. How much bigger is the compressed drive? Not so much as one byte if you ask FDISK, which isn't fooled by *DoubleSpace*. Remember, the disk doesn't really expand; it just looks that way since more data can now be written into the same physical space. How much more data depends on the compression ratio of each file that gets written; since

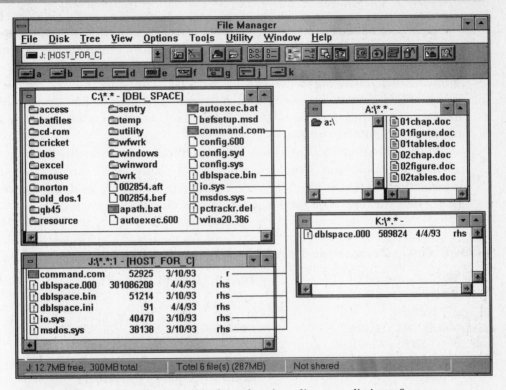

Figure 0.2 A File Manager window showing directory listings for compressed drives C and A. Immediately below are the directory listings for their host drives, J and K.

DoubleSpace is not clairvoyant (yet), it can only guess at what you might be adding in the future. Therefore, it sets up an estimated compression ratio, which affects the total disk space reported by the CHKDSK utility. Refer to the *DoubleSpace Configuration* section later in the chapter for information on reading and/or changing this ratio.

DoubleSpace Reliability. The practice of squishing large data blocks into small spaces is a bit more than some skeptics care to think about. Yet, if you are willing to commit *anything* serious to a coated metal disk, you are already engaged in the practice. If one compares the bulk of any printed hard copy to the space the same data occupies on hard disk, it becomes immediately clear that data compression is hard at work, and has been for some time now. So a utility like *DoubleSpace* is no radical new concept; it's merely an elegant refinement of an old one. Stay away from it if you like, but you may be missing out on a good thing.

DoubleSpace Summary. Table 0.4 presents a typical summary of a compressed drive C and its host drive J. For drive C, the directory listing shows an apparently conventional list of whatever you would expect to find (using DIR /a to show all files, including those usually hidden). The drive J directory listing shows what's *really* there: the critical uncompressed startup files (now including DBLSPACE.BIN), a DBLSPACE.INI file (see *DoubleSpace Configuration*), and the large DBLSPACE.000 file.

This explanation of *DoubleSpace* omits much detail, since this is, after all, a Windows book, and *DoubleSpace* is a DOS utility. For more background information, refer to the *MS-DOS 6 Technical Reference,* and to the brief *DoubleSpace Configuration* section later in this chapter.

TABLE 0.4   Compressed and Host Drive Comparison

Drive C: (Compressed)			Drive J: (Host for Drive C)			
Directory Listings:						
COMMANDCOM	52,925		COMMAND	COM	52,925	
IO SYS	40,470		IO	SYS	40,470	
MSDOS SYS	38,138		MSDOS	SYS	38,138	
(others, plus			DBLSPACE	BIN	51,214	
subdirectories)			DBLSPACE	INI	91	
			DBLSPACE	000	301,086,208	
xx file(s)	*xxxxxx*		6 file(s)		301,269,046 bytes	
					13,320,192 bytes free	
CHKDSK Reports:						
528,588,800			314,613,760		Total disk space	
147,456			301,236,224		In hidden files	
573,440			–		In 68 directories	
98,574,336			57,334		In user files	
429,293,568			13,320,192		Available on disk	
Hidden Files:	**Actual**	**Uses**[†]		**Actual**	**Uses**[†]	
SMART.PAR	268	8,192				
IO.SYS	40,470	40,960	IO.SYS	40,470	40,960	
MSDOS.SYS	38,138	40,960	MSDOS.SYS	38,138	40,960	
			DBLSPACE.INI	91	8,192	
			DBLSPACE.000	301,086,208	301,088,768	
DBLSPACE.BIN	51,214	57,344	DBLSPACE.BIN	51,214	57,344	
		147,456			301,236,224	

[†] Additional space due to rounding up to nearest allocation unit boundary (8,192 bytes).

Setup Procedure for DOS 6.0 and Microsoft Tools

The Setup procedure described here is for a system that already has a valid version of DOS installed, and this version is to be upgraded to DOS 6.0. If your computer does not have a previous version of DOS installed, then refer to the manuals accompanying your system for assistance in getting started. Refer to the instructions which follow when you are ready to upgrade to DOS 6.0. If you need additional assistance, refer to the DOS 6.0 *User's Guide* instead.

Presetup Procedures. DOS 6.0 Setup is reasonably painless, but there are a few precautions to take before getting started.

Prepare Uninstall Diskette(s). Set aside a blank diskette and label it "Uninstall." You will need this diskette during the Setup procedure, and it will be used later on if you decide to restore your previous DOS version, or if there is a problem during the Setup procedure. If you use 360 Kbyte diskettes, you'll need two uninstall diskettes.

Early in the Setup Procedure you will be prompted to insert the Uninstall diskette in drive A. Note that even if you are running Setup from drive B, you must still insert the Uninstall diskette in drive A, so that it can be formatted (if necessary) and used later on as a boot diskette, should the need arise.

Disable Network Message Service. Disable any network messaging service which might interfere with the Setup procedure by popping up at the wrong time.

Unload VSAFE.COM. If you are about to rerun Setup, and the DOS 6.0 *VSafe* utility was previously installed, make sure you disable it (type VSAFE /U at the DOS prompt) before continuing. Otherwise *VSafe* will detect Setup's legitimate attempts to write to the hard disk boot sector area and to change COMMAND.COM and executable programs (for example, QBASIC.EXE and EMM386.EXE). If you forgot to disable the utility, select the Continue option every time *VSafe* flashes a warning message.

Disable Disk-Caching, Delete Protection, Anti-Virus Utilities. In addition to disabling *VSafe* (if appropriate), disable any lines in your CONFIG.SYS or AUTOEXEC.BAT files that load other such programs. However, it is not necessary to disable the DOS 5.0 *SmartDrive* utility.

Begin Setup. If you modified your CONFIG.SYS and/or AUTOEXEC.BAT files, reboot your computer so that the revised configuration is in place. Do not run a DOS shell or open Windows. Insert Setup Disk 1 in drive A or B, log onto that drive, and follow the instructions given here, as appropriate.

Select Setup Option. Table 0.5 lists the various switches that may be used to modify the Setup procedure. A few routine procedures are described here. For a quick review of all the possibilities, type SETUP /? at the DOS prompt. Refer to the DOS 6.0 *User's Guide* for assistance with options not described here.

Run Setup for the First Time **(SETUP).** If you are running the DOS 6.0 Setup procedure for the first time, simply type SETUP at the DOS prompt, press the Enter key, and refer to the *Welcome Screen* below.

Run Setup, Do Not Create Uninstall Diskette **(SETUP /g).** If you know you will not need an uninstall diskette later on, type SETUP /g at the DOS prompt to bypass that phase of the Setup Procedure.

Run Minimum-Configuration Setup **(SETUP /m).** If space is tight, you can install a minimum configuration of DOS 6.0 by typing SETUP /m at the DOS prompt. However, when DOS 6.0 says minimum, it *really* means minimum. Before even thinking about typing SETUP /m, read the *Minimum Configuration Considerations* section found at the conclusion of this Setup section.

TABLE 0.5 DOS 6.0 Setup Switches

Setup Switch	Purpose
/B	Display Setup screens in monochrome.
/E[†]	Install *Microsoft Tools* for Windows and/or DOS.
/F	Install minimal-configuration DOS 6.0 system on diskette.
/G	Do not create an Uninstall diskette during Setup procedure.
/H	Use default Setup options.
/I	Disable hardware detection.
/M	Install minimal-configuration DOS 6.0 system on hard drive.
/Q	Copy DOS 6.0 files to hard disk.
/U	Install DOS 6.0 even if incompatible partitions are detected.

[†] Use after initial Setup procedure to install *Microsoft Tools*, if not done previously.

***Rerun Setup to Install Microsoft Tools for Windows and/or DOS* (SETUP /e).**
If you did not install the Microsoft Tools when you first upgraded to DOS
6.0, you may do so later on. Insert DOS 6.0 distribution diskette 1 in drive
A, type SETUP /e at the DOS prompt, and refer to the *Welcome Screen* section
which follows.

NOTE: **Neither SETUP nor SETUP /e installs the DOS *VSafe* utility
or the *VSafe Manager for Windows* applet. Both must be installed
separately, as described in the *VSafe Installation* section which follows
this description of the DOS 6.0 Setup Procedure.**

Welcome Screen. Figure 0.3(a, b, c) shows the first Setup screen, whose
appearance varies slightly, depending on whether you typed SETUP or
SETUP followed by the /m or /e switch at the DOS prompt. In any case,
you can now press function key F1 or F3 to show one of the additional
screens illustrated in Figure 0.4(a, b, c).

But assuming you typed SETUP because that's what you want to do,
press the Enter key to begin doing it, and continue reading. If you are
running SETUP /e, skip ahead to the *Specify Tools to Install* section.

System Settings Screen. The next screen shows the system settings that
Setup proposes to use, as illustrated in this typical example:

Setup will use the following system settings:
DOS Type: MS-DOS
MS-DOS path: C:\DOS
Display Type: VGA
The settings are correct.   *(This line is highlighted.)*
If all the settings are correct, press ENTER.
To change a setting, press the UP ARROW or DOWN ARROW key until the set-
ting is selected. Then press ENTER to see alternatives.

If any displayed system setting is not correct, highlight the appropriate
line and press the Enter key. Scroll through the list of alternative settings,
highlight the one you want, and press the Enter key again. When the list
is correct, highlight the "Settings are correct" line and press the Enter key
one more time.

If you are running the minimal-configuration SETUP /m, skip to the
Begin DOS 6.0 Upgrade section below. Otherwise, continue reading here.

(a)
Microsoft MS-DOS 6 Setup

Welcome to Setup.
The Setup program prepares MS-DOS 6 to run on your computer.
- To set up MS-DOS now, press ENTER.
- To learn more about Setup before continuing, press F1.
- To quit Setup without installing MS-DOS, press F3.

(b)
Microsoft MS-DOS 6 Setup

Welcome to Setup.
You have chosen to perform a minimal installation of MS-DOS 6. During a minimal installation, Setup copies only the MS-DOS System files to your hard disk.
- To install MS-DOS on your hard disk now, press ENTER.
- To learn more about Setup before continuing, press F1.
- To quit Setup without installing MS-DOS, press F3.

(c)
Microsoft MS-DOS 6 Setup

Welcome to Setup.
You have chosen to install optional programs on your computer.
- To install the programs in your MS-DOS directory now, press ENTER.
- To learn more about Setup before continuing, press F1.
- To exit Setup without installing programs, press F3.

Figure 0.3 The first DOS 6.0 Setup Screen, as it appears if you type (a) SETUP, (b) SETUP /m (minimum configuration), or (c) SETUP /e (install *Microsoft Tools*).

Specify Tools to Install. The next screen lists the three Microsoft Tools that may be installed, either as part of a first-time Setup procedure, or later on if the SETUP /e option is selected. In either case, the following information is displayed:

Column 1. The three Microsoft Tools that may be installed are listed here.

Column 2. All three entries in the *Program for* column will be "Windows only" if Windows 3.1 is already installed, or "MS-DOS" only if it is not. Follow the on-screen directions to revise the entries as desired. However, do not select an option that includes a Windows tool if Windows itself is not yet installed.

Column 3. The *Bytes used* column indicates the amount of space required for each tool, and varies from zero to maximum depending on which configuration (none, Windows, DOS, both) you have selected.

(a)
Setup Help

  Using Setup

Setup installs MS-DOS 6 on your computer's hard disk. The Setup program:
- Identifies your computer's components (display, keyboard, mouse, network, and so on).
- Copies MS-DOS files to your hard disk.
- Copies the original programs you select to your hard disk.
- Updates your CONFIG.SYS and AUTOEXEC.BAT files.

(b)
Setup Help

  Installing MS-DOS 6 Optional Programs
- When you type "setup /e" at the command prompt, Setup installs optional programs on your computer.
- You can choose the programs you want during Setup. Setup displays the choices in the screen that follows the Welcome screen.
- For help during Setup, press F1.

(c)
Exiting Setup

  MS-DOS 6 is not completely installed. If you exit Setup now, you will need to restart Setup to install MS-DOS.
- To exit, press F3 again.
- To return to the previous screen, press ESC.

Figure 0.4 The Setup Help Screens for (a) regular Setup and (b) installation of *Microsoft Tools*. If you decide to exit before completion, the Exiting Setup Screen (c) appears.

In the example shown in Figure 0.5, each tool shows a different configuration option, which of course will vary depending on your own choices. Furthermore, the information in the "Bytes used" column is, at best, an approximation. The file sizes are hard-coded in a DOSSETUP.INI file on distribution diskette 1, and probably don't match the sum of the actual file sizes that will be installed.

As a typical example, if you decide to install none of the *Microsoft Tools* during the initial Setup Procedure, the "Space required for MS-DOS and Programs" line reports 4,200,000 bytes needed for DOS 6.0 alone. And so it might be, if all the files were transferred. However, some of these files (startup and setup files, etc.) are not copied at all, while others depend on system configuration requirements. As shown earlier in Table 0.1, a typical DOS-only installation might take up only about 3 Mbytes—still a rather hefty package, especially for those who can remember when DOS came on one 5¼-inch diskette.

If you selected one or more Windows tools, the screen will be as shown in Figure 0.6a. Verify that the information is correct, press the Enter key, and skip ahead to *Begin DOS 6.0 Upgrade.* However, if Windows itself is not yet installed, the DOS 6.0 Setup procedure can't install a Windows Tool, and therefore the screen in Figure 0.6b appears.

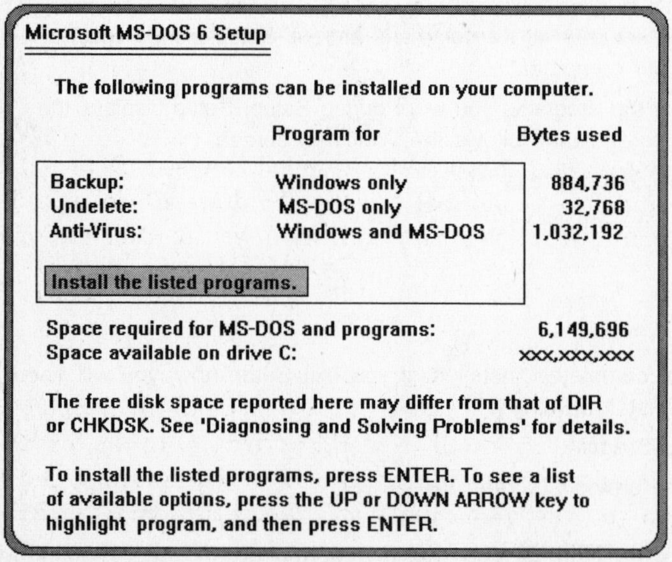

```
┌─────────────────────────────────────────────────────────┐
│ Microsoft MS-DOS 6 Setup                                 │
│                                                          │
│   The following programs can be installed on your computer. │
│                                                          │
│                     Program for          Bytes used      │
│   ┌──────────────────────────────────────────────────┐   │
│   │ Backup:          Windows only          884,736    │   │
│   │ Undelete:        MS-DOS only            32,768    │   │
│   │ Anti-Virus:      Windows and MS-DOS  1,032,192    │   │
│   │                                                  │   │
│   │ ┌──────────────────────────────┐                 │   │
│   │ │ Install the listed programs. │                 │   │
│   │ └──────────────────────────────┘                 │   │
│   └──────────────────────────────────────────────────┘   │
│   Space required for MS-DOS and programs:   6,149,696    │
│   Space available on drive C:               xxx,xxx,xxx  │
│                                                          │
│   The free disk space reported here may differ from that of DIR │
│   or CHKDSK. See 'Diagnosing and Solving Problems' for details. │
│                                                          │
│   To install the listed programs, press ENTER. To see a list │
│   of available options, press the UP or DOWN ARROW key to │
│   highlight  program, and then press ENTER.              │
└─────────────────────────────────────────────────────────┘
```

Figure 0.5 Change the installation options to install each *Microsoft Tool* for Windows, MS-DOS, both, or neither, as required.

(a)
Microsoft MS-DOS 6 Setup

Setup has found Microsoft Windows in the following directory:

C:\WINDOWS

To confirm that this is your Windows directory, press ENTER. To specify a different directory, type its path, and then press ENTER.

If your computer does not have WIndows, neither Backup, Undelete, nor Anti-Virus for Windows can be installed. Press ESC to return to the previous screen and change your selections.

(b)
Microsoft MS-DOS 6 Setup

Setup has not found Microsoft Windows on your computer.

Type the path to your Windows directory, and then press ENTER.

If your computer does not have WIndows, neither Backup, Undelete, nor Anti-Virus for Windows can be installed. Press ESC to return to the previous screen and change your selections.

Figure 0.6 The next Setup Screen reports (a) the location of your Windows directory, or (b) that Setup did not find Windows on your computer.

In the unlikely event that Windows is installed, but the DOS 6.0 Setup procedure didn't find it, type the path to the Windows directory and press the Enter key to continue. If that path is invalid, yet another message will advise that

Setup did not find Windows in the path specified.

Press the Enter or Escape key, then the Escape key again to return to the screen shown in Figure 0.5, which now displays "MS-DOS only" for all Tools that you had wanted to install. If you'd rather not install an MS-DOS version, change the appropriate line to "None," then continue the Setup procedure. Later on you can install the Windows Tools by running SETUP /e *after* installing Windows itself.

Once you have successfully concluded specifying the Microsoft Tools to install as part of the Setup procedure, press the Enter key to continue.

Begin DOS 6.0 Upgrade. The screen shown here appears immediately before the actual Setup procedure begins.

Setup is ready to upgrade your system to MS-DOS 6.
Do not interrupt Setup during the upgrade process.
- To install MS-DOS 6 files now, press Y.
- To exit Setup without installing MS-DOS, press F3.

Assuming you are ready to continue the procedure, press the Y key to begin. Follow the on-screen prompts to complete the installation.

Insert Uninstall Diskette. While diskette 1 is still in the drive, you will be prompted to insert your Uninstall diskette in drive A. Follow the on-screen prompts to prepare the Uninstall diskette, then continue with the regular Setup procedure.

Conclude DOS 6.0 Upgrade Procedure. If all goes well, the DOS 6.0 upgrade procedure should conclude successfully. When it does, remove the final distribution diskette from drive A and reboot to being operation under DOS 6.0. When it doesn't, refer to the *Troubleshooting* or *Error Messages* sections below for assistance.

VSafe Installation

Although the *VSafe* utility files—VSAFE.COM (DOS 6.0) and MWAVTSR.EXE (Windows)—are placed in the DOS directory if the *Anti-Virus* Tools are installed, *VSafe* itself is not automatically loaded when the system is booted on. To load *VSafe* automatically every time you turn the system on, add the following line to your AUTOEXEC.BAT file:

```
VSAFE
```

If you'd rather not run *VSafe* at all times, leave the line out of AUTO-EXEC.BAT and just type it at the DOS prompt when you need it. In either case, *VSafe* is loaded as a TSR program. Refer to the *VSafe Configuration* section below for information about the various switches which can be appended to the command.

VSafe Manager for Windows Installation. If you make a practice of loading *VSafe* prior to opening Windows, then *VSafe Manager for Windows* should be loaded as Windows opens, so that messages are reliably displayed during the Windows session. However, if you do not always load *VSafe,* then *VSafe Manager* should not be loaded automatically. Refer to one of the following procedures, as appropriate for your setup.

Load **VSafe Manager** *Automatically.* If you want the applet to run automatically every time Windows opens, install it in the StartUp Group Window. If you need assistance doing so, follow the procedure described in the *Setup Windows Applet* section of Chapter 1, select the *StartUp* Group Window, and type MWAVTSR.EXE in the Command Line: box described in that section.

Or if you prefer, edit the indicated section of the WIN.INI file, as shown here.

```
[windows]
load=mwavtsr.exe
```

Remember that if you want *VSafe Manager* to load automatically as Windows opens, you must load *VSafe* itself prior to opening Windows.

Load **VSafe Manager** *as an Option.* If *VSafe* is not always loaded prior to opening Windows, then you should not install *VSafe Manager* for automatic loading. If you do, a *VSafe Program is not loaded* error message will appear as Windows opens, and the *VSafe Manager* applet will not open. To avoid this annoyance, install the *VSafe Manager for Windows* in the Microsoft Tools Group Window (or elsewhere if you like), so that it will be available if and when you need it, but won't be loaded automatically every time Windows is opened.

DOS 6.0 Supplemental Program Installation

The *DOS 6.0 User's Guide* includes a coupon for a supplemental diskette which contains the following utilities and files:

> *AccessDOS* (public domain utilities to aid users with physical handicaps)
>
> Three keyboard utilities
>
> DBLBOOT.BAT (creates a bootable compressed diskette, using *DoubleSpace*)
>
> DOS 5.0 utilities not included with DOS 6.0
>
> Network drivers that may be required if upgrading from DOS prior to version 5.0

Insert the supplemental diskette in drive A or B, log onto that drive, and type SETUP C:\DOS at the DOS prompt. Follow the on-screen instructions to expand and copy some or all of the files to your hard disk. If you would rather place the supplemental programs elsewhere, type SETUP with some other destination drive letter and/or path.

Table 0.6 lists the files on the supplemental diskette. Refer to the three text files (ADOS.TXT, AREADME.TXT, COMMANDS.TXT) for further details about the included programs and utilities.

TABLE 0.6 Supplemental Diskette Files*

Filename	Ext.	Size	Filename	Ext.	Size
Access DOS:					
ADOS	CFG	61	ADOS	TXT	103011
ADOS	COM	31086	AREADME	TXT	26235
ADOS	OVL	92154	FAKEMOUS	COM	307
All Transfers Include:					
CHOICE	COM	1754			
Bootable Diskette Utilities:					
DBTBOOT	BAT	1965	DBLBOOT	INI	91
DOS 5.0 Files:					
4201	CPI	6404	GRAFTABL	COM	11205
4208	CPI	720	JOIN	EXE	16576
5202	CPI	395	LCD	CPI	10753
ASSIGN	COM	6399	MIRROR	COM	18201
BACKUP	EXE	35146	MONEY	BAS	46225
COMMANDS	TXT	74282	MSHERC	COM	6934
COMP	EXE	13084	NIBBLES	BAS	24103
CV	COM	716	PRINTER	SYS	18804
EDLIN	EXE	12626	PRINTFIX	COM	234
EXE2BIN	EXE	8424	REMLINE	BAS	12314
GORILLA	BAS	29434			
Keyboard Utilities:					
DVORAK	SYS	2441	KBDBUF	SYS	880
DVORAK	TXT	8542			
Network Drivers:					
NET	EXE	10806	REDIR	1XE	28046
NETBEUI	DOS	30480	REDIR	2XE	28544
NETWKSTA	1XE	62400	SETNAME	EXE	4640
NETWKSTA	2XE	101608			

*Use coupon in *DOS 6.0 User's Guide* to order this diskette.

Delete Old DOS Files and Directory

As noted earlier, the DOS 6.0 upgrade procedure saves your previous DOS files in a directory named OLD_DOS.1. Once you're comfortable with DOS 6.0, you can erase the old directory and its contents. In fact, there's even a DOS 6.0 utility (DELOLDOS.EXE) that will do the job for you. Just type DELOLDOS at the DOS prompt and follow the on-screen prompt. The utility erases all the old files, removes the old directory, then commits suicide, as you'll discover if you try to find it after the job is done.

DOS 6.0 and Microsoft Tools Configuration

This section offers a few thoughts on a DOS 6.0 minimum-configuration, and then gets down to business with a description of the various menu and configuration options within the three *Microsoft Tools* and the *VSafe* utility. Operational aspects of each applet are covered only to the extent needed to get through the configuration details. Consult the *MS-DOS User's Guide* for more details about the actual use of any of the tools described here.

Most chapters in this book have a separate section devoted to the menus available within the applet under discussion. However, the present chapter attempts to describe four distinct applets, each with its own menu set and configuration requirements. And here it's especially hard to separate the menus from the configuration. Therefore, no attempt is made to do so: Each subsection begins with a menu description, followed by configuration details. For general information about the buttons which appear below the Menu Bar on various Help Menus, refer to the *Pushbutton Bar* in the *Help Screen Features* section of Chapter 4.

Minimum Configuration Considerations

As noted earlier, the SETUP /m procedure installs a minimum configuration of DOS 6.0. In fact, SETUP /m is equivalent to the simple DOS SYS command in that it writes only the three new system files (COMMAND.COM, IO.SYS, MSDOS.SYS) to your hard disk. If you need—and have room for—any additional DOS 6.0 files, you'll need to expand them from the distribution diskettes into your DOS directory.

In addition to installing the system files, SETUP /m does something else: it removes your existing CONFIG.SYS and AUTOEXEC.BAT files! Fortunately, these are saved as CONFIG.DAT and AUTOEXEC.DAT on the uninstall diskette. If there's anything important in either, you'll have to copy them back to your hard disk and edit them, as required. If you were using DOS 5.0's HIMEM.SYS and EMM386.EXE, don't forget to expand copies of the new versions from the DOS 6.0 diskettes.

Right about now is a good time to think about where all this is leading (or perhaps, where it is *not* leading). If your hard disk is so cramped for space that you can't install a complete DOS 6.0 in all its glory, you will not be a happy Windows camper later on. If your hard disk is littered with "stuff" that you don't really need any more, now's the time to do a little housecleaning.

In addition to erasing all those old backup files and other useless leftovers, you may want to examine the size of your Windows permanent swap file. If it's on drive C, and is unnecessarily large, perhaps it can be trimmed down a bit (actually, *many* bits). Or maybe you can move it to another partition, if there is one.

As another consideration, remember that the DOS 6.0 upgrade saves your old DOS files in an OLD_DOS.1 directory, which eats a fair amount of hard disk space. If the existence of *two* DOS directories contributes to the bottleneck, perhaps you can back up (to diskettes, or to another partition) some non-essential directory, then delete it from drive C. Once you're confident enough in DOS 6.0 to erase that OLD_DOS.1 directory, you can bring the other directory back to drive C.

Also keep in mind that once you get DOS 6.0 up and running, you can run the Double Space utility to gain more space on your hard disk.

If all these suggestions are not enough to resolve the minimum-configuration blues, then you probably need a new (read, *bigger*) hard disk. And don't even *think* about OS/2.

Anti-Virus

The *Anti-Virus* Applet Window shown in Figure 0.7a may be opened by clicking on the *Anti-Virus* icon in the Microsoft Tools Group Window, or from the File Manager (see Chapter 6) by selecting the Antivirus... option on the Tools Menu.

Anti-Virus Overview

The first configuration step is to specify the drive you wish scanned for viruses by highlighting it in the Drives: window. As you do so, *Anti-Virus* reads that drive's directories and updates the list shown in the Status: section of the Figure. Repeat as required to add additional drives. Then use the Scan Menu's Detect or Clean options described in the *Anti-Virus Menus* section to begin the virus-scanning operation. When you do, the Microsoft Anti-

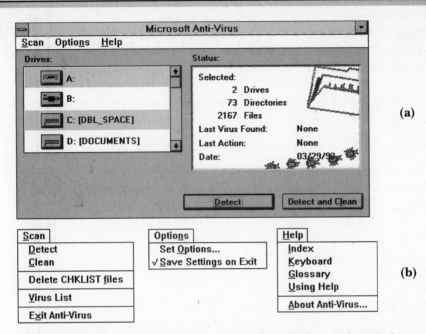

(a)

(b)

Figure 0.7 The *Anti-Virus* Applet, showing (a) the applet window and (b) the three *Anti-Virus* menus

Virus screen shown in Figure 0.8 appears. As *Anti-Virus* scans each directory on the selected drive(s), it displays a Virus Found or Verify Dialog Box if necessary. In addition, a Checklist File is written into each scanned directory. At the conclusion of the scanning operation, a Statistics screen is displayed. Each of these *Anti-Virus* components is described here.

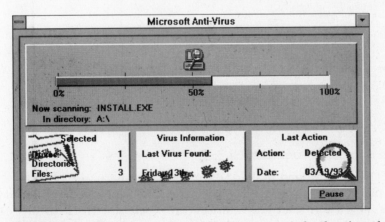

Figure 0.8 The Microsoft *Anti-Virus* screen tracks the virus-detection progress on the selected drive(s).

Virus Found Dialog Box. If a known virus is detected, the Virus Found dialog box shown in Figure 0.9a reports the name of the virus and the file in which it was found.

Verify Error Dialog Box. The Verify Error dialog box (Figure 0.9b) appears if the following four conditions are met:

1. The scanned directory contains a Checklist file.
2. The Verify Integrity and Prompt While Detect boxes are checked.
3. The Scan Menu's Detect or Clean option is selected.
4. A file change is detected.

Refer to the appropriate menu option below for further information about the items mentioned here.

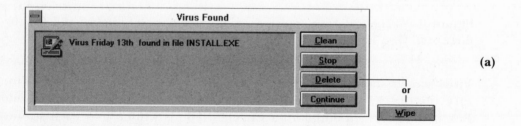

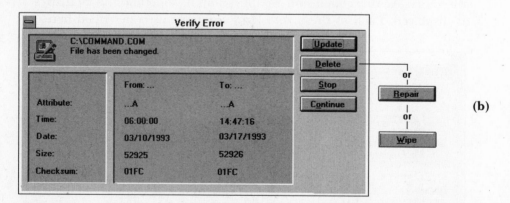

Figure 0.9   The Virus Found dialog box (a) reports the name of a detected virus and the file in which it was found. The Verify Error dialog box (b) reports a file change that may indicate the work of a virus. In this example, *Anti-Virus* has detected a one-byte size change in the COMMAND.COM file.

Statistics Screen. At the conclusion of the scanning operation, the Statistics Screen shown in Figure 0.10 appears. Click on the OK button to clear the screen and return to the *Anti-Virus* window.

Anti-Virus Menus

The *Anti-Virus* applet's menus shown in Figure 0.7b provide access to the applet's operational and configuration options, as described here.

Control Menu. The options which appear on this menu are described in the *Control Menu* section of Chapter 3.

Scan Menu. In addition to performing their indicated functions, the Scan Menu's Clean and Detect options can also be configured to report changes made to executable files. For further details, refer to the Verify Integrity option described in the *Options Menu* section. Before selecting either option, or the Delete CHKLIST files option, one or more drives must be selected, as described in the *Anti-Virus Configuration* section.

Clean. Select this option to automatically remove any known virus that is detected during the Scan procedure. This menu option is duplicated by a Detect and Clean button in the lower righthand corner of the *Anti-Virus* Window shown in Figure 0.7a.

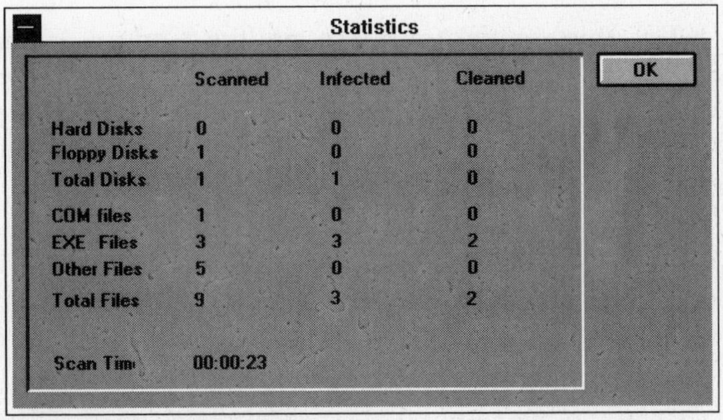

	Scanned	Infected	Cleaned
Hard Disks	0	0	0
Floppy Disks	1	0	0
Total Disks	1	1	0
COM files	1	0	0
EXE Files	3	3	2
Other Files	5	0	0
Total Files	9	3	2
Scan Time	00:00:23		

Figure 0.10 The Statistics Screen summarizes the actions taken during the virus-tracking procedure.

Delete CHKLIST files. If there are many directories on a scanned drive, many CHKLIST.MS files (described below) are written. Although most are quite small—a few thousand bytes or so—each wastes a fair amount of space: the difference between one allocation unit and the files-times-27 product.

To assess the situation, log onto the root directory and type DIR CHK-LIST.MS /s at the DOS prompt. Then multiply the number of files reported by the size of your allocation unit. If that works out to more space than you want to give up, select this option to delete all Checklist files on the specified drive.

> **NOTE:** The CHKLIST.MS file in the DOS directory is not deleted if this option is selected.

Detect. If this option is selected, a Virus Found dialog box is displayed if a known virus is detected, but the virus is not automatically removed. This option is also duplicated in the *Anti-Virus* Window, by the Detect button.

Virus List. This option opens the Virus List dialog box shown in Figure 0.11a. The list shows the name, type, size, and number of variants for viruses recognized by *Anti-Virus*. Use the arrow buttons to scroll through the list, or type the name of a virus in the Search for: box at the bottom of the dialog box. For additional information about the selected virus, click on the Info button to open an Information About Virus Screen such as the one shown in Figure 0.11b. Click on the Print button to print the information.

Exit Anti-Virus. Select this option (or Close on the Control Menu) to close *Anti-Virus*. Unlike the *VSafe* utility described below, there is no reason to keep *Anti-Virus* open when you are done with it. In fact, it's a good idea to make sure you close it after use, since it has been known to interfere with the operation of other applets.

Options Menu. The Options Menu is a bit of a nuisance, in that it offers only two options, one of which leads to a dialog box which offers. . . more options. But that's the way it is, so the menu's own options are described here.

Save Settings on Exit. A check mark next to this option indicates that the current settings will be saved when you exit the *Anti-Virus* applet.

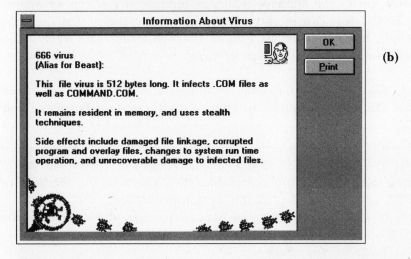

Figure 0.11 The Virus List (a) displays the names of viruses that are known to *Anti-Virus*. Click on the Info button to display the Information About Virus Screen (b), which summarizes the characteristics of the selected virus.

Set Options.... Select this option to get at the configuration options described in the *Anti-Virus Configuration* section below.

Help Menu. For assistance with Help Menus in general, refer to the *Windows Help System* section in Chapter 4. The options on the *Anti-Virus* Help Menu are sufficiently self-explanatory to require no description here. Or, just click on any one of them to find out what it does.

Anti-Virus Configuration

Anti-Virus configuration begins at the Options Menu. Open the menu and select Set Options... to display the Options dialog box shown in Figure 0.12 and described here.

Options Dialog Box. Note that in eight of the nine categories shown in the figure, the listed option is enabled if its check box has an "X" in it. But to make sure you're paying attention, one category is *dis*abled by an "X" in its check box. Each option is described here. A parenthetical reference (on/off) indicates the default status of each option.

Anti-Stealth **(off).** Although the Verify Integrity option (described below) should alert you to file changes that may indicate the effects of a virus, a so-called *Stealth* virus can modify a file in such a manner that the change is not caught by Verify Integrity. Enable the Anti-Stealth and Verify Integrity options to protect against this type of virus.

Check All Files **(on).** In the default configuration, all files are checked for viruses. Disable this option to check only the executable files listed in Table 0.7.

> **NOTE:** The Help Screen *(Check All Files)* states that files with a PIF extension are among the executable files checked for viruses. In fact, PIFs are only checked if this option is enabled.
> *Check All Files* has no effect on files checked by the **Verify Integrity** option. Regardless of its status, *Verify Integrity* checks only the files listed in Table 0.7 for change.

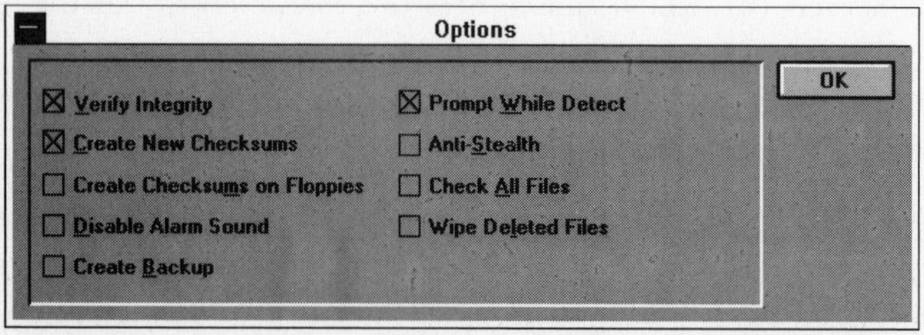

Figure 0.12 The Options dialog box displays the options that may be enabled/disabled to configure *Anti-Virus* as required for your system. In this example, the checked boxes indicate the default configuration options.

TABLE 0.7 Files Checked for Changes by *Anti-Virus* Scan*

Extension	Extension	Extension	Extension
386	DLL	OV1	OVY
APP	DRV	OV2	PGM
BIN	EXE	OV3	PRG
CMD	FON	OVL	SYS
COM	ICO	OVR	

*Data about these files is written to CHKLIST.MS file. Subsequent directory scan triggers a "Verify Error" warning message for each file changed since the previous scan.

Create Backup (**off**). This option creates a backup file with a VIR extension before cleaning the infected file. This offers the dubious advantage of preserving the "original" infected file, for possible use or reuse if the cleanup attempt fails.

Create Checksums on Floppies (**off**). By default, a CHKLIST.MS file (described below) is *not* written to diskette during a virus scan. Enable this option if you want the Checklist file to be created.

Create New Checksums (**on**). By default, a CHKLIST.MS file (described below) is written into each scanned directory if this option is enabled. Disable the option if you don't want these files to be written. However, a Checklist File is written into the DOS directory regardless of the status of this option.

Disable Alarm Sound (**off**). If you *don't* want to hear an alarm every time *Anti-Virus* finds an infected file or detects a file change, place an "X" in this check box (or as they may say in Redmond, "Enable the Disable").

Prompt While Detect (**on**). Under default conditions, the Virus Found or Verify Error dialog boxes shown in Figure 0.9(a and b) appear if a virus or an integrity error is encountered. However, if this option is disabled neither warning appears. If both this prompt and the Alarm Sound (see above) are off, then there will be no evidence of a detected file change. Detected viruses will still be tabulated in the Statistics box shown in Figure 0.10.

Verify Integrity (**on**). In addition to scanning directories for virus-infected files, *Anti-Virus* can also be configured to detect changes to executable files. Since such files rarely change during routine operations, a detected alteration may indicate that a virus is currently active.

Wipe Deleted Files **(off).** If this option is checked and a virus-infected file is discovered, the Delete button shown in Figure 0.9(a and b) is replaced by a Wipe button.

Dialog Box Buttons. The buttons at the right of each dialog box in Figure 0.9 perform the functions described here.

Continue. Choose this option to resume the scan without taking any action on the current file.

Delete. If the Verify Error data indicates that the changed file is corrupt (note, for example the one-byte file size difference seen in Figure 0.9b, you can click on this button to delete the file. Don't forget to locate a valid copy of the file and copy it into the correct directory.

Repair. If the only difference to the file is a change in its creation date and/or time, this button appears in place of the Delete button. Click on it to restore the original file creation data.

Stop. Click on the Stop button to halt the virus scan without taking any further action.

Update. If the change reported in the Verify Error dialog box is acceptable, click on this button to revise the CHKLIST.MS file to accept the change. Doing so prevents the same message from reappearing the next time the directory is scanned.

Wipe. Click once on this button to overwrite the infected file. The following prompt appears, to make sure you really mean it:

Are you sure you want to wipe the file?

If you click the Wipe button in the message box, the entire file is over-written by zeros.

Anti-Virus Support Files

Anti-Virus writes the following files into the DOS directory for the reasons described here.

The Checklist File (CHKLIST.MS). By default, *Anti-Virus* looks for file changes whenever the Scan Menu's Detect or Clean option is selected. The first time either is selected, a special Checklist file (CHKLIST.MS) is written into each scanned subdirectory. The file contains a 27-byte record for each executable file, which includes filename, attributes, creation date, and a checksum. On subsequent scans a new record is calculated for each file, and compared to the corresponding CHKLIST.MS record. If there is a difference—thus indicating a file change—the Verify Error dialog box appears, subject to the conditions described above.

Configuration Options (MWAV.INI). If no default options are reconfigured, the DOS directory will contain an MWAV.INI file with only the following information in it:

```
[options]
auto_save=1
```

If you clear the Save Settings on Exit check mark on the Options Menu, the "1" is of course replaced by "0." However, if you reconfigure any of the other options listed above, then these and still other undocumented options are written into the file, as shown by the list in Table 0.8. To reconfigure any option seen there but not described above, edit the MWAV.INI file as desired.

Infected File (*filename*.VIR). If you enabled the Create Backup option described above, and an infected file was found, *Anti-Virus* saves a copy of that file with a VIR extension. It's not exactly a virus "support" file, but if you find one you'll know what it is. Think about erasing it.

Virus Signature Update Files. Microsoft maintains a bulletin board with updated virus signature data files available for downloading. Refer to *Appendix D* in the *MS-DOS 6.0 User's Guide* for logon and download information. The downloaded files enable Anti-Virus to detect new viruses, but not to remove them. In order to do the latter, the Anti-Virus program itself must be updated. Refer to the update coupon in the *User's Guide* for further details.

Backup

The *Backup* applet is shown in Figure 0.13. As with the *Anti-Virus* applet described above, it may be opened by double-clicking on its icon in the Microsoft Tools Group Window, or via the File Manager's Tools Menu.

TABLE 0.8 Configuration Options in MWAV.INI File*

[options] Line	Default	Access via:*	Description of Option
anti_stealth	= 1	Dialog box	Anti-Stealth
auto_save	= 1	Options Menu	Save Settings on Exit
check_all_files	= 1	Dialog box	Check All Files
create_backup	= 0	Dialog box	Create Backup
create_infreport	= 1[†]	INI only	Create Infection Report
custom_message	= [‡]	INI only	Line 1 of custom message
custom_message2	= [‡]	INI only	Line 2 of custom message
detection_only	= 0	INI only	Disable Clean buttons, Clean Option on Scan Menu
disable_alarm	= 0	Dialog box	Disable Alarm Sound
disable_hotkey	= 0[†]	INI only	Disable Shortcut key
network_access	= 1	INI only	Disable network access
network_message	= [†]	INI only	Network message
new_checksums	= 1	Dialog box	Create New Checksums
new_floppies	= 0	Dialog box	Create Checksums on Floppies
no_continue	= 0	INI only	Disable Continue button
no_scan_stop	= 0	INI only	Disable Pause button (button itself appears enabled)
no_update	= 0	INI only	Disable Update button
prompt_while_detect	= 1	Dialog box	Prompt While Detect
verify_integrity	= 1	Dialog box	Verify Integrity
wipe_files	= 0	Dialog box	Wipe Deleted Files

* If INI only, indicated line in MWAV.INI must be edited to reconfigure option. Note that on some lines, a "1" *disables* the option.

[†] Unimplemented feature.

[‡] Custom message appears in Virus Found and Verify Error dialog boxes, as in Figure 0.9.

Backup Buttons and Menus

The *Backup* applet performs the three separate functions of backup, compare, and restore, selected as described below. Choose the desired function first, then open the appropriate menu to select the option you wish to use.

Backup Buttons. Click on the appropriate large button immediately below the Menu Bar to select one of the following functions. If any menu option is disabled (grayed), that option is not available within the selected function.

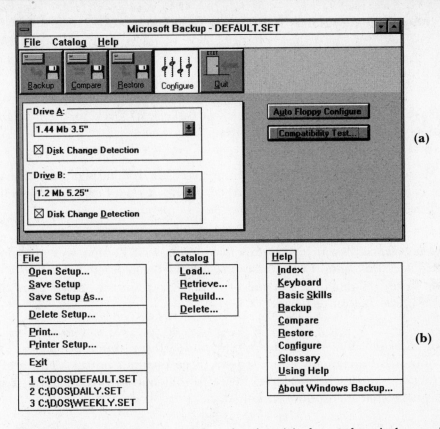

(a)

(b)

Figure 0.13 The *Backup* Applet, showing (a) the applet window and (b) the three *Backup* menus.

Backup. Back up your hard disk to diskettes or to another hard drive partition or MS-DOS medium—local or network; in other words, to just about anything that has a drive letter (except CD-ROM of course). Note that tape backup is not supported.

Compare. Compare the files on the backup diskette(s) with the original source.

Configure. Configure the *Backup* applet as described in the *Backup Configuration* section below.

Quit. This is the fastest way out. Click on the button to display the Exit dialog box with the following two check boxes:

Save Configuration
Save Settings in *filename*.SET

If you made changes to your backup configuration, or to a Setup file, but have not yet saved these changes, one of these lines will be enabled. Clear the check box if you don't want to save the indicated change, then click on the OK button.

Restore. Copy the files on the backup diskette(s) back to their original location on the hard disk, or elsewhere.

File Menu. The options on this menu are used for routine setup file management. The Setup File itself is described in the *Backup Configuration* section which follows this explanation of the *Backup* menus.

Delete Setup.... If you have setup files (*filename*.SET) that you no longer want, select this option to display the Delete Setup Files dialog box (not shown here). Highlight the name of the file you want to erase, then click on the Delete button to get rid of it.

Exit. Backup offers the same option under three different names: This Exit option is functionally equivalent to Close on the Control Menu and to the Quit button described above. Refer to that button's explanation if you can't guess what the option actually does.

Open Setup.... The easiest way to make changes to a Setup File is to simply highlight that file in the drop-down list under the Setup File: box, so that it appears in the box itself. Then make the changes as required in the other parts of the Microsoft Backup dialog box. However, if the Setup File you want is not listed, then select this option to gain access to the directory where the file is located.

Print. Select this option to print the file whose name appears in the Setup File: box.

Printer Setup.... This option is equivalent to the Setup button on the Printers dialog box, which is described in the *Printer Setup* section of Chapter 9.

Save Setup. Select this option if you have made configuration changes and want to save them to the file whose name appears in the Setup File: box.

DOS 6.0 and Windows 41

Save Setup <u>A</u>s.... Before you start an actual backup, you must configure the *Backup* utility, as described in the *Backup Configuration* section later in the chapter. If you want to use the same setup in the future, save it with a distinctive name (DAILY.SET, MONDAY.SET, WEEKLY.SET, etc.) by selecting this option after making your setup choices.

Setup File List. The bottom of the menu lists the various Setup Files that are available. In the example shown in Figure 0.13b, the default file (DEFAULT.SET) has been supplemented by two custom files, for daily and weekly backups. Refer to *Setup Files* below for further details.

Catalog Menu. Configuration information required for a restore operation is written into a backup catalog whenever a backup is done. In fact, two catalogs are created: one in the DOS directory as a file, the other appended to the data written to the final backup diskette. Use the options on this menu for catalog file management, as described here. Refer to *Backup Catalog* in the *Backup Configuration* section for information about the format used to name this file.

<u>D</u>elete.... If you have a catalog file that is no longer needed, select this option to get rid of it. Highlight the filename in the Delete Catalog dialog box (not shown) and click on the OK button to delete it.

<u>L</u>oad.... Select this option to display the Load Catalog dialog box (not shown), which lists the currently available catalog files. Highlight the desired file and click on the OK button to load the file.

<u>R</u>ebuild.... If the catalog file on your hard disk is corrupted or missing, and the last diskette in the backup set is also unavailable, insert the first diskette in your drive and select this option to rebuild the catalog. Damaged diskettes in the backup set may be discarded, but the valid diskettes must be inserted in the correct sequence.

<u>R</u>etrieve.... If the final diskette in the backup series is available, select this option instead of Rebuild... to retrieve the catalog data from that diskette. Once the catalog is retrieved, normal restore operations can begin.

Help Menu. The Help Menu offers the options listed here. Select the appropriate option for a brief survey of that function. For assistance with Help

Menus in general, refer to the *Windows Help System* section in Chapter 4, or select the index option for an outline of the complete *Backup* applet, including its Compare and Restore features.

About Windows Backup	*Glossary*
Backup	*Index*
Basic Skills	*Keyboard*
Compare	*Restore*
Configure	*Using Help*

Backup Configuration

You must configure the *Backup* applet so that it recognizes your system hardware. Therefore, when you open the applet for the first time, the following message appears:

Microsoft Backup has not been configured.
Do you want to automatically configure it now?

Click on the Yes button and the next message prompts you to remove diskettes from all drives (even if no diskettes are in those drives). Click on the OK button to begin the compatibility test described below.

Compatibility Test. The Compatibility Test dialog box shown in Figure 0.14 prompts you to select one of your diskette drives for compatibility testing. Select the desired drive and diskette format, click on the Start button and, after reading a warning message about drive access during backup, click on the OK button to begin the test.

> **NOTE:** If you previously opened the Backup applet but closed it before performing the Compatibility Test, a *Compatibility Test . . . Not Performed* message may be seen the next time you open the applet. However, the message may lead directly to the backup procedure. If this happens, click on the large Configure button, then on the Compatibility Test... button to begin the test. Or, simply do the backup and take your chances.

The Backup Progress screen (Figure 0.15) expects to find a diskette in the selected drive, but if you've been following instructions, you just removed all diskettes. If you don't insert one within about 10 seconds, a message box appears prompting you to do so. If the diskette you insert already contains

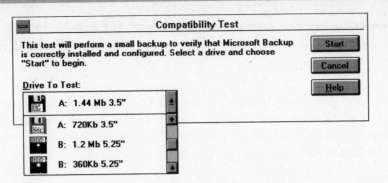

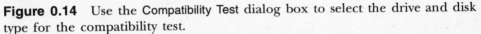

Figure 0.14 Use the Compatibility Test dialog box to select the drive and disk type for the compatibility test.

files or previous backup files, a warning message gives you the opportunity to replace it with another diskette, or to overwrite it.

Once you've made your decision, the Compatibility Test begins. The test backs up slightly more than one diskette-worth of data, so that a diskette swap operation is included in the test.

At the conclusion of the backup, you are prompted to reinsert diskette #1 so that the Compare phase of the test can begin. At its successful conclusion, a final message advises that you can now make reliable disk backups.

Auto Floppy Configure. Although this button appears in the Backup Window (Figure 0.13a), you probably won't have much reason to use it. As a result of your regular configuration, the Drive boxes to the left of the button should accurately report the diskette capacity and size for your drives, and there

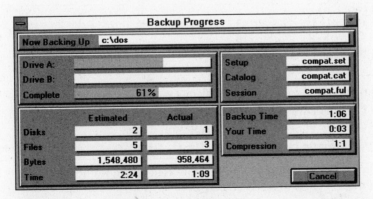

Figure 0.15 The Backup Progress screen reports the status of the compatibility test, or of subsequent backups.

should be checks in the Disk Change Detection boxes. If for some reason the information seen there is inaccurate, click once on the Auto Floppy Configuration button to correct it.

Backup, Compare, Restore Options. Table 0.9 lists additional configuration options that are accessed via the Options... button in the applet window. Note that the option list varies according to which large button (Backup, Compare, Restore) was clicked before clicking the Options... button itself.

Save Configuration. When you exit *Backup* after completing the Compatibility Test, the Save Configuration check box is enabled. Leave the check mark in place and exit, so that the results of the configuration and compatibility test are saved in the MWBACKUP.INI file for future reference. Refer to the *Backup Configuration Record* section below for further information about this file.

TABLE 0.9 Backup Configuration Options*

Function Button	
Configuration Options	**Configuration Options**
Backup	
Always Format Diskettes[†]	Prompt Before Overwriting Used Diskettes[†]
Audible Prompts (Beep)	Quit After Backup
Compress Backup Data	Use Error Correction
Keep Old Backup Catalogs	Verify Backup Data
Password Protection[‡]	
Compare	
Audible Prompts (Beep)	Quit After Compare
Restore	
Audible Prompts (Beep)	Quit After Restore
Prompt Before Creating Directories	Restore Empty Directories
Prompt Before Creating Files	Verify Restored Files
Prompt Before Overwriting Files	

[*]Click indicated Function Button, then Options Button in applet window.
[†]Options disabled if backing up to MS-DOS Path.
[‡]Password data is written into backup file only.

Setup Reconfiguration. If you make changes to the configuration specified in DEFAULT.SET, it's a good idea to save these changes in a new file (DAILY.SET, WEEKLY.SET, or whatever), so that the default settings remain available for future reference.

NOTE: If the Save Configuration option is disabled (grayed), you can re-enable it as follows:

1. Click on the Cancel button to return to the *Backup* window.
2. Click on the Configure button immediately below the Menu Bar.
3. Click on the Auto Floppy Configure button.

Step 3 simply rewrites the existing diskette configuration, thereby enabling the Save Configuration option and sparing you the bother of rerunning the Compatibility Test.

Automated Setup

If you regularly perform daily, weekly, or other backup procedures, you may want to set up a dedicated icon to launch that task, such as the one described here for a daily backup.

First, save the required configuration to a DAILY.SET file, as described immediately above. Then create a new Program Item with the following information in the Program Item Properties dialog box:

Description: Daily Backup
Command Line: MWBACKUP.EXE DAILY.SET

Revise the lines as required to suit other backup routines that you regularly perform. Refer to the *Setup a New Program Item* section and Figure 1.14 in Chapter 1 for assistance, if needed.

When you double-click on the new Daily Backup icon, *Backup* will open with the DAILY.SET configuration in place.

NOTE: This procedure is described in the online Help, under Command-Line Options. However, the descriptive syntax shows a file called WINBACK.EXE. This is a typo, and should read MWBACKUP.EXE instead.

Backup Support Files

Information required by *Backup* is written into several files, as described here. The explanation assumes a full backup was made. If not, the references to an extension of FUL (full) will be INC (incremental) or DIF (differential) instead.

Setup File (*filename*.SET). *Backup* configuration information is stored in a Setup File in the DOS directory. Table 0.10 summarizes the contents of the Microsoft default (DEFAULT.SET) file, which is created during the initial *Backup* configuration session. The table is based on two data sets; one is taken from a printout of the file via the Print option on the File Menu, the other from direct observation of the file contents. Note that in a few cases the printout does not agree with the actual file, and the file itself appears to be the more accurate indicator of actual configuration status. Therefore, in case of an apparent discrepancy in the printed word, refer to the corresponding entry in the file for verification.

TABLE 0.10 DEFAULT.SET Printout and File Contents*

Section and Contents	Printout	File Contents and Comments
Last Update:	*(today's date and time)*	
Last Full Backup:	0/00/80 0:00:00	0/00/80 0:00:00
Last Backup:	0/00/80 0:00:00	0/00/80 0:00:00
General Settings		
File Sort Type:	By file name	0 0=Name, 1=Extension, 2=Size, 3=Date, 4=Attribute
Show Selection Statistics:	†	No
Group Selected Files:	No	No
Print To File:	No	No
Exclude Copy Protected Files:	No	No
Copy Protected File 1:		
Copy Protected File 2:		
Copy Protected File 3:		
Copy Protected File 4:		
Copy Protected File 5:		
Show Directories Above Files:	No	No
File List Width:	0	0
File List Height:	0	0
Selection Window Maximized:	Yes	Yes
Show File Size	†	Yes

TABLE 0.10 *(continued)*

Section and Contents	Printout	File Contents and Comments
Show File Date:	†	Yes
Show File Time:	†	Yes
Show File Attributes:	†	Yes
General Backup Settings		
Backup Type:	Full	0 0=Full, 1=Incremental, 2=Differential
Backup To:	Drive A	1 1=A, 2=B, 3=Both, 4=MS-DOS Device
Backup System Files:	Yes	Yes
Backup Hidden Files:	Yes	Yes
Backup Read-Only Files:	Yes	Yes
Backup Using Date Range:	No	No
Backup Date Range:	†	1/01/80 to 12/31/99
Disk Backup Settings		
Backup Device Path:		
DOS Device Path 1:	C:\DOS\	
DOS Device Path 2:		
DOS Device Path 3:		
DOS Device Path 4:		
DOS Device Path 5:		

Section and Contents	Printout	File Contents and Comments
Backup Diskette Size:	1.44 Mb 3.5"	4 0=360K, 1=720K(5¼), 2=720K(3½), 3=1.2Mb, 4=1.44Mb
Diskette Format Option:§	Only when needed	0 0=Only when needed, 1=Always
Diskette Overwrite Warning:§	On	3 0=None, 3=All disks
Data Verification:§	Off	0 0=None, 3=Read and compare
Data Compression:§	On	1 0=Off, 1=On
Error Correction:§	Yes	Yes
Audible Backup Prompts:§	1	1 0=Off, 1=On
Keep Old Backup Catalogs:§	Yes	Yes
Quit After Backup:§	No	No
General Restore Settings		
Restore Using date range:	No	No
Backup Date Range:	†	1/01/80 to 12/31/99
Restore From:	Drive B	1‡ 1=A, 2=B, 3=Both, 4=MS-DOS Device
Restore To:	Original Locations	0 0=Original, 1=Alt Drives, 2=Alt Directories
Restore System files:	No	No
Restore Hidden files:	No	No
Restore Read-only files:	No	No

TABLE 0.10 *(continued)*

Section and Contents	Printout	File Contents and Comments
Disk Restore Settings		
Restore Device Path:		
Data Verification:§	0	0 0=None, 3=Read and compare
Audible Restore Prompts:§	No	1‡ 0=Off, 1=On
Prompt Before Creating Dirs:§	No	No
Prompt Before Creating Files:§	No	No
Prompt Before Overwriting:§	No	No
Restore Empty Directories:§	No	No
Quit After Restore:§	No	No
General Compare Settings		
Compare With:	Drive A	0 0=Original, 1=Alt Drives, 2=Alt Directories
Compare From:	Alternate Drives	1‡ 1=A, 2=B, 3=Both, 4=MS-DOS Device
Disk Compare Settings		
Compare Path:		
Audible Compare Prompts:§	1	1 0=Off, 1=On
Quit After Compare:§	No	No
Include & Exclude Specifications for Backup:		
(none written during initial configuration)		

* DEFAULT.SET file is generally more reliable indicator than printout.

† This line does not appear in printout.

‡ Printout does not agree with DEFAULT.SET file contents.

§ Select desired function, then click Options button in applet window to change indicated option.

Backup Catalog (*filename*.FUL). The Backup Catalog referred to in the *Catalog Menu* section is stored as a file in the DOS directory, where its filename appears in the following format:

xy01234a.ext

where	*x*	First drive backed up	*ext*	DIF	Differential
	y	Last drive backed up		FUL	Full
	0	Last digit of the backup year		INC	Incremental
	12	Month			
	34	Day			
	a	Backup sequence on indicated date (a = first backup, b = second, . . .)			

Thus, the Backup Catalog filename CE30323B.FUL contains data for a backup of drives C through E, made in 1993, on March 23rd, and is the second full backup made on that day. Note that the Backup Catalog does not record the drive in which the backup diskettes were created.

Master Catalog (*filename*.CAT). The Master Catalog is a 66-byte file containing the following information:

Description (if any) taken from Backup Catalog.

Backup Catalog filename (*filename*.FUL) for last backup under specified Setup File.

Date/Time stamp of Backup Catalog.

For example, if the last backup was run on July 25, 1993 at 2:30PM, the contents of the Master Catalog file might look like this:

Weekly backup of drive C. *(or other description, as written in Backup Catalog)*
CC30725A.FUL, 7/25/93, 2:30P

The Master Catalog filename is the same as the Setup File that was used for the backup, and its extension is CAT. During a restore session, the Master Catalog is read and the Bac<u>k</u>up Set Catalog: window shows the information from line 2, above. Prior Backup Catalogs, if any, are viewed in the pull-down window.

Backup Data File (*filename*.00x). As files are backed up to diskette, they are written into a single file that occupies the entire diskette data area. Therefore, a CHKDSK report will always show the following information, regardless of the actual space occupied by the backed up files:

730112 bytes total disk space *(example is for a 720-Kbyte diskette)*
730112 bytes in 1 user files
       0 bytes available on disk

The Backup Data File's filename matches that of the corresponding Backup Catalog, as described above. The filename extension is 00*x*, where *x* indicates the number (1, 2, 3, . . .) of that diskette in the complete backup set.

Backup Configuration Record (MWBACKUP.INI). A record of the applet's configuration and the Compatibility Test is written into the MWBACKUP.INI file, as shown in Table 0.11. You may want to edit one or both of the lines shown below if you know the recorded values are incorrect, as might happen if you rerun a test and interrupt it before completion.

TABLE 0.11   MWBACKUP.INI File Contents*

[MWBACKUP]	Comments		
Lines written during Initial Configuration & Compatibility test			
Setup File Path = C:\DOS			
Setup File Name = DEFAULT.SET			
Setup File 1 = C:\DOS\DEFAULT.SET			
Setup File 2 =			
Setup File 3 =			
Setup File 4 =			
Setup File 5 =			
Floppy Compatibility Test = 2	0=test not run,	1=test failed,	2=test passed
Lines appended during Subsequent Exit if Save Configuration box is checked			
Drive A Capacity = 5	0=not installed,	1=360Kb,	2=720(5¼),
Drive B Capacity = 4	3=720(3½),	4=1.2Mb,	5=1.44Mb
Change Disk Detect (A) = 1	0=no,	1=yes	
Change Disk Detect (B) = 1	0=no,	1=yes	
Program Configured = 1	0=no,	1=yes	
Video/DMS Compatibility = 0			
System ID = 7742			
Window Left = 124			
Window Top = 95			
Line appended during Backup session			
Show Disable Floppies Message			
= 1			

*Spaces around equal signs added here for clarity. Not present in actual INI file.

```
Floppy Compatibility Test=2
Program Configured=1
```

Temporary Restore File (~WINBACK.TMP). Restored files are written back to disk as ~WINBACK.TMP, then renamed as required. If the restore operation is cancelled, you may find such a file in the target directory on your hard disk. If so, it can be erased before retrying the restore.

DOS Backup Selection File (*filename*). This file is created during a DOS backup session to hold directory and file selection data. Although not further discussed here, this brief mention is made in case you run across an SLT file and wonder what it is.

Undelete

The final Microsoft Tool is *Undelete*. Like its companions described above, you can open it by double-clicking its icon in the Microsoft Tools Group window. Although the other two tools can also be accessed via File Manager's Tools Menu, *Undelete* is different: It appears instead as an added option on File Manager's File Menu. There may be a very good reason for this, but then again there may not. The *Undelete* applet window and its menus are shown in Figure 0.16.

Undelete Buttons and Menus

The large buttons immediately below the Menu Bar duplicate various menu options, as indicated by a parenthetical reference in the menu descriptions which follow. The middle of the applet window shows the list of erased files that *Undelete* has detected on the selected drive, and reports the condition of each. Table 0.12 lists the five conditions that may be seen in the "Condition" column.

File Menu. The options on this menu are described below. To enable the Undelete options, first select (highlight) one or more deleted files in the list which appears in the applet window. If the Purge option is disabled, none of the highlighted files are protected by the Delete Sentry. Although the File Info... option will have no information to report if a file has not been selected, the option remains enabled on the menu, perhaps to see if you're paying attention.

Change Drive/Directory (Alt+D, or Drive/Dir button). Select this option to change to the drive and directory containing the file(s) you want to undelete.

Exit. Select this option, or Close on the Control Menu, to close the *Undelete* applet.

File Info... **(Alt+I, or Info button).** Although the *Undelete* window itself provides deleted-file information, some of that information may be misleading. For example, Figure 0.17a shows an applet window with two files highlighted for undeleting—one in good condition, the other perfect. Yet the bottom of the screen refers to a file that cannot be undeleted. The discrepancy arises because only one file can be reported there at a time, and that file is the *last* one selected (or in this case, *de*selected). In the figure, this happens to be the one in poor condition, which lies between the two selected

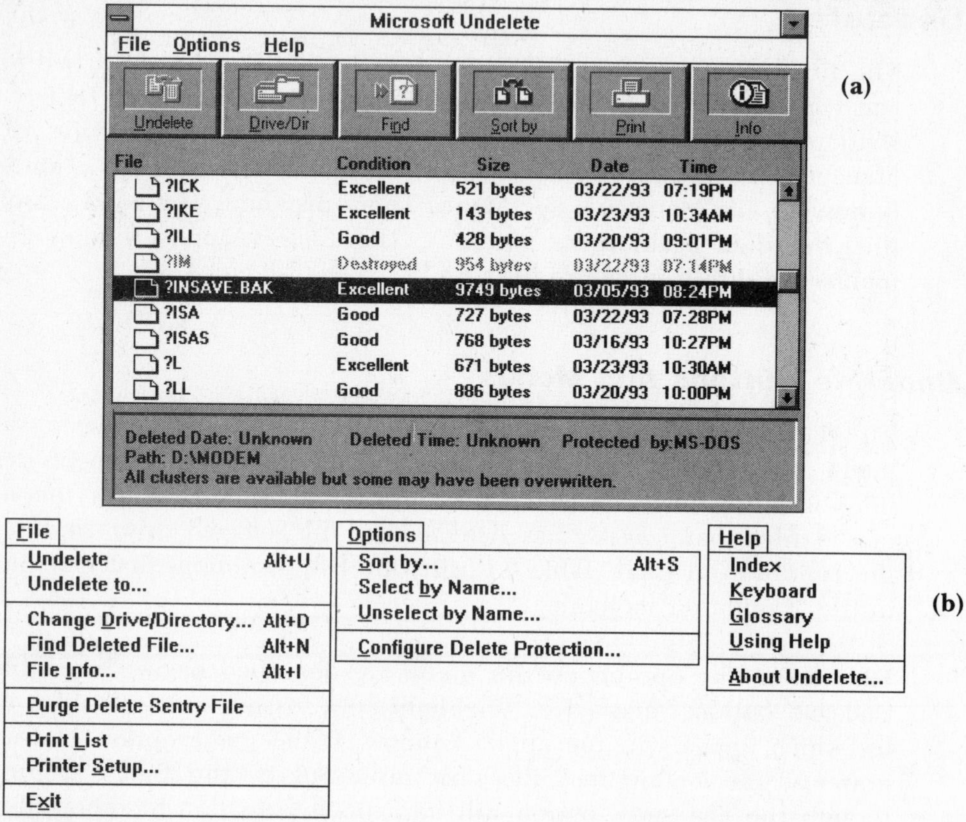

Figure 0.16 The *Undelete* Applet, showing (a) the applet window and (b) the three *Undelete* menus.

TABLE 0.12 Undelete File Status Reports*

Condition	Comment*
Destroyed	This file cannot be automatically undeleted.[†]
Poor	This file cannot be automatically undeleted.
Good	One or more clusters are in use by other files.
Excellent	All clusters are available but some may have been overwritten.
Perfect	This file can be 100% deleted.[‡]

[*] Comment appears at bottom of *Undelete* Window and also on Information Screen.

[†] Message is correct, but should read All clusters for this file are in use by other files.

[‡] File protected by the Delete Sentry.

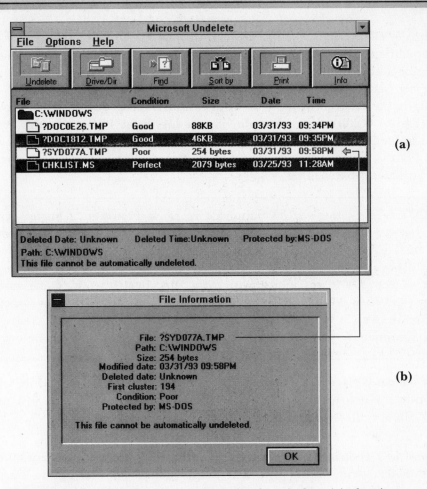

Figure 0.17   The Microsoft Undelete applet window (a) showing two files selected for undeleting. Since the information at the bottom of the screen does not identify the file being reported, refer to the File Information Screen (b) for an unambiguous report. (Click on the Info button to display the screen.)

files. To resolve such ambiguities, select the File Info... option. The File Information screen shown in Figure 0.17b lists the selected filename at the top of the report, so there is no doubt about the source of the information.

Find Deleted File... (Alt+N, or Find button). Select this option if you're not sure where a specific deleted file is hiding, or if you want to find all deleted files with a specific filename or extension, all files associated with a specific applet or application, or all files containing a specified text string.

Search by File Specification. In the Find Deleted Files dialog box, enter the file specification you wish to search for. To find all files associated with selected Windows applets, click on the Groups... button shown in the Find Deleted Files dialog box shown later in Figure 0.20a. Next, highlight the desired applets or applications in the Search these groups: box (Figure 0.20b). For example, if you highlight PBRUSH (the Paintbrush applet) and click on the OK button, the File specification: box will show *.pcx + *.bmp. Click on the OK button to begin the search for all files with these extensions.

> **NOTE:** That's the way it's supposed to work. However, a buglet gets in the way. The search engine will only find file specifications entered in ALL CAPS. Therefore, if you want to find all Paintbrush files, you'll have to change *.pcx + *.bmp to *.PCX + *.BMP before starting the search. Or if you enter your own file specification, make sure you type it in ALL CAPS. Otherwise, deleted files with that specification won't be found. For a workaround, refer to *Search Configuration Techniques* in the *Undelete Configuration* section below.

The Ignore Case option described immediately below is valid only when searching for text within deleted files, and has no effect on the just mentioned file-specification problem.

Search for Text String. If you wish to confine the search to files containing a certain text string, enter that text in the Containing: box before starting the search. If either check box is enabled, a search for the word "Test" will be as described here:

Ignore Case   All occurrences of "Test" are found, regardless of case (for example, TEST, Test, test, TesT, and so on). Also found are words which contain the search text (attest, testing, testament, testy, etc.).

Whole Word   Only occurrences of the word "Test" (as above) are found. Longer text strings containing that word are ignored.

In the example shown in Figure 0.20a, the search engine will look for all deleted files with a DOC extension (note ALL CAPS) that contain the word "Test" or any other text string in which that word is embedded.

Print List (or Print button). The option prints a list of the deleted files in the current directory, as shown in this typical example:

File:	Condition	Protection:	Size:	Modification Date:
C:\DOS				
?OUSE.GRP	Destroyed	MS-DOS	2324 bytes	07/10/93 10:23AM
?EADME.EXE	Poor	MS-DOS	2556 bytes	07/21/93 01:10PM
AUTOEXEC.BAK	Poor	Delete Tracker	473 bytes	07/15/93 09:15AM
?OUSE.INI	Good	MD-DOS	1219 bytes	07/26/93 10:33AM
FOOBAR.DOC	Good	Delete Tracker	2567 bytes	07/29/93 12:01PM
?AILY.CAT	Excellent	MS-DOS	66 bytes	07/30/93 03:30PM
CHKLIST.MS	Perfect	Delete Sentry	108 bytes	07/23/93 08:40PM

Note that filenames are intact if protected by the Delete Tracker, although the files themselves may or may not be in good shape. A file protected by the Delete Sentry is always in Perfect condition, since in fact it has not been erased at all but is simply in hiding, as explained in the *Undelete Configuration* section.

Printer Setup.... This option is equivalent to the Setup button on the Printers dialog box, which is described in the *Printer Setup* section of Chapter 9.

Purge Delete Sentry File. If this menu option is enabled, then one or more of the highlighted files are protected by the Delete Sentry. If the option is selected, the protected highlighted files are removed (purged) from the Sentry directory, thus permanently erasing them. In other words, the selected files are deleted, not *un*deleted.

Note that this option purges only those files protected by the Delete Sentry. Other files that may also be highlighted are not affected, and may be undeleted—subject to their reported condition of course.

Undelete (**Alt+U**). Choose this option to begin undeleting the selected file(s). If a selected file is not protected by the Delete Tracker or Delete Sentry, you will be prompted for the first letter of the filename. In either case the file is restored to its former location. If more than one file was highlighted for undeleting, the files will be sequentially processed.

Undelete to.... You may want to select this option if you know the deleted file is an earlier version of a currently valid file with the same name. You will be prompted to specify a new drive and/or filename, so that the undeleted file does not overwrite the existing file. However, even if you select the regular Undelete option above, you will be prompted for a new filename if required to prevent overwriting an existing file. If you really don't want the existing file, undelete the desired file and give it a new name anyway. Then erase the just-mentioned current file and rename the undeleted one as desired.

Options Menu. Open this menu to access the configuration options listed here.

Configure Delete Protection.... Select this option to configure the level of delete protection you require, as explained in the *Undelete Configuration* section below.

Select by Name, Unselect by Name.... If your list of deleted files is long, use the appropriate option to select or unselect a group of files by filename and/or extension. For example, if you recently deleted all your INI files (!!), you can select all of them by typing *.INI in the File specification: box. Then open the File Menu to undelete the selected group. Use the same general procedure to unselect a file group.

Sort by.... (**Alt+S, or Sort by** button). This option opens a Sort By dialog box (not shown) that offers the following sort choices:

Condition	Name	Date and Time deleted
Extension	Size	Date and Time modified

If the Sort files by directory box is checked, the name of the currently displayed directory appears at the top of the list of deleted files. Deleted subdirectories (if any) within the current directory appear near the top of the list, regardless of the status of the check box. Despite the online "explanation" for this option, a deleted directory must be recovered before the files within it can be recovered.

Help Menu. As with the other *Microsoft Tools* Help Menus, these options require no description here. For assistance with Help Menus in general, refer to the *Windows Help System* section in Chapter 4.

Undelete Configuration

The *Undelete* utility offers the three levels of delete protection described below. To configure it for the desired level, open the Options Menu and select the Configure Delete Protection... option to display the Configure Delete Protection dialog box shown in Figure 0.18. Click on one of the radio buttons shown in the figure and follow the appropriate configuration instructions below.

If either the *Delete Sentry* or *Delete Tracker* mode is selected, an UNDELETE /LOAD command is written into your AUTOEXEC.BAT file, and you must reboot in order for the command to take effect. If you'd rather not bother rebooting, exit Windows anyway, and type the appropriate command(s) at the DOS prompt, as described here.

UNDELETE/UNLOAD   Use at DOS prompt, only if you have just reconfigured from one previously installed mode to another; that is, from *Delete Sentry* to *Delete Tracker*, or vice versa.

UNDELETE/LOAD   Load the specified mode *(see Undelete Configuration)*.

UNDELETE/S*X*   Force *Undelete* to load in the *Delete Sentry* mode for drive *X*.

UNDELETE/T*X*   Force *Undelete* to load in the *Delete Tracker* mode for drive *X*.

As *Undelete* loads—either at the DOS prompt or as the system boots on—the following message is seen:

Delete Sentry Mode	**Delete Tracker Mode**
UNDELETE—A delete protection facility.	UNDELETE—A delete protection facility.
(Central Point Software copyright notice)	*(Central Point Software copyright notice)*
UNDELETE loaded.	UNDELETE loaded.
Delete Protection Method is Delete Sentry.	Delete Protection Method is Delete Tracking.
Enabled for Drives : *X Y*.	Enabled for Drives : *X Y*.
Initializing SENTRY control file on drive *X*.	

NOTE: The **UNDELETE /LOAD** line mentioned above is written at the end of your **AUTOEXEC.BAT** file, and therefore has no effect if an earlier line automatically loads Windows, or otherwise re-routes program execution before this line is encountered. In case of doubt, have a look at the batch file and make the appropriate changes if necessary.

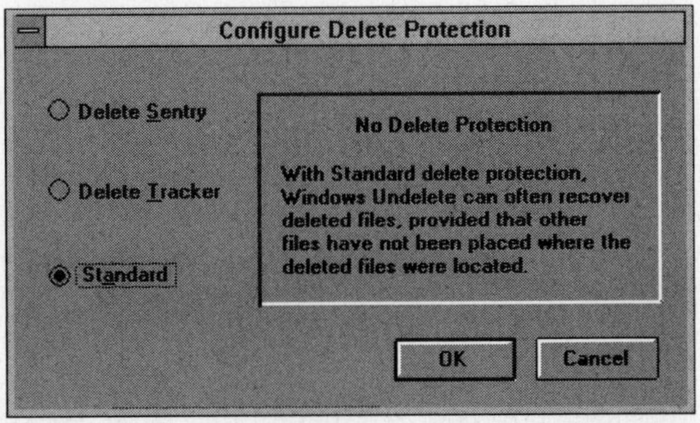

Figure 0.18 The Configure Delete Protection dialog box. Click the appropriate radio button to enable Delete Sentry, Delete Tracker, or Standard protection.

Delete Sentry. This is the highest level of delete protection. In fact, if a file is deleted while this option is enabled, the chance of undeleting it is perfect, provided you remember to do so within say, one week. The reason for such favorable odds is, you only *think* the file is deleted. But instead, the Delete Sentry has simply moved the file into a hidden Sentry directory and changed its name, as described in the *Delete Sentry Protected File* section below. To verify that a file is protected by the Delete Sentry, look for the following information when that filename is selected.

Condition: Perfect
Protected by: Delete Sentry *(bottom of applet window, or see File Information screen)*

By default, the Delete Sentry saves files in the Sentry directory until seven days have passed, or 20 percent of the available disk space is occupied by such files, whichever comes first. Then, the earliest files are discarded. To revise the configuration, click on the Delete Sentry button to open the Configure Delete Sentry dialog box shown in Figure 0.19a.

All Files **or** *Only specified files:.* By default, the Only specified files: button is enabled, and the Include and Exclude boxes (see below) list the files that will and won't be protected. Click on the All files button only if you want to protect all files. Note however, that doing so erases the default list of excluded files. Refer to the *File Exclusion List* section below for a review of the default settings, and a way to restore them if needed later on.

Include: **and** *Exclude: Buttons.* Use wildcards (* and/or ?) to tailor the delete protection as required. The default status is to include all files (*.*), except those whose extensions are listed in the Exclude: box. Note that if you want to exclude a file, the file specification should begin with a minus sign.

Do not save archived files. This option has two strikes against it. First, it's one of those wretched examples of Microspeak—in effect, you must respond "yes, I don't" or "no, I do" (want to save archived files). Once you've decided what you want to do, you must then do the opposite. That is, check the box if you *do* want to save archived files, clear the box if you *don't* want to save them. In other words, the legend next to the box is reversed: It should read simply "Save archived files?" Put a check in the box for "yes," clear it for "no."

Clear the check box if you don't want to protect files that are already backed up (archived) and have not been changed since that backup. If you need to undelete such a file, and the standard mode undelete won't do it, restore the file from the backup diskettes instead.

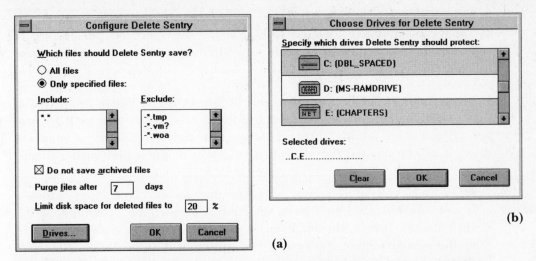

Figure 0.19 If the Delete Sentry mode is selected (see Figure 0.18), the Configure Delete Sentry dialog box (a) displays the current configuration for this mode. Click on the Drives... button to access the Choose Drives dialog box (b). If the Delete Tracker mode was selected, the Title Bar changes to Delete Tracker instead.

Archive Check Box Workaround. Readers who don't mind meddling with file innards can revise the Do not save archived files legend so that it matches the action indicated by the check box. First, make a backup copy of MWUNDEL.EXE. Then use the Norton Utilities *Disk Editor* or similar utility to edit the original MWUNDEL.EXE. Search for the following string and rewrite it, as shown here:

```
Do not save &archived files
Save &archived files?------
```

Don't overlook the "&" character which signifies that the first letter in "archived" will appear underlined in the screen display. Type six spaces in place of six hyphens at the end of the second line to erase the end of the previous message.

If all goes well, you can erase the backup copy. Or if it doesn't, erase the edited version and restore the backup copy.

Purge files after **X** *days* (**default = 7**). A file is automatically tossed out of the Sentry directory after it sits there for seven days without being un-deleted. Any files older than the specified day are deleted regardless of the amount of space they occupy. Therefore you may want to increase the default deadline if you fear having second thoughts after a week has passed, and the available disk space is there.

Limit disk space for deleted files to **xx** *percent* **(default = 20 percent).** If the space occupied by deleted files exceeds the specified percentage of available disk space, early files are discarded in order to stay within the available allocation.

Drives *button.* Click here to open the Choose Drives for Delete Sentry dialog box shown in Figure 0.19b, then highlight the drives you wish to protect. If a hidden Sentry directory does not already exist on a specified drive, it will be created there the first time you delete a file on that drive.

> **NOTE:** If you subsequently discover that Delete Sentry protection is not enabled after you have selected it, repeat the operation and click on the Drives button. Even if you don't want to make changes to the selected drives, selecting this option will force Delete Sentry protection to be enabled.

Delete Sentry and Network Drives. The Delete Sentry is able to protect network drives, as may be noted by the presence of a network drive icon in Figure 0.19b. As a possible source of confusion, the Delete Sentry also recognizes a local CD-ROM drive as a network drive and will offer to protect its files for you. Don't bother though: If you know how to delete a CD-ROM file, no doubt you also know how to undelete one.

File Exclusion List. By default, *Undelete* excludes files with certain extensions from protection by the Delete Sentry, as indicated by the list shown on the sentry.files line in Table 0.13. If this list is lost and you want to recover it, open a DOS window and type ERASE C:\DOS\UNDELETE.INI at the DOS prompt. Then reopen *Undelete* and once again configure it for the Delete Sentry. The default values, including the list of files to be excluded, will be written back into the UNDELETE.INI file and will reappear in the Exclude: box shown in Figure 0.19a.

Delete Tracker. If this mode is selected, Windows keeps track of the full name and location of each deleted file, but such files are not protected from overwriting. Click on the Delete Tracker button to select this mode. The Choose Drives dialog box matches that in Figure 0.19b, except that *Delete Sentry* becomes *Delete Tracker.*

Standard. This is the default level of delete protection, equivalent to the conventional MS-DOS (pre-DOS 6.0) UNDELETE command. If you have

TABLE 0.13   UNDELETE.INI File Contents*

Section and Contents	File Contents	Comments[†]
[configuration]		
archive	= FALSE	Default Value
days	= 7	Default Value
percentage	= 20	Default Value
[sentry.drives]		Drives protected by Delete Sentry
C	=	and/or others, as specified by user
[mirror.drives]		Drives protected by Delete Tracker
C	=	and/or others, as specified by user
[sentry.files][‡]		
sentry.files	= *.* -*.dov, -*.img, -*.rmg, -*.spl, -*.swp	
	-*.thm, -*.tmp, -*.vm?, -*.woa	
[defaults][§]		
d.sentry	= TRUE	Delete Sentry enabled
d.tracker	= FALSE	Delete Tracker disabled

* Spaces around equal signs added here for clarity. Not present in actual INI file.

[†] Most lines written into file only if a default value is changed.

[‡] The "*.*" indicates all files are protected by Delete Sentry, *except* those whose extension is listed on the same line, preceded by a minus sign. Default exclusions listed in Table.

[§] TRUE indicates the enabled protection mode. Both FALSE if Standard mode protection is enabled.

never upgraded to *Delete Tracker* or *Delete Sentry* mode, the UNDELETE /LOAD line does not appear in your AUTOEXEC.BAT file, since it is not needed for *Standard* mode protection. However, if you have upgraded, then returned to *Standard* mode, the line is not deleted. Instead, the [defaults] section of UNDELETE.INI (described below, and in Table 0.13) contains the necessary information to enable *Standard* mode.

Search Configuration Techniques. The fastest way to find an undeleted file is to select the File Menu's Fi̱nd Deleted File... option, then simply enter the desired file specification (CONFIG.* , *.INI, for example) in the F̱ile specifications: box. However, if you regularly need to find all files associated with a specific application, then you may want to reconfigure the list of search groups, as described here.

Edit Search Groups List. To begin, click on the Groups... button at the bottom of the Find Deleted Files dialog box to open the Search Groups dialog box, both of which are shown in Figure 0.20(a and b). Now click on the Edit... button at the bottom of the Search Groups dialog box to open the Edit Search Groups dialog box shown in Figure 0.20c.

In this specific example, the Paintbrush applet is selected and therefore the File Specification: box at the bottom of the dialog box shows *.pcx + *.bmp, since these extensions are associated with that applet. *Undelete* knows these extensions are associated with Paintbrush, since it found the following information in the indicated section of WIN.INI:

```
[extensions]
bmp=pbrush.exe ^.bmp
pcx=pbrush.exe ^.pcx
```

But, as previously noted, a buglet prevents the search engine from finding deleted files when the search specification is entered in lowercase letters. An obvious solution suggests itself: Simply edit WIN.INI to change bmp and pcx to BMP and PCX, and that should take care of it. It should, but it doesn't. *Undelete* has a mind of its own, and transforms the extensions into lowercase, regardless of what it finds in WIN.INI. Since the search engine can't find lowercase file specifications, the subsequent find operation fails.

The easiest solution may be to forget about the Search Groups feature. If you want to find deleted files, just enter the desired file specification in ALL CAPS and do it. Use Search Groups only if you're not sure of all the extensions associated with a particular applet or application. Once you transfer the extensions into the File specification: box, overtype each one with its uppercase equivalent.

Search Group Workaround. However, if you regularly search for deleted files with certain file specifications, and can't bear the thought of entering that specification every time you need it, you may want to go through the following workaround procedure. This may come in handy when searching for all files associated with say, Excel (XLC, XLS, XLW, and so on—it's a bit much to reenter every time you open *Undelete*).

To begin, click on the Edit... button (Figure 0.20b) to open the Edit Search Groups dialog box shown in Figure 0.20c. If you want to modify an existing group, highlight its name in the Edit Search Groups window. As soon as you do, that name and its associated extensions are displayed in the Group name: and File specification: boxes at the bottom of the dialog box. Temporarily change the drive letter, or make any other trivial modification to the group name. Then overwrite each displayed extension with its uppercase equivalent.

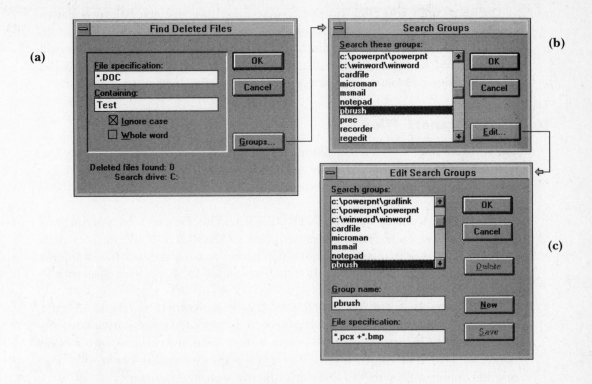

Figure 0.20 Find Deleted Files options for Undelete: (a) shows the initial dialog box, (b) shows the group search box, and (c) shows how you can edit the search groups or modify their search properties.

If you'd rather create a completely new group, click on the New button to clear the Group name: and File specification: boxes. Now type in a new group name and the file specifications associated with that group. In Figure 0.20c, a new Paintbrush group has been entered, with a distinctive (PTbrush) name and the extensions in ALL CAPS (*.PCX + *.BMP).

When you're done, click on the now-enabled Save button to write the data into a Custom Search Record for future use. The slight name or other change is needed to trick *Undelete* into agreeing to save your modifications. In this example, the "new" specification serves as a workaround for *Undelete*'s inability to find its own lowercase Paintbrush extensions. As a final step, open the Custom Search Record file (described below) and locate the information you just entered. Having fooled *Undelete* long enough to save the changes, you can now edit the incorrect PTbrush back to its correct PBrush (or correct whatever other modification you made).

The next time you click on the Groups... button and select Excel, Paint-brush, or whatever, the File specification: box will show the desired extensions, just as you wrote them in ALL CAPS. At the tail end of the list will be all the old lowercase extensions. They'll be ignored as before, but with the new extensions in place, *Undelete* will now find what you want it to find.

Undelete Support Files

The *Undelete* applet uses the following files to maintain a record of every deleted file and, in the case of *Delete Sentry,* the deleted file itself. In each section below, a parenthetical reference indicates the name of the file that is described.

Delete Sentry Control File (CONTROL.FIL). The Delete Sentry maintains a control file in each Sentry directory. This CONTROL.FIL file has a system attribute, and it contains the original filename for each deleted file, together with the code name under which that file resides in the Sentry directory.

Delete Sentry Protected File (#A1B2C9X.MS, or similar). If a file is deleted while the *Delete Sentry* mode is enabled, it is actually moved intact into a hidden Sentry directory and protected with a hidden attribute and a code name, such as that shown above. The code name is cross-referenced to the original name within the CONTROL.FIL file described above.

Delete Tracker Control File (PCTRACKR.DEL). The Delete Tracker also maintains its own control file, named PCTRACKR.DEL. This file also has a system attribute and is located in the root directory of the drive. When a file is deleted, PCTRACKR.DEL records the filename and location of the deleted file, and can use this information to recover the file provided you remember to do so before any of its clusters are overwritten by other files.

Standard Delete Protection (*none*). In this default protection mode, no control files are maintained. You can recognize a deleted file protected by *Standard* mode, by the "?" that appears as the first character in its filename. If you attempt to undelete such a file, you will be prompted for a new first letter.

Undelete Configuration Record (UNDELETE.INI). The current *Undelete* configuration is written into the UNDELETE.INI file, whose contents are summarized in Table 0.13. As noted earlier, the file contains a list of file extensions that are to be excluded from delete protection, and the protection mode that is currently enabled.

Custom Search Record (CPSTOOLS.INI). If you add new file search specifications to *Undelete*'s Search Group, this information is written into a CPSTOOLS.INI file, in the following format:

```
[groups]
z:\excel\excel = *.XLS + *.XLC + *.XLW + ...
d:\custom\myapp = *.XYZ + *.JMW +...
```

The Excel line shows an invalid drive letter, entered so that *Undelete* would accept the line as a new specification, as described in the *Search Group Workaround* section above. Edit the line to indicate the correct drive, and the extensions will be added to the Excel search group.

VSafe

VSafe monitors your computer for various changes which may (and often, *do*) indicate the presence of a virus. It also reports any viruses that it actually finds while monitoring your system. As noted earlier, it is not installed automatically as part of the *Microsoft Tools* group.

VSafe Manager Menus

The *VSafe Manager* window shown in Figure 0.21 may be initially confusing, in that it shows both an Options Menu (described here) and an **Options** button. Refer to the *VSafe Configuration* section which follows for information about the latter.

Control Menu. The options that appear on this menu are described in the *Control Menu* section of Chapter 3.

Help Menu. There isn't any. For assistance with various *VSafe* options, open a DOS window and type HELP VSAFE at the DOS prompt. The Help Screen cautions: "Do not use the VSAFE command when you are running Windows." This means, don't open a DOS Window and type VSAFE at the DOS prompt.

Options Menu. Although Windows may contain many VIMs (very important menus), this is not one of them. It does provide access to the three options listed here, but there's not much reason to select any of them. However, here they are, just in case you get the urge. Remember, the *real* options are accessed via the **Options** button.

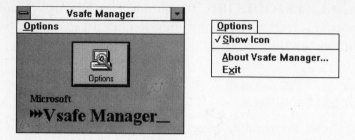

Figure 0.21 The *VSafe Manager* applet window and its lone Options Menu.

About VSafe Manager.... For general information on the various "About..." options that usually show up on Help Menus, refer to the *About... Screen* section in Chapter 4. Like most others, this one displays copyright information about the *VSafe Manager*.

Exit. Catch-22: If you select this option, a warning message advises against selecting this option. The same message appears if you select the Control Menu's **C**lose option. To avoid potential DOS TSR problems, minimize the *VSafe Manager* instead of exiting.

Show Icon. If a check mark is placed next to this option, then the *VSafe Manager* icon appears at the bottom of the Windows Desktop when the utility is minimized. If the check mark is cleared, the icon does not appear. In this case, you can gain access to the utility via the File Menu's **R**un... option, or by double-clicking on the *VSafe Manager* icon if you've installed it in one of your Group Windows.

VSafe Configuration

As you load *VSafe* at the DOS prompt, as described earlier in the *VSafe Installation* section, a message such as that shown in Figure 0.22 should appear on screen. The indicated memory usage will of course vary (to 44K and 0K) if you use the /NX switch. If you would rather not load *VSafe* automatically every time you turn the system on, yet still use it within Windows, write (or modify) a batch file as shown here:

VSAFE / (optional switches)	*Load VSafe prior to opening Windows.*
WIN	*Run Windows.*
VSAFE /U	*Unload VSafe after exiting Windows.*

```
                      VSafe (tm)

             Copyright (c) 1991-1993
           Central Point Software, Inc.
              Hotkey:    <Alt><V>



         VSafe successfully installed.
         Vsafe is using 23K of conventional memory,
                       23K of XMS memory,
                        OK of EMS memory.


         C:\WINDOWS>_
```

Figure 0.22 When *VSafe* is loaded at the DOS prompt prior to opening Windows, this screen reports its status.

Table 0.14 lists the optional switches that may be added to configure *VSafe* as desired. Each switch may be followed by a plus sign to enable that option or a minus sign to disable it. However, no switch is needed if the indicated default mode is acceptable. If more than one switch is added to the command line, separate each switch by a space, not a comma. As noted earlier, the command line may be added to your AUTOEXEC.BAT file or entered later on, at the DOS prompt.

Once *VSafe* is loaded, you may reconfigure it by pressing Ctrl+V to display the VSafe Warning Options dialog box shown in Figure 0.23a. Press any of the listed number keys to toggle the corresponding option on/off. In the Figure, the four "Xs" in the ON column indicate the options enabled by default. Each option shown in the Figure is described in the *VSafe Options Configuration* section below.

VSafe Manager for Windows Configuration. If *VSafe* is loaded prior to opening Windows, then you should load *VSafe Manager for Windows* when Windows opens. Switch settings appended to the VSAFE command line, or changed via Ctrl+V, remain in effect during Windows operations. If you wish to reconfigure these settings while in Windows, double-click on the *Vsafe Manager* icon to open the applet window, then click on the Options button (not the Options *Menu*) to open the VSafe Options dialog box shown in Figure 0.23b. Configuration changes made from within Windows remain in effect after Windows closes. Each configuration option is described immediately below.

VSafe Options Configuration. The *VSafe* options shown in Figure 0.23(a and b) are listed here. A parenthetical reference (3, off) indicates the

TABLE 0.14 VSafe Configuration Switches

	Default Mode[†]			
Protect Against	**Enabled**	**Disabled**	**Other Switches[‡]**	
Hard disk low-level formatting	/1+		/A*x*	Define hotkey as Alt+*x*
Stay-resident programs		/2–		(default is Alt+V)
General write-protect		/3–	/C*x*	Define hotkey as Ctrl+*x*
Executable file check	/4+		/D	Disable checksum creation
Infected boot sector	/5+		/N	Monitor network drives
Hard disk boot sector, partition table write	/6+		/NE	Don't use expanded memory
Diskette boot section write		/7–	/NX	Don't use extended memory
Executable file modification		/8–	/U	Unload VSafe[§]

[†]Append switch only if indicated default mode is not acceptable.
[‡]Append as desired to further modify configuration.
[§]If VSafe is already unloaded, this switch is equivalent to typing VSAFE /? (switch list appears).

DOS number and the default status (for DOS *and* Windows) for each option. To change an option, press the indicated number key at the DOS prompt, or enable/disable the check box from within Windows.

Remember that *VSafe Manager* does not have its own Help Menu (yet). To review the options on line, open a DOS window and type HELP VSAFE on the command line.

Boot sector viruses (5, on). *VSafe* checks the boot sector for viruses.

Check Executable Files (4, on). The executable files whose extensions were listed in Table 0.7 are scanned for viruses or other changes. Note that the *Anti-Virus* applet's Check All Files option does not have a *VSafe* counterpart. Therefore, *VSafe* never scans document and other nonexecutable files for changes.

General Write Protect (3, off). If this option is enabled, *VSafe* warns you of every attempt to write to a hard disk or diskette. Use this option only if you're skilled at virus-snooping, since it interferes with every disk-write

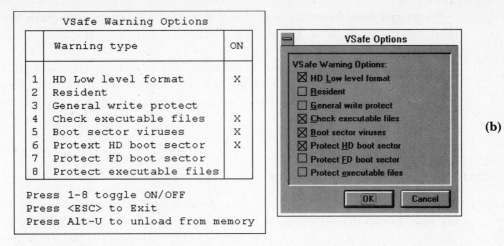

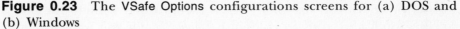

(a)

(b)

Figure 0.23 The VSafe Options configurations screens for (a) DOS and (b) Windows

operation. About the only time you might want to try it is before running an executable program that is not supposed to write to disk. If it tries, then you've caught it red-handed.

Routine operation from within Windows is just about impossible if this option is enabled: In most cases, Windows won't open at all. If you enable the option from within Windows, you'll get a warning message about not doing so, followed by various error messages if you don't take the hint.

HD Low Level Format **(1, on).** By default this option is enabled to warn you of any attempt to format your hard disk—generally considered a bad idea unless you really mean it. In that case, disable *VSafe* (or this option) before proceeding.

Protect Executable Files **(8, off).** This option warns of any attempt to write to an executable file, provided that file's extension is listed in Table 0.7.

Protect FD Boot Sector **(7, off).** *VSafe* warns of an attempt to write to the boot sector on a diskette.

Protect HD Boot Sector **(6, on).** *VSafe* warns of any attempt to write to the hard disk boot sector or partition table.

Resident **(2, off).** *VSafe* issues a warning if a program attempts to load and stay resident in memory. Since many legitimate programs do just that (PRINT.EXE, for example), such a warning is not a reliable virus indicator.

DoubleSpace Configuration

Under normal circumstances, your *DoubleSpace* hard disk should need no configuration, other than what is accomplished automatically when you first install it. However, you may want to change the letter of a host drive, or adjust the size of the CVF (compressed volume file) on a host drive. You'll also need to configure *DoubleSpace* if you want to compress a diskette, or access a diskette that was compressed during a previous session. To do either, refer to *Diskette Mounting* below.

To perform any of the *DoubleSpace* configuration procedures described here, the first step is to exit Windows. Then type DBLSPACE at the DOS prompt to display a screen that lists the status of the various *DoubleSpace* drives on the system, as summarized here for two compressed diskettes and a typical hard disk.

Drive	Description	Free Space (MB)	Free Space (MB)
A	Compressed floppy disk	1.00	1.00
B	Compressed floppy disk	2.18	2.18
C	Compressed hard drive	395.36	501.48

Note that only a few configuration procedures are described here. Refer to the *MS-DOS 6 User's Guide* index for information about other configuration details. In a break from tradition, *DoubleSpace* is listed there under the letter D. Perhaps M was too busy.

Review Compressed and Host Drive Characteristics. For more information about any compressed drive, highlight the drive on the screen, open the Drive Menu, and select the Info... option. The Compressed Drive Information screen will show information such as the following:

Compressed drive C is stored on uncompressed drive J in the file J:\DBLSPACE.000.

Space used:	106.13 MB
Compression ratio:	1.6 to 1

Space free:	395.36 MB
Est. compression ratio:	1.8 to 1
Total space:	501.48 MB

Use this option if necessary to verify the host drive letter for any compressed drive. To display a list of all drives and their *DoubleSpace* status, type DBLSPACE /LIST at the DOS prompt to display a list such as the following:

Drive	Type	Total Free	Total Size	CVF Filename
A	Compressed floppy disk	0.45 MB	0.86 MB	K:\DBLSPACE.000
B	Compressed floppy disk	0.99 MB	0.99 MB	I:\DBLSPACE.000
C	Compressed hard drive	394.84 MB	501.38 MB	J:\DBLSPACE.000
D	Local hard drive	56.23 MB	203.03 MB	
E	Local RAMDrive	0.41 MB	0.99 MB	
G	Available for DoubleSpace			
H	Available for DoubleSpace			
I	Floppy drive	0.60 MB	1.16 MB	
J	Local hard drive	12.70 MB	300.04 MB	
K	Floppy drive	0.82 MB	1.39 MB	
L	Available for DoubleSpace			

From this report it may be deduced that the 501-Mbyte compressed drive C is in fact a CVF on the 300-Mbyte drive J.

Review DoubleSpace Info from File Manager. For a graphical view of any compressed drive, open File Manager's Tools Menu and select the DoubleSpace Info... option. Refer to the *Tools Menu* section of Chapter 6, and to Figure 6.14, for more information.

Review Compression Ratios. To examine the compression ratios for each file in a directory, or for selected files, type DIR /C or DIR /CH at the DOS prompt to display a list such as that shown in Table 0.15. The difference, if any, between these two directory switches is explained here.

DIR /C Report. The compression ratio is based on an 8-Kbyte cluster. Thus, if a very small file (say, 28 bytes) occupies one such cluster, and is subsequently compressed into a *DoubleSpace* 512-byte allocation unit, the compression ratio is 8,192:512, or 16:1.

TABLE 0.15   Comparison of DIR /C and DIR /CH Reports

Filename	Extension	Size	DIR /C	DIR /CH [†]		
				300 MB	720 KB	1.44MB
ALPHABET	TXT	28	16.0:1.0	16.0:1.0	2.0:1.0	1.0:1.0
AUTOEXEC	BAT	265	16.0:1.0	16.0:1.0	2.0:1.0	1.0:1.0
COMMAND	COM	52925	1.4:1.0	1.4:1.0	1.3:1.0	1.3:1.0
CONFIG	SYS	486	16.0:1.0	16.0:1.0	2.0:1.0	1.0:1.0
EDIT	COM	413	16.0:1.0	16.0:1.0	2.0:1.0	1.0:1.0
MAIN	GRP	13644	3.6:1.0	3.6:1.0	3.1:1.0	3.0:1.0
MSD	EXE	158470	1.0:1.0	1.0:1.0	1.0:1.0	1.0:1.0
WIN	INI	15536	1.9:1.0	1.9:1.0	1.9:1.0	1.8:1.0
WIN	COM	53096	2.2:1.0	2.2:1.0	2.0:1.0	2.0:1.0
WINA20	386	9349	5.3:1.0	5.3:1.0	3.3:1.0	3.2:1.0
WINGDING	TTF	71052	1.3:1.0	1.3:1.0	1.3:1.0	1.3:1.0
Average compression ratio:			1.4:1.0	1.4:1.0	1.3:1.0	1.3:1.0
Allocation unit size, in bytes			8,192	8,192	1,024	512

[†]Files written to CVF on hard drive or diskette of indicated size.

DIR /CH Report. The compression ratio is based on the size of a cluster on the host drive. Table 0.16 shows how the reported compression ratio therefore varies from one host drive to another.

Compress/Mount a Diskette. A compressed hard disk partition or diskette is said to be *mounted* when its CVF has a valid drive letter and its host drive has another letter. The mounting ceremony for your compressed hard drive partition(s) occurs automatically as the system is booted on. However, if you subsequently insert a compressed diskette in a drive, that diskette is not automatically mounted, and consequently its CVF is not immediately accessible. To mount the diskette, type DBLSPACE at the DOS prompt, then open the Drive Menu and select the Mount... option. *DoubleSpace* will scan your system and mount any compressed drives that it finds. The mounted diskette's CVF is now accessible for conventional read/write operations.

Edit DoubleSpace Configuration File (DBLSPACE.INI). When the system is booted on, *DoubleSpace* reads the read-only/hidden/system DBLSPACE.INI file for its configuration instructions. The contents of the file are described below, in the *DoubleSpace Support Files* section. The best advice about this

TABLE 0.16   DoubleSpace Reports for Compressed Diskettes*

	720 KB		1.2 MB		1.44 MB	
Compressed Drive A or B						
Total disk space *(no hidden files)*	1,048,576	1,327,104	1,040,384	2,285,568	1,040,384	2,777,088
Available on disk	1,048,576	1,327,104	1,040,384	2,285,568	1,040,384	2,777,088
Allocation unit	8,192	8,192	8,192	8,192	8,192	8,192
Units on disk	128	162	127	279	127	339
Current drive size	1.00	1.27	0.99	2.18	0.99	2.65
Current free space	1.00	1.27	0.99	2.18	0.99	2.65
Estimated C.R.	2.1:1	2.0:1	2.1:1	2.0:1	2.1:1	2.0:1
Host Drive X[†]						
Total disk space	730,112	730,112	1,213,952	1,213,952	1,457,664	1,457,664
1 hidden file[‡]	589,824	730,112	589,824	1,213,952	589,824	1,457,664
Available on disk	140,288	0	624,128	0	867,840	0
Allocation unit	1,024	1,024	512	512	512	512
Units on disk	713	713	2,371	2,371	2,847	2,847
Current drive size	0.70	0.70	1.16	1.16	1.39	1.39
Current free space	0.13	0.00	0.60	0.00	0.83	0.00

[*] Information based on DIS CHKDSK and *DoubleSpace* Drive Menu's Change Size reports.

[†] Host drive letter varies according to system configuration. Reported values match those of conventional diskette of indicated size.

[‡] Under each diskette size, first column shows minimum possible CVF (always 589,824 bytes); second column shows maximum possible CVF.

little file is: Leave it alone. However, if you must make changes, such as those described below, first type the following line at the DOS prompt to clear the file attributes and make it available for editing.

```
attrib -s -h -r DBLSPACE.INI
```

Then edit the appropriate line in the file as desired. After doing so, reboot the system for the change to take effect. Strictly speaking you should reset the attributes after completing the edit. However, the next time you run DBLSPACE this task will be performed automatically.

Change File Fragmentation Index. Under normal circumstances there should be no reason to edit the File Fragmentation Index which appears in the DBLSPACE.INI file. However, if there is a problem mounting a fragmented CVF, you may be able to resolve it by increasing the number listed on the following line of the file:

MaxFileFragments=

Change Host Drive Letter. Since there's little reason for the user to refer to the host drive, there's little reason to worry about what its letter is, and perhaps even less reason to want to change it. However, if you get the urge, it's easy enough to do so. Exit Windows, log onto the host drive, and edit the following line as desired:

ActivateDrive=J,C0

This example shows that drive letter J is assigned to the host drive containing the CVF identified as drive C. Change the "J" as required, save the file, and reboot for the new drive letter to take effect.

Change Compressed Volume Size. When *DoubleSpace* compresses a hard drive or diskette for the first time, it allocates most of the space for the CVF, while leaving a smaller portion uncompressed. Uncompressed space is required on a boot partition for the startup files, and is also required for your Windows swap file, which is not happy if it gets compressed. You may also want additional uncompressed space for other files that should not be compressed.

You can reconfigure the size of an installed CVF if you need additional uncompressed space on the host drive. Or you can reconfigure if you *don't* need the uncompressed space that *DoubleSpace* has set aside and want to make some or all of it available to the CVF. In either case, highlight the drive, then open the Drive Menu and select the Change Size... option to display a Change Size screen such as that shown in Figure 0.24. In this example, the screen shows the characteristics of a previously compressed 720-Kbyte diskette in drive A, along with its host drive K. Refer to Table 0.16 for a summary of *DoubleSpace* compression applied to diskettes of different capacities. In these examples, the diskettes were newly formatted without transferring the system files, and no files have been written to any diskette yet. Two columns appear under each diskette type; the first shows the minimum possible CVF size, which is always 589,824 bytes. The second column shows the effect of allocating the entire diskette space to a CVF. If you plan to reconfigure something serious, like a hard drive partition, you may want to experiment with a test diskette before doing so.

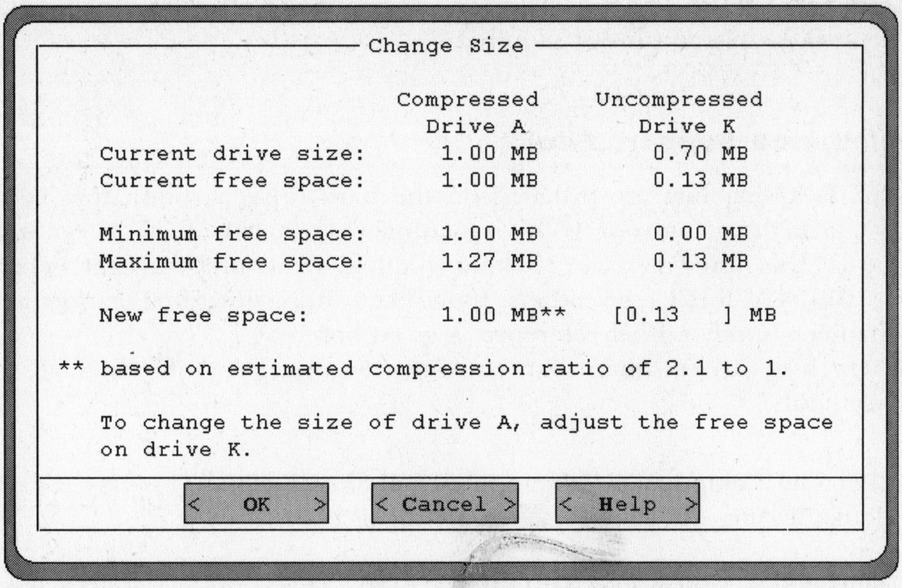

```
┌──────────────── Change Size ────────────────┐
│                                              │
│                  Compressed    Uncompressed  │
│                   Drive A        Drive K     │
│   Current drive size:   1.00 MB      0.70 MB │
│   Current free space:   1.00 MB      0.13 MB │
│                                              │
│   Minimum free space:   1.00 MB      0.00 MB │
│   Maximum free space:   1.27 MB      0.13 MB │
│                                              │
│   New free space:      1.00 MB**  [0.13   ] MB│
│                                              │
│ ** based on estimated compression ratio of 2.1 to 1. │
│                                              │
│   To change the size of drive A, adjust the free space │
│   on drive K.                                │
│                                              │
│   <   OK   >   < Cancel >   <  Help  >        │
└──────────────────────────────────────────────┘
```

Figure 0.24 The *DoubleSpace* Change Size Screen allows the user to change the size of the CVF.

DoubleSpace Size Limitations. As noted above, the minimum size for a compressed volume file is 589,824 bytes. Therefore, it is not possible to apply *DoubleSpace* compression to a 360-Kbyte diskette. Also note that as a CVF fills up with compressed files, it will not be possible to change its size below that required to accommodate the files already present in the volume.

SmartDrive Considerations. If your *SmartDrive* command line in AUTO-EXEC.BAT contains an explicit reference to a drive that is now compressed, you'll need to edit the line to refer to the host drive instead. For example, assuming drive H is the host for drive C, edit the line as shown here, then reboot the system.

```
Change:    C:\DOS\SMARTDRV.EXE C+
To:        C:\DOS\SMARTDRV.EXE H+
```

To verify that all's well, type SMARTDRV at the DOS prompt. The on-screen report should include the following information:

```
drive
C:*
*DoubleSpace drive cached via host drive.
```

If your SMARTDRV line does not contain the explicit reference described here, then this edit is not required.

DoubleSpace Support Files

The following files are installed on the hard drive partition that becomes the host drive for your CVF containing your startup files. The attributes for all files listed here are: system, hidden, read-only. With the exception of DBLSPACE.INI, the others have been fully described earlier in the chapter, so only a brief reference is given here.

On host drives other than the one for drive C, only the CVF file is installed.

CVF: The Compressed Volume File (DBLSPACE.000). This is the large file containing the compressed contents of a drive.

DoubleSpace System File (DBLSPACE.BIN). This is the new DOS 6.0 system file, which supplements MSDOS.SYS and IO.SYS, both of which remain in service.

DoubleSpace Configuration File (DBLSPACE.INI). This file contains configuration data used during system bootup to configure the *DoubleSpace* drive or drives. Typical file contents are shown here.

DBLSPACE.INI Contents	Comments
MaxRemovableDrives=*x*	The number of additional *DoubleSpace* drives you can mount without rebooting.
FirstDrive=	The first drive letter available for *DoubleSpace* use.
LastDrive=	The last drive letter available for *DoubleSpace* use.
MaxFileFragments=	Index of permissible file fragmentation.
ActivateDrive=*X,Yn*	*X* host drive letter.
	Y compressed drive letter.
	n CVF number (= 0 if DBLSPACE.000, = 1 if DBLSPACE.001, etc.).
ActivateDrive=J,C0	*(sample line, specifying host drive J which contains CVF drive C, identified as DBLSPACE.000).*

> **NOTE:** An on-line Help Screen describes the DBLSPACE.INI file.
> Open the Help Menu, select the Index option and double-click on
> "Using the DBLSPACE.INI File." Note, however, that in the
> ActiveDrive= description, the *X* and *Y* definitions are inverted.

DOS 6.0 and Microsoft Tools Troubleshooting

If you experience any difficulty in rebooting immediately after upgrading to DOS 6.0, and an error message is not seen, then there is probably
a problem that can be traced to one or more lines in your CONFIG.SYS
or AUTOEXEC.BAT files. Fortunately, DOS 6.0 adds a handy troubleshooting tool to help isolate the problem. Refer to the *DOS 6.0 Startup
File Configuration* section above for further details. Use the appropriate
techniques described there to isolate any component that you suspect
is causing trouble. Once you identify the line, or lines, that prevent successful system operation, you can take the appropriate action to remedy
the problem(s).

DOS 6.0 Troubleshooting

This section reviews a few troubleshooting procedures that may come in
handy if a DOS-related problem shows up after upgrading to DOS 6.0.

Startup File Troubleshooting. Sooner or later—sooner, if the system won't
start immediately after upgrading to DOS 6.0—you may need to reconfigure
your CONFIG.SYS and/or AUTOEXEC.BAT files. Once DOS 6.0 is installed,
use one of the following procedures to selectively disable one or more
lines in these startup files as you reboot the system. By doing so, you can
observe the effect on the system as each line is executed, and/or temporarily disable any line that is a potential source of trouble. Once you've
isolated a trouble source, take the appropriate action to resolve the problem.

Command Line Bypass **(F8).** When you reboot, watch the screen for a
Starting MS-DOS... message. As soon as it appears, press function key F8
once to display the following message:

    MS-DOS will prompt you to confirm each CONFIG.SYS command.
    DOS=HIGH,UMB [Y,N]?

The startup procedure will pause until you type "Y" or "N" to determine if
the DOS= line should be executed. Then the next line in your CONFIG.SYS

appears and you are again prompted for a decision. The routine continues until every line in CONFIG.SYS has been examined. The final question is:

Process AUTOEXEC.BAT [Y,N]?

The entire file is bypassed if you type "N." Otherwise, it is executed in its entirety.

Selective Command Line Bypass **(device?=).** To confine the selective bypass option to only certain lines in your CONFIG.SYS file, rewrite each such line as shown here:

Change command line from: device=C:\DOS\ . . .*(whatever)*
To: device?=C:\DOS\ . . .*(same as before)*

Note the insertion of a question mark immediately before the equal sign. Next time you reboot, there's no need to press function key F8: normal line-by-line program execution occurs until the line with the question mark. Then execution pauses as described in the previous section above.

You can insert the question mark in any line that you may want to bypass. Or as an alternative, insert it in the line immediately below. Doing so gives you time to examine messages placed on the screen when the previous command is executed.

Startup File Bypass **(F5).** To carry out the command-line bypass procedure, press function key F5 when the Starting MS-DOS... message appears. This displays the following line on screen:

MS-DOS is bypassing your CONFIG.SYS and AUTOEXEC.BAT files.

Note that this option completely bypasses both startup files. Therefore, no devices, TSRs, etc. are loaded, and environment variables are set to their defaults. In addition, the DOS prompt will display the current drive and directory—something it may not do if your regular configuration specifies some other command-line prompt.

Startup Bypass Considerations. In analyzing your overall system configuration, don't overlook the possible effect of one command line on another. As an obvious example, if you bypass the EMM386.EXE line, all devices normally loaded into upper memory blocks will load into conventional memory instead.

Memory-Management Troubleshooting. If the system locks up after the EMM386.EXE line, or displays any memory-related error messages, refer to the *DOS 6.0 Memory Maker (MEMMAKER.EXE)* section of Chapter 13 for assistance in resolving the problem. Refer to other troubleshooting sections of that chapter, or to its *Error Messages* section, for related help as required.

AUTOEXEC.BAT File Troubleshooting. If nothing obvious turns up during the initial run through CONFIG.SYS, type "N" to the final (Process AUTOEXEC.BAT) prompt to bypass the AUTOEXEC.BAT file. If the system starts properly, then the problem originates somewhere within that file, and there are several ways to isolate the culprit.

Apply a little Napoleonic justice by assuming a suspicious command line is guilty until proven innocent. Edit the file to disable any such lines by inserting "rem" (less the quotes) at the head of the line, then type AUTOEXEC at the DOS prompt. If all goes well, then you are an astute judge of character and the disabled line is indeed guilty.

If you disabled more than one line and now need to determine which of them causes the problem, try typing the most suspicious one as a command line at the DOS prompt. If nothing bad happens, try another one until you're able to identify the problem source.

However, if you really have no idea where the AUTOEXEC problem originates, it's time to apply binary logic: Disable half the lines and reboot. If the problem is gone, reenable half the lines you just disabled and try again. Or if the problem is not gone, reenable all the disabled lines, then disable half the other lines. Keep at it until you find the culprit.

Additional DOS 6.0 Startup Troubleshooting. If all else fails, review Chapter 8 in the DOS 6.0 *User's Guide* for additional troubleshooting assistance. Or if you want something in English, try *DOS 6.0 Power Tools,* which, by absolutely no coincidence whatever, is also published by Random House.

Anti-Virus and VSafe Troubleshooting

In addition to problems that occur while using anti-virus software, other problems may show up much later on, and it might not be immediately apparent that the anti-virus software is a factor. For example, the following operational quirks have been discovered (the hard way) during routine Windows operations after using virus detection.

1. Type VSAFE /3+ at the DOS prompt, then open Windows. In enhanced mode, a *Corrupt Swap-File Warning* message appears. Press the "N" key to continue. In either mode, a *Serious Disk Error* message appears. The

message repeats if any key is pressed. In standard mode, the hour-glass is seen and only the "r" key repeats the message. Press Ctrl+ Alt+Del twice to recover. (A message may not be seen between the two sequences.) In standard mode, a cold reboot may be required.

2. Open Windows and open the *Clock* applet. Then open the *Anti-Virus* applet and scan any drive for viruses. When the Statistics screen appears, click on the OK button. Leave the Anti-Virus dialog box on screen and close the *Clock* applet. System will lock up for 10 or more seconds. (Try to move a group or applet window and watch for the appearance of the hourglass.) When system operation returns, try to reopen *Clock*. The *An error has occurred in your application* message appears, followed by a *General Protection Fault* message. The *Clock* applet will not open, but a second attempt to open will sometimes succeed.

In repeated tests on several systems, all the above-cited messages have fortunately proven to be erroneous. They're also easy to avoid—just don't repeat the sequence that caused the problem in the first place. In the cases given above, that too is easy since neither one is really necessary. However, still other unlikely combinations may be encountered (again, the hard way) which don't immediately point to the source of the problem. Therefore, if any unexplainable quirk shows up during routine operations, think back to the last time you used some of the virus-detection software. If it was during the current session, you may want to close and re-open Windows before doing anything really serious.

Selecting the Continue Option Repeats Error Message. In some cases, *VSafe* keeps repeating its warning message even though you've clicked on the Continue button. You may have to click it several times before *VSafe* wakes up and permits the write operation to proceed. If the operation is attempting a diskette write, an erroneous *write protect error* message may appear. If *VSafe* is particularly stubborn, you may have to disable it in order to continue.

File Copy Operation Locks System. During a copy operation, if the source drive spins continuously and you must do a cold reboot to recover, the file that was being copied may be infected with a virus. The *VSafe* utility should warn you of the virus, but there may be a conflict with another virus utility. For example, if your AUTOEXEC.BAT file has the following line in it (or similar), the symptoms described here will occur:

```
SET CPAV=C:\WINDOWS\CPAV.INI
```

The line refers to Central Point Software's full-scale *Anti-Virus for Windows,* and it seems to prevent *VSafe* from functioning properly. If you have a similar AUTOEXEC.BAT line, temporarily disable it. Or, disable *VSafe* (type VSAFE /u) and retry the copy operation. If it succeeds, then the copied file is probably infected. Erase the suspect copy, resolve the conflict, and retry the copy operation. If necessary, do a clean boot and run the *Anti-Virus* utility to check the source file.

Errors Seemingly Unrelated to Virus Watching. If you run up against any unpredictable system behavior after using *Anti-Virus,* exit Windows (Ctrl+Alt+Del, if you must) and, if *VSafe* is loaded, unload it (type VSAFE /u at the DOS prompt). Then reopen Windows and retry the problematic operation. If it succeeds, then the problem was probably caused by the virus-detection software.

Volume Label Garbled in Drives Window. If the *Anti-Virus* applet Drives: window shows a garbled volume label next to a drive, that drive may actually lack a label, or the label may have spaces in it. If this minor cosmetic buglet bugs you, give the drive a new label and/or replace each space with an underscore character.

VSafe Message Buttons Are Missing. If a VSafe Warning message appears as Windows opens, the buttons that are supposed to appear in the message box may be missing. The problem is sometimes caused by a VSAFE switch (/3+, for example) that should be disabled prior to opening Windows.

Press the "B" (boot) key to reboot, disable VSAFE (if it's enabled: type VSAFE /u), and reopen Windows. If all goes well, troubleshoot the VSAFE line in your AUTOEXEC.BAT file to determine which switch causes the problem. If you want to continue using that switch for DOS operations, then write a batch file such as shown here to open Windows. The file disables the problem switch(es) before opening Windows, then restores the switch settings when you exit Windows.

Batch File	Comments
VSAFE /u	*Unload* VSafe, *thereby disabling its switch settings.*
VSAFE	*Reload, if you want* VSafe *(less switches) for Windows operations.*
WIN	*Open Windows.*
VSAFE /u	*Unload* VSafe *(if used with Windows).*
VSAFE /(switches)	*Reload* VSafe *with switches used for DOS operations.*

Backup Troubleshooting

With the exception of the few symptoms described here, most *Backup* problems are accompanied by an error message, as described in the *Backup Error Messages* section later in the chapter.

Backup Compatibility Test Does Not Begin. If you click on the Compatibility Test... button and, after a few message screens, you wind up back at the same spot again, the Backup applet is not yet configured for your system's diskette drives. Click on the Auto Floppy Configure button, remove all diskettes from your drives, and click on the OK button. The Drive A: and Drive B: boxes should now accurately list your drive configurations, and the Compatibility Test can be executed.

Backup Compatibility Test Fails. If the system locks up during the compatibility test, or at the end of it, you may have to reboot to recover. The next time you open *Backup* you'll find a message that the test failed. If so, try editing the following line in your CONFIG.SYS file, as shown here:

```
device=C:\DOS\EMM386.EXE (switches, parameters as before) D=32
```

The D=32 increases the DMA buffers from its default of 16 Kbytes. The maximum value is 256.

Catalog Menu Options Are All Disabled. These options are only enabled if the Compare or Restore are selected. If all the options are grayed, it's probably because Backup or Configure have been selected.

Start-Backup Button Disabled. The most likely problem is that the file listed in the Setup File: box is DEFAULT.SET, which does not specify the files to be backed up. Either select another Setup File or click on the Select Files... button to select the files you wish to back up.

Undelete Troubleshooting

This section describes a few problems that are not accompanied by an error message. If an error message *is* seen, then refer to that error message for assistance.

Archived File Protection Problem. If the Delete Sentry's Do not save archived files option (Figure 0.19a) seems to be working in reverse, it is. Check the box *if you do* want to save archived files. Refer to this option in the *Delete Sentry* section for further details, and for a workaround.

Delete Sentry Mode Is Not Enabled. If the Delete Tracker mode is enabled, and you switch to the Delete Sentry mode, the new mode may not be enabled. To force the change to Delete Sentry mode, click on that radio button, then click on the D̲rives... button at the bottom of the Configure Delete Sentry dialog box (Figure 0.19a), even if you do not need to change the selected drives. Then click on the OK buttons to return to the *Undelete* window.

Erroneous Report of File Condition or Protection Method. The reported condition of a deleted file is most reliable if the report states *Destroyed, Poor,* or *Perfect.* In other cases, the report may be a bit misleading. For example, if an attempt is made to copy a file into a space that is too small, both DOS and File Manager will display the appropriate error message, indicating the copy was not made. Yet the *Undelete* window may report a deleted file in the desired destination, and in *Excellent* condition. The file—such as it is—can be undeleted, but of course it won't be usable. If the Delete Tracker mode was enabled, but a Delete Tracker Control File not yet written, *Undelete* may write such a file and immediately erase it, leaving a PCTRACKR.DEL file in the root directory. Although this file too can be undeleted, the information in it is invalid and may only cause further confusion. As a final example, you may find a short deleted file—say, a few hundred bytes or so—in which some clusters "may have been overwritten."

In cases such as these, it's best to proceed with caution. In most cases, you'll probably recognize the error for what it is. However, it's quite possible to discover a "deleted" file several days after the fact; that is, several days after you've forgotten about that failed copy attempt. So, if an undeleted file doesn't work properly, there's probably a good reason for it. Now all you need to do is figure out what it is.

Exclude Files List Is Lost. If the E̲xclude: box in the Configure Delete Sentry dialog box is empty (shows "-*." only), the All files radio button was enabled during a previous session. If you want to restore the default list of excluded files, refer to *File Exclusion List* in the *Undelete Configuration* section above.

DoubleSpace Troubleshooting

Only a few *DoubleSpace* problems are discussed here. For more assistance, review section 7 of the README.TXT file in the DOS 6.0 directory or consult the separately available *MS-DOS Technical Reference.*

Startup Files Are Not Executed at System Boot. If your system boots with date and time prompts, and your CONFIG.SYS and AUTOEXEC.BAT files are ignored, there is probably a problem with either the DBLSPACE.INI or DBLSPACE.BIN file. At the DOS prompt, type DIR /a to see if one or both are missing, then take the appropriate action as described here. If both are missing, follow both procedures in the sequence listed here.

DBLSPACE.INI file Corrupted or Missing. If a DBLSPACE.INI file is listed, type TYPE DBLSPACE.INI and make sure the following line is present and that the specified letter for drive *x* (i.e., the host drive) is valid.

    ActivateDrive=*x*,C0

If the file is missing, create a new one containing a valid ActiveDrive=*x*,C0 only. (The other lines will be recreated automatically the next time you run DBLSpace, so you needn't worry about them now.) Refer to the *DoubleSpace Configuration* section above for more details about the DBLSPACE.INI file.

DBLSPACE.BIN Corrupted or Missing. If DBLSPACE.INI is in good order and the bootup problem persists, then DBLSPACE.BIN is the most likely suspect. If it's missing, then of course you know what the problem is. If it's present, then either it, or one of the other system files, is causing the problem. In any case, reboot from a valid DOS 6.0 diskette and make sure drive C is now available. If it is, then log onto the host drive and type SYS *x:* (where *x* is the host drive letter) to transfer a fresh set of system files to that drive.

Trouble Mounting a Compressed Volume File. If a compressed volume file is badly fragmented and subsequently unmounted, there may be a problem remounting it. If an *Unrecognized Error #109* message is seen, try increasing the File Fragmentation Index, as described above in the *Edit DoubleSpace Configuration File* section. If that doesn't do it, then more drastic measures are needed.

Since the CVF can't be mounted, it needs to be defragmented prior to mounting. To do so, first clear its attributes by typing the following line at the DOS prompt:

    attrib -s -h -r *X:*DBLSPACE.000

where *X* is the letter of the drive containing the CVF. Now run the DOS defragmentation utility (type DEFRAG *X:* at the DOS prompt). After you're finished, reset the attributes and reboot.

Diskette Mounting Problem. If you try the above procedure on a compressed diskette and the Defrag utility complains that it needs at least one free cluster in order to work, the entire diskette space was previously allocated to the CVF. As a result, the Defrag utility can't do its work. However, all is not yet lost. Copy the DBLSPACE.000 file to the C:\TEMP directory or to a RAM drive and defragment it from there. When you're done, copy it back to its original location, reset the attributes and try to mount it. If your luck holds, it will work.

> **NOTE:** The DOS Defrag utility is not further discussed here. If you need general operating assistance, refer to the *MS-DOS 6 User's Guide.*

Error Messages

The error messages listed here are grouped into the following sections:

DOS 6.0 Setup	Backup	Undelete
Anti-Virus and VSafe	DoubleSpace	

Refer to the appropriate section for details about any error message that shows up. With luck, it will be listed here.

DOS 6.0 Setup Error Messages

This section reviews a few of the error messages that may be encountered during the DOS 6.0 Setup procedure. In addition to the messages listed here, others may cite incompatible hard disks, device drivers, partitions, etc. In this case, refer to the DOS *User's Guide* for assistance.

If an unexpected (is there any other kind?) error message shows up during the Setup procedure, and that message is not covered here or in the DOS *User's Guide,* it is probably a function of some device or TSR loaded via your startup files. Depending on the severity of the problem, you may be able to select an option to continue the Setup. Otherwise, you may have to abort the Setup and run the Uninstall diskette to restore the previous version of DOS. Once things are back to normal, reboot with a very clean CONFIG.SYS and AUTOEXEC.BAT file, then run Setup again from the top.

Error. This is not the correct disk. Press ENTER to continue. If this message keeps repeating when you insert an Uninstall diskette in drive A, try using an unformatted diskette, or any other diskette that can be spared. If this doesn't work, refer to *Setup repeatedly prompts you for the Uninstall disk* in the DOS 6.0 *User's Guide* for assistance in creating a Startup disk.

The root directory of your hard disk contains some of your original DOS files. You must remove these files before you can continue installing MS-DOS on your hard disk. The DOS 6.0 Setup procedure gets upset if it finds certain DOS files in the root directory on your hard disk (FORMAT.COM and GWBASIC.EXE, for example). These files shouldn't really be there in the first place, so you may want to move them into your existing DOS directory, then delete them from the root directory. If you need assistance identifying the specific files that need to be removed, refer to this error message in the DOS 6.0 *User's Guide*.

There is not enough free space on drive C to install MS-DOS. You cannot install MS-DOS unless your computer has at least 4,200,000 bytes of free space on drive C. Although a full installation of DOS 6.0 itself needs only ("only"?) about 3 Mbytes, the additional space is needed during the installation. Exit Setup, type CHKDSK at the DOS prompt, and note the xxxxxx bytes available on disk line. Then do what needs to be done to free the additional space that is needed.

You must have 431K of conventional memory free to install MS-DOS 6. If you see this one, edit your present CONFIG.SYS and/or AUTOEXEC.BAT file to disable TSRs and nonessential devices occupying conventional memory. Once DOS 6.0 is installed, edit the startup files again to re-enable the same devices.

Your computer does not have enough available space to install the selected programs. In this case, there is enough disk space to install DOS 6.0 itself, but not enough to install the complement of Microsoft Tools that you specified. Follow the on-screen instructions to delete some or all of these options, or exit Setup to free up additional space.

Your computer uses a disk-compression program.... If any message begins with this phrase, the Setup procedure has detected a third-party disk-compression system. In this case Setup will not create an Uninstall diskette, nor will it be possible to restore your previous version of DOS. Although you may not want to restore your previous version after DOS 6.0 is safely up and running, you certainly will want to if the Setup procedure sinks in midstream. Therefore, make doubly sure you have backed up your hard disk before continuing with the DOS 6.0 Setup.

If the message also goes on about not enough free disk space, refer to the *not enough free space* message above for additional assistance.

Your computer uses SuperStor disk compression. You need to run SuperStor's ADD2SWP program prior to running Setup. Locate the SuperStor distribution diskette that contains ADD2SWP.EXE, insert it into drive A, and type A:ADD2SWP C: at the DOS prompt.

Anti-Virus Messages

In addition to the messages reviewed here, still others may show up due to interactions between Anti-Virus and other applets. As a typical example, if the Clock applet is open and the Anti-Virus <u>D</u>etect or <u>C</u>lean option is selected, a subsequent attempt to close the Clock applet may display various Clock-related error messages, and system operation may be suspended for several seconds. Once the Clock does close, it won't open again until Windows is closed and reopened. As another possibility, erroneous print-related error messages may be seen if you attempt to print while the Anti-Virus applet remains open.

No attempt has been made here to catalog the error messages that may result from such strange interactions. About the only thing that can be suggested is that if the system goes weird after using Anti-Virus, exit Windows and reopen it before doing anything serious.

Cannot access this file. Please verify security privileges on the network drive. If the message makes sense, then do it. But if it doesn't, then Windows may be having a bit of trouble with the *VSafe* utility. If VSAFE /8+ was set prior to opening Windows, then this message may be seen if the *VSafe Manager for Windows* is not loaded, and a Windows applet or application tries to modify an executable file. To verify the problem, open the *VSafe Manager* applet, then repeat the action that caused the message to appear. If you see a *Microsoft Anti-Virus Warning*, then that's what the real problem is.

Closing this application may not allow MS-DOS TSRs to function properly in Windows. If you have loaded the *VSafe Manager for Windows*, this message is seen if you try to close it. You may want to minimize it instead.

Drive was not logged. Or, in English, there is no diskette in the drive you are trying to read. Insert a diskette and try again.

EMM386: Unable to start Enhanced Mode Windows due to invalid path specification for EMM386. If the message appears when you open Windows after working with the Anti-Virus utility, type VSAFE /u, then try to reopen Windows. If this works, then the CHKLIST.MS file in the DOS directory is probably corrupt. Exit Windows, type VSAFE again, erase the CHKLIST.MS file (a new one will be created automatically) and reopen Windows.

Microsoft Anti-Virus Warning: Program is trying to write to Hard Disk. If you see this one prior to opening Windows, then take the appropriate action. If the message appears within Windows, then the odds are that Windows is just doing its thing, and the *VSafe Manager* has one of the nondefault options checked. If possible, open the *VSafe Manager* applet, click on the <u>O</u>ptions button, and clear the check marks next to <u>G</u>eneral write protect and/or Protect <u>e</u>xecutable files. Or, exit Windows and make sure these options are cleared on the VSAFE command line before reopening Windows.

Permanent Swap File is corrupt (additional information here). Do you want to delete the corrupt swap file? Well, it's possible the swap file really is corrupt, in which case refer to this message in Chapter 13 for assistance. But if the message appears shortly after installing *VSafe,* there's more likely a problem with its command-line switches. Answer "no" to this message prompt, and standby for a *Serious Disk Error* message, after which you may have to do a three-finger salute to escape. If your AUTOEXEC.BAT File contains VSAFE with optional switches appended to its command line, type VSAFE /U at the DOS prompt to clear those switches, then VSAFE again (this time with *no* switches). Reopen Windows, and if the *Swap File is corrupt* message reappears, then it probably really is corrupt. Otherwise, the problem is one of those switches on the VSAFE command line.

Serious Disk Error: A serious disk error has occurred while writing to drive *x*. Continue will retry this operation. Press any key to continue. This message may show up if you open Windows after enabling the *VSafe* utility's General Write Protect option (VSAFE /3+). *VSafe* detects Windows' attempt to write to disk, but gets a little confused over what to do about it. You *should* have the option to continue, but may get this message instead. If so, you'll probably have to force a reboot to continue. Before reopening Windows, make sure the /3+ switch (or any other suspicious switch) is *not* enabled.

The message will also show up if you try to exit Windows after enabling the General Write Protect option from within Windows. Pressing any key won't do a thing either—other than repeating the message over and over again. You'll have to press Ctrl+Alt+Del (a few times, in fact) to recover from this one.

Virus List File: MSAVIRUS.LST not found. The cited file holds the information displayed in the Virus List dialog box shown earlier in Figure 0.11. If this message appears when you select the Scan Menu's Virus List option, expand a fresh copy from the DOS 6.0 distribution diskettes into the DOS directory on your hard disk.

VSafe Manager Warning: It is not recommended to use General write protect in Windows. This message should win some kind of award for best programming understatement. You'll see it if you check the General write protect box in the VSafe Options dialog box (see Figure 0.23), then click on the OK button. Since just about anything you do in Windows causes a hard-disk write, *VSafe* will get very busy warning you over and over again. If you ignore the warning and leave this option enabled, then the next time you try to do just about anything, *VSafe* will display a *trying to write to hard disk* message. If you click on the Cancel button that appears in the message box, you'll probably be rewarded with a *Serious Disk Error* message, while clicking on the OK button may lock the system. In either case you'll have to reboot and remember not to enable this option again.

Vsafe program is not loaded. You must load Vsafe before starting Windows. If the VSafe Manager utility (MWAVTSR.EXE) automatically loads as Windows opens, this error message indicates that VSAFE.COM was not loaded prior to starting Windows. Click on the OK button to continue. If you want to use the utility, exit Windows, type VSAFE at the DOS prompt, then reopen Windows.

VSafe Warning: File *filename.ext* was changed. Do you wish to continue? If you know the change to the cited file is valid, select Continue (press C key) or Update (U key) to register the change. Otherwise, select Stop and take the necessary corrective action.

VSafe Warning: File WIN.COM was changed. Do you wish to continue? If you see this message, don't panic (yet). If you changed screen resolutions recently, that would account for it. If so, select Update (U key) and continue.

VSafe Warning: Other TSRs loaded—cannot unload VSafe. Press S to stop unloading. The message means that other TSRs are loaded *above VSafe*. Type mem /d at the DOS prompt to see what's in conventional memory immediately after *VSafe*. If you see a WIN entry, you're trying to unload *VSafe* from within a DOS window. If you really want to get rid of it, exit Windows first.

VSafe Warning: Program is trying to write to Hard [or Floppy] disk. Do you wish to continue? If you started *VSafe* with the /3+ switch, the utility watches for any attempt to write to the hard disk and flashes this warning if such an attempt is made. The message box should display three buttons (Stop, Continue, Boot). Press the first letter of the desired button text to take that action. If the buttons do not appear, then type the appropriate letter anyway, and hope for the best. Refer to the *Serious disk error* message above if necessary.

Backup Error Messages

If an opening error message appears, and you know the message is incorrect, you can either spend the time necessary to repeat the configuration or test, or edit the MWBACKUP.INI file to prevent the message from repeating itself. Refer to the *Backup Configuration Record* section for further details.

Backup has not been configured. Do you want to automatically configure it now? This message appears the first time you open the Backup applet. Click on the Yes button and follow the instructions in the *Backup Configuration* section of this chapter.

Compatibility test for floppy disks failed on this system. Press F1 for more information. Actually, press F1, then click on the Search button to look up "compatibility test." Or don't bother, since the Help (?) Screen just says that the test should complete successfully, and if it doesn't you should follow the directions on the screen (presumably, not the directions that just told you to press F1).

If the message appears while the Compatibility Test is running, try repeating the test, or running it on a different diskette drive. If the system locks up during the test and the message appears the next time you open *Backup*, refer to *Compatibility Test Fails* in the *Backup Troubleshooting* section for assistance.

Compatibility test for floppy disks has not been performed on this system. Reliable backups cannot be guaranteed until the compatibility test is completed successfully. Despite the warning, you can begin backing up by clicking on the OK button, which is the only choice anyway. Better yet, at the next screen click on the Compatibility Test... button and refer to the *Backup Configuration* section above for assistance.

Compression header for the catalog is corrupt. Use rebuild to reconstruct the catalog. This message may appear if you use the Catalog Menu's Retrieve... option to recover the catalog appended to the backup file. If it does, try the Rebuild option, which should work if the damage is not extensive.

Invalid volume information block detected. The component cannot be used. The "component" referred to is the diskette file from which you are trying to restore files. Before assuming the worst, make sure it's really part of the backup set, since this message also appears if an invalid diskette is in the drive. If the diskette is indeed the right one, then the message is correct and the file is defective.

MS-DOS Path has not been specified. Please specify the desired MS-DOS path and restart backup. The Backup To: box probably shows "MS-DOS Path" but no path is listed immediately below. Either type in the path to the backup medium, or click on the larger of the two down-arrows and select a diskette path instead.

You have inserted a *xxx* Kb diskette. The backup settings require a *yyy* Kb diskette. Please replace the diskette (during Compatibility Test). If the message is valid, then do as it says. Otherwise exit the test, click on the Auto Floppy Configure button, and verify that the diskette capacity and size reported in the Drive A: and Drive B: boxes are accurate. Then retry the Compatibility Test.

Undelete Error Messages

The *Undelete* utility doesn't really have many error messages associated with it. However, here are two of them that may show up.

Cannot unload. UNDELETE is not the last resident program. Others must be unloaded first. If you must unload it anyway, type MEM /d at the DOS prompt to see who needs to be unloaded first. Once you unload *Undelete*, reload whatever you had to unload to get to it.

No deleted files found. There are two possibilities. The first is that there really are no deleted files in the selected directory. The second is that you've selected the File Menu's Fi<u>n</u>d Deleted File... option. Unfortunately, this option is not yet implemented, so the erroneous error message appears even if there are deleted files that match your search criteria.

DoubleSpace Error Messages

Most *DoubleSpace* error messages are reasonably self-explanatory and require no explanation here. As a typical example, if you enter an invalid value when trying to change the size or compression ratio of a CVF, the message will say as much and probably give the range of acceptable values that may be entered. However, there are a handful of messages that may or may not be comprehensible. See the following for typical examples.

Unrecognized Error #109 (when trying to mount a compressed volume file). It's not the most informative error message you'll ever see, but it probably means the CVF is badly fragmented. You can't select the DEFRAG option on the *DoubleSpace* Tools Menu, since the fragmented drive must be mounted before you can run the defragmenter. But you can't mount it until it's defragmented. To break the loop, refer to *Trouble Mounting a Compressed Volume File* in the *DoubleSpace Troubleshooting* section above.

Volume in drive C is HOST_FOR_C. It's not a conventional error message, but if this information appears as the first line in a drive C directory listing, the drive contains an unmounted CVF (compressed volume file). In most cases you can recover by pressing the Ctrl+Alr+Del keys; as the system files reload during the reboot, drive C is mounted. If this doesn't work, the DBLSPACE.BIN file on your hard disk is probably corrupted or missing. Reboot with a valid DOS 6.0 boot diskette in drive A. After doing so, drive C should be back in business. If it is, then log onto drive A and type SYS *X*: at the DOS prompt to transfer fresh copies of the system files to host drive *X*. (Substitute the letter of your own host drive for *X* or this won't work at all.)

You are running the MS-DOS Shell. To run DoubleSpace, you must first quit the MS-DOS Shell. Either that, or you're trying to run *DoubleSpace* from within a DOS Window. Exit the window, close Windows, and rerun *DoubleSpace* at the DOS prompt.

You cannot access any DoubleSpace compressed drives because DBLSPACE.BIN is not loaded. (DBLSPACE.BIN is the portion of MS-DOS that provides access to DoubleSpace compressed drives.) This message is embedded in the DBLSPACE.SYS file, which is loaded from your CONFIG.SYS file. Therefore, if DBLSPACE.BIN is not loaded, you shouldn't see this message because your CONFIG.SYS file remains hidden away in the CVF. Since it is thus unread, how can an unloaded DBLSPACE.SYS be smart enough to rise out of the compressed DOS directory in the CVF and tip you off?

All this could happen under the following unique conditions: Your CONFIG.SYS and DOS directory are *not* in a compressed volume file, the former tries to load the DBLSPACE.SYS from the latter, and the DBL-SPACE.BIN file is indeed not loaded. If all these conditions are satisfied, either you know what's going on already, or your CONFIG.SYS file has a DBLSPACE line that needs to be deleted.

You must specify the host drive for a DoubleSpace Drive (seen during system boot). This message appears if the SmartDrive command line in your AUTOEXEC.BAT file tries to cache a CVF. Refer to *SmartDrive Considerations* in the *DoubleSpace Configuration* section for assistance in resolving the problem.

Windows Setup Procedures

This chapter covers the installation of Windows on an IBM-compatible personal computer. Unless otherwise noted, the procedures described here, and in the other chapters, apply to both Windows version 3.1 and Windows-for-Workgroups.

The first section introduces a few of the terms that will be encountered later in the chapter, reviews system requirements, and offers a bit of presetup information that may be helpful to first-time Windows users. Much of the information presented in the included tables may be ignored for the moment, but will be helpful later on should it become necessary to review or change your basic Windows configuration.

The Presetup and Setup sections cover the procedures for getting ready to install Windows, and for actually doing it—either for the first time or as an upgrade to a previous version. This is followed by a Postsetup Review and a Postsetup Modifications section which describes the installation of various additional components once Windows itself is successfully installed. The next section covers troubleshooting all the little things that might go wrong during any installation. With luck, you won't need it, but it's there just in case. The chapter concludes with a look at the error messages which may show up during any Windows Setup procedure.

Once Windows is successfully installed, refer to the Startup chapter (Chapter 2) for suggestions on resolving problems that may come up as you begin your first few Windows sessions. The chapter covers only those problems that appear as Windows begins operation. After that, if you need configuration and troubleshooting assistance for a specific Windows item, refer to the appropriate chapter for assistance.

Definitions

To begin, a few important terms are given brief definitions. Readers who are already familiar with PC jargon may safely skip ahead without fear of missing anything interesting.

Applications and Applets

Windows, or any of the major programs designed to run under its guidance, are commonly referred to as *applications*. Thus, Excel, Word-for-Windows, Ami Pro, and their competitors are all applications. Within Windows itself are a variety of less-ambitious applications, such as Card File, Paintbrush, Write, and others. Current usage generally refers to these as *applets*.

Distribution Diskettes

These are the diskettes included in your Windows 3.1 package or with any other software that you may be using in conjunction with Windows. The Windows distribution diskettes contain several hundred separate files, but only those required for your specific configuration will be transferred to your hard disk.

Expand Utility

Almost all the files on your Windows distribution diskettes are stored in a compressed format. As the files are transferred to your hard disk, each one is automatically expanded to its full operational size. If you later upgrade your hardware system, you'll probably need to transfer additional files from the distribution diskettes to your hard disk. If so, it is important to remember *not* to use the DOS copy command. Instead, use the Expand utility included with Windows 3.1. Complete details are found in the *Expand* section of Chapter 4.

Microprocessors

In the discussion that follows, a 286 system refers only to a personal computer which uses the Intel 80286 microprocessor. By contrast a 386, or 386 enhanced, system refers to any computer using any version of Intel's 80386 or 486 microprocessors, or their equivalents.

Operating Modes

Windows 3.1 may be operated in two of the three modes described here. In each definition, the parenthetical expression shows the optional switch(es) that force Windows to open in the indicated mode, if that mode is not the default for the system, and if the system is capable of running in that mode.

Real Mode (WIN /r). Effective with Windows 3.1, this operating mode has been discontinued and, with one exception, is not described here. If Windows 3.0 is currently installed on your system, you may want to open it in the real mode to remove the permanent swap file (if any) prior to upgrading to version 3.1.

Standard Mode (WIN /s or WIN /2). This is the default mode for 286 systems, and for 386 systems with less than 2 Mbytes of memory. Expanded memory can be accessed by non-Windows applications, provided the memory is physically present on an expanded-memory adapter. Only one non-Windows application at a time can be active, and that application runs in the foreground on the full screen. To run another non-Windows application, the current one is moved from the foreground to the background; that is, from conventional memory/full-screen operation, into extended memory. When an application is in the background, its program execution is suspended.

Windows applications run faster in standard mode than in enhanced mode, so it is preferred if you do not need to run multiple DOS windows.

Enhanced Mode (WIN /3). This is the default mode for 386 systems with 2 Mbytes or more memory. In enhanced mode, the available memory may be increased by assigning hard-disk space to a swap file. When Windows runs out of physical memory (RAM), the swap file space is used as virtual memory. Thus, it is possible to run multiple applications whose combined memory requirements exceed the installed RAM in the system. Virtual machines and virtual memory are described in Chapter 13.

Setup

Forget "installation." Windows, and many applications designed to run under it, includes a "Setup" program specifically designed to transfer the program from its distribution diskettes to your hard drive.

Hardware System Requirements

Table 1.1a lists the hardware system requirements for running Windows 3.1 in both standard and enhanced modes. Although most of the requirements should be taken seriously, the memory requirements are little more than general guidelines. Further information about some of the system requirements follows.

Microprocessor

Enhanced mode operation demands an Intel 80386, 486, or equivalent microprocessor, while standard mode operation requires an 80286 or better microprocessor. Occasionally there will be a problem with an early version of the 80386 chip, if Windows is started in the enhanced mode. Refer to the *Enhanced Mode Troubleshooting* section later in the chapter for further details.

BIOS

In some cases, your BIOS chips may need to be upgraded. Microsoft suggests that any BIOS dated 1987 or earlier should be regarded with suspicion. If you have any doubts about the BIOS in your system, continue reading. Otherwise you can skip the rest of this section.

BIOS Date. In most cases, the date of your installed BIOS may be seen as the computer is turned on. If necessary, turn your monitor on first so that it has a chance to warm up before the message appears. Or better yet, use the

TABLE 1.1a   Windows 3.1 System Requirements

System Component	Windows Operating Mode	
	Standard	Enhanced
MS-DOS	3.1	3.1
Microprocessor	80286	80386
BIOS	Refer to Table 1.1b	
Free conventional memory	256 KB	256 KB
Free extended memory		
minimum	192 KB	1024 KB[†]
recommended minimum	1408 KB	3456 KB
Free hard disk space[‡]		2 MB

[†] If slightly less, system may be forced into enhanced mode by typing WIN /3 (not recommended).

[‡] In addition to space occupied by Windows itself (see Table 1.1c).

undocumented diagnostics utility included with Windows 3.1. Refer to Appendix A to find the diskette containing the MSD.EXE file, place that diskette in drive A and type A:MSD at the DOS prompt. Next, click on the Computer box (or press the "p" key). The screen will display information about your system, including BIOS data such as that seen in this typical example:

```
Computer Name:      Dell
BIOS Manufacturer:  Phoenix
BIOS Version:       80486 ROM BIOS PLUS version 1.00 A07
BIOS Date:          04/08/92
```

If the BIOS date indicates a potential problem, contact your computer or BIOS manufacturer to see if an updated BIOS set is available. There are also a few post-1987 BIOS sets that are known to cause problems with Windows 3.1. Refer to Table 1.1b for a summary of those problems known to exist at this time.

TABLE 1.1b   BIOS/Windows 3.1 Compatibility Problems

Manufacturer	Date, Model, BIOS	Comments
ALR		Microchannel BIOS incompatible with Seagate hard disks.
AMI	1987	System reboots when diskette drive is accessed via File Manager.
	1989	Intermittent errors, system lockups.
	1991	Serial port (mouse, modem) problems.
AST	Premium 286	System, keyboard, network lockups, general protection faults.
Award	Prior to 3.05	Diskette drive read errors.
Chips & Tech.		
PEAK/DM	1.10	General Protection faults. Requires BIOS version 1.30 or later.
DTK	Prior to rev. 35	No IDE drive support in enhanced mode.
	Revision 35	Enhanced mode inoperative.
	Revision 36	Must disable CMOS Setup utilities.
Phoenix	Prior to 1988	Contact computer manufacturer for specific information.
Quadtel		Requires BIOS version 3.05.*xx* or later.
Tandon		Keyboard failures indicate need for BIOS upgrade.
	386sx Laptop	Requires Tandon BIOS.
Toshiba	T3100/20	Requires BIOS version 4.2 or later.
	TS100a	Requires BIOS version 1.70 or later.
Zenith	386/16	Requires BIOS version 2.6E or later.
	TurboSport 386	Requires BIOS version 2.4D or later.

Memory

As for conventional memory, the critical quantity is the amount free just before you start Windows. Microsoft documentation does not always agree on how much is needed, and reality does not always agree with any of Microsoft's figures. Much depends on your particular system's hardware configuration, and the specific device drivers that you will be using. The various published specifications might best be regarded as little more than an indication of what you might expect on the off chance your system matches that of the person who wrote the specification. Perhaps the best advice is: Make sure you have a full 640 Kbytes of conventional RAM installed, and use the DOS memory management utilities (or someone else's, of course) to keep as much of it free as possible.

Hard-Disk Space Requirements

The amount of hard-disk space required by Windows version 3.1 depends on how many of its features you want to install. If you have very little space available, you can squeeze a minimal configuration into about 6 Mbytes on a 286 or 386 system. For a full configuration, you'll need about 9 Mbytes on a 286 system and 10 Mbytes on a 386 system. To any of these figures, printer support adds about 150 Kbytes for an old IBM Proprinter, about 512–780 Kbytes for a laser printer, and some in-between amount for most other printers. Furthermore, Windows would like to have at least 2 Mbytes of free space available (more is better).

To install a complete set of the 461+ files on the Windows distribution diskettes requires some 16 Mbytes of hard-disk real estate. However, for all but network administrators, doing so is unnecessary, since the complete set includes drivers for every printer and video system supported by Windows 3.1, along with screen fonts for such systems as VGA, SVGA, and 8514/a. Unless you have a *very* fancy system, you won't need all those files on your hard disk.

For future reference, Appendix A lists the name, size, and distribution-diskette location for each file, along with a one-line description of its function.

Configuration Overview

Table 1.1c summarizes the hard-disk space requirements for the minimum and full system configurations which are briefly described below. If you have more than the minimum required, but not quite enough for a full-configuration installation, you can elect to omit various components during the Setup procedure.

TABLE 1.1c **Windows 3.1 Hard Disk Space Requirements***

| System | 286 Configuration | | 386 Configuration | |
Installation Type	Full	Minimum	Full	Minimum
Single User				
2.*x* upgrade†				
3.0 upgrade‡	5.5	5.0	5.5	5.0
New	9.0	6.144	10.0	6.144
Network				
2.*x* upgrade†				
3.0 upgrade‡	0.3	—	0.3	—
New	0.3		0.3	—
Network Administrator				
All	16.0	—	16.0	—

* Requirements given in Mbytes (1Mbyte = 1,048,576 bytes).
† Cannot be directly upgraded. Delete and set up version 3.1 as new installation.
‡ Indicates additional space required for version 3.1 update.

NOTE: If you are upgrading from Windows 3.0, and decide to omit various components that you know you'll never use, make sure to read the *Upgrade from Version 3.0* section below before starting Setup. If a version 3.0 component is *not* upgraded during Setup, the old component will remain in your new configuration, which is probably not what you want.

Minimum Configuration

If you decide to do a minimum-configuration installation, your Windows desktop will contain only three group windows (Main, Accessories, and Startup). The applets and help screens available within these windows are listed in Table 1.2.

The minimum configuration installs the complete set of 14 TrueType fonts included with Windows 3.1. If space is really at a premium, you can erase them from your Windows\System directory after Setup is finished. Look for two sets of 14 files each, with extensions of FOT and TTF. Refer to Chapter 11 for further details about TrueType fonts.

TABLE 1.2   Windows 3.1 Group Windows and Applets*

Group Window Applet Name	Minimum Config.		Full Config.	
	Applet	Help	Applet	Help
Accessories	✓	•	✓	•
Calculator	—	—	✓	✓
Calendar	—	—	✓	✓
Cardfile	—	—	✓	✓
Character Map†	—	—	✓	✓
Chat×	—	—	✓	✓
Clock	—	—	✓	•
Media Player†	—	—	✓	✓
Net Watcher×	—	—	✓	✓
Notepad	—	—	✓	✓
Object Packager†	—	—	✓	✓
Paintbrush	—	—	✓	✓
PIF Editor‡				
Recorder	—	—	✓	✓
Sound Recorder†	—	—	✓	✓
Terminal	—	—	✓	✓
WinMeter×	—	—	✓	✓
Write	✓	✓	✓	✓
Games	—	•	✓	•
Minesweeper†	—	—	✓	✓
Reversi§				
Solitaire	—	—	✓	✓
Main	✓	•	✓	•
Clipboard Viewer	✓	—	✓	✓
Control Panel	✓	✓	✓	✓
Desktop				
Patterns	✓	•	✓	•
Screen Saver	—	•	✓	•
Wallpaper	—	•	✓	•
DOS Prompt	✓	•	✓	•
File Manager	✓	—	✓	✓
Mail×	—	—	✓	✓
PIF Editor‡	✓	—	✓	✓
Print Manager	✓	—	✓	✓
Read Me	—	•	✓	•
Schedule+×	—	—	✓	✓
Windows Setup	✓	✓	✓	✓

TABLE 1.2 *(continued)*

Group Window Applet Name	Minimum Config.		Full Config.	
	Applet	**Help**	**Applet**	**Help**
Program Manager	✓	—	✓	✓
Startup[†] (empty)	✓	•	✓	•
Task Manager	✓	•	✓	•
Unassigned Applets[†]				
Dr. Watson	—	•	✓	•
System Editor	—	•	✓	•
Registration Editor	—	—	✓	✓
Windows Help	—	—	✓	✓

[†] New.
[‡] PIF Editor moved from Accessories (WIN 3.0) to Main Group Window (WIN 3.1).
[§] Windows 3.0 only.
[×] Windows-for-Workgroups applet.
✓ Indicated feature (group window, applet, help file) is installed.
— Indicated feature is not installed.
• Indicated help file does not exist.

Intermediate Configuration

The contents of the group windows will of course be a function of the components you decide to include during the Setup procedure. One or more additional group windows may also be opened, depending on the additional applications that you decide to install during Setup.

Full Configuration

In a full-configuration Setup, additional applets are inserted in the Main and Accessories Group Windows, and a Games Group Window is added to the Desktop. In addition, three unassigned applets are installed, along with such assorted features as screen savers, wallpaper bitmaps, and Read-me files. Refer to Table 1.2 for a complete list of these additions.

Augmented Configuration

Near the conclusion of both the Express and Custom Setups, you will be asked if you want to install additional applications as part of the Setup procedure. If you decide to take advantage of this feature, Setup will search your hard disk for applications that it recognizes. If it finds any, it will add an Applications Group Window to your desktop, and insert an icon for each application that it finds.

Since the applications that Setup finds are obviously already in place on your hard disk, no additional space is required, other than a small amount to accommodate the additional group window and the icons within it.

You may want to consider *not* installing any additional applications during your first time out with the Setup utility, thus keeping your WIN.INI and SYS-TEM.INI files free (for the moment, that is) of all third-party amendments. Then, immediately after concluding Setup, run off a hard copy of both files for future reference, and/or make backup copies of the files. The advantage of doing this is that you now have a permanent record of what is *supposed* to be in your INI files. Many Windows and other third-party applications have the habit of adding their own lines to your INI files. If you remove such applications later on, the lines in your INI files remain in place, and eventually the files are cluttered with lots of useless information. Then, when it is time to do a little housekeeping, you'll be challenged to guess what each line really means and wish you had something to refer to.

A Presetup Overview

Anyone who would actually buy a book about configuring Windows doesn't need to be told that there may be a bit more to the product than meets the eye (to Windows, that is, certainly not to this book). In any case, you may want to spend a bit of time *thinking* about installing Windows before actually starting the Setup procedure. This section offers a few suggestions to help your Windows Setup go a bit smoother than it would otherwise.

Upgrade from Versions Predating Windows 3.0

After carefully reading all the documentation, one might get the idea that version 3.0 was Microsoft's very first commercial Windows product. Perhaps it was: It depends on how one defines "commercial." In any case, if you're currently using a version older than 3.0, the answer to the upgrade question is: Don't even think about it. The Windows 3.1 Setup procedure to be described in this chapter does a reasonably good (but not always perfect) job of upgrading a version 3.0 configuration, but there are too many compatibility problems in the way of upgrading from anything earlier. The best procedure is to simply make a fresh start.

Upgrade from Version 3.0

This section should be reviewed if you're thinking about installing Windows 3.1 as an upgrade over an existing 3.0 version. Otherwise, skip ahead to the next section, or read this section anyway to find out what you might have missed.

Although it's possible—in fact, it's quite easy—to upgrade from Windows version 3.0 to 3.1, there are a few things to think about before doing so. Consider the following worst-case scenario if you decide to take the upgrade path. Based on your previous experience with version 3.0, you know you may never use various accessories and a few Main Group Window applets. So you elect to do a Custom setup, and specify that certain items be omitted from the new Setup. Since we're dealing with a computer here, Setup does just what you ask: It omits certain items from the new Setup. But you didn't ask it to remove the version 3.0 items that you never used, did you? Of course not: Setup doesn't offer this option. As a result, your new Windows 3.1 contains everything you want, and a whole lot more. It also contains all the old version 3.0 applets that you wanted to omit.

To further examine 3.0-to-3.1 upgrade implications, Appendix B compares typical directory listings before and after a minimum-configuration upgrade from version 3.0 to 3.1. The Appendix also shows listings for a completely new 3.1 installation. This information is relegated to an Appendix so as not to get in the way of readers who simply want to get through Setup and on to more rewarding tasks. But it may be a convenient reference source later on, if and when it becomes necessary to figure out how a certain file wound up in one of your Windows directories. For the moment, though, consider this: A completely fresh minimum-configuration installation will place about 37 files in your Windows directory. If that installation is done instead as an upgrade over an existing version 3.0, there will be about 76 files in the same directory. The additional files are all those old applets that Setup left undisturbed during the upgrade.

Of course, a real-world installation won't show such a discrepancy, since few if any systems will be set up with a minimum configuration. The point here is to remember that if you don't upgrade to a full-configuration Windows 3.1, quite a few version 3.0 files will be left over in your Windows and System directories. You can dump all of them by erasing your old Windows 3.0 first, then installing a completely new Windows 3.1. The surgery is drastic, but it's clean.

In addition to potential driver problems, an upgrade may also retain information in your various INI files about other third-party software, and this may come back to haunt you later on. It may be days, weeks, or months before you get around to trying some unique combination of ingredients that will invoke a dusty old 3.0 component that won't be pleased about waking up in a 3.1 environment. At that time, it will be up to you to try to guess what the problem is. Although this book should help you figure out what's wrong and how to right it, you may spare yourself a little heartburn by doing the completely new installation now, then reinstalling your various Windows applications one by one after you've got Windows 3.1 tweaked into shape and uncluttered by ghosts of Windows past.

New Installation

This is the safest, most reliable way to get Windows 3.1 running on your computer. In many cases the time you "save" by upgrading over an existing version of 3.0 will be more than spent later on, trying to figure out what did and what didn't get upgraded.

Reinstallation of Version 3.1

If, after using Windows 3.1 for some time, you decide to run a complete new Setup procedure, you may want to retain soft font information that you've added to your WIN.INI file since you first began using Windows 3.1. If so, refer to the *Soft Font Recovery after Windows Reinstallation* section of Chapter 11 for complete details. Do this before starting the new Setup.

Multimedia Installation

If you run a first-time Setup from a CD-ROM disk supplied with a Multimedia upgrade kit, simply follow the general instructions found here for a new installation.

If you are upgrading an existing Windows 3.1 system to include multimedia, the Setup procedure will leave your existing configuration intact, while adding the necessary components for multimedia operation. Typically, you'll find a few extra applets in the Accessories Group Window, and a MIDI Mapper icon added to the Control Panel in the Main Group Windows.

Windows-for-Workgroups Installation

If you are setting up Windows-for-Workgroups as a new or upgrade installation, simply follow the normal setup procedures given in this chapter. A few minor variations are described at the appropriate points in the setup procedure. In addition to the regular Windows 3.1 applets, two more (Mail and Schedule+) will be found in the Main Group Window and three (Chat, WinMeter, Net Watcher) in the Accessories Group Window.

Once Windows-for-Workgroups is separately installed on each system in the workgroup and the necessary support hardware is installed, the contents of any drive may be shared by any computer in the workgroup. Although the additional features of Windows-for-Workgroups cannot be used on a computer that is not part of a workgroup, all the other Windows applets will function as they normally do.

Network Card Installation. In order to take full advantage of Windows-for-Workgroups, a network adapter card must be installed in each computer in the workgroup, and the adapters must of course be linked via the appropriate cable. Refer to the network adapter *User's Guide* for the necessary installation instructions.

Cable Types. The following information may be of some use to first-time installers of networked systems, but safely ignored by anyone who has already installed a working system.

Depending on the specific adapter card design, one of three cable types may be required to link the systems. Each is briefly described here. Many adapter cards have connectors for two of the three listed types—typically, a BNC connector and one of the others.

Cable Type	Description	Connectors
Thin Ethernet	Coaxial	BNC (requires terminator)
Thick Ethernet	Multiconductor	DIX (15-pin D connector)
TPE (Twisted-Pair Ethernet)	4-conductor	RJ-45 (telephone style)

BNC Cable and Terminator Considerations. Note that the coaxial system requires a terminator at either end of the cable; that is, at the adapter card in the first and last computer in the workgroup. The terminator is an additional BNC plug with an internal 50-ohm impedance and (usually) a separate grounding wire.

Connecting the cable/terminator combination, or simply two cables, to a network adapter card is simple in theory, but difficult—or at least awkward—in practice. You'll need to place a 2-to-1 BNC connector on each network card, then plug both the terminator and the cable (or the two cables) into that connector. Since most such connectors were designed by Edsel Murphy, the cables will get in the way of every other adapter card in the system if a conventional "T" style 2-to-1 connector is used. Other 2-to-1 connectors place their sockets on such close centers that two cables cannot possibly be connected if either has a protective rubber hood on it, as so many of them do. Therefore, you may want to review all these physical constraints (and have a long look at the back of each computer) before rushing out to buy the necessary components.

Dual-Version (3.0 and 3.1) Operation

If your hard-disk space is greater than your confidence in Windows 3.1, you can set up an all new version in its own directory and leave the old one intact. If so, you may want to prepare the batch file described in the *Dual-System Operation (SWAP.BAT)* section of Chapter 2 before installing Windows 3.1.

DOS 6.0 Considerations

If you plan to upgrade your operating system to DOS 6.0, run the Windows 3.1 Setup procedure first. With Windows installed, the DOS 6.0 Setup procedure will offer the following options for installing three new utilities (Anti-Virus protection, Backup, Undelete).
Install the following utilities:

1. Windows utilities in a new Microsoft Tools Group Window
2. DOS-equivalent utilities in the DOS 6.0 directory
3. Both sets
4. Neither set

If DOS 6.0 is installed before Windows, then only the DOS utilities are made available, and you'll have to separately install the Windows equivalents later if you decide you'd like to use them. If so, refer to the *Setup DOS 6.0 Applets* section later in this chapter for assistance.

Presetup Procedures

Assuming you're going to like Windows 3.1 enough to keep it around for a while, it's well worth the effort to take a little time *now* to get your hard disk in order. The following suggestions should go a long way in simplifying the installation, to say nothing of computer life in general. Experienced hackers can skip some or all of this, but readers with little previous experience are urged to follow as much of the following as possible.

The first few procedures may be skipped if Windows 3.0 is not presently installed on your system.

Remove SETUP.EXE from Windows Directory. During installation, Setup should copy a version of itself from distribution diskette 1 into your Windows directory. It *should,* but sometimes it doesn't. If an old SETUP.EXE is already in place, Setup may not overwrite it with the new one. This can cause trouble midway through the installation procedure, when Setup looks to the version it finds on the hard disk for further instructions.

Remove Windows 3.0 Permanent Swap File. If you have been using a permanent swap file with Windows 3.0, you can let the Setup procedure get rid of it. However, it would be best to do this yourself before running Setup, so that the space it occupies can be integrated with other free space when you de-fragment your disk surface (as described below). To do so, run Window 3.0 in its real mode (type WIN /r) and select the Run option on the Program Manager's File menu. Then type SWAPFILE and press the Enter key. Follow the on-screen instructions to delete the current swap file.

Uninstall Third-Party Drivers. It is important to make sure Windows finds and replaces all of its default 3.0 drivers with their 3.1 equivalents. This is a routine part of the normal Setup procedure: As Setup scans your present INI files, it finds, removes, and replaces each listed driver. However, Setup knows better than to meddle with things (that is, with devices) it does not understand. So, if you have a third-party driver that it doesn't recognize, Setup will a) leave it alone, and b) not install the appropriate 3.1 driver, even if one is available on the distribution diskettes. Therefore, it is quite possible that an inactive Windows 3.0 driver will be overlooked during the Setup procedure. This may cause a problem later on.

For example, if Bitstream's *Facelift* is installed, your WIN.INI file will contain several references to Bitstream's own printer driver, which will not be disturbed as Setup upgrades your installation. But, as a consequence, Windows does not find its own 3.0 printer driver, and doesn't replace it with the new 3.1 driver. This means that if you subsequently uninstall *Facelift,* Windows will once again use the old 3.0 driver. Therefore, TrueType fonts will not be available to your applications, since they are not supported by version 3.0 drivers.

To safeguard against this and other potential problems, uninstall any third-party drivers before starting the Setup upgrade procedure. The most likely candidates for future problems are your printer and video drivers, which may be temporarily replaced by their Windows 3.0 equivalents as described here.

Printer Drivers. If you have installed any third-party soft fonts (other than Hewlett-Packard), refer to the soft font documentation for instructions on how to disable third-party printer drivers that may have been included with the font software.

Video and Other Drivers. To make sure that Windows 3.0 drivers are in place, double-click on the Windows Setup icon from the Main Group Window, then select the Options menu. Review the settings displayed by the Change System Settings dialog box. If any third-party drivers are listed, make the appropriate changes back to the Windows default drivers.

Disable Windows 3.0. If you want to leave Windows 3.0 intact and install Windows 3.1 in its own WIN31 (or similar) directory, you can insure the older version's safety by renaming its WIN.COM as WIN30.COM. This will prevent Setup from finding it by chance and accidentally installing version 3.1 in the wrong location. It will also prevent you from running the old version inadvertently later on.

Delete Windows 3.0. If you have decided to do a completely new installation of Windows 3.1, as mentioned above, then perform the following operations now, as appropriate to your system.

Save Important Windows 3.0 Files. You may want to save copies of your old INI and GRP files for future reference. If so, place them in a BACKUPS directory so they won't get lost. In addition, save your existing soft font files (if you want them), and anything else that found its way into your version 3.0 Windows and System directories.

Erase Windows 3.0 Files. Once you have saved what you may need elsewhere, delete the contents of the WINDOWS and SYSTEM directories. If either directory contains subdirectories, these may be left intact, along with the two Windows directories themselves. Or you can delete both directory names and Setup will create a new set. Do this if you plan to install Windows in a directory with some name other than WINDOWS. Otherwise, Setup will simply find the now-vacant directories and move in without asking your permission.

Remove Backup and Temporary Files. First, get rid of all those old backup files that clutter your hard disk. You can find all of them by using the DOS

5.0 DIR command. At the DOS prompt in your drive C root directory, type the following command:

DIR *.BAK /s

The command displays all files with a BAK extension, and the "/s" switch instructs the DIR command to examine all directories and sub-directories. (See page 51 in the revised second edition of *DOS Power Tools* for a QuickBASIC program to quickly remove all such files.)

If you have a TEMP (or TMP) directory, it should—but may not—be empty. Have a look; if you see anything there, get rid of it. However, if there are files with a very recent date on them (like today, for example), make sure they're not important before dumping them.

Clean Up Your Root Directory. Ideally, your root directory should contain almost nothing except the names of various directories. However, things happen, and it's not unusual to find your root directory cluttered with an odd assortment of files that really belong elsewhere. If this describes your system, now's the time to do some reorganization work.

Revise your CONFIG.SYS and AUTOEXEC.BAT Files. The Windows Setup procedure will revise these files as needed, but it's not a bad idea to go into Setup with a so-called "plain-vanilla" configuration, since there are a number of drivers and TSRs (terminate-and-stay-resident) programs that may cause a system hangup or crash during Setup, or when running Windows later on.

Problem Applications. Tables 1.3a and 1.3b list programs that Windows knows it doesn't like, some of which are listed in the SETUP.INF file on distribution diskette 1. If Setup finds any of the files on this list in your CONFIG.SYS or AUTOEXEC.BAT, it will either remove them (see Table), or display a warning message such as the one seen here:

Setup has found the programs listed below on your system. When Setup or Windows runs with some versions of these programs, your system may fail. It is recommended that you quit Setup now and . . . (more, but you get the idea).

PYRO.EXE	In AUTOEXEC.BAT	Pyro! Screen-Saver
DESKTOP.EXE	In CONFIG.SYS	PC Tools Desktop TSR
PRINT.EXE	In memory	MS-DOS PRINT utility

The message may also be seen if a problem utility was loaded after booting by typing its name at the DOS prompt prior to starting Setup (see PRINT.EXE, above).

TABLE 1.3a **Incompatible Drivers, TSRs, and DOS Utilities***

Filename	Ext.	Description
386MAX[†]	COM	Qualitas Memory Manager
ALLEMM4[†]	SYS	All Charge 386
APPEND[§]	COM	MS-DOS Utility
ASPLOGIN[§]	EXE	ASP Integrity Toolkit
ASSIGN[•]	COM	MS-DOS utility
BOOT[†]	SYS	
CACHE[†]	EXE	Disk cache
CACHE[‡]	SYS	
CMEDIT[†]	COM	
DESKTOP[§]	EXE	PC Tools Deluxe TSR
DISKMON[§]	EXE	Norton disk monitoring TSR
DISKREET[†]	SYS	Norton Utility
DOSCUE[†]	COM	Command-line editor
DUBLDISK[§]	SYS	Double Disk data compression
EP[†]	EXE	Norton Desktop for Windows
FAST512[†]	SYS	Secretdisk II disk cache utility
FASTOPEN[†]	EXE	MS-DOS utility
FLASH[†]	EXE	Disk cache utility
GRAPHICS[§]	COM	MS-DOS utility
HPEMM386[‡]	SYS	
HPEMM486[‡]	SYS	
HPMM[†]	SYS	H-P Memory Manager
ICACHE[‡]	SYS	Disk cache utility
IBMCACHE[‡]	SYS	IBM disk cache utility
ILIM386[†]	SYS	Intel Exp. Mem. emulator
IEMM[†]	SYS	Memory manager
JOIN[§]	EXE	MS-DOS utility
KEYB[†]	COM	MS-DOS utility
LANSEL[§]	EXE	Lansight network utility
LE[§]	COM	Le Menu menuing package
LSALLOW[§]	EXE	Lansight network utility
MCACHE[§]	SYS	Mace disk cache utility
MAXIMIZE[§]	COM	Memory manager
MIRROR[†]	COM	MS-DOS utility
NCACHE[§]	EXE	Norton utility
NDOSEDIT[†]	COM	
NEWRES[§]	EXE	Newspace compression utility
NEWSPACE[§]	EXE	Newspace compression utility
PA[§]	EXE	Printer Assist

TABLE 1.3a *(continued)*

Filename	Ext.	Description
PCK[†]	EXE	
PSKSCRN[†]	EXE	
PCKEY[†]	COM	
PCKEY[†]	EXE	Multisoft keyboard enhancer
PC-CACHE[†]	COM	
PC-KWIK[†]	EXE	Disk cache utility
PCPANEL[§]	EXE	Lasertools prn. control panel
PCSXMAEM[†]	SYS	
PCSX2EMS[‡]	SYS	
PRINT[§]	EXE	MS-DOS print utility
PYRO[§]	EXE	Pyro! Screen Save
QCACHE[†]	EXE	Qualitas disk cache
RAMTYPE[‡]	SYS	AST RAMpage! utility
RM386[†]	SYS	Netroom memory manager
S-ICE[§]	EXE	SoftIce debugger
SK[§]	COM	Sidekick version 1.0
SK2[§]	EXE	Sidekick version 2.0
SKPLUS[§]	EXE	Sidekick Plus
SPEEDFXR[§]	COM	SpeedFXR
SUBST[§]	EXE	MS-DOS utility
SUPERPCK[†]	EXE	PC-Kwik disk cache utility
TSCSI[§]	SYS	Trantor T100 SCSI driver
VACCINE[§]	EXE	Vaccine anti-virus program
VDISK[‡]	SYS	IBM RAM disk
VSAFE[†]	COM	Central Point Anti-Virus
VSAFE[†]	SYS	Central Point Anti-Virus
VIRALERT[§]	SYS	Data Physician Plus TSR
VIREXPC[†]	COM	
XGAAIDOS[§]	SYS	8514 emulation driver
XMAEM[†]	SYS	
XMA2EMS[†]	SYS	

[*] Refer to SETUP.TXT file for additional information about each file listed here.

[†] Setup does not warn of presence of this file.

[‡] Listed in [compatibility] section of SETUP.INF file. If present, Setup removes these drivers from CONFIG.SYS file.

[§] Listed in [incompTSR1 (or 2)] section of SETUP.INF. If present, Setup offers warning message.

[*] Listed in [incompTSR2] section of SETUP.INF, but not included in SETUP.TXT file.

TABLE 1.3b   Incompatible Drivers, TSRs, and DOS Utilities*

Program Description	Program Description
Anarkey versions 4.00, 4.01	Norton Anti-Virus version 1.0
Artisoft KBFLOW TSR	PCED version 2.00
Autocon version 2.0e	PC-Kwik disk accelerator
Bootcon version 1.60	PC Tools Deluxe version 7.1
CED version 1.0e	QMAPS memory manager version 5.16
Cubit version 3.01	UMB PRO version 1.07
Hyperdisk disk cache utility	Virus Presention Plus version 5.0
LOCKIT version 3.3	Virusafe version 4.0
Logitech Mouse software versions 5.0, 6.0	

*Listed in SETUP.TXT file, but filename omitted or incomplete.

NOTE: Some of the files listed in Tables 1.3a and 1.3b present problems only during the Setup procedure. Once Setup has successfully concluded and Windows 3.1 is up and running, such files may be reinstated in your CONFIG.SYS or AUTOEXEC.BAT file. In case of doubt, observe the performance of Windows with, and without, the file in question. If there are no performance problems, just remember the name of the file in case you need to rerun Setup later on. If there are problems, contact the appropriate manufacturer to see if an upgraded version is available.

A companion SETUP.TXT file (also on distribution diskette 1) offers information about the files cited in SETUP.INF, and also includes information about many other programs that may cause problems during Setup. Table 1.3 lists all of these files—if you are using any of them, the best course of action is to quit Setup, remove the cited programs, reboot (if necessary), and rerun Setup.

Disk-Caching Software. If the message cites a disk-caching utility such as PC-Kwik's SUPERPCK.EXE, and you want to continue using that utility, you may continue running Setup without taking any action. However, at the conclusion of Setup, exit to DOS (do not reboot). Edit your AUTOEXEC.BAT file to remove the reference to Windows' SMARTDRV.EXE disk-caching utility, then reboot.

> **NOTE:** The Setup warning may be disabled by appending the "/c"
> switch to the Setup command, as described later on in the *Setup
> Switches* section. A complementary "/t" switch enables the feature,
> but is not required for routine operation, since it simply mirrors the
> just-described default condition.

DOS Screen-Savers. It's a good idea to disable any screen-saver applications that you may have running. Some are known to cause problems during Setup, while others are merely distracting if they go into action while Setup is running.

Other Problem Programs. There may be other programs that Windows doesn't know about (yet). So, to eliminate all shadow of a doubt, reboot with as clean a set of files as you can manage. But first, review your present files to see if they contain anything that you really don't need anymore. If they do contain needed material, edit as needed, then make file copies as say, XONFIG.SYS and XUTOEXEC.BAT, so that you'll have them on hand for future reference. Now re-edit the existing files to disable anything that may cause grief during Setup—just insert REM at the beginning of each line to be disabled. Later on, you can restore these lines one at a time, once you've got Windows up and running successfully.

Stacks=x, y *Line (where* x *= number of stacks,* y *= size of each stack, in bytes).* Note the values on this line in your CONFIG.SYS file. If the line is not present, then the default MS-DOS 5.0 values of 9, 128 are used. The Windows Setup procedure will probably change or add the line (if necessary) to read Stacks=9, 256. If you encounter a postsetup *Stack Overflow* error message, and your previous values were greater than those currently in place, you may want to restore the original values. So, it's a good idea to jot them down now, just in case you need them later.

Basic CONFIG.SYS and AUTOEXEC.BAT Files. In case of any doubts about what may or may not get in the way of Setup, try stripping your files down to the basic minimum listings shown in Table 1.4a. As an alternative to editing your present hard-disk boot files, you may prefer to put these plain-vanilla files on a system-formatted boot diskette in drive A, and use it for booting just before running Setup. Keep the diskette on hand for subsequent use should it become necessary to do any troubleshooting.

If you have trouble booting your system with the basic CONFIG.SYS file shown in Table 1.4a, you may need to append a /machine switch to the HIMEM.SYS line. Refer to the *Windows 3.1 HIMEM.SYS Extended Memory Manager* section of Chapter 13 for details about the use of this switch.

Tables 1.4b and 1.4c list various items that may need to remain in—or be deleted from—your basic startup files, depending on your system's specific configuration. Use both lists as guides for tailoring your own startup files. If your system contains items similar to those listed here, retain or delete them as appropriate.

Run CHKDSK/F. Once your hard disk is as clean as you can make it, run the DOS check-disk utility by typing the following line at the DOS prompt:

```
CHKDSK /f
```

The "/f" switch converts any lost chains into one or more files with a name of FILE*xxxx*.CHK, where *xxxx* = 0000, 0001, 0002, and so forth. If any such files are found, you can review, then erase them if they contain nothing worth saving.

TABLE 1.4a   Basic Startup Files*

Before Installing Windows 3.1	After Installing Windows 3.1
CONFIG.SYS	**CONFIG.SYS**
files=40	files=30
buffers=20	buffers=20 (=10, *if* SMARTDRV *is installed*)
	device=C:\WINDOWS\HIMEM.SYS†
	shell=C:\COMMAND.COM /e:1024 /p
(Third-party disk partitioner)	*(Third-party disk partitioner)*
(Third-party disk compression driver)	*(Third-party disk compression driver)*
(Other third-party device drivers)	*(Other third-party device drivers)*
AUTOEXEC.BAT	**AUTOEXEC.BAT**
path=C:\DOS	path=C:\WINDOWS;C:\DOS
prompt PG	prompt PG
	set TEMP=C:\TEMP

*Refer to Tables 1.4b and c for partial lists of other essential and nonessential items.
†Use device=C:\DOS\HIMEM.SYS with DOS 6.0.

TABLE 1.4b Essential Startup Files*

Hard Disk Drivers	Disk Partitioners	Disk Compression Utilities
AH1544.SYS	DMDRVR.BIB	DEVSWAP.COM
ASPI4DOS.SYS	EDVR.SYS	SSTOR.EXE
ATDOSXL.SYS	ENHDISK.SYS	SSWAP.COM
ILIM386.SYS	FIXT_DRV.SYS	STACKER.COM
NONSTD.SYS	HARDRIVE.SYS	
SCSIDSK.EXE	LDRIVE.SYS	
SCSIHA.SYS	SSTOR.SYS	
SKYDRVI.SYS		
SQY55.SYS		
SSTBIO.SYS		
SSTDRIVE.SYS		

* If any of these files are listed in your basic startup files, do not remove them.

TABLE 1.4c Nonessential Startup Files*

Command Lines	DOS Commands	Device Drivers	Miscellaneous
dos=HIGH, UMB	APPEND	CD-ROM	Data acquisition units
device=EMM386.EXE	GRAPHICS	Fax	Disk cache
install=SHARE.EXE	JOIN	Mouse (DOS)	Keyboard accelerator
install=FASTOPEN.EXE	MODE (*prtr. redir.*)	Network	Keyboard buffer
path=(*multiple lines*)	PRINT	RAM disk	Memory manager
	SUBST	Scanner	TSRs
			Virus checker

* If any of these command lines or files are listed in your basic startup files, remove them.

> **NOTE:** Do *not* use CHKDSK's "/f" switch when running CHKDSK from within Windows. If you do, it may find and "fix" some open Windows files that don't need fixing.

Back Up Your Hard Disk. Have you been backing up as often as you should? Whatever the answer, with your hard disk now in reasonably good order, this is a very good time to do a complete backup. With luck you'll never need it, but it may come in handy if you want to return your system to its pre-Windows condition, or if you decide not to skip the next step.

Reformat Your Hard Disk. No doubt you'll want to ignore this step. But if you have any lingering doubts about the general condition of your hard disk, *and* you've just finished a complete backup, you can do a reformat now with minimal disruption to your operations.

If you've divided your hard disk into two or more DOS partitions, you may want to rethink their relative sizes. If your present drive-C partition has gotten rather crowded (it happens), consider using the DOS FDISK utility to allocate more space to it.

Defragment Your Hard Disk. If you have not done a complete backup/ restore procedure, then use a good hard-disk defragmenter (Norton *Speed Disk,* for example) to place all your files into a contiguous area on your hard disk. Doing so will optimize your system's hard-disk space, both for use by Windows and for anything else that comes along in the future.

Running Setup

Survivors of the *Presetup Suggestions* and *Procedures* sections above are almost ready to begin. Before actually doing so, however, review the following sections at least once to get a general idea of what to expect. Although you can always go back later and undo any mistakes you make, you may be able to avoid at least some of them by understanding what will happen *after* you make any decisions.

This section describes the Setup procedure to follow when installing Windows 3.1 for the first time, or when upgrading from Windows 3.0 or an earlier version of 3.1. If Windows 3.1 is already up and running, and all you want to do is make a minor change (for example, from VGA to super-VGA), then refer to the *Making Postsetup Modifications* section later in this chapter.

The Setup Switches

For most routine operations, the Setup procedure begins as described in the *Begin Setup* section which follows. However, there are several switches that may be appended to the Setup command:

/a	Administrative Setup. Expand all files on all distribution diskettes into a Network directory and set all files as read-only. Use this switch to place the entire Windows system on a network server.
/b	Set monochrome display attributes.
/c	Disable the *Problem Applications* search described earlier.
/h:*filename*	Batch mode for automated Setup. *Filename* is a user-prepared system-settings file that contains the desired configuration settings. A model file (SETUP.SHH) on distribution diskette 1 may be used as a template to create your own settings file.
/i	Ignore Setup's hardware detection feature.
/n	Setup a shared copy from a network server previously installed using /a switch.
/o:*filespec*	Specify a custom replacement for SETUP.INF file.
/p	(undocumented) Construct a new group file to replace one that is damaged or missing. Refer to the *Setup /p Switch* section of Chapter 3 for further details.
/s:*path*	Specify a path to the Setup diskettes.
/t	Enable the *Problem Applications* search described earlier.

Begin Setup

If you have any difficulty running Setup, make a note of the problem and refer to the Setup Troubleshooting section later in this chapter for assistance.

To begin, log onto drive A, insert disk 1 in the drive, type **setup** and press the Enter key to display the first Welcome to Setup screen. Select one of the following options by pressing the appropriate key.

Press	**To Do the Following:**
F1	Learn more about Setup.
Enter key	Begin the Setup procedure.
F3	Return to the DOS prompt without installing Windows.

If you press function key F1, several information screens present a brief overview of the Setup procedure.

Setup Method. Assuming you press the Enter key, the *Windows Setup* screen offers two choices of setup methods:

Press	To Do the Following:
Enter key	Begin the Express Setup procedure, in which most decisions are made by the Setup utility itself.
C (or c)	Begin the Custom Setup procedure, which will ask you to specify the Windows components to be installed on your system.

Both Setup options are reviewed here. Once you have made your choice, note that each major section heading below includes a parenthetical reference to an "Express" and/or a "Custom" Setup. Even if you decide on an Express Setup, you may want to review the Custom sections to get an idea of what's going on.

Express Setup. Although Microsoft recommends using Express Setup, there are several reasons to consider using the Custom option instead, even if you are not that familiar with how these things work.

Hardware Compatibility. The Express Setup procedure may fail if certain hardware system components are not correctly recognized. However, the appropriate corrections may be made as part of a Custom Setup procedure. For further information on this subject, refer to the *Hardware Compatibility List* section later in this chapter. If you need to revise this list to take into account some component in your system, then you should select the Custom Setup option.

Permanent Swap File and 32-bit Disk Access. As another consideration, Express Setup does not install a permanent swap file, nor does it enable 32-bit disk access. You may add one or both of these options later on, but you may want to do it now (that is, during initial setup), before your hard disk gets fragmented again, thereby cutting down on the space available to the swap file. If you need more information on this subject, refer to the Swap File and 32-bit Disk Access sections of Chapter 13.

Printer Installation. The Express Setup allows you to install one printer only. Additional printers may be added later, of course, but if you already know you'll be using more than one printer, you can take care of this now by selecting the Custom option.

Windows Accessories. The Express Setup automatically installs thirteen Windows applets in the Accessories Group Window which appears on your Desktop. If you already know you don't want some of them, the Express option does not give you the opportunity to omit the applets you don't want.

> **NOTE:** If you install Windows from a CD-ROM disk supplied with a Multimedia system, a few additional accessory icons (Pro Mixer, Mixer, etc.) will also be available.

Windows Applications. The Express Setup finds every Windows application on your hard disk and includes them all in your Applications Group Window. At first glance, this may seem like a nice feature, but you may regret it later on. Many Windows applications add their own little sections to your WIN.INI and SYSTEM.INI files, which means that if you decide to delete them later on, you'll have to do a line-by-line check of your INI files to search out whatever won't be needed anymore. It would help to have a nice clean record of WIN.INI and SYSTEM.INI made *before* any application gets a chance to put its droppings in them. To do so, select the Custom Setup option, and temporarily exclude all applications until Setup is finished. After you make copies of your INI files for future reference, you can start adding the applications you need. The procedures for doing all this are described at the appropriate places in this chapter.

If you do decide on an Express Setup, the procedure quickly installs all the components included with Windows 3.1, and automatically modifies your AUTOEXEC.BAT and CONFIG.SYS files.

Custom Setup. Choose this option to tailor the Windows Setup to better meet your specific needs. The various steps in the Custom Setup procedure are each described in detail here.

Directory Selection (Express, Custom). Regardless of which option you choose, the Setup procedure will search your hard disk for an existing Windows directory, then for a copy of WIN.COM. If one does not exist in the Windows directory, then it extends the search to the rest of the hard disk. Based on what it finds, Setup will follow one of the courses described here. Review the appropriate section, then proceed to the *File Transfer* (Express) or *System Information Review* (Custom) section below.

New Installation. If neither a Windows directory nor a WIN.COM file is found, Setup assumes this is to be a completely new installation and displays the following message:

Setup is ready to set up Windows version 3.1 in the following directory, which it will create on your hard disk:

C:\WINDOWS

If you'd rather use some other directory, simply follow the on-screen instructions to change the path and/or directory name as required. Then press the Enter key to continue the installation.

New Installation in Existing Windows Directory. During an Express Setup, if Setup finds an empty Windows directory, it will assume this is where you want it to install itself; it will not ask you for instructions on where to do its work. In a Custom Setup, you will be given the option of specifying some other location, as described above.

Upgrade Installation. If a WIN.COM file is discovered, Setup offers the following advice:

Setup has found a previous version of Microsoft Windows on your hard disk in the path shown below. It is recommended that you upgrade this previous version to Windows version 3.1.

To upgrade, press ENTER.

If necessary, you can keep your older version of Windows and add Windows version 3.1 to your system. Press the BACKSPACE key to erase the path shown, then type a new path for version 3.1. When the correct path for Windows 3.1 is shown below, press ENTER.

C:\WINDOWS

NOTE: If you set up Windows version 3.1 in a new directory instead of upgrading, you will not maintain any of your desktop settings or any Program Manager groups and icons you set up. Also, you must make sure that only version 3.1 is listed in PATH in your **AUTOEXEC.BAT** file.

If you decide to follow Setup's recommendation to upgrade, the following message is displayed to give you a chance to reconsider:

You have told Setup to upgrade your previous version of Windows to Windows version 3.1. Please verify that this is what you want to do.

- To have Setup perform an upgrade (recommended), press ENTER.
- To keep your previous version of Windows and add Windows version 3.1 to your system, press ESC.

> **NOTE:** If keeping both versions, PATH in your AUTOEXEC.BAT file should only list version 3.1, to avoid running older Windows system files with 3.1. Also, any applications already set up for use with Windows must be set up again from version 3.1.

If you do decide to keep your previous version intact, press the Escape key to return to the previous screen. Then type in a new directory name to continue the Setup procedure.

Reinstallation after Incomplete or Aborted Setup. If you ran Setup previously, but pressed function key F3 before finishing, you probably have an incomplete set of Windows files in one or both of the Windows directories. Or Setup may have self-destructed because of some hardware or software problem it encountered. In either case, when you try to run Setup again you will see the following message:

Setup has detected a failed Microsoft Windows 3.1 installation in the C:\WINDOWS directory.
It is recommended that you try to recover this Microsoft Windows 3.1 installation now in order to retain previous settings.
To have Setup try to recover this Microsoft Windows 3.1 installation now, press ENTER.
To continue Setup without trying to recover this Microsoft Windows 3.1 installation, press N.

If earlier you elected to terminate Setup and now simply want to resume, just press the Enter key and Setup should pick up where it left off. However, if the previous Setup aborted due to some problem it encountered, then press the "N" key instead and try again. Refer to the *Setup Troubleshooting* section later in this chapter if you are not sure why the previous Setup failed.

System Information Review (Custom). Once you've made your choice of the Setup options described above, Setup examines your current hardware/ software system. If you're riding the Express, Setup simply uses this information to continue its work. Otherwise, a *System Information screen* displays its findings, as shown by the typical example in Figure 1.1a. On some network installations, the "Network:" line does not appear, and network setup takes place after printer setup as described below in the *Network Driver Installation* section.

The Hardware Compatibility List. Note that the screen refers to a Hardware Compatibility List. This is a separate enclosure bundled in your Windows package, which identifies computers and components compatible with Windows 3.1. A system or component not on the list will nevertheless be compatible, if it is fully compatible with a similar listed device. In case of doubt, contact the appropriate manufacturer for the latest word on the subject. If your specific hardware is not listed, make sure that each line on the System Information Screen shows the name of the device that is the closest possible match to your component.

To do this, use the up/down arrow keys to select any item, then press the Enter key to display a list of alternative choices. Highlight the appropriate item and press the Enter key again to insert that item into your list. When you do this, Setup consults the [machine] section of its SETUP.INF file to see if any system cookies are required.

```
Windows Setup
=============

    Setup has determined that your system includes the following hardware
    and software components. If your computer or network appears on the
    Hardware Compatibility List with an asterisk, press F1 for Help.

        Computer:         MS-DOS System
        Display:          VGA
        Mouse:            Microsoft, or IBM PS/2
        Keyboard:         Enhanced 101 or 102 key US and Non US keyboards
        Keyboard Layout:  US
        Language:         English (American)
        Network:          No Network Installed

        No Changes:       The above list matches my computer.

    If all the items in the list are correct, press ENTER to indicate
    "No Changes." If you want to change any item in the list, press the
    UP or DOWN ARROW key to move the highlight to the item you want to
    change. Then press ENTER to see alternatives for that item.


    ENTER=Continue  F1=Help  F3=Exit
```

Figure 1.1a The System Information Screen, as seen during initial setup.

```
Windows Setup

     If your computer or network appears on the Hardware Compatibility List
     with an asterisk next to it, press F1 before continuing.

     System Information
         Computer:          MS-DOS System
         Display:           VGA
         Mouse:             Microsoft, or IBM PS/2
         Keyboard:          Enhanced 101 or 102 key US and Non US keyboards
         Keyboard Layout:   US
         Language:          English (American)
         Codepage:          English (437)
         Network:           No Network Installed

     Complete Changes:  Accept the configuration shown above.

     To change a system setting, press the UP or DOWN ARROW key to
     move the highlight to the setting you want to change. Then press
     ENTER to see alternatives for that item. When you have finished
     changing your settings, select the "Complete Changes" option
     to quit Setup.

     ENTER=Continue  F1=Help  F3=Exit
```

Figure 1.1b The System Information Screen, as seen when run from the DOS prompt after Windows is installed.

TABLE 1.5   System Setup Options*

System Component[†] Manufacturer or Type	System Component[†] Manufacturer or Type
Computer [Machine]	**Computer [Machine]**
AST Premium 386/25 and 86/33 (CUPID)	MS-DOS System with APM[‡]
AT&T NSX 20: Safari Notebook	NCR: all 80386 and 80486 based machines
AT&T PC	NEC PowerMate SX Plus
Everex Step 386/25 (or Compatible)	NEC ProSpeed 386
Hewlett-Packard: all machines	Other
IBM PS/2 Model L40sx	Toshiba 1200XE
IBM PS/2 Model P70	Toshiba 1600
Intel 386SL Based System with APM[‡]	Toshiba 5200
MS-DOS System	Zenith: all 80386 based machines

TABLE 1.5 *(continued)*

System Component[†] Manufacturer or Type	System Component[†] Manufacturer or Type
Display [display]	**Display [display]**
8514/a	Video 7 1Mb 800 × 600, 256 colors
8514/a (Small fonts)	Video 7 1Mb, 1024 × 768, 256 colors (Lg. fnts)
Compaq Portable Plasma	Video 7 1Mb, 1024 × 768, 256 colors (Sm fnts)
EGA	Video 7 512K, 640 × 480, 256 colors
Hercules Monochrome	Video 7 512K, 720 × 512, 256 colors
Olivetti/AT&T Monochrome or PVC Display	VGA with monochrome display
Other	XGA (Small fonts)
QuadVGA, ATI VIP VGA, 82C441 VGAs	XGA (640 × 480, 16 colors)
Super VGA (800 × 600, 16 colors)	XGA (640 × 480, 256 colors)
TIGA (Large fonts)	XGA (Large fonts)
TIGA (Small fonts)	
VGA	
VGA (version 3.0)	
Mouse [pointing.device]	**Mouse [pointing.device]**
Genuis serial mouse on COM1	Mouse Systems serial mouse on COM2
Genius serial mouse on COM2	Mouse Systems serial or bus mouse
HP Mouse (HP-HIL)	No mouse or other pointing device
Logitech	Olivetti/AT&T Keyboard Mouse
Microsoft, or IBM PS/2	Other
Keyboard [keyboard.types]	**Keyboard [keyboard.types]**
All AT type, 84–86 keys	Olivetti 83 key
AT&T 301	Olivetti 86 key
AT&T 302	Olivetti M24 102 key
Enhanced 101, 102 key US & non-US	PC-XT 83 key
Hewlett-Packard Vectra (DIN)	PC/AT-type, 84 keys
Olivetti 101/102 A	Other

Layout [keyboard.tables]

Belgian	French-Canadian	Swedish
British	Icelandic	Swiss French
Canadian Multilingual	Italian	Swiss German
Danish	Latin American	US
Dutch	Norwegian	US-Dvorak
Finnish	Other	US-International
French	Spanish	Other

TABLE 1.5 *(continued)*

System Component[†] Manufacturer or Type	System Component[†] Manufacturer or Type	
Language [language]		
Danish	French Canadian	Portuguese
Dutch	German	Spanish
English (American)	Icelandic	Spanish (modern)
English (International)	Italian	Swedish
Finnish	Norwegian	Other
French		
Code Page [codepages]		
Canadian-French (863)	Icelandic (861)	Nordic (865)
English (437)	Multilingual (850)	Portuguese (860)
Network [network]	**Network [network]**	
3Com 3+Open v. 2.0 Basic	IBM PC LAN Program all v.	
3Com 3+Open v. 2.0 Enhanced	Microsoft LAN Manager v. 2.0 Basic	
3Com 3+Open v. 1.X	Microsoft LAN Manager v. 2.0 Enhanced	
3Com 3+Share	Microsoft LAN Manager v. 2.1 Basic	
Artisoft LANtastic v. 3.X	Microsoft LAN Manager v. 2.1 Enhanced	
Artisoft LANtastic v. 4.X	Microsoft LAN Manager v. 1.X	
Artisoft LANtastic v. below 3.0	Microsoft Network or 100% compatible	
Banyan Vines v. 4.1	No Network Installed	
Banyan Vines v. 4.0X	Novell NetWare shell v. 3.21 and above	
Banyan Vines v. below 4.0	Novell NetWare shell v. 3.26 and above	
DEC Pathworks v. 4.0	Novell NetWare shell v. below 3.01	
DEC Pathworks v. 4.1 or higher	Other	
DEC Pathworks v. below 4.0	TCS 10Net v. 5.0	
IBM OS/2 LAN Server v. 1.2 or 1.3	TCS 10Net v. 4.1X with DCA 1M card	
IBM OS/2 LAN Server v. 1.3 CSD 5015/5050	TCS 10Net v. 4.1X	
IBM OS/2 LAN Server v. 2.0	TCS 10Net versions 4.2 and above	
IBM OS/2 LAN Server v. below 1.2	TCS 10Net versions below 4.1	
IBM OS/2 LAN Server without /API option		

[*] Listed components may be selected via System Information List screen during Custom Setup.

[†] Name [in brackets] indicates section of SETUP.INF file containing listed information.

[‡] APM: Advanced Power Management.

The System Cookie. Cookie is a technical term used to describe any special-purpose device driver or other modification required to adapt Windows to suit your particular system requirements. If you don't believe this (who would?), you can look into the various cookie boxes [*name*_cookz] which follow the above-mentioned [machine] section.

Depending on the item you select, you may be prompted to insert a distribution diskette containing files required to support that component. However, in some cases the selected component requires nothing more than a revision to your SYSTEM.INI file; this is handled automatically. In any case, make sure your System Information List is accurate before continuing Setup. Otherwise, you'll lose your cookies.

Once you have made all the necessary changes, highlight the No Changes: (or, the Complete Changes:) line to accept the configuration and continue. For reference purposes, Table 1.5 lists the options that are available for each line listed in Figure 1.1.

The first time you run a new or upgrade Setup, it's not a bad idea to stick with a "plain-vanilla" configuration in order to install a complete set of Microsoft drivers in your Windows directories. By doing so, the drivers will be readily available later for use as a reference system, should you have doubts about the compatibility of some third-party driver.

> **NOTE:** Once Windows is installed, Setup may be rerun to revise the components list to take into account changes you make to your system configuration. In this case, Setup is run by exiting Windows, logging onto the Windows directory, and typing SETUP. Again, a *System Information screen* displays your present configuration. However, the screen is slightly revised, as shown in Figure 1.1b.

File Transfer (Express, Custom). At this point, Setup searches the distribution diskettes for the files required for your system configuration, and copies them to your hard disk. During the file-transfer operation, the screen displays the following message:

Please wait while Setup copies files to your hard disk. To exit Setup without installing Windows, press F3.

Setup is copying files...

xx%

| Copying : *filename.ext*

A moving horizontal bar offers a visual progress report. When Setup finishes with each distribution diskette, it prompts you to insert the next one in the drive. Immediately before displaying the user-name prompt (described below), you may notice a brief "Please wait while Setup loads Windows" message. This marks Setup's transition from DOS into Windows itself. If Setup fails at or after this point, refer to the *Windows-Mode Setup Failure* section below for assistance.

> **NOTE:** Most of the files on the distribution diskettes are stored in a compressed format, and each required file is automatically expanded before it is copied to your hard disk. Although the expansion/copy procedure requires no user intervention during a routine Setup, you may want to use it later on if troubleshooting suggests that a Windows file needs to be replaced with a fresh copy. For further details, refer to the *File Expansion* section of Chapter 4.

Add User's Name and Company (Express, Custom). Many software applications ask you to "personalize" the installation by inserting your name and company during Setup. (Quarterdeck's *QEMM386* wants to know where you live, too.) Microsoft apparently feels its customers are bright enough to figure out what all this really means, so it skips the euphemism and just prompts you to insert your name and your company's name. On some network and CD-ROM-based installations, only your name is requested. On others, you may be asked to supply network identification details.

On Express setups, file transfer continues without interruption (other than to change disks) until the *Printer Installation* dialog box is seen. All sections before the *Printer Installation* section below refer to Custom installations only. On an Express *Upgrade* Setup, your existing printer configuration will be updated automatically, and applications previously installed will be retained in the Applications Group Window. If you are doing an Express Upgrade Setup, skip ahead to the *Exit Windows Setup* section.

Component Selection (Custom). The next *Windows Setup* screen prompts you to specify which of the following items should be installed:

☒   Set Up Only <u>W</u>indows Components You Select

☒   Set Up <u>P</u>rinters

☒   Set Up <u>A</u>pplications Already on Hard Disk(s)

If you wish to set up all components in the Windows package, clear the first check box. This option is disabled during a network Setup, since all components are accessible via the network server. To install a printer or applications already on your hard disk, do *not* clear the other boxes. Depending on your response, one or more additional screens will be seen during the remainder of the Setup procedure.

As noted earlier, you may want to consider installing no applications during the initial Custom Setup, so that your INI files will contain only those lines necessary to run Windows itself. You can start adding applications later, after you've made backup reference copies of these files.

In Figure 1.2a, each of the listed component groups may be omitted from your installation by clearing the check box to the left of the Group name. Or, you may click on the appropriate Files... button to display a list of the individual files within that Group, as shown by the Accessories group in Figure 1.3. The available files in this and the other groups are listed in Table 1.6.

To determine the actual effect of adding/omitting files from the group, highlight one or more files in either box. Below each box, the cumulative size of the selected file(s) is displayed, along with the total space required to accommodate all the files listed in the Install these files box. Click on the appropriate button between the boxes to add/remove the highlighted files, then click on the OK button to return to the previous screen. Click on the Continue button to proceed with the Setup.

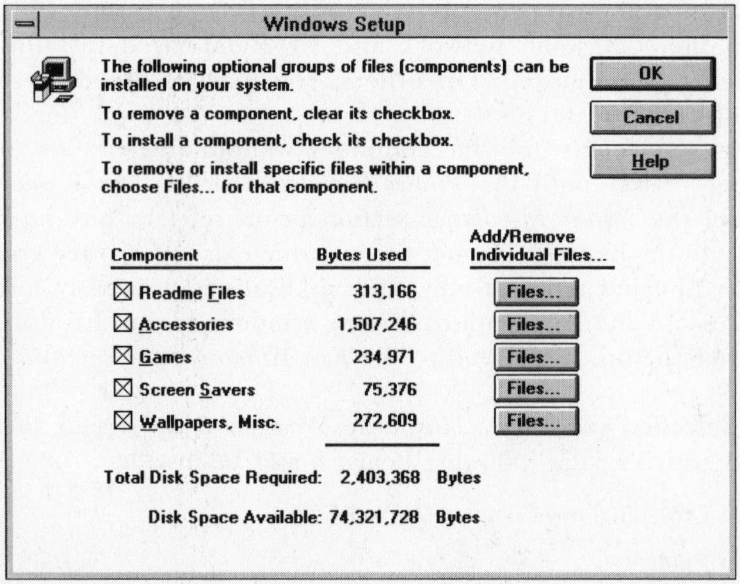

Figure 1.2a The Windows Setup dialog box, as seen during initial Setup.

NOTE: Figure 1.2b is described much later in the chapter, in the *Add/Remove Windows Components* section. The Figure is included here so that the two versions of this *Windows Setup* screen can be easily compared.

Windows Setup

The following optional groups of files (components) are installed on your system.

To remove a component, clear its check box.

To install a component, check its check box.

To remove or install specific files within a component, choose Files... for that component.

Component	Bytes Used	Add/Remove Individual Files...
☐ Readme Files	0	Files...
☐ Accessories	1,247,624	Files...
☐ Games	194,441	Files...
☒ Screen Savers	75,376	Files...
☒ Wallpapers, Misc.	272,609	Files...

Disk Space Currently Used by Components: 4,055,162

Disk Space Freed by Current Selection: 3,856,619

Total Available Disk Space: 414,367,744

[OK] [Cancel] [Help]

Figure 1.2b The Windows Setup dialog box, as seen when run from the Windows Setup applet in the Main Group Window.

Accessories

To install files, select files on the left, then choose Add.

To remove files, select files on the right, then choose Remove.

When finished selecting, choose OK.

Do **not** install these files:

```
Cardfile Help (25K)
Notepad (32K)
Notepad Help (14K)
Windows Tutorial (122K)
```

[Add ->] [Remove <-] [Add All ->]

Install these files on the hard disk:

```
File Expansion Utility (15K)
File Manager Help (76K)
Glossary Help (46K)
Help Utility Help (27K)
Media Player (33K)
Media Player Help (13K)
Object Packager (75K)
Object Packager Help (21K)
```

[OK] [Cancel] [Help]

1 file(s) selected: 13,894 Bytes   2 file(s) selected: 46,208 Bytes

Total Disk Space Required: 1,311,390 Bytes

Figure 1.3 The Accessories dialog box

TABLE 1.6 Custom Setup: Operational Component Files

Component Group Description	Memory Required Listed	Actual	Filename
Readme Files			
Application Compatibility Help	16K	15694	APPS.HLP
General Readme	98K	99584	README.WRI
Networks Readme	67K	68096	NETWORKS.WRI
Printers Readme	44K	44928	PRINTERS.WRI
System.ini Readme OS utility	53K	53760	SYSINI.WRI
Win.ini Readme	31K	31104	WININI.WRI
Accessories			
Calculator	43K	43072	CALC.EXE
Calculator Help	18K	18076	CALC.HLP
Calendar	59K	59824	CALENDAR.EXE
Calendar Help	21K	20656	CALENDAR.HLP
Cardfile	91K	93184	CARDFILE.EXE
Cardfile Help	25K	24810	CARDFILE.HLP
Character Map	22K	22016	CHARMAP.EXE
Character Map Help	11K	10797	CHARMAP.HLP
Clipboard Viewer Help	13K	13071	CLIPBRD.HLP
Clock	17K	16416	CLOCK.EXE
Dr. Watson System Utility[†]	27K	26864	DRWATSON.EXE
File Expansion Utility	15K	15285	EXPAND.EXE
File Manager Help	76K	76855	WINFILE.HLP
Glossary Help	46K	46570	GLOSSARY.HLP
Help Utility Help	27K	26960	WINHELP.HLP
Media Player	33K	33312	MPLAYER.EXE
Media Player Help	14K	12896	MPLAYER.HLP
Notepad	32K	32736	NOTEPAD.EXE
Notepad Help	14K	13894	NOTEPAD.HLP
Object Packager	75K	76480	PACKAGER.EXE
Object Packager Help	21K	21156	PACKAGER.HLP
Paintbrush	180K	183376	PBRUSH.EXE
Paintbrush Help	40K	40269	PBRUSH.HLP
PIF Editor Help	33K	33270	PIFEDIT.HLP
Print Manager Help	40K	40880	PRINTMAN.HLP
Program Manager Help	31K	30911	PROGMAN.HLP
Recorder	39K	39152	RECORDER.EXE
Recorder Help	18K	18200	RECORDER.HLP
Registration Editor[†]	32K	32336	REGEDIT.EXE

TABLE 1.6 *(continued)*

Component Group Description	Memory Required		Filename
	Listed	**Actual**	
Registration Help	23K	22681	REGEDIT.HLP
Registration Help, Advanced	16K	15731	REGEDITV.HLP
Sound Recorder	51K	51305	SOUNDREC.EXE
Sound Recorder Help	18K	17686	SOUNDREC.HLP
System Editor[†]	18K	18896	SYSEDIT.EXE
Terminal	145K	148160	TERMINAL.EXE
Terminal Help	37K	36279	TERINAL.HLP
Windows Tutorial	122K	124416	WINTUTOR.EXE
Games			
Minesweeper	28K	27776	WINMINE.EXE
Minesweeper Help	13K	12754	WINMINE.HLP
Solitaire	177K	180668	SOL.EXE
Solitaire Help	14K	13753	SOL.HLP
Screen Savers			
Default Screen Saver	6K	5328	SCRNSAVE.SCR
Flying Windows Screen Saver	16K	16160	SSFLYWIN.SCR
Marquee Screen Saver	17K	16896	SSMARQUE.SCR
Mystify Screen Saver	19K	19456	SSMSYT.SCR
Starts Screen Saver	18K	17536	SSSTARS.SCR
Wallpapers, Misc.			
256-Color Wallpaper	5K	5078	256COLOR.BMP
Arcade Wallpaper	1K	630	ARCADE.BMP
Arches Wallpaper	1K	10358	ARCHES.BMP
Argyle Wallpaper	1K	630	ARGYLE.BMP
Canyon MIDI song	34K	33883	CANYON.MID
Cars Wallpaper	1K	630	CARS.BMP
Castle Wallpaper	1K	778	CASTLE.BMP
Chimes Sound	16K	15920	CHIMES.WAV
Chitz Wallpaper	20K	19918	CHITZ.BMP
Chord Sound	25K	24982	CHORD.BMP
Ding Sound	12K	11598	DING.WAV
Egypt Wallpaper	1K	630	EGYPT.BMP
Flock Wallpaper	2K	1630	FLOCK.BMP
Honey Wallpaper	1K	854	HONEY.BMP
Leaves Wallpaper	15K	15118	LEAVES.BMP
Marble Wallpaper	27K	27646	MARBLE.BMP

TABLE 1.6 *(continued)*

| Component Group | Memory Required | | |
Description	Listed	Actual	Filename
Red Brick Wallpaper	1K	630	REDBRICK.BMP
Rivets Wallpaper	1K	630	RIVETS.BMP
Squares Wallpaper	1K	630	SQUARES.BMP
Tartan Wallpaper	33K	32886	TARTAN.BMP
Thatch Wallpaper	1K	598	THATCH.BMP
Trumpet Sound	28K	27804	TADA.WAV
Windows Logo Wallpaper	38K	38518	WINLOGO.BMP
Zigzag Wallpaper	1K	630	ZIGZAG.BMP

[†] Undocumented applets may be separately installed after completing Setup. Refer to index for details.

Virtual Memory Configuration (Custom). Since virtual memory is only accessible when Windows is running in 386 enhanced mode, this option is not seen when running Setup on a 286-based system.

After concluding the Component Selection procedure described above, the Custom Setup procedure displays a Virtual Memory dialog box, such as the one shown in Figure 1.4a. You may either accept the displayed settings or click on the Change>> button to make revisions. If you are updating a previous Windows installation, the dialog box shows the settings from that installation, which you may accept (Continue button) or change. If you are unsure of what to do here, you have three choices:

1. Review the *Virtual Memory* section of Chapter 13 before continuing.

2. Accept the listed settings and worry about it later on.

3. Adjust the virtual memory setting to a reasonable size for your hard disk.

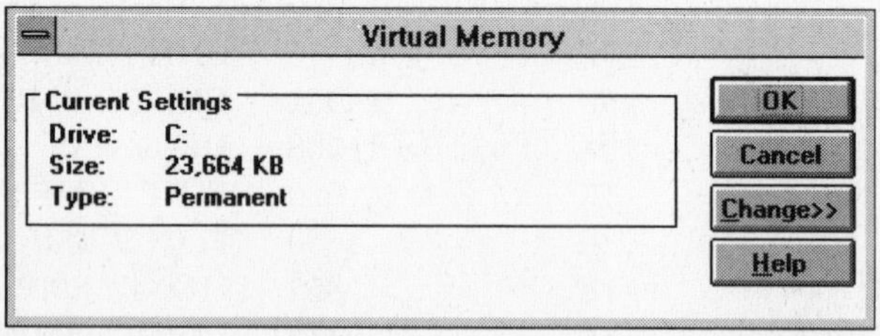

Figure 1.4a The Virtual Memory dialog box, showing the Current Settings section.

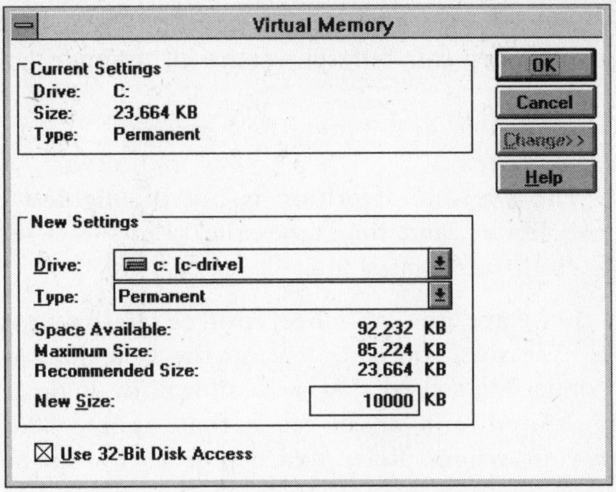

Figure 1.4b   The Virtual Memory dialog box, showing the additional New Settings section which appears if the Change>> button is clicked.

The first two choices are self-explanatory. However, if you'd rather not pause to absorb the finer points of virtual memory, yet suspect that the recommended setting is inappropriate, you may want to make the following adjustments now, and reserve a final adjustment for later on, once you're more familiar with virtual memory.

Briefly stated, Setup is supposed to apply the following two rules to determine how much hard-disk space to set aside for virtual memory:

The 50 Percent Rule. 50 percent of the available contiguous hard-disk space.

The 4× Rule. Four times the available free RAM in the computer.

Whichever rule yields the smaller figure defines virtual memory size. For most routine applications the memory so reserved should be about 6 to 10 Mbytes. However, Setup grabs what it can, so if the listed setting is significantly more than 10 Mbytes, you may want to reduce it to that amount so as not to waste space that might be put to better use.

If the listed setting is either too high or too low, there are several possibilities to consider:

1. You have lots of RAM and so much free hard-disk space that Setup is grabbing an unreasonable amount of it for virtual memory.
2. Your hard disk really does not have more space available for virtual memory.

3. Additional space could be made available by running a defragment utility (since virtual memory can only be set up in a single contiguous space).
4. There is more space available in another DOS partition, or on a second hard drive in your system.
5. Setup is confused. The swap-file algorithm is not the tightest bit of code in the Windows library, and sometimes the swap file is set to a size that contradicts both rules stated above.

For each possibility, there are one or more choices. If the proposed virtual memory space is excessive, you can click on the <u>C</u>hange>> button to display the larger Virtual Memory dialog box shown in Figure 1.4b. Change the settings as desired, and at the same time enable 32-bit access, if it's available on your system. Refer to Chapter 13 for further details about this.

On the other hand, if your hard disk really doesn't have much space available, then simply accept the current setting and continue running Setup. If de-fragmenting the disk would free additional space, you have two choices: Click on the <u>C</u>hange>> button, set virtual memory to none, run a defragment utility later on, then use Setup from within Windows to reenable virtual memory. Or, you can simply accept the current setting, and at some time after Setup remember to disable virtual memory, then reenable it after running the defragment routine. As a final possibility, if you know there is ample space on another DOS partition, or on another hard disk, now's the time to switch to that location.

If you have made any virtual-memory changes, Setup won't let you continue without reconsidering. The following two warning shots are fired across your screen:

Are you sure you want to make changes to virtual-memory settings?

Unless you were only fooling, answer "yes," then respond to the next message:

Using 32-bit access on some battery-powered portable computers may be unreliable when the computer's power-saving features are enabled.
Do you want to use 32-bit disk access?

Answer "yes" or "no" to continue transferring files to your hard disk.

Virtual Memory Configuration Quirks. Don't be surprised if Setup bends its own rules—free RAM permitting; it has been known to create a virtual-memory area that exceeds the 50 percent rule. Or, it may suggest a size that is too small by a power of 10 (for example, 4MB instead of 40MB, when about 80MB is available). Setup will also modify just about any value you enter. For example, select any value at all and Setup will probably announce that it will create a virtual-memory area that is slightly different from that value. After rebooting, if you return to the Virtual Memory dialog box to double-check, don't be surprised to find yet another value in place. No doubt this quirk will be taken care of in a subsequent release. Meanwhile, don't spend too much time trying to second-guess the system.

Misleading Virtual Memory Error Message. If you select a swap file size that exceeds the recommended value, but is less than (or equal to) the listed maximum size, an error message will advise that Windows will not use more than the recommended size. Disregard the message, which is in itself an error. Refer to Chapter 13 for additional information.

> **NOTE:** If you're wondering what the connection is between virtual memory and 32-bit access, the correct answer is "none." Perhaps the 32-bit access check box hides at the bottom of the final *Virtual Memory* dialog box simply to prevent the casual user from enabling it by accident. In any case, its use is not affected by virtual memory settings.

Modify CONFIG.SYS and AUTOEXEC.BAT Files (Custom). The next screen displays the following message:

> To set up Windows correctly, Setup needs to modify your CONFIG.SYS and AUTOEXEC.BAT files. Select the method you want, and then choose Continue or press ENTER.
> Setup can:
>
> ⦿ make all modifications for you
>
> ◯ let you review and edit changes, before modifications are made
>
> ◯ let you make the modifications later

If you select either of the first two options, Setup will update the files and save the old versions with OLD extensions. If you elect to make the modifications later on, Setup will offer to save its recommendations in two files with WIN extensions, which it places in your Windows (not root) directory. Refer to the *File-Editing Utilities* section of Chapter 4 if you need assistance editing these, or any other, files.

> **WARNING:** If you decided to leave your old version 3.0 (or earlier) in place and install version 3.1 in a separate location on your hard disk, make sure your AUTOEXEC.BAT file's PATH statement refers to the version of Windows that you want to execute. If it does not, then Windows will search the wrong path for any files that it needs. The results may be harmless, or disastrous, depending on what's needed at the moment. For details on setting up a dual-system batch file, refer to the *Dual-System Operation (SWAP.BAT)* section near the end of Chapter 2.

Printer Installation (Express, Custom). As the Setup procedure continues, the Printers dialog box shown in Figure 1.5 is displayed. Use the arrow keys to scroll through the list of supported printers. To jump ahead in the list, type the first letter of the desired printer name, then use the arrow keys to continue. (A complete list of supported printers may be found as Table 9.2 in Chapter 9). With the desired printer name highlighted, click on the Install... button to continue.

The next Printer Installation dialog box may list the ports available to your printer. If so, highlight the desired port (usually LPT1:) and again click on the Install... button to conclude this section of Setup. Or, if the

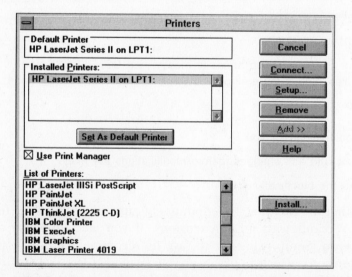

Figure 1.5 The Printers dialog box. To install a printer, highlight its name in the List of Printers section, then click on Install... button.

installed printer appears with the port already listed next to its name (as in the figure), click on the Connect... button if you would like to install it to some other port.

You may also wish to click on the Setup... button to review the various options that are available for the selected printer. Note the listed Memory specification (if available). Setup really has no idea how much memory you may have installed in your printer, so it just takes a guess. If the amount listed is incorrect, change it before continuing.

For more extensive printer setup assistance, refer to Chapter 9. Or, just continue with the regular Setup procedure and leave all this for later on.

Printer Installation (Custom). On Custom Setups, additional printers may be installed by selecting another printer and again clicking on the Install... button. After installing the desired printers, click on the Connect... and Setup... buttons to specify the port and other parameters for each printer.

If more than one printer has been installed, highlight one of them and click on the Set As Default Printer button. When you are finished, click on the Continue button.

Network Driver Installation (Express, Custom). At this point on some network installations, Setup will report that it found a network adapter card in your computer, as shown by this example:

> Windows Setup has detected the Intel EtherExpress 16 or 16TP network adapter in your computer. Do you want to installed the driver for this adapter now?

Next, Setup will recommend settings for the adapter. The proposed settings for the adapter listed above are:

Interrupt (IRQ)   5
Base I/O Port (hex): 0×300
Base Memory Address: (Automatic or Unused)

At this point, a network administrator may modify protocols and/or advanced settings by clicking on the appropriate button and making the necessary changes.

The next *Network Adapters* dialog box shows the name of the Network Adapter(s) in use. If necessary, click on the Setup... button to return to the recommended settings (as shown above).

A *Compatible Networks* dialog box shows a list of Available Network Types that may also be supported. Highlight any of these, click on the Add>> button to transfer them to the "Other Networks in Use" box, then click on the Continue button.

NOTE: If the DOS 6.0 Memory Maker (MEMMAKER.EXE) utility was run prior to running a Windows 3.1 network setup procedure, an "invalid parameter" message may be seen when the system is rebooted. This is due to a conflict with one or more of the parameters on the EMM386.EXE line in CONFIG.SYS. If you see this message during bootup, rerun the MEMMAKER utility. For assistance, refer to the *DOS 6.0 Memory Maker* section of Chapter 13.

Desktop Preparation (Express, Custom). The Windows desktop is briefly seen, along with the Program Manager Window and the Main, Accessories, Games, and Startup Windows which are placed within the Program Manager.

Application Selection (Express). Next, Setup searches your entire hard disk for applications, and installs all of them in your Applications Group Window. However, Setup may pause to ask you about any application whose identity is uncertain. If this happens, refer to the Custom section immediately following for details on the procedure.

Application Selection (Custom). Setup offers to search various areas of your hard disk(s) for Windows and non-Windows applications, which you may want it to install in an Applications Group Window. Figure 1.6 shows the Setup Applications dialog box, which lists only the drives Setup recognizes as being part of a hard disk. In the example shown in the figure, the missing drives A and B are of course diskette drives, and drive G is a Bernoulli box with removable media. Drive J is a RAM drive which should not be selected, unless you make a point of loading applications there prior to starting Windows.

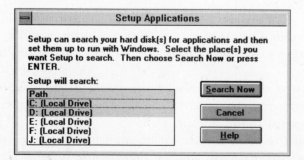

Figure 1.6 The Setup Applications dialog box. Highlight Path and/or the drives that should be searched for applications.

Once you have selected the search areas, Setup refers to the following two sections of its own APPS.INF file for advice on what to do with the files it may find on your system. As the search progresses, Setup builds itself a list of all applications that it finds, then presents the list to you for your review.

[dontfind] Section. This section lists Windows' own applets, each of which was (or later, can be) installed in the Accessories or some other group window. As the section name implies, Setup ignores the names on this list, so these applets do not get installed in the Applications Group Window. The complete list of [dontfind] files is given here in Table 1.7.

[pif] Section. The [pif] (Program Information File) section contains the long list of non-Windows applications listed in Table 1.8, together with the parameters Windows needs to run each one within a DOS window. For detailed information about Program Information files, refer to the *PIF Editor* section of Chapter 7.

TABLE 1.7 Applets Excluded by Setup*

Filename

apm.exe	ftp.exe	mxwin.exe	reversi.exe	win2wrs.exe
calc.exe	graph.exe	note-it.exe	sdkpaint.exe	winbbs.exe
calendar.exe	graflink.exe	notepad.exe	setup.exe	wincbt.exe
cardfile.exe	heapwalk.exe	packager.exe	shaker.exe	winfile.exe
charmap.exe	imagedit.exe	paint.exe	shed.exe	winhelp.exe
clipbrd.exe	implibw.exe	pbrush.exe	sol.exe	winmine.exe
clock.exe	jfprint.exe	pifedit.exe	soundrec.exe	wintutor.exe
control.exe	libw.exe	play.exe	spooler.exe	winver.exe
control3.exe	linkw.exe	pptgraph.exe	spy.exe	wordart.exe
cvpackw.exe	lwinhelp.exe	printman.exe	stress.exe	wpcdll.exe
ddespy.exe	macrode.exe	progman.exe	swapfile.exe	wpwinfil.exe
dewproj.exe	mapsym32.exe	aq.exe	sysedit.exe	write.exe
dialog.exe	mcwin.exe	rcppw.exe	taskman.exe	zoomin.exe
digedit.exe	mmsetup.exe	rcw.exe	tbook.exe	
drwatson.exe	mplayer.exe	recorder.exe	terminal.exe	
eqnedit.exe	msdos.exe	regedit.exe	trans.exe	
fontedit.exe	msdraw.exe	regload.exe	whelp.exe	

*Filenames are listed in [dontfind] section of APPS.INF file.

TABLE 1.8 Applications Recognized by Setup*

Filename	Ext.	Application(s)
123	COM	Lotus 1-2-3
123	EXE	Lotus 1-2-3 2.3, 3.1
ABPI	COM	ACCPAC BPI
ACAD	EXE	Autocad
ACAD386	BAT	Autocad (Batch File)
ACCESS	COM	PFS: Access, Symphony
ACCESS	EXE	Access for DOS
ADMIN	EXE	Microsoft Mail - Admin
AGENDA	EXE	Lotus Agenda
AP	EXE	APPLAUSE II
B	EXE	Brief 2.1/3.0, 3.1
BASIC	COM	Microsoft Basic
BASICA	EXE	Microsoft Advanced Basic
BC	EXE	Borland C++, MS BASIC compiler
BOOKS	EXE	Microsoft Bookshelf
CADD	EXE	Generic CADD
CALC	EXE	WPOffice Calculator
CHART	COM	Microsoft Chart
CL	EXE	Microsoft C Compiler 6.0, WPOffice Calendar
CLOUT	EXE	Microrim R:Base Clout
CPAV	EXE	CP Anti-Virus
CS3270	BAT	Comm Server 3270
DBASE	EXE	Ashton Tate dBase III, IV
DE16M	EXE	DataEase
DEASE	EXE	DataEase
DESKTOP	EXE	PCTools Desktop 5.5, 6.0, 7.0
DM	EXE	PCTOOLS: Directory Maintenance
DOSHELP	EXE	Learning MS-DOS Quick Reference
DP	COM	DataPerfect
DR	EXE	DrawPerfect
DW3PG	COM	DisplayWrite 3
DW4	BAT	DisplayWrite 4
DW5	BAT	DisplayWrite 5
DWA	BAT	DisplayWrite Assistant
DWDOS286	EXE	DWDOS286
DWDOS386	EXE	DWDOS386
DWINF02	EXE	DWINF02
DWINF03	EXE	SWINF03

* Filenames are listed in [pif] section of APPS.INF file.

TABLE 1.8 *(continued)*

Filename	Ext.	Application(s)
ED	EXE	WP Office Editor
EDIT	COM	MS-DOS Editor
EDIT	EXE	IBM Professional Editor
EDITOR	EXE	XY Write
EXPRESS	BAT	Lotus Express
EXTRA	BAT	Extra! for MS-DOS
FG	EXE	PFS: First Graphics
FILE	EXE	IBM Filing Assistant
FIRST	COM	PFS: First Choice 3.1
FIRST	EXE	PFS: First Choice 3.0
FL	COM	Freelance Plus 3.0, 4.0
FL	EXE	Microsoft Fortran Compiler 5.1, Norton File Find
FM	EXE	WPOffice File Manager
FORMTOOL	EXE	Formtool
FOX	EXE	FoxPro (Max. Config.)
FOXPLUS	EXE	Foxbase Plus
FP	EXE	PFS: First Publisher
FS3	EXE	Flight Simulator 3.0
FS4	EXE	Flight Simulator 4.0
FTPSRV	EXE	FTP FTPSRV Utility
FW	EXE	Framework II, III
GAMESHOP	EXE	Microsoft Game Shop
GW	COM	GraphWriter
GWBASIC	EXE	GW BASIC
HG	EXE	Harvard Graphics 2.0, 2.1, 2.3
HG3	EXE	Harvard Graphics 3.0
HGG	EXE	Harvard GeoGraphics
HPM	EXE	Harvard Project Manager
HTPM	EXE	Harvard Total Project Manager
HW	EXE	HotWire
ILEAF	EXE	Interleaf 5 for MS-DOS
INSIGHT	BAT	Insight
KIDPIX	EXE	Kid Pix
KPDOS	EXE	KnowledgePro (MS-DOS)
LEARN	EXE	Learning Microsoft: Quick Pascal Express, Works, Word 5.0, 5.5
LLPRO	EXE	LapLink Pro
LOTUS	COM	Lotus Access System
LP	EXE	LetterPerfect, Norton Line Printer

TABLE 1.8 *(continued)*

Filename	Ext.	Application(s)
LPQ	EXE	FTP LPQ Utility
LPR	EXE	FTP LPR Utility
LRNDOS	EXE	Learning MS-DOS 3.0
LW	EXE	LotusWorks 1.0
MAIL	EXE	Microsoft Mail, PCSA Mail, cc:Mail, XcelleNET X/MAIL
MAKE	EXE	Microsoft Make Utility
MASM	EXE	Microsoft Macro Assembler
MFT	EXE	Manifest
MGMOUSE	EXE	Magellan 2.0
ML	EXE	WPMail, Microsoft Macro Assembler
MM	EXE	MultiMate 4.0
MP	COM	Microsoft Multiplan
MP	EXE	Microsoft Multiplan
MYM	EXE	Managing Your Money
NB	EXE	WPOffice NoteBook
NCP	EXE	Network Control Program
NI	EXE	Norton Utilities 4.5
NORTON	EXE	Norton Utilities 5/6.0
NOW	EXE	Now!
ONLINE	COM	Microsoft Online 1.0
OPTUNE	EXE	OPTune
PAINT	BAT	PC Paintbrush IV Plus
PARADOX	EXE	Paradox 3.5
PARADOX2	EXE	Paradox
PARADOX3	EXE	Paradox 3.0, SE
PC3270	COM	PC3270
PCCONFIG	EXE	PC Config 7.x
PCMAIL	EXE	FTP PCMAIL Utility
PCPLUS	EXE	Procomm Plus, Plus 1.1B
PCSHELL	EXE	PCTools PCShell 5.5, 6.0
PE	EXE	IBM Personal Editor
PF	EXE	Professional File
PING	EXE	FTP PING Utility
PL	EXE	Microsoft Pascal Compiler, Planperfect, PFS: Professional Plan
PLAN	EXE	PFS: Plan
PLUS	EXE	ACCPAC Plus
PN	EXE	PFS: Professional Network
PROCOMM	EXE	Procomm
PRODIGY	EXE	Prodigy

TABLE 1.8 *(continued)*

Filename	Ext.	Application(s)
PROJ	COM	Microsoft Project
PW	COM	Professional Write
PWB	EXE	Programmer's WorkBench
Q	EXE	Quicken, Quattro 1.0, 2.0, Quattro Pro, Pro 1.0
QA	COM	Q & A Report Writer
QB	EXE	Microsoft QuickBASIC
QBASIC	EXE	Microsoft QBASIC
QBX	EXE	Microsoft QuickBasic Extended
QC	EXE	Microsoft Quick C, with QASM
QD3	EXE	Q-DOS 3
QMODEM	EXE	QModem
QP	EXE	Microsoft Quick Pascal
QV2	EXE	Quick Verse 2.0
R1	EXE	Reflection 1
R2	EXE	Reflection 2
R2CALL	EXE	Remote 2 call
R4	EXE	Reflection 4
R7	EXE	Reflection 7
R8	EXE	Reflection 8
RB5000	EXE	Microrim R:Base 5000
RBASE	EXE	Microrim R:Base, R:Base System V
READY	EXE	Ready!
REFLEX	EXE	Reflex 2.0
RELAY	COM	Relay Gold
RIGHT	EXE	RightWriter
RLOGINVT	EXE	FTP RLOGINVT Utility
RSH	EXE	FTP RSH Utility
SAS	EXE	SAS 604
SC	EXE	Scheduler
SC4	COM	Supercalc 4.0
SC5	COM	Supercalc 5.0
SCOM	EXE	Smartcom II
SEDT	EXE	SEDT Editor
SETHOST	EXE	Sethost Terminal Emulator
SHELL	EXE	WordPerfect Office
SK	BAT	Soft Kicker
SK	COM	Sidekick 1.0
SK2	EXE	Sidekick 2.0

TABLE 1.8 *(continued)*

Filename	Ext.	Application(s)
SKETCH	EXE	Autosketch 2.0, 3.0
SKETCH3	BAT	Autosketch 3.0 (batch file)
SKPLUS	COM	Sidekick Plus
SKPLUS	EXE	Sidekick Plus
SKPROF	BAT	Soft Kicker
SPAWNER	EXE	Decnet Job Spawner
SPELL	COM	Microsoft Spell
SPSSPC	COM	SPSS/PC+
SUPPORT	EXE	Close-Up 4.0
SYMPHONY	EXE	Symphony 2.2
TM	EXE	TeleMate
TN	EXE	FTP TN Utility
TTAX	EXE	Turbo Tax
TURBO	EXE	Turbo Pascal 5.0, 6.0
VIEW	EXE	PCTOOLS - View
VMAIL	EXE	FTP VMAIL Utility
VP	BAT	Ventura Publisher
VW3	EXE	Volkswriter 3.0
WORD	COM	Microsoft Word 4.0
WORD	EXE	Microsoft Word 5.0
WORKS	EXE	Microsoft Works 1.*x*, 2.0
WP	EXE	WordPerfect, Multimate, OfficeWriter, 6.2
WR	EXE	Writer Rabbit
WRITE	COM	IBM Writing Assistant 2.0
WS	EXE	WordStar Professional 6.0
WS2	EXE	WordStar 2000
XTALK	EXE	Crosstalk-XVI 3.71
XTG	EXE	XTree Gold

When Setup searches your hard disk and finds a file listed in the [pif] section, it can install that application in the Applications Group Window. In some cases, Setup may find a non-Windows application with an ambiguous filename. As a typical example, WP.EXE might be (*gasp!*) Word Perfect, Multimate, OfficeWriter, or some other DOS word processor. In such cases, you will be prompted to specify the correct identity of the file by a dialog box such as the one shown in Figure 1.7. If no listed application name is correct, highlight "none of the above" and remember to install whatever-it-is later on, as described in the *Setup Non-Windows Application* section later in this chapter.

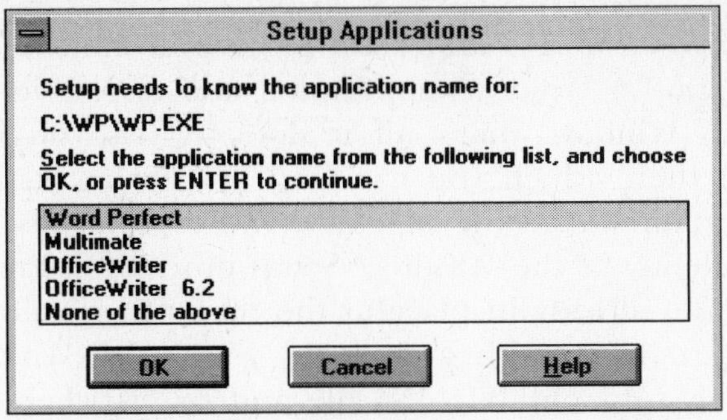

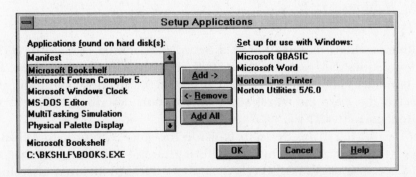

Figure 1.7 If multiple applications with the same filename are shown, Setup needs to know which application it found.

Windows Applications. Setup also finds all Windows applications that reside on your hard disk. Programs such as Excel and Word-for-Windows are automatically added to the list of found applications.

Applications-Found List (Custom). After Setup completes its search, it presents a list of the applications it has found, as shown by the typical example in Figure 1.8. Review the lefthand Applications Found box, highlight those you want to install, and press the Add -> key to transfer these names into the righthand Set Up box. Use the Add -> and <- Remove buttons to refine the list, as required, then click on the OK button to continue. If you're unsure of the identity of any file listed in the Applications Found box, highlight that application and review the information presented below the box, which may help you to recognize what it is.

Figure 1.8 Highlight any applications found that you want to set up for Windows, then click on the Add –> button.

A Windows Application Precaution. It is important to keep in mind that although Setup may indeed find a Windows application and display its icon in the Applications Group Window, that's all it does: It lets you know there's an application out there which you can find by clicking its icon. Whether the found application works will depend on whether it has been properly installed independently of the Windows Setup procedure. Presumably, any Windows application already in place at the time you install Windows itself, is one you were using with a previous version of Windows. However, references to it in your old WIN.INI file and/or elsewhere may no longer be valid, or may have gotten lost during Setup. If it turns out that such applications don't work properly once Windows 3.1 Setup has concluded, the most reliable course of action is to delete the application icon from the group window, then refer to the application's User's Guide for instructions on setting it up again as new. After concluding Windows Setup, refer to the *Setup Windows Application* section below for further assistance.

A Windows Tutorial (Express, Custom). Setup now offers a short tutorial on how to use Windows and the mouse, which you may run or skip, as you like. You can also run the tutorial later on, after Windows has been installed. To do so, click on <u>H</u>elp in the Program Manager's menu bar, then select the <u>W</u>indows Tutorial option. For further information about this and other help screens, refer to the *Help screen* section in Chapter 4.

Exit Windows Setup (Express, Custom). After running (or skipping) the Tutorial, the Exit Windows Setup dialog box is displayed, offering you the following choices:

Reboot
Restart Windows
Return to MS-DOS

The Reboot choice is not offered if Setup determined that no modifications were required to your CONFIG.SYS and AUTOEXEC.BAT files. The Restart Windows choice is not offered if either file needed upgrading, but you selected the make the modifications later option described earlier in the Setup procedure.

If you decide (or if the decision is made for you) to return to MS-DOS, remember to reboot the computer before running Windows, so that the changes made to your AUTOEXEC.BAT and CONFIG.SYS files may take effect.

If you restart Windows, the Windows desktop shown in Figure 1.9 will be displayed, and you are ready to begin your first Windows 3.1 session. For

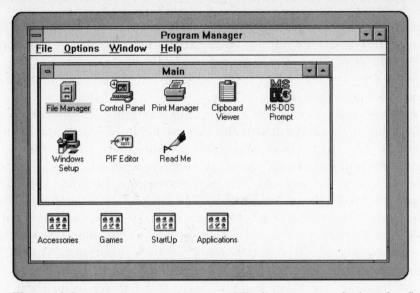

Figure 1.9 The Program Manager Window, as seen during the final phases of the Setup procedure.

assistance in changing the appearance of the Desktop, refer to the *Configuring the Windows Desktop* section in Chapter 3.

Postsetup Review

Once the Windows Setup procedure has successfully concluded, it's a good idea to spend a little time reviewing the contents of your Windows and System directories, and making backup copies of the more critical files.

File Creation Date Check. If you installed Windows version 3.1 over a previous version 3.0, now is the time to take a close look at your Windows directory to see if there are any little surprises there. Ideally, all files in the directory will have one of the following dates:

3-10-92   All files on the distribution diskettes. (If Windows 3.1 was installed from a CD-ROM disk, or from distribution diskettes issued after the initial release, then of course this date will be different. However, it should not be significantly earlier than that indicated here.)

Today's date   Various files created during Setup.

To check for anything else, type "DIR /o-d" (without the quotes) and press the Enter key. This displays a directory listing, sorted in descending order by date, with files created prior to 3-10-92 at the bottom of the list. If any such files are seen, they are leftovers from version 3.0 and may or may not cause problems later.

Some leftovers are reasonably benign: For example, REVERSI.EXE and REVERSI.HLP are associated with the Reversi game which is not included with version 3.1. Other than taking up a little space, these files won't cause you any problems when you try to run Windows 3.1.

However, if you see any old files with extensions of GR2, GR3, DRV, DLL, and so forth, these are version 3.0 files which *should* have been replaced with their version 3.1 counterparts. The reason they were not replaced is that they were not in use by version 3.0 at the time you upgraded to 3.1. Therefore, Setup was not aware of their existence, and of the need to replace them.

For the moment, no harm is done: Since you weren't using these files, their presence in your Windows directory is unimportant. The harm comes later on, when and if you reinstall whatever it was that used these files. To prevent future problems, review all these old files *now* and make a decision what to do with them. If you're not sure what one of them is, refer to Appendix A for a brief description of each Windows file. If the file is not listed in the Appendix, then it probably represents some third-party application or driver that is not part of the Windows installation itself. If you have problems with any such files later on, contact the appropriate software manufacturer to see if there is an updated version of the program or driver available.

As a very brief guide to the identity of some of the files you may find, Table 1.9a compares selected versions 3.0 and 3.1 filenames. The Table also summarizes the nomenclature Microsoft uses to identify various data-exchange support files. Note that with the discontinuance of Windows' real mode, the old real-mode WINOLDAP.MOD file is erased

TABLE 1.9a   Comparison of Selected Files in Win 3.0 and 3.1

3.0 Filename	3.1 Filename	Comments
filename.GR2	*filename*.2GR	286 Grabber files
filename.GR3	*filename*.3GR	386 Grabber files
WINOLDAP.MOD	None (unsupported mode)	Real-mode support
WINOA286.MOD	WINOLDAP.MOD	Standard-mode support
WINOA386.MOD	WINOA386.MOD	Enhanced-mode support

and replaced by a new standard-mode file with the same name. If you have just upgraded from version 3.0, the old standard-mode file (WINOA286.MOD) is left undisturbed in your System directory. It doesn't do any harm there, but it doesn't do any good either, so you might as well erase it. If you discover any other 3.0 file in your Windows directory, note the equivalent 3.1 filename, and find that file on the distribution diskettes.

Table 1.9b lists Windows files that are not found on any distribution diskette, but are instead created from other files during the Windows Setup procedure.

Print Directory Contents. Immediately after installing Windows, run off hard copies of the Windows and System directories. Sooner or later you'll want to uninstall some third-party software that you added after the initial installation. Many such applications add their own files to your Windows or System directories. Few inform you what these files are called, so it's up to you to find them yourself if you want to clean out your disk space. When the time comes for housecleaning, you'll be glad to have a printed baseline reference that shows the basic Windows files. If you're really conscientious, it wouldn't hurt to print additional copies after each installation of a third-party application.

Prepare Backup Files. As another precaution, it's a good idea to create a new directory (WINBAK-A, for example) and copy all *.INI and *.GRP files into it. When you install a new third-party application, copy the revised INI and GRP files into a WINBAK-B directory. For the next application, overwrite the files in the WINBAK-A directory and keep alternating directories as you add more goodies. If you do this faithfully (you won't), you'll be able to restore the system to its recent pre-install configuration if the latest treasure doesn't work out. If you don't do this faithfully, sooner or later you'll wish you had.

TABLE 1.9b   Files Created During Windows 3.1 Setup Procedure

Filename	Created From
CONTROL.INI	CONTROL.SRC
SYSTEM.INI	SYSTEM.SRC
WIN.COM	WIN.CNF + *xxx*LOGO.LGO + *xxx*LOGO.RLE[†]
WIN.INI	WIN.SRC

[†] *xxx* = EGA, VGA, etc., depending on installed video system.

Making Postsetup Modifications

Sooner or later you'll also want to set up additional hardware and/or software to run within Windows. It would be convenient—in fact, it might even make sense—if there were a single entry point through which one would pass to do whatever it is that needs to be done to accommodate anything from a revised video display to a new printer. For the moment, though, there is not one such door, but four. These are:

1. The Setup applet in the Main Group Window
2. The Program Manager's File Menu
3. The DOS prompt (from outside Windows itself)
4. The Control Panel in the Main Group Window

The following sections review the procedures required in examples 1–3. The Control Panel Setup procedures are described in later chapters.

Since the procedures described here are not followed until Windows is up and running, some familiarity with the Windows Desktop is assumed. If necessary, refer to Chapter 3 and elsewhere for general information about these components, then return here for help in completing the desired Setup procedure.

Startup File Modifications by Third-Party Setups. Many third-party setup procedures will make modifications to your CONFIG.SYS and AUTOEXEC.BAT files, with varying degrees of success. A well-behaved setup routine will save copies of your present files, sometimes with a distinctive extension, and sometimes just as BAK files. However, unless you *know* the application will do this, it's not a bad idea to make a set of backup files yourself, just in case.

The modifications made to your startup files may not always work as intended, and are sometimes unnecessary. For example, many applications feel compelled to add themselves to your PATH statement. Some are reasonably modest and simply add a new path line to your AUTOEXEC.BAT file, as shown below. Later on, another application may find these lines and insert itself at the front of *both* of them.

```
path (your existing path, left undisturbed)
path %path%;C:\NEWAPP (this simply appends C:\NEWAPP to your path)
```

Still other applications will add a load line at the beginning or end of your AUTOEXEC.BAT file, without regard for whatever else is there. That means that, if the last presetup line branches to another batch file, the new additions will be ignored.

As another consideration, the new device or file will probably not be loaded into upper memory, assuming that's where you want it to go. Nor will it make use of your third-party memory management system.

All of this means you may need to run a postsetup cleanup operation. In many cases, you can delete the addition to your path line. First, click once on the new application's icon, open the File menu and select the Properties... option. The command line should show the complete path and filename. If it does, then you might not need that path in your AUTOEXEC.BAT file. If it does not, then add the path to the command line and remove it from the path line in the batch file.

The Windows 3.1 Setup Applet

Once your basic Windows 3.1 system is successfully up and running, you will want to make changes, either to accommodate new system hardware and/or third-party device drivers, to set up additional Windows and non-Windows applications, or to revise the Windows components that were installed during the initial Setup procedure. To begin, open the Main Group Window and double-click on the Windows Setup icon. This opens the Windows Setup dialog box shown in Figure 1.10a. The dialog box lists your current display, keyboard, mouse, and network. To change any of these settings, or to gain access to other Setup options, select the Options menu. This displays the setup options shown in Figure 1.10b. Highlight the desired option, then refer to the appropriate section which follows for assistance.

Change System Settings. Select this option to change any of the components listed in the Windows Setup dialog box shown in Figure 1.10a. When

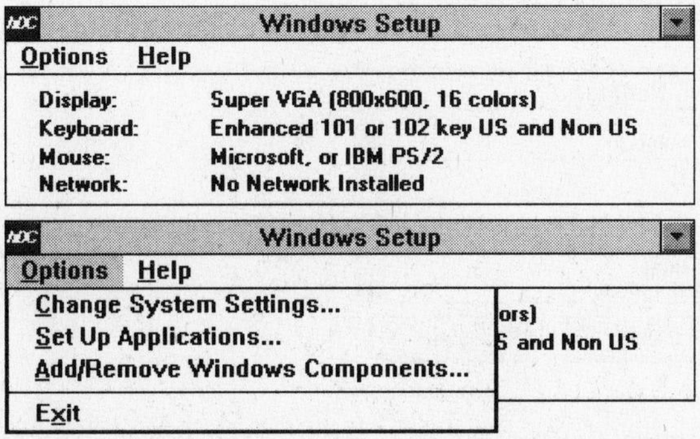

Figure 1.10 Use the Windows Setup dialog box (a) to review your current hardware configuration. Open the Options Menu (b) to make changes, as required.

you do, the Change System Settings dialog box in Figure 1.11a appears. Click on any down arrow to display a list of available changes, such as that shown in Figure 1.11b. Highlight the one you'd like to use, click on the OK button, and one of the following messages should be seen, depending on the specific change you want to make:

A driver for this display *(or other device)* is already on the system. Do you want to use the currently-installed driver or install a new driver?

Insert disk with display driver provided by the hardware manufacturer.

Please insert the Microsoft Windows 3.1 Disk #x.

Follow the appropriate instructions to complete the configuration change.

> **NOTE:** When installing many third-party drivers, the procedure described here will fail, even though the desired system component is listed in a **Change System Settings** dialog box such as that shown in Figure 1.11b. In this case, exit Windows and rerun Setup as described in the *Setup Third-Party Drivers* section later in this chapter.

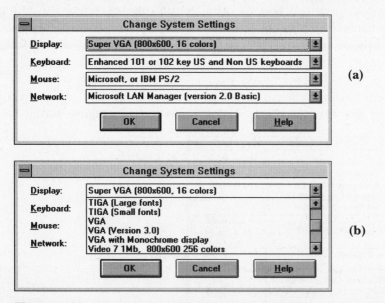

Figure 1.11 The Change Systems Settings dialog box. (a) Highlight the item you wish to change and click on the arrow button to display the list of available choices (b).

Setup Applications. If you know the application is one that Windows Setup will recognize (that is, a Windows applet or application, or a non-Windows application listed in the [pif] section of the APPS.INF file), then select the Set Up Applications... option shown in Figure 1.10b.

The first Setup Applications dialog box displays the following choices, both of which are described below:

- ◉ Search for applications.

- ◯ Ask you to specify an application.

Search for Applications. If you want to install multiple non-Windows applications that are already resident on your hard drive, select the first option and follow the *Application Selection (Custom)* instructions seen earlier in this chapter.

Ask You to Specify an Application. In most postsetup cases you'll be installing a single application, so there's little point in selecting *Search for applications*—you already know where the application is. Click the radio button labeled "Ask you to specify an application" instead. When you do, the *Setup Applications* dialog box in Figure 1.12 is displayed. In the illustration, the path and filename for the undocumented System Edit utility (SYSEDIT.EXE) have already been entered in the "Application Path and Filename" box. If all goes well, the specified application will be installed within the Accessories Group Window, as indicated by the highlighted "Accessories" in the "Add to Program Group" box.

But if all does not go well, Setup displays the following error message; then it's up to you to guess what the problem is.

Setup can't set up this application. Use Program Manager to set up this application.

The reason "Setup can't set up" is simple enough, once you know what it is: The program is a DOS application not listed in the APPS.INF file

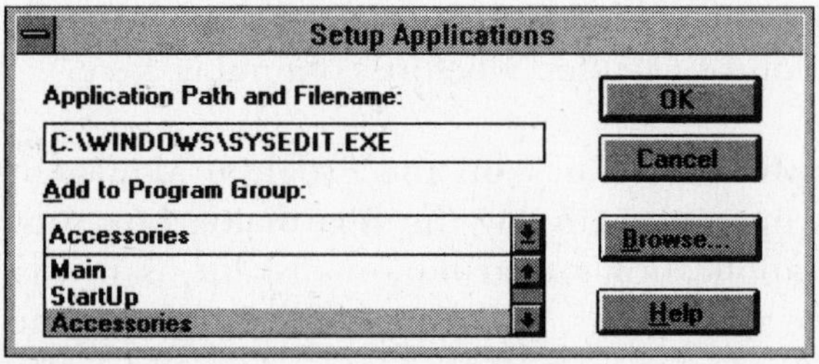

Figure 1.12 The Setup Applications dialog box is used to install the selected application in the desired group window.

(described earlier, in the *Application Selection [Custom]* section). Therefore, Setup can't complete the installation because it has no idea what to do. In other words, if a non-Windows application is not listed in the APPS.INF file, then Setup cannot be used as described above. In this case, follow the installation procedures described in the *Setup Non-Windows Application* section below.

> **NOTE:** As described earlier in the chapter, a Windows application installed via the **S**et Up Applications... option may not work if it has not been properly installed via its own Setup procedure.

Add/Remove Windows Components. During the initial Setup operation, various Windows components (applets, readme files, screen savers, etc.) were installed, as described in the *Component Selection (Custom)* section earlier in the chapter. To revise this list of components after Windows is up and running, select the **A**dd/Remove Windows Components... option shown in Figure 1.10b. This displays the Windows Setup dialog box shown in Figure 1.2b earlier in the chapter. Note that one check box (Readme Files) is blank, indicating that none of these files are presently installed. Two check boxes (Accessories and Games) are shaded, signifying that some, but not all, applets within these two component categories are installed. Follow the instructions given in the *Component Selection (Custom)* section to add or remove items in each of the component categories.

Setup via Program Manager

Perhaps the most reliable way to install a new Windows application is via the **R**un... option which is accessible through the Program Manager's File Menu. Or, the **N**ew... option on the same menu may be used to add a new group window or to insert a new application (which Windows calls a *Program Item*) into an existing group window. The appropriate procedures are described here. If you need assistance negotiating Windows' menus, refer to the *Menus and Menu Options* section of Chapter 3 before continuing here.

Set Up a New Windows Application. Click on the Program Manager's File Menu and select the **R**un... option to display the Run dialog box shown in Figure 1.13. Assuming the application's distribution diskette is in drive A, simply type A:\SETUP (or in a few cases, A:\INSTALL) in the command line box. Then click on the OK button or press the Enter key and follow the on-screen instructions to complete the installation. Of course, if all else fails, read the User's Guide for specific setup/install details.

```
┌──────────────────────────────────────────────┐
│ ═                    Run                       │
│ Command Line:                      ┌──────┐    │
│ ┌──────────────────────────────┐   │  OK  │    │
│ │A:\SETUP                       │   └──────┘    │
│ └──────────────────────────────┘   ┌──────┐    │
│                                    │Cancel│    │
│ ☐ Run Minimized                    └──────┘    │
│                                    ┌──────┐    │
│                                    │Browse…│   │
│                                    └──────┘    │
│                                    ┌──────┐    │
│                                    │ Help │    │
│                                    └──────┘    │
└──────────────────────────────────────────────┘
```

Figure 1.13   To set up an application after Windows is installed, select the Run option on the Program Manager's File Menu to display the Run dialog box.

The application will probably reward itself with its very own group window, which is OK if it's a major word processor or spreadsheet and you plan to surround it with various support applications. In this case, a dedicated window makes some sense and you can just leave things as they are. However, you may think things have gone a bit too far when even the new screen-saver shows up in its own group window. In this case, open your Accessories or Applications Group Window, drag the new application's icon into one of those windows, then delete the now-vacant window. If you need assistance doing all this, refer to the *Icon Management* section of Chapter 3 for detailed instructions.

If you want the application—a screen-saver for example—to run every time you start Windows, refer to Chapter 5 for instructions on using the StartUp Group Window.

Note that the "Setup" described in this section refers to a SETUP.EXE (or INSTALL.EXE) utility which accompanies the Windows application you are installing, and *not* to Windows' own Setup utility. If you accidentally omit the path to the desired SETUP.EXE file by typing SETUP in the Run box (Figure 1.13), the Windows Setup dialog box shown earlier in Figure 1.10a will unexpectedly show up. Since this is probably not what you expected, make a dignified exit and try again.

Another possible error is to insert Windows distribution diskette 1 in drive A instead of the application's own diskette. In this case, the following error message is seen:

You are attempting to set up Windows 3.1 from within Windows. Quit Windows and type 'setup' at the MS-DOS command prompt.

Assuming you really meant to install a new Windows application, remove the Windows distribution diskette from the drive, insert the application's own diskette, and try again.

Reactivate a Previously Installed Windows Application. If the icon representing a Windows application has been deleted from a group window but the application itself is still physically present on the hard disk, follow the instructions found below in the *Select a Group Window* section to return the application's icon to the desired group window.

Set Up a New Group Window. If you want to create a new group window in which to install applications or applets, select the New... option in the Program Manager's File Menu. When the New Program Object dialog box shown in Figure 1.14a appears, click on the radio button next to the Program Group option. This displays the Program Group Properties box shown in Figure 1.14b. In the Description box, enter the name you would like to appear in the new group window's Title Bar.

Each group window is assigned its own group file (*filename*.GRP), which later on will contain information about the applets installed in the group window, including a copy of the icon to be associated with each applet. If you would like to specify the path and name for this group file, enter the appropriate information in the Group File box. Otherwise, Windows

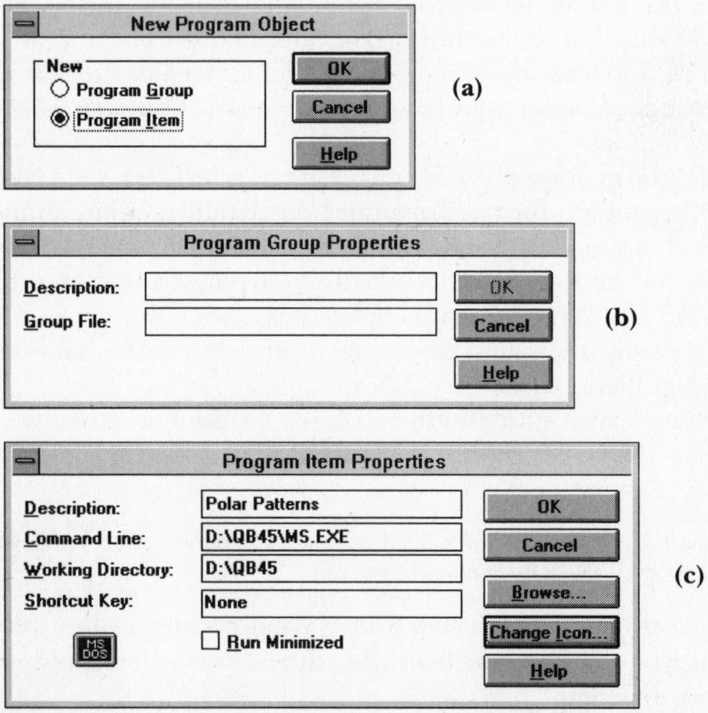

Figure 1.14   The New Program Object dialog box (a). Depending on which radio button is clicked, either the (b) Program Group Properties, or (c) Program Item *(applet)* Properties dialog box is displayed.

will create the group file as C:\WINDOWS*filename*.GRP, where *filename* is the first eight characters in your Description box.

When you click on the OK button, a new group window will appear in the Program Manager area. To install applets within the window, refer to the next section.

Set Up a New Program Item. Occasionally you may want to install a single Windows applet that is not accompanied by its own Setup utility, or a DOS program that you would like to execute from within Windows. For setup purposes, Windows refers to such programs as program *items*. Refer to the appropriate sections which follow for setup instructions.

Set Up a Windows Applet. As a typical example, consider that your present configuration lacks the Windows 3.1 PaintBrush applet, and PBRUSH.EXE is not present in your Windows directory. In this case, expand a fresh copy of PBRUSH.EX_ into the Windows directory as PBRUSH.EXE. Also, look for accompanying files with the same name but a different extension (PBRUSH.DL_, PBRUSH.HL_, for example). If you find such files, expand them into the same directory also. Sometimes an accompanying DLL file will have a name quite different from the EXE file. For example, Central Point Software's anti-virus *TSR Manager* (WNTSR-MAN.EXE) needs an accompanying WNGRAFIC.DLL file in order to run. (This Windows applet is also supplied with DOS 6.0.) In this case, you may not realize the latter file is missing until you try to execute the former one. A "cannot find" error message will advise you of the name of the missing file, which you'll need to find and expand (if necessary) into the same directory.

If the Windows applet file is not compressed, then simply make sure it is present in the desired directory before proceeding.

Once you have the necessary Windows file (or files) in place, refer to the *Select a Group Window* section below.

Set Up a Non-Windows Applet. When setting up a conventional DOS application to run within Windows, the first thing to do is follow the manufacturer's instructions to install the application on your hard drive. Do this at the DOS prompt, just as you might have done in the old non-Windows days. After testing the application to make sure it actually works, follow the procedures listed here.

Select a Group Window. The next task is to decide in which group window you want the application's icon to appear. Click anywhere within that window to make it active, then click on the Program Manager's File menu. Next, select the **New...** option from the pull-down menu to display the **New Program Object** dialog box shown earlier in Figure 1.14a. To install your application, first click on **Program Item** radio button, then click on **OK**. This displays the **Program Item** Properties dialog box in Figure 1.14c. Type in the following information, as appropriate to your application. Or, if you prefer, click on the <u>B</u>rowse... button and search your directories and files for the required information. Highlight any item and double-click on it to insert it into the currently selected box.

Press the Tab key to toggle between boxes, or move the cursor into the desired box and press the primary mouse button.

Box Name	Enter the Following Information:
Description:	A brief description of the application. This information will appear later on under the icon associated with the application.
Command Line:	The complete path and filename for the application.
Working Directory:	(Optional) If the application (a word processor, for example) will regularly refer to files located elsewhere, enter the path and directory name where these files are located, or leave the entry blank.
Shortcut Key	(Optional) If you wish to execute the application from the keyboard, press any key ("K" for example). The box will display "Ctrl + Alt + K." If you press this unique Shortcut key combination later on, the application will execute. Press the Backspace key to clear the Shortcut Key box.
Run Minimized	(Optional) Select this check box, then click the mouse button or press the space bar to toggle "Run Minimized" on (an "X" in the box) and off. After installation, if "Run Minimized" is on, clicking the application's icon displays a duplicate icon on the desktop, and the application runs unseen in the back-ground. Double-click on the icon to bring the application to the foreground.

If no icon is seen in the lower lefthand corner of the Program Item Properties dialog box, you may want to refer to the *Icon Selection Procedure* section of Chapter 3 for instructions on changing the application's icon. Otherwise, just click on the OK button to complete the installation. A simple MS-DOS icon will show up in the Accessories Group Window, and the Program Description you entered (above) will appear directly under the icon. If you highlight the icon by clicking on it once, then reopen the Program Item Properties dialog box, the selected icon will appear, as seen in the lower lefthand corner of Figure 1.14c.

Setup at the DOS Prompt

This section describes how to change any of the system components listed on the *System Information* screen seen earlier in Figure 1.1. It is often safest to make these changes by running Setup at the DOS prompt, and not from within Windows itself.

Begin by exiting Windows, then log onto the Windows directory and type SETUP. You'll see a warning message if one of the programs listed in Table 1.3 is installed on your system, as described earlier in the *Problem Applications* section. In this case, you can ignore the message: Since you're only going to change a driver, the presence of one of these applications should not be a problem. Just press the "C" key to continue.

You should now see the *System Information* screen (Figure 1.1). If instead you see any other screen ("Welcome to Setup" for example), then refer to the *DOS-Prompt Setup Problem* section below. Assuming all is well, highlight the component you wish to change, press the Enter key, and scroll down to the Other option at the bottom of the list. Press the Enter key once again to display the following message:

Please insert the (*selected component*) driver disk provided by the hardware manufacturer. If the files from this disk are located on a different drive and/or directory, type the path where the files can be found.
A:\

Generally, the files you need are on a distribution diskette supplied with the component you want to install or modify. In some cases the diskette contains multiple files that may need to be expanded before use. In this case, first follow the manufacturer's own Setup (or Install, Go, whatever) instructions, then run the Setup procedure described here.

If the above procedure writes the needed files to a directory on your hard disk, then change the "A:\" seen above to the drive and path where these files may now be found. You may need to do this more than once if the Windows Setup procedure makes additional requests for more files. Furthermore, you may need to make a few trial runs if it is not clear which file is really needed. For example, sometimes the installation of a third-party driver brings with it the need for additional files from the Windows distribution diskettes. Therefore, if this Setup procedure can't seem to find what it wants on the manufacturer's diskette, or on the drive and path specified above, then try the Windows distribution diskettes.

Sometimes you'll be assisted by the message content. If you're asked to insert Windows disk #x, then do so. Otherwise, try the third-party diskette first.

Set Up DOS 6.0 Microsoft Tools Applets

If DOS 6.0 was installed prior to running the Windows 3.1 Setup procedure, then the three Windows applets included with DOS 6.0 were not installed. To install them now, exit Windows and log onto drive A. Insert DOS 6.0 (not Windows 3.1) distribution diskette 1 in the drive and type the following command at the DOS prompt:

SETUP /e

Press the Enter key a few times to toggle past the *Welcome* screen and the first MS-DOS 6 *Setup* screen. The second screen lists the following information:

Option	Program for	Bytes Used
Backup:	Windows only	1,081,344 bytes
Undelete:	Windows only	262,144 bytes
Anti-Virus	Windows only	1,292,640 bytes
No Changes:	Accept the above list	

Assuming you want to install all three applets (if one may call anything that eats 1 Mbyte an "applet") then simply press the Enter key to continue. Otherwise, follow the on-screen directions to make changes as desired, then press the Enter key. When you do, the applets will be installed in a new Microsoft Tools Group Window which will appear the next time you open Windows.

Refer to Chapter 0 for detailed information about these applets.

Two Setup Examples

Finally, a few variations in the regular Setup procedure are described here. As appropriate, some of this information may be modified to suit other requirements.

Set Up Application to Run at Startup. In Windows 3.0, the customary way to run an application at Startup was to include its name in one of the following two lines in the [windows] section of your WIN.INI file.

load=*(path and filename.ext)*
run=*(path and filename.ext)*

Any program listed on the load= line will run in the background, while a program listed on the run= line will run full-screen. Although the same general procedure may be followed in Windows 3.1, there is another way that may be more convenient, as described here.

The StartUp Group Window. Note that the Windows Desktop shown earlier in Figure 1.9 contains several minimized group icons, one of which is labeled "StartUp." To open the StartUp Group Window, double-click on this icon and note that the window contains—nothing. However, you may now insert any application you like in this window, and the next time you start Windows the applications now in this window will begin running. The application(s) will run full-screen or minimized, according to the way you have set their respective Program Item Properties. Refer to the *Move Applet to a Different Group Window* section of Chapter 3 for complete details on how to move applets from one window to another. The StartUp Group itself is covered in detail in Chapter 5.

Set Up Undocumented Windows Applets. The four undocumented Windows applets listed here are transferred to your hard disk during Setup, but do not appear on the Windows Desktop.

Filename	Description
DRWATSON.EXE	Diagnostic Utility
REGEDIT.EXE	Registration Editor
SYSEDIT.EXE	Edit utility for SYSTEM.INI, WIN.INI, CONFIG.SYS, and AUTOEXEC.BAT files only
WINHELP.EXE	Master Help Utility

Refer to Chapter 4 for details about these applets (except REGEDIT.EXE, which is in Chapter 6). Although all of them are Windows applications (applets, that is), they must be installed (if you choose to do so) by following the directions in the *Setup Non-Windows Applications* section above. The *Setup Windows Applications* procedure cannot be used, because each of their names is listed in the [dontfind] section of the APPS.INF file described earlier in the chapter.

Setup Troubleshooting

This section contains troubleshooting suggestions only for those problems encountered while running any version of Setup. If you were able to conclude the Setup procedure, but are now having problems getting Windows itself to start, then refer to Chapter 2 for assistance. For help troubleshooting a specific component problem that does not affect the overall operation of Windows, consult the appropriate chapter in this book for assistance. For example, if the Desktop color scheme is just awful, refer to the *Color* section of Chapter 11. Or check the Index if you are not sure where to find the necessary information.

The suggestions found in the *Upgrade Setup* section below apply only to problems encountered when upgrading an existing version of Windows to Windows 3.1. However, if nothing in this section is appropriate to the encountered problem, then refer to the *New Setup* section for additional assistance. Many of the problems described there may also show up during an upgrade Setup.

BOOTLOG and READTHIS Files. As an aid to troubleshooting, Windows 3.1 includes an option to write a boot log file named BOOTLOG.TXT whenever you begin a new Windows session. The procedure is mostly used for troubleshooting after Windows has been successfully set up, and is described in Chapter 2. However, since a boot log file is automatically created during the initial Setup procedure, you may wish to review the *BOOTLOG.TXT* section of Chapter 2 if you experience difficulties during Setup.

Also see the *READTHIS File* section which shows an alternative method of troubleshooting startup problems.

Troubleshooting an Upgrade Setup Procedure

The Setup procedure may fail during an upgrade if the [boot] section of an old SYSTEM.INI file in your Windows directory contains a reference to an invalid (for version 3.1) device driver. In this case, you may see an error message such as:

error loading *filename*.DRV

or,

error loading *(blank)*

The filename (or lack thereof) represents a driver listed on one of the device driver lines. If the system returns to the DOS prompt or hangs up without displaying an error message, have a look at the BOOTLOG.TXT file in the Windows directory. It will probably contain the following lines, in addition to other pairs representing any drivers that did load successfully.

```
[boot]
LoadStart =filename.DRV
LoadFail = filename.DRV Failure code is 02
```

If the LoadStart and LoadFail lines both omit a filename, then one of the following lines in SYSTEM.INI will also be truncated after the equal sign:

```
comm.drv=comm.drv
display.drv=xxx.drv (xxx = EGA, VGA, etc., as appropriate to system)
keyboard.drv=keyboard.drv
mouse.drv=mouse.drv
system.drv=system.drv
```

Edit the appropriate line in the [boot] section of SYSTEM.INI so that the expression on the righthand side of the equal sign matches that on the left. The exception is the display driver line, where the filename should be whatever is required for your system. Then erase the BOOTLOG.TXT file and rerun Setup.

DOS-Prompt Setup Problem. As described earlier in the chapter, you may also run Setup at the DOS prompt to make changes to your system configuration. This is usually the most convenient way to change such elements as video resolutions and mouse drivers.

When you log onto the Windows directory and type SETUP at the DOS prompt, you should see the *System Information* screen shown in Figure 1.1b. If instead you see a *Welcome to Setup* screen, then it's quite likely that the SETUP.EXE file in your Windows directory is the wrong one. If you've recently upgraded from Windows 3.0 to 3.1, or from 3.1 to a CD-ROM or network version of 3.1, it's possible that the SETUP.EXE accompanying the latest upgrade was not copied from distribution diskette 1 (or the CD-ROM disk) to your Windows directory. Therefore, when you attempt to make a minor configuration revision, Setup will instead attempt to run a new installation procedure.

However, no harm is done (yet). To prevent anything unpleasant from happening, press the F3 key to exit Setup. Note the date of the SETUP.EXE file in your Windows directory, which should be 3-10-92 or later. However, if you installed Windows 3.1 from a third-party CD-ROM disk, the date may be a week or so earlier. In any case, the safest course is to locate SETUP.EXE on whatever distribution media you used to install Windows 3.1, and copy a fresh version into your Windows directory. Then run Setup again from the DOS prompt, and you should see the *System Information* screen.

If you still see the *Welcome* screen, then there is something else wrong with your installation. You will probably need to exit Setup again, then rerun it from the distribution diskette.

Troubleshooting a New Setup Procedure

This section describes problems that may be encountered during an attempt to run the Setup procedure. If Setup has concluded successfully, then refer to Chapter 2 for assistance with problems that come up when you try to run Windows.

Defective Distribution Diskette. If there seems to be a problem with a specific distribution diskette, you can request a new copy from Microsoft. But before doing so, try using the DOS 5.0 XCOPY command to copy the diskette contents to another diskette, then use that one in place of the problem diskette. Of course this won't work if the original diskette is seriously damaged, but it has been known to succeed often enough to be worth trying, at least once.

DOS-Mode Setup Failure. Setup begins at the DOS prompt and switches into the Windows mode after the first few procedures have been successfully concluded. You'll recognize the DOS-to-Windows transition point by the "Please wait while Setup loads Windows" message which appears immediately before the prompt to insert your name and company.

If Setup fails before reaching this point, the most likely cause is a hardware-detection error during an Express Setup. Or you may have specified an incorrect or defective component during a Custom Setup. In either case, try running Setup again by typing the following line at the DOS prompt:

    Setup /i

The "i/" switch forces Setup into the Custom mode, and the first screen you see will be the one described earlier, in the *Reinstallation after Aborted Setup* section. Next, you will be asked to specify your hardware system, as described in the earlier *System Information Review* section. Or you can simply rerun Setup, and remember to specify the Custom option. In either case, make sure the equipment list is correct. If you are uncertain what the problem is, make sure your list does not specify any third-party video (or other) drivers. Once you have Windows successfully running with its own default drivers, you can experiment with other drivers.

A notable exception here is the fact that some video adapters will not function with the Windows default drivers in modes beyond plain-old VGA (640 × 480). In this case, you can try again with the third-party driver and hope the problem lies elsewhere. Better yet, specify the default basic VGA display and stay with it until you are satisfied that Windows is running correctly.

Windows-Mode Setup Failure. Once Setup enters its Windows-mode phase, it refers to the copy of itself that is now in your Windows directory (which makes sense, because the earlier version on diskette 1 is now lying on your table somewhere). If it picks up some other SETUP.EXE file by mistake, then anything can happen, and probably will. The most likely suspect is an old Setup file left over from the days of Windows 3.0, or possibly someone else's SETUP.EXE. To restore order, have a look at the file creation date for SETUP.EXE in your Windows directory, and SETUP.INF in the System directory. If either turn out to be the wrong one, erase one or both and rerun Setup. However, if the Setup files seem to be in order, then have a look in your root directory, and in any other locations specified in your PATH statement. If you find another file with the same name, give it some other name and try again.

Setup Error Messages

This section lists many of the error messages that are apt to be encountered during Setup. For every message listed here, there are probably several variations on the same theme. Therefore, find the message here that is the closest match to what you see on screen.

> **NOTE:** The meat in some Setup error messages is submerged in a layer of "Setup has encountered . . ." or "You are attempting . . ." or some other basket of words. As an aid to faster problem-solving, such messages are brought to the top here by a descriptive word or phrase that sums up the nature of the problem. This description is not a part of the message seen on screen.

Cannot find the file *filename.ext.* If the cited file can't be found, it's probably missing from the distribution diskette, or the diskette itself is defective. Check the diskette for the file, and if it really is missing, order a replacement diskette from Microsoft. If the file is present, refer to the *Defective Distribution Diskette* section above for suggestions on recovering the missing information.

Cannot load the file *filename.ext*. If a file can't be loaded, it's probably due to a shortage of conventional memory. If some application is taking up too much space, quit the application (reboot, if necessary), and run Setup again.

Cannot read the file *SETUP.INF*. In this case, the SETUP.INF file on distribution diskette 1 is present but may be defective. Order a replacement diskette, or refer to the *Defective Distribution Diskette* section above for assistance.

Can only run one copy of Setup at a time. It is probable that you're only *trying* to run one copy. The message may be seen if a previously-aborted Setup procedure left a temporary file or directory on your hard disk. For example, Microsoft *Excel 4.0* creates an MS-SETUP.T directory, which it erases at the successful conclusion of Setup. If the directory is not erased, then a subsequent Setup will find it and deliver the error message. The solution is to find the directory, erase its contents (if any), and remove it.

If this message (or a variation on it) appears under similar circumstances with some other application, you may have to do a little snooping to find either a file, or a directory, that needs to be erased.

Disk Drive: Problem with disk drive *x*: Please check to see that the disk is properly inserted in the drive and the drive door is closed. If a physical check of the diskette and drive does not turn up the problem, there may be something wrong with the diskette itself. In case of doubt, double-check the drive by experimenting with a diskette that is known to be good, run Setup from a different drive, and/or refer to the *Defective Distribution Diskette* section above.

> **NOTE:** This message is sometimes seen while attempting to revise the System Equipment list, even though drive *x* (usually, *A*) is not being used. For some reason, Setup wants to see something in drive *x* anyway, and won't continue unless you oblige it by inserting a diskette. To do so, press the Enter key and the setup procedure should continue.

Control Panel: The currently installed (*filename.ext*) is newer than the one you are attempting to install. Do you still want to install the file? This is one of a series of such messages that may be seen if you attempt to install a version of Windows that is older than the version already installed. This message format is seen during the printer configuration segment of Setup. For further details, refer to the *Setup has detected the following conflict(s) . . .* message described below.

Disk Drive: Setup has encountered a serious problem while identifying the type of disk on your machine. To correct this problem, you need to restart your computer. After restarting, run Setup again by typing Setup /i, to skip automatic hardware detection. Note you will need to choose Custom Setup so you can specify your hardware. You may see this message if you tried to run a Custom Setup, and Setup did not correctly identify your system hardware components. If you do rerun Setup with the /i switch, you can just ignore the last sentence in the message above: The switch forces Setup into Custom mode, so there's nothing for you to choose. If you omit the switch by accident, then it will be up to you to choose Custom Setup.

Disk Drive: Your system does not have enough disk space to set up Windows. Windows requires a minimum of *xxx* bytes of disk space. You can specify a directory on another drive if you have one with the required space. Or you can quit Setup, delete files from the current drive, and then run Setup again. The message is self-explanatory. However, if space is really that tight, you may be able to do a minimal-configuration Setup by temporarily removing some files from your hard drive, then trying Setup again. Select the Custom Setup option and omit every component you don't absolutely need. Once Windows is installed, you can restore the files you removed.

Although this may actually work, you probably won't be pleased with Windows' performance, especially if there is not enough free hard-disk space for it to use during routine operations. If you can't free up sufficient space to give Windows the elbow room it needs (it *does* have big elbows), you may want to think about getting a larger-capacity hard drive before going any further.

Divide by 0 (not Zero). A divide-by-zero error message may indicate any number of problems. However, since the "0" message is found only in the LZEXPAND.DLL file which is called late in the Setup procedure, it probably means that a corrupted installation was detected. Review the BOOTLOG.TXT file for clues and, in the absence of any definitive information, try rebooting with a minimal-configuration CONFIG.SYS and AUTOEXEC.BAT file, then rerunning Setup by typing SETUP /i. Choose the Custom Setup option and carefully review the components listed in the *System Information* screen shown earlier in Figure 1.1.

Memory: (any of several "Not Enough Memory" messages). The on-screen message usually contains sufficient information to identify the specific problem area.

Conventional Memory. You should have a full 640 Kbytes installed in your system. If that is not the problem, then perhaps some application is taking up too much space. Either quit the application, or simply reboot to free up the conventional memory area.

TSR Programs. Don't overlook the possibility that you have too many TSR (terminate-and-stay-resident) programs sitting in conventional memory. In this case, rebooting will just reload the TSRs, so you have to edit your CONFIG.SYS and AUTOEXEC.BAT files to temporarily turn them off. Refer to the Basic Startup Files shown in Table 1.4a for suggestions.

Memory Management: The version of *(third-part memory manager)* **that you are running is incompatible with enhanced mode Windows. You will need to upgrade** *(third-party memory manager)* **to run enhanced mode Windows. Or:**
The XMS driver you have on your system in not compatible with Windows. You must remove it before Setup can successfully install Windows. In either case, try editing your CONFIG.SYS file to specify the HIMEM.SYS and EMM386.EXE files included with Windows 3.1. Once you have successfully installed Windows you can experiment with third-party memory-management software.

Message Number: If you are installing Windows, write down the number of this message, then call product support for assistance. With luck, this depressing suggestion is accompanied by other information that will help you resolve the problem without trying to get through to Microsoft Product Support. Review the rest of the message for other clues (cannot find a file, insufficient memory, etc.) before assuming the worst.

Microprocessor: Make sure your computer has an Intel 80286, 80386, or 80486 processor. Or:
You attempted to install Windows 3.1 on a computer with an 8086 or 8088 processor. Windows requires an 80286 processor (or higher). You may run into this sort of advice in the unlikely event that you try to install Windows

3.1 on a system that falls short of an 80286 microprocessor. If you can figure out a workaround, go for it. Otherwise, it's time to get a new computer.

OEM.INF File: Setup is unable to open the OEMSETUP.INF file at the location you specified. Some third-party drivers are accompanied by a file named SETUP.INF, which Setup doesn't recognize. If this message occurs when you try to install such drivers, log onto the System directory and type DIR OEM*.INF at the DOS prompt. If any files are listed, note the one with the highest number following the OEM in the filename. Then copy the third-party SETUP.INF file into your System directory as OEM*x*.INF, where *x* is the next highest number (which of course would be *1* if there are no such files already present). Then retry the installation.

Operating System: Windows does not run with the version of MS-DOS you have on your computer. The obvious problem here is that the computer was booted with a copy of MS-DOS earlier than version 3.1. Upgrade to DOS 5.0, then run Setup.

It's also possible that your computer has a 3.1 or later DOS installed, but it is an OEM DOS version that is not designed for your system. In this case, you should replace it with the correct version, then try again.

Operating System: You are attempting to set up Windows 3.1 from an OS/2 DOS session. Now why would you want to do a thing like that? Quit OS/2 (if not forever, then at least for as long as it takes to install Windows).

Read-Only File. If Setup complains about encountering a read-only file, clear the read-only attribute for that file and rerun Setup. If you need assistance, refer to the DOS *User's Guide* for information about using the ATTRIB command to reset the read-only attribute.

Setup Error #S020. Setup is unable to make changes to the Windows configuration file, SYSTEM.INI (followed by additional information). This message may be seen if your Windows directory already contains a WIN.INI (*not* SYSTEM.INI) file with zero bytes (perhaps a result of a previous failed Setup). The fix is easy enough: Erase the bad WIN.INI file and rerun Setup.

The message may also be seen if there is not enough room in conventional memory for SYSTEM.INI and WIN.INI. In this case, free some conventional memory by rebooting from the basic startup files seen in Table 1.4a. Then run Setup again.

Setup has detected the following conflict(s) between the version of *(filename.ext)* **currently on your system and the version that Setup is attempting to copy. You can choose to use the currently installed file or replace it with the file Setup is trying to copy:**

Current file:	Version: 3.10a	Language:	US English
	220800 bytes	09/14/92	12:02
Proposed file:	Version: 3.10	Language:	US English
	220800 bytes	03/10/92	3:10

- **The replacement file is an older version than your current file.**
- **To keep your currently installed driver file, press ENTER.**
- **To replace the currently installed driver file, press ESC.**

This message (or similar) will be seen one or more times if you set up a version of Windows that is older then the presently installed version. In most cases, this is your clue that something is amiss. Presumably you would want to retain the newer file(s) already installed on your hard disk. However, in the specific example shown here, Windows-for-Workgroups is currently installed, and the Setup procedure is being used to restore Windows version 3.1. Since the version 3.1 files are indeed older than the Workgroups files, you *do* need to replace the installed new files with the older ones. In a case such as this, press the Escape key every time the message is seen.

In other situations, you may want to keep the current (newer) file, so press the Enter key instead. Or press function key F3 to exit Setup if the message tips you off that you shouldn't be trying to install an older version of Windows.

Setup is unable to install the file *filename.ext* **because the file is currently in use by Windows. To upgrade the driver and related files you have selected, quit Windows, then run Setup by typing 'Setup' at the MS-DOS prompt.**
Once Windows is installed, and you run *Windows Setup* from the Main Group Window, you may see this message if you attempt certain system changes. The message may be followed by another, proposing that a needed file may be write-protected. In any case, the first message is a bit confusing because, if a file is already in use by Windows, then it certainly doesn't need to be installed. The actual problem is probably that a file that needs to be replaced is currently in use, and/or the needed file is not yet available in the System directory, as might be the case if you had initially installed say, the default VGA-system drivers, and now wanted to upgrade to Super-VGA (800 × 600) mode.

Exit Windows and run Setup at the DOS prompt from within the Windows directory. Have your distribution diskettes ready, and feed them to drive A, as prompted. If you had previously transferred the needed files into a directory on your hard drive, change the prompt to show that directory, then continue.

Setup must update or change some of the files used by the following application(s):
Viewer Quickeys *(or some other application)*. **Please close these application(s) and run Setup again.** The most likely occasion for a message such as this is if you rerun a previously installed application's Setup procedure. The application cited in the message is currently active, perhaps as an icon at the bottom of the screen. Exit the Setup procedure, close the application, and rerun Setup.

When in doubt about what needs to be closed, exit Windows and reopen it. Hold down the Shift key until the Program Manager screen is seen. This prevents all applets in the StartUp group from being executed. Now try running the Setup procedure again.

Stack Overflow. If you encounter this error message on rebooting after the Windows Setup procedure concludes, then edit the following line in your CONFIG.SYS file:

Stacks = x, y

Try the following values:

x	y	Comments
x	*y*	Restore whatever values were in use prior to running Setup.
0	0	Use only if this indicates the previous values.
9	128	Use if the Stacks line did not previously appear in CONFIG.SYS.
9	256	Recommended setting for most configurations.
9	512	The maximum permissible stack size.

If the 0, 0 combination works, it suggests that some installed software is not compatible with DOS's stack-switching system. There may be occasional stack overflow errors until the incompatible software is removed or updated, and some nonzero values can be used instead.

In some cases, a stack-related problem may cause the system to behave erratically, yet not display a stack error message. If you suspect this is a problem (typically, with a specific application), increase the stack size to the 512-byte maximum.

Stack Overflow: Internal stack overflow. System halted. If this message is seen, then the number of stacks is insufficient. Increase the x value, reboot, and repeat if necessary.

Standard Mode: Fault in MS-DOS extender. This message may be seen while attempting to run Setup on a computer using Digital Research's DR DOS 6.0 operating system. In most cases, the problem is that the DR DOS version predates Windows 3.1 and is not fully compatible. Digital Research has issued a free upgrade which is available to all registered DR DOS owners. Contact the company for ordering instructions.

SYSTEM.INI File Is Unusually Large (above 32K). This message might be seen during an upgrade Setup if your existing SYSTEM.INI file is too big to accommodate further changes. However, 32 Kbytes is one *big* INI file, so it's more than likely that the file contains a lot that could be deleted. If this applies to your system, open SYSTEM.INI and delete comments, unnecessary sections, or whatever else it takes to trim it down to a more reasonable size.

The contradiction notwithstanding, this message may also be seen during a post-installation Setup if there is a problem with your WIN.INI file, or if SYSTEM.INI is completely missing. In the first case, refer to the *Setup Error #S020* message above. Or, have a look at the *Reconstruct INI Files* section of Chapter 14 for suggestions about how to reconstruct that file.

Upgrade: You can only upgrade from version 3.0. You'll meet this message if you attempt to upgrade any version of Windows that pre-dates Windows 3.0. Although you can upgrade from that version to 3.0, then upgrade to 3.1, why bother? It's quicker and cleaner to install a fresh version of Windows 3.1

Version Conflict: The following file conflicts with the version already on your system:

File: *(filename.ext)*

Description: *(file description)*

The new version of the file (*version number*) **you are trying to install is older than the currently installed version** (*version number*)**. Do you want to replace the file that is already on your system?** The message is functionally equivalent to the Setup has detected the following conflict(s)... message described above. This version may appear during the Windows segment of Setup; the other version may appear during the DOS segment. Refer to the other version for further details.

Wassily Kandinsky was the great painter who participated in the Expressionist movement in Germany, taught at the Bauhaus, and edited the Blue Rider Almanac. Apparently, it's not *all work and no play* in Redmond, Washington. This little bit of inside information is tucked away in the long list of error messages. If you have the CD-ROM *Grolier Encyclopedia* on hand, you can verify its accuracy. Otherwise, its significance to Windows troubleshooting is beyond the scope of this book.

Windows 3.1 could not be located on your computer. This version of Windows-for-Workgroups requires that Windows 3.1 already be installed. You must either install Windows 3.1 onto your computer, or purchase the complete version of Windows-for-Workgroups. For the Windows 3.1 user who wants to upgrade to Windows-for-Workgroups 3.1, Microsoft markets an upgrade version at about half the retail price of the full Windows-for-Workgroups. Although both versions offer the same features, the upgrade can only be installed over an existing version of Windows 3.1.

Look for the phrase "Add-On" in the title text on distribution diskette 1. If you find it, you need to follow the message instructions above to successfully install Windows-for-Workgroups.

You are attempting to run Setup from within Windows. You'll see this message if you attempt to run Setup from within a DOS window. Exit the DOS window, then click on the Windows Setup icon in the Main Group Window, or exit Windows itself, log onto the Windows directory, and run Setup from there.

2

Windows Startup and Exit Troubleshooting

This chapter describes the problems that may be encountered when you attempt to run Windows after the Setup procedure has successfully concluded. It is assumed here that the system itself is operational, and that a problem occurs only when you attempt to open or close Windows. If you are having system trouble before opening Windows, then that problem should be resolved first, since it has nothing to do with Windows 3.1. If a problem shows up during a Windows session, refer to one of the other chapters in this book for assistance.

If a system bootup problem arises immediately after installing a new memory manager, refer to the *Memory-Management Troubleshooting* section of Chapter 13 for suggestions. Once the system is fully operational, return to this chapter for help with other Windows 3.1 startup problems.

Depending on the nature of the problem, Windows may run in standard mode only, may run after displaying an error message, or may not run at all. Refer to the appropriate section below for suggestions on how to proceed.

In addition to the troubleshooting sections which follow, an error message section lists the messages that may appear as Windows opens. If you see such a message, then refer to the appropriate error message section for assistance.

The final section of the chapter describes a few batch files that may help you configure Windows to better suit your specific needs.

Preliminary Troubleshooting Notes

If the nature of the startup problem does not make it clear where the trouble lies, review the suggestions found in this section to help isolate the source of the problem.

Windows Essential Files

Table 2.1 lists the rather small handful of files that must be present in order to open Windows and display the Program Manager and group windows on the Desktop. With these files present and in good order (and assuming your hardware system is also in good order), Windows will open, although you may still see error messages along the way. If so, make a note of them,

TABLE 2.1   Windows 3.1 Essential Files*

Directory Filename	Ext.	Comments
Windows		
filename	GRP	One for each group or third-party equivalent.
HIMEM	SYS	
PROGMAN	EXE	
PROGMAN	INI	
SYSTEM	INI	
WIN	COM	
System		
filename	DRV	One for each driver listed in [boot] section of SYSTEM.INI.
DOSX	EXE	Standard mode only.
GDI	EXE	
KRNL286	EXE	Standard mode only, but Windows will still open if it's missing.
KRNL386	EXE	Enhanced mode only.
SHELL	DLL	
SYSTEM	DRV	
USER	EXE	
xxx	DRV	(*xxx* = installed video system prefix)
*xxx*FIX	FON	(*xxx* = installed video system prefix)
*xxx*OEM	FON	(*xxx* = installed video system prefix)
*xxx*SYS	FON	(*xxx* = installed video system prefix)
WIN386	EXE	Enhanced mode only.
WSWAP	EXE	Enhanced mode only.

*The presence of these files represents the minimum requirement to successfully open Windows and display the Program Manager on the Windows Desktop. See text for further details.

then exit Windows to take the appropriate action(s). Once this is done, you should be able to open Windows without getting in trouble. However, your subsequent success in opening various applets and applications will depend on the presence of still other files, memory configuration, and so on.

The BOOTLOG.TXT File

If you try to run Windows and nothing much happens, there may not be an obvious clue as to what the problem is. In this case, you may be able to write a log of the startup procedure by restarting Windows as follows:

```
WIN /b
```

The /b switch instructs Windows to write a BOOTLOG.TXT file to the Windows directory during startup. If you have other switches on the WIN command line, make sure they appear before the /b switch. The bootlog file contains a record of operations performed during the startup procedure. Review the file after Windows unsuccessfully loads to see what problems were encountered.

Table 2.2 shows the contents of a typical bootlog file, and Table 2.3 lists the various failure codes that may be seen within the log. If the file itself is not available, then the error occurred during a very early stage, before the file-writing procedure began. If the file is present, make sure the file-creation time is correct. Otherwise, it may be a leftover from a previous session, with information not related to the present problem. If the file contains no error messages, then the specific problem was not detected by the error-logging system, even though it may be serious enough to prevent successful operations. In this case, you'll need to follow more traditional troubleshooting procedures, as described below.

If it's necessary to reboot the system to recover, the last line of BOOTLOG.TXT should yield a very good clue as to the problem. For example, here's an excerpt from such a file created during an unsuccessful startup:

```
LoadStart = system.drv
LoadSuccess = system.drv
LoadStart = keyboard.drv
LoadSuccess = keyboard.drv
. . .
. . .
INIT=Mouse
STATUS=Mouse driver installed
INITDONE=Mouse
. . .
. . .
LoadStart = comm.drv
LoadFail = comm.drv Failure code is 02
```

TABLE 2.2   Contents of Typical BOOTLOG.TXT File*

Section and Contents		Section and Contents	
Kernel (hardware resources)		**User** *(continued)*	
[boot]		INITDONE	= Mouse
LoadStart	= system.drv	INIT	= Display
LoadSuccess	= system.drv	LoadStart	= DISPLAY.drv
LoadStart	= keyboard.drv	LoadSuccess	= DISPLAY.drv
LoadSuccess	= keyboard.drv	INITDONE	= Display
LoadStart	= mouse.drv	INIT	= Display Resources
LoadSuccess	= mouse.drv	INIT	= TSRQuery
LoadStart	= vga.drv	INITDONE	= TSRQuery
LoadSuccess	= vga.drv	INITDONE	= Display Resources
LoadStart	= mmsound.drv	INIT	= Fonts
LoadSuccess	= mmsound.drv	LoadStart	= SERIFF.FON[†]
LoadStart	= comm.drv	LoadSuccess	= SERIFF.FON[†]
LoadSuccess	= comm.drv	INITDONE	= Fonts
		INIT	= Lang Driver
System Fonts		INITDONE	= Lang Driver
LoadStart	= vgasys.fon	LoadSuccess	= USER.EXE
LoadSuccess	= vgasys.fon		
LoadStart	= vgaoem.fon	**Program Manager**[‡]	
LoadSuccess	= vgaoem.fon	LoadStart	= progman.exe
		LoadStart	= SHELL.DLL
GDI: Graphic Display Interface		LoadSuccess	= SHELL.DLL
LoadStart	= GDI.EXE	LoadSuccess	= progman.exe
LoadStart	= FONTS.FON		
LoadSuccess	= FONTS.FON	**Setup Section**[‡]	
LoadStart	= vgafix.fon	LoadStart	= setup.exe
LoadSuccess	= vgafix.fon	LoadStart	= LZEXPAND.DLL
LoadStart	= OEMFONTS.FON	LoadSuccess	= LZEXPAND.DLL
LoadSuccess	= OEMFONTS.FON	LoadStart	= VER.DLL
LoadSuccess	= GDI.EXE	LoadSuccess	= VER.DLL
		LoadSuccess	= setup.exe
User			
LoadStart	= USER.EXE	**Final Checks**	
INIT	= Keyboard	INIT	= Final USER
INITDONE	= Keyboard	INITDONE	= Final USER
INIT	= Mouse	INIT	= Installable Drivers
STATUS	= Mouse driver installed	INITDONE	= Installable Drivers

[*] Section headers and indents added here for clarity; not seen in actual file.

[†] These lines repeated for each font listed in [fonts] section of WIN.INI. Not included during initial Setup.

[‡] Setup section appears instead of Program Manager section during initial Setup only.

TABLE 2.3   Bootlog Failure Codes*

Failure Code	Meaning
00	Out of memory.
02	File not found.
03	Path not found.
05	Attempt to dynamically link to a task.
06	Library requires separate data segments for each task.
08	Insufficient memory to start application.
10	Incorrect Windows version.
11	Invalid EXE file.
12	OS/2 application.
13	MS-DOS 4.0 application.
14	Unknown EXE file type.
15	Protected mode attempt to load EXE file created for earlier version of Windows.
16	Attempt to load second instance of EXE file containing multiple writable data segments.
17	Large-frame EMS mode attempt to load second instance of application that links to certain non-shareable DLLs already in use.
18	Real-Mode attempt to load application marked for protected mode only.

*Type WIN /b to create BOOTLOG.TXT file.

In the specific BOOTLOG.TXT example given above, the next step is to look for a COMM.DRV file, which should be in the System directory. If it's missing, you'll need to replace it. If it's present, it's probably corrupted. In either case, use the Windows Expand utility (described in Chapter 4) to transfer a fresh copy to your hard disk. If the failure message refers to a garbled filename, then check SYSTEM.INI for that name and edit the line to correct the name.

NOTE: A BOOTLOG.TXT file is created automatically during the initial Setup procedure described in Chapter 1. At other times, you must type **WIN /b** when you begin Windows to write a bootlog.

Each bootlog file is *appended* to the previous bootlog (if any). Therefore, you may wish to erase the previous bootlog before writing a new one. The WIN.BAT file described near the end of this chapter does this automatically.

A READTHIS Error Message File

As another troubleshooting aid, don't overlook the possibility of writing error messages to a disk file. Sometimes when Windows fails to open, a message flashes on and off so fast that you can't read it. In this case, try again by typing the following line at the DOS prompt:

```
WIN > C:\READTHIS
```

This simple step should write the unseen error message into a file named READTHIS, which you can quickly review by typing TYPE READTHIS at the DOS prompt. It's not high-tech, but it works (sometimes).

Windows Mode Test

If you open Windows by typing WIN without appending a mode switch, Windows should automatically open in the mode appropriate for your system. If the nature of a startup problem is not immediately apparent, you may want to force Windows to open first in one mode, then in the other by appending a mode switch to the WIN command, as shown here:

Type	To Force Windows Operating Mode
WIN /s (*or* WIN /2)	Standard
WIN /3	386 Enhanced

 NOTE: The former Enhanced Mode /e switch is no longer supported. Make sure you type WIN/3 to test Enhanced Mode operation.

If only one Windows mode fails, and no on-screen message appears, then one of the Standard Mode or Enhanced Mode EXE files listed below may be defective. Try replacing one, then the other. If the WINSTART.BAT file listed below (Enhanced Mode only) is present, temporarily disable it and try again. If this solves the problem, refer to the *WINSTART.BAT* section near the end of this chapter.

Standard Mode	Enhanced Mode
DOSX.EXE	WIN386.EXE
KRNL286.EXE	KRNL386.EXE
	WINSTART.BAT

If an error message is seen, then refer to the *Standard Mode* or *Enhanced Mode* error message sections below, as appropriate.

Windows Memory Check

In some of the tests described below, Windows may not open in the selected mode, even with the use of the /s or /3 switch. In case of doubt about the current operating mode, click on the Help menu bar and select the About Program Manager... option to display the "About Program Manager" screen shown in Figure 2.1. The bottom of the screen lists the current operating mode, free memory, and system resources. If the screen reports less than about 1,000KB free, then either you really don't have enough memory to feed the Enhanced Mode's appetite, or something else has eaten it first.

If a quick review of the following sections doesn't resolve the problem, refer to Chapter 13 for more information about memory matters.

Conventional Memory Check. Use the DOS MEM /c command to examine the contents of your conventional memory area. If the report scrolls off screen, retype the command as shown here:

    MEM /c | more

Note the "Total FREE" report. If the figure is 300K or less, then you probably don't have sufficient free conventional memory to permit Windows to run. In this case, you'll probably see an application listed that is occupying a significant amount of conventional memory. Be prepared to remove the application if Windows won't run.

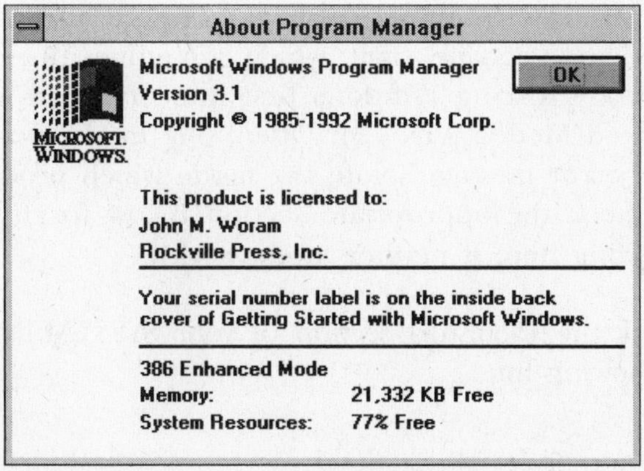

Figure 2.1 The About Program Manager screen displays Windows version, copyright, and licensing information. The bottom of the screen lists operating mode, memory, and system resource data.

Extended Memory Check. If you really don't have much extended memory, you'll have to run around to the memory store and buy some more. However, if you know there should be enough memory to go around, then look to see where it's hiding. Log onto your RAM disk (if any) and run the DOS CHKDSK utility. If it reports several Mbytes of total disk space, edit the RAMDRIVE line in your CONFIG.SYS file to trim it down to a reasonable size, reboot, and reopen Windows. Check the About Program Manager Screen again and the free memory figure should have risen accordingly.

StartUp Troubleshooting

With luck, an error message as Windows opens clearly identified the source of the problem, in which case you're not reading this sentence. Otherwise, review the suggestions found here before trying anything drastic.

The absence of an error message does not necessarily mean that all is well. Windows may not run at all or, to make matters worse, the system may reboot itself, or it may open but not well. A few of the things that can go wrong during startup are described here.

Windows Does Not Run

If Windows won't start when you type WIN and press the Enter key, then review whichever section below best describes what happens.

The DOS Prompt Reappears. An error message is not always seen if a missing or damaged file prevents Windows from running. If this is the problem, try opening Windows a second time, which sometimes does produce an error message. Or try forcing Windows first into Standard Mode (WIN /s), then into Enhanced Mode (WIN /3). Often, one mode succeeds, while the other displays an error message. Note the mode which produced the error message, then check the appropriate section below for further assistance. Or continue reading here if neither mode works.

The System Reboots. Check the [386Enh] section of your SYSTEM.INI file for the presence of the following line:

```
device=*dosmgr
```

If the line is garbled or missing, edit SYSTEM.INI to correct it. If the line is present, then your WIN386.EXE file may be defective. Try installing a fresh expanded copy from your distribution diskettes.

The system may also reboot if there is an upper memory conflict. If this is a possibility, then check the appropriate troubleshooting section of Chapter 13 for assistance.

The System Locks Up. The problem may be due to an incompatible device driver added since running the original Setup procedure. Reboot the system, don't start Windows, but log onto the Windows directory and run Setup at the DOS prompt. Carefully examine the System Information List (refer to Figure 1.1b) and change any references to third-party drivers back to their original Microsoft equivalents.

If the problem persists, try one or more of the following measures, as appropriate to your system:

1. Reboot the system with a minimal-configuration CONFIG.SYS and AUTOEXEC.BAT file (see Table 1.4a). If this cures the problem, restore the HIMEM.SYS, EMM386.EXE and dos= lines (or the equivalent third-party memory management lines). If the problem returns, refer to Chapter 13 for assistance with memory-management details. If not, then restore the other lines, one by one until the problem returns.

2. Disable the Load= and Run= lines in WIN.INI by inserting a semicolon at the beginning of each line.

3. Disable the StartUp group by holding down the Shift key as Windows opens. This prevents the files in the group from being executed.

4. Disable any multimedia devices that you recently installed or reconfigured.

If any of these procedures isolate the problem to a specific item, then refer to the chapter of this book in which that item is discussed in detail. If a multimedia device is a suspect, refer to Chapter 4 for IRQ conflict information.

Troubleshooting Display Problems

Windows may *think* it opened successfully, yet a look at the monitor screen shows that something is clearly (or perhaps unclearly) wrong. If so, the following sections may offer some help in cleaning things up.

Size and Position of Windows 3.1 Logo and/or Desktop Displays Are Incorrect. As Windows opens, the 3.1 logo may be displayed at one video resolution, after which the Desktop is displayed in another. If one or both are off-size or poorly centered, then the alignment of the respective video mode needs adjustment. If your monitor's video modes are separately adjustable, press the Pause button when the distorted screen is seen. Make the necessary adjustments and save the settings by following the instructions in the monitor User's Guide. Then press any key to continue.

Wrong Windows Logo Appears. If the wrong Windows logo screen appears, then the logo file (RLE extension) embedded in your WIN.COM file is the wrong version—either the old 3.0 logo, or the Windows 3.1 instead of the Windows-for-Workgroups 3.1 (or vice versa). It's easy enough to fix this problem. Find the appropriate file (listed below) on your distribution diskettes and expand a fresh copy into the System directory.

CGALOGO.RLE　　　　HERCLOGO.RLE
EGALOGO.RLE　　　　VGALOGO.RLE
EGAMONO.RLE

Next, log onto the System directory and create a new WIN.COM file by typing the following line at the DOS prompt:

```
copy /b WIN.CNF + xxxLOGO.LGO + xxxLOGO.RLE C:\WINDOWS\WIN.COM
```

Replace *xxx* with CGA, EGA, HERC, or VGA, as appropriate. When you press the Enter key, you should see the following screen display:

```
WIN.CNF
xxxLOGO.LGO
xxxLOGO.RLE

1 file(s) copied
```

The **1 file(s) copied** message really means *three* files copied into one file.

This should cure the logo problem, but does not answer the question: Why was the old logo there in the first place? In the case of Windows 3.0, make sure its presence is not an indication that other 3.0 files are still lying around in your Windows directories. If you find any, replace them with their version 3.1 equivalents.

Windows Logo Appears Off-Center and Colors Are Wrong. In this case, the old VGALOGO.LGO file is the culprit. Follow the directions immediately above for creating a new WIN.COM file, and double-check for other 3.0 files in your Windows directories.

Brief On-Screen Message Follows Windows Logo, then Desktop Appears. Some third-party video drivers display a brief configuration message immediately after the appearance of the Windows logo. However, the normal Desktop display may overwrite the message before it can be read, leaving one to wonder what it said, and if the news was bad.

In order to read the message, press the Pause key as soon as it is displayed. You'll probably see product information, current video resolution, copyright notices, and a version number. Press any key and next time just ignore the message.

Distorted Display, Followed by Normal Windows Desktop. Sometimes the initial Windows logo screen resembles a defective TV display, yet it is followed by the regular Windows Desktop, and subsequent Windows operations are not affected.

The problem may show up if system video resolution is downgraded after previous configuration at a higher resolution, especially if a third-party video driver is involved. For example, a super-VGA system may switch through several video modes as it opens: The pre-Windows DOS screen is at 640×400, followed briefly by the Windows logo at 800×600, then the Windows Desktop at 1024×768 (or other). If the system is subsequently downgraded/reconfigured for a conventional VGA monitor, there may be momentary distortion as the system switches into 800×600 mode (without success), then back to conventional VGA mode.

To fix the problem, copy a new WIN.COM file, as described above in the *Wrong Windows Logo Appears* section. Next, check your startup files and remove any third-party video-mode drivers or TSRs that may no longer be required. Or, if the downgraded video system is to be temporary, just ignore the distorted screen.

Distorted Display. If the correct logo is followed by a screen that is either completely blank or otherwise incorrect (flashing colors, horizontal lines, you name it), there may be a video-mode incompatibility that Windows is unaware of.

Press the Ctrl+Alt+Del keys to do a local reboot. This should result in a display that offers two options: press any key to return to Windows, or press Ctrl+Alt+Del to reboot your computer. (Refer to Chapter 4 if you need more information about this procedure.)

No harm is done by rebooting, since no applications are active yet. If you prefer, press any key to return to Windows, do a blind exit by pressing Alt+F4, then press the Enter key. Log onto the Windows directory, type "Setup" and, when the System Information list is displayed, make sure the Display line agrees with your installed video system. If it does, and you are still experiencing a problem, then select a default EGA, VGA (or other, as appropriate) display. If this cures the problem (it should), then the driver you were trying to use may be defective or incompatible with either Windows 3.1, or with your installed video system.

Incomplete Desktop Display. If a top or bottom section of the Windows Desktop is missing, there may be a problem with your system's video RAM. For example, if your memory manager has converted some of the video RAM in the A000-AFFF block into free upper memory blocks, some or all of the Windows display may be missing (screen will be black) or distorted. Try pressing the Enter key a few times and/or force the system into standard, then Enhanced Mode and look for a specific error message that may give more information.

Some conflicts force the system to reboot, in which case you don't need to do any further testing. Just go to your CONFIG.SYS and make sure there are no references to the A000-AFFF block. If there are none, then also check for references to any blocks in the B000-BFFF and C000-C800 areas, and remove them.

Desktop Fonts and/or Colors Are Incorrect. If Windows opens successfully, but the icon font and/or Desktop colors are incorrect, it's possible your WIN.INI file is either corrupt or missing entirely. If the file is present, you'll need to edit it to fix the errors. Refer to Chapter 10 if the fonts are wrong.

If Desktop colors are incorrect, you can change them as desired, by following the instructions in the *Color Applet* section of Chapter 11. Or, to return to the Windows default color set, just delete the entire [colors] section of your WIN.INI file.

StartUp Group Problem

If a startup problem seems to be related to something in the StartUp Group Window, try restarting Windows without loading the group. To do so, hold down either Shift key when the Windows logo is displayed, then release the key when the Desktop appears. If Windows opens successfully, then there is indeed a problem with one of the applets in the StartUp group. If you're not sure which one, move half of them into any other group window, then close and reopen Windows. Repeat, as necessary, until the problem goes away. Then return half of the just-removed group. Keep at it until the guilty applet is identified. Refer to Chapter 5 for further details about the StartUp Group Window.

WIN.INI Problems

If you suspect that your WIN.INI file is causing you grief, but aren't sure what to do about it, try killing it. But make it a temporary death by simply renaming it as say, X-WIN.INI. With the file now "lost," Windows will probably still run anyway. However, information about your specific font configuration, color scheme, installed printer(s), and such will be unavailable. In addition, applications listed on its load= and run= lines will not run.

If WIN.INI's departure cures a startup problem, then revive it by renaming it back to WIN.INI and check the section that contains information related to whatever the problem is. To troubleshoot further, you may want to disable some of the lines in a problem section. You can do so by editing the line(s) to insert a semicolon as the first character. All such lines are ignored the next time you start Windows. You may also want to review the entire contents of WIN.INI, line by line. Some third-party Setup routines have been known to disgrace themselves within the file, leaving all sorts of garbled text droppings behind them. Usually, WIN.INI just ignores anything that doesn't make sense, but now and then a line of garbled text could cause a problem. Remove such lines and try again.

If WIN.INI was accidentally erased and can't be unerased, then refer to the *Reconstruct INI Files* section in Chapter 14 for suggestions on how to rebuild it without running a complete new Setup procedure, or simply rerun Setup.

Enhanced Mode Startup Troubleshooting

Review this section if Windows opens successfully in Standard Mode, but you experience problems starting it in Enhanced Mode.

WIN (no switch) Opens Standard Mode, WIN /3 Opens Enhanced Mode. As noted earlier, Windows should open in the mode appropriate for your system. If Windows opens by default in Standard Mode, but you are able to force it into Enhanced Mode by typing WIN /3, then you probably have a marginal amount of free memory available. Working in this condition is not recommended, other than to verify that no other problem prevents enhanced-mode operation. Refer to the following section for further assistance.

WIN (or WIN /3) Returns DOS Prompt. In this case, try opening Windows in Standard Mode in the hopes that an error message will show up. If it does, then follow the Standard-Mode troubleshooting procedures to cure the problem. Otherwise, check the following lines in the [386Enh] section of your SYSTEM.INI file. If any of these virtual device-driver lines are garbled or missing, edit SYSTEM.INI as required.

```
device=*biosxlat
device=*v86mmgr
device=*vdmad          (requires cold reboot if missing)
device=*vsd            (requires cold reboot if missing)
device=*wshell
```

If all these lines are present and in good shape, edit your CONFIG.SYS file to disable the EMM386.EXE line, reboot, and try opening Windows by typing the following line:

WIN /3 /d:xvsf

If this works, then try each of the switches separately to determine which one solves the problem. The switches are listed in the order that is most likely to produce results.

WIN /3 /d:x. The /d:x switch excludes the entire UMB (upper memory block) region, and is the functional equivalent of inserting the following line in the [386Enh] section of your SYSTEM.INI file:

EMMExclude=A000-EFFF

Add this line, reboot, and try starting Windows in the Enhanced Mode again (with the EMMExclude line in place it is not necessary to include the /d:x switch). If this solves the problem, then there is some memory conflict within the excluded UMB area. Refer to Chapter 13 for suggestions on how to narrow down the excluded range, so that nonproblem areas can be reutilized.

WIN /3 /d:v. An optional line in the [386Enh] section of SYSTEM.INI may be inserted to determine how interrupts from the hard disk controller are handled. The line is shown here, and the /d:v switch is the functional equivalent of the disabled (0) state.

[386Enh] line	Meaning
VirtualHDIrq=0	*ROM routine handles interrupts*
1	*Windows can terminate hard disk controller interrupts*

If the /d:v switch solves the problem, then add the VirtualHDIrq=0 line to the [386Enh] section of your SYSTEM.INI file.

WIN /3 /d:s. In Enhanced Mode, Windows searches the memory area beginning at F000:0000 for a break-point instruction in system ROM. However, if this space is occupied by something else, then Windows may get itself in trouble by finding the wrong information. The following optional line in SYSTEM.INI determines whether this area will be searched, and the /d:s switch is the functional equivalent of the disabled (0) state.

[386Enh] line	Meaning
SystemROMBreakPoint=0	*Don't search F000:0000*
1	*Search F000:0000*

If the /d:s switch solves the problem, then add the SystemROM-Break-Point=0 line to the [386Enh] section of your SYSTEM.INI file.

WIN /3 /d:f. This switch turns off 32-bit access. If it cures the problem, then your system hard drive controller does not support 32-bit access, and this mode should not have been enabled. To permanently disable 32-bit access, find the following line in the [386Enh] section of SYSTEM.INI and edit it to read as follows:

```
32BitDiskAccess=off
```

To prevent future accidents, remove the line entirely, and also delete the following two lines:

```
device=*int13
device=*wdctrl
```

To do all of this from within Windows, double-click on the 386 Enhanced icon in the Control Panel, then click on the Virtual Memory... and Change>> buttons. Finally, clear the Check box next to "Use 32-Bit Disk Access" at the bottom of the screen.

Windows Exit Troubleshooting

If your Setup procedure was a technological triumph, and your Windows session was notable for the flawless operation of every applet and application, you still might not be home free. There are at least a few bugs that don't come out to play until you try to exit Windows. Typical examples are given here.

System Locks Up

If this happens, there is probably some conflict with a program loaded as Windows is opened. To track down the problem, examine the following files.

WIN.INI Load= and Run= Lines. Disable both of these lines and try again. If this solves the problem, then test the files listed on both lines until you find the culprit.

WINSTART.BAT File. In Enhanced Mode, it's possible that some element of the WINSTART.BAT file (if present) is causing a problem. Try starting Windows in Standard Mode. If this solves the problem, then disable WINSTART.BAT and try opening and closing Windows again, this time in Enhanced Mode. If the problem is gone, then examine the batch file for anything related to network operation. Disable any such line and try again.

If the problem can be isolated to a specific program, or programs, loaded via WINSTART.BAT, try loading those programs via your AUTOEXEC.BAT file instead. If the trouble goes away, then it is due to a known problem with WINSTART.BAT itself. For the moment the workaround solution is to use AUTOEXEC.BAT instead of WINSTART.BAT to load whatever it is that triggers the system lockup.

If the trouble persists even though the program is loaded via AUTOEXEC.BAT, then contact the manufacturer of the software called on that line to see if there is either an upgrade or a workaround available.

PS/2 System Lock Up

If a PS/2 computer seems to lock up on exiting Windows, wait at least one minute (!) for the DOS prompt to appear. If it finally shows up, refer to the *Exit to DOS Prompt* section below for suggestions.

System Reboots

A system reboot when you exit Windows suggests there may be a shortage of extended memory, or possibly some other memory-related problem. If Smart Drive is installed, remove it and see if this cures the problem. If it does, then reinstall it, but set the Windows cache size to a lower value. Or, reduce the size of your RAM drive, if this is using extended memory.

If neither action cures the problem, then try the Windows HIMEM.SYS extended-memory manager in place of whatever third-party software you're using. Finally, if all else fails, strip your startup files down to the configurations suggested in the *Basic CONFIG.SYS and AUTOEXEC.BAT Files* section of Chapter 1 (see Table 1.4a). If this solves the problem, then begin replacing lines in these files until you localize the one that is causing the reboot.

Exit to DOS Prompt Takes Too Long

When you exit Windows, it should take only a second or so to return to the DOS prompt. If the exit takes forever (that is, more than a very few seconds), then review the suggestions listed below for a remedy. If all else fails, try removing all third-party drivers from your CONFIG.SYS file. Refer to the *Basic CONFIG.SYS and AUTOEXEC.BAT Files* section of Chapter 1 (Table 1.4a) for suggestions. Once the problem is isolated, begin restoring the other components in these two files. Then contact the supplier of the problem software to see if an upgrade is available.

Fragmented Hard Disk. The Windows files on your hard disk may be fragmented. Run a defragmenting utility, then try again.

Temporary Swap File. You may also notice an exit speed improvement on exiting the Enhanced Mode by creating a permanent swap file.

PS/2 Systems. On some PS/2 systems, a slow exit from Windows occurs because the PS/2 mouse port takes a very long time to reinitialize. If this is the case, try entering the following line in the [386Enh] section of SYSTEM.INI:

```
InitPS2MouseAtExit=0
```

The line stops Windows from reinitializing the PS/2 mouse port. If this speeds up the exit process, then experiment with the mouse after exiting Windows to see if the line has introduced any further problems. If so, you may want to remove the line and just put up with the slow exits.

Stacker Drives. If you're using Stac Electronics' *Stacker* data compression hardware and/or software, make sure your swap file is not on the stacker volume. If it is, you will have problems exiting Windows, in addition to other problems within Windows.

Ctrl+Alt+Del Causes Post-Windows Lockup

Before starting, or after exiting Windows, if a "three-finger salute" locks up your system instead of rebooting it, there may be a conflict with BIOS and/or video RAM shadowing. As a quick fix, disable one or both of these options and try again. If that fixes the problem, then the first thing to do is contact the manufacturer of your PC to see if they have already solved the problem. The fix may involve little more than editing your EMM386.EXE line, or there may be a BIOS upgrade available for your system. If the manufacturer swears this is the first time anyone has complained of this problem, then you're on your own.

Startup Error Messages

If an error message contains a reference to either the standard or the enhanced mode, then refer to the appropriate section later in this chapter for further assistance. If the error message refers to memory, then check the error messages in Chapter 13 for assistance. Otherwise, find the error message in the following section and follow the suggestions given there.

Call to Undefined Dynalink. If this message is seen during start up, the most likely cause is an old copy of TOOLHELP.DLL in the Windows directory. Windows 3.1 installs the new version of this file in the System directory, so if you find an old TOOLHELP.DLL in the Windows directory, just erase it and the problem should go away. While you're at it, make sure the new version is in the System directory. If it's not, then expand a fresh copy from the distribution diskettes.

If this does not solve the problem, examine your Windows Desktop for a missing icon. If you're not sure what's missing, look at the load= and run= lines in the [windows] section of WIN.INI, and also review the contents of your StartUp Group Window. The programs listed on the WIN.INI lines, or associated with the StartUp Group icons, should all be running on your Desktop. If one of them isn't, then that's the one whose DLL file is probably corrupt. If necessary, refer to Table 4.8 in Chapter 4 for a list of DLL files included with Windows 3.1 and Windows-for-Workgroups. Once you have identified the problem file, expand a fresh copy of it from the distribution diskettes.

"Cannot Find . . ." Messages. Windows has a large repertoire of messages for display when it can't find something during its opening ceremonies. Some messages include superfluous and/or redundant information, such as "Cannot find or load *filename*. The file was not found." In many cases the message is self-explanatory and, with luck, will even include the name of whatever it is that couldn't be found. The solution is almost always the same: Locate a fresh copy of the missing file on the distribution diskettes and expand it into the Windows or System directory. The representative examples seen here always begin with the "Cannot Find" phrase.

 . . . File '/S' (or '/3'). If you need to force Windows into Standard or Enhanced Mode, the /S or /3 switch must be the first switch following the WIN command. If some other switch precedes it (WIN /b /3, for example), then a misleading "Cannot find file" message will be seen,

and Windows will open in its default mode with Program manager minimized. Or it won't open at all if there are problems associated with the default mode.

. . . *File 'Filename' specified in WIN.INI (or one of its components). Check to ensure the path and filename are correct and that all required libraries are available.* As Windows opens, it looks for programs listed in the following two lines in the [windows] section of your WIN.INI file:

```
load=(path\filename(s))
run=(path\filename(s))
```

The error message is displayed if a listed path and/or filename cannot be found. To correct the problem, make sure that path and filenames are valid, and that each listed file is present in the specified directory.

. . . *File 'Filename.ext' specified in the startup group.* In this case, the missing file is one contained in the StartUp Group Window. Follow the directions immediately above to fix the problem.

. . . **Filename.ext** *(additional information may follow).* Depending on the nature of the missing file, Windows may successfully open when you click on the OK button. However, operation of the component that depends on the missing file will of course be unreliable or impossible.

. . . **Filename.ext** . . . *(or one of its components)* . . . *Check that all required libraries are available.* If the cited file appears to be present and in good order, don't overlook the hints given in the rest of this message. Unfortunately, the message doesn't suggest *what* library file(s) might be missing, so you'll have to do a little detective work. In Chapter 4, Table 4.8 lists the dynamic link library files that are supplied with Windows 3.1. If one of these is not among the missing, then the library file may be one that came with a third-party application. Check the appropriate User's Guide, or the distribution diskettes for the missing file.

. . . *Files needed to run in either standard or 386 Enhanced Mode.* (The needed files are not identified.) The message may be seen if multiple files are missing, usually from the System directory. Try forcing Windows into either standard or Enhanced Mode and look for specific information about missing files. If an error message is *not* followed by the DOS prompt, jot down the information, then press the Enter key. Jot down any additional error messages and repeat until one of the following things happens:

The DOS prompt reappears
The system locks up
Windows opens

Whatever happens, expand fresh copies of all cited files and try again.

On a network client system, the message may indicate the client system's PATH statement (in AUTOEXEC.BAT file) does not include a path to the network server where the needed files are to be found. The message may also be seen on a 286 system if the DOSX.EXE file is missing or defective.

. . . System initialization file needed to run Windows. You need to run the Setup program again. Well, maybe not. The message refers to a missing SYSTEM.INI file. If your Windows configuration is new, you can rerun Setup without losing much besides the time it takes to do so. But, if your present configuration has been massaged into shape over a long period of time, you probably won't feel like dumping the whole works just to rebuild SYSTEM.INI. With some luck, you remembered to save a backup copy which you can now recover. With no luck, refer to the *Reconstruct INI Files* section of Chapter 14.

Cannot Load MMTLHI.DRV. This is a variation on the *Error Loading MMTLHI.DRV* message described below. Follow the directions given there to resolve the problem.

Contact Beta Support. If this phrase is part of an error message, one or more of your Windows files were not correctly upgraded or installed. Call Microsoft Technical Support for confirmation.

DOS Version Is Incorrect or Unsupported. Several error messages include a reference to a DOS version that is either incorrect or unsupported. Most such messages are seen when a computer requiring a system-specific DOS version has been booted from a Microsoft MS-DOS package that predates DOS 5.0, or from some other version not designed for the computer. In some cases, Windows may open in Standard Mode but not in Enhanced Mode. If the system-specific DOS is not available, try upgrading to Microsoft's version 5.0 DOS, or to the new version 6.0.

If the message refers to just "DOS" (not *MS*-DOS), then there may be an additional problem: The installed WIN386.EXE file is probably the old one from version 3.0. Double-check its file-creation date and replace it if necessary. Then reboot using the version of MS-DOS designed for that system.

Error Loading *Filename (no extension listed).* This message may be seen if a file required for both operating modes is missing. If the problem file is GDI.EXE, then refer to the section immediately following for assistance.

If the screen clears before you can read the name of the problem file, try running Windows in Standard Mode. The message may now remain on the screen; once you know what file is causing the problem, expand a fresh copy of it from your distribution diskettes. (Or try writing a *READTHIS* file, as described earlier in the chapter.)

Error Loading *Filename.Ext (other than those listed below).* The cited file is either missing or defective. In either case, expand a fresh copy from your distribution diskettes and try again.

Error Loading GDI.EXE. An obvious cause of the message is a defective or missing GDI.EXE file. A not-so-obvious cause is that a missing *xxx*FIX.FON file will create the same message, with no hint of the *real* problem.

To help problem-solve, type WIN /s /b to try to open Windows in standard mode, and create a bootlog. Next, type TYPE BOOTLOG.TXT, press the Enter key, and examine the last line of the file. Take the appropriate action as described here.

    LoadFail = GDI.EXE Failure code is 00.

This error is probably preceded by another LoadFail line which lists the name of the missing font file. In this case, disregard the erroneous 00 failure code and expand a fresh copy of the listed file into your System directory. Then try again.

    LoadFail = GDI.EXE Failure code is 02.

If this is the only error seen, then GDI.EXE is among the missing. Expand a fresh copy from your distribution diskettes and try again.

Error Loading MMTLHI.DRV. The cited file is the display driver for ET4000 800×600 and 1024×768 video systems (256 colors, large fonts). If the message is seen on an upgrade (not new) installation of Windows-for-Workgroups, the driver on the upgrade distribution diskettes is defective and cannot be used. You can order a replacement from the Windows Driver Library (see Appendix D). As an interim measure, rerun Setup and select one of the following display drivers or any other display driver, as appropriate for your system:

SVGA	800×600	16 color
ET4000	800×600	256 color, small fonts
ET4000	1024×768	256 color, small fonts

NOTE: The MMTLHI.DRV file supplied with new versions of Windows-for-Workgroups—and presumably, with the latest upgrade versions—is not defective and should not cause the problem described here. In case of doubt, check your version of the file against those listed in Appendix A, or compare its file size against the MMTLHI.DR_ file on your own distribution diskettes. If the expanded version is *smaller* than the original, then both are defective.

Error Loading PROGMAN.EXE. There are a few possible causes of this message. First, make sure the following line in the [boot] section of the SYSTEM.INI file is present:

SHELL=PROGMAN.EXE *(or some other valid shell; FILEMAN.EXE, for example)*

If there is any doubt about the validity of the cited file, expand a fresh copy of PROGMAN.EXE into the Windows directory and edit the line (if necessary) to refer to that file. If doing this solves the problem, then the previous shell was defective.

If the problem continues, than an incorrect version of SHELL.DLL is probably the culprit. Expand a fresh copy of SHELL.DL_ into the System directory and try again.

Error Loading SYSTEM.DRV. This message appears if Windows finds a copy of the KRNL286.EXE or KRNL386.EXE files in the Windows directory. These files must be in the System directory only. If you find either in the Windows directory, check the file date to make sure it is a version 3.1 file. If it is, move it into the System directory. In case of doubt, erase the KRNL*x*86.EXE file(s) in the Windows directory, and expand fresh copies from the distribution diskette.

Error Loading USER.EXE. This error message is usually related to an incompatible Windows 3.0 driver. Log onto the Windows directory and run SETUP. Look for any line that may suggest the presence of a third-party driver, as for example, a non-Windows display driver that is not compatible with Windows 3.1. Change such lines back to their Windows default settings and try again. If the change requires the installation of additional files from the Windows distribution diskettes, follow the on-screen directions to add these files to your Windows directories.

If the above suggestion does not apply to your system, then check your Windows and System directories for the presence of version 3.0 files that did not get replaced by their 3.1 counterparts during Setup.

Finally, don't overlook the obvious: Is USER.EXE itself present and in good shape? If all else fails, expand a fresh copy from the distribution diskettes into your System directory.

Error occurred while trying to unlock the password-list file for *(computer name).* **Error 2: The specified file was not found. For more information, choose the Help button.** If this message appears when you open Windows-for-Workgroups, the password-list file for your user name (*username*.PWL) is missing. Even if you don't want your system to be password-protected, this file must be re-created so as not to encounter the message every time you reopen. Refer to the *Create New PWL File* section of Chapter 8 for the procedure to write the required PWL file.

Exception Error #*nn* **@** *(code segment:instruction pointer)* **CODE** *xx.* This message indicates that the system has detected an invalid memory access. Try deleting EMM386.EXE from your CONFIG.SYS file and rebooting. If some other error message is seen, take the necessary action, then restore the EMM386.EXE line and try again.

If the message persists, there is probably a hardware compatibility problem in your system. Contact the manufacturer to see if a modified version of the EMM386.EXE file is available. The following list of exception error numbers may aid in tracking down the specific source of the problem.

0	Divide error	8	Double fault
1	Debugger interrupt	9	Coprocessor segment overrun
2	Nonmaskable interrupt	10	Invalid task state segment
3	Breakpoint	11	Segment not present
4	Overflow interrupt	12	Stack exception
5	Array boundary violation	13	General protection violation
6	Invalid opcode	14	Page fault
7	Coprocessor not available	16	Coprocessor error

Filename.ext **is write-protected. New settings cannot be saved.** This is simply an advisory message, letting you know that changes can't be made to the cited file. Press the Enter key to continue; to disable write protection, type the following command at the DOS prompt:

```
attrib -r filename.ext
```

Filename **was not found or is corrupt.** This one is easy enough: Simply find the missing file on your distribution diskettes and expand it into the correct directory.

Group File Error: Cannot open program-group file 'C:\WINDOWS\ filename.GRP.' Do you want Program Manager to try to load it in the future? This message appears if Windows cannot find the cited group file in the Windows (or perhaps some other) directory. If you have intentionally erased the GRP file that Windows is looking for, then click on the No button, and neither message nor group will be seen again. Or, if you know the file is available but located elsewhere, click on the Yes button, exit Windows, and transfer it back into the Windows (or other) directory.

If the group file is indeed missing and unaccounted for, click on the No button, and refer to the *Group Window Troubleshooting* section of Chapter 3.

Group File Error: Program-group file 'C:\WINDOWS*filename*.GRP' is invalid or damaged. Re-create the group. In this case, the cited group file is present but probably corrupt, or there is a discrepancy between the group filename and the way that name appears in the PROGMAN.INI file. In either case, when you click on the OK button Windows will continue loading, but the cited group window will be missing from the Desktop.

Group File Error: Program group file 'C:\WINDOWS*filename*.GRP' is write-protected. Its icons cannot be updated for the new display device. If after write-protecting a group file, you change your system's video display configuration, you'll see this message the next time you open Windows. To help keep things confusing, the icons *will* be updated (that is, resized) to suit the new display when you click on the OK button. But the update is not permanent, so the message reappears every time you reopen Windows. To make it go away and stay away, disable the group file's write protection and once again open Windows so that the icons can be permanently updated. Then reenable the write protection if you still want it.

Out of Environment Space. The MS-DOS 5.0 default environment size is 256 bytes. Since Windows adds its own variable to the environment, this error message may be seen if there is insufficient space available. If so, add or edit the following line in your CONFIG.SYS file:

```
SHELL=C:\DOS\COMMAND.COM C:\DOS\ /p /e:xxxx
```

The /e:*xxxx* switch specifies environment size, which should be increased from its current value. Or, if the switch does not appear at all, add it with a value greater than 256. If the present SHELL= line contains information other than that shown above, then leave that information intact and only edit the /e switch, as required.

Path *'path and filename.ext'* **specified in the** *group name* **group is invalid.** This message may be seen in an *Application Execution Error* box during startup. When you click on the OK button (or press the Enter key), startup should conclude successfully anyway. To resolve the problem, review the information in the message. Correct the path and/or filename, or move the cited file into the path where Windows expects to find it.

Video Device Conflict (with Qualitas *386MAX*). If this message is seen on a VGA system with Qualitas' *386MAX* memory management installed, there is a memory conflict due to the automatic remapping of video ROM into RAM. To disable this feature, add the following line to the 386MAX.PRO file in the 386MAX directory:

```
RAM=C000-C800
```

For further details about the 386MAX.PRO file, refer to Chapter 13.

Working directory is invalid. As Windows begins, it checks the working directory specified for each applet that you installed in the StartUp group. This error message is seen if Windows can't find the proper directory for one of these applets. Now all you have to do is guess *which* working directory is invalid.

For the moment, the application with the invalid working directory does not appear on your desktop, so if you're reasonably familiar with what should be there, you'll recognize it by its absence. Now click once on the OK button, and the application icon will appear. When Windows finishes opening, open the StartUp Group Window and click once on that applet's icon. Now select the Program Manager's File Menu and highlight the Properties option. When the Program Item Properties dialog box appears, make the necessary correction in the Working Directory box.

Real Mode Error Messages

Windows 3.1 does not support real-mode operation, so it's unlikely that you'll ever see either message listed in this section. However, . . .

Windows Will not Run in Real Mode. The one-and-only error message associated with this non-problem is:

```
This version of Windows does not Run in Real Mode.
```

There's not much mystery here: The Real Mode has been discontinued, as you'll discover if you attempt to open Windows 3.1 by typing WIN/r at the DOS prompt.

Any Other Message Containing the Words "Real Mode." If you see such a message, then there's a little something left over from Windows 3.0 in one of your Windows directories. The primary suspects are the programs listed in the *Windows Mode Test* section found earlier in this chapter. Check the file-creation dates of these and any other Windows files and replace them, as necessary, with their version 3.1 equivalents.

Standard Mode Error Messages

If your system is configured to open in Standard Mode, or if your attempt to force Windows into Standard Mode (WIN /s) fails, then one of the following messages may be seen.

Cannot find Filename.ext needed to run in Standard Mode; check to ensure the path is correct or reinstall Windows. As with any *cannot find* message, the usual solution is to expand a fresh copy of the file from the distribution diskettes. You may also want to try opening in Enhanced Mode, just to make sure the problem is confined to Standard-Mode operations. If the Enhanced Mode displays a similar message but cites a different filename, then more than one file is missing.

Cannot find files needed to run Windows in Standard Mode. Run Windows Setup again, or try starting Windows in 386 Enhanced Mode by typing win /3 . If this message is seen on a 286 system, the probable cause is a missing or damaged KRNL286.EXE file. In this case the suggestion to try the Enhanced Mode does not apply.

> **NOTE:** If this file is missing on a 386 or 486 system, Windows will still open in the Standard Mode, and will not display an error message.

Cannot run Windows in Standard Mode; check to ensure you are not running other protected-mode software, or run in Real Mode. The reference to the Real Mode is a dead giveaway that some ghost of Windows 3.0 remains in your system. The most likely culprit is an old DOSX.EXE file. Check its file creation date, and replace it with the correct Windows 3.1 file. While you're at it, check the entire System directory for other 3.0 files that may need to be replaced with their 3.1 counterparts.

Cannot start Windows in Standard Mode. Make sure you are not running other protected-mode software, or try starting Windows in Enhanced Mode by typing win /3. The probable cause of this message is a lack of extended memory, in which case Windows won't run in Enhanced Mode either. Double-check this by trying to run it, then follow the suggestions given in the enhanced-mode section.

Executable Not Found. Check the System directory for the presence of the WSWAP.EXE file. If present, it is probably defective. In any case, install a fresh expanded copy from the distribution diskettes.

Standard Mode: Fault outside of MS-DOS Extender. Here, the "Standard Mode:" phrase is part of the error message itself, which is followed by additional data:

EC= *xxxx* CS= *xxxx* I P = *xxxx* AX=*xxxx* BX=*xxxx* CX=*xxxx* DX=*xxxx*
S I = *xxxx* D I = *xxxx* BP=*xxxx* DS=*xxxx* ES=xxxx SS=*xxxx* SP=*xxxx*

In this case, the probable problem is that the KRNL386.EXE file from Windows 3.0 is present in the System directory instead of the correct 3.1 version. Check the file-creation date, which is probably 10-31-90. If so, find the KRNL386.EXE file on your Windows 3.1 distribution diskettes and expand it into the System directory.

If the wrong KRNL386.EXE is present and you attempt to open Windows in Enhanced Mode, you may see a *KRNL386: Unable to enter Protected Mode* message or just the DOS prompt.

Enhanced Mode Error Messages

The following messages indicate a problem running Windows in the 386 Enhanced Mode. To verify that the problem is confined to this mode, try opening Windows in Standard Mode by typing WIN /s. If Windows fails to open in Standard Mode too, then you may see a different error message. Once you've resolved the Enhanced-Mode problem, try Standard Mode again, and refer to the *Standard Mode Error Messages* section above for troubleshooting suggestions.

Bad command or filename. If this message is seen briefly as Windows opens, there is a problem with the optional WINSTART.BAT file that may be executed when Windows starts in Enhanced Mode. Or, if you are using some other batch file to start Windows, there may be a problem with a line in that file. In most cases, one of the programs listed in the batch file is either missing or defective. If necessary, exit Windows, run WINSTART.BAT from the DOS prompt and note the error message(s). Or, rerun your own batch file and note the line that produces the error. Then edit the batch file or replace the problem program, as required. If necessary, refer to the *WINSTART.BAT File* section near the end of this chapter for further details.

Cannot find a device file that may be needed to run Windows in 386 Enhanced Mode. You need to run the Setup program again.

filename.ext (or a name with no extension)

Press a key to continue. Note that the next-to-last line usually shows a filename. Before running the entire Setup again, expand the missing file from your Windows distribution diskettes, then try running Windows again.

If a name appears without an extension (VDDVGA, for example), then the "missing" file is an integral part of the WIN386.EXE file, and is probably damaged. Replace it with a new expanded copy from your distribution diskette.

The "Cannot Find" message may flash several times, then disappear if your WIN386.EXE file is the old one from Windows 3.0, *and* the DOS 5.0 WINA20.386 file is still in your root directory. If it is, temporarily disable it and try again. If you see the *You must have the file WINA20.386* message (see below), then your WIN386.EXE is indeed the wrong one. Replace it and try again.

Cannot find WIN386.EXE needed to run in 386 Enhanced Mode. Check to ensure the path is correct or reinstall Windows. This message will be seen on a 386 or better system if WIN386.EXE is not in the System directory and you use the /3 switch to try forcing Windows to open in Enhanced Mode. Expand a fresh copy into the System directory and try again.

Cannot run in 386 Enhanced Mode. Enter WIN to run in Standard Mode. This message is seen if you attempt to force Windows into Enhanced Mode on a 286 system. Try again by typing WIN without the /3 switch, and start saving for a 386 system.

Cannot run Windows because of Video Device Conflict. Run Setup again. This message indicates a conflict with an installed virtual display device required for Enhanced-Mode operation. To verify, try running Windows again in Standard Mode.

Instead of rerunning the entire Setup procedure, you can probably resolve the problem by reinstalling the required file in your System directory.

If you are not sure how to proceed, look in the [386Enh] section of SYSTEM.INI for a display= line in one of the following formats:

display=VDD*xxx*.386

If the line shows one of the files listed here, then find that file on your distribution diskettes and expand it into the System directory.

VDD8514.386	VDDEGA.386	VDDVGA30.386
VDDCGA.386	VDDHERC.386	VDDXGA.386
VDDCT441.386	VDDTIGA.386	

If some other file is specified, then that file is from a third-party video system and should be available on the diskettes supplied with that system. If the required file is unavailable, then log onto the Windows directory, run SETUP, and change the Display line to the nearest equivalent Windows default display device. Doing so should permit Windows to run successfully until you can locate the file required to support your system.

display=*VDD*xxx*   *(note asterisk, and no extension)*

The asterisk indicates that the virtual device (*VDDVGA, for example) is an integral part of the WIN386.EXE file. In this case WIN386.EXE is probably present, but defective. Replace it with a fresh expanded copy from your distribution diskettes.

Cannot Run Windows in 386 Enhanced Mode with. . . . The remainder of this message indicates the system component that prevents Enhanced Mode operations, as indicated here.

. . . *Extended Memory Driver.* Refer to the User's Guide for the extended memory manager that you are using. If the problem cannot be easily resolved, try using the Windows 3.1 HIMEM.SYS file instead.

. . . *Installed Version of MS-DOS.* In the unlikely event that this message is seen, some DOS-compatibility problem that escaped detection during the Setup procedure is now preventing Windows from opening. The probable suspect is an OEM DOS version that is not designed for your system. In this case, you should replace it with the correct version, then try again.

. . . *Protected-Mode Software.* If you're running some program that fits this description, then you'll have to quit it before running Windows.

A device has been specified more than once in the SYSTEM.INI file, or a device specified in SYSTEM.INI conflicts with a device which is being loaded by an MS-DOS driver or application. Remove the duplicate entry from the SYSTEM.INI and restart Windows.

Duplicated Device: C:\WINDOWS\SYSTEM*devicename.ext*. The obvious reason for this message is there are two versions of the cited file in the [386Enh] section of SYSTEM.INI. However, one version may be in the format of say, *devicename*.386, while the other is **device* with no extension. If you're not sure of the identity of *devicename*.386, the safest course is to disable it in favor of **device*, which is embedded in the WIN386.EXE file. Later on, if some Windows applet really needs *devicename*.386, it will let you know about it. If that happens, restore it and disable or remove **device* instead.

Duplicated device: C:*(path)*\CMSDTAPE.386. In this specific example, you have probably installed the Microsoft Tools *Backup* applet on a system that already has a Colorado Tape backup system installed. If so, examine the indicated section of your SYSTEM.INI file for the following two lines:

[386Enh]	**Line required by:**
device=C:\DOS\VFINTD.386	Microsoft *Backup*
device=C:*(path)*\CMSDTAPE.386	Colorado Tape Backup

Place a semicolon at the head of the line (or delete the line) that specifies the device you do not wish to use.

Device file specified in SYSTEM.INI file is corrupt. It may be needed to run Windows in 386 Enhanced Mode. You need to run the SETUP program again. (*filename.ext*). Press a key to continue. If the message includes the name of the problem file, then try expanding a fresh copy of that file before rerunning the Setup procedure. See also the *Invalid VxD dynamic link call* message below, if that message follows the one described here.

Invalid COMMAND.COM. Cannot load COMMAND.COM, system halted (on exiting Windows). When Windows closes, it looks for a valid copy of COMMAND.COM. Obviously your system had one, or it wouldn't be operating at all. The problem may be that there are *two* versions of COMMAND.COM on your hard disk, and Windows has just discovered the wrong one. Reboot and log onto your root directory. Then type the following line at the DOS prompt:

```
DIR COMMAND.COM /s
```

The /s switch instructs DOS to search all subdirectories for the specified file. If you find more than one version, erase the older one(s). Note the location of the remaining COMMAND.COM file, and make sure the following line in your CONFIG.SYS refers to its actual location, which in this example is the DOS directory.

```
shell=C:\DOS\COMMAND.COM
```

or

```
shell=C:\COMMAND.COM
```

Invalid VxD dynamic link call to device number *xxxx*, service *yyyy*. Your Windows configuration is invalid. Run the Windows Setup program again to correct this problem. Before you do this, check the [386Enh] section of your SYSTEM.INI file for any lines that meet the descriptions given here. The listed file may be the source of the problem. To verify this, expand a fresh copy from the appropriate distribution diskette and try again.

device=**xyz.386** *(where* **xyz** *is any alphanumeric string).* This represents a virtual device driver supplied with Windows 3.1 or installed by a third-party application.

device=**xyz.abc** *(where* **abc** *is* **not 386).** This too is a third-party file which may be causing the problem.

device=***xyz** *(note asterisk and no extension).* This is a virtual device driver embedded in the WIN386.EXE file. A few of the device and service numbers that may comprise part of the error message are listed here.

Device Number	Service	Virtual Device Line
0003	0001	device=*vpicd
0004	0001	device=*vdmad
0005	0001	device=*vtd
000A	0007	device=*vddvga
000D	000E	keyboard=*vkd
0010	8001	device=*BLOCKDEV
0021	8006	device=*PAGEFILE

If one of these pairs of numbers is seen, make sure the listed virtual device line is present in the [386Enh] section of SYSTEM.INI. If the line is garbled or missing, edit SYSTEM.INI as required. What is more likely though, is that your WIN386.EXE is present, but defective. Replace it with a fresh expanded copy from your distribution diskettes.

display=VDDxyz.386 *(where xyz may be any alphanumeric string).* If the file was not listed in the *display=VDDxxx.386* section above, then it is a third-party virtual display driver. If the file is missing, its name will probably be seen as part of an error message. However, if the file is present but defective, then its name may not be seen. If this is a possibility, refer to the *Cannot run Windows because of Video Device Conflict* message above for instructions on how to replace the problem file, or use a Windows default driver listed in that section if the required file is unavailable.

KRNL386: Unable to Enter Protected Mode. This Protected-Mode error message is sometimes accompanied by a system hangup requiring a warm reboot. As in the Standard-Mode DOS Extender error described earlier, the problem is related to the KRNL386.EXE file. To verify this, try starting in Standard Mode, and refer to the *Standard Mode: Fault outside of MS-DOS Extender* error message above for further details.

Unfortunately, a problem with KRNL386.EXE may also show no error message at all: The system simply returns to the DOS prompt.

KRNL386: Unable to Load KRNL386.EXE. If 32-bit access is enabled, FastDisk may have detected a virus in your system which prevents it from loading. Although you can disable 32-bit access and try again, you should really run a virus-detection utility first and take whatever action is appropriate.

Windows may not run correctly with the 80386 processor in this computer. Upgrade your 80386 processor or start Windows in Standard Mode. This is another of those messages that you should never see. Your computer may have a preproduction processor in it, or an early ("b-step") chip that had a problem with 32-bit accessing. In any case, report this error message to the manufacturer of your computer (not to Microsoft) and insist on an upgrade. If your computer came from an unidentified island somewhere in the South Pacific, you may need to buy your own replacement.

You must have the file WINA20.386 in the root of your boot drive to run Windows in Enhanced Mode. The WINA20.386 file is a virtual device driver required for Enhanced Mode operation with the DOS 5.0 HIMEM.SYS file. Although the error message clearly indicates the file is lost, you needn't bother finding it, for the real problem lies elsewhere. Review the following procedures and take whatever action is appropriate to your system.

The file is not required with the HIMEM.SYS supplied with Windows 3.1 or DOS 6.0, so it's possible that a line in your CONFIG.SYS files needs to be edited. If you are using DOS 5.0 and your HIMEM.SYS line matches line 1 (below), then edit it to match line 2 so that the new HIMEM.SYS will be used in place of the old one. (Do *not* follow this instruction if DOS 6.0 is installed: In this case the line-1 listing is correct.)

Change: device=C:\DOS\HIMEM.SYS
    To: device=C:\WINDOWS\HIMEM.SYS

Also, make sure the Windows 3.1 HIMEM.SYS file is available in your Windows directory (or the DOS 6.0 file in the DOS directory). If it is not, then expand a copy from your distribution diskettes. If this does not cure the problem, then you may have an old WIN386.EXE file in your System directory that needs to be replaced with the new version. As soon as you do so, the message should leave and never return.

It should, but maybe it won't. In this case, some third-party application may be asking DOS for the WINA20 file, as illustrated by two typical examples. If the "noems" parameter is used with versions of Quarterdeck's QEMM386 earlier than 6.0, the message will appear if WINA20.386 is not available. If the DOS screen saver in Berkeley System's popular *After Dark* utility is enabled, the message appears when you press any key after the DOS screen goes to black.

In such cases, there are two fixes: If an application upgrade is available, get it. Or, even easier, create a dummy file with the WINA20.386 name. On startup or when you restore the screen, the file will be found, DOS will be happy, Windows will open or continue successfully, and only you will know the truth.

You need an Intel 80386 processor to run Windows in 386 Enhanced Mode. You may see this message on some 80286 systems if you attempt to force them into Enhanced-Mode operation. So far, the only known cure is to move up to a 386 system.

Running Windows with Batch Files

The final section of this chapter offers a few suggestions for using batch files to make life with Windows a bit easier on the system.

Windows Startup (WIN.BAT)

The model batch file listing in Figure 2.2 illustrates how various house-keeping chores can be handled as Windows begins. Among other things, the batch file writes a small marker file to disk before Windows opens, then erases the file when Windows closes. The presence/absence of the file indicates the current status of Windows. If you prefer to set/reset an environment variable instead of writing/erasing a marker file, use the three lines that begin with "*(or)*" instead of the lines immediately above them. Include as many of the other lines shown here as you need for your particular requirements.

To see if Windows is currently open, the "if exist" line checks for the presence of a small marker file (or, the "W" environment variable is checked to see if it is set to "Y"). If the file is present (or if the variable is "Y"), then Windows is already open, and program execution jumps to the :WARNING line near the bottom of the file.

The two lines following :WARNING advise that Windows is active, as would be the case if you accidentally tried to open another Windows session from within a DOS window. When you press any key, the "exit" line closes the DOS window and restores the Windows Desktop.

However, if Windows is not already open, program execution continues and the next two "if" lines check your command for the presence of the "/b" switch, which is used to write a bootlog file as Windows opens. If the switch is found, then the previous bootlog file (if any) is erased. If you have not selected the /b switch, then program execution jumps to the :MARKER line.

Following the :MARKER line, a small file containing a single "X" is written to disk (or the "W" environment variable is set to "Y"), signifying that Windows is open (or will be shortly). If you subsequently try to reopen Windows from within a DOS window, the marker file (or environment variable) will now be noted the next time the batch file is executed. Next, any temporary files (TMP extension) left over from previous Windows sessions are erased, and Windows (MYWIN.COM) is executed.

At the conclusion of the Windows session, the marker file is erased (or the environment variable is cleared), the Smart Drive buffers are flushed as a safety precaution, and program execution jumps around the :WARNING section. The final "exit" line has no effect unless the batch file was accidentally executed from within a DOS window. In this case it serves to close the DOS window and restore the Windows Desktop.

Program Listing	Comments
@echo OFF	
c:	
cd \WINDOWS	
if exist C:WINDOWS\MARKER goto WARNING	Windows is already open.
(*or*) if "%W%"=="Y" goto WARNING	Windows is already open.
if "%1"=="/b" goto EraseLog	Check for /b switch to write new BOOTLOG.TXT file.
if "%2"=="/b" goto EraseLog	
goto MARKER	
:EraseLog	
if exist BOOTLOG.TXT erase BOOTLOG.TXT	If creating a new bootlog, erase prior one, if any.
:MARKER	
echo X>C:\WINDOWS\MARKER	Write MARKER file, denoting Windows is open.
(*or*) set W=Y	"Y" in environment indicates Windows is open.
if exist C:\TEMP*.TMP erase C:\TEMP*.TMP	Erase previous TMP files (if any) in the C:\TEMP directory.
MYWIN	Run Windows (WIN.COM renamed as MYWIN.COM).
erase C:\WINDOWS\MARKER	Erase MARKER file when Windows closes.
(*or*) set W=	Clear environment variable when Windows closes.
SMARTDRV /c	Flush Smart Drive buffers.
goto END	
:WARNING	
echo Hey! Windows is already open!	Display warning message, followed by a "Press any key . . ." message.
pause	
:END	
exit	Return to Windows if it's active; otherwise ignore.

Figure 2.2 The WIN.BAT file. A program listing such as this can be used to open Windows and perform various housekeeping operations before and after the Windows session.

> **NOTE:** If a Windows session is aborted (power failure, system reset, etc.), then the marker file is not removed and will have to be erased manually. Otherwise, its presence will prevent Windows from being reopened when the batch file is next executed. If the environment-variable technique is used instead, then this is not a consideration.
>
> The erasure of TMP files is more than just good housekeeping: On some (but not all) systems, Windows gets a little confused when it finds leftovers in the C:\TEMP directory, and may add one lost cluster every time Windows closes. In this specific case, these clusters contain spurious data, and can be erased without fear of losing something important.
>
> The SMARTDRV /c line in the batch file is a precautionary measure. Some third-party memory managers may not clear the write cache when Windows is closed, so this line makes sure the task gets done.
>
> As written, the batch file always opens Windows in the default mode for the system on which it is run. To open in either mode, additional lines (not shown here) would have to test for the presence of an /s or /3 switch.

Windows Mode Checking (WINMODE.BAT)

The batch file listing in Figure 2.3b displays the current mode of Windows versions 3.0 or 3.1 and will also detect the presence of the MS-DOS task swapper. The file runs a small WINCHECK.COM utility, then displays a status message which varies depending on the error-level code returned by the utility.

To begin, use any convenient ASCII text editor to write the program listing seen in Figure 2.3a. The listing appears as multiple columns in the figure, but should be written as a single column: Thus, TEST AL, 7F (column 2 in the Figure) should appear on the line immediately below INT 2F, and so on. When you type the "W" shown in the next-to-last line, the file is saved as WINCHECK.SCR. Now, use the DOS 5.0 Debug utility to create the WINCHECK.COM file that will be used with the batch file. At the DOS prompt, type the following line:

```
DEBUG<WINCHECK.SCR
```

Having done this, you should find a file named WINCHECK.COM in your directory listing. Now write the batch file listed in Figure 2.3b. When this file

Program Listing

A 100	TEST AL,7F	MOV ES, BX	INT 2F
MOV AX, 160A	JZ 0124	INT 2F	MOV AL, 02
INT 2F	MOV AL, 04	OR AX, AX	MOV AH, 4C
OR AX, AX	JMP 0159	JNZ 0144	INT 21
JNZ 0117	MOV AX, 4680	MOV AL, 01	(*insert blank line here*)
XOR CX, 0003	INT 2F	JMP 0159	RCX
JNZ 0113	OR AX, AX	MOV AX, 1605	5D
MOV AL, 06	JZ 0131	INT 2F	N WINCHECK.COM
JMP 0159	MOV AL, 00	CMP CX, 01	W
MOV AL, 05	JMP 0159	JNZ 0152	Q
JMP 0159	MOV AX, 4B02	MOV AL, 03	
MOV AX, 1600	XOR BX, BX	JMP 0159	
INT 2F	MOV DI, BX	MOV AX, 1606	

Notes: Use text editor (EDIT.COM, for example) to create and save a file named WINCHECK.SCR containing these lines. Then at DOS prompt, type DEBUG< WINCHECK.SCR to create WINCHECK.COM file.

Figure 2.3a   Use a text editor to write this WINCHECK.SCR file.

is run, it executes the WINCHECK.COM utility and displays the appropriate status message. Note that each error line in the batch file can be changed so that some action is initiated if the error level cited on that line is detected.

For further details about this batch file/utility combination, download the Q85469 document from the Microsoft Knowledge Base (go MSKB). Refer to Appendix D if you need assistance doing so.

Enhanced Mode Operations (WINSTART.BAT)

If you have TSR utilities that are only required by Windows applications, you can keep them out of the DOS environment by loading them from an optional WINSTART.BAT file. If this file is present in your Windows directory, it is automatically executed only when you start Windows in the Enhanced Mode. Programs cited in the file are available to Windows applications, but not to non-Windows applications running in a DOS window.

Program Listing

```
@echo OFF
CLS
(path) \WINCHECK.COM
if ERRORLEVEL 0 if not ERRORLEVEL 1 echo Nothing detected.
if ERRORLEVEL 1 if not ERRORLEVEL 2 echo Task swapper enabled.
if ERRORLEVEL 2 if not ERRORLEVEL 3 echo Windows 3.0 real mode.
if ERRORLEVEL 3 if not ERRORLEVEL 4 echo Windows 3.0 standard mode.
if ERRORLEVEL 4 if not ERRORLEVEL 5 echo Windows 3.0 enhanced mode.
if ERRORLEVEL 5 if not ERRORLEVEL 6 echo Windows 3.1 standard mode.
if ERRORLEVEL 6 if not ERRORLEVEL 7 echo Windows 3.1 enhanced mode.
```

(revise each line above, as required)
```
if ERRORLEVEL x if not ERRORLEVEL x + 1 goto XMODE
. . .
:XMODE
; (List actions to take if this mode is detected.)
```

Note: Run this batch file in DOS window to display current Windows mode or to take some action appropriate to the current mode.

Figure 2.3b A batch File for detecting the current Windows operating mode. Use the WINMODE.BAT file to determine the operating mode.

If there is a problem with any of the programs listed in the WINSTART.BAT file, a "bad command or filename" error message will be seen, as noted earlier in the *Enhanced Mode Error Messages* section of this chapter. In this case, the solution is to examine the WINSTART.BAT file for the line that is causing the problem. Either edit the line, or make the necessary corrections to the program listed on that line.

NOTE: If your system locks up when you exit Windows, there may be a compatibility problem with one of the elements within WINSTART.BAT. Refer to the *System Lockup* section above for further details.

Dual-System Operation (SWAP.BAT)

If you plan to maintain separate versions of Windows 3.0 and 3.1 on your hard disk, it is important to make sure that the current path refers to the version you are actually using at the moment. In addition, device drivers and other utilities associated with the selected version should be loaded before starting Windows.

The general procedure is to prepare a unique set of CONFIG.SYS and AUTOEXEC.BAT files for each Windows version, put the appropriate set in place, reboot, then open Windows. The SWAP.BAT file listing in Figure 2.4 will do all of this for you.

Assuming your existing files (prior to installing WIN 3.1) are correctly configured for version 3.0, run the batch file prior to installing Windows version 3.1, to save them for future use. After doing this, the file looks for previously-saved W31 files, but doesn't find them—just disregard the two "File not found" messages. Finally, it writes a marker file named 31FLAG to your hard disk, simply to indicate version 3.1 files are now in place. (Actually they're not, but will be soon.)

Program Listing	Comments
If exist C:\31FLAG goto SETUP30	31Flag file indicates system is set for WIN 3.1.
copy CONFIG.SYS CONFIG.W30	Save current 3.0 files for future use.
copy AUTOEXEC.BAT AUTOEXEC.W30	
copy CONFIG.W31 CONFIG.SYS	Install 3.1 files in their place.
copy AUTOEXEC.W31 AUTOEXEC.BAT	
echo 31 > 31FLAG	Write flag file to indicate system is set for WIN 3.1.
echo Please reboot to use Windows 3.1.	
goto END	
:SETUP30	
copy CONFIG.SYS CONFIG.W31	Save current 3.1 files for future use.
copy AUTOEXEC.BAT AUTOEXEC.W31	
copy CONFIG.W30 CONFIG.SYS	Install 3.0 files in their place.
copy AUTOEXEC.W30 AUTOEXEC.BAT	
erase 31FLAG	Erase flag to indicate system is set for WIN 3.0.
echo Please reboot to use Windows 3.0.	
:END	

Figure 2.4 The SWAP.BAT file toggles between two versions of Windows. To change versions, run SWAP.BAT, reboot, then open Windows.

After you install Windows 3.1, every time you rerun the batch file it looks for the 31FLAG marker. If it finds it, it assumes you want to switch back to version 3.0, and program execution jumps to the SETUP30 section. Your existing 3.1 files are saved, so as not to lose any revisions you may have made. Then the version 3.0 files are copied and the 31FLAG is erased. When you reboot, the system will be set up for version 3.0 use.

The next time you run the batch file, it again looks for the 31FLAG file and, not finding it, assumes you want to replace the current 3.0 files with the 3.1 files. It does so, then writes the 31FLAG file to your hard disk to indicate version 3.1 is again in place. Once again, reboot to begin using version 3.1.

With each subsequent running of the batch file, the files are swapped from 3.0 to 3.1, or vice versa, as appropriate.

The Windows Desktop

If you have just completed a successful Windows Setup procedure, a display similar to the one seen in Chapter 1 (Figure 1.9) should appear. It may look a bit friendlier than a DOS prompt, but it's probably not quite what you expected, especially if you've been reading all the Windows ads.

This chapter shows how to whip your own Windows screen into something a little more presentable than Figure 1.9. The first part of the chapter describes the various Window components, after which some general Desktop configuration techniques are reviewed. The chapter continues with a section on Desktop and Program Manager troubleshooting, covering some of the problems that may come up while trying to optimize the configuration. Note that the troubleshooting suggestions offered here are just those affecting the appearance of the Desktop. For problems with a specific application running on that Desktop, refer to one of the other chapters instead.

Since most error messages related to the Desktop and Program Manager occur as Windows is opened, they are covered in Chapter 2 instead of here. However, those few messages that may appear during routine operations are listed at the end of this chapter.

A Windows Overview

When Windows is running, your monitor's entire display area is referred to as the Windows *Desktop,* an analogy to the conventional desktop as an area where most business is transacted. The items on the Windows Desktop may be neatly arranged or piled one on top of another.

In Figure 3.1a, the Windows Desktop is the shaded rectangular area that represents the entire display on your video monitor screen. In this example, the Program Manager (described below) occupies most, but not all, of the Desktop. For future reference, Figure 3.1b offers a detail view of the components found at the top of the Program Manager and most other open windows, and Figure 3.1c shows examples of various icons. The items seen in these illustrations are described in detail below.

The Windows within Windows. During any Windows session, the Desktop is occupied by one or more of those things that make Windows what it is—its *Windows*. For example, the Desktop in Figure 3.1a reveals several

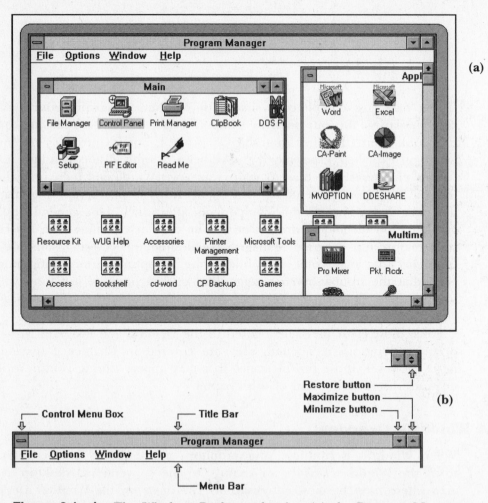

(a)

(b)

Figure 3.1a, b The Windows Desktop, showing (a) the Program Manager and various window components. The detail view below shows (b) components found at the top of the Program Manager and other group windows.

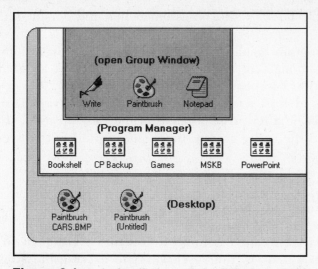

Figure 3.1c A detail view of the Windows Desktop, showing program-item, group, and application icons.

open Windows, the largest of which is the Program Manager. Within that large window, parts of a few smaller group windows may be seen.

In the discussion which follows, frequent reference is made to Windows *applications*. Unless otherwise mentioned, the same information applies as well to Windows *applets*.

The Program Manager

Occupying much of the desktop is Windows' answer to the old-fashioned blotter, now known as the *Program Manager*—the portion of the desktop set aside as the workspace. As the default Windows shell, Program Manager (PROGMAN.EXE) is automatically executed every time you open Windows. You can replace Program Manager with some other shell (Windows' own File Manager is one example) by editing the following line in the SYSTEM.INI file:

Default Setting	**Alternate Setting**	
[boot]	[boot]	
shell=progman.exe	shell=winfile.exe	(if winfile.exe is listed, File Manager becomes the Windows shell)
	shell=ndw.exe	(if *Norton Desktop for Windows* is installed)

For the purposes of this book, it will be assumed that the default setting remains in place.

In Figure 3.1, the Program Manager is the large open window occupying most of the Desktop. Although the size of this window could be adjusted to fill the entire screen (thus completely concealing the Desktop), it is generally a good idea to let at least some of the Desktop remain visible, since later on there surely will be a few icons located on the Desktop itself. If the Program Manager filled the entire screen, these icons would not be seen.

Group Windows

Again referring to Figure 3.1a, the open Program Manager Window shows a smaller Main window and fragments of two other windows. Each of these is an open *Group Window,* so-called because it contains a group of icons, any of which may be selected (by double-clicking) to execute the application associated with that icon. The icons at the bottom of the Program Manager represent various group windows that are currently closed.

When Windows 3.1 is first installed, five group windows appear on the Desktop, as was illustrated by Figure 1.9 in Chapter 1, which showed an open Main Group Window and the others (all closed) represented by their Group Icons.

User-Specified Group Windows. In addition to the group windows that appear automatically when Windows 3.1 is installed, other group windows will show up in the Program Manager area as various third-party applications are installed. The user may also want to add a custom group window to accommodate a group of applets that seem to belong together. Refer to the *Setup a New Windows Application* or *Setup a New Program Group* sections of Chapter 1 for details on how to do either.

The Application Window. When any Windows application or applet is executed, that application runs in its own *Application Window,* which opens to fill part or all of the Windows Desktop. By suitably sizing the application window (as described later), two or more windows may be visible on the Desktop.

The Document Window. Within the Application Window there may be one or more smaller windows. For example, if a Windows word processor is running, and more than one document is visible, each document will occupy its own *Document Window,* which may be resized, closed, or reopened, all within the larger Application Window associated with the word processor. Figure 3.1d is an example of two document windows occupying most of the space within an application window, which in turn sits on top of the Program Manager window.

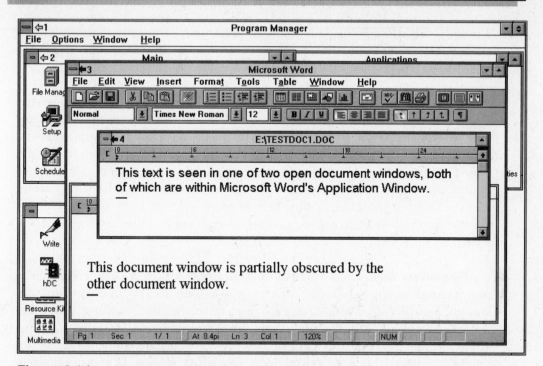

Figure 3.1d A detail view of the Windows Desktop, showing a Microsoft Word application window in which two document windows are open. (Also see Figure 3.7 for Control Menu box details.)

The Active Window. The term is often used to identify the window in which the currently running application appears. When any applet in an open group window is highlighted (by clicking once on its icon), that group window becomes the active group window. Usually, the window border and title bar switch to a distinctive color to visually indicate the active window. Such colors are specified via the Control Panel's *Color* applet, as described in Chapter 11.

Window Components

This section reviews the various Windows components that were shown in the detail views in Figures 3.1b and 3.1c.

Windows Icons. In Windows jargon, an icon is a miniature graphics picture that may represent an application, document, or a closed Group Window. The icon may be found within an open group window, near the bottom of the Program Manager Window, in the File Manager, or lying on the Windows Desktop beneath the Program Manager. In earlier versions of Windows, every icon in the Program Manager required some user heap space. Consequently the more icons, the less system resources were available. In

Windows 3.1 these icons are handled separately, so system resources are no longer affected by the number of icons on the Desktop. (Refer to Chapter 13 for more information on heaps and resources.)

Application Icon. If a Windows application is active (that is, if it is running on the screen), it may be minimized in order to clear the screen for use by some other application. In this case, the still-active application is represented by an *Application Icon* which appears at the bottom of the screen (Figures 3.1c, d). If some other application is opened and sized to occupy the entire Desktop, these application icons will not be seen. (Refer to *View Open Applications* in the *Task Manager* section later in this chapter for the method to view other currently active applications and application icons.)

Program-Item Icon. Each application contained within a Group Window is represented by its own icon, such as those seen in the open group window in Figure 3.1c. Note that each icon is distinctive, making identification a bit more user-friendly than for Group Icons. In this context, Microsoft documentation calls such a device a *Program-Item icon,* to distinguish it from the Application Icon described above. The program-item icon represents an application that is closed. The application it represents is available, but for the moment is not running.

How to Tell an Application Icon from a Program-Item Icon. Since the Application Icon and the Program-Item Icon are visually identical, they are distinguished by their positions on the screen. The former always appears at the bottom of the screen, outside the area occupied by any open window, including the Program Manager. The latter appears within an open group window, where it represents an application that is available, but not running at the moment.

Note that the same icon might appear two or more times on the screen. For example, if the Windows Paintbrush applet is opened, then minimized, its *Application Icon* appears on the Desktop, while the Paintbrush *Program-Item Icon* remains visible in the Accessories Group Window (assuming that window is open of course). A second Paintbrush applet might be opened and minimized, in which case there would be two *Application Icons* on the Desktop, and so on. If a file is open within the minimized application, the name of the file appears as part of the text below the Application icon. Figure 3.1c shows examples of three Paintbush icons: a program-item icon within the Accessories Group Window, and two application icons at the bottom of the screen.

File Manager Icon. These icons are described separately in Chapter 6.

Group Icon. When any group window is closed, it is replaced by a small rectangular Group Icon, several of which are seen near the bottom of the Program Manager Window in Figure 3.1c. Note that the only way to distinguish one group icon from another is by its title, which appears directly beneath the icon. With luck, this visual limitation will be removed in a future version of Windows.

Application Workspace. As its name suggests, an application workspace is that part of an open window immediately below the Menu Bar, in which the application performs its work. Figure 3.2 shows the application workspaces for the Program Manager and for an open Write applet.

Window Background. The area enclosed by a group window might also be thought of as a workspace, but Microsoft refers to it as a *Window Background,* as also illustrated in Figure 3.2. About the only reason for caring about this is that the window background color may be set to a different color than the application workspace. (Refer to Chapter 11 for assistance with these and other Desktop colors.)

Title Bar. This is the bar at the top of any window, in which the name of that window appears. In Figure 3.1a, the Title Bars in the Program Manager and Main Group Windows may be seen. Place the mouse pointer anywhere on the Title Bar to perform the following two actions, both of which are described in the sections listed here.

Click	The Following Action Occurs	Refer to Section
Once	The window becomes the active window	*Active Window*
Twice	Maximize the window	*Maximize Button*

Control Menu Box. At the lefthand corner of the Title Bar is perhaps the only button in all of Windows that is not called a button. For some reason (it's best not to ask), this button is the Control Menu *Box.* Place the mouse pointer on the Control Menu Box to perform the following two actions.

Click	The Following Action Occurs	Refer to Section
Once	Open the Control Menu	*Control Menu*
Twice	Minimize the window	*Minimize Button*

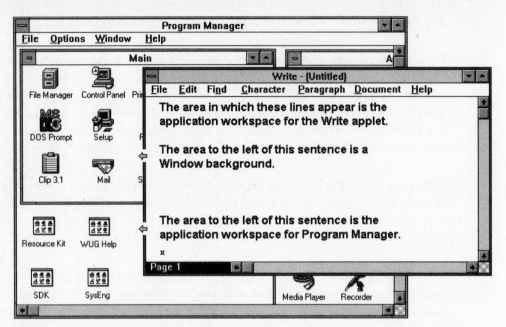

Figure 3.2 The Windows Desktop, showing application workspaces for the Write applet and for Program Manager and the window background in the Main Group Window.

Window Sizing Buttons. Two buttons at the righthand side of the Title Bar provide the means to reconfigure the size of almost any Window. The buttons are also seen in the detail view in Figure 3.1b, and are described here.

Minimize Button. Click once to close any open window and replace it by its group icon, which will appear within the Program Manager area, as shown in Figure 3.1a. Or double-click on the **Control Menu** box to do the same thing. If an icon is not visible, it's probably hiding beneath one of the remaining open group windows. Refer to the *Icon Configuration* section later in this chapter for suggestions on arranging the Program Manager so that all icons are visible.

Maximize Button. If you click on any **Maximize** button, the window expands to fill the entire available area. Thus, to fill the entire Desktop area with the Program Manager window, click once on its **Maximize** button. Or, click once on any group window's **Maximize** button, and that window expands to fill the entire area occupied by the Program Manager, which is not necessarily the entire Desktop.

When you click on any Maximize button, not only does the window expand, but the button also changes to the Restore button, which is seen in the upper righthand corner of Figure 3.1b. An alternative means of maximizing a window is to double-click anywhere in the window's Title Bar.

Screens with No Minimize or Maximize Buttons. Some screens do not have a Maximize button, and some lack both buttons. For example, the upper right-hand corners of the Control Panel and Windows Setup windows show a Minimize button only. The size of windows such as these is usually fixed at whatever you see when the window first opens. However, if the Maximize option is enabled in that window's Control Menu, you may use that option if you feel the need to do so, although sometimes it doesn't do what you might expect it to do. The following three applications illustrate three possibilities.

Applet or Application	Maximize Option	Comments
Control Panel	Yes	Functions as normal
Windows Setup	No	
Central Point Backup	Yes	Moves window to upper left-hand corner of Desktop, without changing its size

Some screens, such as those associated with the Control Panel applets, have neither Minimize nor Maximize buttons on their Title Bars. In cases such as these, the Control Menu usually offers only the Move and Close options, and perhaps About too (for example, if Mouse version 8.20 is installed). The buttons are omitted on purpose: The screen is usually nothing more than a dialog box (described below), and there's no reason for it to occupy a larger area, or to be minimized to an icon.

Restore Button. When the Restore button appears in place of the Maximize button, click once on it to restore the window to its former size.

Scroll Bars. If a window is sized in such a manner that its entire contents are not visible, scroll bars appear along the right and/or bottom edge of the window. Click on the arrow button at either end of the scroll bar, or move the button within the scroll bar to shift the contents of the window as required to view that part which is currently out of sight. In Figure 3.1a, the Main Group Window is a bit too small to see all the icons in the first row; therefore, a horizontal scroll bar appears at the bottom of the window.

The Program Manager Window shows both horizontal and vertical scroll bars so that the two group windows at the right of the screen may be moved into view.

The Menu Bar. Immediately below the Title Bar, the Menu Bar displays the names of any menus available within the current active application, which at the moment is Program Manager. Note that a Menu Bar appears beneath the Program Manager Title Bar, but not beneath the Title Bar of a group window. A Menu Bar will also appear in any application window. For example, see the Word-for-Windows Menu Bar which is visible in Figure 3.1d. To display any menu, place the mouse pointer on the Menu name and click the primary button once. The specified menu opens immediately below the Menu name.

The following section provides details about Windows menus in general, and about the Program Manager's menus in particular.

The Windows Menu Structure

Briefly stated, a menu is a list of one or more options that may be selected when that menu is open. Figure 3.3 illustrates the menus that are part of the Program Manager. To open a menu, move the mouse pointer to any menu name found on the Menu Bar, or to the Control Menu Box, then click the primary mouse button once. When the menu opens, its first option is highlighted. There are several ways to select a menu option:

1. Place the mouse pointer on the option and click the primary button once.

2. Hold the primary mouse button down, drag the highlight bar to the option, release the mouse button.

3. Press the down- or up-arrow keys to highlight the option and press the Enter key.

4. Note the letter in the option that is underlined, and press that letter key.

Shortcut Keys. The underlined key in each menu option is valid only when that menu is open. However, the righthand menu column may list another key, or key combination. If so, this is the *Shortcut Key* for the indicated option, so-called because it offers a shortcut to enable that option. For example, if any applet icon is highlighted, you may simply press the Enter key to open the applet represented by that icon.

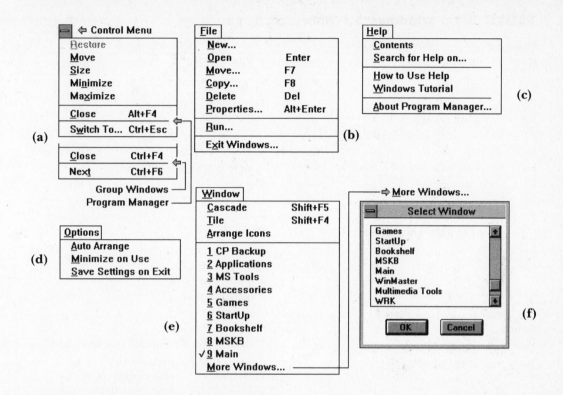

Figure 3.3   Menus accessible via the Program Manager's Menu Bar. (a) Control Menu, (b) File Menu, (c) Help Menu, (d) Options Menu, (e) Window Menu, and (f) More Windows... Menu.

The default Windows shortcut keys are listed in Table 3.1, and are also indicated by a parenthetical reference next to those menu options that support a shortcut key. The menu on which that shortcut key is listed need not be open at the time.

Custom Shortcut Keys. If a unique shortcut key is assigned to an applet, it may be used later to open the applet. The shortcut key will work even if the group window in which that applet resides is closed, or if the window is open and some other icon is highlighted. Refer to the *Shortcut Key Configuration* section later in the chapter for further details.

Task Manager Shortcut Keys. The shortcut keys used in conjunction with the Task Manager are described separately, in the *Task Manager* section later in this chapter.

TABLE 3.1 Windows 3.1 Shortcut Keys

Shortcut Key	Group Window				File Manager			
	F Key	Alt+	Ctrl+	Shift+	F Key	Alt+	Ctrl+	Shift+
F1	Help				Help	—	—	—
F2	—	—	—	—	Drive selector box (1)	—		—
F3	—	—	—	—	—	—	—	—
F4	—	Close (2)	Close (3)	Tile	—	Close (4)	Close (3)	Tile
F5	—	—	—	Cascade	Refresh Window	—		Cascade
F6	—	—	Next	—	Toggle Highlight bar	—		
F7	Move	—	—	—	Move	—	—	—
F8	Copy	—	—	—	Copy	—	—	—
F9	—	—	—	—	—	—	—	—
F10	File Menu highlighted				Same (5)	—	—	—
F11	—	—	—	—	—	—	—	—
F12	—	—	—	—	—	—	—	—
+					Expand one level			
*					Expand branch			
-					Collapse branch			
Enter	Open	Properties			(6)	Properties		
Delete	Delete				Delete (Ctrl+N= Expand one level and display directory tree for drive N. Ctrl+Shift+N= Same as Ctrl+N, but expand all branches. Ctrl+Alt+N= Collapse all branches, except for that displayed in Current Directory Window.)			

Menus

Alt+N	Opens specified menu, where N is any underlined letter on Menu Bar.
N	Opens specified option, where N is any underlined letter in a Menu option.

Properties Dialog Box

Alt+	Selects...	Alt+	Selects...
B	Browse button	I	Change Icon button
C	Command line box	R	Run Minimized checkbox
D	Description line box	S	Shortcut Key box
H	Help button	W	Working Directory box

Task Manager

Alt+Tab	Toggle between all open applications.
Alt+Esc	View all open applications.
Ctrl+Esc	Display Task List dialog box.

(1) Windows-for-Wkgrps only. (2) Exit Windows, if Program Mgr is Windows shell; otherwise, minimize Program Mgr. (3) Exit Windows, if File Mgr is Win shell; otherwise minimize File Mgr. (4) Close active window (only if more than one window is open). (5) Or highlight Control Menu Box, if it appears on Menu Bar. (6) In Directory Tree window: Toggle expand/collapse branches (as $\pm$ keys). In Current Directory window: Execute highlighted file.

Hot Keys. The Shortcut key combination, custom or otherwise, is often referred to as a "hot" key.

Cascading Menus. Windows 3.1 provides a cascading menu option, in which a right-pointing triangle (▶) next to a menu option indicates that if this item is selected an additional menu will appear. So far, implementation within Windows 3.1 is limited to the Edit option on the DOS window's Control Menu (which comes up in Chapter 7). As another example, the hDC *First Apps* utility provides a cascading menu for its MicroApp Manager, as shown by the example in Figure 3.4.

Cascading Menu Delay Time. An optional line may be added to WIN.INI to set a cascading menu delay time, as shown here:

```
[Windows]
MenuShowDelay=xxx (where xxx is the delay time, in milliseconds)
```

If the highlight bar is dragged to a cascading menu option and held there, the cascade menu appears after the specified delay time. But if the highlight bar scrolls beyond the option before the delay is over, the cascading menu does not appear. Therefore, the feature simply keeps cascading menus from popping up when not wanted (for whatever that's worth). Regardless of delay time, the cascading menu appears instantly if the option is directly accessed by clicking on it, or if the primary mouse button is released while the highlight bar is over the cascading menu option.

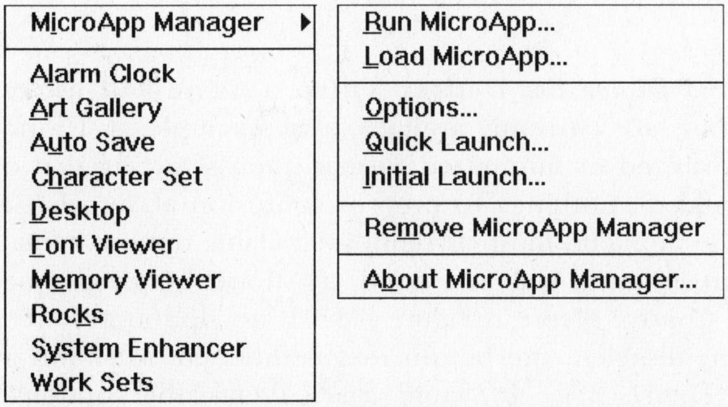

Figure 3.4 A Typical Cascading Menu. Click on the right-pointing triangle to open the cascading menu shown to the immediate right of the triangle symbol.

NOTE: The cascading menu described above is not related to the Cascade option on the Window menu.

Dialog Box. A dialog box is just another kind of menu. Instead of simply clicking a menu option, the dialog box presents its options in one or more of the formats listed here:

Data Entry Box	Type the appropriate information into the box.
Scrolled List Box	View the contents in the list box and highlight the desired item. Use the scroll bar to move through any list too long to fit in the box.
Button	Click once on any enabled button to select the action indicated by the button text.
Radio Button	So-called for its simulation of a radio push-button. When you click on a button, that option becomes enabled and other options in the same box are usually disabled.
Check Box	If you click on any check box, the "X" in that box is cleared and the indicated option is disabled. Click again to re-enable the option.

Figure 3.5 shows a few dialog box examples. The Exit Windows dialog box (a) offers a two-button dialog, while the Browse dialog box (b) confronts the user with a data entry box (immediately below Filename:), a few scrolled lists, and a trio of buttons. The Search dialog box (c) shows a pair of radio buttons in the Look At: box, a disabled Search... button, and five check boxes.

Disabled Menu and Dialog Box Options. Often a menu will list one or more options that are not currently available. For example, if a window is currently in its maximized or minimized format, then selecting that option from the menu would do nothing. To prevent confusion about what is and is not available at the moment, most currently-unavailable options remain visible, but the option lettering will be grayed, as shown by the dimmed Restore option on the Control Menu in Figure 3.3a. If an option accessed by a dialog box button is disabled, the button text is dimmed, as shown by the Search button in Figure 3.5c. In some cases unavailable options—and sometimes, entire menus—completely vanish when not available. As a final point, some options may be permanently disabled, to prevent busy little fingers from running amok.

Refer to the *Menu Troubleshooting* section later in the chapter for assistance if you think your menu options aren't behaving themselves (even though they probably are).

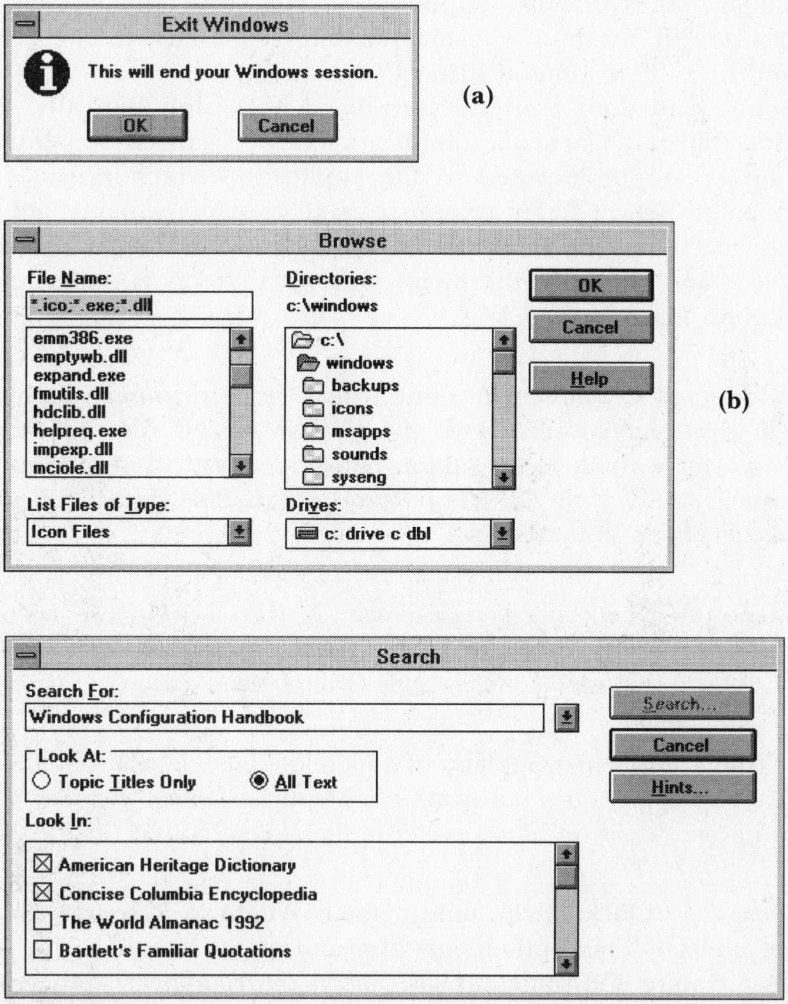

(a)

(b)

(c)

Figure 3.5   A few dialog box examples. (a) The Exit Windows "dialog" consists of clicking on one of two buttons. (b) The Browse dialog box presents several file and directory-selection boxes. (c) The Search dialog box offers a collection of radio buttons, check boxes, and buttons.

Menus and Menu Options

Each Windows application or applet has its own repertoire of menus with options specific to itself. For example, the options associated with the Program Manager menus shown in Figure 3.3 are briefly described in one of the following sections. Although these descriptions are specific to Program Manager, many of the options described in this context may also show up on equivalent menus in other applications. Therefore, when reviewing a menu elsewhere in Windows, you may want to refer back to the descriptions found here for a general idea of what to expect.

The menus, and their contents, are listed here alphabetically. Menu options specific to a particular application are discussed separately in the chapter or section devoted to the application which provides that option. A parenthetical letter reference next to a menu name indicates its location in Figure 3.3. If the menu option is accessible by pressing a key (which is underlined in the menu option), that key is underlined in the description given here.

Menu Restrictions. Certain menu options may be permanently disabled by editing the [restrictions] section of the PROGMAN.INI file. A bracketed [R] next to a menu or a menu option below identifies those options that may be disabled. Refer to *Set Menu Restrictions* in the *Menu Configuration* section for details on how to do so.

Control Menu (a). Except as otherwise noted (in parentheses), each option described here is available on all Control Menus. For the special-case Control Menu in the enhanced-mode DOS window, refer to the Control Menu section of Chapter 7.

About... **(some third-party applets).** This option may appear on the Control Menu if the applet does not provide a Menu Bar which includes a Help Menu. For further details on *About...*, refer to the *Help* section in Chapter 4.

Always on Top **(Clock, Help utility, some Windows Resource Kit and third-party applets).** This option only appears on the menu if the applet supports the feature. On some applets, *Always on Top* appears in a separate dialog box which is accessed by selecting *Options* on the applet's Control Menu. If the undocumented Windows help utility (WINHELP.EXE) is installed, *Always on Top* appears as an option on its own Help menu, as separately described in the *Help Screen* section of Chapter 4.

If *Always On Top* appears on the Control Menu, a check mark in the left column indicates the option is enabled, and the applet remains visible at all times; that is, it is "always on top" of anything else that may be on the Desktop.

The option is often found on diagnostic utilities that monitor system resources. For troubleshooting purposes, enable *Always On Top*, then minimize the applet to an icon, which appears at the bottom of the screen. The icon, or the icon title, displays pertinent information (CPU time, free memory, GDI resources, etc.). Since it is always on top, the meter can be monitored as other tasks are performed.

The Windows Clock applet also provides this option, so that time and date are always visible. The clock applet may run as a minimized icon, or it can run in an open application window suitably sized to occupy a very small portion of the screen.

Representative examples of Always-On-Top applets are listed here, with typical icons shown in Figure 3.6.

Applet	Filename	Source
Clock	CLOCK.EXE	Windows 3.1
Help	WINHELP.EXE	Windows 3.1 (refer to Chapter 4)
PC-Kwik Applets	KWIKINFO.EXE	PC-Kwik *WinMaster*
Smart Drive Monitor	SMARTMON.EXE	Windows 3.1 Resource Kit
Resource Meter	SYSMETER.EXE	Windows 3.1 Resource Kit
Top Desk	TOPDESK.EXE	Windows 3.1 Resource Kit
WinMeter	WINMETER.EXE	Windows-for-Workgroups

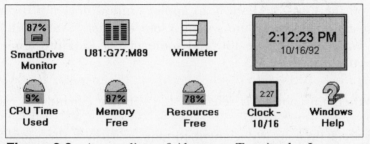

Figure 3.6 A sampling of Always-on-Top Applet Icons.

> **NOTE:** Some resource-monitoring applets may interfere with the normal operation of a Windows applet. If an applet is performing erratically, and a resource monitor is running as an icon (or is open on the Desktop), try closing the resource-monitor applet to see if that clears up the problem with the other applet.

Close **(Ctrl+F4 in Program Manager) [R].** In the specific case of Program Manager, select the Close option to exit Windows. The Exit Windows dialog box appears and prompts you to confirm that you really mean it. Click on the OK button if you do, or the Cancel button if you don't.

Close **(Ctrl+F4 in Group Window).** The Close option in any group window simply closes that window. If the window is already closed, then selecting the Close option just closes the Control Menu.

Windows Exit Procedure. If you attempt to exit Windows while an active application contains a file that has not yet been saved, the following prompt appears:

Do you want to save changes to *filename.ext?*

If a DOS window is open, a different message is displayed:

Application still active.

Quit the application before quitting Windows.

In this case, you must return to the DOS window and close it (type EXIT at its DOS prompt), then go back and close Windows itself.

Help **(some third-party applets).** The Windows Help system may appear as an option on the Control Menu if an applet window does not include a Menu Bar. Typical examples are the system resource meter (SYSMETER.EXE) utility in the Windows Resource Kit, and some of the KwikInfo applets in PC-Kwik's *WinMaster* software.

Maximize. When this option is selected, the window expands to fill the entire Desktop area.

If the Maximize button in a document window is clicked, the window expands to fill the entire application window. A Control Menu box for the document window appears at the lefthand side of the Menu Bar, immediately below the Control Menu box for the application itself. To return the window to its former size, click on the double-arrow Restore button in the upper righthand corner of the document window, or open the Control Menu box and select the Restore option, which is described below.

Minimize. Select this option to reduce an open window to its icon, such as the group icons seen at the bottom of the Program Manager Window in Figures 3.1a, c.

Note that if an application or applet is running and its Minimize button is clicked, the application itself runs in the background, and its Application Icon appears not at the bottom of the Program Manager Window, but at the bottom of the Windows Desktop. The corresponding Program-Item icon remains visible in the appropriate group window (if that window is open). Remember that the former represents the active application, while the latter is available to start a second instance of the same application.

Move. The easiest way to move a window is to simply pick it up and move it. Place the mouse pointer anywhere in the Title Bar, press and hold the primary mouse button as you drag the window wherever you want it to go. The window outline moves accordingly, and when you release the mouse button the window itself appears in the new location.

As for the File Menu's Move option, it does more or less the same thing. Click once on this option and the mouse pointer changes to a four-headed arrow. However, moving the arrow does nothing *until* you press any key (except Enter). When you do, the pointer changes back to its single-arrow format and the window outline follows the pointer. When the outline is in the desired location, press the Enter key to transfer the window to the new location. To control the smoothness with which the window outline moves across the screen, refer to *Granularity* in the *Desktop* section of Chapter 11.

 NOTE: The Move option described here should not be confused with the File Menu's option of the same name, which is used to move a file from one location to another.

Next (Ctrl+F6) (Group Windows only). In the [Settings] section of PROG-MAN.INI, the Order= line lists your group windows in the order in which they were opened, with the last-opened window at the end of the list. If you click on any Control Menu's Next option, Windows reads the Order= line and the active window becomes that which appears at the end of the list. If you click on the same option in that window, the preceding window becomes active, and so on.

In this case, the equivalent key combination (Ctrl+F6) is more efficient. Hold down the Ctrl key and press F6 to toggle through all windows large and small (that is, opened or closed). In each open window, the last-used applet is highlighted.

Options **(Some third-party applets).** If *Options* appears on the Control enu, select it to open a dialog box which offers still more options.

Restore. When the Program Manager Window is open this option is grayed, which indicates it is currently not available. If the window is mini-mized later on, this menu option will be enabled, and may be se-lected to restore the window to its former size.

Size. Select this option and the mouse pointer again changes to a four-headed arrow. Press any arrow key and the pointer moves to the appropriate window edge and changes to a double-headed arrow pointing east/west or north/south. Now move the mouse pointer in either indicated direction and the window frame edge moves accordingly. Move it in any other direction and nothing happens.

If two adjacent arrow keys are pressed sequentially immediately after se-lecting the Size option, the pointer moves to a window corner and points northwest/southeast (or northeast/southwest).

Switch To... **(Program Manager, Applets, not Group Windows).** This option enables the Task Manager. For details and more efficient ways to accomplish the same thing, refer to the *Task Manager* section later in this chapter.

A Control Menu and Maximize/Minimize/Restore Button Summary. A busy Win-dows Desktop will often display multiple Control Menu boxes, and sets of Maxi-mize/Minimize/Restore buttons, as seen in the detail view in Figure 3.7. The significance of each of these boxes and buttons is briefly summarized here.

Control Menu Box	Window
1	Program Manager
2	A group window
3	An application window
4	Active document window within the application window

At the right-hand side of the Figure, the presence of each Maximize (up-arrow) or Restore (double-arrow) button is determined as follows:

Program Manager. The Restore button is seen because the Program Manager currently occupies the entire area available to it; that is, the entire Desktop.

Group and Application Windows. Both windows are open, but not yet maximized; therefore, their Maximize buttons are shown. If the Group Window's Maximize button were clicked, that window would occupy the entire Program Manager area. If the Application Window's Maximize button were clicked, it would expand to fill the entire Desk- top, regardless of the current size of the Program Manager Window.

Document Window. The open document within the Word-for-Windows Application Window is currently maximized to occupy the entire available area. Since it cannot be any larger than the Application Window itself, its Restore button is displayed.

File Menu (b) [R]. The first menu on most application Title Bars is the File Menu which is, in effect, a "File Manager" for that application. The menu offers the basic options needed to open, save, delete, close, or otherwise manage whatever it is that needs to be managed. It also provides the

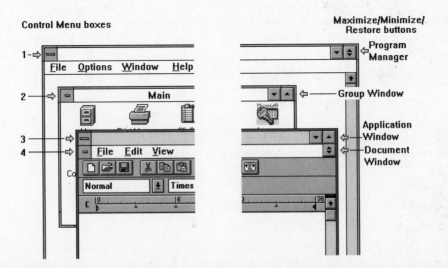

Figure 3.7 Control Menu boxes; Maximize/Minimize and Restore buttons.

means to close the application and either return to the Windows Program Manager or, in the case of Program Manager itself, exit Windows.

If a File Menu option is not currently available, that option may either be dimmed, or it may disappear from the menu until such time as it becomes available. The Excel 4.0 File Menu is a good (or possibly, bad) example of the latter: Depending on context, the Links... option may be dimmed when there is nothing to link, or it may not be seen at all.

If an application supports printing, several print-related options appear on its File Menu. In the case of full-scale Windows applications (such as Word-for-Windows and Excel), a list of the most recently opened files will appear near the bottom of the menu. Simply highlight the desired filename, and that file will be opened within the application.

Copy... **(F8) [R].** This menu option can be used to copy a highlighted applet from its present group window into another group window, as shown by the Copy Program Item dialog box in Figure 3.8. The name of the highlighted file (program item) and its group window are listed near the top of the box. The To Group: box lists the destination group window, which may be changed by clicking on the box's down arrow. As shown in the Figure, an alphabetically sorted scroll list of groups appears. Highlight the desired group name, then click on the OK button to complete the operation.

Delete **(Del) [R].** Use this option to delete an applet or an entire group window. To delete an applet, click once on its icon to highlight it, then select the Delete option. To delete an entire group window (along with all the applets it contains), first close the window. If it is already closed, click once on its Group Icon. Ignore the Control Menu that appears next to the icon, and select the Delete option. One of the following messages appears:

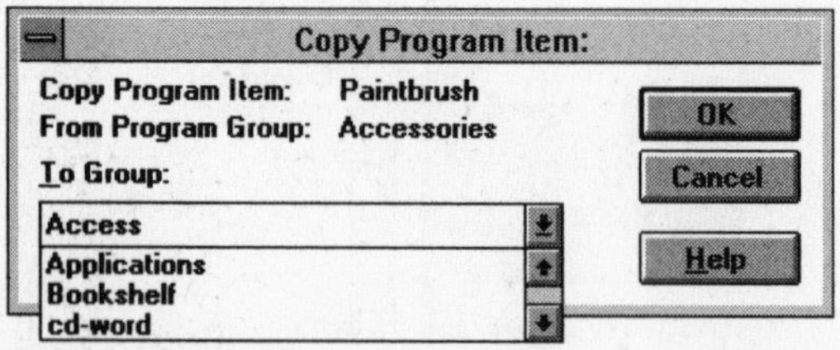

Figure 3.8 The Copy Program Item dialog box. To copy the indicated program item (applet), highlight the desired destination group and click on the OK button.

Are you sure you want to delete the item '(*applet description*)'?
or
Are you sure you want to delete the group '(*group description*)'?

Click on the Yes button if you really mean it. Otherwise, click on the No button to return to the Program Manager without taking any action.

Exit. On File Menus other than Program Manager's, the final option is simply *Exit*, which exits (closes) the application and returns to the Program Manager. However, if the File Manager is the Windows shell, then the Exit option described here does appear on the Program Manager's File Menu in place of the Exit Windows option described immediately below.

Exit Windows...[R]. This one is easy. Click on the option; when the Exit Windows dialog box appears, click on the OK button to complete the exit. As noted in the *Windows Exit Procedure* described above, various prompts appear if an open file needs to be saved, or if a DOS window is open.

If the Windows File Manager is the shell, then its Exit option functions as described here, even though it is not identified as *Exit Windows*.

NOTE: The Save Settings on Exit check box that appeared as part of the version 3.0 exit procedure is now found on the Options Menu, as described below.

<u>***Move***</u>***...(F7) [R].*** This option is equivalent to the Copy option described above, except that the selected file is moved, rather than copied, from one window to another.

If both group windows are currently open, it is perhaps easier simply to pick up the applet icon and drag it from one window into another, as described in the *Icon Configuration* section later in this chapter.

<u>***New***</u>***... [R].*** Use this menu option to add a new group window, or to add a previously installed application to an existing group window. Refer to the *Setup a New Group Window* or *Setup a New Program Item* section in Chapter 1 for detailed instructions on how to proceed.

<u>***Open***</u>***... (Enter).*** Click on this option to execute whatever applet is highlighted in the currently active group window. If all group windows are closed, then click once to open the highlighted group window, and a second time to run the highlighted applet within that window.

The Open option is far more useful when selected from within an application that supports it. For example, if selected on the Sound Recorder applet's File Menu, the Open dialog box shown in Figure 3.9 is displayed. In this example, the WAV files available in the Windows directory are listed in the dialog box. Highlight the desired file and double-click on it to load that file into the Sound Recorder. The same general procedure would be used to load a document file in a word processor, a spread sheet in Excel, and so on.

Properties... (Alt+Enter) **[R]**. Select this option to display the operational properties associated with the highlighted group window or applet. (To display group window properties, first close the window, then highlight it.)

The properties are listed in a **Program Group**, or **Program Items**, **Properties** box. Refer to the *Properties Configuration* section later in this chapter for assistance in changing any of the listed properties.

Run... **[R]**. Once Windows is installed, the Run option is frequently used to begin the installation of a new Windows application, as was described in the *Setup a New Windows Application* section of Chapter 1.

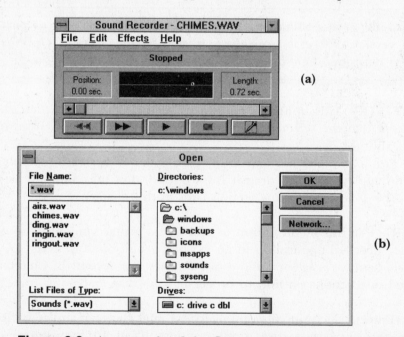

Figure 3.9 An example of the Open option found on the File Menu. If the Sound Recorder applet (a) is open, its Open dialog box (b) lists WAV files appropriate for use with this applet.

The same option may also be used to run any application that is already set up. Enter the path and filename of the desired application, then click on the OK button to run the application. This may be of some use in troubleshooting (if double-clicking on the application's icon doesn't work), or if the desired application is not represented by an icon in one of the group windows. However, for most routine operations, it is a lot quicker to simply double-click on the appropriate icon.

Help Menu (c). The entire Windows 3.1 Help System is described separately in Chapter 4.

Options Menu (d). As its name suggests, this menu lists the various options available within the currently active application. Depending on that application, the Options Menu may be extensive (Excel 4.0, for example), limited (Program Manager), nonexistent (many applets), or hard to find (Word-for-Windows Options are accessible by selecting Options... near the bottom of the Tools Menu).

The selections on Program Manager's Options Menu are described here. In each case, a check mark appears to the left of the menu option when that option is enabled, as may be seen by the check mark next to the Save Settings on Exit option in Figure 3.3d.

Auto Arrange. When this option is enabled, program-item icons arrange themselves automatically every time a change is made. If an icon is moved slightly, it will snap back into place as soon as the mouse button is released. If the icon is moved to another location within the group window, or from one window to another, all icons will realign themselves as required.

Since icons do have a way of "wandering" within a group window, enabling this option will keep the icons arranged in orderly rows and columns. The Auto Arrange option has no effect on the icons at the bottom of the Program Manager which represent closed group windows. Refer to the Arrange Icons option on the Window Menu (described below).

Minimize on Use. When any application is executed, Program Manager will reduce itself to an icon if this option is enabled. Therefore, when you close the application, you will find a Program Manager icon at the bottom of the Desktop, along with any other application icons that may be active.

The Minimize on Use option may be convenient if you customarily run applications on less than a full screen. With the Program Manager icon visible at the bottom of the screen, you can easily switch back to it by dou-ble-clicking on the icon. However, it's probably just as easy to leave Pro-gram Manager open at its normal size, and toggle back to it, as needed, by pressing the Alt+Tab Shortcut key, as described in the *Task Switching via the Alt+Tab Keys* section below.

Save Settings on Exit [**R**]. Prior to Windows 3.1, the Exit Windows dialog box prompted the user to save settings on exit. Now, this feature is rele-gated to the Options menu. If you don't want to save settings automatically on exit, clear the check mark next to this option before closing Windows. The status of this option is recorded in PROGMAN.INI, as shown here:

```
[Settings]
SaveSettings=x (x=1, save settings enabled, x=0, disabled)
```

NOTE: If a **NoSaveSettings=** line is specified in the [restric-tions] section of PROGMAN.INI, that line takes precedence over this **SaveSettings=** line. (Refer to *Set Menu Restrictions* for more details.)

Save Settings without Exiting Windows. Hold down the Shift key and select the Exit Windows option on Program Manager's File Menu. Your settings are saved, but the Exit Windows dialog box does not appear and the Win-dows session continues. As an alternative, select either the Close option on Program Manager's Control Menu, or the Exit Windows option. When the Exit Windows dialog box appears, click on the Cancel button.

You may want to leave the Save Settings option disabled, so configura-tion changes made during any one session will not be carried over to the next one. Then use the Shift+Exit technique to save settings (when you want to save them) without reenabling the option.

NOTE: When settings are saved, they may not take effect until you close and reopen Windows. Although the settings are written to the appropriate INI file, that file may only be read again the next time Windows opens. Therefore, if you are uncertain about the effect of any editing change, take the time to close and reopen Windows while that change is still fresh in your mind. If it's not quite what you expected, you can change back again before you forget what needs to be done.

Window Menu (e). If you have taken great care to configure your Desktop exactly the way you want it, you may want to stay away from this menu. If you do experiment with it and wind up demolishing some carefully crafted configuration, disable *Save Settings on Exit* on the Options Menu, close Windows, and reopen it. Your original settings should be restored.

Arrange Icons. Click on this option to align all the icons in the active group window into orderly rows and columns (not necessary if *Auto Arrange* is enabled on the Options Menu described above).

To arrange closed group icons at the bottom of the Program Manager, click once on any closed icon and then select the *Arrange Icons* option.

Cascade **(Shift+F5).** This option resizes all your open group windows and cascades them one on top of another, as shown in Figure 3.10a. With the exception of the uppermost window, only the Title Bars can be seen. Initially, the arrangement may be satisfactory, since you can at least see the names of the cascaded windows. However, if you select any background window (click once on its Title Bar), it comes to the foreground and blocks some or all the other windows. To restore order, exit Windows (without saving your settings) and reopen it.

Group Window List. The numbered list immediately under the Arrange Icons option shows the names of all (or most) open and closed group windows, and the check mark in the left margin indicates the currently active (open) or highlighted (closed) window. Double-click on any name in the list to make that window active. If the selected window is closed, it opens automatically.

The windows are listed on the menu in the sequence given on the Order= line, in the [Settings] section of PROGMAN.INI.

More Windows... **(Dialog Box (f)).** If there are more windows than can fit on the list, select the More Windows... option at the bottom of the list to display the Select Window dialog box. Use the scroll bar to review the entire list and highlight the desired window.

Tile **(Shift+F4).** Select this option to arrange the open windows in tile fashion, with closed group windows remaining at the bottom of the Program Manager, as shown in Figure 3.10b. If you like this configuration, but want to rearrange the window order, close all the windows, then reopen them in reverse sequence. For

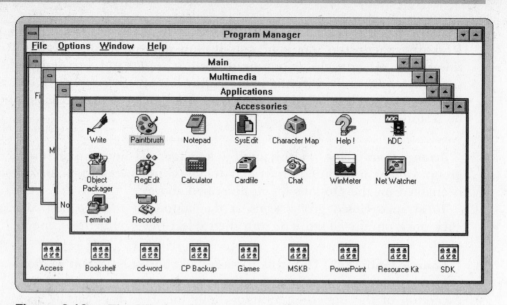

Figure 3.10a The Window Menu offers (a) Cascade and (b) Tile options to display the currently open group windows. In either case, group icons remain at the bottom of the Program Manager window.

example, the alphabetical sequence seen in the Figure was created by opening the windows in reverse ABC order. Once you've opened the windows in the desired sequence, click once on the Tile option to arrange them.

Note that the space allocated to each open window does not take its contents into account. Thus, the three- and four-icon windows get more space than they need, at the expense of others that could use the excess. Of course, you can do a bit of resizing, then save your configuration when you get it the way you want it.

The Task Manager

The Task Manager is an iconless applet (TASKMAN.EXE) that quietly runs unseen in the background. It provides several means for moving from one Windows application to another: "task-switching" as it's called. The Task Manager may be activated by any of the following procedures, each of which opens the Task List dialog box, as shown in Figure 3.11a and described below.

Keyboard Access: The Task Manager Shortcut Key. As one means of activating the Task Manager, press the Ctrl+Esc keys to open the Task List dialog box.

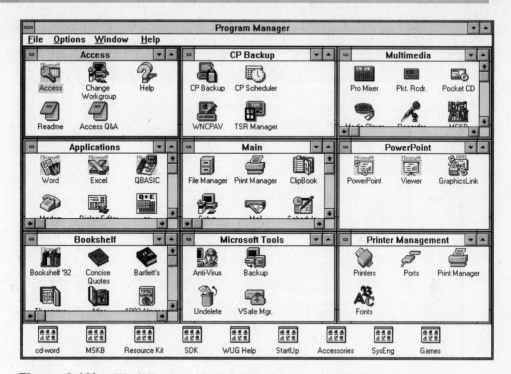

Figure 3.10b The Window Menu's Tile option, showing group icons beneath the tiled windows.

Or, the Alt+Tab sequence may be used instead to toggle directly between applications, by disabling the Cool Switch (yes, that's what it's called). Refer to the Desktop section of Chapter 11 for instructions on how to do so.

Mouse Access: The Desktop Double-Click. To use the mouse instead of the keyboard, simply move the mouse pointer to any free Desktop space; that is, any area not occupied by the Program or File Manager. Then double-click to open the Task List dialog box. This action opens the Task List dialog box regardless of the *Cool Switch* setting.

Applet Icon for Task Manager. In systems where the Task Manager is rarely needed, some users prefer to reassign its shortcut key and mouse access to the File Manager applet, as described in Chapter 6. In this case, you may want to set up a Task Manager icon in one of the group windows so that the applet may be accessed if you do decide to use it every now and then. To do so, simply install Task Manager as you would any other Windows applet. If you need assistance doing so, refer to the *Setup a New Program Item* section in Chapter 1.

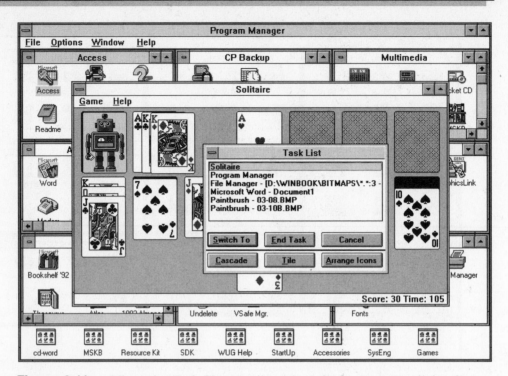

Figure 3.11a When the Task Manager is activated, the Task List dialog box opens to display a list of currently active applets (tasks).

The Task List Dialog Box. When the Task Manager is activated by any of the techniques listed above, the Task List dialog box (Figure 3.11a) appears on the Desktop, and displays the names of all currently active applications. Note that the list shows currently open applets (Solitaire and Program Manager in this example) and also those represented by application icons at the bottom of the Desktop. As each additional application is opened, its name appears at the top of the list.

The six buttons at the bottom of the dialog box perform the following functions:

Task List Button	Performs This Action
Arrange Icons	Align application (not group) icons at the bottom of the Desktop.
Cancel	Close the Task List dialog box.
Cascade	Cascade only those applications that are currently open.

End Task	Close the highlighted applet.
Switch To	Open the highlighted applet.
Tile	Tile only those applications that are currently open.

The Task List is probably best used to review the applets on a cluttered Desktop. But to open the Task List, scroll down to an applet and click once on the Switch To key—certainly not the fastest way of switching from one applet to another, especially when there's an easier way.

Task-Switching via the Alt+Tab Keys. For faster task-switching, hold down the Alt key and press the Tab key once. Under default conditions, this displays a box in the middle of the screen, in which an application icon and its name are displayed, as shown in Figure 3.11b. Toggle the Tab key to sequentially show the names of the other available applets. When the desired name appears, release the Alt key and that applet will open. To quit without making any change, press the Escape key, then release the Alt key.

In Windows 3.0, the Alt+Tab combination sequentially opened each active application window, but did not show the contents of that window until the Alt key was released. If you prefer this feature to the version 3.1 display shown in Figure 3.11b, refer to *Applications* in the *Desktop Applet* section of Chapter 11 for instruction on how to make the necessary changes.

View Open Applications with the Alt+Esc Keys. From time to time you may want to review all the applications that are currently open. For example, if your word processor presently occupies the entire screen, and you want to have a look at everything else without resizing the word processor, simply press the Alt+Esc keys. This brings every other application and minimized application icon to the foreground so that you quickly see who's hiding under the word processor window. If more than one such application occupies the entire screen, other full-screen applications will not be seen, but the minimized icons along the bottom of the Desktop will all show up.

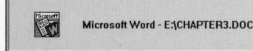

Figure 3.11b   When the Alt+Tab keys are used to toggle between applications, the name of each available application is sequentially displayed on the Desktop.

Subsequent presses of Alt+Esc sequentially hide each application. When the key press hides a full-screen application, the next full-screen application is seen, and so on until all applications are again hidden.

Task Manager Shortcut Key Summary. The three shortcut key combinations described above are summarized here.

Shortcut Key	Function
Alt+Esc	Toggle between all open applications
Alt+Tab	Toggle between all active applications
Ctrl+Esc	Open Task List dialog box

Configuring the Windows Desktop

When Windows is first installed, the Desktop is not very well configured, as was shown by Figure 1.9 in Chapter 1. The Program Manager is probably too small, and the Main Group Window within it, too big. A few suggestions are given here to help reconfigure it into something a bit more presentable. Although the Cascade and Tile options on the Window Menu (described above) offer some rudimentary configuration possibilities, sooner or later you will probably want to work out your own configuration. The procedures described here will help you do so.

In addition to the general window-sizing and placement procedures described in this chapter, the Windows Desktop itself may be further configured with patterns, wallpaper, and screen-savers. These options are accessed via the Control Panel applet, as described in the *Desktop Applet* section of Chapter 11.

Once you have configured a group window to the way you want it to be, you can prevent unauthorized changes from being made by enabling the group file's read-only attribute. Refer to the *Disable Window Configuration* section later in this chapter for assistance if needed.

Window Configuration

Various components of any window may be changed as required to set up your own Desktop configuration. Many of these changes are described in this section, while a few are described elsewhere, as indicated by the references found here.

Colors. The colors of various window components may be changed via the *Control Panel* applet. Refer to the *Color Applet* in Chapter 11 for details.

Location. The simplest way to move any open window is to place the mouse pointer anywhere in its Title Bar, hold down the primary mouse button, and drag the window outline to its new destination. When you get it where you want it, release the button and the window jumps to its new site; or select the Move option on the window's Control Menu, as described earlier in the chapter.

Size. To change the size of an open window, first make sure the button in the upper right-hand corner of the window is the Maximize button described earlier in the chapter. If the double-arrow Restore button appears instead, click once on it to put the window into an adjustable mode.

Now place the mouse pointer on any window border and note that the pointer changes to a double arrow which straddles the border. Hold down the primary mouse button, drag the border to wherever you want it, then release the button to fix the border at its new location. Repeat if necessary on the adjacent border.

To precisely align one group window with another, open the Control Menu for that window, select the Size option, then press the left or right arrow key. The pointer moves to the left or right window edge. Now move the pointer into some other window, as shown by the example in Figure 3.12. Note that the double-arrow is directly below the outlined edge of the window above. Move the pointer until it straddles the edge of this window, then press the Enter key. The other window is now aligned with this one. Fortunately, the action takes far less time to do than to explain.

Title Bar Font. Title Bar text is displayed by the font specified on the fonts.fon= line in the [boot] section of SYSTEM.INI. To change this text to some other font style and size, refer to the *Non-Default Variable-Width System Font* section of Chapter 10.

Title Bar Text. The same text also appears under the Group Icon when that window is closed. To change it, follow the procedure described in *Description Box* in the *Group Window Configuration* section later in the chapter.

Program Manager Configuration

Like any other window on the Desktop, the Program Manager's color, location, and size can be adjusted via the techniques described above. The current size and status of the Program Manager are stored in the [Settings] section of the PROGMAN.INI file.

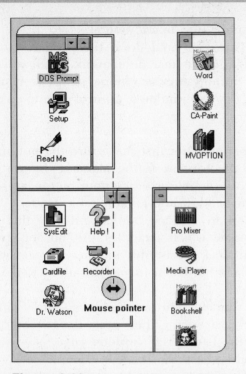

Figure 3.12   Use the Control Menu's Size option and the mouse pointer to precisely position one window border with respect to any other.

When configuring the size of the Program Manager Window, it's usually a good idea to leave a bit of room at the bottom of the screen, so that application icons on the Windows Desktop can be seen.

For additional Program Manager configuration suggestions, refer to the *Assign Shortcut Key to Program Manager* section later in the chapter.

Menu Configuration

A few characteristics of the Windows menus can be modified, as described in this section.

Alignment. Under the default setup, every open menu appears directly under its Title Bar name, and is left-aligned with that name. To right-align the menu, add the following line to the [Windows] (not [Desktop]) section of WIN.INI:

```
[Windows]
MenuDropAlignment=1
```

If space permits, the open menu box will be right-aligned with the menu title. However, if this alignment would force part of the menu off-screen (the File Menu, for example), then the menu position automatically adjusts so that the entire menu may be seen. To return the menu to its default alignment, either change the "1" to "0," or erase the entire line from WIN.INI. Examples of left- and right-aligned menus are shown in Figure 3.13.

Menu Font. Menu text is displayed by the font specified in the fixedfon.fon= line in the [fonts] section of WIN.INI. To change this text to some other font style and size, refer to the *Use of non-Default System Font* section of Chapter 12.

Set Menu Restrictions. As indicated by a bracketed [R] next to many of the menu descriptions earlier in this chapter, the Program Manager menu system can be configured to exclude selected options, or in the case of the File Menu, the entire menu. The procedure is to add a [restrictions] section to the PROGMAN.INI file in which to specify the options you wish to disable, as shown here:

```
[restrictions]
    EditLevel=n   (n=0–4)
    NoClose=1
    NoFileMenu=1
    NoRun=1
    NoSaveSettings=1
```

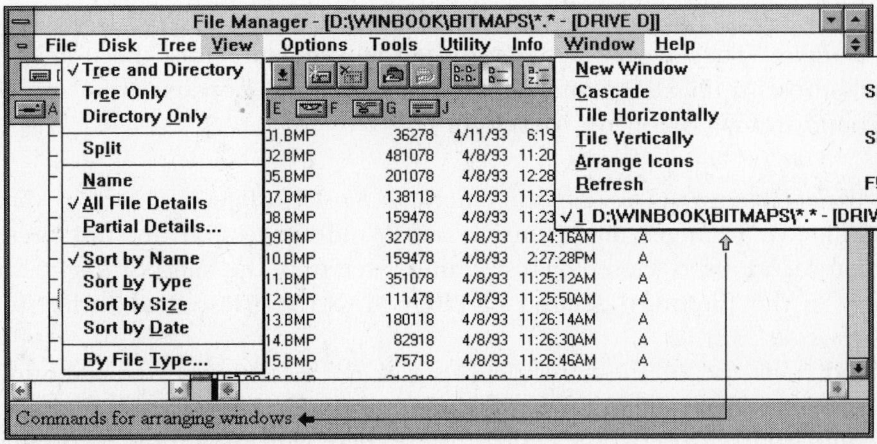

Figure 3.13 Menu Drop Alignment, showing a right-aligned View Menu and a (default) left-aligned Window Menu.

The listings in this section impose certain operational restrictions on the Windows configuration. Since neither the Control Panel nor any other Windows applet provides a means for editing this section, each line must be inserted via the Windows System Editor, the DOS edit utility, or some other ASCII editor. A brief description of each line is given here.

EditLevel=. One of five edit levels may be imposed, as listed here. At each succeeding edit level, new editing restrictions are introduced, and restrictions imposed by lower levels are continued.

Edit Level	Disables These Options
0	No options disabled.
1	New, Move, Copy, Delete a group.
2	New, Move, Copy, Delete a program item.
3	Command line in Properties box.
4	All items in Properties box.

NoClose=. When enabled, the File menu's Exit Windows and the Control Menu's Close options are both disabled (dimmed), and Alt+F4 will not exit Windows either.

NoFileMenu=. The File menu is removed from the Program Manager's Menu Bar, and thus all its options are unavailable. However, the user may still exit Windows by pressing the Alt+F4 keys (unless *NoClose* is also enabled). The File Manager's File Menu is not affected by this setting.

NoRun=. The File menu's Run option is disabled. Thus, the user can run only those applications and applets for which an icon exists in one of the group windows or on the Desktop.

NoSaveSettings=. The Option menu's *Save Settings on Exit* is disabled (dimmed). Changes made during any Windows session are not preserved when Windows is closed. This setting overrides the *Save Settings=* line (if any) in the [Settings] section of PROGMAN.INI (described earlier in *Save Settings on Exit*).

Judicious use of these restrictions can go a long way in preventing the casual user from "fixing" your configuration when you are not around to defend yourself, or it. Of course, the expert will know how to disable the restrictions, but most such experts are usually too busy fouling up their own systems to bother with yours.

Properties Configuration

The procedures for installing a new group window or applet were described in the *Setup a New Group Window* and *Setup a New Program Item* sections of Chapter 1. In those examples, the File Menu's New option was selected, which in turn leads to the appropriate Properties dialog box. If you are installing a new group window or program item (that is, an applet), refer to the appropriate sections of Chapter 1. Otherwise, continue reading here.

After a group window or program item is successfully installed, its properties may be reconfigured by selecting the Properties... option on the File Menu. The procedures for reconfiguring a group window or program item are described in the following two sections.

Group Window Configuration

The first step in reconfiguring a group window's properties is to close the window by either double-clicking on its Control Menu box or by clicking once on its Minimize button. Next, locate the minimized icon and click once on it to highlight the icon text. Make sure the text is highlighted, and disregard the Control Menu that pops up when you do this.

On the Program Manager's File Menu, select the Properties... option, which opens the Program Group Properties dialog box shown in Figure 3.14a. Revise the information listed in the two boxes, as described here.

Description Box. The text in this box appears in the group window Title Bar, and also under the group icon when the window is closed. Make the necessary changes, then move to the Group File box, or click on the OK button to close the dialog box.

To assign a custom title to the Program Manager's Title Bar, refer to the *Change Text in Program Manager's Title Bar* section later in the chapter.

Group File Box. This box contains the path and name of the group file, as it was specified when the group was initially installed. Assuming the group is not defective, there is little need to change the group filename. However, if you have moved the file to another location, be sure to change the path so that Windows can find it. When you are finished, click on the OK button to close the dialog box.

Program Item Configuration. To change the properties of any program item, first open the group window in which that applet resides, then click once on the applet icon to highlight the icon text. Now select the Properties... option

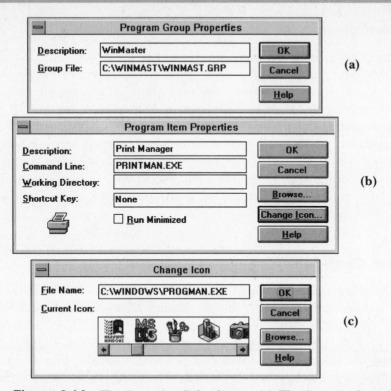

Figure 3.14   The Properties dialog boxes. (a) The Program Group Properties dialog box lists the group window title and the path and filename for the group file. (b) The Program Item Properties dialog box lists the applet's icon title, the command that begins program execution, and other applet properties. (c) The Change Icon dialog box displays the icons that are available within the indicated file.

on the File Menu, which in this case opens the Program Item Properties dialog box shown in Figure 3.14b. The information displayed in this box is slightly different from that for a program group, and is described immediately below.

Description Box. As before, the box shows the text that appears as the program-item icon title. You may want to revise the description, especially in the case of a lengthy title which takes up too much room. For example, many application descriptions begin with the name of the manufacturer, followed by the complete name of the application itself. Even some applet titles are a bit too long; "Windows Setup" for example. Shorten it to plain "Setup," unless you fear someone will confuse it with an OS/2 setup applet.

When a Windows applet or application is run as a minimized application icon on the Desktop, the title under that icon is taken from the applet itself, and so does not show any of the changes you make in the Description box.

Command Line Box. This line is the functional equivalent of a DOS command line that might be typed to launch the application (that is, if it were not a *Windows* application). However, the path need not be included, if the executable file is in the Windows or System directory, or in any other directory specified in the PATH statement in your AUTOEXEC.BAT file. Some users prefer to list the complete path here, and leave it out of the PATH statement, in order to keep the length of that statement within reason.

Immediately after installing some new application, you might want to check your PATH statement. In many cases the setup procedure modifies the statement, often putting your latest treasure at the head of the line. Unless the application is more important than DOS or Windows itself, its proper place is probably at the end of the line or better yet, out of the line completely. Edit the PATH statement accordingly, and make sure the complete path is listed here in the Command Line box. The manufacturer need never know, and your PATH statement will remain under control.

Working Directory Box. This line is often overlooked, but it's quite helpful to fill it in. For example, if your word processor document files are in a separate Document directory on drive D, just type D:\DOCUMENT on the line. Next time you open the word processor, this will be its default directory.

Shortcut Key Box. The shortcut key (actually, *keys*) box lists a keystroke combination that will execute the application, even if the group window in which the applet icon appears is closed. The default is "None," but you can change it by following the directions in the *Shortcut Key Configuration* section later in this chapter.

Run Minimized Check Box. If this box is checked, the application will run in the background, with its minimized application icon seen at the bottom of the Desktop, as was shown earlier by the two Paintbrush icons on the Desktop in Figure 3.1c.

Change-Icon Button. The procedure for changing an application icon is described in the *Icon Selection Procedure* section below.

Icon Configuration

This section reviews the many options available for changing icons and icon titles and also describes how to move an icon from one window to another. Although the discussion is presented here in terms of the icon, it should be understood that what applies to the icon also applies to the applet represented by that icon.

Icon Sources. The icon associated with an applet or application may be found in one of the several files listed here.

filename.CPL	Control panel icons
filename.EXE	The application's own executable file
other.ICO (or DLL)	An icon file that accompanies the executable file
PROGMAN.EXE	The Windows 3.1 Program Manager file
MORICONS.DLL	An additional icon library file supplied with Windows 3.1
Commercial software	Several commercially available utilities contain icon collections
Shareware	Icon files are often available on Windows-related bulletin boards

For future reference, the icons contained in the current versions of PROGMAN.EXE and MORICONS.DLL are shown in Figure 3.15. Any of these icons may be used for any Windows applet or application, or for any non-Windows application that will run in a DOS window. For example, the Windows "Write" applet displays the icon embedded in its own executable file (WRITE.EXE). This icon—a pen and the letter "A"—also appears as the "Read Me" icon in the Main Group Window and may be shared by still other readme files as other applets are installed. For a bit of variety, assign the newpaper icon in PROGMAN.EXE to "Read Me." The procedure for doing so is described below.

NOTE: When the "Read Me" applet's properties are examined, the Command Line in the **Program Item Properties** dialog box shows the name of a document (README.WRI), and not the name of an executable file (WRITE.EXE). The reason a double-click on the Read Me icon automatically loads the former into the latter is that Windows recognizes any file with a WRI extension as being associated with the Write applet. Refer to the *[extensions]* section of Chapter 6 for an explanation of how all this works.

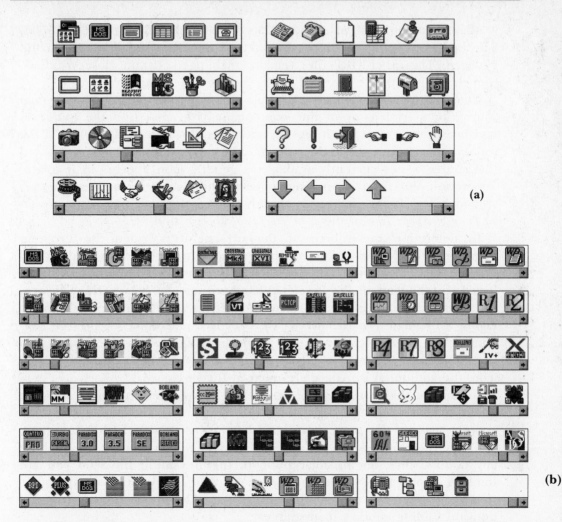

Figure 3.15 The Windows 3.1 Icon Files, showing icons in the (a) PROG-MAN.EXE and (b) MORICONS.DLL files.

Icon Selection Procedure. When an application is installed in a group window or moved from one window to another, the applet's icon is embedded in the appropriate group file (*filename*.GRP). To embed the icon in the group file, Windows searches the application's EXE file, or one of the accompanying icon files listed above. If Windows can't find an icon for the applet, it supplies a generic icon from its own PROGMAN.EXE file. In either case, it is the icon copy in the group file—not the one in the original source—that is displayed in the window. The path and filename for the original icon are also embedded in the group file for future reference.

After changing an icon, go to DOS prompt and look at the *.GRP files. The one containing the recently changed icon has its time/date stamp changed. The other GRP files remain unchanged. If you close Windows, though, all groups are changed to the closing time/date.

Whenever Windows adjusts a group window, it goes back to the original source for a fresh copy of the icon. Again, if it can't find the source as specified in the group file, it digs up one of its own instead. Therefore, if the source icon is on a CD-ROM disk or some other removable medium, and that source is not currently available, a generic icon appears in its place. To prevent this from happening, refer to the *Setting up an Icons Directory* section below. If the damage is already done, refer to *Generic Icon Appears in Place of Applet Icon* in the *Icon Troubleshooting* section.

To determine the source of the present icon, open the Program Manager's File Menu and select the Properties... option. This displays the Program Item Properties dialog box shown in Figure 3.14b. The currently selected icon appears in the lower left-hand corner of the box. Now click on the Change Icon... button to display the Change Icon dialog box shown in Figure 3.14c. The File Name box lists the path and name of the file containing the present icon, and that icon is highlighted in the Current Icon box immediately below the filename. If the file contains more than one icon, the additional icons are also seen in the box.

To change the icon, use the scroll bar (if required) to move through the icon collection, and highlight the desired icon. The highlighted icon appears against the same background color used with highlighted text, and may therefore look a bit different than it will in context. If you have any doubts, click on an adjacent icon, then examine the icon you are thinking about using. If it's not what you want, and there are no other suitable icons in the present file, review the following sections for suggestions on finding another icon source.

Use Browse... Button to Review Other Icon Sources. If the File Name in the Change Icon dialog box contains no icons, or does not contain the one you want, click on the Browse... button to open the Browse dialog box, which was shown earlier in Figure 3.5b. Note that the File Name box shows *.ico; *.exe; and *.dll extensions, as these are the most likely files to contain icons.

If you select a file that contains no icons, the following message is seen:

There are no icons available for the specified file.
You can choose an icon from those available for Program Manager.

The first line really means "There are no icons *in* the specified file." That being so, click on the OK button (it's your only choice) and the

Current Icon box displays the first six icons in PROGMAN.EXE. Use the arrow keys to see the other icons in this collection. If none are suitable, type in the name of some other file containing icons, such as MORICONS.DLL (see Icon Sources section above).

Enter an Icon Filename. If you already know the location of the desired icon file, there's no need to browse; just type the necessary information into the File Name box. If you type an invalid path or filename, the following error message appears:

The path (*path and filename.ext*) is invalid.

Click on the OK button (again, your only choice), make the necessary corrections, and try again.

Install the New Icon. Once you have found and highlighted the right icon for the applet, click on the OK button. The Change Icon dialog box closes and the newly selected icon appears in the lower left-hand corner of the Program Item Properties dialog box. Close the dialog box and the icon appears in the designated group window.

Icon Capacity of a Group Window. A Group Window accommodates only as many icons as will fit into 64 Kbytes of memory, and the maximum number of icons therefore varies according to the installed video system. In any icon file (*filename*.ICO), the icon data itself describes a 32×32-pixel matrix. When the icon is copied into the appropriate group file (see *Icon Selection Procedure* above), each pixel gets 4 to 24 bits, depending on the number of currently supported colors (screen resolution is not a factor). Therefore, since each icon now occupies 512 to 4096 bytes in the group file, as indicated in Table 3.2, the maximum number of icons in the group window varies from 128 to 16, as also shown in the Table. In practice, the icon limit may vary slightly depending on the specific video adapter card.

Note that some 24-bit (3-byte) color systems actually store each pixel in 4 bytes, with the fourth byte reserved. Therefore, the icon limit may be less than what one might expect when a 24-bit color card is installed.

Setting Up an Icons Directory. To discourage Windows from substituting one of its own generic icons (in PROGMAN.EXE) if it can't find the right one, you may want to place copies of removable media icons in a permanent ICONS directory within your Windows directory. To do so, find the location of the current icon, using the *Icon Changes* section above as a

Table 3.2 Group Window Icon Limits

Colors Supported by Video Adapter	Bytes per Pixel[*]	Bytes per Icon[*]	Icons in 64 Kbytes
16	0.5 (4 bits)	512	128
256	1	1024	64
32.8 K	2 (15 bits)	2048	32
16.7 M	3	3072	21.33 (=21)
16.7 M	4	4096	16

[*] Figures indicate icon requirements when stored in a group file.

guide. Once you find the icon's current location, insert that icon source file in the appropriate drive and copy it into a permanent WINDOWS\ICONS (or similar) file on the hard disk. Then enter this new location in the Current Icon box, as described above.

Having done all this, Windows will have no trouble finding the right icon whenever it needs it, even if the original source file is currently unavailable.

This technique is only practical if the icon is in a dedicated icon file (ICO or DLL, for example). If the icon is embedded in an EXE file, it's a bit of a space waster to put a copy of that file into an icons directory.

Changing the Icon Title. In most cases, the title under each icon and the font used to display that title can be easily changed. This section reviews the various font-configuration options that are available in Windows 3.1.

Windows Application Icon Title. The icon title that appears under a minimized application icon on the Desktop is embedded in the application's executable file. Although there are usually multiple appearances of the program name within the file, the first or second is the one that is used. Windows provides no means to change the icon title; such changes should only be attempted by those with sufficient programming experience to do it without wrecking the file itself.

DOS Application Icon Title. By contrast, a minimized DOS application icon shows the same title that appears under the equivalent program-item icon in the group window. To change the title text, refer to the *Description Box* in the *Program Item Configuration* section above.

Group Icon Title. The title under a minimized group icon is the same as that which appears in the Title Bar when that window is opened. To change the title, refer to the *Description Box* in the *Group Window Configuration* section above.

Program-Item Icon Title. To change the title under a program-item icon in an open group window, refer to the *Description Box* in the *Program Item Configuration* section above.

Icon Text Font and Size Selection. By default, icon text is displayed in an 8-point, normal weight, MS Sans Serif font (SSERIF*x*.FON). Refer to *Icon Title Font* in the *WIN.INI Font Changes* section of Chapter 10 for assistance if you would like to change any of these font characteristics.

Icon Text Color Scheme. The text immediately below an icon and its background color are listed here for application, group, and program-item icons:

Icon	Text Color	Background Color
Application, highlighted	Active Title Bar text	Active Title Bar
Application, all others	Black or white	Desktop
Group, highlighted	Active Title Bar text	Active Title Bar
Group, all others	Black or white	Program Manager
Program item, highlighted	Active Title Bar text	Active Title Bar
Program item, all others	Black or white	Window background

Note that when an icon is not highlighted, its text color is either black or white, as required for visibility against its background color. Refer to the *Color Applet* section in Chapter 11 for assistance in changing the icon text color scheme.

Change Icon Spacing. By default, the horizontal distance between icons is 77 pixels, and the vertical distance is determined by the icon title font and the current video resolution. If you would like to change this spacing, edit the following lines in WIN.INI:

```
[Desktop]
IconSpacing=n
IconVerticalSpacing=n
```

where n is the desired spacing, in pixels. To accommodate more icons in an open group window, edit each icon's title so that it fits on one horizontal line, then adjust the vertical space accordingly.

Close and reopen Windows, then select the Arrange Icons option on the Program Manager's Window Menu. The icons in the currently active window will realign themselves according to the pixel spacing specified above. If Auto Arrange on the Options Menu is checked, the realignment takes place automatically.

NOTE: Horizontal spacing (only) may also be adjusted via the *Desktop* applet in the Control Panel, as described in Chapter 11.

Use Drag-and-Drop to Move Icons. In Figure 3.16, the Accessories and StartUp Group Windows are both shown open. In the Accessories Group Window, the empty space between the Calculator and Object Packager icons was recently occupied by the Clock icon now seen in the StartUp Group Window. The icon was transplanted from its former home by using the Windows drag-and-drop procedure. Simply place the mouse pointer over any icon, hold down the primary mouse button, "drag" the icon across the Windows Desktop, and "drop" it in some other group window by releasing the button. If you'd rather drag a copy of the icon (leaving the original in place), hold down the Ctrl key while performing the drag-and-drop routine. In this case, there will be two versions of the applet available: the original one in the Accessories Group Window, and the copy in the StartUp Group Window.

Arrange Group Icons at Bottom of Program Manager. Group icons can be rearranged by using the drag-and-drop procedure described above to move them into the desired order. When you are finished doing so, highlight any one of them, open the Window Menu, and select the **Arrange Icons** option. Doing so aligns all the group icons in a neat horizontal row along the bottom of the Program Manager window.

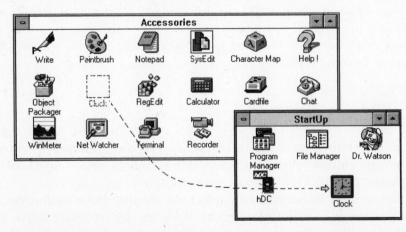

Figure 3.16   The Drag-and-Drop feature. The Clock icon has been moved from the Accessories Group Window to the StartUp Group Window.

Shortcut Key Configuration

Although the customary way to open a Windows application is to click on its icon, the group window in which the icon appears must be open in order to do this. To save a bit of time and mouse movement, a shortcut key combination may be assigned to an applet. When that key combination is pressed, the applet opens even if the group window is closed.

To assign a shortcut key combination, open the group window in which the applet icon appears, click once on its icon, then open the Program Manager's File Menu. Select the Properties... option, move the cursor into the Shortcut Key box, and press any key. When you do, the legend in the box changes to Ctrl + Alt + N, where N is the key you pressed. To specify Ctrl + Shift + Alt + N, hold down either shift key and press the desired letter. To return to "None," press the Shift, Alt, or Backspace key. When you're finished, click on the OK button to close the Program Item Properties dialog box.

Now all you need to do is remember the shortcut key combination, and use it the next time you want that application to open.

Shortcut Key Precautions. If you do use Shortcut Key combinations to execute some of your Windows applets, keep the following precautions in mind as you make your assignments.

Duplicate Shortcut Key Assignment. If you try to use a previously assigned shortcut key, a warning message will be displayed. If a duplicate shortcut key is used anyway, then the application that opens will be either:

1. The application in the active group window that uses that shortcut key

    or

2. The last-opened application that uses that shortcut key.

Shortcut Key Overrides. If a Windows applet makes use of a certain Shortcut Key combination, then this assignment takes precedence over your custom assignment whenever that applet is open. Some of these reserved assignments are reasonably easy to spot: For example, the File Menus in both Excel and Word-for-Windows reveal that Ctrl + Shift + F12 is the Print short- cut. So this combo won't do anything else if either application is active.

Other combinations are not so obvious: File Manager uses Ctrl + *N*, and Ctrl + Shift + *N*, to display directory listings for drive *N* (where *N* is any valid drive letter). Therefore, if File Manager is active, and you expect either combination to open your favorite applet, it won't. If there's no diskette in the specified drive, you'll get an error message and probably wonder why.

For further assistance, refer to Table 3.1 for a list of some Shortcut keys to avoid in making your custom assignments.

Assign Shortcut Key to Program Manager. When many applications are open on the Windows Desktop, you may want to return quickly to the Program Manager without hunting for its icon if it's minimized, or clearing the rubble away if it's not. A convenient way to do this is to assign Program Manager its own shortcut key combination, as described here.

First, open the StartUp Group Window. Then open Program Manager's File Menu, select the New... option, then click on the Program Item radio button. When the Program Item Properties dialog box (Figure 3.13b) appears, enter the following information:

Description:	Program Manager (Or, *use any custom name instead. The name you select will appear in the Program Manager's Title Bar.*)
Command Line:	PROGMAN.EXE
Shortcut Key:	Ctrl+Alt+P (or other, as desired)

When you click on the OK button to close the dialog box, a Program Manager icon appears in the StartUp Group Window. Now close the StartUp Group Window (unless you customarily leave it open) and exit Windows.

The next time you open Windows, Program Manager shows up as it always has. The addition of its icon to the StartUp Group Window has no apparent effect, since Program Manager is one of those "single instance" applications; that is, an application that can only open once, no matter how many times you try to reopen it.

Now do whatever you want to do; when you're ready to go back to Program Manager, press the Shortcut key combination that you specified above. The Program Manager window immediately comes to the foreground, regardless of whether it was minimized, or simply buried under everybody else. The only thing that might get in its way is an applet whose Always-on-Top option has been enabled. If such an applet currently occupies most, or all, of the Desktop, then Program Manager won't be seen.

Change Text in Program Manager's Title Bar. If you'd rather call your Program Manager by some other name, enter that name in the Description box in the Program Item Properties dialog box. When you click on the OK button, the Program Manager Title Bar will display the text you entered, instead of its default "Program Manager" title.

Assign Shortcut Key to a Screen-Saver. Refer to the *Desktop* section of Chapter 11 for suggestions on assigning a shortcut key to a screen saver. If this is done, the screen-saver may be launched at any time, simply by pressing the shortcut key combination that was assigned to it.

Disable Window Configuration

The DOS ATTRIB command can be used to restrict editing access to a specific group window, or windows, without affecting any other part of the Desktop. For example, to prevent anyone from fooling around with something important—your Games Group Window, for example—change its group file attribute to read-only by typing the following command at the DOS prompt:

```
attrib +R GAMES.GRP
```

Now the icons within the group can neither be arranged, moved elsewhere, nor deleted, and these options on various menus will be disabled. Although any icon in a write-protected group window can be copied into another group, no icon from elsewhere can be moved/copied into the protected group window. However, the window itself may be moved, resized, opened, or closed as before.

If the Program Manager file (PROGMAN.INI) is enabled as read-only, a *new settings cannot be saved* warning will be seen every time Windows is opened. You'll have to click on the OK button to continue.

Desktop Troubleshooting

In most cases, a Desktop problem will manifest itself by an error message as you open Windows. In this case, refer to the StartUp error messages in Chapter 2 for assistance. However, there are a few problems that won't be caught as Windows opens; some of these are described here.

Group Window Troubleshooting

When Windows opens, the Program Manager should appear on the Desktop, and your open and closed group windows should be seen in whatever format you left them the last time. If all that doesn't happen, then review some of the topics discussed in this section.

Menu or Title Bar Text Is Missing. No it isn't—it just looks that way. The problem is that the text color is the same as its background color, thus rendering it invisible. Refer to the *Color Applet* section of Chapter 11 for assistance in changing the text or background color.

Window Position Varies as Each Application Opens. When any applet opens, its window is lower than, and to the right of, the position at which the previous applet opened. The effect is seen even if the previous applet was closed before the current one was opened.

This position shift is by design, so that open windows are cascaded on the Desktop. Thus, as each succeeding applet opens, the Title Bars of previous applets remain visible, as was shown previously in Figure 3.10a. However, if a major application (Word-for-Windows or Excel, for example) is opened, it does not follow this sequence.

Unless otherwise noted (the Help Screen for example—see Chapter 4), the opening position of an applet window is not adjustable.

All Group Windows Are Missing. The problem here is that the PROGMAN.INI file is missing. In its absence, Windows creates a new one as it opens, but that one contains only a [Settings] section, in which the name of your current display driver is listed.

The easiest fix is to simply copy the backup PROGMAN.INI file that you cleverly remembered to store elsewhere. Or if this is not your day for clever solutions, then refer to *PROGMAN.INI* in the *INI File Reconstruction Techniques* section of Chapter 14 for assistance getting PROGMAN.INI back in shape.

Group Window Is Damaged or Missing. If an opening error message indicates that a group file (*filename*.GRP) is invalid or damaged, there are several ways in which the file and its group window can be reconstructed, as described here.

The **Setup /p** *Switch: Reconstruct Main, Accessories, Games Groups.* The easiest way to restore any one of these groups is to open the Program Manager's File Menu, select the Run option, and type the following line in the Command Line box:

Setup /p

The undocumented "/p" switch instructs Setup to read the appropriate [group*x*] section of the SETUP.INF file, which contains the names of all files that were installed in the group window during the regular Windows Setup procedure. Setup uses this information to construct a new group file to replace one that is damaged or missing. The newly restored group will not contain changes you may have made since running Setup when you first installed Windows. In other words, if you added, changed, or removed icons within the group, you will have to make the same changes again, once the group is reconstructed by Setup /p.

If one of these damaged groups contains important information that you would like to recover, refer to the *Restore Damaged Group File* section below for suggestions on using the DOS Debug utility to examine the contents of the file. Do this before running Setup /p, so that you can retrieve critical information (if any) from the damaged file before it is overwritten by Setup /p.

You may also run Setup /p on a group that is not damaged. As before, the group will be restored to its initial configuration, but this time any additions you may have made will be preserved within the group. For example, if you had renamed the Clipboard Viewer as simply "Clipboard," and added the SysEdit utility to the Main Group Window, Setup /p would install a new Clipboard Viewer in the window, while leaving your revised "Clipboard" and the SysEdit icon undisturbed.

When Setup /p concludes its work, the hourglass icon may remain on screen until you move the mouse or click one of its buttons. However, make sure you do not move or click the mouse, or touch a key on the keyboard, while Setup /p is working. Otherwise, the procedure may fail, or an icon may be placed in the wrong group window. If this happens, rerun Setup /p and make sure you don't touch the mouse or keyboard until all groups are restored.

Reconstruct Any Other Group File. Since the SETUP.INF file does not contain information about group files other than the ones mentioned above, Setup /p can't reconstruct such groups. In this case, follow the suggestions in one of the following sections.

If you would like to modify SETUP.INF so that in the future Setup /p will restore other groups, refer to the *Recreate StartUp Group* section in Chapter 5, which explains how to do that.

Restore Undamaged Group File. If the group file is present and you have reason to suspect that it is not damaged, try the following procedure. When the error message asks if you want Program Manager to try to load the file in the future, answer "no" so that the reference to that file will be removed from PROGMAN.INI. When Windows opens, double-click on the Program Manager's File menu and select the Ne̲w... option. When the New Program Object screen appears, select Program G̲roup, then type in a brief description of the group (Applications, Spreadsheets, Projects, etc.). In the G̲roup File box, enter the filename for the missing group (*filename*.GRP), then click on the OK button or press the Enter key. Assuming that *filename*.GRP is present in the Windows directory and in good shape, the group window or icon will appear on the Windows Desktop, and PROGMAN.INI will be revised to recognize the revived group in the future.

If this doesn't work, then the cited group file is indeed damaged or missing. Keep reading here.

Restore Damaged Group File. If you recall the contents of the damaged window, simply follow the instructions in the *Setup a New Group Window* section of Chapter 1. However, if you can't recall all the applets that were in the window, you may be able to find their names by examining the damaged group file. Use the DOS Debug utility to open it by typing DEBUG*filename*.GRP at the DOS prompt. When the Debug hyphen prompt appears, search for the hexadecimal string "00 0C 00 80" by typing the following sequence:

```
-s cs:100 fffe 00 0C 00 80
```

Press the Enter key to display a hexadecimal listing in *segment:offset* format, such as the following:

xxxx:0144
xxxx:018C
xxxx:01D5
(and so on)

In each case, the listed *segment:offset* indicates a location in the group file where this unique string occurs. Since the string precedes every icon in the group file, you can display information about each icon/applet by typing "d *xxxx:yyyy*" where *xxxx* is whatever segment appears in every listing above, and *yyyy* is any listed offset. On the right-hand side of the screen you should see information such as that shown in these examples:

```
.File Manager.WI        .........Control        .........Read Me
NFILE.EXE.C:\WIN        Panel.CONTROL.E        .README.WRI.C:\W
DOWS\WINFILE.EXE        XE.C:\WINDOWS\CO        INDOWS\PROGMAN.E
                        NTROL.EXE.......        XE.............
```

Jot down the information required to recreate each new program item. For example, the right-hand listing above contains the following sequential information:

Read Me	Applet description (appears under its icon)
README.WRI	Applet filename (includes path, if necessary)
C:\WINDOWS\PROGMAN.EXE	Path and filename to icon for this applet

The first two items contain all the information you need to add this program item to a new program group. When you do, its default icon should show up in the group window.

Find Icon Previously Used for Applet. Use this procedure if you want to go to the bother of finding the specific nondefault icon formerly used with an applet.

In the first two examples above, note that the icon file is the same file as the applet itself (WINFILE.EXE and CONTROL.EXE). But in the Read Me example, the default icon (in WRITE.EXE) had been replaced by an icon taken from PROGMAN.EXE. Since PROGMAN.EXE contains some 47 icons, it's not immediately clear which one was being used. If it matters, you can find it via the debug utility described above. When the "d *xxxx:yyyy*" command shows the details for the Read Me applet, subtract 1 from the *yyyy* offset and retype the command. The first hexadecimal digit displayed is the icon number, which in this specific example is hexadecimal 18 (the newspaper icon in PROGMAN.EXE). To make sure you're looking at the right number, it should be immediately followed by the "00 0C 00 80" string mentioned above.

Once the applet is reinstalled in the appropriate group window, follow the directions given in the *Change Icon* section (earlier in this chapter) to change its icon. With the PROGMAN.EXE icons displayed in the Change Icon dialog box, highlight icon 18 (decimal 24) and click on the OK button. (Remember to start counting at zero, not one.)

Shortcut Key Troubleshooting

If you press a shortcut key combination and the wrong application shows up, the problem is probably that two (or more?) applications share the same shortcut key. In this case, the application that opens is either the one in the currently active group window, or the last application that was opened.

To resolve the problem, assign different shortcut keys to each application, as described in the *Shortcut Key Configuration* section above.

Menu Troubleshooting

This section reviews a few of the reasons why a menu option may not be available. Review the information offered here, then take the appropriate action.

Entire Menu Is Missing. Sooner or later you'll open a menu and the option you want won't be there, or you may look to an application's Menu Bar for a menu you used a few minutes ago, and the entire menu will be gone. In either case, the solution is to do whatever needs to be done to reinstate the option, or the menu.

As a typical example of what to expect, if a Microsoft *Excel* window shows a spreadsheet and an overlayed chart, the Menu Bar may list one of the following sequences:

Edit, Formula, Format, Data, Options, Macro *(and others)*

or perhaps

Edit, Gallery, Chart, Format, Macro *(and others)*

The specific Menu bar depends on whether the spreadsheet or the chart is highlighted. Therefore, to make certain changes to the chart, you need to highlight it first by double-clicking anywhere within the chart. To return to the spreadsheet, a single click anywhere within its area should do it and the appropriate menus will make their appearance.

Menu Option Is Missing. In some Windows applications, a menu option may be removed from the menu if that option is currently unavailable. Although this does cut down on unnecessary menu clutter, it can be confusing when first learning how an application is supposed to work. To recover the missing option, think about why you need it. Then do whatever you need to do to set up the conditions that would make that option viable. Chances are, you'll find it on the menu the next time you look.

Menu Option Is Dimmed. The usual reason for a menu option to appear dimmed is that the option is currently unavailable. The remedy is to take whatever action is required to enable the option, then reopen the menu on which that option is listed. If you're sure the option should be available under the present circumstances, refer to the section immediately following.

Menu Option Appears Available, but Doesn't Function. If some menu options don't function, it may be that they are currently unavailable, but that the color used to denote disabled text is such that the dimmed-text feature isn't apparent. In case of doubt, examine the Restore option on the Control Menu of any window that currently shows a Maximize button. The option should be dimmed. If it is not, then refer to the *Color Applet* section of Chapter 11 for instructions on how to change the "Disabled Text" screen element.

Option Access Restricted. If an option is disabled when you know it shouldn't be, check the [restrictions] section of your PROGMAN.INI file. If the section exists, one of the lines in it may be restricting access to the option, which accounts for it appearing dimmed on the menu. To reinstate the option, either remove the line or set the EditLevel=n to a lower level, as appropriate. Refer to the *Set Menu Restrictions* section of this chapter for assistance if needed.

Group File Is Write-Protected. As another possibility, if a group file is write-protected, the Move, Delete, and Arrange Icons options will be disabled for all applets within that group. Also, all information displayed in the Program Item Properties dialog box for any applet within that window, and in the Program Group Properties box for the group window itself, will be dimmed.

To verify that this is the problem, open a DOS window (or exit Windows), log onto the Windows directory, and type ATTRIB *.GRP at the DOS prompt. If you see an "r" ahead of any listed file, that file is write-protected. Type ATTRIB -r *filename*.GRP to disable the write-protection for that file (or ATTRIB -r *.GRP to disable it for all group files).

Icon Troubleshooting

This section describes a few of the problems that may affect the icons seen in an open group window or on the Windows Desktop.

Icon Appears as a Black Box. If this happens on a 24-bit color system, note the number of good icons in the group window, which is the limit that Windows can support with the installed video hardware (typically, 15 to 21 icons). Drag each black icon into another group window and drop it off there. As you do, its former appearance should be restored. Make sure the icon count in each window does not exceed the limit for your system. Do not follow the instructions in the next paragraph, which will simply remove the icon and its applet from the group window; this will require you to reinstall the applet as a new program item.

On a system that does not use a 24-bit color card, highlight the black icon, open the File Menu, and select the Properties option. Then press the OK button in the Program Item Properties dialog box. Alternately, you can highlight the icon, press Alt+Enter, then press the Enter key a second time. In either case, the icon should be restored to its former self. If this doesn't work, try dragging the icon into another group window, as just described, or contact the appropriate manufacturer to see if an updated video driver is available.

Application Icon Begins Flashing. If an application icon begins flashing, there is a status or error message associated with that icon's applet. Click on the icon to see the message, then take whatever action is appropriate.

Application Icon Title Illegible. If the title beneath an application icon at the bottom of the Desktop is illegible, chances are a background pattern is conflicting with it. To verify this, click on any such icon to highlight it. Its title color and background should now match that of the Title Bar in your active group window, and therefore be readable.

If you like the idea of the other application icons being illegible, then leave well enough alone. Otherwise, refer to the *Desktop Applet* section of Chapter 11 for instructions on changing the Desktop pattern to something simple: "None" is probably the best choice.

Application Icon Title Missing. If the title beneath a minimized icon is completely missing, it's probably because the colors for the icon title text (Window Text) and background (Desktop) are the same. Refer to the *Color Applet* section of Chapter 11 for assistance in changing one or both to contrasting colors.

Duplicate Icons in Group Window(s). If you upgrade a Windows application, the upgrade Setup procedure may install a duplicate icon (or icons) in a new group window, or in the existing group window. If so, compare the Properties dialog boxes for both icons. Chances are they are identical, and either one may be deleted. Or, simply delete the older icon and relocate the new one, if necessary, in the same group window or elsewhere, according to your preference.

Generic Icon Appears in Place of Applet Icon. Every now and then a Program-Item icon will disappear from a group window, and its place will be taken by one of those drab generic screen icons from the PROGMAN.EXE collection. Typically, this happens as an applet is moved from one window to another, or perhaps when the video mode is reconfigured. The problem occurs because Windows could not find the correct icon, whose location is embedded in the group-window file.

To fix the problem, click once on the generic icon. Then open Program Manager's File Menu, select the Properties... option and click on the Change Icon button. If the error message shown here appears, follow the directions immediately following it. Otherwise, skip ahead to the next paragraph.

The path *(drive, path and filename.ext)* is invalid.

When you click on the OK button, Windows replaces the specified source listed in the message with its own C:\WINDOWS\PROGMAN.EXE. There are two reasons why this might happen: either the cited drive and/or path is unavailable, or the icon file listed after the path is missing. This is a frequent occurrence if that file is on a removable medium (CD-ROM disk, for example) which is currently not in the specified drive. To restore the correct icon, find the disk or diskette medium on which it is stored, and insert it into the designated drive. Then return to the Program Item Properties dialog box and click again on the Change Icon button. You should now see the Change Icon dialog box and, in it, the correct icon. Click on the OK button and the icon should be restored to the group window.

As another possibility, if you know the information in the error message is wrong, and that the desired icon file is already available elsewhere on the hard disk, then enter the correct information into the Filename box and press the Enter Key. Then close the Change Icon dialog box, as described above.

To prevent this sort of nuisance from reoccurring, consider setting up the Icons directory as a Windows subdirectory, and copy such transient icons into it. The procedure was described earlier in the chapter, in the *Setting Up an Icons Directory* section.

Icon Locked in its Present Position. If an icon in a group window cannot be moved from its present position, the group file associated with that group window is probably write-protected. Refer to the *Group File Is Write-Protected* section above if you need assistance in clearing the write-protect attribute.

Desktop Error Messages

Most error messages related to the Desktop or to Program Manager appear when you open Windows, and are covered in the Error Message section of Chapter 2. However, there are a few messages that may show up after Windows has successfully opened, and these are described here.

Call to Undefined Dynalink. If this message shows up for no apparent reason, the SHELL.DLL file in the System directory is probably invalid. One way to verify this is to attempt to change an icon. If the message appears, then replace the SHELL.DLL file with a fresh expanded copy from the distribution diskettes.

If this does not solve the problem, then some other dynamic-link library (DLL) file may be the problem. Refer to this error message in Chapter 4 for further assistance.

Cannot find any icons in this file. This one should be self-explanatory. Click on the Browse... button to search for some other file that may contain an icon selection.

Duplicate Shortcut Key: Item *(applet description)* **is using the same short-cut key. Press OK to accept this or Cancel to select a new key.** Help stamp out confusion by clicking on the Cancel button, then selecting some other Shortcut key combination.

Insufficient memory to perform this operation. Quit one or more Windows applications and try again. If the message appears when you drag an icon from one group window to another, the actual problem is that in the present video mode, the action would place more icons in a group window than Windows can support. Refer to the *Icon Appears as a Black Box* section for more details about the problem.

The file progman.ini is write-protected. New settings cannot be saved. If PROGMAN.INI's read-only attribute is enabled, you'll have to put up with this message every time Windows opens. Just click on the OK button to continue, and think about disabling the read-only attribute. To do so, log onto the Windows directory and type the following command at the DOS prompt:

```
attrib -r PROGMAN.INI
```

The path *(drive, path and filename.ext)* **is invalid.** If this message appears when you try to change an applet's icon, refer to the *Generic Icon Appears...* section earlier in the chapter for assistance.

There is not enough memory to convert all the program icons. The icons which are not converted will appear black. You can fix this by choosing FILE.PROPERTIES from the program manager. If this message appears when you modify your video setup, refer to the *Icon Appears as a Black Box* section above.

4

General Trouble-shooting Tips and Techniques

The chapter begins with a look at Windows' extensive help system. When all else fails, and the User's Guide says nothing, the Help screen may be the place to go for assistance. In fact, the Windows help system can be configured (up to a point) to make it a bit more responsive to the user's needs. Since "configuration" is our middle name, the various techniques are described in the Help Screen Configuration section which follows.

Next comes a look at some maintenance techniques and procedures that may come in handy during routine Windows operations. This is followed by an extensive troubleshooting section, and finally, a section on those error messages that are not usually related to a specific applet or application.

The Windows Help System

An online help system is made available as part of practically every Windows applet or application. The help level is context-sensitive, and thus varies from general to specific, depending on what is on screen at the time help is sought. Access to the appropriate help file is via a Help Menu or a Help button. In some cases, help is available as an option on a Control Menu. The help system may also be accessed by pressing function key F1.

In addition to these means of getting help, Windows 3.1 includes an un-documented help applet as part of the WINHELP.EXE file. This file is the engine that drives all the help screens. Although it includes its own icon for direct access from the Windows Desktop, its installation is not part of the regular Setup procedure. Refer to the *Using the Winhelp Applet* section below for further details on this applet.

Table 4.1 lists the help files included with Windows 3.1 and Windows-for-Workgroups, as well as a few examples of help files supplied with various Windows applications.

TABLE 4.1 **Windows 3.1 Help Files**

Group Window Applet	Help Screen Title	Help File	Notes
Accessories			
Calculator	Calculator	CALC.HLP	
Calendar	Calendar	CALENDAR.HLP	
Cardfile	Cardfile	CARDFILE.HLP	
Character Map	Character Map	CHARMAP.HLP	
Chat	Chat	WINCHAT.HLP	1
Media Player	Media Player	MPLAYER.HLP	2
Net Watcher	Net Watcher	NETWATCH.HLP	1
Notepad	Notepad	NOTEPAD.HLP	
Object Packager	Object Packager	PACKAGER.HLP	
Paintbrush	Paintbrush	PBRUSH.HLP	3
Recorder	Recorder	RECORDER.HLP	
Registration Info Editor	Registration Info Editor	REGEDIT.HLP, REGEDITV.HLP	
Sound Recorder	Sound Recorder	SOUNDREC.HLP	
System Editor	(none)	—	
Terminal	Terminal	TERMINAL.HLP	
Windows Help	How to Use Help	WINHELP.HLP, GLOSSARY.HLP	
WinMeter	(none)	—	1
Write	Write	WRITE.HLP	
Games			
Hearts	Hearts	MSHEARTS.HLP	1
Minesweeper	Minesweeper	WINMINE.HLP	
Solitaire	Solitaire	SOL.HLP	
Main			
Clipboard Viewer	Clipboard Viewer	CLIPBRD.HLP	
Clipbook Viewer	Clipbook Viewer	CLIPBRD.HLP	1
Control Panel	Control Panel	CONTROL.HLP	
All applets, ex. as noted	Control Panel	CONTROL.HLP	
Mouse	Mouse Control Panel	POINT.HLP	4

TABLE 4.1 *(continued)*

Group Window Applet	Help Screen Title	Help File	Notes
Main *(continued)*			
Printers	Control Panel	CONTROL.HLP	
Setup	Universal Driver	UNIDRV.HLP	
Options	Universal Driver	UNIDRV.HLP	
Fonts	Windows	FINSTALL.HLP	
File Manager	File Manager	WINFILE.HLP	
Mail	Help for Mail	MSMAIL.HLP	1
MS-DOS Prompt	*(none)*	—	
PIF Editor	PIF Editor	PIFEDIT.HLP	
Print Manager	Print Manager	PRINTMAN.HLP	
Read Me	(see *Write* in Accessories Group Window)		
Schedule+	Help for Schedule+	SCHDPLUS.HLP	1
Windows Setup	Setup	SETUP.HLP	
Program Manager	Program Manager	PROGMAN.HLP	
Microsoft Tools			5
Anti-Virus	Microsoft Anti-Virus	MWAV.HLP	
Backup	Backup	MWBACKUP.HLP	
Undelete	Microsoft Undelete	MWUNDEL.HLP	
Other			
Application Update Info	Application Compatibility	APPS.HLP	6
Windows for Workgroups	Windows for Workgroups	WFWNET.HLP	1, 6

1. Applet and help available in Windows-for-Workgroups only.
2. Help Screen not directly accessible if MCI drivers are not installed.
3. Help file must remain in Windows directory.
4. Help Screen title bar lists name of help file.
5. Supplied with DOS 6.0. Help files located in DOS 6 directory.

The Help Menu

For most applications, a Help Menu is one of the choices listed on the menu bar at the top of the screen. Table 4.2 lists examples of the pull-down Help Menus available with typical Windows applets and applications. In many cases, the user must descend through a few help levels to reach the desired topic. Table 4.3 lists the help levels found on a few representative help systems. Most of the options available via the Help Menu are described here. Needless to say, not all options are available on all Help Menus.

TABLE 4.2 **Typical Windows 3.1 Help Menu Options**

Application Menu options	Application Menu options	Application Menu options
Word-for-Windows	**Excel**	**Central Point Backup**
Help Index	Contents	Index
Getting Started	Search...	Keyboard
Learning Word	Product Support	Commands
WordPerfect Help	Introducing Microsoft Excel	Procedures
About...	Learning Microsoft Excel	Glossary
	Lotus 1-2-3...	Using Help[†]
	Multiplan...	About Backup...
	About Microsoft Excel...	

Applet Menu options	Applet Menu options	Applet Menu options	Applet Menu options
Program Manager	**Most Applets[‡]**	**Selected Applets[§]**	**PIF Editor**
Contents	Contents	How to Use Help[†]	Contents
Search for Help On...	Search for Help on...	Always on Top[•]	Search for Help on...
How to Use Help[†]	How to Use Help[†]	About Help	Standard Options
Windows Tutorial	About (applet name)...		386 Enhanced Options
About Program Manager...			Advanced Options
			How to Use Help[†]
			About PIF Editor...

[†] Opens WINHELP.HLP file.

[‡] Help not available for DOS prompt, System Editor.

[§] Character Map, Help, *WRK* SysMeter applets.

[•] If enabled, applet screen always visible over any other selected application/applet.

The About... Screen. Figure 4.1 shows a few typical *About...* Screens, which are accessible via the Help Menu on most Windows Menu Bars. The top of the screen displays version and copyright information pertaining to the active application or applet, followed by general licensing information.

If the *About...* screen is accessed from the Program Manager, or from any Windows 3.1 applet, a three-line listing at the bottom of the screen shows current operating mode, memory, and system resources. Whenever you want to check these items, simply access this screen via any Windows 3.1 Help Menu. Refer to Chapter 13 for further details about memory and system resources.

A Help Menu's own About option identifies the currently active application as described immediately below.

TABLE 4.3 **Typical Help Levels***

Application Help Level	Application Help Level
Program Manager Help Menu	**Word-for-Windows Help Menu**
1 Arrange Windows and Icons	1 Alphabetic Listing
1 Change an Icon	2 Addresses (labels)
1 Organizing Applications and Documents	3 Printing Envelopes
2 Arranging Window and Icons	3 Printing Mailing Labels
2 Changing Properties	1 Chapter Listing
2 Copying Program Item	2 2:1 The Word Workplace
1 File Menu Commands	3 Choosing a menu command
1 Options Menu Commands	3 Closing a menu

*Selected examples. Most levels offer additional choices.

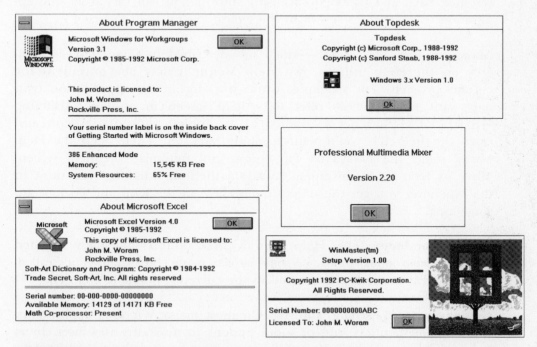

FIGURE 4.1 A collection of "About..." screens, from (a) Program Manager, (b) Microsoft Excel, (c) Topdesk (in *Windows Resource Kit*), (d) Media Vision *Mixer*, (e) PC-Kwik's *WinMaster*.

About Help.... This Help Menu option is seen if you run WINHELP.EXE, either by clicking on a Help icon that you have installed in one of your group windows, or by running it from the Program Manager's File Menu. In either case, About Help... displays version and copyright details pertaining to the Help applet, followed by general licensing and memory information.

If you access any help screen by clicking on any other help screen's File Menu, highlighting the Open... option, then selecting one of the displayed HLP files, the About Help... option described here will still be seen on the Help Menu, even though the help screen title bar correctly lists the selected help file.

About **(applet or application name)....** To view version and copyright information related to a specific Windows applet, open that applet in the usual manner, then click on its Help Menu and select the About (*applet name*)... option. The version number and copyright information for the selected applet now appears on the About Screen.

Third-party applications usually do not display memory and system resource data, and copyright/licensing information will vary from one application to another, as shown by the typical examples in Figure 4.1.

Always on Top. This option—which was described in Chapter 3—is available on the Help utility's own Help Menu; it may be convenient for certain projects. For example, while working in one application, you may want to repeatedly refer to a help screen in another. Assuming WINHELP.EXE has been installed as an applet, click on its icon and open the help file you'll want to study later on. Then open the Help Menu, select the Always on Top option and minimize the help screen. Move its icon to a convenient location, then do whatever you want to do. Whenever you get the urge, double-click on the icon and go look up something.

Contents or Index. The Help Menu's first option is usually labelled Contents, Help Index, Index, or some similar name. But whatever it's called, it offers a list of the topics covered in the currently available Help File.

Getting Started/Learning/Tutorial. On most major Windows applications, the help menu offers one or more options to assist the new user. In at least a few cases, there'll be a little something to ease the transition pain from a rival application. For example, the following applications offer these extra options.

Windows	**Word-for-Windows**	**Excel**
How to Use Help	Getting Started	Product Support
Windows Tutorial	Learning Word	Introducing Excel
	Product Support	Learning Excel
	WordPerfect Help	Lotus 1-2-3
		Multiplan

Search/Search for Help on.... This option displays a list of the topics available within the current help file. You can scroll through the list, or type a search word in the box at the top of the screen. As you type each letter, the highlight bar moves to the word in the list that is the closest match to your word. After you've selected an available search word, click on the Show Topics button to see a list of what's available. Usually it's a one-item list, but now and then there's a choice (try "starting applications" in the Program Manager's Search box). Highlight the topic you want, then click on the Go To button to move directly to that topic.

The Help Button

In contrast to the multilevel help menu system described above, some application/applet screens display a Help button, which may be in a row or column of other buttons. In either case, a single click on the button displays help options specifically related to the screen on which the help button appears.

Control Menu Help

As an alternative to the Help button, help is sometimes available as an option on an applet's Control Menu. This may be the case when the applet's screen format is not suitable for the display of a help button. A typical example is the System Resource Meter applet that is part of the *Windows Resource Kit.*

Once the Control Menu's Help option is selected, the applet's help screen is displayed. That screen's own menu bar may in turn offer an additional Help Menu, one of whose options may lead to yet another help screen. Again using the System Meter as an example, the Help Menu that appears on its own help screen offers a How to Use Help option. If selected, this takes the user back to the same How to Use Help option that is available via the Program Manager's Help Menu. In fact, many other help screens offer the same option.

Function Key (F1) Help

Press Function key F1 for context-sensitive access to the Windows Help system. For example, double-click on the Control Panel icon, click once on any icon in the Control Panel, then press F1 to show the help screen related to the selected Control Panel applet.

In some cases, Function Key F1 opens a help screen that is even more specific. The PIF Editor applet is one of the best examples: Click once on any item in any PIF Editor box, then press F1 to show help for only that item.

Help Screen Features

Most Windows help screens can provide additional information beyond that seen on the current screen by means of one or more of the following devices.

Pushbutton Bar. Buttons on a horizontal bar directly below the Help Screen's Menu bar may offer some of the following selections:

Back. This button is enabled if the present help screen has been accessed from a previous screen. Otherwise, the button is disabled (dimmed). If enabled, click on the button to return to the previous screen.

Contents. Click on this button to display the Table of Contents for the current help file.

Glossary. This button accesses the Windows Glossary file (GLOS-SARY.HLP).

History. Click on this button to display a sequential list of all the help screens you have viewed during the current help session. To directly return to an earlier screen, move the mouse pointer to that entry and double-click the primary button.

Index. If this button appears, an Index dialog box is available for the application. You can type in the word or phrase you want to find, or scroll through the alphabetical list of entries that also appears in the dialog box. Depending on the specific application, the index may offer help items, or lead to topics covered in the application.

Search. This button accesses the Search system described in the *Search/Search for Help on...* section above.

<< *or* >>. These buttons are seen in some applications (Word-for-Windows, for example), where they enable you to skip to the previous (<<) or next (>>) related topic. When you reach the first (or last) topic, the << (or >>) button is disabled (dimmed). The << key is the functional equivalent of the *Back* pushbutton, but only when its use would lead back to a related topic.

If neither button appears on the Pushbutton bar, then the current application does not support this feature. If both buttons are dimmed, then the feature is supported, but is not appropriate for the current screen.

Help Screen "+" Pushbuttons. In some cases, the current help screen shows a row of additional help topics, each accessible by clicking on a "+" pushbutton next to the topic. The button activates a PopUp screen with information about the selected topic. Click anywhere to clear the PopUp screen.

Help Screen Underlining. An underlined word or phrase also indicates that more information is available. Depending on the nature of the new information, it may be located within the current help file, or in some other help file. In either case, the requested information may comprise another full screen of text, or be a simple glossary definition.

A solid line indicates that an additional text screen is available; a dashed line means the item appears in a glossary. To get help, place the mouse pointer over any underlined word or phrase and watch it turn into a pointing hand. Then click the primary mouse button to display the desired help information.

Using the WINHELP Applet

On the Menu Bar that appears within many help screens, the File Menu offers an Open... option, usually as the first option on the menu. For example, Figure 4.2 shows an open Write document in the background. With the document on screen, Write's Help Menu was opened, and the Contents option selected. This opened the Write Help screen which is also seen in the Figure, with its own File Menu shown. If the Open option on that menu is selected, this in turn leads us to the Open dialog box which likewise appears in the Figure. The dialog box lists help files (HLP extension) available in the current directory. In this example, the current directory is a custom Helpfile directory in which most help files have been stored (as described below). As seen in the Figure, the dialog box also allows the user to switch to any other drive and directory to view other help files.

As an alternative (and certainly less confusing) means to the same end, a WINHELP applet may be set up as a free-standing accessory, as follows. Click anywhere within the Accessories Group Window (or if you prefer,

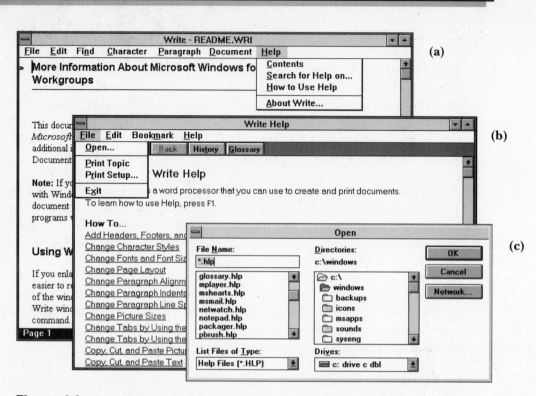

Figure 4.2 An application and its help system. (a) An open Write document, showing its Help Menu. Select the Contents option to display (b) the Write Help Table of Contents. Select the Open option to display (c) the Open dialog box with a list of other help files.

some other window). Then set up a new WINHELP.EXE program item. If necessary, refer to the *Setup a Windows Applet* section of Chapter 1 for assistance doing this. Describe the applet as "Help!" (or similar), then type WINHELP.EXE in the Command Line box and press the Enter key. You should now see a question-mark icon in the group window you selected, as shown in Figure 4.3. Double-click on this icon to gain direct access to the main Windows Help screen, which is also shown in Figure 4.3, along with its About Help screen. On the Help screen's Menu Bar, open the File Menu and select the Open... option to access the desired help screen.

The Help applet offers convenient access to any help file, without the need to open the application to which that file belongs. In fact, if an application is missing or defective, its help file may still be opened via the Help applet. You can also read the help file of an applet such as the Media Player (MPLAYER.HLP), even if the applet itself won't open because the required device drivers have not yet been installed.

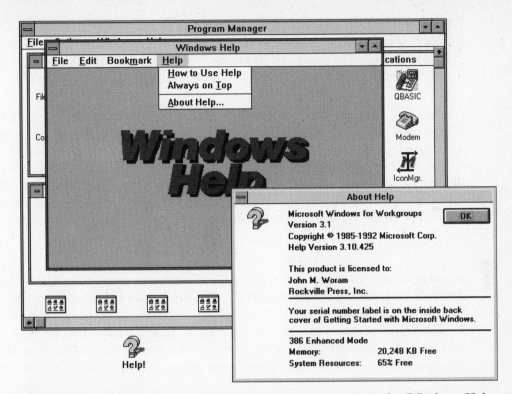

Figure 4.3 Double-click on the Help applet icon to open the Windows Help Application Window. The About Help screen displays the Help Version number and other information.

Help Screen Configuration

By default, the underlined items are displayed as green text against the help screen's white background. The color of each help category may be changed by adding a line to the [Windows Help] section of the WIN.INI file. In each example given below, the three values (R, G, B) indicate the proportion of red, green, blue that is to be used. Thus, 0 0 0 is black; 255 0 0 is bright red, and so on. For assistance mixing your own custom colors, refer to the *Color Applet* section of Chapter 11, and to Table 11.5 which lists various color combinations that may be tried.

Jump Text (Solid Underline)

When you click on a help-screen entry with a solid underline, the Windows help engine "jumps" to a text screen related to the subject of that entry.

This information is usually contained within the currently active help file, although occasionally it may be located elsewhere. To distinguish one category of jump text from the other, the distinctive color of either one may be changed from the default (and sometimes, hard to read) green, as described here.

JumpColor. Most (but not all) help items listed on any help screen's table of contents are contained within the current help file. When any such item is selected, the help engine jumps directly to the appropriate help screen. Within any help screen, a "see also..." reference may lead to an additional screen of text within the current help file. To further identify such entries by a distinctive color, add or edit the following line in the [Windows Help] section of WIN.INI:

    JumpColor=R G B

IFJumpColor. Occasionally, an underlined item may lead to a screen in a different help file. As a typical example, the first table-of-contents item on the Microsoft Excel Help screen (EXCEL.HLP) is "Product Support" (PSS.HLP). If that item is selected, the Help engine jumps from EXCEL.HLP to PSS.HLP. To distinguish these items from the local jump items described above, specify a different IFJump (interfile jump) color on the following line:

    IFJumpColor=R G B

Popup Glossary (Dashed Underline)

When you click on a word or phrase with a dashed underline, a glossary entry "pops up" with a brief definition of the selected item. In some cases, the definition comes from a local glossary within the current help file, while at other times the entry comes from the larger glossary within the GLOSSARY.HLP file. You can change the highlight color for either category, as described here.

PopupColor. The color of a popup item contained within the current help file is specified by the following line:

    PopupColor=R G B

IFPopupColor. If the popup item is located in the GLOSSARY.HLP file, then the color of that item will be as specified by the following line:

    IFPopupColor=R G B

The Windows Help Macro

Windows provides support for Help macros, although this feature is not yet implemented within any help files in Windows 3.1 itself. (Several macro examples may be found within Word-for-Windows, in the PSS.DOC file in the WINWORD directory. In each example, click on the colored Run button to execute the specified macro.)

MacroColor. If an application's help system should include help macros, the presence of these macros may be indicated by a word or phrase in a distinctive color, and that color may be specified by the following line:

    MacroColor=R G B

Click on the macro text to execute the macro associated with that text. Note that some help screens employ a distinctive color for headings; if that color coincides with the one specified above, it may appear that the heading is a macro. It's not, as you'll find out when you click on it and nothing happens.

Size and Position of Help Screens

Several lines in the [Windows Help] section of WIN.INI define the size and position of various Help Screen components. There's no need to edit these lines though, since you can accomplish the same thing by opening the indicated help screen and sizing it as required.

[Windows Help]	**Screen Parameters for**
A_WindowPosition= [x, y, width, height, 0]	Annotate screen
C_WindowPosition= [x, y, width, height, 0]	Copy screen
H_WindowPosition= [x, y, width, height, 0]	History screen
M_WindowPosition= [x, y, width, height, 0 *or* 1]	Main Help screen

x, y	Coordinates of upper lefthand corner of screen
Width	Screen width, in pixels
Height	Screen height, in pixels
0	Open help window as specified by x, y, width, height parameters
1	Open maximized help window

[Note use of brackets around parameters above]

Note that "1" is a valid parameter for the main help screen only. The other screens can be neither minimized nor maximized, and both these options are disabled (dimmed) on their respective Control menus.

Organizing the Windows Help Files

Most of the Windows 3.1 help files are placed in the Windows directory during Setup, although printer help winds up in the System directory. As each additional application is installed, its help file is usually located in whatever directory is associated with that application. All this means that eventually there are help files scattered from one end of your hard disk to another. (Type DIR *.HLP /s at the DOS prompt to find them all.) This in turn may suggest the idea of creating a Helpfile subdirectory and moving all HLP files into it. As an obvious advantage, the working directory of the Help applet (described in the next section) might list this directory, thus making all help files conveniently available for one-stop browsing.

However, not all help files are created equal. For example, some applications search only the specified PATH (in AUTOEXEC.BAT) for their own help file. Even if that file remains in the same directory as the application, it won't be found unless the directory is listed in the PATH statement. Fortunately, not too many applications make this demand— otherwise there could be some very long PATH statements required. This characteristic makes a good argument for setting up a Helpfile directory, moving all help files into it, and including a single reference to it in the PATH statement.

Unfortunately, other applications ignore the PATH statement, and only look in their own directory for their help file. Typical examples include Microsoft Excel, the Windows Paintbrush applet (the only applet that does this), and Central Point's Backup/Restore software. If you do decide to move your help files into a separate directory, you'll need to try each one's help system to see if it still works. If it doesn't, move it back into the directory where the application expects to find it.

Editing a Help Screen

The following two options allow the user to custom-configure the help system, either to add supplementary information or to make returning to a found item a bit easier the next time.

Annotate. After reading a help screen and finally figuring out how to accomplish a desired task, you may wish to insert an annotation—a little note to yourself for future reference. To do so, open the Help Screen's Edit menu, select the <u>A</u>nnotate option, and write yourself a note in the Annotation section of the Annotate dialog box which appears within the Help

Screen area. When you save your annotations, a little paper clip appears to the immediate left of the help topic. To read the annotation later on, place the mouse pointer on the paper clip and watch it change to a pointing finger. Click the primary button once to see your annotation.

Your annotations are stored in a separate file in the Windows directory. For example, if you annotate a PIFEDIT.HLP help screen, you'll find a new PIFEDIT.ANN file in the directory. If you write additional annotations later on, PIFEDIT.ANN will be appended to include them.

Bookmark. On meandering through the various levels of help, you may come across an item that you know you'll want to come back to again. You can either hope you'll remember where it is, or click now on the Bookmark Menu at the top of the help screen. When you select the Define... option, the name of the present help topic appears in a Bookmark Name box. Change the name to something you'll remember with ease, and that name is added to your own custom bookmark list which appears directly below the Bookmark Name box. To return to this spot later on, reopen the Bookmark menu. The list of your own bookmarks appears immediately below the Define... option. Select any one and the help system jumps immediately to the desired screen.

Bookmark information is written into a file with a BMK extension.

Routine Maintenance Techniques and Procedures

Sooner or later you'll need to edit an INI or other file, expand a file from a distribution diskette, and (of course) backup your Windows and other directories. And unless you're a personal friend of Edsel Murphy, there will come the time when a setup procedure will configure an IRQ, I/O port address, or DMA channel (all explained below) in a way that can't possibly work on your system. Since these chores may be required for just about any application, they are covered here so that you can find them whenever you need them.

Editing Utilities

Throughout this book, the solution to a configuration problem often includes the phrase "edit the (*whatever*) to do (*something or other*)." If you're well acquainted with editing procedures, then that suggestion is all you need to begin resolving the problem at hand. However, if you are *not* familiar with editing procedures, the suggestion is one more of those infuriating "solutions" that are almost worse than the problem itself. In that case, the present section makes amends by offering a quick review of some of the editing tools that are readily available to any Windows user.

Line-Disabling Techniques. While troubleshooting, you'll frequently want to remove a line from one of your startup files, or from an INI file, then see what happens. Since you may want to restore the line later on, it's often more convenient to disable it, rather than to remove it entirely (then forget how to replace it).

Unfortunately, there are several ways to disable a line, and each technique works only within the files specified here.

Disabling Mechanism	Insert at Head of Line:	Use in:
rem device=	The word **rem**	CONFIG.SYS, AUTOEXEC.BAT
;device=	A semicolon	An INI file
'A = 3 * B	An apostrophe	BASIC program

The disabling mechanism (shown underlined here) is inserted at the head of the line that is to be temporarily disabled. Once you're satisfied the line is really not needed, you can permanently disable it by removing it from the file in which it appears. But until you're sure about this, it's easy enough to re-enable the line by simply removing the "rem" or punctuation mark.

The Windows System Configuration Editor (SYSEDIT.EXE). Windows version 3.1 includes its own editing utility, in the form of an applet whose filename is SYSEDIT.EXE. For some reason the applet is undocumented in the Windows User's Guide, perhaps to keep the casual user from demolishing his INI files. However, the applet is briefly mentioned in the separately available Windows Resource Kit.

To use the System Configuration Editor, open the Program Manager's File Menu, and select the Run... option. When the Run dialog box appears, type SYSEDIT in its Command Line box, then click on the OK button. When you do this, the System Configuration Editor Application Window shown in Figure 4.4a appears on the Desktop. Note that the application window contains four cascaded document windows. These windows contain the SYSTEM.INI and WIN.INI files, plus your CONFIG.SYS and AUTOEXEC.BAT files. These are the only files available to this configuration editor.

In most cases, you will open the System Configuration Editor to work on a specific file; click on the Maximize button in the appropriate document window to bring that file to the foreground. Of course, you can click on the various Minimize buttons to reduce the other document windows to icons at the bottom of the Editor's application window, in which case the icon titles will probably overlap each other.

The System Configuration Editor's facilities are limited. For example, the Search Menu offers a Find, but not a Replace, option. Nevertheless, the Editor is convenient for reviewing, and making quick changes to, the four files listed in its document windows.

Setup Configuration Editor As a Windows Applet. If you would like to make the editor available as an applet, open the Accessories (or any other) Group Window, then install SYSEDIT.EXE as a new applet, as described in the *Setup a Windows Applet* section of Chapter 1. The System Editor applet (also shown in Figure 4.4a) will appear in the designated group window, and may be used to open the editor for subsequent editing sessions.

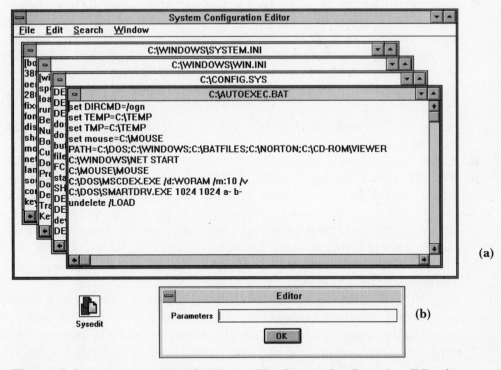

(a)

(b)

Figure 4.4 Windows and DOS Editors. The System Configuration Editor's application window (a) opens with four cascaded document windows containing SYSTEM.INI, WIN.INI, CONFIG.SYS, and AUTOEXEC.BAT. The Editor's icon is shown below the open window. The Editor dialog box (b) allows the user to enter the name of the program to be edited with the DOS Edit utility.

The Configuration Editor Backup File. Whenever you edit a file with this editor, your old file is saved as a backup with an extension of SYD.

The MS-DOS Editor (EDIT.COM). For greater editing power, or to edit files not available through the Windows System Configuration Editor, use the EDIT.COM utility in the DOS directory. If it is not already available as an applet in one of your group windows, write a PIF file to open EDIT.COM and set up the required operating environment, as described in the *PIF Editor* section of Chapter 7. The MS-DOS editor requires the presence of the Microsoft QBASIC.EXE file in your DOS directory. If you're one of those who still believes that real programmers don't use BASIC, and therefore erased this file, you'll have to unerase it to use the EDIT.COM.

Bypass Editor's Opening Screen. If you double-click on the Editor's icon, a "Welcome to the MS-DOS Editor" screen is seen, and you must press the Escape key to get rid of it. With repeated use, this minor distraction gets annoying. To bypass the screen, enter a question mark in the Optional Parameters box in the PIF Editor dialog box. The next time you double-click on the Editor icon, the Editor dialog box shown in Figure 4.4b will appear. In the Parameters box, enter the name of the file to be edited. Then click on the OK button. The editor will open with that file loaded and ready for editing.

The MS-DOS Editor Backup File. There isn't any. If you want a backup copy of your original file, make one *before* using the editor.

The MS-DOS Edlin Utility (EDLIN.EXE). One sure way to identify a DOS power user is to say the word "edlin" out loud. Those who fancy themselves a cut above the crowd will sneer, while the real power user will quietly go on using EDLIN whenever it's necessary to do some really fast and simple editing work. It's a bit awkward on any but the simplest of INI files (not SYSTEM.INI or WIN.INI though), but for quickie changes to your startup files, it's the best game in town.

EDLIN was dropped from early DOS 6.0 beta versions, which prompted at least a few howls from some beta testers. It is now available again, however, on the separate *Microsoft MS-DOS 6 Supplemental Kit* (diskette, that is). You can either order that diskette from Microsoft (see Appendix D), or rescue the old EDLIN from your DOS 5.0 diskettes. Or copy it out of your OLD_DOS.1 directory if you haven't already erased it.

The EDLIN Utility Backup File. EDLIN saves a backup copy with an extension of BAK.

Using DOS 5.0 EDLIN. In order to use the DOS 5.0 EDLIN with DOS 6.0, type the following line at the DOS prompt:

SETVER edlin.exe 5.0

Add the following line to your CONFIG.SYS file if it is not already there:

device=C:\DOS\SETVER.EXE

or

devicehigh=C:\DOS\SETVER.EXE

The next time you boot the system, SETVER will be loaded and DOS 6.0 will not complain if you run DOS 5.0 EDLIN.

Using DOS 6.0 EDLIN. If you have not installed the DOS 5.0 EDLIN utility as just described, you can use the DOS 6.0 version just as soon as you get your hands on it. However, if you did add the SETVER line described above in order to use DOS 5.0 EDLIN, you'll have to remove it if you upgrade to the newer version. To do so, type the following line at the DOS prompt:

SETVER edlin.exe 5.0 /D

This deletes the version 5.0 reference in the SETVER table, so that DOS 6.0 won't have trouble running the new EDLIN. If you don't need the SETVER.EXE utility for any other applications, you can remove it from your CONFIG.SYS file.

File Expansion Utilities

In addition to all those admonitions to go edit something, there are those many occasions when a suggestion is made to go back to the Windows (or other) distribution diskettes for a fresh copy of a critical file. Most such files are stored in a compressed format to save diskette space. In order to use them, each one must be expanded to its normal size as it is transferred to your hard disk. The expansion action takes place automatically during a routine Setup procedure, or later on if you use Setup to make additional changes to your system configuration.

But sooner or later you'll probably want (or need) to expand a file or two without running Setup, as for example to overwrite a recently corrupted file on your hard disk, or to add a missing file to one of the Windows directories. This section reviews the necessary procedures, the first of which is to make sure you're using the correct expand utility.

Since compatibility between an expansion utility and a compressed file is a sometime thing, it pays to make sure you're using the right utility for the file that needs to be expanded. The possibility that you're not is made all the more likely by the presence of *three* expand utilities on your hard disk; one each in the DOS, WINDOWS, and WINWORD (if you have it) subdirectories. Needless to say, each of these utilities works in its own way, and for each compressed file only one of them is correct.

To illustrate the effect of using various expand utilities, several attempts were made to expand the following three files:

File	Description	Location
FENCES.TT$	TrueType font	Word-for-Windows diskette
MOUSE.CO$	Mouse driver	Microsoft Mouse Setup diskette
NOTEPAD.EX_	Notepad applet	Windows 3.1 diskette

Each file was expanded with four commonly available expansion utilities. The resultant on-screen messages are shown in Table 4.4a. Note that each

TABLE 4.4a File Compression Utilities and Error Messages

Decompression Utility Compressed File	On-Screen Message
DECOMP.EXE (Word-for-Windows)	
FENCES.TT$	Wrote 13992 bytes to output file 'FENCES.TTF'[†]
MOUSE.CO$	Error — Unknown compression algorithm
NOTEPAD.EX_	Error — No header in the file (file might not be compressed)
EXPAND.EXE (Dos 5.0, 6.0)	
FENCES.TT$	Input file 'FENCES.TT$' already in expanded format
MOUSE.CO$	Input file 'MOUSE.CO$' already in expanded format
NOTEPAD.EX_	(DOS 5.0) (no message given, but file is correctly expanded)[†]
	(DOS 6.0) NOTEPAD.EX_ → NOTEPAD.EXE 1 file expanded[†]
EXPAND.EXE (Microsoft Mouse version 8.20 Setup diskette)	
FENCES.TT$	Error — Unknown compression algorithm
MOUSE.CO$	Wrote 56425 bytes of output file 'MOUSE.COM'[†]
NOTEPAD.EX_	Error — No header in file (file might not be compressed)
EXPAND.EXE (Windows 3.1)	
FENCES.TT$	Copying FENCES.TT$ to FENCES.TTF.
	FENCES.TT$ 6632 bytes copied
MOUSE.CO$	Copying MOUSE.CO$ to MOUSE.COM.
	MOUSE.COM 30989 bytes copied
NOTEPAD.EX_	Epanding NOTEPAD.EX_ to NOTEPAD.EXE[†]
	NOTEPAD.EX_: 20018 bytes expanded to 32736 bytes, 63% increase

[†] Indicates correct expansion of indicated compressed file.

TABLE 4.4b   File Creation Data for Microsoft Compression Utilities

Filename	Source	File Size	Date	Time
DECOMP.EXE	Word-for-Windows 2.0	39121	10-21-91	12:00 pm
DECOMP.EXE	Word-for-Windows 2.0a	39121	02-13-92	2:00 am
DECOMP.EXE	Word-for-Windows 2.0b	39121	08-31-92	12:00 pm
EXPAND.EXE	DOS 5.0	14563	04-09-91	5:00 am
EXPAND.EXE	DOS 6.0	16129	02-12-93	6:00 am
EXPAND.EXE	Mouse Setup	17820	03-10-92	8:20 am
EXPAND.EXE	Windows 3.0	18337	10-31-90	3:00 am
EXPAND.EXE	Windows 3.1	15285	03-10-92	3:10 am
EXPAND.EXE	Windows-for-Workgroups	15285	09-14-92	12:02 pm

file-expansion utility correctly expanded only one of the files, as indicated by an asterisk. In some cases, an error message indicates that the operation did not succeed. However, some of these messages are wrong (*filename* already in expanded format) or misleading (file might not be compressed). Table 4.4b lists file-creation details for some Microsoft file-expansion utilities, which may be helpful in identifying such utilities on your hard disk.

File Size Comparisons. In a few cases, an "expanded" file is actually *smaller* than its source file on the distribution diskette, as illustrated in the following example of three compressed files. In each case the file is compressed by a 2:1 ratio, with header data added during compression and removed during expansion. Note that if the file is rather large, the effect of the header is negligible. But if the file is quite small, the presence of the header negates the effect of the compression.

Original file size	10000	1000	100	
2:1 compression	5000	500	50	
Add 100-byte header	5100	600	150	(*file size on distribution diskette*)
1:2 expansion	10100	1100	200	
Strip header	10000	1000	100	(*file size after expansion*)

The few Windows files which show this effect are indicated in the Table in Appendix A.

Compressed File Extensions. Note that compressed files supplied on Microsoft and many other distribution diskettes are identified by an extension in which the last character is either a "$" sign or an underline (_) character. If a file on a distribution diskette has a complete extension (EXE or COM, for example), that file is ready to run as is; that is, it does not need to be expanded first.

Downloading Compressed Files. If you need to download a file from CompuServe or elsewhere, be aware that many such files are stored in a compressed format. Often (*too* often, in fact), a "helpful" message will inform you of a utility called *file*.EXE or *filename*.COM, but when you search for a file by that name, it isn't there. If that happens to you, look for a filenamed *file*.ZIP. The ZIP extension indicates the file is compressed, and will have to be expanded by a shareware (usually) file-expansion utility, which is probably available from the same service that provides the file you downloaded. Once you've expanded it, the file will appear with the correct extension.

As another variation, the filename for any file stored in a CompuServe library can have a length of only six characters (plus three-character extension of course). If someone refers you to an eight-character filename, that is the name the file will take when it's expanded. You'll either have to guess at what its compressed name is, or ask for clarification.

As a final point of confusion, some downloaded files with an EXE extension are self-expanding: The first time you execute the file, it expands itself into one or more other files, which may then be used to do whatever they're supposed to do. In case of doubt, download an EXE file into an empty directory, execute it once, then look in the directory. If you find multiple files there, they all came out of the EXE file, which may be discarded (once you make sure the expanded files are operational).

Expand Batch File (X.BAT). If you're a frequent user of the Windows 3.1 expand utility, the following one-line batch file will speed up the chore.

```
EXPAND -r A:%1 %2
```

The -r parameter instructs EXPAND.EXE to automatically give the expanded file the correct name, and is valid only for Windows 3.1 (or other) files that were originally compressed using that parameter.

The A:%1 instructs the expand utility to look to drive A for the compressed file identified by %1 and to expand it to the path specified by %2. Thus, to expand VGA.3G_ to your Windows System directory, type the following line (assuming you've named your batch file X.BAT):

```
X VGA.3G_  C:\WINDOWS\SYSTEM
```

Backup and Restore Procedures

If you're using backup and restore software that runs under Windows, you may not discover a little Windows "gotcha" until it's too late. For example, consider the following worst-case scenario: Last night you made a full backup of your hard drive. This morning, something terrible happened. Never mind what—the bottom line is that you need to reformat the drive. So you do. Now, it's time to restore all your files. But:

1. You can't run the Windows restore software: It isn't on your hard drive anymore.
2. You can't install it: Windows isn't on your hard drive either.
3. You can't install Windows: DOS is not on your hard drive.

Working backwards, you'll have to reinstall DOS first, then Windows, and finally, the Windows backup/restore utility. Somewhere along the way, you'll no doubt wonder if there isn't an easier way. Doing a complete Windows reinstallation so you can reinstall the backup utility is a nuisance to say the least, especially since the version of Windows that you *really* want to install is reposing on your backup media, where for the moment it is inaccessible.

Before the next disaster strikes, consider locating your backup/restore software on drive D; that is, in a different partition than your DOS/Windows drive-C partition. Also, consider using a utility which can backup from within Windows, and later on restore from the DOS prompt (for example, Central Point's *Backup* version 7.0, or similar). With such a utility on drive D, you can restore Windows directly from the backup media to drive C, thus sparing you the hassle of doing a new Windows Setup, followed by a reinstallation of the backup/restore software.

If your utility can backup from either the DOS prompt or from Windows, you might want to try both methods. The former may be a lot faster, in which case there's not much point in backing up from within Windows, unless you like to watch the screen display.

Some backup utilities (again, using Central Point's *Backup* as a typical example) do not make a backup copy of a permanent swap file (if any), thus saving considerable space on the backup medium.

IRQ, I/O, and DMA Channel Assignments

Various devices make use of hardware interrupts, input/output ports, and direct memory access channels. Although you needn't know all the details about this, it is important to keep a device from trying (often, without success) to use the same parameter assigned to some other device.

The best course of action is to maintain a list of devices, along with the parameters assigned to each one. Whenever you add another little something to your system, make sure its settings do not conflict with whatever is already installed. If you see a potential conflict, change the appropriate settings on one of the devices to avoid that conflict. If one device is not adjustable, then you'll need to reconfigure the other one.

Tables 4.5 through 4.7 list typical IRQ, I/O and DMA settings for some of the devices that one might find in any computer. Note however that word "typical." The specific settings on your device will no doubt be different; if not on every item, then at least on one or two. Maintain your own list, and consult it before installing anything new.

If you suspect a problem is related to one of these settings, refer to the *IRQ, I/O, and DMA Troubleshooting* section later in this chapter. For a bit more general information on the subject continue reading here.

IRQ. In computer jargon, there are interrupts, and then there are interrupts. An IRQ signifies an *interrupt request line,* an actual physical circuit on which the system prioritizes actions that are to be performed. For example, whenever the hardware performs some action, an interrupt request is transmitted on one of eight or sixteen lines, according to the priority required for that action (0 highest, 7 or 15 lowest). This hardware interrupt in turn signals a software interrupt, according to the following convention:

IRQ (Decimal)	Software Interrupt (Hexadecimal)	Used on:
0–7	08–0F	All systems
8–15	70–77	80286 or better

TABLE 4.5a   Typical IRQ Line Assignments

IRQ	Device	IRQ	Device
0	Timer tick	8	Real-time clock
1	Keyboard	9	Redirected IRQ2
2	On 8086 systems; cascaded to IRQ 8-15 on 80286 or greater	10	Sound card
3	COM2, COM4, bus mouse, LAN adapter, SDLC, tape ctrlr.	11	
4	COM1, COM3, bus mouse	12	PS/2 style mouse
5	Hard disk, LPT2, LAN adapter, tape, sound card	13	Math coprocessor
6	Diskette	14	Hard disk
7	LPT1, GPIB, Sound Blaster	15	

TABLE 4.5b IRQ Reports by Selected Utilities

IRQ		Microsoft MSD Utility		Quarterdeck*		Qualitas*	
	Detected?	Description	Handled by	Title	Name	Title	Name
0	Yes	Timer Click	MOUSE.COM	System Timer	MOUSE	Time of day	MOUSE
1	Yes	Keyboard	Block Device	Keyboard Event	SMARTDRV	Keyboard	SMARTDRV
2	Yes	Second 8259A	Default Handlers	IRQ 2	DOS Stacks	Cascade	DOS Stacks
3	COM2	COM2: COM4	Default Handlers	IRQ 3	DOS Stacks	COM2	DOS Stacks
4	COM1	COM1: COM3	Default Handlers	IRQ 4	DOS Stacks	COM1	DOS Stacks
5[†]	No	LPT2:	EXP16$	IRQ 5	EXP 16	Alt. Printer	SD
6	Yes	Floppy Disk	Default Handlers	Diskette Event	DOS Stacks	Diskette	DOS Stacks
7	Yes	LPT1:	System Area	IRQ 7	IO	Printer	IO
8	Yes	Real-time Clock	Default Handlers	Real-time Clock	DOS Stacks	CMOS RTC	DOS Stacks
9	Yes	Redirected IRQ2	BIOS	IRQ2 Redirect	System ROM	IRQ 2 Redir.	System ROM
10[‡]		(Reserved)	Default Handlers	IRQ 10	DOS Stacks	IRQ 10	DOS Stacks
11		(Reserved)	Default Handlers	IRQ 11	DOS Stacks	IRQ 11	DOS Stacks
12	PS/2 Mouse	(Reserved)	MOUSE.COM	Mouse Event	MOUSE	Mouse	MOUSE
13	Yes	Math Co-processor	BIOS	Coprocessor	System ROM	Coprocessor	System ROM
14	Yes	Fixed disk	Default Handlers	Hard Disk Event	DOS Stacks	Fixed Disk	DOS Stacks
15	Yes	(Reserved)	BIOS	IRQ 15	System ROM	IRQ 15	System ROM

* IRQ 0-7 shown at software interrupts 08h–0Fh; IRQ 8-15 at software interrupts 70h–77h.

† Installed device is EXP16.DOS (Windows-for-Workgroups network device).

‡ Installed device is Media Vision PAS 16 card (not detected because card is inactive when report is generated).

In order to help keep users properly confused, IRQs are usually stated in decimal notation, and software interrupts are given in hexadecimal. Although this is not supposed to be a programming book, a nodding acquaintance with IRQ lines comes in handy, since there can be trouble if two active devices contend for the same IRQ line at the same time. However, a certain amount of sharing can be tolerated without bringing the system to its knees. For example, your printer and multimedia sound card might share IRQ 7, provided you remember not to try printing and playing audio at the same time.

Some IRQs are permanently assigned, while others may be reassigned (on an adapter card for example) via jumper placement, switch setting, or software configuration. As an example of the latter, the Intel *EtherExpress16* LAN adapter card comes with a SOFTSET.EXE utility, which is used to set and display its IRQ and I/O port assignments. For some Windows applications, a device's IRQ setting is written into the SYSTEM.INI file.

Some memory management utilities (see Chapter 13) provide an IRQ report which may offer limited information. Table 4.5b summarizes information provided by three such utilities. Note that detection of installed adapter cards may be either ambiguous, or nonexistent. Therefore, if you know an adapter uses a certain IRQ line, but that device does not appear when you run an IRQ-reporting utility, you'll have to refer to the appropriate *User's Guide* for hardware or software configuration information.

I/O Ports. About the best way to check I/O (input/output) port assignment is to trot out all those User's Guides and see what the default configuration is for each of your adapters. If two adapters are both assigned to say, input/output port 300–30F, one or both, or your entire system, will not be happy about it.

Once in a while, a thoughtful piece of hardware will announce itself during system bootup. For example:

```
SCSI host adapter detected at address 388h.
```

But more often than not, the only reliable way of checking I/O ports is via paperwork. If you changed a setting during installation, perhaps you made a note of the new assignment. If you changed it but didn't make a note, perhaps you should pull the card right now and see what the jumpers are set at.

Table 4.6 lists some typical I/O port address assignments.

DMA. Disk drives and other devices may use DMA (direct-memory access) channels to pass information back and forth without going through the microprocessor. Some early PCs had a single four-channel DMA controller chip, but most systems built since the days of the IBM PC AT have two such chips. DMA channel assignments are listed in Table 4.7a, and a representative sampling of DMA assignments for various adapter cards is given in Table 4.7b.

General Windows Troubleshooting

If a problem is clearly the fault of a specific Windows applet or procedure, then refer to one of the other chapters for troubleshooting assistance. However, if the trouble-du-jour can't be pinned to a specific source, then this section may be helpful in finding out what's wrong.

TABLE 4.6   Typical I/O Port Usage

I/O Port		Device	I/O Port		Device
180	18F	Colorado tape			
200	20F	Game port	300	30F	Some hard disk, CD-ROM controllers, Intel EtherExpress, Tecmar, Wangtek
210	21F		310	31F	
220	22F	Sound Blaster, Thunder Board	320	32F	
230	237		330	33F	
238	23F	Bus Mouse			
240	24F		340	34F	Alloy tape
250	25F		350	35F	
260	26F		360	36F	
270	277		370	377	Irwin tape
278	2FF	LPT2	378	37F	LPT1
280	28F	Artisoft LANtastic	380	387	
			388	38F	SCSI host adapter
290	29F		390	39F	
2A0	2AF		3A0	3AF	
2B0	2BF		3B0	3BF	
			3BC	3BE	LPT1 on IBM monochrome/printer adapter
2C0	2CF		3C0	3CF	EGA/VGA
2D0	2DF		3D0	3DF	EGA/VGA in color video modes, CGA/MCGA
2E0	2E7		3E0	3E7	Mountain, Summit (@ 3E7)
2E8	2FF	COM4	3E8	3EF	COM3
2F0	2F7		3F0	3F7	Diskette drive controller
2F8	2FF	COM2	3F8	3FF	COM1, bus mouse

TABLE 4.7a DMA Channel Assignments*

Controller 1[†]		Controller 2[‡]	
Channel	Function	Channel	Function
		4	
0	Reserved		Controller 1 (DMA 0-3) cascade
1	SDLC (synch. data link control)	5	Reserved
2	Diskette	6	Reserved
3	Reserved	7	Reserved

*Functions as listed in IBM documentation.
[†] For data transfer between 8-bit I/O adapters and 8/16-bit memory.
[‡] For data transfer between 16-bit I/O adapters and 8/16-bit memory.

TABLE 4.7b Typical DMA Channel Default Assignments

Channel	Function
0	Microsoft Windows Sound System
1	Sound Blaster compatibility, tape controller
2	Tape controller
3	Amdek CD-ROM drive (old)
	Media Vision PAS 16, tape controller
4	(Unavailable)
5	
6	
7	

The section begins with a look at a few diagnostic aids, followed by an overview of the local reboot procedure. Next come a handful of trouble-shooting suggestions, arranged according to the nature of the trouble, and including everyone's favorite—the general protection fault.

Application Compatibility Check

In case of doubt about an application's ability to perform under a variety of circumstances, you may want to check it against the appropriate items in Table 4.8. The Table is based on a Microsoft checklist for Windows 3.1 compatibility. If an application fails one or more of the checklist items, it may help you to pinpoint the problem, or at least give you some ammunition before calling Tech Support.

TABLE 4.8   Application Compatibility Check List*

Feature and Checklist

Application Color Check
  Against Windows defaults
  Against other color setup
  Against custom color setup

Application Window
  Maximize, minimize application Window.
  Move window horizontally, vertically in small increments.
  Resize application window. Use mouse to drag borders.
  Minimize application, start another application, restore first application.
  Open application, bring any Windows accessory (Write, Paintbrush, etc.) to
  Foreground, switch back to first application.
  Open multiple applications. Use Alt+Tab to switch between them. Repeat with Clock
  Applet set to Always on Top mode.
  Open application, use horizontal and vertical scroll bars.

Document
  Open Write, view application file.
  Open other applet, as appropriate, view application file.

File Manager Drag-and-Drop
  Drag file icon to application icon.
  Drag file icon to Print Manager.

Miscellaneous
  Start application in more than one DOS window and switch between them.
  Read and write application files to diskette, with and without caching enabled.
  Do local reboot (Ctrl+Alt+Del). Verify normal Windows operation after application
  terminates.
  Run application with screen saver enabled.
  Install application on a compressed drive.
  Exit Windows with application running. Verify that save files prompt is seen.
  Open application, read file containing OLE object.

Multimedia
  Check all audio functions under MS-DOS.
  Same, under Windows.
  Same, in DOS window.
  Same, with any nonstandard drivers.

Run Application
  From File Manager with network installed, not installed.
  Same, from Program Manager.

TABLE 4.8 *(continued)*

Feature and Checklist

Setup or Install
  Run Setup at DOS prompt.
  Run Setup at DOS prompt from within Windows.
  Run Setup from File Manager.

System Resources
  Check Memory and System Resources before, during, and after running application.

TrueType Fonts
  Enable "Show Only TrueType Fonts in Applications" (Control Panel/Fonts). Check
  application font box to verify that non-TrueType fonts are not available.
  Check font box for only one occurrence of font name (not *fontname* bold, *fontname*
  italic, etc.).
  Check fonts in dialog boxes, Toolbars, sample files, etc. for readibility.
  Use Character Map applet to paste nonstandard ASCII characters into document.
  Create document with text close to screen edges. Scroll document and look for
  broken characters.
  Highlight text block, examine coverage of text, especially first and last characters.
  Print document with multiple fonts, nonstandard ASCII characters.

*Test application against only those checklist items that are appropriate to it.

Diagnostic Aids

If you need help localizing the source of a problem, perhaps one of the
following readily available diagnostic utilities may help.

Dr. Watson. The "doctor" is a Windows undocumented diagnostic utility, which
you'll find in your System directory (DRWATSON.EXE). When installed,
Dr. Watson monitors system activity; in the event of a general protection
fault, he (or rather, it) should write a diagnostic report in your Windows
directory, in a file named DRWATSON.LOG.

Although you may install Dr. Watson in any group window, his admirers
usually set him up in the StartUp Group Window (see Chapter 5), so that
every time Windows opens, Dr. Watson runs too. If you install him in some
other group window, you'll have to remember to double-click on his icon *before* you get into trouble—a neat trick if you can do it. Dr. Watson always runs
as a minimized icon at the bottom of the Desktop, as shown in Figure 4.5a.
If you double-click on the icon before there's any trouble, the message box
shown in Figure 4.5b is displayed. However, if the doctor has already found
problems, the message box in Figure 4.5c appears instead.

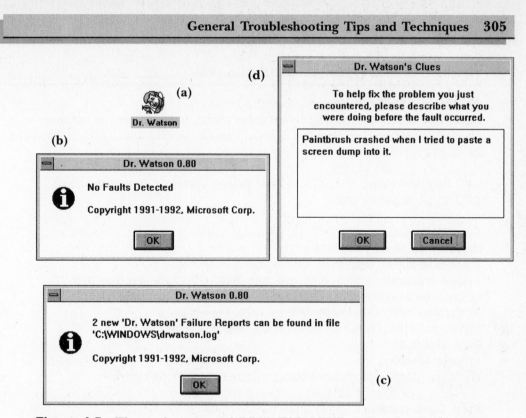

Figure 4.5 The undocumented DRWATSON.EXE utility, showing (a) the applet icon, (b) the report seen if Dr. Watson detects no errors. (c) If the doctor detected a system failure, this advisory message appears when you double-click on the Dr. Watson icon. (d) The Dr. Watson's Clues dialog box can be used to append supplementary information to the log.

A sample of one of Dr. Watson's diagnoses is shown in Figure 4.6. As is common with those of his profession, the Doctor's notes are hard to read, unless you too are a PC doctor. Nevertheless, the log may be useful when it becomes necessary to call someone's technical support line. With luck, the support personnel will know how to interpret the log, if only from having seen many others like it.

The log may also be helpful to the nontechnical user, in that it does provide a bit of information that won't require expert interpretation. An error description is listed at the top of the log, which may be convenient if you didn't jot it down when it appeared on screen. The System Info section lists memory statistics, system resources data (explained in Chapter 13), and the number of tasks in operation at the time of the problem. The tasks themselves are listed near the bottom of the report, and the list may be a bit longer than you would have expected: There's always a little something or other running in the background that you'd completely forgotten about.

Start Dr. Watson 0.80 - Mon Oct 26 16:19:36 1992
****

Dr. Watson 0.80 Failure Report - Mon Oct 26 16:25:21 1992
PBRUSHX had a "Exceed Segment Bounds' (Read) fault at Unknown address
tagPBRUSHX$Exceed Segment Bounds (Read)$Unknown address$lodsb$Mon Oct
26 16:25:21 1992

CPU Registers (regs)   *(These sections contain CPU register data)*
CPU 32 bit Registers (32bit)

System Info (info)   *(Windows version, user name, company, etc.)*
System Free Space 11890944
Stack base 20532, top 28574, lowest 26246, size 8042
System resources: USER: 80% free, seg 06af GDI: 73% free, seg 04ff
LargestFree 21430272, MaxPagesAvail 5232, MaxPagesLockable 1472
TotalLinear 7900, TotalUnlockedPages 1479, FreePages 0
TotalPages 2106, FreeLinearSpace 5365, SwapFilePages 2498
Page Size 4096
11 tasks executing.
WinFlags - Math coprocessor,80486,Enhanced mode,Protect mode

Stack Dump (stack)
Stack Frame 1 is GDI 1:2ec3
Stack Frame 2 is GDI 1:3125   ss:bp 2497:6bac
Stack Frame 3 is GDI 1:2ffd   ss:bp 2497:6bca
Stack Frame 4 is PBRUSHX 31:0f9b   ss:bp 2497:6bf0
(Additional Stack Frame data here.)

System Tasks (tasks)
Task DRWATSON, Handle 23bf, Flags 0001, Info   26864 09-14-92 12:02
    FileName C:\WINDOWS\DRWATSON.EXE
Task PROGMAN, Handle 053f, Flags 0001, Info 115312 09-14-92 12:02
    FileName C:\WINDOWS\PROGMAN.EXE
Task PBRUSHX, Handle 2e6f, Flags 0001, Info 183376 09-14-92 12:02
    FileName C:\WINDOWS\PBRUSH.EXE
(Other active tasks are likewise listed in this section.)

(User comments follow.)
1> Paintbrush crashed when I tried to paste a screen dump into it.

Figure 4.6 Excerpts from a typical DRWATSON.LOG file

In the event of a problem, and after the usual error messages are seen, the Dr. Watson's Clues dialog box shown in Figure 4.5d appears on screen. If you're planning to send the log to someone else for interpretation, or want to jot down a plain-English account of what happened, enter your own words in the dialog box, then click on the OK button. Your description is appended to the log, as shown at the bottom of Figure 4.6.

Unfortunately, Dr. Watson does not offer cures for the diseases he catches. He simply lists the symptoms and leaves the rest to you, or to whomever looks at the report. Nor does Dr. Watson catch every bug flying through the system. Sometimes the nature of the problem is such that the doctor himself is laid low, in which case there'll be no report at all (for example, see the *Call to Undefined Dynalink* error message).

To prevent confusion later on, you may want to rename the Dr. Watson log each time one is generated (or erase it after you read it). If a DRWAT-SON.LOG file exists in the Windows directory, the newest information is appended to the end of it. After a few problems the log can get rather long, and contain much information that is no longer relevant. In Chapter 2, the WIN.BAT startup file listed in Figure 2.2 contains an if exist line that erases the previous DRWATSON.LOG, if there is one.

Troubleshooting Dr. Watson. As noted above, the doctor is good but not infallible. If a DRWATSON.LOG is not created, the problem is one of those that the utility can't find, and you'll have to find a cure on your own.

If you open Dr. Watson and get a *Call to Undefined Dynalink* error message, refer to that message in Chapter 2 for assistance.

System Monitors. Since so many Windows problems are related to system resources, (GDI, User, Memory, as explained in Chapter 13), it's often handy to have a system resource meter running on the Desktop as a minimized icon. The System Resource Meter (SYSMETER.EXE, also in Chapter 13) included with the Windows Resource Kit is one such utility that may prove useful during a troubleshooting session. With the meter visible (Always on Top), you may spot a potential problem before it happens, or use it to keep any eye on how applications make use of your system resources. However, some meters may also cause problems under certain unique conditions. Refer to the *Troubleshooting the More Obscure Problems* section later in the chapter for more details.

Local Reboot Procedure

Most DOS veterans are already familiar with the "three-finger salute" in which you press and hold down the Control, Alternate, and Delete keys— a very effective cure for many PC illnesses, providing you don't mind the side-effect of killing the patient. But sometimes it's the only way to recover the system when an application hangs it up. If the troublesome application is but one of several that are currently running under Windows, the annoyance of a reboot might turn into a catastrophe if the other applications are vaporized at the same time.

As protection against such unpleasantness, the *Local Reboot* procedure (enhanced-mode only) allows you to close a single application while leaving the rest of the Windows Desktop intact. The idea is that Ctrl+Alt+Del will terminate the problem application, but other applications will not be disturbed. However, the procedure is not foolproof. Therefore, if any of the following local reboot procedures do not behave as described here, refer to *Local Reboot Configuration* at the end of this section for a few suggestions.

Windows Application Running Correctly. If you press the Ctrl+Alt+Del keys when there is no Windows application that needs rebooting, the following advisory message is displayed:

> Although you can use CTRL+ALT+DEL to quit an application that has stopped responding to the system, there is no application in this state.
> To quit an application, use the application's quit or exit command, or choose the Close command from the Control menu.
>
> • Press any key to return to Windows.
>
> • Press CTRL+ALT+DEL again to restart your computer. You will lose any unsaved information in all applications.

As already noted, this message is occasionally seen if Windows doesn't recognize an application that is in trouble. In this case the only way out is the old way; press Ctrl+Alt+Del again to reboot the system.

Busy or Unstable Windows System. If you initiate a local reboot while the system is performing an operation or while some error messages are displayed on screen, the following message is displayed:

> Warning!

The system is either busy or has become unstable. You can wait and see if the system becomes available again and continue working or you can restart your computer.

- Press any key to return to Windows and wait.
- Press CTRL+ALT+DEL again to restart your computer. You will lose any unsaved information in all applications.

If appropriate, return to Windows and wait for the weather to clear, or take care of the error message, if any. Otherwise, you'll just have to reboot.

Failed Windows Application. This message may appear if you attempt a reboot after a Windows application fails. It may also appear after the message above, if you return to an unstable application and click on an Ignore button (if one is available within an on-screen error box). The first option below returns you to the failed Windows application.

This Windows application has stopped responding to the system.

- Press ESC to cancel and return to Windows.
- Press ENTER to close this application that is not responding. You will lose any unsaved information in this application.
- Press CTRL+ALT+DEL again to restart your computer. You will lose any unsaved information in all applications.

Non-Windows Application. If you attempt a local reboot while a DOS application is running in an active DOS window, the following message is seen:

You can use CTRL+ALT+DEL to quit an application that has stopped responding to the system. When possible, you should quit the application by using the method recommended in the documentation provided with the application.

- Press ESC to cancel and return to the non-Windows application.
- Press ENTER to close this application that is not responding. You will lose any unsaved information in the application.
- Press CTRL+ALT+DEL again to restart your computer. You will lose any unsaved information in all applications.

Non-Windows Background Application. As a final possibility, this message may be seen if there's a problem with a DOS application running in the background at the time you attempt a local reboot.

This background non-Windows application is not responding.

- Press any key to activate the non-Windows application.
- Press CTRL+ALT+DEL again to restart your computer. You will lose any unsaved information.

Local Reboot Configuration. Refer to one of the following sections if there are consistent problems with any of the procedures described above, or if you want to disable local rebooting or change its screen colors.

Allow Local Reboot to Cancel Applet that Has Not Failed. Just before Windows 3.1 was released, it was discovered that a local reboot could circumvent a password-protected screen saver. When prompted for the password, all one needed to do was execute a three-finger salute and press the Enter key to close down the screen saver and return to the Windows Desktop. So much for password protection.

The problem was fixed, and the Ctrl+Alt+Esc combination should close down an application only if it has really failed. Since screen saver action does not signify a failure, the three-finger salute will simply display the message described above, in the *Windows Application Running Correctly* section.

That's the theory. In practice, Windows sometimes misjudges other situations and insists all's well, even when it is not. Therefore, you may be confronted on one hand with a real applet failure, and on another with Windows insisting there is no problem. In this case, you'll need to grit your teeth and do another salute to terminate the whole works. If this becomes a chronic problem, you may want to add the following line to the indicated section of SYSTEM.INI:

```
[386Enh]
DebugLocalReboot=True
```

Now a Ctrl+Alt+Del will close *any* applet or application, including the password-protected screen saver, regardless of its actual status. If a beep is heard, it signifies that the applet would not otherwise have been terminated.

If you don't use password protection, then its being defeatable is of no consequence and you can add this line without worrying about it. Otherwise, you'll have to decide which aspect of local rebooting is more important to you.

Disable Local Reboot. If for some reason you'd like to disable this feature, you may do so by adding the following line to your SYSTEM.INI file:

```
[386Enh]
LocalReboot=Off
```

With this line in place, a three-finger salute will reboot the system, as in the old days.

Change Message Color. The messages described below appear as white text against a blue background. If you think some other color scheme will ease the pain, add one or both of the following lines to the indicated section of SYSTEM.INI.

```
[386Enh]
MessageTextColor=x          Message text color
MessageBackColor=x          Message background color
```

x	Color	x	Color
0	Black	8	Dark Gray
1	Blue (*default for background*)	9	Light Blue
2	Green	A	Light Green
3	Cyan	B	Light Cyan
4	Red	C	Light Red
5	Magenta	D	Light Magenta
6	Brown	E	Yellow
7	Gray	F	White (*default for text*)

Help Screen Troubleshooting

This section describes various troubleshooting techniques if a help-related problem occurs within any Windows application or applet, or when running WINHELP itself as an applet.

Jump and PopUp Help Troubleshooting. As noted earlier, you can change the various colors to indicate whether Jump or PopUp help for a highlighted word or phrase is contained in the current help file, or in another file, but doing so may be more trouble than it's worth. What difference does it make where the help comes from? What matters is that it's there when you need it. However, if it's not there when you need it, then color-coding may help with troubleshooting.

If an error message ("cannot open," or "does not exist," for example) appears when you click on an underlined word or phrase, it may help to know where the missing item is supposed to be found. If it should be in the current file, and that file is otherwise functional, then it's safe to assume the missing item was not written into the file at the time of its release. Contact the software manufacturer to see if an updated help file is available.

However, if color-coding indicates the lost item lies elsewhere, then perhaps some other help file was accidentally erased. In this case, compare your list of help files with the list given in Table 4.1. If you should have one of these files and you don't, then expand a fresh copy from the distribution diskettes and try again.

The following color scheme provides a reasonably clear indication of the source of any color-coded item on a help screen.

[Windows Help]				Color	Comments
JumpColor=	0	0	0	Black	Text screen in current file
PopUpColor=	255	0	0	Red	Glossary item in current file
IFJumpColor=	0	128	0	Dark Green	Text screen in another file
IFPopUpColor=	0	0	255	Blue	Glossary item in another file

Or to keep things a bit simpler, use one color to indicate items contained in the current file, and another for items in another file.

PopUp Window Shows Word but No Definition. In the unlikely event that a PopUp item is selected from within a very small help window, the chosen word may appear in a PopUp window minus its definition. The solution is to click once, expand the help window slightly and try again.

Troubleshooting General Protection Faults

Some problems are easier to troubleshoot than others. For example, if an error message clearly states that your hard disk just experienced meltdown, you know exactly what happened (if not quite *why* it happened). However, if your system doesn't seem to know what's wrong with itself, but you can tell that something is amiss, then it's likely that some application is making improper use of your system's resources, and a general protection fault may be in the works. If the problem is clearly memory-related, then Chapter 13 is the better place to search for solutions. But if you can't immediately diagnose the problem as originating in the depths of memory, then continue reading here.

According to a Microsoft application note (WW0524, available via CompuServe), a general protection fault occurs "only in standard and 386 enhanced-mode Windows." This is no doubt comforting to those who know how to run Windows 3.1 in some other mode, but to everyone else it's not much help. Therefore, a few general protection possibilities are listed below.

If all else fails, don't overlook the possibility of a consultation from Dr. Watson. The doctor usually detects a general protection fault and writes up a detailed diagnosis, if not a prescription for cure, in a DRWATSON.LOG file in the Windows directory. Refer to the *Dr. Watson* section in this chapter for more information on how this diagnostics system works.

Specific General Protection Fault Conditions. A general protection fault message will usually be accompanied by additional information to help track down the source of the problem. The following sections review some of the possibilities.

Dialog Box Suggests Real Mode. If a dialog box suggests running the application in real mode, then the problem is that the application is not capable of running within Windows version 3.1. You'll need to contact the software manufacturer to see if there is either a workaround solution, or an upgraded version of the application that will run with Windows 3.1.

Incorrect A20 Line Handler. During Setup, Windows determines the correct method for accessing the 64 Kbyte high memory area and may append the /m:*n* or (machine:*n*) switch (if required) to the HIMEM.SYS line in your CONFIG.SYS file. But sometimes Windows guesses wrong and sets the wrong switch, which may result in generally erratic performance, if not an actual system lockup. Although this is a memory-related problem, it is covered here since the symptom does not give evidence of being a function of memory management.

If erratic performance can't be blamed on anything obvious, try changing the machine switch. Refer to Table 13.2 in Chapter 13 for a list of currently available settings.

Device Driver Cited. In cases where a general protection fault message includes a reference to a device driver (*filename*.DRV), then the first step is to identify the driver and replace it with its Microsoft equivalent. If you're not sure of the significance of the driver, then look for that filename in the [boot] section of the SYSTEM.INI file. With luck, you'll find it listed on a line such as:

```
display.drv=filename.drv
mouse.drv=filename.drv
network.drv=filename.drv
```

Once you've identified the problem driver, replace it with its Windows equivalent and try again. If you're not sure which driver needs to be replaced, then replace all third-party drivers with their Windows equivalents. For assistance replacing one or more such drivers, refer to Step 2 in the *General Protection Fault of Uncertain Origin* section below.

Excel 3.0 or 4.0 on Any System. If a general protection fault occurs when you open either version of Excel, rename the EXCEL.XLB file as EXCEL.OLD and try reopening Excel. If this cures the problem, the XLB file was probably corrupt, and in its absence Excel creates a new one on startup. The OLD file can now be erased.

Intel i387 Math Coprocessor Installed, Excel 4.0 Running. On some systems, this combination of ingredients can cause one or more of the following problems:

General Protection fault in WIN87EM.DLL.
General Protection fault in an unknown module when Excel opens.
Windows exits to DOS prompt when Excel is closed.
Floating-point calculation causes hardware error.
Crosstabs failure occurs during a calculation.

If any of these symptoms show up, there's a timing problem between the WIN87EM.DLL file and the math coprocessor. You need an updated version of this file, which is available on the Intel bulletin board (modem (503) 645-6275), or from CompuServe (go MSEXCEL, library 3, download WIN87.DLL, and rename as WIN87EM.DLL).

Intel i387 Math Coprocessor Installed, After Dark, AMI Pro, Lotus 1-2-3, Quicken Running. If the coprocessor is installed and one of these applications is running, the general protection message may refer to a fault in WIN87EM.DLL. As a temporary fix, either remove the math coprocessor, or try using the WIN87EM.DLL file from Window version 3.0. But first, check with the appropriate manufacturer to see if upgraded software is available.

Word-for-Windows 2.0 Running. A general protection fault may occur under certain unique conditions, such as this one:

1. Type C:\WINWORD\WINWORD.EXE /n to open Word without opening a default document.

2. Double-click on any empty space on the toolbar to open the Options screen.

3. In the Category box, select "View" but do not make any changes.

4. Click on the OK button.

It's easy enough to avoid this problem: simply don't do all of the above. However, certain other unique, and as-yet undiscovered, combinations may cause the same problem. This particular one was resolved in the version 2.0b maintenance upgrade, but others may still lurk. If you discover a unique, and repeatable, circumstance that brings on the general protection fault, you may want to contact Microsoft to a.) report it, and b.) see if there's a workaround available yet.

General Protection Fault of Uncertain Origin. If it's uncertain what is causing the general protection problem, you may have to do a bit of configuration housecleaning to track down the culprit. If nothing else works, try going through the following steps. You may want to retry Windows after completing each step, to avoid going further than necessary to find the problem.

1. Reboot the system, using the basic startup files listed in Table 1.4a.

2. Log onto the Windows directory and run SETUP at the DOS prompt. When the *System Information Screen* appears (see Figure 1.1), set all components to the Microsoft-supplied device (VGA display, Microsoft mouse, try no network installed, etc.). Or, if you already know which one is causing the problem, then change that one.

3. Disable the load= and run= lines in the [windows] section of WIN.INI.

4. Open Windows and hold down the Shift key until the Program Manager screen appears (to disable any applets in the StartUp group).

5. If any diagnostic utilities or third-party applets are running as minimized icons, close them.

If the general protection fault problem is gone, reinstate the deleted items one-by-one until it comes back again. However, if the problem persists, try opening Windows by typing WIN /d:xvsf. If this works, refer to the *WIN (or WIN /3) Returns DOS Prompt* section in Chapter 2 for information about the /d switches.

Troubleshooting the More Obscure Problems. Note that item 5 above suggests shutting down any diagnostic utilities that may be running on the Desktop. Although such utilities are valuable for routine troubleshooting, they can cause problems of their own from time to time. Sometimes that trouble occurs only in the presence of some obscure combination of ingredients. As a typical example, if you add text to a full-screen Paintbrush image, the system may lock up if you attempt to change the font immediately *after* typing the text. What causes the crash? The hDC *FirstApps* utility (version 1.0) must be installed, and the System Resource *and* Smart Drive monitors (from the *Windows Resource Kit*) must be active.

If you attempt a local reboot, Windows may report that there are no application problems (see *Windows Application Running Correctly* in the *Local Reboot* section of this chapter). Or it may report a problem with some device not at all related to the real problem (the mouse pointer or Smart Drive, for example). In cases such as this, a bit of common sense and some sophisticated detection skills should be enough to keep your system out of action for hours, if not for days. The best fix is to stop thinking and close down applets until the problem goes away.

The above is one example of a kind of bug that only shows up under a unique set of circumstances. With luck, you'll never encounter this one. But you will probably discover your own special family of buglets, as you try various combinations that are a bit off the beaten Windows track. If there's no rational explanation for the problem, then eliminate all doubt by trying to replicate the problem on the cleanest Desktop possible. Once the problem is eliminated, be on the lookout for unique combinations of applets that may bring the problem back again. In the above-cited example, no combination of three applets causes a problem. But when all four are active, so is the problem.

To get to the bottom of such mysteries, once you've identified applet X as a primary suspect, try (if you have the patience) reinstating it and removing everything else. If the problem remains, then you know applet X is guilty. But if the problem is not back again, then applet X is only half of the problem. With luck and time, you'll eventually find some X-Y (or in this case, X-Y-Z) combination that triggers the problem. With even more luck, it will be some combination that can be easily avoided, until such time as an upgrade is available.

File Expansion Troubleshooting

If you have lingering doubts about the status of a file on your hard disk, compare its size with that of the equivalent file on the distribution diskette. The hard disk file should be significantly larger. If it isn't, then pick the correct expand utility and try again. If you are not sure of your file-expansion utility's origin, compare its file characteristics with those listed in Table 4.4b. If necessary, replace the utility with the one that is correct for the DOS or Windows (or whatever) version you are currently using.

Backup and Restore Troubleshooting

If there's trouble during either operation, an error message should give you some idea of what's wrong. Either refer to the representative messages in the *Backup and Restore Error Messages* section below, or to the appropriate User's Guide for more detailed information.

If you have reason to doubt the validity of your backup, use the utility's *Compare* option to see if the backup copy compares well with the original, or conduct your own tests by restoring a few sample files to your temporary directory. Then compare them with the originals. If there's a problem, now's the time to find out about it. You will not be pleased if you wait until after a disaster to discover that your backup insurance policy lapsed.

IRQ, I/O, and DMA Troubleshooting

If two (or more) devices try to access the same IRQ line, I/O port, or DMA channel at the same time, there will probably be no message advising you of the problem. Instead, the system will simply clam up, or go into oscillation (a sound board, for example), or do something else that isn't very nice.

If you're lucky, this sort of problem will show up immediately after installing some new device, so you'll have a pretty good idea what caused it. To verify the source, try removing the device and see if the problem goes away. If it does, then either the removed device is defective, or there's a conflict between it and some other device. If the problem is caused by an IRQ, I/O port, or DMA channel conflict, then review the settings in the appropriate Table (4.5, 4.6, 4.7) and reconfigure the new board, or the old one with which it conflicts.

Drive-Related Troubleshooting

If a problem appears related to a diskette or hard drive, the first order of business is to make sure it does not exist outside of Windows. If you're not sure about this, exit Windows and try a few write and read operations on the suspect drive. If the problem persists, then there is a DOS- or system-related problem that needs fixing. If necessary, contact the computer (or drive) manufacturer for assistance.

If the drive problem only shows up in Windows, then this may be the place to look for help.

Diskette Drive Access Problems. If the nature of the problem does not make its source obvious, see if it occurs in one or both operating modes, as described here.

Standard Mode Problem. If the problem occurs in this mode only, there may be a BIOS incompatibility problem. Review the information in Table 1.1b, or contact the manufacturer of your computer or of its BIOS.

Enhanced Mode Problem. If the problem occurs in Enhanced Mode, edit your SYSTEM.INI file as shown here:

Change This	To This
[386Enh]	[386Enh]
device=vdmad.386	device=*vdmad *(note asterisk, no extension)*

This editing change replaces the indicated driver with a virtual device driver embedded in the WIN386.EXE file. If the problem persists, add the following lines to the same section of SYSTEM.INI. After adding each line, retest the system before continuing.

```
IRQ9Global=yes
EMMExclude=E000-EFFF (add these two lines at the same time)
HighFloppyReads=no
VirtualHRIrq=off
```

If these lines don't help, remove all of them. Then open WIN.INI and disable the load= and run= lines. If there's still no relief in sight, then there may be a BIOS (see Table 1.4b) or diskette driver incompatibility. Contact the appropriate manufacturer to see if an upgrade is available.

Some Files Are Corrupted After a System Crash. If Smart Drive's write-caching feature was enabled when the system failed, it's quite possible that a FAT (file allocation table) was corrupted during the crash. Try using the Norton Utility's *Disk Doctor* (or similar) to repair the FAT and then, to prevent history from repeating itself, disable write-caching for the affected drive by editing your AUTOEXEC.BAT file as follows:

```
C:\WINDOWS\SMARTDRV N (other parameters, as before)
```

where *N* is the letter of the drive (or drives) whose write-caching is to be disabled. Refer to the *Smart Drive* section in Chapter 13 for more information, if needed.

Troubleshooting Other Problems

This final troubleshooting section reviews a mixed bag of problems that may come up during a Windows session.

Application Does Not Run when Its Icon Is Clicked. If you double-click on an icon whose applet is already running (as for example, any applet in the StartUp Group Window), then you may see one of the following messages:

Applet	Advisory Message
Dr. Watson	A copy of "Dr. Watson" is already running on the system.
Other applets	*Applet name* is already running.
Clock, Mouse, Program Manager, some others	*(None)*

In most cases the message itself is sufficient. In a few cases no message appears; but, if the applet is already running, you'll probably realize it anyway. However, if the applet is *not* running, then there's a problem that needs to be corrected.

It's always possible that the applet was installed under a previous version of Windows, and some needed INI-file references to that applet are either missing or invalid. Try reinstalling the application, and if that works, then delete the icon associated with the previous version.

If that doesn't work, then there's probably some incompatibility between the applet and Windows 3.1. Contact the appropriate manufacturer to see if there's an upgrade or a workaround solution available.

CHKDSK /f Shows Lost Cluster(s) after Exiting Windows. Every now and then it's a good idea to run CHKDSK /f immediately after exiting Windows. If CHKDSK reports any lost clusters, then run CHKDSK /f again the next time you exit Windows. If more lost clusters are reported, it's possible that your TEMP directory is not empty. For some reason, the presence of *any-thing* there can interfere with routine Windows operations, even if whatever it is has nothing to do with Windows itself. For example, if you recently used the directory as a work space for expanding a zipped file, and a few files remain in it, you can expect CHKDSK to report one more lost cluster every time you exit Windows.

The "fix" is simply to keep an eye on things and if this quirk shows up (it doesn't always do so), clean out the TEMP directory.

Ctrl+Alt+Del Locks System, Does Not Reboot. When Windows is not open, if a "three-finger salute" locks the system instead of rebooting it, there may be a conflict between your computer's video BIOS shadowing and your memory-management configuration. If you suspect such a problem, refer to the *System Reboot Failure* section of Chapter 13 for suggestions.

Cursor Visibility Is Poor. The Windows cursor and mouse pointer are displayed in a color that contrasts with its background (black on white background, white on black background, and so on). Regardless of the selected background color, the mouse pointer is usually visible due to its size. However, if certain background colors are selected, the cursor seen in the Write applet and elsewhere may be difficult to find. As a typical example, if the Window Background color is an off-white, the cursor becomes pale blue and almost invisible. If this is the problem, refer to the *Color* section of Chapter 11 for information about the Color applet in the Control Panel. Set the Background Color to pure white (the last box in the last row of the Basic Colors matrix), exit the applet and open the Write applet. The cursor should now be a dark and readable black against a white background.

Shortcut Key Problems. If a custom shortcut key combination does not produce the expected results, the currently active application may have reserved that combination for its own use, which takes precedence over your assignment. Note the action that occurs when you press the shortcut key combination, and if necessary, consult the appropriate User's Guide for verification. However, since some shortcut key assignments are undocumented, you may not find what you're looking for.

In any case, you'll need to change your custom shortcut key assignment, or else get along without it while the present applet is active. You may want to refer to Table 3.1 for a list of shortcut keys reserved by selected Windows applets and applications.

System Clock Runs Off Speed during Windows Session. If your system time is noticeably off-speed, look for the following line in the [386Enh] section of your SYSTEM.INI file:

```
TrapTimerPorts=0
```

Some applications run faster if the line is present, but as a result Windows may be unable to keep accurate system time. If this appears to be the problem, change the "0" to "1," or remove the line completely. Or leave the line as is, and add or edit the following line in the same section of SYSTEM.INI:

```
SyncTime=1
```

This forces Windows to periodically synchronize itself with the system's CMOS clock.

System Locks Up or Reboots When Application Is Run. This kind of problem is particularly hard to troubleshoot, since there are no error messages to suggest the source of the trouble. Before calling the company's tech support line, try rebooting with the startup files described in the *Basic CONFIG.SYS and AUTOEXEC.BAT Files* section of Chapter 1. If that solves the problem, then there's a conflict with something loaded by one of your startup files.

A primary suspect is a third-party memory management system. If you are using one, try returning to your regular startup files, but replace the third-party memory management software by the regular Windows 3.1 (or DOS 6.0) HIMEM.SYS and EMM386.EXE files. Or, refer to the *Qualitas* or *Quarterdeck* sections of Chapter 13 for suggestions, if you're using one of these programs.

If this suggestion does not apply (or doesn't work) on your system, then there may be a TSR program that's causing the trouble. Try eliminating them, one by one, until the problem goes away. Once the problem file is identified, try contacting tech support for either the TSR, or the application that won't run properly when that TSR is installed. With luck, one or both companies will have an upgrade or workaround available. But if each blames the other for the problem, then you'll have to do without one or both of the troublesome components.

Text in Write, SysEdit, Other Applets Is Missing. If the cursor moves across the screen as you type, but nothing shows up in the applet or application window, and error message boxes are likewise blank, the problem is probably that the text (Window Text) and its background (Window Background) are the same color. Open the *Color* applet and change one or both to contrasting colors. Refer to the *Color Applet* section of Chapter 11 if you need assistance doing so.

When-All-Else-Fails Troubleshooting

If it still won't work after you've tried everything that makes sense, and a few things that don't, you could do worse than having a look at how

the adapter card is seated in the slot on the motherboard. It is not unknown for a card to partially unseat itself, especially if that card is a 16-bit
ISA adapter sitting in an EISA slot. The screw at the top of the adapter card
may firmly hold the front of the card in place, yet allow the back of the
card to wander out of the slot—not all the way of course, but enough so that
part of the edge connection does not make contact. Sometimes, putting a
slight bend in the adapter card's metal bracket is enough to keep the entire card well seated. It's worth a look (the voice of experience here).

If you have a multimedia card installed, but the present trouble is
completely unrelated to multimedia, turn on the speakers anyway. It is not
unknown for a sound card to go into oscillation during, say, a network
log-on. The oscillation may or may not interfere with other operations,
but until you are sure such problems are not happening on your system, it
wouldn't hurt to double-check. With luck, you won't hear anything.

Error Messages

The final section of the chapter reviews some of the error messages that
may be encountered during routine operations. As usual, if a message im-
plicates a specific applet or application, you may find better information
in some other chapter.

Help Screen Error Messages

Some error messages are more informative than others. Unfortunately, there
is no help screen available to explain a help error message, so you may
need outside help to figure out what the message really means. For example, if the WINHELP.EXE file is missing, one of the following messages
may be seen, depending on which application is calling for help.

Application	Error Message if WINHELP.EXE Is Missing
Excel, other applications	No response.
Help buttons (most)	No response.
Paintbush	Not enough memory for this operation. (Hourglass remains on-screen until OK button is clicked.)
Program (or File) Manager	Unable to show Help information.
Word, other applications	Word (*or other application*) is unable to start Help.

If one of these messages (or nonmessages) is seen, various nonhelp options on the Help Menu are probably still available. To verify this, click on the About... option. If it works, then a missing WINHELP.EXE is the most likely suspect. Of course, it's possible that memory really is running low; but if so, you'd probably have discovered it before trying to access a help screen.

Check the Windows directory for a copy of WINHELP.EXE. Missing or not, expand a new one into the directory and try again.

Examples of typical error messages related to the Help Screen are given below.

Annotations damaged; please exit *(help screen name)***, delete** *filename.***ANN, and recreate annotations.** If this message appears when you select a help screen's Annotate... option (described earlier in the *Annotate* section), then the separate file containing your annotations has become corrupt. In order to write additional annotations, you'll have to erase the file and begin a new one from scratch.

(Application Name) **is unable to start Help.** This is one of several "unable to" messages that may be seen if the WINHELP.EXE file is missing. Expand a fresh copy into the Window directory and try again.

Bookmarks are damaged; please exit *(help screen name)* **and delete** *filename.***BMK.** This message appears when you select the Bookmark Menu if an existing bookmark file is corrupt. You'll have to erase the damaged BMK file and rewrite your bookmarks.

Cannot Open Help File. When you click on the OK button, if the Windows main help screen remains, open the File Menu and select the Open... option to review the list of available help files. Presumably, the one associated with the current application will not be seen in the list. (Perhaps this error message should be rewritten as Cannot *find* Help File.) If this is the case, then expand a fresh copy from the distribution diskettes and try again.

If the help file is present and apparently in good order, it's possible the application just doesn't know where to find it. A few applications will only search their own directory for a help file. If that file has been moved elsewhere—for example, into a separate Helpfile directory—the application won't find it, even though the PATH statement lists the path to the HelpFile directory. Within Windows itself, this characteristic seems to be limited to the Paintbrush applet. All others have no difficulty finding their help files, provided the PATH statement leads the way.

In some cases, a setup procedure will install an application in a custom subdirectory without complaint (for example C:\CD-ROM\APPNAME). However, when you attempt to access the application's help screen, a *help text file not found* (or similar) message will be seen. You'll probably need to reinstall the application in a directory (not subdirectory), as for example C:\APPNAME instead of the longer path shown above. You'll either have to experiment with this, or call tech support for information.

A little experimenting may also be needed to determine if a full-scale Windows application will tolerate being separated from its help file. Word-for-Windows doesn't mind, Excel does. In any case, if the PATH statement is in order, and the application still can't find its help file, you'll have to move that file back into the same directory as the application—so much for good housekeeping.

***Filename*.HLP not found in your path. Windows searches your PATH environment variable for help files, so you need to copy *Filename*.HLP to a directory included in your PATH if you wish to obtain help while running *Filename*.** In most cases, a Windows application will open successfully even if its help file is defective or missing. However, if the application is designed to look for its own help file as it opens and can't find it, a message similar to this one will be displayed. In this case, the help file is probably in the same directory as the application itself, but the path to that application is not included in the AUTOEXEC.BAT file's PATH statement.

To resolve the problem, either edit the PATH statement as required, or move the help file into the Windows directory, or into a separate Help File directory that is named in the PATH statement.

Help application corrupt; reinstall WINHELP.EXE. In this case, WINHELP.EXE is present but defective. When you click on the OK button an "Unable to show help information" message may be seen. But you know this already, so hit the OK button again, then expand a new copy of WINHELP.EXE from the Windows distribution diskettes.

Help is unavailable while printers are being set up, [*or*] while printing. Wait until the setup procedure or print job concludes, then try again.

Help not available. This message shows up if the help file associated with the current application is missing. If you can't find the required help file on your hard drive, expand a fresh copy from the appropriate distribution diskette.

Help Text file not found. This is just another variation on the *Cannot Open Help File* message described above, as found on some DOS applications. Although the help file (wherever it is) can't be accessed via the Windows help engine, it nonetheless should be available within the application's own system. If it's not, the file is either missing or more likely in a directory where it can't be found. If that's the case, refer to the *Cannot Open Help File* message above for suggestions on how to enable it.

Help topic does not exist. If this message appears when you click on a Help button, the appropriate section of the application's help file has not yet been written. Contact the software manufacturer to see if an updated help file is available now, or will be soon.

If the message is seen when you click on an underlined word or phrase, then either the same problem exists, or the selected item is located in another file, and that file is missing. If the selected item is shown with a dashed underline (indicating a glossary item), try clicking the Glossary button located in the bar just under the Help File's regular Menu bar. If you see the *Cannot Open Help File* message, then that confirms that the GLOSSARY.HLP is among the missing. Expand a fresh copy from the distribution diskettes and try again.

Not enough memory available to perform this operation. Quit one or more applications to increase available memory, and then try again. It's always possible that you are indeed running low on memory, in which case you know what to do. However, this message is also seen if the WINHELP.EXE file is missing. If you know your memory resources are OK, then expand a fresh copy of WINHELP.EXE into your Windows directory and try again.

This file is not a Windows Help File. Unfortunately, the HLP extension is often applied to non-Windows help files, as for example, those found in the DOS 5.0 directory and some of those in the DOS 6.0 directory. The error message will be seen if you try to open any of these or similar files from within Windows. The solution is to access the help file via the application for which it was written.

The message is also seen if a Windows help file was accidentally copied from the distribution diskettes, but not expanded.

This version of Help File not supported. If you see this message, you'll need an updated version of the help file that prompted the message. Before you go much further though, check the release date of the application itself. If its help file doesn't work, then it's quite possible the application itself may have some other compatibility problems as well, but you just haven't encountered them yet. Depending on what you discover, contact the software manufacturer for information on updating the application and/or its help file.

Unable to show help information. Now all you need to do is guess why. Probably, the WINHELP.EXE file is missing. Expand a fresh copy from the distribution diskettes and try again.

Unable to start the Windows help system. Available memory may be too low. As with other "unable to" messages, the problem is probably due to a missing WINHELP.EXE file. Expand a fresh copy; if that doesn't cure the problem, then check your memory resources.

File Expansion Error Messages

Refer to the messages in this section if an error message appears while you are expanding a file from one of your Windows 3.1 (or other) distribution diskettes. If the message itself appears to be in error, the problem is probably caused by trying to expand a file that requires a file-expansion utility other than the one you are using. In this case, refer to the *File Expansion Utilities* section earlier in this chapter for a guide to the various currently available utilities.

Error decompressing file. The wording suggests that the message appears during a file-restore operation. Refer to this error message in the *Backup and Restore Error Messages* section below for assistance.

Input file *'filename.ext'* already in expanded format. If you know the file is *not* in its expanded format, you are probably using the wrong expand utility.

No header in file (file might not be compressed). The parenthetical phrase is part of the error message, one of several such messages that may appear if you use the wrong expansion utility.

Packed file is corrupt. Although the "packed file" phrase suggests a problem related to a file compression utility, it is usually a symptom of a conventional memory problem. For more details, refer to the *Packed File Is Corrupt* error message in Chapter 13.

This program or one of its components is compressed. Use the MS-DOS Expand command to copy the file from the Windows Setup disks. You must follow the message's advice and use the expand utility.

Unknown compression algorithm. This message appears if you attempt to expand certain compressed files with the wrong expand utility.

Backup and Restore Error Messages

A few error messages associated with backup operations are listed here. However, since most such messages are associated with a specific backup software package, the best place to look for help is in the User's Guide accompanying the backup software. If neither the User's Guide nor the messages listed here are of any help, it's possible that a device or TSR in your startup files is causing a conflict problem. Try rebooting the system with the basic startup files listed in Table 1.4a.

Error decompressing file. If this message is seen while restoring files to a hard disk, the backup medium was probably damaged at some time after the backup was made. If so, you may be able to rescue the file, or part of it, by using the Norton Utility's *Disk Doctor* (or similar) after the rest of the restore operation has concluded.

General Hardware Failure xx. If there are no hardware problems outside the backup utility, then carefully check the backup drive to make sure the diskette, tape, or cartridge is seated properly, and that the drive latch (if any) is closed. Also check the utility's setup configuration to make sure the correct drive and backup medium are listed.

Insufficient disk space for temporary file. Some utilities write data to a temporary file during the backup process. For example, Central Point Software's *Backup* needs about 20 Kbytes of temporary disk space for each 20 Mbytes that is to be backed up. If this message (or a variation on it) is seen, make sure your AUTOEXEC.BAT file contains a set TEMP=C:\TEMP (or similar) line, and that the indicated directory has sufficient space available.

Track 0 Bad. The obvious problem is a defective backup cartridge, diskette, or tape. However, if the backup medium is known to be in good order, there may be a TSR conflict. Reboot with the basic startup files (Table 1.4a), then try the backup operation again.

IRQ, I/O Port, and DMA Channel Error Messages

More often than not, a problem with one of these parameters will simply lock up the system or cause some other problem not accompanied by an error message. However, some applications will display an error message such as that shown here.

Invalid [IRQ, I/O port address, DMA channel] specified. If this message, or some variation on it is seen, refer to the *IRQ, I/O, and DMA Trouble-shooting* section found earlier in this chapter.

Drive-Related Error Messages

In addition to the messages seen here, refer to Chapter 6 if a drive-related error message pops up while using the File Manager.

Error reading (or writing to) drive *N* (where *N* is any drive letter). Refer to the *Drive-Related Troubleshooting* section earlier in this chapter for suggestions.

Not ready reading drive C. If this message appears while Windows is open, the first order of business is to make sure drive C is OK (it probably is, or Windows wouldn't be open in the first place). To verify this, exit Windows, write a file to the drive, then read it back again. If all goes well, follow the appropriate instructions below. If not, there may be a compatibility problem that requires a call to the drive manufacturer for resolution.

IBM PS/2 Computer. Copy the DASDDRVR.SYS file from the IBM reference diskette that came with the computer to the root directory on drive C. Then add the following line to your CONFIG.SYS file:

```
device=C:\DASDDRVR.SYS
```

If you put the file elsewhere, then change the line to indicate the correct path.

Plus Hardcard installed. Make sure that the following line is in your CONFIG.SYS file:

```
device=C:\ATDOSXL.SYS
```

The file must be in your root directory, and should be version 1.70 or later. Also add the following lines to the indicated section of SYSTEM.INI:

```
[386Enh]
EMMEXCLUDE=C800-C9FF
virtualHDIrq=OFF
```

Other Hardware Configurations (especially some IDE or SCSI drives, Intel *snapin* 386). Add the following line to the indicated section of SYSTEM.INI:

```
[386Enh]
virtualHDIrq=OFF
```

Serious disk error on file *filename.ext*. Chances are the diskette (or other removable medium) on which the file resides has been removed from the drive, or is not seated properly, or the drive door has popped open. Make sure the diskette is in place and try again.

Unrecoverable disk error on file *filename.ext*. If the *Serious disk error* message above is not resolved, this message may appear when the OK button is clicked. More often than not, the message will keep repeating until the problem is resolved. If you can't do this, you'll have to try a local reboot to escape from the error message.

A Few More Error Messages

The messages which follow are a few of those that can't be pigeonholed into a specific category. For messages seen when you press Ctrl+Alt+Del, refer to the *Local Reboot Procedure* section earlier in this chapter.

An error has occurred in your application. If you choose Ignore, you should save your work in a new file. If you choose Close, your application will terminate. Depending on the severity of the error, the Ignore option may allow you to continue, in which case you should save your work, then try to troubleshoot the problem. If the error is severe, the Ignore option will have no effect and you will have to click on the Close button to clear the message.

When you do, an application error message will probably refer to a General Protection Fault and specify the location at which the fault was detected. The only option available now is to close the application. Jot down the message information first, because when you do click on the Close button, the message clears and the application itself closes. If Dr. Watson is running, a Dr. Watson's Clues dialog box appears. Refer to the

Dr. Watson section in Chapter 5 for further details about this aspect of troubleshooting. Also refer to the *General Protection Faults* section of this chapter for help in tracking down the source of the problem.

Call to Undefined Dynalink. At times this error message is easier on the nerves than at others. For example, if it's seen when you attempt to open an applet, then the dynamic-link library file associated with that applet is either corrupt, or is an old one left over from Windows 3.0. If you are not sure which file may be the culprit, refer to Table 4.9 for a list of DLL files supplied with Windows 3.1 and Windows-for-Workgroups. Find the name of the applet, device, or whatever was active when the error message appeared and note the name of the DLL file. Then replace that file with a freshly expanded version from the distribution diskettes and try again.

TABLE 4.9 Dynamic-Link Library File*

Library File for	DLL Filename	Library File for	DLL Filename
80×87 math co-processor	WIN87EM	LAN Manager API	NETAP120
Adv. Power Mgmnt.	SL	LAN Manager Printer API	PMSPL20
Belgian keyboard layout	KB3GR	Latin-American keyboard layout	KBDLA
British keyboard layout	KBDUK	MultiMedia System	MMSYSTEM
Canadian multilingual keyboard layout	KBDDV	Norwegian keyboard layout	KBDNO
Common Dialogs	COMMDLG	OLE client	OLECLI
Danish keyboard layout	KBDCA	OLE server	OLESVR
DDE Management	DDEML	Olivetti/AT&T keyboard mouse driver	KBDMOUSE
Dr. Watson	TOOLHELP	Paintbrush	PBRUSH[†]
Dutch keyboard layout	KBDNE	Portuguese keyboard layout	KBDPO
Dutch language driver	LANGDUT	Recorder	RECORDER[†]
File expansion	LZEXPAND	Shell	SHELL
Finnish, Icelandic, Norwegian, Swedish	LANGSCA	Soft Font installer, HPPCL5/A printer driver	FINSTALL

TABLE 4.9 *(continued)*

Library File for	DLL Filename	Library File for	DLL Filename
Finnish keyboard layout	KBDFC	Spanish keyboard layout	KBDSP
French keyboard layout	KBDFI	Spanish language driver	LANGSPA
French language driver	LANGFRN	Swedish keyboard layout	KBDSW
French-Canadian keyboard	KBDBE	Swiss German keyboard layout	KBDSG
General International language driver	LANGENG	Swiss-French keyboard layout	KBDSF
Generic printer driver	GENDRV	Tool Helper	TOOLHELP
German keyboard layout	KBDFR	Universal color printer driver	DMCOLOR
German language driver	LANGGER	Universal printer driver	UNIDRV
H-P keyboard driver	KBDHP	Version Resource and File Installation	VER
Icelandic keyboard layout	KBDIC	US keyboard layout	KBDUS
Icon file	MORICONS†	US-Dvorak keyboard layout	KBDDA
Italian keyboard layout	KBDIT	US-International keyboard layout	KBDUSX

* In case of *Call to Undefined Dynalink* error message, a DLL file associated with the active application may be corrupt.

† These DLL files are located in the Windows directory. Most others (if present) are in the System directory.

Now let's look at those other times. If the error message appears in the middle of some routine operation, there may not be a clue as to what went wrong. If your luck is really bad, the entire Program Manager disappears from the Desktop when you click on the Close button in the error message screen. If this happens, the first order of business is to close any application whose minimized icon appears on screen. Double-click on each such icon, save, and close the application, and repeat for any other icon that represents an active application or applet.

This leaves you (maybe) with a smiling Dr. Watson icon at the bottom of the screen. Needless to say, the Doctor thinks everything is just fine;

if you attempt a second opinion by pressing Ctrl+Alt+Del, you'll again discover that no error has been detected. Press Ctrl+Alt+Del once again to restart your computer. Or if that won't do it, you'll have to do a cold reboot. If you fear you may have lost anything, run CHKDSK /f at the DOS prompt before opening Windows again or doing anything else. Refer to the *Run Chkdsk* section in Chapter 1 for assistance if needed.

If no specific DLL file comes to mind, and Table 4.9 doesn't help you identify the file that may be causing the problem, type DIR *.DLL at the DOS prompt. Do this in both the Windows and the System directory, and note any DLL files that predate the release date of Windows 3.1 (3-10-92) or Windows-for-Workgroups (10-01-92). Any such files should be replaced with their newer equivalents. If all else fails, expand a fresh copy of SHELL.DLL into your System directory.

If all else *still* fails, get in touch with the software manufacturer to see if an updated version is available.

Cannot find *filename.ext*. This message may be seen if you attempt to run an application that requires a support file, and that support file is among the missing. Typically, the Windows hourglass will remain onscreen until you click on the Close button in the error box. Then a second *Cannot find file* filename.ext *(or one of its components)* message appears. In this case, the parenthetical remark reveals the actual problem. If the cited file itself were missing, the present message format would not appear at all and only the second message would be seen.

Chances are the missing component is a DLL (or similar) file. Expand a fresh copy of the file into the appropriate directory and try again. If you are not sure of the directory in which the file should be placed, click once on the applet's icon, then click on the File menu and select the Properties option. The command line box should specify the correct directory.

Cannot find *(filename or description)* file. Use the File Open command and specify the correct disk and directory. You may see this message when you attempt to open a Windows application, if that application cannot find a resource that it needs. In this case, open the File menu and select the Open option. At the bottom of the screen, the List Files of Type: box will probably show a brief description and the extension for the missing file type. The Directories and Drives boxes will indicate where Windows is looking for the missing file. Armed with that information, you may be able to track it down and place it in the right location.

Cannot find file *filename.ext* (or one of its components). Check to ensure the path and filename are correct and that all required libraries are available. If you need more information to track down the problem, open the File menu, select the Properties... option and review the information in the Command line: and Working Directory boxes. Edit one or both lines, as required, or check the specified path(s) and filenames to make sure the specified paths and files are valid.

Divide by Zero. There's only one reason for a divide-by-zero error message; something just tried that impossible mathematical stunt and got caught in the act. If it happens when some application is in the middle of a calculation, then probably that application's programming code does not protect against such operations. In this case, the manufacturer needs to upgrade the product, and in the meantime you need to avoid doing whatever it is that caused the illegal division.

However, the same error might be traced to a TSR, an incompatible disk-partitioning system, a memory problem, or a corrupted Windows setup. Try booting from the basic startup files (Table 1.4a again) and see if that helps. Or, if you did not use the DOS FDISK utility to partition your hard drive, check with the appropriate manufacturer to see if your partitioning software is Windows-compatible. The next step is to carefully review your system memory configuration. If the problem still persists, and can't be localized to a specific area, then rerun the Windows Setup procedure. Perhaps some file has become corrupted, in which case Setup should overwrite it with a fresh copy and cure the divide-by-zero error.

Error Message of Unknown Origin. Sometimes an error message is seen that does not give sufficient information to trace its origin. If the message does not appear in a message box that clearly identifies the application that caused it, and the context in which the error occurred does not immediately suggest where it originates, then some detective work may be in order.

Examine the message for some unique word or phrase that is not likely to be found in other error messages. Then use the Norton *Text Search* (or similar) utility to search for the file containing that word/phrase. As an obvious example, "open a valid bitmap image" shows up multiple times in PBRUSH.EXE (the Windows Paintbrush applet) but not elsewhere. Therefore, if this message appears it's reasonably certain the problem is related to PBRUSH.EXE. Of course, this message would only show up (one hopes) during a Paintbrush session, so there would be no need to wonder where it came from. However, the same procedure can be used to track down some other message whose origin is not so obvious. Once you know where the message originates, it may be a bit easier to trouble-shoot its cause.

This procedure may be helpful if the message can be traced to a third-party application. When tech support swears you're the first person to re-port a problem, you can ask them why then is the message embedded in one of their files? If you're lucky, they may have an answer.

Exception Error 12. On the off-chance you don't immediately know what this means, refer to the *Stack Overflow* message below.

***Filename* could not be opened. It may have been deleted.** If this message—or some variation on it—is seen, the obvious first step is to verify that the cited file is indeed missing. If it is, then the obvious second step is to find it on the distribution diskettes that accompanied the application. If you do find it, remember that it may be in a compressed format which needs to be expanded. Look on the application's distribution diskette 1 for an expand utility; if you find one, use it instead of the Windows expand utility.

However, if the "missing" file is not really missing at all, then the not-so-obvi-ous source of the problem may be a driver or DLL file that needs to be in-stalled and included in your SYSTEM.INI (or some other INI) file. The absence of the file(s) is what causes the erroneous error message. If this is a likely source of the problem, contact the company's tech support, describe the problem, and mention the version number of the application. There may be an updated version that includes files necessary for operation with Windows 3.1.

General Protection Fault. If this phrase appears in an error message, refer to the *General Protection Faults* section in this chapter for assistance.

Network Path Specified: The specified path points to a file that may not be available during later Windows sessions. Do you want to continue? You may see this message when editing a command line in the Program Item Properties box (accessible via the Properties... option in the File menu). In addition to cautioning you about specifying a network path, the message is also seen if the command line refers to a file on a CD-ROM disk. In this case, click on the Yes button, since the specified disk must be in the CD-ROM drive in order to run the application anyway.

Packed File Is Corrupt. If this message is seen during system bootup, or later on when you attempt to load a DOS application, refer to the *Packed File Is Corrupt* error message in Chapter 13.

Removable Path Specified: The specified path points to a file that may not be available during later Windows sessions. Do you want to continue? You'll see this message if you try to create an icon for an application that resides on a diskette in one of your diskette drives. If you decide to continue, and later on some other diskette is in the same drive, you'll get a *Cannot find file* error message when you try to run the application.

If the application is one you regularly use, consider transferring it to your hard disk so it will always be there when you need it. Otherwise, don't set it up with an icon. Instead, use the File menu's Bun... option whenever you want to run it.

Stack Fault. This is usually the result of some faulty code in the application you're trying to run. See the next message for some suggestions, then call the software manufacturer for an upgrade.

Stack Overflow (or exception error 12). Someone is trying to pour too much information into your stacks. Refer to the *Stack Overflow* error message in Chapter 1 for suggestions on editing your CONFIG.SYS file to increase the stack capacity. If problems persist, try stacks=0, 0, then try eliminating the line completely.

System Integrity Violation. If the error message includes the phrase "system integrity," the problem is usually caused by a DOS application. But sometimes the message is seen when the error-handling mechanism gets confused. For example, if a system integrity error message shows up while running a Windows applet, such as Write or Paintbrush, the applet's executable file is probably corrupted in such a way that the file has been mistakenly identified as a DOS application—hence the potentially confusing error message. Therefore, if this message is seen while running any Windows applet or application, the problem can usually be resolved by expanding a fresh copy of the appropriate EXE file into the Windows directory, then running the program again.

System Integrity: This application has violated system integrity due to *[see list]* and will be terminated.

Execution of a privileged instruction
Execution of an invalid instruction
An invalid fault
An invalid general protection fault
An invalid page fault

These phrases are contained in the WINOA386.MOD file only (see Table 1.9a), and so suggest an enhanced-mode problem, probably with a non-Windows application running in a DOS window. Try Standard Mode and repeat the conditions that caused the error message. If a different message is seen, then troubleshoot that error first. Then retry the operation in Enhanced Mode. If problems persist, there is a memory-related problem or the application itself is faulty. To eliminate the former, review the troubleshooting section of Chapter 13 for suggestions. Then attack the manufacturer of the application if you are still unable to resolve the problem.

You must have the file WINA20.386 in the root of your boot drive to run Windows in Enhanced Mode. The WINA20.386 file is a virtual device driver that was required for Enhanced Mode operations prior to DOS 5.0. If you're using DOS 5.0 or greater, and this message appears, it's probably due to an application that doesn't know WINA20.386 is no longer needed. Refer to this error message in the *Enhanced Mode Error Messages* section of Chapter 2 for suggestions on how to get rid of it.

5

The StartUp Group Window

This little chapter takes a brief look (which is all that's necessary) at a new feature in Windows 3.1 and Windows-for-Workgroups: the StartUp Group Window. In previous versions of Windows, an application could be run as Windows opened by specifying its filename on one of the following lines in the WIN.INI file:

```
[Windows]
load=filename.ext
run=filename.ext
```

A file listed on the load= line would run as a minimized icon on the Desktop, while an application on the run= line would run in an application window.

Although the procedure still works in Windows version 3.1, the new Start-Up Group Window may be used for the same purpose, as described in this chapter. Except as otherwise noted, the information presented here applies to both the StartUp group, and to applications listed on the WIN.INI lines above.

A StartUp Group Window is automatically created when Windows 3.1 or Windows-for-Workgroups is initially installed. However, Setup does not install any applets within that window; it simply creates it for future use, along with an empty STARTUP.GRP file, as will be seen by examining the following section of the PROGMAN.INI file:

```
[Settings]
Group4=STARTUP.GRP
(other group windows)
```

When Windows opens, it looks for a STARTUP.GRP file; if one is found, the programs listed in that group are executed.

StartUp Group Applet Selection

Although you may of course place any applet you like in the StartUp Group Window, there are a few Windows applets that are especially suited for this use. The installation of each of these applets in the StartUp Group Window is briefly reviewed here. In many cases, the configuration techniques described here can be applied—perhaps with some modification—to other applets in the StartUp Group.

In each example presented here, the applet's filename is given in parentheses. The procedures for moving or copying a previously installed icon and its applet from one group window to another were described in detail in the *Use Drag-and-Drop to Move Icons* section of Chapter 3. In that chapter, Figure 3.16 showed an icon recently transplanted from one window to another. If necessary, review that section for assistance in setting up the StartUp Group applets described below.

Calendar (CALENDAR.EXE). To start each Windows session with a look at your personal calendar, the first step is to have a personal calendar to look at. Open the Accessories Group Window, double-click on the Calendar icon and make a few entries, as appropriate. Save the calendar as CALENDAR.CAL, for example, then close the applet.

Open the StartUp Group Window and place a copy of the Calendar icon in that window. Click on that icon once, open the File Menu and select the Properties... option. In the Program Item Properties dialog box, edit the Command Line as shown here:

Change This: **To This:**
CALENDAR.EXE   C:\WINDOWS\CALENDAR.CAL

The next time you open Windows, today's calendar will appear on screen. For the moment, the size and position of the Calendar window cannot be set, so what you see is what you get. If you want a different size or position you'll have to change it after the Calendar appears on the Desktop.

Clock (CLOCK.EXE). The Windows clock is another applet that may be worth installing in the StartUp Group. You may want to move it out of the Accessories Group, since it's unlikely you'll want to run it a second time. Even if you do, you can't: The clock is another of those single-instance applets (like Program Manager) which will only run once.

Fortunately this applet can be sized and placed wherever you want it; every time Windows opens, it will remember its place and stay there. To get rid of the Clock Title Bar and the Settings Menu immediately below it, open that menu and select the No Title option. As soon as you do, the Title and Menu Bars disappear, leaving just the clock face. To restore both (in order to make further revisions), double-click anywhere within the Clock Window.

If the Clock obscures some other item on the Desktop, you can of course move it to have a look. Or, just hold down the secondary mouse button to make the clock disappear entirely. Release the button and it comes back again.

Dr. Watson (DRWATSON.EXE). The Dr. Watson utility was described in Chapter 4. Its one-and-only purpose is to monitor system activity so that it can prepare a report (DRWATSON.LOG) if it discovers a problem. In order to do this, Dr. Watson has to be active before a problem comes up so, unless you're clairvoyant, the most reliable way to take care of this is to load it automatically every time Windows opens.

After you've run Windows for awhile—long enough to work out any buglets—you can always retire the doctor by moving him out of the StartUp Group Window. If you transfer the utility into the Accessories Group Window, for example, Dr. Watson will remain available should you want to run the utility prior to doing some experimenting.

File Manager (WINFILE.EXE). If you're a regular user of the Windows File Manager, you may want to copy its icon into the StartUp Group and set it to run minimized. That way there'll be a handy File Manager icon on the Desktop, which you can open by assigning it a Shortcut key, as described in the *Shortcut Key Configuration* section of Chapter 3. The File Manager itself is covered in Chapter 6.

hDC First Apps. This third-party application is briefly reviewed here, due to its unique method of installing itself. The *First Apps* "icon" is no icon at all: Rather, the applet takes over the Control Menu box, which it colors red. The usual horizontal bar in the middle of the box is replaced by the *hDC* initials. If you click once on the Control Menu box, the appropriate Control Menu opens and the *First Apps* Menu appears to its immediate right.

The *First Apps* Menu was used earlier (Figure 3.4) to illustrate the Cascading Menu option, and a *First Apps* Memory Viewer screen will be seen later on, in Figure 13.6.

Program Manager. As already noted in Chapter 3, it's easy for the Program Manager to get buried under the general litter of multiple open windows on the Desktop. To quickly bring it to the top of the heap, install it as a new program item in the StartUp Group, as described in the *Assign Shortcut Key to Program Manager* section of that chapter. This places a Program Manager icon in the StartUp Group Window, but has no apparent effect on routine operations. However, whenever you want to return directly to the Program Manager Window, just press the Shortcut key combination that you assigned to its applet in the StartUp Group. Refer to the above section for further details.

System-Monitoring Utilities. If you want to run the System Resource (SYSMETER.EXE) or Smart Drive (SMARTDRV.MON) monitors included with the *Windows Resource Kit* (and described in Chapter 4), install their icons in the StartUp Group Window. For routine operation, you will probably want both utilities to run as minimized icons, so in each case check the Run Minimized box in the Program Item Properties box.

StartUp Group Window Configuration

To install any of the above-listed applets (or any others) in the StartUp Group Window, open the Program Manager's File Menu, select the New... option, and add the applet (or application), just as you would in any other group window. Or, move (or copy) an icon from any other group window into the StartUp Group Window. The next time Windows opens, the applet will run automatically.

Run StartUp Applet As Minimized Icon

Unless otherwise specified, the applet will run in its own application window. To run the applet as a minimized icon, click once on its icon, then open the File Menu. Select the Properties... option and check the Run Minimized box that appears in the Program Item Properties dialog box.

Loading Sequence for StartUp Group Applets

The applets within the StartUp Group Window are executed in the order in which their icons appear in the group window (Row 1 left-to-right, Row 2 left-to-right, and so on). However, the complete sequence may be carried out in two or three passes according to the following priority list:

1. All Windows applets and applications.

2. DOS applications 2, 3, 4, . . .

3. DOS application 1.

In other words, the *first* DOS application is the *last* to be executed. And since Windows insists on loading all Windows applications first, you can't force such an application (or applet) to be the last item loaded.

For example, if you customarily begin your Windows sessions by reviewing your Calendar, you may want to position the Calendar icon as the last one in the window, so that it is not obscured by other applets open during startup. When you close (or minimize) the Calendar, the other active applets (if any) will be seen. If you want to do something like this, you'll have to remove all DOS applications from the StartUp group.

Use Any Group Window as StartUp Group

If you would rather use some other group as a startup group, add the following line to your WIN.INI file:

[Settings]
Startup=*(name of the group window)*

Note that the Startup= line above lists the *name* (not the *filename*) of the desired group, as listed in the existing Title Bar for that group window. If no name appears on the line, or if the line is missing completely, then the applets contained in the default StartUp Group Window are executed, as if a Startup=StartUp line appeared in the [Settings] section.

Remember that *all* applets in the designated startup group are executed as Windows opens, so there's not much point in adding this line, other than to be different.

Use Always-on-Top Option

If you use the StartUp Group Window to load diagnostics applets (for example, SMARTMON.EXE), as minimized icons, you may want to open each such applet and—if available—enable its Always-On-Top option (described in Chapter 3).

Disable StartUp Group

To open Windows without executing any StartUp Group applets, hold down the Shift key when the Windows logo appears and release it when the Program Manager is seen. Having done that, you may execute one or more StartUp applets by opening the group window and double-clicking on the appropriate icon(s).

If you need to temporarily disable a single applet in the StartUp Group, simply move its icon into some other group window. The next time you open Windows, that applet will not be executed.

Re-create StartUp Group

As previously noted in Chapter 3, the Setup /p procedure will restore the Main, Accessories, and Games Group Windows, along with the applets that were in each of these windows immediately after running the initial Windows Setup procedure. Setup /p also creates a new StartUp Window but, since nothing was loaded in that Window during the initial setup, the window is again present, but empty.

If you've subsequently added multiple applets to the StartUp Group, and would like to take out an insurance policy against their accidental demise, you can edit your SETUP.INF file (in the Windows System directory) as illustrated here. Use the same general procedure to protect other applets in other windows, and/or to include some other group window under the Setup /p protection policy.

Figure 5.1 shows the contents of a typical StartUp Group Window. To add the information required to protect this window, first make a backup copy of the SETUP.INF file (unless your editor does this automatically). Then open SETUP.INF for editing, and search for the [progman.groups] section, which should list four groups (Main, Accessories, Games, StartUp). The contents of each group are listed in the next four sections. Find the [group1] section, which initially lists only "Dr. Watson" with no supporting information. Edit the section as shown here:

Description	Filename	Icon File	No.
[group1]			
"Program Manager",	PROGMAN.EXE	,	,
"File Manager",	WINFILE.EXE,	,	3,
"hDC",	C:\HDC\MICROMAN.EXE,	,	,
"Dr. Watson",	DRWATSON.EXE,	,	,
"Clock",	CLOCK.EXE,	,	,
"SMARTDrive Monitor",	C:\WRK\SMARTMON.EXE	,	,
"Sys Resources",	C:\WRI\SYSMETER.EXE	,	,
"After Dark",	C:\AFTERDRK\AD.EXE	,	5,

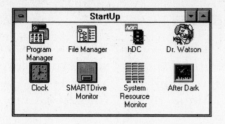

Figure 5.1 The contents of a typical StartUp Group Window. The applets seen here will run automatically every time Windows is opened.

The spacing between commas is added for clarity and need not be included. The four columns provide Setup /p with the following information:

Description	The icon title
Filename	The name (and path if required) of the applet's executable file
Icon File	the name (and path if required) of the icon file for the applet
No.	the number of the icon within the Icon File

An Icon File entry is not required if the icon is contained within the applet's own executable file. Nor is a number required, unless the desired icon is other than the first one in the file (as it is in all files above, except the Mouse applet).

Revise the information presented here as required to suit the contents of your own StartUp Group Window, to add applets to another group window, or to extend Setup /p protection to a group window not included by default.

You can also edit an existing group in SETUP.INF to prevent restoring unwanted applets the next time you run Setup /p. For example, if you have transferred say, the Sound Recorder and Media Player applets into a custom Multimedia Group Window, you won't want them reappearing in the Accessories group later on. Disable the appropriate lines in the [group4] section of SETUP.INF by placing a semicolon at the beginning of each line, or delete an entire line if you're really sure about this.

StartUp Group Troubleshooting

Most problems associated with the StartUp Group Window are similar to those that might show up in any group window, so they are covered by the *General Window Troubleshooting* section of Chapter 3. However, a few potential problems that are unique to the StartUp Group are described here.

Not All Applets Are Executed. If an applet in the StartUp Group does not execute when Windows opens, open the StartUp Group Window and make sure the applet's icon is not obscured by some other icon. Although it's quite unlikely for this to happen by accident, if any icon, *A,* is placed on top of another icon, *B,* only applet *A* will execute. In case of doubt, enable the Auto Arrange option on the Program Manager's Window Menu.

StartUp Applet Obscured by Some Other StartUp Applet. If multiple applets are in the StartUp Group, it's possible that as each applet is opened, its application window obscures the applet that opened before it. Or, one of the applets may have its Always-on-Top option enabled, in which case it will appear on the top of the Desktop.

Rearrange the icons in the StartUp Group Window so that the one you want to see is loaded last. If the Always-on-Top option is enabled for an applet that loads early in the sequence, either disable it or check that applet's Run Minimized box, so that the applet runs as a minimized icon instead of taking up space on the Desktop.

StartUp Group Applets Are Not Executed. The StartUp Group is designed to work in conjunction with Windows' Program Manager shell, as specified in SYSTEM.INI:

```
[boot]
shell=PROGMAN.EXE
```

The Program Manager shell may be replaced with either the Windows File Manager, some Microsoft applications (Excel 4.0 or Word-for-Windows, for example), or certain third-party applications. However, these shells may ignore the StartUp Group, and any items listed on the load= and run= lines in the [Windows] section of WIN.INI, as shown here:

Application	shell=	StartUp Group	load=, run= lines
File Manager	WINFILE.EXE	Ignored	Executed
Excel 4.0	EXCEL.EXE	Ignored	Ignored
Word-for-Windows	WINWORD.EXE	Ignored	Ignored
Third-party	*(refer to User's Guide or contact manufacturer for information)*		

Refer to the *Assign File Manager as Windows Shell* section of Chapter 6 for further details about using the File Manager as the shell.

> **NOTE:** In Windows version 3.0, the Microsoft applications cited above could not be used as the Windows shell. Either one would produce an *Unrecoverable Application Error* if it was specified on the shell= line in SYSTEM.INI.

StartUp Group Error Messages

Most error messages associated with the StartUp Group are no different from the messages seen if some other group window presents a problem as Windows opens. Therefore, the best place to look for help is in Chapter 2.

StartUp Application Error. Application requested abnormal termination. If this message appears, an applet in the StartUp Group Window, or the StartUp Group itself, may be damaged. If you need to verify this, restart Windows and hold down either Shift key until the Program Manager appears. If no error message is seen, then there is a problem within the StartUp Group. However, if the message does appear, then there is a problem with some application listed on the load= or run= lines in the [Windows] section of WIN.INI which will have to be corrected. If you're not sure which line is causing the problem, disable either one and restart Windows.

The File Manager

As its name suggests, the Windows File Manager provides a wide variety of file-management services, which are available via its Menu Bar. The chapter begins with a description of the File Manager's Application and Directory windows, followed by a look at the icons and menus that are available. The next two sections cover File Manager and Network configuration, and are followed by a look at the undocumented *Registration Info Database* — an applet that may be useful for custom configuration of some File Manager functions. Troubleshooting sections follow, and as usual, the chapter concludes with a look at error messages that may be encountered during File Manager operations. These are subdivided into subsections according to the source of the error.

Some Windows Nomenclature. There are several notable differences between the File Manager in *Windows* and in *Windows-for-Workgroups*. In addition, the utilities included with the optional *Windows Resource Kit* and the *Windows-for-Workgroups Resource Kit* are also different. Therefore, if any window component described below is unique to a specific Microsoft product (including DOS 6.0 support for Windows), it is so identified by one of the following parenthetical references in the section heading:

(DOS 6.0)	MS-DOS 6.0
(Windows 3.1)	Windows version 3.1
(Windows Resource Kit)	Windows Resource Kit utilities
(Workgroups)	Windows-for-Workgroups version 3.1
(Workgroups Resource Kit)	Windows-for-Workgroups Resource Kit utilities

347

Since this chapter is the place where most of those differences show up, the comparisons would be even more tedious if the full names for all of the above were used over and over again in the text. In the interests of tedium-reduction, both *Windows-for-Workgroups* and the *Windows-for-Workgroups Resource Kit* with its utilities are now-and-then referred to as simply, *Workgroups* and the *Workgroups Resource Kit*.

The File Manager Windows

When the File Manager opens for the first time, a File Manager Application Window such as that shown in Figure 6.1a is seen on the Desktop. The Application Window contains a smaller Directory Window, which is in turn subdivided into a Directory Tree Window and a Current Directory Window. In this illustration a single Directory Window occupies the entire available area within the Application Window. Refer to the *File Manager Configuration* section later in the chapter for instructions on how to adjust the size of the Directory Window and open additional directory windows within this area.

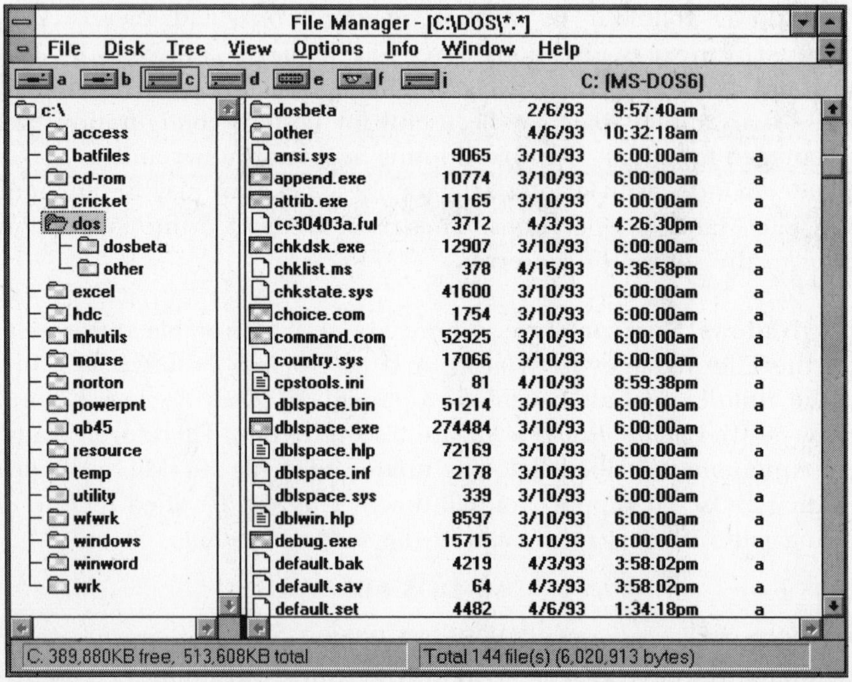

Figure 6.1a The File Manager's Application Window, showing a maximized Directory Window which contains a Directory Tree Window on the left, and a Current Directory Window on the right.

Figures 6.1b and c present detail views of the upper section of the Workgroups Application Window. The various components are described in detail in the appropriate sections later in the chapter.

For future reference purposes, all components of the File Manager's Application Window are described in the following section. If some of the network descriptions are not immediately as clear as they should be, you may want to come back to them later, after reviewing the *Network Configuration* section. Or, ignore them if your system is not part of a network.

Application Window

Like any other Windows applet, the File Manager opens in its own Application Window, which is subdivided into two smaller windows, separately described below.

Title Bar. As with any other applet, the Title Bar lists the application name (File Manager). If any Directory Window (described below) is maximized, the Application Window Title Bar also lists the drive letter and path for that window. If Workgroups is installed, the volume label (if any) for the active drive is also given. However, if a Directory Window is not

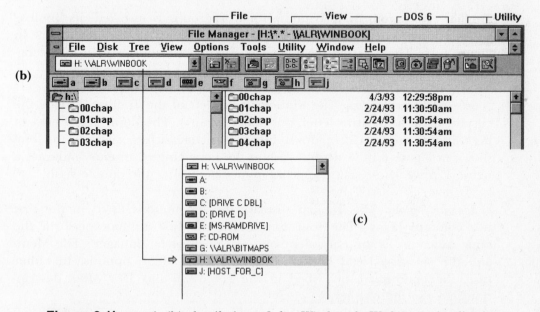

Figure 6.1b, c A (b) detail view of the *Windows-for-Workgroups* Application Window. The text above the window identifies the menus corresponding to the Toolbar buttons. A (c) drop-down list of available drives.

maximized within the Application Window, then the drive letter, path, and volume label information appears instead on the Directory Window's own Title Bar (see below).

Menu Bar. The Menu Bar is functionally equivalent to the Program Manager's Menu Bar described in Chapter 3. However, the Control Menu box and the Restore button seen at opposite ends of the Menu Bar are only visible when a single maximized Directory Window is present, as it is in Figures 6.1a and 6.1b.

Resource Kit Utility Menus. If the utilities supplied with either of Microsoft's optional resource kits adds are installed, one of the following menu names appears on the Menu Bar:

Menu Name	Adds Utilities Supplied with:
Info	*Windows Resource Kit*
Utility	*Windows-for-Workgroups Resource Kit*

In Figure 6.1a, the Info Menu appears on the Menu Bar, while Figure 6.1b shows the equivalent Utility Menu name.

Toolbar (Workgroups). If Windows-for-Workgroups is installed, its Toolbar appears immediately below the Menu Bar, as shown by the detail view in Figure 6.1b. The Selected Drive Window and Toolbar buttons seen in the figure are described here.

Selected Drive Window. The window at the left of the Toolbar displays the current drive icon, drive letter, and label (if any). The down arrow next to the window opens a drop-down list of available drives, such as the one shown in Figure 6.1c. A double slash at the beginning of an entry indicates a network drive whose name appears immediately after the double slash.

Toolbar Buttons. The Toolbar displays the ten buttons listed in the first two columns below. The four buttons in the first column perform the same functions as the equivalent options on the File Manager's File Menu and the six View Menu buttons duplicate View Menu options. In either case, the options are described in the *File Menu* and *View Menu* descriptions later in the chapter.

The four additional buttons in the third column appear if the DOS 6.0 Windows applets are installed. Refer to the *Microsoft Tools* section of Chapter 0 for details about these applets. The two buttons in the fourth column are added to the Toolbar if the *Workgroups Resource Kit* is installed, and their functions are described in the *Utility Menu* section below.

File Menu	View Menu	DOS 6.0 Applets	Utility Menu
Connect Network Drive	View Name	Run Backup	File Size Information
Disconnect Network Drive	View All File Details	Run Anti-Virus	Find File
Share As	Sort by Name	Double Space Info	
Stop Sharing	Sort by Type	Run Undelete (also on File Menu)	
	Sort by Size		
	Sort by Date		

To add additional buttons to the Toolbar, or to remove some of these, refer to the *Toolbar Configuration* section later in the chapter.

Drive Bar (Workgroups). A single Drive Bar shows a Drive Icon for each available drive, and the drive displayed in the Current Directory Window is outlined. Unlike the Windows 3.1 Drive Bar (described below), the Workgroups Drive Bar does not show the drive letter and volume label for the currently selected drive.

Status Bar. At the bottom of the File Manager's Application Window, the Status Bar panels display the following information.

Panel 1. Active drive letter, free space, total disk (or diskette) capacity. The panel is empty if the Directory Tree does not appear in the Current Directory Window.

Panel 2. Number of files in the Current Directory Window and the space occupied by those files. If the Current Directory Window is turned off (via the View Menu), the panel data refers to the last window that was displayed and does not change if some other directory is highlighted in the Directory Tree Window. Therefore, make sure the Current Directory Window is open to verify the validity of this panel.

Status Bar *(Panel 3, Workgroups)*. If Workgroups is installed, a *Network Shared Status* panel also appears in the Status Bar. This additional panel reports the status of the highlighted directory in the Directory Tree Window, as shown here:

Computer	Status Bar Reports:
Local	Not shared, *or*
	Shared as \\(*local computer name*)\(*directory name*)
All others	Not shared

Note that the shared status is only reported on the local computer; that is, the one doing the sharing. As far as the others are concerned, the current directory is always just another directory. However, the Selected Drive Window on the Toolbar does indicate the remote source of the current directory.

A Status Bar Error. If a local directory is shared, then all subdirectories within it are also shared. However, if the local computer displays the contents of one of those subdirectories, the Network Shared Status panel reports it as "Not shared," even though it is.

Status Bar Menu Description **(Workgroups).** If a File Manager menu or menu option is highlighted, or a Toolbar button is clicked, the Status Bar displays a one-line description of the menu or selected option. This feature is also seen on the Control Panel's Status Bar in both versions of Windows.

Directory Window

Within the File Manager's Application Window, one or more Directory Windows may be opened. Each such window has its own Title Bar and (Windows 3.1 only) Drive Bar.

Title Bar. If a Directory Window is maximized, the Application Window's Title Bar displays information about that window, and the Menu Bar shows the Control Menu box and Restore buttons for the Directory Window. However, if the Directory Window is not maximized (click once on the Restore button), then a new Directory Window Title Bar appears. This Title Bar contains the Control Menu box, Restore button, and the Title for the window.

If more than one Directory Window is open, the appropriate controls and title are found at the top of each window.

Drive Bar (Windows 3.1). Each open Directory Window displays its own Drive Bar immediately below the Title Bar. In addition to showing the available drive icons, each Drive Bar lists the drive letter and volume label (if any) for the selected drive.

File Manager Icons

The File Manager has its own set of icons to display drive, directory tree, and file information. These icons, shown in Figure 6.2, are briefly described here. If your File Manager Application Window does not display both a directory tree and a directory listing, open the View Menu and select the Tree and Directory option at the top of the menu.

Drivebar Icons
  a Diskette
  c Hard disk
  e Ram disk
  f Removable media
  h Network drive

File Manager · [C:*.*· [DRIVE C]]   **(a)**

(b)

Figure 6.2 File Manager Icons, showing (a) Drivebar icons and a minimized Directory Window icon, and (b) an open Directory Window in which each icon type is identified.

Drivebar Icons

The Drivebar displays an icon and drive letter for each local and network drive. Figure 6.2a shows examples of the following five icon types that may be seen on the Drivebar:

Diskette drive   RAM drive   Removable media (CD-ROM, for example)
Hard disk   Network drive

Network Drive Icon. The network drive icon identifies any remote network drive, but does not reveal whether the remote device is a diskette, CD-ROM, or other drive. If the icon faceplate is grayed, the drive was accessed during a previous session, but you have not yet logged on to the network during the current session.

Directory Tree Window Icons

In the discussion which follows, it is assumed that the *Indicate Expandable Branches* option on the Tree Menu has been enabled. If this option is not enabled, then the minus and plus signs described here will not be seen.

In Figure 6.2b, the Directory Tree Window is seen on the left side of the File Manager's Application Window.

Directory Icon. The Batfiles directory near the top of the Directory Tree is one of many directories which displays a conventional Directory Icon. The icon is a closed folder with no markings on it, thus indicating the directory contains no subdirectories, and is also not the currently selected directory.

Collapsible Directory Icon. A directory folder marked with a minus sign indicates one whose subdirectories are also displayed, as shown by the Windows directory in Figure 6.2b. It is called a *collapsible directory* because these subdirectories could be concealed by collapsing the display, as in the next example.

Expandable Directory Icon. The Backups subdirectory immediately below the Windows directory is marked with a plus sign to indicate it is an expandable directory; that is, it contains its own subdirectories which may be displayed by expanding it. The Winword directory at the bottom of the directory tree is also an expandable directory.

Shared Directory Icon. A directory designated as shared is identified by a tiny hand under the directory folder, offering it to all who might want it.

Note that although a shared directory may be collapsible or expandable (as for example, the collapsible shared MSAPPS directory in the figure), no minus or plus sign is seen. Perhaps the host's thumb erased it.

Current Directory Icon. The current directory is the one whose contents are displayed in the Current Directory Window to the immediate right of the Directory Tree Window. Its icon is an open folder, as shown by the Winword directory icon at the bottom of the Directory Tree. In this specific example, the Current Directory is also an Expandable Directory, as indicated by the plus sign on the open folder.

Current Directory Window Icons

In Figure 6.2b, the right-hand side of the File Manager Application Window is occupied by the Current Directory Window, which displays the contents of the highlighted directory in the Directory Tree Window.

Directory Icon in Current Directory Window. A Directory Icon may also appear in the Current Directory Window, if the current directory contains subdirectories. In the example in Figure 6.2b, note that the Directory Tree shows the current (WINWORD) directory as expandable; therefore, its subdirectories do not appear as part of the tree. However, these subdirectories are visible in the right-hand Current Directory Window, immediately below the up-arrow icon near the top of the window.

Document Icon. A file that may be opened by a Windows applet or application is identified by a dog-eared page icon with a few lines of text on it. However, the file is not necessarily a traditional document—for example, a bitmap file created under the Paintbrush applet is displayed with a document icon. In fact, the document icon is assigned to every file extension listed in either the [Extensions] section of your WIN.INI file, or in the registration database. When you double-click on any document icon, the associated applet opens and the file is loaded within that applet.

Hidden or System Icon. For the purposes of the illustration in Figure 6.2b, the hidden system files were "borrowed" from the root directory. Such files are identified by a document-style icon which displays an exclamation mark instead of text.

Other File Icon. A file which does not fit any of the other categories in this section is identified as an "other" file, whose icon is a blank sheet of paper.

Program Icon. A program icon identifies any executable program, which may be directly executed by double-clicking on the icon. Windows assigns a program icon to any program whose extension is listed in the following section of WIN.INI:

```
[windows]
Programs=com exe bat pif
```

The line shown here is the default listing created when Windows is installed. Even if it is erased, files with these extensions are still identified by the Program Icon. Additional extensions may be added by the user, and files bearing these extensions will be treated as executable programs.

Up-Arrow Icon. An up-arrow at the top of any Current Directory Window is your clue that the window displays the contents of a subdirectory. Double-click on the arrow to ascend to the next level in the directory tree. As you do so, the highlighted directory in the Directory Tree Window to the immediate left changes accordingly. The up-arrow icon disappears when the Current Directory Window displays the contents of the root directory.

Minimized Directory Window Icon

Within the File Manager's Application Window, any Directory Window may be minimized to an icon, which may be convenient when working with multiple Directory Windows. A minimized Directory Window Icon is also shown in Figure 6.2a.

File Manager Menus

The File Manager's menu structure is similar to that described in the *Windows Menu Structure* section of Chapter 3. However, the specific menus and menu options are slightly different; these differences are described here.

Menus and Menu Options

As in Chapter 3, the menus and their contents are listed alphabetically. A parenthetical letter reference next to a menu name indicates its location, as shown in Figure 6.3, or in the case of the Control Menu, as shown in Figure 3.3. If the menu option is accessible by pressing a key (which is underlined in the menu option), that key is underlined in the description given here.

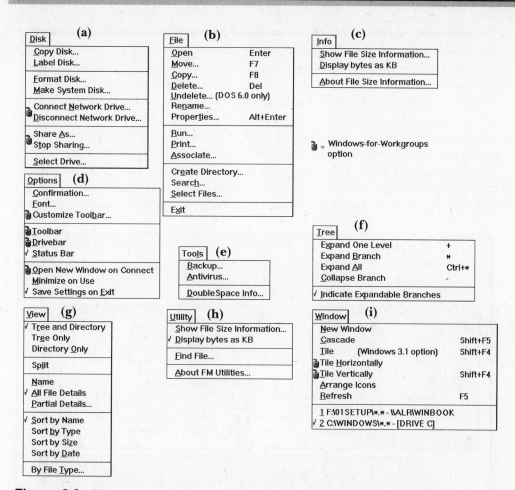

Figure 6.3 Menus accessible via the File Manager's Menu Bar. (a) Disk Menu, (b) File Menu, (c) Info Menu *(Windows Resource Kit)*, (d) Options Menu, (e) Tools Menu, (f) Tree Menu, (g), View Menu, (h) Utility Menu *(Workgroups Resource Kit)*, (i) Window Menu.

Setting Menu Restrictions. In Chapter 3, a bracketed [R] next to a menu or a menu option below identified an option that may be disabled, as described in the *Set Menu Restrictions* section of that chapter. Note that any restrictions set in that section have no effect on the equivalent File Manager menus.

Control Menu (Figure 3.3a). Two or more Control Menu boxes may be visible when the File Manager is open on the Windows Desktop. In the upper left-hand corner is the Control Menu box for the File Manager's own Application Window. If any Directory Window is maximized within that Application Window, its own (and slightly smaller) Control Menu box appears at the left-hand side of the Menu Bar. If no Directory Window is maximized, then a Control Menu box appears in the upper left-hand corner of each open Directory Window within the larger Application Window. For example, Figure 6.4 shows the File Manager's Application Window and two smaller Directory Windows, each with its own Control Menu box. Note that both Directory Windows display the same Directory Tree and Current Directory Windows. For comparison purposes, the upper window is taken from a Workgroups screen, while the lower window shows how the same information would appear on a Windows version 3.1 screen. Note that the lower window has its own Drivebar.

The Application Window's usual Control Menu box has been replaced with the hDC *First Apps* logo. However, the Control Menu is still available

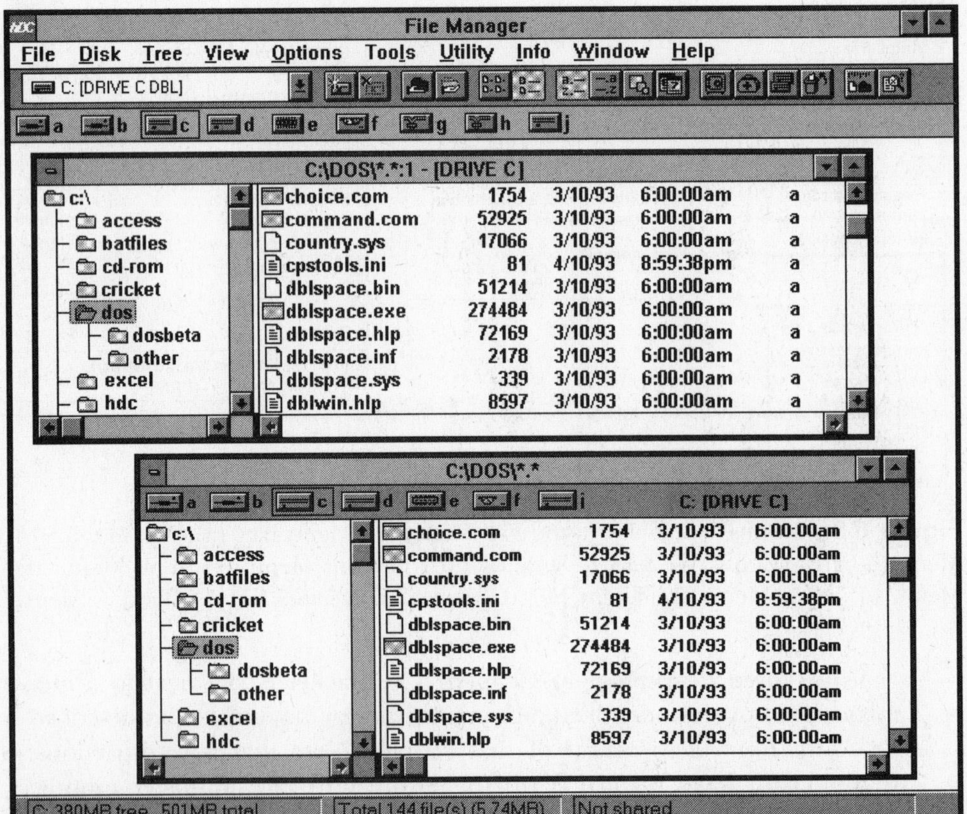

Figure 6.4 A File Manager Application Window in *Windows-for-Workgroups*. Note that the Menu Bar shows both the Info Menu (from *Windows Resource Kit*) and the Utility Menu *(Workgroup Resource Kit)*. For comparison purposes, the upper Directory Window is taken from *Windows-for-Workgroups*, while the lower one is from *Windows*. Note the duplicate Drive Bar on the latter.

by clicking on that box. (Refer to the *h*DC First Apps section of Chapter 5 for an explanation of this.)

The File Manager's Control Menus (all of them) are quite similar to those described for the Program Manager in Chapter 3. With the exception of the Close option described here, refer to the *Control Menu* section of that chapter for a description of the other menu options.

The Close Option. This option performs slightly different actions, depending on which Control Menu is open, and on whether the File Manager is the current Windows shell. In the discussion which follows, note that the Shortcut key combination is different for each window.

Application Window (Alt + F4). If the File Manager is the Windows shell, then the Close option is functionally equivalent to the Exit option on the File Menu. If you click on either one, the Exit Windows dialog box appears. Otherwise, the option simply closes the File Manager and the Program Manager again occupies the Desktop.

Directory Window (Ctrl + F4). If there is only one Directory Window within the File Manager's Application Window, then that Directory Window cannot be closed. Therefore, the Close option will be grayed, indicating its disabled status. To close the File Manager itself, open the Application Window's Control Menu and use that menu's Close option instead.

Disk Menu (Figure 6.3a). This menu provides various disk and diskette utilities, including network drive management facilities.

> **DIRECTORY SHARING NOTE:** If Workgroups is installed, the **Share As...** and **Stop Sharing...** menu options described below require a 386 (or better) microprocessor. In standard mode, these options do not appear on the menu, nor are the equivalent Toolbar buttons seen. To permanently disable these options on 386 systems operating in Enhanced Mode, refer to *Disable File Sharing* later in the chapter.

Connect Network Drive... **(Workgroups).** Select this option to assign a logical drive letter on your computer to a shared directory located elsewhere on the network system. The Connect Network Drive dialog box in Figure 6.5 displays the following information.

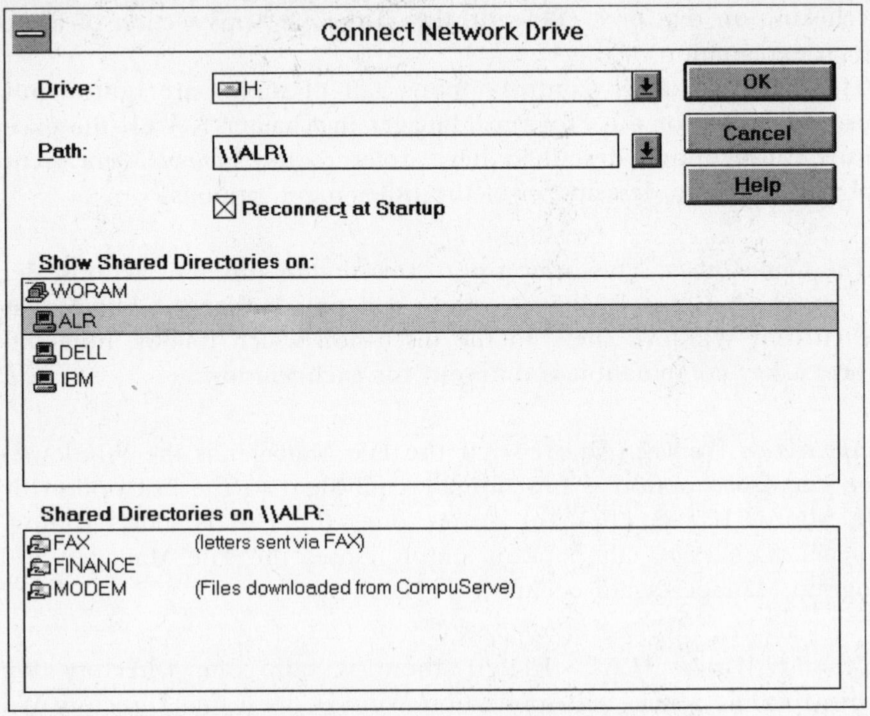

```
┌──────────────────────────────────────────────────────────┐
│ ▭              Connect Network Drive                      │
├──────────────────────────────────────────────────────────┤
│ Drive:      ▭H:                              ▼  │ ┌─ OK ──┐│
│                                                 │         ││
│ Path:       \\ALR\                          ▼   │┌ Cancel┐││
│                                                 │         ││
│             ☒ Reconnect at Startup              │┌ Help ─┐││
│                                                             │
│ Show Shared Directories on:                                │
│ ┌────────────────────────────────────────────────────────┐│
│ │ 🖳WORAM                                                  ││
│ │ 🖳ALR                                                    ││
│ │ 🖳DELL                                                   ││
│ │ 🖳IBM                                                    ││
│ │                                                          ││
│ └────────────────────────────────────────────────────────┘│
│                                                             │
│ Shared Directories on \\ALR:                               │
│ ┌────────────────────────────────────────────────────────┐│
│ │ 📁FAX          (letters sent via FAX)                    ││
│ │ 📁FINANCE                                                ││
│ │ 📁MODEM        (Files downloaded from CompuServe)        ││
│ │                                                          ││
│ └────────────────────────────────────────────────────────┘│
└──────────────────────────────────────────────────────────┘
```

Figure 6.5 The Connect Network Drive dialog box

Drive. The next available local drive letter is displayed here. Click on the down-arrow to show a list of all other available drive letters, through drive Z. Currently assigned letters do not appear in the list, as may be verified by noting the presence of these letters on the Drive Bar.

If you select a drive letter that is beyond that specified by the LASTDRIVE= line in your CONFIG.SYS file, an error message will appear if you attempt to assign that letter to a shared network directory.

Path. If your computer was previously connected to a network drive, the names of the shared directories you accessed are listed in the [MRU_Files] (that is, Most Recently Used Files) section of your own WIN.INI file, as shown here:

```
[MRU_Files]
Order=agebfdc      (the order in which the files were accessed)
a=\\(Computer Name)\(Directory Name)
b=\\(Computer Name)\(Directory Name)
. . . (others)
g=\\(Computer Name)\(Directory Name)
. . . (and so on)
```

Click on the down arrow next to the Path box to show a list of these directories.

Reconnect at Startup. By default, this box is checked the first time you log onto the network so that you will not have to repeat the logon procedure the next time you open Windows. Clear the check box if you do not wish to log onto the network the next time Windows opens.

Show Shared Directories on. This box lists the name of a workgroup and the names of the computers within that group. If necessary, double-click on a workgroup to display the computer names.

Shared Directories. Double-click on any computer name (above) to display a list of the directories on that computer that have been designated as shared. The name of any shared directory may be followed by a comment, if the operator on the remote computer added one when that directory was designated as shared (see *Share As* below). To assign a local drive letter to any listed directory, double-click on that directory name.

Figure 6.6 shows an Excel 4.0 directory tree as it appears (a) on a remote computer which has designated it as a shared directory, and (b) as it appears on the local computer. Note that on the latter, the name of the shared Excel

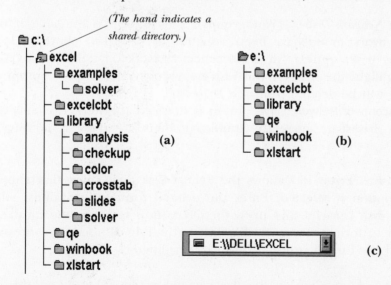

Figure 6.6 A Directory Tree Window sample, as it appears on (a) the host system and (b) the client system. On the latter, the Selected Drive Window (c) shows the host computer name and the Share Name assigned to the directory by the host.

directory is missing from the directory tree, where it is now identified as the root directory of network drive E. However, the missing Excel name is seen in the Toolbar's Selected Drive Window as shown in part (c) of the Figure, which also identifies the computer on which the directory is actually located.

The plus and minus symbols identifying expandable/collapsible directories do not show up on the network drive's directory tree, even though these directories may be expanded or collapsed as on the local system itself.

Copy Disk.... This option copies the entire contents of a source diskette to a destination diskette, both of which must be the same format. If multiple diskette drives are available, a prompt will ask you to specify the source and destination drives. Otherwise, a drive A-to-drive A copy is assumed.

As the source diskette is read, the following message is seen:

Now copying disk in Drive A:. *xx*% completed.

If necessary, the destination diskette is formatted during the copy procedure. If you do use the same drive for both diskettes, a prompt will advise you when to insert the destination diskette. Although the above message remains on screen, it should be interpreted as "Now Copying *to* the disk in Drive A."

Disconnect Network Drive... **(Workgroups).** This option is available if one or more network drives have been assigned, as described above. If so, a list of these drives appears in a Disconnect Network Drive dialog box (not shown). Highlight the drive(s) you wish to disconnect, and the appropriate drive letters will be deleted from the Drivebar.

If the Disconnect Network Drive option is disabled (grayed), it means that no network drives are currently connected; therefore there is nothing to disconnect.

Format Disk.... Figure 6.7 shows the Format Disk dialog box that appears when this option is selected. Enter the desired formatting options, select the desired disk capacity, and press the OK button to begin the format. If you attempt to format say, a 720 Kb diskette at 1.44 Mb, an error message appears and the format procedure will be terminated.

Label Disk.... First, click on the drive icon for the diskette or hard disk partition that you wish to label. Then select this option to display the current label (if any). Enter the new label and click on the OK button to conclude the procedure.

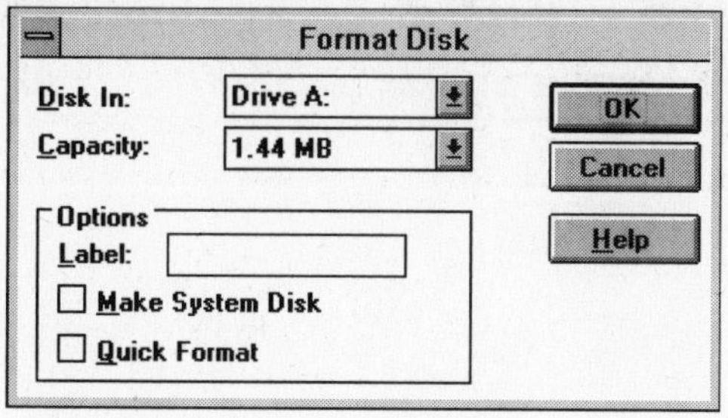

Figure 6.7 The Format Disk dialog box

Make System Disk.... This option copies the DOS system files to a diskette, which must be formatted before making the transfer. If the diskette is not formatted, an error message appears and the procedure is terminated.

Select Drive.... This option displays a Select Drive dialog box, similar to that shown in Figure 6.8. Double-click on any listed drive to display the contents of that drive in the Directory Window. You can accomplish the same thing much faster by simply clicking on the appropriate drive icon on the Drivebar. However, the Select Drive option may be useful if you want to review the identities of the available drives before making a selection.

Share As... (**Workgroups**). Before a drive on your computer can be accessed by others on the network, you must agree to share it. To do so, select the Share As option to open the Share Directory dialog box shown in Figure 6.9a.

Share Name. By default, the name in this box matches the name of the directory to be shared. However, you can change it to some other name up to 12 characters long.

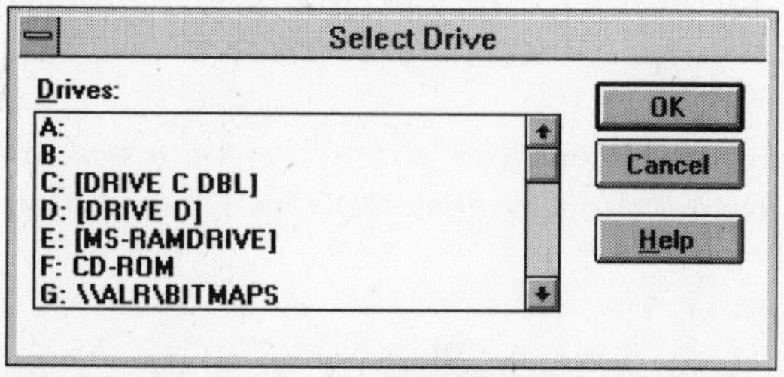

Figure 6.8 The Select Drive dialog box. The double-slashes identify a remote network drive that is currently available on the local computer.

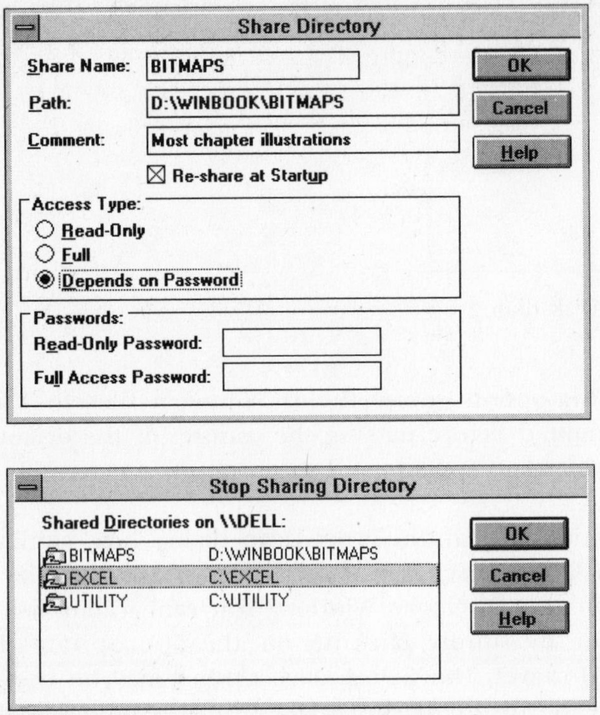

Figure 6.9 The (a) Share Directory and (b) Stop Sharing Directory dialog boxes are accessed from the File Manager's Disk Menu.

If you don't want the directory name to appear automatically as a Shared Directory on other computers, use a $ sign as the last character. Although the directory name will not be seen, it may still be accessed by anyone who knows of its existence.

Path. This box shows the complete path to the directory you wish to share. Although you could certainly change the path by typing in a new one, the usual way to do this would be to return to the File Manager, highlight the directory you wish to share, and reopen the Share Directory dialog box.

Comment. If you type in a brief comment (48 characters or less), this will appear after the directory name in the Connect Network Drive dialog box (see Figure 6.5).

Reshare at Startup. Once you designate a local drive as shared, it will be available to others every time Windows is opened on your computer. Clear this check box if you do not wish this to happen.

Access Type. Depending on your generosity level, you can grant read-only or full (read and write) privileges to others on the network by clicking the appropriate radio button in this section. To allow read-only access to some and full access to others, click on the Depends on Password button, and assign different passwords in the next section.

Passwords. One or both of these boxes can be enabled, depending on which button you clicked in the "Access Type" section above. If you enter a password in one or both boxes, the remote user will have to know the password(s) to gain access to your shared directory.

S_top Sharing... (Workgroups). If you select this option, the Stop Sharing Directory dialog box shown in Figure 6.9b lists the local directories you have designated as shared. Each Share Name appears in the left-hand column, followed by the local directory path for the shared directory. Highlight one or more directories, then click on the OK button to stop sharing them.

If you elect to stop sharing a directory to which other computers are currently connected, an advisory message will prompt you to verify that you really mean it.

File Menu (Figure 6.3b). The menu offers the basic file management options as described in Chapter 3. However, there are some significant differences in, and additions to, the File Manager's File Menu, as described here.

A_ssociate.... As an aid to routine operations, this option associates a file with a specific Windows applet or application, according to that file's three-letter extension. As an obvious example, any document written under the Windows Write applet has an extension of WRI, and that extension is therefore associated with the Write applet. During the Windows Setup procedure this association is automatically recorded in the WIN.INI file, as shown here:

```
[Extensions]
wri=write.exe ^.wri
```

The unique nomenclature shown here means that any file (note "^." instead of the customary "*.") with an extension of WRI is to be associated with the Write applet (WRITE.EXE). Therefore, if a directory window shows a file named *filename*.WRI and you double-click on that filename, the Write applet opens and *filename*.WRI is automatically loaded.

Table 6.1 lists the contents of the [Extensions] section, along with some additional files that may be added as selected Windows applications are

TABLE 6.1 Windows File Associations*

WIN.INI [Extensions] Section Listing		Applet or Application	File Description
bmp = pbrush.exe	^.bmp	Paintbrush applet	Bitmap
cal = calendar.exe	^.cal	Calendar applet	Calendar
crd = cardfile.exe	^.crd	Cardfile applet	Cardfile
doc = C:\WINWORD\winword.exe	^.doc	Word-for-Windows	Document
dot = C:\WINWORD\winword.exe	^.dot	Word-for-Windows	Document template
hlp = winhelp.exe	^.hlp	Help applet	Help
ico = C:\MSU\ICONVIEW.EXE	^.ICO	Icon View utility	Icon
ini = C:\DOS\EDIT.COM	^.INI	DOS Edit utility	Windows initialization
ma = microman.exe	^.ma	PC-Kwik *Winmaster*	
mvb = viewer.exe	^.mvb	Various multimedia	Viewer document
pcx = pbrush.exe	^.pcx	Paintbrush applet	PCX graphics
rec = recorder.exe	^.rec	Recorder applet	
reg = regedit.exe	^.reg	Registration Editor applet	Registration data
rtf = C:\WINWORD\winword.exe	^.rtf	Word-for-Windows	Rich text format
shg = shed.exe	^.shg		
tbk = toolbook.exe	^.tbk	Assymetrix ToolBook	Book
trm = terminal.exe	^.trm	Terminal applet	
txt = notepad	^.txt	Notepad applet	Text
wav = mplayer.exe	^.wav	Media Player applet	WAV audio
wav = prec.exe	^.wav	Media Vision Pocket Recorder	
wri = write	^.wri	Write applet	Text file
xla = C:\EXCEL\EXCEL.EXE	^.xla	Excel	Add-in macro
xlb = C:\EXCEL\EXCEL.EXE	^.xlb	Excel	Toolbar data
xlc = C:\EXCEL\EXCEL.EXE	^.xlc	Excel	Chart
xll = C:\EXCEL\EXCEL.EXE	^.xll	Excel	Crosstab add-in
xlm = C:\EXCEL\EXCEL.EXE	^.xlm	Excel	Macro sheet
xls = C:\EXCEL\EXCEL.EXE	^.xls	Excel	Worksheet
xlt = C:\EXCEL\EXCEL.EXE	^.xlt	Excel	Template
xlw = C:\EXCEL\EXCEL.EXE	^.xlw	Excel	Workbook

*Spacing between inserted here for clarity.

installed. As various third-party applets and applications are installed, their Setup procedures may make other additions to the [Extensions] section of WIN.INI, as also shown in the Table. Note that the various setup utilities don't agree on the use of upper- and lowercase letters. Refer to the *Reconfigure File Association* section later in this chapter for assistance in reconfiguring the [Extensions] section.

NOTE: If you write a new line in the [Extensions] section, and that line has no effect, there is probably a conflict with the Registration Database, which takes precedence over your new line. Refer to *Wrong File/Applet Association* in the Troubleshooting section for further details.

Copy... **(F8).** This menu option can be used to copy a highlighted file, or the contents of an entire directory. Unlike the Program Manager, where the equivalent option only copies a highlighted applet into a specified group window, here the Copy option may be used to copy any source file to any target directory, or to the Clipboard. Accordingly, the Copy dialog box shown in Figure 6.10 is slightly different from the Program Manager's Copy Program Item box (Figure 3.8).

Create Directory.... Before using this option, select the drive and directory in which you wish to create a new subdirectory. Then click on this option to open the Create Directory dialog box (not shown), which displays the drive letter and complete path of the selected directory. Type in the name for the new directory, which is created in the indicated location.

Delete **(Del).** Be careful: You *could* delete the contents of an entire directory by accident, although the File Manager does ask you to confirm your choice before it takes any action.

To begin, highlight the desired directory name, or filename, then select this option. The Delete dialog box displays the name of the item to be deleted and, if you click on the OK button, a Confirm Directory Delete dialog box offers a few choices. For example, if you elect to delete a directory, the following choices are presented:

Button	Action Taken
Yes	You'll be prompted to confirm the deletion of each file and subdirectory in that directory.
Yes to All	All files, the directory itself, and any subdirectories, are deleted.
No	The presently highlighted file or directory is not deleted.
Cancel	Quit the deletion procedure. (Files already deleted remain deleted.)

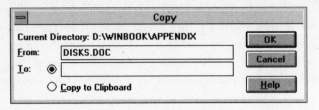

Figure 6.10 The Copy dialog box

Before reaching for that Yes-to-All button, remember that all directories within any deleted directory are likewise deleted.

If you decide to delete, say, the TEST1 directory which contains a few files and a TEST2 subdirectory, the first prompt will ask if you want to delete the TEST1 directory. If you click on the Yes button, the next prompt asks the same question about the TEST2 subdirectory, and so on through other subdirectory levels, if any. When you reach the lowest-level subdirectory, the files within that directory are erased one by one (assuming you continue to click on the Yes button). Once the lowest-level directory is empty, the directory itself is deleted, and the process repeats for the next highest-level directory, and so on until all directories have been cleared and deleted.

If at any stage in this procedure you click on the No button, then that file and the directory in which it resides are preserved, as is any higher-level directory.

Before using the delete option to do serious housekeeping, it's not such a bad idea to create a few levels of test directories, toss a few files in each one, then experiment. Once you're confident about navigating the directory structure with your trigger-finger on the Yes button, you can try your luck on more critical files and directories.

Exit. The File Menu's final option closes the File Manager and returns to the Program Manager. However, if you have made the File Manager the Windows shell (see *Assign File Manager as Windows Shell* in the *File Manager Configuration* section below), then this option displays the Exit Windows dialog box. Click on the OK button to close Windows and return to the DOS prompt.

Move... **(F7).** This option is similar to the Copy option described above, except that the selected directory or file is moved, rather than copied, from its present location to the one specified in the Move dialog box.

If you attempt to move a file that is currently in use, a *Cannot Move* error message will be displayed and the file will remain in its current location.

Open... **(Enter).** This option performs one of two functions, depending on the current location of the highlight bar.

Directory in Directory Tree Window. If the highlight bar is on a directory listing, then the Open option acts as a toggle, alternately expanding and collapsing that directory. If the directory contains no subdirectories, then toggling the Open option has no effect.

File in Directory Window. If the highlight bar is on a file in this window, the Open option opens the applet associated with that file, then opens the highlighted file. If the highlighted item is an executable file, then the Open option executes that file.

Properties... **(Alt+Enter).** Select this option to display the operational properties associated with the highlighted directory or file. Figure 6.11 shows the Properties dialog box if more than one file was highlighted. A shaded attribute box indicates the attribute is not set for all the selected files. If a single file is highlighted, then a larger dialog box lists properties, including attributes, for that file. Figures 6.11a and b show the Properties dialog box as it appears in Windows 3.1 and Windows-for-Workgroups.

The _O_pen by... button is seen only if network software is successfully installed, either during system bootup or prior to opening Windows.

Version Information. The Version Information at the bottom of the dialog box in Figure 6.11b may be enabled if the selected file contains the appropriate information, as in this SETUP.EXE example. Highlight any item in the left-hand box to display the associated information in the right-hand box. For example, "File Description" shows that SETUP.EXE is a "Windows Setup application file" (but you probably knew that already).

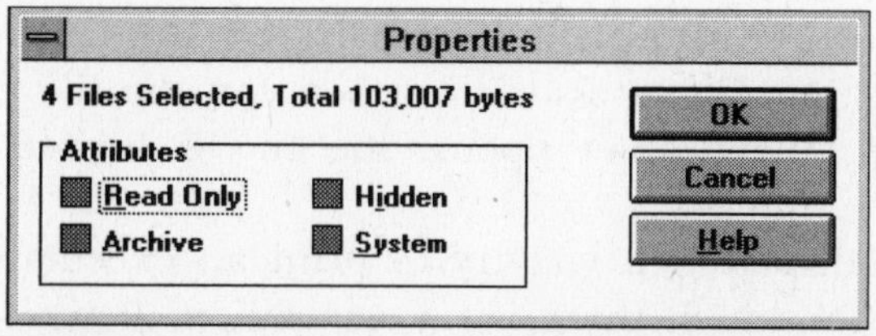

Figure 6.11   The Properties dialog box as it appears if more than one file is highlighted prior to selecting the Properties option.

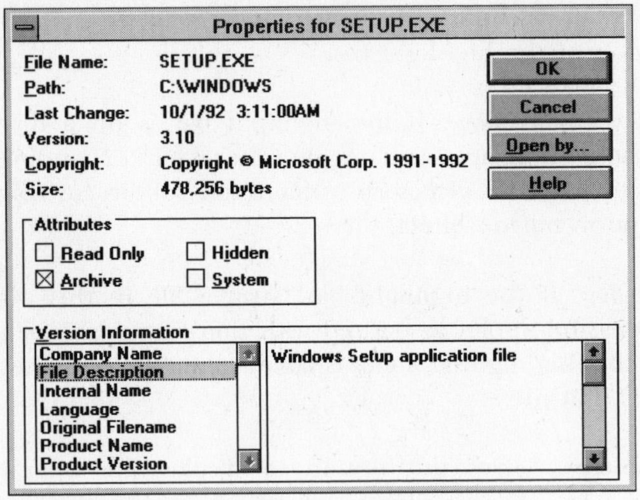

Figure 6.11a,b The Properties dialog box as it appears if a single file is high-lighted in (a) *Windows* or in (b) *Windows-for-Workgroups*.

Print.... The Print option is only enabled if the highlight bar is on a file in the Directory Window. If it is, click on this option to open the Print dialog box (not shown), which displays the name of the file. The file should be printable from within an installed applet (Notepad or Paintbrush, for example) or application (Excel, Word, etc.). If so, click on the OK button to begin printing. Assuming there is an association between the file extension and a Windows applet, that applet opens, the file is loaded, and printing begins.

An error message will be displayed if you try to print an executable or batch file, or any other file for which there is no association. Refer to the *Associate* option on this menu, and to the *Reconfigure File Association* section later in the chapter for further details on file associations.

*Re**n**ame*.... Highlight any file or directory, then select this option to open the Rename dialog box (not shown). Enter the desired new name, then click on the OK button to conclude the Rename process.

*R**u**n*.... Once Windows is installed, the Run option is frequently used to begin the installation of a new Windows application, as was described in the *Setup a New Windows Application* section of Chapter 1.

The same option may also be used to run any application that is already set up. Enter the path and filename of the desired application and then click on the OK button to run the application. This may be of some use in troubleshooting (if double-clicking on the application's icon doesn't work), or if the desired application is not represented by an icon in one of the group windows. However, for most routine operations, it is a lot quicker to simply double-click on the appropriate icon.

*Searc**h***.... Click on this option to open the Search dialog box shown in Figure 6.12. The Figure also shows a Search Results report at the end of a search of all directories for backup files (BAK extension). The option provides a convenient way to find either a specific file that has gotten lost or—as in this example—a collection of files with a common extension. For

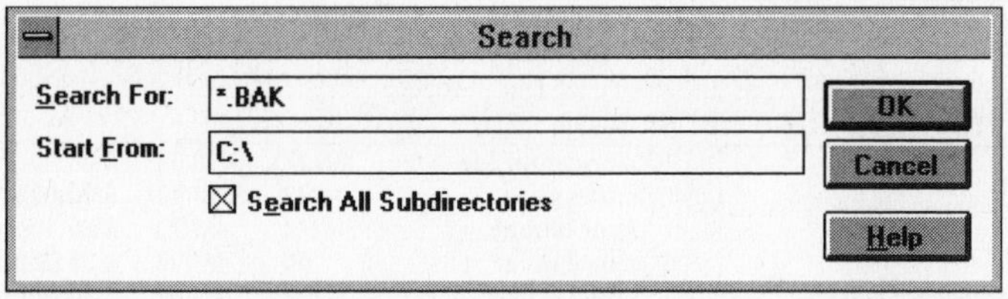

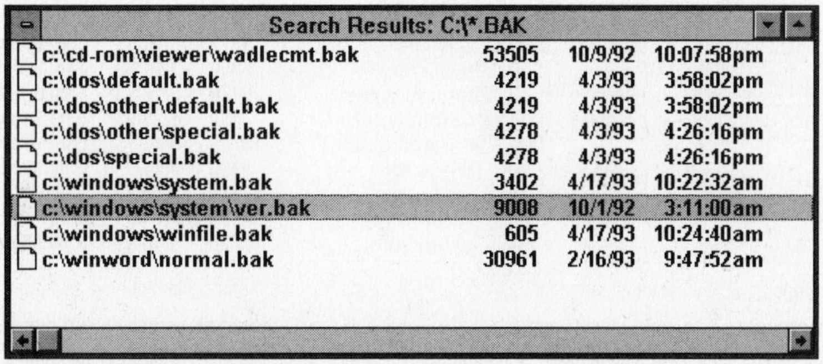

Figure 6.12 The (a) Search dialog box. The (b) Search Results Window shows the results of a search for files with a BAK extension.

housekeeping, use the Search option to find all backup files, then the Delete option to get rid of all of them.

Select Files.... This option opens the Select Files dialog box shown in Figure 6.13. To select a file (or file extension, etc.), type the appropriate information in the File(s) box, then click on the Select button. The Cancel button is replaced by a Close button, and the files which meet the selection criteria are outlined. If necessary, repeat the procedure to select other files, then click on the Close button to conclude the selection process. When you do, the selected files are highlighted (as also shown in the figure), and you may now perform some operation that will affect all of them (copy, delete, etc.).

Undelete... **(DOS 6.0).** This menu option appears if DOS 6.0 and the Microsoft Windows Tools group are installed. These tools accompany DOS 6.0, and were described in Chapter 0. Refer to that chapter for assistance in using the undelete utility.

Help Menu. Refer to Chapter 4 for information about the Windows Help system.

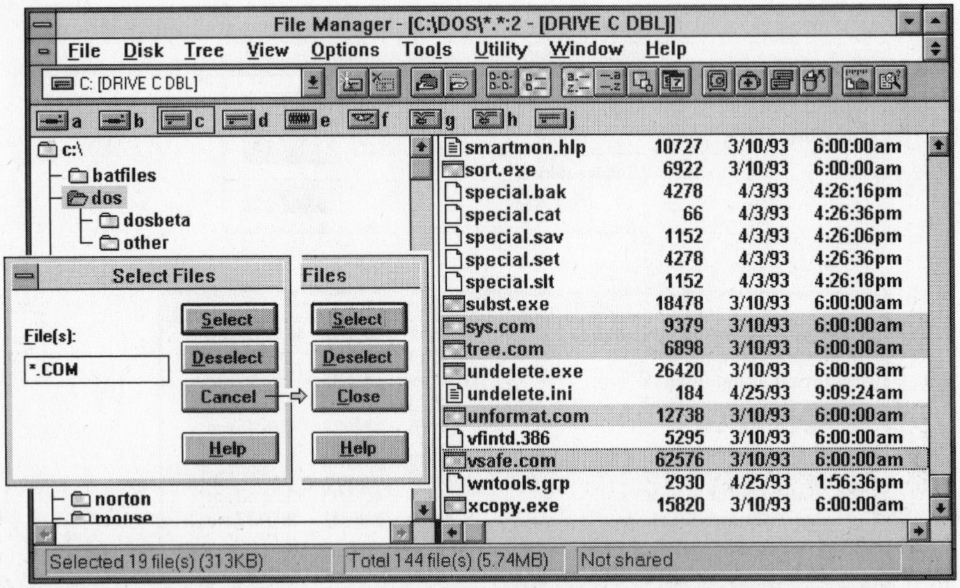

Figure 6.13 A small Select Files dialog box is shown here overlaying the Directory Tree. After clicking on the Select button, the Cancel button is replaced by a Close button.

Info Menu *(Windows Resource Kit)* **(Figure 6.3c).** If the *Windows Resource Kit* is installed, a FILESIZE.DLL file is installed in the Windows directory, an Info Menu appears on the File Manager's Menu Bar, and the menu options described below are available. The installation adds the following line to the indicated section of your WINFILE.INI file:

```
[AddOns]
File Size Extension=C:\WINDOWS\FILESIZE.DLL
```

 NOTE: The *Utility Menu* (see below) is the *Workgroups Resource Kit* equivalent to the Info Menu.

About File Size Information.... As with other About options, this one displays version, description, and copyright information for the *File Size* utility.

Display bytes as KB. This option simply divides the Total File Size (see next entry) by 1024 to display the size as *xx* KB.

Show File Size Information. Highlight a directory icon, then select this option to display a report such as that seen here for the Windows directory.

Number of Files:	571
Number of Directories:	13
Total File Size:	30,973,917 bytes
	30,248 KB (if *Display bytes as KB* is enabled)

If nothing else, this gives you an idea of how much disk space Windows (or your favorite other application) *really* takes up.

Options Menu (Figure 6.3d). This menu offers various configuration options, most of which will help you customize the look of your File Manager's windows.

Confirmation.... If you select certain actions, Windows asks for a confirmation to make sure you really mean it. You can disable various confirmation messages by selecting the Confirmation option and clearing the check box next to one or more of the following options:

Disk Commands	File Delete	Mouse Action
Directory Delete	File Replace	

Customize Toolbar.... (Workgroups). Select this option to add or remove buttons on the Toolbar, as described in the *Toolbar Configuration* section later in the chapter.

Drivebar **(Workgroups).** Although the Drivebar is a part of both Windows 3.1 and Windows-for-Workgroups, only the latter application allows it to be disabled by clearing the check mark next to this option.

Font.... Select this option to open the Font dialog box, which may be used to select any available font, font style, or point size for the display of the directory tree and directory information. On higher resolution displays, you may want to select a larger point size and different font than the default 8-point MS Sans Serif (try Arial, Bold, 10 points).

Minimize on Use. The phrase means that File Manager will be minimized if you execute (or "use") a program file. Therefore, when the program closes, the File Manager will appear as an icon on the Windows Desktop.

Open New Window on Connect **(Workgroups).** If this option is enabled, then whenever you access a network drive, a new Directory Window opens to display the Directory Tree and Directory Windows for the selected drive. Refer to the *Network Operations* section later in the chapter for further details.

Save Settings on Exit. If you've spent considerable time customizing the look of your File Manager display, make sure this option is checked before exiting, so that your changes will be preserved. Later on, you may want to clear the checkmark so that minor changes made during a File Manager session do not overwrite your basic starting configuration.

Status Bar. The Status Bar at the bottom of the File Manager's Application is toggled on and off by clicking on this option.

Toolbar **(Workgroups).** Clear the checkmark next to this option if you'd rather not see the Toolbar during routine File Manager operations.

Tools Menu (DOS 6.0) (Figure 6.3e). This menu offers access to two of the Windows applets supplied with DOS 6.0. If DOS 6.0 is installed and this menu is not available, refer to the *Setup DOS 6.0 Applets* section of Chapter 1 for help in setting them up. (The *Undelete* applet is available separately, as an extra option on the File Menu, as described earlier in the chapter.)

Anti-Virus and *Backup* *Options*. Select either option to run the indicated applet. Refer to the *Microsoft Tools* section of Chapter 0 for details about these applets.

DoubleSpace Info.... If the drive whose directory tree is currently displayed was compressed via the DOS 6.0 Double Space applet, this menu option will display a report such as that shown in Figure 6.14. If the selected drive is not compressed, then an error message will suggest that you select a compressed drive.

Tree Menu (Figure 6.3f). This menu provides various options to modify the appearance of the Directory Tree Window. If all options are disabled, open the View Menu and select either the **Tree and Directory** or **Tree Only** option.

If a directory tree displays a root directory with multiple subdirectories, and some of these show sub-subdirectories, the tree may be pruned via the menu options below to eliminate some, or all, of the lower-level branches. Unlike gardening elsewhere, the branches may be unpruned at will, as described here.

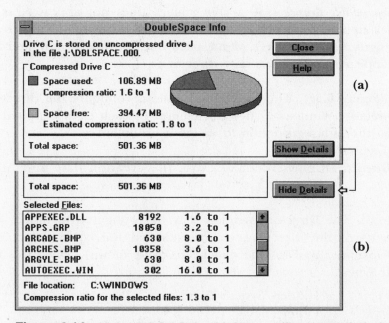

Figure 6.14 If the DOS 6.0 DoubleSpace utility is installed, the Double Space Info screen (a) can be displayed via the Tools Menu. If any files in the Current Directory Window are selected (via Select Files option on File Menu), click on the File Details button to show compression details (b) about the selected files.

Collapse Branch (-). To hide the subdirectories branching out of any directory, highlight that directory, then select this menu option. Better yet, just double-click on the directory icon to collapse it.

Expand All (**Ctrl + ***). This option displays the complete directory structure for the drive in the active Directory Tree Window. (The equivalent keyboard option does not work with the asterisk on the numeral-8 key.)

NOTE: This option must be re-enabled every time you open the File Manager, since it cannot be saved when you close the File Man-

Expand Branch (*****). This option expands all branches of the highlighted directory only. Other expandable directories remain unchanged. (The keyboard option *does* work with the asterisk on the numeral-8 key.)

Expand One Level (+). Highlight any directory and select this option to expand it by one level only.

Indicate Expandable Branches. If a check mark does not appear next to this option, your collapsible/expandable directories are not identified by minus/plus signs. Open the Tree Menu, click once on this option, and the signs will reappear in the appropriate directories.

View Menu (Figure 6.3g). The View Menu options configure the Directory Tree and Directory Windows as described here. In each case, highlight or click once on the indicated option to toggle it on or off.

All File Details. Displays filename, size, file creation date and time, attributes.

By File Type.... The Directory Window may be configured to display the entire contents of the directory, or just selected file types. Select this option to display the By File Type dialog box (not shown), which lists the following file types:

Directories	Hidden/System Files	Programs
Documents	Other Files	

Clear the check box next to each file type that you do not wish to display.

Directory Only. Displays only the Directory Window.

Partial Details. This option opens the Partial Details dialog box (not shown) which displays the following file details:

File Attributes   Last Modification Time
Last Modification Date   Size

Clear the check box next to each file detail that you do not wish to display.

Sort by Date, Sort by Name, by Size, by Type. Toggle the desired option to sort the files in the Directory Window as required.

Split. Select this option to place a double-headed arrow on the Split Bar in the active Directory Window, then use the arrow keys to move the bar to the left or right, as desired. Better yet, simply place the mouse pointer on the Split Bar, press and hold the primary mouse button down, then drag it wherever you want it to go.

Tree and Directory. The active Directory Window displays both the Directory Tree and the Directory Windows.

Tree Only. Displays only the Directory Tree Window.

Utility Menu *(Workgroups Resource Kit)* **(Figure 6.3h).** A File Manager Utilities Menu is added to the Toolbar if the *Workgroups Resource Kit* utilities are installed. With the exception of the options described here, the others are equivalent to those on the *Info Menu* which comes with the version 3.1 *Windows Resource Kit.* Refer to that menu above for a description of these options.

If you previously installed the version 3.1 *Windows Resource Kit* utilities, you may want to delete its Info Menu and erase the FILESIZE.DLL file, since the newer *Workgroups Resource Kit* utilities duplicate the former's options and add the Find File option described below. If so, edit your WINFILE.INI file to remove the File Size Extension= line shown here. The FMUtils Extension= line is automatically inserted when the *Resource Kit* utilities are installed.

```
[AddOns]
File Size Extension=C:\WINDOWS\FILESIZE.DLL    (delete this line and erase file)
FMUtils Extension=C:\WINDOWS\FMUTILS.DLL       (this line added by WfWRKit)
```

Find File.... Figure 6.15a shows the Find File dialog box that appears if you select this option on the Utility Menu, or click on the last button on the Toolbar. Enter the following information in the indicated boxes.

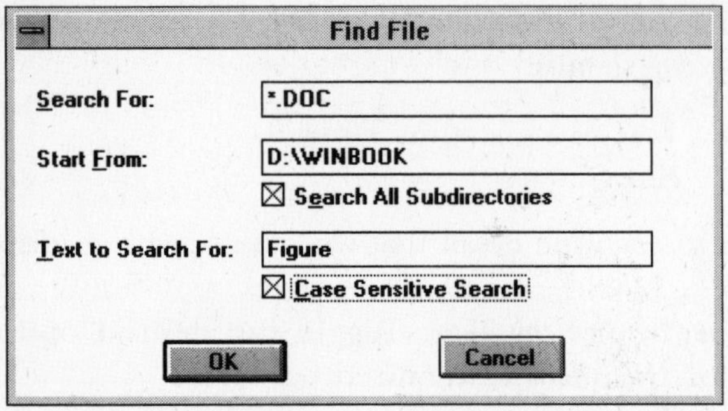

Figure 6.15a Select the Find File option to open the Find File dialog box.

Search For:. Enter the file-search criteria, as shown by these typical examples:

A*.*   All files beginning with the letter "A"
*.DOC   All document files
.   All files

Start From:. The search begins in the drive and path entered in this box. Check or clear the Search All Subdirectories box, as required.

Text to Search For:. If you want to find a specific word or phrase in the searched files, enter the appropriate information here. If the box is left blank, the search will simply find all files that meet the file-search criteria specified in the first box.

As the search progresses, the Find File screen shown in Figure 6.15b keeps a running tally of the files searched, and the number of files found.

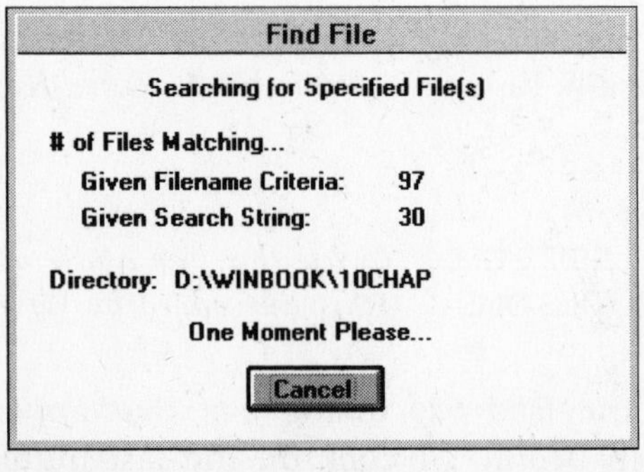

Figure 6.15b The Find File report appears during the search process.

At the end of the search, the Find File Results dialog box shown in Figure 6.15c lists the names of all files found and summarizes the search criteria. In this example, 30 document files contained the word "figure." Double-click on any found file to open it, and click on the Return to File Manager button when you are ready to close the Find File utility.

**Show File Size Information.** This option performs the same function as that described on the Info Menu earlier in the chapter. In addition, the option is made available via the next-to-last button on the Toolbar.

Window Menu (Figure 6.3i). Use this menu to configure the Directory Windows and icons that appear in the File Manager's Application Window.

**Arrange Icons.** If any Directory Windows have been minimized to Directory Icons at the bottom of the Application Window, click on this option to arrange them in an orderly horizontal row. Chances are the icon titles will overlap, since the displayed directory paths and names are usually on the long side. You can always use the Control Panel's _Desktop_ applet (described in Chapter 11) to increase the horizontal spacing, but since this adjustment also affects all the icons in your Program Manager's group windows, it's probably not worth the bother.

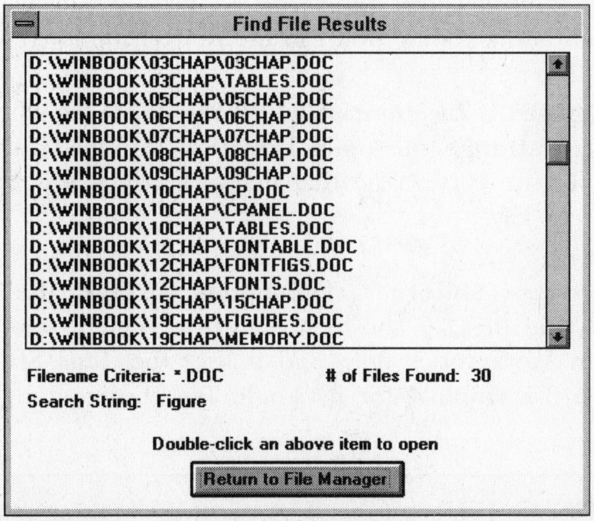

```
Find File Results

D:\WINBOOK\03CHAP\03CHAP.DOC
D:\WINBOOK\03CHAP\TABLES.DOC
D:\WINBOOK\05CHAP\05CHAP.DOC
D:\WINBOOK\06CHAP\06CHAP.DOC
D:\WINBOOK\07CHAP\07CHAP.DOC
D:\WINBOOK\08CHAP\08CHAP.DOC
D:\WINBOOK\09CHAP\09CHAP.DOC
D:\WINBOOK\10CHAP\CP.DOC
D:\WINBOOK\10CHAP\CPANEL.DOC
D:\WINBOOK\10CHAP\TABLES.DOC
D:\WINBOOK\12CHAP\FONTABLE.DOC
D:\WINBOOK\12CHAP\FONTFIGS.DOC
D:\WINBOOK\12CHAP\FONTS.DOC
D:\WINBOOK\15CHAP\15CHAP.DOC
D:\WINBOOK\19CHAP\FIGURES.DOC
D:\WINBOOK\19CHAP\MEMORY.DOC

Filename Criteria: *.DOC        # of Files Found:  30
Search String:  Figure

Double-click an above item to open
Return to File Manager
```

Figure 6.15c The Find File Results dialog box lists the files that meet the search criteria.

Cascade **(Shift+F5).** This option resizes all your open directory windows and cascades them within the Application Window, as was shown in Figure 3.10a in Chapter 3.

Directory Window List. The numbered list immediately under the Refresh option shows the names of all open and closed directory windows, and the check mark in the left margin indicates the currently active (open) or highlighted (closed) window. Double-click on any name in the list to make that window active. If the selected window is closed, it opens automatically, and is displayed in the center of the larger Application Window.

New Window. Click on this option to open another Directory Window within the Application Window. When the new window opens, it displays the same contents as the previously active window. However, either one may not be changed without affecting the other.

Refresh **(F5).** The first time you click on a drive icon, the contents of that drive are displayed in a directory window. If you click on a different drive icon, the display changes as you would expect it to. However, if you display the contents of a diskette (or any other removable media), then replace that diskette with another, subsequent clicks on the drive icon will simply redisplay the old information, which is no longer valid. Instead, make sure the active Directory Window is set to the desired drive, then select this option to refresh the display. Just press the F5 key—it's faster than opening the Window Menu and scrolling down to the Refresh option.

Tile **(Windows 3.1—Shift+F4),** *Tile Horizontally* **(Workgroups—no Shortcut key).** Select this option to arrange the open Directory Windows in horizontal tiles, as shown in Figure 6.16. Note that in Workgroups this option does not support a Shortcut key.

Tile Vertically **(Workgroups—Shift+F4).** This option arranges the open Directory Windows in vertical tiles, as shown in Figure 6.17. The Tile Vertically option is available in Workgroups only, and it uses the same Shortcut key that Windows version 3.1 employs for its single Tile (horizontally) option.

 WORKGROUPS NOTE: For some configurations of four or more Directory Windows, both Tile options may produce the same display.

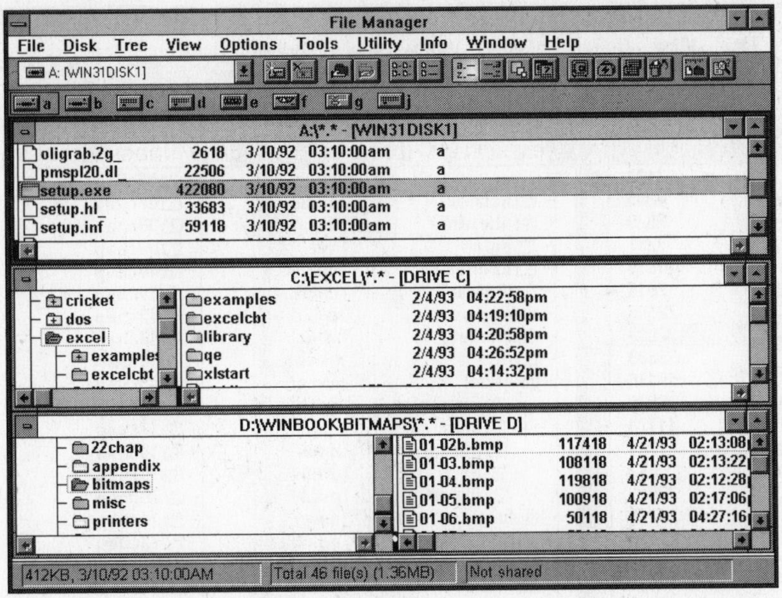

Figure 6.16 Three Directory Windows, as displayed by the Tile *(Windows)* or Tile Horizontally *(Workgroups)* option.

File Manager Configuration

This section reviews some of the procedures that may be used to configure the File Manager's Application Window to better suit individual preference.

Assign File Manager As Windows Shell

By default, the Program Manager is seen when Windows first opens. If you would rather use the File Manager as the Windows shell, edit the following line in the SYSTEM.INI file, as shown here:

```
[boot]
shell=winfile.exe
```

The next time Windows opens, the File Manager will appear on the Desktop instead of the customary Program Manager.

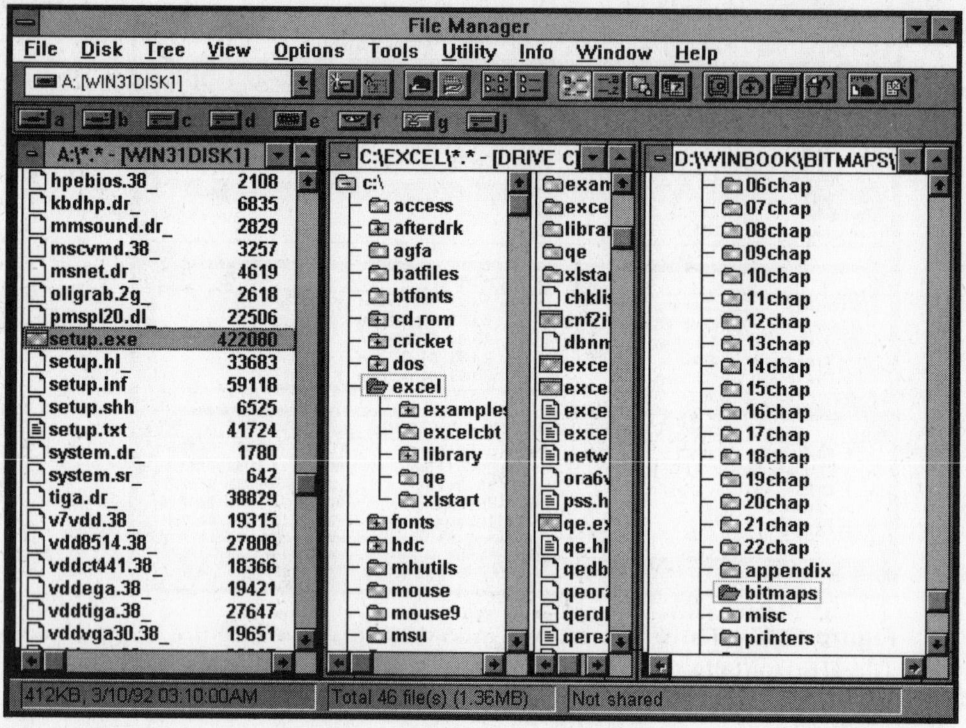

Figure 6.17   The three Directory Windows shown in the previous figure, after selecting the Tile Vertically option.

NOTE: If you elect to make this change, remember that doing so disables the StartUp Group. Refer to the *Load Startup Applets via WIN.INI* section which follows for further details.

Load Startup Applets via WIN.INI. If the File Manager is the Windows shell, the StartUp Group (described in Chapter 5) is ignored. Therefore, if you want to start selected applets as Windows opens, edit one of the following lines in your WIN.INI file:

```
[Windows]
load=PROGMAN.EXE filename.EXE
run=filename.EXE
```

In this example, the Program Manager is loaded as a minimized icon so that it is readily available if needed. Replace each *filename*.EXE above with the name of any other program you wish to load/run as Windows opens.

Reconfigure File Manager Access

When the File Manager is not the Windows shell, some users reassign the Task Manager's Ctrl+Esc shortcut keys to it by adding the following line to the SYSTEM.INI file:

```
[boot]
TaskMan.Exe=WINFILE.EXE
```

Also, drag a copy of the File Manager icon into the StartUp Group Window, and set its properties for Run Minimized. The next time Windows opens, the File Manager's minimized icon appears on the Desktop. If you press Ctrl+Esc or double-click on any unoccupied Desktop space, File Manager comes to the foreground. When you're finished with it, click on its minimize button if you expect to use it again during the current Windows session. If you close it instead, then you will have to press Ctrl+Esc twice to reopen it—once to reopen it as an icon, a second time to open its Application Window.

This procedure may be worthwhile if you never use the Task Manager. Otherwise, set the File Manager's Shortcut keys to Ctrl+Alt+F (or whatever) and leave Task Manager alone. That way, you have both capabilities available.

Configure Multiple Directory Windows

As shown earlier in Figure 6.1, the initial File Manager Application Window is good enough to illustrate various window components, but not very practical for much else. However, it's quite easy to configure a few Directory Windows so that File Manager can be used for real work. The following sections show how to configure four Directory Windows—two open and another two as minimized icons at the bottom of the Application Window. It might be worth the bother to run through this entire procedure at least once, then modify it as required to suit you own needs.

First, make sure that only one Directory Window is open within the File Manager's Application Window. In case of doubt, hold down the Ctrl key and repeatedly press F4 a few times, until doing so has no further effect. Each time you do this, one of the Directory Windows closes. When the keys have no further effect, then only one window remains open. Thus, you can click Ctrl+F4 repeatedly to select a single drive and directory (C:\WINDOWS, for example), then maximize it. Now open the Window Menu and select the New Window option three times. As you do, the File Manager's Title Bar changes as shown here.

```
File Manager - [C:\WINDOWS\.* - [DRIVE C]].
File Manager - [C:\WINDOWS\*.*:2 - [DRIVE C]].
File Manager - [C:\WINDOWS\*.*:3 - [DRIVE C]].
File Manager - [C:\WINDOWS\*.*:4 - [DRIVE C]].
```

Note that when only one Directory Window is open, no number appears in the display, but as each successive window opens, a number indicates that this is the *n*th window displaying this directory. Now click on the Restore button on the Directory Window's Menu Bar to see all four open Windows displayed in cascaded format within the File Managers' Application Window.

Configure Directory Windows 1 and 2. Minimize Window 3, then Window 4, both of which now appear as icons near the bottom of the Application Window. Click once on the C:\WINDOWS*.*:1 window, and select some other directory to display in it (C:\DOS, for example). Now open the Window Menu and select the T̲ile (Windows 3.1) or Tile H̲orizontally (Workgroups) option. Since the C:\DOS window was active when you selected the Tile option, it appears above the C:\WINDOWS*.*:2 window.

Having done all this, your File Manager Application Window should resemble that shown in Figure 6.18. In the figure, several application icons are seen at the bottom of the Windows Desktop, one of which is the minimized Print Manager icon. This will be put to use later on, for drag-and-drop printing as described in the *Setup Print Manager for Drag-and-Drop Printing* section below.

Change Directory Window Font. Refer to the F̲ont... option on the Options Menu (described earlier) for instructions on changing the font which displays directory and file information in the Directory Window.

Change Horizontal Icon Spacing. Chances are the titles under the minimized Directory Window icons overlap, since icon spacing appropriate within the Program Manager's open group windows may be a bit too tight to display lengthy path information. If this is a problem, you can change the following line in WIN.INI:

```
[Desktop]
IconSpacing=n
```

where *n* is the desired spacing, in pixels (try 150 or greater). However, this may be more trouble than it's worth, since the same pixel spacing affects application icons in the Program Manager's open group windows. Probably the best compromise is to optimize icon spacing for Program

Manager displays, and just drag minimized File Manager icons around as required, if their titles overlap.

Configure Directory Windows 3 and 4. Once the above display is more-or-less presentable, minimize the two open directory windows, then open the other two (that is, ":3" and ":4"). Reopen the Window Menu and select the Tile option described above. The Application Window should again resemble that shown in Figure 6.18, except that the two open directory windows show the C:\WINDOWS directory (assuming that's the one you used initially). Change both to display other directories that you frequently use.

Save Configuration. So that you won't ever have to go through this routine again, open the Options Menu and make sure the Save Settings on Exit option

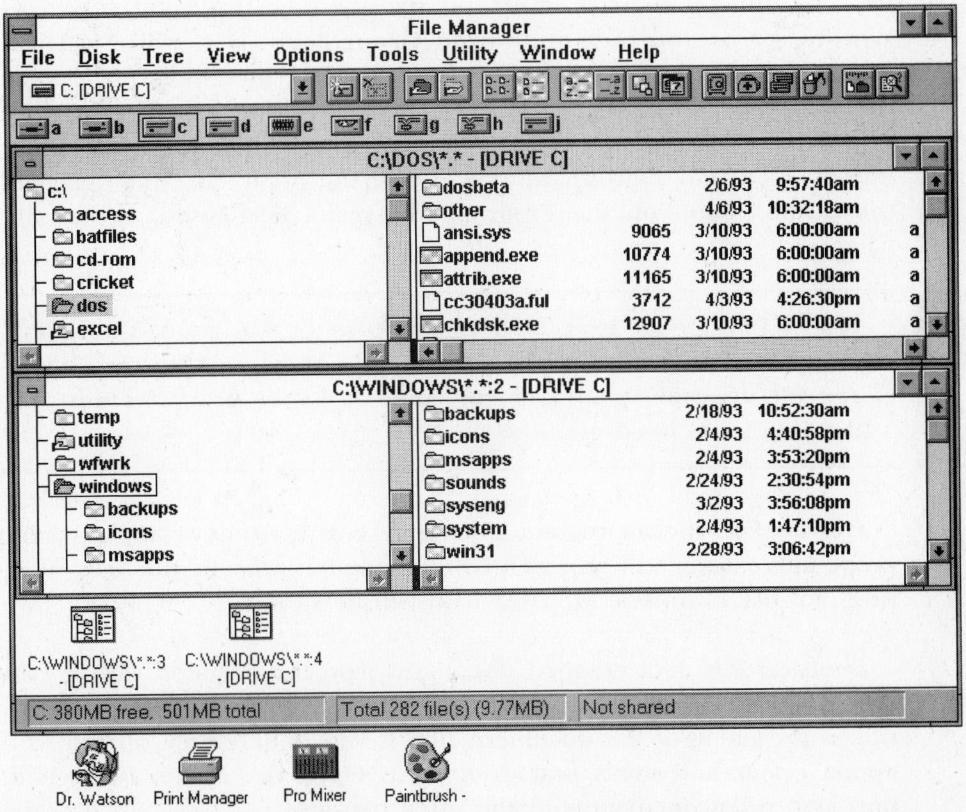

Figure 6.18 A typical File Manager Application Window showing two open Directory Windows and two minimized Directory Windows icons.

is checked. Then close and reopen Windows, return to the File Manager (which should look exactly like it did when you closed Windows), and clear the check mark next to the Save Settings on Exit option. With your current settings preserved for posterity (or until you change your mind), subsequent rearrangements will not override the configuration described here.

Drag-and-Drop Configuration Procedures

This section describes the ways in which the Windows drag-and-drop feature may be put to use within the File Manager.

Setup Applet in Program Manager. The drag-and-drop feature can be used to install an applet by dragging a program or document icon from any File Manager Directory Window into the Program Manager Application Window. The icon must be dropped either in an open Group Window or on top of a minimized Group Icon. Depending on the type of icon that is dragged into the Program Manager, the result will be as described below.

The drag-and-drop procedure cannot be used to delete an applet that was dragged into a group window. Once the applet is safely installed, use the Delete option on the Program Manager's File Menu, as described in Chapter 3.

> **NOTE:** When an icon is dragged into the Program Manager, the original icon remains in place in the File Manager Directory Window, and the appropriate applet icon appears in the group window where the icon is dropped off.

Program File. If the program icon represents a Windows applet, the appropriate applet icon will appear in the group window. In the case of a DOS program file, a generic MS-DOS icon will be shown.

Document File. If a dragged document icon is associated with a Windows applet, the icon for that applet appears in the group window, and the icon title is the name of the document file. If you double-click on the icon, the applet opens and loads that document. Once the applet is opened, you may load other documents in the usual manner.

If the dragged document icon is not associated with a Windows applet, an *Invalid Path* error message will be seen.

Setup Print Manager for Drag-and-Drop Printing. In addition to double-clicking on a document icon to open the associated application and load the selected document, that document also can be printed by dragging its icon to the Print Manager, as described here.

The first step is to open the Print Manager applet in the Program Manager's Main Group Window, then minimize it. The Print Manager Icon should now appear near the bottom of the Windows Desktop, as shown in Figure 6.18. Now open the File Manager, highlight the document you wish to print, and hold down the primary mouse button. Drag the document icon over to the Print Manager icon and "drop" it by releasing the mouse button. The Print Manager should open the associated applet (the Notepad or Write applet, for example), load the document file, print it, then close the applet.

If the drag-and-drop procedure doesn't work, the required information for the file type you want to print is probably not registered in the registration database. Refer to the *Install File Association* section below for assistance.

Embed Object Package in Document. You can use drag-and-drop to embed one file within another. For example, consider a Write document (say, TEST.WRI) and a Paintbrush image (IMAGE.BMP, for example). Open TEST.WRI and size its application window so that the File Manager can also be seen. Locate the document icon for IMAGE.BMP, drag it into the Write document, and drop it at the desired location. A Paintbrush icon will appear there and its title will be IMAGE.BMP (or whatever you called it). Double-click on the icon to automatically open Paintbrush and display the IMAGE.BMP file.

Copy File or Directory. There are several methods to copy a file or the contents of an entire directory from one location to another.

Copy Source Icon to a Directory on the Same Drive. Select the source file or source directory icon, hold down the Ctrl key, drag the icon to the desired destination directory, and release the Ctrl key. If you dragged a directory icon, a copy of that directory is set up as a subdirectory at the target location, and copies are made of all the files in the source directory.

Copy Source Icon to a Directory on Another Drive. Simply drag the source icon to the desired location and drop it there. The file, or directory and its contents, are copied to the target location.

You can also copy to another drive by dragging the source icon to one of the Drive Icons on the File Manager's Drive Bar. However, you should first make sure that the selected Directory Window on the target drive is the one you want. Otherwise, the copied material may wind up in the wrong location.

Move File or Directory. To move a file or directory, follow one of the procedures described here.

Move Source Icon to Another Location on the Same Drive. Select the source file or source directory icon, and drag it to the new location. Release the primary mouse button to complete the transfer.

Move Source Icon to Directory on Another Drive. Select the source file or directory icon and hold down the Shift key while dragging it to the desired new location. You can drag the source icon to either a directory that is visible in another Directory Window, or to a Drive Icon on the File Manager's Drive Bar.

Select Multiple Files

You may want to copy, delete, or move more than one file at a time. To do so, use any of the following procedures to highlight the desired files, then perform the desired operation.

Highlight Selected Files. Hold down the Ctrl key and move the mouse pointer to any file icon. Click once to select it, then move to another icon and click again. When you have finished selecting files, release the Ctrl key.

Highlight Sequential List of Files. Select the first file in the list by clicking once on its icon. Then move the mouse pointer to the last file in the list. Hold down the Shift key and click once on the primary mouse button. All the files between the first and the last will be highlighted.

Exclude File(s) within Highlighted Group. Move the mouse pointer to the file that you do not want to include in an already highlighted list. Hold down the Ctrl key and click on the primary mouse button to deselect that file. Repeat as required to exclude other files from the list.

Disable Confirmation Messages

In these days of unerase and unformat utilities, you may feel that some of Windows' confirmation messages are no longer needed, or you may be one of those superconfident people who never make a misteak. If so, select the Confirmation... option on the Options menu and disable one or more of the available choices. The Mouse Action refers to the message which appears if you move or copy a file by dragging its icon with the mouse. Since it's difficult to make such a move by accident, it's probably safe enough to clear this one. As for the others, proceed at your own risk.

Disable File Sharing

The Disk Menu's Share As... and Stop Sharing;... options may be disabled by adding the following section and line to the WINFILE.INI file.

```
[restrictions]
NoShareCommands=1
```

With the line in place, neither option appears on the menu and the equivalent Toolbar buttons are deleted from the Toolbar.

Reconfigure File Associations

This section reviews the procedures used to install, change, or remove a file association. To begin each procedure, open the File Manager's File Menu and select the Associate... option to open the Associate dialog box shown in Figure 6.19. Then follow the instructions in the appropriate section below. Refer to the *Registration Database Applet* section of this chapter for additional information about the REG.DAT file mentioned here.

Editing the [Extensions] Section of WIN.INI. If you use the Windows System Editor (or similar) utility to edit the [Extensions] section, the edit will have no effect if the same information is also contained in the registration database file (REG.DAT). Therefore, use the Associate... option to make sure that both the WIN.INI and REG.DAT files are modified as required.

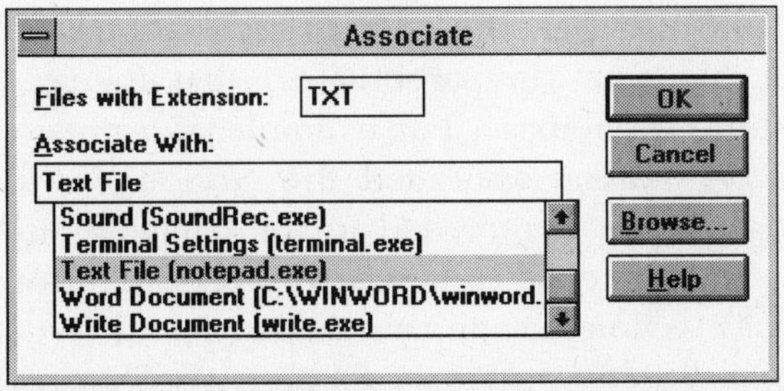

Figure 6.19 The Associate dialog box displays the file type currently associated with the extension shown at the top of the box.

If you know the file association information is found only in the [Extensions] section, and/or you don't want to modify the registration database, then use your editor instead of the **Associate** option to make the required changes. Remember, however, that registration database information (if any) takes precedence over the WIN.INI file.

Install New File Association. Type the new file extension in the <u>F</u>ile with Extension: box, then scroll through the list of executable file types and highlight the desired selection. The selected file type appears in the <u>A</u>ssociate With: box.

The list of file types is taken from the Registration Database's REG.DAT file (not from the [Extensions] section of WIN.INI), and it might not contain the executable file type you are looking for. If it doesn't, click on the <u>B</u>rowse... button, search for the appropriate executable file, and double-click on it. Its path and filename will appear in the <u>A</u>ssociate With: box. Click on the OK button to conclude the procedure. From now on, if you double-click on any document icon with the extension you specified, the executable file you just selected will open and load the document file.

If you had to use the <u>B</u>rowse... button to find an executable file, then you can't take advantage of the drag-and-drop print feature, although you can open a document file as just described. If the new document file is printable, and you need drag-and-drop printing, then refer to the *Registration Info Editor* section later in this chapter for instructions on editing the REG.DAT file to enable this feature.

Change or Review File Association. Type the appropriate file extension in the <u>F</u>iles with Extension: box, or highlight any file with that extension before selecting the <u>A</u>ssociate... option. The box at the top of the <u>A</u>ssociate With: area will show the file type currently associated with that extension, and both the file type and filename will be highlighted in the list of file types. To change the association, scroll the highlight bar to some other file type/name. Or, leave it alone if you simply want to review the current association.

If you need to change the filename (in parentheses) that follows a file type, you must edit the registration database. For example, if a previous installation of Norton's *Desktop for Windows* associated the Norton diskedit.exe applet with "Text File," that association is recorded in the database and cannot be changed back to "Test File (notepad.exe)" via the Association option. Refer to the *Registration Info Editor* section later in this chapter for more details.

Remove File Association. To cancel a file association, type the three-letter extension for the file type. As you enter the final letter of the extension,

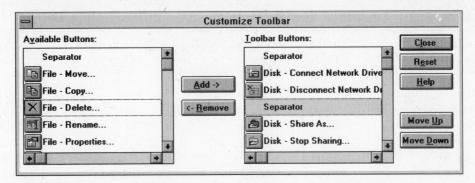

Figure 6.20   The Customize Toolbar dialog box is used to configure the buttons that appear on the *Windows-for-Workgroups* Toolbar.

the current association appears in the Associate With: box. Scroll to the top of the list, highlight (None), and click on the OK button to complete the procedure. The association is deleted from the list in the [Extensions] section of WIN.INI, and also from the registration database.

Toolbar Configuration

The arrangement of buttons on the Toolbar may be easily reconfigured to suit the user's individual needs. To begin, double-click on any unoccupied area on the Toolbar to open the Customize Toolbar dialog box shown in Figure 6.20. The Available buttons seen on the left-hand side of the dialog box are listed in Table 6.2, along with the default Toolbar buttons. To add an available button to the Toolbar, first highlight an existing button in the Toolbar Buttons box. Then highlight any available button and click on the Add–> button to insert it immediately before the highlighted button in the right-hand box. Use the <–Remove button to delete an existing Toolbar button. To adjust the spacing between buttons, add and/or remove the Separators seen in the Toolbar Buttons box. The Separators at the beginning and the end of the list are not removable.

The current Toolbar configuration is recorded in the WINFILE.INI file as shown here:

```
[Settings]
ToolBar=1                      0 = disable, 1 = enable Toolbar
NumButtons=xx00                xx = hexadecimal number of buttons
ToolbarWindow=wxyzwxyzwxyz….   wxyz = a hexadecimal code of each button
```

Each separator (except the first and the last) is counted as a button, and the code for each button is listed in the Toolbar code column in Table 6.2.

TABLE 6.2 **Available and Default Toolbar Buttons***

Menu and Options	Toolbar Code	Menu and Options	Toolbar Code	Menu and Options	Toolbar Code
Disk		**File (cont.)**		**View**	
Connect Network Drive[†]	CE00	Properties	6E00	All File Details	9201
Disconnect Network Drive[†]	CD00	Rename	6D00	by File Type[†]	9901
Share As[†]	FE00	Search	6800	Name only[†]	9101
Stop Sharing[†]	FF00	Select Files	7400	Partial Details	9301
				Sort by Date[†]	9701
DOS 6.0		**Help**		Sort by Name[†]	9401
Compression info[‡]	FB02	Contents	4D04	Sort by Size[†]	9601
Run Anti-virus[‡]	FA02			Sort by Type[†]	9501
Run Backup[‡]	5902	**Options**			
Run Undelete[‡]	5C02	Font	FE01	**Window**	
				Cascade	E903
File		**Separator**	FFFF	New Window	EE03
Copy	6B00	(not a menu item)		Tile Horizontally	EB03
Create Directory	6F00			Tile Vertically	EA03
Delete	6C00	**Utility** [§]			
Move	6A00	File Size Info.	2103		
Print	6600	Find File	2203		

[*] Each button duplicates an option on indicated File Manager menu.
  Toolbar code appears on ToolbarWindow= line in [Settings] section of WINFILE.INI.
[†] Default Toolbar buttons.
[‡] Additional default buttons, if DOS 6.0 Windows applets are installed. Undelete
  option also appears on File Manager's File Menu.
[§] Menu and Toolbar buttons included with Windows-for-Workgroups Resource Kit.

Status Bar Text Configuration

To change the font and point size for the Status Bar text, refer to the section with this name in Chapter 10.

Network Configuration

This section reviews configuration and a few operating procedures that become available if Windows-for-Workgroups is installed on two or more computers that are linked by a network.

VERSION NOTE: The very first edition of Windows-for-Workgroups was launched as "version 3.1" so that future—and presumably, simultaneous—updates of the two Windows products might bear the same version number.

Network Definitions

It's just about impossible to get through the following descriptions without lapsing into a bit of network jargon. Therefore, this section offers the briefest of explanations of the terms encountered later on.

Client. Any computer that accesses files stored on some other computer on a network.

Computer Name. A unique alphanumeric string of one to fifteen characters assigned to each computer on the network, for purposes of identifying it to other computers on the network.

Local Computer. A term used here to identify the computer that the reader is currently using, regardless of its current status (client or server).

Network. The hardware/software required to link two or more computers.

NetBIOS (Network Basic Input/Output System). The NetBIOS interface establishes logical names for network drives and oversees data exchange between network computers.

NetBEUI (NetBIOS Extended User Interface). This is the network protocol supported by Windows-for-Workgroups.

Network Drive. On any local computer, each shared directory (and subdirectories, if any) is identified on a remote computer by its own drive letter, and is referred to as a network drive. Thus, a local C:\WINWORD\DOCUMENT shared directory might be network drive x on one remote computer, and network drive y on another. In each case, network drive x or y is simply the next available drive letter on that computer.

NOTE: The Windows Smart Drive utility does not cache network drives.

Peer-to-Peer. A phrase used to identify a network system in which each computer may function as both a client and a server.

Redirector. A network redirector determines whether "drive x" is an actual physical drive on the local system, or a logical (network) drive located elsewhere. If it's the latter, the redirector arranges an SMB (server message block) protocol to transmit data to and from the network drive.

Remote Computer. A term used here to identify any computer on the network other than the one the reader is currently using.

Server. Any network computer on which one or more local directories may be shared with client computers. Each such shared directory becomes a network drive on the client computer.

Shared Directory. On the local (server) computer, any directory that has been made available for the user by remote (client) computers.

Workgroup. Two or more computers linked by a network.

Workstation. Any computer linked to others on a network.

Software Configuration

The Workgroups Setup procedure adds its share of device drivers and a TSR to your startup files; these additions are briefly reviewed here. Much of the information presented here is based on Microsoft's *Windows for Workgroups Resource Kit*, which should be consulted by anyone in search of an in-depth discussion of network matters.

CONFIG.SYS. In order to open Workgroups in any mode, the Setup procedure adds the following lines to your CONFIG.SYS file:

```
device=C:\WINDOWS\PROTMAN.DOS /i:c:\WINDOWS    (protocol manager)
device=C:\WINDOWS\filename.DOS                 (NDIS driver)
device=C:\WINDOWS\WORKGRP.SYS                  (MS-DOS device driver)
```

The purpose of each line is briefly described below.

Protocol Manager. The PROTMAN.DOS file is the network protocol manager. The /i: switch above specifies the directory in which it looks for the

PROTOCOL.INI file. The file provides configuration information for the network adapter and device driver.

NDIS Driver (**filename.***DOS*). Table 6.3 lists the NDIS (network device interface specification) drivers that are supplied with Workgroups. The name of one of these drivers appears on the second CONFIG.SYS line above.

TABLE 6.3   NDIS Device Drivers Supplied with Windows-for-Workgroups*

Adapter Card	Device Driver	netcard= (PROTOCOL.INI)
3Com EtherLink II	ELNKII.DOS	ms$elnkii
3Com EtherLink III	ELNK3.DOS	ms$elnk3
3Com EtherLink 16	ELNK16.DOS	ms$elnk 16
3Com EtherLink/MC	ELNKMC.DOS	ms$elnkmc3
3Com EtherLink Plus	ENLKPL.DOS	ms$elnkpl
3Com TokenLink	TLNK.DLS	ms$toklnk
Advanced Micro Devices AMC100/PCnet	AM2100.DOS	ms$am2100
Cabletron E2010-X	E20NDSI.DOS	ms$cb120
Cabletron E2112	E2INDIS.DOS	ms$cb121
CDA 10 Mb˙	MAC586.SYS	ms$dca10
DEC EtherWorks	DEPCA.DOS	ms$depca
Everex SpeedLink /PC16 (EV2027)	EVX16.DOS	ms$spdlk16
Hewlett-Packard LAN	HPLANB.DOS	ms$hp272_
IBM Token Ring	IBMTOK.DOS	ms$ibmtr_
Intel EtherExpress 16	EXP16.DOS	ms$ee16
Intel Motherboard Module	182593.DOS	
Intel TokenExpress 16/4	OLITOL.DOS	ms$intisa
NCR Token Ring	STRN.DOS	ms$ncrtr_
Novell/Anthem NE1000	NE1000.DOS	ms$ne1000
Novell/Anthem NE2000	NE2000.DOS	ms$ne2000
Proteon ISA Token Ring	PRO4.DOS	ms$pro_
Proteon Token Ring	NDIS39XR.DOS	ms$pro_
Racal-Interlan N16510	N16510.DOS	ms$ni6510
SMC (WD) EtherCard Plus	SMCMAC.DOS	ms$smc_
SMC 3000 series	SMC3000.DOS	ms$smc3k
SMC ArcNet	SMC_ARC.DOS	ms$smc_
Thomas Conrad TC6_4_	TCCARC.DOS	ms$tc6_4_
Xircom Pocket Ethernet II	PE2NDIS.DOS	ms$xirc

* Underline indicates character/number which depends on specific adapter card model number. Additional drivers are available through the Windows Driver Library (see Appendix D).

MS-DOS Device Driver. This real-mode driver is in turn used by the VNB.386 (NetBEUI transport) and VREDIR.386 (network redirector) virtual device drivers.

AUTOEXEC.BAT. The Setup procedure adds a command line which sets up the network drivers specified in the CONFIG.SYS file and loads network software:

C:\WINDOWS\NET start

The following reports should be seen as the line is executed:

Microsoft Netbind version 2.1
Microsoft NetBEUI version 2.1   *(on 286 systems only)*
The command completed successfully.

> **NOTE:** The command line above releases some 100 Kbytes of conventional memory that the CONFIG.SYS drivers occupy until NET.EXE is executed for the first time. Therefore, this line should remain in the AUTOEXEC.BAT file even if you don't open Workgroups every time you turn on the computer.

Standard Mode on 286 Systems. The NET start command automatically loads the required net BIOS interface and redirector into conventional memory, where they take up about 38 (NETBEUI) and 84 (REDIR) Kbytes, respectively.

In order to release this memory at the conclusion of a Windows session, type NET STOP at the DOS prompt. Just remember to type NET START again if you want to reopen Workgroups.

Standard Mode on 386 Systems. Workgroups may of course be opened in Standard Mode by typing WIN /s at the DOS prompt. However, on 386 systems the NET start command does not automatically load the Net BIOS interface and network redirector required for standard-mode operation. The following batch file will load the required software, run Workgroups in Standard Mode, and unload the network software when Windows closes.

NET start workstation
WIN /s
NET stop

SHARE.EXE and Windows-for-Workgroups. In Enhanced Mode operation, the DOS Share (SHARE.EXE) utility is not required, since the equivalent functions are built into Word-for-Windows. If your AUTOEXEC.BAT file loads SHARE.EXE, you can delete it unless you need it for DOS applications or for use in Standard Mode.

Shared File Report. If the Status Bar (described earlier) reports a directory as shared, you can see if any remote computer is currently accessing that directory by opening the File Menu and selecting the Properties... option (see *Properties...* section earlier in the chapter). When the Properties dialog box shown in Figure 6.11b or c appears, click on the Open by... button to display one of the dialog boxes described below. In each dialog box, you may highlight one or more files, then click on the Close Files button to sever the remote user's connection to that file or files. An advisory message prompts you to confirm that you really want to close the file.

 NOTE: If you know a remote user is accessing a shared file in one of your directories, but the dialog box does not report that usage, it may be due to a bug in Workgroups version 3.1. Refer to the *Inaccurate Usage Report* in the *Network Troubleshooting* section below for further details.

Open Files Dialog Box. If you highlighted a shared directory prior to opening the Properties dialog box, the Open Files dialog box shown in Figure 6.21a reports the following information:

Share Name:	The directory Share Name
Path:	The complete path for the shared directory
Open Count:	The number of local files currently open on remote systems
Open Files Box:	For each open file, the following information is listed:
Open by	Remote user name
Access	File Status
Filename	Local directory and filename

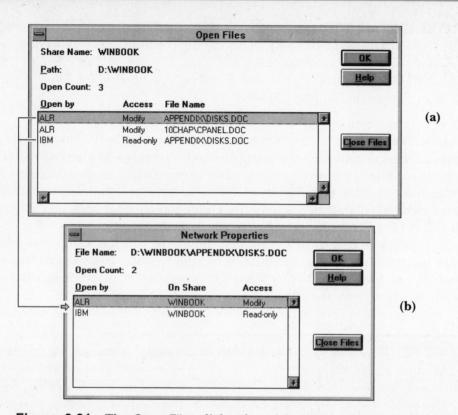

Figure 6.21 The Open Files dialog box (a) reports the names of any remote users who are accessing a file in a local shared directory. The name of each open file is also seen. The Network Properties dialog box (b) reports remote usage information about a specific file in the local shared directory. The arrow points out how the same information appears in both dialog boxes.

Network Properties Dialog Box. If you highlight a shared file instead of a directory, this box (Figure 6.21b) displays a similar report in a slightly different format.

Filename:	The path and name of the shared file
Open Count:	The number of users currently reading the shared file
Open Files Box:	For each open file, the following information is listed:
Open by	Remote user name
On Share	The directory Share Name (same as Share Name, above)
Access	File Status

Registration Database Applet

This section describes the *Registration Database* Applet, for the possible benefit of readers adventurous enough to use it and for the certain confusion of everyone else. Skip ahead to the *Troubleshooting* section if you're not that interested in fine-tuning the File Manager. For most routine operations, the information presented here is not really needed.

In order for the File Manager to open or print a document file, it needs to identify the applet or application with which that file is associated. Given that information, File Manager opens the appropriate application, loads the highlighted file, and if so instructed, prints it. The data that make all this happen are maintained in the Registration Info Database file (REG.DAT) found in the Windows directory.

Under normal circumstances, the database is maintained by Windows itself, and the appropriate information is added to the REG.DAT file as various applets and applications are installed, or when executed for the first time. However, if it should become necessary to modify this information, a *Registration Info Editor* applet may be added to the Accessories (or any other) Group Window.

The Registration Info Editor. The *Registration Info Editor* applet (REG-EDIT.EXE) is undocumented in the Windows *User's Guide,* and is not installed as part of the regular Setup procedure. Therefore, if you want to use it, you'll have to install it as described in the *Setup non-Windows Applet* section of Chapter 1. After you've done this, click on the editor's icon to open the Registration Info Editor Window. Both the icon and the window are shown in Figure 6.22. The first eleven entries are written to the database during the regular Windows Setup procedure (Windows 3.1 omits the Microsoft Mail entry). Additional entries appear as Windows applications are installed, as shown by *Word, Excel,* and other examples in the figure. In actual practice, the complete list is in alphabetical order and, of course, will vary from one system to another.

Modify File Type Dialog Box. You may want to edit the registration database to change the way File Manager reacts when you either open a document file for editing or drag it to the Print Manager for printing. This section describes the procedure for doing so by first reviewing the component parts of the Modify File Type dialog box and then by actually editing the database.

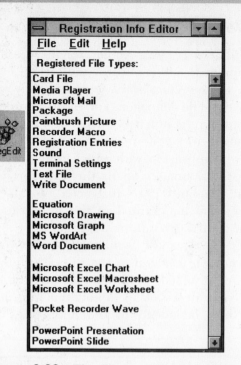

Figure 6.22 The Registration Info Editor's applet icon and applet window. The first group of file types are installed during the Windows Setup procedure. Others are added as applications are installed.

To open the Modify File Type dialog box shown in Figure 6.23, double-click on the appropriate entry in the Registered File Types: list (Figure 6.22), or open the Edit Menu and select the Modify File Type... option. The components shown in the dialog box are described here.

Identifier: This unique keyword describes the file type within the database, and cannot be changed within this dialog box (see *Add New File Type* below for information on changing this parameter while creating a new database entry).

File Type: This is the file-type description as it appears in the following locations:

Dialog Box	Data Entry Box	See Figure
Associate	Associate with:	6.19
Modify File Type	File Type:	6.23

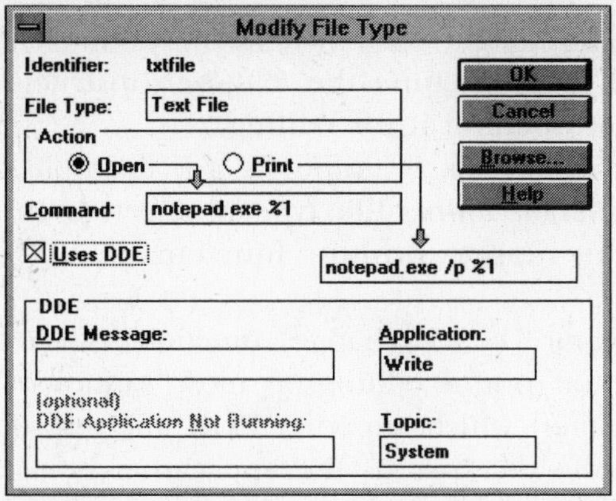

Figure 6.23 Use the Modify File Type dialog box to edit the registration database.

Action. As noted above, the File Manager can perform two actions on a highlighted file in its Current Directory Window. These actions are defined by the Command: box described below. Click on the desired radio button and note the command listed in the box.

Radio Button	Command: Box shows action taken if you:	Typical Example
Open	Double-click on a document icon	notepad.exe %1
Print	Drag-and-drop icon to the Print Manager icon	notepad.exe /p %1

Command:. As you click on either radio button described above, the command line changes to show the action that will be taken, as in the typical examples shown above, and in the composite illustration in Figure 6.23. Each command line is described immediately below.

Open Command. The arrowhead leading from the Open radio button points to the actual location of the Command: box, and that box shows the default *Text File* entry. Under default conditions, if you double-click on the document icon for any text file (TXT extension), the *Notepad* applet (notepad.exe) will be executed. The name of the highlighted document takes the place of the %1 parameter on the command line, and that file is automatically loaded for editing.

Print Command. The figure also shows how the command entry would change (slightly) if the Print radio button were clicked instead. If you drag the document icon to the Print Manager icon instead of double-clicking on it, *Notepad* is again executed, but this time the /p switch instructs it to load and print the file, instead of opening it for editing.

In several cases the P̲rint command box is empty, as for example, if either the *Recorder Macro* or *Registration Entries* file type is selected. In both cases, the selected applet does not support printing functions.

DDE Support.   The DDE (Dynamic Data Exchange) functions are not covered here, nor are they required for routine editing of most Windows applet entries. In the case of an application which supports DDE, the appropriate information will be written into the database as the application is installed. For example, if *Excel, Word,* or some other major application is already entered in the database, select that file type and review the entries seen in the DDE boxes. Refer to the on-line Help system for additional details.

Editing the Database.   The following examples show how the registration database might be edited to modify an existing entry, add a new one, or delete an entry if an application is removed.

Modify an Existing Database Entry.   As an example of database modification, consider a user who prefers to edit text files with the DOS Edit utility (EDIT.COM) instead of *Notepad*. To begin, open the *Registration Info Editor* applet and double-click on the Text File entry to open the Modify File Type dialog box shown in Figure 6.23. Make sure the O̲pen radio button is selected, and then edit the C̲ommand: line as shown here.

Change:	To:
notepad.exe %1	C:\DOS\EDIT.COM %1

Click on the OK button and then close the Editor applet. The next time you open File Manager and click on a text file, that file will be loaded into the DOS Edit utility instead of into *Notepad.*

If you don't use drag-and-drop to print text files, you can always leave the default O̲pen command intact and edit the P̲rint box instead. Click on that radio button and replace the command line with the DOS command shown above. Now if you drag the document icon to the Print Manager, EDIT.COM loads the file for editing. It's not exactly standard operating procedure, but it is one way to choose between two edit utilities, to say nothing of discouraging casual users away from your system.

Add a New Database Entry.   There are two ways to add a new entry to the database. The obvious technique is to open the Edit Menu, select the Add File Type... option and go to it. The Add File Type dialog box (not shown) is similar to the Modify File Type box shown in Figure 6.23, except that the Identifier: entry at the top of the box also must be specified. If you wish, you can create a completely new category by entering the appropriate information in each entry box.

A slightly faster alternative may be to highlight a similar file type first, and then select the Copy File Type... option instead. When the Copy File Type dialog box (also not shown) opens, the parameters for the selected file type are already in place. Use them as a guide in creating the new entry, then give the whole works a distinctive name in the Identifier: box. When you're finished, click on the OK button to save the new file type to the database.

Delete a Database Entry.   If you remove an application from your system, you may want to open the *Registration Info Editor* and delete its file-type references, if any. For example, the three *Excel* file types seen in Figure 6.22 are not needed if that application is deleted. To purge each one from the database, highlight it and then open the Edit Menu and select the Delete File Type option. Repeat the procedure for every other file type to be deleted. This operation is certainly not critical, but it is just one more way to save a few bytes.

Advanced Database Editing.   For a closer look at the registration database, open the *Registration Info Editor* in its "verbose" mode by opening the Program Manager's File Menu and selecting the Run... option. Type REGEDIT /v in the Command Line: box to open the advanced Registration Info Editor dialog box shown in Figure 6.24. In actual practice, the entire database appears in one, long, continuous line that requires a fair amount of scrolling to review. In the figure, the contents have been split into three columns so that the basic 11 entries can be seen. For comparison with the simpler dialog box shown earlier in Figure 6.22, the entries have been arranged in the same order and each File Type is highlighted by a box around it. Needless to say, neither of these amenites is actually present in the on-screen display (maybe next year). To edit any entry, highlight it and make the necessary changes in the Full Path: and Value: boxes at the top of the dialog box. In Figure 6.24, the *Paintbrush* applet's Open command line (in column 2) is highlighted.

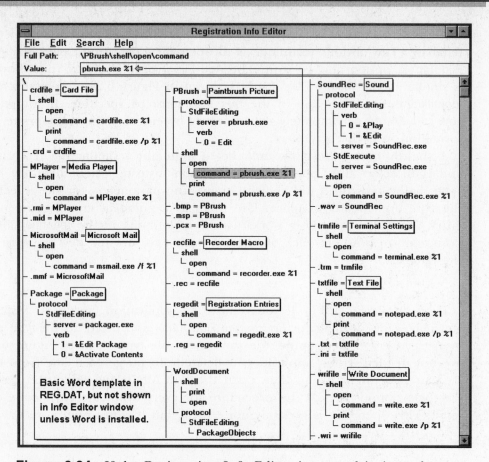

Figure 6.24   If the Registration Info Editor is opened in its verbose mode, this much expanded application window is seen.

If you regularly use the verbose mode, you can, of course, modify the applet's command line so that the Editor always opens in this mode. To do so, open the Program Item Properties box and rewrite the Command line as shown here:

REGEDIT.EXE /v

Or set up two applets, one with and the other without the /v switch.

Database Support in WIN.INI. As the Registration database is created, equivalent entries are added to the indicated section of WIN.INI as shown here. The first three entries are written as Windows is installed, or rewritten later if the database needs to be rebuilt (see *Build New Registration Info*

Database below). Other entries may be added as various Windows applications are installed, executed, or merged into the database. A few typical examples are also shown here.

```
[embedding]
SoundRec    = Sound,              Sound,              soundrec.exe,       picture
Package     = Package,            Package,            packager.exe,       picture
PBrush      = Paintbrush Picture, Paintbrush Picture, pbrush.exe,         picture
Equation    = Equation,           Equation,           (path)\eqnedit.exe, picture
ExcelChart  = MS Excel Chart,     MS Excel Chart,     C:\EXCEL\EXCEL.EXE, picture
MPlayer     = Media Clip,         Media Clip,         mplayer.exe,        picture
```

The [embedding] section is required only for compatibility with Windows 3.0 applications. You might want to delete it if space is tight and you know you are not using any such applications.

Registration Info Editor Support in WIN.INI. There's not much of it, but the applet window dimensions are preserved as shown here:

```
[RegEdit]
width=xxx      (width, in pixels)
height=xxx     (height, in pixels)
```

Build New Registration Info Database. This section describes how to build a new registration database, as might be required if the present one is corrupt or missing. If an error message indicated *There is a problem with the REG.DAT file,* exit Windows, erase that file from the Windows directory and reopen Windows. As you do, entries already listed in the [embedding] section of WIN.INI are automatically written into a new REG.DAT file, and this may be sufficient to resolve the problem. To find out, try to open the *Registration Info Editor* applet. If it opens, and the first eleven entries shown in Figure 6.22 are seen, skip ahead to the *Reinstall Other Database Entries* section. Otherwise, continue reading here.

Reinstall Basic Database. If the Registration Info Editor window shows an empty list of *Registered File Types:*, or if the list does not include the 11 items listed at the top of Figure 6.22, then open the applet's File Menu, select the <u>M</u>erge Registration File... option and then select the System directory. The SETUP.REG file should appear in the <u>M</u>erge Registration File dialog box (not shown). If it does not, then expand a fresh copy from the distribution diskettes into the System directory. Once the file is available, select it. An on-screen message should report that "Information in

C:\WINDOWS\SYSTEM\SETUP.REG has been successfully registered in the registration database." Click on the OK button and the Registration Info Editor dialog box will show the 10 (Windows 3.1) or 11 (Workgroups) applet entries from the above file.

Reinstall Other Database Entries. If you're not sure about other entries that may belong in your database, you can do a directory search for any files with a REG extension. If the search finds anything, merge the file(s) into the database by repeating the procedure described above for each file. For example, the second group of entries shown in Figure 6.22 (*Equation* through *Word Document*) were added when a WW20.REG file from the C:\WINWORD directory was merged. This file is included with Word-for-Windows version 2.0b and later releases for the purpose of rebuilding the database if that becomes necessary.

If you don't find other REG files, chances are that additional entries will be automatically added to the database as you run various Windows applications. For example, the three *Microsoft Excel* entries in Figure 6.22 are added the first time *Excel* is executed. A few other entries also are shown in the figure and, of course, your own list may contain still other entries.

File Manager Troubleshooting

This section describes a few File Manager problems that may not be accompanied by an error message.

Directory Tree Does Not Show Branches when File Manager Opens. If   you enable the Expand All option on the File Manager's View Menu, the expanded directory tree will not be seen the next time you open the File Manager, even if you have also enabled the Save Settings on Exit option. You'll just have to put up with this quirk until it gets fixed (maybe) in a future Windows update.

Diskette Directory Window Shows Incorrect Listings. If you swap diskettes in a drive, then click on that drive's icon, File Manager redisplays the directory of the just-removed diskette, instead of the current diskette. The cure for this File Manager quirk is to press function key F5 to display the correct directory. This is equivalent to, and faster than, selecting the Refresh option on the Windows Menu.

If the problem persists, the drive's diskette-changed sensing mechanism may be faulty. To verify this, exit Windows and try the same operation at the DOS prompt. If the system still fails to recognize a changed diskette, then the drive system needs to be repaired.

Diskette Drive Accessed As File Manager Reopens. If you close File Manager while a diskette directory is displayed, then reopen it, File Manager accesses that drive as it reopens. If a diskette is present, its directory is displayed; otherwise, the drive C directory is seen. Or, if File Manager closed while displaying more than one Directory Window, the space formerly occupied by the now-empty drive is simply left blank.

If you don't want File Manager to look at your diskette drives the next time it opens, close all diskette drive windows before exiting File Manager.

Diskette Drive Problems with DRIVER.SYS File. Windows does not get along very well with the DRIVER.SYS file that is sometimes used to create a logical disk drive. For example, if you install DRIVER.SYS in your CONFIG.SYS file so that your physical drive A also can be used as logical drive B, the drive A or B icon may not appear on the Drive Bar. Or, the icon may be present but File Manager can't access the drive anyway. Other problems include erroneous error messages and system hangups.

Until an upgraded DRIVER.SYS becomes available, the solution is to remove this driver from your CONFIG.SYS file.

Document File Cannot Be Viewed. There are a few cases in which a document file will not appear to open within an associated applet. As a specific example, the Word-for-Windows WINWORD.INI file is unlike most other INI files, in that it is not a conventional ASCII text file. If you've created an association between INI files and say, the Windows Notepad applet, this INI file will be displayed as a long single line of meaningless symbols, along with some text fragments.

If you encounter a similar association problem, try opening a few other files with the same extension as the problem file. If all other files are properly displayed, then the one that isn't is simply one of those files that bears an extension usually associated with text files. However, if there's a problem between an applet and all files with a certain extension, then either the association is invalid, or the applet itself is defective.

Double-Click on Document Icon Has No Effect. In this case, there is probably an incorrect association between the document icon and an executable file. To verify this, highlight the document icon, open the File Menu, and select the Associate... option. Note the name of the executable file that appears in the Associate With: box. It is probably not the correct file for use with the highlighted document icon. Select the proper file type, click on the OK button, and try again.

File Manager Application Window Is Offscreen. If you double-click on the File Manager icon and its Application Window does not show up on the Desktop, it may actually be open but offscreen. To retrieve it, minimize all open application Windows, then open the Task Manager (press Ctrl+Esc) and click on either the Cascade or Tile buttons. The File Manager Application Window should now be seen. Adjust its size as required, then enable the Save Settings on Exit option on the Options Menu.

Garbled Directory Tree Display. Certain Directory Window configurations may leave garbled text fragments in the Directory Tree Display. For example, if the vertical scroll bar is moved until part of the Directory Tree is obscured, and the right scroll arrow is used to view the hidden segment, text fragments will be seen if the vertical scroll is moved back to the right. You'll have to work at it to reproduce this quirk, but it's mentioned here in case you discover it by accident.

PIF Editor's Optional Parameters Ignored. If you create an association between certain document files and a DOS applet or other utility called by a PIF file, the optional parameters in the PIF file are ignored. For more details on this, refer to the *PIF Editor Configuration* section of Chapter 7.

Search Option Always Displays Hidden Files. Even if the Show Hidden/ System Files check box is cleared, the Search... option will display any hidden or system file that meets the search criteria.

StartUp Group Applets Are Not Executed. If the File Manager is used as the Windows shell, the StartUp Group is ignored. Therefore, you'll need to use the load= and run= lines in WIN.INI to open applets that you want to run as Windows opens.

Status Bar Reports Very Low Bytes Free. If the Status Bar report is suspiciously low (say, 10KB instead of 10,000KB free), refer to the *International Applet* section of Chapter 11. The "1000 Separator" is probably missing and, as a result, the bytes-free report is incorrectly truncated. This quirk is not found in Workgroups.

Network Operations Troubleshooting

Most network-related problems are accompanied by an error message which should help track down the source of the problem. However, there are those times when no error message appears, or worse—the error message that does show up doesn't seem related to the actual problem. If no message appears, then this section may help track down the source of the problem. It may also be of some use if the message is misleading and the *Error Messages* section doesn't contain enough information to resolve the problem.

Association (File/Applet) Is Incorrect. When you click on a document icon, the applet associated with that file should open and load the selected document. If the [Extensions] section of WIN.INI shows the association you want (for example, ini=C:\DOS\EDIT.COM ^.ini, to edit INI files with the DOS Edit utility), but some other applet opens instead (for example, Notepad), there is probably a conflict between the [Extensions] section and the registration database. To verify this, open the File Menu and select the <u>A</u>ssociate... option. Scroll through the list and look for the appropriate file type, which in this example would be "Text File." Note the accompanying filename in parentheses next to it. This is the executable file that opens when you double-click on the file icon. This information is taken from the Registration Database's REG.DAT file, and it takes precedence over your own instructions in the [Extensions] section of WIN.INI.

To resolve the conflict, you can either erase your new [Extensions] line and forget about it, or edit the registration editor's REG.DAT file so that the desired applet opens when you double-click on a document icon. To do the latter, refer to the *Registration Info Editor* section earlier in this chapter for assistance.

Delay in Closing Windows. If one or more network drives are enabled when you close Workgroups, there may be a delay until the DOS prompt appears. Wait at least 30 seconds before assuming the system has locked up. Sometimes, a three-finger salute will hasten the return of the DOS prompt.

File on Network Drive Doesn't Open when Local Document Icon Is Double-Clicked. If your Directory Window lists the contents of a network drive, but nothing happens when you double-click on an icon in that directory, the drive may no longer be available. To verify this, press function key F5 to refresh the Directory Window. If a *Shared directory cannot be found* message appears, then the drive's shared status has probably been disabled at the remote site.

File on Network Drive Opens As Read-Only, Despite Valid Full-Access Password. The most likely cause of this problem is that some other computer on the network has the same file open, and that computer has read-only access. To verify this, open another file on the same network drive. Unless that file is also in use elsewhere, you should get full access to it. If you want to make changes to the read-only file, you'll have to save it under a new name, or wait until the other computer is finished reading it.

If the other computer had full access to the file you wanted to read, you would have seen a message asking if you wanted to make a copy of the file instead of getting read-only access.

File Save Problem with Network Drive. If the system locks up when you attempt to save a file to a network drive, or the hourglass appears and won't go away, the most likely suspects are a busy system or the physical connection to the remote site. If you try a local reboot, you may see a message warning that *The system is either busy or has become unstable.* If you suspect a connection problem, try to resolve it, then press the Enter key. If this doesn't work, try another local reboot. If the same message reappears, then you'll probably have to press Ctrl+Alt+Del one more time to restart the whole works. But if you see a *This Windows application has stopped responding to the system* message, it's possible that the physical connection is now in order. Try pressing the Escape key to return to the application. If this actually works, save the file immediately, then try to figure out what the problem really was. Or, you may have to press the Enter key to terminate the current application.

Refer to the *Local Reboot Procedure* section of Chapter 4 if you need more information about the various messages that may be seen when you do a three-finger salute.

Log-On Problems. If you have problems logging on to the network and the *Network Error Messages* section of this chapter doesn't offer sufficient help, you may want to refer to the *Network Applet* section of Chapter 11 for additional assistance.

Remote Computer Not Available. If the local computer is having trouble connecting to a network drive, don't overlook the possibility that the computer on which that drive is located is among the missing—either the computer is not powered on, or Windows is not running. Before tearing your own configuration apart, make sure that all remote system components are powered on and network-ready. If more then two computers are on the network, try connecting to one of the others. If you can, then the problem is either at one of the remote computers, or in the connection leading to that computer. If you are unable to connect to any other computer, then the problem is either with your own network card, or with the cable leading to the other systems. Refer to the *Network Applet* section of Chapter 11 for assistance with network hardware and cabling.

Share Options Do Not Appear on Toolbar or Disk Menu. If you can't find the Share As... or Stop Sharing... options on either the Toolbar or the Disk Menu, your system is running in Standard Mode. If you have a 386 or better system, exit Windows and reopen it in Enhanced Mode. If you're using a 286 (IBM PC AT or equivalent), now's the time to think upgrade.

Usage Report Inaccurate in Network Properties or Open Files Dialog Box. In early releases of Workgroups, these dialog boxes don't report remote usage of certain shared files (with BMP, COM, EXE extensions for example). Therefore, about the only reliable way (short of a telephone call) to determine if a remote user is accessing such a file on your computer is via the Toolbar's Stop Sharing button (or that option on the Disk Menu). If you attempt to close a local directory that is currently in use, a warning message will appear. If the shared directory is not currently accessed, it closes without displaying a message.

Error Messages

The error messages are divided into several sections to make it a bit easier to find what you're looking for. If the message shows up when you attempt drag-and-drop printing, or is clearly related to network operations, then refer to either section below. Otherwise, continue reading right here.

General Error Messages

The error messages listed here are those most often associated with routine File Manager operations. If an error message refers to a specific Windows applet, then you may find additional help in the chapter in which that applet is described.

Access Denied. Make sure the disk is not full or write-protected. When trying to create a new directory, make sure the directory name is not already in use, that the disk is not write-protected, and so forth.

Cannot Copy *(filename.ext)*: Access denied. Source file may be in use. This message indicates you're trying to copy or move a file that is currently open in some Windows application. To do either, close the file from within the application that is using it, then try again.

Cannot Delete *(filename.ext)*: **Access denied. Make sure the disk is not full or write-protected.** If the file you want to delete is not write-protected, then it's possible that access is denied because the file is currently open. If so, you'll need to find the application that is using it, close the file, then delete it. Don't try to figure out that "is not full" phrase: It's part of a stock error message and doesn't have a thing to do with file deletion.

Cannot Move *(filename.ext)*: **File in use by Windows.** The message clearly explains why the file can't be moved. Depending on what it is you're trying to move, you'll either have to exit Windows, or close the applet you're trying to move.

Cannot Print File: There is no application associated with this file. Choose Associate from the File menu to create an association. To print a file, the File Manager's Print option (on the File Menu) opens the associated applet or application, loads the specified file, and commences printing. The error message is seen if the required association does not exist.

The File Menu's Associate option described earlier in the chapter shows how to add the required association to the registration database and to the [Extensions] section of the WIN.INI file.

Create Directory: File Manager cannot find the specified path. Make sure the correct path is specified. Although the message should be self-explanatory, it may also appear erroneously if you try to create a directory name that contains invalid characters. Try again, using valid characters for the directory name.

DblSpace Error: This drive is not compressed. Select a compressed drive before choosing DblSpace Info. If the DOS 6.0 applets are installed on a Windows system, the File Manager's Menu Bar offers a Tools Menu, and a Double Space Info option appears on that menu. If the error message appears when that option is selected, then the current drive is not compressed. Either compress the drive, or select another drive that has been compressed.

Directory does not exist. Do you want to create it? If this message makes some sense, then you don't need outside help to answer the question. But if the message makes no sense at all, it's probably because you are trying to rename a file on a write-protected diskette. Remove the write protection, try again, and you won't be troubled by this confusing message.

Drive I does not exist (or, some other error message referring to drive I). This puzzling message may show up if your AUTOEXEC.BAT file loads a version of GRAPHICS.COM that predates DOS 5.0. If you don't need GRAPHICS.COM, erase it and remove the offending line from AUTO-EXEC.BAT. Otherwise, update to DOS 5.0 or 6.0.

Cannot Run Program: File Manager cannot open or print the specified file. Start the application used to create this file, and open or print it from there. If this message shows up when you try to run a program (applet or application) by double-clicking on a document icon, then the "or print" phrase is a tip-off that there are two problems: Both the [extensions] section of WIN.INI and the registration database lack information Windows needs to open and to print (via drag-and-drop) the file.

There are two solutions: If you don't care about the drag-and-drop feature, all you need to do is edit the [Extensions] section of WIN.INI to create an association between the document file you tried to open and the applet required to do that. Or, use the Associate... option to provide drag-and-drop support too. In either case, refer to the *Reconfigure File Association* section earlier in the chapter for assistance.

Cannot Run Program: There is no application associated with this file. Choose Associate from the File menu to create an association. If you double-click on a file in the Directory Window, the application associated with that file should open; then load the selected file. If it doesn't, the File Manager hasn't been set up to recognize the extension of the file you selected. Refer to the *Install File Association* section for assistance.

File Manager cannot [copy *or* move] *(path and directory name)*: **This destination directory is a subdirectory of the source directory.** The "This destination" phrase refers to the directory into which you are trying to copy or move an icon, and the message explains why the operation can't be performed.

Source and Destination Drives Are Incompatible. The Copy option on the File Manager's File Menu can only copy a diskette to another diskette of the same format. If you have more than one diskette drive, and the drives are of different formats, this message is seen if you attempt to copy from one drive to the other.

Reselect the Copy option and set the *Source* and *Destination* drives to the same drive letter. Insert the source diskette in the selected drive, begin the copy procedure, and swap diskettes when the prompt to do so appears.

Program Not Found: Cannot find *filename***.exe. This program is needed to run files with extension '***EXT***'. Location of** *filename***.exe:** *(drive letter and path).* The message box identifies the name of a missing applet or application, explains why it's needed, and shows the location where Windows went to find it. Chances are the file was accidentally erased and you need to unerase it (if possible) or else install a fresh copy. Or, if you know the file is located elsewhere, then enter the correct path (but not the filename) and click on the OK button. Windows will open a [programs] section (if one does not already exist) and add the information it needs to find the file in the future.

Unable to Copy Disk. This message follows the *Source and destination drives are incompatible* message described above. Click on the OK button and try again, as described in the earlier message section.

Registration Database: There is a problem with the REG.DAT file. Quit Windows, delete REG.DAT, and then restart Windows *(instructions follow).* If this message is seen, the REG.DAT file is present but probably defective. Quit Windows, erase it, and refer to the *Build New Registration Info Database* section above for assistance if needed.

Drag-and-Drop Error Messages

This section describes error messages that may be seen if you drag a file to the minimized Print Manager icon, or to a group window in the Program Manager. Since some of these messages may also be seen if you double-click on a file icon, refer to the *File Manager Error Messages* section above for assistance if you are not using the drag-and-drop procedure when the message appears.

Cannot Print File: There is no application associated with this file. Choose Associate from the File menu to create an association. If this message appears when you drag a file to the Print Manager Icon, there are several possibilities.

Unprintable File. As a typical example, if an executable file (COM or EXE extension) is dragged to the Print Manager icon, it won't print. The solution is easy: Don't try.

Printable File. If a valid document file won't print, highlight its icon, open the File Menu and select the Associate... option. In the Associate dialog box, the <u>A</u>ssociate With: box may show a file*name*—not a file *type*—or the legend (None). If a name appears, then that name is taken from the [Extensions] section of WIN.INI. As a typical example, the box might show notepad.exe instead of Text File. This means that although a double-click should open the Notepad applet and load a highlighted TXT file, the system is not properly set up for drag-and-drop printing. To correct the problem, note the displayed filename (notepad.exe) and use the up- and down-arrows to scroll through the list of available file types, looking for the one that shows that filename in parentheses. Highlight it, and the legend in the <u>A</u>ssociate With: box changes from (in this example) notepad.exe to Text File. The system is now properly set up for drag-and-drop printing.

If the <u>A</u>ssociate With: box shows (None), then follow the scroll procedure above to find the appropriate executable file for the document you want to print. If you can't find what you need, then you'll need to use the *Registration Info Editor* to edit the registration database. Refer to the *Registration Info Editor* section earlier in this chapter for assistance if needed.

Cannot Print File (*or,* Cannot Run Program): File Manager cannot open or print the specified file. Start the application used to create this file, and open or print it from there. You can of course print the file by following the message's advice. The drag-and-drop print procedure didn't work because of a problem with the registration database. Refer to the *Install File Association* section above for assistance in setting up the required association.

Invalid Path: There is no association for *path\filename.ext.* This message is seen if you drag a file icon from the File Manager into the Program Manager, and there is no executable program associated with that file. Create the required association, then try again. Or, if the file cannot be associated with a Windows applet, then don't try again.

Problem with Object/Link. Now all you need to do is figure out *what* problem—the message doesn't even offer a clue. If the message shows up when you attempt to drag an icon into an open document, or later on if you double-click on an already-embedded icon, the problem is probably with your registration database. Refer to the *Registration Database Applet* section for assistance.

Program Not Found. Cannot find *filename*.exe. Refer to this message in the *File Manager Error Messages* section above.

Other Print-Related Error Messages

If any error message appears when File Manager tries to print a file within an associated Windows applet (Cardfile, Paintbrush, Write, for example), the applet may be left over from an earlier version of Windows. Check the file creation date for the appropriate applet; if it predates Windows 3.1, replace it and try again.

Network-Related Error Messages

The messages listed here may appear if there is a problem related to network operations. Unfortunately, at least a few of them are ambiguous, or have little or nothing to do with the real problem. Fortunately, many can be avoided by convincing your co-workers not to play with menu options while the network is up and running.

If all else fails, don't overlook the possibility of a faulty physical connection between your computer and others on the network. A loose connection or missing terminator (required on BNC links) is enough to cause all sorts of error messages, none of which even hint at a loose connection or a missing terminator.

Some messages listed here contain a bracketed message number, such as [SYS0053]. Although the displayed text should convey sufficient information to interpret the message, Table 6.4 lists these operating system numbers, along with the equivalent MS-DOS LAN Manager number.

NOTE: Many network error messages begin with "There is/are...," "You are...," or some other lengthy phrase which makes it difficult to list messages in strictly alphabetical order. To help get to the point, such messages are seen here with an introductory word or two to describe the specific error category. Therefore, if you see an overly chatty on-screen message, note the message subject, then look here for a key word or phrase.

Communication Terminated: This application was communicating on the network when you terminated it. This is the first line in one of the following messages:

Windows was unable to restore the state of the network. You need to restart your computer. The name of the application is given above the message, which may be seen if you attempt to reboot while network communications are in progress. Since Windows has determined that the termination adversely affected network software, you should follow the message's advice.

TABLE 6.4   Operating System Message Numbers

[SYS]*	Problem Description	Net†	[SYS]*	Problem Description	Net†
0050	Network request not supported	809	0062	Not enough print space for file	813
0051	Remote computer not listening	801	0063	Print file was cancelled	814
0052	Duplicate name on network	802	0064	Network name was deleted	815
0053	Network path not found	803	0066	Network device type incorrect	817
0054	Network busy	804	0067	Network name not found	818
0055	Network device no longer exists	805	0068	Network name limit exceeded	819
0056	Net BIOS command limit exceeded	806	0069	Net BIOS session limit exceeded	820
0057	Network adapter hardware error	807	0070	Sharing temporarily paused	821
0058	Incorrect response from network	808	0071	Network request not accepted	823
0059	Unexpected network error	810	0072	Print or disk redirection paused	822
0060	Incompatible remote adapter	811	0088	Network data fault	825
0061	Print queue full	812			

* [SYS*nnnn*] number which appears in some network-related error messages.
† Equivalent NET8*nn* message issued by MS-DOS LAN Manager.

Although Windows attempted to restore the state of the network, you may have problems with network communications until you restart your computer. In this case, Windows isn't sure about the reliability of the network. The safest course is to exit Windows and reboot the system.

Disk Error: There is a serious [*or* unrecoverable] disk error on file *filename.ext*. This message may be seen if a shared network drive is disconnected during a read or write operation. If clicking the OK button simply redisplays the message, and there appears to be no escape, try moving the mouse pointer up to the File Menu. Press the Enter key and click the primary mouse button before the message has a chance to repeat. This may kill it and allow you to select the Close option to conclude the operation. The next step is to restore the connection and try again.

Drive Letter: Specified drive letter is invalid. If you specified a drive, it may be past the value specified by the LASTDRIVE command in the CONFIG.SYS file. In many cases you can resolve this problem by disconnecting a network drive you are no longer using, thus freeing the drive letter for a new connection. However, if you do need to maintain all present connections, then you'll have to edit the LASTDRIVE line in your CONFIG.SYS file, reboot, reopen Windows, and try again.

Drive Read Operation: An error occurred reading drive x:. If network drive x was accessed during the previous session, but was not disconnected prior to closing Windows, this message may appear in the Current Directory Window the next time Windows is opened. It indicates that drive x is still shared but currently unavailable, as for example an empty diskette (or other removable media) drive. Ask the remote system operator to insert a diskette in the drive and try again, or disconnect if you no longer need to access the drive.

If the message appears when you try to read a network CD-ROM drive, the MSCDEX line in the remote system's CONFIG.SYS file may not include the /s (share) switch.

Driver Missing: The following error occurred while loading the device VNETSUP: Error 6111: Could not locate driver WORKGRP.SYS (MS-DOS error 2). The missing WORKGRP.SYS should have been loaded in your CONFIG.SYS file. In its absence, Windows displays this message, then opens without the Workgroup features. Make sure all three CONFIG.SYS lines described in the *Software Configuration* section above are in order, then reboot and try again.

File Access: Cannot access this file. Please verify security privileges on the network drive. You may indeed want to do that. But first, if you are trying to read a file, make sure that file is really there. This message is sometimes encountered if you enter the name of a file that doesn't exist on a read-only network drive. You may also see it if you attempt to save a file under a new name on a read-only network drive. In this case, temporarily save the file on a local drive, or on some other network drive that is not read-only.

File Access: *(Network drive letter):\\(filename.ext)* **is being used by** *(user name)*. **Do you want to make a copy?** If another computer has full access to a file, this message appears if you try to open that file on the local computer. Click on the OK button to make the copy, or else click on the Cancel button.

File Close: Closing the selected file may cause the user to lose data. Are you sure you want to close the file? If you decide to close a local file (by exiting Windows) that is currently accessed by a remote user, this message warns you about the consequences. Click on the OK button to complete the closure, or click on the Cancel button if the remote user is your boss or anyone else who can cause you pain.

File Find: Cannot find this file. Either something has happened to the network or possibly the file has been renamed or moved. Do you want to try again? If you're trying to save a file to a remote network drive, the "something" is probably a recent status change or similar action that prevents you from completing an action. If you can't arrange for the network drive system to take the appropriate corrective action, you'll have to exit without saving your changes.

File is in use. Use a new filename or close the file in use by another application. If you attempt to open a file on a network drive, and that file is in use by someone else, this message lets you know about it. The "Use a new filename" really means "Go read some other file until this one is free."

File is read-only. Use a different filename. If you are working on a file located on a network drive directory, and the host computer is sharing that directory as read-only, then you can't save changes to that drive. You'll have to save it to a local directory or to some other network drive that is not designated as read-only. However, you can use the same filename; it's the path that must be different.

Filename is not valid. Well, maybe it isn't, if you made a typing error while trying to save a file. But what may be more likely is that the network drive is no longer available. For some reason, this misleading message may be seen if you attempt to save a read-only file with a new name to a disconnected drive.

File Open: Not able to open this file. Make sure that the path and filename are correct. If you loaded a file from a network drive, and that drive has recently been disconnected, this message may be seen when you try to save the file back to that drive. If you can't resolve the problem with the network drive, save the file locally (use your File Menu's Save As... option).

File Operation: Cannot operate on file. Make sure the file or disk is not damaged or write-protected. If this message appears when you attempt to save a file to a network drive, it suggests the drive status was just changed from full to read-only. (If the network drive had been read-only from the start, a *This file is read-only* message would have been seen instead.) To confirm this, click on the OK button. You should see a *Cannot find this file* message, which is described above.

File Operation: This document is a copy of a file that was being edited by another Word session. Changes may have been saved to the original file. Do you want to save the document using the original name and overwrite other possible changes? If you tried to open a file that was in use by someone else, you were given the option to make a copy of that file for local use. If you now attempt to save the file under its original name, you run the risk of overwriting changes being made elsewhere on the network. If you don't care, then go ahead and do it. Otherwise click on the No button to open the Save As dialog box, which lets you save your edited copy under a new name.

Log Off: Continuing will cancel these operations:

   x: \\(computer name)\(directory)   (where x: is the network drive letter)

Do you want to continue this operation? (Y/N) [N]: If you guessed that "this operation" in the last line refers to "these operations" in the first line, you are both logical and wrong. Press the "y" key to continue the operation of logging off.

Log On: You are not logged on. You must log on to connect to a shared resource. Do you want to log on now? This message appears if you select the Disk Menu's Connect Network Drive... option before logging on to the network. Click on the appropriate button, as listed here:

Yes   Log on procedure begins. Enter password information (if
        required) and normal network operation should begin.

No   A second error message appears. See *Log On: You are still not
        logged on,* below.

Log On: You are still not logged on. You must log on before you can connect to a resource. This advisory message appears if you click on the No button when asked if you want to log on. It's a bit redundant, but you'll have to put up with it. Click on the OK button to continue.

Network drive is not available. This one-liner appears in the File Manager's Directory Window if you click on a network drive icon and the specified network drive has been disconnected since the last time you accessed it.

Operation cannot be performed to your own computer. This message appears in the Connect Network Drive dialog box (Figure 6.5) if you attempt to show the shared directories on your own computer. Select some other computer on the network and try again.

If you do want to review your own shared directories, then click on the Toolbar's Stop Sharing Directory button instead. This displays a list of the directories you have currently designated as shared.

Password: If you change the password, users who are currently using this resource may not be able to reconnect to it and may lose data. Are you sure you want to change the password? You'll see this message if you try to change *any* status of a shared drive, even if the password itself is not part of the change. In fact, the message is seen even if no passwords are used at all.

Note that the message is advisory only: It doesn't indicate if any remote users are currently logged on to the shared directory. If you have doubts about who's out there, select the Stop Sharing... option on the Disk Menu, then highlight the directory whose status you're about to change. If a remote system is logged on, a *There are* x *users connected...* message will warn you. Refer to that message for further information, and details about yet another message that may be waiting for you.

Protocol Manager: Error 3653: The protocol manager could not be found. The protocol manager is the PROTMAN.DOS file that should be loaded from your CONFIG.SYS file during system bootup. In its absence this message is seen if the NET START command is executed, either from your AUTOEXEC.BAT file or later on, at the DOS prompt. Edit your CONFIG.SYS file (see *Software Configuration* above), reboot, and try again.

Protocols: Network functionality will not be available because network protocols were not loaded. Choose the Network option in Control Panel to check adapter and protocol settings. The Windows for Workgroups network driver was unable to load. Before you do that, check your AUTO-EXEC.BAT file for the NET START command described in the *Software Configuration* section earlier in the chapter. If the line is missing, exit Workgroups, type NET START at the DOS prompt, then reopen Windows. If it works, then fix your AUTOEXEC.BAT file, as required. If it doesn't, then follow the advice given in the error message.

Reconnect Error: An error occurred while reconnecting *(drive letter)* **to ***(Computer name\path)***:** Refer to one of the following messages, each of which may be seen after this opening statement.

The computer name specified in the network path cannot be located. [SYS0053]. Do you want to continue restoring connections? If your computer was connected to a network drive during a previous Windows session, this message indicates that the specified network drive is currently unavailable. If the local computer is set for Log On at Startup (via the Control Panel's *Network Applet*—see Chapter 11), the message appears the next time you open Windows. Otherwise, it shows up later on if you log on during a Windows session.

If you click on the Yes button, the first part of the message repeats, with the last sentence replaced by *The connection has not been restored*. The File Manager's Directory Window reports *The network drive is not available* in the Directory Window. As appropriate, take one of the following actions:

1. Persuade the remote system operator to turn the system on and/or make the network drive available for sharing.

2. Open your own Disk Menu, select the Disconnect Network Drive... option, and sever the connection to the unavailable drive so the message won't be seen the next time you open Windows.

3. Ignore the problem and try again later.

The specified share name cannot be found. [SYS0067]. This connection has not been restored. If you click on a network drive icon and this messages appears, the remote directory associated with that network drive is no longer available as a shared directory. If you do need to access the directory, ask the remote operator to reshare it.

You are still not logged on. You must log on before you can connect to a resource. This connection has not been restored. If you decide not to log on to a network after seeing a previous error message, Windows tries to reconnect anyway, and fails. In this case, just ignore the message. The File Manager's Directory Windows displays an empty directory window, with *Network drive is unavailable* in the window. To get rid of the erroneous network drive icon and window, open the Disk Menu and select the Disconnect Network Drive... option.

Saved Connection: You have a saved connection on x: to \\(computer name)\(directory). Do you want to replace it with a saved connection to \\ (computer name)\(directory)? For more information choose the Help button. (Yes, No, Cancel, Help buttons are shown.) If your local drive *x* is already assigned as a network drive, this message appears if you attempt to reassign that letter to a different network drive. If you click on either the Yes or the No button, the new assignment takes effect for the duration of the current session. Click Yes if you want the assignment saved for the future,

No if you only want it for the present session, or click on Cancel if neither option is appropriate.

If you click on **Yes** or **No**, the Current Directory Window may show a *drive not available* message if the drive specified as the previous saved connection is currently off-line. Press function key F5 (Refresh Window) to update the Directory Window to show the new assignment.

Shared directory cannot be found. If you previously connected to a network drive, and that drive has been disconnected at the remote site, this message appears in the local Directory Window if you attempt to read the directory.

Sharing: An error occurred while trying to share *(directory name)*. **Error 5291: The path x:***(directory name)* **does not exist. Do you want to continue to share** *(directory name)* **each time you start Windows-for-Work-groups?** Chances are, the nonexistent path is to a diskette drive with no diskette in it, or to a hard disk directory that no longer exists. You may have been sharing the directory during a previous session and didn't stop sharing it before exiting Windows. If that's the case, then this message appears the next time you open windows. Click on the No button to get rid of it. Otherwise, click on the Yes button and try to find out where the missing path went.

Sharing: You are already sharing the directory *(drive letter and directory name)* **using the name** *(share name)*. **Do you want to share it using the name** *(new share name)* **instead?** If you really want to change the name under which a directory is being shared, go ahead. Otherwise, click on the No button and select the new directory that you want to make available for sharing.

Sharing: You are sharing the directory *(path and directory name)* **as** *(share name)*. **The directory will not be shared after you move or rename it. Are you sure you want to continue?** This message warns you of the potential consequences of moving or renaming a shared directory. If you really do want to do it anyway, click on the OK button. If anyone is actually accessing the directory, a *There are* x *user(s) connected* message will let you know about it.

Sharing: You can only share resources that are on your computer. If you are trying to share a printer, make sure that it is a local printer and that the TEMP directory is on a local drive. If a local Directory Window shows the contents of a network drive, this message appears if you attempt to share that drive. The drive is, of course, already being shared. Besides, it's not yours to share anyway.

Standard Mode: The Windows-for-Workgroups network was not started. To use networking features in Standard Mode, you must type NET START WORKSTATION before starting Windows-for-Workgroups. The Windows for Workgroups network driver was unable to load. If you want to open in Standard Mode on a 386 system, type NET START WORKSTATION at the DOS prompt and try again. You will also see this message on a 286 system if you typed NET STOP at the DOS prompt prior to opening Windows. In either case, click on the OK button to open without network support. Then exit and try again if you want to join the network.

Startup: You started the workgroup software for MS-DOS before you started Windows. To make more memory available to your applications and use the network components built into Windows-for-Workgroups instead, type NET STOP before starting Windows. Do you want to display this message in the future? If you see this message, it means you typed NET START WORKSTATION at the DOS prompt before starting Windows, thus taking a sizable chunk out of your conventional and upper memory supply (see *AUTOEXEC.BAT* in the *Software Configuration* section).

If Windows-for-Workgroups is on a remote (network server) system, you must load this local workgroup software in order to establish a connection to the server. In this case, the message will appear every time you open Windows, unless you click on the No button to dispense with it. This adds the following line to the WIN.INI file:

```
[windows]
NetMessage=No
```

If the above is not the case, then on a previous session you probably typed NET START WORKSTATION at the DOS prompt before opening Workgroups in Standard Mode on a 386 system. In this case the message is seen the next time you open in Enhanced Mode. To release the memory occupied by the workgroup software, and dump the message, type NET STOP at the DOS prompt to release the memory occupied by the workgroup software, then open Windows.

Unrecoverable error on *filename.ext*. This message probably indicates a severed connection to a network drive during a file read/write operation. If you were trying to write to a network drive, try saving the file locally until you can resolve the network problem.

Users Connected: There are *x* file(s) open by users connected to *(directory)*. If you stop sharing *(directory)*, the files will close, which may cause these users to lose data. Do you want to continue? This message follows the *There are* x *user(s) connected* message if one of those remote users is currently accessing a local file in the directory you are trying to close. Click on the Yes or No button, depending on your attitude towards the remote user.

Users Connected: There are *x* user(s) connected to *(directory)*. If you stop sharing *(directory)*, they will be disconnected. Do you want to continue? If you try to stop sharing a local directory that is currently connected to a remote computer, this message appears before the connection is terminated. Click on the Yes button if you really do want to stop sharing, or click on the No button to leave the connection in place.

This message does not indicate if a connected user is actually accessing a file on your shared directory. If a user is in fact doing so, an additional *file(s) open* warning message will be seen if you click on the Yes button.

7

The DOS Window

This chapter describes procedures and configuration techniques that may be used to run DOS applications within Windows. To accomplish that, the MS-DOS Prompt and PIF Editor applets located in the Main Group Window are described, along with suggestions for optimizing the Windows environment for each DOS application that is installed on the system.

The first section offers a few definitions and an overview of the various modes under which such DOS applications can be executed, followed by sections describing the DOS Application Window's Control Menu and the DOS Window Fonts. Next, the Program Information File and the PIF Editor are described, followed by sections on DOS Window, General Session, and PIF configuration techniques.

The final sections cover DOS Session Troubleshooting and the Error Messages that one is liable to encounter during a DOS session.

Definitions

This short section defines one term that will—and one that won't—be encountered in this chapter.

Non-Windows Application. A non-Windows application is any program that is executed by typing its filename on a command line at the DOS prompt. Although such programs were not written for use with Windows, many can nevertheless be executed from inside Windows, as will shortly be explained. But first, we need to do something about that *non-Windows application* phrase. If nothing else, it can lead to a very awkward description of a *non-Windows* application running in a *window* within *Windows*. If it's a non-Windows application, what's it doing in a window? And if it is in a window, doesn't that mean it's a window (if not, *Windows*) application? One day Russell Baker will work all this out in *The New York Times,* but, in the meantime, this book takes the easy way out by offering the following alternative.

DOS Application. A *DOS application* is any program that is executed by typing its filename at the DOS prompt. If that definition sounds vaguely familiar, there's good reason (see previous paragraph). Therefore, this book follows Groucho Marx's advice on ducks: "If it looks like a DOS app, it's a DOS app." Instead of calling it by what it is not, we call it here by what it is.

DOS Video Modes within Windows

The manner in which a DOS application may be run within Windows depends on the current Windows operating mode, as described in the next two sections. For the purposes of the following explanation, the MS-DOS Prompt applet in the Main Group Window will be used for our DOS examples.

Windows Enhanced Mode. If Windows is opened in enhanced mode, one or more DOS applications may be active at the same time. As each DOS application opens, Windows sets aside 1 Mbyte of memory in which it creates a *virtual machine*, which is—as far as the application is concerned—a separate computer, complete with its own copy of the operating system, and all the device drivers and TSRs that were loaded when the system was booted. To save memory, that 1 Mbyte can be adjusted downward, as explained later in the *PIF Editor* section.

DOS Full-Screen Video Mode. In this mode, the DOS application takes over the entire screen; the Windows Desktop is not seen and the application appears as it would if Windows itself were not there. However, the user may toggle back and forth between the DOS application and other DOS and/or Windows applications that are also active at the same time.

DOS Window Video Mode. In order to keep an eye on multiple applications running simultaneously, a DOS application may be run within its own DOS Application Window (or *DOS Window* for short), as shown by the two open DOS Windows in Figure 7.1. Each such window may be sized and positioned on the Windows Desktop as described in the *DOS Window Configuration* section later in this chapter.

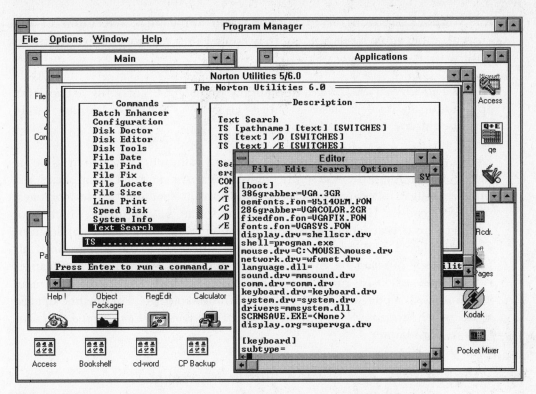

Figure 7.1   The Windows Desktop, showing two open DOS Windows.

Color Values in DOS Window Video Mode. If a DOS application makes any use of color, the color values seen in a DOS Window are not the same as those seen if the application runs in full-screen mode. To illustrate the color shift, run the following BASIC program to display fifteen horizontal color bars. Then press Alt+Enter to toggle back and forth between Full-Screen and DOS Window modes.

```
FOR x = 1 to 15
COLOR x
PRINT STRING$(80,219)
NEXT x
```

To further illustrate the phenomenon, change COLOR x to COLOR 4 (or 6), two colors which exhibit perhaps the greatest change.

Windows Standard Mode. If Windows opens in standard mode, only one DOS application may be active at a time. When the user switches back to the Windows Desktop, or to another DOS application, execution of the current application is suspended; it is copied into memory where it resides until it is again summoned.

DOS Full-Screen Video Mode. In standard mode, the currently active DOS application always occupies the entire screen, and the DOS Window Mode described above is not available.

Exclusive Mode. Under default conditions, computer processing time is distributed among the currently active Windows and DOS applications, with time slices allocated according to priorities that may be set for each such application. However, an *exclusive mode* can be set up in which processing time is reassigned according to the current foreground application. For example, if a Windows application is running in the foreground, all DOS applications can be suspended. Or, if a DOS foreground application is run in an exclusive mode, execution of all other DOS applications may be suspended, along with all—or most—Windows activity. For further details, refer to *Set Exclusive Mode Options* in the *DOS Window Configuration* section later in the chapter.

Executing a DOS Application within Windows

Some DOS applications can be executed after double-clicking on the DOS Prompt Icon in the Main Group Window. When the DOS prompt appears, enter the application's filename and press the Enter key, just as you would if Windows were not running. This procedure is used in the following discussion to illustrate some of the basic techniques for running a DOS application from within Windows.

Begin DOS Session. When you double-click on the DOS Prompt Icon, the Windows Desktop is replaced by a screen showing a boxed introductory message, DOS version and copyright information, and the DOS prompt itself, as shown in Figure 7.2. The switching options cited in the message are described here, in the order they appear on screen. In each case, the parenthetical reference lists the keystrokes required to execute the option.

Close DOS Session ("exit"+Enter). If a DOS prompt is visible, either on the full screen or within a DOS Window, type EXIT at the prompt and press the Enter key to close the DOS session and return to the Program Manager.

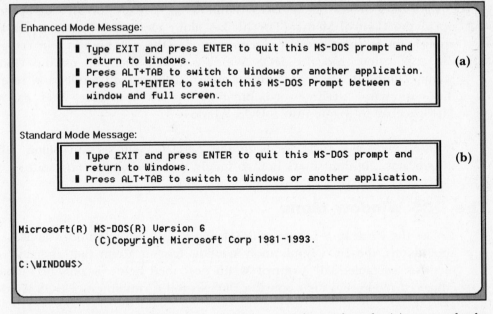

Enhanced Mode Message:

> ▌ Type EXIT and press ENTER to quit this MS-DOS prompt and
>   return to Windows.
> ▌ Press ALT+TAB to switch to Windows or another application.
> ▌ Press ALT+ENTER to switch this MS-DOS Prompt between a
>   window and full screen.

(a)

Standard Mode Message:

> ▌ Type EXIT and press ENTER to quit this MS-DOS prompt and
>   return to Windows.
> ▌ Press ALT+TAB to switch to Windows or another application.

(b)

```
Microsoft(R) MS-DOS(R) Version 6
         (C)Copyright Microsoft Corp 1981-1993.

C:\WINDOWS>
```

Figure 7.2 When a DOS session begins, an enhanced-mode (a) or standard-mode (b) opening message appears at the top of the screen, followed by version and copyright information and the DOS prompt.

 NOTE: If the DOS prompt does not appear within the DOS Window, and the Title Bar text shows Inactive *(application name)*, open the **Control Menu** box and select the **C**lose option to close the DOS Window. Refer to the **C**lose option described below for further details.

Switch to Another Application (Alt+Tab). Use this keystroke combination to toggle between the current DOS application, the Program Manager, and any other active applications, as described in the *Task Switching via the Alt+Tab Keys* section of Chapter 3.

Toggle DOS Video Modes (Alt+Enter). If Windows is operating in enhanced mode, this keystroke combination toggles the display between Full-Screen and DOS Window modes.

Alternate Video Mode Toggles. The following combinations can also be used to toggle between Full-Screen and DOS-Window modes.

Open DOS Window. If a DOS Window is already open, Alt+Spacebar opens the Control Menu. (The Alt key alone closes it.) However, if a DOS application is running in full-screen mode, the combination first toggles the application into the DOS Window mode, then opens the Control Menu. Therefore, if an application opens in full-screen mode, and reserves the customary Alt+Enter combination for its own use, you can use Alt+Spacebar to toggle into a DOS Window.

Enable Full-Screen Mode. Refer to the *Control Menu* section below, where the Settings... option shows how to toggle back to Full-Screen mode.

The DOS Window Menu

Unlike the Program Manager, File Manager, and most Windows applets and applications, the DOS Application Window has no Menu Bar, and only one menu is available. The Control Menu described below is only accessible in enhanced mode, and then only if a DOS session is running in a DOS Window.

The Control Menu. Most options are identical to the equivalent options on the Program Manager's Control Menu, as described in Chapter 3. Refer to the *Control Menu* section of that chapter for information about options not described here. Figure 7.3a illustrates the Control Menu as it appears in a DOS Window.

Close. As shown in the figure, this option is disabled (grayed) if you began the DOS session by clicking on the DOS Prompt icon in the Main

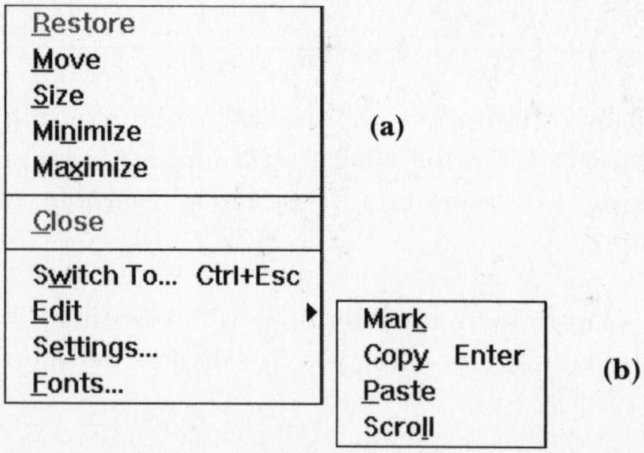

Figure 7.3 The DOS Window's Menu System. (a) The Control Menu. (b) The Edit option's Cascading Menu shows four edit options.

Group Window. To close the window in this case, first quit the application running in that window (if any), then type EXIT at the DOS prompt.

However, if a DOS application is configured so that the DOS session does not close when the application concludes, then an inactive window in enhanced mode remains on the Windows Desktop, and its Title Bar displays the following text:

(Inactive *application name*)

To close the inactive window, open the Control Menu and select the Close option which, under these conditions, is enabled. In standard mode, an inactive full-screen display is seen, with a Press Any Key to Exit prompt in the lower right hand corner.

The inactive modes may be helpful if a DOS application leaves information on the screen that you want to study after the application concludes. Refer to the *PIF Editor* section for information on how to set up an application so that it either does, or does not, close the DOS session when it concludes.

NOTE: If the Close option is not disabled, it's also possible that the Allow Close When Active option for the current DOS Window has been enabled. Refer to the *PIF Configuration* section later in the chapter for further details on this.

Edit. Select this option to open the cascading menu shown in Figure 7.3b. Use the options on this menu to select, copy, and paste information from the DOS Window to the Clipboard, as described here. As in other menu descriptions, a parenthetical reference identifies a key stroke that performs the same function as the indicated menu option. When an option is selected, the menu closes and the Title Bar includes a keyword to remind you of the current edit status. The keywords are shown below in brackets. (See Chapter 3 for information about *Cascading Menus*.)

Copy **(Enter).** Once a section of the DOS Window is highlighted, you can copy it to the Clipboard by reopening the Control Menu, reselecting the Edit option, then selecting the Copy option on the cascading menu. However, it's far simpler to just press the Enter key immediately after using the Mark option.

Mark **(Mark, Select).** Choose this option to begin marking a section of the DOS Window for copying to the Clipboard. Note the blinking square box in the upper left-hand corner of the window, and do one of the following to select the desired area:

Drag the box across and down the screen so that the desired screen section is highlighted.

Move the mouse pointer to one corner of the desired section and press the primary mouse button. Hold the button down and drag the pointer as required.

Move the mouse pointer to one corner of the desired section and press the primary mouse button. But this time move (do not drag) the pointer to a diagonal corner, hold down the Shift key, and press the primary mouse button again. The rectangular area defined by the two corner points will be highlighted.

When the primary mouse button is initially pressed, the Title Bar keyword changes from *Mark* to *Select*. Follow the appropriate actions above, then press the Enter key to copy the selected area to the Clipboard.

> **NOTE:** The Mark option is disabled if the Scroll option is enabled. Therefore, if the latter option is enabled first, you'll have to disable it to begin marking a section. Note the *Scroll* keyword in the Title Bar and press the Escape or Enter Key to clear it and disable the option.

Paste. As elsewhere in Windows, this option pastes the Clipboard contents into the open application Window. You may, of course, use it to paste information copied from elsewhere into a DOS Window. For example, if a word processor document includes a lengthy batch file listing, select and copy the listing to the Clipboard from within the word processor application. Then open a DOS Window, type COPY CON TEST.BAT (or similar) at the DOS prompt, and press the Enter Key. Now paste the clipboard contents into the DOS Window and press Function key F6 to conclude. The selected document text is now available as an executable TEST.BAT file.

Scroll **(Scroll, Scroll Select).** This option is only enabled if a Scroll Bar appears at the side and/or bottom of the DOS Window. If you select it, you can mark a corner of the DOS Window, then use the keyboard arrow keys to scroll to another segment of the Window. If the Scroll option is not selected, the arrow keys have no effect.

**Fonts...** This is actually a font _size_ option. In enhanced mode, Windows provides a selection of ten character matrixes, varying in size from 4×6 to 16×12 pixels. Refer to the _DOS Window Fonts_ section below for information about these font matrixes.

**Settings...** Select the Settings... option to open the DOS Prompt dialog box shown in Figure 7.4. Any changes made to the displayed settings will affect the way the DOS application utilizes system resources during the current session, but these changes will not be saved when the DOS Window is closed. To assign permanent changes to a DOS application, refer to the _PIF Editor_ and _PIF Editor Configuration_ sections later in the chapter.

Display Options. On opening the dialog box, the display option is always "Window" since this is the only mode in which the menu system can be accessed. Of course, you can switch to Full Screen, but it's hardly worth the bother of opening this dialog box to do so. It's far easier to simply press Alt+Enter to toggle into the DOS Window mode. However, if the application has reserved Alt+Enter for its own use, then this method may be convenient for occasional use.

Priority and _Tasking Options._ These choices are equivalent to those selected in the _Multitasking Options_ and _Execution_ sections of the PIF Editor's dialog box, which are described in the _PIF Editor_ section later in this chapter.

Special (Terminate... button). This is a very serious button. Click on it to terminate the active DOS application and simultaneously close the window in which it is running. A warning message lets you know that if you insist

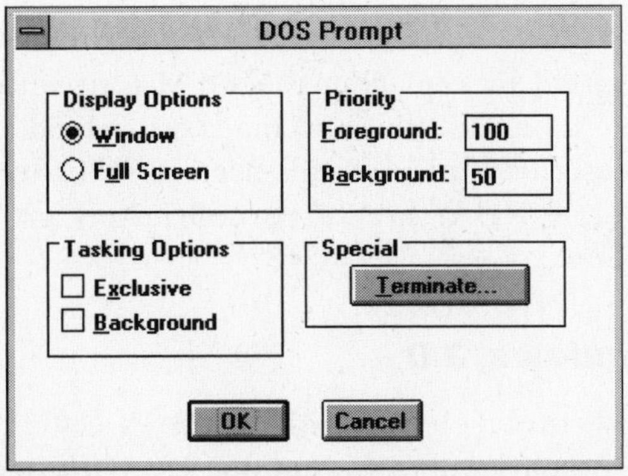

Figure 7.4 The DOS Prompt dialog box is accessed via the Settings... option on the Control Menu seen in Figure 7.3.

on going through with this, any unsaved information will be lost. Click on the OK button to finish the termination job, or if you're intimidated, click on the Cancel button to return to the application.

DOS Window Fonts

When you click on the DOS icon in the Main Group Window, the DOS prompt appears, the entire screen is made available to display DOS applications, and there should be no visible evidence of Windows' presence. However, the whole point of running a DOS application within Windows is so that it can be treated as an integral part of the Windows desktop. If you don't need this feature, you might just as well not bother loading Windows in the first place.

Assuming you are going to run an application in a DOS Window, you can vary the size of the text seen in that window by making changes to the Terminal Font which is described here.

Terminal (OEM) Font

If you have not yet made adjustments to the DOS Window, the default OEM font specified by the oemfont.fon= line in the [boot] section of SYSTEM.INI displays text within that window. The font is usually referred to as the *terminal font,* or *OEM font.* As for *OEM,* it stands for Original Equipment Manufacturer, a term borrowed a bit hastily from the hardware industry, where it identifies suppliers of components which a manufacturer assembles into a finished product. In Microspeak, the terminal font is an OEM font because it is a component whose origins may be traced back to the venerable IBM PC-8 font.

WOA Fonts

DOS Window text size may be varied by replacing the OEM font with one of nine WOA (Windows Other Applications) font matrixes, which come from a variety of font sources described later in this section. This total of ten font matrixes (one OEM, nine WOA) are often collectively grouped under the *Terminal Font* designation.

Terminal Font Sources in Windows 3.0

A brief review of DOS Window font selection in Windows 3.0 is presented here, for purposes of comparison with version 3.1. This section can be skipped by anyone not that interested in fontsmanship within a DOS Window.

Four font type=font name lines in the [386Enh] section of the SYSTEM.INI file specify the files containing the font matrixes available within the DOS Window. The lines are listed here, along with the horizontal and vertical font matrix in each file, the DOS video mode command that would enable that matrix, and the number of vertical lines in the resultant screen display. In the default VGA setup shown here, the "80" or "40" in each font name indicates the number of characters-per-line displayed in a maximized window if that font is selected. Note that in this default configuration, each font type and the actual filename are identical.

[386Enh]	H	V	DOS Mode	Screen Lines
EGA80WOA.FON=EGA80WOA.FON	8	12	Mode 80, 25	300
CGA80WOA.FON=CGA80WOA.FON	8	8	Mode 80, 43	344
EGA40WOA.FON=EGA40WOA.FON	16	12	Mode 40, 25	300
CGA40WOA.FON=CGA40WOA.FON	16	8	Mode 40, 43	344

As the video mode changed (either manually, or by the application running in the window), the font matrix would change accordingly. In addition, the vertical size of a maximized window would change, to display either 300 (12×25) or 344 (8×43) screen lines.

On 600×800 or 1024×768 video systems, the size of even a maximized DOS Window was therefore quite small: on the former system, a 25-line display took up less than 40 percent (300/768) of the vertical screen size. On the latter, a 43-line display used 57 percent of the available vertical dimension.

Some improvement could be realized by replacing the 8×12 matrix above with the 16×20 matrix found in the 8514FIX.FON file, thereby giving 500 lines to the same 25-line display. In like manner, the 8×8 matrix might be replaced by the now-unused 8×12 matrix, thus allocating 516 lines to a 43-line display. To accomplish these reassignments, two of the lines above could be rewritten as follows:

[386Enh]	H	V	DOS Mode	Screen Lines
EGA80WOA.FON=8514FIX.FON	16	20	Mode 80, 25	500 (formerly 300)
CGA80WOA.FON=EGA80WOA.FON	8	12	Mode 80, 43	516 (formerly 344)

Some texts have suggested using the 8514FIX.FON file in both lines above, but doing so would require 860 screen lines to display 43 lines of text—a neat trick when only 768 or 600 screen lines are available. If this or some other impossible suggestion is followed, the 8×12 matrix above is usually replaced by the 16×12 matrix from the EGA40WOA.FON file, which might not produce the expected results.

The above procedures are valid in Windows 3.0 only. Refer to the section immediately following for a discussion of version 3.1 font selection methods.

Terminal Font Sources in Windows 3.1

Five lines in the [386Enh] section of the SYSTEM.INI file specify the files containing the ten font matrixes listed in the Font box. As above, the following four lines specify files containing one font each, while a fifth line (described below) identifies a new file containing six more fonts.

[386Enh]	H	V	Comments
EGA80WOA.FON=EGA80WOA.FON	8	12	Same matrix as VGAOEM.FON
CGA80WOA.FON=CGA80WOA.FON	8	8	Same matrix as EGAOEM.FON
EGA40WOA.FON=EGA40WOA.FON	16	12	
CGA40WOA.FON=CGA40WOA.FON	16	8	

Note that two of these font matrixes are duplicated in the OEM font files used by VGA and EGA displays. If either is installed in your system, that matrix will be taken from the listed OEM font instead of the WOA font. However, since the OEM font is identical to the WOA font it replaces, there is no difference in the on-screen display. At 800×600 and 1024×768 resolutions, the 8×12 matrix is supplied by the EGA80WOA.FON file listed above.

Some Windows 3.1 documentation suggests the EGA files are for DOS applications that display more than 25 lines, while the CGA files are for displays of 25 or fewer lines. In fact, either set of files may be used to display 25 or more lines, according to the current DOS display mode of the system. On a conventional DOS 25-line screen, all four font files above display 25 lines of text in a maximized window. And, of course, the window's vertical dimension may be reduced as desired to display less than 25 lines.

The WOAFont File. The following line in the [386Enh] section of SYSTEM.INI specifies the multifont file which supplies the other six font matrixes for the DOS Window.

```
WOAFont=DOSAPP.FON
```

Table 7.1 lists these matrixes, plus those in the four WOA fonts described above. The offsets at which the DOSAPP.FON file matrixes begin are also given. For comparison purposes, Figure 7.5 shows the letter "E" as it is stored in each of these files. The four-digit hexadecimal number to the right of each file name indicates the offset where the 6 to 18 bytes required for that letter begin.

Terminal Font Character Set

The installed Terminal font's complete character set may be viewed via the Character Map applet in the Accessories Group Window. The applet is described in Chapter 10, and the Terminal font character set itself is shown later in this chapter, as Figure 7.9a.

Since the character set is the same for each of the ten WOA fonts (in a default US English setup), the Character Map displays the size most appropriate for your video system, according to which OEM file you are using, as specified in the OEMFONT.FON= line in the [boot] section of SYSTEM.INI. Highlight the listed Character Map font name to view the character set, whose font matrix and OEM filename are given here.

Character Map	Font Matrix	OEMFONT.FON=
Terminal	8 × 8	EGAOEM.FON
Terminal	8 × 12	VGAOEM.FON
8514oem	16 × 20	8514OEM.FON

In most cases, if a nondefault OEM font is specified, the Character Map will still display the appropriate Terminal font, as listed above.

TABLE 7.1 Terminal Font Matrixes for DOS Window Applications

Matrix		Matrix Is in	Matrix Begins	Aspect Ratio[‡]		
H	V	Font File	at Offset[†]	%	H	V
4	6	DOSAPP.FON	05A7	100	96	96
5	12	DOSAPP.FON	1060	100	96	96
6	8	DOSAPP.FON	2266	100	96	96
7	12	DOSAPP.FON	2EF2	100	96	96
10	18	DOSAPP.FON	3F86	100	96	96
12	16	DOSAPP.FON	681C	100	96	96
		EGA Systems	**VGA Systems**			
8	8	EGAOEM.FON[§]	CGA80WOA.FON	200	96	48
16	8	CGA40WOA.FON	CGA40WOA.FON	200	96	48
8	12	EGA80WOA.FON	VGAOEM.FON[§]	200	96	48
16	12	EGA40WOA.FON	EGA40WOA.FON	133	96	72

[†] Indicated offset applies to Windows version 3.1 DOSAPP.FON file.

[‡] Font may be printed if installed printer specs match (or approximate) these values.

[§] This OEM font is substituted for WOA font when indicated video system is installed.

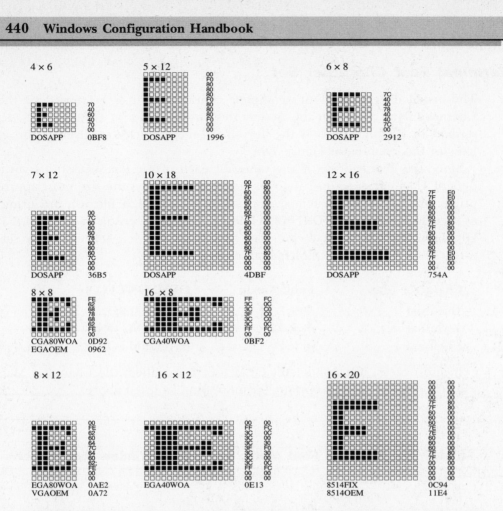

Figure 7.5 The letter "E" as it appears in various DOS font matrixes. The font file(s) containing the indicated font matrix are listed under each character box. A four-place hexadecimal number indicates the offset at which the letter begins in the indicated Windows version 3.1 files.

Terminal Font List

Chapter 10 discusses the fonts used elsewhere on the Windows Desktop, and that chapter's Table 10.2 lists the various Terminal fonts supplied with Windows versions 3.0 and 3.1. Only the fonts appropriate to your system configuration are copied into your System directory during the Windows Setup procedure.

PIF: The Program Information File

In order to run a DOS application from within Windows, a virtual machine must first be set up. The machine is, in effect, a separate computer in which the application will be loaded and executed. Each such virtual machine may be optimized to take into account the application's memory requirements, video modes, and other operating parameters, either as required by the application or as specified by the user. These settings are stored in a PIF, or Program Information File, whose filename is generally the same as the DOS executable file, but with an extension of PIF instead of COM or EXE.

When you double-click on a DOS application icon, Windows reads the same command line that may be seen by examining the Properties... option for that application. If that command line specifies *filename*.PIF, Windows sets up the virtual machine parameters listed in that PIF, then executes the application filename specified by the PIF. In fact, even if the Properties... option specifies *filename*.EXE (or *filename*.COM), Windows still looks for a *filename*.PIF file, and sets up the memory, video, and most other parameters specified in that PIF. In this case, the executable filename specified in the PIF is ignored.

If no *filename*.PIF can be found, then Windows uses settings stored in a special _DEFAULT.PIF file in the Windows directory. This is a generic PIF, with settings that should work for most routine DOS applications. However, since no single PIF can possibly provide optimal settings for every possible application, this file should only be used as a starting point, from which to build a properly configured PIF for each application, as described in the *PIF Editor Applet* section below.

The [pif] section of the Windows APPS.INF file contains settings required for many popular DOS applications that run within Windows. Those applications recognized by the current versions of Windows were listed in Table 1.8. If one of these programs was on your hard disk at the time Windows was installed, it may have been installed in your Applications Group Window. If so, click once on the application's icon, open the File Menu and select the Properties... option. The Command Line in the Program Item Properties dialog box should list *filename*.PIF. If no DOS applications are yet installed, click on the DOS Prompt Icon in the Main Group Window and the Command Line will show DOSPROMPT.PIF. To view the contents of this or any other PIF, or to create a new one, use the PIF Editor applet which is described below.

The PIF Search Path

When you double-click on a DOS application's icon, Windows searches the following locations, in the order shown here, for the PIF for that application.

Path specified (if any) on Command Line in Program Item Properties dialog box

Windows directory

System directory

Working Directory specified in Program Item Properties dialog box

Application's own directory

The PIF Editor Applet

Double-click on the PIF Editor applet in the Main Group Window to open one of two PIF Editor dialog boxes shown in Figure 7.6a and c and described here. The File and Help Menus are similar to those in the Program Manager or File Manager and are not further discussed here.

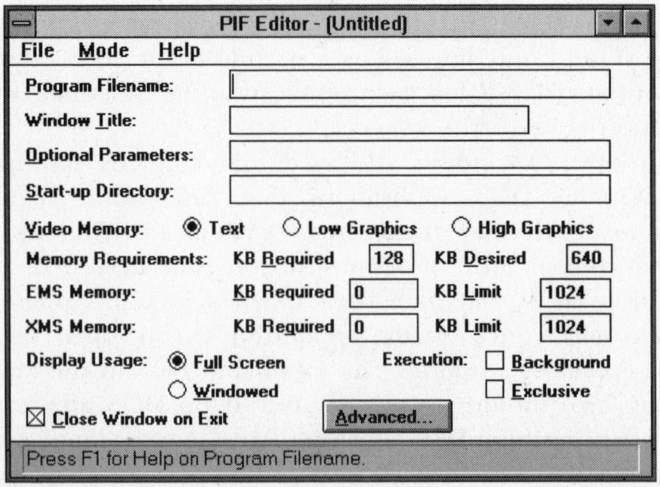

Figure 7.6a The PIF Editor dialog box for Advanced mode

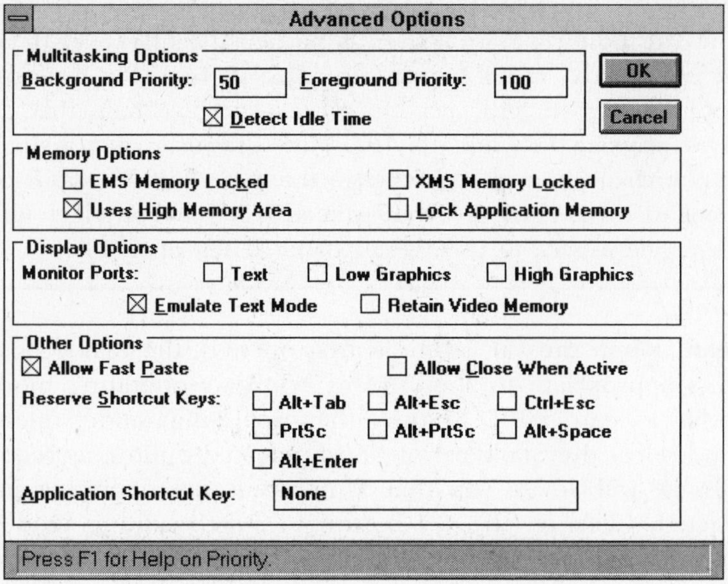

(b)

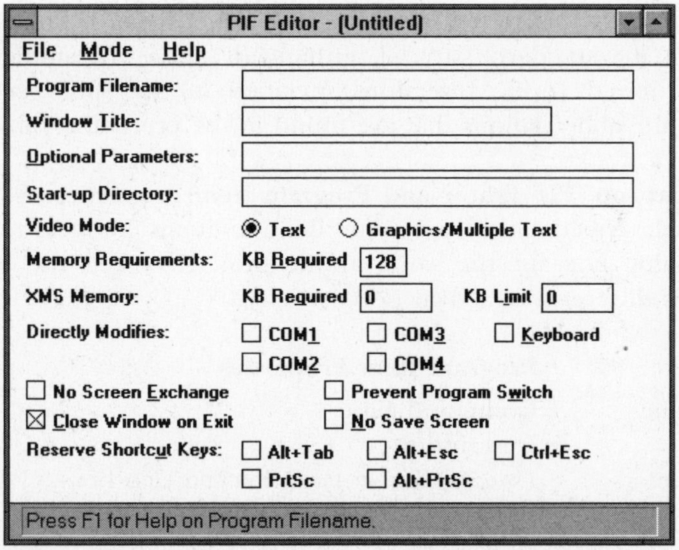

(c)

Figure 7.6b, c The PIF Editor dialog boxes for (b) Advanced-mode options and (c) Standard mode.

> *NOTE:* The PIF Editor's Help system is particularly effective. If you click on any check box, radio button, or adjacent text, the legend at the bottom of the screen indicates the context-sensitive help that can be accessed by pressing Function Key F1. Note, however, that a single-click toggles the check box or may change the radio button status. So, if all you want to do is read the Help screen for that option, double-click on it to toggle it back to its original status. Then press F1.

The Mode Menu. When the PIF editor is first opened, the dialog box displays parameters appropriate to the current Windows operating mode. If you would prefer to edit a PIF in the other operating mode, open the Mode Menu and select the Standard or 386 Enhanced option, as required. A warning message will advise you that Windows is not operating in the mode you selected. Click on the OK button to switch editing modes, or otherwise click on the Cancel button.

Typical PIF Settings. As noted earlier, the [pif] section of the APPS.INF file contains settings for selected DOS applications. For future reference, a few representative examples are shown in Table 7.2. Tables 7.3 and 7.4 illustrate typical contents of the standard [std_...], enhanced [enha_...], ambiguous [amb_...] and optimized [opt_...] sections specified in the [pif] section, and Table 7.5 lists the abbreviations that are found in the preceding Tables.

Dialog Box Comparison: PIF Editor and Program Item Properties. Several PIF Editor items described below are equivalent to items in the Program Item Properties dialog box for the same application. However, the name assigned to each is different, as shown here:

PIF Editor	**Program Item Properties**
Program Filename	Command Line
Window Title	Description
Optional Parameters	(*specify them in the* Command Line box)
Startup Directory	Working Directory

Enhanced Mode PIF Editor Dialog Box

If you open the PIF Editor in enhanced mode, the first of two dialog boxes appears on screen, as illustrated in Figure 7.6a. Edit the following parameters as required, and/or open the Advanced Options dialog box described below to access additional PIF settings.

TABLE 7.2   PIF Data Stored in APPS.INF File*

DOS Application	PIF File-name	DOS Window Title Bar Text	CWE †	Icon file	No.	Parameters‡ Standard	Enhanced	Other Data§
123.COM	123,	"Lotus 1-2-3",	, cwe,	,	3,	std_gra_256,	enha_123c	
123.EXE	123,	"Lotus 1-2-3 3.1",	, cwe,	moricons.dll,	50,	std_123,	enha_123,	amb_123
FOX.EXE	FOX,	"FoxPro (Max. Config.)",	, cwe,	moricons.dll,	91,	std_FOXPRO1,	enha_FOXPRO1,	opt_foxpro
HG.EXE	HG,	"Harvard Graphics 2.3",	, cwe,	moricons.dll,	59,	std_HG23,	enha_HG23,	amb_hg
HG3.EXE	HG3,	"Harvard Graphics 3.0",	, cwe,	moricons.dll,	60,	std_HG3,	enha_HG3	
HGG.EXE	HGG,	"Harvard GeoGraphics",	, cwe,	moricons.dll,	61,	std_HGG,	enha_HGG	
LOTUS.COM	LOTUS,	"Lotus Access System",	, cwe,	,	3,	std_gra_256,	enha_256	
NI.EXE	NI,	"Norton Utilities 4.5",	, cwe,	,	21,	std_NI,	enha_NI	
NORTON.EXE	NORTON,	"Norton Utilities 5/6.0",	, cwe,	,	21,	std_NORTON,	enha_NORTON	
PAINT.BAT	PAINT,	"PC Paintbrush IV Plus",	, cwe,	moricons.dll,	88,	std_PAINTE,	enha_PAINTE	
PARADOX.EXE	PARADOX,	"Paradox 3.5",	, cwe,	moricons.dll,	27,	std_PDOX35,	enha_PDOX35	
PRODIGY.EXE	PRODIGY,	"Prodigy",	, cwe,	moricons.dll,	98,	std_prodigy,	enha_prodigy	
QBASIC.EXE	QBASIC,	"Microsoft QBASIC",	, cwe,	moricons.dll,	15,	std_QBASIC,	enha_QBASIC	
SCOM.EXE	SCOM,	"SmartcomII",	, cwe,	,	5,	std_SCOM,	enha_SCOM	
TURBO.EXE	TURBO,	"Turbo Pascal 6.0",	, cwe,	moricons.dll,	25,	std_BTURBO,	enha_BTURBO,	amb_turbo
WP.EXE	WP,	"Word Perfect",	, cwe,	moricons.dll,	81,	std_WP,	enha_WP,	amb_wp

* Spacing added here for clarity. CWE column: cwe = Close Window on Exit flag. Default icon file is PROGMAN.EXE unless otherwise noted. No. column:=Icon number in specified icon file.

† Startup Directory Name can be inserted here.

‡ Standard and Enhanced mode parameters stored in indicated sections which follow. See Table 7.3.

§ amb_123 (or similar) specifies section containing additional data to clarify selected application. See Table 7.4. opt_foxpro (or similar) specifies additional section with optimization data.

Text Entry Section. The first four lines, at the top of the PIF Editor dialog box, are used to specify parameters for the executable file associated with the PIF.

Program Filename:. The filename listed here will be executed after the DOS virtual machine is configured according to the settings which follow. The filename should be that of the executable program, exactly as you would type it on a command line at the DOS prompt if Windows were not running. However, do not append the switches and parameters which might follow the filename. These will be entered in the Optional Parameters box, as described below.

TABLE 7.3   Typical Additional Sections Specified in [PIF] Section of APPS.INF File

Section and Contents		PIF Editor Section	Selected Option, Check Box
[std_dflt]	*(Standard Default)*		
miniconvmem	= 128	Memory Requirements	128 KB required
videomode	= txt	Video Mode	Text
xmsmem	= 0,0	XMS Memory	0 KB required, 0 KB limit
checkboxes	=	Check Boxes (13 of 14)	No boxes checked
[enha_dflt]	*(Enhanced Default)*		
convmem	= 128, 640	Memory Requirements	128 KB required, 640 KB desired
emsmem	= 0, 1024	EMS Memory	0 KB required, 1024 KB desired
xmsmem	= 0, 1024	XMS Memory	0 KB required, 1024 KB desired
dispusage	= fs	Display Usage	Full screen mode
execflags	=	Execution	None specified
dispoptvideo	= txt	Video Memory	Text mode
(advanced Options follow)			
multaskopt	= 50, 100	Multitasking Options	Priority: 50 bkgrnd, 100 foregrnd
procmemflags[†]	= dit, hma	Multitasking Options	Detect idle time
		Memory Options	Uses high memory area
dispoptports	= hgr	Display Options/Mon. Ports	High graphics
dispflags	= emt	Display Options/others	Emulate text mode
otheroptions	= afp	Other Options	Allow fast paste

TABLE 7.3   *(continued)*

Section and Contents		PIF Editor Section	Selected option, check box
[std_MSEDIT]	*(MS-DOS Editor)*		
minconvmem	= 330	Memory Requirements	350 KB required
videomode	= gra	Memory Requirements	Graphics/Multiple Text
[enha_MSEDIT]	*(MS-DOS Editor)*		
convmem	= 330, 640	Memory Requirements	330 KB required, 640 KB desired
emsmem	= 0	EMS Memory	None required
xmsmem	= 0	XMS Memory	None required
dispoptports	=	Display options/Mon. Ports	No boxes checked
[std_NORTON]	*(Norton Utilities, version 5.0, 6.0)*		
minconvmem	= 350	Memory Requirements	350 KB required
[enha_NORTON]	*(Norton Utilities, version 5.0, 6.0)*		
convmem	= 350, 640	Memory Requirements	350 KB required, 640 KB desired
execflags	= exc	Execution	Exclusive
dispoptports	=	Display options/Mon. Ports	No boxes checked
otheroptions	= aen, aes, afp, asp, ata, ces	Other Options	(see list in Table 7.5)

[†] Note procmemflags line includes *Detect Idle Time* from Multitasking Options section, plus all check boxes in Memory Options section.

TABLE 7.4   Typical Ambiguous and Optimized Sections Specified in [PIF] Section

Section and Contents

[amb_wp]
;WordPerfect, Multimate and OfficeWriter all use WP.EXE

WP.EXE	WP,	"Multimate",	*(additional data follows here)*
WP.EXE	WP,	"OfficeWriter",	*(additional data follows here)*
WP.EXE	WP,	"OfficeWriter 6.2",	*(additional data follows here)*

[opt_foxpro]
FOX.EXE   FOX, "FoxPro (Min. Config.)", , cwe, moricons.dll, 91, std_FOXPRO2, enha_FOXPRO2[†]

[†] enha_FOXPRO2 (or similar) section contains parameters to optimize PIF environment.

TABLE 7.5   Abbreviations Used in [enha_...] and [std_...] Sections of APPS.INF File

Abbreviation and Meaning	Dialog Box	Section
aen Alt+Enter	Advanced Options	Other Options: Reserve Shortcut Keys
aes Alt+Escape	Advanced Options	Other Options: Reserve Shortcut Keys
	PIF Editor (standard)	Reserve Shortcut Keys
afp Allow Fast Paste	Advanced Options	Other Options
aps Alt+Print Screen	Advanced Options	Other Options: Reserve Shortcut Keys
	PIF Editor (standard)	Reserve Shortcut Keys
asp Alt+Spacebar	Advanced Options	Other Options
ata Alt+Tab	Advanced Options	Other Options: Reserve Shortcut Keys
	PIF Editor (standard)	Reserve Shortcut Keys
bgd Background	PIF Editor (enhanced)	Execution:
cl-4 COM1, 2, 3, 4	PIF Editor (standard)	Directly Modifies:
ces Ctrl+Escape	Advanced Options	Other Options: Reserve Shortcut Keys
	PIF Editor (standard)	Reserve Shortcut Keys
cwa Allow Close When Active	Advanced Options	Other Options
cwe Close Window on Exit	PIF Editor (both)	Close Window on Exit (PIF section)
dit Detect Idle Time	PIF Editor (enhanced)	Multitasking Options
eml EMS Memory Locked	Advanced Options	Memory Options
emt Emulate Text Mode	Advanced Options	Display Options
exc Exclusive	PIF Editor (enhanced)	Execution:
fs Full Screen	PIF Editor (enhanced)	Display Usage[†]
gra Graphics/multiple text	PIF Editor (standard)	Video Mode[†]
hgr High Graphics	PIF Editor (enhanced)	Video Memory[†]
	Advanced Options	Monitor Ports
hma Uses High Memory Area	Advanced Options	Memory Options
kbd Keyboard	PIF Editor (standard)	Directly Modifies:
lam Lock Application Memory	Advanced Options	Memory Options
lgr Low Graphics	PIF Editor (enhanced)	Video Memory[†]
	Advanced Options	Monitor Ports
nse No Screen Exchange	PIF Editor (standard)	No Screen Exchange
nss No Save Screen	PIF Editor (Standard)	No Save Screen
pps Prevent Program Switch	PIF Editor (standard)	Prevent Program Switch
psc Print Screen	Advanced Options	Other Options: Reserve Shortcut Keys
	PIF Editor (standard)	Reserve Shortcut Keys
rvm Retain Video Memory	Advanced Options	Display Options
txt Text	PIF Editor (enhanced)	Video Memory[†]
	PIF Editor (standard)	Video Mode[†]
	Advanced Options	Monitor Ports

TABLE 7.5   *(continued)*

Abbreviation and Meaning	Dialog Box	Section
win Windowed	PIF Editor (enhanced)	Display Usage[†]
xml XMS Memory Locked	PIF Editor (enhanced)	Memory Options

[†]Radio button. All others are check boxes.

Window Title. The text in this window appears in an application's DOS Window Title Bar *only* under the following unique conditions:

- Windows creates a PIF for a DOS application as part of its Setup Procedure, using information stored in the [pif] section of the APPS.INF file.
- You write a new application PIF before installing that application. When you do install the application as a New Program Item in a group window, you leave the Description box blank.

Under either of these conditions, Windows copies the *Window Title* text from the PIF to the Description box in the Program Item Properties dialog box; from there it finds its way into the Title Bar whenever the application runs in a DOS Window. However, if you edit the Description text later on, then that new text is used instead. Subsequent edits to the *Window Title* text are ignored unless you open the Program Manager's File Menu, select the Run... option and type *filename*.PIF in the Command Line box.

Optional Parameters:. If the DOS command line entered in the Program Filename box is customarily followed by a switch and/or other parameters, enter those instructions on this line, instead of in the Program Filename box.

Startup Directory. This is equivalent to the Working Directory that may be specified in the application's Properties dialog box. It specifies the directory that the application will initially use for reading and writing files. If the Start up directory name differs from the Working Directory, the latter takes precedence.

Radio Buttons, Memory Specification, and Check Boxes. The remainder of the PIF Editor dialog box contains the following selection of radio buttons, data entry, and check boxes.

Video Memory:. The three radio buttons in this section select the amount of memory allocated to the application for the initial screen display. In most cases, Windows can adjust the allocation upwards if the application requires additional video memory later on. The amount of memory reserved by each button is as follows:

Text	16 Kbytes
Low Graphics	32 Kbytes
High Graphics	128 Kbytes

Memory Options. The PIF Editor provides the means for setting the amount of conventional, extended, and expanded memory that will be made available to an application, as described here. And, as if the subject weren't complicated enough, the screen nomenclature makes it even more so: The first set of boxes is ambiguously labeled *Memory Requirements*. It should in fact be *Conventional Memory Requirements,* or better yet, just *Conventional Memory,* to match the *EMS* and *XMS* sections which follow it.

In each case, an *Insufficient Memory* error message appears if the specified amount of memory is not available. If an invalid number is entered in any box, an advisory message lists the valid range for that box. Valid numbers are given in parentheses in the explanations that follow.

Memory Requirements. For the purposes of the following explanation, consider a system in which the DOS MEM command shows that device drivers and TSRs occupy 60 Kbytes of conventional memory immediately after booting the system. When Windows is opened and the DOS Prompt icon double-clicked, the MEM command shows 75 Kbytes used. (The additional memory is occupied by WIN386, WIN, and a second COMMAND.COM.) If you want to run a DOS application that needs no more than say, another 65 Kbytes, then this virtual machine with its 640 Kbytes conventional memory wastes some 500 Kbytes of RAM resources.

A Windows virtual machine can trim the size of its conventional memory block so as not to waste such unused memory. In the example given here, the conventional memory allocation might be set for 65 Kbytes (in the KB Desired box described below). When the DOS Window is opened, the DOS 5.0 MEM command will show 140K total conventional memory, and 65K available (on the largest executable program size line). The DOS 6.0 MEM command shows 140K Total, 75K Used, 65K Free—figures which will vary from one system to another, depending on the memory required for device drivers and TSRs, and the amount set aside for the application.

With this brief summary of memory utilization as background, enter one of the following values in each box, as appropriate to the application.

−1   Windows allocates as much conventional memory as possible, up to the 640 Kbyte limit for conventional memory.

 0   The application has no minimum conventional memory requirements.

xxx   Windows allocates *xxx* Kbytes of conventional memory.

KB Required (−1, 0–640). The figure in this box is the minimum that must be available in order for the application to be executed.

KB Desired (−1, 0–640). This figure specifies the maximum that is added to the conventional memory block. Thus, if device drivers, TSRs, and Windows itself take up 75 Kbytes and the box shows 65, then this virtual machine gets 140 Kbytes of conventional memory. In this specific example, any value over 565 would be accepted but truncated at 565 (since 75 + 565 = 640, and that's all there is to conventional memory). If the specified amount is not currently available, then Windows supplies whatever it can find.

KB Desired Lower Limit. Although the lower KB Desired figure is listed as zero, in practice it must be set to at least 40–60 Kbytes (figure varies according to system configuration). Windows needs the extra headroom to set up another virtual machine. However, once the DOS session is up and running, most of that space is made available to the application. If you enter a KB Desired value lower than that required by your system, an *Insufficient memory* error message appears when you try to begin the DOS session.

EMS and XMS Memory. A separate set of boxes is provided for EMS (expanded) and XMS (extended) memory requirements. Enter one of the following values in each box, as appropriate to the application.

−1   Windows allocates as much memory as possible, up to the limit of system memory.

 0   The application does not use expanded or extended memory.

xxx   Windows allocates *xxx* Kbytes of memory.

KB Required (0–16384). Enter the amount of memory that must be available in order for the application to be executed. Unless you know the application must have a certain amount of expanded or extended memory, this setting can be left at zero. If the application asks for memory, it gets it—up to the limit imposed by the KB Limit setting.

KB Limit (−1, 0–16384). This is the limit to the amount of expanded or extended memory that the application can receive, assuming the specified amount is available. If it is not, Windows gives the application as much as it can.

Display Usage:. This one is easy: Click the Full Screen or Windowed radio button to specify the screen mode in which you want the application to open.

Execution. The options provided here determine how the application runs when other DOS and Windows applications are also active. Either or both may be checked.

Background. Check this box if you want the application to continue running in the background when some other application is in the foreground. If the check box is cleared, then program execution is suspended whenever some other application is in the foreground.

Exclusive. If this box is checked, it overrides every other application's Background check box. In other words, when any Exclusive application is in the foreground, all other applications are suspended, regardless of their own background status.

NOTE: If a windowed application is running in Exclusive mode, Windows still holds on to a bit of processing time for maintaining the Windows Desktop. Therefore, if you want to be *really* exclusive, run the exclusive application in full-screen mode.

Close Window on Exit. Depending on circumstances, you may want the DOS Window—or in standard mode, the full-screen display—to remain in place after you exit the application. This would be convenient if the application leaves information on the screen that you would like to review. In this case, clear the check box. Otherwise, when the application closes, so does the DOS session, and the Program Manager once again appears.

If the Close Window on Exit box is cleared, use one of the following procedures to exit the DOS session and return to the Program Manager.

Enhanced Mode. If your DOS application runs in full-screen mode, the DOS session switches into an inactive DOS Window when the application closes. The inactive session cannot be toggled back into full-screen mode. Open the Control Menu and select the Close option to close the window.

Standard Mode. When the application closes, a Press Any Key to Exit prompt appears in the lower righthand corner of the screen. When you do so, the inactive DOS session closes and the Program Manager reappears.

Advanced... Button. Click once on this button to open the Advanced Options dialog box, which is described immediately below.

Enhanced Mode PIF Editor: Advanced Options Dialog Box

Use the Advanced Options dialog box shown in Figure 7.6b to make additional edits to the enhanced-mode PIF. The dialog box options are divided into the four sections described here.

Multitasking Options. When multiple applications are simultaneously executed, Windows assigns processing time to each one according to a priority system. All active Windows applications equally share the priority assigned to Windows, which is described in the *386 Enhanced* section of Chapter 13. If Windows-for-Workgroups is installed, a priority is also assigned to the server process, as described in the *Network Settings* section of Chapter 11. Priorities for each DOS application are specified in that application's PIF, as described here.

Foreground and Background Priorities. When a DOS application runs in the foreground, it is allocated a percentage of the total available processing time according to the following formula:

PT = A/B

PT   Processing time, expressed as a percentage of total available processing time

A   This application's *foreground* priority

B   A + sum of all other *background* priorities

For example, consider four DOS applications, whose foreground and background priorities are set as shown in Table 7.6. For the purposes of this illustration, the Table also lists the default priorities for Windows itself. The network server priority (if any) is not considered in this example.

When an application runs in the foreground, it receives the indicated percentage of the processing time, while the background applications share the remainder according to their background priorities. Therefore, in this example, if application 1 runs in the foreground, it receives 29 percent of the processor's time, while applications 2–4 receive 12.4, 8.3, and 4.1 percent, respectively. Since Windows has the same priorities as application 3, it also receives 8.3 percent of the processor time.

TABLE 7.6 Typical Allocations of Processing Time

Application	Priorities[*]		Processing Time					
	Foreground	Background	Foreground		Background			
Windows	100	50	29[†] (100/350)[‡]		8.3	11.8	15.2	15.5
1	400	100	67 (400/600)		—	23.6	28.4	30.9
2	200	75	47 (200/425)		12.4	—	21.3	23.2
3	100	50	29 (100/350)		8.3	11.8	—	15.5
4	50	25	15 (50/325)		4.1	5.9	7.1	—

[*] Priorities set by each application's PIF. Windows priorities set via *386 Enhanced* applet in Control Panel (see Chapter 11).

[†] Foreground application receives indicated percentage of processing time. Remainder is allocated to each background application according to its background priority.

[‡] Numerator = foreground priority. Denominator = foreground priority, plus sum of all other background priorities.

Detect Idle Time. A certain amount of processing time is wasted if the active application isn't doing anything while waiting for user input. If this box is checked, idle time is detected and the CPU is made available to other applications. For most applications, idle-time detection should be enabled, so that background applications can run faster when the foreground application isn't doing anything. One notable exception is any communication program where there is no keyboard action during a modem transmission. To make sure such inactivity is not detected as idle time, clear the check box.

Memory Options. The options in this section provide additional control over the conventional, expanded, and extended memory resources specified in the previous PIF Editor dialog box.

EMS and XMS Memory Locked. If either box is checked, the application's expanded and/or extended memory allocation is permanently assigned, as may be required by some TSRs. Unless your application needs to hold onto its expanded or extended memory, leave these boxes cleared so that the memory resources can be made available to other applications.

Uses High Memory Area. If you load part of DOS into the 64 Kbyte high memory area during system startup (via dos=HIGH in CON-FIG.SYS), or some network or other software uses it, then the status of this box is unimportant, since the area is unavailable to any

DOS application running in a virtual machine. However, if the high memory area is not otherwise used, then a check mark gives the application access to this 64 Kbyte block. If you know the current application cannot use the area either, then clear the check box. Otherwise, check it if you know the area is available.

Lock Application Memory. Perhaps this check box should be labeled "Lock *Conventional* Memory," since that's what it does. If the box is checked, the application is not swapped to hard disk, which may speed it up at the expense of slowing down everything else. If the application doesn't work properly when parts of it get swapped back and forth to disk, then put a check in the box. Otherwise, do or don't, depending on how the rest of the system behaves.

Display Options. Use these options to optimize the video performance of the DOS application, as described here.

Monitor Ports: Text, Low Graphics, High Graphics. If there is a full-screen cursor or other display problem, check the box that matches the current operating mode, which may help resolve a video conflict between the application and the video adapter. The check boxes have no effect on DOS Window operations, and may also have no effect with certain video adapters.

Full-screen access is usually faster if these boxes are not checked, so unless there's a problem, leave them all cleared.

Emulate Text Mode. Screen updates are usually fastest if this box is checked. However, you may need to clear it if screen display is garbled or cursor location is incorrect.

Retain Video Memory. During normal operations, an application should be able to switch between text and video modes with no problem. However, if there is a display problem when an application switches into a higher video mode, it may be because other applications have swiped all the available memory. In this case, toggle the Video Memory button one position to the right (on the first PIF Editor dialog box), and put a check in the Retain Video Memory box. This reserves the indicated amount of video memory for the current application.

Other Options. The final section of the Advanced Options dialog box offers the following additional options.

**Allow Fast Paste.** If you need to paste information into the application from the Clipboard, this option should speed up the process. However, it does not work well with some applications, so clear the check box if there's a pasting problem.

**Allow Close When Active.** If this box is checked, you can close Windows without exiting the DOS session, which is a convenience or a disaster, depending on what's going on in that session. If the application writes to disk, then you run the risk of file demolition, or possibly just some data loss, in which case this option is not a very good idea. Although the Help Screen says closure is automatic, it isn't: A warning message lets you know what's about to happen. If you're not sure about the implications of it all, leave the check box cleared. However, if you do decide to check it, a warning message tells you you're asking for trouble. Click on the message's OK or Cancel button, then press Function Key F1 to read the Help Screen for more information.

**Reserve Shortcut Keys.** Some DOS applications assign various functions to shortcut keys that may otherwise be assigned to Windows. For example, in the DOS Norton Utilities the Alt+Enter keys open one of the drop-down menus, thus precluding the use of these keys to toggle between full-screen and DOS Window modes. To prevent the application from taking over these keys, clear the check box next to Alt+Enter. Note the status of the following check boxes, and clear a box if you'd rather let Windows control that key combination.

Alt+Enter	Alt+PrtSc	Alt+Tab	PrtSc
Alt+Esc	Alt+Space	Ctrl+Esc	

**Application Shortcut Key.** Use this box to specify a shortcut key combination that will bring the application—_if_ it is already open—to the foreground. Hold down one of the following combinations and press any letter or number key to assign that combination.

Alt	Ctrl	Alt+Ctrl
Alt+Shift	Ctrl+Shift	Alt+Ctrl+Shift

> **NOTE:** The interaction between a Shortcut Key assigned in a PIF and the same Shortcut Key assigned via the **Program Item Properties** box is potentially confusing, to say the least. Refer to the _Shortcut Key Configuration_ section later in the chapter for further details and suggestions for staying out of trouble.

Standard Mode PIF Editor Dialog Box

In standard mode, there is only one dialog box for PIF settings, as shown in Figure 7.6c. Since some of the standard mode parameters are significantly different from those in the enhanced-mode PIF, make sure to edit this section too.

Text Entry Section. The entries in this section match those in the equivalent enhanced-mode section described above. Any change made in that section will automatically appear here as well, and vice versa.

Radio Buttons, Memory Specification, and Check Boxes. Many of the items in this section are not found in the enhanced-mode PIF Editor, and of those that do appear in both, the settings are not necessarily the same.

Video Mode. The two radio buttons in this section specify the amount of video memory that Windows should reserve for the application, *and* for copying the screen contents to the Clipboard. (See also *No Screen Exchange* below.)

Text. Select this option if your application runs exclusively in text mode, using a single video page.

Graphics/Multiple Text. This option sets aside sufficient video memory for more than one video page, and for graphics applications.

Memory Requirements. As in the enhanced-mode PIF, this section specifies conventional memory requirements. Note, however, that only one entry box is provided.

KB Required (–1, 0–640). The figure in this box is the minimum that must be available in order for the application to be executed.

XMS Memory. Refer to the enhanced-mode *EMS and XMS Memory Requirements* section for details about these settings.

Directly Modifies. The check boxes in this section reserve the specified communications port(s) and keyboard for the exclusive use of the application. If any box in this section is checked, all Shortcut Keys throughout the system are disabled.

COMx. If the application uses a communications port, check the appropriate box for the port that is used. Otherwise, leave all COM*x* boxes cleared.

Keyboard. Check this box if your application requires exclusive access to the keyboard. If you aren't sure about this, leave the box cleared.

No Screen Exchange. Check this box if memory is tight and you have no need to copy the screen to the Clipboard. The screen-exchange memory usually reserved for Print-Screen operations (to the Clipboard) is made available to the application instead.

Close Window on Exit. Clear this box if you want the DOS screen to remain after you exit the application, as described in the enhanced-mode section above. In standard mode, a Press Any Key to Exit prompt appears in the lower right-hand corner of the screen. Do so when you are ready to return to the Program Manager screen.

Prevent Program Switch. This option prevents Windows from switching back to the Program Manager or to other applications, thus freeing memory usually allocated for program-switching for use by this application.

No Save Screen. Windows usually saves current screen information in memory when you toggle between applications in standard mode. You can save this memory by checking this box, *if* you know your application is capable of retaining, and redrawing, its screen when it is toggled back into active mode. In case of doubt, leave the box cleared.

Reserve Shortcut Keys. This standard-mode option is functionally equivalent to that described in the enhanced-mode section above, except that fewer key combinations are listed. Note the status of the following check boxes, and clear the box if you'd rather let Windows control that key combination.

Alt+Esc	Alt+Tab	PrtSc
Alt+PrtSc	Ctrl+Esc	

DOS Window Configuration

This section is limited to a description of the procedures by which the size and position of an open DOS Window may be adjusted. Refer to the *DOS*

Session Configuration section which follows for additional information that may be applied to both DOS-Window and Full-Screen modes.

Window Size Adjustments

The size of the DOS Window may be adjusted as required, either by adjusting the window borders, changing the Terminal font matrix that displays text within the window, or via the DOS MODE command.

Adjust Window Borders. To directly change the size of the DOS Window, move the mouse cursor across any horizontal or vertical window border; when the cursor shape changes to a double arrow, hold down the primary mouse button and move the border in the desired direction. If necessary, repeat the operation for the other border. Or, place the pointer in a window corner to move the two adjacent borders, as indicated by a diagonal double-arrow. Note, however, that the window may only be adjusted within certain limits. The minimum area contains nothing but the three ribbon buttons and a fragment of the title bar text. The maximum area is defined as the space required to display 25 lines of 40- or 80-character text, which in many cases is somewhat less than the entire Windows Desktop area. If you attempt to move either border beyond its limit, it will "snap back" to its predefined limit as soon as you release the mouse button.

A shortcut method to maximize the window is to simply click on the Maximize button (Up arrow) at the upper right-hand corner of the DOS Window. The screen immediately expands to the maximum size, the Maximize button is replaced by the Restore button (Up and Down arrows), and the border-adjustment function is disabled. If you would rather set the window to some intermediate area, click on the Restore button to return to the previous window area, then use the border adjustment technique described above.

The procedures just described change the size of the DOS Window, but have no effect on the text within that window, other than to allow more or less of it to be seen, depending on the size of the window.

Change Terminal Font Matrix. In addition to the window border adjustments described above, the DOS Window size may also be indirectly varied by changing the font that displays text in the window. Briefly stated, as the font matrix changes, so does the window size, since different fonts require different areas to display the same information.

To change the font matrix, and therefore the window size, click on the Control Menu box in the upper left-hand corner of the DOS Window. When the pull-down Control Menu appears, highlight the Fonts... option to display the Font Selection dialog box shown in Figure 7.7. The Font box at the left of the screen lists the font matrixes available to form characters within the DOS Window. (The matrixes are displayed by the font specified in the fixedfon.fon= line in WIN.INI, which is described in Chapter 10.) The Window Preview box illustrates the relative size of the DOS Window if the highlighted matrix is selected. Simply move the highlight bar up or down, note the effect on the size of the window, then click on the OK button to return to the DOS Window. Scroll bars appear at the bottom and/or right side of the window if it is not large enough to display 25 lines of 40 or 80 characters each.

If the Fonts... option does not appear as a menu choice, then refer to *Missing DOS Fonts* in the Troubleshooting section later in this chapter.

Change DOS Display Mode (Screen Lines). The size of an open DOS Window can also be varied by changing the number of lines displayed in the window. Under default conditions, 25 lines of text are displayed when you begin a DOS session in either full-screen or DOS-Window mode. Add the following line to display 43 or 50 lines instead.

```
[NonWindowsApp]
ScreenLines=43 (or 50)
```

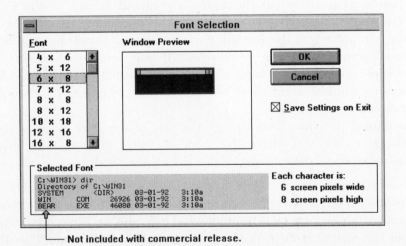

Figure 7.7   The Font Selection dialog box is accessed via the Fonts... option on the Control Menu seen in Figure 7.3.

If you prefer, the number of lines may be changed within a specific DOS session by using the DOS MODE command, as shown here:

mode con lines = 25 (*or* 43, *or* 50)

or

mode *width, height*

where

width	Screen width, in characters (40 or 80)
height	Screen height, in lines (25, 43 or 50)

The number of lines actually seen on screen is a function of the selected DOS display mode, the font matrix, and the installed video system. A few VGA examples are given here.

Mode Command	Full Screen Lines	DOS Window Mode Lines	Matrix	Comments
MODE, 25	25	25	8 × 8	
			8 × 12	Default DOS mode
MODE, 43	43	43	8 × 8	All 43 lines visible
		37	8 × 12	Use scroll bar to view lines 38–43
			12 × 16	Use scroll bar to view lines 28–43
			10 × 18	Use scroll bar to view lines 25–43
MODE, 50	50	50	8 × 8	
		37	8 × 12	Use scroll bar to view lines 38–50

Figure 7.8 shows the effect of changing the DOS Window font matrix. The Windows desktop (Figure 7.8a) is shown with an open DOS Window occupying most of the area. The 25-line directory listing is displayed in the 8 × 12 font, so the maximized window seen in the figure takes up 300 (25 × 12) vertical lines on the 480-line (VGA graphics) screen. To verify that this is indeed the largest DOS Window possible (in this display mode and font matrix), measure the vertical dimensions of the DOS Window and of the Windows Desktop. The ratio should be 30:48 (that is, 300 DOS lines; 480 VGA graphics lines). If another matrix is chosen, the maximum window size will vary, as shown by the 4 × 6 and 7 × 12 matrixes in Figure 7.8b.

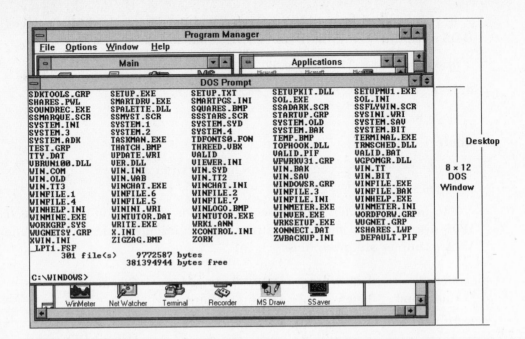

Figure 7.8a The effect on Window size of changing the font matrix. A DOS directory listing is shown in an 8 × 12 matrix.

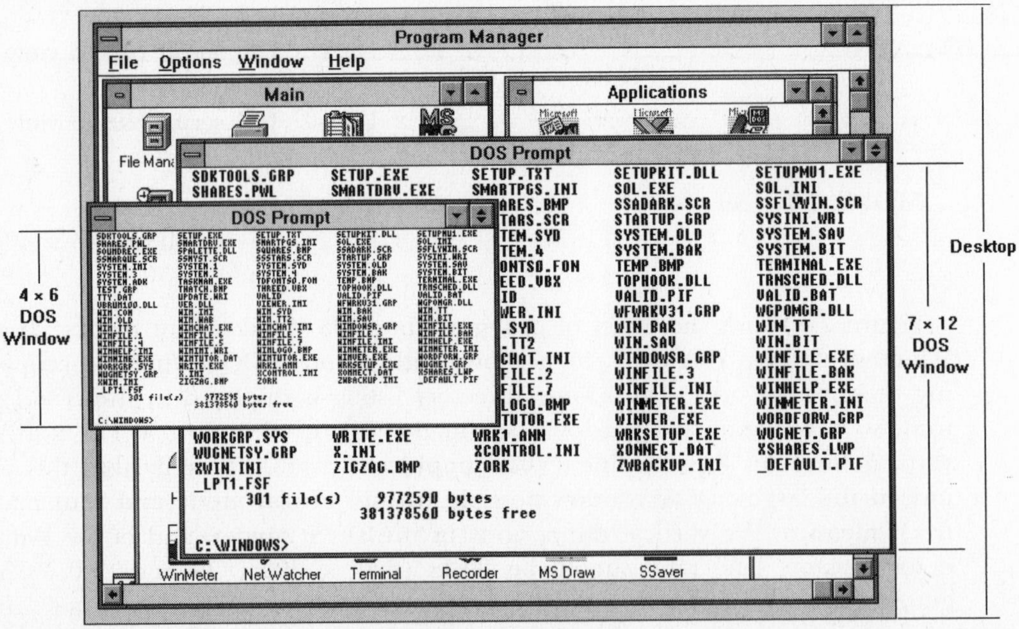

Figure 7.8b A DOS directory listing is shown in 4 × 6 and 7 × 12 matrixes.

For future reference, Table 7.7 shows the video resolution required to display 25, 43, or 50 lines of text in a DOS Window at each of the ten available font matrixes.

A DOS Window Display Mode Test. The DOS 5.0 or 6.0 shell utility (DOS-SHELL.EXE) offers a convenient way to check the display modes that will, or won't, work at your current video resolution. From within Windows, double-click on the DOS Prompt Icon and, in full-screen mode, type DOSSHELL and press the Enter key. When the MS-DOS Shell appears, select the Display... option on the Options Menu. Select any of the graphics modes, click on the Preview button, then press the Alt+Enter keys to try to display the selected graphics mode in a DOS Window. Table 7.8 lists the display modes that are available through the MS-DOS shell.

Character Set (Code Page) Configuration

If you configure Windows for a language other than US-English, you may also specify a "code page" to display a different character set than the default PC-8 set described above. Since a complete initiation into the mysteries of the code page is well beyond the scope of this chapter (and its author), only the effect of code-paging on DOS-window fonts is described

TABLE 7.7   Resolution Required to Display 25–50 Lines in Maximized DOS Window*

Font Matric H × V	25 Lines (Mode, 25)	43 Lines (Mode, 43)	50 Lines (Mode, 50)
4 × 6	320 × 150	320 × 258	320 × 300
5 × 12	400 × 300	400 × 516	400 × 600
6 × 8	480 × 200	480 × 344	480 × 400
7 × 12	560 × 300	560 × 516	560 × 600
8 × 8	640 × 200	640 × 344	640 × 400
8 × 12	640 × 300	640 × 516	640 × 600
10 × 18	800 × 450	800 × 744	800 × 900
12 × 16	960 × 400	960 × 688	960 × 800
16 × 8	1280 × 200	1280 × 344	1280 × 400
16 × 12	1280 × 300	1280 × 516	1280 × 600

* Select Font Matrix and use DOS Mode, *xx* command to specify horizontal lines.
  Screen resolution must be equal to, or greater than, indicated values to show all lines in maximized DOS Window.

TABLE 7.8   DOS Resolutions Available in DOSSHELL Utility

Screen		Text Modes			Graphics Modes		
Lines & Resolution		Pixel	Matrix	Freq. (Hz)	Pixel	Matrix	Freq. (Hz)
25	Low	640	400	70	640	350	70
30	Medium	—	—	—	800	600	60
34	Medium	—	—	—	800	600	60
43	High	640	350	70	640	350	70
50	High	640	400	70	—	—	—
60	High	—	—	—	800	600	60

here. Briefly stated, different code pages display different character sets for some (but not all) of the DOS-window fonts. If you have no need to experiment with this feature, the following paragraphs can be safely skipped.

To install a code page other than standard US-English (code page 437), exit Windows, log onto the Windows directory, and run the Setup program. On the System Information Screen shown in Figure 1.1b, the Code Page entry near the bottom of the list shows the current code page. Highlight this entry and press the Enter key to display the following list of available code pages. For each code page, the OEM font column (not seen on the Setup screen) lists the font file that will be specified in the OEMFONT.FON= line in the [boot] section of SYSTEM.INI. Refer to the appropriate part of Figure 7.9 in the right-hand column for the character set used for the 8×12 font in the DOS Window.

Language	Code Page	OEM (8×12) Font	See Figure 7.9
English	437	VGAOEM.FON	(a)
Multilingual	850	VGA850.FON	(b)
Portuguese	860	VGA860.FON	(c)
Icelandic	861	VGA861.FON	(d)
Canadian-French	863	VGA863.FON	(e)
Nordic	865	VGA865.FON	(f)

In addition, if any code page other than 437 is selected, a different set of WOA files will be specified in the [386Enh] section of SYSTEM.INI, as shown here:

[386Enh]	H	V	Comments
CGA80WOA.FON=CGA80850.FON	8	8	Same character set as APP850.FON
EGA80WOA.FON=EGA80850.FON	8	12	Replaced in DOS Window by VGA8nn.FON, as specified by the selected Code page above

CGA40WOA.FON=CGA40850.FON	16	8	Same character set as APP850.FON
EGA40WOA.FON=EGA40850.FON	16	12	Same character set as APP850.FON
WOAFont=APP850.FON			Character set shown in Fig. 7.9b

As a result of these changes, all DOS-window font matrixes except 8 × 12 display the Multilingual character set seen in Figure 7.9b. The 8 × 12 matrix displays the language-specific character set contained in the appropriate VGA8*nn*.FON file, and this font also appears as the Character Map's Terminal font. The same remarks apply to an EGA system, except that the 8 × 8 matrix displays the language-specific character set.

Use of Foreign-Language Character Set for Selected Font Sizes. Within reason, one or two foreign-language character sets may be used within the DOS Window for selected font matrixes, while the default character set is retained for the others. For example, if the following SYSTEM.INI edits are made to an otherwise conventional US-English installation, the results will be as indicated.

SYSTEM.INI File	**Specifies Code Page**	**Code Page Used for DOS Font Matrix**
[boot]		
oemfonts.fon=vga861.fon	861 (Icelandic)	8 × 12 (also seen as Terminal font in Character Map)
[386Enh]		
woafont=app850.fon	850 (Multilingual)	4 × 6, 5 × 12, 6 × 8, 7 × 12, 10 × 18, 12 × 16
(other lines unchanged)	437 (PC-8)	8 × 8, 16 × 8, 16 × 12

Use of WOA Terminal Fonts in Windows Applications

One or more of the WOA font matrixes resident in DOSAPP or APP850 may be made available to Windows applications (for example, WRITE or Word-for-Windows) if your installed printer offers the necessary support. If it does, then the primary Terminal (*xxx*OEM.FON) font

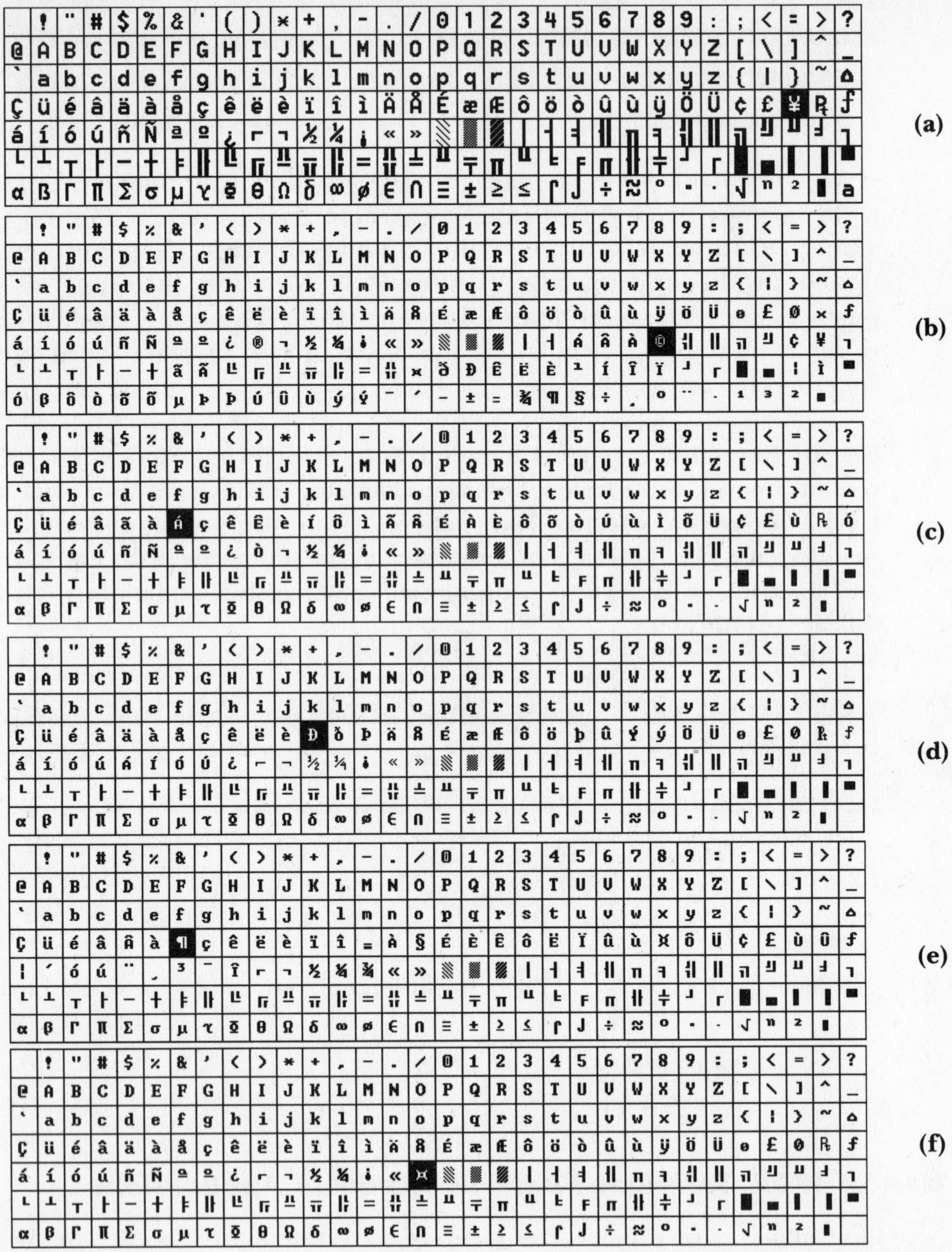

Figure 7.9 DOS Terminal Font character set and code page. The shaded box in each character set identifies a character whose position is unique to that set. (a) US-English; 437, (b) Multilingual; 850, (c) Portuguese; 860, (d) Icelandic; 861, (e) Canadian-French; 863, (f) Nordic; 865.

size is augmented by up to five additional sizes taken from the DOSAPP or APP850 file. The additional font sizes may be configured as temporary or permanent, as described here:

Temporary Terminal Fonts. Open WRITE, select the Terminal font, and note the available font size. Now open a DOS Window, return to WRITE, and observe the selection of Terminal font sizes, which should be greater than it was prior to opening the DOS Window. In Word-for-Windows and some other applications, you'll have to exit the application and reopen it to gain access to the additional fonts made available when a DOS Window is open. The additional Terminal fonts are temporary: available only while a DOS Window remains open.

Permanent Terminal Fonts. To make the additional Terminal font sizes permanently available to your Windows applications, open the Control Panel, click on the Fonts icon, then click on the **Add...** button. Select the System directory and look for an "MS DOS Code Page 437" entry. Highlight the entry, then add it to your list of installed fonts. The additional Terminal fonts are now permanent: available whether a DOS Window is open or not.

Note that the addition of "MS DOS Code Page 437" does not introduce a new font with that name. It merely makes additional font sizes in the DOSAPPS.FON file available when you select the Terminal font. The actual number of sizes depends on the installed printer.

For occasional use of the international character set (Figure 7.9b) on a US-English system, copy the APP850.FON into your System directory, then add the "MS DOS Code Page 850" font as described. The additional Terminal font sizes will now display the international character set.

DOS Session Configuration

The procedures described in this section may be applied to all DOS sessions, either to limit the video mode in which some or all of them operate, or to set operating parameters for some or all such DOS sessions.

Limiting Access to Full-Screen or DOS Window Modes

If it is important to prevent anyone from running some DOS applications in a DOS Window, or others in full-screen mode, use one of the following procedures, as appropriate.

Disable Full-Screen Mode for Selected Applications. Although there's probably little reason to do so, edit these PIF settings to limit access to Full-Screen mode:

Option	Choose:	Comments
Display Usage:	Windowed	Application will open in DOS Window mode.
Reserve Shortcut Keys:	Alt+Enter	Click on check box to disable mode toggling.

NOTE: These settings do not prevent Full-Screen mode from being accessed via the Settings... option on the Control Menu. When the DOS Prompt dialog box appears, simply click on the Window radio button, then click on the OK button. Once in Full-Screen mode, press Alt+Space to return to the DOS Window.

Disable DOS Window for Selected Applications. If a DOS application is executed in enhanced mode, then the Alt+Enter key combination toggles back and forth between full-screen and DOS Window modes, as already described. To prevent the application from running in a DOS Window, edit the following lines in the application's PIF.

Option	Choose:	Comments
Display Usage:	Full Screen	Application will open in full-screen mode.
Reserve Shortcut Keys:	Alt+Enter Alt+Space	Click on each check box. "X" reserves these keys for application's internal use, thus disabling them as screen mode toggles.

Disable DOS Window for All Applications. To prevent all use of the DOS Window mode, refer to *DOS-Exclusive Foreground Mode* in the following section.

The Exclusive Mode Options

As previously noted, Windows usually distributes application processing time to the various applications that are currently running, according to the Priority settings in the active PIFs (see *Priorities* in the *PIF Configuration* section). This section describes two lines that may be added to your

SYSTEM.INI file so that foreground DOS and/or Windows applications will run in an exclusive mode, in which all or most processing time is given to the foreground application.

DOS-Exclusive Foreground Mode. If the following line is added to SYSTEM.INI, only one DOS application can be run at a time, and that application will only run in full-screen mode.

```
[386Enh]
AllVMsExclusive=1 (or ON, TRUE, YES)
```

Any attempt to switch the application into a DOS Window displays an error message, and the DOS application will be minimized to an icon at the bottom of the Desktop. With the DOS application thus minimized, another DOS application may be opened, but it too will only run in exclusive full-screen mode.

Windows-Exclusive Foreground Mode. If a Windows application is in the foreground, the following line reserves all processing time for Windows applications.

```
[386Enh]
WinExclusive=1 (or ON, TRUE, YES)
```

Note that although this line suspends execution of background DOS applications, background Windows applications continue to share processing time with the foreground application. Furthermore, if a DOS application is in the foreground, background DOS applications are not affected.

Environment Size

The default environment for each DOS session is the same size as that of the DOS operating system (160 bytes in versions 2.0–4.0, 256 bytes in versions 5.0–6.0), or it may be some other value specified by the /e switch on the following CONFIG.SYS line:

```
shell=C:\DOS\COMMAND.COM /e:xxx    (other switches, parameters not shown here)
```

where *xxx* is the desired environment size.

To set a different environment size, follow the directions in either or both of the following sections, as required for your applications.

Set Global Environment Size. To specify an environment size for all DOS sessions, add or edit the following line in your SYSTEM.INI file:

[NonWindowsApp]
CommandEnvSize=*xxx* (where *xxx* = 0, or 160 to 32768)

If *xxx* is zero, or any value less than the actual size of the current environment, the line is ignored and the current size remains in place. If your CONFIG.SYS contains the shell= line shown above, then a CommandEnvSize= line is already present in the [NonWindowsApp] section, and the value is that seen on the shell= line.

Set Environment Size for Single Application. If you want to set an environment size for a specific application, open that application's PIF and edit the following lines as shown here:

Program Filename: COMMAND.COM   *(instead of application filename)*
Optional Parameters: /e:*xxxx* /c *filename*.EXE

Note the presence of the /c switch, which is required in this context. It specifies that the command interpreter is to run the executable filename which follows.

Verify Environment Size. To verify the environment size for the foreground DOS session, run the DOS MEM command from within that session—assuming the application provides means for accessing a DOS prompt: some do, some don't. For example, the DOS Norton Utilities *Disk Editor's* Quit Menu has a Shell to DOS option. Ignore the warning messages when you start *Disk Editor,* immediately open the Quit Menu, and select the Shell option. Many DOS word processors have a DOS-access option, as does Quick BASIC and some other DOS applications.

At the DOS prompt, type one of the MEM commands shown in Table 7.9. The screen display will show two COMMAND environments, along with other memory listings. The first COMMAND environment is that created when the system was booted; the second is for the current DOS session—its size should be either the same as the first, or agree with whatever changes you have made, as described above.

A Few Other Configuration Suggestions

The Configuration section concludes with a look at a few additional configuration techniques that may be useful in optimizing the look of your DOS sessions.

TABLE 7.9   Typical MEM Reports of Environment Size*

DOS Version	MEM Command		

DOS 5.0   **MEM /p**

Address	Name	Size[†]	Type
006490	COMMAND	000100	Environment
. . .	*(other lines here)*		
00EA60	COMMAND	000400	Environment

DOS 6.0   **MEM /d**

Segment	Total[‡]		Name	Type
00672	272	(0K)	COMMAND	Environment
. . .	*(other lines here)*			
011B5	1040	(1K)	COMMAND	Environment

DOS 6.0   **MEM/m COMMAND**

Segment	Region	Total[‡]		Type
005C8		2640	(3K)	Program
00672		272	(0K)	Environment
00683		80	(0K)	Data
01100		256	(0K)	Data
01110		2640	(3K)	Program
011B5		1040	(1K)	Environment
Total Size:		6928	(7K)	

* Second environment listing is for current DOS session.
† Size in hexadecimal notation.
‡ Size in decimal notation includes 16-byte memory control block.

Enable DOS PrintScreen Directly to Printer. Under default conditions, pressing the PrintScreen key copies the current screen display to the Clipboard—very nice if that's what you want to do, but a nuisance if you want a quick screen dump to the printer. To get it, open the PIF Editor applet and load DOSPRMPTPIF (In enhanced mode only, click on the Advanced... button shown at the bottom of the dialog box in Figure 7.6a. Next, check the PrtSc and Alt+PrtSc buttons (Figure 7.6b or c) to reserve these Shortcut keys for the DOS Window.

Save the changed PIF under a new name if you don't want to change the default DOSPRMPT.PIF. Or, follow the same procedure for any other PIF that you want to modify.

This feature may not operate as described here in early standard-mode versions of Windows 3.1.

Remove Screen Message. If you get tired of the opening screen message shown earlier in Figure 7.2a, it can be disabled by adding the following line to the indicated section of SYSTEM.INI:

```
[386Enh]
DOSPromptExitInstruc=Off
```

Note that the line is in the [386Enh] section of SYSTEM.INI, and not in the [NonWindowsApp] section, where you might have expected to find it. Also, the line has no effect on standard mode operation.

Insert a Windows "Reminder" in DOS Prompt. After working at the DOS prompt for awhile, it's easy enough to forget that Windows is active, and to type WIN to reopen Windows. There's no great harm in doing so: The worst that happens is a reminder message.

There are several ways to avoid this minor annoyance. For example, the WIN.BAT batch file described in Chapter 2 (Figure 2.2) closes the DOS Window whenever WIN is typed in that window. As shown in the figure, a warning message appears and you must press any key to continue, or remove the pause line and the Program Manager returns without waiting for you to do anything.

As an alternative, you can add the following line to your AUTOEXEC.BAT file:

Environment Variable	**Sets DOS Prompt As:**
set WINPMT=$p[WIN]$g	C:\WINDOWS[WIN]>

The WINPMT (Windows Prompt) environment variable sets the DOS prompt in a DOS Window as specified by the environment string on the righthand side of the equal sign. The $p[win]$g variable inserts a [WIN] reminder into the prompt, as shown above. Of course, you can insert your own reminder between the $p and $g if you like.

Set Cascading Menu Delay Time. If you click on the Edit option on the DOS Window's Control Menu, the cascading menu shown earlier in Figure 7.3b appears immediately. However, if you drag the highlight bar down to the Edit option, there may be a delay before the cascading menu appears. To set the desired delay, edit the following optional line in WIN.INI:

[Windows]
MenuShowDelay=*xxx* *(where xxx is the delay time, in milliseconds)*

Refer to the *Cascading Menu Delay Time* section in Chapter 3 for more information about this feature.

PIF Configuration

This section describes a few configuration techniques which may be useful in optimizing the performance of a DOS application running in Windows.

Configure Conventional Memory. If memory is tight and you're not sure of a DOS application's conventional memory requirements, try dropping the KB Desired value until you get an *Insufficient memory* message when you try to run the application. Once you know the minimum requirement to run the application, enter that value in the KB Required box. On subsequent sessions the application will not open unless the KB Required value can be satisfied by the available memory resources. Next, increase KB Desired until you can exercise all program options without getting into trouble. If you can manage with less than 640 Kbytes Desired (actually, 640 Kbytes *maximum*), then the surplus is available for use elsewhere.

Set Screen Mode. Given the inevitable system overhead (read, processing time) required to maintain an active DOS Window *and* the Windows Desktop, it's not surprising that a DOS application performs better in full-screen mode, which cuts down some of that overhead. Therefore, you may want to configure your important application PIFs to open in full-screen mode. You can always toggle into DOS Window mode when you need to do something else, but in the meantime your application will get the most processing time it can.

If you want to run a DOS communications application in the background during a lengthy modem data transfer, run it as a minimized icon rather than in a DOS Window.

Shortcut Key Configuration. Two dialog boxes—one in Program Item Properties, the other in PIF Editor Advanced Options—offer a Shortcut Key option. Under certain conditions, the information entered in one of these may be affected by the other. For example, consider the same Alt+Ctrl+*key* combination assigned to two applications, as follows:

Application	Dialog Box in:	Data Entry Box
X	PIF Editor: Advanced Options	Application Shortcut Key
Y	Program Item Properties	Shortcut Key

Depending on the Program Manager status, and the application(s) currently open on the Desktop, the Shortcut Key has the effect listed here:

Program Manager Status	Application Open	Effect of Shortcut Key
Background or minimized	None	No effect.
Open	None	Application X opens.
Open	X, in foreground	No effect.
Open	X, in background	Application X comes to foreground.
Open	X, Y in background	Application X comes to foreground.
Open	Y minimized	Application Y comes to foreground, regardless of X status (open, closed or minimized).

One easy way to avoid such confusion is to assign a PIF Shortcut Key combination that can't possibly be used in the Program Item Properties dialog box. For example, Alt+*key* or Ctrl+*key* are both valid PIF Shortcut Keys, but neither will be accepted in the Program Item Properties dialog box. Therefore, if either combination is used in application X's PIF, it can't possibly conflict with application Y's Program Item Shortcut Key.

As a final Shortcut point, note that if the application X Program Item Properties box lists a Shortcut Key, then that application's PIF Shortcut Key is disabled.

Display DOS Prompt at Application Exit. By clearing the Close Window on Exit box in an application's enhanced-mode PIF, an inactive DOS Window remains on the Windows Desktop when the application exits. Although this is convenient if you need to view the final application screen, you can't access a new DOS prompt within that window.

When the application closes, if you'd rather remain in either full-screen or DOS Window mode with an active DOS prompt available, add the following two lines to the batch file described above:

```
cls            Clear screen when application closes
command.com    Display DOS prompt
```

When your application closes, the screen clears, and a new copy of command.com leaves the DOS prompt at the top of the screen. Do what you

need to do, then type EXIT when you're ready to return to Windows. In the
MYAPP.PIF file cited above, do not clear the Close Window on Exit check box.

PIF and Batch File Techniques

This section offers some suggestions for using a batch file in conjunction
with the PIF for further optimization of the DOS session environment.

PIF Execution from a Batch File. The Windows 3.0 PIF Editor help file
(PIFEDIT.HLP) stated that a PIF could be run from a batch file. You
might try this to load various TSRs prior to starting a DOS application.
However, there *is* one little problem: It doesn't work. Although Windows
regards a file with a PIF extension as an executable application, DOS doesn't.
So, if you insert a *filename*.PIF command in a batch file, you will be rewarded with a "bad command or filename" message when that line is read.

The version 3.1 help file corrects this error, which is cited here for the
benefit of readers who may have encountered this excellent suggestion,
then wondered why it didn't work. To set up TSRs before executing a
DOS application, refer to the following instructions.

Load TSRs before Executing DOS Application. If you want to load one or
more TSRs before running a DOS application from within Windows, you
can do so by writing a PIF and a batch file, as shown here:

MYAPP.PIF

Program Filename: MYAPP.BAT
(*Set other parameters as required by your application.*)

MYAPP.BAT

@echo OFF	Do not display command lines on screen.
. . .	TSRs you want to load before running DOS application.
myapp.EXE	Execute DOS application.

Now install the DOS application as a New Program Item in your
Applications (or other) Group Window. In the Program Item Properties
dialog box, enter MYAPP.PIF in the Command line: box. Later on, when
you double-click on the application's icon, Windows reads the MYAPP.PIF
and sets the parameters you've specified. Then it executes the MYAPP.BAT
file which in turn loads the TSRs and executes the application.

DOS Session Troubleshooting

The following sections review some of the problems that may be encountered when running a DOS session within Windows. Refer to the appropriate section here if a problem occurs and is not accompanied by an error message. If an error message does show up, then refer to the *Error Messages* section which follows this one.

General DOS Application Problems

This section lists a few of the problems that may be encountered when trying to begin a DOS session, regardless of whether that session is to run in a DOS Window, or in Full-Screen mode.

Application Won't Run in Background. If, regardless of PIF settings, the execution of any DOS application is suspended when it runs in the background, Windows has probably reserved all processing time for the application running in the foreground. Refer to *Set Foreground Processing Time* in the *DOS Window Configuration* section for more information.

Application Icon Doesn't Work. If double-clicking on an application icon momentarily clears the screen, then returns the Program Manager, it's possible that the Optional Parameters box in the application's PIF lists an invalid switch. In case of doubt, open a DOS session (if necessary, exit Windows) and type filename /? to review the list of valid switches for the application; that is, if the application supports this help feature. If not, check the appropriate User's Guide, or just remove the suspect switch and try again.

All Application Icons Don't Work (standard mode only). If double-clicking on any application icon momentarily clears the screen, then returns the Program Manager, the DSWAP.EXE file may be missing or defective. This file is needed only in standard mode. Enhanced mode works fine without it. Expand a fresh copy into the System directory and try again.

Data Transfer Errors. If a background application experiences errors during data-transfer operations, it may be because the application's priority allocation does not give it sufficient time to keep up with the transfer. Make sure the Background execution box is checked in the application PIF, increase the application's background priority, and clear the Detect Idle Time check box.

Noise Level on Sound System Affected by DOS Mode Changes. If you have a sound card installed, or there is a radio near your computer, you may notice changes in the noise level as you switch from full-screen to DOS Window mode, and again as you open the Control Menu. If the noise level is excessive, try moving your sound card away from your video card. Or, if video is a sub-system on your computer's motherboard, try moving the sound card to a different slot that may be farther from the video system. If radio interference is the problem, try moving the radio away from the computer, or turn it off.

Screen Display Missing or Garbled when Switching Back to Application. Chances are, the application is unable to retain its video information, and the No Save Screen box in the standard-mode PIF is checked. Open the PIF in standard mode, clear the box, and try again. Refer to *No Save Screen* in the *Standard Mode PIF Editor Dialog Box* section for more details.

Shortcut Key Problems

If you press a Shortcut Key combination and something unexpected happens (or doesn't happen), one of the following symptoms may explain the problem and its solution.

Shortcut Key Doesn't Work. If the Shortcut Key specified in an application's PIF has no effect, the application's Program Item Properties dialog box probably has an entry in its Application Shortcut Key box that disables the PIF setting. Also keep in mind that the PIF Shortcut Key will only bring an application to the foreground if that application is already open and running in the background—either hidden behind some other application or at the bottom of the Desktop as a minimized icon.

Shortcut Key Doesn't Work (standard mode only). If you open a DOS application in standard mode and can't toggle back to the Program Manager via the Alt+Tab Shortcut keys, there are a few suspects: Either the Alt+Tab combination is reserved for the application's use, or a box in the *PIF's* Directly Modifies or Prevent Program Switch sections has been checked. In any case, you'll have to exit the application in order to return to the Program Manager. Then refer to *Directly Modifies, Prevent Program Switch,* and/or *Reserve Shortcut Keys* in the *Standard Mode PIF Editor Dialog Box* section for assistance if needed.

Shortcut Key Produces Unexpected Action. If a Shortcut Key does something other than what you expected it would do, the application PIF probably reserves that combination for its own use. Open the PIF and clear the appropriate check box to return the Windows use of that Shortcut Key combination.

Shortcut Key Does Not Toggle Video Modes. As in the example immediately above, the application has probably reserved the Alt+Enter combination. However, you may be able to toggle between video modes by using the methods described in the *Alternate Video Mode Toggles* section. If the Alt+Spacebar toggle does not work, then that combination is also reserved by the application's PIF.

 NOTE: If your DOS application's PIF leaves an inactive DOS Window on the Desktop when the application closes, that window cannot be toggled into full-screen mode. If you need to access DOS in full-screen mode, close the inactive window and double-click on the DOS Prompt Icon.

Shortcut Key Changes Sound System Level. If you're listening to a compact disc or other audio playing as a background application, you may notice the playback level changes whenever you press a Shortcut Key combination. This is usually a function of the sound card drivers, and may or may not be fixed with an upgraded driver. Contact the sound card manufacturer to see if upgrade software is available.

Shortcut Key (Alt+Tab) Locks System. Refer to *System Lockup when Alt+Tab Is Pressed* in the *Mouse Troubleshooting* section for a possible cause of this problem.

DOS Window Problems

This section describes a few problems that may be noted when running an application in a DOS Window. For problems with fonts displayed in a DOS Window, refer to the separate *DOS Font Troubleshooting* section which follows this one.

NOTE: Remember that the DOS Window option may be enabled only when Windows is running in the 386 enhanced mode. Therefore, if the entire DOS Window option is not available, exit Windows and reenter in enhanced mode.

Application Is Sluggish in DOS Window. If you run an application in a DOS Window, Windows must spend a certain amount of time maintaining the surrounding Desktop display, and possibly other applications as well. Therefore, program execution will not be as fast as it might be in full-screen mode. To whip the windowed application along at a faster clip, you may want to edit the foreground and background priorities for all the applications that you customarily run at the same time. Refer to *Multitasking Options* in the *Enhanced Mode PIF Editor* section for assistance if needed.

Application Stops and System Beep Is Heard. The application probably wants to switch into a graphics mode that cannot be run in a DOS Window. An error message appears the first time this happens, but on subsequent attempts only the beep lets you know there's a problem. Press Alt+Enter to switch to full-screen mode and the application should resume.

Application Won't Run in DOS Window. Some DOS applications are just not happy in a window, and there's nothing you can do about it except cave in and run them full-screen. If it's vitally important to get the application to behave in a window, exit Windows and run Setup at the DOS prompt. Install the Windows 3.1 VGA or SVGA video driver, then try again. If this works, contact the manufacturer of your previous driver to see if an updated version is available. If it doesn't work, then you'll just have to get along in full-screen mode.

Color Values Shift between Full-Screen and DOS Window Modes. Unfortunately, this is "normal." If a full-screen display is compressed into the smaller area of a DOS Window, color values shift accordingly. If the color shift is distracting, there are two solutions: Run the application full-screen, or run it in a window and convince yourself that the new color scheme is an improvement. Possibly, it is. For further details, refer to the *Color Values in DOS Window Video Mode* section at the beginning of the chapter.

Cursor Difficult to See in DOS Window. A dim or invisible cursor may be a function of color shift when an application is "squeezed" into a DOS Window, especially on LCD screens. Open the Control Panel's Color applet and select one of the LCD color schemes, which may make the cursor easier to see. If you can't stand the color scheme (some are worse than others), try experimenting with other colors until you find something that works well on your system.

Cursor Missing on DOS Prompt Line. If the DOS prompt is on the last screen line, it's possible that the cursor may not be visible because it lies too far below the line to be seen. This is one of those pesky little "on again/off again" bugs which may only occur if the DOS Window is maximized and then, only if certain font matrixes are selected. To verify the problem, type CLS and press the Enter key to clear the screen and place the DOS prompt at the top of the window. The cursor should now be seen, lying below the line on which it is supposed to appear.

If the above, or some variation on it, describes the problem, then your installed video driver is not fully compatible with Windows 3.1. In this case, contact the manufacturer to see if an updated driver is available. If the manufacturer denies ever hearing of this problem before, you can do a double-check by reinstalling the Microsoft Windows 3.1 VGA driver (or some other Microsoft driver). If doing so clears up the problem, then the third-party driver is indeed the culprit.

Cursor Missing in 43-Line DOS Window. On some systems the cursor may disappear if the DOS screen is set for 43 lines. If this occurs, try typing MODE 80, 43 at the DOS prompt, which sometimes restores the cursor. If it doesn't, then you'll have to get along without the 43-line mode, or try another video driver, if possible.

DOS Window Display Is Garbled. If you open a DOS Window and the display within it is garbled, either the selected screen font is defective, or there is an invalid font size listed in the DOSAPP.INI file. Open the Control Menu and select the Fonts... option. Simply make a note of the highlighted matrix and click on the OK button. If that clears up the problem, then the DOSAPP.INI file was at fault, but that fault is now corrected. If the problem remains, then there's a problem with the selected font. Refer to Table 7.1 and select a font matrix that is not in the same file as the suspect matrix. If that clears up the problem, then the file containing the matrix should be replaced with a freshly expanded copy.

With some combinations of video driver, opening window position, and low conventional memory specified in a PIF, a DOS Window may open with a transparent horizontal band running through it, in which the Program Manager background can be seen. Or, there may be a black band running throughout the Title Bar. In most cases this can be cured by such procedures as minimizing and reopening the window or running a directory listing. However, the quirk is a clue that memory settings are not what they should be, and you may want to have a look at the PIF's conventional memory settings.

As a final possibility, open the application PIF and clear the Emulate Test Mode check box. If doing so has no effect on the problem, then recheck the box.

DOS Window Is Locked in Place. Under certain unique conditions, you may not be able to drag an open DOS Window to another location on the Desktop. To see if your system is affected, select the 10 × 18 font matrix and drag any two adjacent borders outward until the window is at its maximum size. Click on the Maximize button at the upper right-hand corner of the DOS Window, then try to drag the Window. If the Window won't budge, click on the Restore button, adjust one of the borders inward, and click on Maximize again. This time, the Window should respond when you try to move it.

Although the 10 × 18 matrix seems most sensitive to this operational quirk, the same phenomenon may appear at other matrixes, which will vary according to the current video resolution. There's no workaround, but there's also no reason to go to so much trouble to create a problem. If your DOS Window locks up when you do all this, then don't do it again.

Session Switches from DOS Window to Full-Screen Text Mode. The most common cause of this problem is a diskette drive: For example, Windows may have tried to access a diskette that is not present in the drive, or perhaps it tried to write to a write-protected diskette. In most cases, a DOS error message indicates the cause of the problem. The cure is to resolve it, switch back to DOS Window mode, and resume operations, if possible. If not, then resolve the problem and restart the application.

DOS Font Troubleshooting

The following font problems may be noted after switching to a DOS Window. Neither the problems nor the solutions discussed here apply to full-screen DOS operations.

Fonts Option Not Listed on Control Menu. If this option is missing from the Control Menu, it indicates that your enhanced-mode grabber file predates Windows version 3.1. If your version of Windows 3.1 was installed over a previous version, it's possible that the video files listed in Table 1.9a were not upgraded during Setup. Check your system directory against the information listed there. If either of the version 3.0 files are found, insert the appropriate version 3.1 diskette in drive A, and use the Windows expand utility to transfer the 3.1 file(s) into your System directory.

Note that the extension on the video grabber filename has changed from GR3 (in 3.0) to 3GR (in 3.1). Therefore, you should also check the following line in the [boot] section of SYSTEM.INI to verify that it lists the correct 3.1 extension, as shown here for a VGA system:

```
[boot]
386grabber=filename.3gr
```

The 3GR (or 2GR) extension is a good, but not infallible, indication of a version 3.1-compatible grabber file: There are a few third-party files that retain the old GR3 style (as does the Workgroups VGACOLRX.GR2 file), yet work with version 3.1. However, if an upgrade is needed but you don't have it yet, add the following line to SYSTEM.INI:

```
[NonWindowsApp]
FontChangeEnable=1
```

Close and reopen Windows, and try again. If this line fixes the problem, contact the appropriate manufacturer for an updated grabber file. If you actually get one, you can remove this line. Otherwise, leave it in place for the time being.

> **NOTE:** The FontChangeEnable line does not work with all systems, and it may affect the appearance of the mouse pointer.

Font List Does Not Show Ten Matrixes. If the Font Selection dialog box does not list 10 font matrixes, compare the existing list with that shown in Figure 7.1. Then study the list below, which gives the names of the five files which contain all 10 font matrixes. The file containing the missing font matrix is either defective or missing. In either case, expand a fresh copy of that file into the System directory.

[386Enh]	Font Matrix	
CGA80WOA.FON=CGA80WOA.FON	8	8
CGA40WOA.FON=CGA40WOA.FON	8	12
EGA80WOA.FON=EGA80WOA.FON	16	8
EGA40WOA.FON=EGA40WOA.FON	16	12
woafont=dosapp.fon	All others	

In each line above, the filename appears to the right of the equal sign. The names shown here are valid for most systems, but may vary in some.

Font Change Has No Effect. If you select a new font matrix and nothing happens when you click on the OK button, the current DOS Window is probably displaying a graphics-mode image and program execution has been suspended. Take whatever action is needed to return the application to a text mode (or close it), then try again.

Wrong Extended Character Set. The APP850.FON file contains the six WOA fonts used in international configurations. With the exception of the 4 × 6 matrix, the other five in this set use the character set shown in Figure 7.9b. However, the 4 × 6 matrix uses the same extended character set that is found in the US-English WOA font file (DOSAPP.FON, Figure 7.9a). Therefore, if you use an international font set, don't be surprised if the 4 × 6 matrix displays a different extended character set (128–255).

Mouse Troubleshooting

Although mouse operations are described in Chapter 11, the following section reviews a few mouse-related problems that only show up during a DOS session. For the purposes of the troubleshooting suggestions seen here, it is assumed the DOS application itself supports mouse operations. If it doesn't, then running the application in a DOS session within Windows isn't going to change things. In case of doubt about an application's mouse support, run the DOS edit utility (EDIT.COM) while troubleshooting. If the mouse works properly in all modes, then it should do the same with any other application. If it doesn't, then the application is probably the problem.

Mouse Inoperative in Full-Screen Mode. If the mouse works in Windows, but not in either DOS mode, then you need to load a valid mouse driver in your AUTOEXEC.BAT file. Make sure the file contains a line such as the following:

```
C:\WINDOWS\MOUSE
```

Refer to the *Mouse* section of Chapter 11 for further details about mouse configuration, or for assistance if the mouse also does not work elsewhere on the Windows Desktop.

Mouse Inoperative in DOS Window Mode. The first order of business is to see if the mouse works in full-screen mode. If it doesn't, then refer to the previous section for suggestions. Once the mouse does function in full-screen mode, return to this section for assistance.

Application Does Not Support Mouse Operations in a DOS Window. Some older DOS applications may support a mouse in full-screen mode but not in a DOS Window. If this is a possibility, contact the software supplier for verification before spending too much time tearing Windows apart.

Outdated Grabber File. Some mouse problems are caused by a grabber file that predates Windows version 3.1. If an updated grabber file (386GRABBER.3GR) is not available, then add the following line to the indicated section of SYSTEM.INI:

[NonWindowsApp]
MouseInDosBox=1 *(do not use* On, True *or* Yes *on this line)*

If this line doesn't do anything, exit Windows, log onto the Windows directory, and run Setup. Change the display to VGA, then reopen Windows. Doing so installs the Microsoft VGA.3GR file, which should work. If it does, then the previous grabber file is indeed at fault.

System Lockup When Alt+Tab Is Pressed. If a version 5.00 or earlier Logitech mouse driver is installed, your system may lockup when you press Alt+Tab to toggle between full-screen and DOS Window modes. If so, replace the driver with the newer one included with either Windows or Windows-for-Workgroups.

PIF Troubleshooting

As described elsewhere in this Troubleshooting section, many DOS-related problems are solved by editing the PIF associated with the application that is having trouble. However, there are those times when a PIF edit produces no visible effect on the DOS session; a few typical examples are described here.

PIF Window Title Ignored. The text entered in the PIF's Window Title box will only appear in the Title Bar of a DOS Window under the following conditions:

1. Open the Program Manager's File Menu.
2. Select the Run... option.
3. Type *filename*.PIF and click on the OK button.

As you might expect, the DOS Window's Title Bar displays the text entered in the Window Title box. However, if you follow the conventional method of simply double-clicking on the appropriate DOS application icon, the Title Bar text is taken from the Description box instead (as seen in the Program Item Properties dialog box). If the text in the Window Title and Description boxes is identical, then this little bit of trivia is unimportant. However, many users place a short title under the application icon, and may wonder why the longer title from the PIF can't be used for the Title Bar. If you don't mind going through the three-step procedure above, it can. Otherwise, you'll have to put up with the icon title text showing up in the Title Bar.

PIF Edits Are Ignored. If PIF edits have no effect, it's possible that the PIF you edited is not the one used to start the application. As an obvious example, you may have edited the PIF in standard mode, but are now running the application in enhanced mode, or vice versa. In either case, the edits made in one mode have no effect on the other, even though both are stored in the same PIF. This would account for the edit seeming to have no effect. Reopen the PIF and make sure the desired setting is correct in both modes. Of course, this applies only to those settings (Optional Parameters, for example) that appear in both enhanced and standard mode PIF Editor dialog boxes.

As another possibility, there may be two PIFs with the same name, and the one you edited is not the one that is used. To check on this, click once on the application's icon, then open the File Menu and select the Properties... option. If the Command Line explicitly cites a path to the PIF, then make sure that you edit that PIF. When you open the PIF Editor and select the Open option on its File Menu, the listed PIFs are those in the Windows directory. Make sure you don't edit one of those PIFs if the Command Line points to one that lies elsewhere.

To prevent further confusion, search all directories for PIFs with the same name (dir *filename*.PIF /s), and delete all but one.

PIF Optional Parameters Ignored. Under certain conditions, the optional parameters specified in a PIF are ignored. As a typical example, consider the MS-DOS edit utility (EDIT.COM) which may be installed as a DOS applet in one of your group windows. The following sections illustrate conditions in which the optional parameters in the PIF have no effect.

File Association Override. If you place a question mark in the EDIT.PIF file's Optional Parameters: box, then a message box prompts you to name the file you wish to edit when you double-click on the Editor Icon. Assuming you prefer to edit your INI files with EDIT.COM instead of NOTEPAD.EXE, you may have revised the following association in your WIN.INI file:

[Extensions]
ini=EDIT.PIF ^.INI *(instead of the default* ini=NOTEPAD.EXE ^.INI)

Now when you double-click on any INI document file icon in File Manager, EDIT.COM opens and loads that file. Since you've just specified the file you want to edit (by clicking on its icon), that optional question-mark parameter in the PIF would defeat the purpose of the file association by needlessly prompting you for the same information you've already given. Therefore, optional parameters are ignored if you open a file for editing by clicking on its icon in the File Manager. As a consequence, other parameters—such as /h to open the editor in high-resolution (43-line) mode—are also ignored.

If you open the editor by double-clicking on its own icon in a group window, then the optional parameters in the PIF are used, and the above-mentioned file association has no effect. (Refer to the <u>A</u>ssociate... option in Chapter 6, and/or the *MS-DOS Editor* in Chapter 4 for more information on these subjects.)

Command Line Override. When you open the Program Item Properties dialog box for any DOS application, the command line box may show one of the following formats:

C:\DOS\EDIT.COM   *(no switches, parameters)*
EDIT.PIF   *(no switches, parameters allowed)*
C:\DOS\EDIT.COM /h   *(or other switches, parameters)*

In the first example, even though EDIT.PIF is not explicitly specified, Windows still looks at it and uses any optional parameters it finds there. This command line is therefore functionally equivalent to the EDIT.PIF line in the second example. In the third example, the presence of the /h switch on the command line has the effect of disabling any optional parameters specified in the PIF.

Error Messages

The chapter concludes with a look at some of the error messages that may be encountered when running a DOS application from within Windows.

Error Message when Trying to Start a DOS Application

This section reviews error messages that may be seen when you double-click on an icon that should start a DOS application. Some of these messages may also show up if you try to execute an application after starting a DOS session in full-screen or window mode.

No application is associated with the specified file. Create an association by using File Manager. If this message is seen when you try to execute any DOS application, Windows does not recognize the PIF extension as an executable program. Do *not* follow the advice given in the message. Instead, edit the following line in WIN.INI as shown here:

```
[windows]
Programs=com exe bat pif
```

Make sure the pif extension is there, and that there is a single space between each extension (on some systems, more than one space between each extension can cause problems).

Cannot execute *filename.ext*. Now all you need to do is figure out *why?* Chances are, there's not enough conventional memory to load the program in the current virtual machine. Run the PIF Editor applet, load the application's PIF, and in the Memory Requirements section raise the KB Desired value. However, if the current value is at or near the 640 Kbyte maximum, or if you know it should be sufficient to run the application, then there is not enough memory available in the system to supply the desired amount. You'll have to close some other application(s) to free up more memory.

Cannot find WINOLDAP.MOD (or WINOA386.MOD) (hourglass remains on screen). When you click on the Close button, an *Unexpected DOS error:23* message appears. Click on the OK button, then expand a fresh copy of the cited MOD file into the system directory.

Cannot find file. Check to ensure the path and filename are correct. (Filename appears at top of message box.)Check the Command Line entry in the Program Item Properties dialog box. If the extension is BAT, COM, or EXE, make sure the cited file is where it's supposed to be. If the extension is PIF, use the PIF Editor applet to open that PIF and make sure the executable file in the Program Filename box is correct. (If Windows could not find a file with a PIF extension, then the message which follows is seen instead of this one.)

Cannot find file *filename.ext* (or one of its components). Check to ensure the path and filename are correct and that all required libraries are available. The obvious procedure is to make sure the filename and path specified in the PIF are correct, and that the cited file is where it's supposed to be. If all appears to be in order, then try to open some other DOS applications, or simply double-click on the DOS Prompt Icon. If the message reappears for all applications, then continue reading here. If only one application is having a problem, then refer to *Not Enough File Handles* below.

Missing or Old Grabber File. Check the following section of SYSTEM.INI:

```
[boot]
386grabber=filename.3GR
```

If the extension is GR3 instead of 3GR, the file is probably left over from Windows version 3.0, or a third-party grabber that predates version 3.1. In any case, you'll need the version 3.1 file. If this is not available, then exit Windows, log onto the Windows directory, and type SETUP at the DOS prompt. When the System Information Screen (Figure 1.1) shows up, change the display to VGA, press the Enter key, and conclude the Setup procedure. This will install the Windows 3.1 video grabber, which should work until you can locate a good copy of the one you need for your video system.

Files= Is Set Too Low. Another possibility is that the Files= statement in your CONFIG.SYS is set too low. Edit the value to say, 60—or at least, 45—reboot the system, and try again.

Not Enough File Handles. If the *Cannot Find* problem is limited to a specific DOS application, then add the following line to your SYSTEM.INI file:

```
[386Enh]
PerVMFILES=xx
```

The line specifies the number of file handles per virtual machine, and the default value is 10. Set the value to a number greater than 10 and try again.

Cannot find the file WINOLDAP.GRB. Make sure that the file is in the path defined by '286grabber=' value in SYSTEM.INI. Of course Windows can't find it: There's no such thing. What it all really means is that the file specified on the 286grabber= line is missing or invalid, or perhaps the line itself is missing. Make sure the line is there, then look for the file specified after the equal sign. If expanding a fresh copy doesn't cure the problem, exit Windows, log onto the Windows directory, and run Setup at the DOS prompt. Change the Display type to VGA, conclude the Setup procedure, and try again. If the problem is gone, then the previous 286 grabber file probably predates Windows version 3.1 and needs to be updated.

Cannot run a non-Windows application from the second instance of Windows; Exit this instance of Windows and run your application from the original instance. In the unlikely event that this message actually makes sense, stop trying to run two versions of Windows at the same time. However, if you're only running one Windows session in standard mode, the *real* culprit is probably an outdated copy of WINOLDAP.MOD in your System Directory. In the days of Windows 3.0, this file supported real-mode operations. However, the current (and probably, missing) WINOLDAP.MOD offers *standard* mode support (see Table 1.9a). Expand a fresh copy from the distribution diskette and try again.

Error Reading from Drive *X* (where *X* is the current drive). If this message appears when you try to execute a DOS application on drive *X,* and the drive functions properly outside Windows, the DOSAPP.INI file is probably corrupt. Erase or rename it, and try again. Windows will create a new DOSAPP.INI file. If you wish to recover information stored in the old one, make a note of the single line in the new INI file, and edit the equivalent line in the old one to match it. Then erase the new file and rename the old one back to DOSAPP.INI. However, unless there's some important reason for doing this, it's probably not worth the bother: Let Windows build a new DOSAPP.INI as you open further DOS applications.

Incorrect System Version; reinstall the 386 enhanced mode of Windows [*or* Run the Windows Setup program again]. Before doing so, you may want to check the following areas for trouble.

Video Problem. There may be a conflict in the following sections of your SYSTEM.INI file:

```
[boot]
386grabber=
display.drv=
[386Enh]
display=
```

To verify this, open Windows in standard mode and try the DOS prompt again. If it works, then the video grabber above does not match the virtual display device listed in the [386Enh] section. If the 386grabber filename has an extension of GR3, it is probably a leftover from Windows version 3.0. Expand a copy of VGA.3G_ to the System directory as VGA.3GR (note change of extension from the old GR3 to the new 3GR), and change the 386grabber line above from VGA.GR3 to VGA.3GR. However, if the grabber was some other third-party file, exit Windows and run Setup at the DOS prompt. On the System Information Screen (Figure 1.1), change the Display to VGA, and press the Enter key. Conclude the Setup procedure, reopen Windows, and try the DOS prompt once more.

Outdated WINOA386.MOD File. If the video grabber file appears to be correct, check the file creation date of the WINOA386.MOD file. If it predates your other Windows files, expand a fresh copy from your distribution diskette and try again.

Insufficient disk space on drive X. Desired disk space: *xxx* K. Delete one or more files to increase available disk space. If a DOS application is run in standard mode, there must be sufficient swap disk space available for that application, in case you decide to switch to another application. Windows looks to the following locations for the space it requires:

The TEMP directory

The root directory on your first hard drive (or on drive A if no hard drive is present)

The message appears if neither location has the desired free disk space listed in the message. If more space is available on another drive, either change the set TEMP line in your AUTOEXEC.BAT file to specify that drive, or add the following line to the indicated section of SYSTEM.INI:

```
[NonWindowsApp]
SwapDisk=X:directory        (the desired drive letter and directory name)
```

The error message also appears if the above line refers to an invalid drive or directory.

Insufficient memory for application requested space. Decrease PIF KB required and try again. This message may be seen on systems with an acute RAM shortage (about 2 Mbytes and no permanent swap file). Since such a system is almost running on empty, the best solution is to increase system memory and install a permanent swap file. As a temporary fix, try decreasing the KB Required in the Memory Requirements section of the application PIF.

Insufficient memory for application's required space. Decrease PIF KB Required, or quit one or more applications, or free up disk space, to increase available memory. Then try again. The "required space" refers to the amount of conventional memory specified in the application's PIF. If you're not able to free up some memory by closing other applications, edit the application's PIF and put a "–1" in the KB Required and KB Desired boxes. Windows will try to make do with whatever is available; this might work if the application has a modest appetite.

Insufficient memory for application's required EMS [*or* XMS] memory. Decrease PIF EMS [*or* XMS] KB Required, or quit one or more applications, or free up disk space, to increase available memory. Then try again. The amount of expanded (EMS) or extended (XMS) memory specified in this application's PIF is not currently available. Check the appropriate KB Required box in the application's PIF and, if possible, reduce the value seen there. However, if you know the application really requires the specified amount of memory, then you'll have to close other applications, or make a trip to the memory store.

Insufficient memory to run application. Quit one or more applications, or free up disk space, to increase available memory. Then try again. This message appears if the application PIF's (conventional) Memory Requirements: KB Required value is set too low. Either the application itself needs more conventional memory, or Windows requires more space in order to open a DOS session.

Insufficient memory to run the application. Check the memory requirements in the program information file (PIF) and change if necessary. In standard mode, this message appears if there is not enough conventional memory to meet the KB Required figure. (In enhanced mode, a *KB Required value* message appears.) If you know that figure is correct, then you'll need to free up some conventional memory by removing device drivers or TSRs and rebooting the system. But before doing that, open the DOS Prompt applet, type MEM, and note the figure reported on the following line:

DOS 5.0	Largest executable program size	Line 3
DOS 6.0	Conventional (free)	Line 1, Column 3

Now open the application PIF, set KB Required to a value lower than that reported, then try to run the application again.

KB Required value is too large. Decrease PIF KB Required. The message is functionally equivalent to the *Insufficient memory to run the application* message above. Refer to that message for more information.

One of the libraries needed to run this application is damaged. Please re-install this application. If this message is seen when you double-click on the DOS Prompt Icon, one or more of the following files may be missing or defective:

Mode	Look for these files in System directory:
Standard	WINOLDAP.MOD, 286grabber (2GR extension)
Enhanced	WINOA386.MOD, 386grabber (3GR extension), WOA font files

Refer to the *Terminal Font Sources in Windows 3.1* section for assistance in identifying the WOA font files for your system.

This application is now running in exclusive mode because of insufficient memory. Other background applications are suspended. In full-screen mode, the message concludes with "Press any key to continue." If the application is running in a DOS Window, the message box includes an **OK** button instead of that line. In either case, the active application's appetite for memory has forced Windows to suspend execution of background programs. Now that you know what's up, continue program execution, but next time try to avoid RAM cram by running fewer applications.

Unexpected MS-DOS Error #11. Depending on the current operating mode, one of the following files is probably corrupted.

Standard Mode	Enhanced Mode
WINOLDAP.MOD	WINOA386.MOD
286 grabber file	386 grabber file

Expand the appropriate MOD and grabber files from your distribution diskette into the System directory. If you're not sure of the grabber filename, check the following lines in SYSTEM.INI:

```
[boot]
286grabber=filename.2GR
386grabber=filename.3GR
```

Error Messages during a DOS Session

The following error messages usually appear after a DOS Application Window has opened. However, it's also possible for some of these messages to show up when you first try to open a DOS application.

An error has occurred in your application. If you choose Ignore, you should save your work in a new file. If you choose Close, your application will terminate. Depending on the nature of the error, the Ignore button itself may be ignored, and you'll have to click on the Close button to get rid of the message.

The most likely cause of the problem is a memory conflict. When you click on the Close button, a second message may give additional information. If not, try executing the application in full-screen mode. If the message persists, and you're not sure what's causing it, exit Windows and retry the application at the DOS prompt. If it works, contact the software manufacturer to see if a Windows-compatible version is available, or if there is a Windows workaround.

Cannot switch to a full screen. Cancel your selection or scroll command before switching to a full screen. If you encounter this message when you attempt to return to full-screen mode, note the DOS Window Title Bar. If the title includes the word "Select," click on the OK button, and cancel the selected option. If you're not sure what the problem is, try pressing the Escape key. When the Title Bar displays only the name of the DOS application (or "DOS Prompt"), try pressing Alt+Enter again to enable full-screen mode.

This application attempted to access a device that is being used by another application. If you continue running this application it might cause your system to lock up. Type Y or press ENTER to continue running this application. Type N to end this application. [*followed by*] This application has violated system integrity and will be terminated. Quit all applications, quit Windows, and then restart your computer. The usual reason for this message sequence is that a DOS application made an illegal memory access. If the application runs in standard mode, then add an x=A000-EFFF parameter to the EMM386.EXE line in CONFIG.SYS. If that works, then try excluding smaller regions until the problem area is isolated. (See Chapter 13 for all the gory details about upper memory management.)

If the application does not run in standard mode, then either it is incompatible with Windows, or there may be a hardware conflict.

This application has insufficient memory for its display *or* This application was unable to access the video display. Its display was not updated. *Both followed by:* **Check the PIF settings to ensure they are correct. If the display is erratic, redraw the display or restart the application.** Messages such as these may show up when running multiple DOS applications, especially when switching between application windows. Chances are, one

DOS application requires a certain amount of video memory, and that quantity is no longer available due to the other applications that were subsequently opened.

Edit the PIF for the application that displayed the error message. Raise the initial *Video Memory* setting from Text to Low Graphics, or to High Graphics, and also check the **Retain Video Memory** box in the *Display Options* section of the **Advanced Options** dialog box. This allocates more video memory for the application, and makes sure that that amount of memory is set aside so other applications cannot swipe it for their own use.

WINOLDAP caused a Page Fault in module *xxxxx.ext.* at *segment:offset.* (A Close button is the only option.) The page fault indicates that an application tried to make an invalid access to video memory. If this happens when the application is executed in a DOS Window, try again in full-screen mode. If that works, edit the PIF so that the application opens in full-screen mode and cannot be toggled into a DOS Window. For assistance, refer to the *Disable DOS Window for Selected* (or, if necessary, *All*) *Applications.*

You can run this application only in a full screen because the All-VMsExclusive entry in SYSTEM.INI is set to True. If this message appears when you try to switch a DOS application into a DOS Window, you'll need to edit the AllVMsExclusive line in SYSTEM.INI, as described in the *DOS-Exclusive Foreground Mode* section earlier in the chapter.

You cannot run this application while other high-resolution applications are running full screen. The application will be suspended until a low-resolution or text application is running full screen. Check the PIF settings to ensure they are correct. If you're running an application in a DOS Window, you'll meet this message if that application switches from text to graphics mode, and it may not make very much sense. If you think you don't have another high-resolution application running, think again: Windows, itself, is that application. Instead of trying to figure out what that second sentence really means, press the Alt + Enter keys to run the DOS application in the full-screen mode. Once the program concludes, you can press Alt + Enter again if you wish to view the application's screen in a DOS Window.

During any DOS Window session, if an application tries more than once to switch into graphics mode, this message is not seen. Instead, the system just beeps at you.

You cannot run this application in a window or in the background. You can display it in a window, but it will be suspended until you run it full screen. If your CONFIG.SYS or AUTOEXEC.BAT file loads the Microsoft mouse driver version 7.04 or later, add the /y switch to the appropriate line, as shown below. Then reboot the system and try again.

in CONFIG.SYS: or, in AUTOEXEC.BAT
device=C:\WINDOWS\MOUSE.SYS /Y   C:\WINDOWS\MOUSE.COM /Y

It's also possible that system resources are running low. If this is a possibility, close a few applications, then try again. In case of doubt, close and reopen Windows to make sure that system resources have been released.

Your program cannot be swapped out to disk. There is not enough space on your disk. For assistance, refer to this message in Chapter 13.

Error Messages when Exiting a DOS Application

The final few error messages are those that may be seen when you try to close a DOS session.

Application still active. Choose OK to end it. If the Allow Close When Active box is checked in the Advanced Options section of an application PIF, you may close the DOS Window without closing the application running in that window. However, this message warns you that the application is still active. Click on the OK button to close the window anyway, or click on the Cancel button, exit (and save, if appropriate) the application, then close the window.

Extremely Low on Memory. Close an application and try again. If the message makes sense, then do what it says and try again. However, you may run into the message when you try to exit Windows after encountering some other problem, even if no applications are open. In this case, you'll have to reboot to get out. After doing so, do whatever needs to be done to fix the original problem. Once that's resolved, you should have no further problems exiting Windows.

WARNING! Use the Terminate button only as a last resort to quit an application that has stopped responding to the system. To quit an application, use the application's quit or exit command. This message appears if you select the Settings... option on the Control Menu, then click on the Terminate button in the DOS Prompt dialog box (Figure 7.4). If you really want to close the DOS Window, you don't need to go to all this trouble to do so unless some problem prevents a more orderly exit. In that case, go ahead and quit. Otherwise, return to the DOS Window, close the application, then close the Window.

If the Allow Close When Active box is checked in the Advanced Options section of the current application's PIF, then the *Application Still Active* warning is seen instead.

8

The Clipboard and Clipbook Viewers

The Clipboard Viewer applet, or *Clipboard* for short, is part of Windows version 3.1. In Windows-for-Workgroups, it is replaced by the Clipbook Viewer applet, or *Clipbook,* which offers the same basic Clipboard services, plus additional support for features described later in the chapter. Although Windows 3.1 users can safely skip the *Clipbook* sections, Windows-for-Workgroups users might want to review both sections since, unless otherwise noted, all references to the Windows Clipboard refer as well to the Clipboard section of the Workgroups Clipbook.

Briefly stated, the Clipboard/Clipbook is the medium by which data moves, or is copied, from one location to another. Data is transferred from a source file to the Clipboard, then from the Clipboard to a destination file. The transfer may take place under one or more of the following conditions:

Transfer	Typical Example
Between similar files	Text block moved from one Write file to another Write file.
Within same file	Text block moved from page x to page y in the same file.
Between different file types	Bitmap image copied from Paintbrush to Write document.
Across a network	Data block copied from server file on Computer A pasted to client file on Computer B.

The complete procedure may be summarized as a five-step operation. When the operation is completed, the data block from the source file should appear in the destination file.

1. Select the desired data block (text, graphics image, spreadsheet excerpt, etc.) in the source file.

2. Open the source application's File Menu and select the Cut or Copy option to place a copy of the data block onto the Clipboard.
   a. If the destination file is on a remote computer, then the Clipboard must be copied to the Local Clipbook and made available for sharing, so that it may be accessed at the remote computer.
   b. The remote user connects to your Clipbook and copies the data to the remote Clipboard, making it available for use at that computer.

3. Open the destination application.

4. Select the insertion point—the location at which to insert the Clipboard data.

5. Open the destination application's File Menu and select the Paste or Paste Special option.

The Clipboard also serves for more prosaic chores: Any object cut from a Windows file lands on the Clipboard, where it remains until some other object is cut. At that point it gets tossed off the Clipboard, never to be seen again.

During most routine operations, the Clipboard functions invisibly in the background and, if all goes well, the user should be all but unaware of its existence. However, when all does not go well, it helps to have some idea of what's going on behind the scenes—hence this look at Clipboard operations.

It's difficult to describe something as "simple" as a Clipboard without referring to the various Windows applets and applications which it serves. The Clipboard is also an important part of OLE (object linking and embedding). Therefore, one must have a basic understanding of say, the Write and Paintbrush applets, plus a few full-scale applications that take advantage of Clipboard services, before taking on the Clipboard itself. A nodding acquaintance with the fine (and often obscure) points of OLE is also useful. But the user also should have some basic understanding of the Clipboard before tackling these applets and applications. Since there is no neat way to solve this little problem in logistics, this book takes the easy way out by simply jumping into the loop at the Clipboard, then referring elsewhere as required. Therefore, if some part of this chapter is initially unclear, you may want to coast through it for the moment, then return later on after covering a few of the other bases.

Definitions

The entries in this section may help clarify already-familiar terms as they apply to Clipboard operations.

Client. The term is often used—especially in network operations—to identify either the computer, or the application or file, that will receive information from a *server* (via the Clipboard of course). In DOS terms, the client would be known as the destination, or target, file.

Destination. There's not much mystery here: The term refers to the computer and/or file that receives the pasted object.

Local Clipbook. As the term suggests, this is the Clipbook on the user's own computer, and is labeled as such on this Clipbook's Title Bar.

Object. An *object* is simply anything (text block, bitmap, spreadsheet, whatever) that can be cut or copied from one location and pasted to another.

Remote Clipbook. When the Clipbook Viewer accesses Clipboard files on some other computer to which it is connected, those files are displayed in a *Remote Clipbook Window*. However, the text in that window's Title Bar is "Clipbook on \\(*computer name*)" rather than "Remote Clipbook." The latter term is used here as a generic identifier of all such windows, so as to avoid references to windows whose names are unknown.

Server. The *Server* may be the computer on which the object originates or in more specific circumstances, a *Server Application* or *Server File*. Of course, these are the application and the file, in which the source object resides.

Source. This term usually refers to the specific file from which the object is, or will be, taken.

Clipboard Object Formats. When an object in a server file is copied or cut to the Clipboard, it is automatically stored there in more than one format, so that it may be pasted into a client file in a format most appropriate for that client. In a simple *Paste* operation the object is inserted into the client file in the default format for that client. Other available formats (if any) are accessible via the Paste Special or Paste Link options as described in more detail later on.

Some frequently encountered Clipboard object formats are listed in Table 8.1 and briefly described here. A list of object formats currently stored on the Clipboard may be displayed via the *Display* (Windows 3.1) or *View* (Workgroups) Menus, which are described in the *Clipboard and Clipbook Menus* section below. Since not all these formats are suitable for direct Clipboard viewing, some will appear disabled (grayed) on the

TABLE 8.1   Typical Clipboard Object Formats*

Format	Description
Biff, Biff3, Biff4	Binary Interchange File Format
Bitmap	Bitmap (device dependent)
Clipbook Preview	Thumbnail sketch
Csv	Comma separated values
DIB, DIB Bitmap	Device-Independent Bitmap
DIF	Data Interchange Format (Software Arts)
Display Text	Text description of Excel chart
Link	DDE (dynamic data exchange) link data (*Windows*)
	NDDE (network dynamic data exchange) link data (*Workgroups*)
Lnk Copy	Link Copy
Native	Source application's data format
ObjectLink	DDE/NDDE and OLE link data
ObjLnkCpy	Object Link Copy
OEM Text[†]	MS-DOS character set
Owner Display[‡]	Formatted text in source document (*Windows 3.1*)
OwnerLink	Linked or embedded object, with source/class ID
Palette	RGB Table color palette
Picture	Metafile Picture structure
Rich Text Format	Text formatting saved as ASCII character instructions
RIFF	Resource-Interchange File Format
Sylk	SYmbolic LinK format (Microsoft)
Text	ASCII Text only (default Clipboard text format)
TIFF	Tagged Image File Format
Wave Audio	RIFF audio waveform
Wk1	Lotus 1-2-3 Worksheet
Word (or other) Formatted Text	Formatted text in source document

* Boldface indicates format may be viewed on Clipboard.

[†] Source application must remain open for this format to be available.

[‡] Same as above, or data must be saved as CLP file while source application was open.

Display or View Menu. These options are available, however, to any application that can use them. Unless otherwise noted, an underlined letter in an option name identifies the keyboard key that accesses that option.

Table 8.2 lists the formats seen when data is copied to the Clipboard data from various Windows applets, and Table 8.3 is a cross-reference to show which formats will be available for pasting within selected applications.

TABLE 8.2 Typical Formats Available on Clipboard*

Word-for-Windows	Write	Paintbrush	Excel 4.0
Word Formatted Text[†] *(Workgroups)*	**WRITE Formatted Text** *(Workgroups)*	—	**Picture**
Owner display[†] *(Windows 3.1)*	**Owner display** *(Windows 3.1)*	—	**Bitmap**
—	—	**Bitmap**	Biff4, Biff3, Biff
Rich Text Format	—	**Palette**	Sylk
Text	**Text**	—	Wk1
Native	—	Native	DIF
OwnerLink	—	OwnerLink	**Text**
Picture	—	**Picture**	Csv
Link	—	ObjectLink	Rich Text Format
ObjectLink[‡]	—	—	Native
OEM Text	**OEM Text**	—	OwnerLink
LnkCpy[§]	—	—	Link
ObjLnkCpy[§]	—	ObjLnkCpy	ObjectLink
			Display Text
			OEM Text
			LnkCp[§]
			ObjLnkCpy[§]
			DIB Bitmap[§]

* Boldface indicates enabled Menu options. Others are present but unavailable for Clipboard viewing.

† Option removed from menu when Clipboard data is saved as *filename*.CLP.

‡ This option appears on Windows-for-Workgroups View Menu only.

§ Options added to Windows-for-Workgroups View Menu when Clipboard data is saved as *filename*.CLP.

TABLE 8.3 Clipboard Data Formats Available to Selected Applets and Applications*

Server Application Clipboard Formats	Client Format Options	Client Format Available for Pasting into:					
		Card-file	Note-pad	Paint-brush	Write	Excel	Word
Cardfile (text)							
Text	Text	Yes	Yes	Yes	Yes	Yes	No
OEM Text	Unformatted Text	No	No	No	No	No	Yes
Notepad (text)							
Text	Text	Yes	Yes	Yes	Yes	Yes	No
OEM Text	Unformatted Text	No	No	No	No	No	Yes
Paintbrush (bitmap)							
Bitmap	Bitmap	Yes	No	Yes	Yes	Yes	Yes
Picture	Picture	Yes	No	No	Yes	Yes	Yes
DIB Bitmap	Device-Independent Bitmap	No	No	No	Yes	No	Yes
	Paintbrush Picture Object	Yes	No	No	Yes	Yes	Yes
Write (text)							
Write Formatted Text		No	No	No	†	No	No
Text	Text	Yes	Yes	Yes	†	Yes	No
OEM Text	Unformatted Text	No	No	No	No	No	Yes
Excel (worksheet)							
Picture	Picture	Yes	No	No	Yes		Yes
Bitmap	Bitmap	Yes	No	Yes	Yes		Yes
Text	Text	Yes	Yes	No	Yes		No
Display Text	Worksheet Object	Yes	No	No	Yes		Yes
OEM Text	Unformatted Text	No	No	No	No		Yes
	Formatted Text (RTF)	No	No	No	No		Yes
Word-for-Windows (text)							
Word Formatted Text		No	No	No	No	No	Yes
Text	Text	Yes	Yes	Yes	Yes	Yes	No
	Unformatted Text	No	No	No	No	No	Yes
Picture	Picture	Yes	No	No	Yes	Yes	No
OEM Text	Word Document Object	Yes	No	No	Yes	Yes	No
	Microsoft Word Object	No	No	No	No	No	Yes

† Write Formatted Text available if Server file remains open, otherwise Text is available instead.

***Biff, Biff3, Biff4* (Binary Interchange File Format, in Microsoft Excel).** For the benefit of Clipboard scholars, the Microsoft *Excel User's Guide I* index entry is reproduced here in its entirety:

BIFF format *Refer to BIFF file format (Book 2 index)*

Needless to say, there is no such entry in *User's Guide 2,* and the closest approximation (*BIFF Clipboard Format*) simply refers to two pages on which the initials "BIFF" appear. In any case, this is the format for the following Excel documents:

BIFF	Excel version 2.20
BIFF3	Excel version 3.*x*
BIFF4	Excel version 4.*x*

<u>B</u>*itmap*. A pixel-by-pixel description of a rectangular graphics image residing on the Clipboard. The bitmap size depends on the dimensions of the rectangle and the number of colors supported by the current video adapter. The bitmap stored in the CLP file is a replica of the bitmap data section in the source bitmap file (*filename*.BMP), or whatever portion of it was copied to the Clipboard. However, the CLP file's bitmap section is reformatted, as appropriate, to meet the requirements of the current color system, which may be different from that under which the original bitmap was created.

***Clipbook Preview* (Workgroups).** This 512-byte segment contains a rough (sometimes, *very* rough) black-and-white sketch of the Clipboard data. If the Clipboard data is subsequently pasted to the user's Local Clipbook, this sketch is displayed there whenever the Thumbnail viewing option is selected, as described later on in the *Clipbook Thumbnails* section.

Although a *Clipbook Preview* format is written into every saved CLP file (except audio files), it should never appear as a View Menu option since it is intended solely for internal use by the Clipbook. However, if a Workgroups CLP file is opened on a Windows 3.1 Clipboard, *Clipbook Preview* does appear on the Display Menu as a disabled option. Just ignore it.

***Csv* (Comma-Separated Values).** Similar to the Text format, except that the field separator is a comma instead of a tab.

<u>D</u>*IB*, <u>D</u>*IB Bitmap* (Device-Independent Bitmap Bitmap). Redundancy notwithstanding, this is simply the bitmap again, but modified so that it may be displayed on any system, without regard to the number of colors supported.

**DIF** **(Data Interchange Format).** (Software Arts.) File format for transferring data to or from _Visicalc._

**Display Text.** This is a brief text description of an Excel chart. For example, Copy 9R × 5C to describe a copy of a 9-row/5-column chart.

**Link, LnkCpy.** Source application and filename, DDE link data. The additional _LnkCpy_ (Link Copy) section is added to the Clipboard data if that data is saved to a CLP file.

**Native.** This is a replica of the source application's own (or "native") data format, containing all the formatting codes or other instructions present in the original.

**ObjectLink, ObjLnkCpy** **(Workgroups only).** Object linking data. The additional _ObjLnkCpy_ (Object Link Copy) section is added to the Clipboard data if that data is saved to a CLP file.

**OEM Text.** This is an unformatted text rendition of the source object text, displayed in the monospace system font specified on the fixed.fon=_xxx_ fix.fon line in the [boot] section of SYSTEM.INI. To examine the entire character set displayed by the _OEM Text_ format, open the Character Map applet and select the _Terminal_ or _8514oem_ font. Refer to _Text Format Comparisons_ below for additional information.

**Owner Display.** In Windows 3.1, this term describes the format in which the object appears in its source file. For example, an excerpt from a word processor document would be seen if this option is selected. This option is only present while the source application remains open.

In Workgroups, this option may appear on the View Menu if a graphics image has been copied to the Clipboard from a server file other than the one in which the image actually originated. For example, if a bitmap is copied directly from Paintbrush, it will be available on the Clipboard in Bitmap, Palette, or Picture formats. However, if the same bitmap is pasted into a Write file, then copied back to the Clipboard, the enabled menu options will be Owner Display and Picture only.

**OwnerLink.** This gives information about the source (or owner) of the Clipboard object. For example, if a 100 × 50 pixel section of ARCHES.BMP is copied to the Clipboard, the OwnerLink might contain:

PBrush C:\WINDOWS\ARCHES.BMP 0 0 100 50

This shows that the owner is the Paintbrush applet and the object was copied from ARCHES.BMP in the Windows directory. The four numbers indicate the upper left-hand and lower right-hand corners, expressed in pixels.

If you subsequently select the Paste Special option on any application's Edit Menu, the Paste Special dialog box would show:

Paintbrush Picture
ARCHES.BMP 0 0 100 50

If the Clipboard contained data from an unsaved bitmap, similar information would be found in the OwnerLink section of the Clipboard, less the filename section.

> **NOTE:** The OwnerLink section is only saved in the CLP file if the source file is open when the Clipboard data is saved.

Palette. This option appears within the list of formats only if the Clipboard data is taken from a bitmap, and that bitmap originated in a previously saved file. In that case, the option provides a means of viewing colors that are available (but not all necessarily used) in the bitmap file. The Palette option does not appear on the menu if an original Paintbrush drawing is copied to the Clipboard before the drawing is saved as *filename*.BMP.

If data copied from a valid bitmap file is saved from the Clipboard, as *filename*.CLP, the palette section of that file stores the following data:

Save As:	Palette Contains:
16-Color bitmap	16 available colors, + 28-color Paintbrush applet's color matrix
256-Color bitmap	256 available colors, + 28-color Paintbrush applet's color matrix
24-bit bitmap	256-color palette

Each palette color is stored as four bytes: R, G, B, *x*, where *x* is reserved (0). The same information is stored as an RGB Table (described below) within the bitmap file (*filename*.BMP) where—to help keep things confusing—the data is stored in reverse sequence (B, G, R, *x*).

Although the Clipboard Palette may be pretty, its further explanation is not, and so is reserved for inclusion within *The Bitmap File* section, which may be skipped by anyone whose patience wears thin by tiresome rubs against the bits and bytes of bitmaps.

Picture (a/k/a *Metafile*). Going from simplistic to Greek, *picture* and *Metafile* describe a data format in which an object is drawn via GDI (Graphics Device Interchange) commands, not unlike a vector font. As a practical consequence, a picture/Metafile might be considerably smaller than a bitmap of the same object, although it will take longer to paste it into a file.

For those who worry about such things, the closest applicable definition of *meta* may be "more comprehensive."

Rich-Text Format. Word processor text formatting is saved as ASCII character instructions, instead of in the word processor's own native format. For example, the following word-processor excerpt:

"The word *italic* is in italics.
This is line 2."

would be stored as:

\ldblquote-The-word-{\i-italic}-is-in-italics.-<u>0D</u> <u>0A</u> \par-This-is-line-2. \rdblquote

In the above example, each hyphen is actually a space character, the underlined *0D* and *0A* are the ASCII carriage return (*0D*) and line feed (*0A*) characters, and unmarked spaces are added here for clarity but do not appear in the rich-text format. Since all rich-text characters are ASCII standard characters (32–127), the format can be used for straight ASCII transfers (via modem, for example) and it is accepted by most modern word processors.

> **NOTE:** Text documents saved in rich-text format use an RTF extension, not to be confused with the RFT extension, as in DCA-RFT (Document Content Architecture-Revisable-Form Text).

RIFF (Raster Image/Resource Interchange File Format). Various Microsoft documentation alternately offers two RIFF acronyms, neither of which is explained. The former (Raster Image) describes a family of formats that includes TIFF, while the latter (Resource Interchange) includes the *Wave Audio* format.

Sylk **(SYmbolic LinK).** This is used for transferring Excel files to other applications, such as Microsoft *Multiplan* or *Excel for the Macintosh*, versions 1.50 or earlier.

Text. This is an unformatted text rendition of the source object text, displayed in the variable-width system font specified on the fonts.fon=*xxx*sys.fon line in the [boot] section of SYSTEM.INI. To examine the entire character set displayed by the *Text* format, open the Character Map applet and select the *System* font. Refer to *Text Format Comparisons* below for additional information.

TIFF **(Tagged Image File Format).** A graphics file format.

Wave Audio. The data was copied to the Clipboard from a waveform (WAV extension) file. The option is always disabled (grayed) since the format—binary (digital) audio—is not viewable. Although the underlined "W" implies keyboard access, this feature is not presently implemented. Perhaps in some future Clipboard, one will be able to select this option and hear something, but not today.

Wk1 **(Worksheet).** This is a Lotus 1-2-3 release 2.*x* file format.

Word **(or other application)** *Formatted Text.* This is the Windows-for-Workgroups equivalent of the Windows 3.1 **Owner Display** option described above. It is available only while the source application remains open.

Text Format Comparisons. Typical examples of three text formats (Write-Formatted Text, Text, OEM Text) are illustrated in Figure 8.1. If either of the latter two options are selected, the display may or may not be faithful to the formatted-text option, depending on the similarity between the respective character sets, as may be seen by examining Figure 8.1. (Readers who find hidden meaning, other than literary, in the Write-Formatted Text might want to call a psychiatrist for further "assistance.")

The Bitmap File

Although the Clipboard can usually cope with just about anything that gets copied to it, the bitmap format deserves a little extra attention, since a bitmap created on one system can quite often cause grief on another. Therefore, this section takes a rather long look at bitmap innards, for the benefit of those readers who may need to do a little (or a lot of) bitmap

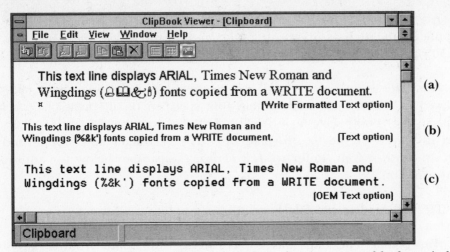

Figure 8.1 A composite Clipbook window, showing a text block copied from a Write file. Use the View option to display the text as (a) Write-Formatted Text, (b) Text, and (c) OEM Text.

troubleshooting. Readers who have no interest in the subject can skip the entire section without fear of missing anything critical.

Table 8.4 lists the component parts of a bitmap file and, for the sake of covering one more base, also shows the 16-bit (64K color) Targa format. One component of some bitmap formats is an RGB Table containing the palette introduced in the *Clipboard Object Formats* section above. The structure of the bitmap file itself, and its palette, varies according to several factors, such as the installed video adapter, color depth, and bitmap dimensions. The following sections review a few color issues and then tackle the bitmap's RGB Table and Bitmap Data Section. The file header information listed in the Table is not further discussed here.

Color Depth

A system's color depth refers to the number of colors that may be displayed, and is independent of the system screen resolution. The latter defines the pixel matrix (640×480, 800×600, 1024×768, etc.) and is not further discussed in this section.

Currently available color depths are briefly described here in terms of the bitmap files that may be created at each depth. Depending on the depth, the bitmap file may contain an RGB Table and a Bitmap Data Section, or just the latter, as described here.

TABLE 8.4   Component Parts of Bitmap (BMP) and Targa (TGA) Files*

Component	Contents	Color Depth				
		Mono	16	256	64K	16.8M
File Header	"BM," file size, etc.	14	14	14	18[†]	14
Information Header	Width, height, bits/pixel, etc.	40	40	40	0	40
RGB Table (palette)	4 bytes per color	8	64	1024	0	0
Bitmap data [‡]	For a 16 × 16 bitmap:	32	128	256	512	768
Padding bytes [§]		32	0	0	0	0
Total		126	246	1334	530	822

[*] 64K color column shows original (pre-Sept. 1989) Targa (TGA) format. All others are Bitmap (BMP).

[†] Targa File Header includes data contained in Bitmap Information Header.

[‡] Size of this section varies according to actual bitmap dimensions.

[§] As required in BMP format, to make each pixel row a multiple of 4 bytes. Not part of actual bitmap data.

Palette-Based Bitmaps. In some bitmap files, an *RGB Table* near the beginning of the file contains a palette of the colors that appear in the bitmap itself. The table is followed by a *Bitmap Data Section* which comprises a sequence of pointers. Each pixel has its own pointer, which refers to the RGB Table location at which the palette color for that pixel is defined. Depending on the number of bits allocated to each pointer, it may point to any location in an RGB Table containing the following number of colors:

Pointer Bits	Colors in RGB Table
1	2
4	16
8	256

TrueColor Bitmaps. In contrast to the palette-based bitmaps described above, the TrueColor bitmap dispenses with the RGB Table. Instead, each pixel color is directly defined by 2 or 3 bytes in the Bitmap Data Section.

The RGB Table (RGBQuad, Color Map)

The RGB Table described in this section is often referred to by programmers as an RGBQuad (since it's based on a 4-byte structure, and *RGBQuad* is less likely to be understood by the unwashed). Or it may be identified as a *Color Map*. This book sticks with *RGB Table,* since that's what it is.

For palette-based bitmaps, each color that will appear in a bitmap is stored in the RGB Table as 3 bytes in reverse sequence (B, G, R), followed by a reserved (zero) byte. For example, the following three colors can be represented in hexadecimal notation as shown here:

dark red, green, yellow   **00 00 80** 00   **00 FF 00** 00   **00 FF FF** 00
                                B G R —   B G R —   B G R —

Table 8.5 shows the RGB Table contents as it appears in bitmap files saved at various color depths supported by Windows. In each case the Windows 256COLOR.BMP file was loaded into the Paintbrush applet, then saved at the indicated color depth on a system in which the appropriate video driver was installed.

Palette-Based Bitmaps. Depending on the current color depth, the RGB Table structure will be as follows.

1 Bit (Monochrome). The Table contains only two 4-byte sequences; black (00 00 00 00) and white (FF FF FF 00).

4 Bit (16 Color). The RGB Table in a 16-color bitmap contains 16 such sequences, for a total of 64 bytes. The default values represent the following colors (reserved zero byte omitted here), which are stored at the indicated *location* in the Table.

Location	Color	B	G	R	Location	Color	B	G	R
0	Black	00	00	00	8	Gray	C0	C0	C0
1	Dark red	00	00	80	9	Red	00	00	FF
2	Dark green	00	80	00	A	Green	00	FF	00
3	Brown	00	80	80	B	Yellow	00	FF	FF
4	Dark blue	80	00	00	C	Blue	FF	00	00
5	Dark magenta	80	00	80	D	Magenta	FF	00	FF
6	Dark cyan	80	80	00	E	Cyan	FF	FF	00
7	Dark grey	80	80	80	F	White	FF	FF	FF

8 bit (256 Color). The RGB Table contains 256 4-byte sequences, for a total of 1,024 bytes. If the bitmap actually used 256 different colors, then each sequence would represent one of those colors. In practice, however, multiple Table locations may show black (00 00 00 00) if the bitmap area is occupied by very few colors as in a simple three-color banner, for example.

TABLE 8.5   RGB Table Colors in Various Copies of 256COLOR.BMP File

| B G R — | | | B G R — | | | B G R — | | | B G R — | | |

Copy, saved as 1-bit/monochrome bitmap[†]

| 00 | 00 00 00 00 |
| 01 | FF FF FF 00 |

Copy, saved as 4-bit/16-color bitmap[†]

00	00 00 00 00	04	80 00 00 00	08	C0 C0 C0 00	0C	FF 00 00 00
01	00 00 80 00	05	80 00 80 00	09	00 00 FF 00	0D	FF 00 FF 00
02	00 80 00 00	06	80 80 00 00	0A	00 FF 00 00	0E	FF FF 00 00
03	00 80 80 00	07	80 80 80 00	0B	00 FF FF 00	0F	FF FF FF 00

Original 8-bit/256-color bitmap[‡]

00	00 00 00 00	08	04 08 00 00	10	00 00 8D 00	18	89 24 44 00
01	00 00 FF 00	09	00 00 71 00	11	00 00 59 00	19	71 28 61 00
02	00 FF 00 00	0A	6D 08 10 00	12	75 2C 6D 00	1A	71 28 69 00
03	FF 00 00 00	0B	91 34 7D 00	13	A5 34 7D 00	1B	59 24 48 00
04	00 FF FF 00	0C	61 24 44 00	14	55 10 55 00	1C	55 24 4C 00
05	FF FF 00 00	0D	00 55 00 00	15	71 24 69 00	1D	DE 38 B6 00
06	FF 00 FF 00	0E	AE 34 A5 00	16	59 28 50 00	1E	50 24 48 00
07	FF FF FF 00	0F	65 2C 30 00	17	7D 30 75 00	1F	95 40 81 00

Copy, saved as 24-bit/16.8M-color bitmap

(No RGB Table. Pixel colors stored directly in file's Bitmap Data Section.)

[†]Complete RGB Table contains these colors.

[‡]Only the first 32 colors are shown. Complete table contains 256 different RGB values at hexadecimal addresses *xxxx*:0136 - *xxxx*:0536 (1024 bytes).

The Windows 256COLOR.BMP File. Perhaps this should really be called *247*COLOR.BMP: although its RGB Table does store 256 different colors, the bitmap data which follows ignores nine of them (at locations 01–07, 28, 8C).

TrueColor Bitmaps. As previously noted, an RGB Table does not appear in the bitmap file. Pixel color information is stored directly in the Bitmap Data Section, as described below.

Viewing the RGB Table Palette. The contents of the RGB Table may be seen by opening the Display or View Menu and selecting Palette from the list of Clipboard Object Formats. As previously noted, this format is available only if the Clipboard image is taken from a previously saved bitmap file.

Figure 8.2 shows how the palette display varies according to the number of colors stored in the RGB Table.

Bitmap Data Section

The RGB Table is followed by a sequence of bytes which store a pixel-by-pixel description of the bitmap. The sequence begins in the lower left-hand corner of the bitmap, moves upward line by line, and concludes in the upper right-hand corner of the bitmap. For monochrome, 16- and 256-color bitmaps, the bitmap section of the file contains the pointers to the RGB Table described above.

Table 8.6 shows how the data for the first 32 pixels in the bitmap data section of 256COLOR.BMP are written into copies of that file saved under various color depths.

Palette-Based Bitmaps. In each of the three color depths listed here, the pointer bits vary as follows.

1 Bit (Monochrome). In a monochrome system, each bitmap pixel is allocated a single bit, which points to one of two locations in the RGB Table. Therefore, you can have any colors you like, provided you only like black and white.

4 Bit (16 color). The first byte represents the RGB Table locations of the first and second pixel (4 bits each), starting at the lower left-hand corner of the bitmap. The final byte represents the last two pixels, at the upper right-hand corner. For example, the bitmap section of the 16-color CARS.BMP file begins with a sequence of 88 88 88, . . . (medium gray is

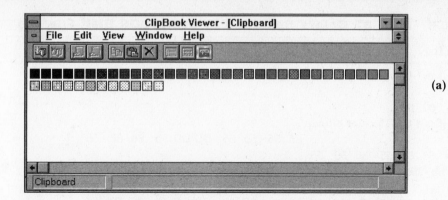

(a)

(b)

(c)

Figure 8.2   A Palette display of a bitmap image saved in (a) 16 colors, (b) 256 colors, and (c) 16.7 million colors.

at position 8 in the Table above) and concludes with FF FF FF, . . . (white is at F). Thus, we can surmise that there is a strip of medium gray at the bottom of this bitmap and one of white at the top. To verify this, open the Paintbrush applet's File Menu, select its Open... option, load the CARS.BMP file, and have a look.

TABLE 8.6 First 32 Colors Specified in 256COLOR.BMP File*

Segment:offset   Data Bytes

Copy, saved as 1-bit/monochrome bitmap[†]

xxxx :0130	..	..	..	..	..	..	..	..	..	-	..	..	..	..	..	..	00	60
xxxx :0140	00	00														

Copy, saved as 4-bit/16-color bitmap[‡]

xxxx :0170	..	..	..	..	..	..	55	55 - 55	55	DD	DD	55	88	88	55
xxxx :0180	55	55	55	55	55	55								

Original 8-bit/256-color bitmap[§]

xxxx :0530	..	..	..	..	..	..	16	15 - DC	50	50	DC	1A	48	AA	3A
xxxx :0540	3A	92	55	F1	A8	35	35	71 - DB	23	CC	CC	15	2F	C1	D0
xxxx :0550	1B	1B	1B	1B	16	2F								

Copy, saved as 24-bit/16.8M-color bitmap[††]   **Pixel No.**

												Pixel No.
xxxx :0130	..	..	..	..	..	..	..	59	28 - 50	71	24	69	79	2C	71	85	00 - 03
xxxx :0140	38	7D	85	38	7D	79	2C	71 - 71	28	69	81	30	79	CE	44	03 - 08
xxxx :0150	BE	EA	50	DE	EA	50	DE	DE- 40	CE	C6	38	B6	AE	40	99	08 - 0D
xxxx :0160	AA	48	91	AA	4C	91	AA	4C - 91	AA	44	91	A5	3C	95	AE	0E - 13
xxxx :0170	34	9D	BA	34	AA	BA	34	AA - 71	24	69	6D	24	5D	9D	30	13 - 18
xxxx :0180	91	65	28	5D	59	24	48	59 - 24	48	59	24	48	59	24	48	18 - 1D
xxxx :0190	59	28	50	6D	24	5D										1E - 1F

*All versions shown here refer to first 32 pixels at bottom of bitmap.

[†]Each bit points to location 0 or 1 in 2-color RGB Table (in Table 8.5). Monochrome copy is very poor rendition of original.

[‡]Each hexadecimal number points to a location in the 16-color RGB Table (in Table 8.5).

[§]Each byte points to a location in 256-bit RGB Table (in Table 8.5).

[††]Each underlined 3-byte sequence directly defines a pixel color.

8 Bit (256 Color). Since there are now 256 possible colors, each byte represents a single pixel. As above, the byte specifies the position in the RGB Table at which the color for that pixel is stored. The system is supported by various third-party drivers, and also by the Windows Paintbrush applet.

Use of Padding Bytes. In a palette-based bitmap, each horizontal row of pixels is rounded upward, as required, to the nearest 4-byte multiple. For example, the monochrome 16×16 pixel bitmaps listed in Table 8.7 require only 2 bytes to define the 16 pixels in each row. Therefore, two padding bytes are added to each row, as indicated by the *xx* bytes in the Table.

TrueColor Bitmaps. The color depths described here do not make use of an RGB Table.

TABLE 8.7   Specifications for a 16 × 16 Pixel Bitmap File*

Color Depth	Bits per Pixel	Color	Pointers in Each 16-Pixel Row		File Size (Bytes)
			Odd Rows	**Even Rows**	
Mono— chrome	1[†]	Black	00 00 *xx xx*	00 00 *xx xx*	126
		White	FF FF *xx xx*	FF FF *xx xx*	
		Gray	55 55 *xx xx*	AA AA *xx xx*	
16	4	Red	99 99 99 99 99 99 99 99	99 99 99 99 99 99 99 99	246
		Green	AA AA AA AA AA AA AA AA	AA AA AA AA AA AA AA AA	
		Blue	BB BB BB BB BB BB BB BB	BB BB BB BB BB BB BB BB	
		Brown	31 31 31 31 31 31 31 31	13 13 13 13 13 13 13 13	
256	8	Red	01 01 (× 8)	01 01 (× 8)	1334
		Dark red	11 11 (× 8)	11 11 (× 8)	
		Brown[‡]	03 01 (× 8)	03 01 (× 8)	
16.8M	24	Red	00 00 FF (× 16)	00 00 FF (× 16)	822
		Dark red	00 00 80 (× 16)	00 00 80 (× 16)	
		Brown	00 80 80 00 00 80 (× 8)	00 80 80 00 00 80 (× 8)	

* Entire bitmap is in indicated color. Except as noted ([†]), refer to appropriate RGB Table in Table 8.5 to verify color.

[†] Each pointer bit is either 0 or 1, thereby pointing to Table locations 0(00 00 00 00) or 1 (FF FF FF 00). *xx* is padding byte inserted to create multiple of 4 bytes per row, but not part of actual bitmap data.

[‡] Cited RGB Table colors are: @03; 00 80 80 00 (dark green, dark red), @ 01; 00 00 80 00 (dark red).

16 Bit (32K Color). If a video adapter card/driver combination supports 32,768 (2^{15}) colors, each pixel in the bitmap file is represented by 2 bytes, with 5 bits each for red, green, and blue. The sixteenth bit is reserved for video overlays, which are not further discussed here. This is the 16-bit implementation most often encountered, but is not directly supported by Windows.

However, the format is supported by various third-party Windows graphics applications. As a typical example, Computer Associates' *Cricket Image* can convert any Windows bitmap file into the popular Targa (Truevision Advanced Raster Graphics Adapter) 16-bit format. Such files are identified by a TGA extension.

16 Bit (64K Color). If all 16 bits are allocated to color definition, 65,536 (2^{16}) colors are possible. This format (5 red, 6 green, 5 blue) is supported by XGA (Extended Graphics Array) video, which IBM introduced in its PS/2 series. Although Windows does support four XGA video modes (listed below), this 16-bit format is not one of them. It is mentioned here simply to illustrate how 64K color depth is achieved by those who might want to achieve it.

Resolution	Color Depth	Driver
640 × 480	16	vga.drv
640 × 480	256	xga.drv
1024 × 768	256 small fonts	xga.drv
1024 × 768	256 large fonts	xga.drv

24 Bit (16.7M Color). The ultimate (so far, that is) in Windows color depth, a 24-bit color system allocates 3 bytes to each pixel.

Bitmap Comparisons

Except as indicated, the RGB Tables and Bitmap Data Sections described here were created using the Microsoft VGA and SuperVGA 4-bit/16-color video drivers. If either is replaced by a driver that supports a greater color depth, the position of colors within the RGB Table may shift from that shown in the various tables in this chapter, even though the bitmap is saved in the 4-bit format. Therefore, the pointers in the Bitmap Data Section will likewise be different.

This can be demonstrated on any system that supports an 8-bit/256-color driver. Open the Paintbrush applet and load the 4-bit/16-color CARS.BMP file. Then save it as CARS2.BMP. Although Paintbrush saves the copy at the same color depth as the original, the RGB Table color palette is written in a slightly different sequence. And because of that, the pointers in the Bitmap Data Section are also revised, to point to the appropriate new locations in the table. As a result, a DOS file comparison (fc /b CARS.BMP CARS2.BMP) will show multiple differences between the two files. Nevertheless, there should be no visual difference between them.

The Windows 3.1 Clipboard Viewer

Figure 8.3 shows the Application Window for the Windows version 3.1 Clipboard. A bitmap file (CARS.BMP) was previously opened within the Paintbrush applet and copied to the Clipboard, where it is currently displayed in the Clipboard's *Picture* format, as indicated by the check mark next to that option on the Display Menu. Refer to the *Display Menu* section below for further details about this and other menu options. As for the other basic window components, they're no different from those described in the *Window Components* section of Chapter 3.

The Workgroups Clipbook Viewer

Figure 8.4 shows the Windows-for-Workgroups Clipboard Viewer as it might appear on a typical local computer. The component parts of its Application Window are described here, and this explanation is followed by a description of the formats in which each Clipboard or Clipbook may be displayed.

Application Window

The Clipbook Viewer's Application Window is similar in concept to that of the File Manager, in that it may contain several smaller windows. The com-

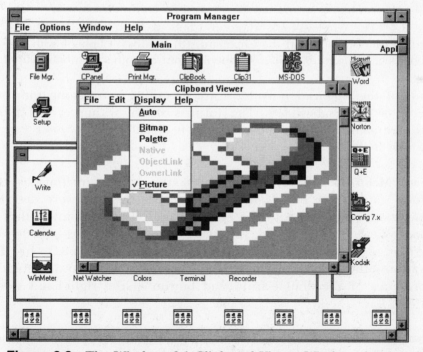

Figure 8.3 The Windows 3.1 Clipboard Viewer Window, showing the CARS.BMP file via the Display Menu's Picture option.

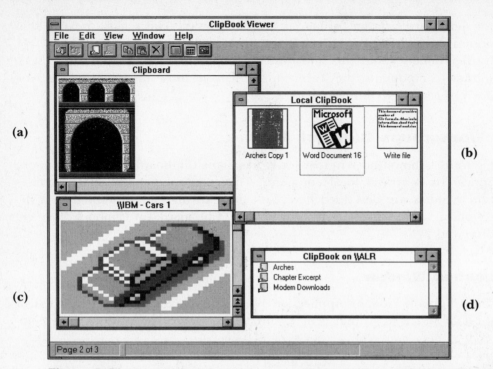

Figure 8.4 The Windows-for-Workgroups Clipbook Viewer Window. The application window shows (a) the Clipboard, (b) the local Clipbook with three Clipbook pages, (c and d) remote Clipbooks from two other network computers.

ponents of the Application Window are described here, along with a description of each subwindow. The formats shown within each Clipbook window are identified here and described in detail in the *Clipbook Page* section which follows.

Title and Menu Bars. Both bars perform the same functions as their Program Manager or File Manager counterparts, which were described in Chapters 3 and 6. As with the File Manager, if any window within the Clipbook Viewer is maximized, the name of that window is added to the Title Bar text, as may be seen in Figures 8.1 and 8.2. In these illustrations, the Clipboard Window is maximized, as may be noted by the presence of the double-arrowhead button at the right-hand side of the Menu Bar.

Toolbar and Toolbar Buttons. The Clipbook Viewer's Application Window displays a Toolbar immediately below the Edit Menu. The 10 buttons on the Toolbar are shown in Figure 8.5 and listed in the three columns

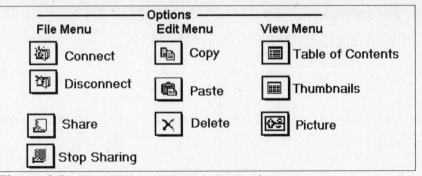

Figure 8.5   The Clipbook Viewer's Toolbar buttons

below. The four buttons in the first column perform the same functions as the equivalent options on the Clipbook Viewer's File Menu. The three buttons in the second column duplicate Edit Menu options and those in the last column match View Menu options. Refer to the appropriate menu descriptions later in the chapter for information about these options.

File Menu	Edit Menu	View Menu
Connect	Copy	Table of Contents
Disconnect	Paste	Thumbnails
Share As	Delete	Picture
Stop Sharing		

Clipboard Window. The window shown here in the upper left-hand corner of Figure 8.4 is the Clipbook Viewer's own Clipboard (a), which is functionally equivalent to the one in Windows version 3.1 (as shown in Figure 8.3). Whenever an object is cut or copied within an application, that object appears in this window. For future reference, the Windows ARCHES.BMP file is displayed via the Bitmap option in the Figure.

Local Clipbook Window. This window (Figure 8.4b) may hold one or more previously saved files, and these may also be shown in any of the Formats listed on the View Menu. In this illustration, the pages are shown as *Thumbnails*.

Remote Clipbook Window. There may be one or more additional windows within the Clipbook Viewer, such as the two shown at the bottom of Figure 8.4(c and d). The Title Bar of each such window may display the following information:

Title Bar Displays	**See Figure 8.4**
Remote computer and displayed page names	(c)
Clipbook on \\(*remote computer name*)	(d)

The latter style (d) appears if the Remote Clipbook pages are displayed in *Thumbnail* or—as in this example—*Table of Contents* format.

Status Bar. At the bottom of the Application Window, the Status Bar panel identifies the highlighted Thumbnail or icon in the active window. In the example shown in Figure 8.4b, the *Word Document 16* Thumbnail in the Local Clipbook Window is highlighted, so the panel shows "Page 2 of 3" since this is the second of the three Thumbnails in that Window.

The Clipbook Page A Clipbook *page* is simply any Clipboard image that has been placed on the local or remote Clipbook, using the techniques described in the *Edit Menu* section below. Although each Clipbook can only show one complete page at a time, alternate View Menu options permit it to display the entire set of Clipbook pages, either as *Thumbnails* or as *Icons*.

Clipbook Thumbnails. A *Thumbnail* is a miniature black-and-white sketch of a currently available Clipbook page. As noted earlier, it is stored in a 512-byte *Clipbook Preview* segment in the CLP file, and despite its diminutive size may be almost readable if the Clipboard data itself is text, as may be noted in the *Write File* Thumbnail seen in the Local Clipbook in Figure 8.4b. However, color-graphics images do not fare as well and may be all but unrecognizable, as may be noted by the *Arches Copy 1* Thumbnail in the same Figure.

Figure 8.6 shows a few Thumbnail variations which may be encountered, as described here.

Missing Page. If a Local Clipboard page was erased prior to the current Windows session, but not deleted from the Clipboard itself, a blank Thumbnail appears with a padlock in the upper right-hand corner, as shown by the *Chart 1* Thumbnail in Figure 8.6.

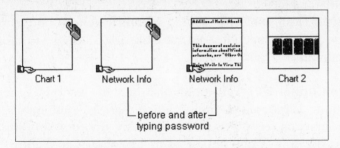

Figure 8.6   These Thumbnails may appear on a Local or Remote Clipbook.

 NOTE: A local computer cannot restrict its own access to its own Local Clipbook via password protection. Therefore, the appearance of a padlock on a Local Clipbook is an indication of trouble.

Password-Protected Page. On a Local Clipbook, there is no indication that a page is password-protected. However, if that page is displayed as a Thumbnail on another computer's Remote Clipbook, a padlock appears in the upper right-hand corner of that Thumbnail, as shown by the first *Network Info* Thumbnail in Figure 8.6. Here, the padlock/blank page indicates that the user has not yet been granted access by typing the required password. After doing so, the Thumbnail image changes, as shown by the next *Network Info* Thumbnail: The padlock is removed and a simulation of the remote page format appears within the Thumbnail.

 NOTE: Password protection is initiated via the **Share...** option, as described below: Refer to *Access Type* in the File Menu section for further details. See also *Passwords* and *Clipbook Sharing* in the Configuration section.

Shared Page. A small hand in the lower left-hand corner of a Local Clipbook Thumbnail indicates that the local computer has made this page available for sharing with remote systems.

All Thumbnails in any Remote Clipbook Window show a sharing hand in the lower left-hand corner of the Thumbnail, which in this context is redundant: The very presence of a Thumbnail indicates a shared page is available. If the remote computer did not want to share that page, it wouldn't be there in the first place.

Unshared Page. If no little sharing hand is outstretched under the Thumbnail, the page has not been made available for sharing, as shown by the *Chart 2* Thumbnail in Figure 8.6.

Clipbook Icons. The ClipBook Viewer applet also may display the contents of its Local and Remote Clipbooks as icons rather than as Thumbnails, or any of its windows may be reduced to an icon at the bottom of the Viewer's Application Window. Examples of each are shown in Figure 8.7 and described here.

Table of Contents Icon. If the Table of Contents option on the View Menu is selected, the Clipbook Window displays a page as a miniature spiral notebook icon, followed by the Page Name.

Password-Protected Page. Unlike the Thumbnail displayed on a Remote Clipbook, a Table-of-Contents icon gives no indication if a Clipbook page is password-protected.

Shared Page. If the Clipbook Page is available for sharing, a sharing hand appears in the lower left-hand corner of the icon. As with the Thumbnails described above, all Table-of-Contents icons on the Remote Clipbook show the sharing hand under the notebook.

Unshared Page. If a Local Clipbook page is not available for sharing, the sharing hand is omitted from the icon.

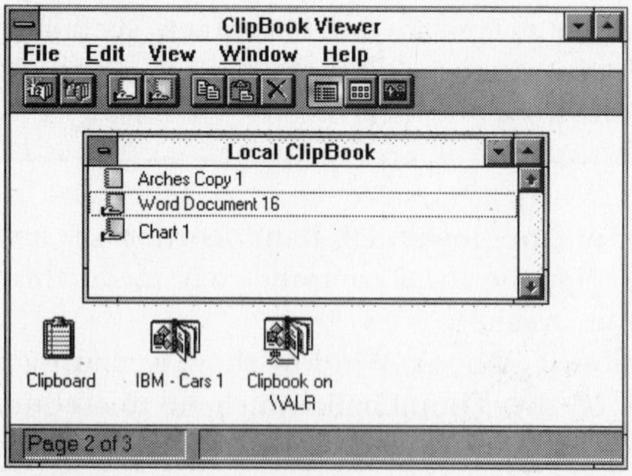

Figure 8.7 Clipbook Icons. The Local Clipbook shows Document and Shared-document icons. Minimized Clipboard and Clipbook icons appear underneath the Local Clipbook Window.

Minimized Clipboard or Clipbook Icon. Note that each window within the Clipbook Viewer has its own Minimize button, as may be seen in all four windows in Figure 8.4. If any such button is clicked, the window is reduced to a minimized icon, as shown by the examples at the bottom of Figure 8.7.

Clipboard and Clipbook Menus

Unless otherwise noted by a parenthetical reference, the menus and menu options described in this section are found on both the Clipboard and Clipbook Menu Bars. Typical Menus are illustrated in Figure 8.8. As usual, a letter in parentheses next to a menu name indicates its location in the figure, and if the menu option is accessible by pressing a key (which is underlined in the menu option), that key is underlined in the description given here.

Control and Help Menus. Refer to the *Control Menu* or *Help Menu* sections of Chapter 3 for a discussion of the options found on these menus.

Display (a) (*Windows*) Menu. As noted earlier, an object copied to the Clipboard may exist there in more than one format, so that when an application pastes that object into a client file, it can select the format most compatible with itself. The currently available formats appear as options on the Display or View Menu; when any such option is selected, the Clipboard displays the object in that format. This display is solely for the benefit of the user, and has no effect on subsequent pastes to any application.

Auto. When you first open the Clipboard, information is automatically displayed in the format of the file in which the information originated, as indicated by a check mark next to this option. The actual format is one of those in the list of Clipboard Object Formats which follow, but it's up to you to guess which one. To try your luck, select the one you think it is. If the on-screen image does not change, you win. If it does change, reselect the Auto option and try again.

Clipboard Object Format List. The remainder of the Display Menu lists the object formats currently stored on the Clipboard. The specific formats seen on any menu are determined by the server file from which the object was taken. A list of frequently-encountered formats was given in Table 8.1, and the formats themselves were briefly described in the *Clipboard Object Formats* section above.

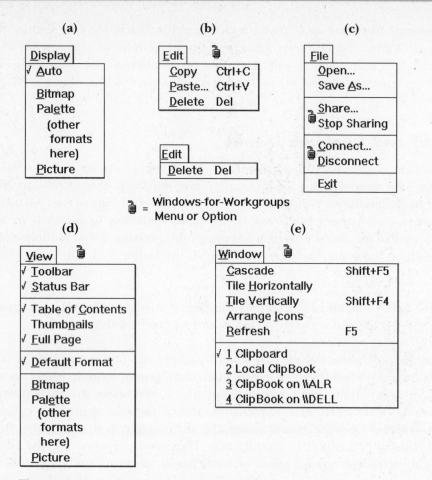

Figure 8.8 Clipboard and Clipbook Menus

If a format may be directly viewed on the Clipboard, it appears in the list as an enabled (boldface) option, which may be selected in the usual manner. If a format appears but is disabled (grayed), it is unsuitable for direct viewing on the Clipboard, but is available to any application that can use it (via the Paste Special... option on the application's Edit Menu).

Edit Menu. For the moment, Clipboard edit functions are limited to the few simple operations described here. More sophisticated editing may show up on the next version of Windows.

Copy (**Ctrl+C**) *(Workgroups)*. When the Copy option on any applet or application Edit Menu (*not* File Menu) is selected, the user is not asked to specify a destination. The selected data is always copied to the Clipboard, where it remains available to the same, or any other, application that can use it.

The Clipbook Viewer's own <u>C</u>opy option is enabled only if there is a Clipbook Page available in the active (local or remote) ClipBook Window. Highlight the desired page on the active Clip*book*, then select the <u>C</u>opy option to copy that page to the Clip*board*. Once on the Clipboard, the data may be pasted into any application on the local computer.

<u>D</u>elete (Del). This option is enabled if the Clipboard contains data. In most cases it is not necessary to open the Clipboard and select this option, since whatever is on the Clipboard can stay there until it gets deleted automatically by something else. However, if there is a problem within some other application that relates to the contents of the Clipboard, you may want to open the Clipboard in order to have a look. In this case you can save the Clipboard, then delete its contents without returning to the application.

<u>D</u>elete **(Del)** *(Workgroups).* In addition to the regular Windows function just described, you may also delete a highlighted Clipbook Page on your Local Clipbook. If the Page is available for sharing, and a remote application currently shows the Page on its own Remote Clipbook, the Page automatically disappears without notice at the remote location when you delete it from your Local Clipbook. Needless to say, the <u>D</u>elete option is never enabled if your own Remote Clipbook Window is active. If you think a Remote Clipbook Page should be deleted, you'll have to persuade the remote operator to do it.

<u>P</u>aste **(Ctrl+V)** *(Workgroups).* If the Clipboard contains data, the <u>P</u>aste option is enabled on the Edit Menu if either the Clipboard itself, or the Local Clipbook, is the active window. In either case, the option pastes a copy of the Clip*board* to the Local Clip*book*.

Page Name. If you do select the <u>P</u>aste option, the <u>P</u>aste dialog box shown in Figure 8.9 prompts you for a *Page Name,* which will appear under the Thumbnail or next to the Page Icon in the Local Clipbook Window. The name may be up to 47 characters in length.

The dialog box also provides a <u>S</u>hare Item Now check box. If you check it, the Share ClipBook Page dialog box appears. This dialog box is fully described below, in the description of the File Menu's <u>S</u>hare... option.

File Menu (c). The File Menu contains the applet's file-access options, as well as the network sharing and connection options included with Windows-for-Workgroups.

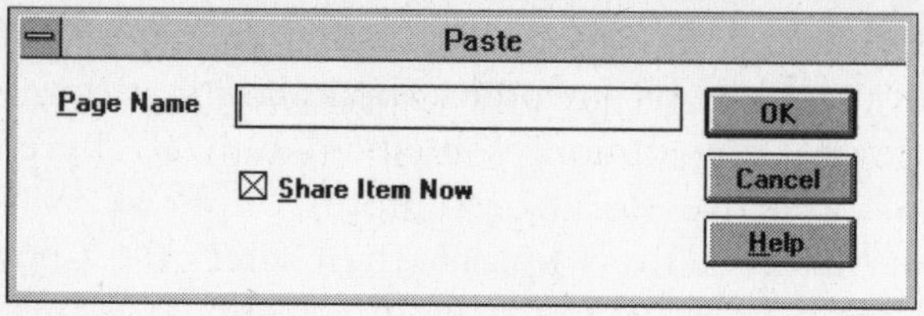

Figure 8.9 Use the Paste dialog box to specify the name for a Clipbook page.

Connect... **(Workgroups on Enhanced-Mode Systems).** Select this option to connect to a remote computer's Local Clipbook. When you do so, the Select Computer dialog box shown in Figure 8.10 appears. The Computers: box lists the Workgroups, and the computers within each such group.

Connect... **(Workgroups on Standard-Mode Systems).** In Figure 8.10, the Computers: box does not show the IBM (AT 286) computer that is part of the network. Nor would it show any 386 (or better) computer currently running Workgroups in standard mode. However, if you know there are pages available for sharing on a remote 286 or other standard-mode system, you can type the name of that computer into the Computer Name: box. (Note the presence of \\IBM in the pull-down list.) A new Remote Clipbook Window will open within your Clipbook Viewer, and those pages will be available.

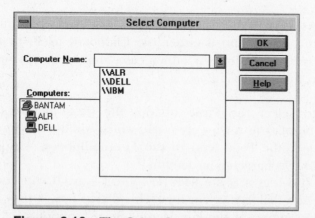

Figure 8.10 The Select Computer dialog box lists the names of the computers on the network. Although an icon and name for a 286 computer (\\IBM) does not appear in the Computers: box, its name may be typed into the Computer Name: box (see drop-down list) if the computer has a Local Clipbook available for sharing.

Disconnect **(Workgroups).** Once you've grabbed what you need from a Remote Clipbook, select this option to do exactly what it says. Otherwise, the next time you open the Clipbook Viewer, it will try to re-establish the connection, and pause with an error message if it can't.

Exit. The option closes the Clipboard or Clipbook Viewer.

Open.... This option is enabled only if the Clipboard is the active window within the Clipboard Viewer or Clipbook Viewer. Use it to load a previously saved CLP file into the Clipboard. No error message is seen if you attempt to open a non-CLP file. However, nothing shows up on the Clipboard, and no _Clipboard Object Format List_ appears on the Display/View Menu.

Save As.... The customary Save option does not appear on the Clipboard's File Menu, since the Clipboard is not the medium for saving the contents in the same format as the source file. Instead, Save As... saves the Clipboard contents to a file (_filename_.CLP) which contains all the formats currently stored on the Clipboard. For further details about the CLP file, refer to _CLP File Characteristics_ in the _Clipboard and Clipbook Configuration_ section later in the chapter.

Share... **(Workgroups).** Select this option if you want to share a Local Clipbook Page with remote users. First, highlight the Page you want to share, then select the option to open the Share Clipbook Page dialog box shown in Figure 8.11. The dialog box also shows up if you clicked on the Share Item Now check box mentioned above in the description of the Edit Menu's Paste option.

Sharing Options: Start Application on Connect. This one takes a bit of explaining: Consider a Local Clipbook Page on the DELL computer which contains a section of an Excel spreadsheet. Assume a user at a remote ALR computer copies this page to ALR's own Clipboard, then opens a Write file and Paste-Links the page (or _object_) into that file.

Later on, the remote user double-clicks on the linked object in the Write file, expecting it to be updated from the original spreadsheet on your computer. If the local Excel is currently open, _and_ the spreadsheet is loaded, then there's no problem—all this happens as it should. However, if Excel is not open, or it's open but the spreadsheet is not loaded, then nothing at all happens, _unless_ you checked the Start Application on Connect box when you made the Clipbook page available for sharing. If you did,

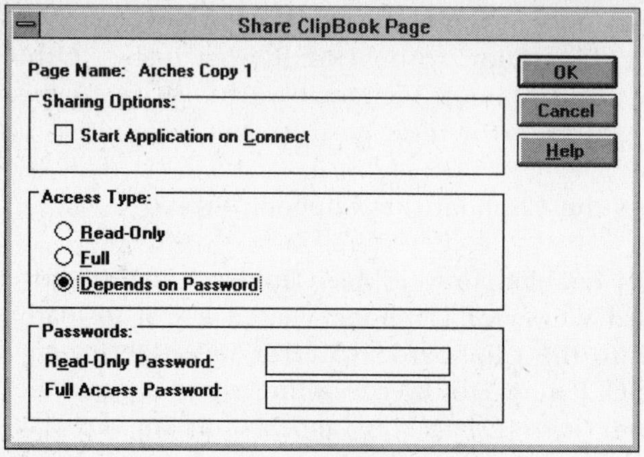

```
┌─────────────────────────────────────────────┐
│ ─            Share ClipBook Page              │
├─────────────────────────────────────────────┤
│ Page Name:  Arches Copy 1       ┌──────────┐ │
│ ┌─Sharing Options:──────────┐   │    OK    │ │
│ │                           │   └──────────┘ │
│ │ ☐ Start Application on Connect │ ┌────────┐ │
│ │                           │   │  Cancel  │ │
│ └───────────────────────────┘   └──────────┘ │
│                                 ┌──────────┐ │
│ ┌─Access Type:──────────────┐   │   Help   │ │
│ │ ○ Read-Only               │   └──────────┘ │
│ │ ○ Full                    │                │
│ │ ⦿ Depends on Password     │                │
│ └───────────────────────────┘                │
│ ┌─Passwords:────────────────────────────────┐│
│ │ Read-Only Password:    [              ]   ││
│ │ Full Access Password:  [              ]   ││
│ └───────────────────────────────────────────┘│
└─────────────────────────────────────────────┘
```

Figure 8.11 Use the Share Clipbook Page dialog box to specify the sharing options for a local Clipbook page.

then when the remote user double-clicks on the object in his Write file, your local Excel opens, the spreadsheet loads, and the remote user gets an updated copy of the object. If you're in the middle of something else when a remote user decides to update a link back to your system, you may be momentarily startled to see an Excel spreadsheet (or whatever) pop up on your screen without being invited.

Access Type: and *Passwords:* Boxes. Before spending too much time assigning unique read-only and full-access passwords, refer to *Passwords and Clipbook Sharing* in the *Clipboard and Clipbook Configuration* section later in the chapter for information about currently-available password implementation.

Share... (Workgroups, on 286 System). Forget what you've read about not being able to share resources while running Windows in standard mode—which is all there is on a 286 computer. Although that limitation is imposed on disk drives, it is lifted for the Clipboard. The option appears on the File Menu, and all the various procedures described above may be utilized.

If a remote user opens the Clipbook Viewer's File Menu and selects the Connect... option, the name of the 286 computer does not appear in the Computers: list in the Select Computer dialog box shown earlier in Figure 8.10. However, if the remote user enters the 286 computer name into the Computer Name: box, the shared 286 Clipbook pages will appear in a new Remote Clipbook Window. In other words, the remote system user must know that your 286 system has Clipbook pages available for sharing.

Stop Sharing (Workgroups). Highlight any shared page on your own Local Clipbook and select this option to quit sharing it. As soon as you do, the page disappears from the Remote Clipbooks on all the other computers on the network.

View Menu *(Workgroups).* This menu is similar in function to the Display Menu in Windows version 3.1. However, the listed options vary according to which window is currently active, as shown here. Any option listed in boldface type may be selected. Grayed text identifies an option not available within the current active window, but which will be available in the other windows.

Clipboard	Local Clipbook	Remote Clipbook
Window Options		
Status Bar	**Status Bar**	**Status Bar**
Toolbar	**Toolbar**	**Toolbar**
Viewing Options		
Full Page	**Full Page**	Full Page
Table of Contents	**Table of Contents**	**Table of Contents**
Thumbnails	**Thumbnails**	**Thumbnails**
Clipboard Object Format List		
Default Format	—	—
(format list varies)	—	—

Each of these options is described in the alphabetical listing which follows.

Clipboard Object Format List. As on the Display Menu in Windows 3.1, the lowest section of the View Menu lists the various formats currently stored on the Clipboard. Refer to *Clipboard Object Format List* in the *Display Menu* section above for further details, or to the *Clipboard Object Formats* section for a description of the formats that may be listed here.

Default Format. This is the Workgroups equivalent of the Windows 3.1 Auto option described earlier in the Display Menu section. When you first open the Clipboard, information is automatically displayed in the default format of the file in which the information originated, as indicated by a check mark next to this option. To determine the actual name of that format, refer to the previously described Auto option.

Full Page. This viewing option displays the selected Clipbook page as a full-page image in the active window, and is the only viewing option available in the Clipboard. In either case, the full-page image does not necessarily occupy the entire window. For example, Figure 8.12 shows two windows open in the Clipbook Viewer applet. The image in both windows was copied to the Clipboard from the ARCHES.BMP file, via the Paintbrush applet. The Clipboard Window shows a full-page view as it appears if the Picture option is selected. Since a Clipboard picture expands to fill the entire active window, the full-page picture shows horizontal distortion due to the dimensions of the Clipboard Window. In contrast, the Local Clipbook Window shows a full-page in which Bitmap is the selected viewing option. Since this window happens to be somewhat larger than the actual bitmap image, this full-page viewing option shows some white space in the window.

Status Bar. The Status Bar at the bottom of the Clipbook Viewer Window may be toggled on and off by selecting this option. The Status Bar's panel identifies the active Clipboard Window (Clipboard) or the selected page in the active Clipbook Window (Page *x* of *y*).

Table of Contents. This option displays the names of the currently available local or remote Clipbook pages, as shown by the Local Clipbook examples in Figure 8.7.

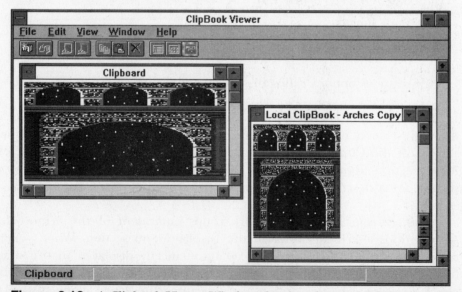

Figure 8.12 A Clipbook Viewer Window showing the same bitmap as a Picture in the Clipboard and as a bitmap on the Local Clipbook.

Thumbnails. If you select the Thumbnails option, the Clipbook Viewer Window displays its contents as Thumbnails, such as those shown in Figure 8.6.

Toolbar. The Toolbar described earlier in the chapter may be toggled on and off via this option.

Window Menu *(Workgroups).* The Clipboard and Clipbooks that may be viewed are described here. The other Window Menu options are similar to those described in the *Window Menu* section of Chapter 6. Refer to that section for a complete description.

The Clipboard and available Clipbook Windows are listed in the lower section of the Window Menu, as shown by the representative examples below. Example 3 appears only if the local computer is connected to a Remote Clipbook. If the local computer is connected to more than one Remote Clipbook, Example 3 is repeated as *4, 5, . . .* and so on, for each connected Clipbook.

<u>1</u> **Clipboard.** Select this option to view the conventional Clipboard, such as the one (and only) Clipboard available in Windows 3.1.

<u>2</u> **Local ClipBook**   *If Local Clipbook displays Table of Contents or Thumbnails, or is empty.*

or

<u>2</u> **Local ClipBook - (***page name***)**   *If Local Clipbook displays a full-page image.*

<u>3</u> **Clipbook on \\(***computer name***)**   *If Remote Clipbook displays Table of Contents or Thumbnails.*

or

<u>3</u> **\\(***computer name***) - (***page name***)**   *If Remote Clipbook displays a full-page image.*

Clipboard and Clipbook Configuration

This section reviews a few procedures and techniques that may be useful in routine configuration and use of the Clipboard Viewer and Clipbook Viewer applets.

Basic Copy/Paste Test Procedure

The following test procedure may be used to verify that the Clipboard's basic Copy/Paste functions work properly when transferring data between files. As described here, the procedure copies a portion of a bitmap from a saved Paintbrush (server) file into a Write (client) file. The server and client files may be on the same computer, or on two computers linked via Windows-for-Workgroups and the appropriate hardware.

On the server computer:

1. Open Paintbrush and load any Microsoft bitmap file found in the Windows directory.

2. Open the File Menu, select the **Save As**... option and make a copy of the file as TEST.BMP (to avoid accidentally changing the original bitmap file).

3. Copy some or all of TEST.BMP to the Clipboard.

   If server and client files are on the same machine, skip to Step 4 in the following section. Otherwise, continue reading here.

4. Open the Clipbook Viewer and Select the Local Clipbook.

5. Open the Edit Menu, select the **Paste**... option, and check the **Share Item Now** box.

6. In the **Paste Dialog** box, enter a suitable Page Name (*Test Page*, for example). The bitmap is now present as *Test Page* on the Local Clipbook.

On the client computer:

1. Open the Clipbook Viewer and select the appropriate Remote Clipbook Window.

2. Double-click on the *Test Page* icon or Thumbnail. Enter password if necessary.

3. Open the Edit Menu and select the **C**opy option to place a copy of *Test Page* on the Clip*board*. Check the Clipboard to make sure the desired image is really there, and then proceed to step 4.

   If server and client files are on the same machine, begin here.

4. Open the Write applet, write a few sample text lines, then select a suitable insertion point.

5. Open the Edit Menu and select the **Paste Link** option.

The Paintbrush bitmap should now appear in the Write file at the selected insertion point, thus indicating that the basic Clipboard/Clipbook functions are in good order. However, if the correct image does not appear, then review the various symptoms listed in the *Troubleshooting* section. If an error message appears, then refer to the *Error Messages* section for further assistance.

Copy/Paste Text Configuration

If your idea of a game of chance is guessing what pasted text is going to look like, the following section may help remove the guesswork—or at least improve your odds on getting it right the first time. Although the examples below use Write, Word-for-Windows, and Paintbrush, the same general principles should be valid for most other applications too.

Select Font for Pasted Text. When text is pasted into a client file, it may or may not appear in the font and/or point size you expected. As a typical example, consider a copy/paste operation in which a 10-point Arial text block copied from document A is pasted into a 12-point Times New Roman text block in document B. If the pasted text does not appear in the font format you wanted, it's easy enough to change it as required. However, the following sections may help explain why the text appears the way it does.

Copy/Paste between Two Write Files. The pasted text font will appear in either of the following formats:

Pasted Text Appears As:	Using Font in:	Conditions during Paste:
10-pt. Arial	Document A	Document A is open
12-pt. Times New Roman	Document B	Document A is closed

Therefore, if you want the pasted text to retain the font and point size under which it was created, open a second Write applet window. Leave document A open and paste the desired text into document B.

However, if you want the pasted text to assume the characteristics of the text currently in use in document B, close document A after copying the text and before pasting it. If you would rather not close document A, then just open the Clipboard and use the Save As... option. As noted earlier, this action clears the Write formatted text from the Clipboard, leaving unformatted text in its place. Then go to document B and paste the now-unformatted text into the file at the desired location.

Copy/Paste between Two Word (or other) Files. Open the Edit Menu, select Paste Special..., then choose the text option shown here, as desired.

Pasted Text Appears As:	Using Font in:	Use Paste Special Option:
10-pt. Arial	Document A	Formatted text
12-pt. Times New Roman	Document B	Unformatted text

Copy/Paste into a Paintbrush Window. Text pasted into a Paintbrush Window always appears in the current Paintbrush font, regardless of whether the source document is open or closed.

Insert Text in Client File as an Object Icon. If a server text block is pasted into a client file as an *object* (Microsoft Word Object, for example), the client file displays an icon at the insertion point instead of the text itself. This feature may be convenient for inserting supplementary information into a document: The extra information is available if one wants to read it, but it doesn't take up screen space unless it's actually needed. In order to see the text represented by the icon, double-click on it and the text should appear.

Presumably, the text should be displayed as it appears in the server file. Usually it does, but sometimes it doesn't. For example, if text is copied from one new document and pasted into another as a Microsoft Word Object, a subsequent double-click on the icon may show the text in a smaller point size, and sometimes with a different font. This appears to be a minor buglet, which may be squashed in a subsequent upgrade. Refer to the *Object Text Displayed in Wrong Format* in the Troubleshooting section for a workaround solution.

Determining Bitmap Color Depth

If a bitmap file was created elsewhere, the following techniques may be used to determine the color depth.

First, load the bitmap into Paintbrush. If the color palette at the bottom of the window changes to black-and-white, then the bitmap is obviously monochrome and no additional testing is needed. Otherwise, select the Save As... option, and note the Save File as Type: box. If the type is *less* than the current system's own color depth then, it is a reliable indication of the file's actual color depth. However, if the type is the same as the system color depth, then although the file may have been created at that depth, it may also have been created at a greater color depth, which the present system does not fully support. As an example, open 256COLOR.BMP on a 4-bit/16-color system, and the Save File as Type: box shows "16 Color bitmap" even though the file itself is known to have been created on a 256-color system. In this case, further testing is necessary.

Use the Paintbrush Save As... option to make a copy of the bitmap, then compare the size of the original and the copy. If they match, then the original was indeed created at the same color depth as the copy. As a further test, use the DOS fc /b command to compare the files. If no more than two differences are reported, the original was created on a system that was set at the same color depth as the present system. If there are more than two differences then, although both files are at the same color depth, the original was created on a system that was set at some other color depth.

If the sizes of the original and the copy are unequal, and the first Paintbrush test did not reliably specify the original's color depth, then the original was created at a color depth greater than that of the present system.

BASIC Program for Finding Color Depth. If all else fails, the following short BASIC program will report the color depth of any valid BMP file. If the file was created or modified under a third-party application, such as Computer Associates' *Cricket Paint* or *Cricket Image,* and has an extension of TGA (Targa—Truevision Advanced Raster Graphics Adapter), substitute the lines shown in the right-hand column.

```
OPEN "filename.ext" FOR RANDOM AS #1 LEN = 1
FIELD #1, 1 AS A$
                                    (For TGA Files)
GET #1, 29                          GET #1, 17
K = 2 ^ ASC(A$)                     K = ASC(A$)
PRINT USING "##,###,###"; K;
PRINT "-color bitmap."
CLOSE : END
```

Passwords and Clipbook Sharing

As shown earlier in Figure 8.11, it's possible to assign separate read-only and full-access passwords to a shared Clipbook Page. Since the existence of the latter certainly implies some sort of read/write capability, the reader may very well wonder what sort of power is actually conferred when full-access privileges are enabled. After all, one can't even edit one's own Clipboard, so how can a full-access password make it possible to edit a Remote Clipboard? The quick answer is, it can't.

Once you've accessed a password-protected Remote Clipbook page, you can do what you please without regard to the password you used to get it. Copy it to your own Clipboard—if the object is a text block, you can paste it into the appropriate applet or application and edit it beyond recognition if you want to. Or do the same with a bitmap image. But having done all that, you have a Clipboard object which you can certainly paste to your own Local Clipboard (in case anyone else wants it), but you can't sneak it back onto the remote computer. If the remote user wants it, he'll have to access your Local Clipboard.

For the moment, there is no distinction between read-only and full-access privileges. Either grants you access to the remote Clipbook; neither prevents you from editing the page (once you paste it into the appropriate applet), and neither lets you edit the remote user's original anyway. In the future, there may be an application that permits Clipboard/Clipbook editing and at that time a read-only password should protect your Clipbook pages from being edited by others. In the meantime, it's a feature ahead of its time.

Password Assignment. To assign a password to a local Clipbook Page, enter the desired password in the Full Access Password: box seen at the bottom of Figure 8.11. Or, once a Clipboard-editing utility becomes available, assign read-only and full-access passwords as required.

Password Access. If a remote user has assigned a password to a page on his or her local Clipbook Page, then that page appears on your own Remote Clipbook as a blank Thumbnail with a padlock in the upper right-hand corner, as was seen in Figure 8.6. If your Remote Clipbook displays Table-of-Contents icons, then the password-protected status is not indicated. In any case, when you double-click on the Thumbnail or icon, the Enter Network Password dialog box in Figure 8.13 shows up. To gain access, type the required password into the Password: box.

Add Password to Password List File. If you do not clear the "X" in the Save This Password in your Password List check box, the password you entered is written to an encoded password-list file (*username*.PWL) in the Windows directory, where *username* is your network user name. If you subsequently view the Thumbnails on your Remote Clipbook, the blank padlocked Thumbnail will be replaced with a sketch of the Clipbook page, and you will not have to retype the password to gain access again.

```
┌─────────────────────────────────────────────────────────┐
│ ▬ │           Enter Network Password                     │
├─────────────────────────────────────────────────────────┤
│ You must supply a password to make this connection:  ┌────────┐ │
│                                                      │   OK   │ │
│ Computer Name:    ALR                                └────────┘ │
│                                                      ┌────────┐ │
│ Share Name:       $CONFIDENTIAL STUFF                │ Cancel │ │
│                                                      └────────┘ │
│ Password:      │ ········              │                        │
│                                                      ┌────────┐ │
│ ⊠ Save This Password in Your Password List           │  Help  │ │
│                                                      └────────┘ │
└─────────────────────────────────────────────────────────┘
```

Figure 8.13   If a remote Clipbook page is password-protected, the Enter Password dialog box appears on the Local system if an attempt is made to access that page.

Create New PWL File. If the just-described blank padlocked Thumbnail reappears every time you select the Thumbnails viewing option, then the above-mentioned PWL file is probably defective or missing. To create a new one, exit and reopen Windows. When the opening *Error occurred* message appears, click on the OK button and enter a logon password. Or just click on OK again if you don't want one. In either case, the following message appears: *There is no password-list for the user (user name). Do you want to create one?* Click on the Yes button, and then re-enter your logon password, or click OK again if you still don't want one. After doing all this, a new PWL file is written into your Windows directory and you can now save the passwords you need to gain access to Remote Clipbooks, as described immediately above.

Displayed Clipboard Formats

The Clipboard display formats are not always what you might expect. For example, the Word- or Write-formatted text option (both identified as *Owner Display* in Windows 3.1) will disappear from the menu if the source application closes. Although Word-formatted text remains on the Clipboard in a Rich-Text Format, this format is not available for subsequent Clipboard viewing, although it is available to those applications that can use it.

If an object containing a bitmap and text, or a bitmap only, is copied from a Word document, the Display/View Menu options listed in Column 1 below produce the Clipboard displays listed in Column 2. Later on, if the Paste Special option is selected from within the same or another applet, the Clipboard data will be available in the options listed in Column 3, which will produce the displays listed in Column 4.

Clipboard Display/View Menu Option	Clipboard Displays	Available to Other Applets As	Applet Displays
Word-Formatted Text	Bitmap & Text	Formatted Text	Bitmap & Text
Text	Text only	Unformatted Text	Unformatted Text only
Picture	Word Icon	Microsoft Word Object	Word Icon
OEM Text	Text only		

Note that if the pasted object is a bitmap only, the Formatted Text option will display that bitmap, but the Unformatted Text option displays nothing at all. If the Word icon is pasted into a client file, then double-click on that icon to open a Word Application Window in which the object (bitmap, or whatever it is) will be displayed.

CLP File Characteristics

As noted above in the description of the File Menu's Save As... option, the contents of the Clipboard can be saved to a file for subsequent use later on. The file is saved with the default Clipboard extension (CLP), and its unique characteristics are reviewed here. Note especially that the size of a CLP file may be many times larger than the source file from which it came.

The Save As... Option. The option does exactly what you might expect: It saves the Clipboard contents to a file with a CLP extension. What you might not expect is the size of the saved file. Remember that although the Clipboard displays only one format at a time, there may be quite a few others lurking in the background, as noted earlier in Table 8.2. For example, Table 8.8 shows how data copied to the Clipboard from selected sources is stored in various formats when that data is saved to a CLP file. Therefore, the Clipboard file may be considerably larger than the source from which it originated. Although the Paintbrush applet provides means for omitting the Picture format cited in the table (select Omit Picture Format on its Options Menu), the saved CLP file is still quite a bit larger than the original.

To give an idea of the size implications of pasting a Clipboard object into a client file, consider a very simple Excel 2 × 3-cell worksheet copied to the Clipboard and saved as say, EXCEL.CLP. Among the 20 (!) formats saved in the CLP file will be *Text*, *Picture*, and *Bitmap* formats. The size of the original spreadsheet is given below, along with the size of the saved CLP file. The third line compares the size of the text, picture, and bitmap formats within the CLP file, and the last two lines compare the size of Write documents containing nothing but the indicated object.

	Text	**Picture**	**Bitmap**
Small spreadsheet saved as: EXCEL.XLS 2,181			
Same, saved from Clipboard as: EXCEL.CLP 63,303			
Size of the indicated format within EXCEL.CLP	288	3,432	21,934
Write file with pasted text, picture, or bitmap object	896	4,096	22,528
Same, paste-linked picture, or bitmap object	n/a	4,096	22,656

TABLE 8.8   Comparison of Saved CLP File with Original Source*

Format Stored in CLP File	Video Driver 16	256	Format Stored in CLP File	Video Driver 16	256	Format/Other in CLP File	Video Driver 16	256
CARS.BMP (630 bytes)[†]								
Bitmap	526	1038	OwnerLink	64	64	DIB Bitmap	640	—
Palette	184	184	Picture	1032	2504	File header	4	4
Native	640	640	ObjLnkCpy	64	64	8 format headers	—	712
ObjectLink	96	96	Clipbook Preview	512	512	9 format headers	801	—
						CLP File Size	**4563**	**5818**
Write test document (640 bytes)[‡]								
Text	32	32	Clipbook Preview	512	512	File header	4	4
OEM Text	32	32				3 format headers	267	267
						1 empty header	89	89
						CLP File Size	**936**	**936**
Word-for-Windows test document (2016 bytes)[‡]								
Rich Text Format	704	704	Link	288	288	Clipbook Preview	512	512
Text	32	32	ObjectLink	288	288	File header	4	4
Native	1984	1984	OEM Text	32	32	11 format headers	979	979
OwnerLink	256	256	LnkCpy	256	256	1 empty header	89	89
Picture	2280	5288	ObjLnkCpy	256	256	**CLP File Size**	**7960**	**10968**
Excel Worksheet (1708 bytes)								
Picture	1736	1736	Text	32	32	OEM Text	32	32
Bitmap	7742	15470	Csv	32	32	LnkCpy	32	32
Biff4	1696	1696	Rich Text Format	1216	1216	ObjLnkCpy	64	64
Biff3	1600	1600	Native	1696	1696	Clipbook Preview	512	512
Biff	1056	1056	OwnerLink	64	64	DIB Bitmap	7840	—
Sylk	800	800	Link	64	64	File Header	4	4
Wk1	288	288	ObjectLink	96	96	20 format headers	—	1780
DIF	224	224	Display Text	32	32	21 format headers	1869	—
						CLP File Size	**28727**	**28526**

* Microsoft SUPERVGA.DRV 16-color or Tseng VGA468S.DRV 256-color video driver installed, as indicated.

† Entire CARS.BMP file copied to Clipboard via Paintbrush applet.

‡ Document consists of "This is a test." Text and OEM Text formats increase in 32-byte increments.

Figure 8.14 shows other text, bitmap, and picture objects pasted into the same Write file, to illustrate their physical appearance on the printed page. Note that the headings in the Text sample need to be realigned, but this minor annoyance may be more than offset by the savings in file space.

Load CLP File Automatically when Clipbook Viewer Opens. For most Windows applets, the Command Line in the applet's Program Item Properties box can be written to open the applet and load the specified file. The line is shown here as it might be written for the Clipbook Viewer:

C:\WINDOWS\CLIPBRD.EXE C:\WINDOWS*filename*.CLP

The above line only works with Windows-for-Workgroups. If there is already something on the Clipboard, a *Do you want to clear the contents of the Clipboard?* message will appear. If you click the Yes button, the specified file will be loaded.

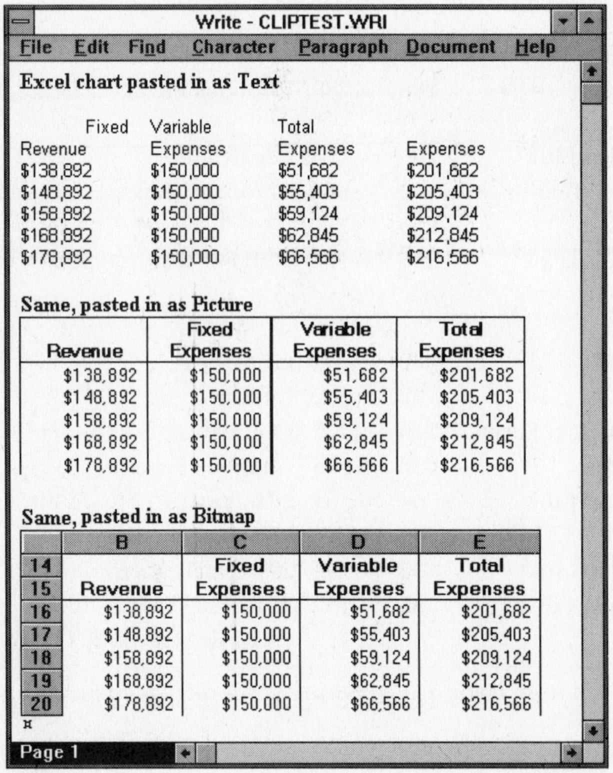

		Write - CLIPTEST.WRI				

File Edit Find Character Paragraph Document Help

Excel chart pasted in as Text

	Fixed	Variable	Total		
Revenue	Expenses	Expenses	Expenses		**(a)**
$138,892	$150,000	$51,682	$201,682		
$148,892	$150,000	$55,403	$205,403		
$158,892	$150,000	$59,124	$209,124		
$168,892	$150,000	$62,845	$212,845		
$178,892	$150,000	$66,566	$216,566		

Same, pasted in as Picture

Revenue	Fixed Expenses	Variable Expenses	Total Expenses	
$138,892	$150,000	$51,682	$201,682	**(b)**
$148,892	$150,000	$55,403	$205,403	
$158,892	$150,000	$59,124	$209,124	
$168,892	$150,000	$62,845	$212,845	
$178,892	$150,000	$66,566	$216,566	

Same, pasted in as Bitmap

	B	C	D	E	
14		Fixed	Variable	Total	
15	Revenue	Expenses	Expenses	Expenses	
16	$138,892	$150,000	$51,682	$201,682	**(c)**
17	$148,892	$150,000	$55,403	$205,403	
18	$158,892	$150,000	$59,124	$209,124	
19	$168,892	$150,000	$62,845	$212,845	
20	$178,892	$150,000	$66,566	$216,566	

Page 1

Figure 8.14 Three views of the same thing. The same small Excel chart has been pasted into a Write document as (a) Text, (b) a Picture, and (c) a Bitmap.

In Windows 3.1, the instruction to load *filename*.CLP is ignored. However, this should not be a serious problem since it's unlikely you will want to load the same CLP file every time the applet opens.

The SYSTEM.INI [ClipShares] Record. If you copy Clipboard data to a page on your Local Clipbook, Windows saves the page as a CLP file in the Windows directory, and records its presence in your SYSTEM.INI file. If you decide to share a Local Clipbook Page, the SYSTEM.INI entry for that page changes. Typical examples are shown here:

```
[ClipShares]
C:\WINDOWS\CBKxxxx.CLP=*Page Name (* indicates Page Name is not shared)
C:\WINDOWS\CBKxxxx.CLP=$Page Name ($ indicates Page Name is shared)
```

Clipbook Page Review. If you need to verify the contents of a CBK*xxxx*.CLP file, display your Clipboard, then select the File Menu's Open... option. The Open dialog box should display the list of CLP files currently in the Windows directory. Double-click on any such file to display it on the Clipboard.

Use of Save As... for Multiple Copies. If the Clipboard's Save As... option is used to make more than one copy of the same data, the size of the first, second, and succeeding copies may be slightly different. Or, the copies will be the same size, yet a byte-by-byte comparison will show multiple differences within the files.

In the following example, a file was created and saved using the indicated application. Then a portion of the saved file was copied to the Clipboard, and from the Clipboard three sequential copies were made as TEST1.CLP, TEST2.CLP, TEST3.CLP. The sizes of the second and third copies, with respect to the first, are shown here.

Application	Copy Size			Comments
	1	2	3	
Excel	x	x	x	
Notepad	x	x	x	
Paintbrush bitmap	x	$x + 64$	$x + 128$	32 bytes added to ObjectLink and to ObjLnkCpy formats
Word	x	$x - 89$	$x - 89$	Empty 89-byte header omitted
Write	x	$x - 89$	$x - 89$	Empty 89-byte header omitted

The file size changes noted above are limited to Windows-for-Workgroups files. When the same test is performed under Windows version 3.1, file size remains constant. In most cases, slightly different results are obtained if the Clipboard data is copied from an applet file *before* the file itself is saved.

As a further observation, if the TEST1.CLP file is erased or renamed before the Save As... option makes additional copies, the operation will conclude without an error message, yet the additional copies will not, in fact, be made.

These anomolies are a function of Windows linking/embedding characteristics, and although not further described here, they do not affect the useability of any of the copies (with the obvious exception of the ones that don't get made of course). To minimize confusion later on, if you need more than one copy of a CLP file, you may want to make the additional copies from the first one, rather than via the Save As... option described above.

Video Driver and Clipboard File Considerations. If a Clipboard file is saved, its size and internal format varies according to the currently installed video driver. As a typical example, Table 8.9 lists the results if the Windows CARS.BMP file is opened in the Paintbrush applet, saved as CARS-*xxx*.BMP, then copied to the Clipboard and saved as CARS*xxx*.CLP, where *xxx* indicates the current video color depth.

If a 16-color Clipboard file is subsequently opened on a system with a 24-bit color driver installed, the Clipboard may not be able to show the device-*dependent* bitmap (that is, the regular bitmap). For example, Figure 8.15(a) shows the error message that may appear on the Clipboard if the Bitmap option is selected, and various effects that may be noted if the message is ignored and the bitmap is pasted into a Word-for-Windows file (b) or into the Paintbrush (c) or Write (d) applets.

If such a CLP file is opened from the Clipboard, it is the Picture option that appears in the Local Clipboard Window; therefore the potential problem may be overlooked unless one takes the time to select—or, to *try* to select—the incompatible Bitmap option. If this bitmap is pasted into a client file, a further warning error message often does not appear: A distorted image just shows up in the document with no explanation of what's wrong.

As a further consideration, if you load a CLP file containing an incompatible bitmap, then try to save the Clipboard as a new CLP file, you probably will encounter a General Protection Fault error message.

TABLE 8.9   CARS.BMP Saved As Clipboard File with Selected Video Drivers

Bitmap Source*	Original 16-Color CARS.BMP		256-Color Copy	24-Bit Color Copy
Video Driver†	16-Color	———— 256-Color ————		24-Bit Color
CLP File contents				
Bitmap‡	526	1038	1038	4110
Palette§	184	184	184	1032
Native	640	640	2112	3136
ObjectLink	64	96	96	64
OwnerLink	32	64	64	32
Picture	1032	2504	2504	4360
ObjLnkCpy††	32	64	64	32
Clipbook Preview	512	512	512	512
DIB Bitmap	640	—	—	—
format headers	805	716	716	716
Total File Size	4467	5818	7290	13994

* Indicated bitmap source file copied to Clipboard, then saved as CARS.CLP with indicated driver installed.

† Drivers are: 16-color Microsoft SUPERVGA.DRV, 256-color Tseng VGA468S.DRV, 24-bit Hercules TIGA24.DRV with Hercules Chrome video adapter.

‡ Bitmap size = 32 (bytes/pixel) + 14-byte section header.

§ Palette size (16-, 256-color) = (16 + 28 colors) 4 bytes/color + 8-byte section header/footer.

†† For bitmap, ObjLnkCpy is actually a copy of OwnerLink.

Clipboard File Restoration Techniques

Figure 8.16 shows how the 16-color CARS.BMP file might appear if saved as a CLP file on a 24-bit color system, and that file is subsequently loaded to a Clipboard on a 256-color system. Under the circumstances, the file appears useless if viewed via the Picture option, and it can't be displayed at all via the Bitmap option, which simply offers an error message.

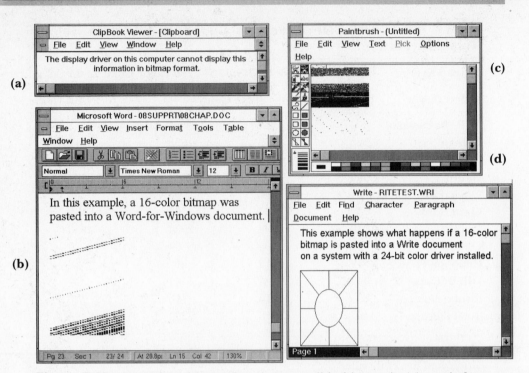

Figure 8.15 Typical problems if an incompatible bitmap is (a) copied to the Clipboard, then pasted into (b) a Word-for-Windows file, (c) the Paintbrush applet, and (d) a Write file.

If the image is pasted into say, Paintbrush or Word-for-Windows, it doesn't get any prettier. In fact, it may become little more than a black blob (Paintbrush) or just a miniature version of its distorted self (Word). However, paste the same image into a Write or Notepad Application Window, and it returns to its former 16-color glory. It's still not great art, but at least it's there; with the bitmap restored to its proper condition, it can now be copied *back* to the Clipboard, then pasted into Paintbrush, Word, or wherever else it's needed.

The file-transfer characteristics described above vary from one color depth to another, the Clipbook Picture option is not always as distorted as that shown in Figure 8.15, and the image may not always fail in the same applications. Therefore, if it is really important to rescue an apparently demolished CLP file, try pasting it into at least a few applications before giving up.

Status Bar Text Configuration

To change the font and point size for the Status Bar text, refer to the section with this name in Chapter 10.

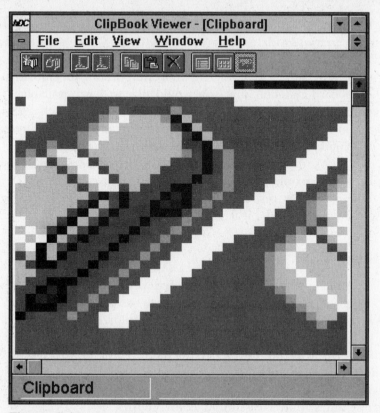

Figure 8.16 Another bitmap problem. Here, a CLP file saved on a 24-bit color system has been loaded to the Clipboard on a 16-bit system. Compare this version of CARS.BMP with the one in Figure 8.3 or 8.4c.

Windows Video Driver Installation

Since video driver-swapping plays such an important role in getting the Clipboard to behave itself, a brief review of the general procedure is given here.

Exit Windows and log onto the Windows directory. Type SETUP at the DOS prompt, and when the System Information Screen (see Figure 1.1b) appears, highlight the entry in the Display column. For future reference, make a note of the current entry, then press the Enter key to show the list of available display drivers. Select one of the VGA display options or the **Super VGA (800x600, 16 colors)** option. Press the Enter key and follow any on-screen prompts to complete the installation of the selected driver. When changing from one driver to another, you may be prompted for various Windows distribution diskettes if fonts required by the new configuration are not already on your hard disk.

Now open Windows and retry the operation that caused the problem. If it is resolved, then the previous video driver was the culprit. Contact the manufacturer to see if an upgraded driver, or a workaround for the problem, is available. If not, you'll have to decide which is more important: the incompatible driver or the Clipboard function that you would like to have available. If the function is important but seldom used, you can always switch back and forth between drivers until the day when a satisfactory upgrade becomes available. Not the best of solutions, but sometimes it's the only one that works.

Obviously, if the Windows VGA or Super VGA driver does not solve the problem, then further troubleshooting is required. Stick with the Microsoft driver until the problem is resolved, then go back to the driver you really want to use. If your luck holds, it'll work now.

Troubleshooting

Table 8.10 lists some of the Clipboard-related problems that may be encountered during a paste operation between a server and a client file, most of which may be traceable to incompatible color depths between two systems. No doubt the easiest way to stay out of trouble is to make sure that all machines on a network support the same color depth. However, if the server and client files are both on the same machine and there is still a cut/paste problem, don't overlook the possibility that the files were created at different times, under dissimilar color depths.

TABLE 8.10 Effect of Typical Copy/Paste Operations between Server and Client

Selected Data Type:	Paste Displays: [†]		Paste Link Displays: [†]	
Paintbrush bitmap pasted into Word Document				
Server, Client at differing color depths				
Bitmap	*General Protection Fault* or distorted bitmap	[1.]	*General Protection Fault* or distorted bitmap	[2.]
Device Independent Bitmap [‡]	bitmap	[1.]	nothing	
Paintbrush Picture Object	picture	[2.]	option disabled	
Picture	picture	[1.]	picture	[2.]
Server, Client at same color depth				
Bitmap	bitmap	[1.]	bitmap	[2.]
Device Independent Bitmap [‡]	picture	[1.]	nothing	
Paintbrush Picture Object	picture	[2.]	option disabled	
Picture	picture	[1.]	picture	[2.]

TABLE 8.10 *(continued)*

Selected Data Type:	Paste Displays: †		Paste Link Displays: †	
Paintbrush bitmap pasted into Write Document				
Server, Client at differing color depths				
Bitmap	*Problem drawing or printing object*		*Problem drawing or printing object*	
Paintbrush Picture Object	Picture	[2.]	*Problem drawing or printing object*	
Picture	Picture	[3.]	Picture	[2.]
Server, Client at same color depths				
Bitmap	Bitmap	[3.]	Bitmap	[2.]
Paintbrush Picture Object	Picture	[2.]	Picture	[2.]
Picture	Picture	[3.]	Picture	[2.]
Word text block pasted into Word Document				
Server, Client at differing or same color depths				
Formatted Text [RTF]	Formatted Text		Formatted Text	
Picture	Word icon	[1.]	Word icon	[2.]
Unformatted Text	Text in client font		Text in server font	
Word Document Object	Word icon	[4.]	Option disabled	
Word text block pasted into Write Document				
Server, Client at differing or same color depths				
Picture	Word Icon	[3.]	Word Icon	[2.]
Text	Text in client font		Option disabled	
Word Document Object	Word Icon	[4.]	Word Icon	[2.]

* For reported effect to be observed in client file, server applet must be open with server object loaded.

† Column indicates what is seen in client file when indicated paste option is selected. [Bracketed number] refers to action taken if Paintbrush image or icon in client file is double-clicked.

‡ Device Independent Bitmap Data Type not available at all server color depths.

Double-click on Paintbrush image or Word icon produces the following results:
1. MS Draw opens (if available), with Paintbrush object loaded for viewing or editing. Otherwise *Word cannot locate the server application for Microsoft Drawing Objects* error message appears.
2. Server file opens, with pasted object loaded for viewing or editing.
3. Error message: *This is not an embedded or linked object. You cannot activate it.*
4. Text displayed in Word window, sometimes with wrong point size.

As another possibility, if a problem cannot be solved while using a third-party video driver, it's worth the bother to install either the Microsoft VGA (VGA.DRV) or SVGA (SUPERVGA.DRV) driver supplied with both Windows 3.1 and Word-for-Windows. To avoid repeating the same old procedure over and over again, refer to the *Windows Video Driver Installation* section above if you need assistance installing one of these drivers.

Bitmap Object Is Distorted. There are two conditions under which a bitmap may appear distorted, as in the examples shown in Figure 8.15. You may encounter such a problem when you paste a bitmap into a file on your system, or when you open a file created elsewhere which already contains a bitmap. In either case, the problem bitmap was probably created (or inserted) on a system whose video adapter supports a different number of colors. Depending on specific system and application details, an error message may or may not accompany the distorted image.

If you want to double-check a problem encountered while trying to paste a bitmap into a file, open the Clipboard's Display or View Menu and see if a DIB, DIB Bitmap, or Picture option is available. If so, that option should display the bitmap on the Clipboard. In the file itself, highlight the distorted image and press the keyboard delete key to remove it. Do *not* use the Edit Menu's Cut option, as doing so will cut the image back to the Clipboard, thereby discarding all other versions. Now open the Edit Menu, select the Paste Special... option, then select any Data Type *except* bitmap.

If the problem occurs when you open a file created elsewhere, and bitmap is the only format available for pasting, then the only solution is to install a video driver that supports the same number of colors as the driver on the other system. If the distorted bitmap is really critical, Murphy's Law clearly states that the desired color depth will be unknown. In this case, you can guess at it until you get it right, or refer to the *Determining Bitmap Color Depth* section above for some workaround suggestions.

Clipboard Does Not Automatically Load CLP File. If the command line in the Clipboard or Clipbook Viewer's Program Item Properties dialog box specifies a CLP file to be loaded automatically every time the applet opens, that instruction will only work with Windows-for-Workgroups; Windows version 3.1 ignores it. Refer to the *Load CLP File Automatically* section above for further details.

Clipboard Does Not Display Data Format Selected via Display/View Menu. If a data format is listed as an enabled option on the Display or View Menu, then the object should of course be displayed in that format when the option is selected. If it is not, there are two possibilities, both described here. Read both before taking any action.

Incompatible Video Driver. There may be a compatibility problem with the installed video driver. To verify this, reinstall the Microsoft VGA (VGA.DRV) or SVGA (SUPERVGA.DRV) video driver and try again. If the Clipboard is now able to display its data in every enabled option, then there was indeed a problem with the driver you were previously using. Contact the manufacturer to see if an updated version is available, or live with it.

Basic Clipboard Limitation. If you're doing extensive cutting and pasting, it's possible to confuse the Clipboard applet. As a test case, copy a text block from one Word-for-Windows (or other application) document to the Clipboard, then insert it into another document, or elsewhere in the same document. To do so, open the application's File Menu, select the Paste Special... option and review the data types listed in the dialog box. Highlight the one labeled "Word Document Object" or "Microsoft Word Object" (or some other text type with that word "Object"). When you do so, an icon should appear at the insertion location. Highlight that icon, copy or cut it back to the Clipboard, then open the Clipboard's Display or View Menu. If you select either the Text or OEM Text options, the Clipboard displays a blank screen.

In a unique circumstance such as this, the real problem is that the Clipboard's Text or OEM Text options should not really be enabled. The item currently on the Clipboard is an icon which *represents* a text block, but of course is not the text block itself. You can see it (the icon) by selecting the Formatted Text or Picture options. In fact, even the former option is a bit of a misnomer; *Owner Display* would be more appropriate. In fact, if you perform the above operation between Word-for-Windows and Write, that's just what you'll see when you copy the object icon back to the Clipboard from Write.

Clipboard Does Not Display Correct Font. If you copy a text block to the Clipboard, then open the Clipboard, that text should be seen in the font style and point size of the original, and the Display or View Menu list should show the following option, plus others.

Source Document	Windows 3.1 Display Menu	Workgroups View Menu
Write	Owner display	WRITE Formatted Text
Word	Owner display	Word Formatted Text

However, the above option disappears from the menu list and the text display changes to unformatted text under either of the following conditions.

Source Applet Closes. The problem is that the Clipboard itself does not have the capability to display all the formatting unique to Write or to Word-for-Windows, and therefore requires the presence of the source applet to maintain that display. When the applet is closed, the formatted display is lost.

In the case of a text block from a Write file, the lost formatting stays lost. However, Word-formatted text instructions remain on the Clipboard—and in the CLP file if one was saved—as the rich-text format. If the Clipboard data is subsequently pasted back into a document that supports the rich-text format, it should appear in that document with its formatting intact.

Clipboard's Save As... Option Used. The same phenomenon is observed on the Clipboard and once again, Write-formatted text is lost while Word-formatted text is retained.

Network Password Dialog Box Problems. The following quirks may be noticed when the Enter Network Password dialog box shown in Figure 8.13 is on screen:

Computer Name: and Share Name: entries are out of alignment.
Help Button is inoperative.
Help is not available via Function key F1.

For the moment there are no fixes for these minor problems; perhaps there will be solutions in the next upgrade.

Open... Option on File Menu Inoperative. If you attempt to open a file and nothing happens, either the CLP file you are trying to load is corrupt, or you tried to load a non-CLP file. In either case, no error message appears. To verify that nothing is there, open the Display or View Menu and look for the *Clipboard Object Format List.* Chances are, it's not there; but if it is, try selecting the Picture option if it's available. If that works, then refer to the *Text Option Problems* section below for further troubleshooting suggestions.

Padlock Reappears on Remote Clipbook Thumbnail, Despite Use of Valid Password. If you enter a valid password, gain access to a Remote Clipbook page, then have to re-enter the same password the next time you select that remote page, your password list file (*username*.PWL) is probably missing. Refer to the *Create New PWL File* section above for assistance in resolving the problem.

Paste Option Doesn't Work. If a third-party application has a problem pasting a Clipboard image that originated in Paintbrush, reopen Paintbrush and enable the Omit Picture Format option on its Options Menu. Then recopy the image to the Clipboard and try the Paste operation again. If this actually works, contact the application's manufacturer to see if an update is available.

Rectangular Image Appears Instead of Bitmap. A rectangular image, such as that shown in Figure 8.15d, indicates that although the basic network copy/paste operations are in good working order, there is a color depth compatibility problem between the two computers that prevents the link from working. Highlight the rectangle and press the Delete key to get rid of it. To double-check the basic operation of the Clipboard itself, reopen the Edit Menu and select the regular Paste option, which should simply paste your local Clipboard into the Write document.

To resolve the linking problem, exit Windows on either system and log onto the Windows directory. Run Setup and change the display driver to match the number of colors supported on the other system, as described earlier (pixel resolution is not critical, just color depth).

Save As... Option Doesn't Work. If you save a CLP file, then can't find it, there is probably not enough space in the destination path to accommodate the file, or the path and/or directory you specified does not exist. Unfortunately, the Clipboard does not warn you when it can't save a file, so it's not a bad idea to check the destination directory before moving on. If you can't find the file, try saving it to another location with more space available.

Text: Formatted-Text Option Displays Bitmap. If the formatted-text option displays a bitmap instead of text, the Clipboard object is a bitmap copied to the Clipboard from a text document, rather than from the applet in which it was originally created. Since the Clipboard found the object in a text file (for example, in a Word document), it thinks it's dealing with formatted text, hence the potentially misleading option descriptor. If the object contained text in addition to the bitmap, then that text would be seen on the Clipboard.

Text: Object Text Displayed in Wrong Format. If server text is pasted into a client file as an object icon, a double-click on that icon may display the server text in the wrong font and/or at the wrong point size. If this happens, the following workaround may solve the problem.

Highlight the text block in the server file and select a different font, then reselect the desired font and copy the block to the Clipboard. Repaste the block into the client file as an object. When the object icon in the client file is subsequently double-clicked, the text should appear in the correct font and point size.

Text: Unformatted Text Option Displays Blank Screen. As in the previous example, the Clipboard object is a bitmap. However, since this option displays text only, and there is no text available, the screen shows nothing.

Text Pasted into Document Shows Wrong Font and/or Point Size. If the inserted text retains its original formatting or takes on the formatting in place at the insertion point, and you wanted the opposite effect, refer to *Copy/Paste Text Configuration* in the *Configuration* section above for assistance.

Text Pasted into Paintbrush Displayed As Application Icon. If a text block is copied from a Word-for-Windows (or similar) file into Paintbrush, the Paintbrush Window will display a Microsoft Word icon instead of the desired text block. If you wanted to paste the actual text into Paintbrush so that you could use it as part of a bitmap, the icon representation isn't going to do you much good.

To get the text instead of the bitmap, first open the Write applet, select the Edit Menu's Paste Special... option, then select the Text data type. When the actual text appears in the Write Window, select it and copy it back to the Clipboard. Now open Paintbrush's Text Menu and select the font characteristics you want. Duplicate those from the original Word document, or select some other style, as appropriate.

Move the mouse pointer to the position where you want the text to begin, then open the Edit Menu and select the Paste option. The text should appear now.

Error Messages

In the error messages which follow, frequent reference is made to an incompatible video system. Rather than repeat the same tired explanation over and over again, it is given once here.

An incompatible video system is one in which the system's current color depth (4-, 8-, 24-bit color, for example) is different from that under which a file was originally created. If you try to open, copy, or paste such a file, one or more error messages may be encountered. Chances are neither the current video driver nor the file itself is defective—it's just that the one doesn't like the other very much. The Clipboard either can't open the file in the first place, or once open, can't perform various routine functions. In all such cases, the solution is to either change the installed video driver, or get a new version of the file that was created at the same depth as is in use on the current system.

Action cannot be completed because the application needed is busy. You may 'Switch to' the object's application and try to correct the problem. If the application in question is on your own computer, then you can switch to it and see what's up, or wait for it to finish whatever is keeping it busy. However, if the application is on a remote computer, then it might be that the remote computer itself is busy and will get around to you as soon as it can. In case of doubt, wait a few moments to see if the situation resolves itself. If not, then get in touch with the remote user to see what needs to be done, or try again later.

Cannot display. Data is in binary format. Since conventional binary files (COM and EXE files, for example) are indeed viewable on the Clipboard (though not in a very useful display), the message implies that some other binary format, such as a waveform file, is on the Clipboard. To verify this, open the Display or View menu, either of which should display a single Wave Audio (or similar) option, and that option is disabled (grayed). In this case, the data can only be accessed via the applet from which it was copied to the Clipboard.

Cannot read from drive x *(when attempting a Paste operation).* This message may be seen under the following unique conditions: Clipboard data previously saved to diskette is loaded back to the Clipboard, and the diskette is removed from drive *x* before pasting the data into a file. Under the circumstances, Windows should not need to read drive *x* again, since the required data is now on the Clipboard where it belongs. This quirk has been frequently observed when working with bitmap data, while text is less apt to cause the problem. To try to clear the message, click the Cancel button two or three times. Or reinsert the diskette in the drive and try again.

Clipboard information is not available in this format. If this message appears when you select one of the enabled formats listed on the Display or View Menu, it's possible that format contains some internal errors. If other formats are correctly displayed, then the format that displays this message is indeed corrupt. If possible, return to the original source document, re-copy the information to the Clipboard, and try again.

ClipBook Viewer cannot currently access the information (when opening Clipbook File). This message will appear under the following circumstances, when trying to open a Clipbook file via the View Menu's Table of Contents or Thumbnails options. If the message appears within the former option, select the Thumbnails option so that the images described below can be seen.

Blank Thumbnail Sketch with Padlock in Corner **(on Remote Clipbook).** The presence of the padlock indicates the Clipbook file is password-protected, and the message appears if you enter an incorrect password. You'll need a valid password to open the file. If you know your password is valid, there may be a problem with the PWL (password list) file in your Windows directory. To resolve this problem, disconnect from the remote computer, reconnect, and try again. If this doesn't work, then you may need to rebuild the PWL file, as described in the *Create New PWL File* section above.

Blank Thumbnail Sketch with Padlock in Corner **(on Local Clipbook).** The Clipbook file was probably erased prior to the current Windows session, but the filename was not deleted from the Local Clipbook. If it's important to recover the missing file, make a note of the filename under the Thumbnail. Open your SYSTEM.INI file for editing and search for the following section, which should be at the end of the file.

```
[ClipShares]
C:\WINDOWS\CBKxxxx.CLP=*Page Name   (* indicates Page Name is not shared)
C:\WINDOWS\CBKxxxx.CLP=$Page Name   ($ indicates Page Name is shared)
```

Find the missing filename (ignore the leading $ or *) and jot down the CBK*xxxx*.CLP on the left-hand side of the equal sign. Then exit Windows, log onto the Windows directory, and unerase that file. If you're successful in doing this, the blank Thumbnail should be replaced by the correct sketch. However, if the missing file cannot be unerased, then highlight the blank Thumbnail, open the Edit Menu, and select the Delete option to get rid of it, or delete the appropriate [ClipShares] line to accomplish the same thing.

Valid Thumbnail Sketch with no Padlock in Corner **(on Local Clipbook).** In the unlikely event that the above error message is seen when the Thumbnail sketch appears to be in order, then the corresponding Clipbook file was probably erased during the current Windows session, but its name was not deleted from the Local Clipbook. Unfortunately, clicking on the OK button does nothing—the message just keeps repeating and you'll have to do a warm reboot to recover. When you reopen Windows, and the Local Clipbook, the missing Clipbook file will appear as a blank Thumbnail sketch with padlock. Follow the procedure at the end of the previous paragraph to get rid of it.

Clipbook Viewer cannot currently access the information (when closing Windows). This message may also show up if you try to close Windows after connecting to a Remote Clipbook, if that remote system is no longer on the network. Repeated clicks on the OK button should eventually clear the message.

Connection could not be established to the specified computer. If you see this message when you open the Clipbook Viewer, the applet may have tried to access a Remote Clipbook to which you were previously connected, and that Clipbook is no longer available. The message does not identify the specified computer, so you'll have to recognize it by its omission from your Clipbook window.

If the message shows up while trying to load a CLP file stored on your own computer, either the file's bitmap color depth is incompatible, or a previous file that you tried to load was incompatible. In either case, the message doesn't have much to do with the problem. To verify the problem, close and reopen Windows, reopen the Clipboard and reload the CLP file. If the load succeeds, open Paintbrush and select the Paste option. The image will probably be distorted, thereby confirming that the file is incompatible with the currently installed color depth.

If possible, go back to the original file which contains the bitmap that was copied to the Clipboard and saved in the problem CLP file. Copy that bitmap back to the Clipboard, then use it as required, instead of the CLP file. Or, save it as a new CLP file for future use on the present system.

Display driver on this computer cannot display this information in bitmap format. If a Clipboard file is saved, the bitmap within that file may not open reliably on a system whose video driver supports a different number of colors. For example, this message may appear if you select the Bitmap option to examine a previously saved 16-color Clipboard file on a system with a 24-bit color driver installed.

The device-*dependent* bitmap (that is, the regular bitmap) does not display on the Clipboard; if you subsequently paste that bitmap into a client file anyway, it may appear there in one of the distorted formats shown earlier in Figure 8.15. An additional error message may or may not accompany the pasted image. In any case, refer to *Pasted Object Is Distorted* in the *Clipboard Troubleshooting* section above for a workaround suggestion.

You may also see a highly distorted Clipboard rendition of the bitmap if you select the View Menu's P̲icture option.

Error has occurred. Clipbook Viewer cannot complete this procedure. It's not the most informative of messages, but you can probably figure out what it means from the context in which it happened. For one reason or another, Clipboard couldn't do whatever you wanted it to do. The most likely suspect is a driver-related incompatibility involving Clipboard and the file from which you were trying to copy data. If possible, install the driver that was in place when that file was created and try again.

Error has occurred in your application. If you choose Ignore, you should save your work in a new file. If you choose Close, your application will terminate. One of the following conditions is probably the source of the problem.

Clipboard Copy/Paste Operations. You are probably working on a CLP file that is incompatible with the currently installed video system. If so, a *General Protection Fault* (see below) message will appear when you click on the Close button, and the Ignore button will live up to its name: It will be ignored. If possible, install the video driver that was in place when the CLP file was created and try the operation again.

Scrolling Operations on VGA System. If you discover the error message during some scrolling operations, the problem is probably a function of the current version of VGA.DRV, and a workaround or upgrade is not yet available. Regardless of the outcome, the safest course is to save the Clipboard file (if you want it), then close and reopen Windows.

To test your system for the problem, first make sure nothing important is going on, then press the Print Screen key to capture a full screen. Open the Clipboard and click on the Maximize button. Move the vertical Scroll-Bar button to its lowest position, then move the horizontal Scroll-Bar button to its rightmost position. As the button approaches the end of the Scroll Bar, the above message appears. When you click on one of the buttons, the following actions occur:

Close:. A new message shows up—*CLIPBRD caused a General Protection Fault in module VGA.DRV at 0001:0CA2*—and the Clipboard closes without any apparent further problem. However, if you immediately reopen the Clipboard, the system may reboot itself.

Ignore:. The Clipboard returns to normal. If you save the current Clipboard and repeat the scrolling experiment, the problem does not recur.

Error occurred while trying to unlock the password-list file for (*computer name*). Error 2: The specified file was not found. For more information, choose the Help button. If this message appears when you open Windows-for-Workgroups, the password-list file for your user name (*userame*.PWL) is missing. Even if you don't want your system to be password-protected, this file must be recreated so as not to encounter the message every time you reopen. The file must also be in place so that passwords used to access Remote Clipbooks can be saved, if desired. Refer to the *Create New PWL File* section for the procedure to write the required PWL file.

General Protection Fault: (*Application Name*) caused a General Protection Fault in module (*video driver name*) at *xxxx:yyyy*. If you discover this one while trying to paste a bitmap into a file, the current color depth probably differs from that under which the bitmap was created. The message may be followed by a system lockup which requires a cold reboot.

Once you're back in business—and if you're willing to try this again—select the Paste Special option on the application's Edit Menu and see if *Device Independent Bitmap* or *Picture* is available. If so, use either in place of *Bitmap* and the object should be inserted without further problem.

General Protection Fault: CLIPBOOK (*or* CLIPBRD) caused a General Protection Fault in module GDI.EXE at *xxxx:yyyy*. If this message appears when you attempt to display/view a bitmap on the Clipboard, that image was probably created under a different color depth than that presently installed on your computer. When you click on the Close button, the Clipboard/Clipbook closes and the Clipboard image is lost. Reinstall the video driver that supports the required color depth and try again.

Information is in a binary format. Clipbook Viewer cannot display this format. To view the information, try pasting it into a document. This is the Workgroups equivalent to the *Cannot Display* message described earlier. Refer to that message for assistance.

Memory: Error Messages, such as—
Low Memory. Save the document now.
There is not enough memory for such a large Clipboard.
There is not enough memory to complete this operation.

A *not enough memory* message may be followed by the *An error has occurred* message described above. Any of these messages may very well be true and, if so, you know what to do about it. But if the message appears to be erroneous, there is probably a compatibility problem with the installed video driver. As usual in such cases, install one of the Windows drivers (VGA.DRV or SUPERVGA.DRV) and try again.

Memory: (*Application name*) does not have enough memory for the large Clipboard. Do you want to discard it? You may see this message when you try to close a Windows application. If there is indeed a lot of information on the Clipboard, or you're not sure what it contains, click on the Cancel button, minimize the application, and open the Clipboard applet to examine its contents. If the application is Word-for-Windows, you can open its Control Menu and select the Run option to gain direct access to the Clipboard. If the Clipboard contains something you want to save, do so, then return to the application in which the message was seen. Otherwise, open the Clipboard's Edit menu and select the Delete option. Or, just return to the application and, when the message reappears, click on the OK button to discard the Clipboard contents.

If this message appears when there is very little in the Clipboard, there's probably an incompatibility with your video driver. To verify this, copy or cut a single letter to the Clipboard, then try to close the application. If the message still appears, contact the supplier of your video driver to see if an upgrade is available. As a double-check, try the same operation with the Windows VGA driver installed. If the problem goes away, then it's definitely a driver-related problem.

Problem drawing or printing object. This message is seen in some applications if there is a color depth problem. As usual, the solution is to install a video driver compatible with that used to create the file that can't be pasted or printed.

Problem with Object/Link. This message is sometimes seen when attempting to paste a high-color depth bitmap into a Write file, or it may be encountered later on if you try to print the file. In the latter case the file may print satisfactorily, but without the bitmap. So far, there is no permanent solution to the problem, although the following workaround may be tried.

First, cut the pasted image from the Write file, then paste it into the Paintbrush applet and save it. Now mark the desired portion of the image, copy it back to the Clipboard, and paste it back into the Write file. Save the file and print it. If all goes well, both operations should work. Otherwise, paste the bitmap into a Word-for-Windows (or other) word processor and use that one in place of Write.

9

Printer and Port Configuration

For one reason or another—or possibly for many reasons—Windows places its printer management functions in several locations. One is the Print Manager applet in the Main Group Window. The others—Printers, Ports, and Fonts—are contained in the Control Panel. Of course, the Control Panel is itself an applet, so the Printers/Ports/Fonts trio might be considered as sub-applets within that applet. For the purposes of this book, however, they are treated as though they were just a few more applets. In fact, the chapter begins with a procedure for creating a new Printer Management Group Window in which the Print Manager and the other printer-support applets may be placed for convenience. Although such information would usually be found in a *Configuration* section later on, it is placed up front for the benefit of readers who want to put all their printer management tools in one box before getting down to work.

As for the tools themselves, this chapter describes Printers, Ports, and the Print Manager, which is more than enough for one chapter. The Fonts applet gets its own chapter, which follows this one. The Control Panel itself and its remaining tenants are described in subsequent chapters.

Printer Management Group Configuration

In addition to the Printers, Print Manager, and Ports applets described below, the Fonts applet in the Control Panel might be considered as a fourth part of a Printer Management Group. If you find yourself making extensive use of these applets, you might want to create a new Printer Management Group Window in which all are conveniently located, possibly along with any other print-related applets that you acquire. This section describes the general procedure for doing so.

Create Printer Management Group Window. The first step is to open the Program Manager's File Menu and select the Ne̲w... option. When the New Program Object dialog box appears, click on the Program G̲roup radio button. Type the following information into the Program Group Properties dialog box (shown earlier, in Figure 3.14a), then click on the OK button.

D̲escription: Printer Management
G̲roup File: PTR-MGR.GRP

This creates an empty Printer Management Group Window, which must now be populated as described below.

Install Printer Management Applets. The next step is to install copies of the four Printer Management utilities in the group window, as shown in Figure 9.1. The icons are arranged in the sequence in which they are described here. Later on you can add other printer utilities, as desired. For example, the figure also shows that Agfa's *Discovery Font Guide* and Bitstream's *FaceLift 2.0* have been included in the group. Both are described in the following chapter.

Install Control Panel Applets. Reopen the Program Manager's File Menu, again select the Ne̲w... option, and this time click on the Program I̲tem radio button. When the Program Item Properties dialog box (Figure 3.14b) appears, enter the information given here in the *Printers Applet* column. The MAIN.CPL row identifies the file containing 10 of the Control Panel icons, and gives the position in that file for each icon that you may want to use in this new group.

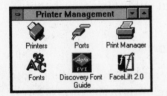

Figure 9.1 The four print management applet icons, shown here in a new Printer Management Group Window. Also seen are two third-party font-management applet icons, which are described in Chapter 10.

	Printers Applet	**Ports Applet**	**Fonts Applet**
Description:	Printers	Ports	Fonts
Command Line:	CONTROL PRINTERS	CONTROL PORTS	CONTROL FONTS
MAIN.CPL icon	5	6	4

Select Applet Font. Click on the Change Icon... button, then on the Browse button in the Change Icon dialog box (Figure 3.14c). When the Browse dialog box appears, type SYSTEM\MAIN.CPL into the File Name: box. Select the Printers icon and press the OK button twice to exit.

Repeat these procedures, but this time enter the information in the *Ports Applet* column above. Finally, repeat for the *Fonts Applet* column.

Move or Copy Print Manager Applet. Open both the Main Group Window and the new Printer Management Group Window, and drag the Print Manager applet from the former to the latter. Or hold down the Control key while dragging if you want a copy of the Print Manager in the new window, while leaving the original in place.

Printer Management Group Summary. The procedures described above have created a new group window containing the Printers, Ports, Fonts, and Print Manager applets—all of which come in handy when overhauling your printer configuration. Although clicking on any of the Control Panel icons opens the Control Panel, the desired applet appears immediately on top of it. When you close the applet, the Control Panel closes with it.

The dedicated group window makes it a bit easier to access all of these applets from a single source; when not in use, the window can be closed to put it out of sight.

Printer Management Group Flow Chart. After spending a bit of time navigating the printer management applets, you may discover more than one path from where you are to where you want to be. For example, here are four ways to access a network printer:

	Windows	**Workgroup**	**Both**	**Both**
Open...	Print Manager	Print Manager	Print Manager	Printers Applet
Open...	Options Menu	Printer Menu	Options Menu	

	Windows	Workgroup	Both	Both
Select...			Printer Setup	
Select...			Connect	Connect
Select...	Network Connections	Connect Network Printer	Network	Network

For future reference, Figure 9.2 presents a flow chart through the various applets described here and in the next chapter. Each shaded area represents the Title Bar of an applet window or a dialog box. Each boxed word or phrase identifies a button or menu option that leads to the next access level. The chart also indicates the two entry points at which the Print Setup... option on many application File Menus provides access to the printer management functions.

In case you don't find the chart confusing enough, note that there are two sections labeled *Fonts*. In the *Printers Setup* section, a Fonts button appears if the printer associated with the installed printer driver supports downloadable soft fonts. The *Fonts* applet is used to add fonts to Windows itself, and to configure TrueType font usage.

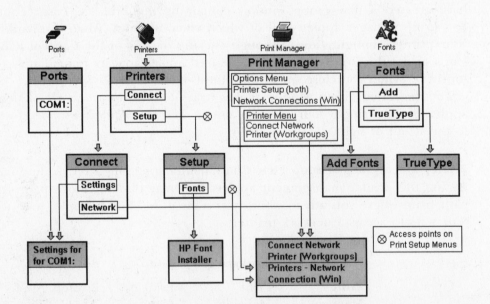

Figure 9.2 A printer management flow chart. Each shaded area represents a Title Bar in an applet window. Boxed text within each window is a button or menu option.

You may want to refer to the flow chart every now and then, especially if you get lost in the labyrinth of buttons below. The chart is valid whether the applets are copied into a dedicated printer management window as described above, or accessed from their default locations.

Definitions

A few new terms to be encountered in this chapter are given brief definitions here. Fortunately, there aren't too many of them this time.

Local User. In the *computer name* section of the print queue (defined below), the term identifies a print job originating on the computer whose name is at the head of the queue. Since this name, and the print queue itself, is displayed in all Print Manager Windows, it should be kept in mind that in this context, "Local User" often refers to a *remote* location, where the cited file happens to be *local* to the printer. It's not often that a *local* user is *remote,* but this is one of those times.

Network Printer. When a local computer's Print Manager is configured to accept print jobs from computers other than its own, the printer attached to that computer is identified here as a *Network Printer.*

Print Queue. This refers to any list of files displayed in the Print Manager Window. Each print queue appears immediately below the name of the printer to which the files have been routed.

The Printers Applet

The Printers applet handles printer installation, connection, setup and removal, default printer selection, and other chores. Since the applet is used for configuration only, further description will come in the *Printers Applet Configuration* section.

The Print Manager

The Print Manager Help Screen says "If Print Manager is not activated, you can print only one document at a time," which is true. The Printers Applet Help Screen says "When Print Manager is activated, you can print several documents at a time," which is *not* true. If you can figure out how to do the latter, call Hewlett-Packard and make your fortune overnight.

In fact the Print Manager is, as its name implies, a print management utility. If enabled (as it is by default), then when you open any applet's File Menu and select the Print... option, your file is sent to the Print Manager, which stores it in your temporary directory. During this operation, an onscreen report, such as that shown in Figure 9.3 may be initially confusing, since it clearly states "Now printing Page *xx*" or perhaps just "Printing" (it depends on the application). What it really means is that the indicated page is being "printed" into a temporary file. The *real* printing comes later: When the printer is ready to receive the file, Print Manager sends it out for actual printing.

At first glance the Print Manager may seem a bottleneck, since it delays delivery of the actual printed page. However, a large document sent to the Print Manager gets there in a fraction of the time it would take to actually print it. And once the Print Manager has the document in its clutches, it returns control of the computer to the user who may then go on to do something else—either print another document (again, to the Print Manager) or open another applet while the Print Manager takes care of the print job in the background.

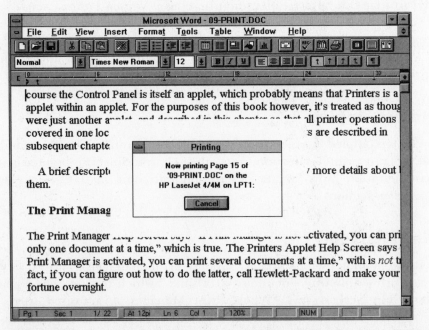

Figure 9.3 An onscreen Printing box overlays an application window's workspace. The print job is actually being "printed" to the Print Manager.

Files may be sequentially sent to the Print Manager from a variety of sources, such as other computers on a network or from one or more applets. The Print Manager will send them to the printer in the order received. If multiple documents await printing, the sequence of those documents can be revised, and/or certain documents can be deleted from the print queue (explained below) or temporarily taken out of the queue.

If the Print Manager is disabled, the Print option sends the selected print job directly to the printer. The job itself is completed faster, but other use of the computer must wait until printing is completed. In addition, the printer will not be available to other computers on a network.

By default, the Print Manager is enabled. To disable it, or to re-enable it later on, open the Control Panel's Printers applet (not the Print Manager itself), as described in the *Print Manager Configuration* section later in the chapter.

Applet Window

Figure 9.4 a and b shows the Print Manager Applet Window as it appears in Windows and Windows-for-Workgroups. The component parts for each window are described here. In cases where there is a significant difference between the corresponding Windows and Workgroups component, each is described separately, as indicated by a parenthetical reference in the heading.

Title Bar and Menu Bar. The Program Manager's Title Bar and Menu Bar are functionally equivalent to those bars found in almost every other Windows applet. Refer to Chapter 3 or 6 for detailed descriptions of these components.

Toolbar (Windows). Microsoft documentation refers to the three objects at the left-hand side of the horizontal bar immediately below the Menu Bar as "These buttons." And that they are; but for reference purposes here, they are collectively identified as a *Toolbar.* The three Toolbar buttons are shown in the detail view in Figure 9.5a. Although pretty much self-explanatory, refer to the equivalent functions on the Workgroups Toolbar (and its Document Menu) for additional details, if needed.

Toolbar (Workgroups). The Toolbar contains the 12 buttons shown in Figure 9.5b. The buttons duplicate various options on the Document and Printer Menus, as indicated here. Refer to the appropriate menu description later in the chapter for an explanation of each option.

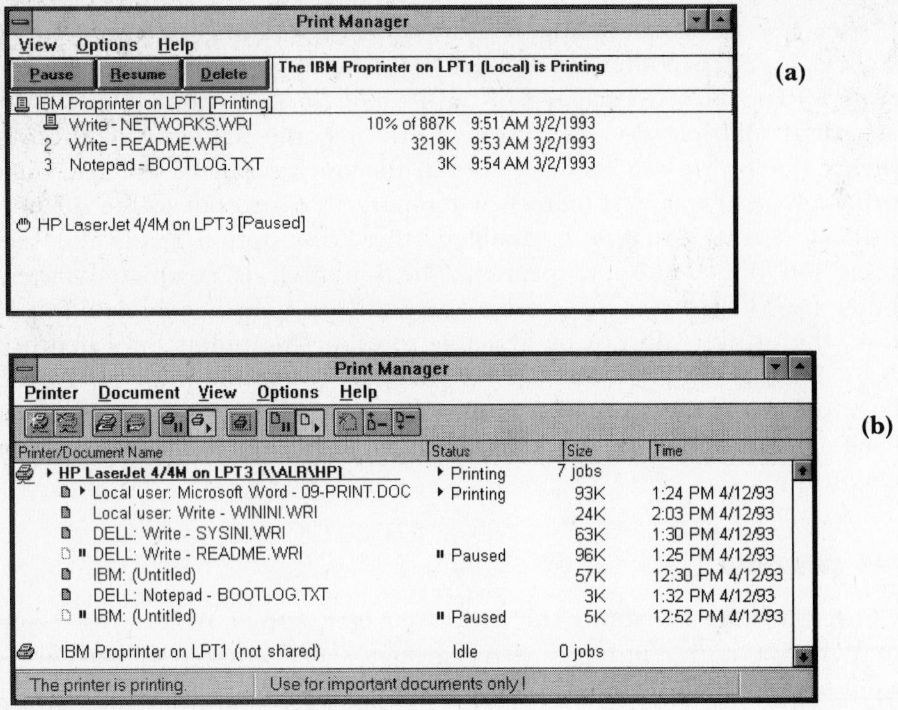

(a)

(b)

Figure 9.4 The Print Manager Application Window in (a) Windows 3.1 and (b) Windows-for-Workgroups.

Document Menu	Printer Menu	Printer Menu
Delete Document	Connect Network Printer	Set Default Printer
Move Document Down	Disconnect Network Printer	Share Printer As
Move Document Up	Pause Printer	Stop Sharing Printer
Pause Printing Document	Resume Printer	
Resume Printing Document		

Message Box (Windows). The Windows 3.1 Print Manager does not have a Status Bar such as that described below for Workgroups. However, similar printer status messages are displayed in the *Message Box* to the immediate right of the three Toolbar buttons, as may be seen in Figure 9.4a.

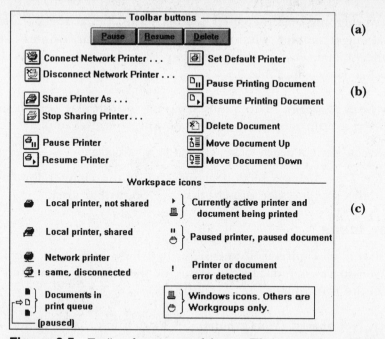

```
┌──────────── Toolbar buttons ────────────┐
│         [ Pause ] [ Resume ] [ Delete ]       │                          (a)
│                                               │
│  🖳 Connect Network Printer . . .    🖳 Set Default Printer       │
│  🖳 Disconnect Network Printer . . .                              │
│                                    🗎ǁ Pause Printing Document    │      (b)
│  🖨 Share Printer As . . .          🗎▸ Resume Printing Document  │
│  🖨 Stop Sharing Printer. . .                                    │
│                                    🗎 Delete Document             │
│  🖨ǁ Pause Printer                  🗎 Move Document Up           │
│  🖨▸ Resume Printer                 🗎 Move Document Down          │
│                                               │
└──────────── Workspace icons ────────────┘
```

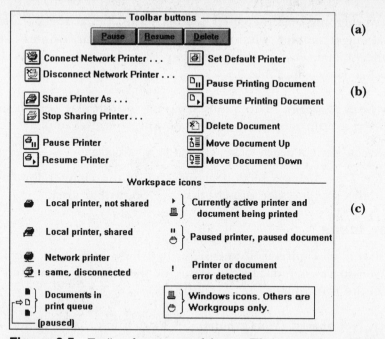

Figure 9.5 Toolbar buttons and icons. There are three Toolbar buttons in (a) Windows 3.1 and 12 in (b) Windows-for-Workgroups. (c) The Workspace icons.

Header Bar (Workgroups). Immediately below the Toolbar is a narrower bar which displays the following text:

Printer/Document Name   Status   Size   Time

Although the Windows-for-Workgroups *User's Guide* does not identify, name, or describe the bar, its purpose is reasonably obvious: These are column headings for data that will appear below. With the exception of the first header, the horizontal position of the others, and the entries which appear beneath them, may be adjusted. Refer to the *Header Bar* section in the *Print Manager Window Configuration* section later in the chapter for details on how to do so, and to the *Header Bar Troubleshooting* section for assistance if the column headers exhibit problems (or don't exhibit at all).

Workspace. Another important part of the Print Manager window remains unnamed: the large white area between the Header Bar above and the Status Bar below. To avoid referring to it as "it," this book dubs it the *Workspace,* if only to keep the word count down.

The Workspace displays a dynamic report on the installed printers, print queues, and the status of print jobs in progress or awaiting the printer.

Status Bar (Workgroups). Two panels in the Status Bar at the bottom of the Print Manager applet window display the current printer status (printing, idle, stalled, etc.) and information about the print queue. Typical messages are shown in Table 9.1.

Status Bar Error Messages. The Status Bar may also display certain error messages during a print job, such as the following typical example:

The port settings may not match those required by your printer.

Refer to the *Error Messages* section at the end of the chapter for an explanation of any error message displayed in the Status Bar area.

Print Manager Icons

The icons shown in Figure 9.5c and described here appear in the Print Manager's Workspace to indicate the status of the listed printers and the documents in the print queue.

Local Printer, Not Shared (Workgroups). A local printer is identified by a small printer image.

Local Printer, Shared (Workgroups). If the local printer is available for sharing, a hand appears underneath the printer icon.

Network Printer (Workgroups). A network printer is identified by a horizontal "cable" underneath the printer, which may be almost invisible if the network printer is highlighted.

TABLE 9.1 Typical Status Bar Messages*

Panel 1	Panel 2
The printer is idle,	Printer is not shared with the network
paused,	Microsoft Word - *filename*.DOC is Printing on LPT1
printing,	Notepad - *filename*.TXT is Queued
stalled, etc.	(Untitled) is Paused [†]
	Write - *filename*.WRI is Paused
	(*comment from* Comment *box in* Share Printer *dialog box*)
	(*blank, if printer is shared and no comment has been entered*)

* Status Bar may also display a printer error message.

[†] (Untitled) if document is not yet saved, or if remote computer is in standard mode.

Disconnected Network Printer.   If a remote user stops sharing a network printer, the Network Printer icon in the local Workspace changes to a grayed icon.

Active Printer and Document.   A printer image (Windows) or right-pointing solid arrowhead (Workgroups) identifies the currently active printer and the first document in the print queue.

Paused Printer and Document.   An upraised hand (Windows) or vertical dual-bar symbol (Workgroups) identifies a paused printer and the document (if any) that is also paused.

Print Queue Documents.   A number (Windows) or document icon (Workgroups) identifies each document in the print queue. The document icon is shaded if the file is available for printing, or unshaded if marked as paused. Windows documents are numbered sequentially, while Workgroups documents are not. However, Workgroups users can probably guess the printing sequence simply by looking at the queue.

Error Symbol (Workgroups).   An exclamation mark identifies a printer or document in which an error has been detected. The nature of the error should be displayed in the Status Bar at the bottom of the Printer Manager Applet Window.

Print Manager Menus

The Print Manager menus are illustrated in Figure 9.6 and described here. A parenthetical letter next to a menu name indicates its position in the figure. If a Shortcut Key exists for a menu option, it is given in parentheses next to that option.

Document Menu (Figure 9.6a) (Workgroups).   Use the options on this menu to manage the print jobs listed in the Print Queue for any local or network computer listed in the Print Manager's Applet Window. Each menu option is briefly described here. For further details, refer to *Print Queue Management* in the *Print Manager Configuration* section later in the chapter.

Delete Document **(Del).**   To remove any document from the print queue, highlight it, then select this option or press the Delete key.

Move Document Down, Up.   Select either option, as appropriate, to relocate a highlighted document in the print queue.

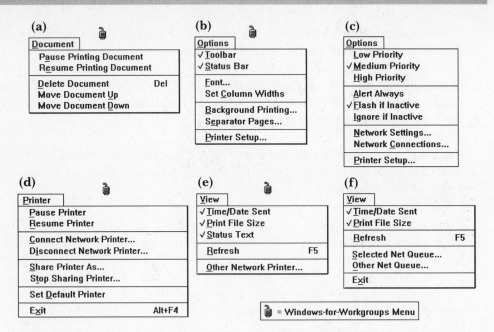

Figure 9.6 Menus accessible via the Print Manager's Menu Bar. (a) Document Menu, (b) Workgroups and (c) Windows Options Menu, (d) Printer Menu, (e) Workgroups and (f) Windows View Menu.

Pause, Resume Printing Document. If a document has not yet begun printing, use either option to determine whether it will be printed when its turn comes up in the print queue. If a document is paused, this does not affect the printing of any document(s) following it in the queue.

Options Menu (Figure 9.6b, Workgroups; Figure 9.6c, Windows 3.1). These menus provide access to options for configuring the general appearance of the Print Manager Applet Window, print job management, and printer setup, as described here.

***Alert Always, Flash if Inactive, Ignore if Inactive* (Windows).** Refer to *Message Notification* in the *Background Printing Configuration* section below for information about each option.

Background Printing... (Workgroups). This Workgroups selection incorporates many items found on the Options Menu in Windows. Refer to *Background Printing Priority* in the *Print Manager Configuration* section later in the chapter for assistance with configuration options.

Font... **(Workgroups).** The selected font displays the text in the Print Manager's Workspace. To change from the default MS Sans Serif (SSERIF*x*.FON) to some other font, select this option to open the Font dialog box (not shown here—see Figure 10.16).

The Print Manager always displays the default printer in a bold font style. Therefore, you might want to select any other style for everything else, so as to maintain the default printer's distinctive font style. If you do use this option to select a Workspace font, the following line is written into the indicated section of WIN.INI:

```
[spooler]
font=F3FF9001 . . . . (or similar long hexadecimal string)
```

 NOTE: The MS Sans Serif font is also used in Windows 3.1, but there is no option to change it from within the Print Manager. To do so, you must change the font used for icon titles, as described in _Icon Title Font_ in the _WIN.INI Font Changes_ section of Chapter 10.

Low, Medium, High Priority **(Windows).** These options determine how processing time is distributed between the Print Manager and other applications. If you need assistance in selecting one of these options, refer to _Background Printing Priority_ in the _Print Manager Configuration_ section below.

Network Connections... **(Windows).** Select this option to connect or disconnect a network printer. The Printers - Network Connections dialog box is shown later on (Figure 9.14) in the _Network Printer Configuration_ section.

Network Settings... **(Windows).** Select this option to open the Network Options dialog box (not shown) which contains the two check boxes described here.

Update Network Display. If this box is checked, the current status of the network printer is reported in the Message Box, where it is continuously updated as required. If the box is cleared, the Message Box simply reports what the network printer _should_ be doing, even if it isn't. Refer to the _Print Manager Configuration_ section for further details about these check boxes.

Print Net Jobs Direct. Check this box to send documents directly to the network Print Manager. Refer to _Bypass Local Print Manager_ in the _Print Manager Configuration_ section for additional configuration information.

Printer Setup... (both). This selection accesses printer configuration options described in the *Printers Applet Configuration* section later in the chapter. The only difference is that the Printers applet itself (in the Control Panel) must be used to disable or re-enable the Print Manager. All other features may be accessed from within the Print Manager by choosing this option.

Separator Pages... (Workgroups). An optional separator page can be printed before each print job, which may be convenient if a network printer is handling print jobs from a variety of sources. Click on one of the following radio buttons, as desired.

No Separator Page. This radio button is enabled by default, and no separator page is printed at the head of each print job.

Simple Separator Page. The following information appears on the separator page in a Courier (monospaced) font:

```
Microsoft (R) Windows (TM) for Workgroups
- - - - - - - - - - - - - - - - - - - - - - - - -
Document:        Notepad - README.TXT
Printed By:      Local User (or remote computer name)
Date and Time:   4:08 PM  6/20/93
```

Standard Separator Page. The same information is printed, but with the first line in a large boldface font complete with the Microsoft Windows logo. On a laser printer, this looks better than the separator page described above.

Custom Separator Page. Choose this option if you want to replace either of the above with one of your own. But first, you'll have to create a custom file, as described in the *Custom Separator File Preparation* in the *Print Manager Configuration* section. Once the file is available, enter its name in the text box within the **Separator Page Options:** section, click on this radio button, then on the **OK** button to close the dialog box.

> **NOTE:** The desired Separator Page must be specified at the local Print Manager for the printer that is handling the print jobs. If a user sends print jobs to a network printer, that user's Separator Page mode has no effect at the remote site.

***Set Column Widths* (Workgroups).**   Click on this option to reposition the three column headers (Status, Size, Time) seen at the top of the Workspace in Figure 9.4b. Refer to *Header Bar* in the *Print Manager Window Configuration* below for further details.

***Status Bar, Toolbar* (Workgroups).**   If you don't regularly use the Status Bar and/or Toolbar described earlier, clear the check mark next to either option to remove it from the applet window.

Printer Menu (Windows).   Don't look for this one: It isn't there. Instead, some printer controls are located on the Toolbar (described above), while network-related operations are handled via the Printers applet in the Control Panel.

Printer Menu (Figure 9.6d—Workgroups).   The options on this menu are used to set network connection and sharing configurations, and to specify the local default printer and pause or resume printing operations.

Connect Network Printer....   There are two ways to establish a connection to a network printer. One is by selecting this option; the other is via the Printers applet. Since the configuration procedure is identical in either case, it is described under this heading in the complete *Network Printer Configuration* section below.

Disconnect Network Printer....   Select this option to disconnect your computer from a shared network printer. A Disconnect Network Printer dialog box (not shown) lists the present network printer connections. Highlight one or more of the listed printers and click on the OK button to sever the connection(s).

Note that this option appears enabled even if no network printers are connected.

***Exit* (Alt+F4).**   Click here to close the Print Manager. If a local printer is currently shared, a message appears to warn you that print sharing will be disabled.

Pause, Resume Printer.   Highlight any local printer, then click on either button, as appropriate, to pause or resume printing. These menu options are disabled if a network (remote) printer is highlighted, since it is not possible to interfere with a printer connected to someone else's computer.

Set Default Printer. Highlight any local or network printer, then click on this option to use that printer for all local print jobs.

Share Printer As.... (Enhanced mode only.) Select this option if you want to make a local printer available for sharing by others on the network. Refer to the *Printer Sharing Configuration* section below for assistance with the printer sharing parameters, or with disabling this option.

Stop Sharing Printer.... (Enhanced mode only.) Unlike the Disconnect Network Printer... option described above, this option is disabled if no local printers are currently shared. If the option is enabled and you select it, a Stop Sharing Network Printer dialog box appears. Select the printer, or printers, you wish to stop sharing and click on the OK button.

View Menu (Figure 9.6e, Workgroups; Figure 9.6f, Windows). The options on this menu determine the appearance of the data displayed in the Print Manager's Workspace.

Exit (Alt+F4) (Windows). Click here to close the Print Manager. If a local printer is currently shared, a message warns that print sharing will be disabled.

Other Net Queue... (Windows). This option is equivalent to the *Other Network Printer* option which follows.

Other Network Printer... (Workgroups). Select this option if you are not connected to a network printer, but want to view its print queue anyway. When the Other Network Printer dialog box shown in Figure 9.7 appears, enter the name of the network computer and its printer in the Network Printer: box, then click the View button. The figure shows four documents in the print queue. Note that the name of the final document in the print queue is not shown.

Print File Size, Time/Date Sent (Windows). These options determine whether the indicated information will appear next to each file in the print queue.

Print File Size, Status Text, Time/Date Sent (Workgroups). These options determine whether the Header Bar and Workspace will display the indicated information.

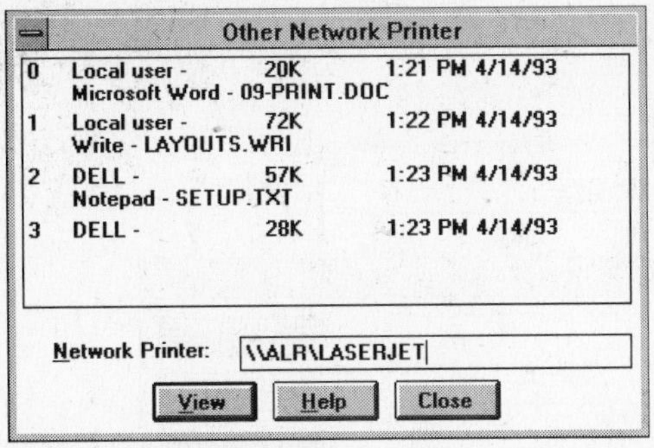

```
┌─────────────────────────────────────────┐
│ ═                 Other Network Printer   │
├─┬───────────────────────────────────────┤
│0│ Local user -        20K      1:21 PM 4/14/93 │
│ │ Microsoft Word - 09-PRINT.DOC           │
│1│ Local user -        72K      1:22 PM 4/14/93 │
│ │ Write - LAYOUTS.WRI                      │
│2│ DELL -              57K      1:23 PM 4/14/93 │
│ │ Notepad - SETUP.TXT                      │
│3│ DELL -              28K      1:23 PM 4/14/93 │
│ │                                          │
│ │                                          │
│ │                                          │
├─┴───────────────────────────────────────┤
│ Network Printer:   \\ALR\LASERJET|        │
│                                            │
│        [ View ]  [ Help ]  [ Close ]       │
└─────────────────────────────────────────┘
```

Figure 9.7 The Other Network dialog box shows the print queue for a network printer to which the user is not connected.

Refresh **(F5).** As changes occur at the network printer, the local Workspace is periodically refreshed to indicate those changes. However, if you just can't wait for the next Refresh cycle, click on this option to force an immediate screen refresh.

Selected Net Queue... **(Windows).** By default, the Windows local print queue displays only those files sent by the local system to the network printer. Select this option to display the entire print queue.

Printers Applet Configuration

The Printers applet is accessed through the Control Panel icon in the Main Group Window, as shown in Figure 9.8a–c. To get at it, first open the Main Group Window and double-click on the Control Panel icon (a). Then double-click on the Printers icon (b) to open the Printers dialog box (c). The component parts of the dialog box are briefly reviewed here.

The Printers Dialog Box

This section assumes a printer has been physically connected to one of the computer's printer ports. However, since the physical presence of a printer is not required during this configuration, the procedure may be followed prior to actually connecting, or powering on, the printer.

For the purposes of this explanation, it is assumed that the LPT1 port is, or will be, used for the printer connection. If not, change LPT1 references to LPTx, where x is the port number that is used.

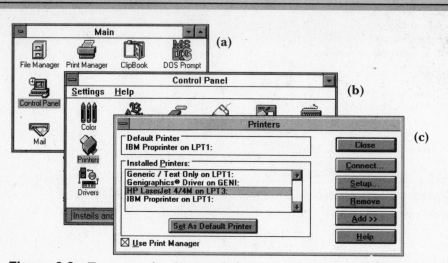

Figure 9.8   To access the Printers dialog box, (a) click on the Control Panel icon in the Main Group Window, (b) click on the Control Panel's Printers icon to open (c) the Printers dialog box.

Installed Printers List.   It might have been better if the Installed Printers: box had been labeled "Installed Printer *Drivers*." Although the list format suggests that certain printers are physically present, in fact it indicates only that *drivers* for the listed printers are installed. The list might suggest that several printers are attached to the same port. What it really means is that drivers for those printers have been configured for a printer on the indicated port. The printer itself may or may not be there.

Default Printer.   The driver for the printer listed in this box is presently configured as the default. Therefore, when a print job begins, the Print Manager (if enabled) will expect to find that printer ready to receive the job.

Set Default Printer.   To specify the printer to be listed in the Default Printer box, highlight its name in the Installed Printers: list. If the desired printer name does not appear in that list, refer to the *Printer Driver Installation* section which follows. Or, if you need to change the listed port, refer to the *Port Configuration* section below.

When the highlighted printer and its port are correct, click on the Set As Default Printer button to assign that combination as the default printer. The highlighted information should now appear in the Default Printer box at the top of the screen.

Printer Driver Installation. To add a printer name to the Installed Printers: box, click on the Add>> button shown in Figure 9.8. When you do, the Printers dialog box expands to include a List of Printers: box, as shown in Figure 9.9a. Scroll through the listed printers and highlight the desired one. Or, select "Install Unlisted or Updated Printer" at the top of the list if you want to install a driver that is not represented in the list, or if you know the driver is already in your System directory. Next, click on the Install... button to begin the driver installation.

The Install Driver dialog box shown in Figure 9.9b prompts you to insert a diskette containing the required driver in drive A. Do so, or—to review drivers already available—type C:\WINDOWS\SYSTEM (or other destination) in the box, then click on the OK button to display the Add Unlisted or Updated Printer dialog box (not shown). Highlight the printer (driver) you wish to install and again click the OK button. At the conclusion of the procedure, the Printers dialog box should reappear, with the new printer added to the Installed Printers: list, as shown here:

(printer name) on LPT*x*:

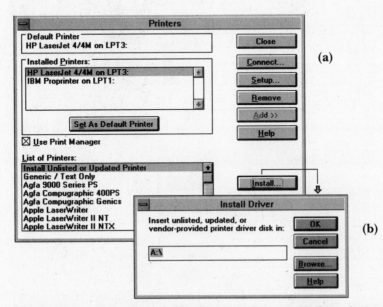

Figure 9.9 The Printers dialog box, (a) expanded to show the List of Printers: box. (b) The Install Driver dialog box prompts for a diskette containing unlisted or updated driver files.

NOTE: Before installing a printer driver that is already available on your hard disk, refer to the *Reinstallation of Printer Driver* section below.

Printer Setup Configuration.   Once you have selected the desired printer driver, you may want to click on the Se*t*up... button to configure various parameters unique to that printer. For example, Figures 9.10 and 9.11 show the Setup dialog boxes for a Hewlett-Packard LaserJet 4/4M and IBM Proprinter. In each case, an *O*ptions... button accesses additional parameters on the appropriate Options dialog box (part b of each figure). If you need assistance configuring any of these Setup parameters, refer to the *User's Guide* for the selected printer. The TrueType check boxes in Figure 9.10 are described in the *TrueType Font Configuration* section of the next chapter.

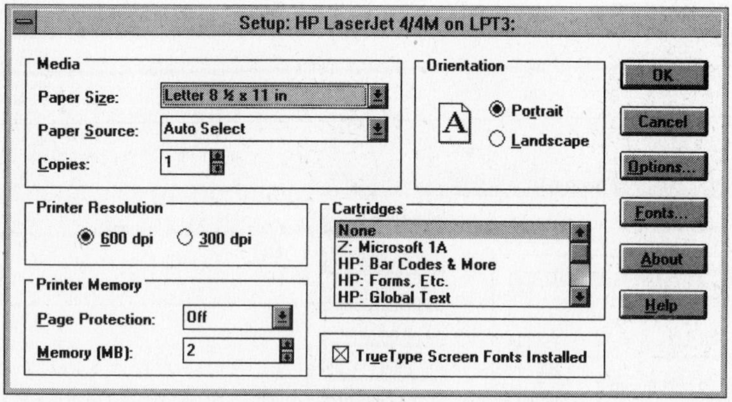

(a)

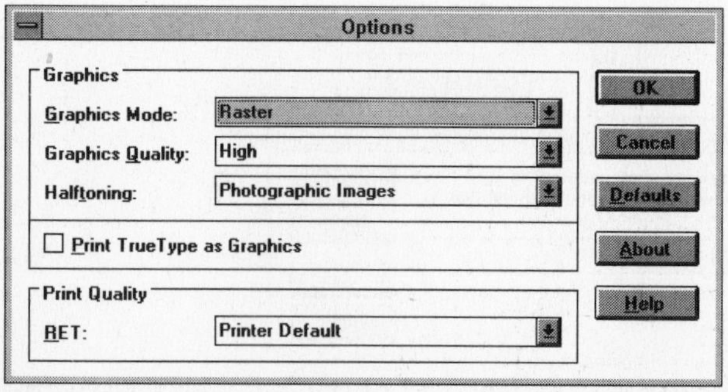

(b)

Figure 9.10   A typical Printer Setup dialog box. (a) Dialog box for a Hewlett-Packard LaserJet 4/4M printer and (b) the Options dialog box.

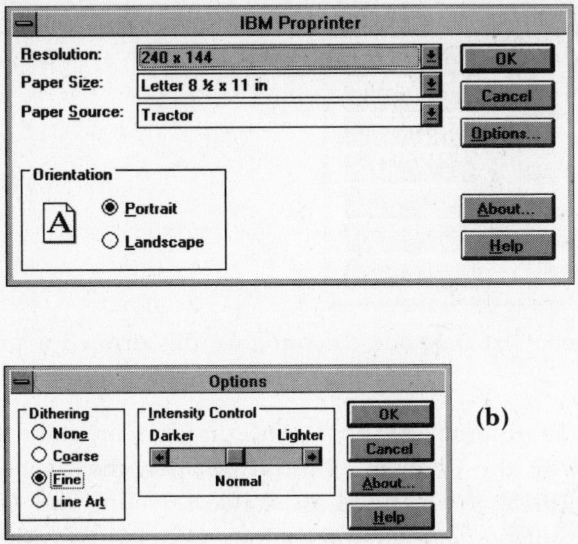

Figure 9.11 A typical Printer Setup dialog box. (a) Dialog box for an IBM Proprinter and (b) the Options dialog box.

PAPER SIZE CHANGE NOTE: After configuring the printer, if you open the *International* applet and change the specified **Country** entry, the information in the **Paper Size:** box (figures 9.10 and 9.11) may change to the default paper size for that country. Refer to *Printer Paper Size* in the *International Applet* section of Chapter 11 for more details.

The Generic/Text-Only Printer Driver **(TTY.DRV).** This driver is often dismissed as the last resort for a printer that isn't quite up to modern standards. However, it's also a handy device (driver) for saving an ASCII file within an application that doesn't otherwise provide such a feature. As a typical example, if you use the *Cardfile* applet's Print option, the printed output will resemble the screen display—a series of cards complete with borders and a double line under each Index line. This is convenient (maybe) if you want to cut them out and save them in a nice little metal box.

However, if you configure the generic driver on the File port (Generic / Text Only on FILE:), the cardfile will print to a diskette file as straight ASCII text, which can then be imported into some other applet for subsequent reformatting as desired. Figure 9.12 shows one of the dialog boxes used to configure the generic driver. Refer to the *Port Configuration* section below for further details about the File port.

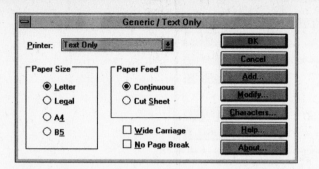

Figure 9.12 Use the Generic/Text Only box to configure this driver for printing ASCII text to a disk file.

Connect Configuration. To change the port configuration or make other connection changes, click on the Connect... button to open the Connect dialog box shown in Figure 9.13. If you need assistance selecting the proper port, refer to the *Port Configuration* section below. Otherwise, review or change the other listed settings as described here.

Timeouts (seconds). This section of the Connect dialog box specifies the interval that Windows will wait for the indicated action to take place before sending an error message. The default timeouts are listed in parentheses. If you specify some other value, it will be rounded up to the nearest 5-second interval.

Device Not Selected: (15 seconds). The printer must be online and ready to print within the time specified in this box.

Transmission Retry: (45 seconds; 90 seconds for PostScript printer). Each page of the print job must be received by the printer within the time specified in this box. You may want to increase the interval if the printer has trouble printing a complex graphics image.

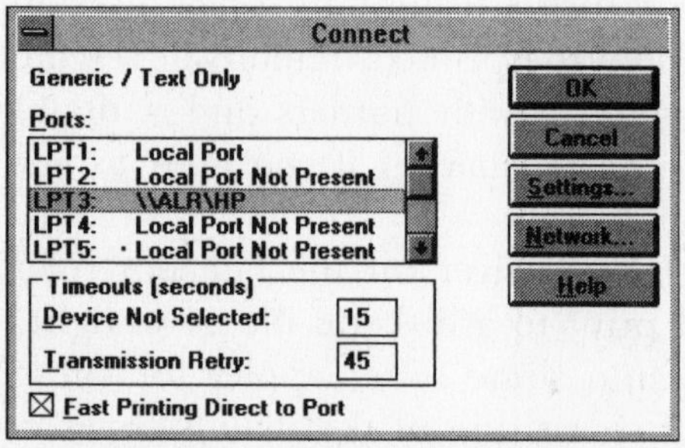

Figure 9.13 The Connect dialog box offers port selection and access to serial port settings and network connections.

Fast Printing Direct to Port. If this option is enabled, Windows bypasses the DOS interrupt routines and your documents print faster. That is, if you believe the online Help Screen. But out there in the real world, *Fast Printing* is sometimes *Slow Printing:* It depends on a variety of factors, including what else is happening while the print job runs in the background. If Print Manager is disabled (foreground printing only), then this option is definitely faster. But if Print Manager is on, then it's worthwhile to run tests under your own typical operating conditions to determine the best mode to use.

Network Printer Configuration. As shown earlier in the Figure 9.2 flow chart, several paths lead to the dialog box used to set up a network printer. And, although both Title Bars use the same three words (well, almost), their sequence is reversed as shown here:

Application	Title Bar Text	See Figure
Windows	Printers – Network Connection	9.14
Workgroups	Connect Network Printer	9.15

Printers–Network Connection (Windows). To establish a connection to a new network printer, enter the appropriate information in the **New Connection** dialog box and click on the **C**onnect button to complete the operation.

Current Printer Connections:. This box should be labeled "Current *Network* Printer Connections:" since that's what appears here. If you have a printer connected to a local port, it is not listed here. The example in Figure 9.14 shows a current LPT3 connection, with a new connection about to be assigned to LPT1.

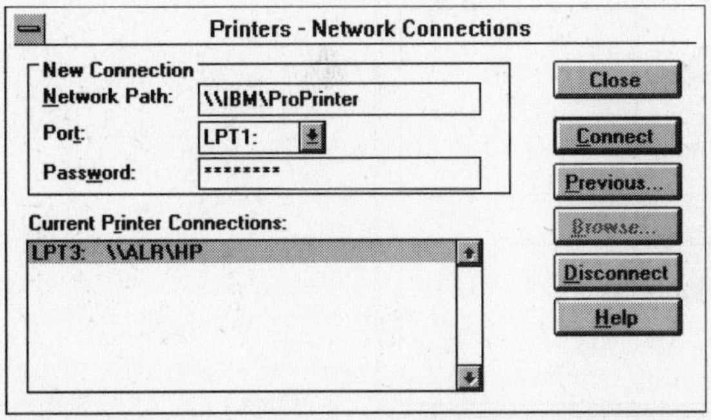

Figure 9.14 The Printers-Network Connections dialog box as it appears in Windows if the **Network** button (Figure 9.13) is clicked.

Network Printer Password. If the network software has assigned a password to the printer, enter it in the Pass<u>w</u>ord: box to complete the connection. Note that Windows itself does not assign network printer passwords.

Disconnect Network Printer. Click on the <u>D</u>isconnect button to disconnect the highlight printer in the Current P<u>r</u>inter Connections: box. The button is disabled if this box is empty.

Connect Network Printer (Workgroups). The Connect Network Printer dialog box shown in Figure 9.15 offers a much improved view of network printer status. The <u>S</u>how Shared Printers on: box lists the network computers currently logged onto the workgroup whose name appears at the top of the list. Highlight any computer in the list (except your own) and that computer's shared printers are listed in the Sha<u>r</u>ed Printers box immediately below. If no printer names appear in the box, try to persuade the remote operator to share one of the printers that you know are available, then try again.

When you highlight a printer in the Sha<u>r</u>ed Printers box, the <u>P</u>ath: box near the top of the Connect dialog box should show the network computer name and the name of the shared printer, as shown in Figure 9.15. As a final step, make sure the <u>D</u>evice Name: box at the top of the dialog box indicates the desired printer port. Of course, you can accept the default LPT1, but before doing so you may want to review *Network Printer Port Selection* in the *Port Configuration*

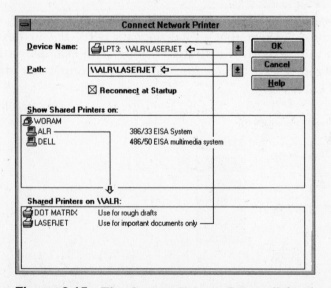

Figure 9.15 The Connect Network Printer dialog box as it appears in Windows-for-Workgroups if the Network button (Figure 9.13) is clicked.

section later in the chapter. Also refer to this section for additional general assistance with port selection and the use of serial ports.

Once you've made the necessary selections described above, click on the OK button. If the Connect dialog box (Figure 9.13) reappears, the Ports: box should show the desired LPT*x*-to-printer association. Make any other configuration changes as required, then click on the OK button to return either to the Printers dialog box or to the Print Manager, as appropriate.

Network Printer Password. If the network printer requires a password, an Enter Network Password dialog box appears (not shown here, but similar to Figure 8.13). Type in the password to complete the connection. Windows-for-Workgroups does provide password security for shared printers, as described under *Passwords* in the *Printer Sharing Configuration* section later in the chapter.

Printer Configuration Considerations

This section offers a few suggestions that may be of some use in keeping track of your Printers applet configuration.

Verify Installed Printer Drivers. The currently installed printer drivers and some (but not all) related files can be tracked down via the WIN.INI and CONTROL.INI files. For example, the [devices] section of WIN.INI lists each printer name, driver, and assigned port, as shown by a few typical examples below. Find the driver name (HPPCL5E, TTY, etc.) in the second column, then look in the [installed] section of CONTROL.INI for other files with the same name and a different extension (DLL, HLP, for example). Or, refer to Table 9.2 for a list of printer drivers and other files required for most popular printers. If UNIDRV files are found in CONTROL.INI, it is not clear which printer requires them, so you'll need to refer to Table 9.2, or to the UNIDRV cross-reference in Table 9.3 for this information. In the examples shown here, only the IBM Proprinter requires these files.

WIN.INI			**CONTROL.INI**
[devices]			[installed]
HP LaserJet 4/4M=	HPPCL5E,	LPT3:	(*none*)
Generic / Text Only=	TTY,	FILE:	TTY.DRV=yes
			TTY.HLP=yes
IBM Proprinter=	proprint,	LPT1:	PROPRINT.DRV=yes
			UNIDRV.DLL=yes
			UNIDRV.HLP=yes

TABLE 9.2 Printer Drivers for Windows 3.1*

Printer Manufacturer Model	Driver Filename	Ext.	Other Filename	Ext.	Filename	Ext.
Agfa						
9000 Series PS	PSCRIPT	DRV				
Compugraphic 400PS	PSCRIPT	DRV				
Compugraphic Genics	HPPCL	DRV	UNIDRV	DLL		
Apple						
LaserWriter, II, II NTX, Plus	PSCRIPT	DRV				
Apricot						
Laser	HPPCL	DRV	UNIDRV	DLL		
AST						
TurboLaser/PS	PSCRIPT	DRV				
AT&T						
435	HPPLOT	DRV				
470/475	CITOH	DRV	UNIDRV	DLL		
473/478	OKI9IBM	DRV	UNIDRV	DLL		
C-Itoh						
8510	CITOH	DRV	UNIDRV	DLL		
Canon						
Bubble-Jet BJ-10e	CANON10E	DRV	UNIDRV	DLL		
Bubble-Jet BJ-130e	CANON130	DRV	UNIDRV	DLL		
Bubble-Jet BJ-300, BJ330	CANON330	DRV	UNIDRV	DLL		
LBP-4, LBP-8	LBPIII	DRV	GENDRV	DLL		
LBP-8 II	LBPII	DRV	GENDRV	DLL		
Citizen						
120D, 180D	CIT9US	DRV	UNIDRV	DLL		
200GX, 200GX/15	CIT9US	DRV	UNIDRV	DLL	DMCOLOR	DLL
GSX-130, 140, 140+, 145	CIT24US	DRV	UNIDRV	DLL	DMCOLOR	DLL
HSP-500, 550	CIT9US	DRV	UNIDRV	DLL	DMCOLOR	DLL
PN48	CIT24US	DRV	UNIDRV	DLL		
Dataproducts						
LZR-2665	PSCRIPT	DRV				

TABLE 9.2 *(continued)*

Printer Manufacturer Model	Driver Filename	Ext.	Other Filename	Ext.
Diconix				
150 Plus	DICONIX	DRV	UNIDRV	DLL
Digital				
Colormate PS	PSCRIPT	DRV	DECCOLOR	WPD
DEClaser 1150	PSCRIPT	DRV	DEC1150	WPD
DEClaser 2150	PSCRIPT	DRV	DEC2150	WPD
DEClaser 2250	PSCRIPT	DRV	DEC2250	WPD
DEClaser 3250	PSCRIPT	DRV	DEC3250	WPD
LN03R ScriptPrinter	PSCRIPT	DRV		
PrintServer 20/turbo	PSCRIPT	DRV	DECLPS20	WPD
PrintServer 40	PSCRIPT	DRV		
Epson				
DFX-5000	EPSON9	DRV	UNIDRV	DLL
EPL-6000, EPL-7000	HPPCL	DRV	UNIDRV	DLL
EPL-7500	PSCRIPT	DRV	EPL75523	WPD
EX-800, 1000	EPSON9	DRV	UNIDRV	DLL
FX-80, 80+, 85, 86e	EPSON9	DRV	UNIDRV	DLL
FX-100, 100+, 185	EPSON9	DRV	UNIDRV	DLL
FX-286, 286e	EPSON9	DRV	UNIDRV	DLL
FX-850, 1050	EPSON9	DRV	UNIDRV	DLL
GQ-3500	HPPCL	DRV	UNIDRV	DLL
JX-80	EPSON9	DRV	UNIDRV	DLL
L-750, 1000	EPSON24	DRV	UNIDRV	DLL
LQ-500, 510	EPSON24	DRV	UNIDRV	DLL
LQ-570 & 870 ESC/P 2	ESCP2	DRV	UNIDRV	DLL
LQ-800, 850	EPSON24	DRV	UNIDRV	DLL
LQ-950, 1000, 1050	EPSON24	DRV	UNIDRV	DLL
LQ-1070 & 1170 ESC/P 2	ESCP2	DRV	UNIDRV	DLL
LQ-1500, 2500, 2550	EPSON24	DRV	UNIDRV	DLL
LX-80, 86, 800, 810	EPSON9	DRV	UNIDRV	DLL
MX-80, 80 F/T, 100	EPSON9	DRV	UNIDRV	DLL
RX-80, 80 F/T, 80 F/T+	EPSON9	DRV	UNIDRV	DLL
RX-100, 100+	EPSON9	DRV	UNIDRV	DLL
SQ-2000, 2500	EPSON24	DRV	UNIDRV	DLL
T-750, 1000	EPSON9	DRV	UNIDRV	DLL

TABLE 9.2 *(continued)*

Printer Manufacturer Model	Driver Filename	Ext.	Other Filename	Ext.
Fujitsu				
DL 2400, 2600, 3300, 3400	FUJI24[†]	DRV	UNIDRV	DLL
DL 5600	FUJI24[†]	DRV	UNIDRV	DLL
DX 2100, 2200, 2300, 2400	FUJI9[†]	DRV	UNIDRV	DLL
Generic				
Generic/Text Only	TTY	DRV		
Hermes				
H 606	PG306[†]	DRV	GENDRV	DLL
H 606 PS (13 Fonts)	PSCRIPT	DRV	HERMES_1	WPD
H 606 PS (35 Fonts)	PSCRIPT	DRV	HERMES_2	WPD
Hewlett-Packard Plotters				
7470A, 7475A, 7550A, 7580A, 7580B	HPPLOT	DRV		
7585A, 7585B, 7586B	HPPLOT	DRV		
ColorPro, ColorPro w/ GEC	HPPLOT	DRV		
DraftPro, DXL, EXL	HPPLOT	DRV		
DraftMaster I, II	HPPLOT	DRV		
Hewlett-Packard Printers				
DeskJet, +, 500	HPDSKJET	DRV	UNIDRV	DLL
DeskJet 500C	DJ500C[††]	DRV		
LaserJet, +, 500+, 2000	HPPCL	DRV	UNIDRV	DLL
LaserJet Series II, IID	HPPCL	DRV	UNIDRV	DLL
LaserJet IID PS	PSCRIPT	DRV	HPIID522	WPD
LaserJet IIP, IIP +	HPPCL	DRV	UNIDRV	DLL
LaserJet IIP PS	PSCRIPT	DRV	HPIIP522	WPD
LaserJet III	HPPCL5A[†]	DRV		
	HPPCL5MS[‡]	DRV		
LaserJet III PostScript	PSCRIPT	DRV	HPIII522	WPD
LaserJet IIID	HPPCL5A	DRV		
LaserJet IIID PostScript	PSCRIPT	DRV	HP_3D522	WPD
LaserJet IIIP	HPPCL5A	DRV		
LaserJet IIIP PostScript	PSCRIPT	DRV	HP_3P522	WPD
LaserJet IIISi	HPPCL5A	DRV		

TABLE 9.2 *(continued)*

Printer Manufacturer Model	Driver Filename	Ext.	Other Filename	Ext.	
LaserJet IIISi PostScript	PSCRIPT	DRV	HPELI523	WPD	
LaserJet 4, 4M	HPPCL5E§	DRV	HPPCL5E*x*	DLL	(*x*=1,2,3,4)
PaintJet, XL	PAINTJET	DRV	UNIDRV	DLL	
ThinkJet (2225 C-D)	THINKJET	DRV	UNIDRV	DLL	
IBM					
Color Printer	IBMCOLOR	DRV			
ExecJet	EXECJET	DRV	UNIDRV	DLL	
Graphics	OKI9IBM	DRV	UNIDRV	DLL	
Laser Printer 4019	IBM4019	DRV	GENDRV	DLL	
LaserPtr 4019 PS17	PSCRIPT	DRV	IBM17521	WPD	
LaserPtr 4019 PS39	PSCRIPT	DRV	IBM39521	WPD	
LaserPtr 4029 PS17	PSCRIPT	DRV	40291730	WPD	
LaserPtr 4029 PS39	PSCRIPT	DRV	40293930	WPD	
Personal Pageprinter, II-30, II-31	PSCRIPT	DRV			
Proprinter, II, III, XL, XLII, XLIII	PROPRINT	DRV	UNIDRV	DLL	
Proprinter X24, X24e, XL24, XL24e	PROPRN24	DRV	UNIDRV	DLL	
PS/1	PS1	DRV	UNIDRV	DLL	
QuickWriter 5204	IBM5204	DRV	UNIDRV	DLL	
QuietWriter III	QWIII	DRV	UNIDRV	DLL	
Kyocera					
F-Series (USA), F-5000 (USA)	HPPCL	DRV	UNIDRV	DLL	
Linotronic					
100 v42.5	L100_425‡	WPD			
200/230	PSCRIPT	DRV	L200230&	WPD	
300 v47.1	L300_471‡	WPD			
300 v49.3	L300_493‡	WPD			
330	PSCRIPT	DRV	L330_52&	WPD	
500 v49.3	L500_493‡	WP			
530	PSCRIPT	DRV	L530_52&	WPD	
630	PSCRIPT	DRV	L630_52&	WPD	

TABLE 9.2 *(continued)*

Printer Manufacturer Model	Driver Filename	Ext.	Other Filename	Ext.
Microtek				
TrueLaser	PSCRIPT	DRV	MT_TI101	WPD
NEC				
Colormate PS/40	PSCRIPT	DRV	NCM40519	WPD
Colormate PS/80	PSCRIPT	DRV	NCM80519	WPD
Pinwriter CP6, CP7, P5XL, P6, P7, P9XL	NEC24PIN	DRV	UNIDRV	DLL
P2200, P5200, P5300	NEC24PIN	DRV	UNIDRV	DLL
Silentwriter LC 860 +	HPPCL	DRV	UNIDRV	DLL
Silentwriter LC890	PSCRIPT	DRV	N890_470	WPD
Silentwriter LC890XL	PSCRIPT	DRV	N890X505	WPD
Silentwriter2 90	PSCRIPT	DRV	N2090522	WPD
Silentwriter2 290	PSCRIPT	DRV	N2290520	WPD
Silentwriter2 990	PSCRIPT	DRV	N2990523	WPD
OceColor				
G5241 PS	PSCRIPT	DRV	O5241503	WPD
G5242 PS	PSCRIPT	DRV	O5242503	WPD
Okidata				
LaserLine 6	HPPCL	DRV	UNIDRV	DLL
ML 92-IBM, 93-IBM	OKI9IBM	DRV	UNIDRV	DLL
ML 192. 192 +	OKI9	DRV	UNIDRV	DLL
ML 192-IBM, 193-IBM, 320-IBM, 321-IBM	OKI9IBM	DRV	UNIDRV	DLL
ML 193, 193 +, 320, 321	OKI9	DRV	UNIDRV	DLL
ML 380, 390, 390 +, 391, 391 +	OKI24	DRV	UNIDRV	DLL
ML 393, 393 +, 393C, 393C +	OKI24	DRV	UNIDRV	DLL
OL-400, 800	HPPCL	DRV	UNIDRV	DLL
Oki				
OL840/PS	PSCRIPT	DRV	OL840518	WPD

TABLE 9.2 *(continued)*

Printer Manufacturer Model	Driver Filename	Ext.	Other Filename	Ext.
Olivetti				
DM 109, DM 309	DM309	DRV	GENDRV	DLL
ETV 5000	HPPCL	DRV	UNIDRV	DLL
PG 108, 208 M2, PG 308 HS	HPPCL	DRV	UNIDRV	DLL
PG 303, PG 308 HS PostScript	PSCRIPT	DRV		
PG 306	PG306[†]	DRV	GENDRV	DLL
PG 306 PS (13 Fonts)	PSCRIPT	DRV	OLIVETI1	WPD
PG 306 PS (35 Fonts)	PSCRIPT	DRV	OLIVETI2	WPD
Panasonic				
KX-P1123, KX-P1124, KX- P1624	PANSON24	DRV	UNIDRV	DLL
KX-P1180, KX-P1695	PANSON9	DRV	UNIDRV	DLL
KX-P4420	HPPCL	DRV	UNIDRV	DLL
KX-P4455 v51.4	PSCRIPT	DRV	P4455514	WPD
PostScript Printer	PSCRIPT	DRV		
QMS				
ColorScript 100	PSCRIPT	DRV		
QMS-PS 800, 800 +, 810	PSCRIPT	DRV		
QMS-PS 820	PSCRIPT	DRV	Q820_517	WPD
QMS-PS 2200	PSCRIPT	DRV	Q2200510	WPD
Seiko				
ColorPoint PS Model 04	PSCRIPT	DRV	SEIKO_04	WPD
ColorPoint PS Model 14	PSCRIPT	DRV	SEIKO_14	WPD
QuadLaser				
QuadLaser I	HPPCL	DRV	UNIDRV	DLL
Tandy				
LP-1000	HPPCL	DRV	UNIDRV	DLL
Tegra				
Genesis	HPPCL	DRV	UNIDRV	DLL

TABLE 9.2 *(continued)*

Printer Manufacturer Model	Driver Filename	Ext.	Other Filename	Ext.
Tektronix				
Phaser II PX	PSCRIPT	DRV	PHIIPX	WPD
Phaser II PXi, III PXi	PSCRIPT	DRV	TKPHZR21	WPD
Texas Instruments				
850/855	TI850	DRV	UNIDRV	DLL
MicroLaser PS17	PSCRIPT	DRV	TIM17521	WPD
MicroLaser PS35	PSCRIPT	DRV	TIM35521	WPD
Toshiba				
P351, P1351	TOSHIBA	DRV	UNIDRV	DLL
PageLaser12	HPPCL	DRV	UNIDRV	DLL
Triumph Adler				
SDR 7706	PG306[†]	DRV	GENDRV	DLL
SDR 7706 PS13	PSCRIPT	DRV	TRIUMPH1	WPD
SDR 7706 PS35	PSCRIPT	DRV	TRIUMPH2	WPD
Unisys				
AP9210	HPPCL	DRV	UNIDRV	DLL
AP9415	PSCRIPT	DRV	U9415470	WPD
Varityper				
VT-600	PSCRIPT	DRV		
Wang				
LCS15, PCS15 FontPlus	PSCRIPT	DRV		
LDP8	HPPCL	DRV	UNIDRV	DLL

[*] Refer to Appendix A for file size and diskette location.
  WPD extension indicates Postscript Description file.
[†] Windows 3.1 only.
[††] Available from Hewlett-Packard.
[‡] Windows-for-Workgroups only.
[§] Separately available from Hewlett-Packard.

TABLE 9.3   Printers Which Require UNIDRV.DLL file*

Mfr.	Printer	Mfr.	Printer	Mfr.	Printer
Agfa Compugraphic Genics		Epson	L -750, 1000	NEC	Pinwriters
Apricot	Laser		LQ series		Silentwriter LC 860+
AT&T	470/475, 473/478		LX, MX, RX, SQ series	Okidata	ML series
C-Itoh	8510		T-750, 1000		LaserLine 6
Canon	Bubble-Jet BJ	Fujitsu	DL series	Olivetti	ETV 5000
Citizen	120D, 180D	HP	DeskJets		PG series
	200GX, 200GX/15		LaserJets series 2, 3	Panasonic	KX-P series
	GSX-130, 140, 145		PaintJets	QuadLaser I	
	HSP-500, 550		ThinkJet (2225 C-D)	Tandy	LP-1000
	PN48	IBM	ExecJet, Graphics	Tegra	Genesis
Diconix	150 Plus		Proprinters	Texas Inst.	TI 850/855
Epson	DFX-5000		PS/1	Toshiba	P351, 1351
	EX, FX series		QuickWriter 5204		PageLaser12
	JX-80		QuietWriter III	Unisys	AP9210
	DLQ-2000	Kyocera	F-, F-5000 Series	Wang	LDP8

*Based on information contained in CONTROL.INF file in System directory.

The CONTROL.INI file does not reveal that the HP LaserJet printer also requires a set of four HPPCL5Ex.DLL files ($x = 1$–4). To track down such examples as this, try typing DIR HPPCL*.* at the DOS prompt to see what other files may show up.

Verify Printer Drivers in System Directory. If you remove an installed printer from your list of printers, the driver for that printer remains in your System directory until you get around to erasing it. If you're not sure what drivers are still available, click on the Printers icon, select "Install Unlisted or Updated Printer," then click on the Install... button. When the Install Driver dialog box appears, type C:\WINDOWS\SYSTEM in the box and click on the OK button. The printer drivers in the System directory will be listed in the List of Printers: box.

Unfortunately, the list identifies each driver by the name of the printer it supports, but does not give the name of the driver file itself. Therefore, if you want to erase the driver, use Table 9.2 as a cross-reference between the printer name and the drivers used for that printer. Just make sure you don't erase a driver that is also used for a printer that you *do* want to retain.

Reinstallation of Printer Driver. If you want to reinstall a printer driver that was previously removed, but not physically erased from the System directory, you can always type C:\WINDOWS\SYSTEM in the Install Driver dialog box (see Figure 9.9b). The procedure will find the existing driver and reinstall it, thus sparing you the bother of locating the appropriate distribution diskettes.

However, there is one potential minor problem that may cause major confusion later on. If the System directory does not also contain the appropriate OEMSETUP.INF file for the driver, it may be reinstalled with a slightly different name. As typical examples, the identification for two reasonably well-known printers varies as shown here:

Printer Identified As:	In File:	Identification Is:
HP LaserJet 4/4M	OEMSETUP.INF	In [io.device] section
HP LaserJet 4	HPPCL5E.DRV	At address cs:0B8F
IBM Proprinter	CONTROL.INF	In [io.device] section
PROPRINT	PROPRINT.DRV	At address cs:0365

When either printer driver is installed, the printer identification is taken from OEMSETUP.INF and written into the WIN.INI file as shown here:

```
[windows]                 (this section lists one default printer only)
device=HP LaserJet 4/4M,HPPCL5E, (printer port)
device=IBM Proprinter,proprint, (printer port)

[PrinterPorts]
HP LaserJet 4/4M=HPPCL5E, (printer port, timeout settings)
IBM Proprinter=proprint, (printer port, timeout settings)

[devices]
HP LaserJet 4/4M=HPPCL5E, (printer port)
IBM Proprinter=proprint, (printer port)
```

However, if OEMSETUP.INF is not available, then the identification is taken from the driver's own internal reference, which is slightly different, as shown above. In the HP example, the apparently insignificant difference may become significant later on, if you try to install the optional Hewlett-Packard *Screen Font Pack* for the printer. Its Setup procedure looks at the [windows] section of WIN.INI to make sure that "HP LaserJet 4/4M=" is there. If it isn't, then the setup procedure is aborted.

As for your own printer, a similar subtle difference may prevent some add-on accessory from being successfully installed if the setup procedure examines WIN.INI and doesn't find what it needs. And in some cases, a Windows application may hang up on opening. Therefore, in case of doubt it's probably worth the bother to trot out the original distribution diskettes whenever you need to reinstall a driver.

Printer Drivers Supplied with Windows. Table 9.4 lists the printer driver files currently supplied with Windows and Windows-for-Workgroups. For file size and location, refer to the Diskette Directory in Appendix A. If you need a driver whose name does not appear on either list, then you may need to contact the printer manufacturer to get it, or refer to the Microsoft Library files, as described immediately below.

TABLE 9.4   Windows Printer Drivers*

Driver Name	Ext.	Driver Name	Ext.	Driver Name	Ext.
40291730	WPD	FUJI24	DRV [†]	L330_52&	WPD
40293930	WPD	GENDRV	DLL	L500_493	WPD
CANON10E	DRV	HERMES_1	WPD	L530_52&	WPD
CANON130	DRV	HERMES_2	WPD	L630_52&	WPD
CANON330	DRV	HP_3D522	WPD	LBPII	DRV
CIT9US	DRV	HP_3P522	WPD	LBPIII	DRV
CIT24US	DRV	HPDSKJET	DRV	MT_TI101	WPD
CITOH	DRV	HPELI523	WPD	N2090522	WPD
DEC1150	WPD	HPIID522	WPD	N2290520	WPD
DEC2150	WPD	HPIIP522	WPD	N2990523	WPD
DEC2250	WPD	HPIII522	WPD	N890_470	WPD
DEC3250	WPD	HPPCL	DRV	N890X505	WPD
DECCOLOR	WPD	HPPCL5A	DRV [†]	NCM40519	WPD
DECLPS20	WPD	HPPCL5MS	DRV [‡]	NCM80519	WPD
DICONIX	DRV	HPPLOT	DRV	NEC24PIN	DRV
DJ500C	DRV [††]	IBM4019	DRV	O5241503	WPD
DM309	DRV	IBM5204	DRV	O5242503	WPD
DMCOLOR	DLL	IBM17521	WPD	OKI9	DRV
EPL75523	WPD	IBM39521	WPD	OKI9IBM	DRV
EPSON9	DRV	IBMCOLOR	DRV	OKI24	DRV
EPSON24	DRV	L100_425	WPD [‡]	OL840518	WPD
ESCP2	DRV	L200230&	WPD	OLIVETI1	WPD
EXECJET	DRV	L300_471	WPD [‡]	OLIVETI2	WPD
FUJI9	DRV [†]	L300_493	WPD [‡]	P4455514	WPD

TABLE 9.4 *(continued)*

Driver Name	Ext.	Driver Name	Ext.	Driver Name	Ext.
PAINTJET	DRV	Q2200510	WPD	TKPHZR21	WPD
PANSON9	DRV	Q820_517	WPD	TKPHZR31	WPD
PANSON24	DRV	QWIII	DRV	TOSHIBA	DRV
PG306	DRV [†]	SEIKO_04	WPD	TRIUMPH1	WPD
PHIIPX	WPD	SEIKO_14	WPD	TRIUMPH2	WPD
PROPRINT	DRV	THINKJET	DRV	TTY	DRV
PROPRN24	DRV	TI850	DRV	U9415470	WPD
PS1	DRV	TIM17521	WPD	UNIDRV	DLL
PSCRIPT	DRV	TIM35521	WPD		

[*] Refer to Appendix A for file size and diskette location.
  WPD extension indicates Postscript Description file.
[†] Windows 3.1 only.
[††] Available from Hewlett-Packard.
[‡] Windows-for-Workgroups only.

Printer Drivers in the Microsoft Library. In addition to the printer drivers supplied on the Windows distribution diskettes, other drivers are available for downloading from the Microsoft Library (GO MSL on CompuServe). The library may also contain drivers that have been recently updated. For example, Table 9.5 lists those drivers currently available for downloading. Compare the listed date for the file of interest and, if it is later than the driver you currently use, it may be worth downloading. Refer to Appendix D if you need more information about downloading these or other files.

Printer Driver Support Files. Every time you change local printer ports and do a print job, your WIN.INI file may grow a few more lines, as shown by this typical example:

```
[HPPCL5E,LPTx]                          x = installed printer port
prtcaps2=13779
FontSummary=C:\WINDOWS\FS5ELPTx.PCL   x = installed printer port
```

The section, or something close to it, is repeated for each printer port ever used with the printer, which in this case is the Hewlett-Packard LaserJet 4. In addition, the Windows directory contains a copy of FS5ELPTx.PCL for each port. If you regularly switch from one port to another, you may as well leave all this in place. However, once you settle on a permanent residence for the printer, you may want to edit WIN.INI to remove the redundant references. You also can erase all but one of the

FS5ELPT*x*.PCL files. Other printers may create similar WIN.INI sections and other support files.

TABLE 9.5 Windows Printer Drivers in Microsoft Library (GO MSL on CompuServe)*

Printer	Filename	Date	Printer	Filename	Date
Agfa Compugraphic			**Epson**		
Genics	HPPCL	10/08/92	ActionLaser II	EPLZR	10/08/92
Apricot Laser	HPPCL	10/08/92	AP-3250, 5000, 5500 ESC/P 2	ESCP2	01/15/93
Brother					
HJ-100, 770	BROHL	10/08/92	DFX-5000	EP9	03/12/93
HL-4, 8, 8d, 8e	BROHL	10/08/92	DLQ-2000	EP24	10/08/92
M-1309, M-1809, M-1909	BRO9	10/08/92	EPL-4000, EPL-7000 ESC/P2	EPLZR ESCP2	10/08/92 01/15/93
M-1324, M-1824L, M-1924L	BRO24	10/08/92	EX-800, EX-1000	EP9	03/12/93
Bull Compuprint series	BULL	10/08/92	FX-80, 80+, 85, 86e	EP9	03/12/93
Canon			FX-100, 100+, 105, 185, 286, 286e	EP9	03/12/93
Bubble-Jet BJ-10, 20, 130 series	CANON	10/08/92	FX-800, FX-850, FX-1000, FX-1050	EP9	03/12/93
Bubble-Jet BJ-200	CANON2	12/09/92	JX-80	EP9	03/12/93
Bubble-Jet BJ-300, BJ-330	CANON3	10/20/92	L-750, L-1000	EP24	10/08/92
			LQ-100 ESC/P 2	ESCP2	01/15/93
Bubble-Jet BJC-800	CANON	10/08/92	LQ-200, 400, 450, 500, 510	EP24	10/08/92
Citizen			LQ-570, 870, 1070, 1170 series	ESCP2	01/15/93
120D, 120D+, 180D, GX series	CIT9	10/08/92			
124D, 224, GSX series	CIT24	10/08/92	LQ-800, 850, 860	EP24	10/08/92
HSP-500, HSP-550	CIT9	10/08/92	LQ-950, 1000, 1010,11050, 1060	EP24	10/08/92
PN48	CIT24	10/08/92			
Prodot 9, 9x	CIT9	10/08/92	LQ-1500, 2500, 2550	EP24	10/08/92
Prodot 24	CIT24	10/08/92	LX-80, 86, 400, 800, 810, 850, 850+	EP9	03/12/93
PROjet	JP350	12/09/92			
Swift 9, 9x	CIT9	10/08/92	MX-80, 80 F/T, 100	EP9	03/12/93
Swift 24, 24e, 24x	CIT24	10/08/92	RX-80, 80 F/T, F/T+, 100, 100+	EP9	03/12/93
Diconix 150 +	DICONX	10/20/92			
Digital			SQ-850	EP24	10/08/92
DEClaser series	DEC1	02/03/93	SQ-870, 1170 ESC/P 2	ESCP2	01/15/93
DECmultiJET 1000, 2000	JP350	12/09/92	SQ-2000, 2500, 2550	EP24	10/08/92
			T-750, 1000	EP9	03/12/93
LA, LJ, LN series	DEC1	02/03/93			

TABLE 9.5 *(continued)*

Printer	Filename	Date	Printer	Filename	Date
Fujitsu			**NEC**		
PrintPartner series	FJ10W3	03/12/93	Pinwriter series	NECP24	02/09/93
Breeze 100, 200	JP350	12/09/92	Silentwriter LC 860	HPPCL	10/08/92
DL 900, 1100, 1200	FUJI24	12/09/92	Plus		
DL 3350, 3450, 3600,	FUJI24	12/09/92	**Okidata**		
4400, 4600			LaserLine 6	HPPCL	10/08/92
DX 2100, 2200, 2300,	FUJI9	10/20/92	ML series	OKI24	10/08/92
2400			Okidata OL-400, OL-	OKILED	10/08/92
Generic Printer Driver	GENDRV	02/03/93	800		
1.68			OL-830	OK830	12/09/92
Hewlett-Packard			DM 124 C	OLIVE	02/03/93
DeskJet series	HPDJET	02/09/93	ETV 5000	HPPCL	10/08/92
DeskJet 500	HPDJET	02/09/93	JP 150, 350, 350S	JP350	12/09/92
LaserJet, LaserJet II	HPPCL	10/08/92	PG 108, 208 M2	HPPCL	10/08/92
series			PG 306, 308	OLIPG	11/16/92
LaserJet III series	HPPCL5	11/16/92	PG 308 HS	HPPCL	10/08/92
LaserJet 4/4M	HPCL5E	03/12/93	**Panasonic**		
PaintJet, PaintJet XL	HPPJET	10/08/92	KX-P1081, 1180,	PAN9	02/09/93
QuietJet, QuietJet +	HPQJET	10/08/92	1695, 2180		
IBM			KX-P1123, 1124,	PAN24	12/09/92
Laser Printer 4029	IB4029	02/03/93	1124i, 1624		
Personal Printer II	IB2390	10/08/92	KX-P2123, 2124, 2624	PAN24	12/09/92
2300 series			KX-P4420	HPPCL	10/08/92
Proprinter, II, III, XL,	PROP9	10/08/92	KX-P4450, 4450i	PANKX	10/20/92
XL II, XL III			**QMS** QMS-PS 200	PS2000	12/09/92
Proprinter X24, X24e,	PROP24	10/20/92	**QuadLaser** QuadLaser I	HPPCL	10/08/92
XL24, XL24e			**Royal** CJP 450	OLIVE	02/03/93
QuickWriter 5204	IB5204	11/16/92	**Seiko**		
QuietWriter III	QWIII	11/16/92	CH 4104, 5504, 5514	SEIKO	02/03/93
Kyocera F-Series	HPPCL	10/08/92	CH 4104 (PS)	PS4104	02/03/93
(USA)			CH 5504 (PS)	SEIKO2	02/03/93
Linotronic 100- 600	LINO	12/09/92	CH 5514 (PS)	CH5514	02/03/93
series			**Sharp** JX-9300, 9500	SHARP	10/08/92
Mannesmann Tally	MANNT	10/08/92	series, 9700		
MT series			**Star**		
Microsoft PostScript	PSCRIP	12/09/92	Laserprinter 4, 8 series	STAR	10/08/92
Driver 3.55			NB24-10, 15	STAR	10/08/92
			NL-10, NX series, SJ-48	STAR	10/08/92
			XB series, XR series	STAR	10/08/92

TABLE 9.5 *(continued)*

Printer	Filename	Date	Printer	Filename	Date
Tandy LP-1000	HPPCL	10/08/92	**Unisys**		
Tegra Genesis	HPPCL	10/08/92	AP-1324, 1337, 1339	UNI24	10/08/92
Texas Instr. Omnilaser	TIOMNI	12/09/92	AP-1371	UN1371	10/08/92
2108, 2115			AP-9205/AP-9210	UNILZ	10/08/92
Toshiba			**Universal** Printer	UNIDRV	10/08/92
ExpressWriter 420, 440	EXPRSS	10/08/92	Driver 3.1.2		
PageLaser12	HPPCL	10/08/92	**Wang** LDP8	HPPCL	10/08/92
P351, P1351	TOSH24	08/12/92			
P351SX	P351SX	10/08/92			

*All files are self-extracting. Download as *filename*.EXE and execute at DOS prompt to expand.

Port Configuration

Although the information in this section is described in terms of printer driver configuration, most of it should hold up reasonably well when configuring just about anything else that needs a parallel or serial port interface (for the latter, a modem comes immediately to mind). Therefore, if you need to configure a port for use with something other than a printer, just follow the procedures described here and make the necessary nomenclature corrections as you go along.

The section also introduces the *Ports* applet which provides separate access to serial port configuration, with more information in Chapter 11.

Network Printer Port Selection (Workgroups)

If there is only one printer on a network system of two or more computers, there shouldn't be much confusion about accessing it. Although the printer is physically attached to LPT1 (presumably) on only one computer, it can also be designated as LPT1 on every other network computer. However, what if two or more computers have printers physically attached to their respective LPT1 connectors?

In the ideal environment, each operator knows what printers are really attached to each local computer, but when was the last time you worked in an ideal environment? Of course, you can always *look* to see what printers are really there, but that's such a low-tech trick that perhaps it shouldn't even be mentioned here. For example, consider a two-computer network in which an HP LaserJet 4 is physically connected to LPT1 on an ALR computer, and an old IBM Proprinter is connected to LPT1 on a DELL computer. The latter computer has drivers installed for both printers, and prints to the remote LaserJet whenever something important needs printing.

Before connecting to the network printer, the Dell Print Manager's Workspace looks like this:

HP LaserJet 4/4M on LPT1 (not shared)
<u>IBM Proprinter on LPT1 (not shared)</u> (*underline indicates current default printer*)

If the Dell user connects to the network printer and makes it the default, the Dell Workspace changes to:

<u>HP LaserJet 4/4M on LPT1 (\\ALR\HP)</u> (*underline indicates current default printer*)
IBM Proprinter on LPT1 (\\ALR\HP)

Both reports are misleading: In the first, there is really no LaserJet on the Dell's LPT1, and in the second, the Proprinter is certainly not attached to the remote ALR's LPT1. Furthermore, in the second example, the icons next to both printers have changed to network printer icons (see Figure 9.5), which suggests that the local Proprinter is actually attached to the remote computer.

All that needs to be done to resolve these potentially confusing reports is to reconfigure the Dell computer's LaserJet printer driver. Disconnect it from LPT1 and connect it to the physically nonexistent LPT3, to produce a Workspace report that looks like this:

HP LaserJet 4/4M on LPT3 (\\ALR\HP) (*icon shows this is a network printer*)
IBM Proprinter on LPT1 (not shared) (*icon shows this is not a network printer*)

When the Dell user subsequently disconnects from the network printer, the first line above changes to:

HP LaserJet 4/4M on LPT3 (not shared)

The LPT3 serves as a visual reminder that this printer is in fact still located elsewhere.

The Ports List

To change the port assigned to the printer listed in the Connect dialog box (Figure 9.13), highlight the new port that you wish to use. The ports listed in the Ports: box are read from the [ports] section of WIN.INI, and include the following listings, each on a separate line:

Parallel	**Serial**	**Other**
LPT1:=	COM1:=9600,n,8,1,x	EPT:=
LPT2:=	COM2:=9600,n,8,1,x	FILE:=
LPT3:=	COM3:=9600,n,8,1,x	LPT1.DOS=
	COM4:=9600,n,8,1,x	LPT2.DOS=

Refer to the following sections for information about each of these port types.

Parallel Ports (LPT1:-3:).   To assign one of these ports to a driver, simply highlight its name in the Ports: box and, if the printer is local, click on the OK Button to close the Connect dialog box. If you need to set up a network printer, click on the Network... button, which is enabled only if a parallel port (LPT*x*:) is selected. Refer to *Network Printer Configuration* above for additional information.

Serial Ports (COM1:-4:). Selection.   If a serial port (COM1— 4) is selected, the Settings... button is enabled instead. In this case, refer to *Serial Port Configuration* below.

EPT:=.   This is a special-purpose enhanced parallel port for the IBM Personal Pageprinter, which requires its own adapter card. Refer to that printer's *User's Guide* for additional information.

File:=.   Select this "port" if you want to write a print job into a printer file on diskette or hard disk instead of sending it to a printer. The next time you select an application's Print option, a Print to File dialog box (not shown) will prompt you to enter a name for the file you wish to create. To send that file later on to a printer on LPT1, type the following command at the DOS prompt:

COPY *filename.ext* LPT1

The printed output should look no different than if it had been printed directly from the application to the printer. This procedure may be convenient if you need to send a file elsewhere for printing; that is, to a printer that is not connected to the network, or to the printer at the site where the document was created. The only limitation is that the printer specified in the Print Setup box must match the one that will later be used for the actual print job.

LPT1.DOS=, LPT2.DOS= (*note absence of colon after* DOS *extension*).   If one of these ports is specified, Windows writes your print job to a file with the indicated name. That file is then sent to the printer, and the Print Manager and normal Windows error-checking system are bypassed. This alternative printing technique may be required if network software does not support the conventional default printing system. However, with error-checking disabled, the resultant print job may be garbled if there is some other problem.

The DOS extension is not critical, and may be replaced by any extension you like. It is the presence of an extension, and not the choice of letters, that determines if this procedure is enabled.

LPT1.OS2=, LPT2.OS2=. If your [ports] section has these lines instead of those described immediately above, you probably upgraded from Windows 3.0, which used the OS2 extension. The upgrade Setup procedure does not change these lines, nor is there any reason to do so, unless you too want to pretend that OS2 does not exist.

Special Purpose Drivers. Some applications add a special-purpose driver to the [ports] section of WIN.INI. For example, Microsoft's *PowerPoint* adds a Genigraphics driver (GEN1:=), which may be used to save files to disk (not to the printer) in a format used by Genigraphic service centers. Such drivers may also provide additional configuration options unique to the application; a few of these are briefly described in *Special Purpose Print Setup* in the *Print Setup Reconfiguration* section later in the chapter.

Special-purpose drivers are not further discussed in this book; this one is mentioned here (and below) just as an example of what may be found in this section of WIN.INI.

Changing the [ports] List. Although Windows supports up to nine parallel ports, only three are listed by default in the [ports] section of WIN.INI. If that's not enough to keep you busy, you can edit the section to specify additional ports (LPT4: through LPT9:). Note, however, that Windows does not support more than 10 installed drivers in this section.

Serial Port Configuration

If you select a serial port for your printer, the Networks... button described earlier is disabled and the Settings... button is enabled instead. Click on that button to open the Settings for COMx: dialog box shown in Figure 9.16a. Click on any of the down-arrows in the dialog box to change settings, as required. Or click on the Advanced... button to open the Advanced Settings dialog box shown in Figure 9.16b.

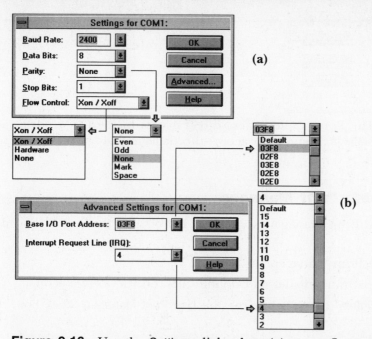

Figure 9.16   Use the Settings dialog box (a) to configure the basic serial port settings. Click on the Advanced... button to open (b) the Advanced Settings dialog box.

Note that these communication-port settings affect any serial device (modem, printer, etc.) connected to the specified COM port.

Direct Serial Port Configuration.   If all you need to do is change the configuration of a serial port, you can access the desired COM*x* port by double-clicking on the *Ports* icon to display the Ports dialog box shown in Figure 9.17. Click once on the desired COM port, then on the **S**et-tings... button to open the Settings dialog box described above.

Print Manager Configuration

This section describes various procedures to configure the Print Manager applet as required for optimum performance. In this section it is assumed that at least one printer is already installed and operational. If this is not the case, then refer to *Printer Driver Installation* in the *Printers Applet Configuration* section above.

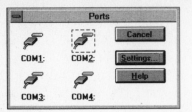

Figure 9.17 The Ports applet offers direct access to the COM ports. Click on the Settings... button to access the Settings dialog box shown in Figure 9.16.

Enable or Disable Print Manager

By default, the Print Manager is enabled. Follow this three-step procedure to disable it:

1. Close the Print Manager.
2. Open the Control Panel and double-click on the *Printers* icon.
3. In the Printers dialog box, clear the Use Print Manager check box.

Load Print Manager at Startup

If you put a copy of the Print Manager icon in the StartUp Group Window, it will be loaded every time Windows opens. However, even if the applet is not placed there, it will still appear as a minimized icon if your system is configured to reshare a printer at startup, as described in *Re-share at Startup* in the *Printer Sharing Configuration* section below.

Print Manager Window Configuration

This section describes the many options that may be used to change the general appearance of the Print Manager Window and its Workspace area. Unless otherwise noted by a parenthetical reference in the section header, the configuration information applies to both Windows and Windows-for-Workgroups.

Header Bar (Workgroups). As noted in the View Menu section earlier in the chapter, the Print Manager display of print queue Status, Size, and Time columns can be independently toggled on and off. In addition, the horizontal position of each of these headers and the column beneath it can be adjusted.

To move all three headers left or right, place the mouse pointer over the vertical bar to the immediate left of the Status column. The pointer should change to a vertical bar and horizontal double arrow. If you hold down the primary mouse button and drag the bar left or right, all three headers will shift accordingly. Release the button when the Status column is at the desired position. To move the Size and Time columns while keeping the Status column fixed, repeat the procedure by placing the mouse pointer over the bar to the left of the Size header, or place it to the left of the Time header to move only that column.

You can accomplish the same thing by selecting Set Column Widths on the Options Menu. In this case, the double-arrow cursor appears in the Print Manager Window, somewhere below the Status header. Drag it left or right as desired, and click the primary mouse button when the three headers are where you want them. To "fine tune" the positions of the other two headers, don't click the primary mouse button yet. Instead, press the Tab key to toggle the mouse pointer to the Size header. Adjust its position as required, then Tab again to adjust the position of the Time header. When all three are where you want them, click the primary mouse button to exit the adjustment mode.

If you really work at it, you can waste an entire afternoon configuring (tweaking, actually) the Header Bar. And it's quite possible to adjust their positions in such a way that unadjusting becomes difficult, if not impossible. If this happens, refer to the *Header Bar Troubleshooting* section for assistance in restoring order.

Message Bar (Windows). The Message Bar (see Figure 9.4a) displays a continuously updated report of printer status. In the case of a network (remote) printer, the update feature may be enabled or disabled by selecting Network Settings... on the Options Menu to display the Network Options dialog box (not shown). Check or clear the check box next to Update Network Display, as desired. For example, if a network printer problem has recently occurred, the message box may or may not report it, as shown in this typical example:

Check Box	Message Box Report
Checked	A general network error has occurred. Try again.
Cleared	The HP LaserJet 4/4M on \\ALR\HP (LPT3) is Printing.

Status Bar Text (Workgroups). To change the font and point size for the Status Bar text, refer to *Status Bar Text Configuration* in the *Font Configuration* section of Chapter 10.

Other Configuration Options

This section describes a few more options that may be helpful in optimizing your printer configuration.

Custom Separator File Preparation (Workgroups). As noted earlier, you can create a file containing a graphics image to be used as a Custom Separator Page between print jobs, using either of the procedures described here. Once you've created or located the necessary CLP or WMF file, refer to Separator Pages... on the Print Manager's Options Menu above for instructions on how to put it to use.

> **NOTE:** Although a Custom Separator Page may be graphically interesting, it's of limited practical value since it doesn't identify the remote printer whose job is about to be printed. If this is no problem, then try it out. Otherwise you may want to stick with one of the other separator options.

Clipboard File As Page Separator (filename.CLP). Although the Print Manager's online Help Screen states that a custom separator file cannot be created via Windows-for-Workgroups accessories, it can. It may not be worth it, but it can. Open Paintbrush, import or create a new bitmap graphic image, and copy it to the Clipboard. Then save that image as CUSTOM.CLP (or as *anything*.CLP).

The Print Manager may take a long time to print a CLP file as a page separator, and your printer may have troubles of its own. For example, a Hewlett-Packard LaserJet 4 may print the separator page but display a W1 IMAGE ADAPT message on its readout, indicating the graphics image was too complex to print. Other printers may not do as well. Therefore, this method may be useful only for general testing purposes.

Metafile As Page Separator (filename.WMF). As a practical alternative, use any available Windows metafile (WMF extension), such as those found in the WINWORD\CLIPART directory and its subdirectories (assuming you have them). Or search your hard disk for any other metafiles, by typing DIR *.WMF /S at the DOS prompt.

Several utilities, such as the Microsoft *MSDraw* applet, or Computer Associates *Cricket Paint,* can import metafiles but can neither create nor save a file in the required metafile format. If you want to create your own custom WMF file, or convert some other image format, you'll need an application such as

Corel's *CorelDRAW!* or Microsoft's *PowerPoint* to do it. The advantage of such a file is that it's reasonably small and prints easily.

Background Printing Priority. Both Windows and Windows-for-Workgroups provide options to specify the amount of CPU time that is allocated to the Print Manager. However, the means of accessing these options varies, as described here.

Set Printing Priority **(Windows).** The Options Menu lists the three priorities described below. Place a check mark next to the priority you wish to enable.

Set Printing Priority **(Workgroups).** Instead of a direct display of the printing priority choices on the Options Menu, click on that menu's Background Printing... option to open the Background Printing dialog box shown in Figure 9.18.

Low Priority. At low priority, maximum CPU time is devoted to running applications. As a practical consequence, print jobs take longer than normal. Select this option if you prefer optimum application performance at the cost of slower printing.

Normal Priority. This is the default setting, which evenly distributes CPU time between applications and print jobs. Use it as the reference point against which to compare the other two priority options.

High Priority. Maximum CPU time is allocated for printing. This option may be preferred when the print job was due yesterday and everything else can wait until its done.

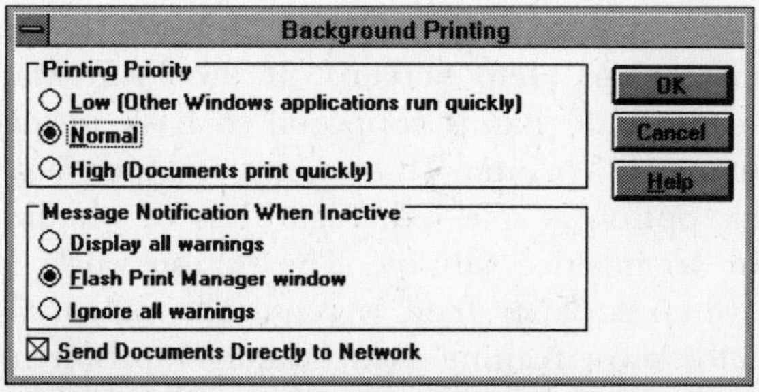

Figure 9.18 The Background Printing dialog box in Windows-for-Workgroups

Message Notification. In most routine operations, the Print Manager runs as a minimized icon while some other application occupies the user's attention on the Windows Desktop. The information presented here allows you to specify the way in which the Print Manager will notify you if it becomes inactive due to a problem that requires attention. As above, the configuration procedure varies between Windows and Windows-for-Workgroups.

Message Notification **(Windows).** The Options Menu lists the three notification formats that are available. Place a check mark next to the one you wish to enable.

Message Notification when Inactive **(Workgroups).** Again, there is an intermediate step. Click on the Options Menu's Background Printing... option to open the Background Printing dialog box shown in Figure 9.18. Then click on one of the radio buttons to select the appropriate option.

> **NOTE:** The specified message notification applies only to the local computer. If a remote computer has sent a print job to the local Print Manager, an error message will be displayed on the remote Print Manager's Status Bar, but that Print Manager window must be open in order to see the message. There is no other warning of trouble at the print site.

Alert Always (Windows); *Display all warnings* (Workgroups). An error message is prominently displayed on your screen, thus interrupting whatever you were doing. In most cases you can click on a Cancel button to clear the message and return to your application.

Flash if Inactive (Windows); *Flash Print Manager window* (Workgroups). In theory, the Print Manager icon flashes if "a situation requires your attention" (according to the Workgroups Help Screen). If the Print Manager window is open but inactive, its Title Bar is supposed to flash instead. In practice, however, most "situations" (printer off-line, out-of-paper, etc.) display an error message if this option is selected, regardless of whether the Print Manager is an icon or an inactive window. The option works as described with some plotters when a paper feed is required, and may work in other isolated cases. But for most routine Print Manager problems, the flashing feature is not yet implemented.

Ignore if Inactive (Windows); *Ignore all warnings* (Workgroups). The printer can go up in smoke and you won't be disturbed with a warning. You'll have to open the Print Manager Window to see how the print job is progressing.

Bypass Local Print Manager. When sending documents to a network (remote) printer, the document makes a few stops along the way. First stop is at the local Print Manager, which sends it on to the network Print Manager, which sends it to the network printer. A bit of time may be saved by cutting out the first stop. But despite what the online Help Screen says, the document is *not* sent directly to the network printer. Instead, it winds up in the remote print queue, just like any other document. If your local queue is paused with several documents in it, you can enable this option to send the next document out ahead of all those in that queue.

In each description given here, it is assumed that a network printer is the local default printer. If a local printer is the default, this option has no effect.

Print Net Jobs Direct **(Windows).** Select Network Settings... on the Options Menu to display the Network Options dialog box (not shown). Check or clear the check box next to Print Net Jobs Direct, as desired.

Send Documents Directly to Network **(Workgroups).** The option appears next to a check box near the bottom of the Background Printing dialog box shown in Figure 9.18. Check or clear it, as desired.

Printer Sharing Configuration. If you wish to share or change the sharing configuration of a local printer, follow the procedures listed here.

Select Printer. Highlight the appropriate local printer in the Print Manager Workspace. If you wish to share the printer immediately without making configuration changes, simply select the Share Printer As... option, and click on the OK button to do so. Otherwise, continue reading here.

Begin Configuration. Open the Printer Menu and select the Share Printer As... option to display the Share Printer dialog box in Figure 9.19. Enter the appropriate information in the four boxes, as described below.

Share Printer	
Printer:	HP LaserJet 4/4M on LPT1 ▾	OK
Share as:	HP	Cancel
Comment:	Use for important documents only.	Help
Password:	SECRET	☐ Re-share at Startup

Figure 9.19   The Share Printer dialog box

Printer:. This box identifies the local printer whose name is currently highlighted in the Print Manager applet's Workspace. If you wish to share some other printer instead, you can click on the down arrow and select that printer. However, the information in the other three boxes does not change accordingly. Therefore, if you wish to make changes to the rest of this configuration, first return to the Print Manager Workspace, highlight the printer you wish to share, then reselect the Share Printer As... option to display the appropriate information for the selected printer.

Share as:. Enter a name (12 characters or less) that will appear in parentheses following the printer name in the Workspace, as shown here:

IBM Proprinter on LPT1 (shared as OLD PRINTER)

Comment:. The text entered here (48 characters or less) appears in the Program Manager Status Bar on the remote system, if the remote user highlights this printer in the Workspace area.

Password:. Enter a password to restrict access to those users who will be given the password. Unlike other password applications, this one remains visible in the box and reappears on subsequent sessions whenever the Share Printer dialog box is opened. Therefore, it you don't want snoopers to see the password, you may want to take advantage of the *Disable Changes to Printer Sharing Configuration* option (see below). This prevents busybodies from accessing the Share Printer As... option, and therefore from seeing the password.

Re-share at Startup. Place a check mark in this box if you want to make the printer available for sharing every time you open Windows. In this case the Print Manager icon will appear on the Desktop every time Windows opens. If the box is cleared, you will have to go through the sharing procedure every time you reopen Windows and want to share the printer.

Save Configuration. The first time you share a printer, clicking the OK button saves the comment and password (if any) in an encoded

SHARES.PWL file in the Windows directory. If you subsequently change either text string and want to save the change(s) for future use, you must also change the re-share status or the text in the Share as: box. If you don't want either of these to be changed, do it anyway. Then close and reopen the Print Manager and change it back to whatever it's supposed to be. If do don't do this, the new comment and/or password are not written into SHARES.PWL and therefore are valid for the present session only. The re-share status itself is saved as reshare=yes (*or* =no) in the [network] section of SYSTEM.INI.

Disable Changes to Printer Sharing Configuration (**Workgroups**). The Share Printer As... and Stop Sharing Printer... options may be removed from the Print Manager's Printers Menu by editing the indicated section of WIN.INI, as described here:

```
[spooler]
NoShareCommands=1
```

When you close and reopen Windows, it will no longer be possible to share a local printer, nor to stop sharing such a printer if it was shared before the line was added. You might want to add this line after setting up the desired printer-sharing configuration so that a user can't alter the sharing status of the local printer(s).

Print Queue Management

If there are multiple documents in the print queue, the techniques described here can be used to resequence, delete, or pause those documents.

Resequencing Print Jobs. The Print Manager Window displays the print queue (if any) on your local printer and also the queue(s) on any connected network printers. With the exception of the first job in the queue (whose position remains fixed until the job is printed) you may use the Document Menu's Move Document Up/Down options to resequence any print queue, subject to the limitations described here.

NOTE: If you resequence a print job, the effect should appear almost immediately in the Print Manager Window at the network printer's computer. However, it may take several seconds until the changes appear in other Print Manager Windows, even the one on the local computer where the changes were initiated.

Resequence Local Print Queue. If it's your own printer, you're in charge and you can resequence the print queue however you like.

Resequence Remote Print Queue. Your resequencing privileges are limited to your own files that await printing, as described here. If you have sent say, three files (*a, b, c*) to the remote print queue, you can only shuffle these files by moving *a* and/or *b* down. If another file (*d*) from elsewhere follows yours, you cannot move any of your files still lower in the queue.

Drag-and-Drop Resequencing. Subject to the limitations described above, you can resequence the files in the print queue by selecting any document icon and dragging it to a new location in the queue. As long as the icon remains in a valid location, an up-and-down arrow is displayed. However, if you drag the icon to an illegal position in the print queue, the arrows are replaced by a circle with a diagonal line through it.

Deleting or Pausing a Print Job. Use the procedures described here to delete or pause a document in the print queue.

Delete File in Local Print Queue. Highlight any file in the queue, then select the Document Menu's <u>D</u>elete Document option to remove that file from the queue. You may delete any document, including those placed in the queue by remote users.

Delete File in Remote Print Queue. You can only delete your own files from a remote print queue. If you highlight someone else's file and open the Document Menu, you'll find that all menu options are disabled.

Pause Local Document. Oddly enough, you can't pause a local document awaiting printing on the local computer. You can pause the printer itself, but that halts printing of all documents in the queue.

Pause Remote Document. If remote users have placed print jobs in your local printer's print queue, you can highlight any such file and select the Document Menu's P<u>a</u>use Printing Document option to suspend printing of that file. When the file reaches the top of the queue, the file immediately below it will be printed instead.

Temporary Directory Location

If you have not already created a temporary directory, now's the time to do it. Many applications use this directory to store temporary files, and the Windows Print Manager makes extensive use of it, as described in the *Print Manager Support Files* section which follows.

To set up the required directory, log onto the drive C root directory and type MD TEMP at the DOS prompt. Then add the lines listed below to your AUTOEXEC.BAT file and reboot. Although the SET TMP= line is not essential, some programs—especially older ones—look for a TMP instead of a TEMP variable.

TEMP directory on Hard drive	On RAM drive (but see text)
	MD X:\TEMP
SET TEMP=C:\TEMP	SET TEMP=X:\TEMP
SET TMP=C:\TEMP	SET TMP=X:\TEMP
	(X = RAM drive letter)

If the Print Manager can't find a valid temporary directory, it writes its temporary files directly into the Windows directory. If all goes well, the files are automatically deleted when no longer needed. But things happen, and sometimes a few such files get left behind. In time, your Windows directory can get rather cluttered with leftovers. Other temporary files may be found in the root directory itself, or in the DOS directory. So it's worth the time it takes to set up a temporary file.

Some users put the temporary file on a RAM drive. The idea is that the files will be written and read faster than on a hard disk, and the leftovers will be conveniently disposed of every time the system is rebooted or turned off. However, such files will be *in*conveniently lost if there's a power failure or if you need to reboot. So you may want to rethink this idea before doing anything that's really important.

Print Manager Support Files

While files await printing, the Print Manager stores them in the temporary directory. With one or more files in the print queue, you can view these temporary files by opening a DOS Window and typing DIR C:\TEMP.

As each file is printed, the associated files in the temporary directory are deleted. Note that the TMP and SPL extensions are included in *Undelete's* File Exclusion List, so that utility's Delete Sentry mode does not offer undelete protection. Refer to the *File Exclusion List* section of Chapter 0 and to Table 0.13 for further details.

Local Print Manager File (~SPL0E68.TMP, or similar). If a file is sent to the local Print Manager from an application on the local computer, it is stored in multiple files under filenames beginning with ~SPL and ending with a TMP extension.

Remote Print Manager File (0002.SPL, or similar). A file sent to the local Print Manager from a remote computer arrives in the temporary directory in one piece. The filename (a number) indicates the order in which it arrived, and the SPL extension distinguishes it from local files.

Share Printer Data (SHARES.PWL). This file in the Windows directory contains encoded comments and the passwords for your shared printers. Comments for the network itself are in the [network] section of SYS-TEM.INI.

Print Setup Re-Configuration from within an Application

The File Menu within many Windows applets and applications contains a Print (not Print*er*) Setup... option which may be used to change the printer driver. Several formats of dialog box may be encountered, and their operational differences are reviewed here. The flow chart seen earlier in Figure 9.2 indicates the two points at which the dialog box buttons provide entry into the printer management system. Refer to the *Printer Setup Configuration* and *Network Printer Configuration* sections above for further assistance if needed.

Temporary Printer Reassignment

If the Print Setup dialog box shown in Figure 9.20a is displayed, the radio button indicates that the default printer is enabled, and its name is listed under the button. Click on the Specific Printer: button to temporarily select another printer, and use the down arrow (if necessary) to make your selection. Click on the Network... button if you need to make new network printer connections. In this case, the dialog box shown earlier in Figure 9.14 (Windows) or 9.15 (Workgroups) will appear.

The printer you select will be used for print jobs within the active application only. Windows itself, and all other applications remain configured to the default printer. In fact, if a second copy of the reconfigured applet is opened, that applet will also remain configured to the default printer. When the reconfigured applet closes, the temporary specific printer setting is discarded.

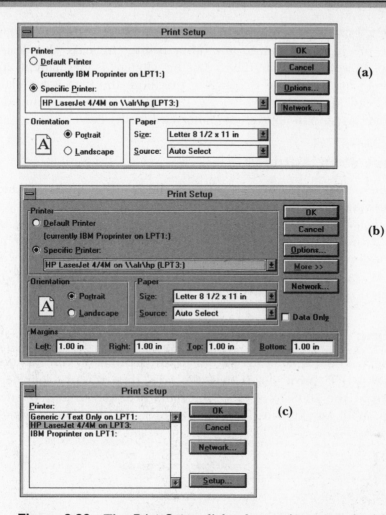

Figure 9.20   The Print Setup dialog box as it appears in (a) most Windows applets, (b) an enhanced version in Microsoft's *Powerpoint* application, and (c) in *Word-for-Windows*.

Some newer applications provide a few additional options in a classier version of this dialog box, such as the example in Figure 9.20b.

Permanent Printer Reassignment

Other applications (Word-for-Windows, for example) offer the dialog box shown in Figure 9.20c. The Setup... and Network... buttons duplicate the previously described functions for these options.

If this dialog box is seen, its Printer: box highlights the current default printer. Move the highlight bar to any other printer to make the desired change. Note, however, that in this case, the change is permanent. You can verify this by arranging the Desktop so that both the Print Setup dialog box and the Print Manager are visible. As the default printer is changed in the former, that change will appear soon afterward in the latter.

Special Purpose Print Setup

As noted earlier, some applications provide a special-purpose driver which, if selected, provides additional configuration options required by the application. As a typical example, Figure 9.21 shows the Print Setup dialog box that appears if the Genigraphic driver supplied with Microsoft's *PowerPoint* is installed. Additional dialog boxes (not shown here) prompt the user for instructions, as appropriate to the application. In this specific example, the file will be saved to hard drive or diskette as *filename*.GNA.

Troubleshooting

Before tearing Windows apart to resolve a printing problem, you may want to exit and try a DOS print job. If that also fails, then the problem needs to be resolved at the DOS level first. Once that's done, reopen Windows and try again. With any kind of luck, the problem will have gone away. If not, keep reading.

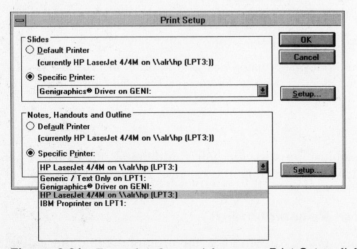

Figure 9.21 Example of a special-purpose Print Setup dialog box, as seen in Microsoft's *PowerPoint*.

Printer Connection Problems

A few problems that may be encountered while trying to establish a connection to a network printer are described here.

Startup Connection Problems. If a printer-related *Error occurred while reconnecting* message shows up when you open Windows, the local computer was configured during a previous session to reconnect itself to a network printer, and for one reason or another that printer can't be found. If you're not sure why that is, then investigate the following possibilities.

Remote Computer Is Not Logged On. This is the easiest one to troubleshoot. If the remote computer is not logged onto the network, then its resources obviously cannot be shared. Check out this possibility before spending much more time wondering what's wrong this time.

Network Printer Is Not Shared. This is also worth investigating. The remote computer user may have disabled printer sharing. It's worth a call to find out.

Network Hardware Problem. There's always the possibility that the physical link has a problem. To verify that the network itself is functioning, open the File Manager's Disk Menu and select the Connect Network Drive... option. Click on any network computer name and a list of its Shared Directories should appear in the Connect Network Drive dialog box (see Figure 6.5 in Chapter 6). If no directories appear, try looking at another network computer. If you can't find any shared directories, it's of course possible that there are none. But what's more likely is that the physical connection at your computer is in trouble. Check the connections carefully and if necessary, the seating of the network card in its slot. Once you've verified that all connections are good, reboot the system and try again.

Connection to a Shared Printer Is Not Successful. If you attempt to connect to a shared network printer and nothing happens when you click on the OK button, then the Path: box probably does not specify a specific printer. Highlight the name of a network printer in the Shared Printers list, or click on the down arrow to the right of the Path: box, and select the computer\printer combination you want and try again.

Header Bar Troubleshooting (Workgroups)

Under certain unique combinations of header positioning, one or more headers may disappear, and toggling the various View Menu options has no visible effect. In this case, try one of the following procedures, as appropriate to the problem. In each case, make sure all three View Menu options are toggled on first. If the Time/Date Sent option will not toggle on, continue reading here.

Time Header Cannot Be Enabled. Due to a minor buglet, the Time header may disappear completely, and toggling the View Menu's Time/Date Sent option will have no effect, as may be noted by a missing check mark next to this option, regardless of how many times it is toggled. In this case, you'll need to edit the WIN.INI file, as described here.

The status of the Header Bar titles is determined by the following line in the WIN.INI file:

```
[spooler]
msctls_headerbar=2C01 6400 6400 6400  (or some other 16-character hexadecimal string)
```

The spaces in the above hexadecimal string are added here for clarity (?) and do not appear in the actual WIN.INI listing. In any case, the entire [spooler] section is an all but undocumented feature. The *Windows-for-Workgroups Resource Kit* concedes that "The [spooler] section is used by Print Manager. Many entries . . . are defined privately [and] . . . should not be changed." Not exactly the last word on configuration, but that's all there is.

A certain amount of trial and error reveals that the three 6400 sequences above determine the condition of the Status, Size, and Time headers. If any one of these headers is disabled by toggling a View Menu option, the equivalent 6400 changes to *xx*FF, where *xx* is some other value, and FF apparently signifies that this header is disabled.

During some Print Manager operations, the above line may be corrupted, introducing a condition in which the Time header becomes disabled, and stays that way. If this happens and no other remedy works, edit the msctls_headerbar line to agree with the string shown above (but without the spaces). This should restore all three headers to their default status and position.

Status and/or Size Header Not Visible. Chances are, the Time header overlays the Size header, or both overlay the Status header. In this case, position the mouse pointer to the right of the vertical header bar that remains visible and move it leftward until the double arrow appears. Then drag the arrows to the right to slide the Size/Time header(s) clear.

All Three Headers Are Missing.   First, maximize the Print Manager Window. Then select Set Column Widths on the Options Menu. The double arrow should appear at the extreme right-hand side of the window. Drag it to the left and the three headers should follow.

Vertical Bars Overwrite Header Bar Titles.   This minor buglet may appear if the View Menu's Time/Date Sent option is toggled off and the right-hand vertical window border is moved while the mouse pointer is on that boarder and also within the Header Bar area. To clean up the Header Bar, just move the mouse pointer out of the Header Bar area and readjust the vertical border again.

Other Print Management Problems

This section contains a mixed bag of print-related problems that may show up during any print job. Although some of these problems are described in terms of a specific applet or application, the same problem may also show up elsewhere.

Application Hangs Up on Opening.   If a previously well-behaved application won't open after you have reconfigured your printer setup, the default printer identification in the [windows] section of WIN.INI may need editing, as described in the *Reinstallation of Printer Driver* section. For example, the apparently minor change from "4/4M" to "4" (for the H-P LaserJet 4) is enough to cause Word-for-Windows to hang up on opening if that printer is the default. If you're not sure of the correct name for your own printer, reinstall it according to the directions in the *Reinstallation . . .* section.

Calendar File Won't Print.   The problem is described in detail in *Notepad File Won't Print* below. However, there is another workaround that is usually successful. Open the File Menu and select the Print Setup... option. Do this twice (the first time, nothing happens). If the Print Setup dialog box shows up the second time around, close it and try the print job again. This time it should work.

Ctrl+Up/Down Arrow Does Not Change Print Job Sequence in Print Queue.   In the Print Manager's Help Screen, the *Changing the Order of Documents* section describes the use of the arrow keys to change the order of jobs in the print queue. This feature is in fact not yet implemented, although it may work in a future release.

Erratic Printer Output. When printing graphics to an IBM Proprinter X24 or XL24, clear the *Fast Printing Directly to Port* check box if the printer output is erratic. Try the same thing if graphics output to other printers is erratic. The *Fast Printing* option was described earlier in this chapter.

Erroneous Error Messages. If a *Printer Stalled, Computer Name Is Invalid* or similar message appears in the Status Bar and the message itself appears to be invalid, it may be caused by a minor buglet in the Network Settings dialog box (which is described in Chapter 11). The erroneous error message appears if a text string of 14 or 15 characters is entered in the Computer Name: box. Reduce the name to 13 characters or less and the problem should go away. If it doesn't, then there is an additional problem that needs to be resolved.

Error Message Does Not Appear in Local Print Manager Workspace. If a local user tries to print a remote file to a network (remote) printer, no error message will appear at the local site if there's a print-related problem.

Garbled Characters at Top of Printed Page. If the print job consists of multiple pages of meaningless characters—often just a line or two at the top of each page—the most likely culprit is an incorrect printer driver. Install the correct driver and try again.

Intermittent Brief System Lockups. If an application on the local computer periodically freezes for a few seconds, the computer may be connected to a network printer on which an error has been detected. The remote computer regularly updates the local Print Manager with an error report, and this may interfere with local keyboard operation. As a typical symptom, a series of keystrokes won't appear immediately on screen, but after a short delay all the characters do show up. If this happens regularly, open the Print Manager and look for an error message. If necessary, disconnect from the network printer until the remote problem is resolved.

Network Printing Problems. If you encounter general print problems during network operations, with no clear indication of the trouble spot, there may be a problem with network software compatibility (presumably, this does not include Windows-for-Workgroups though). If all else fails, open the Printers applet, click on the Connect... button, then clear the

East Printing Direct to Port box. Refer to the section with that name above for further details.

Network Print Job Drops from Print Queue.   If a local printer runs out of paper while printing a local file, the next network file will be discarded from the print queue, although subsequent files will not be affected. The only workaround is for the remote user to resend the print job.

Notepad File Won't Print.   If you attempt to print a Notepad file and nothing happens, it's probably because you changed default printers while Notepad was open. For some reason, it can't cope with this. To verify the problem, open Notepad's File Menu and select the Print Setup... option. If again nothing happens, save the file you are trying to print, exit Notepad, re-open it, and try again. This time it should work. If it doesn't, there is some other Print Manager problem not necessarily related to Notepad.

Print Jobs Don't Print; Separator Pages Do.   If Separator Pages... on the Options Menu is enabled, some printers will print only the first job in the print queue, although separator pages will be dispensed by the printer. This is a known buglet with the following printers:

Canon LBP-4, LBP-8 II, LPB-8 III
IBM Laser Printer 4019
Olivetti DM 109, DM 309

For the moment, the only solution is to disable the Separator Pages... option if one of these printers is to be used.

Print Option on Some File Menus Is Disabled.   The most likely suspect is a missing UNIDRV.DLL file, and a system whose default printer requires that file. In some cases, a *Cannot find UNIDRV.DLL* error message will be seen when you open an applet or application that supports printing, and the File Menu's Print option will be disabled, as shown by the following representative examples:

Applet	*Cannot Find* **Message**	**Print Option Disabled**
Calendar	No	No
Cardfile	No	No
Excel 4.0	No	No
Notepad	No	No
Paintbrush	No	Yes

Applet	*Cannot Find* Message	Print Option Disabled
Word	Yes	Yes
Write	Yes	Yes

In any case, the solution is to exit the applet or application, close Windows and expand a fresh copy of UNIDRV.DL_ into the System directory, as UNIDRV.DLL.

Printout Begins with Multiple Lines of Print-Format Codes. If a document file contains an embedded print field code that the printer driver doesn't support, the printout may begin with multiple lines of printer codes, such as this typical example:

```
gsave
initgraphics
56 512 translate
/wp$xorig 56 def
/wp$yorig 512 def
/wp$(other codes, and so on)
```

There are a few workarounds. If you realize the wrong printer driver is installed by mistake, replace it and try again. However, if the correct driver is installed, you may be able to edit the document to delete the incompatible codes—that is, if you can find them, and there aren't too many of them. In Word-for-Windows, for example, open the View Menu, select the Field Codes option, then look through the document for a "{ *field code* }" such as the example given above.

If that's not practical, then as another alternative edit the document and place a page break at the beginning. Depending on the nature of the problem codes, the document itself may print satisfactorily immediately following the page of codes, which may be discarded. If the printed document is satisfactory except for a certain section, the problem code is probably in that section, and this clue may make it a bit easier to find.

Of course the best solution is to print the file to the proper driver/printer combination; but if that's not possible, then one of these workarounds may be sufficient to produce a readable hardcopy.

Print Queue Is Duplicated in Local Print Manager Workspace. If more than one printer is connected to the same printer port, the same print queue will appear under each printer name in the local Print Manager Workspace. Although each queue is a dynamic "carbon copy" of the one under the default printer name, only the latter is active. The extraneous copies may be ignored.

Share Printer Dialog Box: Comment and/or Password Change Ignored. If you open the Share Printer dialog box (see Figure 9.19) and find that a recent change to the displayed Comment or Password has reverted back to its previous form, it's because your changes were not written into the SHARES.PWL file. To make your desired changes permanent, refer to *Save Configuration* in the *Printer Sharing Configuration* section earlier in the chapter.

Share/Stop Sharing Printer Options Missing from Printer Menu. These options do not appear if Windows-for-Workgroups is running in standard mode. If the options are not available in enhanced mode either, then they have probably been disabled in WIN.INI. Check the *Disable Printer Sharing* section above for further details.

Error Messages

NOTE: Some print-related error messages are not displayed in the usual dialog-box format. Instead, the message appears in the Status Bar at the bottom of the Print Manager Window.

If an error message appears to be erroneous, check *Erroneous Error Messages* in the *Print Manager Troubleshooting* section for a possible solution.

Access has been denied. If you try to move one of your own print jobs up the print queue on a remote printer, this terse message will let you know you're out of luck. Refer to *Resequencing Print Jobs* for further details.

Cannot find UNIDRV.DLL. If this file is missing, this message is seen if you try to open some Windows applets. Click on the Close button a few times and a *Cannot Print* message should appear. Click on that message's OK button and the present message may appear one more time. Another click or two should finally open the applet window. The File Menu's Print... option will be disabled. Exit the applet, close Windows and expand a fresh copy of UNIDRV.DL_ into the System directory, as UNIDRV.DLL.

Cannot Print. Be sure that the printer is connected and set up properly. If it is, then the UNIDRV.DLL file may be missing. If so, some applets—such as Cardfile—display this message instead of the more informative *Cannot find UNIDRV.DLL.* Refer to that message for additional information, if needed.

Cannot Print [*or*, Cannot Print the (*filename*) file]. Be sure your printer is connected properly, and use the Printers option in Control Panel to verify that the printer is configured properly. In addition to following the displayed advice, refer to the *Cannot find UNIDRV.DLL* message above.

Closing Print Manager will cancel all pending print jobs. If you try to close Windows while there are still jobs to be printed on the local printer, this message warns you of the consequences. Click on OK or Cancel, and be prepared to lose a friend or two if you choose the former.

Control Panel cannot perform the current operation because *printer driver*.DRV is not a valid printer-driver file. Make sure that you have a valid printer-driver file, reinstall the printer, then try again. This message may appear during a printer setup operation, even if that operation originated from within the Print Manager instead of the Control Panel. Although the printer-driver file cited in the message may indeed be defective, it's also possible that the UNIDRV.DLL file is missing. In case of doubt, expand fresh copies of both and try again.

Computer name or share name in the specified network path is invalid. Although the obvious solution is to enter the correct information and try again, a more reliable technique is to click on the down arrow to see what printers are available. Double-click on the desired printer and its name will appear in the Path box.

If the printer you want to use does not appear in the list above, then double-click on the appropriate computer name in the "Show Shared Printers on:" box. The list of printers on that computer should now appear in the "Shared Printers on *computer name*" box. If the printer you seek still does not show up, then the remote system is not currently sharing it.

If a *Computer name is invalid* message seems to be erroneous, maybe it is. Check *Erroneous Error Messages* in the *Print Manager Troubleshooting* section for further details.

Computer name specified in the network path cannot be located (*message does not include a* [SYS00*xx*] *notation*). Check one of the following possibilities, as appropriate.

Failed Connect Network Printer Attempt. Refer to this message under the *Error occurred while reconnecting* . . . message below.

Failed View Attempt.   If you are connected to a network printer, you may see this message if you attempt to view its print queue via the View Menu's Qther Network Printer... option and its Yiew button. This option is intended for viewing a remote printer's print list if you are *not* connected to that printer. If you are connected, don't use this option: Look at the Print Manager Window, which should show the appropriate print list. Of course, the message might also appear if you typed the name of a remote computer\printer combination that really does not exist. Check the spelling and message syntax (\\ *computer name\printer name*) and try again.

Connection: You cannot connect the selected port to a shared printer because you already are sharing a printer on that port.   If a printer attached to LPT*x* on the local printer has been made available for sharing, this message appears if you try to connect a network (remote) printer to the cited port. Either select a different port (via the Connect Network Printer dialog box), or stop sharing the local printer, then try again.

Driver: This driver cannot be updated because it is currently being used by Windows. Wait until Windows is finished with the driver, then try again.   If you are indeed trying to update a driver that is currently in use, then do as the message suggests and try again later on. However, if you know the driver is not in use, Windows might not know that, and hence the message. The surest way of continuing is to exit and reopen Windows, which should clear any lingering references to the driver in WIN.INI. Now reinstall the driver and the procedure should conclude successfully.

Error occurred while reconnecting LPTx: to \\(*computer name\printer name*): This sentence is followed by additional information, as listed below. In each case, the message concludes with *Do you want to continue restoring connections?* If you click on the Yes button, Windows tries to restore other connections, if any. A similar message will appear if Windows can't find other devices (network drives, for example) that should be connected. Or, click on the No button if you don't want Windows to try restoring other connections.

   If the information provided below does not lead to a resolution of the problem, refer to *Printer Connection Problems* in the *Print Manager Troubleshooting* section for additional assistance.

   Computer name specified in the network path cannot be located. [SYS0053].   The most likely explanation is that the specified computer is not powered on. Another possibility is that the physical link between your computer and the network is having problems. Of course, it's also possible that the computer name was changed since the previous session, but if that had happened someone should have told you about it.

Specified share name cannot be found [SYS0067].   In this case the specified computer is either not logged on to the network, or its printer is currently not shared. Or as above, there may be a problem with the hardware link between the local computer and the network.

Error printing on *(printer name)* **on LPT**x**:.**   If something happens to interrupt a print job in progress, there should be some evidence other than this vague message to help you troubleshoot. If not, check all the connections and try again.

If the message appears at the beginning of a print job, and the printer is one that requires the UNIDRV.DLL file, that file is probably missing or defective. Expand a fresh copy into the System directory and try again.

File Manager cannot print multiple files. Select only one file, then try again.   You'll see this message if you select more than one file, then drag them as a group to the Print Manager, or to its icon. As a workaround, drag the files to Print Manager one at a time.

General network error has occurred. Try again.   This Windows 3.1 Message Box message is so vague it's just about useless. Before tearing the system apart, select <u>N</u>etworks Settings... on the Options Menu, then clear the <u>U</u>pdate Network Display check box. Now try the print job. If it works, the message is erroneous, and may be caused by a compatibility problem with the network software.

HP LaserJet 4/4M is not set as the default printer in WIN.INI. Use the Printers icon in the Control Panel to set the default printer.   This   message may be seen when installing the Hewlett-Packard *LaserJet 4/4M Printers TrueType Screen Font Pack* which is available to owners of the LaserJet 4 or 4M printer. If the message is valid, you may use either the Control Panel's Printer applet or the Print Manager to set the default printer. If you use the latter, highlight the HP LaserJet 4 printer, then open the Printer Menu and click once on the Set <u>D</u>efault Printer option. Or, if this printer is not listed, select <u>P</u>rinter Setup... on the Options Menu and install it.

However, if you know this printer is already set as your default printer, then refer to the *Reinstallation of Printer Driver* section for assistance in correcting a probable configuration error.

Jobs waiting in this queue. Continuing will delete the jobs. Do you want to continue? The message appears if you attempt to stop sharing a local printer whose print queue is not empty. If you click on the Yes button, the jobs in that queue will be discarded.

LPT*x* is being used by another application. When the application is finished with the port, resume printing. If the first part of the message is valid, then try again later. However, the message is sometimes seen if the Print Manager was turned on (see *Enable or Disable Print Manager*) during the current Windows session. If nothing else works, exit Windows, then re-open it. That usually works.

LPT*x*: There is currently no printer connected to LPT*x*. Do you want to install one? The message does not refer to a physical link between a printer and your computer's LPT1 connector. Instead, it means there is no printer *driver* installed for the cited printer port. You need to install the driver, even if all you want to do is access a printer that is physically connected to another computer on a network. Assuming you want to continue, click on the Yes button and refer to the *Printer Driver Installation* section for further details.

LPT*x* is already connected to \\\\(*computer name*)\\(*printer name*). Do you want to connect LPT*x* to \\\\(*other computer name*)\\(*printer name*) instead? The message just warns you of an existing printer connection which will be broken if you continue. If both computer and printer names are identical, the connection you want to make is already in place.

LPT*x* is not present on your computer. Choose the Printers icon in Control Panel or the Printer Setup command in Print Manager to assign an installed port to your printer. If your local printer is physically attached to a certain printer port, make sure the default printer driver is configured for that port.

If the cited port refers to a network (remote) printer, the most likely explanation of the message is that your local Print Manager has not made a connection to that printer. Make the necessary connection and retry the print operation.

Network error has occurred. Now all you have to do is figure out what error occurred. If you're trying to connect to a network printer, that printer is probably not available for sharing. Either try to connect to another printer, or see if you can persuade whoever needs persuading to share the printer. Then try again.

Network: There are jobs waiting in this queue. Continuing will delete the jobs. Do you want to continue? If you try to stop sharing your printer while there are print jobs in its print queue, this message warns you of the consequences.

Network: There are network jobs waiting to print. Continuing will delete the jobs. Do you want to continue? You'll see this one if you try to close your Print Manager applet while your own printer is in use by others.

Network: There are no network printers currently connected. Unlike most menu options, the Printer Menu's Disconnect Network Printer... option appears to be enabled even if it isn't. Therefore, this message appears if you try to disconnect a printer, and there are none to be disconnected.

Not enough disk space to print *(application name - filename.ext)*. **Delete any unwanted files from your disk, then try printing the document again.** Print Manager is trying to write (not print) the cited file into your temporary directory, and there is not enough room for it. If possible, move the temporary directory to another drive partition where more room is available. Or if it's on a RAM drive, increase the size of that drive. Then reboot and try again.

If your disk resources are truly almost exhausted and you can't free up the needed space, disable the Print Manager and print directly to the printer. While you're at it, think about getting a bigger hard disk, or compressing the one you have.

Port settings may not match those required by your printer. If this message appears while a print job is in progress, it's unlikely that the port settings have mysteriously changed all by themselves. The printer has probably just run out of paper or lost power. (See also *Print Manager cannot print to LPT*x.)

Port with jobs queued was removed (or the printer assigned to the port was changed). These jobs could not be printed and have been deleted. If you see this message after making a printer port change, it's too late to do anything about it. You'll have to resend the deleted jobs to the Print Manager in order to print them.

Print Fields: It will not be possible to send PRINT field data to the printer with the currently installed printer driver. Do you want to continue printing? The message refers to data such as Postscript or printer control codes embedded in a document. As a typical example, the following Postscript code should print the paragraph which follows it on a shaded background:

```
{print \p para "wp$box .99 setgray fill"}
```

If you attempt to print a document containing this (or similar) code, the message appears if the driver/printer does not support such codes. In this specific example, the document will print anyway on some non-Postscript laser printers—the code is ignored and the paragraph prints as normal (un-shaded) text. On other printers (dot-matrix, for example), the code may force the printer to print out a string of print-formatting codes at the head of the document. Refer to *Printout begins with . . . Print-format Codes* in the *Troubleshooting* section for a few workaround suggestions.

Print Manager cannot print to LPT*x*. The port settings may not match those required by your printer. Cancel the print job, or choose the Printers option in Control Panel or the Printer Setup command in Print Manager to specify the correct port settings. Or if none of that does it, check the status of the remote Print Manager. If it has been turned off, this message appears if the local Print Manager attempts to send a job out for printing. Persuade the remote operator to turn the Print Manager back on again, then click on the Retry button. Otherwise, click on the Cancel button and do as the message says.

Print Manager has been disabled. Choose the Printers option in Control Panel to re-enable the Print Manager. After doing so, check the Use Print Manager box at the bottom of the dialog box, then click on the Close button. Print Manager should now open the next time you try to do so.

Print Manager has been turned off. To run the Print Manager, choose the Printers icon in the Control Panel, and then choose the Use Print Manager check box. Every once in a while there's a message that explains itself. This is one of those times.

Print Manager is still running. You must close Print Manager before you can disable it. In order to escape from this message, recheck the Use Print Manager box, close the Printers dialog box, then close the Print Manager. Now you can return to the Printers applet and clear the Use Print Manager box if you really want to stop using it.

Print queue does not exist. You may see this message if you try to view the print queue on a remote printer, and that printer is currently not shared or its name is incorrectly entered. Make the necessary correction(s) and try again.

Print queue does not exist. It may have been removed by an administrator. If you see both sentences when you try to view the print list on a remote computer, make sure you correctly enter both the computer name *and* printer name, as in *\\computer name\printer name.*

Printer is stalled. If it is, then of course you need to fix the problem at the printer and try again. However, if it isn't, then refer to *Erroneous Error Messages* in the *Print Manager Troubleshooting* section for suggestions.

Printer *(printer name)* **on LPT***x* **is shared as** *(share name)***. You must stop sharing the printer before removing it. Any documents sent to this printer will not be printed. Do you want to remove the printer?** In most cases the message should explain itself. You may, however, remove the printer while still sharing it, in which case an additional warning message will appear.

Printer: Do you want to quit printing the document *application name - filename.ext?* The warning appears if you attempt to delete a document in the print queue. Click on Yes or No, depending on what you really want to do.

Printer on this port is . . .
. . . not responding. Check the printer or increase the Transmission Retry value in the Printers Connect dialog box, and then resume the print queue.
. . . is out of paper or is not connected to your computer. Check the printer cable or network connection (etc.). If these messages or variations appear, the first thing to do is check for the problems cited in the message. However, if the printer appears to be in good order and properly connected, then it's possible that the UNIDRV.DLL file is missing. Expand a fresh copy in the System directory and try again.

Printer specified share name cannot be found. If you are sure you selected a valid path and name for the printer you want to access, then that printer is not available for sharing.

Sharing: You can only share resources that are on your computer. If you are trying to share a printer, make sure that it is a local printer and that the TEMP directory is on a local drive. This message warns that you are trying to share a network (remote) printer that isn't yours to share. Although you can print to any printer connected to your computer (physically, or via network connection), you can share only your own local printer(s) with others on the network.

If the message appears when you are indeed trying to share your own printer, you are probably connected to a network printer on the same port. If so, disconnect it and try again.

Temporary file created by Print Manager may be corrupted. Try reprinting the document. Something has apparently happened to the temporary file that the Print Manager wrote to your temporary directory, prior to beginning the actual print job. When you click on the OK button, the filename will no longer be seen in the print queue (if there was one). If repeated print attempts also fail, then try to print some other document. If that document prints satisfactorily, then the first document file is probably corrupted. However, if the second document also fails, then turn off the Print Manager and try again. If that works, then the Print Manager itself is in trouble. Expand a fresh copy of PRINTMAN.EX_ into the Windows directory and try again.

There are *x* user(s) connected to *(printer name)*. If you stop sharing *(printer name)*, they will be disconnected. Do you want to continue? It's just another one of those warning messages to let you know others are using the printer you are about to stop sharing or remove. If you are trying to remove the printer driver, and don't mind losing the print queue—and possibly a few friends—click on the Yes button, then repeat the driver removal procedure.

You are already using [Control Panel *or* Print Manager] to install a printer. Choose the OK button to switch to the dialog box you were using. You may see this message with the bracketed section missing if you attempt to reopen the Printers applet after a failed printer configuration attempt required a local reboot. If you press the OK button and nothing happens, close and reopen Windows, and try again.

If the bracketed section is not missing, then the Print Manager *and* the Printers applet are both open. Click on the OK button to return to whichever applet was opened first.

Fonts

Windows 3.1 offers a wide selection of fonts with which to display text on the screen or print that text on the installed printer. The specific fonts are a function of the installed video system and the printer. In addition to the fonts supplied with Windows itself, additional fonts may be added from a variety of third-party suppliers.

Successful fontsmanship is sometimes as easy as selecting the font you want to use, then using it. And sometimes it's not: A font may "disappear" when some other font is installed. Or, a font formerly displayed in one style will now appear in another style. There may, or may not, be any similarity between the font on the screen and the font on paper. In short, WYSIWYG(m). That's "m" as in "maybe."

A Few Definitions

This chapter tries to sort out some of the configuration variables that affect font usage. For readers unfamiliar with font nomenclature, a few definitions are given first.

Device Font. A *device font* is an integral part of an installed device; that is, of a printer. For example, the Courier and Line Printer fonts built into most laser printers are device fonts, as are fonts resident in a plug-in cartridge. The availability of a device font is indicated by the appearance of a printer icon next to the font name in the Font Box. In addition, dot-matrix device font names include a pitch specification, as *xx*cpi (characters-per-inch), as shown here:

Courier *xx*cpi

The Font box displays a separate font listing for every available pitch on the installed dot-matrix printer.

Support for all Hewlett-Packard device fonts (internal and in font cartridges) is built into the HPPCL driver supplied with Windows. For device fonts not supported by this driver, you will need a separate PCM (Printer Cartridge Metrics) file. Unless otherwise noted, a device font is designed in the raster font format.

> **NOTE:** When a device font is selected, Windows uses the closest screen font it can find to display the selected text on screen. If the screen font so selected contains more point sizes than the equivalent device font, only those sizes contained within the device font will be listed in the **Font Size Box**. For example, the COUR*x*.FON file contains Courier fonts in 10-, 12-, and 15-point sizes, and this font is used to display the Courier device font in the Hewlett-Packard LaserJet series II printer. However, since the device font is available only in the 12-point size, only that size shows up in the **Font Box**.

Font. This is a complete set of characters in one typeface size and style. A Windows font file may contain one to six separate fonts or, in the case of vector and TrueType files (described below), one file contains all the information needed to create a font in any point size. A separate file is supplied for each available font in the specified typeface. See Table 10.1a for a comparison of *Font* and *Typeface*.

Font Box. In the descriptions which follow, frequent reference is made to a *Font Box*. This is an integral part of those Windows utilities and applications which permit the user to select the font to be used for display or printing. The name of the currently selected font appears in this box, which is described in greater detail later in the chapter.

Monospace Font. In a monospace font, the same amount of horizontal space is set aside for each displayed or printed character. Thus, a lowercase "i" and uppercase "W" take up the same space on a line, as shown by the first line in the example given here. For comparison purposes, a variable-width font is also shown in the same point size.

```
monospace font      iiiiWWWW    iWiWiWiW    (Courier New)
variable-width font  iiiiWWWW   iWiWiWiW   (Times New Roman)
```

TABLE 10.1a   Typeface and Font Comparisons

| | Fonts | | | |
Typeface	Roman	Bold	Italic	Bold Italic
Albertus Medium	(regular)	—	—	—
Albertus Extrabold	(regular)	—	—	—
Arial	(regular)	Bold	Italic	Bold Italic
Book Antiqua	(regular)	Bold	Italic	Bold Italic
Bookman Old Style	(regular)	Bold	Italic	Bold Italic
Garamond	Antiqua	Halbfett	Kursiv	Kursiv Halbfett
Letter Gothic	(regular)	Bold	Italic	—
Marigold	(regular)	—	—	—
Times New Roman	(regular)	Bold	Italic	Bold Italic
Univers Condensed	(regular)	Bold	Italic	Bold Italic

Pitch.   This is a measure of the number of characters per horizontal inch (cpi) in a monospace font. The relationship between pitch and point size is usually given as follows:

Pitch (cpi)	Point Size (pts)
10	12
12	10
15	8

Plotter Font.   The three vector fonts supplied with Windows are often referred to as *plotter fonts*, since they are designed primarily for plotter applications.

Point Size.   The vertical size, in points, of the character box in which each font character is printed. A point is about 1/72 of an inch. Within any point size, the height of each character is always less than that size, so that letters on one line will not touch those on another.

Points Box.   As its name suggests, the Points Box lists the currently selected point size for the font listed in the Font Box.

Printer Font.   A *printer font* is simply any device font, or other font that may be downloaded to a printer.

Screen Font.   Any font that is displayed on screen is by definition a *screen font.*

Serif, Sans Serif.   A serif is a decorative line segment that terminates the strokes of a character in some typefaces. If present, that face is known as a serif typeface (Times New Roman, for example). If absent, the face is a sans serif typeface (Arial, for example). Table 10.1b illustrates typical serif and sans serif typefaces.

Style or Attribute.   This is a distinctive characteristic applied to all the characters in a typeface. Windows typefaces are usually available in the following styles: roman, bold, italic or oblique, and bold italic or bold oblique. Strictly speaking, the *roman* style designator refers to any upright typeface that is set without italic or bold attributes. However, due to worldwide recognition of Linotype-Hell's *Times* typeface in its *roman* style, the typeface itself is now popularly identified as *Times Roman.* Monotype's *Times New Roman 327* goes a step further by making *Roman* a part of the typeface name. Thus, we have Times New Roman roman, Times New Roman italic, and so on. To help minimize the confusion, the style properly called *roman* is now often referred to as *regular* or *normal* instead. The term *regular* is used throughout this book to help avoid such apparently contradictory designations as say, Swiss roman.

Symbol Set.   The unique set of printable characters in a typeface is referred to as its Symbol Set, and any typeface may be available with one or more distinctive symbol sets. For example, the PC-8 symbol set identifies a typeface in which the extended characters (128–255) include the familiar IBM PC line-drawing characters, while the Roman-8 symbol set includes extensive foreign-language characters. Both *Facelift for Windows* and *Type Director* (described below) allow the user to create multiple versions of the same typeface, each with a different symbol set. The *Facelift* software refers to the symbol set as a character set.

System Fonts.   The three raster font sets that display most (but not all) text on the Windows Desktop are known collectively as the *system font.* The specific system font set installed during Setup depends on the video system in use at that time, as described later in the chapter in the *System Font Selection* section.

TABLE 10.1b   Typeface Style Comparisons

Typeface Style Examples

Typeface Style	A	B	C	D	E	F	G	H	I	J	K	L	M
Serif [†]	A	B	C	D	E	F	G	H	I	J	K	L	M
Sans Serif [‡]	A	B	C	D	E	F	G	H	I	J	K	L	M
Serif [†]	N	O	P	Q	R	S	T	U	V	W	X	Y	Z
Sans Serif [‡]	N	O	P	Q	R	S	T	U	V	W	X	Y	Z

[†] A–M; Times New Roman   N–Z; Garamond
[‡] A–M; Arial   N–Z; Letter Gothic

Unfortunately, Microsoft further defines the three system fonts as *System, Fixed System,* and *Terminal* or *OEM.* So it's not always clear if *System Font* is a general reference to the three fonts collectively, or to one (possibly two) specific fonts within the set. For the purposes of this book, the term is used as a general reference.

Table 10.2 lists the system fonts supplied with Windows.

Terminal (OEM) Font.   The system font used to display text in a DOS window is usually referred to as the *terminal font,* or *OEM font.* For details about the use of these fonts in a DOS Window, refer to the *Fonts for Windowed DOS Applications* section in Chapter 7.

Typeface.   This is a collection of stylistically consistent letters, numbers, punctuation marks, and symbols. A typeface may be of any size or style. Thus, Arial, Courier, and Lucida Calligraphy are three of the many typefaces available for Windows applications.

Typeface Family.   This is the complete collection of styles available for any typeface. A Windows typeface family may include one, two, or four of the styles listed above. See Table 10.1a for a comparison of *Typeface* and *Font.*

Typeface and Font Nomenclature.   As further confusion factors on typeface nomenclature, the regular font in some typefaces (*Park Avenue, Marigold* for example) is an italic style, and in others (*Albertus Extrabold*) it is bold. In such cases there is no difference between say, Marigold and Marigold italic, or between Albertus Extrabold and Albertus Extrabold bold.

TABLE 10.2   Windows System Fonts

Font Type and Filename	Aspect Ratio	H.	V.	Code Page	Set	Notes
Fixed System						
cgafix.fon	200	96	48	–	#2	(Win 3.0)
egafix.fon	133	96	72	–	#3	
vgafix.fon	100	96	72	–	#6	
8514fix.fon	100	96	72			
System (variable width)						
cgasys.fon	200	96	48	–	#2	(Win 3.0)
egasys.fon	133	96	72	–	#3	
vgasys.fon	100	96	96	–	#6	
8514sys.fon	100	96	96	–	#6	
Terminal, DOS Applications						
dosapp.fon (see Table 7.1)				437	–	
cga40woa.fon	200	96	48	–	–	
cga80woa.fon	200	96	48	–	–	
ega40woa.fon	133	96	72	–	–	
ega80woa.fon	133	96	72	–	–	
Terminal, DOS Applications, International						
app850.fon				850	–	
cga40850.fon	200	96	48	–	–	
cga80850.fon	200	96	48	–	–	
ega40850.fon	133	96	72	–	–	
ega80850.fon	133	96	72	–	–	
Terminal, Hercules						
herc850.fon	133	96	72	–	–	
hercwoa.fon				–	–	
Terminal, OEM						
cgaoem.fon	200	96	48	437	#2	(Win 3.0)
egaoem.fon	133	96	72	437	#3	
vgaoem.fon	100	96	96	437	#6	
8514oem.fon	100	96	96	437		
Terminal, OEM International						
vga850.fon	100	96	96	850	#6	International
vga860.fon				860		Portuguese
vga861.fon				861		Icelandic
vga863.fon				863		French-Canadian
vga865.fon				865		Norwegian

Finally, font suppliers are not always consistent in naming the regular font. Usually, the typeface name alone is used, but sometimes it's not, as illustrated in these examples.

Arial, Courier, Book Antiqua, Courier New, Times New Roman, etc. Here the typeface name applies to the regular font, with *italic, bold, bold italic* appended as appropriate to the font style.

Garamond. In the Hewlett-Packard version of this typeface, the regular font only is *Antiqua.* The others are *Kursiv* (italic), *Halbfett* (bold), *Kursiv Halbfett* (italic bold—which is also a reversal of the customary sequence of these modifiers).

Univers, Univers Condensed. Hewlett-Packard may not be sure what to call these. The LaserJet's internal typeface calls itself *Univers Medium* in its regular and italic fonts, and plain *Univers* in the bold and bold italic fonts. The latter designation is also used for all TrueType versions of the same font. The same pattern applies to the *Univers Condensed* fonts.

Variable-Width Font. In a variable-width font, horizontal space is assigned according to the actual width of the character to be displayed or printed. See *Monospace Font* above for a comparison of variable-width and monospace fonts.

Font Categories

The font files supplied with Windows may be categorized as Raster, Vector, or TrueType, and each is described in this section. These categories refer only to the manner in which font data is stored, displayed and/or printed, but do not describe a specific typeface, style, or point size.

Raster Fonts

In a raster font, the multiple bytes comprising each character are a bit-by-bit "map" of the pixels required to display that character on screen; it is sometimes referred to as a *bitmap* font. (See *The Bitmap File* in Chapter 8 for more on bitmaps.) For example, a monospaced raster font might store each character in 13 bytes, for a width of 8 pixels (one byte) and a height of 13 pixels. Thus, the bytes containing the letter "X" are as listed below. When the hexadecimal notation is converted to binary, it gives a graphic illustration of how the character will look on screen, with each "1" bit representing a pixel that will be illuminated to form the character.

Hex	Binary
00	0 0 0 0 0 0 0 0
00	0 0 0 0 0 0 0 0
77	0 **1 1 1** 0 **1 1 1**
22	0 0 **1** 0 0 0 **1** 0
14	0 0 0 **1** 0 **1** 0 0
14	0 0 0 **1** 0 **1** 0 0
08	0 0 0 0 **1** 0 0 0
14	0 0 0 **1** 0 **1** 0 0
14	0 0 0 **1** 0 **1** 0 0
22	0 0 **1** 0 0 0 **1** 0
77	0 **1 1 1** 0 **1 1 1**
00	0 0 0 0 0 0 0 0
00	0 0 0 0 0 0 0 0

Base and Expanded Raster Fonts. The practical disadvantage of any raster format is that it is optimized for one font size only, referred to here as a *base* font. As the term implies, the base font can be used to create *expanded* fonts, in even multiples of the base size. For example, Figure 10.1a shows the pixel representation of the letter seen above. (The blank bytes at the top and bottom of the pixel matrix are not shown in the Figure.) To increase the displayed font size, an algorithm considers each pixel as a 1×1 matrix, then doubles it to create an expanded 2×2 matrix, as seen in part (b) of the Figure. Another doubling creates the 4×4 matrix in part (c).

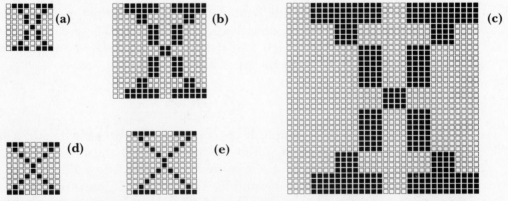

Figure 10.1 Pixel representations of the letter "X" in various COURE.FON font sizes. The 8×13 base font in (a) its actual configuration and at (b) double and (c) quadruple enlargement. The 16×16 (d) and 20×20 (e) base fonts. In each example, the blank lines at the top and bottom of the character box are not included.

The obvious tradeoff is that as the font expands, diagonal lines take on a jagged look. Therefore, additional raster base fonts are often provided, with each one optimized to suit a certain display size. For example, the Windows COURE.FON file contains three complete font sets, as listed in Table 10.3 (The letter "X" described above is taken from the first set.)

As noted, each base font can display even multiples of itself. The figure references show how the letter "X" is created in each of these base fonts. As before, blank bytes at the top and bottom of each matrix, and the additional bits to fill out the character box are not shown in the figure. Additional examples of each font are given in Figure 10.2a, to show how some letters deteriorate more than others as point size is doubled or quadrupled. For comparison purposes, Figure 10.2b and c shows comparable examples of the vector and TrueType fonts described later on.

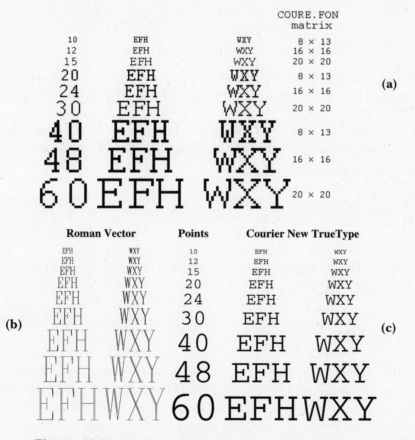

Figure 10.2 Typical examples of font enlargement. (a) The three COURE.FON fonts at base, double, and quadruple enlargement. Comparable Vector (b) and TrueType (c) fonts.

TABLE 10.3   Windows Font Matrixes in COURE.FON File

Font Set	Bytes/ Character W × H	Total	Character Box[†] W × H	"X" Letter Size[†] W × H	Point Sizes Base	Point Sizes Other	See Figure 10.1
1	1 × 13	13	8 × 13	8 × 9	10	20, 40,...	(a)
2	2 × 16	32	16 ö 16	9 × 10	12	24, 48,...	(d)
3	2 × 20	40	16 ö 20	12 × 12	15	30, 60,...	(e)

[†] Width and height in pixels.

The raster font was, and still is, frequently encountered in various applications, from the Windows system and OEM fonts that will be described later in the chapter, to soft fonts created by *FaceLift for Windows, Type Director* and other font utilities.

Raster Font Extension. Since Windows raster and vector (described below) filenames both use FON as their extension, the filename itself provides no clue to the font type it contains. To tell one from the other, refer to the [fonts] section of your WIN.INI files, where raster font listings follow the general formats given here for the Courier font described above:

    Courier 10,12,15 (VGA res)=COURE.FON

Raster fonts display the font style, available point sizes, and video resolution, as seen to the left of the equal sign above. Note that the listed point sizes refer to the internal contents of the cited font, and that not all of these sizes may be available to your system. As another alternative, click on the Fonts icon in the Control Panel to display the list of installed fonts.

Raster, or bitmap, soft fonts supplied by various third-party suppliers are cited elsewhere in WIN.INI, and usually do not use the FON extension. When such a font name does appear in the [fonts] section of WIN.INI, it may be listed with no extension at all.

Windows Raster Fonts. Table 10.4 lists the Windows (and Word-for-Windows) raster fonts found in the [fonts] section of WIN.INI. Additional raster fonts are also supplied for DOS applications, described in the *Fonts for Windowed DOS Applications* section in Chapter 7.

TABLE 10.4 Windows Raster Fonts

Typeface & Filename	Aspect Ratio	H.	V.	Video System	Typeface & Filename	Aspect Ratio	H.	V.	Video System
Arial Arial 8, 10					**Serif** MS Serif 8, 10, 12, 14, 18, 24				
arialb.fon	133	96	72	EGA	serifb.fon	133	96	72	EGA
					serife.fon	100	96	96	VGA
Dialog				All	seriff.fon	100	120	120	8514
dialog.fon (Word dialog boxes)									
					Small (6 sans serif & serif) Small Fonts				
Digital (Win 3.0 digital font)				All	smallb.fon	133	96	72	EGA
digital.fon	100	96	96		smalle.fon	100	96	96	VGA
					smallf.fon	100	120	120	8514/a
Courier Courier 10, 12, 15									
coura.fon	200	96	48	CGA	**Symbol** Symbol 8, 10, 12, 14, 18, 24				
courb.fon	133	96	72	EGA	symbola.fon	200	96	48	CGA
courc.fon	83	60	72	60 dpi	symbolb.fon	133	96	72	EGA
courd.fon	167	120	72	120 dpi	symbole.fon	100	96	96	VGA
coure.fon	100	96	96	VGA	symbolf.fon	100	120	120	8514/a
courf.fon	100	120	120	8514/a					
					Times Roman Times New Roman 8, 10				
Helv Helv 8, 10, 12, 14, 18, 24 (Win 3.0)					timesb.fon	133	96	72	EGA
helva.fon	200	96	48	CGA					
helvb.fon	133	96	72	EGA	**Times Roman**				
helvc.fon	83	60	72	60 dpi	Tms Rmn 8, 10, 12, 14, 18, 24 (Win 3.0)				
helvd.fon	167	120	72	120 dpi	tmsra.fon	200	96	48	CGA
helve.fon	100	96	96	VGA	tmsrb.fon	133	96	72	EGA
helvf.fon	100	120	120	8514	tmsrc.fon	83	60	72	60 dpi
					tmsrd.fon	167	120	72	120 dpi
Sans Serif MS Sans Serif 8, 10, 12, 14, 18, 24					tmsre.fon	100	96	96	VGA
sserifb.fon	133	96	72	EGA	tmsrf.fon	100	120	120	8515 [*sic*]
sserife.fon	100	96	96	VGA					
sseriff.fon	100	120	120	8514					

Microsoft Bookshelf Fonts (in Viewer directory on CD-ROM disc)

Typeface & Filename	Aspect Ratio	H.	V.	Video System	Typeface & Filename	Aspect Ratio	H.	V.	Video System
Lucida Sans B (B1, B2) Lucida Sans 10, 12, 14					**Symbol B** Symbol 10, 12, 14				
vgalsb.fon	100	96	96	VGA	vgasb.fon	100	96	96	VGA
vgalsb1.fon					8514sb.fon	100	120	120	8514
vgalsb2.fon									
8514lsb.fon	100	120	120	8514					
8514lsb1.fon									
8514lsb2.fon									

Raster Font Name Ending. Note that each Windows raster font name ends in a letter (A–F) which identifies the video system or printer for which it was designed. Table 10.5 summarizes these font name endings. Within each font family, only the file with the letter-ending appropriate to the installed video system is transferred during the Windows Setup operation, and listed in WIN.INI.

Word-for-Windows Raster Font. The dialog boxes in Word-for-Windows 2.0 use one of several raster font matrixes found in the DIALOG.FON file in the Winword directory. If you wish to use this font set for other applications, add the following line to the [fonts] section of WIN.INI:

```
MS Dialog (W4W)=C:\WINWORD\DIALOG.FON
```

The font may now be displayed via the Character Map applet (described below), but will only show up in your application's Font Box *if* your installed printer provides the necessary support.

> **NOTE:** Since DIALOG.FON font contains three complete font sets (EGA, VGA, 8514), its name does not end with a system-identifying letter, as do the other raster fonts.

TABLE 10.5   Windows Raster Font Summary

File Name Root[†]	Font Style	Description[‡]	Comments	File End	Video System
COUR*x*.FON	Courier	Courier		A[§]	CGA
HELV*x*.FON	Sans Serif	Helv	Discontinued	B	EGA
SERIF*x*.FON	Serif	MS Serif	Replaces TMSR	C[§]	Printer (60 dpi)
SSERIF*x*.FON	Sans Serif	MS Sans Serif	Replaces HELVD	D[§]	Printer (120 dpi)
SYMBOL*x*.FON	Symbol Set	Symbol		E	VGA
TMSR*x*.FON	Serif	Tms Rmn	Discontinued	F	8514/a

[†] Refer to File End and Video System columns for letter *x* and corresponding video system.

[‡] Font description appears in [fonts] section of WIN.INI, and in applet Font Box.

[§] Windows 3.0 only.

Printing Raster Fonts.   A raster font may be printed only if the specified size is supported on the installed printer. In any Windows application, supported base sizes are listed in the application's Points box. When a listed base font is used to create an expanded font, that font may or may not be accurately printed, depending on the resolution of the printer. For further details, refer to the *Expanded Font Does Not Print Correctly* section later in this chapter.

HPPCL Printer Note.   Despite the possible appearance of a raster font in your font list, the font cannot be printed on an HPPCL (Hewlett-Packard Printer Control Language) laser printer. If you select such a font (Courier, for example), Windows' COUR*x*.FON file displays the font on screen, but the subsequent printout uses the printer's own internal Courier font. For example, the Hewlett-Packard LaserJet series II has an internal 12-point Courier font, while COUR*x*.FON itself supplies 10-, 12-, and 15-point base font sizes. If this printer is installed, the available font in your word-processing application will list the Courier 12-point size, since that's the only one available at the printer.

Vector Fonts

A vector font is so-called because, instead of using the raster font's bitmap format, it contains instructions for drawing line segments between various points. As the distance between the points is increased or decreased, the line connecting them adjusts itself as required. Therefore, multiple font sizes may be generated from a single vector font, with the obvious advantage of saving the hard disk space otherwise required for multiple font sets.

The vector font was designed primarily for plotter applications and, in fact, is often referred to as a "plotter font," and occasionally as a "stroke font." As a text font for word-processing and related applications, it is not always as satisfactory as a raster font, especially if the latter is available in the desired point size. However, the plotter font generally looks smoother than an expanded raster font at larger point sizes. Figure 10.2b shows examples of the Windows Roman vector font.

Vector Font Extension.   As noted earlier, Windows' vector and raster fonts share a common (FON) filename extension. Within WIN.INI such fonts are listed in the format shown here for the Modern or LineDraw fonts.

```
Modern (Plotter)=MODERN.FON
MS LineDraw (all res)=WINLD.FON
```

Windows Vector Fonts. The vector fonts supplied with Windows are listed in Table 10.6, as is the Word-for-Windows font described immediately below.

Word-for-Windows Line-Drawing Vector Font (WINLD.FON). Newcomers to Windows often spend hours looking for a means to display and print the 48 line-drawing symbols that have been an integral part of personal computing since the introduction of the first IBM PC. But until recently, these special characters have not been readily available to Windows applications. However, a special vector font containing nothing but these symbols (176–223) is supplied with the Word-for-Windows upgrade release 2.0a or later. If you've installed this upgrade, your list of available fonts should include a new one called MS LineDraw. The complete font set is also viewable via the Character Map.

If you need help installing this font, refer to *Add New Fonts* section later in the chapter. Or better yet, get Bitstream's *Facelift for Windows* (also described below) and modify one of its fonts to include the IBM PC8 symbol set.

Printing Vector Fonts. Vector fonts may be printed on any laser or other printer. Print time is often longer than when the equivalent raster font is used, due to the time required to generate the specific font size required for the print job.

Vector Fonts on Dot-Matrix Printers. A Table in the *Windows Resource Kit* (p. 317 in Windows 3.1 version) indicates that vector fonts can't be printed on dot-matrix printers, which might surprise anyone who printed one before reading the manual. The vector data is converted into a bitmap image and this is printed. Strictly speaking it's no longer a vector font, so the Table is correct. However, it *looks* like a vector font and, as the

TABLE 10.6 Windows Vector Fonts

Filename	Font Style	Video System	Comments
MODERN.FON	Sans serif	All	
ROMAN.FON	Serif	All	
SCRIPT.FON	Script	All	
WINLD.FON	Sans serif	All	PC-8 line drawing symbols, supplied with Word-for-Windows 2.0a

manual says elsewhere (p. 322), "Vector screen fonts can be printed in any resolution or orientation." You probably won't want to bother though: They're not much to look at.

TrueType Fonts

One of the most popular features of Windows 3.1 is the TrueType family of scalable fonts. For each typeface style, a single TrueType font file and a small font resource file provide all the information necessary to display and print that typeface in any point size.

TrueType fonts are not downloaded to the printer prior to beginning a print job. Instead, the necessary font data is sent to the printer as needed. Furthermore, only those characters needed to print the next page are transmitted. Letters that never appear in a document are not sent to the printer at all. Thus, depending on the content of the document, there may be considerable savings both in production time and in printer memory.

Figure 10.2c shows examples of the TrueType Courier New font, for comparison with the Courier raster font in Figure 10.2a.

TrueType Font Extensions. For each installed TrueType font, you will find two files with the same name but different extensions, as described here.

Font Resource Data (filename.FOT). A small file (typically, about 1200–1400 bytes) with a FOT extension contains font resource data, including an internal reference to the location of the associated TrueType font file. Readers who know their way around the DOS debug utility (or similar) may view this reference, which is found at CS:0500.

For each installed TrueType font, a line in WIN.INI refers to the font resource data file, as shown here:

```
[fonts]
Arial (TrueType)=ARIAL.FOT
Arial Bold (TrueType)=ARIALBD.FOT
Arial Italic (TrueType)=ARIALI.FOT
Arial Bold Italic (TrueType)=ARIALBI.FOT
```

TrueType Font File (filename.TTF). A larger file with a TTF extension is the actual font itself, containing all the data required to display/print the font in any size from 4 to 127 points.

Windows TrueType Fonts. Table 10.7 lists the TrueType fonts included with Windows 3.1, and Table 10.8 lists the additional 44 fonts in the optional *TrueType Font Pack*. Table 10.9 shows a sample of each font in all available styles.

Simulated Typeface Styles. If a font style is unavailable, TrueType can simulate it from information derived from the regular style. For example, the Lucida Blackletter bold, italic, and bold italic fonts are all generated from the regular font. For the script fonts (Lucida Calligraphy and Handwriting, Monotype Corsiva), the bold and bold italic fonts are generated from the regular font, which is italic.

When the regular font itself is neither bold nor italic (for example, all the other fonts in the Table), TrueType can come quite close to simulating any missing font from the regular font. In fact, the visual difference between say, the actual Times New Roman bold font, and a bold font simulated from Times New Roman regular is so slight that it is almost undetectable.

Printing TrueType Fonts. TrueType fonts can be printed to any dot-matrix, HPPCL, or Postscript printer, provided the installed printer driver provides the necessary TrueType support. In order to be printed, a TrueType character is converted into a bitmap which is sent to the printer. In addition, the bitmap is stored in a font cache for future reference. Therefore, the next time the same character is required, Windows will retrieve it from the cache. As a result, subsequent print jobs will be faster than the first one.

TABLE 10.7 TrueType Fonts: Windows version 3.1

Typeface & Filename	Font	Typeface & Filename	Font	Typeface & Filename	Font
Arial		**Courier New**		**Times New**	
arial.ttf	Regular	cour.ttf	Regular	**Roman**	
arialbd.ttf	Bold	courbd.ttf	Bold	times.ttf	Regular
ariali.ttf	Italic	couri.ttf	Italic	timesbd.ttf	Bold
arialb.ttf	Bold Italic	courbi.ttf	Bold Italic	timesi.ttf	Italic
				timesbi.ttf	Bold Italic
Symbol		**Wingdings**			
symbol.ttf	Symbols	wingding.ttf	Dingbats		

TABLE 10.8a   Windows *TrueType Font Pack:* Lucida Set

Typeface & Filename	Font	Comp.	Exp.	Typeface & Filename	Font	Comp.	Exp.
Blackletter				**Handwriting**			
lblack.ttf	Decorative	45267	54072	lhandw.ttf	Decorative Italic	42495	50776
Bright				**Math**			
lbrite.ttf	Regular	47815	59828	lmath1.ttf	Math Extension	33104	45700
lbrited.ttf	Demibold	44182	56056	lmath2.ttf	Bright Math Italic	23236	36704
lbritei.ttf	Italic	47724	59872	lmath3.ttf	Br.Math Symbols	41420	54576
lbritedi.ttf	Demibold Italic	48197	60288	**Sans**			
Calligraphy				lsans.ttf	Regular	42563	53144
lcallig.ttf	Decorative Italic	38332	45440	lsansd.ttf	Demibold	38557	48508
Fax				lsansi.ttf	Italic	42877	53604
lfax.ttf	Regular	40375	50600	lsansdi.ttf	Demibold Italic	43571	54136
lfaxd.ttf	Demibold	41139	50980	**Sans Typewriter**			
lfaxi.ttf	Italic	45042	56124	ltype.ttf	Regular	37377	45040
lfaxdi.ttf	Demibold Italic	47565	59556	ltypeb.ttf	Bold	34472	41912
				ltypeo.ttf	Oblique	39412	53192
				ltypebo.ttf	Bold Oblique	35079	43264

TABLE 10.8b   Windows *TrueType Font Pack:* Monotype Set

Typeface & Filename	Font	Comp.	Exp.	Typeface & Filename	Font	Comp.	Exp.
Arial Narrow				**Century Gothic**			
arialn.ttf	Regular	46783	59708	gothic.ttf	Regular	43125	54200
arialnb.ttf	Bold	46403	59008	gothicb.ttf	Bold	38151	47912
arialni.ttf	Italic	47187	60592	gothici.ttf	Italic	43869	54964
arialnbi.ttf	Bold Italic	48246	61476	gothicbi.ttf	Bold Italic	40236	50244
Bookman Antiqua				**Century Schoolbook**			
antqua.ttf	Regular	50549	59472	schlbk.ttf	Regular	53820	66116
antquab.ttf	Bold	50133	61960	schlbkb.ttf	Bold	55654	68620
antquai.ttf	Italic	47587	57020	schlbki.ttf	Italic	53585	67708
antquabi.ttf	Bold Italic	48228	61076	schlbkbi.ttf	Bold Italic	53548	67660
Bookman Old Style				**Monotype Corsiva**			
bookos.ttf	Regular	53401	64240	mtcorsva.ttf	Decorative Italic	51097	60852
bookosb.ttf	Bold	50477	61648	**Monotype Sorts**			
bookosi.ttf	Italic	52756	64504	mtsorts.ttf	Dingbats	63689	79968
bookosbi.ttf	Bold Italic	55651	67872				

TABLE 10.9   TrueType Font Samples*

Typeface	Bold	Italic	Bold Italic
Arial	**Bold**	*Italic*	***Bold Italic***
Arial Narrow	**Bold**	*Italic*	***Bold Italic***
Book Antiqua	**Bold**	*Italic*	***Bold Italic***
Bookman Old Style	**Bold**	*Italic*	***Bold Italic***
Century Gothic	**Bold**	*Italic*	***Bold Italic***
Century Schoolbook	Bold	*Italic*	***Bold Italic***
Courier New	**Bold**	*Italic*	***Bold Italic***
Lucida Blackletter	Bold	Italic	Bold Italic†
Lucida Bright	**Bold**	*Italic*	***Bold Italic***
Lucida Calligraphy	Bold	—	Bold Italic‡
Lucida Fax	**Bold**	*Italic*	***Bold Italic***
Lucida Handwriting	Bold	—	Bold Italic‡
Lucida Sans	**Bold**	*Italic*	***Bold Italic***
Lucida Sans Typewriter	**Bold**	*Italic*	***Bold Italic***
Monotype Corsiva	Bold	—	Bold Italic‡
Times New Roman	**Bold**	*Italic*	***Bold Italic***

*   All fonts set at same point size.
†   Bold, italic, bold italic fonts generated from regular font.
‡   Regular font is italic. Bold, bold italic fonts generated from regular font.

Refer to the *TrueType Font Configuration* section later in the chapter if TrueType font names are not available within an applet or application Font Box.

WARNING: Deleting a TrueType font listing from WIN.INI may have an unpredictable effect on previously created documents which use TrueType fonts, even if the deleted font itself does not appear in the document. Refer to the *Wrong Font Appears in a Document* section later in this chapter for further details.

Font File Extension Summary

In case of doubt, a font file's extension often gives a clue as to the nature of the file. A list of some frequently encountered extensions is given in Table 10.10.

Fonts on the Windows Desktop

Windows uses its three system fonts and the MS Sans Serif screen font to display text on the Desktop. Table 10.11 summarizes the Desktop locations at which each font appears, and identifies the section of SYSTEM.INI or WIN.INI at which the default font is specified. Figure 10.3 shows representative examples of these and other fonts.

During the regular Windows installation process, the most appropriate fonts for your system are expanded and copied from the distribution diskettes to your Windows SYSTEM directory. Their file names are entered in the SYSTEM.INI and WIN.INI files, and in most cases these default fonts will be satisfactory. However, you may want to change one or more fonts if you change your display system, or to suit personal taste. The procedure for doing so is described in the *Changing Windows System Fonts* section later in this chapter.

TABLE 10.10   Representative Font File Extensions

Extension	Meaning	Comments
ANL	AN(?) Landscape	Hewlett-Packard soft font
ANP	AN(?) Portrait	Hewlett-Packard soft font
CSD	Character Set Descriptor	For Bitstream Speedo character set config.
FON	FONt	A Windows raster (bitmap) or vector font
FOT	FOnT	Font resource data file for a TrueType font.
PCM	Printer Cartridge Metrics	Font metrics for a printer cartridge
PFB	Printer Font, Binary	Soft font; must download prior to print job
PFM	Printer Font, Metrics	Font metrics for a PFB soft font
PSO	Post Script	Post Script
SFL	Soft Font, Landscape mode	
SFP	Soft Font, Portrait mode	
SFS	Soft Font, Scalable	
SPD	Speedo	Bitstream Speedo outline font
TDF	Typeface Definition File	Font metrics for Bitsream Facelift fonts
TTF	TrueType Font	

TABLE 10.11a   Default Screen Font Usage*

Desktop Area	Font Style	INI File	Section	Line
Cardfile, Notepad, Windows ver 2.x Applications				
	Sans Serif	SYSTEM.INI	[boot]	fixed.fon=VGAFIX.FON
Character Map				
Fixedsys	Sans Serif	SYSTEM.INI	[boot]	fixedfon.font=VGAFIX.FON
System	Sans Serif			fonts.fon=VGASYS.FON
Terminal, or	Mixed			oemfonts.fon=VGAOEM.FON, or
8514oem	Sans Serif			oemfonts.fon=8514OEM.FON [†]
Other	Various	WIN.INI	[fonts]	*(various)*
			[*other*]	*(as installed by third-party apps.)*
DOS Window				
Terminal Fonts	Sans Serif	SYSTEM.INI	[386Enh]	*(see Table 7.1)*
File Manager				
Directory	Sans Serif	WIN.INI	[fonts]	MS Sans Serif=SSERIFE.FON
Group, Applet Windows				
Title Bars & Menus	Sans Serif	SYSTEM.INI	[boot]	fonts.fon=VGASYS.FON
Help Screens	Sans Serif	WIN.INI	[fonts]	MS Sans Serif=SSERIFE.FON
Titles	12 pt. font			
Text	10 pt. font			
Icon Titles	Sans Serif	WIN.INI	[fonts]	MS Sans Serif=SSERIFE.FON
Print Manager				
Workspace	Sans Serif	WIN.INI	[fonts]	MS Sans Serif=SSERIFE.FON
Status Bar				
	Sans Serif	WIN.INI	[fonts]	MS Sans Serif=SSERIFE.FON
SysEdit Applet				
Text	Sans Serif	SYSTEM.INI	[boot]	fonts.fon=VGASYS.FON
Word-for-Windows				
Menu Bars	Sans Serif	SYSTEM.INI	[boot]	fonts.fon=VGASYS.FON
Ribbon Boxes	Sans Serif	*(uses DIALOG.FON in WINWORD directory)*		
Doc. Text Area	TrueType	WIN.INI	[fonts]	Various

*VGA system fonts listed here. Figure 10.3 shows onscreen examples of these fonts.
[†] If this line appears in [boot] section, then Character Map shows 8514oem font, as indicated, and Terminal font becomes EGA80WOA.FON.

TABLE 10.11b   Default Screen Font Usage*

SYSTEM.INI [boot] Section		WIN.INI [fonts] Section
fixed.fon=xxxfix.fon	**fonts.fon=xxxsys.fon**	**MS Sans Serif=SSERIFx.FON** [†]
Cardfile text	Character Map: System	File Manager Directory listings
Character Map: Fixedsys	Menus	Help Screens
Notepad text	SysEdit text	Icon Titles [‡]
Windows version 2.*x* applications	Title Bars	Print Manager Workspace [‡]
		Status Bar text

[*] Unless otherwise noted, categories in each column are displayed by font at head of column.

[†] If specified font is not SSERIF*x*.FON, Windows searches for closest available sans serif font, regardless of filename specified on this line.

[‡] If specified font is not SSERIF*x*.FON, icon titles may be MS Serif; Print Manager Workspace uses Small Fonts.

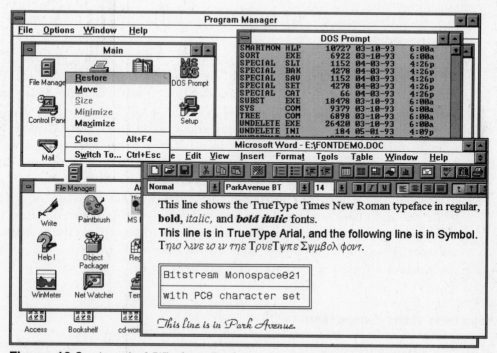

Figure 10.3 A typical Windows Desktop showing various system fonts within the Program Manager and DOS Window, plus TrueType and other fonts in the Microsoft Word application window.

Location of Windows Fonts

Windows assumes all fonts are located in its own SYSTEM directory; therefore, path information need not be included in the various font-specification lines discussed below. However, if you decide to move these or other fonts into their own directory, then the name of that directory must be included in the appropriate line in your SYSTEM.INI or WIN.INI file.

Font Specification Nomenclature.   In SYSTEM.INI and WIN.INI, fonts may be specified in one of the following formats:

Font Specification Format	Used in	Section	Specific Example
1. Fonttype.fon= *filename.ext*	SYSTEM.INI	[boot]	fixedfon.fon=vgafix.fon
2. Font Descriptor= *filename.ext*	WIN.INI	[fonts]	Courier 10,12,15 (VGA res)=COURE.FON
3. Font Usage=Font Descriptor	WIN.INI	[Desktop]	IconTitleFaceName= Courier

Specific Example 1 is particularly confusing, since fixedfon.fon certainly looks like the name of a file. But, appearance notwithstanding, it is simply a *description* of the font type that will be used, while the name of the font file itself appears to the right of the equal sign. Later on, Windows will refer to this line, then use whatever font is listed here. Therefore, you will find a font named vgafix.fon (or similar) in your Windows System directory but you *won't* find one named fixedfon.fon.

In example 3, IconTitleFaceName= describes a specific usage of a font, while the right-hand expression refers not to a font filename, but to a font descriptor which in turn specifies the font file that will be used. Thus, in the specific example, a courier font displays the text under each icon, and the actual font used is COURE.FON (as defined in example 2).

System Font Selection

Three of the fonts that Windows needs for its own use are specified in the SYSTEM.INI file and the fourth is specified in WIN.INI, as described in this section.

The System Fonts in SYSTEM.INI. The three fonts that Windows identifies as its system fonts are specified in SYSTEM.INI, as described below. Each font is specified in the "*fonttype*.fon=*filename.ext*" format, as seen here:

[boot]	**Description**
fixedfon.fon=vgafix.fon	Monospaced system font
fonts.fon=vgasys.fon	Variable-width system font
oemfonts.fon=vgaoem.fon	OEM (Terminal) font

This example shows the default fonts for a VGA video system. Additional details about each of these lines follows. In each case, the *xxx* part of the filename identifies the video system, as CGA (Win 3.0 only), EGA, VGA, or 8514.

Monospaced System Font (fixedfon.fon=xxxfix.fon). This is the monospaced system font used in the following locations:

Cardfile
Character Map: Fixedsys
Notepad Text
DOS Window

The Font Selection dialog box displays the list of pixel matrixes in this font. The fonts themselves are taken from a variety of files, as described in Chapter 7.

The ASCII character set is sans serif, except for lowercase *i, j,* and *l.*

Variable-Width System Font (fonts.fon=xxxsys.fon). This is the variable-width system font seen in the following locations:

Character Map: System
Clipboard Text
Menus
Title Bars
SysEdit Text

The ASCII character set is sans serif (all of it).

OEM (Terminal) Font (oemfonts.fon=xxxoem.fon). Depending on the video system in use, one of the following monospace OEM (Original Equipment Manufacturer) fonts will be listed on this line.

OEM Font	H	V	Used with Video System
egaoem.fon	8	8	EGA
vgaoem.fon	8	12	VGA
8514oem.fon	16	18	Super-VGA, 8514
vga*xxx*.fon	8	12	VGA, where *xxx* is a code page used with various foreign-language setups. See *Character Set (Code Page) Configuration* in Chapter 7.

The OEM font is seen in the following locations:

Character Map: Terminal font
Clipboard OEM Text
DOS Window   Text, only in OEM font matrix listed above. Other matrixes originate elsewhere (see Chapter 7).

The ASCII character set is a mix of serif and sans serif characters.

OEM Font Usage in DOS Window.   Since the OEM font is used primarily to display text in a DOS Window, it is described in greater detail in Chapter 7.

The Fourth "System Font."   In addition to the fonts specified in SYS-TEM.INI, Windows uses one other font to display certain items on the Desktop. That font is specified in WIN.INI, as shown here for a VGA video system:

```
[fonts]
MS Sans Serif=SSERIFE.FON
```

Although the font is not classified as a system font, perhaps it should be since it performs in a similar capacity to the three official system fonts de-scribed above. For example, the MS Sans Serif font is seen in the follow-ing Desktop locations:

Character Map: MS Sans Serif
Help Screen titles and text
File Manager directory listings
Icon Titles
Print Manager Workspace

As the filename suggests, the ASCII character set is all sans serif.

WIN.INI Font Selection

In addition to the System fonts specified in the SYSTEM.INI file, additional fonts are specified in several sections of the WIN.INI file, as described below.

The [fonts] Section. This section lists the raster, vector, and TrueType fonts described earlier in this chapter. A few sample listings are given here for review purposes. The comment lines (beginning with a semicolon) do not appear in the section, but may be added at the user's discretion.

```
;raster fonts (VGA font set listed here)
Courier 10,12,15 (VGA res)=COURE.FON
MS Sans Serif 8,10,12,14,18,24 (VGA res)=SSERIFE.FON
MS Serif 8,10,12,14,18,24 (VGA res)=SERIFE.FON
Small Fonts (VGA res)=SMALLE.FON
Symbol 8,10,12,14,18,24 (VGA res)=SYMBOLE.FON

;vector fonts
Modern (All res)=MODERN.FON
Script (All res)=SCRIPT.FON
Roman (Plotter)=ROMAN.FON

;TrueType fonts
Arial (TrueType)=ARIAL.FOT
Arial Bold (TrueType)=ARIALBD.FOT
Arial Bold Italic (TrueType)=ARIALI.FOT
Arial Bold (True Type)=ARIALI.FOT
```

The [FontSubstitutes] Section. The raster fonts formerly identified as "Helv" and "Tms Rmn" have been renamed in Windows 3.1 as "MS Sans Serif" and "MS Serif." Since it is quite likely you will refer to documents created when the older names were in effect, a [FontSubstitutes] section of WIN.INI provides a cross-reference guide between old and new names, as shown here:

```
[FontSubstitutes]
Helv=MS Sans Serif
Tms Rmn=MS Serif
Times=Times New Roman
Helvetica=Arial
```

For example, if a document created earlier with the Helv font is opened after upgrading your system to Windows 3.1, all text marked as Helv will now be displayed with the new MS Sans Serif font. If your installed printer does not support MS Sans Serif, then the Arial font will be substituted in its place, since that font is the closest available match to MS Sans Serif. Although the Points Box will only list the point size currently in use, if you type another point size in the box, selected text will be displayed and printed in that size.

The substitution just described will not take place if the old font is in fact still available. And in any case, the Font Box will continue to list the name of the old font, regardless of which font is actually in use.

> **NOTE:** If any of the default lines in this section of WIN.INI are changed or deleted, some third-party applications may not display the correct screen fonts. For further details, refer to *Wrong Font Used by Third-Party Application* in the *Troubleshooting* section later in this chapter.

Font Installation Procedures

During the initial Windows Setup procedure described in Chapter 1, the various raster, vector, and TrueType fonts included with Windows were installed in your System directory, with the appropriate lines inserted in the [boot] section of SYSTEM.INI and the [fonts] section of WIN.INI. To identify the currently installed fonts, double-click on the Fonts Applet icon to display the Fonts dialog box in Figure 10.4a. Assuming the TrueType fonts supplied with Windows itself are already installed, the complete Installed Fonts: list should resemble that shown in part b of the figure.

This section describes a few of the ways in which new fonts can be added to those already installed on your system. In addition, certain software-specific configuration problems that may occur during installation of the cited software are described. General font configuration procedures are covered separately in the *Font Configuration* section later in the chapter.

Although you might want to skip one or more of the following subsections if you don't have the software under discussion, some of the procedures may be valid for similar font packages from suppliers other than those specifically mentioned here. In each case, the section header identifies the specific software supplier, so you'll know which sections to read and which to skip.

Add New Fonts (General Information)

To install more fonts, click on the Add... button seen at the right-hand side of the Fonts dialog box. This opens the Add Fonts dialog box shown in Figure 10.5.

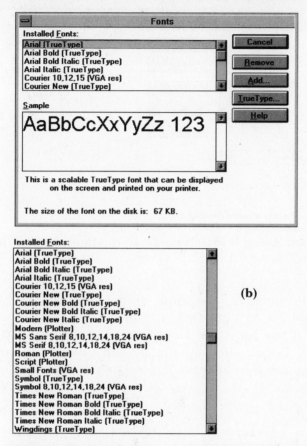

Figure 10.4 The Fonts dialog box (a) shows the list of currently installed fonts. (b) The complete Installed Fonts list as it might appear shortly after installing Windows.

NOTE: If the new fonts are supplied with their own installation software, follow the instructions provided with that software. A few examples of such third-party font installation software are described later in this section.

If you want to install your fonts into a separate directory, then refer to the *Font Relocation* section below and modify the font installation procedure according to the information given in that section. However, if you plan to install all new fonts in the system directory, then simply continue reading here, since that's where they'll land if you don't specify otherwise.

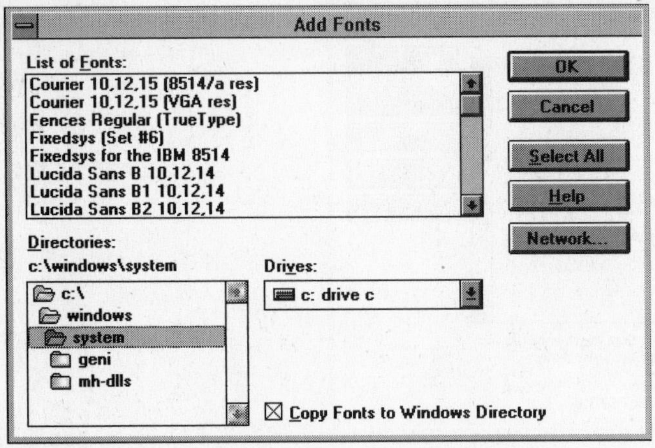

Figure 10.5 The Add Fonts dialog box shows a list of the fonts detected in the indicated subdirectory.

Retrieve Font Names. Presumably, the fonts to be installed are on a distribution diskette in drive A. Therefore, use the Drives: box to select that drive (or another if the fonts are elsewhere). If necessary, change the Directories: box too. Double-click on the desired drive or directory name and the following message appears immediately below the List of Fonts: box:

Retrieving font names: *xx*%

At the end of the search, the List of Fonts: box will display all the fonts that were found on the diskette or other source. To simply test the font-retrieval process, double-click on the Windows\System directory and in a few seconds the List of Fonts: box will show all the fonts in that directory. Presumably these are already installed, but this retrieval test will give you an idea of how the process works.

Accelerating the Font Name Search. If the fonts to be installed are on a distribution diskette that contains many other files, the search can be considerably speeded up by copying only the font files to a RAM disk, then searching that disk instead of the distribution diskette. For example, consider a reinstallation of the TrueType fonts supplied with Windows and Windows-for-Workgroups. On the 1.44 Mbyte distribution diskettes for Windows-for-Workgroups, 11 of 14 TrueType fonts are among 78 compressed files on distribution diskette 7. On a typical 486 computer, it could take almost 5 minutes to search and retrieve the fonts on this diskette, and the list would include the non-TrueType fonts as well. To save time, try one of the following procedures, as appropriate to your needs.

Install Fonts in System Directory.   If you plan to follow the default procedure of installing the fonts in your System directory, simply copy them to an empty RAM drive by typing one or both of the following lines at the DOS prompt:

COPY A:*.TT_ x: *(to copy all TrueType fonts to your RAM disk, drive x)*
COPY A:*.FO_ x: *(to copy all screen fonts to your RAM disk, drive x)*

Now search drive *x* instead of the distribution diskette. The files should be found in a few seconds, rather than in several minutes.

Install Fonts in Some Other Directory.   If you want the fonts to be installed in some other directory, then they must be expanded into that directory prior to installing them. If they are compressed on the distribution diskette (as is likely), then log onto the Windows directory and type the line shown below at the DOS prompt. If the files are not compressed, then simply copy them into the desired directory and proceed to *Select Fonts to Install* below.

expand -r A:*.TT_ C:\WINDOWS\TRUETYPE

The -r parameter is supported by the Expand utility in the Windows directory, but not by the same utility in the DOS directory, so it is important to type this command from within the Windows directory. The parameter specifies that each file will be correctly renamed (in this case, as *filename*.TTF) as it is expanded.

NOTE: The -r parameter is not recognized by all compressed files. To keep things interesting, the TrueType files that accompany Windows do recognize it. The ones in the separately available TrueType Font Pack for Windows don't.

Select Fonts to Install.   If you want to install all the fonts in the List of Fonts: box, simply click on the Select All button. Note the check box next to Copy Fonts to Windows Directory near the bottom of the dialog box (which should really read "Copy Fonts to *System* Directory," since that's where the fonts go unless you clear the check box). In most cases, you will probably want to leave this box checked. However, if you have set up a separate directory for your font collection, then clear this box so that the fonts don't get copied into the System directory.

Install Fonts.   After selecting the fonts you want to install, and making sure the Copy Fonts check box status is correct, click on the OK button to conclude the font installation. As each font is installed, its name will appear highlighted in the Fonts dialog box. If more than one font is installed, then at the conclusion of the procedure the Sample box will be empty, since all the just-installed fonts are highlighted (selected), and the box can only display one file at a time. Click once on any font name to select it and clear all the others at the same time. A font sample should now be seen in the box.

Conclude Font Installation.   When you are finished installing the new fonts, click on the Close button to exit.

If you just installed TrueType fonts, a *filename*.FOT file will be found in your system directory for each font. A *filename*.TTF file will also be in the System directory, or elsewhere if you specified a different destination for the New... files. In either case, the FOT file contains an internal pointer to let Windows know where the equivalent TTF file is located. Refer to *True-Type Font Extensions* above for further details.

Microsoft: TrueType Font Pack for Windows

The *TrueType Font Pack for Windows* is supplied with its own installation software. This setup procedure does not give you the option to select the destination directory for the fonts that will be installed. Like it or not, the fonts are installed in your System directory. If you'd rather have them elsewhere, then follow the procedures described in the *Install New Fonts* section above instead. Or, run the Setup procedure, then relocate the fonts later on, as described in the *Font Relocation* section below.

The typefaces included in the *Font Pack* were listed earlier, in Table 10.8. To begin installing them, open the File Menu, select the Run... option, and type A:SETUP in the Command Line: box. Follow the on-screen prompts to complete the installation.

Agfa: Discovery TrueType Pack

This package contains the TrueType text, headline, and clip art fonts listed in Table 10.12. The *Discovery* installation procedure automatically places the fonts you select into the System directory. Therefore, it you'd rather place them elsewhere, install the *Discovery Font Guide* only. Then install some or all of the fonts as described in *Install Fonts in Some Other Directory* in the *Add New Fonts* section above.

TABLE 10.12 Agfa *Discovery TrueType Pack* Files

Font Box Name	Font	Typeface and Font Name	TTF File[†]	Comments
		Text Fonts		
Garth Graphic ATT	Regular	Garth Graphic ATT Regular	GARTHG	
	Bold	Garth Graphic ATT Bold	GARTHGB	
	Italic	Garth Graphic ATT Italic	GARTHGI	
	Bold italic	Garth Graphic ATT Bold Italic	GARTHGBI	
Garth Graphic Cond. ATT	Regular	Garth Gr. Cond. ATT Reg.	GARTHCD	
	Bold	Garth Gr. Cond. ATT Bold	GARTHCDB	
Nadianne ATT	Regular	Nadianne ATT Regular	NADIAN	Script font
	Bold	Nadianne ATT Bold	NADIANB	Bold script
Nadianne Medium ATT	Regular	Nadianne Medium ATT Reg.	NADIANME	Bold script
Shannon ATT	Regular	Shannon ATT Regular	SHANNO	
	Bold	Shannon ATT Bold	SHANNOB	
	Italic	Shannon ATT Italic	SHANNOO	Oblique font
Shannon Ext. Bold ATT	Regular	Shannon Extra Bold ATT Reg.	SHANNOEB	
Wile ATT	Regular	Wile Roman ATT Regular	WILE	
	Bold	Wile Roman ATT Bold	WILEB	
	Italic	Wile Roman ATT Italic	WILEI	
	Bold italic	Wile Roman ATT Bold Italic	WILEBI	

Clip Art[‡]	TTF File[†]	Headline[‡]	TTF File[†]
Borders & Ornaments 1	BOR&ORN1	Artistik	ARTISTIK
Borders & Ornaments 4	BOR&ORN4	Bernard Fashion	BERNHFA
Borders & Ornaments 5	BOR&ORN5	Bernard Modern	BERNHMO
Communications 1	COMMUNI1	Broadway	BROADWAY
Communications 2	COMMUNI2	Carmine Tango	CARMINET
Communications 3	COMMUNI3	CG Poster Bodoni	CGPOSTER
Communications 6	COMMUNI6	Cooper Black	COOPERBL
Games & Sports 1	GAMES1	Delphian	DELPHIAN
Games & Sports 3	GAMES3	Dom Casual	DOMCASUA

TABLE 10.12 *(continued)*

Clip Art [‡]	TTF File [†]	Headline [‡]	TTF File [†]
Games & Sports 4	GAMES4	Eccentric	ECCENTRI
Holidays	HOLIDAYS	Goudy Handtooled	GOUDYHAN
Industry & Engineering 1	IND&ENG1	Old English	OLDENGLI
Industry & Engineering 2	IND&ENG2	Revue Shadow	REVUESHA
Transportation 1	TRANSPO1	Signet Roundhand	SIGNETRO
Transportation 2	TRANSPO2		

[†] Each filename has TTF extension.

[‡] Regular font only for each listed Clip Art and Headline typeface.

> **NOTE:** Although the Agfa fonts on the distribution diskettes are compressed, they may be mistaken for noncompressed files since their extensions are TTF (not TT_, as is usual for compressed TrueType files).

The Discovery Font Guide. Although any Agfa TrueType font can be viewed via the Character Map applet described later in this chapter, the *Discovery Font Guide* offers a much improved method of viewing Agfa Clip Art fonts. Double-click on the applet icon to open the Discovery Font Guide (not shown here). Then select *Clip Art Keyboard Maps* near the bottom of the screen to display a list of the Clip Art fonts that are represented by keyboard maps. Select the font (map) of interest to display a keyboard map such as that shown in Figure 10.6a. In this and several other Clip Art fonts, two or more keystrokes are required to build a complete illustration. For example, press letter keys "a, b, c" to create a telephone, as shown by the detail view in Figure 10.6b. Some experimentation may be needed, since each "letter" will overlay the others in order to build the composite illustration.

In addition to the keyboard maps described here, the *Discovery Font Guide* offers an excellent tutorial on general font usage. If your documents look like ransom notes, you may want to study it carefully.

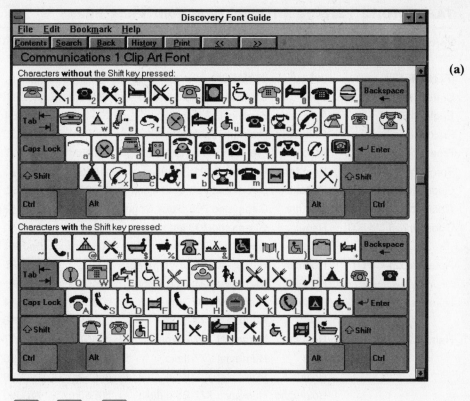

Figure 10.6 The keyboard map (a) for one of Agfa's Clip Art fonts. The graphic on each key is printed when that key is pressed. (b) An "a,b,c," sequence produces the telephone graphic seen here.

Bitstream: TrueType Font Pack for Windows 3.1

To install some or all of these fonts, follow the procedure described in the *Add New Fonts* section above, and repeat it for diskettes 1 and 2. Since the files are not compressed on the distribution diskettes, they may be copied directly into the System or other directory and installed from there. Only the files with TTF (TrueType Font) extensions are required: Although there is a corresponding TDF (Typeface Definition File) file for each font, these files need not be copied from the distribution diskettes. The TPF.CFG (Typeface Configuration) file on each distribution diskette provides cross-reference information between typeface and font names, and TTF and TDF files, as summarized in Table 10.13.

TABLE 10.13 Bitstream *True Type Font Pack* Files*

Font Box Name	Font	Typeface and Font Name	TTF File [†]	TDF File [‡]
[FLNAMES] [§]		[NAMES]	[TTF]	[TDF]
Clarendon Cn BT	Bold	Clarendon Bold Cond	tt0228m_	jx0228
English157 BT	Italic	English 157 Regular	tt0840m_	mw0840
Fraktur BT	Regular	Fraktur Regular	tt0983m_	3n0983
Freehand575 BT	Italic	Freehand 575 Regular	tt1046m_	4f1046
Freehand591 BT	Regular	Freehand 591 Regular	tt1043m_	4g1043
Geometr706 BdCn BT	Regular	Geometric 706 Bold Cond	tt0662m_	6f0662
Geometr706 BlkCn BT	Regular	Geometric 706 Black Cond	tt0663m_	6g0663
Geometr706 Md BT	Regular	Geometric 706 Medium	tt0660m_	6d0660
	Bold	Geometric 706 Black	tt0661m_	6e0661
Humanst521 Cn BT	Regular	Humanist 521 Condensed	tt0495m_	xq0495
	Bold	Humanist 521 Bold Cond	tt0496m_	xr0496
Humanst970 BT	Regular	Humanist 970 Roman	tt0264m_	8c0264
	Bold	Humanist 970 Bold	tt0265m_	8d0265
Humnst777 BT	Regular	Humanist 777 Roman	tt0857m_	ke0857
	Italic	Humanist 777 Italic	tt0858m_	7x0858
	Bold	Humanist 777 Bold	tt0859m_	7y0859
	Bold Italic	Humanist 777 Bold Italic	tt0860m_	7z0860
HuxleyVertical BT	Regular	Huxley Vertical Regular	tt1177m_	581177
Imperial BT	Regular	Imperial Roman	tt0352m_	8i0352
	Italic	Imperial Italic	tt0353m_	8j0353
	Bold	Imperial Bold	tt0354m_	8k0354
Impress BT	Regular	Impress Regular	tt0209m_	8l0209
Incised901 Nd BT	Regular	Incised 901 Nord	tt0469m_	8p0469
Incised901 NdIt BT	Italic	Incised 901 Nord Italic	tt0470m_	8q0470
Informal011 BT	Regular	Informal 011 Roman	tt1115m_	8u1115
Informal011 Blk BT	Regular	Informal 011 Black	tt1116m_	8v1116
Nuptial BT	Italic	Nuptial Regular	tt0981m_	h30981
OzHandicraft BT	Regular	BitsOzHandicraft Roman	tt1178m_	ou1178
PosterBodoni BT	Regular	Poster Bodoni Roman	tt0129m_	sw0129
PosterBodoni It BT	Italic	Poster Bodoni Italic	tt0130m_	sx0130
Revival565 BT	Regular	Revival 565 Roman	tt1068m_	j01068
	Italic	Revival 565 Italic	tt1069m_	j11069
	Bold	Revival 565 Bold	tt1070m_	j21070
	Bold Italic	Revival 565 Bold Italic	tt1071m_	j31071

Table 10.13 *(continued)*

Font Box Name	Font	Typeface and Font Name	TTF File [†]	TDF File [‡]
SquareSlab711 Bd BT	Regular	Square Slab 711 Bold	tt0412m_	o00412
SquareSlab711 Lt BT	Regular	Square Slab 711 Light	tt0410m_	n80410
	Bold	Square Slab 711 Medium	tt0411m_	n90411
Staccato555 BT	Italic	Staccato 555 Regular	tt1153m_	ot1153
Umbra BT	Regular	Umbra Regular	tt1074m_	s61074
Vineta BT	Regular	Vineta Regular	tt0215m_	kb0215

[*] Information based on TFP.CFG file on distribution diskettes.

[†] Each filename has TTF extension.

[‡] Each filename has TDF extension.

[§] Bracketed section headers in TFP.CFG file.

Hewlett-Packard: TrueType Screen Font Pack (for LaserJet 4/4M)

The Hewlett-Packard LaserJet 4 contains 46 internal typefaces grouped in 18 typefaces, as listed in Table 10.14. The fonts are supported by the printer driver (HPPCL5E.DRV), with one Line Printer and 13 Intellifont typefaces appearing in Font Boxes as screen fonts (note printer icon next to font name and W1 after it). The four internal Courier (Intellifont) and 10 TrueType fonts match the equivalent 14 Windows TrueType fonts. If any of these fonts appear in a document, some download time is saved since the complete font is already resident in the printer and need not be downloaded.

An optional *TrueType Screen Font Pack* is separately available from Hewlett-Packard and includes TrueType fonts that match 31 of the 35 internal Intellifonts (the four internal Courier fonts are matched by the Windows Courier New TrueType fonts).

Since the TrueType fonts are resident in two compressed files (TT1.LIB and TT2.LIB), the included installation software must be used to expand the files into the System directory. To begin the installation, open the File Menu, select the Run... option and type A:SETUP in the Command Line: box. Follow the onscreen prompts to complete the installation.

The Setup procedure makes a backup copy of WIN.INI as WIN.TT. If a backup with that name already exists, you will be prompted to enter a new suffix (that is, file extension).

TABLE 10.14 Hewlett-Packard LaserJet 4 Internal Fonts*

Typeface Font	Typeface Font	Typeface Font	Typeface Font

Intellifont

Typeface Font	Typeface Font	Typeface Font	Typeface Font
Albertus Medium	**CG Times**	**Garamond Antiqua**	**Univers**
Regular	Regular	Regular	Regular
	Bold	Halbfett	Bold
Albertus Extra Bold	Italic	Kursiv	Italic
Regular	Bold Italic	Kursiv Halbfett	Bold Italic
Antique Olive	**Clarendon Condensed**	**Letter Gothic**	**Univers Condensed**
Regular	Regular	Regular	Regular
Bold		Bold	Bold
Italic	**Coronet**	Italic	Italic
	Regular		Bold Italic
CG Omega	**Courier**[†]	**Marigold**	
Regular	Regular	Regular (Italic style)	
Bold	Bold		
Italic	Italic		
Bold Italic	Bold Italic		

TrueType

Arial[†]	Times New Roman[†]	Symbol[†]	Wingdings[†]
Regular	Regular	Regular (symbols)	Regular (symbols)
Bold	Bold		
Italic	Italic		
Bold Italic	Bold Italic		

Raster Font

Line Printer
Regular (16.67 pitch, 8.5 points)

---

[*] Unless otherwise noted, TrueType font available from Hewlett-Packard to match internal Intellifont font.

[†] Internal font matches Windows 3.1 TrueType font.

Font Pack Support Files. The Font Pack includes the following INI files:

TTFONTS.INI	Lines to be added to the [fonts] section of WIN.INI. For example: Albertus Extra Bold (TrueType)=ALBERTEB.FOT *(and so on)*
TTINFO.INI	Information required by Setup procedure.
TTSUBS.INI	Lines to be added to the [FontSubstitutes] section of WIN.INI: Albertus Xb (W1)=Albertus Extra Bold Albertus Xb (WN)=Albertus Extra Bold *(and so on)*

Postinstallation Check. Once the TrueType fonts are installed, you may want to open the Printer Setup dialog box shown in the previous chapter as Figure 9.10. Make sure there is an "X" in the check box at the beginning of the TrueType Screen Fonts Installed line. If this option is disabled, the Fonts list or Fonts Box in various Windows applets will list each font twice: one as the internal screen font, the other as the TrueType font. If the box is checked, only the TrueType line appears. If you clear the box and recheck it, or check it for the first time, a warning message advises:

Check this box only if you have the following screen font software installed:
HP LaserJet 4/4M TrueType Screen Font Pack

If at a later date you're not sure about this, check the Windows directory for the presence of a WIN.TT file, which is a backup copy of WIN.INI made during the initial installation of the screen fonts. Its presence indicates that the Screen (that is, TrueType) Fonts are indeed installed on your hard disk.

Microsoft: Equation Editor TrueType Fonts

The Microsoft *Equation Editor* is supplied with Word-for-Windows and some other applications. If it was installed as part of the Setup procedure for that application, then the following TrueType fonts should be available as indicated here.

Installed Fonts List:	**[fonts] Section of WIN.INI**
Fences Plain [TrueType]	Fences Plain [TrueType]=FENCES.FOT
MT Extra Plain [TrueType]	MT Extra Plain [TrueType]=MTEXTRA.FOT

If these fonts are not available, then review the instructions which follow.

Installation Procedure. The following text reproduces the Equation Editor's setup instructions in its entirety:

> If Equation Editor has not been installed, use the Install program for the Microsoft product that it came with to install it (*User's Guide*, p. 1). If you need information about installing Equation Editor, see the installation instructions for the Microsoft product it came with (ditto, p. 3).

On the off-chance that it doesn't tell you everything you need to know about installing the Equation Editor, a few supplementary details follow.

If one of your group windows shows a Word-for-Windows Setup icon, double-click on it to begin the Setup. Otherwise, insert the Word-for-Windows (or other) Setup diskette in drive A, click on File in the Program Manager's Menu bar, select Run, and type A:SETUP to begin the Setup procedure. Assuming you only want to install the Equation Editor at this time, follow the screen directions and select "Custom Installation" when that option is displayed. Then clear the boxes for every other option, so as to install only the Equation Editor.

Once the Equation Editor is installed in the application which it accompanies, it will probably be found in a subdirectory within the Windows directory—not the application's own directory. To set up the Equation Editor as a free-standing applet in any group window, proceed as follows.

Open the Program Manager's File Menu, select the New... option, and click on the Program Item radio button. Type the following information in the Program Item Properties box:

Description: Equations
Command line: C:\WINDOWS\MSAPPS\EQUATION\EQNEDIT.EXE

The command line indicates the usual location for this utility. Revise the line if necessary to indicate some other location.

After concluding this procedure, an Equation Editor icon should be available in the selected group window. To verify or correct the editor's font configuration, double-click on the icon to open the applet. Or if you prefer, open WRITE, Word-for-Windows, or some other application and sequentially choose the following options (or similar) to arrive at the Equation Editor.

WRITE	**Word-for-Windows**
Edit Menu	Insert Menu
Insert Object...	Object...
Equation	Equation

If an error message appears when the Editor opens for the first time, refer to that message in the *Equation Editor Error Messages* section below. If you encounter no messages at all, then the Equation Editor is correctly installed (perhaps). However, you may want to verify this by reviewing the section which immediately follows.

Equation Editor Font Configuration. In addition to its own Fences Plain and MT Extra Plain fonts, the Equation Editor uses (or *should* use) the TrueType Times New Roman and Symbol fonts. To verify that these fonts are specified, open the Equation Editor's Style Menu and select the De-fine... option to display the Styles dialog box shown in Figure 10.7. The various Times New Roman (or other text) fonts are not critical—any text font will do just as well, and these fonts may be changed to agree with the text font used for the body of the document in which the equation will appear. However, the Greek and Symbol fonts *must* use a font that agrees with the symbols in the Equation Editor's palettes. Therefore, the L.C. Greek, U.C. Greek, and Symbol boxes should all list Symbol. If some other font name appears, click on the appropriate down arrow and select the Symbol font.

NOTE: The Equation Editor *User's Guide* (p. 72) incorrectly lists a text font (Times New Roman) in the **L.C. Greek font box**. The correct font is, of course, "Symbol."

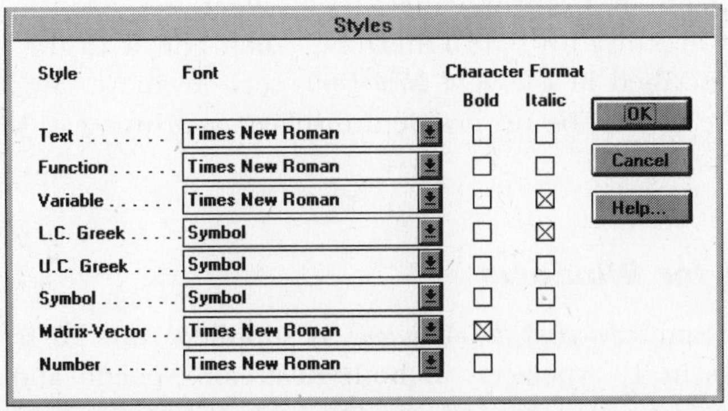

Styles			
Style	**Font**	**Character Format**	
		Bold	**Italic**
Text	Times New Roman	☐	☐
Function	Times New Roman	☐	☐
Variable	Times New Roman	☐	☒
L.C. Greek	Symbol	☐	☒
U.C. Greek	Symbol	☐	☐
Symbol	Symbol	☐	☐
Matrix-Vector . . .	Times New Roman	☒	☐
Number	Times New Roman	☐	☐

OK Cancel Help...

Figure 10.7 The Equation Editor's Styles dialog box lists the fonts that will be used for various equation elements.

Equation Editor Support File (MTFONTS.INI). The names of the eight fonts listed in the Styles dialog box (Figure 10.7) are stored in an MTFONTS.INI file in the Windows directory, as shown here:

```
[(default printer, port)]
TEXT=Times New Roman
FUNCTION=Times New Roman
VARIABLE=Times New Roman, I        (I = italic font)
LCGREEK=Symbol, I                  (I = italic font)
UCGREEK=Symbol
SYMBOL=Symbol
VECTOR=Times New Roman, B     (B = bold font)
NUMBER=Times New Roman
USER1=Times New Roman
USER2=Times New Roman
```

Microsoft: MS Line Draw Vector Font

If you have Microsoft's *Word-for-Windows* and the MS Line Draw font is not available, find the distribution diskette labeled Drawing/Equation Editor and verify that a file named WINLD.FO$ (compressed format) is present. Then use the Word-for-Windows decompress utility (DECOMP.EXE) to transfer it to your system diskette. (Neither the DOS nor the Windows expand utility may be used for the operation, nor the regular Add Fonts option in the Icons section of Windows Control Panel.) If you need help completing the procedure, refer to the *File Expansion Utilities* section of Chapter 4 for further details.

Once the file has been successfully transferred to your System directory, click on the Fonts icon in Control Panel, then select the Add... option. Search your System directory for "MS LineDraw," then add it to the list of installed fonts, as described in the *Add New Fonts* section above. Since this is a vector font, there should be no problem displaying/printing it, regardless of the installed printer.

Bitstream: FaceLift for Windows

Version 2.0 of Bitstream's *FaceLift for Windows* is supplied with 16 scalable (not TrueType) fonts in 10 typefaces, in both Bitstream Speedo and Postscript Type 1 formats. To install *FaceLift* and the fonts themselves, open the Program Manager's File Menu, select the Run... option, and type A:INSTALL in the Command Line: box. Follow the onscreen prompts to complete the installation. In a default installation, Speedo fonts are copied into a BTFONTS directory, and Postscript fonts go to a PSFONTS directory.

Like most other Windows applications, *FaceLift* creates its own group window which displays *FaceLift* and *Read Me* icons. If you created a separate Printer Management group (as described in the previous chapter), you may want to move these icons into that group, then delete the Bitstream Group Window. In any case, Figure 10.8 shows the *FaceLift* application window, and Table 10.15 lists the 10 typefaces and 16 fonts that are included.

Bitstream Display Driver. *FaceLift* revises one line, and adds another, in SYSTEM.INI, as shown here:

```
[boot]
display.drv=shellscr.drv      (revised line, to specify new video driver)
display.org=vga.drv           (new line, to retain original driver name)
```

Bitstream Printer Driver. When *FaceLift* is on, the default printer driver is replaced by a Bitstream driver (SHELLPRT.DRV), and the following line of WIN.INI is revised as shown here:

```
[windows]
device=HP LaserJet 4/4M, SHELLPRT, LPTx:
```

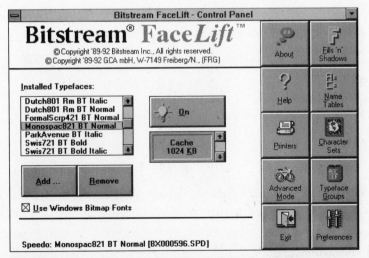

Figure 10.8 The Bitstream *FaceLift* Control Panel. The name of the highlighted font appears at the bottom of the window.

TABLE 10.15 **Bitstream** *FaceLift* **Fonts**

Font Box Name	Font	Typeface and Font Name	SPD †	TDF ‡	PostScript §
BrushScript BT	Regular	Brush Script	BX000199	DC0199	0199A___
Cooper Blk BT	Regular	Bitstream Cooper Black	BX000630	CE0630	0630A___
Dutch801 Rm BT	Regular	Dutch 801 Roman	BX000011	AI0011	0011A___
	Bold	Dutch 801 Bold	BX000013	AK0013	0013A___
	Italic	Dutch 801 Italic	BX000012	AJ0012	0012A___
	Bold Italic	Dutch 801 Bold Italic	BX000014	AL0014	0014A___
FormalScrp421 BT	Regular	Formal Script 421	BX000609	HZ0609	0609A___
Monospac821 BT	Regular	Monospace 821	BX000596	IG0596	0596A___
ParkAvenue BT	Regular	Park Avenue	BX000362	GD0362	0362A___
Swis721 BT	Regular	Swiss 721	BX000003	AA0003	0003A___
	Bold	Swiss 721 Bold	BX000005	AC0005	0005A___
	Italic	Swiss 721 Italic	BX000004	AB0004	0004A___
	Bold Italic	Swiss 721 Bold Italic	BX000006	AD0006	0006A___
SymbolMono BT	Regular	Symbol Monospaced	BX019831	EO9831	9831X___
SymbolProp BT	Regular	Symbol Proportional	BX019830	EN9830	9830X___
ZapfDingbats BT	Regular	ITC Zapf Dingbats	BX028556	EM8556	8556X___

† Each filename has SPD extension.
‡ Each filename has TDF extension.
§ Two files with PFB and PFM extensions for each indicated filename.

A new section retains original default driver data, along with similar information for all other installed printers:

```
[Shelldevices]
HP LaserJet 4/4M=HPPCL5E, , , 1
(others)=(driver name), , , 1
```

In the above examples, *FaceLift* functions are handled by the SHELLSCR and SHELLPRT drivers, after which the default drivers take over. When *FaceLift* is turned off, the device line in the [windows] section is rewritten to its pre-*FaceLift* state.

The [PrinterPorts] and [devices] sections are also revised to specify the Bitstream driver. Refer to the *Reinstallation of Printer Driver* section of Chapter 9 for more information about these sections.

Bitstream Configuration Record (FACELIFT.INI). *FaceLift* follows the admirable practice (others, please note!) of not using WIN.INI as a dumping ground for all its configuration data. In fact, the following one-line section is all that's needed:

```
[Typefaces]
Settings=FACELIFT.INI
```

The cited INI file is located in your Windows directory, and contains complete configuration data for your system. For example, the installed Speedo and Postscript fonts are listed as shown here.

```
[BtFonts]     (Speedo font section)
BTFont001=C:\btfonts\CE0630.TDF, C:\btfonts\BX000630.SPD
BTFont002=... (and so on)

[PsFonts]     (Postscript font section)
BTFont017=C:\PSFONTS\0630A___.PFM, C:\PSFONTS\0630A___.PFB
BTFont018=... (and so on)
```

Extended Character Set Configuration. To change the extended character set (i.e., symbol set) (128–255) associated with any *FaceLift* Speedo (*not* PostScript) font, click on the Character Sets button to open the Speedo Character Sets dialog box shown in Figure 10.9. Use the down arrows to select the typeface and the extended character set you wish to apply to it, then click on the Connect button to specify a custom font, whose name will appear in the Custom Fonts: box. The indicated name will appear as an additional font in the Fonts box and, if selected, the appropriate extended character set will be available.

To create a new font with a specified extended character set, *FaceLift* writes one or more lines into its FACELIFT.INI file, as shown here (spaces added for clarity):

```
[Remapped Typefaces]
Monospac821 PC8 BT = Monospac821 BT, IBM PC,         IBMPC.CSD,   0
Swis721 BSN        = Swis721 BT,      ASCII Business, ASCIIBUS.CSD, 0
```

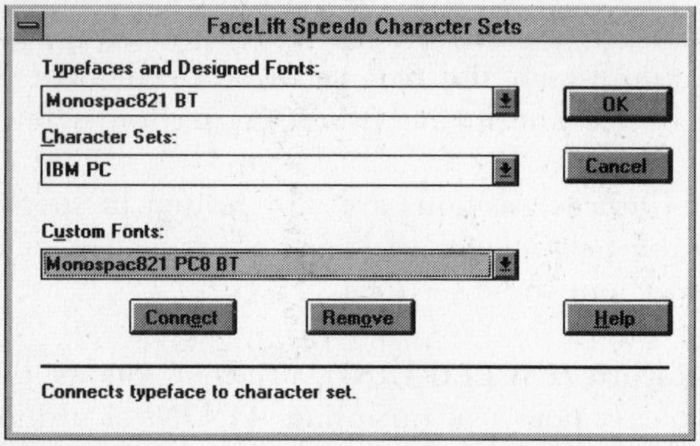

Figure 10.9 Use the Speedo Character Sets dialog box to specify a character set (symbol set) to be associated with one of the Speedo fonts. The name of the new typeface set appears in the Custom Fonts box.

In the first example, a new monospaced font has been specified using the Bitstream monospace font and the IBM PC extended character set (symbol set) file (IBMPC.CSD). The second example adds a Swiss (sans serif) font with the ASCII business extended character set. For comparison purposes, Table 10.16a shows how a [Remapped Typefaces] section might look if a

TABLE 10.16a Bitstream Character Set Specifications*

Font & Character Set code	Base Typeface	Character Set	Filename	Ext.	Win Code
[Remapped Typefaces]					†
Monospace821	BT = Monospace821 BT,	ANSI Extended,	ANSI	.CSD	1 ‡
Monospace821 BSN	BT = Monospace821 BT,	ASCII Business,	ASCIIBUS	.CSD, 0	2
Monospace821 TCH	BT = Monospace821 BT,	ACSII Technical,	ASCIITCH	.CSD, 0	3
Monospace821 HR8	BT = Monospace821 BT,	HP Roman 8,	ROMAN8	.CSD, 0	4
Monospace821 PC8	BT = Monospace821 BT,	IBM PC,	IBMPC	.CSD, 0	5
Monospace821 LTN	BT = Monospace821 BT,	Latin 1,	ECMA	.CSD, 0	6
Monospace821 LB2	BT = Monospace821 BT,	Latin 2,	BTLATIN2	.CSD, 0	7
Monospace821 LB5	BT = Monospace821 BT,	Latin5,	BTLATIN5	.CSD, 0	8

*Typical lines added to FACELIFT.INI if indicated character set (symbol set) is specified. Spaces added for clarity.

† Cross-reference to character set shown in Table 10.14b.

‡ Line shows default font configuration, but does not actually appear in FACELIFT.INI.

complete set of the eight available character set fonts were set up for the Monospace821 font. Table 10.16b shows the extended character set for each of these font sets.

Using *FaceLift* with a New Printer.   A few features may not be available if the installed printer was introduced after *FaceLift* version 2.0. As a typical example, if a Hewlett-Packard LaserJet 4/4M printer is installed, the features listed below will appear disabled, since *FaceLift* does not recognize this printer. In a case such as this, there are two options. The easiest is to install a series II or series III printer driver (either of which *FaceLift* does recognize), utilize the features below, then return to your actual LaserJet 4 driver.

Or you can edit the FACELIFT.INI file so that *FaceLift* will recognize the new driver. To do so, follow the procedures described below. Interim measures such as this will usually work if the new printer is reasonably compatible with one the *FaceLift* does recognize. In case of doubt, contact *Bitstream* to see if an upgrade is available.

Dynamic Downloading.   For faster printing, *FaceLift's* Dynamic Download option can send to the printer only those font characters needed for the current print job (see *User Guide* for more details). If the Dynamic download: button at the bottom of the Printers dialog box (not shown here) is disabled, check the [Drivers] section of FACELIFT.INI for the name of your installed printer. If the name appears in the format shown below for the IBM Proprinter (PROPRINT=1,0), the 0 indicates this feature is not supported. However, if your printer driver name does not appear, and the printer is new, then you may be able to edit the section as shown by the Hewlett-Packard examples. The HPPCL5A line can be changed as shown, or a new line can be inserted.

```
[Drivers]
PROPRINT  = 1, 0                        (IBM Proprinter, DDL not available)
HPPCL5A   = 6, 3,      PCLSOFT.DYN      (H-P LaserJet series III)
HPPCL5E   = 6, 3,      PCLSOFT.DYN      (edit line to identify LaserJet 4 driver)
PSCRIPT   = 6, 3,      T3SOFT.DYN       (Postscript driver)
driver name = a, b,    ddl             (see list below for explanation)
where      a =         1 9-pin printer    4 Inkjet, 300 dpi
                       2 18-pin printer    5 Inkjet, 360 dpi
                       3 24-pin printer    6 Other printer, 300 × 300 dpi
```

TABLE 10.16b Bitstream Extended Character Sets

Dec	1 —	2 BSN	3 TCH	4 HR8	5 LTN	6 LB2	7 LB5	8 PC8
127			▨	▨	▨			⌂
128								Ç
129								ü
130	‚					‚	‚	é
131	ƒ						ƒ	â
132	„					„	„	ä
133	…					…	…	à
134	†					†	†	å
135	‡					‡	‡	ç
136	ˆ					ˇ		ê
137	‰					‰	‰	ë
138	Š					Š	Š	è
139	‹					‹	‹	ï
140	Œ					Ś	Œ	î
141						Ť'		ì
142						ž		Ä
143						Ź		Å
144								É
145	'					'	'	æ
146	'					'	'	Æ
147	"					"	"	ô
148	"					"	"	ö
149	•					•	•	ò
150	–					–	–	û
151	—					—	—	ù
152	~						~	ÿ
153	™					™	™	Ö
154	š					š	š	Ü
155	›					›	›	¢
156	œ					ś	œ	£
157						ť'		¥
158						ž		Pt
159	Ÿ					ź	Ÿ	ƒ
160	SP				SP	SP	SP	á
161	¡	"	+	À	¡	ˇ	¡	í
162	¢	"	–	Â	¢	˘	¢	ó
163	£	©	-	È	£	Ł	£	ú
164	¤	®	×	Ê	¤	¤	¤	ñ
165	¥	™	÷	Ë	¥	Ą	¥	Ñ
166	¦	•	±	Î	¦	¦	¦	ª
167	§	●	∓	Ï	§	§	§	º
168	¨	—	≡	´	¨	¨	¨	¿
169	©	–	≠	`	©	©	©	⌐
170	ª	†	~	^	a	Ş	a	¬
171	«	‡	~	¨	«	«	«	½
172	¬	¶	≥	~	¬	¬	¬	¼
173	-	§	≤	Ù	-	-	-	¡
174	®	°	↓	Û	®	®	®	«
175	¯	□	←	£	¯	Ż	¯	»
176	°		→	–	°	°	°	░
177	±	↑	↑	Ý	±	±	±	▒
178	²	↕	↕	ý	²	‚	²	▓
179	³	↔	°	°	³	ł	³	│
180	´	↨		Ç	µ	´	´	┤
181	µ	∈	ç	ç	µ	µ	µ	╡
182	¶	∩	Ñ	Ñ	¶	¶	¶	╢
183	·	∟	ñ	ñ	·	·	·	╖
184	¸	∮	¡	¸		¸		╕
185	¹	∫	¿	¿	¹	ą	¹	╣
186	º	⌡	¤	°	º	Ş	º	║
187	»	│	£		»	»	»	╗
188	¼	√	¥	¼		Ł'	¼	╝
189	½	—	§	"	½	½		╜
190	¾	∞	ƒ	¾		ł'	¾	╛
191	¿	∝	¢	¿		ż	¿	┐

#	—	BSN	TCH	HR8	LTN	LB2	LB5	PC8
192	À		⌞	â	À	Ŕ	À	└
193	Á		¬	ê	Á	Á	Á	┴
194	Â		⌐	ô	Â	Â	Â	┬
195	Ã		Γ	û	Ã	Ă	Ã	├
196	Ä		Δ	á	Ä	Ä	Ä	─
197	Å		Θ	é	Å	Ĺ	Å	┼
198	Æ		Σ	ó	Æ	Ć	Æ	╞
199	Ç		Φ	ú	Ç	Ç	Ç	╟
200	È		Ω	à	È	Č	È	╚
201	É		α	è	É	É	É	╔
202	Ê		β	ò	Ê	Ę	Ê	╩
203	Ë		δ	ù	Ë	Ë	Ë	╦
204	Ì		∈	ä	Ì	Ě	Ì	╠
205	Í		η	ë	Í	Í	Í	═
206	Î		θ	ö	Î	Î	Î	╬
207	Ï		µ	ü	Ï	Ď	Ï	╧
208	Ð		π	Å	Ð	Đ	Ğ	╨
209	Ñ		σ	î	Ñ	Ń	Ñ	╤
210	Ò		τ	Ø	Ò	Ň	Ò	╥
211	Ó		φ	Æ	Ó	Ó	Ó	╙
212	Ô		ε	å	Ô	Ô	Ô	╘
213	Õ		¹	í	Õ	Ő	Õ	╒
214	Ö		²	ø	Ö	Ö	Ö	╓
215	×		³	æ	×	×	×	╫
216	Ø		⁴	Ä	Ø	Ř	Ø	╪
217	Ù		⁵	ì	Ù	Ů	Ù	┘
218	Ú		⁶	Ö	Ú	Ú	Ú	┌
219	Û		⁷	Ü	Û	Ű	Û	█
220	Ü		⁸	É	Ü	Ü	Ü	▄
221	Ý		⁹	ï	Ý	Ý	İ	▌
222	Þ		⁰	ß	Þ	Ţ	Ş	▐
223	ß		₁	Ô	ß	ß	ß	▀
224	à	2		Á	à	ŕ	à	α
225	á	3		Ã	á	á	á	β
226	â	4		ã	â	â	â	Γ
227	ã	5		Đ	ã	ă	ã	π
228	ä	6		ð	ä	ä	ä	Σ
229	å	7		Í	å	ĺ	å	σ
230	æ	8		Ì	æ	ć	æ	µ
231	ç	9		Ó	ç	ç	ç	τ
232	è	0		Ò	è	č	è	Φ
233	é	¼		Õ	é	é	é	Θ
234	ê	½		õ	ê	ę	ê	Ω
235	ë	¾		Š	ë	ë	ë	δ
236	ì	⅛		š	ì	ě	ì	∞
237	í	¼		Ú	í	í	í	φ
238	î	⅜		Ÿ	î	î	î	ε
239	ï	½		ÿ	ï	ď	ï	∩
240	ð	⅝		Þ	ð	đ	ğ	≡
241	ñ	¾		þ	ñ	ń	ñ	±
242	ò	⅞		•	ò	ň	ò	≥
243	ó	⅓		µ	ó	ó	ó	≤
244	ô	⅔		¶	ô	ô	ô	⌠
245	õ	£		¾	õ	ő	õ	⌡
246	ö	¢		—	ö	ö	ö	÷
247	÷	f		¼	÷	÷	÷	≈
248	ø	Pt		½	ø	ř	ø	°
249	ù	¥		ª	ù	ů	ù	•
250	ú	Fr		°	ú	ú	ú	·
251	û	¤		«	û	ű	û	√
252	ü	ℓ		■	ü	ü	ü	ⁿ
253	ý	‰		»	ý	ý	ı	²
254	þ			±	þ	ţ	ş	■
255	ÿ				ÿ	˙	ÿ	

1. —	ANSI Extended	4. HR8	HP Roman 8
2. BSN	ASCII Business	5. LTN	Latin 1
3. TCH	ASCII Technical	6. LB2	Latin 2

7. LB5   Latin 5
8. PC8   IBM PC

b =	0	DDL disabled	2 DDL on
	1	DDL on each pg.	3 DDL possible

ddl=	PCLSOFT.DYN	Dynamic downloader for PCL IV fonts
	T3SOFT.DYN	Dynamic downloader for PostScript type 3 fonts

Hewlett-Packard Soft Font Creation. If this option does not work, add or edit the following line in FACELIFT.INI as shown here:

```
[Devices]
ValidSoftfont=HPPCL,HPPCL5E (to support LaserJet 4/4M)
```

Agfa, Hewlett-Packard: Type Director

The *Type Director* font-management utility jointly marketed by Agfa and Hewlett-Packard creates bitmap and scalable printer and screen fonts. A brief installation overview is given here—for complete details refer to its *User's Guide.*

To install *Type Director,* insert diskette 1 in drive A, type INSTALL, press the Enter key, and follow the onscreen prompts. In addition to setting up a new directory (default is C:\TD), the install procedure will propose a change to your AUTOEXEC.BAT file, and possibly to your CONFIG.SYS file too, as shown here:

```
AUTOEXEC.BAT    path  %path%;C:\TD;
CONFIG.SYS      files=30
                buffers=20
```

The first line simply appends the *Type Director* path (the default C:\TD is shown here) to your existing path. If environment space is tight, you can probably get along without this addition. The CONFIG.SYS changes are made only if the existing lines specify values less than those shown above.

Configure Environment. After concluding the *Type Director* installation, run the program (type TYPEDIR at the DOS prompt) and at the Main Menu, select the Environment Menu's Set Environment/Defaults option. Check the hardware configuration list for accuracy and make any changes that may be required (select HP LaserJet III for that printer or for any HP printer introduced after it). Next, toggle on down to the *Available Applications* section, highlight *unlisted application,* and press the Enter key. Scroll down the Applications list to *Microsoft Windows v3.0* (a v3.1 option is not yet available, nor is it needed).

Install Typefaces. The next step is to select the typeface(s) you want to install. Open the Typefaces Menu and select the Install Typefaces option. Insert a *Type Director* diskette containing typefaces in drive A, press the Enter key, then press function key F3 to display the list of available typefaces. Highlight any one and press F2 to select it (an asterisk should appear next to the typeface name). Repeat as required, then press F1 to begin the actual installation of the typeface(s). Press the Escape key and F8 to return to the Main Menu.

Make Fonts. Open the Fonts Menu and select the Make Fonts option. Press the Enter key until a blank highlighted bar appears under the Typeface column, then press it again to display the list of installed typefaces. Highlight the desired typeface, then type in the point sizes you wish to create, specify printer and/or screen fonts, orientation (portrait or landscape) and symbol set. Repeat all of this, as required, then press function key F1 to actually make the font(s) in the sizes you selected.

Installation Summary. During the typeface and font creation procedures described above, the appropriate information is written into your WIN.INI file to make the printer and screen fonts available to Windows applications. Although not further described here, the basic procedures are much the same as those described immediately below in the *HP Font Installer* section. Also, refer to the following section for font-downloading instructions.

Windows: HP Font Installer

Windows' HP Font Installer may be used to install most soft fonts that will be used with an HP-compatible printer. To use the Font Installer, open the Windows Control Panel and click on the Printer icon, then on the Setup button. This displays the Printer Setup dialog box such as that shown in Figure 9.10 in the previous chapter. If your printer supports downloadable soft fonts, a Fonts... button will be seen in the dialog box. If the button is not seen, this section does not apply to your printer and may be skipped.

Click on the Fonts... button to display the HP Font Installer dialog box shown in Figure 10.10a. The box on the left side of the dialog box lists fonts already installed for the designated printer. To add additional fonts, click on the Add Fonts button to display the Add Fonts dialog box shown in part b of the figure.

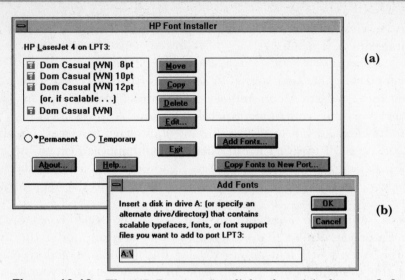

Figure 10.10   The HP Font Installer dialog box (a) shows soft fonts installed for the current printer. Use the Add Fonts dialog box (b) to add additional fonts.

Assuming the new fonts are on a distribution diskette in drive A, press the Enter key to continue, or type in an alternate location, then press the Enter key. In either case, the source location is scanned for available fonts. If none are found, the following message is displayed:

No fonts compatible with this printer found.

This message might be seen if you attempted to install fonts supplied with utilities such as the *Facelift* or *Type Director* font packages. In such cases, quit the Font Installer and refer to the appropriate *User's Guide* for detailed instructions.

If HPPCL fonts are found, the Font Installer lists them in the empty Source box shown on the right side of the Font Installer screen. Highlight the fonts you wish to install for your printer, and click on the Move button to continue. After answering a prompt for the location where you want the fonts to be placed, three things happen:

The fonts are copied into the specified directory.
The Font Installer writes an accompanying printer font metrics file for each font.
The font names are added to the list displayed by the Font Installer.

After either completing the operation just described, or installing the fonts via *Type Director,* a new [HPPCL,LPT1] section will be found in your

WIN.INI file. The fonts listed in that section may be designated as temporary or permanent, as described in the following sections. In the examples given here, the fonts are located in a FONTS directory, in which various subdirectories have been created, including a TYPEDIR directory for the fonts described below. (Some additional font-management instructions in this section of WIN.INI are omitted from this discussion.)

Temporary Soft Fonts. The fonts installed as just described are designated as temporary fonts, and are listed as shown here:

```
[HPPCL,LPT1]
SoftFonts=3
SoftFont1=C:\fonts\typedir\DCR0WUSA.PFM,C:\fonts\typedir\DCR0WUSA.SFP
SoftFont2=C:\fonts\typedir\DCR14USA.PFM,C:\fonts\typedir\DCR14USA.SFP
SoftFont3=C:\fonts\typedir\DCR1CUSA.PFM,C:\fonts\typedir\DCR1CUSA.SFP
```

Note that each font line refers to two files. The PFM (Printer Font Metrics) file specifies general font characteristics, while the SFP (Soft Font, Portrait) file is the soft font itself, which will be downloaded to the printer only when a print job requires it. If a subsequent print job downloads additional fonts to the printer, the fonts listed here will be erased. Therefore, the fonts are considered as temporary.

Permanent Soft Fonts. A permanent soft font need only be downloaded to the printer once, where it remains installed until the printer is either reset or turned off. To designate any soft font as permanent, return to the HP Font Installer described above. When you highlight any one (only) font, the *Permanent and Temporary buttons shown in Figure 10.10a will be enabled. Click on the *Permanent button and an asterisk appears next to the highlighted font, indicating its permanent status. When you exit the Font Installer, you will be prompted to download the permanent font(s), and the [HPPCL,LPT1] section of WIN.INI will be revised as shown here.

```
[HPPCL,LPT1]
SoftFonts=3
SoftFont1=C:\fonts\typedir\DCR0WUSA.PFM,C:\fonts\typedir\DCR0WUSA.SFP
SoftFont2=C:\fonts\typedir\DCR14USA.PFM,C:\fonts\typedir\DCR14USA.SFP
SoftFont3=C:\fonts\typedir\DCR1CUSA.PFM
C:\fonts\typedir\DCR1CUSA.PFM=C:\fonts\typedir\DCR1CUSA.SFP
```

This example shows the effect of designating Softfont3 as permanent. Note that the line on which it first appears has been truncated to show only the printer font metrics file. As a result, the font will no longer be downloaded during a print job, even if it is needed. Instead, Windows expects that the font is already available at the printer, as indicated by the new permanent-font line at the end of the listing above.

If you subsequently redesignate Softfont3 as temporary (again, via the Font Installer), the truncated line above will be rewritten as required. However, the permanent-font line will not be deleted. Therefore, after several status changes, the [HPPCL,LPT1] section may appear to contain conflicting information. However, the first appearance of a font reference takes precedence.

> **NOTE:** After installing any permanent *Type Director* font, refer to the section entitled *Type-Director/TrueType Font Conflicts* later in this chapter if there is a subsequent problem with a TrueType font.

Font-Download Batch File. Another line in the [HPPCL,LPT1] section refers to a batch file (SFLPT1.BAT) that will download your permanent fonts:

    sfdlbat=C:\fonts\typedir\SFLPT1.BAT

Although the line is added whenever you designate a font as permanent, the batch file itself is not written unless you select "Download at Startup." This option appears as you exit the Font Installer, but only if you have designated one or more fonts as permanent. If you select it, the batch file is written and a line appended to your AUTOEXEC.BAT File so that SFLPT1.BAT will be executed every time you boot the system. If you select the "Download Now" option instead, the fonts are immediately downloaded, but the batch file is not written. If a batch file from a previous "Download at Startup" option was written, that file remains in place and will continue to be used every time the system is booted. It will download only those fonts designated as permanent at the time the file was written.

However, the downloading batch file may be more trouble than it's worth. Refer to the *Font-Download Batch File Troubleshooting* section later in this chapter for more details.

HPPCL Screen Fonts. If *Type Director* or some other utility has created screen fonts to match the installed printer soft fonts, a new line should be added to the [fonts] section of WIN.INI for each typeface family that you created. For example, the following line identifies a Dom Casual screen font to accompany the printer soft fonts described above.

```
[fonts]
Dom Casual (WN) 8,10,12 (DCASUAL)=DCASUAL0
```

Assuming the screen font file was written to match the installed printer fonts, it will contain as many complete fonts as you've specified (in this example, three). In the specific *Type Director* example, the usual FON extension is omitted, although it does appear on the font file itself. As an additional consideration, *Type Director* places the screen font in the Windows (*not* System) directory. If, for the sake of good housekeeping, you move it to the System directory after installation, Windows will find it with no trouble but *Type Director* itself won't. Therefore, if you subsequently want to modify the screen font, you'll have to move it back into the main Windows directory so that *Type Director* can find it.

Soft Font Reinstallation after Windows Reinstallation. If you reinstall Windows 3.1, Setup writes files as appropriate for the new installation. One of these will be a WIN.INI containing all the necessary new information, but not a word about all those old HPPCL soft fonts that you may not have wanted to discard. To avoid the hassle of going through yet another session with the Font Installer, you can prepare a font-summary file that contains all the information necessary to recreate the [HPPCL] section of WIN.INI. It's a good idea to take advantage of this undocumented feature every time you make a substantial change to your soft font library.

The FINSTALL.DIR File. The file that will contain your font-summary information is called FINSTALL.DIR and it is created by accessing the HP Font Installer described earlier in the *Windows HP Font Installer* section. When the Font Installer dialog box is seen, make all the displayed fonts temporary (otherwise, the following procedure won't work). Then hold down the Ctrl and Shift keys and click on the Exit button to display the Create installer directory file dialog box shown in Figure 10.11a. The box at the bottom of the dialog box shows where the FINSTALL.DIR file will be written. Press the Enter key to write the file to the specified location. It's a good idea to store the file along with the fonts themselves, but you can write it elsewhere if you wish, by changing the information in the box.

The FINSTALL.DIR file contains font-summary information such as that seen here:

```
FAMILY "PCL / HP LaserJet on LPT1"
"Dom Casual (US)    8pt" = P, DCR0WUSA.SFP, DCR0WUSA.PFM
"Dom Casual (US)  10pt" = P, DCR14USA.SFP, DCR14USA.PFM
"Dom Casual (US)  12pt" = P, DCR1CUSA.SFP, DCR1CUSA.PFM
```

NOTE: The "P" in each line above is for portrait, not permanent.

Begin Reinstallation. When you are ready to reinstall the soft fonts, return to the Font Installer. Again hold down the Ctrl and Shift keys, but this time click on the Add Fonts button instead, to display the revised **Add Fonts** dialog box shown in Figure 10.11b. Revise the information in the boxes as required, then press the Enter key. The names of the fonts will once again appear in the right-hand box on the Font Installer screen. Highlight the fonts you wish to reinstall, then click on the Move button. At the next prompt (not shown in the Figure) specify the directory where the fonts are to be located. When you press the Enter key, the installation procedure described earlier is repeated, and the fonts are again listed as temporary fonts in the left-hand Font Installer box. Again, you may make one or more of them permanent, as required.

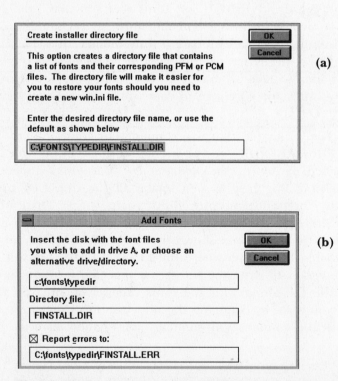

Figure 10.11 Use the Create installer dialog box (a) to write font-summary information to a FINSTALL.DIR file for future reference. (b) Use this **Add Fonts** dialog box to reinstall the fonts listed in the FINSTALL.DIR file.

Font Configuration

If you reconfigure your system from one video resolution to another, the three existing system fonts and the screen fonts (COUR*x*.FON, for example) are automatically replaced by a new font set appropriate to the new resolution. However, you may want to make custom font changes to suit personal preference. For example, an oversize font may be useful for the visually-impaired user, while a smaller-than-normal font may be preferred by others.

To change any screen font, find the location in SYSTEM.INI or WIN.INI at which that font is specified, and edit the file as described below. Each of the following sections lists typical examples of Windows screens in which the default font is used. Note that in some cases a non-default font may be specified simply by editing a line in the appropriate INI file. In other cases, a new line must be added to override the default setting. For reference purposes, Table 10.17 summarizes the INI file changes that are described in this section.

TABLE 10.17   Custom Screen Font Usage*

Desktop Area	INI File	Section	Typical Font Specification Lines
Character Map (*add line, to view* DIALOG.FON)			
	WIN.INI	[fonts]	MS Dialog (W4W)= C:\WINWORD\DIALOG.FON
DOS Window			
Text	DOSAPP.INI	[DOS applications]	
			(*font matrix saved for each window*)
File Manager [†]			
Directory	WINFILE.INI	[settings]	Face=Arial *(or other)*
			Size=10
			LowerCase=0
			FaceWeight=700
Group, Applet Windows [‡]			
Title Bars & Menus	WIN.INI	[windows]	SystemFont=*anyfont*.FON
			SystemFontSize=11
Icon Titles	WIN.INI	[desktop]	IconTitleFaceName=MS Serif [§]
			IconTitleSize=10
			IconTitleStyle=1

TABLE 10.17 *(continued)*

Desktop Area	INI File	Section	Typical Font Specification Lines
Print Manager			
Workspace (Win)	*(changes with* Icon Titles, *above)*		
Workspace (Wrk) [†]	WIN.INI	[spooler]	Font=*(hex character string)*
Status Bar Text [‡](Chat, Clipbook Viewer, File & Print Managers, Net Watcher)			
	WIN.INI	[desktop]	StatusBarFaceName=Arial
			StatusBarFaceHeight=12
System Editor Text	*(changes with* Group, Applet Windows, *above)*		

[*] Unless otherwise noted, add indicated lines to specified section of INI file.
[†] To make changes, open Options Menu and select Fonts... option.
[‡] Undocumented feature.
[§] IconTitleFaceName has no effect on icon titles in Object Packager applet.

To try a different font, use the following procedure. If the new font is already available in your SYSTEM directory, skip to step 4. Otherwise, begin at the beginning.

1. Refer to Appendix A to locate the distribution diskette with the font file you need.

2. Insert that diskette in drive A.

3. Use the Windows EXPAND utility (described in Chapter 4) to copy/expand the desired font file(s) into your SYSTEM directory.

4. To use the new font file(s), edit the appropriate line in your SYSTEM.INI or WIN.INI file, as described below.

5. The new font(s) take effect the next time you start a Windows session.

The Character Map Applet

The complete symbol set for any installed typeface can be conveniently viewed via the Character Map applet in the Accessories Group Window. As shown in Figure 10.12, the applet's dialog box displays a 7 × 32 matrix of the 224 (or less) printable characters (32–255) in the regular (roman) font for the typeface whose name is listed in the Font: box. Since the Character Map display is independent of the default printer, it will display any installed font, even if that font is not supported by the printer. The Character Map also displays printer fonts supported by the default printer driver. It is therefore a handy tool for font configuration and troubleshooting sessions.

Typeface Selection.   There are several ways to select the typeface displayed by the Character Map.

Press Alt+F and any letter key to display the first typeface that begins with that letter, then press the same letter a few times to toggle through other typefaces whose names begin with the same letter. Or, click on the Font: box's down arrow to open the typeface list, then highlight the one you want to view.

The drop-down list under the Font: box shows all currently enabled Raster, Vector, and TrueType fonts, without regard to the font support offered by the currently installed printer.

Character Enlargement.   For an enlarged view of any printable character, move the mouse pointer over that character and hold down the primary mouse button. To sequentially view adjacent characters, hold the mouse button down and drag the pointer as desired. Or—after highlighting any character—press any key to move to that character.

Figure 10.12 shows a sampling of four enlarged characters, although only one will actually appear at a time. The Status Bar panel at the lower right-hand corner of the applet window reports the equivalent keystroke that will display the currently highlighted character. In the figure, the panel shows that pressing the Alt+192 keys will display the Clock character seen near the left edge of the applet window.

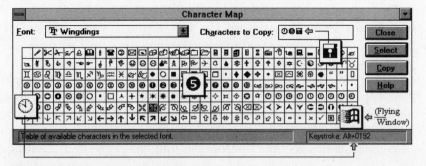

Figure 10.12   The Character Map applet displays the entire symbol set in any installed typeface. Place the mouse pointer over any character to enlarge it, as shown by the four examples in the figure. The equivalent keystroke(s) for the currently highlighted character appears in the Status Box, as indicated here for the Clock symbol.

Copy Characters. The Character Map can be used to copy characters to the Clipboard for subsequent pasting into a document. To begin, open the Character Map, select the desired typeface, and double-click on each character you wish to copy. As you do, the character appears in the Characters to Copy: box at the top of the dialog box. After selecting all the desired characters, click on the Copy button to transfer them to the Clipboard. Now open any applet or application file, select the desired insertion point, and paste the characters into the file.

What you see is what you get, but what you get may not be what you want to see. Sometimes the pasted characters retain the font in which they originated, and sometimes they don't, as summarized here. The first column indicates the Character Map font, and the second specifies the font in use at the insertion point in the document. The third and fourth columns indicate how the pasted characters will appear in the target document.

Character Map Font:	Target Document:	Pasted Font in Word:	In Write:
Arial, Courier New, Symbol, Times New Roman	Any font	Character Map, 12 pt.	Target Document's font and point size
Any other font	The same font	Character Map, 12 pt.	Same as above
	A different font	Times New Roman, 12 pt.	Same as above

As can be seen (perhaps with difficulty), if Wingdings are pasted into a 10-point Arial text block in a Word-for-Windows document, they appear in a 12-point Times New Roman font. In fact, even if you preselect Wingdings in the Word document, the pasted characters *still* appear in 12-point Times New Roman.

To determine how the Character Map copy/paste operation will behave in some other application, make a few test runs. If the desired character gets lost along the way, use the Character Map only to highlight the desired character(s) and note the required keystroke (which appears in the Status Bar). Then return to the application, select the appropriate font, and enter that keystroke.

Display Italic and/or Bold Font. Although the Character Map does not directly display italic, bold, or bold italic fonts, it can, if necessary, be forced to display one of these styles by disabling one or more of the others, as shown here:

Character Map Font	To Display, Disable These Fonts
Regular	(*default*)
Italic	Roman
Bold	Roman, Italic
Bold Italic	Roman, Italic, Bold

Figure 10.13 is a composite illustration of four fonts in the TrueType CG Omega typeface.

Font Leading Gauge

The vertical space between lines on the printed page is referred to as "leading" (pronounced *ledding*). The term is taken from traditional type-setting, in which line spacing was adjusted by inserting a small strip of lead between type lines. In computer printer applications, leading may be set as follows:

Leading	Description
Fixed	Leading is fixed at some value specified by the user
Variable	Leading varies according to the maximum font size used on each line. Use of subscripts and/or superscripts also effects leading.

For routine print operations, the default leading is usually satisfactory and screen-to-printer comparisons present no practical problems, other than that the screen rarely displays a full page of type. However, page breaks are usually indicated clearly, so there should be no little surprises between what you see and what you get.

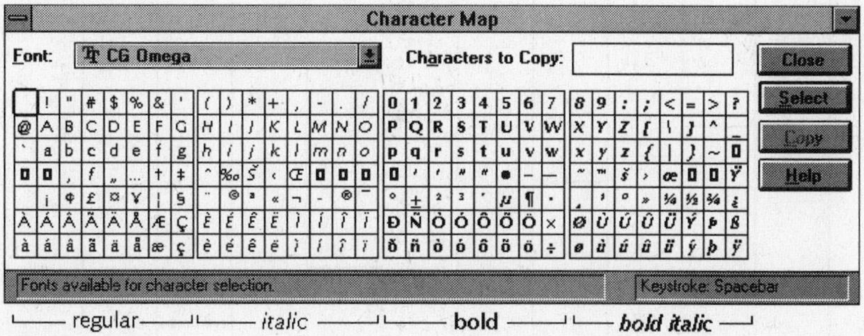

Figure 10.13 A composite view of the Character Map, showing all four fonts in the TrueType CG Omega typeface. Under normal conditions, only the regular font style appears in the Character Map.

However, for some complex applications the screen display may be somewhat misleading. For example, Figure 10.14 shows a printout of a 14-column chart used to verify printer leading. Each column consists of numbered rows of underline characters set in 6-point type. The only difference between columns is the vertical line spacing, or leading, as indicated at the top of each column.

When preparing such a chart, the visual display of the selected leading may not agree with the final printed document. For example, Word-for-Windows provides normal and page-layout viewing modes, in which various adjacent column pairs display the same amount of leading, as indicated here:

Normal View and Magnification

80%		100%		120%	
6.5	7.0	6.5	7.0	6.0	6.5
8.0	8.5	8.0	8.5	8.5	9.0
9.0	9.5	9.5	10.0	11.0	11.5
10.0	10.5	11.0	11.5		
11.0	11.5				

Page Layout View and Magnification

80%		100%		120%	
6.0	6.5	6.0	6.5	7.5	8.0
7.5	8.0	7.5	8.0	9.5	10.0
8.5	9.0	9.0	9.5		
9.5	10.0	10.5	11.0		
10.5	11.0				
11.5	12.0				

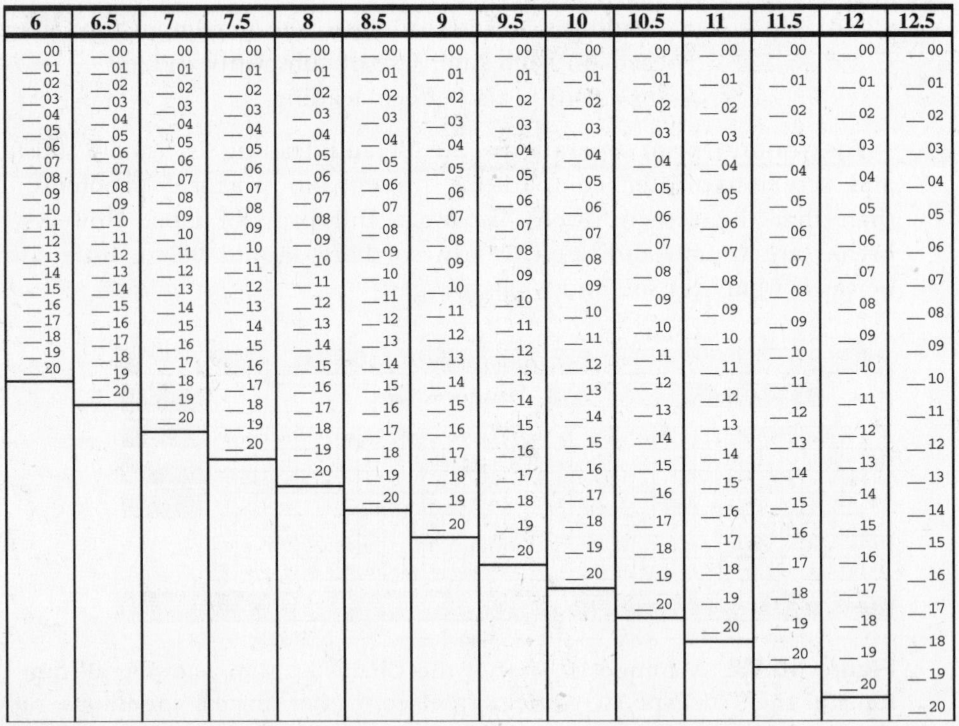

Figure 10.14 A leading gauge such as this can be used to verify how various point sizes appear onscreen.

Only the Print Preview mode accurately displays the columns onscreen as they will be seen on the printed page. Although the comparisons given here may vary depending on video resolution, drivers, and other factors, you might want to make your own tests if you expect to prepare documents in which various line spacings will be applied. Try a few test printouts to compare the screen image to the printed page. Or, you might consider varying leading in increments of at least one point, instead of the half-point increments described here.

As another variable, the leading on the printed page may not always agree with that specified within your Windows applications. Again, make a few trial runs to determine if what you specify is what you get.

Font Relocation Procedures

As already noted, Windows stores its own font files in the System directory, along with many other files essential to routine operation. Some users prefer to move the fonts out of the System directory and into one or more new directories that contain nothing else. For example, a C:\FONTS master directory might be created, with subdirectories containing various font files, according to category. The assorted collection of bitmap fonts might be moved into a BITMAPS directory, while True-Type fonts are placed in a TRUETYPE directory, and so on. This makes it a bit easier to keep track of your font garden, especially when it's time to do a little weeding.

Relocating Raster and Vector fonts. Moving either style font into another directory is a reasonably straightforward operation.

1. Use File Manager to create a new directory, then copy all files with a FON extension from the System directory into the new directory (see Chapter 6 for further details about File Manager).

2. Search your SYSTEM.INI and WIN.INI files for all references to bitmap files (search for ".FON") and edit each line found to include the new path information. Ignore occurrences of ".FON" found on the left side of an equal sign. These are font *descriptions* and not actual bitmap filenames.

3. In the System directory, erase all files with a FON extension.

WARNING: Do *not* use File Manager's Move option for this operation, since many bitmap files cannot be moved while Windows itself is using them. Therefore, some FON files will be moved and some won't.

The four WOA fonts listed in the [386Enh] section of SYSTEM.INI *must* remain in the System subdirectory. Even if the lines are edited to include the path to some other location, three of the four font matrixes will not be available in the Fonts menu. One matrix (EGA 8 × 8 or VGA 8 × 12) will be available, since it is supplied by the OEM font, which is not affected by the limitation described here.

If you do any video-system reconfiguration later on, Windows will load the required fonts into the system directory and rewrite the appropriate lines in your WIN.INI file. Therefore, you'll need to repeat this relocation procedure to move the new fonts into their own directory.

Relocating TrueType Fonts.   The relocation of TrueType fonts takes a bit more work, since there are two files associated with each font, as described in the TrueType Fonts section above.

Move all TrueType Fonts into a New Directory.   If a TrueType font file (TTF) is moved into a new directory, its corresponding font resource file (FOT) must be edited to refer to the new location. Therefore, use the following procedure to transfer TrueType fonts into their own directory:

1. Copy all TrueType TTF (*not* FOT) files into a new TRUETYPE directory.
2. Double-click on the Control Panel icon in the Main Group Window.
3. Double-click on the Fonts icon.
4. Highlight all TrueType fonts, then click on the Remove button.
5. Check the Remove Files from Disk box.
6. Click on the Yes to All button to verify that all highlighted files should be removed.

The above steps delete all WIN.INI references to the TrueType fonts, and physically remove the TTF and FOT files from the system directory. You are now ready to reinstall the TrueType fonts residing in the TRUE-TYPE directory.

1. Repeat steps 2 and 3, above.
2. Click on the Add button.

3. Select the TrueType directory, and when the List of Fonts Box displays the TrueType fonts in that directory, click on the Select All button.

4. Clear the "Copy Fonts to Windows directory" box at the bottom of the screen (so the fonts are not copied back into the System directory again).

5. Click on the OK button.

Relocate FOT Files. The above procedure writes a complete new set of FOT files into the System directory, each of which now contains the appropriate internal reference to the TrueType font in your TRUETYPE directory. The [fonts] section will once more contain a collection of lines referring to the various new FOT files in your system directory. Each line may simply cite the name of a FOT file, or it may also contain explicit path information. If the path is C:\WINDOWS\SYSTEM, you can delete that phrase without affecting operations. If the path points elsewhere (see below), then leave it alone.

To carry the housekeeping one step further, you may wish to move the new FOT files into the new TRUETYPE directory as well. However if you do so, you will have to manually edit each TrueType line in the [fonts] section of WIN.INI, as follows:

Change: Arial (TrueType)=ARIAL.FOT (*or* = C:\WINDOWS\SYSTEM\ARIAL.FOT)
To: Arial (TrueType)=C:\FONTS\TRUETYPE\ARIAL.FOT

Repeat the above procedure for every line referring to a TrueType font. And if you have not already done so, erase the FOT files in the System directory.

NOTE: Although FOT-file relocation may unclutter the System directory, it does increase the size of your WIN.INI file.

Move New TrueType Fonts into an Existing Directory. If a font-installation procedure has just placed new TrueType fonts in your System directory, and you want to move these fonts into a dedicated font directory that already contains other TrueType fonts, you may want to modify the procedure described above.

For example, consider a system in which the basic Windows TrueType fonts were previously moved into a TrueType directory. At a later date, the *TrueType Font Pack for Windows* was installed using the Setup procedure included with that software. Since this procedure automatically places the new fonts in the System directory, your system now has some TrueType fonts in the TrueType directory, and others in the System directory. Follow these steps to transfer the new fonts from the System directory into the TrueType directory:

1. Copy the new TrueType TTF (*not* FOT) files into a new TRUETYPE directory.

2. Erase the just-copied TTF files from the System directory.

3. Erase all FOT files in the TrueType directory.

4. Edit the [fonts] section of WIN.INI. Delete all lines referring to True-Type FOT files.

5. Open Windows, open the Fonts applet, and double-click on the C:\Windows\TrueType directory to retrieve all the TrueType fonts in that directory.

6. Click on the Select All button, clear the Copy fonts to Windows directory box, and click on the OK button to install the fonts.

By following this procedure, you have physically removed the latest True-Type fonts from the System directory and reinstalled the complete set from your TrueType directory. The [fonts] section of WIN.INI will now show an alphabetical list of all your TrueType fonts.

INI File Font Configuration

To modify the way in which Windows displays text on the Desktop, one or more lines in one of the INI files may be edited, as described in this section.

SYSTEM.INI Font Changes. In each of the next three sections, the font specification given in parentheses refers to the line in the [boot] section of SYSTEM.INI which must be changed.

Fixed System Font (fixedfon.fon=). Perhaps the most direct method of showing the effect of changing this line is to click on the Notepad icon in the Accessories Group Window, then open any available document, or create a new one. On a 640 × 480 VGA screen, Notepad text will be displayed in one of the following formats, depending on which font is specified.

Fixed Font Name	Text Rows	Text Columns
cga40850.fon	52	38
cga80850.fon	52	76
egafix.fon	42	76

vgafix.fon (default)	28	76
8514fix.fon	21	61
Other	Varies according to the selected font	

Keep in mind that Notepad's screen display may not compare well with the printed output from a Notepad document if the specified font does not agree with the display system in use. For example, the following two examples show the VGA screen display when Word Wrap is disabled and the indicated monospace font is installed. In both cases, the two complete lines seen in the first example will be printed, but only the first example matches the printed output.

```
1. This sentence shows the number of characters on one
   line of Notepad text. (Appears on one line on-screen.)
2. The installed monospace font is VGAFIX.FON.
1. This sentence shows the number of characters on one line o
2. The installed monospace font is 8514FIX.FON.
```

NOTE: When using Notepad, it is not possible to specify a printer font. The printer's default font is the only one available to Notepad.

Variable-Width System Font (fonts.fon=). To illustrate the effect of changing the variable-width system font, three versions of the Control Panel Settings Menu are seen in Figure 10.15. The composite illustration shows the menu on a VGA system when the system font is changed from VGA to 8514 to CGA. In each case, the actual menu would appear directly under the Settings Menu, as it does here for the default VGA system font.

As an additional point of reference, the number of full-screen text lines displayed by the SysEdit applet varies, as listed here for a VGA (640 × 480) screen resolution.

System Font	SYSEDIT Lines	Comments
cgasys.fon	53	Not included with Windows 3.1
egasys.fon	35	May be preferred for some VGA displays
vgasys.fon	26	Default VGA system font
8514sys.fon	21	Oversize font may be preferred by visually-impaired users

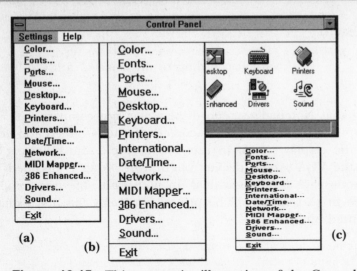

Figure 10.15 This composite illustration of the Control Panel shows how the size of a typical menu varies according to the font specified on the fonts.fon= line. On this VGA system, the specified font is (a) the VGA default, and alternate (b) 8514 and (c) CGA fonts.

OEM Font (oemfont.fon=). The only visible effect of changing the OEM font is to swap one Terminal font for another. For example, if CGAOEM.FON is used on a VGA system instead of the default VGAOEM.FON, the Character Map will display an oversized Terminal font. But within the DOS window, no change will be seen: The default VGA terminal font supplies the 8 × 12 font, while the CGA font supplies an 8 × 8 font. In either case, the other font comes from the appropriate WOA font collection described earlier, so the net effect of the swap is zero. Refer to Chapter 7 for more details about font selection in a DOS Window.

WIN.INI Font Changes. A few lines in WIN.INI may be inserted to change a specific font on the Windows desktop, as described in the following sections.

Icon Title Font. The default font for the text under each Windows icon is a Sans Serif, 8-point, normal-weight typeface specified in the [fonts] section of WIN.INI. The following example shows how the line appears in a VGA system.

```
[fonts]
MS Sans Serif 8,10,12,14,18,24 (VGA res)=SSERIFE.FON
```

To specify some other font instead, leave the above line in place, but add one or more of the following lines to the [desktop] section of WIN.INI.

[desktop]	Comments
IconTitleFaceName=MS Serif	Replaces default sans serif with a serif font
IconTitleSize=10	Replaces default 8-point with 10-point font
IconTitleStyle=1	1 = bold, 0 = normal weight typeface

Experiment with different font names, sizes, and styles to find one that best suits your needs. Note that, unlike other font-change lines, the desired font is specified here by the font description (MS Serif, or similar), not the actual filename (SERIFE.FON).

NOTE: The Windows 3.1 Print Manager uses the **IconTitleFaceName** font to display printer status and print queue documents in the Workspace (see Figure 9.4a). You might want to have a look at the Workspace to see if the font you selected is satisfactory. Small Fonts, for example, shows a broken typeface that may be hard to read, even though it looks fine under icons on the Desktop. In Windows-for-Workgroups, the Workspace font is selected via the <u>F</u>ont... option on the Options Menu (see Figure 9.4b).

Non-Default Variable-Width System Font.   As described earlier, Windows' title bars, menus, and text in the SysEdit applet are displayed in the variable-width system font specified in the fonts.fon= line in the [boot] section of SYSTEM.INI. To use some other font instead, leave that line intact but add one or both of the following lines to the [windows] section of your WIN.INI file:

[windows]	Comments
SystemFont=*fontname*.FON	Must be a raster or vector font (with FON extension).
SystemFontSize=*xx*	xx is point size. This line valid only with raster fonts.

Try SYMBOLE.FON to make your version of Windows useless to all your non-Greek-speaking friends, or SMALLE.FON for a typeface that can only be read by Superman. Vector fonts are likewise impractical: The resultant oversized text is too big to be useful. However, you might choose a serif font (SERIFE.FON, for example) if you don't care for the sans serif default font.

NOTE: Remember the font you select will also be used for text displayed by the SysEdit applet which, as a result, may become useless for editing purposes. To recover from such an editing indiscretion, use the DOS EDIT utility instead, which displays text in the OEM font described earlier in the chapter.

Status Bar Text Configuration (Workgroups). The font and point size for Status Bar text in some Windows applets can be changed by adding the following lines to the indicated section of WIN.INI:

```
[Desktop]
StatusBarFaceName=Arial
StatusBarFaceHeight=12
```

Insert the name and point size for the font you wish to use, as shown by the Arial 12-point example above. The height of the Status Bar automatically adjusts itself to accommodate the new point size. However, if you select a large size, there may not be room within each panel to view the entire message. As a further consideration, italic, bold, and bold italic styles are not supported. If specified anyway, a typeface other than the one specified may appear.

The changes made here affect Status Bar text in the following applets:

Chat   Net Watcher
Clipbook Viewer   Print Manager
File Manager

The Character Map and Control Panel Status Bars are not affected by these changes.

Revising the [FontSubstitutes] Section. In addition to the other font reconfiguration procedures described here, the [FontSubstitutes] section can be edited as required. As a typical example, if a document was created with the Hewlett-Packard "R" cartridge, and that cartridge is no longer available, its Presentations and Letter Gothic fonts will both be displayed and printed by the TrueType Courier New font. Thus, the stylistic differences between the two cartridge fonts will be lost if the document is displayed and/or printed.

To remedy this problem, edit the [FontSubstitutes] section as follows:

```
Presentations=Century Gothic Bold
Letter Gothic=Arial Narrow
```

In the above example, substitute other names as required to approximate the style of other missing fonts. The substitute font must be a Windows vector screen font or a TrueType font. If a non-Windows screen font is specified, it may not be recognized as a valid substitute; in this case Windows will make some other substitution.

Some font software packages (Hewlett-Packard TrueType Screen Font Pack, for example) may make lengthy insertions in the [FontSubstitutes] section, such as seen in this brief excerpt:

```
Albertus (W1)=Albertus Medium
...other lines here...
Univers Cd (W1)=Univers Condensed
```

This set of lines is followed by a duplicate set in which (W1) is replaced by (WN). If you created documents using (W1) or (WN) device fonts prior to installing the Font Pack, then leave these lines in place. Otherwise, they can be removed.

WINFILE.INI Font Changes. The [Settings] section of the WINFILE.INI file contains initialization settings for the File Manager window. In a default setup, the section may contain nothing but a few lines defining window size and directory format. However, additional lines to specify font instructions also may appear, as described here.

File Manager Directory Font. The default font for File Manager's directory listings is the MS Sans Serif raster font in an 8-point, all lowercase type style. To change this selection, open File Manager's Options Menu and select the Font... option to open the Font dialog box. When you change any of the default settings, the appropriate lines are written into WINFILE.INI, as shown here.

```
[Settings]
Face=            font description    Specify desired font.
Size=            xx                  Specify desired point size.
LowerCase=       x                   Select x, y combination from values
                                     below.
FaceWeight=      y                   Select x, y combination from values below.
```

x	y		x	y	
0	400	Uppercase regular	4	400	Uppercase italic
1	400	Lowercase regular	5	400	Lowercase italic
0	700	Uppercase bold	4	700	Uppercase bold italic
1	700	Lowercase bold	5	700	Lowercase bold italic

Additional details about File Manager font selection are given in the *Applet and Application Font Configuration* section which follows.

Applet and Application Font Configuration

Within Windows itself, applets that support font selection provide a menu option to select the font to be used. A few representative examples are described below.

File Manager Font Selection. Open the Options Menu (Figure 10.16a) and select Font... to open the Font dialog box shown in Figure 10.16b. The File Manager's directory listings are for screen display only. Therefore, font selection criteria match those of the Paintbrush utility described immediately below.

Paintbrush Font Selection. Open the Text Menu (Figure 10.16c) and select the Fonts... option to open the Font dialog box shown in Figure 10.16d. Printer font support is not an issue, since text imported into a Paintbrush picture becomes an integral part of that picture. It is no longer regarded as text, and so may be printed by any printer that works with Paintbrush. Therefore, the Paintbrush Font Box lists all currently installed fonts, and the list is completely independent of the installed printer.

However, since printer device fonts are only available at the printer in which they are resident, their names do not appear in the Paintbrush Font Box. If a screen font with the same name is also installed, that name will show up in the list of course, but the printer icon seen next to the same font name in the Write Font Box will not be displayed here.

Write Font Selection. Open the Character Menu (Figure 10.16e) and select the Fonts... option to open the Font dialog box shown in Figure 10.16f. Since any font selected for use within a Write document must also be available for print jobs, the Font Box and Font Size Box list only those fonts and point sizes that are supported by the currently installed printer. Device fonts—such as those found in a printer cartridge—are listed, although the onscreen font may or may not be a close match, depending on what screen fonts are available.

Word Processor Font Selection. For most word processors designed for use within Windows, the font selection criteria are the same as for the

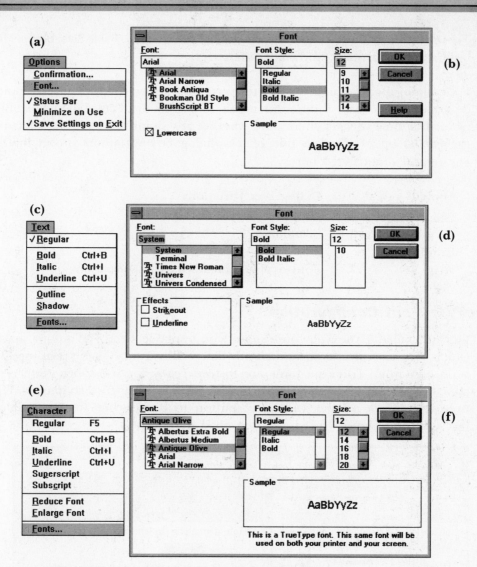

Figure 10.16 The Options Menu and Font dialog box as they appear in (a and b) the File Manager, (c and d) the Paintbrush applet, and (e and f) the Write applet.

Write applet. However, a smaller screen area is usually set aside to display Font and Point Size Boxes, as shown in Figure 10.17. When the down arrow to the right of either box is clicked, a pull-down menu displays the list of available fonts or font sizes, both of which are shown in the figure.

The B, I, and U buttons to the immediate right of the Point Size box select bold, italic, bold italic, and underline styles.

Font Dialog Box Summary. For the sake of variety (maybe), each applet described above uses a different menu to get to the Font dialog box. But no matter how you get there, and whether it's singular or plural, selecting the Font(s) option displays one of the dialog box variations shown in the Figure and summarized here:

Applet	Dialog Box Variations
File Manager	Lowercase check box
	Help button
Paintbrush	Effects box
Write	Font explanation under the Sample box

TrueType Font Configuration

Once installed, TrueType fonts should be available to any Windows application that can use them, and should be readily available for printing. To verify that your TrueType fonts are indeed ready for use, open the Fonts applet to display the Fonts dialog box shown earlier in the chapter as Figure 10.4a. Click on the TrueType... button to display the TrueType dialog box shown in Figure 10.18a and described here.

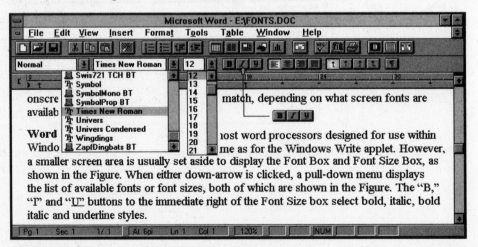

Figure 10.17 In Word-for-Windows and many other applications, the Font dialog box is replaced by a Fonts box and a separate Points box. A down arrow button opens a drop-down list of available typefaces and point sizes. Three buttons on the Toolbar access bold, italic, and bold italic fonts for the selected typeface.

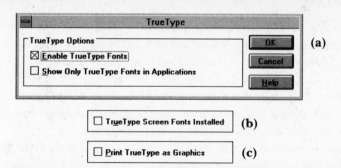

Figure 10.18   Use the TrueType dialog box (a) to specify if TrueType and other fonts are to be made available to your applications. The TrueType Screen Fonts Installed (b) and Print TrueType as Graphics (c) check boxes appear in the Setup (Figure 9.10a) and Options (Figure 9.10b) dialog boxes.

Enable TrueType Fonts.   Under default conditions there is an "X" in the check box and TrueType font names are displayed in the appropriate Fonts Box in any applet or application that supports TrueType fonts. Clear the check box to disable TrueType fonts without physically removing them. If you change the status of this check box, you will be prompted to restart Windows in order for the change to take effect.

TrueType versus non-TrueType Font.   If the same name is used by a True-Type and a non-TrueType font, the former takes precedence and the latter is not seen. If you need to access the latter, you'll have to remove the TrueType font to do so.

> **NOTE:** A **TTIfCollisions** option described in the Windows Resource Kit Manual (available separately; see Appendix D) describes a line that may be added to WIN.INI to assign precedence to either the TrueType or the non-TrueType font. However, the option is not yet implemented and is mentioned here simply to help readers avoid spending hours wondering why it doesn't do anything.

Show Only TrueType Fonts in Applications.   If the Enable TrueType Fonts box is cleared, then this option is disabled (grayed) since the fonts must be enabled in order to show them.

Place an "X" in this box if you want to make sure you only use True-Type fonts in the future. In this case, the names of all other installed fonts will not be displayed and the fonts will not be available for use. It is not necessary to restart Windows after changing the status of this check box.

TrueType Screen Fonts Installed. If the optional *Hewlett-Packard TrueType Screen Font Pack* (described above) is installed for the H-P LaserJet 4/4M printer, the option with this name should be checked on the Setup dialog box shown in Figure 9.10a. The check box is also shown here as Figure 10.18b. If the *Font Pack* has been installed but the check box is cleared, then each font will be listed twice: once as the device (printer) font, and a second time as the True-Type version. Check the box to eliminate the former reference.

Make sure the box is cleared if the *Font Pack* is not installed. Otherwise, the printer's resident fonts will not be available.

Print TrueType as Graphics. Figure 10.18c shows the check box for this feature that appears in a printer's Options dialog box if the printer supports it. For example, see the Hewlett-Packard LaserJet 4/4M Options dialog box in Figure 9.10b in the previous chapter. Other printers (H-P series II, for example) show a dialog box similar to that shown in Figure 9.11b, but with this option displayed near the bottom of the screen.

In most cases, *Print TrueType as Graphics* should be disabled. However, you may want to check the box if the printed output does not match the screen display, as may be the case if a graphics object overlays TrueType text. On screen the text is masked by the image, but on the printout, the text shows through. If the option is enabled, the printout should match the screen, but the print job will take longer.

In case of any discrepancies between what you see and what you get, put a check in the box and try again.

Font Removal Procedures

To remove one or more installed fonts, open the Fonts dialog box (Figure 10.4a) and highlight the font(s) to be removed. If at least one font name is highlighted, the Remove button is enabled. Click on the button to open the Remove Font dialog box shown in Figure 10.19, which shows the name of the first font to be removed.

Delete Font File from Disk. By default, the check box next to this option is clear. If you do not change its status, the font file remains on your disk, and only the reference to it in WIN.INI is removed. This may be convenient if the removal is to be temporary, so that the font can be reinstalled later on without copying/expanding it from the distribution diskette. However, if you know you won't want to use the font(s) again, check the box so that each one is physically deleted during the removal procedure.

Figure 10.19   Use the Remove Font dialog box to remove the specified font.

Remove Some/All Fonts.   If you highlighted several fonts—for example, an entire typeface family—you can click on the Yes to All button to avoid repeating your instructions for every font to be removed. Or, click on the Yes button to remove/delete the listed font and be sequentially prompted for each other highlighted font.

Font Troubleshooting

For those Windows applications which offer a choice of fonts, an onscreen Font Box displays the currently selected font. In some applications a font menu appears immediately below the Font Box. Or you may need to click an adjacent arrow button to display a pull-down font menu. In either case,

1. the menu should offer the font you're looking for,
2. the selected font should appear on screen when you resume typing or, previously highlighted text should now be displayed in that font, and
3. your printer should use the font you selected.

If one or more of these criteria are not met, refer to the appropriate section below for troubleshooting assistance. Refer to the sections on screen and printer problems, screen only or printer only, as appropriate.

General Font Troubleshooting

In most cases, an improper font display or printout can be traced to something reasonably obvious, like an error in the WIN.INI file, a font that really is missing, a permanent font not downloaded to the printer, and so on. But in at least a few cases, the problem will not be solved by checking for obvious errors. For example, the appropriate lines in WIN.INI may all be in order, the font is where it should be, and yet it still won't behave itself. In this case, it's a good idea to go through the WIN.INI file and scout out any line (or whole section) which appears font-related, but which cannot be verified by checking against your plain-vanilla WIN.INI file—the one you printed immediately after installing Windows 3.1 (you did do that, didn't you?).

For example, installation of Bitstream, Hewlett-Packard, or other third-party fonts will add new sections to WIN.INI (Bitstream's [Typefaces], H-P's [HPPCL,LPT*x*], etc.). Sometimes an added line, or perhaps a missing line, will have a completely unexpected effect on font and print operations not really related to the new section. Therefore, if a quick review of the following paragraphs does not offer a solution to a problem, you may want to disable recently added font software, then try again.

Unless you're very well acquainted with third-party installation procedures, resist the temptation to edit WIN.INI by hand. Although it's easy enough to find and remove complete sections added by third-party software installation, it's even easier to overlook other changes that have been made elsewhere. For example, an installation may replace all references to the default Windows printer driver in favor of its own driver. To verify this, check the device=(*printer driver name*) in the [windows] section of WIN.INI to see if the driver name has been changed. Then look for other lines that need to be revised. Or better yet, use whatever uninstall/disable procedure is included (one hopes) with the software in question.

Character Map and Application Font Checks.   For general font troubleshooting, the Character Map's Font Box is often a good place to start. If you can find and display the font there, the font is correctly listed in WIN.INI, and the font file itself is available. However, this does *not* mean the font is available to Windows applications, which will list the same font *only* if your installed printer supports it. A TrueType font with the same name as a non-TrueType font will take precedence in both font lists.

Printer Internal Font Check.   If you need to check the symbol set of an internal printer font, the BASIC program listing in Figure 10.20 will print the complete symbol set (32–255) in seven columns. As shown in the figure, the program prints the IBM PC8 symbol set on most Hewlett-Packard laser printers. To check some other symbol set, substitute its ID number for the 10U seen in the first line of the program listing. Table 10.18 lists the symbol set ID number for most current symbol sets. Refer to your printer *User's Guide* for verification that any code listed in the Table is supported by the printer.

When All Else Fails.   If none of the suggestions given below do anything for you, try enabling the Print TrueType as Graphics option described above (if the printer supports it, of course). Some printers always have trouble with TrueType fonts unless this option is enabled, while others may not print graphics and text properly.

Character Map Troubleshooting

As just noted, the Character Map applet is a helpful tool for viewing the symbol set in any typeface. However, there may be problems associated with the applet itself, and a few of these are reviewed here.

Applet Window Does Not Cascade or Tile Properly. If the Task Manager Tile or Cascade button is clicked while the Character Map Applet Window is open, the window will not properly fit into the normal Cascade or Tile pattern. This is because the size of the Character Map window is fixed and therefore neither option can resize it as required. There is no work-around, other than closing the applet before clicking on either button.

Program Listing[*]

```
LPRINT CHR$(27); "(10U"                    10U is IBM PC-8 symbol set. See Table 10.18
FOR k = 32 TO 63                           and printer User's Guide for valid codes for
                                           selected printer.
LPRINT USING "###  "; k; : LPRINT CHR$(k);
LPRINT TAB(12); USING "###  ";  k + 32;   :  LPRINT CHR$(k + 32);
LPRINT TAB(24); USING "###  ";  k + 64;   :  LPRINT CHR$(k + 64);
LPRINT TAB(36); USING "###  ";  k + 96;   :  LPRINT CHR$(k + 96);
LPRINT TAB(48); USING "###  ";  k + 128;  :  LPRINT CHR$(k + 128);
LPRINT TAB(60); USING "###  ";  k + 160;  :  LPRINT CHR$(k + 160);
LPRINT TAB(72); USING "###  ";  k + 192;  :  LPRINT CHR$(k + 192)
NEXT k
LPRINT CHR$(12);
```

[*] Program produces 7-column printout of complete symbol set in printer's default font. To specify font, change line 1 to read as follows:

```
LPRINT CHR$(27); "(10U" ; CHR$(27); "(font code—see below)"
```

Typical xx-point font codes for H-P LaserJet 4. Do not include spaces, inserted here for clarity.

```
"(s1p xx v1s0b 4168T"      Antique Olive italic
"(s1p xx v1s3b 16602T"     Arial bold
"(s1p xx v0s0b 16901T"     Times New Roman regular
```

Figure 10.20 This short BASIC program will print out the complete symbol set for any internal printer font.

TABLE 10.18 Hewlett-Packard Symbol Set ID Codes*

Character Set	Standard	PCL†	TD‡	Character Set	Standard	PCL†	TD‡
ANSI (see Windows 3.1 Latin 1)				PC-8 (code page 437)		10U	PC
ASCII, JIS	ISO 14	0K		PC-8 Danish/Norwegian		11U	PD
ASCII	ISO 6	0U	US	PC-850		12U	PM
Chinese	ISO 57	2K		PC-852		17U	
Desktop		7J	DT	Pi font	HP	15U	PI
French	ISO 25	0F		Portuguese	ISO 16	4S	
French	ISO 69	1F		Portuguese	ISO 84	5S	
German	HP	0G		PS Math			MS
German	ISO 21	1G		PS Text		10J	TS
Greek-8	HP	8G		Roman extension	HP	0E	
Intl. Ref. Version	ISO 2	2U		Roman-8	HP	8U	R8
Italian	ISO 15	0I		Spanish	HP	1S	
Latin 1	ISO 100, 8859-1, ECMA-94	0N	E1	Spanish	ISO 17	s2S	
				Spanish	ISO 85	6S	
Latin 2	ISO L2	2N		Swedish	ISO 10	3S	
Latin 5	ISO L5	5N		Swedish	ISO 11	0S	
Legal	HP	1U	LG	Symbol		19M	
Line Draw	HP	0B		Technical-7		1M	
Math, PS		5M		Turkish		9T	
Math-7	HP	0A		United Kingdom	ISO 4	1E	
Math-8	HP	8M	M8	Ventura Intl.		13J	VI
MC Text		12J		Ventura Math		6M	VM
Microsoft Pub.		6J	PB	Ventura US		14J	
Norwegian v. 1	ISO 60	0D		Windows 3.0 Latin 1		9U	WN
Norwegian v. 2	ISO 61	1D		Windows 3.1 Latin 1		19U	
OCRA		0O		Windows 3.1 Latin 2		9E	
OCRB		1O		Windows 3.1 Latin 5		5T	
OEM-1		7U		Wingdings		579L	

* Check printer *User's Guide* to verify support for listed character set.
† PCL: PCL Symbol set ID.
‡ TD: Type Director Symbol Set ID.

Bitstream *FaceLift* Fonts Displayed Incorrectly. If a *Facelift* font of 9 points or smaller is installed, the Character Map may show an incorrect display if this font is selected. If so, set *Facelift*'s Threshold parameter to a lower value.

Enlarged Character Is Distorted.   The *Enlarge* mode may have trouble displaying characters in screen fonts which contain special-purpose accented characters and symbols. The "B" series from Microsoft's CD-ROM *Bookshelf* (Lucida Sans B, Symbol B, etc.) are typical examples. If one of these typefaces is selected, the Character Map's 7 × 32 matrix should display the characters properly. However, if the *Enlarge* mode is activated, the character may be displayed with "dirt" in the character box, or there may be a *General Protection Fault* error message. The problem is due to an incompatibility between the Character Map, the font file, and the installed video driver. If you must view enlarged characters when one of these fonts is selected, try using the default VGA or SVGA video driver and/or a different screen resolution.

Enlarged Character Obscured by Mouse Pointer.   If you place the mouse pointer over a character and hold down the primary mouse button, the pointer should disappear. However, sometimes the pointer sits on top of the enlarged character box, partially obscuring the character. This may occur if the Character Map is opened after Berkeley Systems' *After Dark for Windows* screen saver has been active. So far, the only workaround is to close and reopen Windows, then use the Character Map before the screen saver is activated. Or, use the keyboard instead of the mouse to move around the matrix.

Screen Font Troubleshooting

This section describes situations in which a font prints correctly, but the screen display is incorrect.

Deleted Font Still Available.   If you've deleted a font name by removing all references to it in WIN.INI, the font should no longer display or print, nor should its name appear in the Font Box of any Windows application. But sometimes all of that doesn't quite happen: The name is still there and the font still prints if you select it, even if the onscreen display looks like something else. In this case, there is probably some overlooked little file hiding out somewhere on your hard disk, and in that file is the name of the deceased.

As a typical example, if a Hewlett-Packard LaserJet series II printer is installed, a file called HPPCL.P00 in the Windows directory contains the names of fonts available at the printer, such as Courier, Line Printer, and any other fonts installed in a font cartridge. But there's more: The file also lists the path and filename of installed temporary and permanent soft fonts. So if you subsequently delete the name of a soft font from WIN.INI, but forget about HPPCL.P00, the filename will not go away. And, if you select the deleted (from WIN.INI) font, HPPCL.P00 will still track it down (provided you didn't erase the font file too) and use it for the print job.

In this particular case you can erase HPPCL.P00 with no disastrous side-effects. The file will rebuild itself and the file(s) deleted from WIN.INI will at last be really gone. However, in case of doubt about the consequences of similar deletions, the safer course is to use the appropriate utility to delete all references to any font you no longer want. In this case, open the Control Panel and select Fonts to remove any screen font that you don't want to have around. Then return to the Control Panel, and select Printers/Setup/Fonts to remove the printer font, and the references to it in the HPPCL.P00 file. Finally, exit and restart Windows.

Raster Font Missing. If a selected raster font prints correctly but some other font appears on screen, then the required screen font is not available and Windows has substituted something else in its place.

All Vector (Plotter) Fonts Missing. Depending on the installed printer driver, the three Windows vector fonts (Modern, Roman, Script) may not appear in your application's Font Box if the Print TrueType as Graphics option is enabled. Depending on the specific installed printer, the fonts may still be available anyway. The procedure described here works on a Hewlett-Packard LaserJet series III, but not on a series II printer. To determine if your installed printer will display and/or print a "missing" vector font, type the font name in the Font Box. Then select the Font Size box and type the desired point size. Although the list of available point sizes will be empty, you may enter any size and it will take effect immediately.

If you subsequently highlight text for which a vector font was specified, the correct font name and point size will appear in the Fonts and Points boxes. However, that font name will still not appear in the pull-down fonts list, nor will other font sizes appear to be available.

Some Screen Characters Garbled or Missing. If certain characters are either displayed incorrectly or are completely missing, follow the troubleshooting procedures described in the *Typeface Style Incorrectly Displayed* section.

Typeface Style (italic, bold, bold italic) Incorrectly Displayed. If a selected typeface style does not display correctly, there is probably a compatibility problem with the installed video driver. To verify this, try a new point size that is several sizes removed from the one showing the incorrect display, or a different typeface with the same attribute. As another alternative, readjust the page magnification if that feature is available within the current application. If any of these changes clear up the problem, try using one of the default Windows video drivers. If the problem no longer exists, then contact the appropriate manufacturer to see if an update is available.

"windows bug fix=" Line Appears in WIN.INI.   *What* Windows bug fix? This odd line may be inserted into the [fonts] section of WIN.INI if *Type Director* installs screen fonts. Apparently Windows sometimes has trouble reading lengthy screen font descriptions, and this line resolves the problem. If you find it in WIN.INI, just leave it alone. No expression, boolean or otherwise, follows the equal sign.

Wrong Font Displayed on the Windows Desktop.   To display text on-screen, various Windows applets and applications use one or more of the raster fonts listed in the [fonts] section of your WIN.INI file. For example, a VGA system displays the following font matrixes, all taken from the SSERIFE.FON file:

Applet/ Application	Uses This Font	For	Alternate Fonts
Help Screen	12 points (16 × 20)	Titles	Arial, Dom Casual
Help Screen	10 points (16 × 16)	Text	Arial, Dom Casual
Word-for-Windows	8 points (16 × 13)	Ribbon-bar Text	Arial, Dom Casual
Windows	8 points (16 × 13)	Icon Text	Serif, Arial, Times New Roman

If the SSERIFE.FON file is missing, Windows will search for an appropriate substitute, such as one of the alternate fonts listed above. The list will vary depending on the fonts actually available on your system, and the chosen alternate font may or may not be close to the missing font. Therefore, if something quite unexpected shows up in an area such as one of those listed above, it may be that in the absence of a default font, Windows could not find a close approximation (such as TrueType Arial) for it. In this example, verify that the MS Sans Serif= line in WIN.INI's [fonts] section specifies the correct sans serif font for your system. Next, make sure the font is indeed present in the system directory (or elsewhere, if you have moved your fonts into another location). If only the icon text is incorrect, don't overlook the possibility that you added an IconTitleFaceName= line to the WIN.INI [Desktop] section, but the font specified in that line is missing.

Wrong Font Used by Third-Party Application. Even if a third-party application has been updated for Windows 3.1 compatibility, it's still possible that its choice of fonts will be influenced by a listing in the [FontSubstitutes] section of WIN.INI. Therefore, if one or more of the listings shown in this section have been changed, the application may display some or all of its text in the wrong font.

As a typical example, version 1.2 of Central Point's *Backup for Windows* utility contains numerous internal references to the Windows 3.0 *Helv* font. Assuming the [FontSubstitutes] section contains the needed Helv=MS Sans Serif line, the utility's screen displays will all be correct. But if this line is missing, or if a TrueType font has been listed as the Helv replacement, then some fonts will be displayed incorrectly. In this case, the fix is to restore the required line in the [FontSubstitutes] section of WIN.INI. For further details, refer to the *[FontSubstitutes]* section earlier in this chapter.

Screen Leading Does Not Match Printer Leading. If the vertical space between lines on the printed page is not what you expect it to be, it's possible that the screen leading does not agree with the printer. Try viewing the document at some other magnification, or via the Print Preview mode, if your application supports it.

For more details, refer to *Font Leading Gauge* in the *Font Configuration* section earlier in the chapter.

Sluggish Screen Display. As more and more fonts are inserted into a document, the time required to update the screen increases. As an extreme example, if a document contains samples of all the fonts shown earlier in Table 10.9, the screen redraw time will slow to a crawl. It will take so long just to move the cursor from one letter to another that editing will be almost impossible, except for the most patient of typists.

Given a reasonable number of fonts, no lag time should be perceived between striking a key and seeing the letter onscreen. If it is necessary to include an unreasonable number of fonts in a document, then select the Print TrueType as Graphics option described above. This will usually improve the onscreen response time, and may be required anyway, if the number of fonts selected exceeds the printer's soft font limit.

Italic Cursor Missing. Word-for-Windows users may be accustomed to seeing an italic cursor ("/" instead of "|") displayed when text is set in some italic typefaces. This feature is made possible by the application's ability to determine the font style and make the appropriate adjustments, which early versions could not do with some recent font packages. A few representative examples are listed here.

Italic Cursor Displayed With	Italic Cursor Not Displayed With
Atech Publishers' Powerpack	Adobe Type Manager
Bitstream Facelift	Micrologic MoreFonts
Hewlett-Packard Intellifonts	TrueType fonts
Plotter fonts	Zenographics SuperPrint
Windows 3.0 resident screen fonts	

With TrueType fonts, if only the regular style font is available and one of the other styles is generated from the regular font, then the italic cursor may be displayed if the bold italic combination is selected. Therefore, the appearance of an italic cursor over TrueType text is an indication that the selected font style is in fact missing, and TrueType is generating it from the regular font.

This characteristic applies only to Word-for-Windows version 2.0 and earlier. Subsequent updates (2.0a or later) have no problem recognizing italic text.

Printer Font Troubleshooting

This section describes situations in which a font is displayed correctly, but is printed incorrectly.

Wrong Font Printed. If a non-TrueType font is correctly displayed on screen, but some other font appears in the printed document, perhaps a required permanent soft font was not downloaded prior to printing. To verify this, click on Control Panel, Printers, Setup, then on Fonts, to display the Font Installer screen shown in Figure 10.10a. If an asterisk appears next to any font, that font is permanent; therefore, Windows assumes you will download it prior to starting a print job.

As a quick review, here are two lines from the [HPPCL,lpt*x*] section of WIN.INI. The first lists a temporary font, the second a permanent font. The Font Installer display should agree with the format shown here.

```
SoftFont1=C:\TYPEDIR\DCR0WUSA.PFM
SoftFont2=C:\TYPEDIR\DCR14USA.PFM,C:\TYPEDIR\DCR14USA.SFP
```

If text that should be printed with a permanent font is printed incorrectly, then the permanent font is missing at the printer. Perhaps it was not downloaded, or the printer was reset since the download. As a consequence, the text is printed in the nearest available font style, which may or may not be close. In this particular example, if a temporary Dom Casual font is in the same document, it will be used in place of the missing 10-point font, making a reasonably close substitution. But if no temporary Dom Casual font is in the document, then some other font style will be used instead.

If this describes the problem, then download the permanent font(s) before starting a print job which requires them. As an alternative, highlight each permanent font (one at a time) and click on the Temporary button to change its status. Now, the font will be downloaded whenever it is needed.

For further information about downloading soft fonts, refer to the *Font Download Batch File Troubleshooting* section later in this chapter.

Correct Font Printed, but via Screen Font instead of Temporary Printer Soft Font. As noted above, a temporary soft font will (or *should*) be downloaded as needed. However, in some cases the expected download does not occur and the matching screen font is used instead. Since the resultant print quality may be indistinguishable from that which would be produced by the soft font, about the only way to distinguish one from the other is to note how long it takes for the document to print. If it takes too long compared to say, some other document for which you know a permanent font is downloaded, then no doubt the screen font is being used.

There are several fixes available, including the easiest fix of all: Do nothing and let the screen font do its work in peace. Or, reset the font in question to permanent and download it as you exit the Font Installer. But if the font does not appear in the list displayed by the Font Installer, then there may be a conflict between one font source and another. In this case, click on the Font Installer's Add button and select the directory which contains the desired font. Then add it to the directory containing all the other listed fonts and make it temporary or permanent, as desired. Having done all this, there should be a new line in whatever third-party section of WIN.INI contains the listings for the other soft fonts. Within that section, the number in the Softfonts= line should indicate the addition of the new font.

Not All Fonts Printed. Some laser printers have a limit of 16 soft fonts per page. So if your page requires more than that number, the extra fonts will not be printed. There are two solutions to this problem. Find another Art Director, or select the *Print TrueType as Graphics* option described earlier in the chapter.

Expanded Font Does Not Print Accurately.   If you create an expanded raster font by selecting an available font size and doubling (or quadrupling, etc.) it, the screen will display the character distortions described earlier, and illustrated in Figure 10.2a. In addition, very large point sizes may not print correctly. If printed characters are compressed in height or width, or in both, then the specified font size exceeds the capabilities of the printer.

Extended Characters Print Incorrectly.   If characters in an extended symbol set (128–255) print incorrectly, it may be because of an older universal printer driver (UNIDRV.DLL). To verify this, try printing a page that contains only the font in which the problem is noted, or select the *Print True-Type as Graphics* option. If either action clears up the problem, then obtain an updated UNIDRV.DLL file from the Microsoft Windows Driver Library. (GO WDL on CompuServe.) Refer to Appendix D for further details on downloading such files.

Garbled Characters at Top of Printed Page.   If your printer prints a stream of meaningless characters across the top of the page instead of the expected text, the wrong printer driver is probably installed. Refer to the troubleshooting section of Chapter 9 with the same name for further details.

Print Job Takes Too Long.   If routine print jobs take too long, it may be that the *Print TrueType as Graphics* option is enabled. If the option is not required, turn it off before resuming printing.

Double-Underlining Prints as Solid Bar.   On some laser printers (H-P LaserJet, series II for example), if a TrueType font is double-underlined, the underline is printed as a solid bar, even though it displays correctly on screen. Generally, the transition between the double-underline and solid bar occurs in the 10–12 point region. The fix is to either pretend this buglet is a feature, or to wait for the printer manufacturer to supply an updated printer driver. This quirk is not noted with the LaserJet 4/4M driver.

Combination Screen and Printer Font Troubleshooting

This section describes a few problems that may affect both the screen display *and* the printed output.

Wrong Vector Font Displayed and Printed. If a selected vector font does not display or print correctly, there may be a conflict with a third-party font, especially if that font predates the introduction of Windows version 3.1 (April 6, 1992). As a specific example, if Bitstream's Monospace 821 font (in *FaceLift* version 1.2) is installed, and Windows' Modern plotter font is selected, both the screen display and subsequent printout will use the Bitstream font instead of the Windows font. To resolve such problems, use your favorite editor (Windows SysEdit or NotePad, DOS Edit utility, etc.) to insert the following line as line 2 in the [Typefaces] section of your WIN.INI file:

```
NoSubstVectFonts=1
```

In other words, "make no substitutions for vector fonts."

Wrong Font Appears in a Document.   If text created with a certain font is now displayed and printed in some other font, the problem may be traced to one of the following causes.

Selected Font Is No Longer Available.   As an obvious example, text created with the version 3.0 Tms Rmn font should now appear as MS Serif, as explained above in the *Font Substitutes* section. However, if the substitute font is also unavailable, or not supported by the installed printer, then Windows will look for the closest match it can find. In most cases, this means an old Tms Rmn font will appear as either MS Serif or Times New Roman, and so on. If so, the displayed and printed substitute font is reasonably close to the original. But if the old typeface now appears in some style that bears little or no resemblance to it, then it's possible the specified font is not a valid substitute.

Another possibility is that text sections created with two or more currently unavailable fonts are now displayed using the same font, thus losing whatever typographic distinction there was between the sections.

In cases such as these, refer to the [*FontSubstitutes*] section earlier in this chapter for information on how to substitute a new font, or fonts, for one or more missing fonts. In case of doubt, make a trial run using a distinctive TrueType font—Lucida Blackletter, for example. Its presence will be quite obvious, and will prove that the line in the [FontSubstitutes] section is indeed functioning properly.

TrueType Font Deleted from WIN.INI.   In the case of a wrong font appearance, a less-obvious cause is that one or more TrueType fonts have been deleted from the [fonts] section of the WIN.INI file. The effect may be noted even if the deleted font was never used in the document. For example, consider a document file containing only the Arial, Courier New, and Times New Roman font families. The following three lines show two versions of a test document using these fonts.

Test document, as written	Same, after deleting Arial font from WIN.INI	Line now displayed as:
1. Arial test	1. Arial test	Dom Casual
2. Courier New	2. Courier New	Courier New
3. Times New Roman	3. Times New Roman	Courier

Of course it's to be expected that in the absence of the Arial font, line 1 would appear in some other font instead. But what might *not* be anticipated is the effect noted in line 3, where Times New Roman text now appears as Courier. In fact, even if a TrueType font is deleted because it is never used, its removal from the [fonts] section of WIN.INI may have a ripple effect on some, or possibly all, of the other fonts used in your documents. The specific effect will depend on the former position of the deleted font, and on the properties of the remaining fonts.

Type Director/TrueType Font Conflict. Under certain conditions, installing a *Type Director* permanent font will cause a *TrueType* font in a previously written document to be incorrectly displayed and/or printed with the *Type Director* font. As a specific example, if *Type Director's* Dom Casual font is installed in a system which uses a LaserJet series II printer, documents containing TrueType's Arial font will now display that font as Dom Casual, and the Dom Casual name will appear in the Font Box when the affected text is selected.

The remedy described here corrects this specific example, and may be used as a general model to resolve similar conflicts affecting other fonts.

First, open the Printers applet, then click on the Setup... and Fonts... buttons. Highlight the Dom Casual fonts, then delete them, but do not remove them from the disk. Finally, add the just-deleted fonts back again. This procedure rewrites the PFM files for the fonts in question, and in so doing resolves the font conflict.

After completing this procedure, you will probably find *two* sets of PFM files in the directory containing the Dom Casual fonts. Each of the older, and now unused, sets probably has the same filename as the equivalent SFP file. Each newer file has a slightly different name, which probably refers to the actual point size of the equivalent font. Thus, an old DCR1CWNA.PFM is superseded by a new DCPR0120.PFM (0120 = 12 points), and so on.

In case of doubt about which file is which, compare the various PFM files in your *Type Director* fonts directory with the equivalent SFP listings in the [HPPCL,LPT1] section of WIN.INI. Any PFM file now listed in WIN.INI is required. Any PFM file *not* listed there is obsolete and can be erased from the directory. For insurance purposes, you may want to save these old PFM files elsewhere, until you are satisfied that they are indeed not needed.

Listed Point Size Does Not Display or Print. As a result of some installed-font conflicts, the list of font sizes available in the Font Size box may be inaccurate. For example, the Hewlett-Packard LaserJet series II supports a 12-point Courier font (internal), and only that size should appear when the Courier raster font is selected. If you've installed a third-party Softfont (for example, with *Type Director*), only the font sizes actually available for printing should be accessible via the Font Size box. However, if a Bitstream font (in *Facelift* version 1.2) is also installed, the Font Size box may display any point size from 4 through 127 for all raster screen fonts. Needless to say, only the valid size(s) will be displayed and/or printed. In the LaserJet II example, if you select say, Courier 20 (or Courier *anything*), you still get Courier 12.

In this case, the fix is to just disregard the misleading font size information. If you don't recall which listed sizes are valid, look in the [fonts]section of WIN.INI for the appropriate screen font and note the sizes listed there, or disable *Facelift* and re-examine the Font Size box for each vector font.

TrueType Font Troubleshooting

This section describes a few problems that are unique to TrueType font usage.

All TrueType Fonts Missing. There are two areas to check if your True-Type fonts are not available for Windows applications. But first, any doubts about whether the fonts were successfully installed should be resolved, as follows. Verify that the TrueType fonts are indeed in place by opening the Character Map in the Accessories Group Window and examining one or more of them. If the fonts are not available, then there is a problem with the installation. Go back to the Control Panel, select Fonts, and remove the TrueType fonts from the list of installed fonts. Then add them back in again, reboot and try again.

Once the Character Map displays the TrueType fonts, then refer to one of the following sections, as appropriate.

TrueType Fonts Unavailable after Upgrading to Windows 3.1. If your True-Type fonts were installed during an upgrade from an earlier version of Windows, but the font names are not available in your application's Font Box (in WRITE, Word-for-Windows, etc.), then it's quite likely the upgrade procedure neglected to replace an old printer driver with an updated version, and that the old driver does not support TrueType.

Refer to Table 9.2 in Chapter 9 for printer driver information and to Appendix A for date and file size information. If the printer driver presently installed does not match any driver listed in the Table, then it probably does not support TrueType.

TrueType Fonts Disabled. Once you have verified that the correct printer driver is installed, open the Control Panel in the Main Group Window, and click on the Fonts icon to display the Fonts dialog box shown earlier in Figure 10.4a. Then click on the TrueType button to display the TrueType dialog box, which is seen in Figure 10.18a. An "X" in either of the TrueType Options boxes indicates the listed feature is enabled.

To enable TrueType fonts, make sure there is an "X" in the Enable True-Type Font Box. If the box is cleared, TrueType fonts are disabled and the Show only TrueType Fonts option is grayed, so it is not possible to specify contradictory options.

The options described above are recorded in two lines in the indicated section of WIN.INI as listed here.

```
[TrueType]
TTEnable=    1    TrueType fonts are available to your applications (default).
             0    TrueType fonts are not available to your applications.

TTOnly=      1    Only TrueType fonts are available to your applications.
             0    All installed fonts are available to your applications
                  (default).
```

Symbol and Wingdings Fonts Missing. These two fonts were not supported by early versions of Word Perfect for Windows. If they are not available in some other application, check the accompanying *User's Guide* for details. When you can't find any details to check, call the company's Tech Support line (if any) to see if an update is available.

Some non-TrueType Fonts Missing. If your installed font collection contains a TrueType font and a non-TrueType font with the same name, then only the TrueType font will be available.

All non-TrueType Fonts Missing.   If non-TrueType fonts are not available, then disable the S̲how only TrueType Fonts option. The procedure for doing so was described in the *TrueType Fonts Disabled* section above.

Wrong Font Displayed and Printed.   If a TrueType font name appears in the font box, but the wrong face appears on screen, then possibly the font resource (FOT) file for that font is missing, or its internal path does not point to the actual location of the corresponding TrueType font (TTF) file, or the font file itself is missing. In any case the selected font will not be printed. If in doubt as to the source of the problem, open the Fonts applet and remove the problem font. Check the Delete Font File from Disk box to erase the suspect file. Then insert the appropriate TrueType diskette in drive A and add a fresh copy of the font to your system.

Font Looks Slightly Different than on Previous Jobs.   As noted earlier in the chapter, TrueType can create a missing typeface style based on information it finds in another file in the same font family. Therefore, if the file containing a single font style is inadvertently deleted, TrueType may come very close to matching it. However, if the difference is noticeable, it may be that TrueType came close, but not close enough. The discrepancy may be more apparent on screen than on the printed page. The solution is to copy/expand the missing font file back into the System (or True-Type) directory.

Print TrueType as Graphics Is Disabled.   If this feature is grayed in the printer's Options dialog box, then some other option has disabled it. For example, if the Hewlett-Packard LaserJet 4/4M is not set for Raster Graphics Mode *and* High Graphics Quality, then *Print TrueType as Graphics* is disabled. Reset the other options as required, then check this box.

TrueType Fonts Not Available within Application.   If TrueType fonts are not available in the Font Box in the Write applet or in most applications, such as Excel or Word-for-Windows, open the Character Map or Paintbrush applets and see if the missing fonts are listed there. If not, then they really are missing, and need to be reinstalled. If the fonts do appear in either applet, though, then continue reading here.

The following printers do not support TrueType fonts at resolutions other than 300 dots-per-inch or greater. Therefore, if some other resolution is selected, the TrueType fonts are not available for print jobs. However, you can still display the fonts via the Character Map applet, and insert them into bitmap images via the Paintbrush applet.

Canon	Driver Name	Hewlett-Packard	Driver Name
LBP-4, LBP-8 II	LBPII.DRV	Deskjet series	HPDSKJET.DRV
LBP-8 III	LBPIII.DRV		

Wrong Font Displayed at Small Point Sizes. Believe it or not, this is a "feature." When a small TrueType font size is selected, Windows displays a serif or sans serif bitmap font instead of the font actually selected. This is done to improve screen readability—at small font sizes, the bitmap font is easier to read than the TrueType font it replaces. The font swap affects the screen only: If the document is printed, the desired TrueType font is used.

Table 10.19 shows a few examples of screen font substitutions at smaller point sizes. The Table is based on a Word-for-Windows file viewed at normal magnification on a VGA system, and shows that the substitution takes place at font sizes of 7 points or less. Under other conditions, the substitution might occur at some other point size. For example, all else being equal, an SVGA system (800×600) might display TrueType fonts down to about 6 points.

TrueType symbol fonts are not subject to screen-font substitution at small point sizes.

TABLE 10.19   Bitmap Screen Font Substitutes for Small TrueType Font Sizes

Correct TrueType Font (VGA, 8 pts)	Bitmap Substitute Font (VGA, 7 pts)
FONT TEST IS CENTURY SCHOOLBOOK.	FONT TEST IS CENTURY SCHOOLBOOK.
FONT TEST IS GARAMOND ANTIQUA.	FONT TEST IS GARAMOND ANTIQUA.
FONT TEST IS TIMES NEW ROMAN.	FONT TEST IS TIMES NEW ROMAN.
FONT TEST IS ARIAL.	FONT TEST IS ARIAL.
FONT TEST IS ARIAL NARROW.	FONT TEST IS ARIAL NARROW.
FONT TEST IS CENTURY GOTHIC.	FONT TEST IS CENTURY GOTHIC.
FONT TEST IS LUCIDA BLACKLETTER.	FONT TEST IS LUCIDA BLACKLETTER.
FONT TEST IS LUCIDA CALLIGRAPHY.	FONT TEST IS LUCIDA CALLIGRAPHY.
FONT TEST IS LUCIDA HANDWRITING.	FONT TEST IS LUCIDA HANDWRITING.

Equation Editor Font Troubleshooting

This section discusses font troubleshooting the Microsoft Equation Editor bundled with Word-for-Windows and also available elsewhere. If you don't have this utility, the following paragraphs may be skipped.

Due to changes made to Windows 3.1 after the Equation Editor was introduced, the TrueType fonts supplied with the Editor may not have been installed correctly. Although recent Equation Editor upgrades have corrected the problem, this section may be of use if an older version of the editor displays some fonts incorrectly.

Several error messages associated with the Equation Editor are described in the *Equation Editor Error Messages* section of this chapter.

Wrong Symbol Font. If the Lucida Bright Math Symbol font is listed in the Symbol box, the ± symbol is displayed as a triple integral ($\int\int\int$), which doesn't make equation-editing any simpler. So if this or some other erroneous symbol is seen here or elsewhere in your equation, change the Symbol font to Symbol to correct the problem. While you're at it, change the two Greek fonts (if necessary) to Symbol too.

Fences, MT Extra Plain Font Problem. If the letters "b" and "g" (or some other incorrect display) appear in the Equation window when parentheses are selected, the Fences and/or MT Extra fonts are unavailable, even though they may appear to be present. To verify the problem, open the Control Panel, select the Fonts applet, then highlight either font name in the Installed Fonts: list. The Sample display at the bottom of the screen will probably be blank, even though you have (apparently) selected a font for display.

To correct the problem, click on the Add button. At the bottom of the screen, log onto the Windows System subdirectory; when the list of fonts appears, look for "Fences Plain" and "MT Extra Plain" (note the additional word "Plain"). Highlight both entries, then click on the OK button to add them to the list of installed fonts. Finally, highlight the "Fences" and "MT Extra" fonts in that same list, then click on the Remove button.

Having done all that, the Sample box should show a short sample of either the Fences or MT Extra fonts in place of the blank display seen earlier. There should be no further font-related problems with the Equation Editor, once you work up the courage to give it another chance.

Font Download Batch File Troubleshooting

If you chose the Download-at-Startup option as you exited the Font Installer (as described above), Windows wrote a batch file (SFLPT*x*.BAT) containing the necessary instructions, and added a line to your AUTOEXEC.BAT file which calls that file every time the computer is booted—a mixed blessing at best. While a downloading batch file might be nice to have on hand for future use, it's a bit of a nuisance to go through the download procedure every time you reboot the system, especially if the printer is neither always on nor always needed. Therefore, if you'd rather be spared this unwanted help, you may wish to edit the line out of your AUTOEXEC.BAT file, and just use SFLPT1.BAT as a freestanding batch file, when and if you need it.

In any case, SFLPT1.BAT writes a few small files (PCL*x*.TMP) for its own use, then erases them at the conclusion of the download. Although these files should be written into your temporary directory (usually, C:\TEMP), this may not happen. The batch file tries to find that directory by looking in the MS-DOS environment for a location specified by a set TMP= line in your AUTOEXEC.BAT file. However, this line is now usually written as set TEMP=, therefore, SFLPT*x*.BAT won't find what it's looking for. So it writes its temporary files into your root directory instead. This is no great tragedy, provided there is room in the directory for the files. And as noted, the files are erased at the end of the download, so you might not even be aware of what's happening.

However, if there is a problem with the download, there are two solutions to consider: either add a set TMP=C:\TEMP line to your AUTOEXEC.BAT file, or edit SFLPTx.BAT to change all references from TMP to TEMP. If you decide to do the editing, there are a few other revisions that might be considered, especially if you will be running the batch file independently of your regular AUTOEXEC.BAT file. If so, the following three lines can be deleted:

```
C:\(path)\PCLSF0YN.EXE LPT1
if ERRORLEVEL 1 goto nodownload
copy %tmp%\pcl3.tmp LPT1
```

The first line calls a file that asks you if you really want to do this. If you answer "no," the next line aborts the download by jumping to the end of the file. But presumably you wouldn't be going through this little exercise if you didn't want to download, so the question is more hindrance than help. The final line prints out samples of the downloaded fonts. Again, after you've done this a few times, the printout is simply a waste of paper. So remove it and help save a tree.

Error Messages

In most cases, a font-related problem does not produce an error message. Instead, the screen and/or print job does not appear as it should—that's your clue that something's wrong. However, there are a few conditions that may be accompanied by an error message; some of these are listed here.

Character Map Error Messages

The following message(s) may appear if one of several non-TrueType fonts is displayed by the Character Map applet and you attempt to enlarge a character by placing the mouse pointer over it and holding down the primary button. Refer to the *Character Map Troubleshooting* section above for further information.

CHARMAP—An error has occurred in your application. If you choose ignore,... The message indicates an incompatibility between the applet and the video driver. Chances are, if you click on the Ignore button nothing will happen. Click on the Close button and a *General Protection Fault* message identifies the driver (*filename*.DRV), as described in the next message.

CHARMAP caused a General Protection Fault in module *filename*.DRV at *xxxx:yyyy*. This message may be seen by itself, or immediately following the *Error has occurred* message described above. In either case, it confirms the compatibility problem between the cited video driver and the Character Map applet.

Font Installation Error Messages

A few error messages may be encountered during an attempt to install additional fonts in your system.

Check this box only if you have the following screen font software installed: HP LaserJet 4/4M TrueType Screen Font Pack. It's not exactly an error message—just a warning against an accidental box-check prior to installing the Hewlett-Packard optional TrueType Screen Font Pack. Refer to *Post Installation Check* in the *Hewlett-Packard TrueType Screen Font Pack* above for further details.

No fonts found. If this message is seen in the List of Fonts box (grayed), then it's possible the diskette or hard disk path you are searching really doesn't have any fonts on it. However, if you encounter the message while trying to install TrueType fonts, then it's more likely that the TrueType option has been disabled. Refer to *Enable TrueType Fonts* in the *TrueType Font Configuration* section above for instructions on how to re-enable TrueType.

The *fontname* font is compressed and cannot be installed, unless you copy it to your Windows directory. Do you want to copy it to your Windows directory? The message appears if you try to install a compressed font and the Copy Fonts to Windows Directory check box is cleared (see Figure 10.5). Either check the box to copy the font into the *System* directory—not the Windows directory—or expand the font file, then retry the installation.

Your TrueType system was disabled. You will need to quit and restart Windows to enable TrueType and then run SETUP to install the TrueType font pack. This error message is seen if you try to install TrueType fonts while the TrueType option is disabled. All you need to do is exit and restart Windows. When you do this, the TrueType option is automatically re-enabled, and you may now install the fonts without encountering the error message. For further details refer to *Enable TrueType Fonts* earlier in the chapter.

Equation Editor Error Messages

Although recent upgrades have solved most font problems related to the Equation Editor, a few font-related error messages may be encountered when using an older version of the applet. Most such errors can be resolved by upgrading the Equation Editor. If that's not practical, then follow the instructions given here, or in the *Equation Editor Configuration* section.

Font Assignment: Equation Editor will assign fonts available on the default printer to your equation in the appropriate styles. Use the Define command on the Style menu to make sure these assignments are to your satisfaction. This is strictly an advisory message. The Equation Editor makes several default font selections based on the list of fonts that it finds in the [fonts] section of your WIN.INI file. Therefore, some equation elements may be incorrect if the Editor selects the wrong font(s). To verify this, open the Operator Symbols menu and select the "±" symbol in the upper left-hand corner of the pull-down menu. You should see a "±" in the Equation Editor window, which is taken from the TrueType Symbol font file (SYMBOL.TTF). If some other character appears, refer to the *Equation Editor Font Configuration* section above for assistance.

Font Not Available: Equation Editor's (*Fences, or MT Extra*) font is not available on the default printer. Some characters will not display or print. Choose a different printer or reinstall Equation Editor to properly install its fonts. More often than not, if a *Fences* message is seen, it will be immediately followed by an *MT Extra* message. To verify the problem, open the Fence Template menu and select the parentheses pair in the upper left-hand corner. If the letters "b" and "g" (or some other incorrect display) appear in the Equation window instead of the desired parentheses, the Fences and/or MT Extra fonts are unavailable, even though they may appear to be present. Refer to the *Equation Editor Troubleshooting* section for assistance resolving this problem.

Font Not Available: An adequate Symbol font is not available on the default printer. Some characters will not display or print. Choose a different printer or reinstall Equation Editor to properly install its fonts. In this case, the Equation Editor was not able to find a suitable symbol font listed in your WIN.INI file, and it substituted a non-symbol font instead. To verify this, check the Styles dialog box (Figure 10.7) for the font names appearing in the Greek and Symbol boxes. In each case a symbol font should be listed, but there's probably a conventional text font there instead.

Make sure the TrueType symbol files (SYMBOL.FOT and SYMBOL.TTF) are installed, and that the [fonts] section of WIN.INI contains a valid line reference to the SYMBOL.FOT file. Once the symbol font is available, return to the Equation Editor and recheck the Styles dialog box. Edit the Greek and Symbol lines to show the Symbol font.

Font & Style Not Available: The font & style, (*font and style description*) was not available on the default printer: (*another font and style description*) was substituted. When the Equation Editor is opened, it looks for the eight fonts listed in the MTFONTS.INI file, as described earlier in the chapter. If one of these fonts is no longer available, the warning message above is seen, and the name of a substitute font is written into the MTFONTS.INI file in place of the missing file. The new font will be used for this, and all subsequent Equation Editor sessions. In this case you may want to check the Styles list to see if the substitute font is acceptable. If it is, no further action is required. If not, then select an appropriate font in its place.

Printer: Equation Editor's fonts may not have been installed for the default printer [*(default printer name)* **on LPT1:]. Equation Editor will attempt to use available fonts. If any symbols are missing or incorrect, reinstall Equation Editor to properly install its fonts.** This message appears if you've changed your default printer since the last Equation Editor session. If so, the fonts listed on the Style screen may no longer be appropriate. Verify this by experimenting with various symbols. If the symbols are correct, no further action is needed. Otherwise, go back to the Setup procedure and reinstall the Equation Editor to correct the problem.

A Colophon of Sorts

The text you have been reading is set in 10.5-point serif *regular* font, in New Baskerville typefaces. Here and there, computer screen text is represented by a 9.5-point sans serif *regular* font in Helvetica typeface. Table headers are 10-point Helvetica black and figure legends are 10-point New Baskerville.

11

The Control Panel

Various components within the complete Windows system may be modified via the Control Panel applet located in the Main Group Window. To avoid the confusion of discussing the icons within it as "sub-applets" (or something equally unsatisfactory), the Control Panel is promoted here to the status of Group Window, with its occupants identified as applets.

Figure 11.1a shows the Main Group Window, the highlighted Control Panel icon, and the Control Panel itself as it might appear in Windows 3.1 standard mode. In this case, a Network icon would also appear if a network is installed and running. In Windows-for-Workgroups, the Network icon is always visible, regardless of network status.

Figure 11.1b shows the Control Panel with additional icons installed. The presence of the 386 Enhanced icon indicates that Windows is running in enhanced mode, while the other icons support various functions described below and in the next chapter. The detail view in Figure 11.1c shows additional icons that may show up in the window if Windows-for-Pen-Computing and a Sound Blaster Pro Mixer are installed. Finally, Figure 11.1d compares variations on the *Mouse* applet icon and concludes with a *Joystick* icon.

When any icon in the Control Panel is highlighted, a brief description appears in the Status Bar at the bottom of the panel, as may be seen in all parts of Figure 11.1. Table 11.1 gives an alphabetical list of the Control Panel applets, the file in which each icon is located, and the appropriate Status Bar description when that icon is highlighted.

731

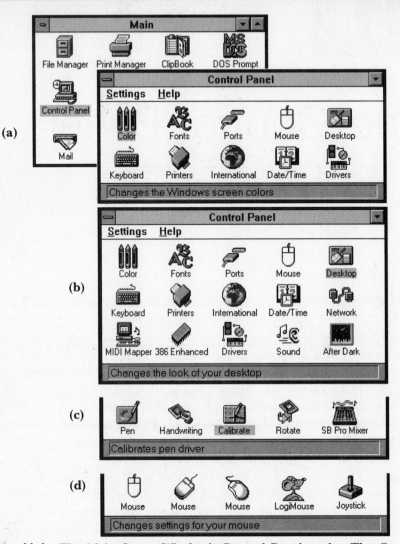

Figure 11.1 The Main Group Window's Control Panel applet. The Control Panel with (a) 10 applets seen in Windows 3.1 standard mode, and (b) in enhanced mode with additional applets installed. (c) Windows-for-Pen-Computing and SB Pro Mixer icons. (d) Typical Mouse applet and joystick icons.

Control Panel Menus

The Control Panel menus are briefly described here, in probably more space than they deserve. You can open the Control or Settings menu to exit the Control Panel, or save a little time by pressing the Alt+F4 keys to do the same thing.

TABLE 11.1   Control Panel Icons and Descriptions*

Icon	Icon Location	Status Bar Description [†]	Notes
386 Enhanced	CPWIN386.CPL	Optimizes Windows for 386 enhanced mode	1
AfterDark	ADCPL.CPL	Configure After Dark by Berkeley Systems	2
Calibrate	CPCAL.CPL	Calibrates pen driver	3
Color	MAIN.CPL	Changes the Windows screen colors	
Date/Time	MAIN.CPL	Changes date and time of computer clock	
Desktop	MAIN.CPL	Changes the look of your desktop	
Drivers	DRIVERS.CPL	Installs, removes, and configures drivers	
Fonts	MAIN.CPL	Adds and removes fonts, sets TrueType opts	
Handwriting	CPHW.CPL	Specifies user preferences for recognition	3
International	MAIN.CPL	Specifies international settings	
Joystick	IBMJOY.CPL	Calibrate joysticks version 1.0	4
Keyboard	MAIN.CPL	Specifies the keyboard repeat rate and delay	
MIDI Mapper	MIDIMAP.DRV	Selects MIDI setup, changes MIDI settings	5
Mouse	MAIN.CPL	Changes settings for your mouse	
	POINTLIB.DLL	Changes settings for your Microsoft Mouse	6
	POINTLIB.DLL	Changes settings for your Ballpoint Mouse	6
	LMOUSE.DLL	Changes settings for your mouse	7
Network	MAIN.CPL	Specifies settings for your network connections	8
Pen	CPPEN.CPL	Changes pen ink and double-tap settings	3
Ports	MAIN.CPL	Specifies communications settings for serial ports	
Printers	MAIN.CPL	Installs and removes printers, sets print opts	
Rotate	CPROT.CPL	Adjusts display orientation	3
Sound	SND.CPL	Assigns sounds to system events	
SB Pro Mixer	SBPMIXER.CPL	Controls Sound Blaster Volumes	9

Files (above) included with Windows, Windows-for-Workgroups

CPWIN386.CPL	MAIN.CPL	SND.DRV
DRIVERS.CPL	MIDIMAP.DRV	

* Seen on all systems, unless otherwise noted.

[†] Description seen when indicated icon is highlighted.

1 386 enhanced mode only.

2 Download ADCPL.ZIP (see text).

3 If Windows-for-Pen-Computing is installed.

4 Download IBMJOY.ZIP (see *Joystick* in text).

5 If MIDI is installed.

6 If optional Mouse software is installed (see text).

7 If Logitech *MouseWare Utilities* version 6.20 is installed.

8 Windows 3.1: Only if network is installed.

   Workgroups: Icon is always visible. Also included in WFWSETUP.CPL.

9 File is in Drivers directory on Windows (*not Workgroups*) Resource Kit diskette.

Control Menu

The standard Control Menu options are described in detail in Chapter 3.

Control Menu within a Control Panel Applet.   In each case, the menu offers only the *Move* and *Close* options, which have been fully covered in the *Control Menu* section of Chapter 3. As an exception to this rule, some third-party applets, such as *After Dark* (described below) offer additional options.

Settings Menu

This menu simply lists the titles of the icons seen in the Control Panel Window. You can select any one to open the corresponding applet, but it would be faster to simply double-click on the icon itself without bothering with the menu. The Settings menu may be seen (if you really do need to see it) by referring back to Figure 10.15, where it was used to illustrate the effect of changing one of the system fonts.

Help Menu

By now you should be thoroughly sick of Help menus. If not, refer to Figure 3.3: The Control Panel's Help menu is essentially the same, except it doesn't offer the *Windows Tutorial* option.

Control Panel Configuration

Unlike conventional group windows, the Control Panel does not permit an icon to be moved by dragging it to another location within the window, and the properties of a Control Panel applet cannot be changed. To illustrate, highlight the *Drivers* (or any other) icon, open the Program Manager's File menu and select the Properties option. The Program Item Properties dialog box will show the properties of the Control Panel itself (CONTROL.EXE), and not those of the highlighted icon within the Control Panel.

As a further point, you cannot minimize any applet within the Control Panel (except *After Dark,* if it's there). Each applet's own window is simply a dialog box which can be moved or closed, but that's it. If you want to minimize the Control Panel itself, first you have to close the Control Panel applet that's currently open.

However, you can do some configuration—including some icon resequencing—by following the procedures described in the following sections.

The [MMCPL] Section of CONTROL.INI

The Windows Resource Kit states that the Multimedia Control Panel [MMCPL] section of CONTROL.INI "specifies values related to the multimedia items in Control Panel." However, since most multimedia data is stored elsewhere, the [MMCPL] section is more likely to comprise only Control Panel size and position data, and perhaps the paths to CPL files. Examples of both are described below.

Window Size and Position

You can change the size of the Control Panel Window by dragging any of its borders around the Desktop, but there is no maximize button to make it fill the screen. Nor would you want to do this, since the window rarely contains more than about 12–15 icons. As you resize the window, the icons automatically rearrange themselves; in effect, the Auto Arrange option (see Program Manager's Options menu) is always enabled within the Control Panel.

To move the Control Panel, place the mouse pointer in the Title Bar, hold down the primary mouse button, and drag it to where you want it to be.

When you close the Control Panel, its position and size are stored in CONTROL.INI, as shown here:

```
[MMCPL]
NumApps=15   number of applets in the window
X=175        x coordinate of upper left-hand window corner
Y=91         y coordinate of upper left-hand window corner
W=362        window width
H=245        window height
```

The next time you open the Control Panel, it will return to the size and position specified here.

Add Applets to Control Panel

In most cases, applets are added to the Control Panel window only if they are designed to do so, in which case the installation may be automatic or optional. See the *After Dark* and *Mouse* descriptions later in the chapter for representative examples.

Although Windows itself installs its own Control Panel files in the System directory, some third-party applets place theirs elsewhere. For example, pen-computing files are often installed in the Windows directory. In cases such as this, the setup procedure adds one or more lines to the [MMCPL] section of CONTROL.INI to let Windows know where to find the file(s). In most cases, each such file could be moved into the System directory, and the equivalent [MMCPL] line removed. However, review the *Relocate Icons* section which follows before doing so. That section also explains the format in which these lines appear.

Resequence Icons within the Control Panel

Within certain limits, icon resequencing within the Control Panel Window can be accomplished by moving CPL files around and by editing the MAIN.CPL file. Examples of both techniques are given here.

Resequence CPL Files. To reorder the sequence in which some individual icons appear in the Control Panel window, move all the CPL files out of the System directory into a new CPLFILE (or whatever) directory. Then add a line for each such file, in the desired sequence, to the [MMCPL] section of CONTROL.INI.

In the following example, a Windows-for-Pen-Computing installation has placed its own CPL files in the Windows directory, and for the purposes of this example they have been left there. The other CPL files have been placed in a new CPLFILE directory.

To arrange the icons in the desired sequence, add a line for each applet or applet group as shown below. Each line begins with a filename (no extension) followed by an equal sign, then the complete path and filename (with extension) for the desired applet. The icons appear in the Control Panel window in the following sequence:

1. All icons in CPL files remaining in the System directory.

2. The MIDI Mapper icon (see text, below).

3. Icons in CPL files specified in [MMCPL] section, in the indicated sequence.

```
[MMCPL]
adcpl=C:\WINDOWS\CPLFILES\ADCPL.CPL        After Dark Screen-Saver
main=C:\WINDOWS\CPLFILES\MAIN.CPL          9 or 10 icons (see Table 11.1)
cprot=C:\WINDOWS\CPROT.CPL                 Pen Rotate Utility
drivers=C:\WINDOWS\CPLFILES\DRIVERS.CPL    Drivers applet
```

Unfortunately, the MIDIMAP.DRV file cannot be relocated, since Windows needs to find it in the System directory when it needs it. Therefore, if this applet is installed, it will show up as the first icon in your Control Panel.

> **NOTE:** If you move MAIN.CPL into a new directory and add the **main=** line shown above, you'll need to add **C:\WIN-DOWS\CPLFILES** to the PATH in your AUTOEXEC.BAT file. The *Print Manager* applet needs to know where to find MAIN.CPL if you use it for printer setup.

Resequence Icons within MAIN.CPL File. Changing the icon sequence within MAIN.CPL is no routine task, but it can be done by anyone who doesn't mind attacking the file with the DOS Debug utility (or similar). If you have no intention of doing so, this whole section can be ignored.

A section of MAIN.CPL contains 10 16-byte segments which specify the order in which the icons appear, as shown in Figure 11.2. This segment can be found and viewed by typing the first two lines shown in column 1 below. When Debug displays the third line, note the value following the colon and enter it on the fourth line, as shown. Press the Enter key to display the code shown in the figure.

```
C:\WINDOWS\SYSTEM>debug main.cpl
-s cs:100 fffe "CplApplet"
24B0:4180
-d cs:4180 422D
xxxx:4180  43 70 6C 41 70 70 6C 65-74 00 00 00 00 00 18 00   CplApplet.......
xxxx:4190  30 00 58 02 00 00 01 00-88 13 00 00 A6 00 1A 00   0.X.............
xxxx:41A0  32 00 5A 02 02 00 01 00-8A 13 00 00 A6 00 1C 00   2.Z.............
xxxx:41B0  34 00 5C 02 04 00 01 00-8C 13 00 00 A6 00 1E 00   4.\.............
xxxx:41C0  36 00 5E 02 06 00 01 00-8E 13 00 00 A6 00 20 00   6.^............ .
xxxx:41D0  38 00 60 02 08 00 01 00-90 13 00 00 A6 00 1D 00   8.`.............
xxxx:41E0  35 00 5D 02 05 00 01 00-8D 13 00 00 A6 00 19 00   5.].............
xxxx:41F0  31 00 59 02 01 00 01 00-89 13 00 00 A6 00 1B 00   1.Y.............
xxxx:4200  33 00 5B 02 03 00 01 00-8B 13 00 00 A6 00 1F 00   3.[.............
xxxx:4210  37 00 5F 02 07 00 01 00-8F 13 00 00 A6 00 22 00   7._...........".
xxxx:4220  3A 00 62 02 0A 00 01 00-92 13 00 00 A6 00         :.b.........
-
```

18	Colors	1E	Mouse	19	Printers	22	Network
1A	Fonts	20	Desktop	1B	International		
1C	Ports	1D	Keyboard	1F	Date/Time		

Figure 11.2 DOS Debug screen dump showing section of MAIN.CPL which specifies icon sequence in Control Panel. Each boldface character indicates beginning of 16-byte section for one applet.

Debug Script	**Comments**
C:\WINDOWS\SYSTEM>debug main.cpl	Debug the MAIN.CPL file.
-s cs:100 fffe "CplApplet"	Search for "CplApplet."
xxxx:4180	Found at *xxxx*:4180.
-d cs:4180 422D	Dump (display) offset 4180 to 422D.

The next-to-last column in Figure 11.2 indicates the locations at which each applet specification begins. Thus, the third applet (Ports) begins at *xxxx*:41AE (bold hexadecimal 1C), and so on. To swap the positions of any two icons, swap their 16-byte segments.

Figure 11.3 shows a resequenced main group, in which the printer-related applets (*Printers, Fonts, Ports*) are placed first, followed by input devices (*Mouse, Keyboard*), desktop applets (*Desktop, Color*), and finally everything else (*International, Date/Time, Network*). The positions of the other applets (*386 Enhanced - SP Pro Mixer*) were arranged by lines in the [MMCPL] section which put them in the sequence shown in the figure. In this specific example, the sequence places all the audio-related applets on their own line. If you regularly switch between standard and enhanced mode operations, you may want to place the *386 Enhanced* icon last (CPWIN386.CPL), so that when it disappears (in standard mode) it won't affect the positions of the other icons.

Figure 11.3   Control Panel after resequencing applets

NOTE/DISCLAIMER: This experimental procedure is neither described, supported, nor recommended by Microsoft. Although it seems to work without problems, it cannot be guaranteed against future revisions. As a further consideration, do not move the position of the *Mouse* icon if you install the optional *Microsoft Mouse* or other mouse software. Most such packages place their own mouse icon (version 9.0 shown in the figure) at position 4, regardless of what's already there.

Don't forget to make a backup copy of MAIN.CPL before making any changes.

Remove Applets from Control Panel

Table 11.1 lists the files that contain the Control Panel icons. If any such file is among the missing, then all the icons within it will not show up in the Control Panel, and the corresponding applets will not be accessible.

To selectively delete one or more applets from the Control Panel, add the following section to your CONTROL.INI file, and include a line for each applet you want to exclude.

```
[Don't Load]
386 Enhanced=True
Drivers=False
AnyIconTitle=anything at all
```

Note that in this section of CONTROL.INI, any expression following the equal sign (*true, false, up, down, apple, orange, 1, 0,* and so on) is sufficient to prevent the applet icon from appearing. If you want to re-enable the applet later on, either erase that expression or delete the entire line.

You might want to add the lines shown above to prevent unauthorized helpers from "fixing" your system for you, or to kill the Color and Desktop icons if you have compulsive interior decorators on board. Refer to Table 11.1 for the name of each applet that may be specified in the [Don't Find] section.

Font Usage in the Control Panel

Unlike the File Manager (Chapter 6) and Print Manager (Chapter 9), there's not much opportunity here for fontsmanship.

Title Bar and Menu Text. The font used here is specified in the [boot] section of SYSTEM.INI (fonts.fon=VGASYS.FON, for example), and may be changed as described in the *Variable-Width System Font* section of Chapter 10.

Status Bar Text. The Status Bar displays its messages via the MS Sans Serif font specified in the [fonts] section of WIN.INI (MS Sans Serif=COURE.FON, for example). Unlike some other applets, this text is not affected by the *Status Bar Text* changes described in Chapter 10 and in Table 10.17.

Applet Configuration within the Control Panel

Most Control Panel applets are described in one of the sections which follow. Each section describes the applet and its configuration procedures. For descriptions of applets not included here, refer to one of the following chapters:

Applet	Chapter	Applet	Chapter
Drivers	12	Ports	9, 11
Fonts	10	Printers	9
MIDI Mapper	12	Sound	12

Up/Down-Arrow Usage. In several of the applets described below, a pair of up/down arrows is used to increment a numeric value in either direction. Unless otherwise noted (in the *Color* applet, for example), the displayed value change depends on which mouse button is pressed, as indicated here:

Mouse Button	Increment
Primary	1
Secondary	5

Slider Bar Usage. Use the primary mouse button to click on either arrow button, or to drag the slider button as required. In some cases, a slider-bar button may not move smoothly within the bar. For example, the *Keyboard* applet's *Delay Before First Repeat* slider has only four valid positions (0–3). Therefore, if you drag the Delay button with the mouse pointer, the button jumps forward or backward to the nearest valid position when you release the mouse button. Click on either the left or right arrow to toggle through the four positions. In most cases, the secondary mouse button has no effect on slider bar movements.

Control Panel Record in CONTROL.INI File

In addition to the [MMCPL] and [Don't Load] sections of CONTROL.INI described above, many Control Panel applets maintain their unique configuration data in various sections of this file, as described below in the sections covering each applet.

386 Enhanced Applet

As its name suggests, this applet's icon shows up only if Windows is opened in enhanced mode. The applet handles the configuration of three enhanced-mode functions: device contention, scheduling, and virtual memory. The first two are discussed here, while virtual memory is covered in Chapter 13.

Device Contention

The online help screen tells all: "To specify device contention for a device, select the port that the device you want to use is connected to." And then what?

Reading between the lines, this option determines how Windows reacts if multiple DOS applications contend with each other, or with a Windows application, for simultaneous access to the same printer, modem, or other device. (Contentions between Windows-only applications are handled separately, by Windows itself.)

Port Selector. For each port, you may specify one of three options to handle device contention. First, select the port, then click the appropriate radio button as described here.

Always Warn. A *device conflict* message appears if an application attempts to access a device that is currently in use by some other application. You will be prompted to specify which application should control the port.

Never Warn. If this option is selected, Windows will try to resolve device contentions but may not succeed in doing so. Since this could result in corrupted print jobs, modem transmissions, etc., select this option only if you are sure that device contention will never be a problem.

Idle. If you select this option, you can specify the interval (in seconds) that must elapse after an application stops using a device, before some other application can gain access to it.

Parallel Port Device Contention. In Windows 3.1, device contention is supported for serial devices only. Consequently, the LPT1 seen in Figure 11.4 will not appear. If you require parallel support, download the compressed self-extracting VPD.EXE file from the Windows Driver Library (GO MSL on CompuServe). Execute the program once and place the expanded VPD.386 file in your System directory. A fully expanded VPD.386 file may also be found in the Drivers directory on the diskette accompanying the *Windows Resource Kit.*

Next, add the following line to the indicated section of SYSTEM.INI:

```
[386Enh]
device=VPD.386
```

This procedure does not apply to *Windows-for-Workgroups,* which includes VPD.386 as part of its setup procedure, with the above line automatically inserted in SYSTEM.INI. The two versions of this file are not compatible.

Scheduling

This section of the dialog box defines how CPU time is distributed between Windows itself and Windows applications, and DOS applications operating at the same time. Briefly stated, Windows allocates timeslices to each application according to the specified scheduling priorities. Those for Windows applications are defined here. However, these priorities are influenced by others set up for DOS applications, so it may help to look back at *Foreground and Background Priorities* in the *Enhanced Mode PIF Editor: Advanced Options* section of Chapter 7.

The DOS application priorities are set as described in the above-cited section, and the Windows priorities are set by the first two options in the Scheduling

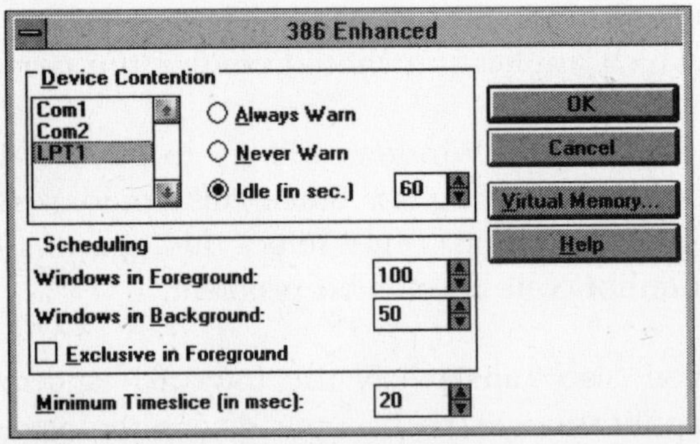

Figure 11.4 The 386 Enhanced applet's dialog box

section, as described here. To relate a Windows or DOS timeslice priority to an actual time interval, refer to *Minimum Timeslice* later in this section.

Windows in Foreground (1-10000). This value specifies the timeslices allocated to Windows and all Windows applications when any Windows application is active.

Windows in Background (1-10000). This value replaces that specified above when a DOS application is active.

Figure 11.5a bakes a timeslice pie chart in which *Windows in Foreground* has been set at 100 timeslices. A Windows application runs in the foreground while three DOS applications run in the background with priorities of 50, 30, and 20 timeslices. Therefore, the total pie contains 200 timeslices, so one doesn't need a rocket scientist to figure out that 50 percent of CPU time goes to Windows and its application(s).

In Figure 11.5b, one of the DOS applications (DOS App 2) is brought to the foreground, which redistributes the pie as follows: *Windows in Background* gets 50, and the three DOS priorities take 50, 100 (App 2 now in the foreground), and 20. The total pie is therefore 220 timeslices (50 + 50 + 100 + 20), so the Windows slice is 50/220, or 22.7 percent, with the three DOS apps getting 22.7, 45.4, and 9.0 percent.

In these specific examples, note that a Windows foreground priority of 100 earns it a 50 percent share of the timeslice pie, while an active DOS App — which also has a priority of 100—gets 45.4 percent. If DOS App 1 had been made active instead, it would have taken 66.6 percent, or 80 percent if it were the only DOS application running. In that case, when Windows returns to the foreground, it gets 66.6 percent of the pie, and DOS App 1 drops to 33.3 percent. Therefore, although the DOS App 1 priorities of 200/foreground and 50/background might suggest a 4:1 ratio, they really translate into a 2:1 distribution due to the influence of the other priority settings.

If you can keep track of all this and still get any work done, you're obviously a power user. Otherwise, you may just want to experiment with different settings and note the effect.

Exclusive in Foreground. If this check box is enabled, all CPU time is allocated to Windows applications whenever any Windows application is active. Therefore, execution of all DOS applications is suspended.

Minimum Timeslice (1-10000 milliseconds). Although located outside the Scheduling box, this option is nevertheless part of the scheduling system. If CPU time has been divided into two or more timeslices, as described above, the minimum timeslice (10 percent in Figure 11.5a, 9 percent in Figure 11.5b) gets the processor time specified here. Therefore, if the four applications specified in Figure 11.5b are running, processor time is allocated as follows:

Application	Timeslice	Percent	Time (ms.)	
DOS App 1	50	22.7	50	
DOS App 2	100	45.4	100	Foreground application
DOS App 3	20	9.0	20	*Min. Timeslice* 9% = 20ms.
Windows	50	22.7	50	

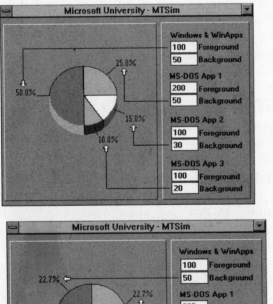

(a)

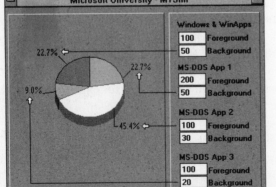

(b)

Figure 11.5 Timeslice pie chart showing (a) Windows running in foreground, with three DOS applications in background and (b) DOS application 2 running in the foreground.

> **NOTE:** As one more scheduling variable in Windows-for-Workgroups, the Network Settings dialog box contains a **Perfor-mance Priority:** adjustment. A slider bar sets the background priority at which the computer handles requests for its shared re-sources. Refer to *Performance Priority* in the *Network Applet* section for further details.

<u>V</u>irtual Memory Button

Click on this button to review or reconfigure your permanent or tempo-rary swap file. Since this action falls under memory management, it is dis-cussed separately in the *Swap File Configuration* section of the Chapter 13, where the Virtual Memory dialog box appears as Figure 13.12.

386 Enhanced Applet Record in SYSTEM.INI

Device contention status and scheduling data are recorded in SYSTEM.INI as shown here. The first three lines illustrate how device contention op-tions are recorded, while the last two lines record the Scheduling sections's foreground, background, and minimum timeslice values.

```
[386Enh]
Com1AutoAssign    =    -1      Always warn
Com2AutoAssign    =     0      Never warn
LPT1AutoAssign    =    60      60-second idle time
WinTimeslice      =   100,50   (foreground, background priorities)
MinTimeslice      =    20
```

After Dark Screen-Saver Applet

This section describes configuration procedures for Berkeley Systems' *After Dark* screen-saver, and may be skipped if this utility is not installed. As de-scribed in this section, there are several ways of setting up the *After Dark* screen-saver. Since one technique is to install it as an applet within the Control Panel, it is discussed here under that category.

During the regular *After Dark* setup procedure, a new directory is created for most of the files associated with this screen-saver. However, a number of files are also placed in the Windows directory, and new lines are written into WIN.INI and SYSTEM.INI. In addition, one or two lines may be added to your AUTOEXEC.BAT file. Table 11.2 summarizes all these modifications.

Control Menu

Regardless of where *After Dark* is installed, its Control Menu displays the options found on the Program Manager's Control Menu, which were described in Chapter 3 and illustrated in Figure 3.3a. The following additional option is also included on the menu.

Utilities. This menu selection opens a cascading menu (see *Cascading Menus* in Chapter 3) with Network Password and Master Password options on it—all this in addition to a plain old Password button on the Setup dialog box. Refer to the applet *User's Guide* for assistance setting up all these passwords.

After Dark Configuration

The various procedures that can be used to configure and operate the *After Dark* screen-saver are described in this section.

Conventional Operation. As part of the regular installation procedure, the load= line shown in Table 11.2 loads *After Dark* and a minimized icon is seen at the bottom of the Windows Desktop. Double-click on the icon to open the After Dark Control dialog box shown in Figure 11.6 and follow the instructions in the *User's Guide* for configuring screen-saver operation. Figure 11.7 shows one of the many screen-savers that are available.

If you are operating another screen-saver via the *Desktop* applet, then open that applet and disable the other screen-saver. Refer to *Screen-Saver* in the *Desktop Applet* section for further details.

Load *After Dark* As Part of StartUp Group. To automatically load *After Dark* as part of your Windows StartUp Group, open that group window and set up a New Program item with the following properties:

Description:	After Dark
Command Line:	C:\AFTERDRK\AD.EXE
Working Directory:	C:\AFTERDRK
Shortcut Key:	*(as desired)*
Run Minimized	*(put an "X" in the check box)*

Refer to Chapter 5 for general information about the StartUp Group Window.

Configure *After Dark* from *Desktop* Applet. As previously noted, your regular Windows screen-saver (if any) should be disabled if you install *After*

TABLE 11.2   Berkeley Systems' *After Dark* **Screen-Saver Configuration**

Filename	Extension	Filename	Extension	Filename	Extension
		Files Added to Windows Directory [*]			
AD	CFG	AD_NVLNW	RTL	ADCPL	CPL [§]
AD	HLP	AD_PREFS	INI	ADCPL	HLP [§]
AD-DOS	COM [†]	AD_RSRC	DLL	ADMODULE	ADS
AD_AILAN	RTL	AD_SND	DLL	AFTERDAR	GRP
AD_GRAPH	TXT	AD_WRAP	COM [‡]	SSADARK	SCR
AD_MESG	ADS				

[*] Additional files are in C:\AFTERDRK directory.
[†] DOS screen-saver
[‡] Password protection
[§] for optional Control Panel icon (see text)

INI File Modifications

SYSTEM.INI

[386Enh]
;VDD used by AD-DOS and After Dark
device=ad.386

WIN.INI

[windows]
load=c:\afterdrk\ad.exe c:\afterdrk\adinit.exe

AUTOEXEC.BAT Modifications

@C:\WINDOWS\AD_WRAP.COM   *(for password protection)*
C:\WINDOWS\AD-DOS.COM   *(for DOS screen saver)*

Dark, or you can configure and operate *After Dark* itself from the *Desktop*. With *After Dark* installed, select the *After Dark Runner* screen-saver, as described in the *Desktop Applet* section below. Having done this, remove the *After Dark* references on the load= line in your WIN.INI file. The *After Dark* icon will no longer appear on the Desktop, but the utility will operate as before, and it may be configured via the *Desktop* applet.

If you also use the *After Dark for DOS* screen-saver, this procedure may be the ideal configuration. For example, if you open a DOS window and disable the DOS screen-saver (before downloading a lengthy file via modem, for example), this action will also disable *After Dark's* Windows screen-saver. However, when you re-enable the DOS screen-saver, the Windows screen-saver

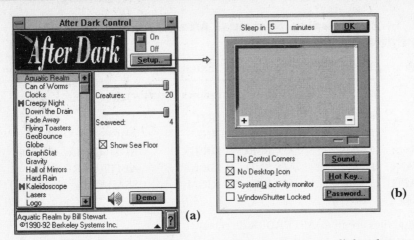

Figure 11.6   Berkeley Systems' (a) After Dark Control dialog box and (b) Setup screen.

Figure 11.7   The *After Dark* Aquatic Realm screen-saver

remains disabled. The only way to get it back is to click on the *After Dark* icon, reset the on/off switch, then minimize the After Dark Control dialog box. This problem does not occur if you use the After Dark Runner option described here.

Configure *After Dark* As a Control Panel Applet.   As yet one more configuration option, *After Dark* may be installed in the Control Panel as an additional applet, which is then used to configure the screen-saver. Begin by downloading the compressed ADCPL.ZIP file (18944 bytes) from the Berkeley Systems library in Vendor Forum C (GO WINAPC, library 4). Expand the file, and place the ADCPL.CPL file in your System directory and ADCPL.HLP in the Windows directory.

Either leave the *After Dark* reference on the load= line in place, or install *After Dark* as an applet in your StartUp Group Window, as described above. In either case, double-click on the Control Panel icon to reconfigure *After Dark*. If you load it via the StartUp group, you can also configure it via that group window.

Hide *After Dark* Icon. If you configured your *Desktop Applet* or Control Panel itself to provide access to the After Dark Control dialog box, you may also wish to delete the *After Dark* icon on the Windows Desktop. To do so, open the After Dark Control dialog box and click on the Setup... button to open the Setup dialog box shown in Figure 11.6b. Put an "X" in the No Desktop Icon box, click on the OK button, then minimize (don't close) the Control dialog box. Having done all this, there will be no trace of *After Dark* until the screen-saver activates at the specified time, as indicated in the Sleep in *x* minutes box in the dialog box.

Configure *After Dark* Audio. As an extra added attraction, *After Dark* has an audio option in which accompanying sound effects can be heard via your PC speaker or multimedia system (if installed). Fortunately, there is a Mute Sound option to kill the audio when the novelty wears off and it gets to be annoying. Five minutes should do it, unless there's a good reason to antagonize your co-workers when you step away from your computer.

After Dark *Audio versus Other WAV Audio*. If you run the After Dark sounds option through a multimedia system, there may be a little surprise waiting for you if you play waveform audio after the screen-saver has activated itself. When *After Dark* operates, it readjusts WAV audio output level according to the settings you made while configuring it. When *After Dark* quits, it does not reset the system to its previous audio level. To verify this, open the After Dark Control dialog box and your Multimedia Mixer dialog box (or equivalent). In the former dialog box, click on the up/down-arrows next to the speaker icon and watch the WAV audio faders in the latter move accordingly. After setting *After Dark* audio as desired, play some other WAV signal to make sure the level is not excessive.

Color Applet

When Windows is first installed, various Desktop elements are displayed in colors defined by Windows' default color scheme. Use the *Color* applet to reconfigure the Desktop to one of the other predefined color schemes, or to set up your own color choices.

Figure 11.8 shows a typical Windows Desktop and identifies 21 elements of the screen display. A brief description of each element is given in Table 11.3.

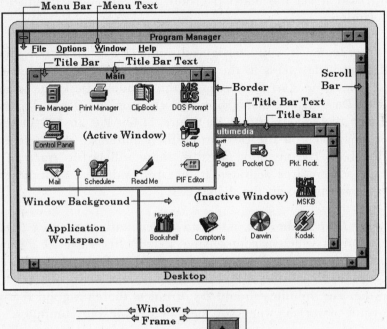

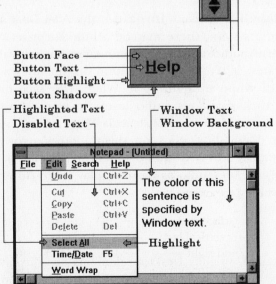

Figure 11.8 A typical Windows Desktop, identifying the 21 Desktop elements whose color can be specified via the Color applet.

TABLE 11.3 Screen Element Guide for Typical Windows Display*

Screen Element	Comments
Menu Bar [†] Menu Text [†]	Most Menu Bars begin with "File" and end with "Help." Other menus are placed between these selections.
Active Title Bar Active Title Bar Text [†] Active Border	The active group window may be identified by the distinctive colors of its Title Bar, Title Bar Text, and/or Active Border. A highlighted icon title displays the same color scheme as the Active Title Bar and Title Bar Text.
Inactive Title Bar Inactive Title Bar Text [†] Inactive Border	Inactive group windows are usually assigned a different set of colors, to prevent confusing them with the active window.
Window Background [†]	All open group windows use the same color. Many Windows applets and applications (Write, Notepad, Word-for-Windows, etc.) also use this background color.
Application Workspace	The area within the Program Manager in which group windows are displayed.
Desktop	The entire active surface of your display screen. The Program Manager and/or various Windows applications usually take up all or most of the Desktop, thereby concealing it from view. Desktop color is also text background color for minimized icons (see text).
Scroll Bar	When the size of an open window is not sufficient to display its entire contents, vertical and/or horizontal scroll bars are displayed.
Highlight Highlighted Text [†] Disabled Text [†]	In a pull-down menu, a highlight bar indicates the selected menu option. Options currently unavailable are displayed in a distinctive gray (usually) disabled-text style.
Window Frame [†]	The fine lines that define the edges of all Window borders.
Window Text [†]	The text within File Manager, SysEdit, most word processors, etc. Does not affect color of icon titles.
Button Face Button Text [†] Button Highlight Button Shadow	Color of button surface and text. Highlight defines the upper horizontal and left vertical button borders. Shadow defines the lower horizontal and right vertical borders. Black-on-gray up/down arrows not affected by button face and text colors.

* Refer to Figure 11.8. Color of each listed element may be changed by the user.

[†] These elements accept solid colors only (from Table 11.4).

The Color Dialog Box

To change the color scheme, double-click on the *Color* icon to open the Color dialog box shown in Figure 11.9a. The three sections of the dialog box are:

1. *Color Schemes.* Use the arrow key to review the names of previously saved color schemes. Windows 3.1 comes with 23 of them, some worse than others. To view a color scheme, highlight its name in the pull-down box. After viewing some of the more garish collections, you can restore the conservative Windows Default set which appears at the head of the list.

2. *Sample Area.* This mid-screen area is a miniature Desktop showing samples of the currently selected color scheme. When you first access the Color dialog box, the colors seen here are those presently in use.

3. *Color Palette Access.* The bottom-screen area is used to open the Color Palette section of the Color dialog box, as described immediately below.

Color-Change Section

If you want to change the color of one or more elements, click on the long Color Palette >> button to expand the dialog box as shown in Figure 11.9b. At the top of the screen, the Screen Element box lists one of the 21 elements identified in the figure and listed in Table 11.3. Immediately below, 48 Basic Colors are displayed in a 6 × 8 matrix. There is a black border around the color currently in use by the element whose name appears in the Screen Element box. The border may not be easy to see if the selected color is very dark. In this case, look carefully for a color box slightly larger than its neighbors.

To change the color of the indicated screen element, move the cursor to any color box and click the primary mouse button. A dotted-line border appears around this color box, and the selected color is immediately applied to the appropriate element in the Sample Area. Repeat, as required, until you are satisfied with the new color. Then select either of the following techniques to choose another Screen Element.

1. Click on the arrow at the right of the Screen Element box to access a pull-down list of screen elements. Scroll through the list and highlight the name of the element you wish to change.

2. Move the cursor into the Sample Area and click on any screen element.

In either case, the name of the selected screen element appears in the Screen Element box, and a black border surrounds the appropriate color box.

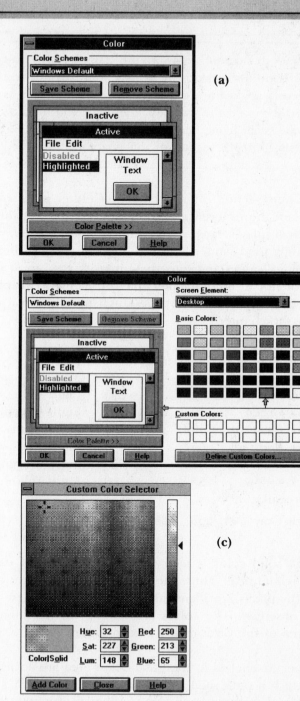

Figure 11.9   The Color applet's dialog box (a) as the applet opens and (b) after clicking on the Color Palette button. (c) The Custom Color Selector is accessed via the Define Custom Colors button.

> **NOTE:** The *Desktop* screen element color in the Sample Area will not appear on the actual Windows Desktop if a tiled Wallpaper option has been selected. However, since the Desktop color is also used as background for minimized icons on the Desktop, the color will be seen behind the text label of any such icon. The fine art of applying wallpaper is described in the *Desktop Applet* section of this chapter.

Basic Colors. The B̲asic Colors section offers a choice of either pure solid or dithered colors. To explain the difference, a VGA video system set for a 4-bit (16-color) color depth display serves as an example. (See *Color Depth* in Chapter 8.) The commonly used names for its 16 colors are given here. The RGB (Red, Green, Blue) values indicate the intensity that must be sent to each phosphor color dot in a color pixel (picture element) to produce the indicated color. The significance of these intensity values will be clarified (perhaps) later in the chapter.

R	G	B	Color	R	G	B	Color
0	0	0	Black	192	192	192	Medium Gray
0	0	128	Dark Blue	0	0	255	Light Blue
0	128	0	Dark Green	0	255	0	Light Green
0	128	128	Dark Cyan	0	255	255	Light Cyan
128	0	0	Dark Red	255	0	0	Light Red
128	0	128	Dark Magenta	255	0	255	Light Magenta
128	128	0	Dark Yellow ("Brown")	255	255	0	Light Yellow
128	128	128	Dark Gray	255	255	255	White

Pure Solid Colors. A pure solid color is seen when the intensity of each enabled RGB component is identical. Thus, the 16 colors listed above are all pure solids. When nearby pixels are identically excited, one of these 16 pure solid colors is seen onscreen. The colors are among the 48 choices seen in the B̲asic Colors area of the Color dialog box in Figure 11.9b.

Dithered Colors. The other 32 choices in the B̲asic Colors area are achieved by a dithering process in which a pure solid color is modified ("dithered") by selecting intensity values other than those listed above. Although it is supposed to be impossible to squeeze 48 pure colors out of a 16-color system, Windows bends the rules by alternately switching the intensity values sent to adjacent pixels. Thus, one pixel might be a pure dark red (128, 0, 0), while its neighbor is black (0, 0, 0), thereby creating a "Darkest Red" shade that subjectively looks like a pure color from a pixel whose RGB values are 64, 0, 0. Depending on the specific intensity pattern sent to adjacent pixels, the subjective color may appear to be a pure solid or a textured color.

Table 11.4 lists 29 solid colors (16 pure solid, 13 dithered solid) that can be displayed on a 16-color system. Each of these dithered colors—set in italics in the Table—is simply named after the subjective solid color seen onscreen. The Basic Colors matrix makes 20 of these solid colors available: 1 Black, 5 Darkest, 7 Dark, 6 Light, and 1 White. The other 28 colors in the matrix are: 25 other Dithered, 2 Special, and 1 Medium.

Table 11.5 lists the RGB values of the 48 Basic Colors. For each, the table also lists the RGB values for the nearest pure color, taken from the list of 16 colors normally available on a 16-color system.

To keep a difficult subject reasonably under control, when a color listed in Table 11.5 is made up of unequal RGB values, its name is simply the word "Dithered" followed by a color name defined by the column(s) containing the highest value. Therefore, there are several colors identified as say, "Dithered Green." The reader who is not yet saturated by color values can work out distinctive names for all of them.

The Basic Colors chart values shown in Table 11.5 are stored in your system's display driver, which is listed in the "display.drv=" line in the [boot] section of your SYSTEM.INI file. For example, the following list gives the offset location for the chart in a few Windows 3.1 display drivers:

Display Driver	Color Table Begins at Offset:
EGA.DRV	11652
SUPERVGA.DRV	11CA2
VGA.DRV	11B72
XGA.DRV	22002

The location may be verified by using a Disk Editor such as that found in the *Norton Utilities*. (The DOS Debug utility may not be used, since it only loads the first 64 Kbytes, and the locations cited above are all beyond that point.) Search the appropriate driver file for a sequence that begins with hexadecimal values FF 80 80. This is the dithered red color found in the first Basic Colors box. If you want to write your own basic colors into this area, make a backup copy of your display driver first.

TABLE 11.4 Color Selection Guide: Pure and Dithered Solid Colors*

Color	(MS Color)[†]	Hue	Sat.[‡]	Lum.	Red	Green	Blue
Darkest Red		0	*240*	*30*	*64*	*0*	*0*
Dark Red	(Maroon)	0	240	60	128	0	0
Medium Red		0	*240*	*90*	*192*	*0*	*0*
Light Red	(Red)	0	240	120	255	0	0
Darkest Yellow		40	*240*	*30*	*64*	*64*	*0*
Dark Yellow	(Olive)	40	240	60	128	128	0
Medium Yellow		40	*240*	*90*	*192*	*192*	*0*
Light Yellow	(Yellow)	40	240	120	255	255	0
Darkest Green		80	*240*	*30*	*0*	*64*	*0*
Dark Green	(Green)	80	240	60	0	128	0
Medium Green		80	*240*	*90*	*0*	*192*	*0*
Light Green	(Lime)	80	240	120	0	255	0
Darkest Cyan		120	*240*	*30*	*0*	*64*	*64*
Dark Cyan	(Teal)	120	240	60	0	128	128
Medium Cyan		120	*240*	*90*	*0*	*192*	*192*
Light Cyan	(Aqua)	120	240	120	0	255	255
Darkest Blue		160	*240*	*30*	*0*	*0*	*64*
Dark Blue	(Navy)	160	240	60	0	0	128
Medium Blue		160	*240*	*90*	*0*	*0*	*192*
Light Blue	(Blue)	160	240	120	0	0	255
Darkest Magenta		200	*240*	*30*	*64*	*0*	*64*
Dark Magenta	(Purple)	200	240	60	128	0	128
Medium Magenta		200	*240*	*90*	*192*	*0*	*192*
Light Magenta	(Fuchsia)	200	240	120	255	0	255
Black	(Black)	§	§	0	0	0	0
Darkest Gray		160	*0*	*60*	*64*	*64*	*64*
Dark Gray	(Gray)	160	0	120	128	128	128
Medium Gray	(Silver)	160	0	181	192	192	192
White	(White)	§	§	240	255	255	255

* *Italic* name identifies a dithered (see text) solid color. To select the desired color, enter the appropriate values in the Hue, Saturation, and Luminosity boxes shown in Figure 11.9c. Or enter color values in the Red, Green, Blue boxes. In either case, values in the other set of boxes will change accordingly.

[†] (MS Color) is name used in *Marquee* Color selector (see text).

[‡] Saturation set at maximum (240) to define pure colors.

[§] Hue and Saturation have no effect on Gray-scale black or white.

TABLE 11.5   Custom Color Cross-Reference: Basic Color and Nearest Pure Color*

Row	Col.	Basic Color	R	G	B	Nearest Pure Color	R	G	B
1	1	Dithered Red	255	128	128	White	255	255	255
1	2	Dithered Yellow	255	255	232	White	255	255	255
1	3	Dithered Green	128	255	128	White	255	255	255
1	4	Dithered Green	0	255	128	Light Cyan	0	255	255
1	5	Dithered Cyan	128	255	255	White	255	255	255
1	6	Dithered Blue	0	128	255	Light Cyan	0	255	255
1	7	Dithered Red	255	128	192	White	255	255	255
1	8	Dithered Magenta	255	128	255	White	255	255	255
2	1	*Light Red*	255	0	0	Light Red	255	0	0
2	2	Dithered Yellow	255	255	128	White	255	255	255
2	3	Dithered Green	128	255	0	Light Yellow	255	255	0
2	4	Dithered Green	0	255	64	Light Green	0	255	0
2	5	*Light Cyan*	0	255	255	Light Cyan	0	255	255
2	6	Dithered Blue	0	128	192	Light Cyan	0	255	255
2	7	Dithered Blue	128	128	192	Medium Gray	192	192	192
2	8	*Light Magenta*	255	0	255	Light Magenta	255	0	255
3	1	Dithered Red	128	64	64	Dark Red	128	0	0
3	2	*Light Yellow*	255	255	0	Light Yellow	255	255	0
3	3	*Light Green*	0	255	0	Light Green	0	255	0
3	4	*Dark Cyan*	0	128	128	Dark Cyan	0	128	128
3	5	Dithered Blue	0	64	128	Dark Blue	0	0	128
3	6	Dithered Blue	128	128	255	White	255	255	255
3	7	Dithered Red	128	0	64	Dark Red	128	0	0
3	8	Dithered Red	255	0	128	Light Magenta	255	0	255
4	1	*Dark Red*	128	0	0	Dark Red	128	0	0
4	2	Dithered Red [†]	255	128	0	Light Yellow	255	255	0
4	3	*Dark Green*	0	128	0	Dark Green	0	128	0
4	4	Dithered Green	0	128	64	Dark Green	0	128	0
4	5	*Light Blue*	0	0	255	Light Blue	0	0	255
4	6	Special Blue	0	0	160	Dark Blue	0	0	128
4	7	*Dark Magenta*	128	0	128	Dark Magenta	128	0	128
4	8	Dithered Blue	128	0	255	Light Magenta	255	0	255
5	1	Darkest Red	64	0	0	Black	0	0	0
5	2	Dithered Red [‡]	128	64	0	Dark Red	128	0	0
5	3	Darkest Green	0	64	0	Black	0	0	0

TABLE 11.5 *(continued)*

Row	Col.	Basic Color	R	G	B	Nearest Pure Color	R	G	B
5	4	Darkest Cyan	0	64	64	Black	0	0	0
5	*5*	*Dark Blue*	*0*	*0*	*128*	Dark Blue	0	0	128
5	6	Darkest Blue	0	0	64	Black	0	0	0
5	7	Darkest Magenta	64	0	64	Black	0	0	0
5	8	Dithered Blue	64	0	128	Dark Blue	0	0	128
6	*1*	*Black*	*0*	*0*	*0*	Black	0	0	0
6	*2*	*Dark Yellow*	*128*	*128*	*0*	Dark Yellow	128	128	0
6	3	Dithered Yellow	128	128	64	Dark Gray	128	128	128
6	*4*	*Dark Gray*	*128*	*128*	*128*	Dark Gray	128	128	128
6	5	Dithered Cyan	64	128	128	Dark Gray	128	128	128
6	*6*	*Medium Gray*	*192*	*192*	*192*	Medium Gray	192	192	192
6	7	Special Gray	130	130	130	Dark Gray	128	128	128
6	*8*	*White*	255	255	255	White	255	255	255

* Row and Column cross-reference to Basic Colors matrix in Figure 11.9b.
Color name is defined by column (s) containing highest value.
Italic row indicates a solid color (see Table 11.4).
Solid-color modifiers are defined by same value in all non-zero columns:

64	Darkest		255	Light
128	Dark		Other	Special
192	Medium			

† Close approximation of orange.
‡ Close approximation of brown.

If this search technique doesn't work, check the RGB values for the color in the first box in your own Color Dialog box's 6 × 8 matrix, as described in the *Red, Green, Blue Boxes (0–255)* section. Then search your installed video driver for the hexadecimal equivalent of those numbers.

Reconfigure Basic Color Matrix. If you want to permanently change one of the colors in the 6 × 8 Basic Colors matrix, you can do so by editing the currently installed video driver. This driver is listed in the following section of SYSTEM.INI:

```
[boot]
display.drv=filename.drv        (on most systems)
```
or
```
display.org=filename.drv        (if Bitstream Facelift for Windows is installed)
```

First, check the RGB values for the color you want to change, as described in the *Red, Green, Blue Boxes* section below (or in Table 11.5 for a 16-color driver). Then exit Windows and make a backup copy of the driver file. Open the original and search for the hexadecimal string that defines the color you want to change. Make sure you find the string that defines that color, and not some other location at which the same sequence appears. In case of doubt about this, search first for FF 80 80, which appears only once in the driver files listed above, and indicates the dithered red in the first box. Then look for the desired sequence in the area following this string.

If all goes well, the new color will appear in the appropriate color box the next time you open the *Color* applet. If all doesn't go well, erase the edited file and rename the backup file to the original name.

Flicker Check.   As a subjective test of worst-case screen flicker, change the Desktop to any Basic Color that exhibits a patterned effect. For example, select the patterned blue in Row 2, Column 6 or 7 of the Basic Colors matrix. Then minimize Program Manager to an icon so the entire Desktop can be seen. At a high video resolution ($1024 \times 768 \times 256$ colors, for example), the screen flicker should be at its worst.

If the flicker is objectionable, the fix is to select a purer color, a lower resolution, or both.

Custom Colors.   Solid, pure, dithered or otherwise, if you can't find what you want among the basic 48 colors described above, you may wish to enable the Windows Custom Color Selector. To do so, click on the Define Custom Colors button at the bottom of the Color dialog box. This opens the Custom Color Selector shown in Figure 11.9c. Using the Color Refiner box and/or the other components, you may specify up to 16 additional choices from a palette of about 17 million colors, which should be sufficient to satisfy all but the most refined tastes.

The Custom Color Selector

The various ways to select a custom color are described in this section. Note that no matter which method you choose, the various components in the Custom Color Selector screen are interactive: As you change one component, the other components vary automatically to track the changes you make.

A Few Definitions.   To take full advantage of the Custom Color Selector, a few definitions and a brief excursion into the world of hue, saturation, and intensity may be helpful, or you can skip the trip and stay with the familiar RGB nomenclature. In the following definitions, a pair of numbers in parentheses indicates the available range.

Color Purity. In theory, this is the degree to which a hue consists of a single primary color (Red, Green, Blue) only. In practice, it is the degree to which a hue consists of equal parts of one or two primary colors. In either case, as the other primary color—or colors—are added, purity decreases and the hue approaches a point on the gray scale.

Gray Scale (0–255). This is a series of achromatic colors ranging from black through gray to white. At every point on the scale, the gray is comprised of equal parts of Red, Green, and Blue. Thus:

	R	G	B		R	G	B
Black	0	0	0	Medium Gray	192	192	192
Darkest Gray	64	64	64	White	255	255	255
Dark Gray	128	128	128				

Hue (0–239). This is the name of a color group (reds, greens, magentas, yellows, etc.), without regard to color purity or intensity. The Custom Color Selector identifies hues by the numbers 0-239, which is a lot easier than giving each a distinctive name.

Luminosity (0–240). The brightness of a color is its *luminosity*. At 50 percent luminosity (120), a color is defined by its hue and saturation. As luminosity decreases, all colors fade to black. As luminosity increases, all colors fade to white.

Saturation (0–240). This is a measure of color purity. On the Custom Color Selector, a pure hue has a saturation of 240. As the saturation value is lowered, the hue fades from its defined color to a point on the gray scale.

Color Refiner Box. To quickly review the available custom colors, use the mouse to move the crosshairs in the Color Refiner box (seen near the upper left-hand corner of the box in Figure 11.9c).

Color|Solid Box. The left side of the box offers a magnified view of the color under the crosshairs, which changes as you move the crosshairs. The right side of the box displays the nearest pure solid color. If you move the cursor over to this side of the box and double-click the primary mouse button, the following events take place:

- The left-side magnified view changes to match the right-side solid color.
- The crosshairs jump to the appropriate position along the edge of the Color Refiner box.
- The numeric values (in the Hue, Sat, Lum, R, G, B boxes) change to indicate the appropriate pure solid-color values.

Luminosity Scale. This is the unmarked vertical bar to the right of the Color Refiner box. You may vary the luminosity of the selected color by dragging the arrow (to the right of the scale) up or down. As you do so, the color will fade towards white (up) or black (down).

Hue, Saturation, Luminosity Boxes. For greater control of the selected color, you may enter the desired values into these boxes. Either highlight a current value and type in a new number, or use the up- and down-arrow buttons, as appropriate. Place the cursor over any arrow button and click the primary mouse button to increment the value by one, or click the secondary mouse button to increment by 40. The latter alternative is useful in toggling through the various solid colors. To do so, set the Saturation and Luminosity to any pair of values listed in Table 11.4. Then set the Hue to zero and toggle through the available solid colors by clicking the secondary mouse button on the Hue up-arrow.

Red, Green, Blue Boxes (0–255). You may enter the desired RGB values into these boxes instead, following the just-described procedures. In this set of boxes, the secondary mouse button increments the displayed value by 32.

For reference purposes, the RGB values of the 48 Basic Colors were listed in Table 11.5. It's a bit of a nuisance to verify these values (as indeed it was to prepare the list in the first place), but it can be done by anyone with the patience to repeat the following three-step procedure 48 times.

1. Close the Custom Color Selector.
2. Click on any basic color.
3. Open the Custom Color Selector. The Red, Green, Blue boxes contain the values of the selected basic color.

Note that the Basic Color in Row 1, Column 2 is barely distinguishable from that in Row 6, Column 8. However, only the latter is a pure white

(255, 255, 255); the blue value of the former is slightly reduced (255, 255, 232), as may be seen by clicking on that box and following the three-step procedure described above. If you can spot the difference between the two halves of the Color|Solid box, you have good eyes *and* a good monitor system. But whether you can see it or not, double-click on the Solid half of the box and watch the movement of the Color Refiner crosshairs and the changing values for Hue, Saturation, and Luminosity.

Save Custom Color. When the left side of the Color|Solid box displays a color that you would like to use, you may save it in one of the 16 Custom Color boxes in the 2×6 matrix seen at the bottom of Figure 11.9b. You may specify which one by clicking on the desired box, which will then be identified by a black border. If no box displays such a border, the color will be saved in the first Custom Color box (column 1, row 1). In either case, subsequent saves will use the next available box, overwriting its present contents.

When you are ready to save a custom color, click on the Add Color button at the bottom of the Custom Color Selector Screen. The selected color now appears in the appropriate Custom Color box, as just described.

Exit Custom Color Selector. When you finish your selection of custom colors, click on the Close button to restore the full Color dialog box.

Applying Custom Colors. To apply a custom color to any Windows Screen element, follow the same instructions given above in the Color-Change Section.

Permannent Color Scheme Storage. If you've finally discovered a color scheme that you can live with, you may want to store it for future reference *before* experimenting with other colors. To do so, return to the Color dialog box seen in Figure 11.9a. If the Save Scheme button is disabled (grayed), click on the Color Palette button to enable it, then click on the Save Scheme button itself. When the Save Scheme dialog box appears, type an easily remembered name for your color scheme (up to 32 characters, including spaces). When you click on the OK button in the dialog box, your color scheme is saved for posterity in the [color schemes] section of the CONTROL.INI file. You may use the same technique to store additional color schemes before exiting the Color dialog box.

Color Scheme Selection.   To select the color scheme to use for the duration of the present Windows session, choose one of the following options.

Option	Procedure
1. Return to the color scheme in use before you made the current changes.	Click on the Cancel button.
2. Adopt the scheme presently displayed in the Color Summary area.	Click on the OK button.
3. Select a previously stored color scheme.	In the Color Schemes box, highlight the name of a previously stored scheme. Then click on the OK button.

Don't worry about making a bad choice (there are many of them); just click on the Cancel button at the bottom of the screen if you don't remember which color scheme was in effect previously.

If you regularly switch between several saved color schemes, you can edit the [colors] section of CONTROL.INI to place the desired lines at the top of the list.

Exiting the Color Dialog Box

After you have finished selecting the colors you want Windows to use, click the OK button to close the Color dialog box. It is not necessary to exit and restart Windows to discover what you have accomplished: Your selections take effect immediately.

Color Scheme Usage by Windows Applications

The current color scheme is used by the various applets included with Windows, and may or may not be used in whole or in part by various third-party Windows applications. After making significant color scheme changes, you may want to look in on various Windows applications to make sure the new colors are satisfactory. If not, you can make the necessary revisions while the new color scheme is still fresh in your mind.

Color Applet Record in INI Files

Color applet data is recorded in WIN.INI and CONTROL.INI as described here.

WIN.INI: Screen Element Colors. It is not necessary to save your Screen Element color choices for future use. When you click on OK to close the Color Dialog Screen, they are automatically written into the [colors] section of the WIN.INI file, as shown in the left-hand column in Table 11.6a. The three numbers following each element name are the decimal RGB values assigned to that element. Note that the element names listed in WIN.INI differ slightly from the corresponding names in the Screen Element box, which are also listed in the Table.

CONTROL.INI: Custom Color Storage. Custom colors are stored separately, in the [Custom Colors] section of the CONTROL.INI file shown in Table 11.6b. Only one set of custom colors may be saved; on subsequent

TABLE 11.6a   Screen Element Colors Stored in WIN.INI File

[colors] Section	R	G	B	Name As Seen in Screen Element Box	Compare with ColorX in CONTROL.INI [†]
Background=	128	0	0	Desktop	A
AppWorkspace=	128	128	0	Application Workspace	I
Window=	0	128	0	Window Background	B
WindowText=	0	128	128	Window Text	J
Menu=	0	0	128	Menu Bar	C
MenuText=	128	0	128	Menu Text	K
ActiveTitle=	255	0	0	Active Title Bar	D
InactiveTitle=	255	255	0	Inactive Title Bar	L
TitleText=	0	255	0	Active Title Bar Text	E
ActiveBorder=	0	255	255	Active Border	M
InactiveBorder=	0	0	255	Inactive Border	F
WindowFrame=	255	0	255	Window Frame	N
Scrollbar=	0	0	0	Scroll Bars	G
ButtonFace=	128	128	128	Button Face	O
ButtonShadow=	192	192	192	Button Shadow	H
ButtonText=	255	255	255	Button Text	P
GrayText=	192	192	192	Disabled Text	
Hilight=	128	0	0	Highlight	
HilightText=	255	255	0	Highlighted Text	
InactiveTitleText=	0	0	0	Inactive Title Bar Text	
ButtonHilight=	255	0	0	Button Highlight	

[†] For comparison purposes, the first 16 lines above are also stored as Custom Colors, as seen in Table 11.6b.

Windows sessions the set will appear each time you return to the Color Dialog Screen. Of course, any custom color actually assigned to a Screen Element is also saved in the WIN.INI file, as just described.

Perhaps to keep snoopers properly impressed with the complexity of Windows, the [Custom Colors] section stores its RGB information in a reversed-hexadecimal format. Thus, RGB values of say, decimal 255, 0, 0 become hexadecimal 00, 00, FF. Once in hex format, leading zeros are truncated and this example is simply stored as FF. Furthermore, although custom colors enter the onscreen 2×6 matrix in a column/row sequence, they are stored in CONTROL.INI in a row/column sequence.

To compare the two storage formats, the first 16 screen-element colors in the [colors] section of WIN.INI (Table 11.6a) were also stored as custom colors in the [Custom Colors] section of CONTROL.INI (Table 11.6b). Therefore, WIN.INI's "Background=128 0 0" becomes CONTROL.INI's "ColorA=80" and "AppWorkspace=128 128 0" is "ColorI=8080." In Table 11.6b, the three sets of RGB values to the right of each color show how a hexadecimal series is converted to decimal format.

TABLE 11.6b   Screen Element Colors Stored in CONTROL.INI File

[Custom Colors] Section		Add Leading Zeros			Reverse			Decimal		
ColorA=	80	00	00	80	80	00	00	128	0	0
ColorB=	8000	00	80	00	00	80	00	0	128	0
ColorC=	800000	80	00	00	00	00	80	0	0	128
ColorD=	FF	00	00	FF	FF	00	00	255	0	0
ColorE=	FF00	00	FF	00	00	FF	00	0	255	0
ColorF=	FF0000	FF	00	00	00	00	FF	0	0	255
ColorG=	0	00	00	00	00	00	00	0	0	0
ColorH=	C0C0C0	C0	C0	C0	C0	C0	C0	192	192	192
ColorI=	8080	00	80	80	80	80	00	128	128	0
ColorJ=	808000	80	80	00	00	80	80	0	128	128
ColorK=	800080	80	00	80	80	00	80	128	0	128
ColorL=	FFFF	00	FF	FF	FF	FF	00	255	255	0
ColorM=	FFFF00	FF	FF	00	00	FF	FF	0	255	255
ColorN=	FF00FF	FF	00	FF	FF	00	FF	255	0	255
ColorO=	808080	80	80	80	80	80	80	128	128	128
ColorP=	FFFFFF	FF	FF	FF	FF	FF	FF	255	255	255

Date/Time Applet

Not everything in Windows is complex: All this little applet does is change the date and time. To do either, open the Date & Time dialog box shown in Figure 11.10. Next, press the Tab key to move the highlight to the segment you want to change. Then type in the corrected value, or use the up- and down-arrows to increment the number as desired.

Although the arrows appear to be enabled at all times, they are not, and neither is the keyboard. Both are enabled only if a date or time segment is highlighted. Thus, if you sequentially press the Tab key until the OK, Cancel, or Help button is selected, there will be no cursor/highlight in either the date or time field, and both arrow pairs and the keyboard (except "H" for Help) will be disabled.

If you enter an illegal date or time value, no error warning is seen. However, if you close the applet before making a correction, the illegal entry is ignored and the previous value is retained.

Date and Time Display Configuration

The date and time are displayed in the format specified in the appropriate sections of the *International* applet's dialog box (described below). Thus, to change the date format from month/day/year to year/month/day, or the

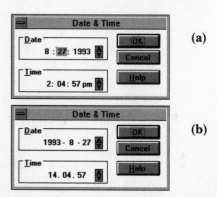

(a)

(b)

Figure 11.10 The Date & Time dialog box, showing two date formats: (a) the 12-hour clock and (b) 24-hour clock formats.

time from a 12-hour to 24-hour clock, open the *International* applet and make the desired changes. Examples of both of these formats are shown in Figure 11.10.

Date/Time Record in INI Files

There isn't any. Changes made within this applet affect the system clock, but since both values are continuously changing, there's nothing to store in an INI file.

Desktop Applet

The *Desktop* applet provides controls for configuring the general appearance of the Desktop itself, plus a few additional functions such as cursor blink rate, icon title and spacing configuration, and a sizing grid. The Desktop dialog box is shown in Figure 11.11 and each of its sections is described here in alphabetical order.

Applications

This section contains the single check box described here.

Fast "Alt+Tab" Switching (the CoolSwitch). Under default conditions, toggling the Alt+Tab combination displays a box in midscreen, in which

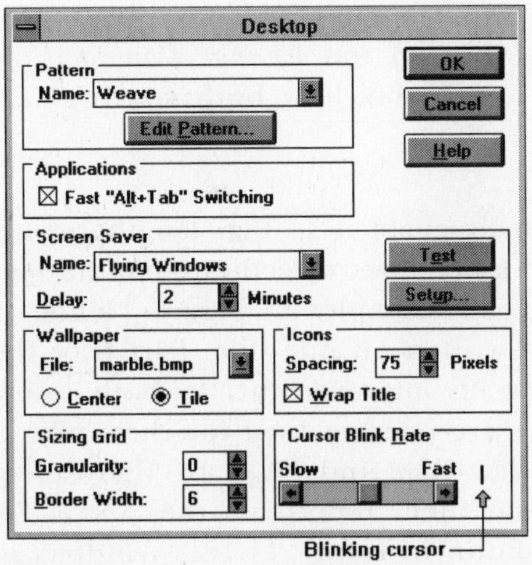

Figure 11.11 The Desktop applet's dialog box

each active application icon and its name are sequentially displayed, as described in *Task Switching via the Alt+Tab Keys* in Chapter 3, and illustrated there in Figure 3.11b. If you prefer the old Windows 3.0 configuration, in which each application appears onscreen (or application icon is highlighted) as you toggle through them, then clear the "X" in the Fast Switching box. The checkbox status is recording in WIN.INI as shown here:

```
[windows]
CoolSwitch = 1   Fast Switching enabled (default)
           = 0   Fast Switching disabled (Windows 3.0 mode)
```

Cursor Blink Rate

Drag the button in the horizontal slide bar to vary the cursor blink rate. A vertical bar to the right of the *Fast* arrow indicates the current blink rate.

Icons

Two controls to vary icon spacing and title wrap are found in this section.

Spacing.   The number in the box indicates the horizontal spacing, in pixels, between icons in each group window. Although vertical spacing is not adjustable from within the *Desktop* applet, it may be changed by editing the WIN.INI file, as described in the *Change Icon Spacing* section in Chapter 3. That section also shows how both spacings are recorded in WIN.INI.

Wrap Title.   This check box is usually enabled so that lengthy icon titles "wrap" on down to occupy two or more lines directly under the icon, as shown by a few good and not-so-good examples in Figure 11.12a. If the check box is cleared, the titles are written on one line. Part b of the figure shows that in this case there's no improvement. In both examples, the real problem is that some titles are just too long for their own good. Unless you need to be reminded that *Word* and *Excel* are Microsoft products, and that the thing in between them represents the *Norton Utilities 5/6.0,* try shortening the titles as shown in Figure 11.12c. Windows is *supposed* to be a graphic environment (graphic user interface, or something like that), so you shouldn't need a mini-essay under an icon to tell you what it means.

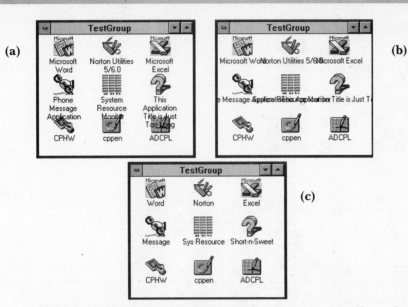

Figure 11.12   A Test Group window, showing the effect of enabling (a) and disabling (b) the Wrap Title check box. (c) The same test group, after cutting the applet titles down to a reasonable size.

Pattern

The solid color usually applied to the Windows Desktop may be replaced by a pattern whose colors are defined by the Window Text and Desktop colors (see Table 11.3 and Figure 11.8).

Name Box and Edit Pattern Button.   To view any pattern, select it in the Name box and click on the Edit Pattern... button. The pattern is displayed in a Sample box in the Desktop–Edit Pattern dialog box, and another box shows an enlarged view of the basic pattern as an 8×8-byte matrix. For example, Figure 11.13a shows how the dialog box displays the *Weave* pattern. The color of any point in the matrix may be toggled between foreground (on) and background (off) colors by selecting it with the mouse pointer and clicking the primary mouse button.

The buttons at the lower right of the dialog box are enabled under the following conditions.

Add.   To add a new pattern, select any existing pattern, including *(None)*, and edit the name in the Name box, as desired. Then click on the Add button to save the pattern under the new name. In most cases you will perform this step after making changes to an existing pattern as described immediately below.

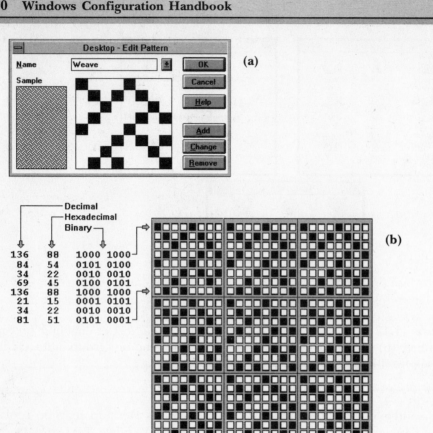

Figure 11.13 The Edit Pattern dialog box, showing (a) the Weave pattern. (b) A 3×3 byte detail view of the weave pattern.

**Change.** As soon as you click on any pixel in the 8×8 matrix, the Change button is enabled. Continue to make changes, then click on the button when you are done. The changes will be written to the pattern whose name is displayed at the top of the dialog box. If you want to save the new pattern under a different name, then edit that name and click on the Add button instead, as described above.

**Remove.** This button is enabled immediately after selecting any pattern, and is disabled if you make any changes to the pattern.

Pattern Record in CONTROL.INI. The 8-byte sequence for each pattern is recorded in the CONTROL.INI file as shown below by a few examples. In each case the numbers are separated by a space (not a comma), with additional spaces added here for readability.

```
[Patterns]
(None)    =   (None)
Paisley   =      2     7     7     2    32    80    80    32
Scottie   =     64   192   200   120   120    72     0     0
Weave     =    136    84    34    69   136    21    34    81
```

In Figure 11.13b, the *Weave* sequence is shown in decimal, hexadecimal, and binary formats, followed by a detail view of a 3×3 block matrix.

If the Sample pattern box shows a solid color, the foreground (Windows Text color) and background (Windows Desktop color) are the same. Use the Colors applet described earlier in this chapter to change one of them to some other color.

If the Wallpaper/tile option (described below) is enabled, the entire Desktop is covered by the selected wallpaper, and therefore the pattern will not be seen. However, the pattern does appear as background for the text under each minimized icon, and may interfere with the legibility of that text, especially on high-resolution screens. To verify that a pattern is interfering with icon text, click once on any minimized icon at the bottom of the Desktop. The text background should change to whatever color is defined by the Active Title Bar color (Table 11.3 and Figure 11.8a). If the icon text is now legible, then change the pattern to something less obtrusive (like "none").

Screen-Saver

Windows is supplied with several screen-saver displays which may be selected by clicking on the down-arrow button to the immediate right of the N<u>a</u>me box. The currently available screen-savers are listed here, along with the filename for each one. The files are located in the Windows directory.

Screen-Saver	Filename	
After Dark Runner	SSADARK.SCR	(see *After Dark* applet)
Blank Screen	SCRNSAVE.SCR	
Flying Windows	SSFLYWIN.SCR	
Marquee	SSMARQUE.SCR	
Mystify	SSMYST.SCR	(not included in Workgroups)
Starfield Simulation	SSSTARS.SCR	

If both keyboard and mouse are idle for the interval listed in the D<u>e</u>lay box, the selected screen-saver will appear.

Screen-Saver File Descriptions.   Each Windows screen-saver is briefly described here, followed by a few configuration notes. For additional details about any screen-saver, select it, then click on the Help button.

After Dark Runner.   This additional choice shows up if you have installed Berkeley Systems' *After Dark for Windows* screen-saver. Refer to the *After Dark Applet* section above for further details.

Blank Screen.   For the more conservative user, this one does nothing. At the appointed time the screen goes black and stays that way.

Flying Windows.   This screen-saver displays 10 to 200 copies of the familiar Windows logo, flying across the screen at whatever Warp Speed you select, which in any case will be slightly less than what Picard gets on the *Enterprise*. Each flying window is actually the last character in the TrueType Wingdings font, as shown in Figure 11.14a. Therefore, if that font is missing you'll see something else instead. Refer to the *Create Other Flying Object* below for a procedure to replace the flying windows with any other character in the TrueType Wingdings font. For comparison purposes, Figure 11.14b shows the effect of replacing the flying window with Wingdings character 60—a 3.5-inch diskette.

Marquee.   The Marquee screen-saver displays an inspiring(?) Windows 3.1 banner which traverses your screen from right to left. Refer to *Marquee Text Formatting* for the procedure to change the message.

Mystify. This one displays one or two polygon strings in two user-selected, or multiple-random, colors. Perhaps its name alludes to the mystery of why it is not included with Windows-for-Workgroups.

Starfield Simulation.   This "Flying Starfield" is a variation on the *Flying Windows* screen-saver.

Setup Configuration.   After selecting the Screen-Saver you want to use, click on the Setup... button if you wish to make adjustments. Figures 11.15a and 11.16 show the Setup dialog boxes for the *Flying Windows* and *Marquee* screen-savers, which are used here to illustrate a few configuration examples.

Screen-Saver Password Protection.   The Screen Savers offer a password protection system that will keep casual snoopers at bay. On any Setup dialog box, click on the Set Password... button to access the Change Password dialog box

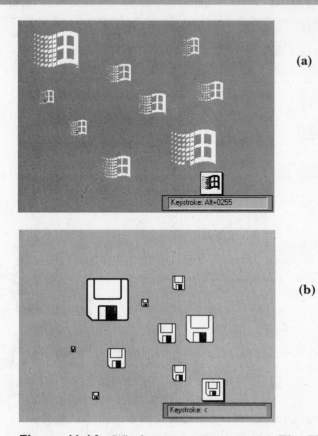

(a)

(b)

Figure 11.14 Windows screen-savers. (a) The Flying Windows screen-saver. The Character Map insert at the bottom shows a detail view of Wingdings character 255. (b) By editing a copy of SSFLYWIN.SCR, a "Flying Floppies" screen-saver can be created.

shown in Figure 11.15b. Enter the password in the New Password: box, press the Tab (*not* Enter) key, re-enter the same password in the Retype New Password: box and now press the Enter key to return to the main Setup dialog box.

Marquee Text Formatting. To replace the *Windows 3.1* banner with your own message, select the *Marquee* dialog box and click on the Format Text... button to access the Format Text dialog box shown in Figure 11.16b. The dialog box is functionally equivalent to those shown in Figure 10.16 in the previous chapter. Edit the Text box to change the banner to "Out to lunch," "Keep your Hands off my computer!" or whatever else you want to say. Then select the font and point size desired. Note, however, that flicker increases with point size.

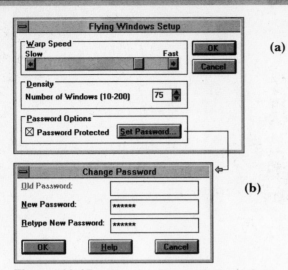

Figure 11.15 The (a) Flying Windows Setup dialog box and (b) Change Password dialog box.

Although the Format Text dialog box is functionally equivalent to the Font dialog boxes shown in Figure 10.16, it does offer one more option: Select the Color box at the bottom of the screen to change the color of the moving text from the default fuchsia (yes, fuchsia) to your own choice. Refer to Table 11.4 for a cross-reference between color names seen in the Format Text dialog box and Windows Desktop colors.

Screen-Saver Configuration Procedures. The following section describes a few techniques to modify the screen-saver feature to suit personal preference.

Install Screen-Saver As an Applet. You may want to set up a Screen-Saver as an applet, in order to activate it by pressing a Shortcut key combination. For example, you may need to leave your computer in the middle of a critical Solitaire game and don't want anyone to finish the game in your absence. If such considerations are of interest, add an SCR extension to the following line in the WIN.INI file, as shown here:

```
[windows]
Programs=com exe bat pif scr
```

In order for this addition to take effect, you'll have to close and reopen Windows. After doing so, open any group window and add a new program item as shown here:

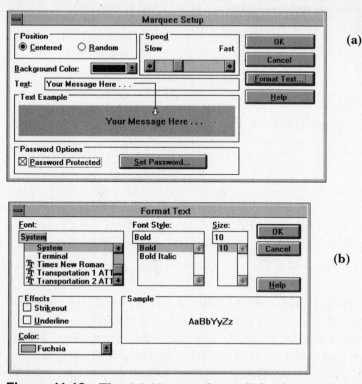

Figure 11.16 The (a) Marquee Setup dialog box and (b) Format Text dialog box. The latter is equivalent to those shown in Figure 10.16.

Description: Screen-Saver
Command Line: ssmarque.scr /S
Shortcut Key: Ctrl + Alt + S

Change ssmarque to the filename for the screen-saver you want to use. The /S switch on the command line instructs Windows to activate the designated screen-saver when you press the Shortcut key combination. Without it, the Shortcut key simply opens the Screen-Saver's Setup dialog box.

Screen-Saver Icons. The Screen-Saver applet icon will be one of those shown in Figure 11.17. If you'd rather use one of the other screen-saver icons, click on the Change Icon... button and browse through the other SCR files.

Start Screen-Saver As Windows Opens. As one more form of system security, put the Screen-Saver applet into the StartUp Group and assign a password to

Figure 11.17 Screen-Saver icons embedded in the Windows screen-saver SCR files.

it. By doing so, anyone who opens your Windows will have to know the password in order to do anything other than watch the flying Windows. Of course, the determined meddler can gain access by simply deleting the password from CONTROL.INI, but this will protect you from the casual user.

Create Other Flying Objects. If you get tired of watching the Microsoft logo warping across the screen, you can replace it with another character in the Wingdings font. For example, to create the "Flying Floppies" screen-saver shown in Figure 11.14b, make a copy of SSFLYWIN.SCR and name it FLOPPIES.SCR (or whatever.SCR). Then at the DOS prompt, type the following debug script:

```
debug FLOPPIES.SCR
-s cs:100 fffe "DISPLAY"
xxxx:2EF3
-d cs:2EF0
```

This should display eight lines of code, the first two of which look like this:

```
xxxx:2EF0 32 00 FF 44 49 53 50 4C-41 59 00 57 69 6E 67 64   2.=DISPLAY.Wingd
xxxx:2F00 69 6E 67 73 00 57 69 6E-67 64 69 6E 67 73 00 25   ings.Wingdings.%
```

The hexadecimal "FF" (shown above in bold) is the extended character 255 (decimal), which is the Microsoft Windows logo in the Wingdings font. Replace it with either hexadecimal 3C or 3D—the characters for a 3.5-inch and 5.25-inch diskette. To do so, continue the Debug script as follows:

```
-f  cs:2EF2  L1  3C  (or 3D)
-w      (to write the change into the file)
-q      (to quit Debug)
```

Now open the *Desktop* applet, click on the down-arrow next to the N̲ame: box, and look for FLOPPIES.SCR (or whatever you called it). Highlight it and click on the T̲est button to make sure it works. If it actually does, click on the OK button to quit. When you get bored with flying floppies, you can try some other character, or graduate to *After Dark*.

Screen-Saver Record in INI Files. The Screen-Saver makes changes to three INI files, as shown by these typical examples.

SYSTEM.INI: Current Screen-Saver. The name of the currently selected screen-saver is recorded in SYSTEM.INI.

```
[boot]
SCRNSAVE.EXE=C:\WINDOWS\filename.SCR
```

WIN.INI: Status and Timeout. Two lines in WIN.INI specify screen-saver status and delay time:

```
[windows]
ScreenSaveActive=x          0, enabled or 1, disabled
ScreenSaveTimeOut=xxx       xxx = delay time, in seconds
```

CONTROL.INI: Screen-Saver Characteristics. Every time a Microsoft-supplied screen-saver is enabled, a description of its characteristics is written into CONTROL.INI. as shown below. As additional screen-savers are enabled, additional sections are written into CONTROL.INI, but the former entries are not removed. If the *After Dark* screen-saver is enabled, its characteristics are saved separately in a small AD.CFG file in the Windows directory.

```
[Screen-Saver.Flying Windows]
Density=xx          (number of flying windows)
WarpSpeed=xx
PWProtected=x       (Password protection: 1 = yes, 2 = no)

[Screen-Saver.Marquee]
PWProtected=x
Text=Out to Lunch - Be Back Soon
Font=Lucida Blackletter
Size=12
Background Color=0 0 0
TextColor=0 255 255
Speed=10
Attributes=10111
Charset=0
```

CONTROL.INI: Password. The password is written in encrypted format in its own section of CONTROL.INI, as shown here

```
[ScreenSaver]
Password=9j/l>{      (if the password is "Secret")
```

Sizing Grid

Use the two controls in the Sizing Grid section to adjust grid spacing and border widths, as described here. The parenthetical values show the default, followed by the valid range for each option.

Granularity (0, 0-49). The Windows Desktop sits on an imaginary (virtual?) 8 × 8-pixel grid, with application window borders aligned with these invisible grid lines. If you move any application window, it jumps one line (8 pixels) if *Granularity* is set at 1, two lines if set at 2, three lines if set at 3, and so on. If the setting is high, the window "leaps" across the Desktop and may in fact get stuck if the top of the window goes off-screen. To disable the grid, set *Granularity* to 0. In this case, the window will move smoothly across the Desktop, which allows greater control over its placement.

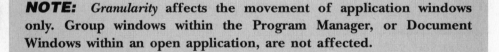

NOTE: *Granularity* affects the movement of application windows only. Group windows within the Program Manager, or Document Windows within an open application, are not affected.

Border Width (3, 1-49). This setting determines the pixel width of the border around each open window. Depending on your video resolution, mouse sensitivity, and other factors, you may want to adjust the border size by a pixel or two to make it easier to drag it around the screen. If you just want to see something positively awful, try a setting of 30 or more.

Sizing Grid Record in WIN.INI. If *Granularity* or *Border Width* values are revised, the following lines are added to the indicated sections of the WIN.INI file:

```
[Desktop]
GridGranularity=x

[windows]
BorderWidth=x
```

Wallpaper

Literary scholars have not yet decided if "Desktop Wallpaper" is an oxymoron, a mixed metaphor, another entry in the lexicon of Microspeak, or perhaps all three. But whatever it is on paper, it's the graphic image that may be used to decorate the Windows Desktop.

Wallpaper Selection and Display. Use the controls described here to select your wallpaper pattern and display method.

File. Any bitmap file (BMP extension) in the Windows directory may be used as wallpaper. Click on the down-arrow to review the available files, which are listed in Table 11.7.

Other Wallpaper Sources. If you want to display wallpaper with a bitmap file not located in the Windows directory, type the complete path and filename into the File: box. You can either create your own with the Paintbrush applet or use a third-party bitmap file. For example, *After Dark* includes two bitmap

TABLE 11.7   Windows Bitmap Files*

Filename	Size	Included with	Filename	Size	Included with [†]
256COLOR	5078		LEAVES	15118	
ADLOGO	17582	*After Dark* [‡]	MARBLE	27646	Win 3.1
ARCADE	630		PAPER	9662	Win 3.0
ARCHES	10358	Win 3.1	PYRAMID	630	Win 3.0
ARGYLE	630		REDBRICK	630	
BOXES	630	Win 3.0	RIVETS	630	
CARS	630		SEA	18550	[§]
CASTLE	778		SQUARES	630	
CHESS	153718	Win 3.0	TARTAN	32886	Win 3.1
CHITZ	19918	Win 3.1	THATCH	598	
EARTH	25702	*After Dark* [‡]	WEAVE	190	Win 3.0
EGYPT	630		WINLOGO	38518	
FLOCK	1630	Win 3.1	ZIGZAG	630	
HONEY	854				

[*] All files have BMP extension.
[†] Column lists last Windows version which includes indicated file.
[‡] Files are in *After Dark* Bitmaps directory. Transfer to Windows directory to use as wallpaper.
[§] Included in Window 3.0 *Resource Kit* only, compressed in WIN3FISH.EXE file.

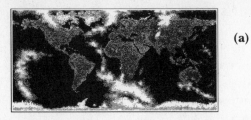

(a)

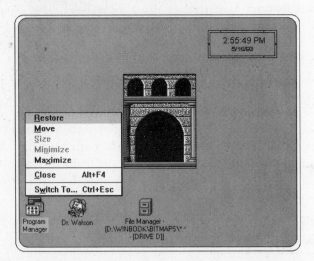

(b)

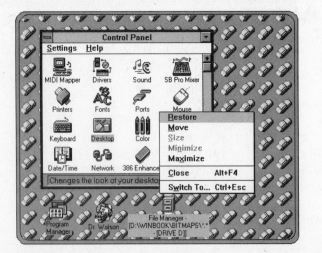

(c)

Figure 11.18 Windows wallpaper selections. (a) The EARTH.BMP bitmap file in the AFTERDRK/BITMAPS directory is an *After Dark* screen-saver, but it can also be used as wallpaper. Other wallpaper examples include Windows' own (b) ARCHES.BMP centered and (c) CARS.BMP tiled.

files in its Bitmaps directory, one of which is shown in Figure 11.18a. Note, however, that if you subsequently select a file that *is* in the Windows directory, the path and name of your previous selection will not be retained. Therefore you'll need to re-enter it if you want it back again, or move the bitmap file into the Windows directory so that it will always be available for selection.

**Center** **and** _**Tile**_ **Buttons.**   Click on either radio button to paste a single centered bitmap, or—if you can handle the semantic challenge of tiled desktop wallpaper—multiple copies on the Desktop. Examples of both are shown in Figures 11.18b and c.

Wallpaper Record in WIN.INI.   Your choice of wallpaper is preserved for posterity by the following lines in WIN.INI:

```
[Desktop]
Wallpaper=filename.bmp
TileWallPaper=1      ( 0 = centered, 1 = tiled)
```

International Applet

Although this applet looks like something that needn't concern the domestic user, you may want to have a look, if only to change the format in which the date and time are displayed.

The International Dialog Box

Figure 11.19 shows the *International* applet's dialog box which displays the current settings, most of which are self-explanatory. However, like most "simple" things, there are a few confusion factors built into this applet; some of those are reviewed here. The good news is that all of this can be ignored if you have no occasion to change the default settings.

_**C**_**ountry:.**   Table 11.8 shows the [country] section of the CONTROL.INF file. When a new country is selected, Windows searches this section of the file for the appropriate format parameters for that country. The values are displayed in the dialog box, except for _Language_ and _Keyboard Layout,_ which are described below.

**Printer Paper Size:.**   The selected country may also change the Paper Si_z_e: entry in your default printer's Setup dialog box (seen in Figures 9.10 and 9.11). For example, the following _C_ountry: change affects paper size (not Page Size, as noted on the Help screen) as shown here.

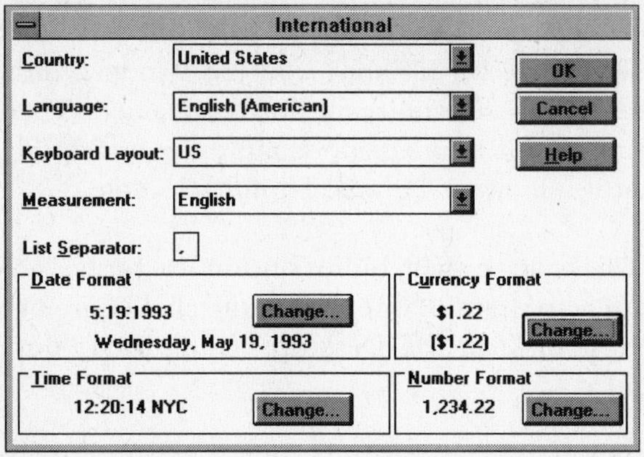

Figure 11.19 The International applet's dialog box

	United States	**United Kingdom**	
Paper Size	Letter 8 × 11	A4	210 × 297 mm

This feature does not work with all printer drivers. To verify its operation, install the Hewlett-Packard LaserJet series II printer driver, make a country change, close and reopen Windows, and view the **Paper Size:** entry. Then repeat the same procedure for your own default printer. If there is no change, and the feature is important to you, contact the printer manufacturer to see if a new driver is available. It probably isn't, since this is a relatively minor problem, unless you take your printer on international flights.

Language: This parameter is set independently, to specify how certain language-specific tasks are handled. When a language is selected, Windows searches the [language] section of SETUP.INF for the required LANG*xxx*.DLL library file (where *xxx* specifies the country). If that file is not in the system directory, an Install Driver dialog box will prompt you to insert the distribution diskette which contains the required file. Table 11.9 lists the languages and support files that are currently supplied with Windows.

Keyboard Layout:. Keyboard layout is also set separately, to specify the keyboard layout for the country of choice. Windows searches the [keyboard.tables] section of SETUP.INF for the required KBD*xx*.DLL library file (here, *xx* specifies the country). As above, an Install Driver dialog box will prompt you if the file can't be found in the System directory. Table 11.9 also lists the available keyboard layouts and support files.

TABLE 11.8   International Formats in CONTROL.INF File*

A	B	C	D	E	F	G	H	I	J	K	L	M	N	O	P	Q	R	S
[country]																		
Australia	61	1	0	2	0	0	0	2	0	0	AM	PM	$	,	.	/	:	,
Austria	43	2	2	2	1	1	0	2	9	1			S	.	,	-	:	;
Belgium (Dutch)	32	1	3	2	1	1	0	2	8	0			BF	.	,	/	:	;
Belgium (French)	32	1	3	2	1	0	0	2	8	0			FB	.	,	/	:	;
Brazil	55	1	2	2	1	1	0	2	0	0			Cr$	.	,	/	:	;
Canada (English)	2	1	0	2	1	1	0	2	1	1			$	,	.	/	:	,
Canada (French)	2	2	3	2	1	1	0	2	8	1			$		,	/	:	;
Denmark	45	1	2	2	1	1	0	2	2	1			kr	.	,	-	:	;
Finland	358	1	3	2	1	1	0	2	8	0			mk		,	.	.	;
France	33	1	3	2	1	1	0	2	8	1			F		,	/	:	;
Germany	49	1	3	2	1	1	0	2	8	1			DM	.	,	.	:	;
Iceland	354	2	3	2	1	0	0	2	8	0			kr	.	,	.	:	;
Ireland	353	1	0	2	1	1	0	2	1	1			£	.	,	/	:	,
Italy	39	1	2	2	1	1	0	0	9	0			L.	.	,	/	.	;
Mexico	52	1	0	2	0	0	0	2	0	0	AM	PM	$	,	.	/	:	,
Netherlands	31	1	2	2	1	1	0	2	10	0			F		,	-	:	;
New Zealand	64	1	0	2	0	1	0	2	0	1	AM	PM	$	,	.	/	:	,
Norway	47	1	2	2	1	1	0	2	2	1			kr	.	,	.	:	;
Portugal	351	1	3	2	1	1	0	2	8	0			Esc.	.	,	-	:	;
South Korea	82	2	0	2	1	0	0	2	1	0			W	,	.	.	.	,
Spain	34	1	3	2	1	0	0	0	8	0			Pts	.	,	/	:	;
Sweden	46	2	3	2	1	1	0	2	8	1			kr		,	-	.	;
Switzerland (Fr.)	41	1	2	2	1	1	0	2	2	1			Fr.	'	.	.	,	;
Switzerland (Ger.)	41	1	2	2	1	1	0	2	2	1			Fr.	'	.	.	,	;
Switzerland (Ital.)	41	1	2	2	1	1	0	2	2	1			Fr.	'	.	.	,	;
Taiwan	886	2	0	2	1	0	1	2	1	0			$	,	.	/	:	,
United Kingdom	44	1	0	2	1	1	0	2	1	1			£	,	.	/	:	,
United States	1	0	0	2	0	1	1	2	0	0	AM	PM	$	,	.	/	:	,
US Metric [†]	1	0	0	2	0	1	0	2	0	0	am	pm	$	,	.	/	:	,
Other Country	1	0	0	2	1	0	1	2	0	0			$	,	.	/	:	,

*A–S Column Headers: Use Table 11.10b as cross-reference. CONTROL.INF uses exclamation point as delimiter between values.

[†] Not part of CONTROL.INF. See *Custom International Format Configuration* in text.

TABLE 11.9 **International Country, Language, Keyboard Formats**

CONTROL.INF	SETUP.INF			
[country]	[language]	Library File	[keyboard.tables]	Library File
Australia				
Austria				
Belgium (Dutch)			Belgian	kbdbe.dll
Belgium (French)				
Brazil	Portuguese	langeng.dll	Portuguese	
Canada (French)	French Canadian	langeng.dll	French Canadian	
			Can. Multilingual	kbdfc.dll
Denmark	Danish	langsca.dll	Danish	kbdda.dll
Finland	Finnish	langsca.dll	Finnish	kbdfi.dll
France	French	langfrn.dll	French	kbdfr.dll
Germany	German	langger.dll	German	kbdgr.dll
Iceland	Icelandic	langsca.dll	Icelandic	kbdic.dll
Ireland				
Italy	Italian	langeng.dll	Italian	kbdit.dll
Mexico			Latin American	kbdla.dll
Netherlands	Dutch	langdut.dll	Dutch	kbdne.dll
New Zealand				
Norway	Norwegian	langsca.dll	Norwegian	kbdno.dll
Other Country				
Portugal	Portuguese	langeng.dll	Portuguese	kbdpo.dll
South Korea				
Spain	Spanish	langspa.dll	Spanish	kbdsp.dll
	Spanish (Modern)	langeng.dll		
Sweden	Swedish	langsca.dll	Swedish	kbdws.dll
Switzerland (French)			Swiss French	kbdsf.dll
Switzerland (German)			Swiss German	kbdsg.dll
Switzerland (Italian)				
Taiwan				
United Kingdom	English (Internatl.)	langeng.dll	British	kbduk.dll
United States	English (American)		(*none*)	(*none*)
			US	kbdus.dll
			US-Dvorak	kbddv.dll
			US-International	kbdusx.dll

Other International Format Options. The International dialog box also displays other format data appropriate to the selected country, as listed here:

Measurement: *(English* or *Metric)*
List Separator
Date, Currency, Time, Number formats

As noted above, default values are read from the [country] section of CONTROL.INF and displayed in the appropriate boxes whenever the selected country is changed. However, any default value can be easily changed to suit the user's personal preference. With the exception of the brief *Time Format* and *Number Format Configuration* notes which follow, the other formatting options are not further described here. To review the options, click on the Measurement: down-arrow or on one of the Change... buttons.

Time Format Configuration. Figure 11.20 shows the International-Time Format dialog box as it appears if either the 12- or 24-hour clock is selected. In the 12-hour example, note that the two boxes in the middle of the dialog box show user-selectable suffixes to denote AM/PM, am/pm, or whatever else you'd like to use with the 12-hour format. The 24-hour format shows only one box, since am/pm clarification is not needed. Enter your local time zone, the time zone where you wish you were, or anything else. In either case, the suffix appears next to each file-creation time in File Manager's directory listings, and in the Clock applet if the digital readout mode is selected.

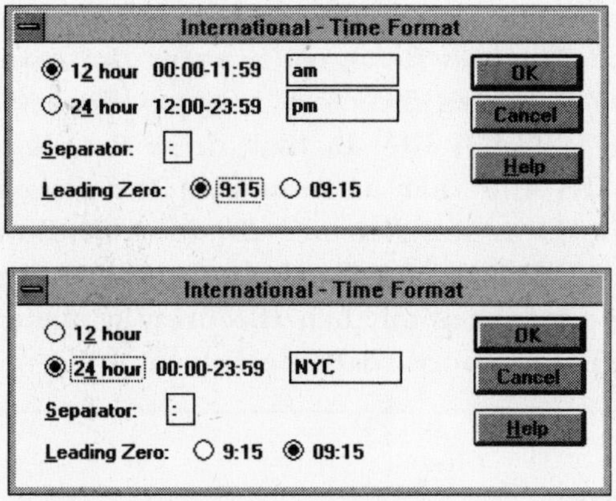

(a)

(b)

Figure 11.20 The International applet provides (a) 12-hour time format with am/pm or other suffixes, or (b) 24-hour time format with a single suffix for time zone or other information.

Number Format Configuration (Windows). If you edit the number format, make sure the 1000 Separator box in the Number Format dialog box contains either a punctuation mark (usually a period or comma) or a space character. If the box is empty, the File Manager's Status Bar incorrectly truncates its *bytes-free* report. This quirk is not found in Windows-for-Workgroups.

Custom International Format Configuration

Although your custom format changes are written into WIN.INI, the basic format settings in CONTROL.INF don't change. Therefore, if you switch to another country, then back again, your custom settings will be lost. If you want to permanently modify the settings for one country (for example, to always use metric measurement when the selected country is the United States), use Table 11.10b as a cross-reference to Table 11.8. In this specific example, Table 11.10b shows *iMeasure* (0 = metric) at position H in CONTROL.INF. Consulting position H in Table 11.8 may make it easier to find the actual position of the number that needs to be edited in the CONTROL.INF file.

If you want to start your own country, copy the [country] line closest to what you want, edit it as desired, and give it a distinctive (or real) name. For example, Table 11.8 shows a new "US Metric" entry, copied from the default United States entry, then edited to specify metric measurement (note boldface **0** in listing). In addition, the uppercase AM and PM were edited to lowercase.

> **NOTE:** Both versions of the *Windows Resource Kit* refer the reader to the WININI.WRI file in the Windows directory for specific details about the [intl] section of the WIN.INI file. In fact, these details are found only in the WININI.WRI file that accompanies the *Resource Kit* for Windows 3.1. This file is in the *Resource Kit* (not Windows) directory, and it is not included with the Workgroups kit. In any case, the file contains no more information than the printed manual, although it is presented in a slightly more readable format.

International Record in INI Files

The values read from SETUP.INF and CONTROL.INF, plus any user-selectable changes, are recorded in the INI files as shown here.

SYSTEM.INI: Language and Keyboard. The support files for the selected language and keyboard are read from the [language] and [keyboard.tables] sections of SETUP.INF and recorded in the [boot] and [keyboard] sections of SYSTEM.INI, with a few typical examples shown in Table 11.10a.

WIN.INI: Country-specific Formatting. The default formats for the selected country are read from the [country] section of CONTROL.INF and recorded in the [intl] section of WIN.INI. However, changes made to the default settings—via the International dialog box—supersede the defaults as the record is written. Table 11.10b shows how the US default is recorded in WIN.INI. For comparison purposes, the table lists the entries in the sequence in which they appear in CONTROL.INF. However, the written WIN.INI sequence is usually as indicated by the numbers in the last column.

Joystick Applet

Joystick support is not included with either Windows or Windows-for-Workgroups and, with the exception of this brief note, is not discussed here.

A joystick support file can be downloaded from CompuServe. The file (IBMJOY.ZIP) is located in Library 6 in the Windows Shareware forum (GO WINSHARE). When it is expanded, it provides the following files:

IBMJOY.DRV	Joystick driver
JOYSTICK.CPL	Joystick calibration applet for Control Panel
JOYSTICK.TXT	Documentation
LICENSE.TXT	License agreement
OEMSETUP.INF	Setup information file

TABLE 11.10a   International Format Record in SYSTEM.INI*

Section	Dialog Box and Entry	Section	Dialog Box and Entry
[boot]	**Language:**	**[keyboard]**	**Keyb. Layout:**
language.dll = (*none*)	English (American)	keyboard.dll = (*none*)	US
= langeng.dll	English (Intl.)	= kbduk.dll	British
= langfrn.dll	French	= kbdsf.dll	Swiss French
= langspa.dll	Spanish	= kbdsp.dll	Spanish

*Table shows typical configurations, which vary according to selected language, keyboard layout.

TABLE 11.10b   International Section Listing for United States Entry in WIN.INI

[intl] Section		Comments	Cross Reference	
Line	Value*		†	‡
sCountry	= United States	Country (other values change to suit)	A	22
iCountry	= 1	Uses intl. telephone code (exception: Canada = 2)	B	1
iCurrency	= 0	Currency format, 0 = $1, 1 = 1$, 2 = $ 1, 3 = 1	C	5
iTLZero	= 0	Leading zero in time, 0 = 7:11, 1 = 07:11	D	4
iDigits	= 2	Digits following decimal point in numbers	E	9
iTime	= 0	Time format, 0 = 12-hour clock, 1 = 24-hour clock	F	3
iLzero	= 1	Leading zero? 0 = .9, 1 = 0.9	G	8
iMeasure	= 1	0 = metric, 1 = English	H	10
iCurrDigits	= 2	Digits following decimal point in currency	I	6
iNegCurr	= 0	Negative currency format.	J	7
iDate	= 0	Date format, 0=11/25/93, 1=25/11/93, 2=93/11/25	K	2
s1159	= AM	Time string, before noon	L	11
s2359	= PM	Time string, before midnight	M	12
sCurrency	= $	Currency symbol	N	13
sThousand	= ,	Separator between thousand, hundred	O	14
sDecimal	= .	Decimal separator in numbers	P	15
sDate	= /	Date separator	Q	16
sTime	= :	Time separator	R	17
sList	= ,	Separator in lists	S	18
sShortDate	= M/d/yy	Short date format	–	19
sLongDate	= dddd, MMMM dd, yyyy	Long date format	–	20
sLanguage	= enu	Language (enu = U.S. English, deu = German, etc.)	–	21

* US default values shown in Table.
† Cross-reference to column in Table 11.8.
‡ Listing sequence in WIN.INI.

Refer to Appendix D for downloading details, and to the *Driver Installation Procedure* section of Chapter 12 if you need assistance installing this or any other driver. If all goes well, a joystick icon will appear in the Control Panel window, as shown at the beginning of this chapter in Figure 11.1d. For hardware-specific configuration details, refer to the *User's Guide* accompanying your joystick.

Joystick Record in SYSTEM.INI

The joystick described here inserts the following data into the indicated sections of SYSTEM.INI.

```
[drivers]                [ibmjoy.drv]
joystick=ibmjoy.drv      axes=3
```

Other joystick software will vary these settings. However, if there's a joystick=whatever.drv in the [drivers] section, there's probably an equivalent [whatever.drv] section later on in the file.

Keyboard Applet

Figure 11.21 shows the Keyboard dialog box with the sliders in their default positions. Each slider sets the time, in milliseconds, before the specified action commences, as described here. The parenthetical values are the default, and the valid range.

<u>D</u>elay Before First Repeat (2, 0-3).   If a key is held down, the first repetition of that character will occur at the indicated elapsed time. Although a zero millisecond delay might suggest that the character repeats instantaneously, in practice there is sufficient time to release the key before punching out a lengthy character string.

<u>R</u>epeat Rate (31, 0-31).   If a key is held down until the character is repeated, subsequent repetitions occur at the rate specified here.

<u>T</u>est: Box.   Type a character string into the box to test the effect of your setting changes. The length of the string varies according to the letters typed.

Keyboard Record in INI Files

Keyboard configuration data is stored in SYSTEM.INI and WIN.INI as follows.

SYSTEM.INI: Keyboard Drivers and Support Files.   The lines listed below are found in SYSTEM.INI file. In most cases, the [keyboard] section specifies a type number, and the other entries are blank.

```
[boot]
keyboard.drv=keyboard.drv
```

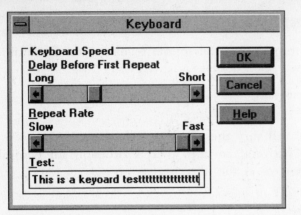

Figure 11.21   The Keyboard applet dialog box

```
[keyboard]
subtype=          (if required, to specify special features)
type=4            (1 = IBM PC, 2 = Olivetti, 3 = IBM AT, 4 = IBM enhanced)
keyboard.dll=     (layout library file, if required for some non-US keyboards)
oemansi.bin=      (OEM/ANSI code-page translation file, if required)

[boot.description]
keyboard.typ=Enhanced 101 or 102 key US and Non US keyboard (or other)

[386Enh]
keyboard=*vkd     (virtual keyboard device driver)
```
or
```
keyboard=C:\MOUSE\mousevkd.386 (MS Mouse version 9.0 software installed)
```

WIN.INI: Default Keyboard Configuration. When Windows is first installed, the default keyboard values described above are copied from the WIN.SRC (WIN.INI template) file into WIN.INI, as shown below. The lines are listed here in the same order described above and shown in the dialog box, and the first set of values (default 2, 31) is used. If the *Keyboard* applet is opened and the OK button is clicked, both lines are rewritten, even if no setting changes were made. If the lines are erased (by editing), then the lines are reinserted with the second set of values (0, 15) the next time the applet's OK button is clicked. User changes take precedence and the value(s) change accordingly.

```
[windows]
KeyboardDelay     = 2     0    (Delay Before First Repeat)
KeyboardSpeed     = 31    15   (Repeat Rate)
```

Mouse Applet

Mouse support software is installed as part of the regular Windows Setup procedure. There are, however, a wide variety of enhanced software packages such as the Microsoft Mouse version 8.20 and more recently, version 9.0. The latter accompanies the new Microsoft Mouse 2.0 and is also available separately for use with other mouse hardware. Of course, there's no shortage of third-party software out there. But regardless of what software is actually installed, the *Mouse* icon usually provides the necessary configuration access.

Given the variety of mouse software/hardware on the market, it's just about impossible to describe configuration details for all of it. However, a few representative examples are covered here.

Mouse Hardware Installation

For the purposes of the discussion which follows, it is assumed that the appropriate mouse hardware (if required) is installed in the system, and that the mouse is operational within DOS applications which support it. Although Windows itself does not require that a mouse driver be loaded prior to opening Windows, that driver will be necessary for mouse operations within a DOS Window and, of course, for DOS operations outside Windows.

Port and IRQ Configuration. Table 11.11 lists the ports to which a mouse may be connected. The ports are searched in the order they appear in the table. If your mouse is connected to a serial port, refer to the *Ports Applet* section below for configuration help.

Mouse Software Installation

This section briefly describes the installation of representative examples of mouse software for use in DOS and Windows operations. In the case of the Microsoft mouse software packages, each succeeding version offers additional configuration options in addition to those offered in earlier versions. To keep repetitive explanations to a minimum, configuration is therefore described later on, after all software versions have been introduced.

DOS Mouse Driver Installation. Not every DOS mouse driver supports mouse operations within a DOS window once Windows itself is opened.

TABLE 11.11a   Mouse Port Connections

Port	Connector	IRQ	I/O Port Address
InPort	9-pin circular	†	23C-23F primary, 238-23B secondary
Bus Card	DB-9	†	23C-23F primary, 238-23B secondary
PS/2 port	6-pin DIN	12	060
COM2	DB-9 or -25	3	2F8-2FF
COM1	DB-9 or -25	4	3F8-3FF
COM3, 4	(invalid for use with mouse)		

† Do not use IRQ listed here, if indicated hardware is installed.

2 EGA, VGA, IBM network adapter, IBM compatible PC.

3 Modem or other device on COM2.

4 Modem or other device on COM1.

5 Many network adapters, IBM compatible PC.

TABLE 11.11b   Mouse Type As Specified in MOUSE.INI

[mouse]			
MouseType	= Bus		Old Bus Mouse card
	= InPort1		InPort card with jumper 3 set to primary
	= InPort2		Same, jumper 3 set to secondary
	= PS2		PS/2 mouse port
	= Serial		Mouse uses either COM1 or COM2
	= Serial1		Mouse uses COM1 port
	= Serial2		Mouse uses COM2 port

Therefore, the Windows distribution diskettes include a few DOS drivers that do offer this support. These drivers are listed here:

Filename	Load in	Provides Support for
LMOUSE.COM	AUTOEXEC.BAT	Logitech
MOUSE.COM	AUTOEXEC.BAT	Microsoft
MOUSE.SYS	CONFIG.SYS	Microsoft
MOUSEHP.COM	AUTOEXEC.BAT	Hewlett-Packard
MOUSEHP.SYS	CONFIG.SYS	Hewlett-Packard

If you find some other driver listed in one of your startup files, it may or may not support mouse usage within a DOS window. If in doubt, contact the appropriate manufacturer for confirmation.

Windows Mouse Driver Installation. During the regular Windows setup procedure, the included mouse driver is installed in the System directory and the first mouse.drv line below is included in the SYSTEM.INI file:

```
[boot]
mouse.drv=mouse.drv        (=lmouse.drv with Logitech mouse software)
mouse.drv=C:\MOUSE\mouse.drv
```

If version 8.20 or 9.0 software is subsequently installed, the mouse.drv line may be rewritten as shown by the second line above, if the mouse software is installed in its own directory. Third-party mouse software may revise the mouse.drv line as shown by the Logitech example above.

Mouse Pointer Support. Mouse software versions 8.20 and 9.0 supplement the mouse driver with additional mouse pointer features, such as mouse trails, pointer size, etc. (described below). These additional features are supported by POINTER.EXE and POINTER.DLL files. The former is usually loaded via WIN.INI, as shown here.

```
[windows]
load=C:\MOUSE\POINTER.EXE
```

This "sub-applet" can be moved into the StartUp Group Window, but there is little point in doing so. The file must be loaded once as Windows opens, in order for the pointer features to be available via the mouse applet icon. But once it loads, a subsequent double-click on a pointer icon in the StartUp group will have no effect. So there's no need to make it available via its own icon. If you don't want the pointer options to be available, refer to the *Disable Mouse Pointer* section below.

Sofware Version Descriptions. Representative examples of Windows mouse software are desribed here. Note that each of these software packages changes the Control Panel's *Mouse* icon to help identify the installed version. In the figures which follow (11.22–11.25), each icon is shown next to the main dialog box for that version.

Windows Mouse. Figure 11.22 shows the default mouse icon in the Control Panel and the dialog box as they appear after a conventional Windows installation.

Microsoft Mouse Version 8.20. The separately available version 8.20 software offers much improved software support. Once installed, the Control Panel's mouse icon changes from the vertically oriented image shown in

Figure 11.22 to the diagonal mouse in Figure 11.23. The same figure also shows the two dialog boxes that offer additional configuration options.

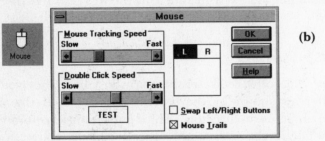

Figure 11.22 The standard-issue (a) Mouse applet icon and (b) Mouse dialog box as they appear in Windows 3.1 and Windows-for-Workgroups.

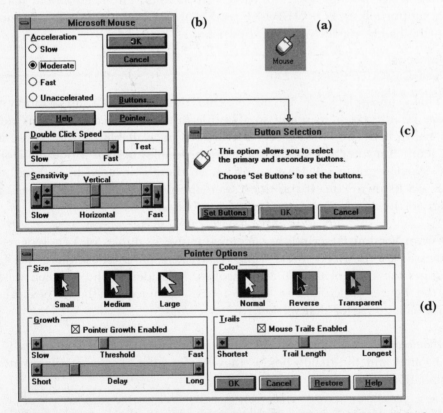

Figure 11.23 Microsoft Mouse version 8.20 software changes (a) the Control Panel icon and (b) the Mouse dialog box. Dialog box buttons provide access to (c) the Button Selection and (d) Pointer Options dialog boxes.

Microsoft Mouse Version 9.0. This latest mouse software accompanies the new *Microsoft Mouse 2.0.* However, it is also available separately for use with other Microsoft and third-party mouse and trackball hardware. The new software features a much enlarged dialog box, now dubbed the *Mouse Manager.* When installed, the Control Panel's *Mouse* icon changes to the new model shown in Figure 11.24. The same figure also shows the new Mouse Manager dialog box and the Orientation and Sensitivity dialog boxes.

Logitech to Microsoft Version 9.0 Conversion Note. If you convert from Logitech version 6.20 (described below) to Microsoft version 9.0 software, the former's LOGIMENU and CLICK command lines in AUTOEXEC.BAT are not deleted during the version 9.0 setup. Therefore, two *mouse driver not loaded* error messages are seen when the system reboots. To get rid of the messages, delete the LOGIMENU and CLICK lines in your AUTOEXEC.BAT file.

If the Logitech Cursor Tracking option was enabled prior to installing the Microsoft version 9.0 software, the *LogiCursor* icon remains onscreen and functional. If you don't want it anymore, remove the following citation from the indicated line in WIN.INI:

```
[windows]
load=C:\WINDOWS\LMOUSE\LCURSOR.EXE
```

Or, if you installed this applet in your StartUp Group Window, delete it. However, you may want to refer to the *Combination Microsoft/Logitech Software Operation* section later in the chapter before doing either.

Logitech MouseWare Utilities Version 6.20. This popular third-party software can be used with a Logitech mouse and with most Microsoft and other mice, trackballs, etc. The Logitech mouse icon and dialog windows are shown in Figure 11.25.

The Logitech *MouseWare* installation may add the following three lines to your AUTOEXEC.BAT file:

```
C:\LMOUSE\MOUSE PS2      (or other type, as appropriate)
C:\LMOUSE\LOGIMENU
C:\LMOUSE\CLICK
```

Mouse Software Configuration

Mouse configuration options vary according to which software version is installed. In this section, the following parenthetical notes are inserted as necessary to indicate that the item under discussion applies only to the indicated software.

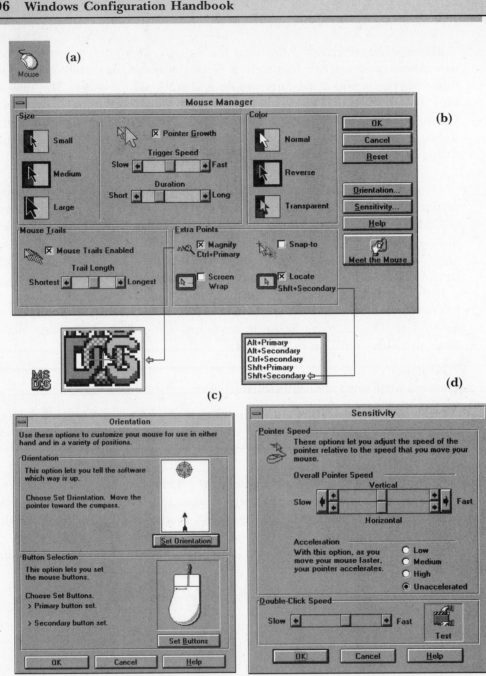

Figure 11.24 Microsoft Mouse version 9.0 software again changes (a) the Control Panel icon and introduces (b) the Mouse Manager dialog box. The detail views at the bottom illustrate the Magnify option and show a pull-down list of key strokes for the Locate option. The Mouse Manager also provides access to (c) the Orientation and (d) Sensitivity dialog boxes.

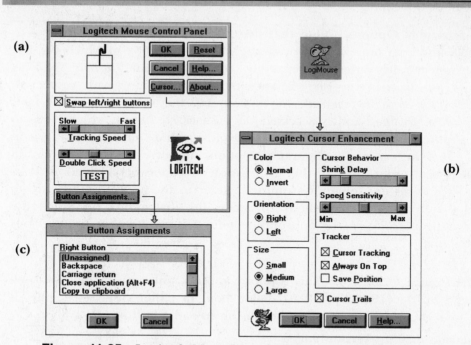

Figure 11.25 Logitech MouseWare Utilities software, showing dialog boxes for (a) the Mouse Control Panel, (b) Cursor Enhancement and (c) Button Assignments.

(Win)   Windows 3.1 and Windows-for-Workgroups
(8.20)   *Microsoft Mouse* version 8.20
(9.0)   *Microsoft Mouse* version 9.0
(Logitech)   *Logitech MouseWare Utilities* version 6.20

In the absence of such a note, the item applies to all software versions.

As usual, an underlined letter indicates the keyboard key which accesses the described option. To adjust slider bars from the keyboard, press the underlined letter, then use the up- or left-arrow to move the button leftward, and the down- or right-button to move it to the right. If no letter is underlined, press the Tab button until the button blinks, then use the arrow keys.

Primary, Secondary Mouse Buttons. In the discussion which follows, as in the rest of this book, the button that does most of the work is referred to as the *primary* mouse button, and the other is the *secondary*. If nothing else, this means the left-handed user (such as the one writing this ms.) doesn't have to read mouse instructions with a mirror. If a button is referred to here as *left* or *right,* the discussion really means the button in that physical location, without regard to the user's preference. The middle button (if there is one) is not discussed here.

Configuration Options. Note that in some cases a feature is renamed as it migrates from one version to another. The dialog box in which the feature appears also varies. For example, Windows' *Mouse Tracking Speed* becomes *Sensitivity* in version 8.2, and its relative position with respect to *Double-Click Speed* is reversed. In version 9.0, the same option becomes *Overall Pointer Speed* and is accessed via a Sensitivity button which leads to yet another dialog box. Therefore, to avoid making some explanations in triplicate, the various configuration options are described here once, in alphabetical order. As a further concession to paperwork reduction, location references are sometimes omitted. Refer to the appropriate figure to find the item being described. To access the dialog box on which the item appears, click on the appropriate button located within the previous dialog box.

Acceleration (8.20, 9.0). This option appears on either the Microsoft Mouse (8.20) or Sensitivity (9.0) dialog box. In either case, select one of the four choices listed here by clicking on its radio button:

Version 8.20	Version 9.0
Slow	Low
Moderate	Medium
Fast	High
Unaccelerated	Unaccelerated

Acceleration Profile. In Microspeak, each option selects a different *Acceleration Profile,* which defines how the screen pointer reacts to physical movement of the mouse. If the mouse moves slowly, the pointer moves at so-called normal speed, regardless of the selected profile. However, if the mouse moves at a faster rate, pointer speed increases according to the selected profile. If none of the profiles are satisfactory, you can create your own, as described in the *Configure Custom Acceleration Profile* section below.

Button Assignments (Logitech). This option can assign certain keyboard commands to the primary and middle (if any) button. The right button assignment is actually the left button, if button swapping is enabled. Refer to the Logitech *User's Guide* for further details about this option.

Button Swapping. Under default conditions, the left mouse button is the primary button. Use one of the following procedures to make the right button the primary.

Swap Left/Right Buttons (Win, Logitech). A simple check box inverts the functions of the left and right buttons, as may be noted by swapped "L" and "R" legends in the Mouse dialog box if the Swap Buttons box is checked.

Set Buttons (8.20). Click on this button to access the Button Selection dialog box shown in Figure 11.23c. Then click on the Set Buttons button. The final step is to click on the button you want to use as the primary button.

Set Buttons (9.0). To find this option, click on the Orientation... button in the Mouse Manager dialog box. When the Orientation dialog box (Figure 11.24c) appears, click on Set Buttons, then on the button that is to be the primary.

Color (8.20, 9.0, Logitech). The color of the mouse pointer may be set as follows:

Color Option	Actual Color
Normal	White pointer, black outline
Reverse	Black pointer, white outline
Invert (Logitech)	Black pointer, white outline
Transparent	Pointer changes from white to gray to black, for best contrast with background color (not available with Logitech software)

Note that this "color" option has no effect on the color of the text cursor seen in Notepad, Write, and most Windows word processors. That color is usually the complement of the Window Background color selected via the *Color* applet described earlier in the chapter.

Cursor Behavior (Logitech). This section controls the *Shrink Delay* (see *Delay*) and *Speed Sensitivity* (see *Pointer Speed*).

Cursor Trails (Logitech). See *Mouse Trails*.

Delay (8.20), Duration (9.0), Shrink Delay (Logitech). After the mouse pointer stops moving, it shrinks back to its original size after the interval set by this slide bar.

Double Click Speed. Believe it or not, this function retains the same name through all four software versions described here. The setting defines the time interval that may elapse between the first and second mouse click in a double-click operation. If the second click comes after that interval, the two clicks are treated as unrelated actions.

NOTE: See also *Double-Click Distance Adjustment* below for additional information on configuring double-click performance.

Duration (9.0). See *Delay* above.

Extra Points (9.0). This section of the Mouse Manager dialog box offers the following configuration options (extra points). Check the appropriate box to enable the option.

Locate. If this option is enabled, the mouse pointer jumps to the center of the screen whenever the key combination listed under the check box is pressed. If no combination is listed, refer to the *Select Key Combination* section below.

Magnify. If the key combination listed under this check box is pressed, the mouse pointer changes into a rectangular magnifying glass, which can be used to take a closer look at any item on the Desktop. For example, the detail view at the bottom of Figure 11.24b shows the magnifier over the MS-DOS icon in the Main Group Window. For comparison purposes, a duplicate icon is also shown in the Figure. Click either mouse button to restore the normal pointer.

Refer to the *Select Key Combination* section below if no key combination is listed under the check box.

Screen Wrap. This one takes a bit of practice. If the mouse pointer moves off-screen when the option is enabled, it immediately reappears on the opposite side of the screen. Perhaps the best part of this feature is that it can be disabled if you can't get used to it.

Snap-to. If enabled, the mouse pointer automatically positions itself over the default button whenever there is one. For example, as you exit Windows, the pointer appears over the OK button in the Exit Windows dialog box. Thus, you can quickly exit Windows by double-clicking on the File Menu's Exit Windows... option: The first click brings up the dialog box, the second closes Windows.

Note that if you open an applet window with a default OK button, an accidental additional click will immediately close the applet again.

Select Key Combination for Locate and Magnify Options (9.0). As previously noted, either option is enabled by pressing the key combination listed under its check box. As you do, a small window displays a list of key combinations, as shown by the detail view at the bottom of Figure 11.24b. Five of the following six choices are available:

| Alt+Primary | Ctrl+Primary | Shift+Primary |
| Alt+Secondary | Ctrl+Secondary | Shift+Secondary |

The missing combination is either assigned to the other option, or was previously assigned to it. Thus, if you want to use, say, Alt+Primary for the Locate option and it's not listed, even though the Magnify check box is clear, temporarily assign any other combination to the Magnify option. Now reopen the *Locate* window and the Alt+Primary combination will be available. After selecting it, the Magnify option can be cleared if you don't want to use it.

Meet the Mouse (9.0). The button with this name runs a semi-animated tutorial. You can recover some 700+ Kb by erasing it after (or possibly, before) you view it. If you erase the ERGODEMO.DLL file in the Mouse directory, the button disappears from the dialog box. If you get the urge to see it again, you can always expand a fresh copy from the distribution diskette, or wait for the movie.

Mouse Tracking Speed (Win). The button on this slider bar may be moved to one of seven positions, arbitrarily labeled 0–6 below. At each position, the values in the next three columns are written into WIN.INI, as shown here:

```
[windows]
MouseSpeed=
MouseThreshold1=
MouseThreshold2=
```

Button Position	Mouse Speed	Threshold1	Threshold2
0	0	0	0
1	1	10	0
2	1	7	0
3	1	4	0
4	2	4	12
5	2	4	9
6	2	4	6

Each threshold above specifies a pixel distance that the mouse may move between consecutive mouse interrupt signals. If movement exceeds a threshold, then pointer speed increases at a rate defined by the Mouse Speed column.

If the Slider Bar button position (1-3) sets Mouse Speed at 1, then pointer speed doubles if Threshold1 is exceeded. If Mouse speed is 2 then pointer speed doubles again if Threshold 2 is exceeded.

If version 8.20 or 9.0 software is installed, the above three lines remain in WIN.INI, but with values set at zero.

Mouse Trails. Enable this option to leave a momentary trail as the mouse pointer moves around the Desktop. The trails consist of multiple pointer images which may make the pointer easier to locate on some screens.

Mouse Trails. For all versions, a check box on one of the dialog boxes enables the Mouse Trails option (*Cursor Trails,* Logitech). If the check box itself is disabled, then the currently installed video driver does not support this option. The Microsoft VGA and SVGA drivers support mouse trails, while many third-party 256-color depths do not. If the box is completely missing (*Win* only), then it's possible that the driver does support the option. To test it, write the line described below into the WIN.INI file.

If mouse trails are supported, and enabled, the following line is written into WIN.INI:

```
[windows]
MouseTrails=x      (x = 1–7; see Trail Length)
```

Trail Length (Win). If the Mouse Trails option is enabled, the value on the MouseTrails= line above is set to 7. To adjust trail length, edit the value between 1 (shortest) and 7 (longest).

Trail Length (8.20, 9.0). Use the slider bar to vary the MouseTrails= line between 1 and 7, as described above.

Orientation (Logitech). The *Right/Left* labels refer to the user's mouse hand, not the mouse pointer. By default (*Right*) its arrowhead points to the upper left. The southpaw mouseketeer may prefer the *Left* option, in which case the arrowhead points to the upper right. In other words, right is left, and vice versa.

Pointer Growth Enabled (8.20), Pointer Growth (9.0). If this box is checked, the mouse pointer grows to the specified larger size whenever it is moved, making it easier to see on some screens. Pointer growth characteristics are adjusted by the two slide bars labeled *Trigger Speed* (see *Threshold*) and *Duration* (see *Delay*).

Pointer Speed (9.0).   At last this feature is properly named. On previous software versions it was known as either *Mouse Tracking Speed* (Windows) or *Sensitivity* (8.20). Now it has been moved to the separate Sensitivity dialog box and labeled *Overall Pointer Speed*. But whatever it's called, it adjusts the speed at which the pointer moves across the screen in response to your mouse movements. In versions 8.20 and 9.0, vertical and horizontal sensitivity (8.20) or speed (9.0) are separately adjustable. Use the large arrow buttons to adjust both, or the smaller buttons for independent vertical or horizontal adjustment.

For the purposes of this book, the option will henceforth be known as *Pointer Speed*.

Pointer Speed Configuration Note.   The optimum setting for any of the mouse options is, of course, whatever works best for you; in most cases, a little subjective testing will help you decide what works. However, you may want to try the following procedure to adjust pointer speed.

Open both the Mouse dialog box and *Paintbrush* applet and size the latter's window so both applets are visible. Adjust mouse pointer speed to its maximum (fast) setting. In the *Paintbrush* applet, draw two very fine horizontal lines. Then try to place one line directly on top of the other, so that only one fine line remains visible. Repeat the test with two vertical lines. If one or both tests fail because the moving line "jumps" from one side of the stationary line to the other, gradually decrease the speed until the test is consistently successful. Any further decrease will simply slow down operations without producing any noticeable improvement in pointer speed. In fact, a pointer speed that works well with *Paintbrush* operations may be a bit too slow for convenient use elsewhere. If so, increase the speed limit as desired, then reduce it again when necessary for critical graphics work.

Reset (9.0).   Click on this button to clear all settings in the Mouse Manager dialog box. The Reset button does not clear orientation or button-swap settings.

Reset (Logitech).   This button resets all options on the Logitech Mouse Control Panel dialog box, including the left/right swap buttons.

Sensitivity (8.20).   See *Pointer Speed* above.

Set Buttons (8.20, 9.0). See *Button Swapping* above.

Set Orientation (9.0). Some users prefer to hold or move the mouse diagonally, thereby skewing the usual up/down/sideways pointer response. To tailor pointer movement to suit personal preference, or to make your mouse useless to anyone else, click on the Set Orientation button on the Mouse Manager dialog box.

To set orientation, move the mouse in any straight-line direction and watch the moving arrow. When the arrowhead reaches the center of the compass, the arrow is immediately disabled and the Set Orientation button is re-enabled. Test the new orientation by moving the mouse around the screen. If it's satisfactory, press the OK button to quit. Otherwise, try again. To quit in mid-test, press the Escape key.

Size (8.20, 9.0). At rest, the mouse pointer is always the size shown in the Small box. But when the pointer is moved, it instantaneously grows to the size shown in whichever check box is enabled, according to the parameters specified in the *Pointer Growth* section of the dialog box. Note, therefore, that if the Small box is enabled, there is no pointer growth; in fact, that option becomes disabled.

Size (Logitech). At rest, the mouse pointer size is either small, medium, or large, depending on which radio button is clicked. If the pointer is moved, it grows to large size, then shrinks back to the selected size when movement ceases. In contrast to the Microsoft Size option described above, the Logitech Cursor Behavior options are disabled if the Large size button is enabled.

Speed Sensitivity (Logitech). This is the Logitech equivalent of the Pointer Speed option described above.

Test (the double-click speed). If you set a very fast double-click speed, it's worthwhile to test it before continuing. Depending on the capabilities of the mouse and your trigger finger, you may not be able to get in a double-click within the designated interval. In Windows or version 8.20 software, the Test Box blinks if you made it. In version 9.2, your iconic assistant alternately opens and closes the clapper on the Take Slate if your double-click is fast enough.

Threshold (8.20), Trigger Speed (9.0). Perhaps the Help Screen is getting too sophisticated for its own good. If you want to know all there is to know about version 9.0's *Trigger Speed*, click on *Improving Pointer Visibility*, then on *Enabling Pointer Growth*. List item 4 states "Adjust Trigger Speed and Duration settings by dragging the scroll box to Slow or Fast." You probably could have figured that much out just by looking at the slow/fast scroll bar under the *Trigger Speed* legend.

Assuming you still don't know what *T. S.* is, try looking under *Pointer Growth* in the *User's Guide* (p. 29). It actually adjusts the pointer growth *threshold,* which is what it's called in version 8.20. In either case, if you move the pointer across the screen at a rate faster than that set on the slide bar, the pointer grows to its maximum size.

Tracker (Logitech). This section is unique to the Logitech mouse software, and offers the following options.

<u>C</u>ursor Tracking. If this option is checked, a *LogiCursor* icon appears near the bottom of the Desktop. The icon consists of a moveable arrow which always points to the current location of the mouse pointer.

<u>A</u>lways on Top. Select this option to keep the *LogiCursor* pointer always on top, so that it doesn't get lost under a full-screen application window.

Save <u>P</u>osition. Check this box if you want the *LogiCursor* to remain at a specified location on the Desktop. Place the *LogiCursor* wherever you want it, and the next time Windows opens it will reappear in that location.

Trigger Speed (9.0). See *Threshold* above.

Custom Configuration Procedures for Microsoft Mouse Software

A few additional configuration options are available for training your mouse to behave properly. A parenthetical note in each heading identifies the required software or Windows version required for that procedure.

Configure Custom Acceleration Profile (8.20, 9.0). If you can't find an acceleration profile that suits you, you can write your own by editing one of the default profiles stored in the MOUSE.INI file. The medium and unaccelerated profiles are listed here.

```
[AccelerationProfile2]
Label       = Medium
Movement    = 1    9    12   15   18   21   24   27   30   33   37   41   46
Factor      = 1.00 1.25  1.50 1.75 2.00 2.25 2.50 2.75 3.00 3.25 3.50 3.75 4.00

[Acceleration Profile4]
Label       = Unaccelerated
Movement    = 1
Factor      = 1.00
```

In each profile, the Movement value is an arbitrary unit specifying a speed at which the mouse moves. The corresponding Factor defines the relative pointer speed when the mouse travels at the specified Movement speed. Thus, in Profile2 above, if the mouse moves slowly (Movement = 1), the pointer moves at normal speed (Factor = 1). But as the mouse moves faster (Movement = 9, 12, 15, . . .), the pointer moves even faster (Factor = 1.25, 1.5, 1.75, . . . times normal speed). In Profile4, both values are set at 1.0, so there is always a 1:1 correspondence between the mouse and the pointer.

To write your own profile, edit any label and change the acceleration profile as desired. Valid entries are listed below.

	Label:	16 character maximum	
		Minimum	Maximum
Movement:		1	127
Factor:		0.1	16
Total Entries:		1	32
Entry Separator:		Space	

Acceleration profiles are set when the mouse driver is loaded, so you'll have to close and reopen Windows if you make revisions. The next time you open the *Mouse* applet, your new label(s) will be seen in the Acceleration section of the dialog box and the new profile will be available for use.

Double-Click Distance Adjustment (Workgroups). If the mouse pointer moves more than four pixels between the two clicks in a double-click action, the double-click is not recognized. To increase the permissible distance, add one or both of the following lines to WIN.INI:

```
[windows]
DoubleClickHeight=4
DoubleClickWidth=4
```

With these lines in place, the pointer can move within the specified vertical and/or horizontal range (default = 4) between clicks. Note that this option is a feature of Windows-for-Workgroups only, and not of the installed mouse software.

Verify Mouse Port Connection (9.0).   Under certain conditions, you can verify the mouse port connection by typing mouse /f at the DOS prompt before opening Windows. However, the switch is valid only if a mouse driver was not loaded during system startup, either on purpose (not listed in CONFIG.SYS or AUTOEXEC.BAT) or by accident (not enough memory, mouse hardware not found, etc.). In either case, mouse /f tries to load the driver and issue a report. If a mouse is connected to a working port, then the driver is loaded, the appropriate MouseType= line is written into MOUSE.INI (see below), and one of the reports listed here is seen. If some other report appears instead, then refer to the *Mouse Troubleshooting* section for assistance if needed.

InPort Mouse enabled on InPort1, Interrupt 3 (default settings; may vary according to jumpers on InPort card).   A bus mouse was detected with the indicated settings. If either is incorrect, then refer to the *InPort* card documentation for assistance.

Mouse driver installed. Mouse Port Device enabled.   A mouse was detected on the PS/2 port.

Serial Mouse enabled on COMx: If the mouse is found on a COM port, the number of that port is included as seen here.

Disable Confirmation Messages.   In File Manager, if you use drag-and-drop to move or copy a file, a message appears to verify that you really mean it. Refer to *Disable Confirmation Messages* in Chapter 6 if you want to get rid of this message.

Disable Mouse Pointer Options (8.20, 9.0).   If you want to disable the pointer options, you can do so by renaming POINTER.EXE to say, XPOINTER.EXE and erasing the reference to it on the load= line in WIN.INI. The next time the *Mouse* applet opens, an *Unable to Access Pointer Options* message appears, and the version 8.20 Pointer... button is disabled. In version 9.0, the pointer options on the Mouse Manager dialog box are also disabled. In either case, previously set pointers are retained.

To temporarily re-enable the options, open the Program Manager's File Menu, select the Run... option, and type XPOINTER.EXE (or whatever you called it) in the Command Line: box. If you give the file some really obscure name, it's unlikely that the casual snooper will take the trouble to find it and redo your settings for you.

Combination Microsoft/Logitech Software Operation. If Logitech version 6.20 software is installed, you can continue to use some of its features after installing Microsoft version 9.0 software. If the Logitech *LogiCursor* applet is active, its Tracker options (see Figure 11.25b) remain enabled; therefore, the *LogiCursor* arrow still points to the mouse pointer location. In addition, the Cursor Trails check box will enable/disable the corresponding version 9.0 Mouse Trails option. Although the Logitech Color, Orientation, and Size options still appear enabled, their radio buttons no longer have any effect.

Configure Windows for No Mouse (the NOMOUSE.DRV driver). If you don't want a mouse in Windows, it's not enough to remove all references to it from your INI files. If you do anyway, the mouse pointer will still be there the next time you open Windows. If you edit the [boot] section of SYSTEM.INI so that the mouse.drv= line shows nothing following the equal sign, Windows won't start at all and you'll be left at the DOS prompt.

If you remove the entire mouse.drv= line mentioned above, Windows gets so upset that it roams through your Windows and System directories, then goes through your entire path looking for a MOUSE.DRV file. If it finds one, it uses it. If it can't find one, then you get the DOS prompt.

To run a mouseless operation, close Windows, and at the DOS prompt, log onto the Windows directory and run SETUP. Highlight the Mouse: box, press the Enter key, toggle down to No mouse or other pointing device, and press the Enter key again. You will be prompted to insert a distribution diskette in drive A. The diskette contains a NOMOUSE.DRV file which, as it installs, writes the following line in SYSTEM.INI:

```
[boot]
mouse.drv=nomouse.drv
```

This special-purpose driver assures Windows that it's OK to operate without a mouse. And it doesn't even ask you why you don't like mice.

Mouse Record in INI Files

The following sections of your INI files contain information about the installed mouse software.

SYSTEM.INI: Driver Information. The boot section specifies the Windows mouse driver, and the line may include a path if the file is located elsewhere than in the System directory. In addition, some third-party software may change the comm.drv and keyboard.drv lines, and/or add a new section.

```
[boot]
mouse.drv=(path, if required\)mouse.drv
comm.drv=comm.drv
keyboard.drv=keyboard.drv

[boot.description]
mouse.drv      = Microsoft, or IBM PS/2
               = Microsoft Mouse version 9.00
               = (or other, from Table 1.5)

[386Enh]
mouse=*vmd
keyboard=(path, if required\)mousevkd.386 (with Microsoft Mouse 9.0 software)

[LogiMouse]      (if Logitech Mouse Software is installed)
Mode=Right
Release=2.20
Type=PS/2
. . . other lines follow
```

WIN.INI: Configuration Data. If the default Windows (or Workgroups) mouse driver is installed, all mouse configuration data (except mouse type) is written into WIN.INI, as described in various configuration sections above. If version 8.20 or 9.0 software is installed, most configuration data goes into the MOUSE.INI file instead. However, a few lines are still written into WIN.INI, such as those shown here.

```
[windows]
load=C:\MOUSE\POINTER.EXE (with MS Mouse versions 8.20, 9.0 software)
DoubleClickWidth=        (workgroups only)
DoubleClickHeight=       (workgroups only)
MouseSpeed=0
MouseThreshold1=0
MouseThreshold2=0
MouseTrails=
```

If Logitech version 6.20 software is installed, an additional section is written into WIN.INI, as shown here.

```
[Logitech Mouse Control Panel]
(Logitech mouse configuration data)
```

MOUSE.INI: Version 8.20/9.0 Configuration Data. If the default Windows (or Workgroups) mouse driver is installed, this file contains only the following section.

```
[mouse]
MouseType=PS2     (or other, see Table 11.11)
```

However, if version 8.20 or 9.0 software is installed, MOUSE.INI contains a detailed configuration record, including the currently installed mouse type, acceleration profiles (described earlier), and other data.

Network Applet

The *Network* applet provides access to network configuration options, including network logon, passwords, and performance priority. You'll need to use the applet to set up your network configuration for the first time, or to make changes later on. Once the network is configured, there's little need to use the applet since most network operations can be handled directly from the File Manager, as described in Chapter 6.

The following section reviews the first-time network logon procedure.

Network Settings

Double-click on the *Network* icon to open the Network Settings dialog box shown in Figure 11.26.

Computer Name: Enter a distinctive name that will identify the computer to other users on the network.

Workgroup: If you wish to join an existing workgroup, enter the name of that group. Or type in a distinctive name if you wish to create a new workgroup.

Comment: If you enter a comment here, it appears next to your Computer Name in File Manager and Print Manager dialog boxes.

Enable Sharing. This box must be checked if you want to share your directories, printer(s), and Clipbook pages. If the box is cleared, then the *Performance Priority* options (see below) are disabled, and the Share options on the File Manager's Disk Menu (Figure 6.3a) do not appear. If you

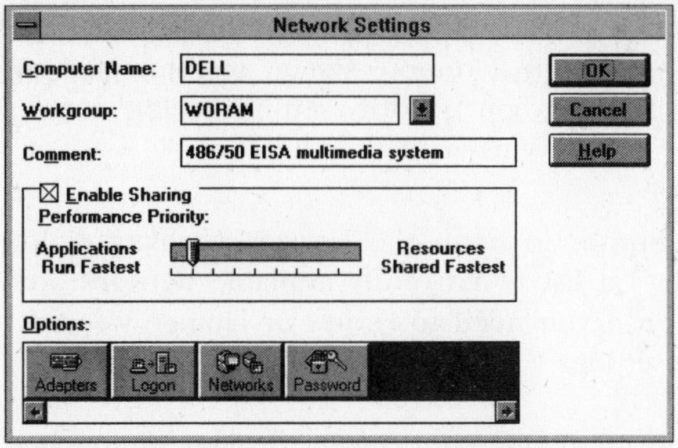

Figure 11.26 The Network Settings dialog box

change the Enable Sharing status, a prompt advises that you must restart
Windows for the change to take effect.

Lock Sharing Status. To prevent the user from changing the Enable
Sharing status described above, add the following line to your SYS-
TEM.INI file:

```
[network]
NoSharingControl=1
```

The current sharing status remains enabled or disabled, so make sure
it's correct before adding this line. To unlock sharing status later on,
change the 1 to 0 or erase the entire line.

Performance Priority: If a remote user accesses your shared resources,
your own computer must allocate a certain amount of CPU time to handle
background server chores, which results in slower performance of local
tasks. Move the slider as required to adjust the allocation of time between
your own work (*Applications Run Fastest*) and that required for resource
sharing (*Resources Shared Fastest*). The 10 slider-bar settings assign the following background priorities to the server function.

40	110	200	300	5000
80	175	250	500	9000

The specified priority setting is written into the SYSTEM.INI file as
shown here:

```
[386Enh]
Priority=250      (or other value listed above)
```

Note that resource sharing is always a background activity, and that the selected setting only takes effect if a remote system is connected to your computer. For more information about priority settings, refer to *Scheduling* in the *386 Enhanced Applet* section earlier in the chapter.

Adapters. Click on this button to open the Network Adapters dialog box (not shown), which displays a list of currently available network adapters. Click on the <u>S</u>etup... button if you need to review or change network IRQ, I/O port or base address settings.

Logon. Click on this button to open the Logon Settings dialog box and refer to the *Logon Settings* section below for further details.

Networks. Windows-for-Workgroups also provides support for the Microsoft LAN Manager and Novell NetWare. If you wish to use either, or some other network software, click on this button to open the Compatible Networks dialog box (not shown). Highlight a listed network type and click on the <u>A</u>dd - > button, or simply drag the network icon into the <u>O</u>ther Networks in Use: box. A prompt will ask you to insert the distribution diskette with one of the following files on it:

Network Type	Filename	Other Files Added
Microsoft LAN Manager	LMSCRIPT.EXE	LMSCRIPT.PIF (in System directory)
Novell NetWare	NETWARE.DRV	NETWARE.HLP, NETX.COM, MSIPX.COM
Unlisted/UpdatedNetwork	vendor-provided network driver disk	

After installing the necessary driver, click on the <u>S</u>ettings... button (if enabled) to access configuration options appropriate to that network. If you add or remove Novell NetWare software, your startup files and PROTOCOL.INI will be modified, and you must reboot for the changes to take effect.

Password. Click on this button to access the Change Logon Password dialog box (not shown). Enter your old password (if any) and press the Tab (not Enter) key to move to the new password box. Enter the new password, then re-enter it for confirmation. The password change takes effect immediately; the next time you open Windows-for-Workgroups, a Welcome dialog box (see Figure 11.27b, below) will prompt you for that password.

To disable the current password without replacing it with a new one, just enter the old password and press the Enter key.

Logon Settings

This dialog box is shown in Figure 11.27a, with current status reported as *Not logged on* or *Currently logged on as* (logon name). The legend on the button under the Default Logon Name: line is Log On... (as in the figure) or Log Off, as appropriate.

Log On.... If you click on the Log On... button, either the Logon Status changes, or the Welcome dialog box shown in Figure 11.27b appears. In the latter case, enter a Logon Name and Password (if desired), then click on the Yes button. If an advisory message (Figure 11.27c) appears, click on the Yes button even if you don't want to use a password. Otherwise, the same message will reappear every time you try to log on.

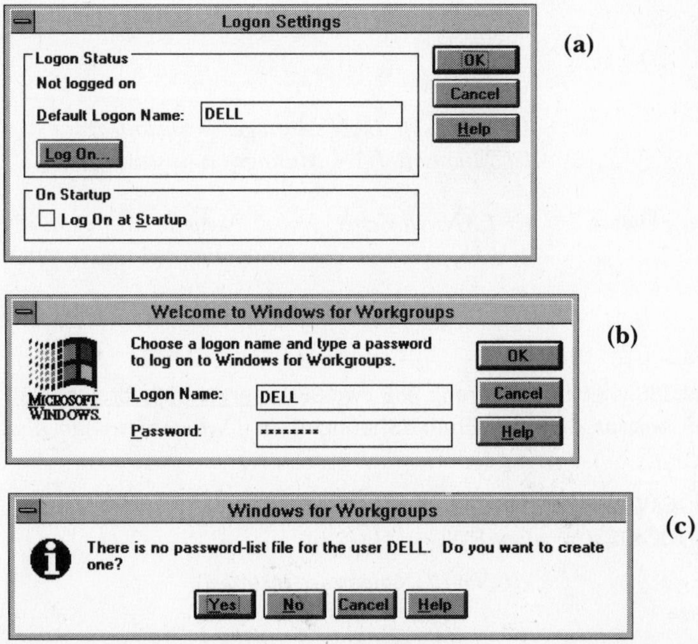

Figure 11.27 The Logon Settings dialog box reports current logon status. When the computer logs onto the network, the button legend changes to Log Off. (b) The Welcome screen appears during initial logon, and Windows opens every time if a password has been specified. (c) Click on the Yes button to create a password list file, which is required even if no password is used.

Log Off. The appearance of this button legend indicates that your system is currently logged on to the network.

Log On at Startup. Enable this check box so that the next time you open Windows-for-Workgroups, your system will automatically log on to the network.

Network Record in SYSTEM.INI

Most network configuration data is saved in the SYSTEM.INI file, as shown by these representative examples:

```
[boot]
network.drv=wfwnet.drv
secondnet.drv=netware.drv        (if Novell Netware is also installed)

[boot.description]
network.drv=Microsoft Windows for Workgroups (version 3.1)

[Network]
AutoLogon=
Comment=
ComputerName=
EnableSharing=
LMLogon=                          (if Microsoft LAN Manager is installed)
LogonDomain=                      (if Microsoft LAN Manager is installed)
logonvalidated=
multinet=lanman, netware          (if LAN Manager, Novell Netware are installed)
Priority=                         (see Performance Priority section, above)
UserName=
Workgroup=

[386Enh]
network=vnetbios.386,vnetsup.386,vredir.386,vwc.386,vserver.386,vbrowse.386
        (underlined segment deleted if EnableSharing=0 in [Network] section above)

[Password Lists]
*Shares=C:\WINDOWS\SHARE000.PWL
Username=C:\WINDOWS\Username.PWL

[NetWare]                         (if Novell Netware is installed)
NWShareHandles=
RestoreDrives=
```

Ports Applet

Although the *Ports* applet was introduced in Chapter 9, some additional configuration information is included here to help resolve conflicts between a serial mouse and a modem and, possibly, clarify communication settings within a DOS window.

Communication Settings Configuration

As Windows opens, it scans the [ports] section of WIN.INI for the following line, which is repeated for COM2, 3 and 4:

COM1:=9600,n,8,1,x   *9600 baud, no parity, 8 data bits, 1 stop bit, Xon/Xoff flow control*

To review or change any communication setting, open the *Ports* applet, select the port, and click on the Settings... button. Figure 11.28a shows the Settings dialog box with the default values listed above.

Baud Rates Greater than 19200. Although the highest baud rate in the Settings dialog box is 19.2 kBaud (19200), some Windows 3.1 and Windows-for-Workgroups applications support rates up to 57.6 kBaud. Contact the software supplier for the required support software.

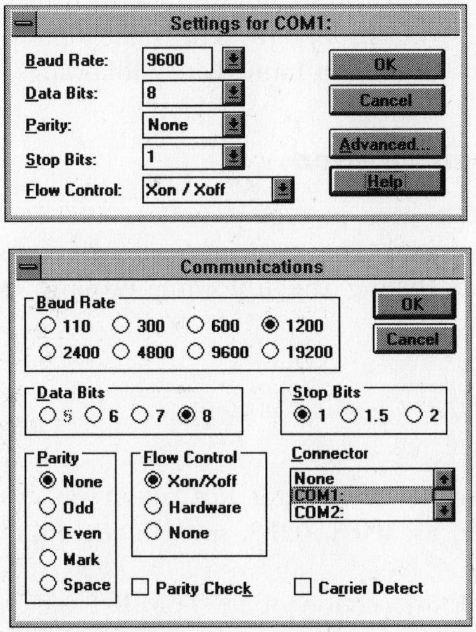

Figure 11.28   A comparison of (a) the Ports applet's Settings and (b) Terminal applet's Communications dialog boxes. The latter settings take precedence within the Terminal applet.

Terminal Applet Settings. If the *Terminal* applet is used, and its communication settings differ from those set via the *Ports* applet, the *Terminal* settings take precedence within that applet. For comparison purposes, Figure 11.28b shows the default COM1 *Terminal* settings.

DOS Communication Settings. For some reason just about every DOS manual states that the *Mode (Configure Serial Port)* default settings are as given in the first line below. However, the actual startup values are listed on line 2.

Baud Rate	Parity	Data Bits	Stop Bits	According to:
Not given	Even	7	1	Any DOS manual
2400	Odd	8	1	Any diagnostic utility

To switch to the claimed default values, type MODE COM*x yy* at the DOS prompt, where *x* is the port number and *yy* the first two digits of the desired baud rate. The screen will report the selected baud rate, followed by the settings listed in line 1 above.

The reason for mentioning all this here is to point out that Windows settings do not apply to communications within a DOS window, and neither do the "default" DOS settings themselves. To verify the current DOS mode settings on your own system, run the DOS 6.0 MSD utility (described in Chapter 13) and have a look at the COM Ports... option. The same option also reports the port address described in the section immediately following.

COM Port Address and IRQ Configuration

As Windows opens, it scans the BIOS area at segment:offset 40:0 for I/O port address information. The first eight bytes provide the settings for COM ports 1–4, as may be seen by typing the following two-line debug script at the DOS prompt:

```
debug
-d 40:0 L8     (to display 8 bytes (L8) beginning at 40:0)
0040:0000   F8  03 F8  02 00  00 00  00
```

The four byte-pairs above (underlined here, but not on-screen) specify the addresses, which are interpreted as; 03F8, 02F8, undefined, undefined for COM ports 1–4, respectively.

Next, Windows searches the [386Enh] section of SYSTEM.INI for entries such as those shown here for COM4:

```
COM4Base   =   base address
COM4Irq    =   IRQ
```

In the absence of such explicit instructions, Windows sets COM1 and 2 to the addresses specified above, and to IRQ 4 and 3. Next, COM3 is set to address 3E8 and IRQ 4. COM4 is not set to the customary 2E8 and IRQ 3, since that address may be in use by an 8514 display adapter or other device.

To review or change the current Windows settings, open the *Ports* applet, select a COM port, followed by the <u>S</u>ettings... button, then the <u>Ad</u>vanced... button. The Windows default values are summarized here:

COM	I/O Port Address	IRQ	
1	03F8	4	
2	02F8	3	*(COM2 and 3 addresses inverted by error in Windows 3.1 User's Guide.)*
3	03E8	4	
4	Default	Default	
	02E8	3	*(customary values for COM4)*

COM4 Configuration Considerations. If your modem or some other serial device is configured for COM4 and your computer does not have a physical COM3 device installed, Windows may get confused and think there is a COM3 device at address 02E8 but with IRQ 4. To restore order, add the first line below to the indicated section of SYSTEM.INI, and make sure lines 2 and 3 specify the correct values—presumably those listed here.

```
[386Enh]
COM3Irq=-1      (the -1 disables the erroneous COM3 configuration)
COM4Irq=3
COM4Base=02E8
```

Mouse Serial Port Configuration. As noted in the *Mouse Applet* section above, Windows looks for a mouse on COM2 before looking at COM1, unless it finds one before getting to either of these serial ports. Therefore, it's not a bad idea to connect a serial mouse to COM2, so Windows doesn't get the chance to make a mistake. With luck it won't make the mistake anyway, but without luck, it will.

Troubleshooting

Troubleshooting suggestions for the applets described in this chapter are covered in this section. The first part covers the Control Panel itself and most of this chapter's applets, and each item begins with a keyword to identify the applet in which the trouble may occur. This is followed by a separate section for troubleshooting the *Mouse* applet and mouse hardware.

Color: Color Refiner Box Color Does Not Appear in Color|Solid Box. If you move the crosshairs around in the Color Refiner box and the Color|Solid box shows only white, the Luminosity is set at maximum (240), in which case all "colors" are white. Drop the Luminosity scale to about 128, then try again, readjusting luminosity as needed.

Color: Color Values Shift between Full Screen and DOS Window Modes. Unfortunately, this is "normal." For further details, refer to the *Color Values in DOS Window Video Mode* section in Chapter 7.

Color: Luminosity Arrow "Stuck" at Top of Scale. If the arrowhead at the top of the Luminosity Scale can't be moved via the mouse pointer, double-click on the arrowhead, then try again.

Control Panel Icons Missing. If you open the Control Panel and only a few icons appear, the COMMDLG.DLL file may be corrupted. If so, only the MIDI Mapper and Sound (if installed) icons appear in standard mode, along with the 386 Enhanced icon in enhanced mode. To restore the missing icons, expand a fresh copy of COMMDLG.DLL into the System directory.

Control Panel Doesn't Open. If you double-click on the Control Panel icon and nothing happens, it's possible that the *x* and *y* coordinates in the [MMCPL] section of CONTROL.INI have placed the Control Panel off-screen. If so, minimize all other open windows to icons, double-click anywhere on the Desktop to open the Task Manager, then click on the Cascade button. This "cascades" the Control Panel back onto the screen, where its size and position can be readjusted as desired. Next, reopen all the recently closed windows. Since these windows were minimized before hitting the Cascade button, each returns to its former size and position unaffected by the recovery operation.

Date/Time: Calendar Displays Time on 24-hour Clock. If you set the *Date/Time* applet to display time on the 12-hour (am/pm) clock, the *Calendar* applet uses the 24-hour clock format anyway. This is because the applet is unable to display the am/pm suffix, and there is presently no workaround.

Date/Time: Clock Applet Shows Erroneous Character between Hours/Minutes/Seconds, no Suffix. If the separator specified in the *International* applet's Time Format dialog box is missing, the *Clock* applet may insert an erroneous character (bracket, or other) as a separator, and the am/pm or 24-hour suffix (if any) will not appear. To make the necessary corrections, open the *International* applet and specify any Time separator, including a space.

Date/Time: File Manager Time Display Is Truncated. If the separator specified in the *International* applet's Time Format dialog box is missing, the File Manager directory listings will truncate the file creation time to show the hour only (minutes, seconds missing). Note that the value is not rounded to the nearest hour. Thus 14:59:03 NYC is shown as simply 14, and so on. To make the necessary corrections, open the *International* applet and specify any Time separator, including a space.

Date/Time: Time, in Seconds, Is Inaccurate. The Control Panel timer reads the system clock to keep track of the passing hours and minutes. The seconds segment does the best it can to keep up, but doesn't always make it. If timing is really critical, buy a stop watch.

Date/Time: Word-for-Windows Default Date/Time Format Does Not Match *International* Applet Settings. Although Word-for-Windows can display date and time listings in many formats (via the Date and Time... option on its own Insert Menu), the default format in a header or footer may be specified separately by the following lines in WIN.INI:

```
[Microsoft Word 2.0]
DateFormat=MMMM DD, YYYY     (example: August 27, 1993)
TimeFormat=HHmm              (example: 1130)
```

Settings such as these take precedence over the format specified in the *International* applet. To match the *International* format, either edit these lines or remove them.

Desktop: Screen-Saver Activates Too Soon, or Wrong Display Is Seen. If you set the *After Dark* screen-saver via its own applet icon (in Control Panel or elsewhere), and also set it or some other screen-saver via the *Desktop* applet, the screen-saver whose delay time is shortest will be activated first. Thus, if *After Dark* is configured in both locations, it will appear at whichever time interval is shortest. If the respective delay times and screen-savers are not the same, the one with the shortest delay time appears at the specified time, and the other does not show up at all. To keep confusion at a minimum, double-check the delay times of all screen-saver utilities.

Desktop: Screen-Saver Suspends DOS Print Job. If a DOS print job is not running as a background application, the print job may be suspended if the *After Dark* DOS screen-saver activates. Either disable the screen-saver, set a longer delay time, or periodically touch the mouse or a keyboard key.

Desktop: Title Bar Off Screen, Window Can't Be Moved. If *Granularity* is set high, it's possible to accidentally move a window so that its Title Bar is no longer visible; therefore, the complete window can't be moved back onto the Desktop. If this happens, follow the procedure described in *Control Panel Doesn't Open* above, which "cascades" the problem application back onto the screen, where its size and position can be readjusted as desired. If the problem frequently recurs, then reset granularity to a lower value.

Desktop: Wallpaper File Not Listed in File Box. You could have worse problems. The Wallpaper File: box lists only those bitmap files currently resident in the Windows directory. If your favorite file lies elsewhere, you'll need to type the complete path and filename into the box in order to access that file.

Desktop: Wallpaper Shows White Space between Tiles. If you use the *Paintbrush* applet to create your own custom bitmap file, then select the Wallpaper Tile option, there may be white space around each tile. If so, the *Paintbrush* image attributes were set to include a larger area than occupied by the bitmap itself. Therefore, the saved bitmap includes a certain amount of white space—probably to the right and beneath the area of interest. To get rid of it, reopen *Paintbrush,* reset the image attributes, and use the Edit Menu's Paste From... option to paste the original file into the smaller area. Once the fit is right, resave the image.

Desktop: Windows Are Blank when Toggling between Applications. If you cleared the Fast Switching check box in the Desktop dialog box (Figure 11.11), then toggling the Alt+Tab combination sequentially brings each background window to the foreground. At some video resolutions, the portion of that window that overlays the active window may appear empty. To see what's really there, release the Alt key.

Desktop: Password-Protected Screen-Saver Defeated by Local Reboot.   If a local reboot closes a password-protected screen-saver and restores the Windows Desktop (it shouldn't), check the indicated section of SYSTEM.INI for the following line:

```
[386Enh]
DebugLocalReboot=True
```

If this line is present, refer to the *Local Reboot Configuration* section of Chapter 4 for further details and performance tradeoffs.

Desktop: Valid Password Doesn't Work.   There is a bug in the password feature that prevents certain passwords from being recognized. When you type in your password, that word is stored in encrypted format in the [ScreenSaver] section of the CONTROL.INI file, as shown in this example:

```
Password="BkhE"
```

If the encrypted password begins and ends with quotation marks, as in this example, the quotation marks are ignored when you type in your password after the screen-saver is activated. As a result, it will be impossible to quit the screen-saver, since even your correctly entered password will not be recognized. The fix is to reboot the system and edit CONTROL.INI to remove the Password= line. Then reopen Windows and try your luck with some other password. Note that you must remove the line; you can't edit it (unless you're an encryption expert), nor can you change to a new password until the old one is physically removed.

386 Enhanced: Device Contention Does Not Show COM Ports.   In Windows 3.1, if the Device Contention area in the 386 Enhanced dialog box shows no COM ports, check the [386Enh] section for a device=*vcd line. This line is required for Windows 3.1, but not for Windows-for-Workgroups.

386 Enhanced: Memory Problems.   If a problem occurs shortly after clicking on the Virtual Memory... button, refer to Chapter 13 for assistance.

Keyboard: Characters Lost while Typing.   If you regularly lose characters while typing in a Windows application, add the following line to the indicated section of WIN.INI:

```
[windows]
TypeAhead=2047
```

Try a larger number if necessary.

Keyboard: Keyboard Locks Up. If the keyboard periodically locks up for no apparent reason, you may need to add (or change) the machine switch (/machine:) on the HIMEM.SYS line in CONFIG.SYS. Refer to *Windows Extended Memory Manager* section for an explanation of this switch. In this specific example, try switch settings of 11, 12, then 13.

Network Problems. Since most problems with network operations are usually encountered within the File Manager, refer to the *Troubleshooting* section of Chapter 6 for assistance in resolving them. However, a few problems that may show up when network hardware is first installed are briefly reviewed here.

Network: Interconnection Problems. In troubleshooting any network problem, don't overlook the obvious: the cables and connectors which link the computers. Figure 11.29 shows a typical Workgroups (or any other) network system linked by coaxial cable and BNC connectors. The first and last computers on such a network require a 50-ohm terminator which, if missing or poorly connected, is enough to bring down the entire system. Make sure that all terminators, BNC connectors, and cables are well connected, and that the BNC connector makes good connection with the adapter card in the computer. Given the usual back-of-the-computer layout, the conventional "T" connector is probably the worst choice. An alternative connector layout is shown in the figure, and others are also available. Try to find one that will cause the least amount of grief on your system(s).

If a connection problem can't be immediately localized, try a simple two-computer link. If that works, reconnect intermediate computers one at ·a time until the problem returns. If network size makes this impractical, then it's time to call the network administrator (unless you *are* the network administrator).

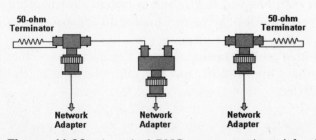

Figure 11.29 A typical BNC connector/coaxial cable link between three computers on a Windows-for-Workgroups network.

Network: New Drive Installation Problems. Before adding a new drive *x* to a local computer, disconnect the network drive (if any) that uses that drive letter. Otherwise, every time you open Windows-for-Workgroups, a *Cannot reconnect x:* message will be seen.

If you've discovered this interesting problem too late, don't bother opening File Manager to disconnect the remote drive *x:* It wasn't reconnected at startup, so it doesn't appear on the list of connected drives. However, there are a few ways to kill the message, as described here. Choose whichever one you like.

Erase the CONNECT.DAT File. The CONNECT.DAT file in the Windows directory contains, in encoded format, the name(s) of the network drive(s) that the local computer was connected to on the last session. If you erase the file, the problem will disappear along with all record of other connected drives. If that's no problem, this is the simplest way of clearing up the problem.

Edit the CONNECT.DAT File. If you want to fix the drive *x* problem yet retain information about other connected drives, you can edit the CONNECT.DAT file. To do so, exit Windows and type the following line at the DOS prompt:

NET USE *x:* /DELETE   (where *x* is the connected drive you wish to delete)

Disregard the following error message:

Error 3: The specified path was not found.

For more information about this procedure, type NET USE /? at the DOS prompt. The "help" screen for the /DELETE option is the next best thing to incomprehensible, but some of the other information may be useful.

Temporarily Disable the New Local Drive x. Edit your CONFIG.SYS and/or AUTOEXEC.BAT file to temporarily disable the new local drive. Then reopen Windows, open File Manager's Disk Menu, select the Disconnect Network Drive... option and disconnect drive *x*. Then exit Windows, reenable the new local drive, and the message should not reappear.

Ports: Modem Dialing/Connection Problems. If your system reboots, or fails to complete a connection after dialing, it's possible that another I/O port in the system is assigned to the same COM port as the modem. If so, reconfigure it to some other port. If necessary, remove the suspect device to see if doing so clears up the problem.

Mouse and Mouse Applet Troubleshooting

If you need to expand a fresh copy of any file on a *Microsoft Mouse* distribution diskette, don't forget to use the expand utility (EXPAND.EXE) on that diskette, not the one in the DOS or Windows directory. The version 8.20 and 9.0 utilities are identical (except for file creation date) and either may be used. Refer to the *File Expansion Utilities* section of Chapter 4 if you need assistance.

General Mouse Troubleshooting. If the source of a mouse problem is uncertain, it's not a bad idea to exit Windows and try using the mouse within some DOS application known to support mouse operations. As a convenient troubleshooting procedure, load the DOS Edit utility (EDIT.COM) and see if the mouse pointer shows up and is functional. If not, check your startup files for one (not all!) of the following lines in CONFIG.SYS:

    device=C:\DOS\MOUSE.SYS

or, in AUTOEXEC.BAT, one of the following (or similar):

    C:\MOUSE\MOUSE.COM   (your path may differ)
    C:\MOUSE\MOUSE.EXE   (Microsoft Mouse version 9.0: note EXE extension)
    loadhigh C:\MOUSE\MOUSE

If no such line is seen, then find the location of your mouse software, insert the appropriate line in CONFIG.SYS or AUTOEXEC.BAT, and reboot the system. At the DOS prompt, type **MEM /c** and verify that the mouse software is loaded. If not, then reboot the system and watch for an error message as the mouse driver is loaded.

If a *Microsoft Mouse Not Found* message appears, then refer to the *Verify Mouse Port Connection* section above for configuration suggestions. However, if you see a memory-related message, or no message at all, then refer to Chapter 13 for memory-related troubleshooting assistance.

Troubleshooting Checklist. Once all this is working, the mouse should be functional within any DOS application that supports it. If not, then review the items which follow. If any item on the checklist resolves the problem, then contact the appropriate manufacturer to see if an upgrade is available.

Mouse Check. It's always possible that the mouse itself is defective. If possible, try using the mouse on another system whose mouse is operational, and/or try that mouse on your system.

Mouse Driver. Make sure your system does not have multiple DOS mouse drivers in various directories listed in your PATH statement. To double-check, log onto the root directory and type DIR MOUSE.* /s at the DOS prompt. If multiple files are found, retain the one that should be used (check your startup file), and delete the others. Or, move them into a directory that is *not* listed in your PATH statement, or rename them.

To minimize potential software conflicts, both the DOS and Windows mouse drivers should come from the same source. If a mouse problem within Windows cannot otherwise be resolved, temporarily disable the DOS mouse driver in your startup files, reboot, and retry the Windows operation. If the trouble is gone, then contact the mouse software supplier to see if a workaround or upgrade is available.

Port Check. Windows looks for a mouse at the locations listed in Table 11.11a, which are scanned in the order given in the table. If a mouse is connected to a COM port on a system with an unused PS/2 port, Windows may mistakenly "find" a mouse on that port. If so, the pointer appears on screen, but it can't be moved. Either disable the PS/2 port (contact the computer manufacturer if necessary), or move the mouse to that port.

If your mouse is connected to COM1 and some other device is connected to COM2, try swapping the devices so that Windows correctly finds the mouse when it checks COM2.

If you'd rather not change your system setup, you can edit the MOUSE.INI file to let Windows know where the mouse is. Refer to the listings in Table 11.11b and insert or edit the MouseType= line as required.

If your system has only one serial port, and that port is used by the mouse, it must be configured at COM1. If it is designated COM2, the mouse probably won't work. In addition, serial mouse performance is not supported on COM 3 or 4.

IRQ Check. Make sure the IRQ setting for the port is correct, as listed in Table 11.11a.

Video Driver. If you are using a third-party video driver, try using the Microsoft VGA or SVGA driver. If that works, it's time to call the manufacturer of the other driver to see if an update is available.

Third-Party Hardware/Software. If possible, try installing a mouse that is known to be compatible with a Microsoft mouse driver.

INI File Check. Verify that the mouse.drv=mouse.drv line in the [boot] section of SYSTEM.INI is correct, including the path (if any is listed). In addition, make sure there is only one MOUSE.INI file and that it is located in the directory cited on the following line in your AUTOEXEC.BAT file:

set MOUSE=C:\MOUSE　　(*or elsewhere, depending on your system configuration*)

If this line does not exist, then your MOUSE.INI file should be in the Windows directory.

Operating Mode Check. Open Windows in standard mode and try the mouse. If it works, then open Windows in enhanced mode by tying WIN /d:X at the DOS prompt. If the mouse works now, then there is a memory conflict problem with the DOS mouse driver. Try forcing that driver to load in conventional memory, or temporarily disable it. If either action cures the problem, then try to resolve the memory conflict. Refer to Chapter 13 for assistance with memory matters if necessary.

Group Window Can't Be Moved. If granularity is set too high, it's possible that a group window cannot be moved, even though its Title Bar remains onscreen. The fix is to lower the granularity setting until the problem goes away.

Double-Click Has No Effect (Workgroups). If a double-click does nothing, it's possible that the value on the DoubleClickHeight= and/or DoubleClickWidth= line is set too low, and mouse pointer movement exceeds that value between clicks. For example, if either value is set to zero, double-clicking is disabled.

Memory Error Messages. If an error message appears when you open Windows immediately after installing new third-party mouse software, there is probably a conflict between the DOS and Windows mouse drivers. Or, there may be a set MOUSE= line in your AUTOEXEC.BAT file that is no longer valid. To resolve the problem, make sure the DOS and Windows mouse drivers are from the same third-party source and edit or disable the set MOUSE= line as required. If a DOS driver is not available, then temporarily disable the existing DOS mouse driver and try to open Windows. If this is successful, then there definitely was a conflict between the two drivers. Contact the supplier of the Windows driver to see if a compatible DOS driver is available, or if there is a known work-around solution.

Mouse Problem in DOS Window. The first order of business is to make sure the application running in the DOS window supports mouse operations. If in doubt about this, run some application known to support a mouse (DOS *Edit* or *Norton Utilities,* for example). If either works with the mouse, then the problem is that the former application does not support mouse operations within Windows. You may want to close Windows and try running the same DOS application again. In at least a few cases, a DOS application that does support mouse operations in DOS will not offer that support within a DOS window. Once you know what all the variables are, contact the manufacturer to see if an upgrade is available, or switch to a Windows version of the software if there is one.

If none of the above resolves your mouse problem, and the mouse does function properly within Windows itself, then refer to the *Mouse Trouble-shooting* section of Chapter 7 for additional assistance.

Pointer Button (8.20) or Functions (9.0) Disabled (grayed). In either case, there should have been an error message as you opened the *Mouse* applet. The most likely problem is that the POINTER.EXE or POINTER.DLL file is missing or corrupt. If so, other mouse functions are still available. In case of doubt, expand fresh copies of each into the directory in which your mouse software is located.

Pointer Cannot Be Removed from Desktop. Running Windows without a mouse is almost like running a car without gas: You can still get from here to there, but it's not easy. Nevertheless, if you delete all mouse references in your INI files, then the next time you open Windows you'll discover. . . a mouse. The only way to permanently kill it is to call in an exterminator: the special no-mouse driver. Refer to *Configure Windows for No Mouse* in the *Mouse Applet* section for more details.

Pointer Missing after Switching to/from DOS Window. If the mouse pointer gets lost when switching between Windows and DOS applications, open the *386 Enhanced* applet, highlight the mouse's COM port, then click on the Never Warn radio button.

Pointer Movement Problem (too fast, too slow, erratic, etc.). If the mouse is working, but it's difficult to place the pointer where you want it because it jumps from one location to another, the pointer speed probably needs adjustment. Refer to *Pointer Speed* above for assistance if needed.

Pointer Movement Is Erratic (PS/2 port only). If your mouse seems to be conducting its own Windows session, there may be a synchronization problem between mouse and microprocessor. If so, the mouse pointer may wander about the screen all by itself or react unpredictably if you try to take control. To verify a sync problem, test the mouse on a serial port. If the mouse behaves itself, then you know what the problem is and mouse software version 8.10 or greater may resolve it. However, if you're already using version 8.20 or 9.0, then there may be some other PS/2 port problem. If you can't resolve it, then you may have to stick with the COM port solution.

Wrong Mouse Icon in Control Panel. If you've installed the *Microsoft Mouse* version 8.20 or 9.0 software, or some other software that comes with its own distinctive icon, that icon should show up in the Control Panel in place of the Windows mouse icon shown in Figure 11.22a. If it doesn't, the set MOUSE= line (if any) in AUTOEXEC.BAT and the mouse.drv= line in the [boot] section of SYSTEM.INI are probably pointing in the wrong direction. Edit one or both to list the correct location for the desired software, reboot and have another look. This time Control Panel should show the correct icon.

Error Messages

If there's a problem with one of the applets described in this chapter, it probably affects the general appearance of the Desktop and may not be accompanied by an error message. However, there are a few error messages associated with general Control Panel operations, and no shortage of them if a mouse or network is involved. Mouse and network messages are therefore found in separate sections following this one. Also, check Chapter 6 for additional network error messages that may show up during File Manager operations.

Application Error: Control caused a General Protection Fault in module MAIN.CPL [*or other*] at *xxxx:yyyy*. This one will take a bit of detective work to figure out. The first thing is to note which Control Panel applet you tried to access when the message appeared. See what happens if you open other Control Panel applets. If the error is confined to one applet, then perhaps some file associated with that applet is defective. For example, if you tried to open the *Desktop* applet, a screen-saver file (*filename*.SCR) may be corrupt. The applet looks at all the SCR files, even if you're not using one. Move all of them out of the Windows directory into a temporary location and try again to open the *Desktop* applet. If it works now, then one of the SCR files is indeed defective. Put any two of them back and try again. If the problem returns, remove one of them. If that takes care of it, then you know who the culprit is. And if it doesn't, you *still* know who's guilty. However, if these two files are both OK, then put back two more. Keep at it until you isolate and exterminate the faulty file. Then expand a fresh copy of that file from the distribution diskettes.

Apply the same general procedure to any other applet that triggers the error message. Needless to say, if the fault is in some module (file) other than MAIN.CPL, that information may help localize the source of the problem.

Control Panel: Not enough memory available for this task. Quit one or more applications to increase available memory, and then try again.   If this message appears as you select a *Desktop Applet* screen-saver, that BMP file is either corrupted or not a valid bitmap file. To verify this, select some other file instead. Of course, it's always possible that there really isn't enough memory available. If so, then follow the advice given in the message.

Control Panel cannot display the International dialog box. The SETUP.INF and CONTROL.INF files may be damaged or may not be in the SYSTEM directory. Copy the original files on Windows Disk 1 to your SYSTEM directory.   The *International* applet needs to read these files as it opens. If either is missing from the System directory, copy a fresh version from the distribution diskette. If neither is missing, then one of them is probably corrupt. If you're not sure which one is bad, copy fresh versions of both. Neither file is compressed, so a simple copy operation is all that's needed. And despite what the message says, only SETUP.INF is on diskette 1. Refer to Appendix A for the location of the CONTROL.INF file.

General Protection Fault in WIN87EM.DLL (*with math coprocessor installed*).   If the *After Dark* screen-saver is installed, try disabling it. If that cures the problem, refer to *Intel 1387 Math coprocessor installed* in Chapter 4's *Troubleshooting* section for additional assistance.

Mouse and Mouse Applet

This section lists some of the error messages that may show up when the *Mouse* applet or the mouse itself is in trouble.

Cannot find file 'C:\(*path*)\POINTER.EXE' specified in [win.ini/startup group] (or one of its components). Check to insure the path and filename are correct and that all required libraries are available. If Microsoft Mouse version 8.20 or 9.0 software is installed, this message appears if the cited file is missing. In the former version, the Mouse dialog box's Pointer... button (Figure 11.23b) is disabled, but all other options are still available. In the latter, all options are disabled, with the exception of the buttons on the right-hand side of the dialog box (Figure 11.24b). In either case, check the load= line in WIN.INI, or the Properties dialog box if the mouse is loaded via the StartUp Group. Then expand a fresh copy of POINTER.EX_ into the specified directory (presumably, C:\MOUSE).

Changes have been written to your MOUSE.INI file. You MUST restart your computer for changes to take effect. Chances are, the message is erroneous. If you type mouse /f at the DOS prompt and the mouse driver loads successfully, the message appears if you type the same command a second time. If so, just ignore it. Otherwise, reboot or the mouse and/or entire system may lock up.

Memory Error: (*Any memory error message immediately after installing Logitech mouse software***).** If a memory error message shows up when Windows restarts after installing third-party mouse software, refer to *Memory Error Messages* in the *Mouse Troubleshooting* section above for assistance.

Microsoft Mouse not found, try another 9 or 25 pin serial port and/or check for interrupt conflicts with other peripherals. Type Mouse /f to check all ports (9.0). If this message is seen during system startup or later on when you type mouse /f, then either the mouse is connected to a PS/2 port, or it was not detected on COM1 or COM2. Take one of the following actions, as appropriate.

Mouse Connected to PS/2 Port. Reconnect the mouse to COM1 or COM2 and try again. If you see the *Serial Mouse enabled on COM*x: message described in the *Verify Mouse Port Configuration* section earlier in the chapter, then there is something wrong with your PS/2 port. If cable-swapping doesn't resolve the problem, then the port itself is probably defective.

Mouse Connected to COM1 or COM2 Port. Try the other COM port or the PS/2 port. If nothing works, then the mouse or its cable is probably defective. If possible, try another mouse and/or cable, or try the same mouse/cable combination on another computer. Once you've located the defective component, repair or replace it.

Mouse Driver for MS-DOS cannot be loaded from an MS-DOS session within Windows. Exit Windows to load the mouse driver for MS-DOS.   You'll see this message if you try to load a DOS mouse driver from within a DOS window. Even if you only need the mouse within one DOS window, you need to load it before opening Windows.

Mouse is not installed. Run Windows Setup to install a mouse.   If the no-mouse driver (nomouse.drv) is specified in SYSTEM.INI, this message appears if you double-click on the *Mouse* icon. Install the required driver and try again.

Orientation (9.00 only): To set the orientation for your mouse properly, move the mouse in as straight a line as possible. Please try again.   In order to set mouse orientation, the Mouse Manager has to know which way is up. You need to move the mouse in a straight line until the onscreen arrow touches the compass. This message appears if you move the mouse in more than one direction.

Unable to access Pointer options (8.20, 9.0).   If this message appears as the *Mouse* applet opens, the POINTER.EXE file is probably missing. When you click on the OK button, the dialog box should appear, but the Pointer... button (8.20) or pointer options (9.0) will be disabled.

Network Applet

The error messages listed here are confined to problems that usually show up when using the Control Panel's *Network* applet. For network-related problems encountered via the File Manager, refer to Chapter 6 instead.

Cannot find NETWORK.DRV.   Check the [boot] section of SYSTEM.INI for a network.drv=*filename*.drv line. Either the filename or the line itself is missing. If you are not using a network, the line must still appear in SYSTEM.INI, with nothing following the equal sign.

Cannot reconnect *x:* to \\(*remote computer*)\(*directory*) because *x:* is already being used by your computer.   This message is seen when Windows opens, if a new drive *x* has been added to the local computer since the last session, and that same drive letter was previously assigned to a network (remote) drive. To get rid of the message, refer to *New Drive Installation Problems* in the *Network Troubleshooting* section.

Device Conflict on LPT*x*. If a network interface card is connected to a parallel port also used for local printing, Windows may display this message because it thinks the local printer and the network are both trying to use the port. If you do not use the port for local printing, then disable the following line in SYSTEM.INI:

```
[386Enh]
device=VPD.386
```

Error occurred while reconnecting LPT1: to \\(*computer name*)\(*printer name*) ON (*computer name*): The specified computer is not receiving requests. [SYS0051]. Do you want to continue restoring connections? At the moment when you tried to reconnect the specified device, the remote computer may have been busy doing something that prevented it from responding properly. Make a note of the reconnection error and retry the operation later on.

Network Driver: The Windows for Workgroups network driver was not loaded. Some of the options in the Network Settings dialog box will not be available. This message is seen if there are no network settings in SYSTEM.INI.

VNETSUP: The following error occurred while loading the device VNETSUP: Error 6101: The string specified by the COMPUTERNAME keyword in the [NETWORK] section of the SYSTEM.INI file was not found. Actually, it's "ComputerName=" and it's unlikely to be the real problem. Click on the OK button, open the Control Panel, and click on the *Network* icon. Chances are, the dialog box entries will be blank, indicating a missing [Network] section. If so, re-enter the required information, then click on the Logon button and do the same. Repeat for the Password button, if desired. The data is written into the [Network] section, but does not take effect until you restart Windows. As you exit the dialog box, click on the Restart Computer or Continue button as desired.

VNETSUP: Network features are not available because the VNETSUP.386 driver did not load. The NETWORK= value in SYSTEM.INI file may be incorrect. Run Setup again to configure your network properly. The Windows for Workgroups network driver was unable to load. Click on the OK button, then check the [386Enh] section of SYSTEM.INI for the following line:

```
network=vnetbios.386, vnetsup.386, vredir.386, vwc.386, vserver.386, vbrowse.386
```

Make sure that VNETSUP.386 is listed, and that it and the other files are available. If in doubt, expand fresh copies and try again, or just rerun Setup as suggested.

VSERVER: The file server encountered a critical error and terminated. Save any unsaved information, quit any running applications, and then restart Windows. Press any key to continue. If this message shows up during routine network operations, there may be a problem with the physical link between computers. Before restarting Windows, check all connections carefully. If the problem persists, turn off the power and check the seating of each network card and the integrity of the cable connections. If possible, try to isolate the problem to a specific computer.

Control Panel: Part II

The Control Panel applets described in this chapter are those used to install multimedia drivers and otherwise meddle with Windows' audio/video capabilities. In addition, the chapter has a look at two Windows applets frequently used in conjunction with the Control Panel applets: These are the *Media Player* and *Sound Recorder*. If nothing else, you can use one or both of them to make sure your a/v system is properly configured.

Since a CD-ROM drive is needed on the video side of audio/video, the MS-DOS CD-ROM extensions driver—better known as MSCDEX.EXE—is also described here.

A Few Definitions

A handful of new terms encountered in this chapter are briefly described here.

MCI: Media Control Interface. The initials are frequently encountered in various INI files. For example, there is an [mci] section in SYSTEM.INI and assorted [MCI] citations in the [drivers.desc] section of CONTROL.INI. The interface is a command set that provides additional support required by multimedia devices and their associated media files. Although not further described here, this definition is included since the initials do show up with some regularity whenever multimedia drivers are configured.

Media File. The term is used here as a catch-all descriptor for any file that can be played back via the *Media Player* and *Sound Recorder* applets, or from a CD-ROM disc.

MIDI: Musical Instrument Digital Interface. The acronym refers to the interface standard that allows one music synthesizer to talk to another, and also lets the PC in on the conversation. The *Standard MIDI Files 1.0* document describes MIDI file specifications, including the binary data stream in the file. The Standard is available from the International MIDI Association in Los Angeles, California.

MSCDEX: Microsoft Compact Disc Extensions. Every drive has its driver, except CD-ROM which needs two of them. Among other things, the directory structure on a CD-ROM disc differs from that on the conventional computer diskette or hard drive; this additional driver (MSCDEX.EXE) handles the necessary translation chores. For more information, refer to the *MSCDEX* section later in the chapter.

Wavefile and Waveform Audio (*filename*.WAV). As a descriptor of digital audio, one of these terms is bad and the other worse. If there is anything a digital signal is *not,* it is a "waveform." An analog audio signal has wavelength, waveform, and all the other characteristics of an audio wave. All of that gets tossed out when an A/D (analog-to-digital) converter encodes the signal. Nevertheless, both terms are used to identify a file in which an audio signal is stored in digital format. Rather than buck the bitstream, this chapter bows to Microspeak and goes along with this usage.

Drivers Applet

During the initial Windows setup procedure, a diverse assortment of drivers is installed in the System directory to provide the required support for your video system, keyboard, mouse, and network (if any). If you subsequently revise any of these system components, the appropriate new drivers are installed, either via the *Windows Setup* applet or at the DOS prompt if you run Setup after exiting Windows.

Sooner or later most users will need to replace one or more of these drivers, if only to switch from one video resolution to another; it would seem logical to use the *Drivers* applet to perform this task. Logic, however, has no place here: The applet is used *only* to install or remove device drivers that support the following applications:

Audio CD (compact disc), MIDI, and other digital audio devices
Video Videodiscs, AVI, and other video, but not drivers for your video adapter
Multimedia Combination audio/video on CD-ROM discs

If you need to install, remove, or reconfigure drivers in any of these categories, then the *Drivers* applet is the place to do it.

The Drivers Dialog Box

Figure 12.1a shows the Drivers dialog box as it appears immediately after
the initial Windows setup procedure has concluded. Windows searches the
[mci] and [drivers] sections of SYSTEM.INI for files with a DRV extension.
Then, it finds the corresponding driver description in the [drivers.desc]
section of CONTROL.INI and displays that information in the Installed
Drivers list. Table 12.1 summarizes the information found in both INI files.
To revise the list, or configure a driver that is already installed, click on
the appropriate button and refer to one of the following sections.

Add a New Driver. To add a new driver to the Installed Drivers list, click
on the Add... button to open the Add dialog box shown in Figure 12.1b.

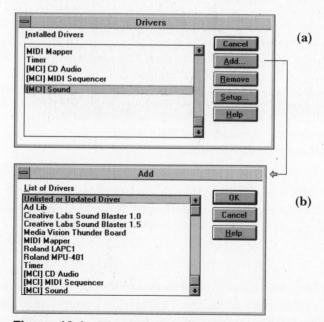

Figure 12.1 The Drivers dialog box, showing (a) drivers installed during Windows Setup. (b) The Add (drivers) dialog box shows the drivers supplied with
Windows.

TABLE 12.1   Drivers Applet: Typical List of Installed Drivers

SYSTEM.INI		CONTROL.INI	Description*	Notes
[mci]		**[drivers.desc]**		
AVIVideo	= mciavi.drv	mciavi.drv	= [MCI] Microsoft Video for Windows	1
CDAudio	= mcicda.drv	mcicda.drv	= [MCI] CD Audio	2
Mixer	= mcimixer.drv	mcimixer.drv	= [MCI] Mixer Control	3
Sequencer	= mciseq.drv	mcisseq.drv	= [MCI] MIDI Sequencer	4
WaveAudio	= mciwave.drv	mciwave.drv	= [MCI] Sound	4
[drivers]				
Aux	= mvproaud.drv	(*see mvproaud.drv*)		
MIDI	= opl3.drv	opl3.drv	= Voyetra OPL-3 FM Driver	3
MIDI*x*†	= mvproad.drv	mvproaud.drv	= Media Vis. Pro Audio/CDPC Wave/MIDI/Aux	3
MIDI*x*†	= msadlib.drv	msadlib.drv	= Ad Lib	5
MidiMapper	= midimap.drv	midimap.drv	= MIDI Mapper	4
Mixer	= mvmixer.drv	mvmixer.drv	= Media Vision Pro Audio/CDPC Mixer	3
Timer	= timer.drv	timer.drv	= Timer	4
VIDC.MSVC	= msvidc.drv	msvidc.drv	= Microsoft Video 1 Compressor	1
VIDC.RT21	= indeo.drv	indeo.drv	= Intel Indeo (TM) Video Driver	1
Wave	= mvproaud.drv	(*see mvproaud.drv*)		
Wave	= tlwave.drv	tlwave.drv	= Media Vision Thunder & Lightning Wave 1.0	5
Wave	= speaker.drv	speaker.drv	= Sound Driver for PC-Speaker	6

* Description appears in *Installed Drivers* box in Drivers dialog box (see Figure 12.1).
† In MIDI*x*, value of *x* increments by 1 for each additional MIDI driver.

Notes: Driver added to list if following software is installed:

1. Microsoft *Video for Windows*
2. Initial Windows setup, if MSCDEX is installed
3. Media Vision *Pro Audio Spectrum PAS-16*
4. Initial Windows setup
5. Media Vision *Thunder & Lightning*
6. Downloaded driver (see text; *Internal PC Speaker*)

The List of Drivers displays descriptions of drivers supplied on the Windows distribution diskettes, and is read from the [Installable.Drivers] section of SETUP.INF file. The data in that section of the file is listed in Table 12.2. Highlight the desired driver, click on the OK button, and insert the distribution diskette specified in the onscreen prompt.

TABLE 12.2   Drivers Supplied with Windows*

Driver	Filename	VxD	Parameter §
Ad Lib	MSADLIB.DRV	VADLIBD.386	
Creative Labs Sound Blaster 1.0	SNDBLST.DRV	VSBD.386	msadlib
Creative Labs Sound Blaster 1.5	SNDBLST2.DRV	VSBD.386	msadlib
[MCI] CD Audio†	MCICADA.DRV		
[MCI] MIDI Sequencer‡	MCISEQ.DRV		
[MCI] Sound‡	MCIWAVE.DRV		4
Media Vision Thunder Board	SNDBLST2.DRV	VSBD.386	
MIDI Mapper‡	MIDIMAP.DRV		
Roland LAPCI	MPU401.DRV		
Roland MPU_401	MPU401.DRV		
Timer‡	TIMER.DRV	VTDAPI.386	

* Data taken from [Installable.Drivers] section of SETUP.INF file.

§ Install driver, then click on *Setup* button to display parameter listed here.

† Installed during initial Windows setup procedure, if MSCDEX is installed.

‡ Installed during initial Windows setup procedure.

Add Unlisted/Updated Driver. In many cases, one or more new drivers automatically appear in the Installed Drivers list as various third-party multimedia software packages are installed. However, if you need to install a new or updated driver not accompanied by its own installation procedure, select Unlisted or Updated Driver at the top of the List of Drivers. At the prompt, type in the drive letter and path where the driver and its accompanying OEMSETUP.INF file are located, then click on the OK button to complete the installation. When you're done, the new driver should be included in the Installed Drivers list.

Remove a Driver. To remove any driver from the Installed Drivers list, highlight its name and click on the Remove button. A potentially confusing *your system may not work properly* message appears, but your system *will* operate properly—except for whatever it is you're about to remove. If you didn't realize that you can't operate a driver that isn't installed, then click on the No button and think about it. Otherwise, read the next paragraph, then click on the Yes button to delete the driver from the list.

The just-removed driver is not really removed. Its name is purged from the list, and the appropriate lines in SYSTEM.INI and CONTROL.INI are deleted, but the driver itself still lurks in the System directory. If you're sure you won't want to reinstall it later on, delete it. If necessary, refer to the CONTROL.INI column in Table 12.1. Find the *driver description* corresponding to that in the Installed Drivers list and note the corresponding filename for the driver. Then go find it in the System directory and delete it. If you can't find the information you need in the Table, then refer instead to your own CONTROL.INI file.

Configure (Setup) a Driver.   If an installed driver can (or must) be configured to optimize its performance, the Setup... button in the Drivers dialog box is enabled. For configuration information about typical audio/video drivers, refer to the *Driver Configuration Procedures* section below.

Driver Installation Record in SYSTEM.INI

During the regular Windows installation, the setup procedure installs the device drivers listed here (whether you need them or not); these are subsequently accessed via the *Drivers* applet, along with any similar drivers installed later on.

[MCI] CD Audio	*(only if MSCDEX.EXE is installed)*
[MCI] MIDI Sequencer	MIDI Mapper
[MCI] Sound	Timer

These and other multimedia drivers are installed in two sections of the SYSTEM.INI file, the first of which lists MCI drivers, while the second lists the others. Typical examples are shown here. Note that some driver lines may show a parameter specific to that driver.

```
[boot]
sound.drv=mmsound.drv

[mci]
CDAudio=mcicda.drv       4          (buffer space, specified in seconds)
Sequencer=mciseq.drv
Videodisc=mcipionr.drv   COM1       (COM port for videodisc player)
WaveAudio=mciwave.drv    7          (buffer space, specified in seconds)

[drivers]
timer=timer.drv
MidiMapper=midimap.drv
```

Configuration information specific to selected Windows drivers is presented in the *Driver Configuration Procedures* section which follows.

Virtual Device Driver.   In addition to the drivers specified above, a virtual device driver may be required for enhanced-mode operations. If so, the driver will be found in the System directory, and listed in SYSTEM.INI as shown for these typical examples:

```
[386Enh]
device=vtdapi.386        Timer
device=vadlibd.386       Ad Lib
device=vpasd.386         Media Vision
device=vsbd.386          SoundBlaster
```

Driver Configuration Procedures

This section describes configuration procedures for a few of the drivers that may be installed via the *Drivers* applet.

Driver File Review

As each device requiring a driver is installed, the appropriate driver is copied into the System directory, and one or more additional files may also be transferred to your system. Unless you write elegant notes to yourself every time you install something, sooner or later you'll wind up with a vast collection of driver files whose names may mean nothing whatsoever to you. If it ever becomes necessary to try to figure out who goes with what, you might review the contents of the various OEM setup files in your System directory, or an OEMSETUP.INF may be found on the distribution diskettes accompanying the installed device.

Table 12.3 shows the contents of the [Installable.drivers] section of typical INF files. For each entry, the first item after the equal sign is the name of the device driver, while the fourth item (if there is one) is the name of a virtual device driver associated with the device. Additional sections may follow, each with a bracketed name that matches one of the entries in the [Installable.drivers] section. If such a section appears for the device you installed, then the files listed there are also required for its operation.

In the event of driver-related trouble, the various OEM.INF files may help you track down the names of every file associated with a troublesome device.

CD Audio

If a CD-ROM drive with CD audio playback capability is installed, the *Drivers* applet's Installed Drivers list should show an [MCI] CD Audio entry. If not, click on the Add... button, highlight this entry, and click on the OK button. At the conclusion of the installation the following message appears:

```
Redbook CD Audio Configuration
One CDROM drive was detected. Installation is complete.
```

TABLE 12.3   Installable Driver Information in OEMSETUP.INF Files*

Filename [†] VxD(s) [†]	Type(s) Def. Parameters	Description (*unspecified*)

[Installable.Drivers]

	Filename [†] / VxD(s) [†]	Type(s) / Def. Parameters	Description (*unspecified*)
adlib [‡]	= 3:adlib.drv, 4:vadlibd.386,	"MIDI",	"Ad Lib",
adlib	= 1:msadlib.drv, "1:vadlibd.386",	"MIDI", ___,	"T & L FM Synthesis (MS/Adlib)", ___,
lapc1 [‡]	= 3:mpu401.drv, ___,	"MIDI",	"Roland MPU401",
mvproauda	= 1:mvproaud.drv, "1:vpasd.386",	"Wave,MIDI,Aux", ___,	"Media Vision Pro Audio/CDPC Wave/MIDI/Aux", "opl3, mvmixer,mixermci"
mvproaudb	= 1:mvproaud.drv, "1:vpasd.386",	"Wave,MIDI,Aux", ___,	"Media Vision Pro Audio (Original) Wave/MIDI/Aux", "opl3,mvmixer,mixermci"
mixermci	= 1:mcimixer.drv, ___,	"Mixer",	"[MCI] Media Vision Mixer Control",
mvmixer	= 1:mvmixer.drv, ___, ___, mvmixer	"Mixer",	"Media Vision Pro Audio/CDPC Mixer",
mpu401	= 1:mpu401.drv, ___,	"MIDI1",	"Roland MPU-401 MIDI I/O Driver",
opl3	= 1:opl3.drv, ___,	"MIDI",	"Voyetra/Media Vision OPL3 Stereo FM Driver",
sbwave	= 1:sbwave.drv, ___,	"Wave", ___,	"Media Vision Pro Audio/CDPC SndBlaster Wave", "mvmixer,mixermci"
timer [‡]	= 4:timer.drv, 4:vtdapi.386,	"Timer",	"Timer",
tlwave	= 1:tlwave.drv, "1:vtbd.386",	"Wave", ___,	"T & L Waveform (SndBlaster)", ___,
wave	= 5:mciwave.drv, ___,	"WaveAudio", 4	"[MCI] Sound",

Additional sections may list other files required for setup.

[mvproauda]	[mvproaudb]	[mixermci]	[opl3]
1:mmmixer.dll	1:mmmixer.dll	1:mmmixer.dll	1:mmmixer.dll
1:promix.exe	1:promix.exe		1:midimap.cfg
1:midimap.cfg	1:midimap.cfg		
	1:mvfm.drv		

---

* Information on single line in INF file. Spaces added for clarity. Underline segments indicate blank entry.

[†] 1: - 5: indicate distribution diskette numbers.

[‡] From Windows SETUP.INF file.

Redbook has nothing to do with a popular magazine. Instead, it's a reference to the color of the CD Audio standard document, a phrase popularly used to distinguish this publication from other CD standards.

CD-ROM Discs and MSCDEX

In order to play any CD-ROM or audio compact disc, you'll need to install the MSCDEX.EXE file, which is loaded via your CONFIG.SYS file. If your excursion into multimedia drivers includes anything pertaining to a CD-ROM system, you'll need to have it installed before doing much else. And since MSCDEX is not your standard driver either, this section briefly reviews some of its configuration details.

CD-ROM configuration requires two drivers: a hardware driver in CONFIG.SYS and the CD-ROM Extensions driver in AUTOEXEC.BAT, as described here.

CONFIG.SYS: The CD-ROM Driver. The CD-ROM hardware driver is loaded via CONFIG.SYS, as shown in this typical example, which assumes the driver is located in a DRIVERS directory.

    device=C:\DRIVERS\TSLCDR.SYS   /D:*signature* (*other switches, as required*)

The /D switch is described in the following section, while the other switches (if any) depend on the specific driver. Refer to the appropriate *User's Guide* (if any) for information about these switches.

To verify that the device driver loads properly, look for the following message (or similar) as the driver loads.

```
TSLCD: Trantor CDROM Driver, version 1.46
Copyright (C) 1989-1992, Trantor Systems, Ltd.
-- For the Media Vision Pro Audio Spectrum --
SCSI host adapter detected at address 388h.
Device 1, Read-Only Optical Device (Removable media)
1 CD ROM Drive found.
```

AUTOEXEC.BAT: The CD-ROM Extensions. The following command line in AUTOEXEC.BAT loads the CD-ROM Extensions:

    C:\DOS\MSCDEX.EXE /D:*signature* /E /K /L:*X*   /M:*xxx* /S /V

The /D switch shown on the command line is critical, while the others are optional. Each switch is briefly described here.

/D:signature. The /D switch appears twice: once in CONFIG.SYS and again here in AUTOEXEC.BAT. The word following the switch can be any convenient

identifier. Since its purpose is to establish a link between MSCDEX and the CD-ROM driver in the CONFIG.SYS file, the same word must appear in both locations.

Multi-Drive Configuration. Append another /D switch to the command line for each additional CD-ROM driver loaded in the CONFIG.SYS file, using some other distinctive name at both locations. In other words, each device driver gets its own line in CONFIG.SYS, but there is only one MSCDEX line in AUTOEXEC.BAT.

/E. This switch instructs MSCDEX to use expanded memory and should be used only if you have expanded memory installed and want to use it for this application.

/K. If you can read this line, you may not need this switch. It instructs DOS to read CD-ROM volumes encoded in Kanji (Japanese) characters.

/L:X. Use this switch if you want to specify the drive letter for the first CD-ROM drive. You may want to do so on a network system, if the drive letter shifts from one letter to another because of varying network drive connections.

/M:xxx. This switch specifies the number of 2 Kbyte sector buffers reserved for CD-ROM usage. The default is 10, for 20 Kbytes (20,480 bytes).

/S. If you're using the CD-ROM drive with Windows-for-Workgroups or MS-NET, use the /S switch to support sharing the drive across the network. The switch was probably inserted during network installation, if a valid MSCDEX line was already in place.

/V. Add this switch if you'd like to coax MSCDEX into its verbose mode, in which a detailed report is displayed during system bootup, such as the example shown here for a one-drive configuration.

```
MSCDEX Version 2.22
Copyright (C) Microsoft Corp. 1986-1993. All rights reserved.
        Drive X: = Driver signature unit 0
xxxxxx bytes free memory
xxxx    bytes expanded memory
xxxxx  bytes CODE
```

```
xxxx    bytes static DATA
xxxxx   bytes dynamic DATA
xxxxx   bytes used
```

MSCDEX Configuration Considerations. During an initial configuration session, you may want to make sure that MSCDEX is loaded into conventional (not upper) memory, and that it is really there after the system is powered on. Due to some memory-management quirks, the system boot procedure may think MSCDEX requires less loading space than it actually needs. Then, DOS goes through the motions of loading it, reports that it is in fact loaded, but when you look for it, it isn't there. To verify that all's well, type MEM /c at the DOS prompt and look for the MSCDEX and TSLCDR (or other driver) entries in the list of modules. If either is missing, then troubleshoot the cause before trying to get anything else to work. Refer to Chapter 13 for assistance with general memory management if needed.

Batch File Loading Sequence. If Windows-for-Workgroups or other network software is loaded in your AUTOEXEC.BAT file, the MSCDEX command line should appear *after* the network-related lines.

MSCDEX Support in SYSTEM.INI. If MSCDEX was installed prior to running the Windows 3.1 or Workgroups setup procedure, one of the following entries will appear in the indicated section of SYSTEM.INI:

```
[386Enh]
device=lanman10.386
networks=lanman10.386 (may be listed here among other network-related drivers)
```

This virtual device driver was required for CD-ROM support with MSCDEX versions prior to 2.2. If you are using MSCDEX version 2.2 or greater (and you should), remove the device=lanman10.386 line shown above. It is unlikely the file will be cited on the networks= line (if there is one), but it's worth having a look.

Internal PC Speaker

For anyone who has seen—or worse, *heard*—the typical internal PC speaker, there's little danger of confusing it with a custom sound system. However, it is possible to squeeze a bit more than the customary beep codes out of it. To do so, a PC speaker driver is required, and one is available for downloading on CompuServe (GO WINAPA, Library 1). The self-extracting SPEAK.EXE file contains the speaker driver, OEM setup information, licensing, and setup information files.

In one of the classic understatements of the computer literature, the SPEAKER.TXT file accompanying the driver notes that "The PC Speaker driver may not produce high quality sound on all computer systems"—or, for that matter, on *any* computer system. However, it does give the user a reasonably painless introduction to digital audio, PC-style. With the driver installed, the *Sound* applet can be used as described in this chapter, and waveform audio can also be played via the *Sound Recorder* applet. However, the driver does not support waveform playback via the *Media Player* applet.

Driver Installation and Configuration. After expanding the SPEAK.EXE file, install the driver (SPEAKER.DRV) as described in the *Add Unlisted/Updated Driver* section above. After doing so, the following line should be seen in the Installed Drivers list:

Sound Driver for the PC-Speaker

Select that line, then click on the Setup... button to open the PC-Speaker Setup dialog box shown in Figure 12.2. The configuration options are briefly described here.

Speed:, Volume:, Limit (playback time). Adjust these slider-bar controls as required for optimum audio reproduction on your system.

Enable interrupts during playback. By default, interrupts are disabled during the interval in which sound is heard. Therefore, keyboard action and mouse pointer movements are momentarily suspended. If you check

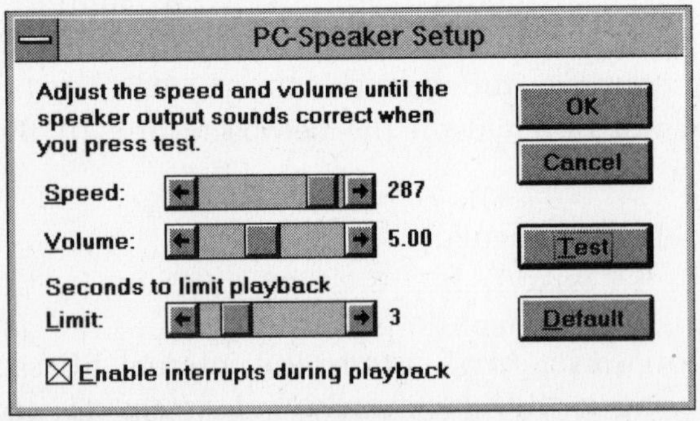

Figure 12.2 The PC-Speaker Setup dialog box accompanies the internal PC speaker driver which can be used if a real sound card is not installed.

this box, these activities continue during playback, but the audio quality suffers as a result. Try enabling/disabling the check box and note the effect on your system.

Test. After adjusting any of the slider bars, click on the <u>T</u>est button to check speaker quality (or lack thereof). The test signal is the wavefile specified as *Default Beep* in the *Sound* applet, which is described later in this chapter.

Default. Click on this button to restore the default settings for your system configuration.

Speaker Driver Record in SYSTEM.INI. Speaker driver information is recorded in the following sections:

```
[speaker.drv]
CPU Speed=
Volume=
Version=
Enhanced=
Max seconds=
Leave interrupts enabled=

[drivers]
Wave=speaker.drv
```

NOTE: If you graduate to a *real* sound system such as the *Media Vision Pro Audio Spectrum 16* described later in the chapter, the Wave= line in the [drivers] section is rewritten as part of the installation procedure. However, the [speaker.drv] section will not be deleted unless you do it yourself.

MCI Sound

The MCI Sound driver supports waveform audio record and playback functions and is installed as part of the regular Windows Setup procedure. To configure the driver (rarely necessary), highlight [MCI] Sound in the <u>In</u>stalled Drivers list, and click on the <u>S</u>etup... button to open the MCI Waveform Driver Setup dialog box shown in Figure 12.3.

Driver Configuration. There isn't much to it: just the one adjustment listed here.

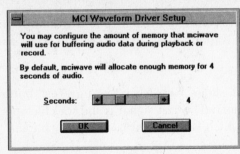

Figure 12.3 The MCI Waveform Driver Setup dialog box configures the amount of memory set aside as a record/playback buffer for waveform audio.

Seconds. By adjusting the slider bar, sufficient memory is allocated to buffer record or playback data for the number of seconds indicated to the right of the bar. The range is 2-to-9 seconds, with a default value of 4 seconds. If a non-default selection is specified, the following line in SYSTEM.INI is modified to show the specified time:

```
[drivers]
WaveAudio=mciwave.drv X   (where X is the specified time, in seconds)
```

Video for Windows

This application is available separately, or you can download a runtime version from the Microsoft Applications Forum (GO MSAPP, Library 3) on CompuServe. Download the compressed VFWRUN.ZIP file (478,575 bytes), and expand it into your C:\TEMP (*not* C:\WINDOWS) directory. Then run the C:\TEMP\SETUP.EXE program from within Windows for a complete installation. If you only want the new version 3.11 *Media Player* applet described earlier in the chapter, then just expand the MPLAYER.EX_ and MPLAYER.HL_ files into the Windows directory, as MPLAYER.EXE and MPLAYER.HLP.

Assuming the runtime or full application setup procedure is executed, the following additions are made to the Installed Drivers list in the Drivers dialog box.

```
Intel Indeo (TM) Video Driver
Microsoft Video 1 Compressor
[MCI] Microsoft Video for Windows
```

Once these drivers are installed, you should be able to view animated AVI and MOV files, as described later on under *Video System* in the *Multimedia System Overview* section of this chapter.

Driver Configuration. Select [MCI] Microsoft Video for Windows and click on the Setup... button to open the Video Playback Options dialog box shown in Figure 12.4. For future reference, the figure also shows other components of the AVI system that will be cited in the following sections. Refer to the online Help screen for additional information, and for a description of options not covered here.

Video Mode. Click on either of the following radio buttons to vary the size of the video display.

Window. The video image fills a small window whose initial size is determined by the *Zoom by 2* option described below. That window size may be readjusted by moving the window borders as desired. However, the image may or may not resize itself to fill the new window. Refer to the *Stretch to Window* option below for details.

Full Screen. If this option is selected, the video window occupies the full screen and the video resolution switches to 640×400 when the video is played. The image may occupy one half, or all, of the screen area depending on the *Zoom by 2* status, as described below.

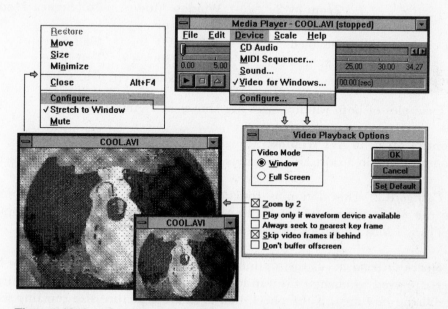

Figure 12.4 Video for Windows components. The Video Playback Options dialog box may be opened from the Media Player or video window Control Menu, as shown here, or via the Setup button in the *Drivers* applet. The video window size is determined by the Zoom by 2 check box.

Play only if waveform device available.   In the default mode, a combined audio/video file will play only if a waveform device is available. If the check box is cleared, then the video portion will play without accompanying audio, if the waveform device is not available.

Set Default.   If any video configuration option is changed, that change is valid only for the current session. If you wish to revise the default configuration and save it for future use, click on this button after making the necessary changes. The new configuration will be written into WIN.INI and used for subsequent sessions. (See *Video Record in WIN.INI*, below.)

Skip video frames if behind.   If the box is checked, video frames will be dropped as necessary to maintain synchronization with the audio segment. If the box is cleared, the audio pauses as required to stay in synch with the video.

Zoom by 2.   If this check box is enabled, the image area changes as determined by the selected *Video Mode* (see above). The video image occupies the area listed here.

Zoom by 2	Window Mode H × V (pixels)	Full-Screen Mode
Disabled	160 × 120	Half Screen
Enabled	320 × 240	Full Screen
Video Resolution	Same as Desktop	640 × 400

Examples of both window sizes are shown in Figure 12.4.

Control Menu in AVI Window.   In addition to its usual menu options, the Control Menu in a video window offers the AVI-specific options described here.

Configure....   This option is functionally equivalent to the same option on the *Media Player's* Device Menu. As shown in Figure 12.4, either option opens the Video Playback Options dialog box.

Stretch to Window.   If this option is checked, and either AVI window border is moved to change the window size, the picture expands or contracts to fill the new area. If the check box is cleared, picture size remains fixed. In this case, the additional window space is black, or the picture itself is clipped, depending on window size adjustment. Note that this option is available only via the Control Menu.

Mute.   Put a check mark next to this option to disable the audio.

Video Record in WIN.INI.   If you click on the Set Default button, your configuration changes are written into WIN.INI and will be used for all subsequent _Media Player_ sessions which utilize _Video for Windows_. The WIN.INI section is summarized here.

```
[MCIAVI]
DefaultVideo            = Window                   (Window video mode)
                        = 240 Line Fullscreen      (Full Screen video mode)
AccurateSeek            = 1
ZoomBy2                 = 0
DisallowSilentPlay      = 0
DontBufferOffscreen     = 0
SkipFrames              = 1
```

Media Player Applet

The _Media Player_ applet is briefly described here, since it is a readily available means of verifying the performance of various devices whose drivers are configured via the _Drivers_ or _MIDI Mapper_ applets.

Applet Versions

There are currently two versions of the _Media Player_ applet (MPLAYER.EXE), both briefly described below. For future reference, file information data is summarized here.

Product	File Size	Date	Version
Windows	33312	03-10-92	3.1
Workgroups	33312	10-01-92	3.1
Video for Windows	113488	10-28-92	3.11

The version number is encoded in the MPLAYER.EXE file, but not otherwise available. A brief description of each version is given here, and in subsequent sections a parenthetical reference identifies information which applies to the specified version only.

Version 3.1.   This is the version included with Windows 3.1 and Windows-for-Workgroups. The applet icon is usually found in the Accessories Group Window, and is shown in Figure 12.5a, along with the fixed-size applet window.

Version 3.11. This updated *Media Player* applet is included with Microsoft's *Video for Windows,* and is also on the Microsoft *Word & Bookshelf* CD-ROM disc (in the WINVIDEO\MPLAYER directory). If neither product is available, refer to the *Video for Windows* section above for information on how to download a runtime version, which includes the new *Media Player.* The same runtime version is also included with the Grolier *Multimedia Encyclopedia* (MSVIDEO directory) and may be supplied with other CD-ROM software as well. The size of MPLAYER.EXE may vary slightly from that given above, if the file is supplied as part of a third-party software package.

Media Player version 3.11 offers OLE and AVI (Audio Visual Interleaved) file support and also provides an enhanced applet window for use with any audio or video device. Its horizontal window size is continuously variable, while vertical size can be switched between the first three configurations listed here.

Full Window. This window shows the slider-bar scale and all playback control buttons, as seen in Figure 12.5b. If the *Intermediate* window is seen instead, drag either horizontal window border slightly to open the *Full* window. Double-click on the Title Bar to switch to the *Small* window described below.

Intermediate Window. This window omits the slider-bar scale, as shown in Figure 12.5c. If the *Full* window is seen, drag either horizontal window border slightly to collapse the window to the *Intermediate* size. Double-click on the Title Bar to switch to the *Small* window described below.

Small Window. The small window shown in Figure 12.5d is only available if a media file is loaded into the *Media Player* applet. If so, double-click on the Title Bar to switch from the *Full* or *Intermediate* window to this one. Double-click again to return to the previous window.

Miniature Control Bar. As yet another option, the small control bar shown in Figure 12.5e appears under a *Media Player* object in a client document, during the interval in which the media file is played from within the client document.

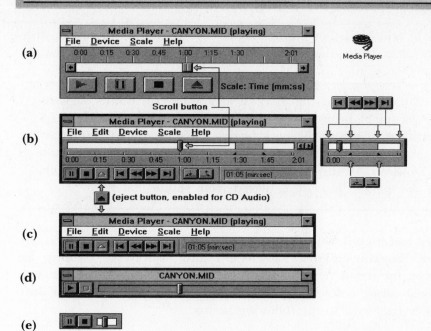

Figure 12.5 The *Media Player* applet. (a) The Windows 3.1 applet window and icon. If a runtime or full version of Video for Windows is installed, the version 3.11 Media Player applet window may be displayed in several sizes: (b) full (inset shows Mark-In and Mark-out, forward and reverse motion details), (c) intermediate, and (d) small. A miniature control bar (e) appears under a Media Player object in a client document.

Playback Control Buttons

A row of buttons near the bottom of the applet window controls the way the applet plays the selected media file. The buttons simulate similar controls found on most audio cassette recorders and, with the exception of the following notes, are not further described here.

Mark-In and Mark-Out Buttons (3.11). This button pair appears at the bottom of the detail view in Figure 12.5b. As any media file plays, click on the Mark-In (left) button to mark the beginning of a section, then on the Mark-Out (right) button to mark the end of the section, or hold down the Shift key and drag the Scroll button to mark a section of the file. If the file is subsequently pasted into an application document file (as described below), the marked section will play when the object icon within that document file is double-clicked.

The Mark-In and Mark-Out points may also be used in conjunction with the Step-Forward and Step-Reverse buttons described immediately below.

> **NOTE:** Although specifying Mark-In and Mark-Out points suggests that playback might begin and end at these points, this doesn't happen. Regardless of where playback begins, it continues without interruption through the end of the file, regardless of the marked interval. However, if the *Media Player* is pasted into a client file, then only the marked interval is played from within that file.

Step-Forward and Step-Reverse Buttons (3.11). These buttons are on either side of the conventional fast-forward and fast-reverse buttons, as pointed out in the detail view in Figure 12.5b. Depending on the selected scale (see *Scale Menu,* below), sequential button-clicks step the Scroll Button forward or backward to the following points:

Frame From beginning of scale, to Mark-in, Mark-out points, to end of scale.
Time Same.
Tracks Same, then to each track, to Mark-in, Mark-out points, to end of scale.

Media Player Menus

This section describes only those menus unique to the *Media Player* applet. Refer to Chapters 3 and 4 for general information about File and Help Menus.

Many of the version 3.11 applet's menu options provide support for OLE functions. If any such option description is not immediately clear, refer to the *OLE/Media Player Summary* which follows this section on menus, or skip the whole works if the subject is of no interest.

Device Menu. This menu provides access to currently available audio and video devices. The list varies according to the installed devices, with a few typical examples given here.

Device	*Configure Option (3.11) Provides Access to:*
CD Audio	Redbook CD Audio Configuration screen
MIDI Sequencer	Option disabled
Sound	MCI Waveform Driver Setup (Figure 12.3)
Video for Windows (3.11)	Video Playback Options (Figure 12.4)

Device Menu <u>C</u>onfigure Option (3.11). If the version 3.11 *Media Player* applet is installed, a <u>C</u>onfigure... option appears at the bottom of the menu. It is enabled if the selected device may be configured *and* a file is loaded or a disc is ready for playback, as summarized in the above list, with additional details following.

CD Audio. Although the option is enabled, all it does is reconfirm the existing CD-ROM drive installation by displaying the *Redbook CD Audio* message cited earlier in the *CD Audio* section. If an [MCI] CD Audio driver is not yet installed, then CD Audio doesn't show up on the Device Menu and, consequently, there is no access to this option.

Sound and *Video for Windows.* If either device is selected, the <u>C</u>onfigure... option opens the MCI Waveform Driver Setup (Figure 12.3) or Video Player Options (Figure 12.4) dialog box. Refer to those sections above for configuration details.

Device Menu Option Sequence. The options listed on the Device Menu are read in reverse order from the [mci] section of SYSTEM.INI. Thus, to arrange the options in the order shown above, the [mci] sequence should be as follows:

```
[mci]
AVIVideo=mciavi.drv
WaveAudio=mciwave.drv 4
Sequencer=mciseq.drv
CDAudio=mcicda.drv
```

The options are listed in this order in the open Device Menu shown in Figure 12.4 above.

Edit Menu (3.11). The options on the Edit Menu (not shown) are enabled only if a media file has been loaded into the *Media Player* via the Device Menu described above. A parenthetical reference indicates the Shortcut key combination for that menu option.

<u>C</u>opy Object (Ctrl+C). This option copies the *Media Player* and selected media file to the Clipboard for pasting as an OLE object into another application.

<u>O</u>ptions.... (Ctrl+O). The options available via this menu choice determine how a media file will be presented if it is pasted into a document file. The Options dialog box is shown in Figure 12.6a, and its selections are briefly described here.

Auto Rewind, Auto Repeat. After the object is played, the media file rewinds and/or repeats, depending on the status of these two check boxes.

Border around Object. The check box status specifies whether a border will be drawn around the object, as shown in Figure 12.6b.

Caption. Enable this check box and type in the desired caption text, which will be displayed under the object, as also shown in Figure 12.6b, or clear the check box to display the icon without any text under it.

Control Bar on Playback. If this check box is enabled, a miniature control bar appears under the object while the media file is playing. If the *Play in...* box is cleared, the *Small Applet Window* (described above) appears instead.

Dither Picture to VGA Colors. If a video media file is pasted into a client file, a single frame appears in the document at the insertion point. Its color rendition may be distorted if the image comes from a 256-color (or greater) media file, and the client document is viewed at a color depth of 16 colors. Enable this check box to provide a 16-color frame image to avoid this potential problem.

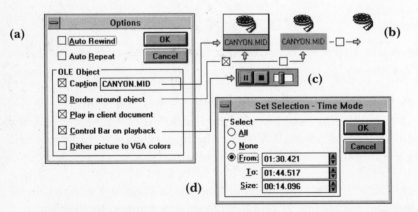

Figure 12.6 The Options dialog box (a) provides configuration settings for AVI, with object format (b) determined by check boxes. A miniature control bar (c) may be included for playback control from within a client document. Use the Set Selection dialog box (d) to specify the file interval to be played from the client document.

Play in Client Document. If this check box is enabled, then either the miniature control bar (Figure 12.6c) appears under the object in the application file, or the *Small Applet Window* appears instead, as determined by the Control Bar on playback check box, above. If the *Play in...* box is cleared, then neither item is displayed.

Selection.... Choose this option to open the Set Selection dialog box shown in Figure 12.6d, which provides options for marking a portion of the loaded media file. The procedure is functionally equivalent to using the Mark-In and Mark-Out buttons described above, except that the two points are now referred to as From and To. You may want to select this option if timing is critical. For example, Figure 12.5b showed a marked 15-second segment between 1:30 and 1:45. On opening the Set Selection dialog box, it is seen that the marked segment begins slightly late and ends slightly early, for a total playing time of only 14.096 seconds. If that's not accurate enough, type in new *From* and *To* settings as needed.

If the *Frame* mode is selected (see *Scale Menu* below), then you can use the Set Selection dialog box to specify a specific frame, or frame range.

Scale Menu. Open this menu (not shown) to select the scale to be displayed above or below the *Media Player's* slider bar. The menu options are a function of the selected media device, as shown by these examples:

Scale in:	AVI	CD Audio	MIDI	Waveform
Frames	Yes	No	No	No
Time	Yes	Yes	Yes	Yes
Tracks	No	Yes	No	No

CD Audio Presence Check. Note that the Scale Menu's Tracks option is available only if the disc in the drive contains one or more CD audio tracks. This characteristic is therefore a convenient means of checking a compact disc for CD audio. Insert the disc in the drive, select the Device Menu's CD Audio option, then open the Scale Menu. If the Tracks option is enabled, the disc contains CD audio; otherwise, it doesn't.

OLE/Media Player Summary

In Figure 12.7, the *Write* applet window displays an open client file (MEMO.WRI). The file consists of two text lines and the boxed graphics image immediately below the text. Previously, the *Media Player* applet was opened and that epic digital ditty, CANYON.MID (described below), was loaded. A 15-second segment between 1:30 and 1:45 was marked, as described above. Then the Edit Menu's Copy Object option was selected to place the *Media Player*/CANYON.MID object on the Clipboard.

Meanwhile, back at the *Write* applet the Edit Menu's Paste option has inserted the CANYON.MID object image in the memo. If the object is double-clicked, a miniature control bar appears under the image, and CANYON.MID begins playing at the 1:30 mark. Fifteen seconds later, playback terminates and the control bar disappears. During the playback interval, the Pause button or the Scroll button can be used as desired. Furthermore, you can drag the Scroll button back to the beginning of the Slider Bar to play the media file in its entirety. Clicking on the Stop button at any time will close the control bar.

To revise the marked section of the media file from within the *Write* applet, open the Edit Menu and highlight the Media Clip Object option. The section of the menu containing this option is also shown in Figure 12.7. If the cascading menu's Edit option is selected, the *Media Player* applet window opens, as also shown in the figure.

MIDI Mapper Applet

The *MIDI Mapper* applet provides configuration access to an installed MIDI device. If no such device is installed, then the *MIDI Mapper* applet icon does not appear in the Control Panel, even though the Installed Drivers list (see *Drivers* applet) indicates a *MIDI Mapper* is installed.

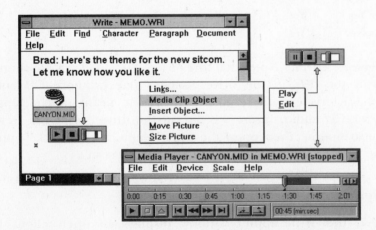

Figure 12.7 An open Write document with a media clip object (MIDI file) inserted in the text. A section of the Edit Menu shows edit options related to the object.

The MIDI File Format

The complete structure of a general MIDI file is described in the *Standard MIDI Files 1.0* specification published by the International MIDI Association in Los Angeles, California. In addition, the *Multimedia PC Specification, version 1.0* (jointly developed by Microsoft, Media Vision, Creative Labs, and others) includes specifications for extended-level and base-level synthesizers.

Much of the background information presented here is derived (and sometimes, translated into English) from these and other MIDI-related documents. Although no attempt is made here to explain MIDI in its entirety, there should be sufficient information to allow the beginner to survive basic MIDI configuration and troubleshooting sessions.

Channel Assignments. Any MIDI file intended for interchange between MPC-compliant systems usually adheres to a dual-level standard, in which the same musical composition is recorded in two versions, on 14 of the 16 available channels. Channel assignment within the file is as follows:

Setup	Channels	For Use by
Extended Level	1–9	Extended multitimbral synthesizers (melodic)
	10	Same (percussion)
—	11–12	Unused in base- and extended-level files
Base Level	13–15	Base multitimbral synthesizers (melodic)
	16	Same (percussion)
General MIDI	1–16	Complete 16-channel MIDI system

MIDI Mapper Overview

As part of the regular Windows setup procedure, the *MIDI Mapper* applet is configured to support several popular MIDI hardware systems. If you subsequently install a sound card that supports MIDI, then the *MIDI Mapper* may be reconfigured during the setup procedure for that card. In either case, the configuration information is stored in a MIDIMAP.CFG file, and the purpose of the *MIDI Mapper* applet is to reconfigure that file as required. Therefore, that file is introduced first, and is followed by a look at the *MIDI Mapper* itself.

The MIDI Mapper Configuration File (MIDIMAP.CFG). The MIDIMAP.CFG file contains the configuration data required to support the installed MIDI Mapper setups. The file is not, however, in a text-only format such as that used for most INI files. As a result, MIDIMAP.CFG editing chores must be done via the *MIDI Mapper* applet. If a configuration change needs to update the MIDIMAP.CFG file, you will be prompted to restart Windows. When you do, the file will be rewritten as required.

MIDIMAP.CFG *Revisions during Upgrade Procedure.*   Any software upgrade that affects MIDI operations will probably modify the existing MIDIMAP.CFG file, sometimes with disastrous results. The usual procedure is to toss out the existing file and replace it with a new one, which may or—more likely—may not preserve existing configuration information that you don't want to lose. Therefore, it's not a bad idea to make a backup copy whenever you have a MIDI configuration that you don't want to lose forever. Make a new backup as often as required to maintain a current version for recovery, should the need arise.

Some well-behaved upgrades will rename your existing MIDIMAP.CFG file, then add a new one in its place. In this case you can review the new file, then rename the original back to MIDIMAP.CFG and incorporate the new information into it, or vice versa, of course. Two typical examples are given here, and there are no doubt others that will do the same thing. But don't count on it. In case of doubt, make your own backup *before* installing anything that might misbehave.

Windows 3.1 Upgrade.   The setup procedure renames the old MIDIMAP.CFG file as MIDIMAP.OLD and writes a new MIDIMAP.CFG which contains the *Ad Lib* patch map.

Windows Sound System.   If you install Microsoft's *Windows Sound System,* your existing MIDIMAP.CFG file is renamed as MIDIMAP.WSS, and a new one takes its place.

MIDI Mapper Configuration

To review or revise the current MIDI configuration, double-click on the *MIDI Mapper* applet icon to open its dialog box, both of which are shown in Figure 12.8. The component parts of the dialog box are described below.

NOTE: If the *MIDI Mapper* icon does not appear in the Control Panel window, a sound card with MIDI support has not yet been installed. Install the necessary hardware and drivers, then reopen the Control Panel, which should now show the icon.

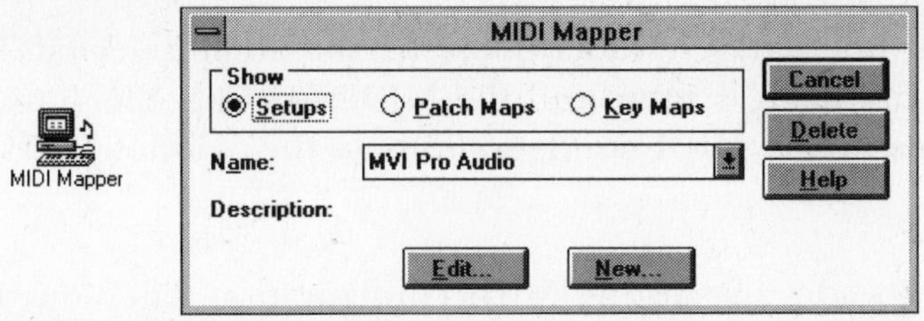

Figure 12.8 The MIDI Mapper applet icon and dialog box. Click on any radio button to select one of the dialog boxes shown in Figures 12.9–11.

Show MIDI Configurations. This section of the dialog box contains three radio buttons for selecting one of the options described here. As each button is clicked, the name and description (if any) of the currently selected item are displayed in the dialog box. (See *Name:* and *Description:*, below.) After selecting the desired item, refer to the appropriate *MIDI Mapper Dialog Boxes* section for a description of the related configuration options.

Setups. A *MIDI Setup* is simply (if that word can be used) a listing of the configuration settings for each of the 16 separate MIDI channels.

Patch Maps. The General MIDI specification has assigned a specific instrument name to each of 128 potential MIDI sources, and each channel in a MIDI file is mapped to one of these sources. If you know the source to which a specific file channel is mapped, you can remap it to some other source via the Patch Map, as described in the PATCH MAP dialog box section below.

Key Maps. The General MIDI specification defines the octave in which each melodic note is to play, and also specifies the percussion instrument sound for each percussive note. Use the Key Map to change these specifications.

The Name: Box. Depending on which Show option is selected, the Name: box lists the item currently available for editing. Make sure you make a note of the current name before changing it, because once you access the drop-down list, the Cancel button disappears. Therefore, if you should want to return to the previous item but can't remember what it was, you'll just have to take a guess at it.

The names listed in the Name: box are read from the MIDIMAP.CFG file in the System directory.

Description:. This line gives a description of the item selected in the
Name: box, if one has been written into the MIDIMAP.CFG file. Table 12.4
lists the descriptions of the MIDI configurations in the Windows version of
MIDIMAP.CFG.

Edit. If you want to edit an existing MIDI configuration, click on the desired radio button, then on the **E**dit button to open the dialog box (described below) for editing.

TABLE 12.4   Configuration Data in MIDIMAP.CFG File*

MIDI Mapper Dialog Box		MIDI Setup Dialog Box		
Setups	Description	Channels	Port Name	Patch Map
Microsoft *Windows* MIDIMAP.CFG file				
Ad Lib	Base-level setup	13–16	Ad Lib	[None]
Ad Lib general	General MIDI setup	1–16	Ad Lib	[None]
Extended MIDI	Extended-level setup	1–10	Creative Labs Snd. Blstr. 1.5	[None]
General MIDI	General MIDI setup	1–16	Creative Labs Snd. Blstr. 1.5	[None]
LAPC1	Extended-level setup	1–8	Roland MPU-401	MT32
		10	Roland MPU-401	MT32 Perc
MT32	Extended-level setup	1–8	ProAudio MIDI Output	MT32
		10	ProAudio MIDI Output	MT32 Perc
Proteus General	General MIDI setup	1–9, 11–16	ProAudio MIDI Output	Prot/1
		10	ProAudio MIDI Output	Prot/1 Perc
Proteus/1	Extended-level setup	1–9	ProAudio MIDI Output	Prot/1
		10	ProAudio MIDI Output	Prot/1 Perc
Media Vision *Pro Audio Spectrum 16* MIDIMAP.CFG file [†]				
Extended FM	(*none*)	1–9	Voyetra OPL-3 FM Synth	[None]
Extended MIDI [‡]	Extended-level setup	1–16	Pro Audio/CDPC MIDI Output	[None]
General MIDI	(*this configuration not included*)			
MVI MVFM	(*none*)	13–16	Media Vision FM Synth	[None]
MVI OPL3 FM	(*none*)	13–16	Voyetra OPL-3 FM Synth	[None]
MVI Pro Audio	(*none*)	1–10	Pro Audio/CDPC MIDI Output	[None]
		13–16	Voyetra OPL-3 FM Synth	[None]

---

* Above information and subsequent additions, revisions, deletions are written into
   MIDIMAP.CFG file in System directory.

† Unless otherwise noted, *PAS-16* file also contains configurations listed in *Windows* file above.

‡ Replaces default *Extended MIDI* above.

New. To create a new configuration, again click on the desired radio button, then on the <u>N</u>ew button. Depending on which button is selected, a dialog box with one of the following titles will appear.

New MIDI Setup...
New MIDI Patch Map...
New MIDI Key Map...

Regardless of which item was selected, the dialog box (not shown) will ask for the following new information:

<u>N</u>ame:
<u>D</u>escription:

After entering a descriptive name (required) and description (optional), click on the OK button to open a new dialog box for that item. Edit the columns in that box, then click on the OK and Yes/No/Cancel buttons, as desired. If you do save your configuration, the name, description, and configuration data is appended to the MIDIMAP.CFG file.

The MIDI Mapper Dialog Boxes

The three MIDI Mapper dialog boxes are briefly described here. To open any dialog box and display the desired configuration data, first click on the appropriate radio button. The name and description (if any) of the currently installed item appear in the dialog box. Click on the down-arrow to select some other item, then on the <u>E</u>dit button, or just click on the New button to begin editing.

Setup. Figure 12.9 shows the MIDI Setup dialog box. The information in columns 2–4 may be edited as described in the following sections.

Source Channel (Src Chan). This column simply lists the 16 channel numbers within any MIDI file. If you click once in this or any other MIDI Setup row, arrow buttons appear in columns 2–4 for that row, as shown by the example in Row 14.

Destination Channel (Dest Chan). This is the channel in your synthesizer to which the source channel is routed. By default, the destination channel matches the source channel, but it can be changed by typing a new channel number, or by clicking on the up/down arrows.

Port Name. The entry in this column specifies the MIDI port to which the Destination Channel signal is routed. Click on any <u>P</u>ort Name box to view a

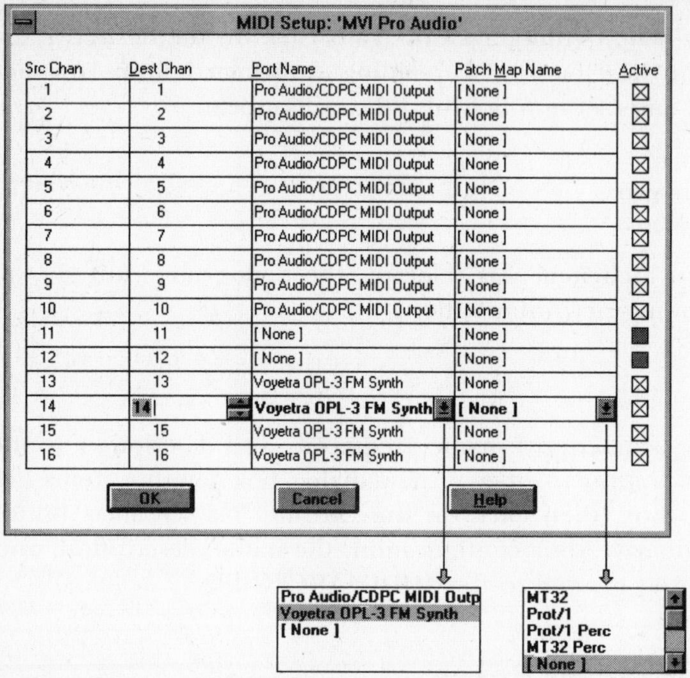

Figure 12.9   Use the MIDI Setup dialog box to set the port, patch map, and destination routing for each source channel.

drop-down list of available ports, as shown at the bottom of Figure 12.9. For a port to appear on this list, the appropriate MIDI driver must have been loaded via SYSTEM.INI, and there must be a corresponding description in CONTROL.INI. If both criteria are met, then the appropriate name appears in the Port Name box. That name, however, may not quite match the CON-TROL.INI description, since it is read from within the cited MIDI driver. A few examples of this three-part driver configuration are given here.

SYSTEM.INI	CONTROL.INI	Port Name
[drivers]	[drivers.desc]	*(embedded in driver file)*
MIDI=opl3.drv	opl3.drv=Voyetra OPL-3 FM Driver	Voyetra OPL-3 FM Synth
MIDI1=mvproaud.drv	mvproaud.drv=Media Vision Pro Audio/CDPC Wave/MIDI/Aux	Pro Audio/CDPC MIDI Output
MIDI2=msadlib.drv	msadlib.drv=Ad Lib	Ad Lib

External Port Name.   Note that in Figure 12.9, extended-level channels 1–10 are all assigned to the *Pro Audio/CDPC MIDI Output* port. If this or some other output port is listed, these channels are routed to an external MIDI device which may or may not be physically available. If not, then no sound will be heard from these channels.

Unassigned Port. Channels 11 and 12 are unused in MPC-compliant MIDI setups, as indicated by None in the P̲ort Name box.

Internal Port Name. Figure 12.9 also shows that base-level channels 13–16 are assigned to the *Voyetra OPL-3 FM Synth(esizer).* This device is built into the Media Vision sound card installed in the computer, and so the base-level channels of any MIDI file will be heard if this configuration is selected.

Patch M̲ap Name. Double-click on any box in this column to open the list of available patch maps, as shown by the example at the bottom of Figure 12.9. The four patch maps in the Windows MIDIMAP.CFG file are listed in the box. These or other patch maps may be edited by clicking on the P̲atch Maps radio button, as described in the next section.

A̲ctive Check Box. An "X" in this box indicates that the MIDI channel is active. Clear the check box if you wish to disable the signal on that channel.

P̲atch Maps. Figure 12.10 shows a custom patch map, whose components are described here.

0/1 Based Patches Button. The 128 names in the General MIDI Patch Name list may be numbered as follows:

Patches	Numbered As:	Patch Map Button Reads:
0-based	0–127	1̲ based patches
1-based	1–128	0̲ based patches

Use the button to toggle the patch numbers from one base to the other, solely for the purpose of matching the screen display with a synthesizer that uses either base system. Note that the button legend identifies the base that is currently *not* displayed. If you click on it, that base is displayed and the legend switches to the other base. It's initially confusing—just remember the legend is always the opposite of the current status.

MIDI Patch Map: 'MyPatch'				
		0 based patches		
Src Patch	Src Patch Name	Dest Patch	Volume %	Key Map Name
1	Acoustic Grand Piano	1	100	[None]
2	Bright Acoustic Piano	2	100	+2 octaves
3	Electric Grand Piano	13	100	[None]
4	Honky-tonk Piano	4	100	[None]
5	Rhodes Piano	5	100	[None]
6	Chorused Piano	6	100	[None]
7	Harpsichord	7	100	[None]
8	Clavinet	8	100	[None]
9	Celesta	9	100	[None]
10	Glockenspiel	10	100	[None]
11	Music Box	11	100	[None]
12	Vibraphone	12	100	[None]
13	Marimba	13	100	[None]
14	Xylophone	14	100	[None]
15	Tubular Bells	15	100	[None]
16	Dulcimer	16	100	[None]

Prot/1
55
79
38
+1 octave
-1 octave
21
+2 octaves
MT32
[None]

OK   **Cancel**   **Help**

Figure 12.10   The MIDI Patch Map dialog box can be used to patch any source signal to a different patch name (instrument) and/or to vary volume or specify a Key Map.

Source Patch.   This column lists the 128 General MIDI patch numbers (0–127 or 1–128) associated with the adjacent *Source Patch Name* column. For each melodic *channel* recorded in a MIDI file, an embedded *Source Patch* number associates that channel with a *Source Patch Name*. If you click once in this or any other MIDI Patch Map row, arrow buttons appear in columns 3–5 for that row, as shown by the example in Row 3.

Source Patch Name.   This column lists the names of the 128 melodic channels, as defined by the General MIDI specification. The names are listed here in Table 12.5. The list is read from the MIDI Mapper driver, as shown in the *MIDI Mapper Record in SYSTEM.INI* section below.

Dest(ination) Patch.   Change the entry in this column to reassign any recorded channel to some other *Source Patch Name*. For example, in Figure 12.10, Row 3 shows that any channel associated with the *Electric Grand Piano* (Source Patch 3) will be associated instead with the *Marimba* (Source Patch 13).

Volume %.   By comparison, this one is easy. Adjust the value up or down to change the output level of the selected instrument.

TABLE 12.5   General MIDI Patch Names*

Source & Patch Name	Source & Patch Name	Source & Patch Name
0. Acoustic Grand Piano	43. Contrabass	86. Synth lead 7–Bright Saw Wave Lead
1. Bright Acoustic Piano	44. Tremolo Strings	87. Synth lead 8–Brass and Lead
2. Electric Grand Piano	45. Pizzicato Strings	88. Synth pad 1–Fantasia Pad
3. Honky-Tonk Piano	46. Orchestral Harp	89. Synth pad 2–Warm Pad
4. Rhodes Piano	47. Timpani	90. Synth pad 3–Poly Synth Pad
5. Chorused Piano	48. String Ensemble 1	91. Synth pad 4–Space Voices Pad
6. Harpsichord	49. String Ensemble 2	92. Synth pad 5–Bowed Glass Pad
7. Clavinet	50. Synth Strings 1	93. Synth pad 6–Metal Pad
8. Celesta	51. Synth Strings 2	94. Synth pad 7–Halo Pad
9. GlockenSpiel	52. Choir Aahs	95. Synth pad 8–Sweep Pad
10. Music Box	53. Voice Oohs	96. Synth SFX 1–Ice Rain
11. Vibraphone	54. Synth Voice	97. Synth SFX 2–Soundtrack
12. Marimba	55. Orchestra Hit	98. Synth SFX 3–Crystal
13. Xylophone	56. Trumpet	99. Synth SFX 4–Atmosphere
14. Tubular Bells	57. Trombone	100. Synth SFX 5–Brightness
15. Dulcimer	58. Tuba	101. Synth SFX 6–Goblin
16. Hammond Organ	59. Muted Trumpet	102. Synth SFX 7–Echo Drops
17. Percussive Organ	60. French Horn	103. Synth SFX 8–Star Theme
18. Rock Organ	61. Brass Section	104. Sitar
19. Church Organ	62. Synth Brass 1	105. Banjo
20. Reed Organ	63. Synth Brass 2	106. Shamisen
21. Accordion	64. Soprano Sax	107. Koto
22. Harmonica	65. Alto Sax	108. Kalimba
23. Tango Accordion	66. Tenor Sax	109. Bagpipe
24. Acoustic Nylon Guitar	67. Baritone Sax	110. Fiddle
25. Acoustic Steel Guitar	68. Oboe	111. Shanai
26. Electric Bass Guitar	69. English Horn	112. Tinkle Bell
27. Electric Clean Guitar	70. Bassoon	113. Agogo
28. Electric Muted Guitar	71. Clarinet	114. Steel Drums
29. Overdriven Guitar	72. Piccolo	115. Woodblock
30. Distortion Guitar	73. Flute	116. Taiko Drum
31. Guitar Harmonics	74. Recorder	117. Melodic Tom
32. Acoustic Bass	75. Pan Flute	118. Synth Drum
33. Electric Bass, Fingered	76. Bottle Blow	119. Reverse Cymbal
34. Electric Bass, Picked	77. Shakuhachi	120. Guitar Fret Noise
35. Fretless Bass	78. Whistle	121. Breath Noise
36. Slap Bass 1	79. Ocarina	122. Seashore
37. Slap Bass 2	80. Synth lead 1–Square Wave Lead	123. Bird Tweet
38. Synth Bass 1	81. Synth lead 2–Sawtooth Wave Lead	124. Telephone Ring
39. Synth Bass 2	82. Synth lead 3–Calliope Lead	125. Helicopter
40. Violin	83. Synth lead 4–Chiff Lead	126. Applause
41. Viola	84. Synth lead 5–Charang	127. Gunshot
42. Cello	85. Synth lead 6–Solo Synth Voice	

* Information taken from 0-based Patch name list in Multimedia PC Specification, Version 1.0.
May 18, 1991. Patch names 80–103 slightly different in MIDI Patch Map dialog box.

Key Map Name. Click on the down-arrow to open the drop-down list of available Key Maps, such as that shown by the inset in Figure 12.10. Note that in that figure, the *Bright Acoustic Piano* (Row 2) was previously assigned to the *+2 octaves* Key Map. Refer to the *Key Maps* section which follows for further details.

Key Maps. By default, any key on a synthesizer keyboard plays the musical note associated with that key, and by convention, middle C (below A-440 = 261.63 Hz) is identified as key 60. If the synthesizer keyboard is set up to play percussion, then each key is instead associated with a specific percussive sound. For example, key 48 is either the melodic note C below middle C, or the High-Mid Tom percussion sound.

The Key Map can be used to remap one or more melodic or percussion keys. For example, Figure 12.11 shows a section of the *+1 octave* key map.

Source Key (Src). This column lists the 128 MIDI keys (0–127) on a synthesizer keyboard, or specified within a MIDI file.

Source Key Name (for percussion). The names in this column identify the percussion instruments associated with synthesizer keys 35–81. It too is read from the MIDI Mapper driver (see *MIDI Mapper Record in SYSTEM.INI*,

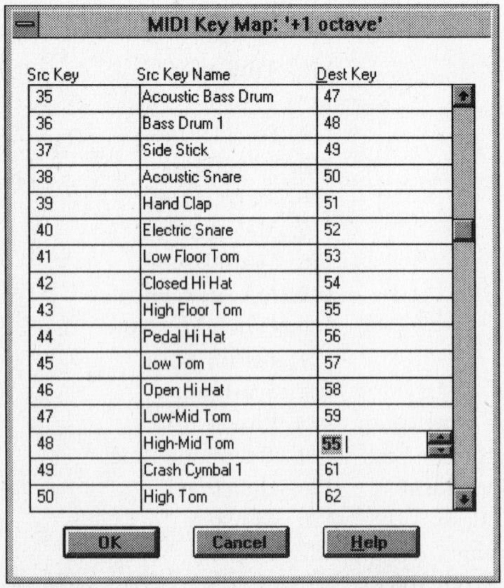

MIDI Key Map: '+1 octave'

Src Key	Src Key Name	Dest Key
35	Acoustic Bass Drum	47
36	Bass Drum 1	48
37	Side Stick	49
38	Acoustic Snare	50
39	Hand Clap	51
40	Electric Snare	52
41	Low Floor Tom	53
42	Closed Hi Hat	54
43	High Floor Tom	55
44	Pedal Hi Hat	56
45	Low Tom	57
46	Open Hi Hat	58
47	Low-Mid Tom	59
48	High-Mid Tom	55
49	Crash Cymbal 1	61
50	High Tom	62

OK   Cancel   Help

Figure 12.11 The MIDI Key Map dialog box lists the percussion sound associated with each synthesizer key.

below). The column can be ignored if using the Key Map for melodic instrument mapping.

Dest(ination) Key. If any *Source Key* is pressed (or specified in a MIDI file), the corresponding *Destination Key* is heard. If no key mapping is specified, then of course source key 35 plays destination key 35, and so on. However, if the *+1 octave* key map shown in Figure 12.11 is used, then every source key is remapped 12 semitones, or one octave, higher. Thus, source key 35 now plays destination key 47, and so on.

In the figure, source key 48 is remapped to destination key 55, thus making it a perfect fifth (7 semitones) higher, instead of one octave. To create a complete "Fifths" Key Map, edit a new Key Map and add 7 to each Destination Key.

Table 12.6 lists the names assigned to source keys 35–81 for percussion applications. In addition, the Table shows how these keys are remapped by the MT32 (Roland) and Prot/1 (Proteus) Key Maps.

Revising the MIDI Mapper Configuration

It's possible to add entries to the available ports list by installing an extra MIDI driver. For example, the Media Vision *PAS-16 (Pro Audio Spectrum 16)* setup procedure installs two MIDI ports: *Voyetra OPL-3 FM Synth* and *Pro Audio/CDPC MIDI Output,* as noted in the *Port Names* section above. The former is an onboard synthesizer and the latter provides output to an accessory MIDI device, but only if you have one installed. Otherwise, it doesn't do a thing.

Install New MIDI Port. The Media Vision *PAS-16* is *Ad Lib* compatible, and there is an *Ad Lib* MIDI driver included with Windows. To install it, open the *Drivers* applet, click on the <u>A</u>dd... button, then select "Ad Lib" in the List of Drivers. Click on the OK button to continue the installation. When the installation concludes, the following lines will appear in the indicated INI files.

SYSTEM.INI	**CONTROL.INI**
[drivers]	[driver.desc]
MIDI2=msadlib.drv	msadlib.drv=Ad Lib

Add New MIDI Setup. With the new driver in place, you can add additional MIDI setups as described here for the just-cited *Ad Lib* driver. To begin, open the *MIDI Mapper* applet and click on the <u>N</u>ew... button. Type the information in the *Base configuration* column below.

Data Entry Box:	Base Configuration	General Configuration
Name:	Ad Lib	Ad Lib general
Description:	Base-level setup	General MIDI setup

Click on the OK button and when the MIDI Setup: 'Ad Lib' dialog box appears, open box 13 in the Port Name column and select the Ad Lib option on the drop-down list. Repeat the procedure for boxes 14–16. This concludes the conventional base-level setup for the *Ad Lib* driver. If you want to setup a general MIDI configuration as well, repeat the just described procedure using the information in the *General configuration* column above. But this time open boxes 1 through 16 and select *Ad Lib* for each one.

Of course, you can make whatever configuration modifications you like, but the procedure described above sets up the two conventional *Ad Lib* setups usually encountered when this driver is installed.

Delete MIDI Mapper Setup. In order to delete a *MIDI Mapper* setup, you must first make sure the setup is not in use. That is, when you open the

TABLE 12.6 MIDI Key Maps*

Source Key & Name [†]	[†]	[‡]	Source Key & Name [†]	[†]	[‡]	Source Key & Name [†]	[†]	[‡]
35 Acoustic Bass Drum	–	–	51 Ride Cymbal 1	–	–	67 High Agogo	–	70
36 Bass Drum 1	–	–	52 Chinese Cymbal	49	49	68 Low Agogo	–	58
37 Side Stick	–	73	53 Ride Bell	51	70	69 Cabase	–	68
38 Acoustic Snare	–	–	54 Tambourine	–	42	70 Maracas	–	66
39 Hand Clap	–	53	55 Splash Cymbal	46	50	71 Short Whistle	–	42
40 Electric Snare	–	57	56 Cowbell	–	94	72 Long Whistle	–	44
41 Low Floor Tom	–	40	57 Crash Cymbal 2	51	49	73 Short Guiro	70	69
42 Closed Hi Hat	–	54	58 Vibraslap	73	71	74 Long Guiro	69	71
43 High Floor Tom	–	41	59 Ride Cymbal 2	51	51	75 Claves	–	63
44 Pedal Hi Hat	–	42	60 High Bongo	–	65	76 High Wood Block	75	63
45 Low Tom	–	43	61 Low Bongo	–	64	77 Low Wood Block	75	61
46 Open Hi Hat	–	56	62 Mute High Conga	–	65	78 Mute Cuica	62	48
47 Low-mid Tom	–	45	63 Open High Conga	–	64	79 Open Cuica	63	45
48 High-mid Tom	–	47	64 Low Conga	–	62	80 Mute Triangle	68	54
49 Crash Symbol 1	–	–	65 High Timbale	–	60	81 Open Triangle	67	56
50 High Tom	–	48	66 Low Timbale	–	59			

* Number in [†] and [‡] column is key remap for indicated Source Key. A "–" indicates no change.
[†] MT32 Key Map.
[‡] Prot/1 Key Map.

MIDI Mapper applet, the setup to be deleted must not be seen in the Name box. If it is, select some other setup, then close and reopen the applet. Now, select the setup you want to delete and click on the Delete key.

MIDI Mapper Configuration Test

This section may be of use to the MIDI beginner who is still trying to figure out what all this really means.

The CANYON.MID File. Windows is supplied with a grand total of one MIDI file, named CANYON.MID. The file makes a convenient configuration tool, since its header contains a text section in which the various channel/patch assignments are listed. Although some Microsoft documentation states that the file contains information on all channels, it doesn't. Refer to Table 12.7 for CANYON.MID file channel assignments. The file will be used here to illustrate various aspects of *MIDI Mapper* configuration.

Although the *Multimedia PC Specification* suggests that "MIDI authors put the most important melodic timbers in lower melodic MIDI channels," this bit of advice is not followed in CANYON.MID, where the base-level melody is on channel 15. Open the MIDI Setup dialog box and clear the Active box for all channels except 15, so that only this melody line is heard when the file is played. Close the *MIDI Mapper* and play a bit of it, to get an idea of what it sounds like. Then stop the playback and reopen the *MIDI Mapper*.

TABLE 12.7   CANYON.MID File: MIDI Channel Assignments

Channel [†]			MIDI Patch Name [‡]	Channel [†]			MIDI Patch Name [‡]
1	Synth Pads	P91	Pad 3 (Polysynth)	9	–	–	Unused
2	Rhythm Guit.	P28	Electric Guitar (Clean)	10	Drums	–	
3	Acous. Piano	P1	Acoustic Grand Piano	11	–	–	Unused
4	Elec. Bass	P34	Electric Bass (Fingered)	12	–	–	Unused
5	Dist.Guitar	P30	Overdriven Guitar	13	Synth	P86	Lead 7 (voice)
6	Glock.	P10	Glockenspiel	14	Rhythm Guit.	P2	Bright Acoustic Piano
7	–	–	Unused	15	Melody	P3	Electric Grand Piano
8	–	–	Unused	16	Drums	–	

[†] Channel information data embedded in CANYON.MID file.

[‡] Equivalent patch name from MIDI Patch Map. 1-based patches selected to agree with "P*xx*" data in CANYON.MID file. See also Table 12.5.

Patch Map Test. Edit a new "MyPatch" patch map, and patch the *Electric Grand Piano* source over to the *Marimba* destination, as was shown in Figure 12.10. This particular source was selected because the CANYON.MID file header data shows "melody C15-P3" (that is, channel 15 to patch 3: electric grand piano).

Next, open the Setup dialog box and in the channel-15 Patch Map Name box, specify your new "MyPatch" patch map. Close the *MIDI Mapper* and replay CANYON.MID. The melody should now bear about as much resemblance to a marimba as it previously did to a piano.

Melodic Key Map Test. Since the CANYON.MID header also reveals that channel 14 is for bright acoustic piano, open your "MyPatch" Patch Map and specify the *+2 octaves* Key Map for that instrument. Next, open the Setup dialog box and re-enable the channel-14 Active check box. The next time you play CANYON.MID, you should hear that marimba accompanied by a high-pitched piano.

Percussion Key Map Test. The percussion channels (base-level 16, extended-level 10) are treated somewhat differently. Listen to channel 16 only, then assign your "MyPatch" patch map to that channel. Edit this patch map and in the Key Map Name column, open the box in the first row and assign any Key Map to it. Note that the Src Patch Name column (Acoustic Grand Piano in this case) has no significance when the patch map is assigned to a percussion channel (16 or 10), but the effect of the assigned key map will be heard on the percussion the next time CANYON.MID is played. If one of the numbered key maps (21, 38, 55, 79) is selected, then all percussion sounds are routed to that key. (Select any such map and note the explanation on the Description line.)

MIDI Mapper Record in SYSTEM.INI

As previously noted, the installed MIDI drivers are listed in the [drivers] section of SYSTEM.INI, with accompanying virtual drivers in the [386Enh] section, as shown by the first four entries below.

```
[drivers]                [386Enh]
timer=timer.drv          device=vtdapi.386      Timer
MIDI=msadlib.drv         device=vadlibd.386     Ad Lib
MIDI=mvproaud.drv        device=vpasd.386       Media Vision
MIDI=sndblst2.drv        device=vsbd.386        SoundBlaster
MidiMapper=midimap.drv                          MIDI Mapper
```

The MIDI Mapper driver itself is also listed in the [drivers] section, as shown above. In addition to handling its other chores, the driver contains the following information:

MIDI Patch Map: Source Patch Names
MIDI Key Map: Source Key Names

 NOTE: The MIDIMAP.CFG file was described near the beginning of the *MIDI Mapper Applet* section.

The Sound Applet

Use the *Sound* applet to specify the wavefile you wish to hear when a certain system event occurs. If you're not sure what a system event is, you're in good company: Read on.

Sounds and System Events

Before a Windows application performs certain tasks, it will often display a message in the form of an advisory note, a warning, or a question. Perhaps to bring multimedia to the masses, Windows 3.1 and Windows-for-Workgroups now offer application programmers the option of supplementing each of these visual messages with an aural message. For example, if the application program code includes a *SystemAsterisk* line, then whenever the user does something to trigger that line, the momentous occasion—or "event"—is celebrated in sound. The *Sound* applet allows the user to assign a distinctive sound to each of seven such message categories. In Windows-for-Workgroups, two additional sounds may be assigned to the *Chat* applet.

Sound Driver Requirements. In order for the *Sound* applet to operate as described here, a sound card with its supporting software must be installed in the system. If a sound card is not available, the internal PC speaker may be used as a poor substitute. In either case, the present discussion assumes that a sound card or PC speaker driver is already installed. Refer to the *Drivers Applet* section above for assistance with driver installation, or to the *Driver Configuration Procedures* later in the chapter if the installed driver needs tweaking.

The Sound Dialog Box. Figure 12.12 shows the applet's dialog box, whose components are described here. The figure also includes a composite Message Box showing the graphics symbols associated with four of these events. Some events are reasonably clear, while others aren't. And for extra points, what on earth is that Asterisk?

Events:. You may have already guessed that *Windows Start* is an event that happens when you open Windows. As for *Asterisk* and some of the others, keep on guessing: It all depends on how the programmer used the available choices. If you really need to know, you can assign a distinctive sound to each event. Then when you hear it, you'll know the event has taken place. Note, however, that if the same action occurs within some other program, it may be interpreted as a different event, depending on the mood of the programmer. Therefore, a *ding* here may get you a *chimes* there. In any case, select an event and refer to the *Files* section which follows.

Files:. This box lists the wavefiles in the Windows directory. Select the file you wish to associate with the highlighted *Event* and click on the OK button to save your choice and exit the dialog box. Or, make other events/files selections before exiting, which, by the way, is not an event worth hearing about.

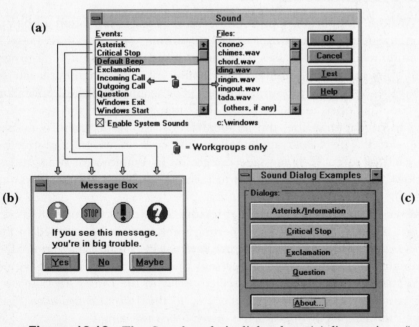

Figure 12.12 The *Sound* applet's dialog box (a) lists various "events" which may trigger a distinctive sound (provided the application makes use of this feature). (b) This composite Message Box shows the characteristic graphics symbols associated with the events. (c) The SOUNDEX applet window's four buttons test the indicated event sounds.

Enable System Sounds.   The audio features described above are heard if this check box is enabled. If you'd rather run a silent session, clear the check box. However, the *Windows Start* and *Windows Exit* sounds are heard regardless of the check box status. If even that is too much racket, highlight each event and select *None* in the Files: box.

Event Usage in Windows.   Windows itself does not yet take advantage of its own audio capabilities, except for opening and closing sounds and a warning for an invalid mouse click or a network printer disconnect. For the other events, you'll have to find a Windows application that supports this feature.

Event-Checking Utility (SOUNDEX.EXE).   To verify that your system supports all Windows sound events, download the compressed SOUNDX.ZIP file from CompuServe's *Windows Fun* forum (GO WINFUN, library 6). The utility consists of a single dialog box (see Figure 12.12c) with four buttons—one for each system event that displays a graphics image in a message box.

Sound Applet Record in WIN.INI

The sound assigned to each system event is written into the WIN.INI file as shown by the following examples:

```
[sounds]
SystemStart=tada.wav, Windows Start
SystemExit=C:\WINDOWS\EXIT.WAV, Windows Exit
```

The first line illustrates the default entry for the *Windows Start* event. (In *Workgroups,* the TADA.WAV is replaced by CHIMES.WAV.) If the *Sound* applet is used to change the sound file associated with any event, the corresponding line in WIN.INI is rewritten as shown by the second line above. Note that the revised line includes the complete path to the waveform file. If that file is located in the Windows directory, the path information is not required and may be deleted.

Table 12.8 lists the seven (nine, in *Workgroups*) events currently supported by Windows.

Waveform Files Supported by Sound Applet

The *Sound* applet will play 8-bit mono waveform files recorded at sampling rates from 8 kHz to 44.1 kHz. In addition, it will play 16-bit mono and 8- or 16-bit stereo files at any sampling rate supported by the installed sound driver, as summarized here for a few typical systems.

TABLE 12.8   Sound Applet: Events List

WIN.INI [sounds]	Waveform (WAV) File		Event (both)	Message Box [*]	Typical Usage Sample
	Windows	Workgroups			
RingIn	–	= ringin.wav,	Incoming Call [†]		*Chat* applet
RingOut System	–	= ringout.wav,	Outgoing Call [†]		*Chat* applet
Asterisk System	= chord.wav,	= ding.wav,	Asterisk	i	MicroHelp *UnInstaller*
Default	= ding.wav,	= ding.wav,	Default Beep		Invalid mouse click, PC Speaker test signal
System Exclamation	= chord.wav,	= ding.wav,	Exclamation	!	Invalid cursor move [‡]
SystemExit	= chimes.wav,	= chimes.wav,	Windows Exit		*Windows* close
SystemHand System	= chord.wav,	= ding.wav,	Critical Stop	STOP	SOUNDEX.EXE
Question	= chord.wav,	= ding.wav,	Question	?	MicroHelp *Uninstaller*
SystemStart	= tada.wav,	= chimes.wav,	Windows Start		*Windows* open

[*] Sound may accompany a Message Box which includes this symbol (see Figure 12.12).
[†] Telephone icon appears at bottom of screen.
[‡] Supported in *Write* applet, *Word-for-Windows, etc*. Not supported in *Notepad, SysEdit*, etc.

Installed Driver	Stereo Playback Support
PC Speaker driver	None, 8-bit mono only
Media Vision *Thunder & Lightning*	22.05 kHz, 8 bits
Media Vision *Pro Audio Spectrum 16*	44.1 kHz, 16 bits

A *Cannot play selected sound* error message appears if you attempt to play a WAV file whose bit rate or stereo sampling rate exceeds that of the installed sound system.

Sound Recorder and Pocket Recorder Applets

This section reviews a few operating parameters of the Windows *Sound Recorder* and the Media Vision *Pocket Recorder* applets.

Sound Recorder

The *Sound Recorder* applet window is shown in Figure 12.13a. The applet will record any audio signal routed to it by a multimedia mixer, such as that described later in this chapter in the *Multimedia System Overview* section. Although the Windows and the Workgroups *User's Guides* both state that you must have a microphone installed in order to record sound files, you can in fact record any mixer output signal, with or without a microphone.

Waveform Files Supported by Sound Recorder. The *Sound Recorder*'s support for playback of WAV files matches that described above for the *Sound* applet. In addition, the applet records in mono only, at a 22.05 kHz sampling rate, provided that rate is supported by the installed sound driver. The recorded bit rate is 8- or 16-bits per sample, as determined by the capabilities of the sound driver.

Pocket Recorder

Media Vision's *Pocket Recorder* applet window is shown in Figure 12.13b. The applet offers more extensive features than the Windows *Sound Recorder*. Refer to the *User's Guide* for information beyond this brief review of record parameters.

Record Parameters. Unlike the *Sound Recorder* applet described above, the applet's record parameters can be selected via the radio buttons shown in the dialog box in Figure 12.13c. To select a sample rate other than the five shown in the figure, click on the lowest radio button and type in the desired rate. The Windows *Sound* and *Sound Recorder* applets will both play back any waveform file recorded by the *Pocket Recorder* at a non-standard sampling rate.

If the *Pocket Recorder* is installed on a system whose sound card offers fewer record parameters than those shown in Figure 12.13c, some of the radio buttons will be disabled. For example, if Media Vision's own *Thunder & Lightning* card is installed, the following buttons will be grayed: 32.0 and 44.1 kHz, Stereo, and 16 bits.

A Multimedia System Overview

When installing and configuring multimedia system drivers, one complex and often confusing variable is the system itself. In at least a few cases it may not be immediately clear whether a problem is due to a driver, to the hardware, to one of the support applets, or to some combination of these ingredients.

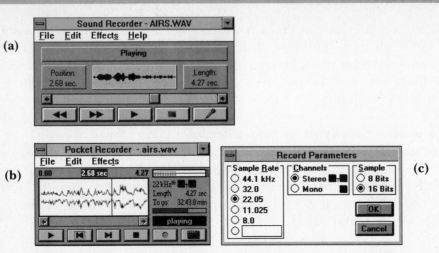

(a)

(b)

(c)

Figure 12.13 The (a) Windows *Sound Recorder* applet window, and (b) Media Vision's equivalent *Pocket Recorder.* (c) Use *Pocket Recorder*'s Record Parameters dialog box to specify sampling rate, channels, and sample size.

Since some (all, possibly?) multimedia packages are not celebrated for the clarity of their documentation, this section offers a quick overview of the basic structure of a typical system. The signal path is shown from a CD-ROM drive to an external stereo amplifier, with stops along the way at the installed sound card and the mixer applet for the audio segment of the program.

Some very basic record and playback operations are reviewed, but only to the extent necessary for a general understanding of the way the system works (or, the way it *should* work).

Media Vision Pro Audio Spectrum 16 (PAS-16) System

A partial listing of the features on Media Vision's *PAS-16 (Pro Audio Spectrum 16)* sound card includes hardware support for 16-bit digital audio recording and playback, plus MIDI and Compact-disc audio reproduction. The latter requires a suitably equipped playback system, such as that incorporated in most modern CD-ROM players. The *PAS-16* card contains a built-in stereo playback amplifier with four-watt-per-channel output. These items are mentioned here since the *PAS-16* serves as the system model in much of the following configuration description. However, the information presented here is intended neither as a complete description of that system, nor a review of its performance.

In some of the illustrations which follow, the actual location of various components has been repositioned (courtesy of *Paintbrush*) for the benefit of the signal-flow description. Perhaps some day the components will be permanently repositioned (courtesy of *software*) for the benefit of the human who must try to run things.

Audio System

The audio signal flow charts in Figures 12.14 and 12.15 may be useful in configuring, testing, and troubleshooting the various hardware and software components in a multimedia system. Figure 12.14 illustrates the relationship between various playback components, while Figure 12.15 adds a few record/playback details. The first figure shows the hardware cables between an internal CD-ROM drive and a sound card, as well as the software "cables" between the card and the applet window used to control playback level. The latter are illustrated by dashed lines between the card and the Multimedia Mixer dialog box. The drive's mechanical functions (start/stop, etc.) are handled separately by the *Media Player* and are not included in the illustration. The second figure details the separate record and playback paths through the Multimedia Mixer dialog box.

The Signal Paths.   In this signal-flow description, keep in mind that the signal may actually be *two* signals: one each for left and right audio channels. In each description below, a parenthetical reference gives the name of the fader pair under discussion.

MIDI and Waveform Audio (SYNTH, WAVE).   If the disc in the CD-ROM drive contains MIDI or WAV audio, these digital audio signals are routed to the sound card through the 50-conductor SCSI cable that links the drive to the card. There, the signals are converted to analog and then sent to the SYNTH and WAVE faders. MIDI and waveform audio signals derived from hard-disk files (*filename*.MID or *filename*.WAV) are also routed to these faders.

CD Audio (CD).   A separate internal audio cable between the drive and the sound card carries the analog (not digital) CD audio output from the former to the latter. This signal path is for conventional compact-disc audio only. The digital MIDI and waveform audio signals are routed separately, as described above. From the sound card, CD audio is routed (dashed line) to the CD fader pair on the Multimedia Mixer. As an alternative route, a stereo cable could be plugged into the front-panel headphone jack on the drive, with the opposite end of the cable inserted in

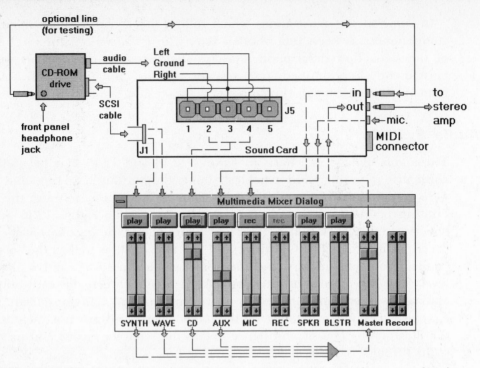

Figure 12.14   Playback components in a mulitmedia sound system, showing mixer control of audio input signals.

the external *Line-In* jack on the sound card mounting bracket. This method might also be used to route any other external *analog* (not MIDI or WAV) audio signal to the sound card.

Auxiliary (AUX).   The sound card's external stereo *Line-in* jack is connected to this fader pair. The input signal should be at line level (typical tape recorder output, for example), and is not suitable for use with a microphone. In Figure 12.14, an external stereo cable links a CD-ROM (or other CD audio player) headphone jack to the *Line-in* jack, an alternate signal path which may be useful in troubleshooting work, or simply to play some external audio signal through the multimedia system.

Microphone (MIC).   The microphone jack on the sound card's adapter bracket is a mono-input device. The single input signal is routed to both left and right MIC faders.

Record-Line Monitor (REC).   If one or more of the other fader pairs are in the *Record* mode, their combined output is routed to the *Master Record*

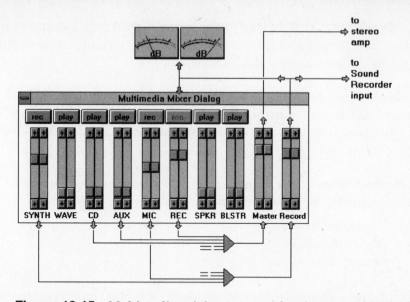

Figure 12.15   Multimedia mixing system, showing record and playback signal paths.

faders and then to the *Sound Recorder* applet for recording. The same signal is also routed back to this fader pair, and adjusted as desired for monitoring purposes. This signal is combined with any other device faders that are in the *Play* mode, routed to the *Master* fader pair, then to the external stereo amplifier. This signal flow path is summarized in Figure 12.15.

Speaker (SPKR).   The internal mono PC speaker signal is routed to the SPKR fader pair, for the benefit of users who want to mix speaker beeps into the external sound system. This signal routing has no effect on normal system beeps sent to the internal speaker. Furthermore, the path is not enabled on all systems. If your internal speaker is functional, but the fader pair is not, then your PC probably does not support this feature. In case of doubt, contact your computer manufacturer, who will probably have no idea what you're talking about.

Sound Blaster (BLSTR).   This fader set controls the signal level from a Sound-Blaster compatible device.

Master Monitor Level (Master).   Assuming the Play/Rec button above the CD faders is in the Play mode, the CD signal is combined with other playback signals (if any), and the combined signal is routed to the Master fader pair. From there it is routed back to the sound card (dashed line) and to the stereo output jack on the external bracket. A stereo cable links this jack to the external stereo playback system.

Master Record Level (Record). Use this fader pair to adjust the level of the combined signal that is to be sent to the *Sound Recorder* applet for recording. The same signal is also routed to the meters, and to the *Record-Line Monitor* faders (see Figure 12.15).

Record/Playback Buttons (Rec, Play). Click the button above any fader to toggle between modes as described here:

Mode	Signal Is Routed to
Record	*Master Record Level*
Play	*Master Monitor Level*

Rec Fader Button. The *Rec/Play* button above the *REC* fader pair is permanently disabled. Since this fader pair simply routes the record signal into the monitor system, the button functions are meaningless.

WAVE Fader Button. If this button is toggled into *Record* mode, the *Sound Recorder* output is routed back to its own input, which is ideal for setting up a feedback squeal, but not for much else. If the button is placed in the *Record* mode, it automatically toggles itself back to *Play* mode if a recording is started. You can toggle it back to *Record* if you want to feed the signal back onto itself, but otherwise just leave it alone.

External Stereo Playback System. Connect the external stereo *Line-out* jack to an auxiliary input on your stereo system. As an alternative, a pair of self-powered speakers may be used. In many cases, the sound card output level is sufficient to drive a *small* set of speakers without installing batteries or using a step-down transformer to power the speakers.

Audio System Check. The procedure given here may be used to verify that the basic audio functions are operational. Each numbered step is valid only if the preceding steps have been successfully concluded. If a problem occurs at any step, troubleshoot that problem before continuing. However, skip any steps that refer to a device not installed on your system.

1. Insert an audio-only compact disc in the CD-ROM Drive, and plug a headphone set into the drive's front panel headphone jack.

2. Open the *Media Player* applet's Device Menu and select the C̲D Audio option. Play an audio-only compact disc and adjust the front panel volume control as necessary for a comfortable listening level in the headphones. Note that this adjustment is for the headphones only, and has no effect elsewhere in the system.

3. Adjust the settings in the Multimedia Mixer dialog box as listed here.

Fader	Fader Setting	Button
CD	$^3/_4$ or higher	Play
Master	$^1/_4$ to $^1/_2$	—
all others	off	—

4. At the external stereo amplifier, select the appropriate auxiliary input and adjust volume control to a low-to-mid-level setting. If the amplifier is also used to play other audio programs (FM tuner, phonograph, etc.), use one of these inputs to set a comfortable listening level, then switch to the auxiliary input for the sound card output.

5. With the compact disc still playing, raise the Master fader pair until the listening level is comfortable. If appropriate, adjust the level to be roughly equivalent to other signal sources (as in step 4) played through the same external stereo amplifier.

6. At the *Media Player* applet, stop the CD playback, then select M̲IDI Sequencer... and load CANYON.MID or any other valid MIDI file.

7. Play the file selected in step 6 and adjust the SYNTH fader pair for a comfortable listening level.

8. Repeat steps 6 and 7, but this time select the S̲ound... option, load any waveform (WAV extension) file, and adjust the WAVE fader pair.

9. Repeat step 6 but select V̲ideo for Windows... and load any video (AVI extension) file.

10. If necessary, readjust the WAVE fader pair for a comfortable listening level.

Audio Sources. Table 12.9 lists some audio sources that may be helpful in verifying the signal flow through various system components.

Video System

Unlike the audio side of the multimedia system, the video system doesn't require extensive mixing support. Therefore, this section simply reviews the video signal path and offers a few video testing procedures.

TABLE 12.9 CD-ROM Media File Sources*

Software Product	Video§		Audio		
	AVI	MOV	CD Audio	WAV	MIDI
Asymetrix Toolbox	—	—	—	(root)	—
Compton's Interactive	AVI	—	—	AUDIO	—
Compton's Multimedia	—	—	Track 2 †	—	—
Grolier Guinness Book	—	M	—	M	—
Grolier MM Encyclopedia	001AVI	—	Track 2 †	—	—
	002AVI	—	—	—	—
Lightbinders Darwin	—	—	Track 2	—	—
McGraw Hill MM Encyclopedia of Mammalian Biology					
	VIDEO (AVS files)	—	—	AUDIO	—
Microsoft Cinemania	—	—	—	CONTENT\HELPANIM & DEMO	
Microsoft Encarta	—	—	—	ENCYC/MM	—
Microsoft Word/Bookshelf	WINVIDEO	—	—	SOUNDS	—
Multimedia Beethoven	—	—	Tracks 2–6 ‡		MIDI

* Unless otherwise noted, entries list directories where files in indicated media format are located. Listings are for system test purposes only. Main program may be located elsewhere on disc.

§ Waveform audio embedded in AVI or MOV file. Use WAVE fader on mixer.

† Track 2 contains separate mono programs on left and right channels.

‡ Tracks 2–5, Ninth Symphony in stereo; Track 6, "Ludwig's" remarks in mono split to both channels.

Signal Path. Video signals on a CD-ROM disc are routed from the drive to the sound card via the 50-conductor SCSI cable, then to the video adapter card, as shown in Figure 12.16. There are no user-adjustable controls that affect the video signal-flow path. The video signal itself can, however, be configured, as was described earlier in *Video for Windows* in the *Driver Configuration Procedures* section.

Video System Check. The most direct method of checking the video system is to execute some application that uses it and see (one hopes) what happens. However, if there's a problem with the application itself, it should be possible to play a video file independently of that application, as described in the following procedures.

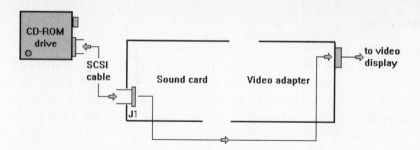

Figure 12.16 The video signal path from a CD-ROM drive to the computer's monitor.

AVI Files. Simply open the *Media Player's* Device menu, select the <u>V</u>ideo for Windows... option and load any AVI file included with the application. If the video plays satisfactorily within *Media Player*, it should be seen with the same quality when viewed from within its parent application.

MOV Files. The video files included in the Grolier *Guinness Multimedia Disc of Records* are played back through the WINPLAY1.EXE file (not the *Media Player* applet). The file is located in the Guinness directory (default name is GGN) on your hard disk. To play any MOV file independently, open the Program Manager's File menu, select the <u>R</u>un... option and type the following line in the Command Line: box:

```
C:\GGN\WINPLAY1.EXE   filename.MOV
```

If you have MOV files accompanying some other application, check the related directory for a WINPLAY1.EXE (or similar) file.

Video Check from File Manager. If you regularly need to review video files without running the related application, add one or both of the following lines to the indicated section of WIN.INI:

```
[Extensions]
AVI=C:\WINDOWS\MPLAYER.EXE ^.AVI
MOV=C:\GGN\WINPLAY1.EXE ^.MOV
```

With these lines in place, open *File Manager* and double-click on any AVI or MOV file to open MPLAYER.EXE or WINPLAY1.EXE and play the selected file. Refer to the *Associate* option in the *File Menu* section of Chapter 6 for additional details on this section of WIN.INI.

Video Sources. Table 12.9 lists some video sources that may be helpful in verifying your system's video configuration.

Troubleshooting

This section offers some troubleshooting assistance for problems that are not accompanied by an error message. Although a few (very few) application-specific problems are covered here, this section makes no attempt at keeping up with every problem in every multimedia software package. Therefore, if you don't find your specific grievance addressed here, it may be worth the time it takes to scan the others. With luck, one or more problems/solutions will come close enough to help you resolve your own trouble.

Determining WAV File Parameters

The information in this section is presented as an aid to configuring or troubleshooting any system component involved in recording or playing back a waveform file. For example, if your entire sound system consists of nothing but the internal PC speaker and the SPEAKER.DRV driver, then the following applet limitations are in effect:

Applet	WAV File Functions
Media Player	Inoperative
Sound	8 kHz to 44.1 kHz mono playback only
Sound Recorder	Same (record function disabled)

The *Sound Recorder*'s Record button is disabled, and the Play button is also disabled if you load either a stereo WAV file or a 16-bit mono file. As noted earlier, in the *Sound* and *Sound Recorder* sections, these limitations are eased if decent sound card hardware/software is installed. Therefore, if a problem related to these operating parameters is encountered, its solution may require a hardware upgrade, or worse, a software downgrade.

If you need to verify the sampling rate and other parameters of a WAV file, the DOS debug script below will display the 44-byte file header which contains this information. The example given here is for the CHIMES.WAV file in the Windows directory.

```
C:\WINDOWS>debug chimes.wav
-d cs:100 12B
12AE:0100 52 49 46 46 28 3E 00 00-57 41 56 45 66 6D 74 20   RIFF(>..WAVEfmt
12AE:0110 10 00 00 00 01 00 01 00-22 56 00 00 22 56 00 00   ........"V.."V..
12AE:0120 01 00 08 00 64 61 74 61-04 3E 00 00               ....data.>..
```

The single underlined byte (22) specifies the recorded channels (1 = mono, 2 = stereo) and the four underlined bytes (24–27) give the sampling rate, in hertz (cycles-per-second). Table 12.10 summarizes all the information contained in a WAV file header.

Better yet, load any unknown WAV file into an applet such as Media Vision's *Pocket Recorder* and note the information displayed in the applet window. Or, click on the File Menu's <u>N</u>ew option. The Record Parameters dialog box (shown in Figure 12.13c) lists the sampling rate, channels, and sample size for the most recently loaded file.

Enhanced-Mode Troubleshooting

If a driver-related problem occurs in enhanced mode, and none of the trouble-shooting procedures below offer a workable solution, it may be worthwhile trying the same operation in standard mode. If it works, then there's probably a problem with a virtual device driver (*filename*.386) listed in the [386Enh] section of SYSTEM.INI. If you're not sure which one to suspect, refer to those listed in Table 12.2. If the table doesn't offer much help, try the *User's Guide* for the installed sound card. If that fails (which is likely), then have a look at the distribution diskettes that accompanied the card. Once you've found the correct filename, make sure it's correctly listed in the [386Enh] section, and expand a fresh copy of the file from the diskette into the System directory.

TABLE 12.10   WAV File Header Details

Bytes		Contents	Bytes		Contents
			Format Chunk Detail		
00–03	4	"RIFF"	20 – 21	2	Data format (1 = PCM)
04–07	4	Length of data following this point	22 – 23	2	Channels (1 = mono, 2 = stereo)
08–11	4	"WAVE"	24 – 27	4	Samples per second[†]
12–15	4	"fmt"	28 – 31	4	Average bytes-per-sec[†]
16–19	4	Format chunk size (10h = 16d)			(sample rate × channels × bits/8)
20–35	16	Format chunk (see Detail column)	32 – 33	2	Block align (channels × bits/8)
36–39	4	Chunk type ("data")	34 – 35	2	Bits per sample (8 or 16)
40–40	4	Data chunk size			

[†] 40 1F 00 00   8,000 (kHz or bytes-per-second)
   11 2B 00 00   11,025
   22 56 00 00   22,050
   00 7D 00 00   32,000
   44 AC 00 00   44,100

Startup Problems

If you've just installed a new driver and the system reboots as you open Windows in enhanced mode, try opening in standard mode. If successful, then a virtual device driver (device=*filename*.386) in the [386Enh] section of SYSTEM.INI is probably corrupt. Expand a fresh copy of the driver into the System directory and try again. If the problem persists, disable the line in SYSTEM.INI and make one more attempt at opening in enhanced mode. If it works, then the driver on your distribution diskette is probably defective. But if Windows still won't open, then the reboot problem does not appear to be related to the virtual device driver.

General CD-ROM Hardware and Software Problems

A few general troubleshooting procedures may help if an error message during a CD-ROM operation does not lead to a resolution of the problem. Try one or more of the following, as necessary.

1. Run some other CD-ROM application. If other applications run successfully, then the basic CD-ROM system configuration is OK, and the application itself is at fault. You may want to check the audio and/or video segments of the disc independent of the application's own software. To do so, refer to *Audio* (and/or *Video*) *System Check* in the *Multimedia System Overview* section earlier in the chapter for assistance if needed. If these checks work, then try reinstalling the application itself.

2. If all CD-ROM applications fail, make sure the CD-ROM drive letter is still valid. If you've recently changed your startup configuration, it's quite possible that CD-ROM drive *X* is now drive *Y*, and your applications don't know about it. Put a CD-ROM disc in the drive and type DIR *X*: at the DOS prompt. If you don't see the correct directory listing, then try other drive letters until you do. Then make the necessary changes to either restore the original letter, or edit each application's Properties dialog box to find the new drive letter.

3. Make sure your MSCDEX driver is properly installed during startup and that it does show up in your memory report. If you need assistance doing this, refer to *CD-ROM Discs and MSCDEX* earlier in this chapter, or to Chapter 13 for general memory-management information.

4. If none of the above works, try falling back to the Microsoft VGA driver. Once you've verified reliable system performance at 640×480

resolution, 16-color depth, then you can upgrade to 800×600 or higher, and finally to the greater color depth you'll want for AVI or another video.

Audio Output Problem. If your CD-ROM drive is connected to a sound card, its audio outputs are usually routed through a multimedia mixer applet, such as that described earlier in the chapter. If no audio output is heard, make sure the appropriate fader pair has not been turned off. Refer to *Audio System* in the *Multimedia System Overview* section and to Figures 12.14 and 12.15 for assistance in verifying the audio signal-flow path.

> **WARNING:** If you use headphones for the tests described below, make sure you follow the 1,2 sequence given here. If you reverse the sequence, *and* are lucky, no harm is done. If you are not lucky, then your computer may be the least of your problems, at least until the ringing stops.
> 1. Plug the headphones into the appropriate jack.
> 2. Place the headphones near, but not on, your ears.

Audio on One Channel Only. The audio program on some CD-ROM discs is recorded in mono, with separate programs on the left and right tracks. Most CD-ROM systems are smart enough to play only the track that should accompany the video, and to route that channel to both left and right speakers. However, some older systems can't handle this and as a result the audio is heard on one side only. If the drive has a front-panel headphone jack, the same problem should be noted there as well. Other audio segments on the same disc will be heard on the opposite speaker.

For troubleshooting purposes, Table 12.11 lists a few CD-ROM sources in which CD audio is alternately recorded on the left and right tracks. Listen to any of the listed audio tracks via the front panel headphone jack on your CD-ROM drive. If audio is heard on the left or right channel only, then the drive does not support the mono-to-stereo switching feature. To further verify that this is indeed the problem, play a conventional music compact disc. If normal stereo reproduction is heard, then the problem is as described here. The fix is either to live with it, or get a new CD-ROM drive. However, if the problem remains, then try the tests listed here.

TABLE 12.11   CD-ROM Audio Sources for Left/Right Channel Check

Software Product	Search Item	Audio Segment Is On:	
		Left Channel	Right Channel
Compton's *Multimedia Encyclopedia*			
	Orchestra	Orchestra	Woodwinds
	Dictionary Help	—	Pronunciation Symbols
	Time Line	1868–14th Amendment	1765–Stamp Act
Grolier *Multimedia Encyclopedia*			
	Animal Sounds	—	All
	Bird Sounds	All	—
	Famous Speeches	All, except:	Bryan, Coolidge, Hoover, Taft, Truman, Wilson
	Musical Instruments	All	—
	Musical Selections	All, except:	Joplin, Sousa

Front-Panel Headphone Test. Plug a headphone set into the CD-ROM drive's front-panel headphone jack. If only one channel is heard, then the drive's basic audio circuitry needs servicing. If normal stereo is heard, then it's time for the next test.

Sound Card Line-Out Test. Plug the headphone set into the stereo *Line-out* jack on the sound card's external bracket. If only one channel stereo is heard, then there may be a problem with the internal cable between the drive and the sound card, or a problem on the sound card itself. Before calling in outside help, you may want to make a visual check of the cable and its connectors. However, if normal stereo is heard, then the problem is in the external stereo system.

Drive Failures. If you are experiencing general drive-related problems within Windows, the first order of business is to make sure the drive is fully operational prior to loading Windows. If not, then the drive or its associated driver needs troubleshooting.

For reliable CD-ROM operation within Windows, you should use MSCDEX version 2.1 or greater. If you have version 2.2 or greater, then make sure there is no device=lanman10.386 line in your SYSTEM.INI file. This virtual device driver was required with earlier versions of MSCDEX, but may cause problems with version 2.2 or greater. Refer to the *MSCDEX Support in SYSTEM.INI* section above for further details.

Generally Sluggish System Performance. If system performance is unacceptably slow, it's possible the *Media Player* is running in the background, and trying to read a CD-ROM disc in a drive that has been turned off. This might happen if you were using an external CD-ROM drive earlier, and turned if off but did not close the *Media Player* applet. If so, either turn the power back on again, or close the applet.

Icon Replaced by Generic DOS Icon. If one or more CD-ROM-based application icons have been replaced by the generic DOS icon, the most likely suspect is a recent change in video resolution. Every time resolution is changed, the icons in all the group windows are redrawn. Windows goes back to each original source for a fresh copy of the icon; if that source is a CD-ROM disc not currently available, then the DOS icon appears in its place. If this is a frequent problem, you may want to copy each CD-ROM icon file into an ICONS directory on the hard disk and specify that location for the icon. If you need assistance doing so, refer to the *Icon Selection Procedure* section of Chapter 3.

Search Function Inoperative. On some CD-ROM software, the search function is inoperative if video resolution is set too high. If you run into this kind of problem, try reconfiguring to VGA mode. If that works, then try SVGA (unless that was the resolution that caused the original problem).

Video Problems. Some CD-ROM discs do not perform reliably at higher video resolutions (especially at 1024×768). If you have any reason to suspect the screen display is not what it should be, try using the Microsoft or some other VGA (640×480, *not* SVGA) driver. If doing so resolves a problem, contact the CD-ROM software manufacturer to see if an upgraded version is available yet.

Product-Specific CD-ROM Problems

This section makes no attempt to catalog all the problems that might show up with all the CD-ROM products listed. Instead, a few typical problems are described. If you encounter a similar problem on some other disc, perhaps the solution offered here will work there too. If not, it may help explain why a certain feature is inoperative.

Compton Encyclopedia Setup Problem. For some system configurations, the Setup procedure will ask for Windows diskette *x*, then keep asking for it. It really wants the Windows version 3.0 diskette containing the old

VGA.GR3 and VGACOLOR.GR2 grabber files. If you have these available, temporarily use them to complete the installation. Afterward, edit SYSTEM.INI and replace both with their 3GR and 2GR equivalents. Then delete the VGA.GR3 and VGACOLOR.GR2 files from the System directory.

[boot]	As Written:	Change to:
386grabber=	VGA.GR3	VGA.3GR
286grabber=	VGACOLOR.GR2	VGACOLOR.2GR

If you don't have the Windows 3.0 files, then copy the Windows 3.1 files to a spare diskette and rename them as shown here:

Rename:	As:
VGA.3G_	VGA.GR_
VGACOLOR.2G_	VGACOLOR.GR_

After installation, edit SYSTEM.INI as described above and discard the files with the GR2 and GR3 extensions.

Guinness Multimedia Disc of Records (1993). There are 37 movie files (*000000xx.MOV*) in the M directory, some of which include audio and some don't. The Speaker button at the lower left-hand corner of the screen is disabled (grayed) if the selected movie does not have a sound track. To verify that the audio is operational, search for *Beatlemania* and view that movie. You should hear sound. Oddly enough the *Howling Monkey* entry, which describes the racket this beast makes, does not include a sound track.

To troubleshoot a file with an MOV extension independent of the application in which it is normally played, refer to the *Video System Check* section earlier in the chapter.

Kodak *Photo CD* Access and Network Access. If you can't access a Kodak *Photo CD* disc across a network, add a set PIX=*x*: line to your AUTOEXEC.BAT file, where *x* is the network drive letter.

Kodak *PhotoEdge* Setup Problem (Workgroups only). When installing this software on a Workgroups system, the setup procedure will probably fail shortly after inserting distribution diskette 2, due to a minor compatibility problem with Windows-for-Workgroups. If so, the following workaround should successfully complete the installation.

Click on the Cancel button a few times, and when the *Insert disk 2...* message reappears, click on its Cancel button. Repeat as necessary until a blank Message box appears. Click on its OK button, then close the PhotoEdge Setup dialog box.

Select the Group Window in which you want to install *PhotoEdge*. Then open the Program Manager's File Menu, and install a new program item, as shown here:

```
Description:        PhotoEdge
Command Line:       C:\P_EDGE\P_EDGE.EXE
```

A new icon should appear in the selected group window. But if you try to run the application, the following error messages appear in succession:

```
Cannot find PCDLIB.DLL
Cannot find RESDLL.DLL
Cannot find C:\P_EDGE\P_EDGE.EXE (or one of its components)
```

To resolve the problem, log onto the DLL subdirectory on Kodak distribution diskette 2 and copy the following files, as indicated here:

```
COPY PCDLIB.DLL      C:\P_EDGE
COPY ENGLISH.DLL     C:\P_EDGE\RESDLL.DLL (note name change)
```

There should be no further problem with the *PhotoEdge* application.

Multimedia Beethoven: *Play from MIDI* Button Has No Effect.   If a section of the score is highlighted but no sound is heard, then the current MIDI setup is not compatible with the *Multimedia Beethoven* MIDI channel (extended-level 1, base-level 13). Change the Setup configuration for one of these channels and try again.

If a section of the score is not highlighted when the button is clicked, then the current MIDI Setup probably specifies a MIDI device that is not installed on your system. Open the *MIDI Mapper* and change the Setup name as required. You'll have to close and reopen *Multimedia Beethoven* for the change to take effect.

Driver Applet Troubleshooting

This section reviews some of the problems that may be encountered while coping with the multimedia drivers that are installed via the *Drivers* applet.

Driver Missing in Installed Drivers List.   If a driver that you need has unexpectedly disappeared from the Installed Drivers list, Windows may have accidentally removed it along with some other driver that you *did* want to remove. As a typical example, the *Ad Lib* driver has been known to leave if a *Sound Blaster* driver is removed. In a case such as this, click on the Add... button and select the driver you want to recover.

Erratic System Performance after Driver Configuration. It's not unusual for the system to perform unpredictably immediately after configuring, or reconfiguring, a DMA or IRQ setting associated with one of the drivers in the Installed Drivers list. Typical symptoms include endless looping of a system sound, and/or unpredictable response to a three-finger salute. There may be a long delay before anything happens, or repeated Ctrl+Alt+Del key presses may have no effect. It may be possible to return to the Program Manager, but not to exit Windows.

Often enough, the only escape route is through the Reset button if your computer has one. Otherwise, you'll have to kill the power, then restart. There's not much point in reopening Windows and trying again. Unless you're just lucky, the erratic performance will still be there.

The problem may be confined to enhanced-mode operation if a virtual device driver is defective, although its more likely traceable to a DMA or IRQ conflict. To rule out the first possibility, open Windows in standard mode and retry the operation that caused the problem in enhanced mode. If the problem is gone, then refer to the *Enhanced Mode Troubleshooting* section above.

However, if the problem occurs in both standard and enhanced modes, open the SYSTEM.INI file and look for a [*filename*.drv] section, such as those shown here for two representative sound cards:

Media Vision	**Media Vision**
Pro Audio Spectrum 16	*Thunder & Lightning*
[mvproaud.drv]	[tlwave.drv]
dma=5	dma=1
irq=10	int=7 (*note* int *not* irq)
	port=220

Note the settings seen in your own SYSTEM.INI, which no doubt will vary from those shown here. If you recognize a setting that conflicts with some other installed device, then change it, either here or at the other device. If you *don't* recognize a setting conflict, it's time to get out a pad and pencil and jot down all the likely combinations. Then start working your way through the list until you find a combination that works. If you have any *User's Guide* documentation, you may want to burn it before beginning, since much of it is slightly to the left of incomprehensible.

For a little DMA and IRQ background information, refer to the *IRQ, I/O, and DMA Channel Assignments* section in Chapter 4, and to Tables 4.5 through 4.7. Once you've found the combination that works, *write it down!*

Media Player

If you're having a problem running a multimedia application, the *Media Player* may be useful as a troublshooting device. If the application's CD-ROM disc has media files that can be played via this applet, try to do so. If the audio and/or video files play without problem here, then a problem within the application may be the result of a defective installation. If you're not able to quickly resolve such problems, the best bet is probably to reinstall the application and try again.

CD Audio Missing on Device Menu. Due to various operational quirks (buglets?), Windows has a positive talent for regularly disabling its own CD audio support. This usually happens when SYSTEM.INI is rewritten to accommodate a new video (or other) driver. At that time, MPLAYER.INI is also rewritten and—if an audio compact disc is not in the CD drive—CD Audio support is disabled.

Although you can open the *Drivers* applet, remove the CD Audio driver and add it back in again, a much faster fix is to edit the MPLAYER.INI file. Find the following line, and change it as shown here:

```
[Devices]
CDAudio=0,
```

change to:

```
CDAudio=17, CD Audio
CDAudio=2553, CD Audio      (variation, noted on some systems)
```

Although a "0" clearly suggests a disabled feature, the significance of "17" and other numbers found next to various items in the [Devices] section is undocumented. In the year-plus that it took to assemble this little opus, no Microsoft representative has been able to explain what it means. But it must mean something, because without it there's no CD audio.

CD Audio Playback Can only Begin at Track 1. If you attempt to start playing an audio-only CD disc elsewhere than at its start, the Scroll Button may jump back to Track 1 as soon as you release it. This is due to a minor compatibility problem between *Media Player* and some CD-ROM drivers. The workaround is to click on the Play button first, then drag the button to wherever you want playback to start. See *CD-ROM Audio Playback Problem* for more details, including information about third-party playback software that does not exhibit this problem.

CD-ROM Audio Playback Problem. If a *problem with your media device* message appears when you try to play an audio track on a CD-ROM disc, that track is probably not an audio track. Track 1 on many CD-ROM discs contains computer data, and CD audio begins at Track 2 or later. Sometimes you can drag the *Media Player* scroll button to other tracks until you find one that contains audio. However, if the scroll button immediately jumps back to Track 1, then *Media Player* does not support this feature with the currently installed CD-ROM driver (Trantor TSLCDR.DRV is one example). In this case, CD-audio tracks on the same disc cannot be played via the *Media Player* applet.

To play CD audio you'll need third-party software such as the Media Vision *Pocket CD* or Animotion *Stereo* applets. Neither has a problem playing CD audio on mixed-media discs. The other alternative is, of course, to play the CD audio segment via the software associated with the disc. In this case, the problem should not occur.

Device Name Missing on Device Menu. If the missing device is CD Audio, refer to *CD Audio Missing on Device Menu,* above. For anything else, check the [mci] section of SYSTEM.INI and the corresponding [drivers.desc] section of CONTROL.INI for the name of the missing driver. Then expand a fresh copy of the cited driver into the System directory. If these INI file sections do not list the missing device, then it needs to be reinstalled via the *Drivers* applet.

Media Player Appears Operational, but No MIDI Output. A likely suspect is a non-functional MIDI port specified in the Port Name column of the selected MIDI Setup. For example, if the name in each row is say, *Pro Audio/CDPC MIDI Output,* and no external MIDI device is connected to that port, then you'll hear silence—and lots of it too. Open the *MIDI Mapper,* make sure the Setups radio button is enabled, note the entry in the Name: box, and click on the Edit... button. Open one of the Port Name entries and change it to one of the other available selections.

MIDI File Playback Problem. If some MIDI files play and others don't, the most likely suspect is the current MIDI Setup. Open the *MIDI Mapper* applet and click on the Edit... button to view that Setup. Chances are, only the base-level ports (channels 13–16) are active or mapped to a valid device, but the loaded file uses the extended-level ports (channels 1–10), or vice versa.

If only one channel set (1–10 or 13–16) is active, play the CANYON.MID file to make sure the specified port is operational. If it is, then create a new setup in which the other channel set is mapped to the same port, or specify an existing setup that does the same thing. In either case, the previously silent MIDI file should now be heard.

Scroll Button Remains at Scale End after Playback. If a CD-audio disc plays to completion, the Scroll Button should move back to the beginning of the horizontal scale. However, in some configurations the button remains at the end of the scale and subsequent clicks on the Play or other buttons have no effect. The only workaround is to eject and reinsert the disc, or switch to another media device and back again.

Shortcut Key Changes Sound System Level. If you happen to be listening to compact disc or other audio playing as a background application, you may notice the playback level changes whenever you press a Shortcut Key combination. This is usually a function of the sound card drivers, and may or may not be fixed with an upgraded driver. Contact the sound card manufacturer to see if upgrade software is available.

Tracks Scale Omits Some Track Numbers. If a CD audio track is very short, its track number may be overwritten by the adjacent lower track. If you have installed the *Media Player* version 3.11 described earlier in the chapter, you can expand the scale by dragging either vertical border outward, thus making more track numbers visible.

Video File Playback Problem. If video playback on an AVI file is not as smooth as it should be, it's possible that your CD-ROM drive's data-transfer rate is not fast enough to keep up. If possible, copy a short AVI segment onto a RAM drive and then play it via the *Media Player* applet. If you can't free up sufficient space to load the file, then try the next best thing: Copy it to your TEMP directory on the hard drive. If you want to get an idea of just how bad video playback can get, copy an AVI file to a diskette and try to play it back. Using the diskette and RAM drives as worst case/best case examples, you can judge the performance of your CD-ROM drive and decide whether it needs to be replaced.

Waveform File Problems. In case of general playback problems with waveform files, refer to *General Troubleshooting Suggestions* in the *Sound Recorder* troubleshooting section below.

MIDI Mapper

MIDI Mapper Icon Is Missing. If you open the *Drivers* applet and note that *MIDI Mapper* is included in the Installed Drivers list, you may wonder why its icon does not appear in the Control Panel. The most likely explanation is that a sound card with the required hardware/software support is not installed. In its absence, the Drivers dialog box may show the presence of a MIDI Mapper, yet its icon remains among the missing. Install the necessary peripheral equipment and the icon will show up. Or if necessary, add the MIDI Mapper *after* installing the sound card and its software.

If the icon still doesn't show up, check the [drivers] section of SYSTEM.INI for a MIDI=*filename*.DRV line. If the line is missing, then the sound card software may need to be reinstalled. If the line is present, then make sure the cited driver file is in the System directory.

MIDI Device Problem. If a *MIDI device . . . not installed* error message appears, the most likely suspect is that missing device. However, there are two other suspects that you might want to consider guilty until proven innocent. This section will help identify which of these items is behind the message. The example given here uses the *Ad Lib* setup to show what might happen if the *not installed* message appears when you try to play a MIDI file via the *Media Player*, or edit a MIDI setup from the *MIDI Mapper* applet.

If the message shows up in the *Media Player*, close it, open the *MIDI Mapper* and try to edit the *Ad Lib* setup. If you're already in the *MIDI Mapper*, then trying to do this is what caused the message. In either case, click on the Yes button to open the MIDI Setup dialog box (see Figure 12.9). Open any of the Port Name boxes and you should see *Ad Lib* listed as one of the available choices.

Now click on the Cancel button, and click on the New button. Give the new (and temporary) setup any convenient name, click on the OK button and open any Port Name box. If *Ad Lib* does *not* appear as a choice, then there are three possibilities, as described below. Click on the Cancel button to discard the setup, which is no longer needed.

Virtual Device Driver Problem. If the problem shows up in enhanced mode, try running in standard mode. If the problem is gone, then a virtual device driver listed in—or perhaps, missing from—SYSTEM.INI is the culprit. Refer to the *Enhanced-Mode Troubleshooting* section above for further assistance.

Defective MIDI Driver. Check the [drivers] section of SYSTEM.INI for any line that begins with MIDI= or MIDIx= (x may be 1, 2, . . .). Copy fresh versions of the cited driver files into the System directory and try again.

Invalid MIDIMAP.CFG File. If the above two procedures did not cure the problem, then the current MIDIMAP.CFG file probably does not contain the information required for the *Ad Lib* setup.

To update the file, you'll need to remove *Ad Lib* and then put it back again. To do so, close the *MIDI Mapper* and open the *Drivers* applet. Remove *Ad Lib* from the Installed Drivers list, and restart the system. Now reopen the *Drivers* applet and add it back in again. You should see a message stating that *The required msadlib.drv driver is already on the system*. If you think the file itself is OK, click on the Current button. If in doubt, click on New to install a new copy of the driver. The final step is to again click on the Restart Now button. Having done all this, the newly rewritten MIDIMAP.CFG file should support the Ad Lib setup.

Sound Applet

A few problems involving the Test button are described here. Aside from that, most *Sound* applet problems are accompanied by an error message.

Test Button Dimmed. If the Test button on the Sound dialog box is dimmed, the [sound] section of WIN.INI is probably missing. If so, the Events: box will show no entries. Refer to the *Sound Applet Record in WIN.INI* and to Table 12.8 above for assistance in adding the section.

Test Button Starts Endless Sound Loop. If you click on the Test button and the sound keeps repeating, you have probably just discovered a DMA or IRQ conflict. Refer to *Erratic System Performance after Driver Configuration* in the *Driver Applet Troubleshooting* section above. Although the Test button has nothing to do with system configuration, the problem is usually traced to the driver configuration details described there.

Sound Recorder

The troubleshooting suggestions offered here may also be applied to third-party waveform recorders, such as the Media Vision *Pocket Recorder* and others.

General Troubleshooting Suggestions. When recording and playing back waveform files, one or more of the problems listed below may be encountered. And if a file is played several times, the same problem may occur intermittently; that is, one playback will work and the next one won't. Typical on again/off again symptoms include the following:

Playback is distorted.
Playback halts before completion.
Meters (if any) continue to flash after playback ceases.
"Playing" readout (if any) does not change to "stopped" when playback ceases.

In cases such as this, a little system housekeeping may be in order, as described in the next few sections.

Increase DMA Buffer Size. Increase the amount of memory reserved for the DMA buffer by adding or editing the following line in SYSTEM.INI:

```
[386Enh]
dmabuffersize=64      (default is 16)
```

The specified value is the memory size, in Kbytes.

Clean Out TEMP Directory. Make sure your temporary directory does not hold a collection of leftovers from previous Windows sessions. In case of doubt, close Windows first, then erase any TMP files in the C:\TEMP directory. If you use the directory as a holding pen for other files, move them elsewhere.

Defragment Your Hard Drive. Sometimes a badly fragmented drive can interfere with smooth recording operations. Exit Windows and run the DOS 6.0 DEFRAG.EXE or similar utility. But first, type CHKDSK /f at the DOS prompt and clean up any lost clusters.

Check Bus Speed. If your sound card is designed to work on a system whose bus speed is 8 MHz, it might get confused on a system whose bus speed is significantly higher. And *you* might get confused trying to find the bus speed of your own computer. You'll have no trouble finding CPU speed—often enough it's even part of the model number. But in the fine art of specsmanship, "25 (or higher) MHz CPU" certainly looks more impressive than "8 MHz bus," and so the latter figure rarely makes it into print.

The bus speed in most older ISA computers is 8 MHz, and EISA systems usually run at 8.25 MHz (33 MHz CPU ÷ 4) or at 8.33 MHz (25 MHz ÷ 3 or 50 MHz ÷ 6). In any case, such minor variations should cause no problems. However, if bus speed is say, 11 MHz or higher, then there may be trouble. Therefore, if you're not sure your bus speed is 8.*xx* MHz, it may be worth a call to the manufacturer to find out. If the speed is 11 MHz or higher, there's good news and bad news: The good news is your system bus runs a bit faster then most; the bad news is that your sound card may not work.

The bus speed on a few computers is user-selectable (5/10 MHz, 8/16 MHz for example). If you have such a system, try running it at the slower speed when using the sound card. It may not be the ideal solution, but it could be the only one.

Play Button Is Disabled. If the Play button remains grayed after loading a waveform file, one or more of that file's parameters may exceed the capabilities of the installed sound card. For example, a file recorded in stereo at a 44.1 kHz sampling rate cannot be played on a system that only supports sampling rates up to 22.05 kHz. In case of doubt, try to play the same file via the *Media Player*. If a *No wave device...* error message appears, then the problem is as described here. If the file does play back through *Media Player*, then the *Sound Recorder* applet itself is defective. Expand a fresh copy of SOUNDREC.EXE into the Windows directory and try again.

Playback Problem with Newly Recorded WAV File. If you record a WAV file and play it back before saving it, the playback is sometimes distorted and/or incomplete. If this happens, save the file, then try again. Sometimes this is all it takes to correct the problem. If not, then try removing the driver and reinstalling it.

When using a third-party recorder (Media Vision *Pocket Recorder,* for example), the "playing" readout may remain displayed and the bargraph meter(s) continue to blink after playback ceases. If a click or two to the Stop button doesn't help, then close the applet and reopen it. This sometimes helps, especially at higher sampling frequencies. To banish the problem permanently, refer to the *General Troubleshooting* section above for some good-housekeeping suggestions.

Error Messages

Error messages pertaining to multimedia drivers are grouped here according to the applet which is most likely to be open when the message shows up. However, if you can't find a message in the section where you would expect it to be, it's worth checking some of the other sections as well.

CD-ROM General and Application-Specific Messages

If the error message itself does not lead to the solution of a problem, then check the *General CD-ROM Hardware and Software Problems* section earlier in the chapter for some troubleshooting suggestions. If an error message appears when playing an audio or video segment via the *Media Player* applet, then check that section below for additional assistance.

Any CD-ROM disc: Network Path Specified: The specified path points to a file that may not be available during later Windows sessions. Do you want to continue? If you open the Program Item Properties box (accessible via the Properties... option in the File menu) to configure a CD-ROM application, this message warns you of the consequences of installing software on removable media. In this case, click on the Yes button, since the specified disc must be in the CD-ROM drive in order to run the application anyway.

(Application name) is already running. If it really is, then you know what to do. But if it isn't, there may have been an earlier load failure. Now, Windows thinks the application is up-and-running, but it isn't. Close Windows and verify that MSCDEX is properly loaded in memory. If it isn't, then refer to the *CD-ROM and MSCDEX* section for configuration assistance. But if it is, then the cited application may need to be reinstalled.

Bookshelf: Out of Memory. Close one or more applications and try again. If the message is valid, then do it. However, you may want to try some other CD-ROM application and see if it works. If it does, then look in the System directory for one of the following screen font file sets, which should have been installed during the *Bookshelf* setup procedure:

EGA System	VGA System	8514 System
EGALSB.FON	VGALSB.FON	8514LSB.FON
EGALSB1.FON	VGALSB1.FON	8514LSB1.FON
EGALSB2.FON	VGALSB2.FON	8514LSB2.FON
EGASB.FON	VGASB.FON	8514SB.FON

If you changed video resolution after installing the *Bookshelf,* then the required font set is probably missing. If so, copy the required set from the VIEWER directory on the *Bookshelf* diskette. If this doesn't cure the "memory" problem, then you may need to reinstall the *Bookshelf.*

Cannot Find Database (or anything else). It's hard to lose a database (or anything else) on a CD-ROM disc, so this message probably indicates trouble with the CD-ROM system itself, unless of course there's a database on the hard disk that has been lost. If that's not the problem, then review the *CD-ROM and MSCDEX* section. If all else fails, try reinstalling the application.

Compton Multimedia Encyclopedia: (smart_init failed) Error #10002: Error Soundex.IDX not found in any read-only directory (.,etc.). If this message appears when you try to run the application, there is a drive-related problem. If other CD-ROM applications also fail, then check the *General CD-ROM Hardware and Software Problems* section earlier in the chapter for suggestions.

Kodak Photo CD and Windows-for-Workgroups: System Error: Cannot read from drive A. This message indicates a minor compatibility problem during the Kodak *PhotoEdge* software setup procedure. Refer to the *Kodak PhotoEdge Troubleshooting* section for a workaround.

Kodak Photo CD: There is not enough memory to start the specified application. Quit one or more applications, and then try again (or any other memory-related message). This message may show up while trying to run *X*:\WINDOWS\SETUP on the Kodak *Photo CD* disc (where *X* is the CD-ROM drive letter). If so, and you know there is sufficient memory, then the CD-ROM drive may not be compatible with the software. For example, early NEC CDR-84 drives need a chip upgrade to cope with Kodak software. In case of doubt, contact the hardware and software suppliers, both of whom will be happy to blame the other.

Movie is still playing! Please close the movie window before continuing. If the message is valid, then follow the advice given. However, if the message appears as you try to close a CD-ROM based application, and a movie window is *not* open, then you'll probably have to reboot to recover. This problem may follow an earlier *Cannot read from drive X* message. If that describes your situation, contact the disc manufacturer to see if an upgrade is available.

MultiMedia Beethoven: The music example could not be played. Check the music synthesizer and make sure other programs are not using the synthesizer. Among those other applications is Windows itself: Make sure the *MIDI Mapper* is not open, and then try again.

Multimedia Viewer: Please make sure the (*application name*) CD is in *X*:\ (*where X: is the CD-ROM drive letter*). If the cited disc is indeed in the specified drive, then it's possible your MSCDEX.EXE file is either missing or defective. If you need assistance verifying the correct configuration, refer to the *CD-ROM Discs and MSCDEX* section earlier in the chapter.

System Error: Cannot read from drive X. If the message cites the CD-ROM drive, and the correct disc is in the drive, eject and reinsert it, then try again. With some software, if you click on the Cancel button, a *Tried to show movie* message will appear. Refer to that message and to *Movie is still Playing!* for additional details.

Tried to show movie: *X*:*path**filename.ext*. This message may follow the *System Error: Cannot read from drive X* message cited above. If you can't continue normal operations, you'll probably have to reboot. Refer to the *Movie is still playing!* message for additional details.

Drivers Error Messages

These messages indicate a driver-related problem that may usually be resolved via the *Drivers* applet, or in the case of MSCDEX, by editing your startup files.

Cannot load the (*driver description*) driver. The driver file may be missing. Try installing the driver again, or contact your system administrator. Unfortunately, the message does not give the name of the file that Windows can't load. If you're not sure what it is, look in the [drivers.desc] section of CONTROL. INI for a line which ends with the *driver description* seen in the message. That line begins with the name of the missing driver file. Install a fresh copy of that file into the System directory and try again.

Cannot share drives. This message may show up during system bootup, if the /S switch is on the MSCDEX command line, and MSCDEX does not load properly. If so, troubleshoot the MSCDEX problem (temporarily disable the /S switch if necessary). Once MSCDEX loads without problems, the message should go away.

Configuration or hardware problem has occurred. Use the Drivers option in the Control Panel to reconfigure the (*sound card name*) driver. This message shows up as Windows restarts, if either problem is encountered. Assuming the card itself is not defective, the most likely suspect is an invalid port or interrupt setting.

Current Sound Device cannot be used, because there are no Multimedia Sound Devices installed. Select another device in the Sound Setup Dialog. (*Message box lists application name.*) If this message appears as Windows opens, some startup application went looking for a multimedia device and couldn't find it. Or, the message might be seen later on, if you try to open such an application after Windows itself has opened. In either case try to identify the missing device, then open the *Drivers* applet and add it.

Driver: This (*driver name*) driver is required by the system. If you remove it, your system may not work properly. Are you sure you want to remove it? This message is seen when removing just about any driver in the *Drivers* applet's

Installed Drivers list. It's true—your system may *not* work properly, but only if you try to use the driver after you've removed it. Consider the message as just a little reminder, or re-read the *Remove Driver* section near the beginning of the chapter.

Driver: No mixer device drivers are available. The most likely reason for this (or a similar) message to show up is that a recent removal of some other driver took the mixer driver with it by accident. Open the *Drivers* applet, click on the Add... button, and scan the List of Drivers box for an entry with the word "Mixer" in it. If there is none, then insert the distribution diskette that came with your sound card into drive A, click on Unlisted or Updated Driver, and search that diskette for the driver. Highlight it and click on the OK button to install it.

Interrupt setting does not match those on the card. Check your hardware settings, and then try again. If you see this message while setting up a sound card via the *Drivers* applet, the easiest fix is to select one of the other Interrupt settings listed in the dialog box. Keep at it until you find one that works. If none do, then make a note of the available interrupts. Exit Windows, turn the power off, open the system, and have a look at the Interrupt jumper on the card. Select a setting that matches one of those previously seen in the dialog box. Make sure the new setting does not conflict with some other device that uses the same interrupt.

Port setting does not match those on the card. Check your hardware settings and then try again. Follow the same general instructions given in the *Interrupt setting* error message above.

There does not exist a mixing device. See *Driver: No mixer device drivers are available.*

Media Player

The syntax of most messages cited here is the same as that encountered while using the Windows *Media Player* applet. If you're using some other applet to play a media file (or, to *try* to play a media file), the wording may vary slightly.

Cannot read drive *x*. Please verify that the drive door is closed and that the disk is formatted and free of errors. If it's a CD-ROM disc, the odds are that it is both formatted and free of errors—or at least of errors that would cause a read failure. What's more likely is that the wrong medium is selected on the *Media Player's* Device menu. Or perhaps there's no disc in the drive. Check both possibilities and try again.

Device cannot play. This message appears if the *Media Player's* Device menu incorrectly lists an item that is not a playback device. Since such devices should not appear on the list in the first place, there is probably an error in the [Devices] section of the MPLAYER.INI file. Open that file and note the number next to the device that cannot play. Then open the *Drivers* applet, remove the device, and add it back in again. This action should correct any errors in the line, and either the device *will* play the next time you open the *Media Player* applet, or its name will no longer appear on the Device menu.

MCI device you are using does not support the specified command. On some CD-ROM drives you can eject the currently inserted disc by clicking on the *Media Player's* Eject button, but a subsequent click on the same button does not reinsert the disc, and instead this message appears. This is a typical condition on a drive that uses a disc caddy to hold the disc. You'll have to reinsert the caddy by hand—not high tech, but it works.

No MIDI devices installed on the system. Use the Drivers option in Control Panel to install the driver. *What* driver? If you installed sound card hardware that supports MIDI playback, the necessary driver should already be in place. In case of doubt, use Table 12.1 as a guide and check the [drivers] section of SYSTEM.INI and CONTROL.INI files for the necessary MIDI driver lines. If they're missing, then you need to reinstall the sound card software, which should take care of the MIDI driver problem.

However, it's also possible that the MIDI Mapper Setup is invalid. If you think the *Media Player* applet should be able to play a MIDI file, open the *MIDI Mapper* and select a Setups option name that is known to be good. If that works, then the problem is probably related to the MIDIMAP.CFG file. Refer to the *MIDIMAP.CFG File Troubleshooting* section for the procedure to update this file.

Multimedia timers are being used by other applications. Quit one of these applications, and then try again (enhanced-mode message). If the message is valid, then follow its advice. However, if there are no other applications using multimedia resources, then the VTDAPI.386 file is probably defective. To verify this, exit Windows, reopen in standard mode, and try the same operation. If it works, then expand a fresh copy of VTDAPI.386 into the System directory and try again.

No wave device that can play files in the current format is installed. Use the Drivers option to install the wave device. The *Media Player* applet displays this message if you open its Device Menu, select the <u>S</u>ound... option, and try to play a WAV audio file on a system that does have the necessary hardware/software support installed. There are a few possibilities to be considered.

PC Speaker Driver Installed. The *Media Player* applet does not support wavefile playback if the PC speaker driver is installed. However, limited WAV audio support is available by loading a WAV file into the *Sound Recorder* for playback.

Sound Card Installed. Check the installation procedure and/or *Drivers* applet to make sure the required software driver is properly installed and configured.

WAV File Recorded at Wrong Sampling Rate. If the WAV file you're attempting to play was recorded elsewhere, it's possible that the recording was made in a format not supported on your computer (for example, wrong sampling rate, stereo instead of mono). In case of doubt, play one of the Windows WAV files, which were recorded in 8-bit mono at a 22,050 kHz sampling rate. If the Windows file plays, then the other wavefile file is incompatible with your system. If the Windows file does *not* play, then the *Media Player* itself may be defective. Expand a fresh copy into the Windows directory and try again.

Problem with your media device. Make sure it is working correctly or contact the device manufacturer. Well now, if the device were working correctly there wouldn't be a problem, would there? If the message appears while trying to play a file via the *Media Player*, note the device listed in the Title Bar. If it is not correct, open the Device menu and select the device you want to use.

If the problem is confined to audio playback on a CD-ROM disc, refer to *CD-ROM Audio Playback Problem* in the *Media Player Troubleshooting* section above.

Problem with your media device. You may have a data disc in your CD ROM drive that does not contain CD digital audio. Put a digital audio disc in your drive and try again. This more informative message appears under the conditions described above, if Media Vision's *Pocket CD* applet is used instead of the *Media Player*.

Specified device is not open or is not recognized by MCI. If you see this message when you select CD Audio on the *Media Player's* Device Menu, make sure an audio disc is properly seated in the drive and that the drive door is closed.

Specified file cannot be played on the specified MCI device. The file may be corrupt, or not in the correct format. To verify the problem, try to play some other media file in the same format. If that file plays correctly, then the first one is indeed corrupt, or perhaps mislabeled as say, a waveform (WAV) file when it is in fact a MIDI (MID) file.

In the unlikely event that every file in the specified format cannot be played, then there's something wrong with the driver associated with the format. Try switching to another format (CD audio instead of WAV or MIDI, for example). If there's no longer a problem, then replace the driver that was in use when the message appeared. But if the problem persists in all media formats, then the *Media Player* itself is defective. This, however, is unlikely, since the message content usually indicates a specific file problem.

Specified MIDI device is already in use. Wait until it is free, and then try again. If this message appears when you try to play a MIDI file, then either the *MIDI Mapper* applet is open, or some other MIDI applet is active. Close whatever it is, then try again.

Undetectable problem in loading the specified device driver. In order to get to the bottom of this one, you have to know *what* specified device driver. The message doesn't say, but you can probably guess at it—it's the driver for whatever device you're trying to use. In case of doubt, refer to Table 12.1 to find the name of the driver associated with various *Media Player* devices. Then expand a fresh copy of the appropriate driver into the System directory and try again.

MIDI Mapper

The messages in this section are directly associated with the *MIDI Mapper* applet. Additional MIDI error messages which may show up while using the *Media Player* were described in the previous section.

Delete Setup: You cannot delete setup '*setup name*' because it is currently in use. In order to delete the selected setup name, choose some other setup, then close and reopen the *MIDI Mapper*. Now select the setup you want to delete and click on the Delete button.

MIDI Mapper could not find a valid MIDIMAP.CFG file in your Windows SYSTEM directory. It cannot run without this file. Do you want to create and initialize a new MIDIMAP.CFG file? If you want to do this, then click on the Yes button to initialize the new file. Its sole entry will be a setup named "Vanilla" which is helpfully (?) described as a "Vanilla setup definition." The MIDI Mapper Setup box will show 16 Ports and 16 Patch Maps, all named [None]. For Patch Maps and Key Maps, you'll find a disabled "No entries found" line.

If that's a bit more vanilla than you can handle, click on the No button instead. Then, expand a fresh copy of MIDIMAP.CF_ into the System directory as MIDIMAP.CFG and retry the *MIDI Mapper* applet. Or, if you installed a sound card that came with its own MIDIMAP.CFG file, expand or copy that file into your System directory.

MIDI Mapper setup refers to a MIDI device that is not installed on the system. Use MIDI Mapper to edit the setup. If the *MIDI Mapper* applet's Setups lists a MIDI device that is not installed, this message appears if an applet tries to play a MIDI file. Open the *MIDI Mapper* and select some other Setups name. If a similar message appears, then the selected device is also not installed. Keep at it until you can close the dialog box without getting an error message.

MIDI setup references a MIDI device which is not installed on your system. Do you want to continue? In trying to make sense out of this message, remember that an installed MIDI device requires several ingredients: one or two valid driver references in SYSTEM.INI, one more in CONTROL.INI, and an up-to-date MIDIMAP.CFG file in the System directory. If you're not sure which ingredient is missing or defective, then review one of the following sections, depending on which button brought up the message in the first place.

Edit... Button. In the MIDI Setup dialog box which is about to open, one or more entries in the Port Name column refer to a MIDI port that is not available on your system. Click on the Yes button if you want to edit the setup to correct this reference or make other changes. Or, click on the No button, then select a different Setups name.

If the ports listed in the Port Name column appear valid for your system configuration, then a driver associated with one of those ports is either missing or defective. If you're not sure which port is causing the problem, refer to the *MIDI Device Problem* section for troubleshooting assistance.

Close Button. The message also appears if you attempt to close the *MIDI Mapper* under the conditions just described. If you click on the Yes button, the applet closes but the *Media Player* will display a *MIDI Mapper setup refers...* error message if you try to play a MIDI file. Refer to that message above for further assistance. Or, click on the No button and make the necessary changes before quitting.

You will not be able to change any settings because the MIDI Mapper is currently being used by another application. If you want to change settings, wait until the application is finished, and then try again. The message appears if you try to open the *MIDI Mapper* applet while the *Media Player* (or some other applet) is playing a MIDI file. When you click on the OK button, the MIDI Mapper dialog box appears, but any changes you make are ignored, and additional OK and New... buttons in the dialog boxes are disabled. To use the *MIDI Mapper* for editing, close the M*edia Player* first.

Sound and Sound Recorder Applets

The error messages seen here apply to the *Sound* applet Sound, *Media Player,* and just about anything else that can—or *should*—play a waveform audio file (WAV extension).

Cannot play the selected sound. Make sure:
- **The sound file exists and is a wavefile.**
- **The sound file is not already being used.**
- **Enough memory is available.**

If the message check list doesn't turn up the problem, then further troubleshooting is needed. For example, the message shows up in the *Sound* applet if you select a wavefile recorded at the wrong sampling rate, in which case none of the above checks are valid. To verify this possibility, try to play the same file via the *Media Player* applet. If a *No wave device...* error message appears, refer to that message in the *Media Player* section above.

Sound Recorder cannot record or play back because a sound driver is not installed. Use the Driver option in Control Panel to install a driver. An [MCI] Sound entry should appear in the *Drivers* applet's Installed Drivers list. If it doesn't, then click on the Add... button and install it.

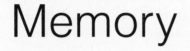

Memory

There are three secret ingredients in the ideal Windows 3.1 configuration: memory, memory, and memory. Windows just loves the stuff and, like other forms of wealth, you (or it) just can't have too much of it. To continue the analogy, you should invest your available memory wisely to maximize your dividends. In this case, the investment is in the form of careful configuration, and the dividend is enhanced system performance.

To help configure your installed memory, this chapter takes a long look at some of the variables involved. The first section offers a few definitions of memory-related terms that appear throughout the chapter. This is followed by an overview of the Windows System Resources structure—a necessary evil since these Resources are not what you might think they are. Next in line is a review of a few memory-management utilities that are all but essential in reviewing any system's memory configuration.

The two sections following present an overview of memory management with DOS and Windows 3.1 software or with typical third-party memory managers. The information in both sections should be supplemented by a careful reading of the appropriate *User's Guide* for the software under discussion.

The chapter continues with a look at some memory-management techniques that may help you to further optimize your memory configuration using whichever software you have selected. This is followed by a look at some of the memory-related features and functions that go a long way toward muddling anyone's memory, in the computer or elsewhere. The topics covered are: virtual memory, swap files, Smart Drive, 32-bit access, and the RAM drive. Since getting all of these items to peacefully coexist takes a bit of doing, these sections offer a few suggestions on how to proceed.

Finally, the section on troubleshooting may come in handy when some of the guns in your system's memory arsenal start misfiring. To get to the root of the trouble with a minimum of grief, the section is divided according to the item causing the trouble.

The chapter concludes (finally!) with a look at some error messages that may be encountered when there's memory trouble. As above, messages are arranged according to the device that is the source of the problem.

> **NOTE:** Unless otherwise noted, all references in this chapter to Windows 3.1 apply as well to Windows-for-Workgroups 3.1.

Definitions

For the purposes of smoothing the way through this chapter, a few memory-related terms are defined here. The described memory areas are all shown on the memory map in Figure 13.1 and are tabulated in Tables 13.1a and b.

Conventional Memory. Also called *lower* memory, this is the area below 640K (hex segments 0000–9FFF).

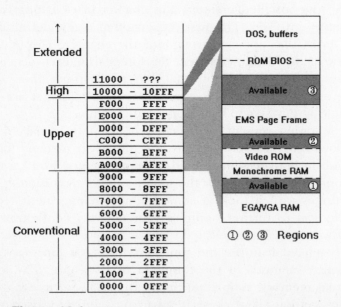

Figure 13.1   Memory Map, showing conventional, upper, and high memory areas.

TABLE 13.1a   Conventional and Extended Memory Details

Memory Type	Size (KB)	Start (KB)	End (KB)	Start[†] (Hex)	End (Hex)	Typical Usage
Conventional	640	0	640	0000	9FFF	Various
Upper	384	640	1024	A000	FFFF	
Upper Memory Blocks	64	640		A000	AFFF	EGA/VGA graphics
	64	704		B000	BFFF	EGA/VGA text (at B800)
	64	768		C000	CFFF	Video ROM (24–32K)
	64	832		D000	DFFF	Adapters, drivers, TSRs
	64	896		E000	EFFF	EMS page frame, etc.
	64	960		F000	FFFF	ROM BIOS
Extended	[‡]	1024	[‡]	100000	[‡]	
High Memory Area	64	1024	1088	100000	110000	DOS 5.0, 6.0, or other

[†] Hex addresses below 100000 (1024 Kb) given in segment format.
[‡] Size and address range depends on system configuration.

TABLE 13.1b   Typical Upper Memory Block Area Usage

Address	Occupied by	Address	Occupied by	Or	Or
FC00–FFFF	ROM BIOS	CC00–CFFF	Unassigned	Unassigned	Network ROM
F800–FBFF	ROM BIOS	C800–CBFF	8514/a ROM	Unassigned	Hard disk ctrlr.
F400–F7FF	ROM BIOS	C400–C7FF	8514/a ROM	VGA ROM	
F000–F3FF	ROM BIOS	C000–C3FF	8514/a ROM	EGA/VGA or other ROM	
EC00–EFFF	Unassigned[†]	BC00–BFFF	EGA/VGA RAM	(Text mode)	
E800–EBFF	Unassigned[†]	B800–BBFF	EGA/VGA RAM	(Text mode)	
E400–E7FF	Unassigned[†]	B400–B7FF	Unassigned	Mono/Hercules RAM	
E000–E3FF	Unassigned[†]	B000–BFFF	Unassigned	Mono/Hercules RAM	
DC00–DFFF	Unassigned	AC00–AFFF	EGA/VGA RAM	(High resolution)	
D800–DBFF	Unassigned	A800–ABFF	EGA/VGA RAM	(High resolution)	
D400–D7FF	Unassigned	A400–A7FF	EGA/VGA RAM	(High resolution)	
D000–D3FF	Unassigned	A000–AFFF	EGA/VGA RAM	(High resolution)	

[†] E000-EFFF additional ROM BIOS on PS/2 systems. May also be unavailable on certain other systems.

Expanded Memory (EMS). Expanded memory is any memory installed on an accessory memory adapter, but that does not have a permanently assigned address in conventional or extended memory. As it is needed, expanded memory is paged in and out of a page frame located within the extended (or occasionally, conventional) memory area.

Extended Memory (XMS). This term describes any memory whose address is at or above the first 1 Mbyte. Thus, extended memory starts at absolute hexadecimal address 100000 (decimal 1,048,576).

High DOS, High DOS Area. More jargon! Some documentation refers to upper memory as a *High DOS* area. And so it is, except that Microsoft documentation calls it upper memory. Try to remember that the *High DOS* area is not the same as the *High Memory Area*. It might help to remember that while *High DOS* does not contain DOS, *High Memory* does. Then again, it might not.

High Memory Area (HMA). Although the term might describe any memory area with a high address, popular usage restricts it to the 64 Kbyte block at the beginning of extended memory (hex 100000–110000). This is the area in which part of DOS 5.0 or 6.0 can be loaded in order to save some conventional memory space.

Kbytes and Mbytes. In this chapter and elsewhere in the book, an uppercase "K" indicates the quantity 2^{10}, or 1024. The *kilo,* or *k,* prefix is reserved for what it really is: the quantity 1000, exactly. Thus, 5 Kbytes is 5120 bytes, while 5 kHz (kilohertz) is 5000 hertz.

Likewise, an Mbyte is 2^{20}, or 1,048,576 bytes, and the *mega* prefix (one million, exactly) is not used to express a memory quantity (or, *shouldn't* be—most people do anyway). Unlike *k* and *K,* an uppercase *M* is used interchangeably to express both Mbytes and MHz. So the reader will have to examine the context to determine if it means a power of 2, or a multiple of one million. For memory matters, it invariably means the former; for everything else, the latter.

Given the ever-increasing interest in matters multimedia, it may be worthwhile keeping the distinctions between *K* and *k,* and *M* and *mega* in mind.

Memory Regions. In the upper memory area, each contiguous block of free memory is a memory *region.* Thus, in a typical VGA configuration, the free memory at B000–B7FF is region 1, and the contiguous memory block from C800 (that is, immediately above the VGA ROM) to EFFF is region 2. However, if an adapter (or EMS page frame, etc.) is installed at D000, then the free memory above it would become region 3, and so on. These three memory regions are indicated in Figure 13.1.

When certain memory management software is installed, each line in the CONFIG.SYS and AUTOEXEC.BAT file shows the region in which the device or TSR on that line is to be loaded, as seen in these two examples:

DOS 6.0   LH /L:2,56928 C:\WINDOWS\MOUSE.COM
Quarterdeck *QEMM386*   C:\QEMM\LOADHI /R:1 C:\WINDOWS\MOUSE.COM

The /L:2 and /R:1 switches indicate that DOS 6.0 will load MOUSE.COM into its region 2, while Quarterdeck loads it into its region 1. Note that such regions are a function of currently available free memory blocks, and vary (as shown) from one memory manager to another, or as other configuration changes are made.

TSRs.   Throughout this chapter there are frequent references to TSR (Terminate-and-Stay-Resident) files. The term refers to any program loaded during bootup for use later on, as required. Since the program may be used several times during any session, it remains in memory when you exit it, so that it may be quickly recalled whenever required.

Upper Memory.   This is the 384 Kbyte area (hex segments A000–FFFF) immediately above conventional memory. Note that some third-party memory-management documentation refers to this area as *high* memory, or as a *high DOS* area. Although the area certainly is high (compared to that which is lower), either term invites confusion with the *high memory area* (see definition).

To further promote confusion, the terms "device*high*" and "load*high*" (in CONFIG.SYS and AUTOEXEC.BAT) are used to load devices and TSRs into the *upper* (not the *high*) memory area.

Upper Memory Block.   The term refers to upper memory segments occupied by RAM or adapter ROM, or available for use. Often the 384 Kbyte upper memory area is described in terms of six 64 Kbyte upper memory blocks, each beginning at hexadecimal $x\,000$ (x = A, B, C, D, E, F).

System Resources

With apologies to J. Caesar, all of Windows is divided into three parts: one kernel, one user interface, one graphics-device interface. Each part has its own DLL (dynamic-link library) file, as briefly described here. A nodding acquaintance with these DLLs may help make the concept of *System Resources* a bit less mysterious.

The Graphics-Device Interface (GDI.EXE). This dynamic-link library controls graphics operations and printing too.

The Kernel (KRNL*x* 86.EXE). Actually, there are two files: KRNL286.EXE for standard mode and KRNL386.EXE for enhanced mode. In either case, the kernel takes care of basic functions such as file input/output, plus memory and application management.

The User Interface (USER.EXE). As the name suggests, USER.EXE looks after the user's needs: keyboard and mouse operations, some drivers, and the communications ports. In addition, this interface handles general window and icon management and the user dialog boxes.

The Heap. Contrary to popular belief, *The Heap* is not a grade-B movie, but a reference to a 64 Kbyte data segment within each of the above. Windows 3.1 adds two more heaps—which some Microsoft documentation refers to as "two new heaps," which is perhaps not the most informative labeling that could be used. Nevertheless, there are now four heaps (two old, two new) that are critical to Windows operations, and these are summarized here.

GDI Heap. This heap holds graphical objects, such as the cursor, fonts, icons, brushes, and pens.

Menu Heap. For the purposes of this explanation, this new heap is christened the *Menu Heap* since it contains data pertaining to menu structures.

Text String Heap. This is the other newcomer, so-called (here, at least) because it contains menu and window text strings.

User Heap. This data segment contains information about all active application usage of open or minimized windows, dialog boxes, and button/check box controls.

System Resource Monitoring. These four heaps are known collectively as the *System Resources* and, although they are indeed comprised of RAM, they are but a very small portion of the installed total. All things considered, *System Resources* is probably not the best term to describe these heaps, but that's the way it is.

The available system resources fluctuate as Windows applets and applications are opened and closed. Some applications use the resources sparingly, while others take a relatively big bite. Depending on what's running, one can run out of system resources long before one runs out of system RAM, in which case you might see an *Out of Memory* error message even though your system has memory to spare. Perhaps a later version of Windows will change this message to *Heap Space Running Low,* or something.

To check system resources, open any Windows 3.1 Help menu and select the <u>A</u>bout... option. At the bottom of the screen, the System Resources line shows a single "*xx*% Free" figure. This is the status of whichever heap presently has the lowest percentage of free space. In most cases this is the GDI heap, although the "About" screen does not identify the heap by name.

To keep a close watch on system resources, use a resource meter provided in one of the memory-management utilities described later in the chapter. In the following section the System Meter in the *Windows Resource Kit* (see Appendix D) is used to monitor system resources. Similar metering is provided in PC-Kwik's *WinMaster* and other utilities.

System Resources Leak.   When an application is closed, it should relinquish its space in the system resources pool. Unfortunately, some do and some don't. To demonstrate this, begin with an uncluttered Desktop and note the figures reported by the System Meter icon (SYSMETER.EXE in *Windows Resource Kit*). Then start opening multiple applications and applets and watch the heaps (especially GDI) run lower and lower. Sooner or later you'll get an *Out of Memory* error message. Then start closing things and watch the meters rise. Although the free memory should return to the value seen at the beginning of the experiment, the User and GDI heaps will not. For the moment, the only "fix" is to close and reopen Windows.

Such resource depletion is usually referred to as a *System Resources Leak,* and is further illustrated in Figure 13.2, which graphs system resources as various applications are opened and closed. For a more complete system-resource analysis, refer to the *PC-Kwik WinMaster* in the following section.

Icons and System Resources.   In earlier versions of Windows, every icon in the Program Manager required some User heap space. Consequently the more icons, the less system resources were available. In Windows 3.1 these icons are handled separately, so system resources are no longer affected by the number of icons on the Desktop.

Selectors and System Resources.   To further complicate system resource watching, every time a Windows application allocates memory to a data object, it eats a small bit of memory for a *selector,* which is a pointer to that data object. Although these selectors are not considered in the System Resources

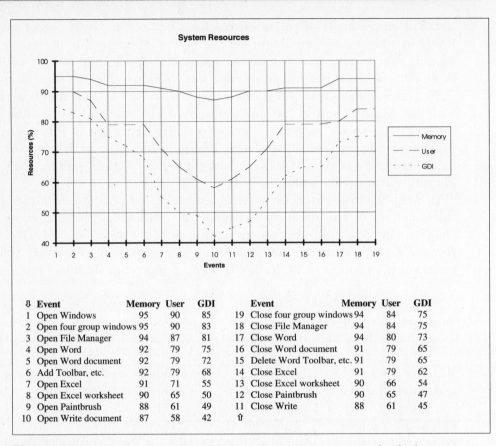

⇩ Event	Memory	User	GDI	Event	Memory	User	GDI
1 Open Windows	95	90	85	19 Close four group windows	94	84	75
2 Open four group windows	95	90	83	18 Close File Manager	94	84	75
3 Open File Manager	94	87	81	17 Close Word	94	80	73
4 Open Word	92	79	75	16 Close Word document	91	79	65
5 Open Word document	92	79	72	15 Delete Word Toolbar, etc.	91	79	65
6 Add Toolbar, etc.	92	79	68	14 Close Excel	91	79	62
7 Open Excel	91	71	55	13 Close Excel worksheet	90	66	54
8 Open Excel worksheet	90	65	50	12 Close Paintbrush	90	65	47
9 Open Paintbrush	88	61	49	11 Close Write	88	61	45
10 Open Write document	87	58	42	⇧			

Figure 13.2 System Resource Usage, showing resource depletion as applications and applets open (1–10), and recovery as they are closed again (11–19).

report, they can contribute to an *out-of-memory* error message if an application allocates many small data objects, each requiring its own selector. Windows allows 4096 selectors in standard mode, 8192 in enhanced mode.

Memory-Management Utilities

In the discussions which follow, frequent reference will be made to utilities which may be used to examine memory utilization. For future reference, the utilities are introduced here, with further details supplied later on, as needed.

The DOS Memory Utility (MEM.EXE)

For a good summary of conventional and upper memory utilization, use the DOS 5.0 MEM.EXE utility and append the /c (classify) switch to the command line, as shown below. Include the | more parameter only if needed to keep information from scrolling off screen.

    MEM /c | more

The MEM /c command lists each program that is permanently resident in conventional and upper memory, and also shows the amount of free space remaining, as shown by the sample report in Figure 13.3a. Values reported will vary from one system configuration to another. Note that MEM /c does not report space occupied by itself while it is producing the report.

Memory Control Blocks. If you add up the various MEM /c program sizes and subtract that total from 640 Kb (655,360), the remainder should be the amount reported on the *Total FREE* line.

It should be, but it isn't. The MEM /c command does not report memory occupied by the various 16-byte MCBs (memory control blocks) that also occupy space in conventional and upper memory. To determine the number of MCBs in conventional memory, type MEM /p instead of MEM /c. Count the number of lines between the second IO entry and the "FREE" entry immediately before the System Program line at 09FFF0. Deduct the 2 MCBs that are currently utilized by the MEM program. If you multiply that remainder by 16, the product should be the few hundred bytes not accounted for in the MEM /c report. All of which may be more trouble than it's worth, unless you want to know where every byte of memory has gone.

NOTE: The DOS 5.0 MEM /c command does not report upper memory usage when some third-party memory managers are installed.

The DOS 6.0 Memory Utility (MEM.EXE)

The DOS Memory utility is substantially revised for DOS 6.0, as shown by the MEM /c report in Figure 13.3b. For comparison purposes, both MEM /c reports were created on the same DOS 6.0 system, with Smart Drive (described later in this chapter) split between conventional and upper memory.

```
Conventional Memory :
  Name                 Size in Decimal          Size in Hex
  -----------          ----------------         -----------
    MSDOS              17392     ( 17.0K)          43F0
    HIMEM               1024     (  1.0K)          400
    EMM386              4080     (  4.0K)          FF0
    COMMAND             2880     (  2.8K)          B40
    SMARTDRV           16384     ( 16.0K)          4000
    FREE                  64     (  0.1K)          40
    FREE              613312     (598.9K)          95BC0
Total  FREE :         613376     (599.0K)

Upper Memory :
  Name                 Size in Decimal          Size in Hex
  -----------          ----------------         -----------
    SYSTEM            168848     (164.9K)          29390
    SMARTDRV           11920     ( 11.6K)          2E90
    SETVER               432     (  0.4K)          1B0
    ANSI                4192     (  4.1K)          1060
    RAMDRIVE            1184     (  1.2K)          4A0
    MVSOUND             9360     (  9.1K)          2490
    NECCDR             12720     ( 12.4K)          31B0
    MSCDEX             27952     ( 27.3K)          6D30
    MOUSE              17280     ( 16.9K)          4380
    FREE                 208     (  0.2K)          D0
    FREE               73392     ( 71.7K)          11EB0
Total  FREE :          73600     ( 71.9K)

Total bytes available to programs (Conv. +Upper):  686976  (670.9K)
Largest executable program size :                  613072  (598.7K)
Largest available upper memory block :              73392  ( 71.7K)

  11534336 bytes total contiguous extended memory
         0 bytes available contiguous extended memory
   8015872 bytes available XMS memory
           MS-DOS resident in High Memory Area
```

Figure 13.3a Typical DOS MEM /c Reports. Smart Drive split between conventional and upper memory (loadhigh SMARTDRV.EXE /L) and listed in boldface for comparison between (a) DOS 5.0 and (b) DOS 6.0 versions.

Not the least of the MEM /c improvements is that the 16-byte memory control block described above is now included in the memory report for each program module.

The Microsoft Diagnostics Utility (MSD.EXE)

This utility is included with Windows, Windows-for-Workgroups, and DOS 6.0, but the only printed documentation is in the MS-DOS 6 *Technical Reference* manual.

```
Modules using memory below 1 MB:
  Name          Total       =  Conventional  +  Upper Memory
  --------      --------       ------------      ------------
  MSDOS         17517  (17K)    17517  (17K)         0   (0K)
  HIMEM          1040   (1K)     1040   (1K)         0   (0K)
  EMM386         4096   (4K)     4096   (4K)         0   (0K)
  COMMAND        2912   (3K)     2912   (3K)         0   (0K)
  SMARTDRV      28336  (28K)    16400  (16K)     11936  (12K)
  SETVER          448   (0K)        0   (0K)       448   (0K)
  ANSI           4208   (4K)        0   (0K)      4208   (4K)
  RAMDRIVE       1200   (1K)        0   (0K)      1200   (1K)
  MVSOUND        9376   (9K)        0   (0K)      9376   (9K)
  NECCDR        12832  (13K)        0   (0K)     12832  (13K)
  MSCDEX        27968  (27K)        0   (0K)     27968  (27K)
  MOUSE         17296  (17K)        0   (0K)     17296  (17K)
  Free         687040 (671K)   613408 (599K)     73632  (72K)

Memory Summary:
  Type of Memory       Size      =     Used      +     Free
  ---------------   ----------      -----------      -----------
  Conventional         655360 (640K)     41952  (41K)   613408 (599K)
  Upper                158896 (155K)     85264  (83K)    73632  (72K)
  Adapter RAM/ROM      234320 (229K)    234320 (229K)        0   (0K)
  Extended (XMS)    11534336 (11264K)  3518464 (3436K) 8015872 7828K)
  Expanded (EMS)            0   (0K)        0   (0K)        0   (0K)
  ---------------   ----------      -----------      -----------
  Total memory      12582912 (12288K)  3880000 (3789K) 8702912 (8499K)

  Total under 1 MB    814256 (795K)    127216 (124K)   687040 (671K)

    Largest executable program size     613312  (599K)
    Largest free upper memory block      73408   (72K)
    MS-DOS is resident in the high memory area.
```

Figure 13.3b

To get an idea of how upper memory is utilized, type MSD at the DOS prompt *before* Windows itself is loaded. When the opening screen appears, select the memory box (or type M) to display memory details. Although MSD can also be run from within a DOS window, a warning message advises that the displayed information may be inaccurate.

Among other things, MSD will display a memory map of the entire upper memory area. The map uses extended character-set graphics symbols to show the areas occupied by ROM, RAM, page frames, and used and free memory blocks.

NOTE: Remember that MSD reports the status of the upper memory area in the current (text) mode only. Therefore, on EGA/VGA systems, the "available" 64 Kb block at A000–AFFF is not really available. This is the high-resolution graphics area that will be used later on when you run Windows.

MSD and 386MAX. When the MSD utility is run, the system may reboot or lock up if the Qualitas *386MAX* memory manager is installed, *and* the 386MAX.PRO file (described below) contains a use=*xxxx-yyyy* line which specifies an address block at or above F000.

MSD and QEMM386. The system may also lock up if the MSD utility is run immediately after installing or editing the Quarterdeck memory manager's QEMM386.SYS line. To avoid the problem, run the *Optimize* utility before running MSD.

MSD File Summary. Table 13.2 summarizes the three current versions of the utility and lists the files that may be viewed via its File Menu.

System Meter Utility (SYSMETER.EXE) in Windows Resource Kit

For troubleshooting purposes, the Microsoft *Windows Resource Kit* comes with a System Meter utility which monitors the User and GDI heaps and system memory, as shown in Figure 13.4. Although the bar graphs clearly show which heap is running lowest, SYSMETER may be most helpful in its minimized format. Its icon (also shown in the figure) continuously reports the status of the heaps, and of memory, as various applications are opened and closed.

TABLE 13.2 Microsoft Diagnostics Utility Summary

MSD.EXE	File Size	Date	Version
Windows	155538	03-10-92	2.00
Workgroups	158413	10-01-92	2.00a
DOS 6.0	158470	03-10-93	2.01

MSD File Menu Display Options

File	MSD Version	File	MSD Version
AUTOEXEC.BAT	All	DBLSPACE.INI	2.01
CONFIG.SYS	All	MEMMAKER.STS	2.01
SYSTEM.INI	All	MSMAIL.INI	2.00a, 2.01
WIN.INI	All	PROTOCOL.INI	2.00a, 2.01

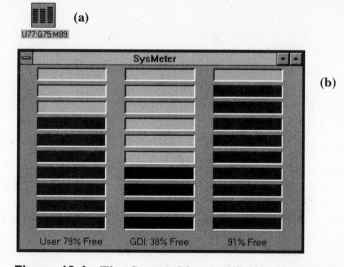

Figure 13.4   The System Meter utility in the Windows 3.1 Resource Kit monitors user, GDI, and memory usage. (a) The minimized icon and (b) open applet window. Column identifications are omitted at smaller window sizes (note missing "Memory" in column 3).

The Memory Report. Windows memory is the sum of actual physical memory and the swap file, less whatever physical memory is used by the system for non-Windows functions (Smart Drive, a RAM disk, DOS, non-Windows applications, and so on). Whatever that figure works out to be, the System Meter icon shows the percentage of it that is still free. So, although you may learn that your free memory is say, 86 percent, you may wonder—86 percent of *what*? If you really want to know, find the Memory figure (in Kb) reported on the About... screen and divide it by the decimal percentage shown by the System Meter (*not* the System Resources percentage reported immediately below the memory figure on the About... screen). Or, use the *WinMaster* utility described in the next section.

> **NOTE:**   If the System Meter described here remains on the Desktop as a minimized icon, Berkeley Systems' *After Dark* screensaver may not function properly. If there is no keyboard or mouse activity for the specified time, the screen-saver is seen briefly, but the Windows Desktop returns almost immediately. This quirk is encountered only if this screen-saver is enabled via *After Dark Runner* in the Desktop screen-saver area.

PC-Kwik WinMaster

The *KwikInfo* applet in the PC-Kwik (formerly, Multisoft) *WinMaster* utility has a Memory Information window that reports both total and free resources for the User and GDI heaps, as shown in Figure 13.5. Note that both heaps are slightly less than a full 64 Kbytes, and that the lowest resource (GDI, in this example) is the one reported as System Resources, both here and on Windows' own <u>A</u>bout... screen.

hDC Memory Viewer

This utility is included in hDC Computer Corporation's *FirstApps for Microsoft Windows* software. An earlier version of the *Memory Viewer* applet was included in the *Windows Resource Kit,* version 3.0. Figure 13.6 shows a typical memory report generated during an enhanced-mode session. The two or three bar graphs display the following information:

Total Memory   This shows how memory is allocated to DOS, device drivers, Windows, and its applications. In enhanced mode, the total includes the swap file.

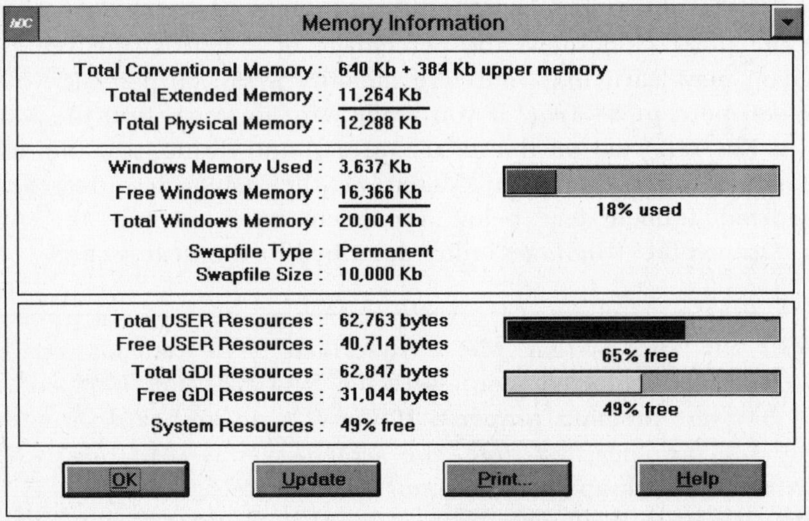

Figure 13.5 A detailed system memory report displayed by PC-Kwik's *WinMaster* utility.

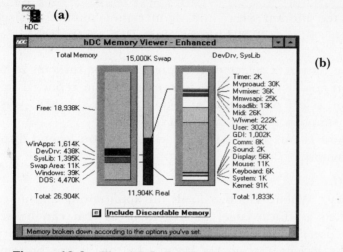

Figure 13.6 The hDC *FirstApps* icon (a) and (b) an enhanced-mode memory report displayed by hDC's *Memory Viewer,* version 2.0.

Swap File & Real memory (Enhanced mode only)	The bar graph illustrates how total memory is divided between your swap file and system RAM.
Options	This bar graph shows one or more of the following resources (selected via **Options...** on HDC Control Menu):

Windows Applications	Fonts
Windows System Libraries	Device Drivers

Memory Viewer Notes. Note that the DOS area includes memory occupied by TSRs and drivers, plus Smart Drive and your RAM drive (if any).

The reported swap file size is generally more accurate than that reported by Windows itself via the Control Panel's *386 Enhanced* icon. For example, when the Virtual Memory screen reports say, a 12,240 Kbyte swap file, the actual swap file size may be 12,244 Kbytes. To double-check the figures on any system, run CHKDSK at the DOS prompt. (Make sure you do *not* append the /f switch to CHKDSK if you run it from within Windows.) Note the number reported in the second row as "*xxxxx* bytes in three hidden files" and deduct the cumulative size of the hidden system files (70,824 bytes for DOS 5.0 IO.SYS and MSDOS.SYS files).

If more than one option is selected, the report may be difficult to read in a high-resolution applet window, due to overlap of the reported items. If this is a problem, select one option at a time, or get the hDC version 2.0 upgrade which supports an adjustable window size.

When *Memory Viewer* is run as a minimized icon, the icon legend displays the current free memory.

Discardable Memory. When Windows loads an application, certain code segments are marked as discardable; that is, as areas that can be relinquished for other use. To determine how much discardable memory is available, toggle the Include Discardable Memory button at the bottom of the Memory Viewer Screen. The button color indicates the status of the report, as follows:

Button Color	Discardable Memory
Yellow	Not reported
Gray	Reported as free (with other areas reduced accordingly)

The memory reported in use by system libraries (User, GDI, Kernel) requires some interpretation. The amount reported for each library includes not only the 64 Kbyte heap associated with that library, but data and code segments as well.

Qualitas ASQ Utility (ASQ.EXE)

The Qualitas *ASQ* utility is supplied with the company's *386MAX* software, or may be downloaded separately from the *Qualitas* forum on CompuServe. A typical *ASQ* Memory Summary report is shown in Figure 13.7a. The utility also provides separate and more detailed reports of conventional and upper memory, with an example of the former given as Figure 13.7b.

Quarterdeck Manifest Utility (MANIFEST.EXE)

For comparison purposes, the same system configuration reported by the Qualitas *ASQ* utility in Figure 13.7 is shown as reported by Quarterdeck's *Manifest* utility in Figure 13.8.

Description	Size
DOS System:	18,432 (18 KB)
Device Drivers:	4,608 (5 KB)
COMMAND.COM:	2,992 (3 KB)
Available:	629,232 (614 KB)
Total Low DOS:	655,264 (640 KB)
Video:	0 (0 KB)
Page Frame:	65,536 (64 KB)
ROM:	48 (0 KB)
SC:	144,464 (141 KB)
SETVER:	432 (0 KB)
ANSI:	4,208 (4 KB)
RAMDRIVE:	1,152 (1 KB)
MVSOUND:	9,376 (9 KB)
NECCDR:	12,736 (12 KB)
MSCDEX:	27,968 (27 KB)
SMARTDRV:	28,320 (28 KB)
MOUSE:	17,296 (17 KB)
Unknown:	240 (0 KB)
Available:	81,456 (80 KB)
Total High DOS:	393,232 (384 KB)
Available Extended:	0 (0 KB)
Total Extended:	11,534,336 (11264 KB)
Total Physical Memory:	12,189,696 (11904 KB)
Available Expanded:	7,962,624 (7776 KB)
Total Expanded:	11,763,712 (11488 KB)
Total EMS+XMS Memory:	7,962,624 (7776 KB)

(a)

Description	Hex Start	Length	Description	Hex Start	Length
Interrupts	0000:0000	1,024	OPT$$$$$	025D:0000	96
BIOS Data	0040:0000	256	EMMXXXX0	0263:0000	63
System Data	0050:0000	512	QEMM386$	0263:003F	3,025
			Ext. BIOS	0324:0000	1,040
IO	0070:0000	2,752	SETVERXX	0365:0000	272
CON	0070:0023	0	CON	0376:0000	272
AUX	0070:0035	0	Drive E	0387:0000	320
PRN	0070:0047	0	MVPROAS	039B:0000	272
CLOCK$	0070:0059	0	NECCD	03AC:0000	256
Drive A-D	0070:006B	0			
COM1	0070:007B	0	55 FILES	03BC:0000	3,280
LPT1	0070:008D	0	4 FCBS	0489:0000	272
LPT2	0070:009F	0	0 BUFFERS	049A:0000	528
LPT3	0070:00B8	0	Drive List	04BB:0000	640
COM2	0070:00CA	0	DOS Stacks	04E3:0000	3,024
COM3	0070:00DC	0			
COM4	0070:00EE	0	RAM	05A0:0000	80
			COMMAND.COM	05A5:0000	2,640
MSDOS	011C:0000	5,104	-Available-	064A:0000	80
NUL	011C:0048	0	COMMAND.COM	064F:0000	272
			COMMAND.COM	0660:0000	80
Device Drvrs	025B:0000	32	-Available-	0665:0000	629,152

(b)

Figure 13.7 Qualitas *ASQ* utility's (a) memory summary report, and (b) low DOS report. Environment and attributes are also reported but not shown here. Reports are for same system configuration reported in Figure 13.8.

Microsoft Memory Managers

This section shows how both the conventional and upper memory areas may be reorganized in order to better utilize the memory resources which lie below the 1 Mbyte barrier. Much of what follows here can be safely ignored by readers who have already skipped down the memory block too many times to need assistance. But for those less familiar with the finer (and often, obscure) points of memory management, each sub-section offers an example of how to free just a bit more memory for use by Windows—or for that matter, by almost anything else.

Both DOS (5.0 and 6.0) and Windows 3.1 divide memory-management tasks between two files; HIMEM.SYS and EMM386.EXE, both described below. Third-party memory-management software often uses a single file to handle the same chores (for example, Qualitas *386MAX* and Quarterdeck *QEMM386*, both described later in the chapter).

> **NOTE:** The Windows Expanded Memory Emulator does more than its name suggests—it also provides access to the upper memory area. Therefore, if you want to load drivers and TSRs into this area, you must include the EMM386.EXE file in your CONFIG.SYS file, even if you have no need for expanded memory. Refer to the *Expanded Memory Emulator* section below for further details.

Excluded UMB Blocks and Windows 3.1 All memory managers provide the upper memory area with RAM, hence the name *UMB (Upper Memory Block) Provider*. For example, the Microsoft EMM386.EXE manager scans certain upper memory blocks and maps RAM into any scanned block that appears to be available. (Refer to the *Windows 3.1 Expanded Memory Emulator* section below.) However, it is possible that a UMB provider will map RAM into a block that should really be reserved for some other purpose. Since this can cause a system crash or other problem, the UMB provider must be excluded from this block. The area to be excluded is either specified by an x=*xxxx-yyyy* parameter, or in the case of the Qualitas *386MAX* utility, the required specification is written into a 386MAX.PRO file (described below). Typical command lines are listed here, with further details in the appropriate sections later in the chapter.

First Meg / Overview		First Meg / Programs	
Memory Area	**Size & Description**	**Memory Area**	**Size & Description**
0000-003F	1.0K Interrupt Area	05A5-0649	2.6K COMMAND
0040-004F	0.3K BIOS Data Area	064A-064E	0.1K [Available]
0050-006F	0.5K System Data	064F-065F	0.3K COMMAND Env.
0070-05A4	20.0K DOS	0660-0664	0.1K COMMAND Data
05A5-0664	3.0K Program Area	0665-9FFE	614.0K [Available]
0665-9FFE	614.0K [Available]	==Conventional memory ends at 640K===	
9FFF-9FFF	0.0K High RAM	D000-D342	13.0K QEMM386
==Conventional memory ends at 640K==		D343-D343	0.0K UMB
A000-AFFF	64.0K VGA Graphics	D344-D35E	0.4K SETVER
B000-B7FF	32.0K Unused	D35F-D465	4.1K ANSI
B800-BFFF	32.0K VGA Text	D466-D4AD	1.1K RAMDRIVE
C000-CFFF	64.0K Page Frame	D4AE-D6F7	9.2K MVSOUND
D000-FFFC	191.0K High RAM	D6F8-DA13	12.0K NECCDR
FFFD-FFFF	0.0K System ROM	DA14-DA22	0.2K [Available]
HMA	64.0K First 64K Extended	DA23-DA26	27.0K MSCDEX
		E0F7-E7E0	27.0K SMARTDRV
		E7E1-EC19	16.0K MOUSE
		EC1A-FFFC	79.0K [Available]

Figure 13.8 Quarterdeck *Manifest* utility's memory report. Program Area and High RAM (UMB area) details are reported on Programs screen.

Memory Manager	**CONFIG.SYS Line**
Windows 3.1	device=C:\WINDOWS\EMM386.EXE x=*xxxx-yyyy*
Qualitas	device=C:\386MAX\386MAX.SYS
	pro=C:\386MAX\386MAX.PRO
Quarterdeck	device=C:\QEMM\QEMM376.SYS x=*xxxx-yyyy*

Regardless of which memory manager is used, it is important to note that the excluded UMB area is—contrary to some Windows documentation—*not* made available to Windows 3.1 for use as a translation buffer area, or for anything else. In enhanced mode, Windows takes its instructions from the UMB provider, and if a certain block has been placed off limits by one of the command lines seen above, then Windows stays out of that block too, regardless of any instructions to the contrary which you may write into your SYSTEM.INI file.

Within SYSTEM.INI, the following lines are often inserted in the indicated section to control Windows' use of sections of the upper memory area.

```
[386Enh]
EMMExclude=          EMMPageFrame=
NoEMMDriver=         UseableHighArea=
EMMInclude=          IgnoreInstalledEMM=
ReservedHighArea=
```

All such lines are ignored if the instruction for the specified area conflicts with a similar instruction in the CONFIG.SYS file. For example, consider a system in which the following lines appear:

CONFIG.SYS:	**Comments**
device=EMM386.EXE noems	Noems provides access to all available space in C000-DFFF (DOS 5.0, Windows 3.1) or C000-EFFF (DOS 6.0) blocks. See i=*xxxx-yyyy* below.

SYSTEM.INI:
[386Enh]

EMMExclude=D800-DFFF	Unnecessary, and ignored anyway, due to noems instruction above.
EMMInclude=B000-B7FF	Accepted, because block is outside the range specified by noems, and is not cited in CONFIG.SYS line.

Upper Memory Block Utilization in DOS Window. Once you've finished filling your system's upper memory area, Windows takes the leftovers for itself when it runs in enhanced mode. Therefore, for each DOS window that you open, the DOS MEM /c command will show zero free memory in its upper memory area. Look for a "win386" entry to see how much upper memory is occupied by Windows.

If you want to load a TSR into the upper memory area of a virtual machine (that is, in a DOS window), add the following line to the [386Enh] section of SYSTEM.INI:

LocalLoadHigh=On

Windows will still occupy a few Kbytes of the available upper memory, but will relinquish the rest.

Managing DOS Itself: The dos= Command Line

The *Memory Management* sections below will show how considerable conventional memory space may be recovered by moving a rather large chunk of DOS out of this area. In addition, various device drivers and TSR programs may also be moved out of conventional memory.

The dos= command line which accomplishes both these tasks may appear in your CONFIG.SYS file in one of the following formats:

dos=HIGH	Move part of DOS into the High Memory Area.
dos=UMB	Give DOS control over Upper Memory Blocks.
dos=HIGH, UMB	(or UMB, HIGH). Do both of the above.

> **NOTE:** The DOS 5.0 *User's Guide* isn't really sure about where the **dos=** command must be placed. Page 447 states you must install HIMEM.SYS first. The next page states the **dos=** command can be placed anywhere in your CONFIG.SYS file. The latter information is correct.

If you install a third-party memory manager, the UMB parameter is usually deleted so that the new manager can take charge of the upper memory area. In addition, if you want to load the high memory area (described below) with something other than DOS, then the HIGH parameter must be omitted.

Windows 3.1 Extended Memory Manager (HIMEM.SYS)

In order for Windows to use extended memory, your CONFIG.SYS file must load an extended memory manager into the conventional memory area. Microsoft's HIMEM.SYS extended memory manager is included with Windows and once installed, it oversees the use of extended memory.

Since Windows and DOS 5.0 and 6.0 are each supplied with a HIMEM.SYS file, make sure the HIMEM.SYS line in your CONFIG.SYS file refers to the latest version, as shown here:

device=C:\WINDOWS\HIMEM.SYS *(switches, as required)*   *(pre DOS 6.0)*

or

device=C:\DOS\HIMEM.SYS   *(with DOS 6.0)*

Some of the switches that may be appended to the HIMEM.SYS line are listed here, with further details immediately following. For switches not listed here, refer to the Windows 3.1 *User's Guide* (pp. 543-546).

/hmamin=*x*   (see *High Memory Area Management* section below)
/int15=*xxxx*
/machine:*name* (*or number*)
/shadowram:on (*or* off)

/EISA. If you have an EISA system with more than 16 Mbytes of memory, add this switch to instruct HIMEM to allocate all available extended memory. The switch is not required on EISA machines with 16 Mbytes or less, or on non-EISA systems.

/hmamin=xx. The 64 Kbyte high memory area can accommodate only one program, regardless of how little space that program requires. Under most routine configurations, some 45 Kbytes of DOS are moved into the HMA by using the dos=HIGH command line described above. Therefore, almost 20 Kbytes of HMA is left unused.

If you have some other program that could make better use of the HMA, you can make the area available to it by leaving all of DOS in conventional memory. To do so, simply omit the HIGH parameter on the dos= line. You can further restrict access to whichever program will use the most of the available 64 Kbytes by first excluding DOS (as just described), then editing the HIMEM.SYS line in your CONFIG.SYS file as follows:

    device=HIMEM.SYS /hmamin=xx

The /hmamin (High Memory Area/MINimum) switch specifies the amount of memory, in Kb, that a program must require in order to qualify for HMA access. The use of the switch will prevent programs with less than that amount from getting there first.

/int15=. HIMEM.SYS cannot provide extended-memory access to some older applications that require it. If you have such an application, use the /int15=xx switch to provide the necessary space, where xx is 64 Kb greater than the space required.

/machine:. If your system requires the use of this switch, you've probably discovered it the hard way long before installing Windows 3.1 However, if you have not used HIMEM.SYS prior to installing Windows, and now your system has trouble booting, it's possible that HIMEM.SYS does not recognize your hardware configuration. If this is a possibility, see if your computer or BIOS is listed in Table 13.3. If it is, then edit your HIMEM.SYS line as follows:

    device=C:\WINDOWS\HIMEM.SYS /machine:*Name*
or
    device=C:\WINDOWS\HIMEM.SYS /machine:*Number*

Enter the name or number listed in the Table and you should see the following message as the system is rebooted:

    Installed A20 handler number *xx*.

TABLE 13.3   HIMEM.SYS /machine Codes*

Computer or BIOS	Name[†]	Number	Computer or BIOS	Name[†]	Number
Abacus 386		1	IBM (continued)		
Acer 1100	ACER1100	6	AT (alternate delay)	AT2	12
AT&T 6300 Plus	ATT6300PLUS	5	AT (alternate delay)	AT3	13
Bull Micral 60	BULLMICRAL	16	PS/2	PS2	2
Chaplet		1	Intel 301z or 302		8
CompuAdd 386		1 or 8	JDR 386/33		1
CSS Labs	CSS	13	OPT 386/25 motherboard		1
Datamedia 386/486		2	Pak 386SX		1
Dell	DELL	17 [‡]	PC 300/33C BIOS revision 1.14		2
Everex AT + 1800		1	PC 350/33C, 380/33C		2
Everex Ntbk. ELX		1	PC Limited		4
Excel Comp. Systs.		13	Philips	PHILIPS	13
Hewlett-Packard			Phoenix Cascade BIOS		1 or 8
Vectra	FASTHP	14	Phoenix Cascade BIOS	PTLCASCADE	3
Vectra A & A+	HPVECTRA4	4	(reserved)		18
Hitachi HL500C		8	Tosh 1200XE, 1600, 5100	TOSHIBA	7
IBM			Tulip SX	TULIP	9
7552	IBM7552	15	Unisys PowerPort		2
AT, 100% compat.	AT	1	Wyse 12.5 Mhz 286	WYSE	8
AT	AT1	11	Zenith ZBIOS	ZENITH	10

* For machines listed above, append /machine:*Name* or /machine:*Number* to HIMEM.SYS line in CONFIG.SYS if system has trouble booting. For machines not listed, or if the listed number does not work, try other numbers in the following sequence: 1, 11–13, 8, 2–7, 9–10, 14–17.

[†] No entry in name column above indicates a system added in DOS 6.0.

[‡] Some Microsoft documentation cites valid switches as 1–16 and 18. Other documentation lists 17 as indicated here.

/shadowram:.   In order to move faster, some computers do a bit of upper memory manipulation independently of the resident extended memory manager. For example, a ROM BIOS or video BIOS *shadow* mode may be enabled, in which case the BIOS is copied into RAM, and that RAM is mapped (shadowed) into the appropriate upper memory area. The good news is that the shadow-RAM BIOS is faster acting than the ROM, so system performance is enhanced. The bad news is that the shadow RAM is requisitioned from your available extended memory, so that resource is diminished accordingly. On a system with minimal memory (2 Mb or less), HIMEM.SYS will attempt to disable BIOS shadowing, in order to preserve as much memory as possible for Windows, at the cost of a system slowdown.

To force HIMEM to leave shadow RAM enabled on a minimal-memory system, append the /shadowram:on switch to the HIMEM.SYS line.

> **NOTE:** On some systems, HIMEM.SYS is not able to control BIOS shadowing, in which case the shadowram switch has no effect one way or the other. To see what the switch is really doing (or not doing), use the MSD utility (described above) to examine the upper memory area. If you want to disable BIOS shadowing, the most reliable way is via the computer's own configuration utility.

Windows 3.1 Expanded Memory Emulator (EMM386.EXE)

If your system has expanded memory, Windows can use that memory in standard mode only, to run non-Windows applications that need it. If such memory is lacking, Windows can simulate it from extended memory, by using its EMM386.EXE expanded-memory emulator. The emulator is also used to provide access to the upper memory area. Therefore, if you want to load device drivers and TSRs into this area, make sure that EMM386.EXE is present in your CONFIG.SYS file. Use the noems parameter described below to disable the expanded-memory option, while still providing upper memory access to the programs that need it.

Even if expanded memory is present, Windows will not use it in enhanced mode. Again, the emulator uses extended memory to simulate expanded memory for those non-Windows applications that require it. In either case, the EMM386.EXE expanded memory emulator creates a 64 Kb page frame in the D000-DFFF upper memory block.

    device=EMM386.EXE (switches and parameters, as required)

One of the switches and several parameters that may be appended to the EMM386.EXE line are briefly described here. For further details and information about other EMM386 settings, refer to the Windows 3.1 *User's Guide* (pp. 552–555).

Note that if neither the noems nor the ram parameter is appended to EMM386.EXE, the expanded-memory emulator assigns a 64Kb EMS page frame, but will not otherwise use the upper memory area.

frame=*xxxx*. By default, the EMS page frame loads itself into the 64 Kb UMB whose base (beginning) address is at hexadecimal segment address D000 (E000 in DOS 6.0). To move the base address elsewhere, use the frame= parameter and specify any base address in the region 8000–9000, or C000–E000. The base address may begin at any increment of hexadecimal 400 (C000, C400, C800, CA00, and so on).

i=*xxxx-yyyy*. By default, EMM386.EXE scans only the UMBs in the default scanning range indicated here:

DOS/Windows Vers. of EMM386.EXE	Default Scanning Range	Optional Scanning Ranges (Others Depend on Hardware)
DOS 5.0, Windows 3.1	C000–DFFF (128 KB)	i=B000–B7FF i=E000–EFFF
DOS 6.0	C000–EFFF (192 KB)	i=B000–B7FF

To include other ranges, such as those shown above, append one or more copies of i=*xxxx-yyyy* to the EMM386.EXE line, where *xxxx* is the start and *yyyy* is the end of each segment to be included.

NOTE: Before using the i=*xxxx-yyyyy* parameter to include areas that the MSD utility reports as "May be available," refer to the Note listed at the end of the *Microsoft Diagnostics Utility* section above.

noems. When this parameter is appended to EMM386.EXE, the expanded memory emulator will not set up an EMS page frame in the upper memory area, thus making the entire area available for other uses.

/nohi. If either the ram or the noems parameter is appended to EMM386.EXE in order to provide access to upper memory blocks, a small portion of EMM386.EXE is loaded into the first three available UMBs. If UMB space is really tight, you can prevent this by appending the /nohi switch.

NOTES: The Windows *User's Guide* incorrectly lists this switch as "/nohigh," but this setting does not work. If you use it, an "Invalid parameter specified. Press any key when ready" error message will be seen during bootup. The boot procedure will pause for a few seconds waiting for you to press any key. If you don't, the system will continue booting anyway.

The /nohi switch is supported by the EMM386.EXE files supplied with Windows 3.1 and DOS 6.0, but was not supported by earlier versions.

ram. Append this parameter to install a 64 Kb EMS page frame in the upper memory area, and to assign free XMS UMBs to any other free upper memory.

win=*xxxx-yyyy*. This parameter may be added by the DOS 6.0 Memory Maker utility (MEMMAKER.EXE), to reserve UMB space for Windows buffers, as described in the *Reserved Buffer Blocks* section which follows.

x=*xxxx-yyyy*. This parameter prevents EMM386.EXE from using the area defined by *xxxx-yyyy*, and may help prevent conflicts if the expanded-memory emulator attempts to use upper memory space that is used by some other device.

DOS 6.0 Memory Maker (MEMMAKER.EXE)

If DOS 6.0 is installed on your system, the MemMaker utility will optimize upper memory utilization to provide a bit more room for device drivers and TSRs. In addition, the utility may reserve UMBs for the exclusive use of Windows 3.1. To run the utility, exit Windows and type MEMMAKER at the DOS (6.0) prompt. After the opening welcome screen, the next screen prompts you to select Express or Custom Setup. Select the latter to display the following list of options.

Specify which drivers and TSRs to include during optimization?	No
Set aside upper memory for EMS page frame?	Yes
Scan the upper memory area aggressively?	Yes
Optimize upper memory for use with Windows?	Yes
Create upper memory in the monochrome region (B000-B7FF)?	No
Keep current EMM386 memory exclusions and inclusions?	Yes
Move extended BIOS Data Area from conventional to upper memory?	Yes

The right-hand column lists the default settings. Follow the onscreen directions to change one or more of them as necessary, then press the Enter key to begin the optimization process, during which the system will reboot several times.

The amount of additional memory that MemMaker makes available will depend on your configuration before running the utility. If you have already tweaked your upper memory into its optimum configuration, then MemMaker won't do much for you, except reserve some space for Windows, as described immediately below.

Reserved Buffer Blocks. In this example, MemMaker options were selected to use the B000–B7FF area and also to optimize for Windows.

These options add the following parameters to the EMM386.EXE line in CONFIG.SYS:

```
device=C:\DOS\EMM386.EXE I=B000-B7FF WIN=aaaa-bbbb WIN=cccc-dddd
```

The first parameter includes the 32-Kbyte block at B000–B7FF and the next two reserve a UMB block (WIN=*aaaa-bbbb*) for API (application program interface) buffers and another (WIN=*cccc-dddd*) for network buffers. Depending on available resources, the two blocks may, or may not, be contiguous. If the blocks are contiguous, they may nevertheless be listed in reverse sequence—for example, B500–B7FF followed by B200–B4FF. In the specific case where two contiguous blocks are reserved within the monochrome B000–B7FF area, Windows may fail to open despite the presence of the device=monoumb.386 line in SYSTEM.INI (the line is described in the *MONOUMB2.386 and MONOUMB.386 Files* section later in the chapter). If so, rewrite the line so that the entire area is defined in a single parameter (WIN=B200-B7FF in this example).

Undo MemMaker.   The MemMaker utility stores your old startup files in the DOS directory as CONFIG.UMB and AUTOEXEC.UMB. To restore your system configuration to its previous condition, exit Windows and type the following command at the DOS prompt:

```
MEMMAKER /undo
```

This copies the UMB files back to the root directory and renames them as CONFIG.SYS and AUTOEXEC.BAT.

Microsoft Memory Manager Summary

If your system began life under DOS 5.0 (or earlier) and then made the transition to Windows 3.1 and still later to DOS 6.0, your hard disk will have a small collection of redundant files on it. Table 13.4 lists those memory-related files that are critical to system performance. As you move from one DOS version to another, make sure your CONFIG.SYS and AUTOEXEC.BAT files always refer to the path for the most recent versions of these files, as indicated in the table. In other words, for DOS 5.0/Windows 3.1 operation, the correct files are in the Windows directory. If you upgrade to DOS 6.0, then the path should lead to the DOS directory. Presumably, all this will be attended to by the appropriate Setup procedure, but it never hurts to double-check. Once you're reasonably sure you're going to stick with your present configuration, you might want to erase the redundant files. Just don't toss out those distribution diskettes.

TABLE 13.4   Microsoft Memory Manager and Smart Drive Summary

Filename	DOS 5.0 C:\DOS Size	Date	Windows 3.1 C:\WINDOWS Size	Date	DOS 6.0 C:\DOS Size	Date
EMM386.EXE	114782	09-01-92	110174	03-10-92	115294	03-10-93
HIMEM.SYS	11552	04-09-91	13824	03-10-92	14208	03-10-93
SMARTDRV.EXE	—	—	43609	03-10-92	42073	03-10-93
SMARTDRV.SYS	8335	04-09-91	—	—	—	—

Third-Party Memory Managers

Several third-party memory-management utilities are available as substitutes for those supplied with Windows 3.1. These utilities usually provide the means for increasing the amount of conventional and upper memory that is available for use by Windows. Two of the most popular memory managers are described below.

Qualitas Memory Manager (386MAX.SYS)

The *386MAX* memory-management utility offers several options to optimize your system's memory resources. One notable feature is its ability to relocate adapter ROM in the upper memory area, thus increasing the size of the largest contiguous free UMB. If necessary, *386MAX* can use the EMS page frame block (if available) as a temporary loading zone for device drivers and TSRs that require extra space during installation. In addition, some conventional memory may be saved, since 386MAX.SYS requires less space than the HIMEM.SYS/EMM386.EXE combination.

This section gives a brief overview of some *386MAX* features that may be useful in configuring memory resources for Windows applications. For more information on any of the subjects covered here, refer to the *386MAX User Guide* and *Reference Guide*. However, if you discover a note buried in the manual that claims *386MAX* is not compatible with Windows standard mode, rest assured that this applies to Windows 3.0 only. *386MAX* *is* compatible with both of WIN 3.1's operating modes.

The Maximize Utility (MAXIMIZE.EXE).   As part of the installation process, the Qualitas Maximize utility rewrites your CONFIG.SYS and AUTOEXEC.BAT files to load device drivers and TSRs into upper memory in a format compatible with *EMM386*. However, if existing memory-management software is detected (DOS HIMEM.SYS and EMM386.EXE, for example), then the initial installation procedure replaces that software with EMM386.SYS, but does not execute the Maximize utility. In this case, you must reboot the system after installing *386MAX*, then log onto the *386MAX* directory and run the Maximize utility separately.

In the following installation description, the CONFIG.SYS and AUTOEXEC.BAT file examples illustrate the changes that occur after the Maximize utility has done its work, either as part of the initial installation, or after rebooting as just described.

386MAX Installation

During installation, *386MAX* makes several changes to your existing CONFIG.SYS and AUTOEXEC.BAT files, as illustrated here. Lines not shown here are left as they are.

Windows 3.1	**Qualitas *386MAX***
CONFIG.SYS	**CONFIG.SYS**
device=C:\WINDOWS\HIMEM.SYS	
device=C:\WINDOWS\EMM386.EXE noems	device=C:\386MAX\386MAX.SYS pro=C:\386MAX\386MAX.PRO
dos=HIGH,UMB	dos=HIGH
devicehigh=(*path and filename.ext*)	device=C:\386MAX\386LOAD.SYS=*xxxx* flexframe prog=(*path and filename.ext*)
or	
device=(*path and filename.ext*)	device=C:\386MAX\386LOAD.SYS=*xxxx* flexframe prog=(*path and filename.ext*)
AUTOEXEC.BAT	**AUTOEXEC.BAT**
loadhigh (*path and filename.ext*)	C:\386MAX\386load size=*xxxxx* flexframe prog=(*path and filename.ext*)
or	
(*path and filename.ext*)	C:\386MAX\386load size=*xxxxx* flexframe prog=(*path and filename.ext*)

Note that the 386MAX.SYS file replaces both HIMEM.SYS and EMM386.EXE in your CONFIG.SYS file. The pro= segment of the line specifies a file containing profile data, which comprises the various configuration options that are to be applied to the memory manager. These are described in the *386MAX.PRO File* section below.

Since *386MAX* takes control of the entire upper memory area, the dos= line is edited to delete the UMB parameter.

The other notable change is that the various lines which load your device drivers and TSRs are rewritten as shown above. In each case, a small 386LOAD entry is made in conventional memory, with the driver or TSR loaded into upper memory. In the examples shown above, each *xxxx* specifies the space initially required to load the listed item, as described in the *Flexframe* section below.

NOTE: When 386MAX is installed, the DOS 5.0 MEM /c command does not report upper memory usage.

The 386MAX.PRO File.   Although the various 386MAX configuration options can be appended to the 386MAX.SYS line in CONFIG.SYS, they are usually handled in a different style. During installation, a profile (386MAX.PRO) file is created, which contains the configuration information that 386MAX.SYS needs. The 386MAX.PRO file can be edited after installation, just as one might edit the HIMEM.SYS and 386EMM.EXE lines in CONFIG.SYS to optimize your system's memory utilization.

Refer to Chapter 2 in the *386MAX Reference Guide* for a complete list of the available options. A few that are of particular concern in a Windows 3.1 system are briefly reviewed here.

EMS=xx.   For normal use of expanded memory, *386MAX* automatically allocates space for an EMS page frame. If you have no need for it, put an EMS=0 line in the profile to disable the page frame and release 64Kb for extended memory or XMS blocks.

FRAME=xxxx.   This is equivalent to the parameter of the same name that may appear on the Windows' EMM386.EXE line. The hexadecimal *xxxx* defines the base address at which the EMS page frame is installed.

HMAMIN=xx.   This is functionally equivalent to HIMEM.SYS's /hmamin switch. It defines the HMA size, in Kb, that a program must require in order to gain access to the high memory area.

NOFRAME.   Some applications, such as Lotus 1-2-3, use expanded memory but do not require an EMS page frame in the upper memory area. If you are using such an application, and no others that do require the page frame, use the NOFRAME parameter to release the 64 Kb page frame block for other uses.

NOROM. This parameter prevents 386MAX from mapping BIOS and video ROM into RAM. You may want to use it to conserve extended-memory resources (see *shadowram Switch* described earlier), or as a troubleshooting aid if the ROM does not function properly when shadowed into RAM. In the latter case, you may want to experiment with the ROM= parameter to determine which ROM block is causing the trouble.

NOWIN3. This parameter saves a bit of conventional memory space by disabling Windows support. If this appeals to you, maybe it's time to take a break.

RAM=xxxx-yyyy. This option prevents 386MAX from mapping RAM into the area defined by *xxxx-yyyy,* and can be used if an error message indicates that an error has occurred at an address within the upper memory area. Both values must lie on 4Kb boundaries (D000, D100, D200, etc.). Refer to the *386MAX Error Messages* section below for further details.

ROM=xxxx-yyyy. 386MAX automatically caches all UMB ROM blocks into RAM for faster system operation. To selectively cache only certain ROM, use rom=*xxxx-yyyy,* where *xxxx-yyyy* is the address of the ROM to be cached. The rom= parameter disables automatic caching, and only those blocks explicitly listed in the parameter will be cached.

USE=xxxx-yyyy. Some upper memory blocks may be available even though they appear to be in use. As a typical example, the 32-Kbyte block at F000–F7FF is usually occupied by ROM that might seem to be off limits as a RAM mapping area. However, this ROM block is sometimes required during system bootup only. Once the system is up and running, RAM could be mapped into this area instead. If you're not sure about the availability of this or other areas, run the Qualitas ROM search utility (ROMSRCH.EXE) at the DOS prompt. If ROMSRCH finds an area that it thinks could be used, it will display the following message:

ROMSRCH would like to suggest that you add the following line(s) to your
386MAX or BlueMAX profile . . .
USE=F000-F800 *(or some other area(s))*

Edit the WIN386.PRO file to include this line and reboot the system, then open Windows and run a few applications. If all goes well, leave the line in place. However, if you run into any problems, either in Windows or at the DOS prompt before opening Windows, then the line will have to be deleted.

The Qualitas *386MAX Reference Guide* suggests adding USE=B000-B800 if your system has an EGA/VGA adapter and no monochrome display. However, the line is often not required since the normal installation procedure discovers that this area is available, and remaps your video ROM here from its customary position at C000.

CAUTION: If you do place the USE=F000-F800 line in your 386MAX.PRO file, avoid using the DOS MSD.EXE utility, which may cause a system reboot or lockup.

Flexframe UMB Loading.   In some cases, a program may require a comparatively large memory area during the loading process, after which much of that space is relinquished. For example, the Qualitas 386UTIL.COM utility displays the initial (during loading) and resident sizes for the following programs:

Program	Available UMB Space	Needed for Loading	Resident Space
386MAX.SYS	65,536	2,768	2,768
ANSI.SYS	62,768	9,040	4,192
RAMDRIVE.SYS	58,576	5,888	1,136
SETVER.EXE	57,440	11,504	400
AD-DOS.COM	57,040	20,736	5,136
MOUSE.COM	51,904	57,072	17,392
SMARTDRV.EXE	34,512	43,360	<u>28,416</u>
Total resident space required			59,440

Note that the 59,440 bytes required by the listed programs should fit comfortably within a UMB area in which only 64 Kbytes are initially available. However, as each program becomes resident, the available UMB space diminishes as indicated. Therefore, neither MOUSE.COM nor SMARTDRV.EXE will load into upper memory, because both require more loading space than is available. To load SMARTDRV.EXE, it could be placed ahead of MOUSE.COM in the AUTOEXEC.BAT file: With 51,904 bytes available, there is sufficient room for its 43,360-byte load space. However, MOUSE.COM would still be excluded from upper memory.

To get around this problem, 386MAX's *flexframe* option temporarily borrows the EMS page frame block during the loading process. Once all programs are installed at their resident sizes, the page frame is restored for EMS use. However, this option is only available if the EMS block itself is available. If you've used the EMS=0 parameter to disable the page frame, then *flexframe* cannot use it as a temporary loading area.

Adding Drivers/TSRs after Installing 386MAX.   At installation, *386MAX* calculates the loading space required for the drivers and TSRs listed in your CONFIG.SYS and AUTOEXEC.BAT files, and rewrites each line as shown in the examples given above. But sooner or later you will want to add a little something to your system, and you probably won't know how much space to specify for *flexframe* loading.

The fastest way to determine the space required is to log onto the 386MAX directory and type the following line at the DOS prompt:

386LOAD GETSIZE prog=C:\WINDOWS\AD-DOS.COM

In this example, the listed program is Berkeley Systems' *After Dark* screen-saver for DOS. Substitute the path and filename for whatever program you wish to load. When you press the Enter key, one of the following messages is seen on screen:

Program loaded in LOW DOS memory for automatic size determination.
If this message is seen, you still don't know how much space to specify. To find out, display a memory report by typing:

386UTIL /s

Figure 13.9 is an example of the Resident Program Memory Summary that will be displayed on screen. Note the AD-DOS.COM program cited above. In both the *Initial* and the *Suggested Action* columns, the required load size is given as 20736 bytes. Therefore, the load line in AUTOEXEC.BAT should be rewritten as:

C:\386MAX\386load size=20736 flexframe prog=C:\WINDOWS\AD-DOS.COM

Program terminated without resident request.   The message means that the automatic *GETSIZE* procedure failed. You may still be able to load the program into upper memory by running the somewhat-longer maximize (MAXIMIZE.EXE) utility instead. The system will reboot three times during the MAXIMIZE procedure, after which the DOS prompt will appear.

```
386MAX  -- Version 6.01 -- A Memory Manager for 386 Systems
        (C) Copyright 1987-92 Qualitas, Inc. All rights reserved.
Serial # 000000000.5 - Licensed to Johannes Gutenberg
```

Device or Program Name	Size Parameters		Allow Flex Frame?	Suggested Action
	Initial	Resident		
RESIDENT PROGRAM MEMORY SUMMARY				
386MAX.SYS	2,768	2,768	No	No SIZE parameter needed
ANSI.SYS	9,040	4,192	Yes	No SIZE parameter needed
SETVER.EXE	11,504	400	Yes	No SIZE parameter needed
RAMDRIVE.SYS	5,888	1,136	Yes	No SIZE parameter needed
SMARTDRIVE.EXE	43,360	28,416	Yes	No SIZE parameter needed
AD-DOS.COM	20,736	5,136	Yes	Remove GETSIZE; use SIZE=20736
MOUSE.COM	57,072	17,392	Req	You *MUST* use SIZE=57072
All programs/environments fit into high DOS memory			Prog/env in use 69,248 Available 61,296	

Figure 13.9 The Qualitas *386UTIL.COM* utility reports initial (while loading) and resident memory requirements. If EMS=0 appears in the Flex Frame column, then 386MAX.PRO has EMS=0 in it, thus disabling FlexFrame.

The appropriate line should now appear correctly in your CONFIG.SYS or AUTOEXEC.BAT file. However, if the line still loads the file into conventional memory, then that's where it will have to stay.

Quarterdeck Expanded Memory Manager (QEMM386.SYS)

Like most other third-party memory managers, *QEMM386* will reboot the computer several times as it installs itself. During the *Stealth* phase of the installation, *QEMM386* will try to make various ROM areas available as upper memory blocks. Although this procedure is usually quite successful, the following message warns you to expected the unexpected.

> During the course of the Stealth process OPTIMIZE will try the methods of ROM memory management. Many strange things may happen during the course of this testing. Do not Worry. If your normal boot process does not complete, just reboot your system (without a DOS disk in your floppy drive). The Stealth process will continue normally after the reboot. You will need a floppy for your A: drive.

During installation, *QEMM386* also makes several changes to your existing CONFIG.SYS and AUTOEXEC.BAT files, as illustrated below. The switches and parameters shown may vary, depending on how your system is configured. At one point in the installation you may be asked to select an M or F option. However, the install process does not indicate what these are, or whether one is preferable to the other. Refer to the *Stealth Mapping and Frame Options* section below for further details.

Windows 3.1	**Quarterdeck** *QEMM386*
CONFIG.SYS	**CONFIG.SYS**
device=C:\WINDOWS\HIMEM.SYS	
device=C:\WINDOWS\EMM386.EXE	device=C:\QEMM\QEMM386.SYS R:1
noems	(*operating parameters*)
dos=HIGH,UMB	dos=HIGH
devicehigh=(*path and filename.ext*)	device=C:\QEMM\LOADHI.SYS /R:1 C:=(*path and filename.ext*)
or	
device=(*path and filename.ext*)	device=C:\QEMM\LOADHI.SYS /R:1 C:=(*path and filename.ext*)
AUTOEXEC.BAT	**AUTOEXEC.BAT**
loadhigh (*path and filename.ext*)	C:\QEMM\LOADHI /R:1 (*path and filename.ext*)
or	
(*path and filename.ext*)	C:\QEMM\LOADHI /R:1 (*path and filename.ext*)

Note that the QEMM386.SYS file replaces both HIMEM.SYS and EMM386.EXE in your CONFIG.SYS file. Some of the switches and parameters that may be appended to the QEMM386.SYS line are briefly reviewed here. For further details, refer to the Quarterdeck *Expanded Memory Manager 386* manual.

Since *QEMM386* takes control of the entire upper memory area, the dos= line is edited to delete the UMB parameter. The other notable change is that the various lines which load your device drivers and TSRs are rewritten as shown above. In each case, a small LOADHI entry is made in conventional memory, with the driver or TSR loaded into upper memory.

QEMM386 **Operating Parameters.** During installation, the following switches and parameters are appended to the *QEMM386.SYS* line, as appropriate to your system configuration. Refer to the Quarterdeck manual for further details, or for information about switches and parameters not listed here.

If you make any post-installation edits to the *QEMM386.SYS* line, it's a good idea to run the *Optimize* utility again so that the changes can be correctly implemented.

AdapterRAM=xxxx-yyyy. You can use this parameter to set aside a memory block that is used by adapter RAM. However, you will only need to do so if *QEMM386* fills the area by accident. The parameter is equivalent to

x=*xxxx-yyyy*, except that the QEMM.COM utility reports the area's status as "Adapter RAM" instead of as "Excluded."

AdapterROM=xxxx-yyyy. This excludes an area occupied by ROM on an adapter card. The QEMM.COM utility marks the area as "ROM."

i=xxxx-yyyy **(or include=*xxxx-yyyy*).** This parameter is functionally equivalent to the same setting in Windows' EMM386.EXE. It instructs *QEMM386* to include the specified upper memory block as a mappable region.

In most cases, **i=*xxxx-yyyy*** need not be used, since Quarterdeck's *Optimize* utility (described below) will find and use all available UMB space. However, *Optimize* does not use the B000–B7FF block, which is used by some video systems when Windows is run. Therefore, you will need to append an **i=B000-B7FF** parameter if you want *QEMM386* to take charge of this area.

If you do decide to let *QEMM386* take over this area, or any other blocks that may be available, rerun the *Optimize* utility after appending i=*xxxx-yyyy* to the **QEMM386.SYS** line. After doing so, if the system locks up when you open Windows, refer to the *Windows cannot set up an upper memory block at segment B000* error message for a few suggestions.

Even if your system does not need expanded memory, do not use **i=*xxxx-yyyy*** to include the page frame block as more UMB space. *QEMM386* needs this space during system startup; if it's not available to it, many devices and TSRs will get left in conventional memory, and you may therefore lose more than you gain.

RAM (or RAM=xxxx-yyyy). This parameter instructs *QEMM386* to fill all available upper memory blocks, or just the area specified by *xxxx-yyyy*, with RAM. Areas not automatically filled may be explicitly included using the **i=** parameter described above.

ROM (or ROM=xxxx-yyyy). This parameter instructs *QEMM386* to copy all ROM, or just that ROM in the area specified by *xxxx-yyyy*, into RAM. The RAM is then mapped into the specified ROM blocks, where it performs faster than the ROM which it replaces.

Stealth Mapping (ST:M) and Frame (ST:F) Options. During installation you will be asked to select an **M** or the **F** option. However, the install process does not indicate what these are, or whether one is preferable to the other. Let the install procedure try the **M** (mapping) option first—

it makes more upper memory available but may not be compatible with some systems. If it fails, the F (frame) option will be used instead. It provides less upper memory space, but should be compatible with systems that do not operate under the M option. In either case, ST:M or ST:F will be appended to the *QEMM386.SYS* line in your CONFIG.SYS file.

x=*xxxx-yyyy* (or exclude=*xxxx-yyyy*). This parameter performs the same function as it does with the Windows 3.1 EMM386.EXE utility. The specified area is excluded from *QEMM386's* control.

The Quarterdeck *Optimize* Utility (OPTIMIZE.EXE). During installation, the *Optimize* utility scans your CONFIG.SYS and AUTOEXEC.BAT files and makes the changes required to load your various device drivers and TSRs into upper memory. If you subsequently change your system configuration (for example, by adding a new driver or removing an old one), you should rerun *Optimize* so that *QEMM386* can make the appropriate changes.

If your AUTOEXEC.BAT file loads a second batch file, the *Optimize* utility will not optimize that file unless it is executed via a *CALL* statement in the first file. If the second batch file loads still other TSRs, you may want it to be optimized too. However, if all it does is say, display a screen menu, then there is nothing to be optimized in it. Depending on its contents, you may want to edit the appropriate line(s) in your AUTOEXEC.BAT file as shown here.

Change

C:\\(*path*)*filename*.BAT

to

CALL C:\\(*path*)*filename*.BAT

The LOADHI.OPT File. This file contains information that may be helpful for troubleshooting purposes. Each device driver and TSR is listed in the following format:

C:*path and filename.ext* /I=*xxxxx* /R=*yyyyy* (*other parameters follow*)

where

/I=*xxxxx*   space required during initialization
/R=*yyyyy*   space required once file is resident

Sometimes a file needs extra space as it is loaded into memory, but once resident it will occupy a smaller area. Certain files (notably, MSCDEX.EXE) may erron eously report an initialization requirement smaller than what is actually required. As a result, *Optimize* may reserve an area too small to accommodate its initialization needs. If so, *Optimize* may appear to conclude successfully, yet the program in question will fail to load into upper memory when the system is rebooted.

If you have a device driver or TSR that fails in this manner, examine the /I and /R values in the LOADHI.OPT file. If the former is *less* than the latter, then erroneous information has been reported and probably accounts for the load failure. Refer to the *Not enough memory to load filename high* error message below for suggestions to resolve this problem.

Smart Drive *and* QEMM386. If you use *QEMM386* prior to version 6.02, Smart Drive does not automatically flush its write buffer when you exit Windows or if you press Ctrl+Alt+Del to reboot the system. Therefore, you should run Windows from a batch file which includes the following line immediately after the WIN.COM command line:

```
C:\WINDOWS\SMARTDRV.EXE /c
```

The /c switch forces Smart Drive to flush its write buffer when you close Windows, thus preventing accidental data loss. Note, however, that this measure does nothing to preclude data loss if the write buffer contains data placed there after Windows was closed.

If an early version of *Optimize* recommends loading SMARTDRV.EXE /double-buffer with the LOADHI.SYS line, do not follow this advice. The double-buffer feature must be loaded into conventional memory, or it will not function properly.

SYSTEM.INI File Changes. During installation, some third-party memory managers will write the following line into the [386Enh] section of your SYSTEM.INI file:

```
SystemROMBreakPoint=FALSE
```

The line specifies that the F000–FFFF address space may contain something other than system ROM. In fact, the space usually does contain such ROM, but both memory managers described above are capable of using some or all of this area as an upper memory block.

If a version of Quarterdeck's *QEMM-386* between 5.1 and 5.12 is in place when Windows is installed, the following line is inserted in the [386Enh] section of SYSTEM.INI:

```
device=*qemmfix     (note presence of asterisk)
```

The line specifies a virtual device driver built into the Windows WIN386.EXE file, which is required for compatibility. The line may be removed if *QEMM-386* is upgraded to a version greater than 5.12.

Memory-Management Techniques

This section describes a few procedures that may help optimize your system's memory configuration, thus enabling you to get the best use out of the available system memory.

System Memory

When figuring out how much memory you have to spare, don't overlook the fact that your computer may be helping itself to a bit of that memory. For example, the conventional and extended memory listed here were reported during bootup on two typical systems. (All figures in Kbytes. 1Kb = 1024 bytes.)

Memory Resources	System A	System B
Installed RAM	5120	12288
Conventional memory	− 640	− 640
Extended memory	− 4352	−11264
Missing	128	384

On both systems, the total reported memory is somewhat less than the installed memory, and the system *User's Guide* may say little or nothing about where it went. Read between the lines though and you'll discover references to various cache and shadow ROM features, each of which requires some RAM. In many cases, the RAM is borrowed from whatever you have in your system, but the amount debited from your RAM resources is neither mentioned nor reported on screen. Therefore, if you find yourself missing some amount between 64Kb and 384Kb, it's a pretty safe bet that the system has swiped it.

Sometimes it's possible to recover this RAM, but doing so may be more trouble than it's worth, even if you don't want to use the feature that requires the RAM. Given the reasonably low prices of RAM these days, buy another 1 Mbyte or more, and just charge the lost RAM against the general cost of doing business with a computer.

Conventional Memory Management

The upper section of Table 13.5a shows how the DOS 5.0 MEM /c utility reports conventional memory usage as various lines in CONFIG.SYS and

TABLE 13.5a Typical DOS MEM /c Reports*

| | DOS 5.0 | | DOS 6.0 | | | | |
	1	2	3	4	5	6 †	7 ‡
Conventional Memory							
MSDOS	59056	17392	17392	17392	17392	17376	17376
HIMEM	3200	1184	1024	1024	1024	1728	1328
EMM386	9424	9424	9072	9072	9072	2064	4112
SETVER	416	—	416	—	—	—	—
ANSI	4192	—	—	—	—	—	—
RAMDRIVE	1184	—	—	—	—	—	—
MVSOUND	9360	—	—	—	—	—	—
NECCDR	12720	—	—	—	—	—	—
MSCDEX	27952	—	—	—	—	—	—
COMMAND	4704	2624	2880	2880	2880	2880	2880
MOUSE	17280	—	—	—	—	—	—
SMARTDRV	28304	—	—	—	—	—	—
FREE	64	—	—	—	—	—	—
FREE	224	64	64	64	64	64	64
FREE	476944	624464	624288	624720	624720	630976	629328
Total Free:	477232	624528	624352	624784	624784	631040	629392
Upper Memory							
SYSTEM	—	163840	163840	163840	155680	131584	131120
QMMXXXX0		—	—	—	—	2784	—
EMM386	—	—	—	—	—	—	13360
SETVER	—	416	—	416	416	432	432
ANSI	—	4192	4192	4192	4192	4208	4208
RAMDRIVE	—	1184	1184	1184	1184	1152	1152
MVSOUND	—	9360	9360	9360	9360	9376	9376
NECCDR	—	12720	12720	12720	12720	12736	12736
MSCDEX	—	27952	27952	27952	27952	28128	27968
MOUSE	—	17280	17280	17280	17280	17456	17296
SMARTDRV	—	28304	28336	28336	28336	28512	28352
FREE	—	—	—	—	32	—	—
FREE	—	224	224	224	224	—	240
FREE	—	—	—	—	6912	—	—
FREE	—	—	—	—	16032	—	—
FREE	—	62016	62416	61984	47040	124080	81440
Total Free:		62240	62640	62208	70240	124080	81680

* Column numbers are cross-referenced to Table parts b and c, Figures 13.10 and 13.11.

† Values in HIMEM and EMM386 rows are for *386LOAD* and *386MAX,*, respectively. MEM /c does not report upper memory usage when *386MAX* is installed. All upper memory values are derived from Qualitas *ASQ* report.

‡ Values in HIMEM and EMM386 rows are for *LOADHI* and *QEMM386,* respectively. MEM /c does not report upper memory usage when *QEMM386* is installed. All upper memory values are derived from Quarterdeck *Manifest* report.

TABLE 13.5b   Memory Summary*

	DOS 5.0		DOS 6.0				
	1	2	3	4	5	6	7
Conventional Memory							
MEM /c †	655024	655152	655136	655152	655152	655088	655088
MCBs ‡	336	208	224	208	208	272	272
MCBs (quan.)	(21)	(13)	(14)	(13)	(13)	(17)	(17)
Total (640K)	655360	655360	655360	655360	655360	655360	655360
Upper Memory	—		—	—	—		—
MEM /c †	—	327488	327504	327488	327360	360448	327680
MCBs ‡	—	192	176	192	320	—	—
MCBs (quan.)	—	(12)	(11)	(12)	(20)	—	—
ROM BIOS at F000	—	65536	65536	65536	65536	32768	—
Page Frame	—	—	—	—	—	—	65536
Total (384K)	—	393216	393216	393216	393216	393216	393216
Upper Memory SYSTEM Line Includes:							
A000–AFFF	—	65536	65536	65536	65536	65536	65536
B000-BFFF	—	65536	65536	65536	65536	65536	65536
C000–C01F	—	—	—	—	—	512	—
FFFD–FFFF(+1)	—	—	—	—	—	—	48
C000–C7FF	—	32768	32768	32768	32768	—	—
i=B000–B7FF	—	—	—	—	–32768	—	—
WIN=B200–B4FF	—	—	—	—	12288	—	—
WIN=B500–B7FF	—	—	—	—	12288	—	—
2 MCBs for WIN blocks	—	—	—	—	32	—	—
Total	—	131104	163840	163840	155680	131584	131120

* Column numbers are cross-referenced to Table parts a and c, Figures 13.10 and 13.11.

† Each value is sum of listings in Table 13.5a.

‡ To calculate MCBs, run MEM /p (DOS 5.0) or MEM /d (DOS 6.0). Count lines, starting at second "IO" entry. Deduct 2 MCBs for MEM.EXE itself. Conventional and upper MCBs listed separately in Table. (*xx*) indicates number of MCBs. *EMM386* and *QEMM386* MCBs not listed separately.

AUTOEXEC.BAT are edited. The columns are numbered for cross-reference to Figure 13.10, which presents a graph of the MEM /c reports. For purposes of scale, the graph shows only the portion of conventional memory that is currently occupied.

The purpose of making the changes described here is to open up as much room as possible in the conventional memory area for Windows (or for anything else of course). As various programs are moved

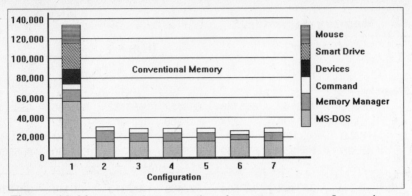

Figure 13.10   Typical conventional memory usage for various system configurations. Refer to Table 13.5c for configuration details.

out of conventional memory, it's a good idea to use MEM /c to make sure the programs have really departed. For example, the devicehigh= and loadhigh lines described below will only have an effect if the upper memory area is available to DOS, and contains sufficient free space to accommodate whatever it is you're trying to move. If the MEM utility shows that either instruction is being ignored, then refer to the *Memory Management Troubleshooting* section later in this chapter for suggestions.

NOTE: The items removed from conventional memory are transferred into the HMA (High Memory Area) or into UMB (Upper Memory Blocks), both of which are described in subsequent sections. For future reference, the lower half of Table 13.5 lists upper memory usage as reported by the DOS 5.0 MEM /c command.

The Memory Summary in Table 13.5b shows how the first 1 Mbyte of memory is always equal to the items reported by MEM /c, plus memory control blocks and other items unreported by DOS 5.0 MEM /c. The summary also itemizes the upper memory components which MEM /c reports on the single **SYSTEM** line.

Basic Configuration.   In Table 13.5 and Figure 13.10, column 1 shows what might be found when the system is booted with all devices loaded in conventional memory. DOS 5.0 grabs a fairly big bite for itself, with Smart Drive and a Microsoft mouse driver taking the next largest chunks. Memory-management software (HIMEM.SYS and EMM386.EXE) swipe their share, other assorted drivers nibble away at the memory pie, and of course COMMAND.COM is in there too. It all adds up to about 130,000+ bytes, as shown graphically in Figure 13.10.

Enable UMB (Upper Memory Block) Area. Column 2 shows the effect of adding a dos=UMB line to your CONFIG.SYS file. This lets DOS take control of the upper memory block area. As a result, Smart Drive automatically moves itself out of conventional memory and into this area. The MEM /c report now shows the status of the Upper Memory area, as will be described in the *Upper Memory Management* section below.

Move DOS into HMA. The next thing to do is get rid of DOS—not all of it certainly, but most of it can be moved out of the conventional memory area by simply adding a dos=HIGH line to your CONFIG.SYS file. (Or, insert a single dos=HIGH,UMB line). Column 2 also shows that MSDOS, HIMEM, and COMMAND(.COM) have all surrendered some of their conventional memory space. These memory segments have been moved into the 64 Kbyte HMA (High Memory Area) immediately above the upper memory area. The last line of any MEM report should now read as follows:

MS-DOS resident in High Memory Area

Move CONFIG.SYS Device Drivers and TSRs into UMB Area. The various device drivers and TSR programs listed in your CONFIG.SYS file can be loaded into the upper memory area by changing each device= line as shown here.
Change

device=C:\(*path and filename*)

to

devicehigh=C:\(*path and filename*)

Column 2 also shows the results of using the devicehigh= line to load device drivers into upper memory. Note that some of HIMEM.SYS and all of EMM386.EXE remain in the conventional memory area. If you attempt to load either or both high, your wishes will be ignored.

Move AUTOEXEC.BAT TSRs into UMB Area. TSR programs loaded by your AUTOEXEC.BAT file can likewise be moved into the UMB area, as shown by this example.

Change

```
C:\MOUSE\MOUSE.COM
```

to

```
loadhigh C:\MOUSE\MOUSE.COM
```

Again, column 2 shows the effect of moving MOUSE.COM out of conventional memory and into the UMB area.

Upgrade to DOS 6.0. In Table 13.5 and Figure 13.10, column 3 shows the initial effect of upgrading to DOS 6.0, which is minimal. And, when the MEMMAKER utility is run, little improvement is noted (see column 4) since all device drivers and TSRs were already in upper memory. In fact, about the only real action seen from columns 2 to 4 is the placement of SETVER.EXE back into conventional memory (column 3), then back into upper memory by MEMMAKER (column 4). However, if MEMMAKER does a full optimization (column 5), it will pick up an extra 32 Kbytes of upper memory and then reserve 24 Kbytes for Windows use. The parameters that MEMMAKER adds to the EMM386.EXE line are shown at the top of column 5.

Use of Third-Party Memory Manager. A slight additional savings in conventional memory may be realized by using third-party memory-management software, such as Qualitas' *386MAX* or Quarterdeck's *QEMM386,* as shown in columns 6 and 7. For additional effects of using third-party memory management, refer to the *Upper Memory Management* section immediately following.

Upper Memory Management

The 384 Kbyte area immediately above conventional memory is referred to as the upper memory area. For convenience it may be divided into six blocks of 64 Kbytes, each occupying a hexadecimal address area of *x*000-*x*FFF, where *x* = A, B, C, D, E, or F (see Figure 13.1). Although some of these blocks are partially or completely occupied, others can be occupied by device drivers and TSRs that are moved out of conventional memory by the devicehigh= and loadhigh lines described in the *Conventional Memory Management* section of this chapter.

TABLE 13.5c   CONFIG.SYS Lines for Memory Summary*

| | DOS 5.0 | | DOS 6.0 | | |
	1	2	3	4†	5‡
device= HIMEM.SYS					
EMM386.EXE	*(none)*	noems i=E000–EFFF	noems i=E000–EFFF /nohi	noems i=E000–EFFF /nohi	i=B000-B7FF /nohi WIN=B500–B7FF WIN=B200–B4FF
dos=	*(none)*	high,umb	high,umb	high,umb	high,umb
	6	Qualitas *EMM386*			
	7	Quarterdeck *QEMM386*			

* Column numbers are cross-referenced to Table parts a and b, Figures 13.10 and 13.11.
† Optimized, but no mono and not optimized for Windows.
‡ Full optimize.

As noted earlier, Table 13.5b also shows how upper memory usage varies as a function of the various conditions described in the *Conventional Memory Management* section above. In Figure 13.11, upper memory utilization is shown graphically. As before, the columns are numbered for cross-reference purposes.

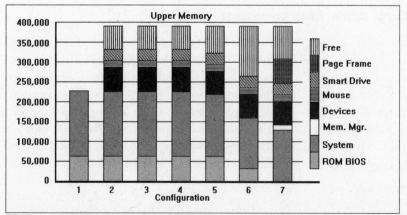

Figure 13.11 Typical upper memory block usage for various system configurations. Refer to Table 13.5c for configuration details.

SYSTEM.INI's EMMExclude=*xxxx-yyyy* and ReservedHighArea=*xxxx-yyyy* Lines.
Once you are done filling the upper memory area, Windows will pick up the leftovers for itself when running in enhanced mode. This might cause a problem if a certain upper memory area appears to be available, but should really be set aside for some adapter that will want to use it later on.

If you have an adapter that you know will use a specific UMB range, you can lock Windows out of that range by inserting one of the lines described below in the [386Enh] section of your SYSTEM.INI file. However, if you have appended an x=*xxxx-yyyy* line to the EMM386.EXE line in your CONFIG.SYS file, that line takes precedence. Therefore, neither of the following lines need be used if the area in question has already been excluded via the EMM386.EXE line. (Refer to the *Excluded UMB Blocks and Windows 3.1* section above for further details.) You may want to use one of them anyway, if only for the sake of redundancy, and to prevent any little surprises while experimenting with various third-party memory managers.

EMMExclude=xxxx-yyyy. This line prevents Windows from using the area defined by *xxxx-yyyy*, where *xxxx* is rounded down, and *yyyy* up, to the nearest multiple of 16 Kbytes. Thus, EMMExclude=C900-CA00 will actually keep Windows out of the 16 Kbyte C800–CBFF area. To exclude an area less then 16Kb, use the ReservedHighArea=*xxxx-yyyy* line instead, as described immediately below.

ReservedHighArea=xxxx-yyyy. This line performs the same function as EMMExclude=*xxxx-yyyy*, except that *xxxx* and *yyyy* are rounded down, and up, to the nearest multiples of 4Kb. Therefore, ReservedHighArea=C900-CA00 will exclude Windows from that 4Kb area only.

High Memory Area Management

As noted earlier, CONFIG.SYS's dos=HIGH line will transfer about 45 Kbytes of DOS out of conventional memory and into the 64 Kbyte High Memory Area, which leaves almost 20 Kbytes left over for other purposes—except for one little thing. It turns out that the HMA can be occupied by only one tenant at a time, regardless of how much space may be left over for something else. This is usually of no practical consequence, since few programs can use this area anyway. However, if you do need to keep DOS out of the HMA so that it can be used for other programs, rewrite the line as follows:

    dos=LOW,UMB

or

    dos=UMB

Or omit the line completely if UMB control is in the hands of a third-party memory manager, in which case the dos=UMB portion is not required either. For further control of the high memory area, refer to the */hmamin Switch* section earlier in the chapter.

Additional Memory-Saving Techniques

Still more memory can be saved by some judicious pruning of those drivers and TSRs that are now hanging out in the upper memory area. Do you really need them? And if so, why? If you routinely open Windows in enhanced mode and run your non-Windows applications from within a DOS window (or windows), consider the following. Every time you open another DOS window, the conventional memory for that virtual machine gets a copy of *everything* you've loaded into your real system, via your CONFIG.SYS and AUTOEXEC.BAT files. Since there's a good chance that not everything so loaded is needed by Windows *and* by each virtual machine, you can do a bit of resource management by making a few changes, as described here.

CONFIG.SYS Management. Anything loaded into memory via the CONFIG.SYS file gets duplicated in each virtual memory machine, and there's no way to avoid this. However, it might be worthwhile to carefully review the drivers being loaded here to see if there's anything that you really don't need. If so, get rid of it.

You may be able to save a few bytes of memory by keeping an eye on the following three lines in your CONFIG.SYS file. The amount of memory taken up by each is briefly described here. Obviously there are a few bytes to be saved here by keeping each setting as low as possible. However, the first consideration for any of these lines is to set the optimum value for Windows 3.1 and your specific system. Try to do your memory saving elsewhere.

Buffers=xx. This line sets aside *xx* 512-byte buffers in which data is cached. The buffer system caches a single disk sector in each buffer, and is most efficient for small-scale caching (30 to 50 buffers). If you are using Smart Drive, use BUFFERS=10 in your CONFIG.SYS file. Otherwise, try BUFFERS=20.

If you load DOS into the high memory area, your buffers are usually loaded automatically into that area too. To verify this, run the DOS MEM /p command and note the amount of space allocated to the BUFFERS= line. If it's only 200 (= decimal 512), then your buffers are indeed located in the HMA. If the number is substantially larger, you may have specified more buffers than can fit in the high memory area. If you have

Quarterdeck's *Manifest* utility, the DOS Overview Screen shows the number of buffers loaded into HMA.

Refer to the *Buffers and Smart Drive* section later in this chapter for more details on the relationship between buffers and Smart Drive.

Files=x. Figure about 60x bytes of conventional memory taken up by this command. For Windows 3.1, the recommended setting is usually Files=30, or higher depending on your specific system requirements.

Stacks=x,y. The space occupied by DOS stacks ranges from zero (stacks=0,0) to about 704 + xy bytes, where x is the number of stacks and y is the size of each stack.

Batch File Management. If you regularly use a TSR program prior to loading Windows, then that TSR must of course be included in your AUTOEXEC.BAT file, or loaded at the DOS command line when you need it. In either case, it will be available to Windows, and a duplicate copy of the program will be found later on, in every DOS window that you open from within Windows. If the program in question is something you do need in every DOS window (for example, a DOS screen-saver), then the AUTOEXEC.BAT file remains the most logical place to load it. However, you may have a TSR that you need only when Windows is running, or only in one of the several DOS windows you may open. In this case, you can make more efficient use of your available memory by deleting the TSR from the AUTOEXEC.BAT file and loading it by other means, as described here.

Table 13.6 illustrates the availability of TSRs loaded into memory by AUTOEXEC.BAT and various application-specific batch files.

The WINSTART.BAT File. The WINSTART.BAT file is a special-purpose batch file that only loads when Windows opens in enhanced mode. Programs loaded via WINSTART.BAT are available only to enhanced-mode Windows, and do not take up space in the conventional memory area of any DOS window. For further details, refer to the *WINSTART.BAT File* section of Chapter 2.

DOS-Window Batch Files. If you need certain DOS TSRs every now and then, and perhaps others at other times, then consider creating a few DOS icons, each tailored to a specific need. For each icon, write a PIF file that calls a batch file. Then let the batch file load only those programs you need to use within that DOS window. If you open another DOS window, memory space in its virtual machine will not be wasted on things you don't need.

TABLE 13.6   Availability of Drivers and TSRs Loaded at Startup

| Filename | | Virtual DOS Machines | |
Contents	Windows	1	2
CONFIG.SYS			
(everything in it)	Yes	Yes	Yes
AUTOEXEC.BAT			
SMARTDRV.EXE	Yes	Yes	Yes
(*anything else*)	Yes	Yes	Yes
WINSTART.BAT			
WHATEVER.COM	Yes	No	No
DOS-1.BAT			
C:\MSCDEX.EXE /d:NECCD	No	Yes	No
DOS-2.BAT			
(*as required*)	No	No	Yes

Program-Loading Sequence. Some drivers and TSRs require a comparatively large block of memory during the loading procedure, after which the resident portion of the program is substantially less. As a typical example, version 8.20 of MOUSE.COM needs 57,072 bytes loading space in order to make itself comfortable in upper memory. However, once loaded it occupies only 17,392 bytes. As an obvious consequence, if the larger amount is not available, MOUSE.COM will load into conventional memory instead.

If you find that this or some other program is not loading into upper memory, try rearranging the load sequence in your CONFIG.SYS and/or AUTOEXEC.BAT files so that such programs are at the head of the line. Once they shrink to their normal resident size, other programs that don't have this problem can be loaded into the remaining space.

Needless to say, the success of this technique will depend on the number of programs that require extra loading space, and the amount of space that is available. You may have to do a bit of experimenting to find a load sequence that works, since a program's file size is not a reliable indicator of its load-space requirements. For example, earlier in the chapter Figure 13.9 gave the initial and resident sizes of several programs, as measured by a Qualitas memory-management utility. The figures show there's no correlation between initial and resident sizes.

Virtual Memory and the Swap File

One of the features of Windows' 386 enhanced mode is its ability to use more memory than has been installed in the system. To accomplish this, the people in Redmond have not found a loophole in one of the laws of Physics. Instead, a little virtual reality is applied to memory management, as described here.

Virtual Memory

The term *virtual* describes just about anything that gives an appearance of being something (or somewhere) it isn't. Thus, you see your virtual image in a mirror, but—unless your name is Alice—it's not really you in there. As for *virtual memory,* it could be just about anything that behaves as if it were real memory. In the specific case of enhanced-mode Windows, the *virtual* definition is bent slightly, to specify one kind of memory that behaves like another; in other words, hard disk sectors that simulate RAM chips. With virtual memory enabled, when Windows runs out of the real stuff (RAM), it looks to the hard disk for *swap file* space in which to work.

The Swap File

For readers who know their way around the English language, a *swap file* might suggest a file that can be swapped. However, software developers have their own dictionary: A swap file is not swapped, nor is it always a file. Instead, it may be a stationary hard disk area into which data can be moved, so that RAM space occupied by that data can be used for other purposes.

If a swap file is enabled, applications continue their read/write data operations in RAM, but when the system runs low on RAM, some of that data is moved into the swap file and the RAM is again available for use. So as far as Windows operations are concerned, the system has, if not a bottomless RAM pit, then at least a lot more of it than the installed chips would suggest.

Windows 3.1 Swap File Types. The several types of Windows swap files are briefly described here. In each case the parenthetical reference gives the name of the swap file that is used. Although the standard-mode *application swap file* is not a virtual memory device, it is described here anyway, for purposes of comparison with the others.

For a discussion of the relationship between a swap file and a RAM drive, refer to the *RAM Drive* section later in this chapter.

Application Swap File (~WOAxxxx.TMP). In standard mode only, when a non-Windows application is opened, Windows sets aside some hard disk space for it. If you switch some other application to the foreground, the former one is temporarily stored in its application swap file area as ~WOA*xxxx*.TMP, where *xxxx* is a distinctive hexadecimal number. The file attributes are marked as hidden, read-only.

Windows looks first to SYSTEM.INI, then to AUTOEXEC.BAT for a suitable location for the application swap files. If it finds neither of the lines shown here, then the swap files are written into the root directory. If either line is present, but the specified site does not have sufficient room, then the files are written to the next available area.

SYSTEM.INI
    [NonWindowsApp]
    SwapDisk=(*path and directory name*)

AUTOEXEC.BAT
    set TEMP=(*path and directory name*)

When you quit an application, Windows deletes its application swap file. Therefore, when you exit Windows, there should be no such files left on your hard disk. However, if a Windows session is aborted, an application swap file may not be deleted. Therefore, you may want to periodically check the appropriate area for hidden, read-only files with the distinctive ~WOA*xxxx*.TMP name. If you find any, clear these attributes (type attrib -h -r ~WOA*.TMP) and erase the files.

Temporary Swap File (WIN386.SWP). In enhanced mode, if you have not installed a permanent swap file (as described in the next section), Windows sets aside a temporary area whose path, name, and size are specified in SYSTEM.INI. As shown here, the swap file is identified as a Paging File. No doubt the name change makes perfect sense to whoever is in charge of these things.

    [386Enh]
    PagingFile=(*path*)\WIN386.SWP
    MaxPagingFileSize=*xxxxx* (*in Kbytes*)

Unlike application swap files, the temporary swap (or paging) file attributes are neither hidden nor read-only. Therefore, the filename and size will show up if you open a DOS window and look at a C:\WINDOWS directory listing (or elsewhere if you've specified a different path). The temporary swap file is deleted automatically when you exit Windows.

An advantage of the temporary swap file is that the space it occupies is available for use by other applications when Windows is closed. However, temporary swap file space need not be contiguous, so its operation may be somewhat slower than that of a permanent swap file.

Permanent Swap File (386SPART.PAR and SPART.PAR). If a permanent swap file is installed, it is marked as a hidden system file, and is always installed in the root directory of the specified drive. The small read-only SPART.PAR file is located in the Windows directory, and contains information telling Windows the location and size of the swap file. The same information is also written into SYSTEM.INI as shown here:

```
[386Enh]
PermSwapDOSDrive=C
PermSwapSizeK=xxxxx (in Kbytes)
```

Since permanent swap file space is not released when Windows is closed, this area is never available to other applications. However, a permanent swap file can only be installed within a contiguous free space on the hard disk, so it should operate considerably faster than a possibly fragmented temporary swap file; this consideration may outweigh this permanent loss of space.

Swap File Configuration. To change swap file configuration, open the *Control Panel* applet in the Main Group Window and double-click on the *386 Enhanced* icon to display the first **386 Enhanced** dialog box. Click on the **V**irtual Memory... button to open the **Virtual Memory** dialog box, then on the **C**hange>> button to display the entire dialog box, as shown in Figure 13.12. The items shown in the **New Settings** box are described below.

Space Available. Despite the name and the context in which it appears, the figure is not necessarily the space available for a swap file. It is actually the total free space on the indicated drive, without regard for file fragmentation. In other words, this space may be broken up by bad clusters or file fragments, thus cutting down on the space available for a swap file. A better name for this area might be "Free space."

Maximum Size. This figure shows the largest contiguous block of free space on the indicated drive. If the hard disk was just defragmented, the figure will match that in the **Space Available** box immediately above. If the figure is considerably smaller, this is an indication that it's time to run a good defragmentation utility. If so, you might want to exit Windows and do this before continuing.

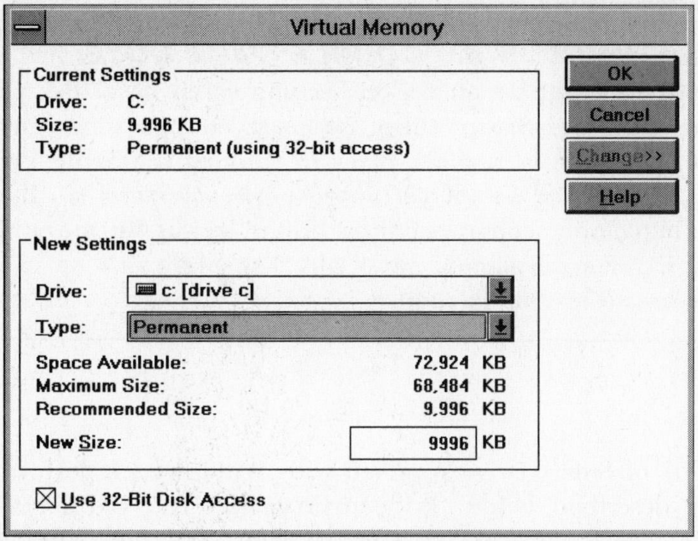

Figure 13.12 The Virtual Memory dialog box is accessed via the Virtual Memory... button on the 386 Enhanced dialog box (shown in Figure 11.4). Click on the Change>> button to open the *New Settings* section of the dialog box. Windows does not warn if a compressed drive is selected, as it is in this example.

Recommended Size. This is the figure that most Windows documentation claims is either one-half the *Space Available,* or four times the available system RAM, whichever is less. However, it never is, and may not even be close. Furthermore, if a permanent swap file already exists (as in Figure 13.12), its size appears in this box, regardless of the space that is actually available. In this or just about any other case, ignore the recommendation and enter whatever size you like.

However, if you do select a size larger than the recommended size, a warning message will advise that Windows will not use more than the virtual memory specified by the Recommended Size. The message is incorrect: Windows will, in fact, use whatever you give it, provided it is less than that listed in the Maximum Size box. However (again), Windows usually adjusts the figure, whatever it is, by a few Kbytes. In fact, even if you accept its own recommendation, you probably won't get it. The actual swap file size will be off by just enough to make you wonder what you did wrong.

Perhaps all this will be fixed in a later Windows release. But until then just enter a reasonable value and expect to get a file size that's close to what you requested.

SWAP FILES AND DOS 6.0 DOUBLESPACE NOTE: A permanent swap file cannot be set up on a compressed hard disk partition, and the DOS 6.0 Setup utility is smart enough to stay away
from a swap file if one is in place prior to running the Setup Procedure. Windows, however, is not yet aware of *DoubleSpace*; so, if you
have a nice big empty compressed partition, it will be more than
happy to use it for a permanent swap file. Therefore, it's up to you
to remember not to let this happen.

Smart Drive

The version (4.0) of Smart Drive supplied with Windows 3.1 performs two
functions, both described below. Prior to Windows 3.1, SMARTDRV.SYS
was loaded as a device driver in your CONFIG.SYS file. The version
shipped with Windows 3.1 is SMARTDRV.EXE (note new extension), and
there may be separate references to it in both CONFIG.SYS and AU-
TOEXEC.BAT, as described here.

Double Buffering (Smart Drive in CONFIG.SYS). Briefly stated, double-
buffering sets aside a small block of conventional memory which may
be needed to prevent memory-addressing conflicts with certain SCSI
hard disk controllers. During Windows 3.1 installation, Setup adds the
following line to your CONFIG.SYS file if it determines that double-
buffering is required.

```
device=SMARTDRV.EXE /double_buffer
```

This line loads only the double-buffer driver segment of Smart Drive,
which must not be loaded into high memory. In other words, do *not* use
devicehigh= with this line.

Double buffering is not required with non-SCSI drives, nor is it needed
with some newer SCSI drives. If the double-buffer line is present in your
CONFIG.SYS file and you are not sure that it is required, type SMARTDRV
at the DOS prompt to display a Smart Drive status report such as that
shown in Figure 13.13. The final column may contain one or more of the
following entries:

Yes   Double-buffering is required.
No   Double-buffering is not required.
—   Smart Drive has not yet determined if double-buffering is required.

```
Microsoft SMARTDrive Disk Cache version 4.0
Copyright 1991,1992 Microsoft Corp.

Room for 128 elements of 8,192 bytes each
There have been 16,664 cache hits
    and 2,473 cache misses

Cache size: 2,097,512 bytes
Cache size while running Windows: 1,048,576 bytes

            Disk Caching Status
drive   read cache   write cache   buffering
-------------------------------------------
  A:        yes          no           no
  B:        yes          no           no
  C:        yes          yes          no
  D:        yes          yes          no
  F:        yes          no           no
  G:        yes          no           no
  H:        yes          no           no
  I:        yes          no           no

For help, type "Smartdrv /?".
```

Figure 13.13 A typical Smart Drive report is displayed by typing **SMARTDRV** at the DOS prompt.

If any entry in the last column is a dash, perform some operation that will use the indicated drive, then try again. If and when there are nothing but "no" entries, then the double_buffer line is either not required, or is not present in your CONFIG.SYS file. If the line is present, it can be removed (all of it). If double-buffering is not required but you leave the line in place, it will be ignored—the double-buffer driver will not be loaded. However, you can force Smart Drive to load it by appending a plus sign at the end of the line (as in /double_buffer+).

If the line is not present, then Setup determined double-buffering is not required, and so did not insert it. If you have doubts about this, insert the line in your CONFIG.SYS file to force double-buffering, reboot, and review the status report just described. Then take the appropriate action, based on that report.

If your system does require the double-buffer option, then Smart Drive's disk cache should be forced into conventional memory, as described in the following section.

Disk-Caching (Smart Drive in AUTOEXEC.BAT). As a disk-caching utility, Smart Drive's default configuration provides read-caching from all drives and write-caching to all nonremovable media, as described here.

Read-Caching. As data is read from a diskette or hard disk, a copy of that data is placed in a read cache. The next time the same data is needed, the system need not go back to the disk to read it. Instead it is read directly from the RAM-resident cache, which is considerably faster than going back to the disk again to retrieve the same data.

Write-Caching. Instead of writing directly to the hard disk, data is written into a RAM-resident write cache, which takes less time than writing it to disk. However, such data must be written to disk in order to be permanently saved, so this operation takes place whenever the system is not otherwise engaged. As a result, system performance is improved since disk-writes do not interfere with other operations. If system activity keeps a data block in a write cache for five seconds, the data is automatically written to the hard disk.

As a disaster-prevention device, write-caching is not enabled for diskette or other removable-media drives. If such write-caching were enabled, a determined user might find the time to swap diskettes before the data was written to the proper destination.

Smart Drive Configuration. During installation, Setup writes the following line into your AUTOEXEC.BAT file to enable Smart Drive caching:

    C:\WINDOWS\SMARTDRV.EXE

Assuming a UMB provider such as EMM386.EXE is installed, Smart Drive is automatically loaded into the upper memory area, provided space is available. Therefore, it is not necessary to use the LOADHIGH command with SMARTDRV.EXE (but see *Smart Drive Loading Techniques* below for an exception).

Smart Drive's default cache size is determined by the installed extended memory, and the size may be reduced automatically when Windows is opened, as shown here:

Extended Memory	DOS Cache	Windows Cache
1 MB or less	All of it	None
1–2 MB	1 MB	256 KB
2–4 MB	1 MB	512 KB
4–6 MB	2 MB	1 MB
6 MB or more	2 MB	2 MB

Several switches and parameters may be appended to the SMARTDRV.EXE line to modify the Smart Drive configuration; a few of these are shown below. For information about those not shown here, refer to the Windows 3.1 *User's Guide* (pp. 539–540).

C:\WINDOWS\SMARTDRV.EXE   C+ D- E   /L *xxxx yyyy*

C+	Enable read- and write-caching for drive C.
D-	Disable read- and write-caching for drive D.
E	Enable read-caching, disable write-caching for drive E.
/C	Flush the write cache to disk (use on command line or in batch file to force a disk write before turning system off).
/L	Force Smart Drive to load into conventional memory (see below).
/S	Display additional information (see below).
xxxx	Specify nondefault size of DOS cache.
yyyy	Specify nondefault size of Windows cache.

Smart Drive Loading Techniques. As noted earlier, Smart Drive automatically loads itself into upper memory (space permitting), so the loadhigh command is not required. However, in order to use the double-buffering option, all or part of Smart Drive must be loaded low by appending the /L switch. There are, therefore, three ways to write the Smart Drive line in your AUTOEXEC.BAT file. Depending on the method selected, Smart Drive will load itself into conventional and/or upper memory as shown by the MEM /c reports listed here:

Command Line in AUTOEXEC.BAT File	MEM /c Report Shows Conventional	Upper
C:\WINDOWS\SMARTDRV.EXE /L	28304	—
loadhigh C:\WINDOWS\SMARTDRV.EXE /L	11920	16384
C:\WINDOWS\SMARTDRV.EXE	—	28304

The second example may be useful if conventional memory space is tight, since it uses only as much as required to accommodate double-buffering, with the rest of Smart Drive loaded into upper memory.

The /S Switch. When you append this switch to the Smart Drive command line, additional information is displayed, as shown here:

Room for 256 elements of 8,192 bytes each.
There have been 22,846 cache hits
and 4,819 cache misses.

The first line indicates that the Smart Drive cache, which in this example is 2MB (2048 Kbytes) has room for 256 elements (that is, tracks). Each track contains 8192 bytes in 32 sectors (8192 bytes ÷ 512 bytes/sector = 32).

Hits and Misses.   The cache hits and misses figures indicate the number of times the cache did (hits) and did not (misses) contain the information needed.

Smart Drive Control.   Once Smart Drive is up and running, it cannot be turned off, nor can its size be adjusted. However, you can control read-and/or write-caching to a specific drive, or drives, by typing SMARTDRV C+ D– (use drive letters, + or – signs as required). For example, if you want to disable drive-C caching during a certain operation, and then restore it, write a batch file as:

SMARTDRV C–

(*command to perform desired operation*)

SMARTDRV C+

The Smart Drive Monitor.   The Windows 3.1 Resource Kit is supplied with a Smart Drive Monitor utility (SMARTMON.EXE), which displays disk-caching information such as that shown in Figure 13.14. Caching for any drive can be controlled via the Drive Controls box. Additional adjustments are available via the SmartDrive Monitor Options dialog box which is also shown in the figure. When SMARTMON.EXE is run minimized, its icon displays the current hit rate.

For troubleshooting, it may be helpful to enable SMARTMON's Always on Top option, so that the hit rate is always visible. Refer to the *Always on Top* section in Chapter 3 for instructions on how to do this.

WARNING: If you use a third-party disk-caching utility, you might want to rename SMARTDRV.EXE as say, XMARTDRV.EXE. Since the presence of two disk-caching utilities will create performance problems, this precaution prevents Smart Drive from being accidentally loaded by typing SMARTDRV at the DOS prompt.

Also, make sure you never install more than one disk cache at a time, since doing so will probably cause data loss problems and possible corruption of the file-allocation table. You can, however, (and should) continue to use the Buffers= line in your CONFIG.SYS file. For further details, refer to the *Buffers and Smart Drive* section which follows.

Buffers and Smart Drive. As noted earlier in the chapter, the Buffers=xx line in your CONFIG.SYS file sets aside xx 512-byte buffers in which data is cached. The buffer system caches a single disk sector in each buffer, and is most efficient for small-scale caching (30 to 50 buffers). By contrast, Smart Drive will cache several thousand sectors: For example, there are 4,096 512-byte sectors in a 2,048 Mbyte Smart Drive cache.

As the buffers fill up, caching chores are passed on to Smart Drive. Consequently, as the number specified in the Buffers=xx line decreases, Smart Drive caching increases. It might, therefore, seem that the fewer buffers the better, because with more data passing in and out of Smart Drive itself, its "hit rate" would go up. (See Hits and Misses, above.) However, performance usually goes down (noticeably too) if there are less than 10 buffers.

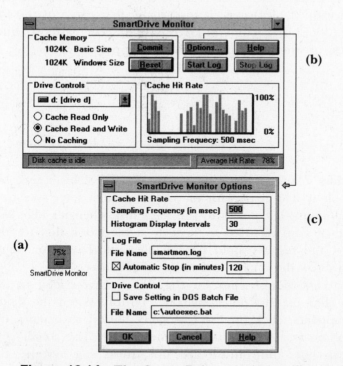

Figure 13.14 The Smart Drive monitor utility in the Windows 3.1 Resource Kit. The icon (a) shows cache hit rate, with more details (b) displayed in the open SmartDrive Monitor dialog box. (c) Click on the Options... button to open the SmartDrive Monitor Options dialog box.

32-Bit Access (FastDisk)

In enhanced mode, 32-bit access is a technology that permits faster disk accesses and allows more and faster DOS applications to run than would be possible without it. To accomplish this, the system BIOS is bypassed during disk-write operations. Although not further described here, this brief mention is given because 32-bit access is enabled via the Virtual Memory Screen, which is in turn accessed through the Control Panel's *386 Enhanced* icon. Since the same screen displays swap file settings (see *Virtual Memory* section above), there is often some confusion about what the one has to do with the other. The short answer is, "nothing." The 32-bit access box may have been "buried" on the Virtual Memory Screen, simply to keep the casual user from finding it and possibly doing some harm.

In Microsoft and other documentation, 32-bit access technology is sometimes referred to as "FastDisk," since that describes part of what it does. During installation, if Setup determines that your system's hard disk controller is compatible with 32-bit access, it inserts the first three of the following lines in the [386Enh] section of SYSTEM.INI. The last two lines are inserted regardless of whether your system can support 32-bit access.

```
32BitDiskAccess=off
device=*int13
device=*wdctrl
device=*BLOCKDEV
device=*PageFile
```

Note that Setup plays it safe: It sets your system up for 32-bit access, but does not actually enable it. The reason for the caution is that some systems—notably, portable computers—cut power to the hard disk when it's idle, as a power-saving measure. If FastDisk tried to write to a hard disk that for the moment wasn't there, the results would not be pleasant. Therefore, Setup leaves it up to you to throw the final switch to turn 32-bit access on.

To enable 32-bit access, double-click on the *386 Enhanced* icon in the Control Panel, then click on the Virtual Memory... button. When the Virtual Memory dialog box appears, click on the Change>> button to expand the screen. Near the bottom is a check box and the phrase "Use 32-Bit Disk Access." If the check box and phrase are not there, it's because the 32BitDiskAccess=off line seen above was not inserted during the Setup procedure. If you want to push your luck, you can edit SYSTEM.INI by hand; however, the missing information usually means that Setup determined your system is not compatible with 32-bit access.

CAUTION: If you are about to enable 32-bit access on a system whose hard disk already contains critical data, back up the hard disk first.

RAM Drives

Before setting up a RAM drive, remember that Windows uses extended memory for application swap files in standard mode, and for virtual machines in enhanced mode. Also, your Smart Drive (or other) disk cache will want some of that extended memory too. Therefore, you may want to review the following sections before determining the optimum size for your own RAM drive.

NOTE: If you routinely copy programs to your RAM drive for faster execution, either insert the RAM drive letter at the beginning of the PATH statement in your AUTOEXEC.BAT file, or include that drive letter in the command line when you execute the program. Otherwise, DOS may find and execute the original program on the hard disk instead of the RAM-drive copy.

Standard Mode Considerations.   At first glance it might seem that a RAM drive would be the ideal site for application swap files. When Windows needs to move an application (or itself) in and out of the background, the transfer would go faster if data were written to RAM rather than to the hard disk. However, if you set your paging file to a RAM disk (see *Temporary File* section above), then when Windows switches an application into the background, the application simply moves from one part of RAM to another, thus defeating the RAM-saving aspect of the application swap file. Therefore, you might want to use this time-saving technique only if you have more RAM than you need to run all your applications, or if you just can't spare the hard disk space for the temporary files.

Enhanced Mode Considerations.   In enhanced mode, Windows turns to the swap file when it runs out of RAM space. Therefore, the more memory assigned to a RAM drive, the sooner Windows will need the virtual memory space in the swap file.

RAM Drive in Expanded Memory.   If your system has an expanded-memory card installed, and you need only some of its memory for DOS applications in standard-mode Windows, then use the remainder for your RAM drive, thus keeping the drive from eating into your extended-memory resources. In enhanced mode, Windows does not use any expanded memory, so all of it can be turned over to the RAM drive. The tradeoff is that an expanded-memory RAM drive may be slower than one that runs in extended memory.

Do not use expanded memory for your RAM drive if that memory is emulated by the EMM386.EXE expanded-memory emulator (or similar). The emulator creates its expanded memory by borrowing some of your extended memory, and it would be more efficient to just assign the extended memory directly to the RAM drive.

Smart Drive and RAM Drive Configuration Table 13.7 shows how extended memory might be allocated to Smart Drive and RAM drive use. However, the figures should be considered only as a convenient reference for a first-time setup. Depending on your specific needs, you'll no doubt want to vary these amounts to optimize your system's performance. For example, if you notice a lot of hard disk activity, that's a reasonable indication that your swap file is overworked. If so, try cutting down on the RAM drive size. If you have the *Windows Resource Kit,* place the Smart Drive Monitor icon in its "Always on Top" mode and keep an eye on the percentage shown as you perform various operations. Then try other Smart Drive and RAM Drive configurations and note the performance change. Sooner or later you'll arrive at the values for both that work best on your system. Finally, put a big "X" through Table 13.7 and stay with your own settings.

Troubleshooting Memory-Related Problems

Memory problems may be caused by something as simple (though unpleasant) as defective RAM, or as obscure as a conflict that only occurs under a certain set of conditions. As a troubleshooting aid, this section lists various problems according to the device that is the most likely suspect.

Memory-Management Troubleshooting

If *any* problem makes its debut immediately after installing a new—or reconfiguring an old—memory-management system, you don't need Sherlock Holmes to find the suspect. However, if a problem does not occur until sometime after your new memory manager is installed, it may not be immediately obvious that the memory manager is at fault.

TABLE 13.7 Typical Smart Drive and RAM Drive Configurations

Extended Memory	Standard Mode			Enhanced Mode		
	Win	SmartDrv	RAM	Win	SmartDRV	RAM
256	256	None	None	—	—	—
1024	768	256	None	1024	None	None
2048	1536	512	None	1792	256	None
3072	2048	512	512	2560	512	None
4096	2048	1024	1024	3072	1024	None
5120	3072	1024	1024	3072	1024	1024
6144	3072	2048	1024	3072	2048	1024
7168	3072	2048	2048	3584	2048	1536
8192	3072	3072	2048	3584	3072	1536
9216	4096	3072	2048	4096	3072	2048
10240	4096	3072	3072	4096	4096	2048
11264	4096	4096	3072	4096	4096	3072
12288	4096	4096	4096	4096	4096	4096

Maybe it is, and maybe it isn't. As a typical example, perhaps you open a DOS window and all seems well. Then you make the window full-screen, type DIR, and nothing happens. Or, something unexpected happens when you open or close a Windows application that used to work just fine. Either the screen display blanks out, or it shows strange graphics and colors. Or perhaps the system reboots itself, or just locks up.

Don't overlook the fact that little surprises such as these may not be the fault of the memory manager. If you're not really sure whether the problem existed earlier but you just didn't run into it, then you may want to double-check elsewhere before pulling your memory configuration apart.

Bootup Problems with New Memory-Management Software

This section describes problems that may occur when you boot your system immediately after installing a third-party memory manager, or after revising the configuration of a previously installed memory manager. Once your system boots successfully, try running a few DOS applications to verify that all is well. If problems persist, then more pre-Windows troubleshooting is required.

When everything else is in working order, try opening Windows. If some new memory-related problem shows up, then refer to the *Memory Problems at Windows Startup* section below for assistance.

Although it's a good idea to have a system boot diskette available at all times, you can probably restart your computer without it, if a just-installed memory manager causes the system to lock up. First, try pressing the Ctrl+Alt+Del keys. If that won't do it, turn the power off and back on again. But before doing either, refer to one of the following sections, as appropriate for your system configuration.

DOS 6.0 Boot Failure. Reboot the system and press function key F5 or F8 when the following message appears on screen:

Starting MS-DOS . . .

The appropriate function key depends on the nature of the problem. For problems that aren't immediately obvious, try function key F5. If you're reasonably sure the problem can be localized to your CONFIG.SYS file, then try F8. Refer to the appropriate section below for further assistance.

Function Key F5. When you press F5, you should see the DOS prompt. If you don't, there is something wrong with the system files (IO.SYS, MSDOS.SYS, COMMAND.COM). Since the F5 key press prevented CONFIG.SYS and AUTOEXEC.BAT from loading, nothing in either of these files could be causing the problem. Try rebooting from a DOS 6.0 boot diskette, and then using the DOS 6.0 SYS command to transfer a fresh set of system files to your hard disk (refer to the DOS 6.0 *User's Guide* for assistance if needed).

If you can't run SYS.COM because you can't access the DOS directory on your hard disk, then boot the system from DOS 6.0 distribution diskette 1, which contains the Expand utility and the SYS.CO_ file. Expand a fresh copy of SYS.CO_ to a system-formatted diskette, then run SYS.COM from that diskette. Then try rebooting from the hard disk, and again press F5 as described above.

If problems persist, there is probably something wrong with your hard disk. To rule out DOS 6.0 as the culprit, use your UNINSTALL diskette to return to DOS 5.0. If this does cure the problem, then it's time to call Microsoft's Product Support Services (see Appendix D).

Function Key F8. When you press this key, each line in your CONFIG.SYS file is displayed on screen, followed by a [Y,N]? prompt. As you respond to each prompt, the next line appears, again followed by a prompt. After all CONFIG.SYS lines are processed, a final prompt offers the option to process the AUTOEXEC.BAT file. If you decide not to do so, the entire batch file is ignored and the DOS prompt appears on-screen.

Figure 13.15 shows a typical screen display during the boot procedure. In this specific example, the DOS 6.0 MemMaker had been run previously. This utility splits the usual DOS=HIGH,UMB line into two separate lines, which allows the option of separately specifying whether either one should be executed, as shown by the first two lines of the figure.

CONFIG.SYS Troubleshooting. During an initial troubleshooting session, answer yes to each prompt and look for an error message that indicates the source of the problem. For example, Figure 13.15 shows an error in one of the parameters following EMM386.EXE (C000–B7FF should be B000–B7FF). As a warning, an *invalid parameter specified* message appears, but it's up to you to identify the specific parameter that is invalid.

If the system locks up while loading HIMEM.SYS, refer to the *Installed A20 handler* error message for assistance.

If no error messages are seen, then answer no to the final prompt (Process AUTOEXEC.BAT [Y,N]?). If the system starts properly, then there is a problem in the AUTOEXEC.BAT file. Refer to the *AUTOEXEC.BAT Troubleshooting* section below. Otherwise, continue reading here.

If disabling AUTOEXEC.BAT (as just described) doesn't cure the problem, then obviously something is wrong in CONFIG.SYS. Repeat the procedure described in this section, but only enable the following lines:

DOS=HIGH,UMB (*or each item separately, as appropriate*)
HIMEM.SYS
EMM386.EXE
(*any essential disk device drivers, disk-compression drivers*)
(*half of the remaining lines in CONFIG.SYS*)

If this cures the problem, then one of the disabled devices is the culprit. If it doesn't, then one of the devices just enabled is guilty. Repeat the procedure and enable/disable half the suspected devices until you have isolated the one causing the problem.

Once you have (finally!) identified the problem device driver, contact the manufacturer to see if an upgrade or workaround is available.

```
DOS=UMB [Y,N]?
DOS=HIGH [Y,N]?
DEVICE=C:\DOS\HIMEM.SYS [Y,N]?

    HIMEM: DOS XMS Driver, Version 3.09 - 07/24/92
    Extended Memory Specification (XMS) Version 3.0
    Copyright 1988-1992 Microsoft Corp.

    Installed A20 Handler number xx
    64K High Memory Area is Available.
```
                                                 ↙ *(invalid parameter)*
```
DEVICE=C:\DOS\EMM386.EXE NOEMS I=C000-B7FF (other parameters follow) [Y,N]?

    Microsoft Expanded Memory Manager 386 Version 4.45
    Copyright Microsoft Corporation 1986, 1992

    Invalid parameter specified.              ⇐    (Note error message)
    Press any key when ready . . .
    EMM386 successfully installed

Expanded memory services unavailable.

        Total upper memory available . . . .
        Largest Upper Memory Block available . . . .
        Upper memory starting address . . . .


BUFFERS=10,0 [Y,N]?
FILES=60 [Y,N]?
LASTDRIVE=G [Y,N]?
DEVICEHIGH=/L:2,11504 =C:\DOS\SETVER.EXE [Y,N]?
STACKS=9,256 [Y,N]?
SHELL=C:\DOS\COMMAND.COM C:\DOS /E:256 /P [Y,N]?
DEVICEHIGH=/L:2,5888 =C:\DOS\RAMDRIVE/SYS 1024 /E [Y,N]?

    Microsoft RAMDrive version 3.07 virtual disk E:
    Disk Size: 1024k
    Sector Size: 512 bytes
    Allocation Unit: 1 sectors
    Directory entries: 64


DEVICEHIGH=/L:2,5888 =(path, other device, parameters) [Y,N]?
    (messages related to device, if any)


Process AUTOEXEC.BAT [Y,N]?
```

Figure 13.15   A typical DOS 6.0 screen display during system bootup, if function key F8 is pressed when the *Starting MS-DOS...* legend is displayed

NOTE: MemMaker adds a device=CHKSTATE.SYS line to CONFIG.SYS for its own use, and then deletes the line at the conclusion of the optimization process. If the line remains in your CONFIG.SYS file, it may indicate a failure during memory optimization. If so, you may want to delete the line and rerun the procedure.

AUTOEXEC.BAT Troubleshooting. If the problem is localized to this batch file, the first thing to do is take a long look at its contents. If there is nothing obviously wrong, then disable half the TSRs by inserting "REM" (without the quotes) at the beginning of the appropriate lines. Reboot and see what happens. (There's no need to press F8, since CONFIG.SYS has already been cleared of suspicion.) If all is well, then one of the disabled TSRs was causing the problem. Or, if the problem persists, then one of the TSRs that was *not* disabled is the culprit. Keep hacking away by halves until you've isolated the problem line.

Disable Function Key Options. Both function-key procedures described below may be disabled by inserting the following line at the beginning of your CONFIG.SYS file:

```
switches /n
```

If this line is added to the file, then pressing F5 or F8 during the system boot will have no effect. You may want to add this line once your system is running reliably, if only to prevent accidents if someone else boots the machine and tries to "fix" things for you.

Qualitas *386MAX* Boot Failure. As the system reboots, hold down the Alt key when you hear the beep, then release the key when the following message is seen:

```
386MAX:  Alt-key pressed. Memory manager NOT installed.
Press any key to continue . . .
```

The following message is repeated each time you press any key, as each device and TSR fails to load.

```
386LOAD
Device=C:\386MAX\386LOAD.SYS SIZE=xxxx FLEXFRAME PROG=(device or
TSR name)
Load failed — not installed.
Press any key to continue.
```

Note that all the listed devices and TSRs are not loaded into conventional or into upper memory. If you attempt to run Windows in either mode, you will see a *Missing HIMEM.SYS* error message and the DOS prompt will reappear. Depending on the nature of the lockup problem, try one of the procedures described below to get the system back into operation.

Alt Key Press Failure. If the Alt key technique suggested above has no effect, you will have to restart the computer from a bootable system diskette. Once you have done so, log onto the 386MAX directory and look for files named CONFIG.00*x* and AUTOEXEC.00*x*, where *x* is any number. The highest-numbered set are the files that were in effect before the most recent installation of *386Max*. Copy these files as CONFIG.SYS and AUTOEXEC.BAT, respectively, and reboot the system. If problems continue after rebooting, then the problem lies elsewhere. Check both files carefully and if necessary, boot again using the basic startup files described in Chapter 1 and listed in Table 1.4a.

Lockup after Installing **386MAX.** If the lockup occurs immediately after installing *386MAX,* log onto the 386MAX directory and run the PREINST.BAT file. This restores your CONFIG.SYS and AUTOEXEC.BAT files to their preinstallation configuration. If you still have trouble, look in the 386MAX directory for files named CONFIG.00*x* and AUTOEXEC.00*x* where *x* may be any number. Find the set with the lowest number and copy them as CONFIG.SYS and AUTOEXEC.BAT, respectively. If problems continue after rebooting, then the trouble lies elsewhere, as described immediately above.

Lockup after Running **MAXIMIZE.** If a failure occurred while running the Qualitas *Maximize* utility, the PREMAXIM.BAT file in the 386MAX directory automatically restores the system to the configuration in effect prior to running this utility. If for some reason *Maximize* seemed to conclude successfully and now the system freezes during bootup, then log onto the 386MAX directory and run the PREMAXIM.BAT file to accomplish the same thing. Or if you prefer, run the PREINST.BAT file described above. If you do so, *Maximize* settings (if any) will also be removed.

Restore Startup Files with **Strip Manager** *Utility.* As an alternative to the methods described above, you can strip your startup files of all *386MAX* references by using the Qualitas Strip Manager (STRIPMGR.EXE) utility.

Assuming your startup files are in the root directory on drive C, log onto the 386MAX directory and type the following line at the DOS prompt:

STRIPMGR C: /s

Note that the utility removes references to the installed memory manager, but does not reinsert references to the Windows 3.1 HIMEM.SYS and EMM386.EXE files, or to any other memory manager that you may have been using prior to installing 386MAX. To preserve references to such items, refer to the STRIPMGR description in the *386MAX Reference Guide.*

Quarterdeck *QEMM386* Boot Failure. If the system locks up when you reboot after installing *QEMM386,* reboot, then press and hold the Alt key when you hear the beep. Release the key when the following message is seen:

QEMM386: Press <ESC> to unload QEMM or any other key to continue with QEMM. . .

When you press the Escape key, the following message is repeated as each device driver or TSR loads into low memory.

There is no high memory available. Loading low: *(device or TSR name)*

Although the Quarterdeck memory manager did not load, all your device drivers and TSRs will be loaded into conventional memory. Depending on the nature of the lockup problem, try one of the procedures described below to get the system back into operation.

Alt Key Press Failure. If the Alt key technique suggested above has no effect, you will have to restart the computer from a bootable system diskette. Once you have done so, refer to the following sections for troubleshooting suggestions.

Lockup after Installing **QEMM386.** If the lockup occurs immediately after installing *QEMM386,* you can recover your original startup files, which were renamed with BAK extensions during the *QEMM386* installation.

Lockup after Running **OPTIMIZE.** When you run the Quarterdeck *Optimize* utility, your startup files are saved with QDK extensions in place of SYS and BAT. In addition, an "unoptimize" file (UNOPT.BAT) is written into the QEMM directory. If a problem with *Optimize* cannot be easily resolved, you can restore your system to its pre-*Optimize* configuration by logging onto the QEMM directory and typing UNOPT at the DOS prompt.

The batch file copies the QDK files as CONFIG.SYS and AUTOEXEC.BAT. Or, to return to your configuration prior to installing *QEMM386* itself, simply copy the BAK files instead.

Resolving Memory Manager Problems.   If you had to use any of the just-described procedures to get your system back in business, then obviously something went wrong with the installation of the memory-management system. Either something in your system doesn't care for the new boss, or an installation glitch slipped by undetected.

Note that when you restart your computer as described above, the memory-manager software will be bypassed during bootup. As a result, Smart Drive will not be loaded, since it requires the presence of either HIMEM.SYS or its Qualitas or Quarterdeck equivalent. An error message will report that HIMEM.SYS is not loaded. Furthermore, Windows itself will not run. If you try anyway, another message will complain about the missing HIMEM.SYS. However, since the system is otherwise more-or-less functional, you can begin troubleshooting the memory-management configuration. Once that's taken care of, Windows should start properly.

In your CONFIG.SYS file, your memory manager should usually appear at the head of the list of devices to be loaded. There are, however, a few devices that should go first. As an obvious example, if your memory-management software is on a drive other than the one used to boot the system, the driver for that hard disk drive must be loaded first and, of course, it cannot be loaded via the memory manager itself. If the recent installation has created such a problem, restore the appropriate device line in CONFIG.SYS to its former state and make sure the line appears ahead of the memory-management line. If this is not appropriate in your system, try disabling other device lines, one at a time, until the problem goes away. Once the system boots normally, restore all other lines that were previously disabled. Then try reloading the troublesome device into conventional memory with the standard device= line. If that actually works, then check with the appropriate hardware/software supplier to see if an updated driver is available, or if there is a workaround solution.

If none of the above works, try disabling anything that loads via your AUTOEXEC.BAT file. As a quick check, disable the entire file by renaming it as say, XUTOEXEC.BAT, then try rebooting. If the system makes it through bootup, then something in AUTOEXEC.BAT is causing the trouble. Disable various lines until you isolate the problem, and take whatever action is appropriate.

Upper Memory Block Conflicts. It's possible that the memory manager it-self is causing a problem by accidentally taking over a block of upper memory required by one of your installed devices. In this case there may not be a problem until the device tries to use that memory block. If the nature of the problem reveals the device that is causing the conflict, then check the *User's Guide* for that device. You should find a reference to the UMB which it uses. Exclude that area by using the appropriate syntax for the installed memory manager and reboot the system.

If you aren't sure which device is causing the problem, try excluding the entire upper memory area by rewriting the appropriate line in CON-FIG.SYS, as follows:

Manager	CONFIG.SYS Line	Utility
Windows 3.1	device=C:\WINDOWS\EMM386.EXE x=A000-FFFF	MSD.EXE
Qualitas	device=C:\386MAX\386MAX.SYS exclude=A000-FFFF	ASQ.EXE
Quarterdeck	device=C:\QEMM\QEMM386.SYS x=A000-FFFF	MFT.EXE

Now use the appropriate utility (listed above) to view the upper memory area, and look for a block that is occupied by some device. If you can identify such an area, then rewrite the exclude line above to keep the memory manager out of just that block (or blocks) of upper memory.

If the above procedure doesn't reveal the problem, it's possible that some device has not yet accessed the memory block in question. As an obvious ex-ample, the Windows MSD utility will show that the A000–AFFF block is avail-able. And so it is—at the moment. That's because this 64 Kbyte UMB is reserved for high-resolution graphics, and MSD runs in text mode. If your memory manager included this area (it won't), your system would lock up whenever you attempt to run a graphics-mode program, Windows or otherwise.

If some less-obvious device causes the UMB conflict, try excluding pro-gressively smaller ranges until the problem occurs again. Then return to the last setting, at which there was no problem. If the problem seems to be video-related, refer to the section immediately following.

Video Problem. If a graphics application's display is corrupted, try ex-cluding the A000–CFFF range. If that solves the problem, try reducing the range until the problem comes back again. Then return to the last setting that did not give trouble.

Upper Memory Load Failure.   Occasionally, a driver or TSR fails to load into upper memory, even though there is plenty of room for it up there. In fact, your memory management software may write the appropriate instruction in CONFIG.SYS or AUTOEXEC.BAT to load the file into upper memory, yet the procedure fails during subsequent system boots.

Some drivers and TSRs just don't like upper memory and refuse to be seen there even if the memory manager doesn't realize there's a problem. At other times the use of the B000–B7FF block causes a conflict that seems to have nothing to do with either the block itself or the program that refuses to load into upper memory. The file may either load into conventional memory, or worse, not get loaded at all. In either case, you'll probably see a misleading "not enough room to load *filename* high" message during boot up. If so, refer to that error message below for suggestions.

Windows Startup Troubleshooting

Assuming you can now turn your system on without getting into trouble, this section describes a few memory-related problems that may show up when you try to open Windows.

WIN /s Locks System, WIN /3 Returns DOS Prompt.   If this problem occurs immediately after installing or reconfiguring your memory manager, then whatever you just did is causing the problem. If you included the B000–B7FF range on your memory manager's command line, refer to the *Windows cannot set up an upper memory block at segment B000* error message for a few suggestions. Otherwise, review the recently made changes and, if necessary, restore the configuration that was in place before the error occurred.

If the problem occurs immediately after running the DOS 6.0 MemMaker utility, then examine the EMM386.EXE line in your CONFIG.SYS file for the presence of WIN= parameters. If there are two such parameters, and both are within the B000–B7FF range, refer to the *Reserved Memory Blocks* section earlier in the chapter for a problem-fix.

MSD.EXE Utility Causes Lockup or System Reboot.   The most likely suspect here is an incompatibility with a third-party memory manager. For example, Qualitas' *386MAX* has a ROM search utility (ROMSRCH.EXE) which will examine the upper memory area for blocks reserved for ROM but currently unoccupied. If it finds such an area, it will write a USE=F000-F800 (or other address range) line into the 386MAX.PRO file. On bootup, the designated block(s) will be added to the available UMB area. This action may cause no problems with most applications, but it will bring the MSD utility (and your system) to a halt. The solution is either to delete the USE= line or to remember not to use the MSD utility while the third-party memory-management system is installed.

Windows Session Troubleshooting

Most memory-related problems that show up during a Windows session may be resolved by noting the error message and taking the appropriate action. However, there are those times when no message is seen; in fact, Windows keeps on working, but it just doesn't seem to be working well enough. For example, if Windows is crawling instead of running, there are several possibilities to be considered.

Add More Memory. Remember that Windows *loves* memory. Without a certain amount of it, one or both modes won't run, period. Then there's that vague area in which Windows can be forced into enhanced mode by appending the /3 switch (see, for example, *Windows Opens in Standard Mode* below). Beyond that, Windows may start in enhanced mode without protest and, although it won't actually growl at you during a session, it's easy to tell that it isn't running full throttle.

The point at which this kind of behavior may be noted varies from one system to another, and depends on what is running at the moment. However, it usually means that Windows could use more memory. If other suggestions in this section do nothing to whip Windows into shape, it may be time to pour a few more Mbytes into its memory tank. For example, if your total system RAM is in the 5-Mbyte region, this should be enough to run Windows without any problems. It should be. But if you can handle say, an additional 4-Mbyte injection, you may be pleasantly surprised at the performance improvement.

Change Permanent Swap File Size. As a rule-of-thumb, a permanent swap file should be about three times the size of the available system RAM. However, this does not mean that a 20-Mbyte system wants a 60-Mbyte swap file. If you have 20 Mbytes of RAM, you may not need a permanent swap file at all, since the RAM gives Windows more than enough room in which to play. In this case you might get better performance by setting the swap file to "none."

The best time to experiment with swap file size is after you've become familiar with Windows' general performance with whatever you're using now. Then adjust the size up or down and see how it goes. After a few experiments, you'll have a better idea of the optimum swap file size for your specific system and operating style.

Run a Disk Defragmenting Utility.   If you use a temporary swap file, remember that its area may become fragmented over time as files are written to, and erased from, the hard disk on which the swap file resides. If regular disk defragmenting noticeably improves performance speed, it may be time to consider setting aside space for a permanent swap file.

Run Windows in Standard Mode.   If you don't need the features offered by enhanced mode, try running Windows in standard mode, which is generally faster. If you can feel the difference, you may want to run in standard mode unless the application requires enhanced-mode support.

Swap File Troubleshooting

Problems related to swap files usually show up during virtual memory configuration. This section describes a few of the most likely problems that will be encountered. If none of this helps, then review the *Windows Session Troubleshooting* section above for additional suggestions.

General Permanent Swap File Setup Problems.   If you experience difficulties setting up a permanent swap file despite the availability of sufficient disk space, it's possible that a third-party video device driver is interfering with the setup. If this is a possibility, exit Windows and run Setup at the DOS prompt. Change the display to the standard VGA, then reopen Windows and try again. After the swap file is properly installed, reset your video configuration as desired.

Maximum Size Is Too Small.   When setting up a swap file, if the Space Available box shows considerable free space on the hard disk, but the Maximum Size box shows an insufficient amount of it available for a permanent swap file, it's possible some unmoveable occupied blocks are in the free space area. For example, if a single lost cluster or other file fragment sits at about midpoint in an otherwise-free 20-Mbyte space, the Maximum Space box will report only 10 Mbytes available for a permanent swap file.

Since a permanent swap file can only be installed in contiguous free space, the fix is to exit Windows, run CHKDSK /f at the DOS prompt and save or erase the FILE*xxxx*.CHK file(s) recovered by CHKDSK. Next, run a defragment utility (Norton *SpeedDisk* or similar) to move any other file fragments. Then reopen Windows and set the desired swap file configuration.

Recommended Size Is Too Small. If a permanent swap file is already in place, its size is listed as the Recommended Size, regardless of the actual space available. Simply disregard the recommendation and the warning message that follows.

Available Memory Does Not Include Permanent Swap File. If you've installed a swap file and yet your free memory does not seem to include its size, check the [386Enh] section of your SYSTEM.INI file for the following line:

```
[386Enh]
Paging=Off (or =False)
```
Change the line to =On (*or* =True), or delete it entirely.

Smart Drive Troubleshooting

This section describes a few problems that may be encountered when Smart Drive is installed, or when its cache size is changed.

General Startup Problems. If your system functions properly when Smart Drive is not installed, then there may be a conflict between it and some device driver listed in your CONFIG.SYS file. Reboot with the basic startup files shown in Table 1.4a, but retain the C:\WINDOWS\SMARTDRV.EXE line in your AUTOEXEC.BAT file. If you can isolate the conflict problem to a specific device driver, contact the supplier of that driver to see if an updated version is available. If you discover a third-party disk cache utility being loaded in your startup files, then you'll have to remove either it, or Smart Drive itself.

Disk Drive Conflicts. Assuming space is available, Smart Drive automatically loads itself into upper memory. If it accidentally occupies a UMB that is required by some other device, disk operations become risky business. If you suspect such a problem, force Smart Drive into conventional memory by appending the /L switch (SMARTDRV.EXE /L), and reboot the system. Then, use the MSD utility (or similar) to inspect the upper memory area. If you see any occupied blocks, append the appropriate x=*xxxx-yyyy* parameter to the EMM386.EXE line in your CONFIG.SYS file to exclude the memory manager from that block. By doing this, Smart Drive (or anything else) won't get loaded into that area again, so you can delete the /L switch to get it back into upper memory.

If loading Smart Drive into conventional memory does not solve the problem, then disable all caching to half of your drive complement, as follows:

C:\WINDOWS\SMARTDRV.EXE A- B- (*and so on*)

If this solves the problem, then re-enable caching to half of the just-disabled drives. Or if it doesn't, disable half of the remaining drives. Continue this process until you've isolated the drive, or drives, causing the conflict.

> **NOTE:** If you use Stacker version 2.0 or later, Smart Drive knows enough to stay away from it, and so it is not necessary to disable caching to that drive. However, you should disable caching to Stacker drives prior to version 2.0.

Enhanced-Mode Problems.   If Windows refuses to open in enhanced mode, or it opens but acts up when you try to run a non-Windows application, then append a "+" sign to the following line in your CONFIG.SYS file:

device=C:\WINDOWS\SMARTDRV.EXE double_buffer+

Also, append the /L switch to the Smart Drive line in your AUTOEXEC.BAT file. This forces the double-buffer feature to be enabled, and may resolve problems with some SCSI and ESDI drive controllers.

Network or Other Device Conflicts.   It's possible that Smart Drive is being loaded into an upper memory block that is subsequently accessed by a network or other device, causing a conflict. In the specific case of a network card, try appending x=D800-DFFF to your EMM386.EXE (or third-party equivalent) line. For other devices, refer to the appropriate *User's Guide* for information about the upper memory area that the device uses, then exclude this area, as just described.

Parity Errors.   If parity errors appear soon after installing Smart Drive, or after changing the cache size, it's likely that the presence of the cache is forcing some application into a memory area that contains defective RAM. To verify the problem is not caused by Smart Drive, disable it and install a RAM drive of the same size (or, increase the size of your existing RAM drive to accomplish the same thing). If the problem remains, then you know it isn't Smart Drive.

Performance Slowdown with Double-Buffering. If the double-buffer option noticeably slows down system performance, contact the manufacturer of your hard drive to see if updated ROM is available. Or, there may be a virtual DMA services (VDS) driver available for use with your controller. In either case, remove the double-buffer line after installing the new hardware or software.

Performance Slowdown with Smart Drive version 4.0. If you notice that the new SMARTDRV.EXE is slower than the previous version, try running it with the /L switch to force it into conventional memory.

System Lockup. If your system locks up during reboot after installing Smart Drive, you may need to increase the number and/or size of the Stacks line in your CONFIG.SYS file, as follows:

    Stacks=9,256

Windows Opens in Standard Mode. If you need to type WIN /3 to force Windows to open in enhanced mode, then it's likely that your Windows cache size is too large, given the amount of extended memory installed in your system. At the DOS prompt, type SMARTDRV and press the Enter key. Note the DOS and Windows cache sizes listed in the report. Then rewrite the Smart Drive command line as follows:

    C:\WINDOWS\SMARTDRV.EXE *xxxx yyyy*

where

xxxx   DOS cache size previously reported
yyyy   Half the previously reported Windows cache size

Repeat the procedure until Windows will open in enhanced mode without using the /3 switch. Then think about getting more memory.

A Final Smart Drive Check. Once you've nailed down the device that Smart Drive doesn't seem to like, you might try going back to the DOS 5.0 version. Disable the SMARTDRV.EXE line in your AUTOEXEC.BAT file and insert the following line in your CONFIG.SYS file:

    C:\DOS\SMARTDRV.SYS (*note* SYS, *not* EXE, *extension*)

If this actually works, you can report to the device manufacturer that the driver needs updating.

32-Bit Access Troubleshooting

If 32-bit access is enabled and there is a startup problem the next time you open Windows, try opening with the WIN /d:F switch. This disables 32-bit access. The next step is to go to the 32-bit access check box described above and disable it.

System Reboot Failure

When Windows is not running, you should be able to reboot the system by pressing the Ctrl+Alt+Del keys. If this well-known "3-finger salute" locks the system instead of rebooting it, there is probably a conflict between your computer's own video BIOS shadowing and your installed memory-management software. Watch for a *Video BIOS Shadowing enabled* or similar message as the system boots. If you see such a message (or even if you don't, but suspect this may be the problem), access your computer's BIOS configuration and disable video BIOS shadowing. Depending on your specific system, you may need to run a diagnostics utility, or press a specific key combination (Ctrl+Alt+Esc, or Ctrl+Alt+Enter, for example) to do this. Once you have disabled shadowing, restart the system and again try a system reboot.

If the reboot problem is gone, then temporarily revise your EMM386.EXE (or equivalent) line to exclude the entire upper memory area (x=A000-FFFF will do it). Then re-enable video BIOS shadowing, reboot the system, and use the DOS MSD utility (or similar) to examine the upper memory area. You'll probably find a 32-Kbyte block identified as ROM at E000, or perhaps elsewhere. In any case, note the location, and rewrite the x=A000-FFFF line to exclude just that block. Now reboot one more time and once the system is running, try the three-finger salute.

If the problem is gone, then run the DOS MEM /c utility to see if the exclusion of the UMB required for video shadowing has forced any of your device drivers or TSRs back into conventional memory. If it has, then you'll have to decide if video shadowing is worth it.

If none of the above solves the Ctrl+Alt+Del lockup problem, then contact the computer manufacturer to see if there's a workaround. In some cases, a BIOS upgrade will take care of the problem. If the manufacturer knows less about the problem than you do, try contacting the BIOS manufacturer directly.

Error Messages

Various memory-related error messages may show up during system bootup, or as Windows opens, closes, or simply goes about its routine operations.

Still others may show up when you attempt to change your swap file configuration. These error messages are described below in three separate sections. But first there are a few words about everyone's favorite: the parity error. For memory-related messages confined to a specific applet or application (for example, opening or closing a DOS window), refer to the chapter in which that application is described.

The Parity Error Message

Windows presents this little bit of bad news against an appropriately blue background. Its eight words can be summarized in just four: "You're out of business."

```
System Error
Memory parity error detected.
System halted.
```

Don't bother with a three-finger salute; the only thing that works here is a cold reboot.

When parity errors show up immediately after installing Windows 3.1, most users find it hard to believe that it's not really a Windows fault. People who have been running Windows 3.0 find it even harder to believe that 3.1 is not the culprit. And those who take the time to do a memory diagnostics test that reports no trouble at all may become hostile when someone else still insists that Windows is not at fault.

Not that it's much consolation, but there are a few factors at work here. One is that many diagnostic routines are not rigorous enough to find all memory faults. So, your system can pass the memory test and still die when Windows gets going. The reason the memory problem did not show up before installing version 3.1, is that Windows 3.0 ignored parity errors, which may have caused UAEs (unrecoverable application errors) that were not recognized for what they really were. As a further consideration, Windows 3.1 allocates memory in reverse order (from high to low), so previously unused (and faulty) RAM may be getting used for the first time. Therefore, if you do encounter a parity error, the odds are that you really do have a faulty RAM chip, most likely near the top of your memory map.

Erroneous Parity Error Messages.   If a parity error shows up only when you change video modes (for example, switching to a full-screen DOS application from within Windows), then the video adapter is probably generating a nonmaskable interrupt, which causes an erroneous parity error message. To verify this, write a PIF file that opens a DOS session in a window. Once the DOS window is open, press Alt+Enter to switch to full screen. If the parity error shows up every time you do this, then the video adapter card is indeed the culprit.

If the parity error is not related to the video adapter, you can probably suppress the error message by disabling the parity line in SYSTEM.INI, as follows:

```
[386Enh]
;device=*parity  (note semicolon at head of line)
```

At best, this is a temporary fix. If the faulty memory area is actually accessed later on, you'll get a general protection error message. However, if this workaround does restore normal operation, then there is probably a problem with the application that originally triggered the parity error message. Contact the manufacturer to see if an upgrade is available.

Error Messages during System Bootup

Error messages unique to a specific memory manager are identified by a parenthetical reference to that system at the end of the error message. Note, however, that the type of error being described might also occur with some other memory manager; therefore, the suggestions that follow may be found useful regardless of what memory manager is in use.

Installed A20 handler number *xx*. It's not exactly an error message, but if the system locks up after displaying this line, then the machine name or number listed on the DOS 5.0 or 6.0 HIMEM.SYS line in CONFIG.SYS is invalid for your system. Insert a system boot diskette in drive A, then press the reset button (if any) or turn the power off and back on again (Ctrl+Alt+Del won't do it this time). Then refer to the discussion of the /machine: switch in the *Windows 3.1 Extended Memory Manager (HIMEM.SYS)* section earlier in the chapter. Or just have a look at Table 13.3 for the correct name/number for your system.

Installed A20 handler number *xx* (where *xx* is not what it used to be). Under certain conditions, the number reported during system bootup may change to a new number after upgrading your DOS version. With each new edition of HIMEM.SYS, one or more new machine handlers may be recognized, and therefore reported. For example, a Dell system running MS-DOS 5.0 might report itself as using handler number 1. The same system reports handler number 17 after upgrading to MS-DOS 6.0. Assuming the system still works, the new number is just a function of the new memory manager. If the system doesn't work, then refer to the message immediately above this one.

Invalid parameter specified. Press any key when ready.   Make a note of the device or TSR listed on the line(s) immediately above the message. Then check the appropriate line in your CONFIG.SYS or AUTOEXEC.BAT file for an incorrect switch or other parameter. For example, the message appears if the /nohigh switch is appended to EMM386.EXE. Although /nohigh is listed in the Windows 3.1 manual, the correct syntax is /nohi.

LOADHI: An invalid region was specified. Please rerun OPTIMIZE. Loading low (QEMM386).   This message may be seen after a device name, if you change one of the parameters on the QEMM386.SYS line in your CONFIG.SYS file. When you rerun the *Optimize* utility, *QEMM386* will make the necessary corrections to once again load the specified device into upper memory (space permitting of course).

Not enough memory to load *filename* high. Loading low (QEMM386).   If this message appears even though there is sufficient upper memory available, there may be a memory-management conflict caused by erroneous file-loading data, as described in the *LOADHI.OPT File* section earlier in the chapter.

Part of the problem may be due to the inclusion of an i=B000-B7FF parameter in your CONFIG.SYS file. If your memory manager reserves this 32-Kbyte block for a device driver that initially requires more than 32 Kbytes, the *not enough memory* error message may be seen and the device will be loaded into conventional memory, even though there is room to spare for it higher up in the UMB area.

There are several solutions to the problem. In the specific case of Quarterdeck's *QEMM386,* the i=B000-B7FF parameter is not really needed, since this area will be utilized anyway. However, the explicit presence of this parameter may lead *Optimize* to erroneously reserve the area for something too big to fit in it. In this case, remove the parameter and rerun *Optimize.*

As another alternative, try rearranging the items loaded in CONFIG.SYS or AUTOEXEC.BAT, so that the problem file is loaded later in the sequence. This may move it into a higher UMB, thus obviating the problem.

If all else fails, it's possible the device driver or TSR is just one of those that doesn't like the upper memory area. In this case, rewrite the appropriate line in CONFIG.SYS or AUTOEXEC.BAT to load it into conventional memory, and rerun *Optimize* (or other). Then contact the driver/TSR supplier to see if an upgrade is available.

Specific MSCDEX.EXE Loading Problem. If the MSCDEX.EXE file is the one that won't load into upper memory, try appending the /M:4 switch and—if expanded memory is available—the /E switch, as shown here:

C:\(*QEMM loadhi, or similar*) C:\(*path*)\MSCDEX.EXE (*existing switches*) /M:4 /E

Refer to *AUTOEXEC.BAT: The CD-ROM Extensions* in the *CD-ROM Driver Requirements* section of Chapter 12 for a description of these and the other switches associated with the MSCDEX.EXE file.

> **NOTE:** The potential B000–B7FF conflict described here refers to a system bootup problem, and is not related to a similar conflict that may show up when Windows itself is run in enhanced mode.

Packed file is corrupt. Some software stays compressed until loaded into conventional memory, at which time it expands automatically. In a few cases, this may cause a problem if the software loads itself in the first 64 Kbytes of conventional memory (hexadecimal segments 0000–1000). Given the ability of modern memory managers to free conventional memory space, it's possible that such a program may find itself loading into this low-memory area, thus causing this error message to appear.

There are a few fixes. Use the DOS 5.0 LOADFIX command, as shown here:

LOADFIX *filename.ext*

This workaround simply wastes some lower-memory space so that the problem program is loaded above the 64-Kbyte boundary. You can accomplish much the same thing by increasing the number of files and/or buffers listed in your CONFIG.SYS file. Or, try loading some other program ahead of the one causing the error message. This may obviate the need to waste space with unneeded files or buffers.

> **NOTE:** The just-described error message has nothing to do with the familiar practice of distributing software in compressed format and expanding it during installation.

Warning: Unable to use a disk cache on the specified drive. SMARTDrive cannot be loaded because the XMS driver, HIMEM.SYS is not loaded. Check the CONFIG.SYS file for a device=himem.sys command line. This message is seen if HIMEM.SYS is missing from your CONFIG.SYS file. If the message appears while you are troubleshooting a third-party memory-management system, it is because that system's extended-memory support was not loaded. In its absence, the Smart Drive utility looks for HIMEM.SYS and doesn't find it—hence the error message.

You are using an expanded memory manager which is not compatible with Windows 3.1, or which is configured incorrectly. If this message appears, check the line in your CONFIG.SYS file which specifies your memory manager and its switch settings. If the problem cannot be easily resolved, then try using the HIMEM.SYS and EMM386.EXE files that come with Windows 3.1 or DOS 6.0.

Error Messages during a Windows Session

The following error messages may be seen as Windows opens or closes, or during routine Windows operations. If the message seems to contradict your own knowledge of how much memory is available, you may want to run the System Resource Monitor (SYSMETER.EXE) utility that comes with the Windows 3.1 Resource Kit (or a third-party equivalent such as PC-Kwik's KwikInfo applet). If you use SYSMETER.EXE, enable its Always on Top option and keep an eye on system resources as you re-create the situation that causes the error message. If one of the resource gauges indicates that the error message is valid, then you either need more memory or you must free up some of what you already have. However, if the utility shows that system resources are not low, then the file causing the error message is either corrupt, or incompatible with something else.

Back Fill: Unable to start Enhanced Mode Windows due to base memory back fill. If your memory manager has taken over an upper memory area that Windows needs, this message will be seen if you attempt to open Windows in enhanced mode. To verify that this is the problem, try opening Windows in standard mode. If you see a *Bad Fault in MS-DOS Extender* message, then there is indeed a problem with the memory manager.

One likely cause is a parameter that incorrectly converts video RAM into a free upper memory block, as might happen if a parameter such as the i=A000-AFFF seen here is appended to your memory manager.

```
device=EMM386.EXE i=A000-AFFF
```

The A000–AFFF area is reserved for EGA/VGA RAM, and must not be assigned for other uses. To cure the problem, edit your CONFIG.SYS file to remove the i=A000-AFFF parameter.

Conventional memory in your system is fragmented and Windows cannot run in 386 enhanced mode. Restart your computer and try again, or try starting Windows in standard mode. You may want to use the DOS MEM /p command (or MEM /d in DOS 6.0) to have a look at your conventional memory and see why it is fragmented. If you can exit an application that is tying up some of this memory, then do so and try running Windows again. Or, just clean out your conventional memory area the easy way: Reboot the system. It's not elegant, but it works.

Insufficient conventional memory to run Windows; reconfigure your system to increase available memory and try again. If this message appears, run the DOS 5.0 MEM /c command to examine the amount of free conventional memory that is available. According to Table 1.1a in Chapter 1, Windows 3.1 should run if there is a minimum of 256 Kbytes of free conventional memory. So much for theory: In practice, Windows may need slightly less than 300 Kbytes in order to get started. If your total free memory falls somewhere in the 200–300 Kbyte range, the first question to ask is, why? The obvious answer is that some DOS application is hogging space. Review the MEM /c utility's conventional memory report and exit whatever DOS application is preventing Windows from getting started. If you really need that application, launch Windows first, then run it from within a DOS window.

Insufficient conventional memory to run Windows in standard mode. Free some conventional memory before starting Windows. As with any message referring to conventional memory, there is probably some DOS application taking up too much space. For further details, refer to the *Insufficient Conventional Memory* error message immediately above.

Insufficient extended memory available. Quit one or more applications to increase available memory or restart your computer. When this message appears, the solution is to free up more extended memory by reducing the size of your RAM disk and/or SMARTDRV, or exit any application that may be occupying extended memory, or buy more memory.

Insufficient extended memory available to run Windows. Quit one or more applications to increase available memory or restart your computer. If this message is seen only when you try to force Windows into enhanced mode, then you have the option of running in standard mode, or taking the appropriate action to free some additional extended memory. If previously loaded applications are the problem, then rebooting the computer is one way to get rid of them all. However, rebooting won't help if the culprit is a too-large RAM or Smart Drive. In this case you'll have to trim one or both down to size, and reboot.

Another possible solution is to disable the EMM386.EXE (or equivalent) line in your CONFIG.SYS file, so that your extended memory resources are not diminished to fill the upper memory blocks. Although this means that programs formerly loaded into this area will now reside in conventional memory, the increased free extended memory may permit Windows to run in enhanced mode, at least until you can buy some more memory.

Insufficient extended memory to run Windows in standard mode. Increase the amount of available extended memory.   If the message is valid, then do whatever needs to be done to free up some extended memory. However, if you've just installed some third-party mouse software, there may be a conflict between the DOS and Windows drivers. Refer to the *Mouse Troubleshooting* section of Chapter 11 for assistance.

Insufficient memory or address space to initialize Windows in 386 enhanced mode. Quit one or more memory-resident programs or remove unnecessary utilities from your CONFIG.SYS and AUTOEXEC.BAT files, and restart your computer.   When this message appears, there may be sufficient memory to run Windows in standard mode. Do so, and check the amount of free memory reported on the About Program Manager screen. The figure should show an amount sufficient for standard mode, but not for enhanced mode.

Reduce the size of your RAM disk and/or SMARTDRV to free up sufficient memory for enhanced-mode operation, or quit any application that is occupying your available extended memory.

Mouse Software Conflict.   If the above message appears immediately after installing third-party Windows mouse software, there may be a conflict between the DOS and Windows drivers. Refer to the *Mouse Troubleshooting* section of Chapter 11 if you need assistance resolving the problem.

Insufficient memory to run application. Quit one of more applications, or free up disk space, to increase available memory. Then try again.   If the message recommendations don't apply to your system, then it's possible the program you are trying to run is defective. In case of doubt, run some other application. If the message persists, then there is indeed a memory-related problem. However, if other programs run without a problem, then the suspect program is probably defective.

Invalid HIMEM.SYS. Windows 3.1 officially requires HIMEM.SYS version 3.01 or higher, although it may open with some slightly earlier versions as well. If you have any doubts about the currently installed version, reboot and watch the opening screen for the version number, or expand a fresh copy from your distribution diskettes. Finally, check your CONFIG.SYS file to make sure the path to your HIMEM.SYS file is correct. Unless you've relocated the file, the line should read as follows:

```
device=C:\WINDOWS\HIMEM.SYS
```

or

```
device=C:\DOS\HIMEM.SYS  (if DOS 6.0 is installed)
```

Missing HIMEM.SYS; Make sure that the file is in your Windows directory and that its location is correctly specified in your CONFIG.SYS file. As noted by the message itself, your CONFIG.SYS file may lack a command line referring to the HIMEM.SYS file, or you may be using a third-party memory manager that is not correctly installed. If you have any doubts about what's wrong, try booting with the basic CONFIG.SYS file listed in Table 1.4a. During bootup, you may see a warning message about Smart Drive, which cannot be loaded if HIMEM.SYS (or a third-party equivalent) is missing.

Not enough memory... (*various phrases follow*). There are so many variations on the "Not enough memory. . . " theme that it would take too much room to list them all separately. Instead, Table 13.8 summarizes the messages as they appear in various Windows applets. Needless to say, still other "Not enoughs" will appear in various other Windows applications. If the context in which the message appears is not clear, refer to the table for help in identifying the source of the message.

Although the theme may vary, the resolution is always the same: You need more memory. Either close some applications, revise your configuration to make more memory available, or go out and buy more of it. However, you might want to refer to the *Out of Memory* message below, if you think you should not be seeing the message. Possibly your other system resources are running low, in which case more memory might not help.

TABLE 13.8   Memory Messages in Windows Applets*

Not enough memory...	Applet	Not enough memory...	Applet
Available	PaintBrush	**To (continued)**	
		Continue	Reg. Editor
Available for		Copy the object	CardFile
Contents of the Clipboard	Write	Cut to the Clipboard	Object Packager
The data	Calculator	Determine link update	CardFile
This operation	Recorder, Terminal	Determine link update	Object Packager
This task	Control Panel	Display card faces	Solitaire
		Display data	Clipboard
Available to		Edit image	PaintBrush
Complete this action	CardFile	Increase Clipboard cont.	Write
Complete this operation	Media Player, NotePad,	Paste Clipboard cont.	Object Packager
	Sound Recorder, Write	Perform this operation	CardFile, Object
Load *filename*	Sound Recorder	Print	Packager, PBrush
Perform this operation	Calendar		CardFile, File Mgr
Print	Calendar	Print picture	NotePad, PBrush
			CardFile
For		Read card	CardFile
This operation	PaintBrush	Read picture	CardFile
Write	Write	Repaginate, print doc	Write
		Retrieve Clipboard	CardFile
Or		Retrieve the object	CardFile
Disk space	Clipboard	Run Cardfile	CardFile
Other system resource	Print Manager	Run program	PaintBrush
Pntr. not installed properly	PaintBrush	Run the Tutorial	Windows Tutorial
		Run this application	Object Packager
To		Save card	CardFile
Cancel the link	CardFile, Write	Start Help	Screen Savers
Complete operation	PaintBrush	Start specified application	File Manager
Complete this operation	Write	Convert all program icons	Program Manager

*Use message text as guide if source of error is not clear from context in which message appears.

> **Out of Memory. Close one or more applications and try again.** The message is self-explanatory—except when you know very well that you've got enough memory to run everything that's running and then some. In this case, the message means that your system resources are running low. To verify this, make your way to any Help menu and select the <u>A</u>bout... option, which will probably show system resources at about 20 percent or less, even though you may have lots of free memory.

If you're wondering what all this means, refer to the *System Resources* section earlier in this chapter for a bit more information. If you'd rather just get on with it, try closing down a few applications—especially anything that uses a lot of graphics. Doing so will release some system resources for whatever you're trying to do at the moment.

Parity Error Message. This unpleasant subject is discussed at the beginning of the chapter's *Error Messages* section.

A [*Privileged Operation Exception, stack fault, internal system error, etc.*] has occurred at address *xxxx:yyyy*. Press any key to restart your computer (386MAX). If this message is seen, and the first *x* is a letter (hexadecimal A-F), *386MAX* may be mapping RAM into an upper memory block that is used by a hardware adapter. To exclude 386MAX from that area, add a ram=*xxxx-yyyy* line to the 386MAX.PRO file, as described in the *386MAX.PRO* section earlier in the chapter. If you're lucky, the documentation for the adapter will explicitly cite the memory block that it uses, and you can set the ram= line as required.

If you're not that lucky, and don't otherwise know what values to assign, exit Windows and run the ASQ.EXE utility supplied with *386MAX*. When the menu bar appears at the top of the screen, select the "Memory" menu and double-click on "High DOS." Look in the Hex Start column for a segment:offset that corresponds to, or is slightly less than, the *xxxx:yyyy* in the error message. Also note the decimal length of the device at that address. Then write the ram= line as follows:

    ram=*xx*00-*yy*00

Replace *xx* with the first two characters in the segment that you just found in the Hex Start column. Replace *yy* with whatever hex value is needed to exclude the range indicated by the decimal length. If the *address xxxx-yyyy* error message occurs as the system boots, then you'll need to reboot and hold down the Alt key (see above) to disable *386MAX* so that the system can start. As soon as the DOS prompt appears, use the ASQ utility as just described to find the values required for the ram= line.

If the first character in the error message is a number (0–9), then there is a problem in conventional memory with the item at that address. If necessary, use the ASQ utility as described above, but double-click on "Low DOS" instead. Check the Name column to determine the identity of the item in the segment:offset reported in the error message. Whatever it is, it's probably not compatible with

386MAX. You can verify this by disabling the appropriate line in CONFIG.SYS or AUTOEXEC.BAT so the device is not loaded during bootup. If that solves the problem, contact the manufacturer to see if an update is available.

Smart Drive is not installed. If the Windows Resource Kit's SMARTMON.EXE utility is loaded in the StartUp group, this error message is seen if Smart Drive itself is missing, or if the installed version of Smart Drive is not recognized by SMARTMON.

Unable to allocate extended memory to run Windows in 386 enhanced mode. Quit one or more applications to increase available memory or restart your computer. Refer to the *Insufficient Extended Memory* messages above for suggestions.

Video Device Conflict (386MAX). If this message is seen on a VGA system, there is a memory conflict due to the automatic remapping of video ROM into RAM. To disable this feature, add the following line to the 386MAX.PRO file in the 386MAX directory:

```
RAM=C000-C800
```

Waiting for System Shutdown. If this message is seen when you try to reboot the system, it simply means that Smart Drive's write cache contains some data that has not yet been written to disk. In most cases, the data will be written to disk before the reboot takes place, so no corrective action is necessary. However, if you use Quarterdeck's *QEMM386* prior to version 6.02, refer to the *QEMM386 and Smart Drive* section for help in avoiding data loss.

Windows cannot set up an upper memory block at segment *xxxx*. Exclude this address space by using the syntax of your memory manager. (If *xxxx* = B000, refer to the error message immediately following this one.) The message indicates the memory area beginning at *xxxx* is occupied by some device that precludes its use as a UMB. To keep Windows out of this area, you'll need to edit your memory manager line in CONFIG.SYS as follows:

```
device=EMM386.EXE  x=xxxx-yyyy
```

where *yyyy* is the address specified in the error message, and *yyyy* is 16 Kbytes higher. Refer to your memory manager's documentation for the specific syntax required, which may vary from that shown here. If the exclusion works, try reducing *yyyy* in increments of 4 Kbytes. If it doesn't, try increasing it in 4-Kbyte increments.

Windows cannot set up an upper memory block at segment B000. Exclude this address space by using the syntax of your memory manager. This message may be seen if both your memory manager and your display driver try to use the 32 Kbyte B000–B7FF range. There are a few solutions to the problem.

MONOUMB2.386 and *MONOUMB.386* **Files.** Windows 3.1 provides a device driver (MONOUMB2.386) that may permit joint access to the B000–B7FF range. To use the driver, find the MONOUMB2.38_ file on the Windows 3.1 distribution diskettes and expand it into the System directory as MONOUMB2.386. Then add the following line to the [386Enh] section of SYSTEM.INI and restart Windows.

    device=monoumb2.386

Unfortunately, this driver does not work with Windows' own EMM386.EXE, and may not work with some third-party memory managers. However, an alternative driver (MONOUMB.386) is available in the Windows Driver Library. You can obtain a copy by contacting Microsoft, or by downloading the self-extracting MONO.EXE file via CompuServe (go MSL), as described in Appendix D.

As another alternative, edit your memory manager's command line to exclude the B000–B7FF region. If you recently appended an i=B000-B7FF parameter, remove it. Otherwise, explicitly exclude the region by appending x=B000-B7FF to the line.

Quarterdeck WINHIRAM.VXD Update. If Quarterdeck's *QEMM386* is installed, check the QEMM directory for a WINHIRAM.VXD file dated 09-17-92 or later. If it is present, then the device=monoumb2.386 line cited above can be deleted from your SYSTEM.INI file. The latest WINHIRAM.VXD is available from the Quarterdeck forum on CompuServe (go Quarterdeck). Download the binary WINHRM.VXD file from Library 3 and rename it as WINHIRAM.VXD. (Refer to Appendix D for general details about CompuServe forums.)

You must have the file WINA20.386 in the root of your boot drive to run Windows in enhanced mode (QEMM386). The message is seen when you open Windows in enhanced mode, if the installed QEMM386.SYS is earlier than version 6.0, and the command line contains the noems parameter. However, Windows opens properly and the message may be ignored. For further information, and ways to eliminate the message, refer to this error message in Chapter 2.

Virtual Memory/Swap-File Error Messages

If there's a problem related to your swap file, one (or more) of the error messages in this section will be encountered the next time you try to change its configuration. Often, the actual problem is with the small SPART.PAR file in the Windows directory. So if for some reason you'd rather not delete and re-create the swap file, you can exit Windows, disable the SPART.PAR read-only attribute (type attrib -r SPART.PAR), then erase it. Reopen Windows and if all goes well, a new SPART.PAR file will be written automatically and your swap file will remain intact. However, all this may be more trouble than it's worth. It takes less time to delete the corrupt swap file (even if it's not) and re-create it.

If the same (or similar) error message reappears after you've taken the indicated action, you may need to close and reopen Windows in order to completely reconfigure your swap file.

A corrupt permanent swap file was found on drive *x*. To get accurate swap-file analysis, the file should be set to zero length. Set corrupt file to zero length now? This message appears if you open the Virtual Memory Screen after ignoring a previous *swap file is corrupt* message as Windows opened, or if something happened to your swap file (most likely, to SPART.PAR) while Windows is running. Click on the Yes button and redo your swap file configuration as desired.

A new permanent swap file cannot be created. Another permanent swap file is in use on one of your drives, or a temporary swap file is in use on the specified drive. This message may show up if you interrupt a swap file configuration to do something else and then return to it. The safest course is to close the Virtual Memory Screens, return to the Program Manager and close any active applications, then go back and try again. In case of any doubts about the real source of the problem, close and reopen Windows first.

A permanent swap file has been found on a drive where one cannot be created. Select a different drive, or change Type to None. Do you want to set the swap file to None? One could spend a lot of time wondering how a swap file was ever created on a drive where one can't be created. However, this message is part of the swap-file repertoire. If you see it, click on the Yes button, then set up a new swap file.

Note, however, that this message may appear in error if you used the keyboard to select a new drive letter. If so, retry the operation using the mouse instead.

A permanent swap file has been found on drive *x*. The installation of Windows that you are using did not create the file. If this file is not used by another installation of Windows, you can delete it. Do you want to delete the file now? This one means that Windows found a permanent swap file not recognized by the current SPART.PAR file. Click on the Yes button to delete it.

The number you specified is too large. The number currently displayed is the largest you can specify. If you attempt to create a swap file larger than that listed in the Maximum Size box, the size seen in that box will appear in the New Size box. Either accept it, or type in a lesser value. If the value in the Maximum Size box is significantly less than that in the Space Available box, refer to the *Swap File Configuration* section earlier in this chapter for an explanation.

A previously created swap file has been found, but it is corrupted. It will be deleted. And there's nothing you can do about it. The only choice is to click on an OK button in the error message box, which returns you to the 386 Enhanced dialog box. The obvious next step—to click on the Virtual Memory button again and create a new swap file—won't work. The message just keeps repeating.

   You'll have to quit Windows and reopen it. When you do, you'll see the *permanent swap file is corrupt* message also described in this section. Follow the directions there to delete the file. If you decide not to do this, you'll see a *corrupt swap file* message the next time you open the Virtual Memory dialog box.

The permanent swap file is corrupt. You need to create a new swap file (*followed by directions how to do so*). Do you want to delete the corrupt swap file? This is just one more variation on the same theme. The best course is to click on the Yes button, then set about creating a new swap file.

Windows will not use more than the virtual memory specified by the Recommended Size. Are you sure you want to create a larger swap file? This message is incorrect: Windows *will* use whatever you give it, provided you do not exceed the Maximum Size specification. Refer to the *Swap File Configuration* section earlier in the chapter for more information on this subject.

Your program cannot be swapped out to disk. There is not enough space on your disk. In standard mode, Windows swaps applications into the area specified by the SET TEMP statement in your AUTOEXEC.BAT file. If this error message is seen, there are a few possibilities.

1. There really is not enough space on your disk to accommodate the application that Windows is trying to store in the temporary directory.
2. The SET TEMP statement specifies an invalid path, or it specifies a RAM drive that is not large enough.

Either make more space available in the hard disk partition where the temporary directory is located, or rewrite the SET TEMP statement to point to another drive or partition. If your temporary directory is on a RAM drive, increase the size of that drive as needed. If you don't have sufficient RAM to do this, then relocate the temporary directory to your hard disk (assuming sufficient space is available).

14

The Windows INI Files

Windows' initialization, or INI, files contain information used by Windows itself and/or by applications that run within Windows. Whenever you open Windows or one of its applications, the information within one or more INI files is used to configure your system as required to suit the application. Some INI file information sets up the various drivers that are required by your printer, video system, and other components, while other information establishes color schemes, group window layouts, and so on.

Much of the information in various INI file sections is described in detail in other chapters of this book, as appropriate to the specific section. For example, various settings affecting the Windows help screen are covered in the *Help Screen Configuration* section of Chapter 4. In the present chapter, an overview of the INI file itself is given; to keep things on a sufficiently grim note, it is assumed the file is either dead or dying. In the former case, the file has passed into the great digital beyond, and there is no trace of its remains in the Windows directory. In the latter, the file is still there but needs major surgery. In either case, this chapter may be useful in restoring the file to its former condition. In fact, some of the general information seen here may even be useful if the file is not yet in trouble.

Many lines below are written as "Feature=1" or "Feature=0," indicating that the listed feature is either enabled (1) or disabled (0). However, the line itself may not appear if that feature's default state has never been modified by the user. For example, the default conditions for two WIN.INI lines are as follows:

```
[TrueType]
TTEnable=1
TTOnly=0
```

If these states have never been changed by the user, then neither line appears in the [TrueType] section. Should it ever become necessary to edit an INI file to reduce its size, any line which lists the default status may be eliminated.

Some other lines are written as "Feature=" with no numeric value following the equal sign. In this case, the actual value depends on the specific system configuration, so it will vary from one system to another, or even from one moment to another if you're making changes.

INI File Size Limitations

Although some third-party applications are unable to read INI files larger than 32,768 bytes (32 Kb), Windows 3.1 and Workgroups 3.1 can read INI files up to 65,536 bytes (64 Kb). If an INI file grows larger than that, the information at the end of the file will be ignored and, depending on its content, may prevent some or all of Windows from functioning properly.

INI File Format

Almost without exception, INI files are saved in an ASCII text format, and may be edited with any good DOS editor, such as EDIT.COM or similar, or with the Windows *Notepad* applet. The SYSTEM.INI and WIN.INI files may also be edited via the Windows System Editor (SYSEDIT.EXE), which was described in the *Windows System Configuration Editor* section of Chapter 4.

If you edit an INI file within your favorite word processor, make sure you save the results as an ASCII text file. If the file is saved in the word processor's own unique format, the embedded formatting codes will make the file unusable by Windows.

Binary INI Files.   As for those exceptions, the WINWORD.INI file in the C:\WINWORD (usually) directory is in binary format. Changes to this file are made as required from within Word-for-Windows, and the file should not be edited in any other manner. Various INI files in the DOS directory may also be written in binary format (MSBACKUP.INI, for example).

If a third-party INI file shows up elsewhere than in the Windows directory, you may want to verify its format before trying to edit it. As a quick test, type TYPE *filename.ext* at the DOS prompt. If recognizable text goes flying by, then the file is in ASCII format. Otherwise, it's probably a binary file.

INI File Reconstruction Techniques

You'll probably never read this section, because you always remember to make backup copies of all your INI files. In case an original gets damaged or lost, all you need do is trot out the backup version and copy it into the Windows directory.

If the above paragraph does not quite fit the immediate situation, all may not be lost. The good news is that many INI files are expendable: They're created or revised as you use various components of Windows and, if one gets lost, it will be rebuilt automatically later on, as needed. The bad news is that there are notable exceptions, such as PROGMAN.INI, SYSTEM.INI, WIN.INI, and to a lesser extent, CONTROL.INI.

The basic information in the first three of these files can be easily restored simply by rerunning the Windows Setup procedure. Although many users regard doing so as a last act of desperation, more often than not the procedure is reasonably benign. In fact, if Setup is run on a fully functional custom-tweaked Windows system, its net effect will usually be about zero. Your previous INI files are left undisturbed, as are your group windows, including the Startup Group.

If you're not sure which INI file is causing trouble, a Setup rerun may be the most expedient way of getting back in business. If so, read the following section, then refer to Chapter 1 if you need assistance. However, if you know that only one INI file needs work, then refer to the *Windows INI Source Files* section below for help in rebuilding only that file. Or, if the file is not one of the gang of three described there, then refer to the section below in which that file is discussed.

A Setup Procedure Review

Although Chapter 1 presents the entire Windows Setup procedure in all its gory details, the present section offers a quick overview of that procedure for the benefit of the user who may think about using it as a means to restore one or more INI files. After reading this section, refer to Chapter 1 for step-by-step assistance if you do decide to rerun the Setup procedure.

Custom Components. During any custom Setup procedure, you can specify the components to be (re-)installed, as described in the *Component Selection (Custom)* section of Chapter 1.

Permanent Swap File. Your permanent swap file will be left intact, or you can change it as desired.

New File Replacement. If you had previously updated a Windows file to a version newer than the one on the distribution diskettes, Setup will pause before overwriting that file. For example, if you installed the improved version 3.11 of MPLAYER.EXE (described in Chapter 12), Setup will ask if you want to overwrite it with the older version on its distribution diskettes. Presumably, you would click on the No button to avoid doing so. Refer to the *Setup has detected the following conflict(s)...* message in Chapter 1 for more details if necessary.

WARNING: As an exception to the above, Setup does not offer this warning with the MIDI Mapper configuration file (MID-IMAP.CFG). If you have a custom version of this file in your System directory, make a copy of it as MIDIMAP.XYZ before running Setup. Then copy MIDIMAP.XYZ back to MIDIMAP.CFG after Setup concludes. See *The MIDI Mapper Configuration File* in Chapter 12 for more details if you need them.

Multiple Printer Configuration. If your previous setup had multiple printers installed, there will be a fair amount of disk-swapping required near the end of the Setup procedure to install fresh copies, the necessary printer drivers, and support files.

Group Windows. Your existing group windows will remain intact, including the StartUp Group, and any applets you may have installed there. About the only exception to this is that if you renamed any Windows applets (*Clipbook Viewer* to just *Clipbook,* for example), you will find an additional copy of that applet in the group window, with its Windows official name under it. Just delete it if you don't want it.

Setup Conclusion. After rerunning Setup, you should note little or no difference in your Windows system, other than the correction of some, if not all, problems that existed in some of your INI files. Setup will have cleaned up Windows' own contributions to these files, while leaving custom additions intact. If these sections need work, then they'll still need it. However, Windows itself will now be back in shape, which may be a good way to start.

The Windows INI Source Template Files (filename.SRC)

The Windows distribution diskettes contain three source template files which may be used to reconstruct three critical INI files. In each case, the file contains the basic structure of the named INI file and the default settings for many of its lines. Needless to say, none of the files contain specific configuration information unique to your system. However, once the basic file structure is restored, you may be able to edit the file to insert whatever information is required to run your system correctly. In addition, much missing information can be reconstructed simply by running various components of Windows, as will be described in the sections below, as appropriate.

The following excerpt from the complete list of files in Appendix A lists the source files and the distribution diskettes on which they may be found. If you decide to use this resource, assign an INI extension to each file as you expand it, instead of using the indicated SRC extension. Or, rename the file with an INI extension once you are finished editing it. In either case, save your existing INI file first, if that file has custom sections that you want to retain. After restoring the basic INI file, use any good text editor to insert sections of the old file into the new one, as needed.

| Filename | Extension | | File Size | | Distrib. Diskette | | | Template for |
	Comp.	Exp.	Comp.	Exp.	1.44	1.2	720	
CONTROL	SR_	SRC	1278	3609	5/7	6/8	9/14	CONTROL.INI
SYSTEM	SR_	SRC	642	1009	1	2	1	SYSTEM.INI for Windows
			755	1196	3	3	5	Same, for Workgroups
WIN	SR_	SRC	1666	2272	1	1	1	WIN.INI for Windows
			1705	2341	3	3	5	Same, for Workgroups

For assistance in preparing any of these files for use, refer to the sections which follow. In each example, the name of the template file is listed in the main header, and each section header lists the name of the section that is to be restored. Sections contained in each template are described first, followed by an alphabetical listing of other sections that may need to be restored. Rather then repeat procedures and descriptions that appear elsewhere in this book, the following sections make frequent reference to other sections in other chapters. By now you may not need to bother with these references, but they're given anyway, in case you need them to finish the job.

> **NOTE:** In the descriptions which follow, section headings are listed alphabetically, as are the listings within each section. This style is followed here to make it a bit easier to find what you're looking for. However, the actual file sections and listings do not follow this style.

CONTROL.INI Reconstruction (CONTROL.SR_)

As noted earlier in the chapter, CONTROL.INI contains information that is not essential to running Windows. In fact, much of it is *so* nonessential that CONTROL.INI may quietly recover most of itself long before you ever realize that it was among the missing. However, there are a few items that will need your assistance in order to return the file to its former condition.

If you have to reconstruct SYSTEM.INI and/or WIN.INI, do that first since CONTROL.INI needs information stored in these files in order to completely restore itself. Assuming you've done so and opened Windows to make sure SYSTEM.INI and WIN.INI are in good shape, you can begin to rebuild CONTROL.INI as described below.

If you open and use Windows prior to restoring CONTROL.INI, you may find a small CONTROL.INI file in your Windows directory. The file may contain one or more sections, depending on what actions you took within Windows. However, it will not contain the default sections described below. When you're ready to completely restore the old CONTROL.INI, erase the existing version (or save it elsewhere if you're nervous about doing so).

CONTROL.INI Default Sections

Locate the template file on the distribution diskette and expand it into the Windows directory as CONTROL.INI. The file should contain the four default sections listed here and tabulated in Table 14.1.

TABLE 14.1 CONTROL.SRC Template File for CONTROL.INI*

Section and Contents		Section and Contents	
[current]		**[Custom Colors]** *(all are white)*	
color schemes	= Windows Default	ColorA = FFFFFF ColorI = FFFFFF	
		ColorB = FFFFFF ColorJ = FFFFFF	
[color schemes] †		ColorC = FFFFFF ColorK = FFFFFF	
Arizona	= 804000,FFFFFF,FFFFFF,...	ColorD = FFFFFF ColorL = FFFFFF	
Black Leather Jacket	= 0,C0C0C0,FFFFFF,0,...	ColorE = FFFFFF ColorM = FFFFFF	
Bordeaux	= 400080,C0C0C0,FFFFFF,...	ColorF = FFFFFF ColorN = FFFFFF	
Cinnamon	= 404080,C0C0C0,FFFFFF,0,...	ColorG = FFFFFF ColorO = FFFFFF	
Designer	= 7C7C3F,C0C0C0,FFFFFF,...	ColorH = FFFFFF ColorP = FFFFFF	
Emerald City	= 404000,C0C0C0,FFFFFF,...		
Fluorescent	= 0,FFFFFF,FFFFFF,0,...	**[Patterns]**	
Hotdog Stand	= FFFF,FFFF,FF,FFFFFF,...	(None)	= (None)
LCD Default Screen	= 808080,C0C0C0,...	50% Gray	= 170 85 170 85 170 85 170 85
LCD Reversed - Dark	= 0,80,80,FFFFFF,...	Boxes	= 127 65 65 65 65 65 127 0
LCD Reversed - Light	= 800000,FFFFFF,...	Critters	= 0 80 114 32 0 5 39 2
Mahogany	= 404040,C0C0C0,FFFFFF,...	Diamonds	= 32 80 136 80 32 0 0 0
Monochrome	= C0C0C0,FFFFFF,FFFFFF,...	Paisley	= 2 7 7 2 32 80 80 32
Ocean	= 808000,408000,FFFFFF,0,...	Pattern	= 224 128 142 136 234 10 14 0
Pastel	= C0FF82,80FFFF,FFFFFF,...	Quilt	= 130 68 40 17 40 68 130 1
Patchwork	= 9544BB,C1FBFA,FFFFFF,...	Scottie	= 64 192 200 120 120 72 0 0
Plasma Power Saver	= 0,FF0000,0,FFFFFF,...	Spinner	= 20 12 200 121 158 19 48 40
Rugby	= C0C0C0,80FFFF,FFFFFF,...	Thatches	= 248 116 34 71 143 23 34 113
The Blues	= 804000,C0C0C0,FFFFFF,...	Tulip	= 0 0 84 124 124 56 146 124
Tweed	= 6A619E,C0C0C0,FFFFFF,...	Waffle	= 0 0 0 0 128 128 128 240
Valentine	= C080FF,FFFFFF,FFFFFF,...	Weave	= 136 84 34 69 136 21 34 81
Wingtips	= 408080,C0C0C0,FFFFFF,...		

* Listings sorted alphabetically within each section. Actual file listings are unsorted. Spaces added here for clarity.

† Refer to SYSTEM.SRC file for complete hexadecimal string following each name.

[current]   [custom colors]
[Color Schemes]   [Patterns]

[current] and [color schemes].   The [current] section contains a single line specifying the current color scheme, which at the moment is the Windows default. The [color schemes] section lists alternate color schemes that are available.

Insert Custom Color Scheme in [color schemes] Section.   The information presented here is valid only if (1) prior to losing your CONTROL.INI file, you had created your own set of custom colors for the Windows Desktop, and (2) these colors were in use on the Desktop. If this is correct, then continue reading here for assistance in restoring the [current] section of CONTROL.INI. Otherwise, this section can be ignored.

Open the Control Panel and double-click on the *Color* applet icon to open the Color dialog box which was seen in Chapter 11 as Figure 11.9a. When you click on the Color Palette > button, the Save Scheme button at the top of the screen is enabled. Since the present color scheme is the one you want to save with a distinctive name, simply follow the instructions in the *Color Scheme Storage* section of Chapter 11 for saving it with the name you choose.

The next time you look into CONTROL.INI you'll see a revised [current] section, plus an addition to the [color schemes] section, as shown here:

```
[current]
color schemes=(the name you selected)

[color schemes]
(default color schemes, as in Table 14.1)
(the name you selected)=(21 hexadecimal strings defining your custom color set)
```

None of the above will make much difference to the grand scheme of things. It merely re-creates a base record of your present color scheme, which may come in handy later on if you make still more color changes, then decide you liked your old colors better.

[Custom Colors].   The restored [Custom Colors] section will offer a choice of 16 colors, each of which is white (see Table 14.1). If you previously defined your own custom colors, you'll have to do it all over again since this information is not otherwise recoverable. Refer to *The Custom Color Selector Dialog Box* in the *Color Applet* section of Chapter 12 for details.

[Patterns]. As noted above, the Windows default patterns are restored when you expand the CONTROL.SR_ file as CONTROL.INI. However, your own custom patterns (if any) are lost and you'll have to re-create them if you can't get along without them.

Other CONTROL.INI Sections

In addition to the default sections described above, your original CONTROL.INI may have contained one or more of the following sections, which can be restored as described here.

[Don't Load]. If your previous configuration disabled certain applets that normally appear in the Control Panel, you'll have to edit CONTROL.INI to once again include a [Don't Load] section. Refer to the *Remove Applets from Control Panel* section of Chapter 11 for assistance.

[drivers.desc]. To restore this section of CONTROL.INI, simply open the *Drivers* applet and review the contents of the Drivers dialog box. The Installed Drivers list should include the five drivers installed during the regular Windows Setup procedure, as shown in Figure 12.1 in Chapter 12. The list should also show all drivers you installed after Windows itself was installed. If the list is correct, close the dialog box and the Control Panel. Having done all this, the [drivers.desc] section of CONTROL.INI should be restored.

However, if any drivers are missing, then they have not yet been reinstalled in SYSTEM.INI. If you do need to reinstall a driver, refer to *Add a New Driver* in the *Drivers Applet* section of Chapter 12 for assistance if required.

[installed] (Windows Version and Printer Files). This section begins with a reference to the installed Windows (or Workgroups) version, then lists the installed printers and supplementary printer files, as shown in this typical example.

```
[installed]
3.1=yes
PROPRINT.DRV=yes
UNIDRV.DLL=yes
UNIDRV.HLP=yes
```

If the section is missing, it can be restored by opening the Control Panel's *Printers* applet and reviewing the list of installed printers. If any previously installed printer is missing from the list, click on the Add... button and look in the System directory for the desired printer (or use the appropriate distribution diskette if necessary). Once you add a printer at some time after the initial Setup procedure, this section is written. Otherwise it doesn't show up, nor is it needed.

[MMCPL] (Multimedia Control Panel). The act of opening and closing the Control Panel rewrites the basic [MMCPL] section, as shown in *The [MMCPL] Section of CONTROL.INI* in the *Control Panel Configuration* section in Chapter 11.

Custom Control Panel Applet Arrangement. If this section of your original CONTROL.INI contained lines that specified the path to certain CPL files, these lines will have to be reinserted via editing. If you need assistance with this, refer to *Resequence CPL Files* in the *Control Panel Configuration* section of Chapter 11.

[related.desc]. See *[Userinstallable.drivers]* below.

[ScreenSaver] and [Screen Saver.*name*]. To restore these sections, open the Control Panel's *Desktop* applet and set the Screen Saver parameters as desired. Refer to *Screen Saver* in the *Desktop Applet* section of Chapter 11 for further details.

[Userinstallable.drivers] and [related.desc]. These sections are added if you reinstall a driver that was lost during the initial recovery operation. For example, if your system had a previously installed CD-ROM drive that supports CD Audio, and the required driver was seen when you reviewed the Installed Drivers list, then probably neither of the sections described here will be seen in CONTROL.INI. However, if you need to reinstall the CD audio driver, then the first line in each of the following sections will be seen after doing so. The second lines illustrate additional items that may be added if a Wave audio device is reinstalled.

```
[Userinstallable.drivers]
CDAudio=mcicda.drv
Wave=mvproaud.drv

[related.desc]
CDAudio=
Wave=opl3.drv,mvmixer.drv,mcimixer.drv,
```

SYSTEM.INI Reconstruction (SYSTEM.SR_)

If this one gets lost, you'll see the *Cannot find the system initialization file* message cited in the Troubleshooting section of Chapter 2 if you try to open Windows. Of course, you can always take the message's advice and rerun Setup for the sole purpose of obtaining a new SYSTEM.INI file. However, if only SYSTEM.INI needs to be revived, you can do so by following the procedures described here.

Locate the SYSTEM.SR_ template file on the distribution diskette and expand it into the Windows directory as SYSTEM.INI. The file contains the default sections and some of their parameters. The sections are listed here.

386Enh	DDEShares (*Workgroups only*)	mci
boot	drivers	NonWindowsApp
boot.description	keyboard	standard

Table 14.2 lists the contents of these default sections, each of which is briefly described here.

SYSTEM.INI Default Sections

The following descriptions review the work that needs to be done to whip the above listed sections back into shape.

TABLE 14.2 SYSTEM.SRC Template File for SYSTEM.INI*

Section and Contents

[boot]

286grabber	=	language.dll	=
386grabber	=	mouse.drv	=
comm.drv	=	network.drv	=
display.drv	=	oemfonts.fon	=
drivers	= mmsystem.dll	shell	=
fixedfon.fon	=	sound.drv	=
fonts.fon	=	system.drv	=
keyboard.drv	=	taskman.exe	=

[keyboard]

keyboard.dll	=	subtype	=
oemansi.bin	=	type	=

[boot.description]   (*SRC template contains header only, no listings. See text.*)

TABLE 14.2 *(continued)*

Section and Contents

	(*Windows*)	(*Workgroups*)		(*Windows*)	(*Workgroups*)
[386Enh] † (*All indicated information is present in SRC file*)					
device =	*biosxlat	*biosxlat	device	= —	vpd.386
device =	*BLOCKDEV	*BLOCKDEV	device	= *vpicd	vpicd.386
device =	*cdpscsi	*cdpscsi	device	= *vsd	*vsd
device =	*combuff	*combuff	device	= —	vshare.386
device =	*dosmgr	*dosmgr	device	= *vtd	*vtd
device =	*PAGEFILE	*PAGEFILE	device	= vtdapi.386	vtdapi.386
device =	*pageswap	*pageswap	device	= *wshell	*wshell
device =	*parity	*parity			
device =	*reboot	*reboot	display	= *vddvga	*vddvga
device =	*v86mmgr	*v86mmgr	FileSysChange	= off	off
device =	*vcd	**vcd 386**	keyboard	= *vkd	*vkd
device =	*vdmad	**vdmad.386**	local	= CON	CON
device =	*vfd	*vfd	mouse	= *vmd	*vmd
device =	*vmcpd	*vmcpd	netheapsize	= —	16
device =	*vmpoll	*vmpoll	network	= *vnetbios, *dosnet	*vnetbios, *dosnet

[standard] (*Empty section*)

[drivers]
midimapper = midimap.drv
timer = timer.drv

[NonWindowsApp]
localtsrs=dosedit,pced, ced (*win*)
localtsrs=dosedit, ced (*wrk*)

[mci]
CDAudio =mcicda.drv
Sequencer =mciseq.drv
WaveAudio =mciwave.drv

[DDEShares] (*Workgroups only*)
CHAT$ =winchat,chat ,,31,,0,,0,0,0
CLPBK$ =clipsrv,system ,,31,,0,,0,0,0
HEARTS$ =mshearts,hearts ,,15,,0,,0,0,0

---

* Listings sorted alphabetically within each section. Actual file listings are unsorted. Spaces added here for clarity.
† Boldface indicates change between Windows and Workgroups listing.
(*win*) Windows 3.1 only.
(*wrk*) Windows-for-Workgroups only.

[386Enh] (386 Enhanced). No decent Windows application setup procedure would be complete without mucking about in this section of

SYSTEM.INI. Almost everybody has a virtual device driver that needs to go in here; it would take a book and a half to list and describe each of them.

Instead of ignoring the entire [386Enh] section, the next few paragraphs describe a few of the more likely entries that may need to be reinserted. For those not listed here, the best way to discover what's needed is the hard way: Run each application at least once and, if it needs something that it can't find, it will surely let you know about it.

In each of the examples given below, add or revise the indicated line in the [386Enh] section of SYSTEM.INI, if the information is appropriate to your system.

Berkeley Systems' After Dark. This popular screen-saver utility adds the following lines to SYSTEM.INI:

```
;Virtual Device driver used by AD-DOS and After Dark
device=ad.386
```

Needless to say, only the second line is essential to normal operations.

DOS 6.0 Backup Utility. If you installed the Windows *Backup* utility included with DOS 6.0, the following line was added during that Setup procedure, as described in *SYSTEM.INI Modification* in the *Microsoft Tools* section of Chapter 0:

```
device=C:\DOS\VFINTD.386      (virtual floppy interrupt)
```

Microsoft Mouse Version 9.0. If you installed this version, find the following default line and revise it as shown here.
Change:

```
keyboard=*vkd
```

to:

```
keyboard=C:\MOUSE\MOUSEVKD.386
```

Revise the path as required to specify the actual location of the indicated file.

MSCDEX Support. If MSCDEX was installed prior to running the Windows 3.1 or Workgroups setup procedure, one of the following entries was in this section of SYSTEM.INI:

```
device=lanman10.386
networks=lanman10.386
```

Refer to *MSCDEX Support in SYSTEM.INI* in the *MSCDEX Configuration Considerations* section of Chapter 12 for information about these lines.

Networks.   If you're using Windows-for-Workgroups, find the following line and revise it as shown here.

Change:

network=*vnetbios, *dosnet

to:

network=vnetbios.386,vnetsup.386,vredir.386,vserver.386,vbrowse.386,vwc.386

Note that the six *filename*.386 entries are on one line, with no spaces between each filename. For assistance restoring other network systems, refer to the *Network Applet* section of Chapter 11, or to the *User's Guide* for the network software.

Norton Desktop for Windows.   The well-known Windows application makes numerous revisions to the SYSTEM.INI file. The version 2.0 changes are listed here:

```
[boot]
SHELL=NDW.EXE

[386Enh]
device=vfintd.386      Floppy interrupt
device=vnavd.386       Anti-virus
device=vndwd.386       SmartErase
device=vnss.386        Screen Saver
DMABufferSize=32       Increased from default of 16
```

Port Settings.   If you changed any of the COM*x* port settings, refer to the *COM Port Address and IRQ Configuration* section in Chapter 11 for assistance in resetting these parameters.

Swap File.   You may want to review the status of the swap file. Start Windows in enhanced mode, open the Control Panel, then the *386 Enhanced* applet. Next, click on the Virtual Memory... button and note the current settings for your swap file, which should be correct. However, the 32-bit access feature will be missing. In order to restore it, you'll need to edit the SYSTEM.INI file, then exit and restart Windows. Or, exit Windows first, then edit SYSTEM.INI. In the [386Enh] section, add the three lines shown here.

```
32BitDiskAccess=on
device=*int13
device=*wdctrl
```

Refer to the *386 Enhanced Applet* section of Chapter 11, and/or to the *32-Bit Access* section of Chapter 13 for additional information if needed.

> **NOTE:** Do not even *think* about doing this if the 32-bit access feature was not previously available on your system. The purpose of this edit is to restore a feature accidentally lost during the demise of your SYSTEM.INI file, not to attempt miracles.

[boot], [keyboard], and [boot.description] Sections. Although the SYSTEM.SR_ file restores the indicated sections of SYSTEM.INI, the first two sections contain nothing but empty entries (with the exception of drivers=mmsystem.dll), and the [boot.description] section consists of the section header only.

It's quite easy to reconstruct most of this information before starting Windows. Simply log onto the Windows directory and run Setup at the DOS prompt. When you do, a System Information Screen similar to that shown in Chapter 1 (Figure 1.1b) is seen. However, the system list now looks like the one seen here as Figure 14.1. To restore the list to its former shape, simply highlight each item in turn, select the appropriate component for your system, and press the Enter key. Repeat for every item on the list; when you are done, highlight the "Accept the configuration" line and again press the Enter key. Next you'll see a series of messages, each beginning as follows:

This driver for (*selected component*) is already installed on your system.

Each message includes data pertaining to the listed driver. Just press the Enter key to accept the current setting and repeat for each message that you see. When the DOS prompt reappears, your SYSTEM.INI file will contain new information such as that shown here for a typical super VGA system (800 × 600 × 16 colors).

Windows [*or* Windows for Workgroups] Setup

If your computer or network appears on the Hardware Compatibility List with an
asterisk next to it, press F1 before continuing.

System Information
Computer:	—	system.drv
Display:	—	display.drv
Mouse:	—	mouse.drv
Keyboard:	keyboard.typ	keyboard.typ
Keyboard Layout:	US	US
Language:	—	language.dll
Codepage:	—	woafont.fon
Network:	—	network.drv (*Windows 3.1 only*)

Complete Changes: Accept the configuration shown above.

To change a system setting, press the UP- or DOWN-ARROW key to move the
highlight to the setting you want to change. Then press ENTER to see
alternatives for that item. When you have finished changing your settings, select
the "Complete Changes" option to quit Setup.

Figure 14.1   The System Information Screen, after expanding SYSTEM.SRC to
SYSTEM.INI. The column 2 entries ("keyboard.typ" and "US" only) are usually
seen, although some column 3 entries may show up if certain lines in the [boot]
section are edited by hand. In either case, highlight each entry and select the
correct information for your system.

```
[boot]
286grabber     =   vgacolor.2gr          language.dll    =
386grabber     =   vga.3gr               mouse.drv       =   mouse.drv
comm.drv       =   comm.drv              network.drv     =
display.drv    =   supervga.drv          oemfonts.fon    =   vgaoem.fon
drivers        =   mmsystem.dll          shell           =
fixedfon.fon   =   vgafix.fon            sound.drv       =   mmsound.drv
fonts.fon      =   vgasys.fon            system.drv      =   system.drv
keyboard.drv   =   keyboard.drv          taskman.exe     =

[keyboard]
subtype        =                         oemansi.bin     =
type           =   4                     keyboard.dll    =

[boot. description]
```
   (*as appropriate for your system*)

Edit Shell Setting.   Note that the Setup procedure has left a few lines
blank, and at least one of these (shell.drv=) is critical to Windows operation.
Edit this line as shown below, or insert some other filename (NDW.EXE,

WINFILE.EXE, for example) if you prefer to use some other shell. Make sure the line is not left blank, or Windows won't open. Refer to the *Program Manager* section of Chapter 3 for additional shell information.

```
[boot]
shell=progman.exe
```

Edit Network Settings. If your system is part of a network, you'll have to restore the appropriate network-related line. On a Windows-for-Workgroups system, edit the network.drv = line as shown here. Also check the network= line in the [386Enh] section, as described above.

```
[boot]
network.drv=wfwnet.drv
```

[DDEShares] Dynamic Data Exchange (Workgroups only). This section is a database of items available for network DDE applications. The Windows (*Resource Kit*) "documentation" says almost nothing, except that the database is currently located in this [DDEShares] section, but that could change in a future version of Workgroups. Furthermore, the section should not be edited by hand—and there's little danger of doing that since the listings are not explained.

As a typical example of what one might find here, if a *Paintbrush* bitmap (CARS.BMP) is copied to the *Clipbook Viewer's* Clipboard, then pasted to the Local Clipbook as "CARSTEST" for sharing across the network, the following lines will appear in this SYSTEM.INI section:

```
[DDEShares]
$CARSTEST=ClipSrv,$CarsTest,,3,,0,,0,0,0
$CARSTEST.OLE=PBrush,C:\WINDOWS\CARS.BMP,,3,,0 0 32 32,0,0,0
```

A related SYSTEM.INI section will contain the name of the file in which the Clipboard image is saved, as shown here:

```
[ClipShares]
C:\WINDOWS\CBK6268.CLP=$CarsTest
```

All these lines will be deleted if the item is subsequently deleted from the Local Clipboard. And, of course, they're all lost if SYSTEM.INI itself is lost. If you need to recover such information, open the *Clipbook Viewer* applet's *Clipboard* and search the Windows directory for files with an alphanumeric filename and a CLP extension. If you find one, load it into the *Clipboard.* If it's what you were looking for, use the Edit menu's Paste... option to restore it to the *Local Clipbook.* By doing so, the appropriate lines in the sections above will be rewritten. Refer to Chapter 8 if you need more information about all this.

[drivers]. If you installed multimedia drivers prior to losing your SYS-TEM.INI file, you'll need to reinstall them now. Refer to the *Add New Drivers* section of Chapter 12 for assistance with this, if needed.

[keyboard]. The restoration of this section was described above, along with the [boot] and [boot.description] sections.

[MCI] (Media Control Interface). This section lists the MCI drivers used by the *Media Player* applet. Each such line should be rewritten as you rein-stall the various drivers associated with this applet. Refer to the *Media Player Applet* section of Chapter 12 for further details.

[NonWindowsApp] (Non-Windows Applications). This section lists config-uration settings for applications running in a DOS Window. The single de-fault listing specifies third-party TSRs that may be copied into each DOS virtual machine without causing problems.

   If you made certain configuration changes to the DOS window, you may need to add one or more additional lines to restore these changes. As typical examples, refer to the following sections, all of which are in Chapter 7.

Change DOS Display Mode
Font Option not listed in Control Menu (in *Troubleshooting* section)
Insufficient disk space on drive X. (in *Error Messages* section)
Mouse Inoperative in DOS Window Mode (in *Troubleshooting* section)
Set Global Environment Size

[standard]. This section is available for standard-mode operation, al-though no Windows application writes entries into it. All such entries must be made by editing SYSTEM.INI, so if you added lines to this section pre-viously, you'll have to add the same lines again if you're restoring SYS-TEM.INI to its former condition.

Other SYSTEM.INI Sections

Having completed the steps described above, Windows should now open, although it's likely that a few network-related error messages will appear if network hardware/software is installed. If so, review the *Networks* section which follows. Otherwise, skip that section and review any of the others which may be relevant to your system.

Mouse Section. If you previously installed third-party mouse software, you may need to reconfigure your mouse parameters, if they were stored in

SYSTEM.INI. For example, the Logitech *MouseWare Utilities version 6.20* adds a [LogiMouse] section to SYSTEM.INI. To restore this or a similar section, reconfigure the mouse as desired.

Multimedia Sections. If you did need to reinstall multimedia drivers, there may be one or more sections added to SYSTEM.INI. As a typical example, the following section defines DMA and IRQ settings used by the Media Vision *Pro Audio Spectrum* system.

```
[mvproaud.drv]
dma=5
irq=10
```

If all goes well, such sections are restored as you reinstall each driver. However, if all went well, you wouldn't be doing this in the first place, so it may be worthwhile to double-check each driver setup as you add it back to your system. Highlight each driver listed in the Drivers dialog box, and if the Setup... button (see Figure 12.1) is enabled, click on it and review the current settings. Make changes as required, then click on the OK button and review the next driver in the list. Keep at it until you've checked each one.

Network Sections and Reconfiguration. You should be able to resolve most opening network-related error messages by opening the *Network* applet and configuring the system as required. If the Log On button in the Logon Settings dialog box is disabled, click on the OK button, then click on the Adapters button, followed by the Setup... button. Check the Interrupt (IRQ) entry and the others to make sure the information is valid. New network configuration information will be written into SYSTEM.INI as required.

In case of doubt about the correct settings, check the appropriate *User's Guide* and/or the *Network Applet* section of Chapter 11 for assistance.

Restore Custom Configuration

The procedures described above should have restored most of your SYSTEM.INI file to its previous configuration. However, if you were previously using third-party printer drivers, these will now have to be reinstalled if you want them back again. For example, if Bitstream's *Facelift for Windows, version 2.0* (described in Chapter 10) was installed, your SYSTEM.INI file would have contained the following variations on the list shown above.

```
[boot]
display.drv=shellscr.drv
display.org=supervga.drv
```

To restore lines such as these, open the appropriate application and try to use it. If the application runs successfully, it will rewrite the SYSTEM.INI and other INI files, as required. However, if the application does not open, or opens but then causes trouble, it may need to be reinstalled. If so, delete its icon, then rerun its own Setup procedure.

Backup Your New SYSTEM.INI File.   Your SYSTEM.INI file is now about as close to its original condition as it is possible to make it. You probably don't need the following advice, but here it is anyway.

Now would be as good a time as any to make a backup copy so you don't have to go through this routine ever again.

WIN.INI Reconstruction

The easy part first: Expand the basic WIN.SR_ template file into your Windows directory and rename it as WIN.INI. The file contains Windows default parameters for the following sections:

Compatibility	International	Sounds
Desktop	mci extensions	TrueType
Extensions	MS Word	Windows
Font Substitutes	Ports	

Table 14.3 lists the contents of these default sections, each of which is briefly described here.

WIN.INI Default Sections

In the following descriptions, it is assumed the reader has some familiarity with the sections which need to be reconstructed. Therefore, only the information required to do the job is presented. If more information is required, refer to the specific chapter in this book in which the subject is covered in detail.

[Compatibility].   This section of WIN.INI is part of the WIN.SRC file and is therefore restored if this template file is used. A brief explanation of the section is given here, simply because no Windows manual, including the *Resource Kits,* gives even a clue as to what it all means.

TABLE 14.3 WIN.SRC Template File for WIN.INI*

Section and Contents

[windows]

Beep=yes	DoubleClickSpeed=452	run=
BorderWidth=3	KeyboardDelay=2	ScreenSaveActive=0
CursorBlinkRate=530	KeyboardSpeed=31	ScreenSaveTimeOut=120
device=*(for installed printer)*	load=	SetupWin=1
DeviceNotSelectedTimeout=15	NullPort=None	Spooler=yes
Documents=	Programs=com exe bat pif	TransmissionRetryTimeout=45

[Compatibility] [†]

_BNOTES=0x24000	ED=0x00010000	PACKRAT=0x0800	TURBOTAX=0x00080000
AMIPRO=0x0010	EXCEL=0x1000	PIXIE=0x0040	VB=0x0200
APORIA=0x0100	GUIDE=0x1000	PLANNER=0x2000	VISION=0x0040
CCMAIL=0x0008	JW=0x42080	PLUS=0x1000	W4GL=0x4000
CHARISMA=0x2000	MCOURIER=0x0800	PM4=0x2000	W4GLR=0x4000
CP=0x0040	MILESV3=0x1000	PR2=0x2000	WIN2WRS=0x1210
DESIGNER=0x2000	NETSET2=0x0100	REM=0x8022	WINSIM=0x2000
DRAW=0x2000	NOTSHELL=0x0001	TME=0x0100	WPWINFIL=0x0006

[Desktop]

GridGranularity=0	Pattern=(None)	Wallpaper=(None)

[Extensions]

bmp=pbrush.exe ^.bmp	ini=notepad.exe ^.ini	trm=terminal.exe ^.trm
cal=calendar.exe ^.cal *(win)*	mmf=msmail.exe /f ^.mmf *(wrk)*	txt=notepad.exe ^.txt
crd=cardfile.exe ^.crd	pcx=pbrush.exe ^.pcx	wri=write.exe ^.wri
hlp=winhelp.exe ^.hlp	rec=recorder.exe ^.rec	

[FontSubstitutes]

Helv=MS Sans Serif	Times=Times New Roman
Helvetica=Arial	Tms Rmn=MS Serif

[intl]

iCountry=1	iMeasure=1	sCountry=United States	sLongDate=dddd, MMMM dd, yyyy
iCurrDigits=2	iNegCurr=0	sCurrency=$	sShortDate=M/d/yy
iCurrency=0	iTime=0	sDate=/	sThousand=,
iDate=0	iTLZero=0	sDecimal=.	sTime=:
iDigits=2	s1159=AM	sLanguage=enu	
iLzero=1	s2359=PM	sList=,	

[mci extensions]

mid=sequence	rmi=sequencer	wav=waveaudio

TABLE 14.3 *(continued)*

Section and Contents

[Microsoft Word 2.0] [‡]
HPDSKJET=+1

[ports]
; A line with [filename].PRN followed by an equal sign causes [filename] to appear in the Control Panel's
; Printer Configuration dialog box. A printer connected to [filename] directs its output into this file.

COM1:=9600,n,8,1,x	EPT:=	LPT1:=
COM2:=9600,n,8,1,x	FILE:=	LPT2:=
COM3:=9600,n,8,1,x	LPT1:DOS=	LPT3:=
COM4:=9600,n,8,1,x	LPT2.DOS=	

[Sounds] [§]

RingIn=ringin.wav, Incoming Call *(wrk)*	SystemExit=chimes.wav, Windows Exit
RingOut=ringout.wav, Outgoing Call *(wrk)*	SystemHand=chord/ding.wav, Critical Stop
SystemAsterisk=chord/ding.wav, Asterisk	SystemQuestion=chord/ding.wav, Question
SystemDefault=ding.wav, Default Beep	SystemStart=tada/chimes.wav, Windows Start
SystemExclamation=chord/ding.wav, Exclamation	

[TrueType]

---

[*] Listings sorted alphabetically within each section. Actual file listings are unsorted.

[†] Undocumented section. Numeric string specifies "compatibility bit" status. If the indicated application is run, windows inititiates certain bug fixes for each compatibility bit that is set (on). See Table 14.4.

[‡] Section and/or line can be deleted if Word and/or HP DeskJet printer are not installed.

[§] chord/ding, tada/chimes indicate Windows/Workgroups filenames.

(win) Windows 3.1 only. *(wrk)* Windows-for-Workgroups only.

Windows has various compatibility problems with some applications that can be resolved by setting a "compatibility bit" to tip off KERNEL.EXE (see *The Kernel*, Chapter 13) that the problem exists and needs correction. A few such problems are listed here, along with the bit that identifies the problem, and a few applications that require its use.

Problem	Compatibility Bit	Application
Font mapping problems	10	Ami Pro, Word Perfect
Duplicated font size, erroneous vector font	200	Visual BASIC, Word Perfect
Point size problem, erroneous TmsRmn font	1000	Excel, Word Perfect

There are three WIN.INI lines which resolve each of the problems listed above, and a fourth line that resolves all of them, as shown here:

```
[compatibility]
AMIPRO    = 0x0010
VB        = 0x0200
EXCEL     = 0x1000
WIN2WRS   = 0x1210
```

Other lines resolve other problems as various Windows applications are loaded. Table 14.4 lists Windows applications that currently make use of compatibility bits.

[Desktop]. Most of the information in this section can be reconstructed via the Desktop dialog box (Figure 11.11) which is accessed by double-clicking on the Control Panel's *Desktop* icon. However, if you previously adjusted icon vertical spacing with the undocumented IconVerticalSpacing= line, you'll once again have to insert this line by directly editing the [Desktop] section. In any case, refer to the *Desktop* section of Chapter 11 for assistance it it's needed.

NOTE: If no patterns are available in the **Pattern** box, the CONTROL.INI file is probably also missing. For the moment, don't worry about it—you've got more important things to do. But once the [Desktop] section is under control, refer to the *CONTROL.INI Reconstruction* section of this chapter for help with this file.

[Extensions]. In most cases you can restore missing lines in this section simply by opening and closing the application which requires them. For

TABLE 14.4   Applications that Require Compatibility Bit(s) Set

Application	Compatibility Bit[†]	Application	Compatibility Bit[†]
AccPack	WINSIM	MGXDraw 3.0	DRAW
Ami Pro	AMIPRO	Microcourier	MCOURIER
Aporia 1.4	APORIA	Milestones	MILESV3
Ascend 3.1	PLANNER	Money	NOTSHELL
CC Mail	CCMAIL	MS Draw 3.0	DRAW, ED
Charisma	CHARISMA	ObjectVision	VISION
Compton's Multimedia	TME	Packrat	PACKRAT
Cricket Presents	CP	Pagemaker 4.0	PM4
Designer 3.1	DESIGNER	Persuasion	PR2
Excel	EXCEL	Pixie	PIXIE
ExploreNet	NETSET2	Publisher	NOTSHELL
Freelance	REM	Spinnaker +	PLUS
Guide	GUIDE	Turbo Tax	TURBOTAX
Ingress	W4GL, W4GLR	Visual BASIC	VB
Just Write	JW	Word Perfect	WIN2WRS, WPWINFIL
Lotus Notes 2.0, 2.1	_BNOTES	Works	NOTSHELL

[†] Cross-reference to [compatibility] section of WIN.INI. See Table 14.3.

example, the following three lines will be added to the [Extensions] section the next time Word-for-Windows is opened:

```
doc=winword.exe ^.doc
dot=winword.exe ^.dot
rtf=winword.exe ^.rtf
```

For assistance with other revisions to this section of WIN.INI, refer to the description of the *Associate* option on the File Manager's File Menu in Chapter 6.

[FontSubstitutes]. This section is described in the *[FontSubstitutes]* section of Chapter 10. If you previously installed third-party font software, such as Hewlett-Packard's *TrueType Screen Font Pack*, the software may have added additional lines to this section, as described in *Revising the [FontSubstitutes] Section* in Chapter 10. Although such lines are not always required—it depends on your previous font usage—you may want to review the indicated sections of Chapter 10 to help decide whether it's worth it to reinstall some of your font software packages.

[Intl] (International). If you had made any changes to the [Intl] section of WIN.INI, you'll need to reopen the *International* applet and make the same changes once again. When you do, this section will be rewritten as required to reflect those changes. Refer to the *International Applet* section of Chapter 11 for assistance if needed.

[mci extensions]. When you open the *Media Player* applet's Device menu and select one of the listed devices, the Open dialog box should show all files whose extensions are listed in this section of WIN.INI. You'll discover a missing entry if you select a device and the File Name: box in the Open dialog box shows a "*.*" instead of the extension(s) normally associated with that device. For example, if Video for Windows is installed, the File Name: box should show the AVI extension. If it doesn't, add the following line to this section:

```
[mci extensions]
avi=AVIVideo
```

Repeat as required to restore any other missing extensions. Refer to the *Media Player Applet* section of Chapter 12 for additional information about the applet itself.

[Microsoft Word 2.0]. This section can be tossed out if you don't use Microsoft's own *Word-for-Windows*. However, if you do use this word processor, the previous section may have contained extensive configuration information, as shown by a few sample lines here:

```
HPDSKJET=+1
AUTOSAVE-path=C:\WINWORD
DOT-PATH=C:\WINWORD
Grammar 1033,0=C:\WINWORD\GRAMMAR.DLL,C:\WINWORD\GR_AM.LEX
Hyphenate 1033,0=C:\WINWORD\HYPH.DLL,C:\WINWORD\HY_AM.LEX, . . . (more)
INI-path=C:\WINWORD
LoadToolbarBitmaps=Yes
programdir=C:\WINWORD
Spelling 1033,0=C:\WINWORD\SPELL.DLL,C:\WINWORD\SP_AM.LEX
Thesaurus 1033,0=C:\WINWORD\THES.DLL,C:\WINWORD\TH_AM.LEX
```

Some of these lines will be restored the next time you use the word processor and the option which writes information into this WIN.INI section. Other lines, however, may not be automatically restored. Therefore, if you discover that a previous feature is no longer available, you may need to reinstall one or more word processor options, or insert the required line, if you can remember it.

[Ports]. If you made revisions to this section, you'll have to make them one more time. Refer to the *Port Configuration* section of Chapter 9 and/or the *Ports Applet* section of Chapter 11 for assistance if needed.

[Sounds]. This section of the restored WIN.INI file lists the default wave-form files associated with various system events, as described in the *Sound Applet* section of Chapter 12 (see also Table 12.8). If you changed any of these files, you'll have to change them again.

[TrueType]. The previous [TrueType] section contained a line or two only if you enabled/disabled the TrueType, or TrueType only, options. To restore these settings, double-click on the Control Panel's *Fonts* icon and click on the Tr̲ueType... button. Then clear or check the two TrueType option boxes, as desired.

[windows]. This section contains (or, contained) all sorts of entries in addition to those listed in Table 14.1. Once your base WIN.INI is back in shape, many will be rewritten as you reactivate your screen-saver, reconfigure your mouse, or restore other settings that were lost during the recent demise of WIN.INI. However, a few lines may need special attention, as shown by these typical examples.

Device=. This line lists the installed default printer in the following format:

   device=*printer name, driver name (less extension), printer port*

   Refer to *Printer Sections* in *Other WIN.INI Sections* below for additional details about printer configuration.

Load= and Run= Lines. If these lines cited programs that were to be loaded or run at startup, you'll have to either edit the lines or reinstall the software that previously appeared on one or both lines.

Mouse Configuration Lines. In the absence of the appropriate mouse lines in the [windows] section of WIN.INI, your mouse pointer will be the default white arrow, with no mouse trails, size changes, or whatever other fancy stuff you had trained it to do. To begin recovery, open Control Panel and double-click on the *Mouse* icon to display the Mouse dialog box (Figure 11.22, 23, 24, or similar). If the simple act of doing this restores your mouse to its former condition, then your MOUSE.INI file was found either in the Windows directory or possibly in a separate C:\MOUSE directory on your hard disk.

However, if the above operation didn't whip some sense into your mouse, then use the Mouse, Pointer, and Button screens to reset its operating parameters as you want them.

Once again, exit *Control Panel* and have a look at your WIN.INI file. The [windows] section will now contain whatever lines are required to control mouse behavior, and/or a MOUSE.INI file will contain the necessary information.

Programs=.   This line lists the file extensions that the File Manager will recognize as executable programs. If you added additional extensions to the default list (com, exe, bat, pif), you'll have to edit the line to add them back again. Refer to the *Program Icon* section of Chapter 6 for general information, and for a specific example, refer to *Install Screen-Saver as an Applet* in the *Screen-Saver Configuration Procedures* section of Chapter 11.

Other WIN.INI Sections

Needless to say, your previous WIN.INI contained sections not described above. Many of these were added as you installed various Windows applications, or used some of the applets included with Windows itself. For the most part, these will be automatically rewritten the next time you do whatever you did in the first place. However, if you experience trouble running a specific feature in an application, or perhaps an entire application, then that feature or application will have to be reinstalled (unless you can remember all the missing lines and insert them via editing).

This section reviews some, but certainly not all, additional information that may be found in your WIN.INI file after Windows has been up and running for some time. The information presented here may be useful in reconstructing such sections after your basic WIN.INI file is operational.

[colors].   The [colors] section of WIN.INI lists the colors currently in use on the Windows Desktop, or at least it did until WIN.INI got lost. If you've been using the regular Windows default (and rather depressing) color set, there's no need to reconstruct this section, since Windows gets along just fine without it. However, if you had previously saved your own custom color set, it's quite easy to recover it. At the moment it's safely stored in your CONTROL.INI file (unless that one was erased too; in which case you're out of luck).

To recover your custom color scheme, and at the same time write it into WIN.INI, open the Control Panel and double-click on the Color icon to display the Color dialog box (Figure 11.9a). At the top of the screen, click on the down-arrow at the right-hand side of the Color Schemes box. Scroll through the list of color schemes and highlight your custom color scheme. Then click on the OK button and exit the Control Panel. The Desktop will now show your favorite color scheme, and it will once again be recorded for posterity (or until the next accident) in a new [colors] section which you'll find at the bottom of WIN.INI.

[embedding] (Embedded Objects). The information in the [embedding] section was included to maintain compatibility with Windows 3.0 and its applications. In Windows 3.1, the undocumented *Registration Database* applet (see Chapter 6) is used instead.

When Windows is first installed, the [embedding] section contains the three entries shown below. However, these entries are not part of the WIN.SRC file and so are not restored if you use that template file as your base WIN.INI file. If you need to restore the [embedding] section, insert the section heading and the following three lines as well as any others you may have added previously.

	Server Object	Description	Program Name	Format
[embedding]				
Package=	Package,	Package,	packager.exe,	picture
PBrush=	Paintbrush Picture,	Paintbrush Picture,	pbrush.exe,	picture
SoundRec=	Sound,	Sound,	SoundRec.exe,	picture

 NOTE: Spaces after equal signs and commas are inserted here for clarity: Do not include in the actual section.

[fonts]. Your installed font collection is (or was) listed in the [fonts] section. In the absence of this section, icon titles are displayed by whatever proportional-spaced system font is specified on the fonts.fon= line in the [boot] section of SYSTEM.INI. To restore the complete [fonts] section, open the Control Panel and double-click on the *Fonts* icon. The following advisory message is displayed:

No fonts are installed. The Add Fonts dialog box will appear so that you can in-stall fonts.

Click on the OK button to display the Add Fonts dialog box, which was shown in Figure 10.5, then use the Drives and Directories boxes to select the Windows System directory. Presumably, all your fonts are intact in that directory and their names will now appear in alphabetical order in the List of Fonts: box at the top of the screen. Click on the Select All button, then on the OK button to reinstall all the fonts. In a few seconds the Fonts dia-log box (Figure 10.4a) will appear with the fonts listed in the Installed Fonts: box. Click on the Close button to conclude the operation.

The next time you open the WIN.INI file, you'll find your complete font collection listed in a new [fonts] section at the end of the file. When you exit and reopen Windows, icon titles will once again be displayed by the 8-point MS Sans Serif font, and all your raster, vector, and TrueType fonts will again be available to your applications.

If you have other fonts located elsewhere than the System directory, sim-ply repeat the instructions given here and select the appropriate path to those fonts. Refer to the *Soft Fonts* section below for further information about font restoration.

[HPPCL] (Soft Fonts). If your previous WIN.INI had an [HPPCL] sec-tion, *and* you saved its contents in a FINSTALL.DIR file, you can easily re-construct this section. Refer to the *Soft Font Reinstallation after Windows Reinstallation* section in Chapter 10. If you did not take advantage of this undocumented Windows 3.1 feature, then you'll have to reinstall all your soft fonts from scratch.

Multimedia Sections. If you installed any multimedia drivers, there were several sections in WIN.INI that specified various settings relating to the applets which use those drivers. As a typical example, two of the Media Vi-sion *Pro Audio Spectrum's* applets use fader configuration settings written into an [mvmixer.drv] section. If the section gets lost, it will be rewritten automatically the next time the applet is used.

Printer Sections. Since the WIN.SRC template has no idea what printers you had installed, you'll need to open Control Panel and double-click on the *Printers* icon to reinstall your printer(s). The basic procedure for doing this was described in the *Printer Installation (Express, Custom)* section of Chapter 1. For further details on refining your printer installation, refer to the *Printers Applet Configuration* section of Chapter 9.

NOTE: During this reinstallation, you will be prompted to insert one of the Windows 3.1 distribution diskettes in drive A. But, assuming the necessary printer drivers are already in place, change the prompt to read C:\WINDOWS\SYSTEM, then press the Enter key. The existing driver will be used. However, read the *Reinstallation of Printer Driver* section of Chapter 9 before doing this.

Examine your WIN.INI file and you'll find a few more additions. The last line in the [windows] section (device= *printer name and port*) lists the default printer that you just installed, as briefly mentioned above. In addition you'll find a [PrinterPorts] and [devices] section added at the bottom of WIN.INI, and both sections will contain printer data.

Word Processor Sections. Your Windows word processor (if any) probably added one or more sections to WIN.INI, such as the [Microsoft Word 2.0] section described above. To restore such sections, check your word processor directory for the presence of its own SETUP.EXE (or similar) file. Then return to the Program Manager, open the File menu, and select the Run... option. Type in the path and name of the word processor's setup file, then click on the OK button or press the Enter key. When the application's own Setup screen appears, select a custom installation and reinstall the spell-checker, thesaurus, file-conversion utilities, and other paraphernalia that you regularly use with that word processor.

Reconstructing Other INI Files

The following sections describe a few other INI files and the procedures that may be used to re-create them if they're missing.

MOUSE.INI

This file contains settings that determine the operating characteristics of your mouse. The file should be in your Windows directory, or in a C:\MOUSE directory if you have one. To reconstruct it, double-click on the Mouse icon and make whatever configuration changes you need.

PROGMAN.INI

If this file is lost, Windows will start without protest but the Program Manager area will be devoid of all group windows. Fortunately, it's quite easy to restore order here, either by using the Setup procedure or by re-creating each group window separately. Both methods are described here.

Restore Primary Group Windows with Setup /p. The undocumented /p switch was described in Chapter 3, in *Setup /p Switch* in the *Desktop Troubleshooting* section. In the present situation, Setup /p restores the four group windows listed here in less time than it takes to read this explanation.

Group Window	Group File Name
Main	MAIN.GRP
Accessories	ACCESSOR.GRP
Games	GAMES.GRP
StartUp	STARTUP.GRP

If you want to quickly restore these groups to their post-Setup state, click on Program Manager's File Menu and select the Run... option. When the command line box appears, type the following command:

SETUP /p

As each group is restored, its window is left open on the screen, with the four windows displayed in cascaded mode. Close and/or resize and re-arrange the windows as required to suit your needs. Refer to the cited section of Chapter 3 for additional information about this procedure.

NOTE: These newly created group windows will contain only those applet icons that are part of Windows itself. If you had previously revised the applets within one of these windows, those revisions will not be restored by the SETUP /p command. If you did make such revisions, you may prefer to use the procedure described below instead of SETUP /p.

Restore Original Primary Groups after Running SETUP /p. If you discover too late that SETUP /p did not restore a primary group to the condition it was in before losing PROGMAN.INI, all may not yet be lost. Close the group window, then highlight its icon title. Open the Program Manager's File Menu and select the Properties... option. The Program Group Properties dialog box should display information such as that shown here for a newly restored Main group.

Description: Main
Group File: C:\WINDOWS\MAINx.GRP

Note the MAINx.GRP filename, where x is probably the number 1. This nomenclature indicates that SETUP /p found an old MAIN.GRP file in your Windows directory, but didn't restore it to use. If there is no such number in the filename, then a previous group file was not found, and the following procedure won't work. But if there is a number in the name, then continue reading here.

If you want to check this group file, change the current description from Main to Mainx, then close the dialog box. From the File Menu, select the New... option and create a new Main Group Window, in which the Group File: is once again MAIN.GRP. When you close the dialog box, your recent Main Group Window should appear. If its contents are correct, then you can discard the MAINx group.

Restore Group Windows with New... Command. To restore a group window individually, and at the same time include all items added to that group since running your initial Setup procedure, select the New... option on Program Manager's File menu. When the New Program Object screen appears (Figure 1.14a), click on the Program Group button, then on the OK button to display the Program Group Properties Screen (Figure 1.14b). In the Description box, enter the name of the group, and in the Group file box enter the name of the group file. If you don't remember the names of other groups that you may have created previously, log onto the Windows directory and do a search by typing DIR *.GRP.

For additional assistance recovering group files—undamaged or damaged—refer to *Reconstruct Any Other Group File* in the *Desktop Troubleshooting* section of Chapter 3.

PROTOCOL.INI (Workgroups)

If this file is among the missing, a long procession of error messages will be seen the next time the system is booted, such as those shown here for a system with an Intel *EtherExpress 16* LAN adapter card installed.

PROTOCOL.INI file open failure.
Protocol Manager did not accept EtherExpress 16 driver.
NDIS environment invalid, Driver not loaded.

Unable to open Protocol Manager.
Error 3653: The protocol manager could not be found.

To restore the PROTOCOL.INI file, open Windows and click on the OK button when the following message shows up:

Networking functionality will not be available because network protocols were not loaded.

Open the Control Panel's *Network* applet and click on the Adapters button near the bottom of the Network Settings dialog box (see Figure 11.26). When the Network Adapters dialog box appears, click on the Add... button to display the Install New Network Adapter dialog box. Highlight the name of the previously installed network adapter which, in this specific example, is Intel EtherExpress 16 or 16TP. A message box should advise that:

A version of the required driver file EXP16.DOS is currently installed on your system. Do you want to replace it with the version you are installing now?

Click on the No button (unless of course you *do* want to replace it). Finally, review the interrupt and I/O port settings, protocols, and advanced settings. If in doubt about any setting, accept the default value, then click on the OK button and finally on the Close button. After all this is done, the following bit of encouraging news should be seen:

Control Panel has modified your PROTOCOL.INI file. The old version has been saved as PROTOCOL.000. You need to restart . . .

Click on the OK button to exit, then on the Restart Computer button. The next time you examine your Windows directory, you'll find that the "old version" is a PROTOCOL.000 with a file size of zero bytes. You can probably erase it without fear of losing anything (except an empty file).

The specific sequence of messages and actions described here may vary slightly depending on your specific system, but the eventual result should be the same: a new PROTOCOL.INI and no more error messages—or at least none relating to this part of the system.

WINFILE.INI

According to the *Windows Resource Kit* manual, this INI file contains but one [settings] section, in which various File Manager options are specified. However, if the utilities which accompany the *Windows* or the *Workgroups Resource Kits* are installed, an undocumented [AddOns] section appears within the file. Both these sections are described in Chapter 6, in the *ToolBar Configuration* and *Info Menu* sections, respectively.

If WINFILE.INI is lost, it doesn't stay lost very long. A new one is written the next time you close Windows if you've opened the File Manager (even as just a minimized icon) during the current session. However, the new version will not contain information previously written into it if either of the *Resource Kits* or DOS 6.0 was installed. Each adds a new menu to the File Manager's Menu Bar, so if that menu is subsequently missing, it's an indication that WINFILE.INI may have been lost and rewritten. To restore the missing menu, add the following line(s) to the indicated sections.

Menu Added by:	WINFILE.INI Section and Line:
	[Settings]
Tools DOS 6.0	UNDELETE.DLL=C:\DOS\MSTOOLS.DLL
Utility Workgroups Resource Kit	AddOns=FMUTILS.DLL
	[AddOns]
Info Windows Resource Kit	File Size Extension=C:\WINDOWS\FILESIZE.DLL
Tools DOS 6.0	MS-DOS Tools Extentions=C:\DOS\MSTOOLS.DLL
Utility Workgroups Resource Kit	FMUtils Extension=C:\WINDOWS\FMUTILS.DLL

If you find the minor spelling error in one of the lines above, you can correct it without bringing the system to its knees, or just leave it alone, as you prefer. For more information about any of the menus listed above, refer to that menu section in Chapter 6.

Third-Party INI File Editors

The final section of this final chapter offers a brief review of two third-party Windows applications that may be useful to any Windows user who spends too much time configuring and troubleshooting INI files. If you've gotten this far in the book, then you know just such a person, or your significant other does—or did.

INI File Comparisons

In troubleshooting any INI file, it's often helpful to pinpoint the most recent change that occurred. If the file size changes by one byte, chances are some parameter changed from "no" to "yes" or vice versa. However, it's a bit of a chore to rummage through the old and new versions searching for whatever it is that's different. Although more extensive changes should be easier to spot, it's still a nuisance to try to pinpoint each and every change that has been made.

DiagSoft's *QAPlus/WIN* has a handy *QAMatch* utility that can be used for such comparisons. As shown in Figure 14.2, the utility displays a line-by-line comparison of any two files in which dissimilar lines are highlighted. The figure shows that the current SYSTEM.INI file has two disabled device= lines and a new keyboard= line.

INI File Housecleaning

So far, this chapter—if not the entire book—has been devoted to configuring Windows and the various applets and applications that have a talent for accumulating in any active Windows system. But not much—in fact, nothing—has been said about *un*configuring the system.

Of course, it's reasonably easy to uninstall any Windows applet or application: Simply delete its icon and it's gone. Or is it? It's a bit of a mixed blessing, but about the only thing that's gone is the icon. Everything else is still there, taking up space on your hard drive and consuming a fair number of lines in one or another INI file. This is all very nice if you're the indecisive type who may have second thoughts about the recently departed icon. With a minimum amount of effort you can get it back again and be none the worse for the experience. However, if you deleted the icon because you really want to be rid of the application once and for all, then it would be nice if something would go through the entire system and toss out everything that belongs to it.

The MicroHelp *Uninstaller* offers just such a utility, which in the following example is used to uninstall Microsoft *Excel version 4.00a*. Before using the utility, make a backup copy of WIN.INI, in case you'd like to make a before-and-after comparison later on.

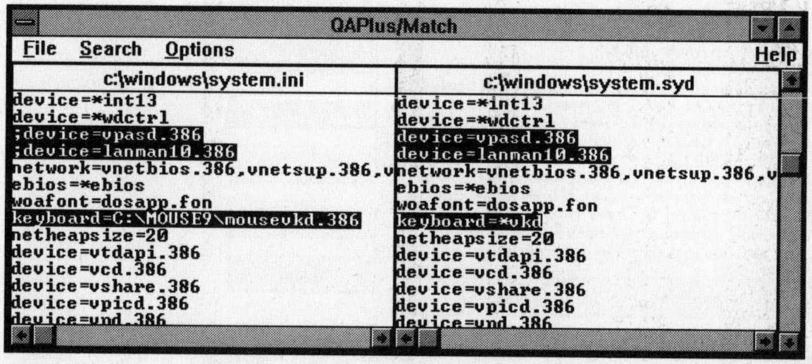

Figure 14.2 The DiagSoft *QAMatch* utility displays a line-by-line comparision of any two INI files. Nonmatching lines are highlighted, as shown by the two device= and one keyboard= lines in the Figure.

The first step is to select Excel in the Select a program dialog box shown in Figure 14.3. Next, click on the Analyze button to display a list of items associated with *Excel*. A portion of the list is shown in the MicroHelp Uninstaller dialog box in Figure 14.4, with an expanded view of some of these lines given in Figure 14.5. Of the total of 34 items found, *Uninstaller* proposes removing 23 of them,

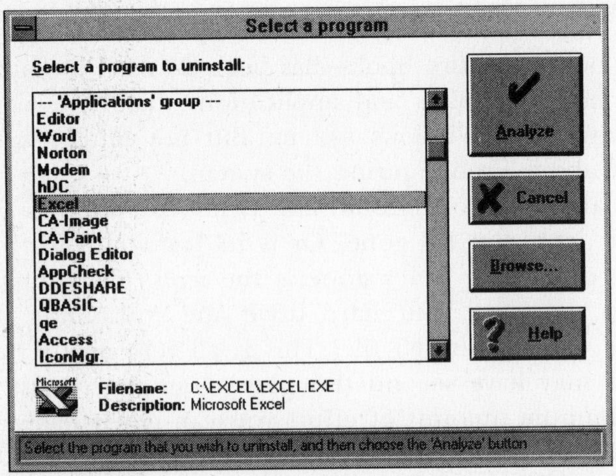

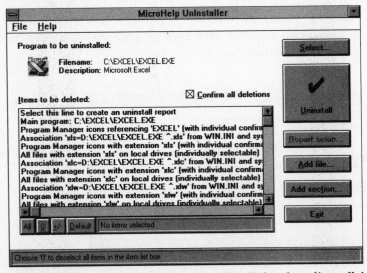

Figure 14.3 The MicroHelp *Uninstaller* utility's Select a program dialog box. Highlight the program to be uninstalled, then press the Analyze button to begin.

Figure 14.4 The MicroHelp Uninstaller dialog box lists all items associated with the program to be uninstalled.

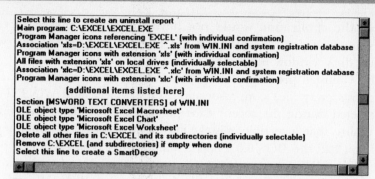

Select this line to create an uninstall report
Main program: C:\EXCEL\EXCEL.EXE
Program Manager icons referencing 'EXCEL' (with individual confirmation)
Association 'xls=D:\EXCEL\EXCEL.EXE ^.xls' from WIN.INI and system registration database
Program Manager icons with extension 'xls' (with individual confirmation)
All files with extension 'xls' on local drives (individually selectable)
Association 'xlc=D:\EXCEL\EXCEL.EXE ^.xlc' from WIN.INI and system registration database
Program Manager icons with extension 'xlc' (with individual confirmation)
              (additional items listed here)
Section [MSWORD TEXT CONVERTERS] of WIN.INI
OLE object type 'Microsoft Excel Macrosheet'
OLE object type 'Microsoft Excel Chart'
OLE object type 'Microsoft Excel Worksheet'
Delete all other files in C:\EXCEL and its subdirectories (individually selectable)
Remove C:\EXCEL (and subdirectories) if empty when done
Select this line to create a SmartDecoy

Figure 14.5 An expanded view of a partial listing of *Excel*-related items that may be deleted during the Uninstall procedure.

thus sparing files with various XL? extensions (XLA, XLB, etc.) which you may not want to lose. In any case, you can review the list and decide which items to delete. If you go for a total purge, the entire Excel directory and all its subdirectories are deleted, as are any other applications related to *Excel*. In addition, the *Excel* references in the Registration database are removed.

At each potentially lethal step in the Uninstall procedure, a prompt asks if you're sure this is what you really want to do. It's a good idea to review each step carefully, since the procedure is good, but not infallible. Although you can probably recover anything deleted by accident (as described below), it's easier on the nerves to prevent accidents from happening in the first place.

At the end of the complete Uninstall procedure, the only *Excel* references left are the following few:

FACELIFT.INI	EXCEL.EXE= line in [ScalingMode] section
MSACCESS.INI	[Microsoft Excel] section
Various EXE files	Any internal references to EXCEL.EXE
SETUP.INF	EXCEL=0x1000 line for WIN.INI [Compatibility] section
WIN.INI	EXCEL=0x1000 line in [Compatibility] section
WIN.SYD (the WIN.INI backup)	Untouched
WINFILE.INI	dir*X*= lines referring to *Excel* directory windows in File Manager

With the exception of the WINFILE.INI lines, all remaining others should not be deleted, regardless of the status of Excel itself, since a subsequent reinstallation of the application would not have sufficient "smarts" to reinsert such references. As for the WINFILE.INI line(s), they will be overwritten when a new dir*X* window is opened in the File Manager.

If desired, the Uninstall procedure will write a report to an UNINSTAL.TXT file. The report lists every file, icon, association, OLE object, and WIN.INI section that was deleted during the recent *Excel* purge. If, on studying the report, you suddenly realize that a terrible mistake has been made, you can unerase the uninstall if you had the DOS 6.0 *Undelete* utility's *Delete Sentry* activated prior to running the Uninstall procedure.

To examine the effect of the Uninstall procedure on WIN.INI, use the DiagSoft *QAPlus/WIN* application's *QAMatch* utility to compare the file against the backup WIN.SYD or WIN.BAK that you made earlier. If you let the Uninstall procedure delete everything it found, the *QAMatch* comparison should show that the following WIN.INI sections were modified, as listed here:

WIN.INI Section	**Deleted Lines:**
[embedding]	Three *Excel* references
[extensions]	xla=, xlb=, . . .
[MSWord Text Converters]	Entire section

The deletion of the [MSWord Text Converters] section was one of those accidents mentioned earlier. This section is a part of the Word-for-Windows application, contains multiple lines, and only one of them pertains to *Excel*. To recover the entire section, run the DOS editor (EDIT.COM) in a DOS Window or full screen, mark the entire [MSWord Text Converters] section, and copy it to the Clipboard. Then open WIN.INI and paste it back where it belongs.

As a final quirk, the Uninstall procedure overlooks the presence of an EXCEL4.INI file in the Windows directory.

Distribution
Diskettes

This Appendix consists of a single multipage table listing all the files on the various distribution diskettes which accompany Windows 3.1 and Windows-for-Workgroups 3.1. Files are listed in alphabetical order, along with the compressed and expanded extension and file size for each file.

The three *Diskette* columns identify the distribution diskette on which each file may be found. In each column, the first number is for the Windows 3.1 diskette, the second is for the Workgroups diskette. A minus sign indicates that the cited file is not supplied with that version of the software. In a few cases, the file size varies slightly between a Windows and a Workgroups file. In this case the latter is listed separately on a second line for that entry.

The final column contains a very brief description for each file, abbreviated as necessary to confine most entries to a single line.

TABLE A.1   Complete List of Windows and Windows-for-Workgroups Files*

Filename	Extension Comp.	Extension Exp.	File Size Comp.	File Size Exp.	Diskette 1.44	Diskette 1.2	Diskette 720	File Description
256COLOR	BM_	BMP	4312	5078	3/7	4/8	6/14	Wallpaper: 256 color
386MAX	VX_	VXD	20237	35167	2/2	2/3	3/4	Virtual Device: Qualitas 386MAX
40291730	WP_	WPD	1105	2941	6/8	6/9	11/15	PS Desc.: IBM LaserPtr 4029 (17)
40293930	WP_	WPD	1741	5411	6/8	7/9	11/15	PS Desc.: IBM LaserPtr. 4029 (39)
8514	DR_	DRV	50425	92032	1/2	1/2	2/3	Display Driver: 8514/a
8514FIX	FO_	FON	3646	10976	2/3	2/3	3/5	System Font: 8514/a fixed
8514OEM	FO_	FON	4237	12288	2/3	2/3	3/4	Terminal Font: 8514/a
8514SYS	FO_	FON	3633	9280	1/3	2/3	2/5	System Font: 8514/a
AB	DL_	DLL	57499	97584	-/5	-/5	-/10	Library: Address Book user interface
AM2100	DO_	DOS	6347	9276	-/8	-/10	-/17	NDIS Driver: Advanced Micro Devices
APP850	FO_	FON	16663	36672	1/3	1/3	4/5	DOS Window Font: code page 850
APPS	HL_	HLP	11491	15694	3/-	3/-	5/-	Help: application compatibility
APPS	IN_	INF	16889	57475	4/-	6/-	6/-	Info: for non-Windows applications
			16953	57650	-/6	-/8	-/14	
ARCADE	BM_	BMP	375	630	4/7	6/8	7/14	Wallpaper: Arcade
ARCHES	BM_	BMP	3137	10358	4/-	4/-	6/-	Wallpaper: Arches
ARGYLE	BM_	BMP	245	630	3/4	3/3	6/14	Wallpaper: Argyle
ARIAL	FO_	FOT	427	1306	5/7	6/8	9/9	TT Font Resource: ARIAL.TTF
ARIAL	TT_	TTF	52532	65692	5/6	6/6	9/9	TT Font: Arial
ARIALB	FO_	FON	10358	22144	5/6	6/8	8/14	Screen Font: Arial 8,10 (EGA)
ARIALBD	FO_	FOT	427	1308	5/7	6/8	9/9	TT Font Resource: ARIALBD.TTF
ARIALBD	TT_	TTF	51841	66080	5/7	6/7	9/9	TT Font: Arial Bold
ARIALBI	FO_	FOT	436	1322	5/7	6/8	10/13	TT Font Resource: ARIALBI.TTF
ARIALBI	TT_	TTF	57729	71880	5/7	6/6	9/9	TT Font: Arial Bold Italic
ARIALI	FO_	FOT	429	1312	5/7	6/8	9/9	TT Font Resource: ARIALI.TTF
ARIALI	TT_	TTF	47643	61656	5/7	6/7	11/11	TT Font: Arial Italic
BANINST	38_	386	992	4861	2/-	2/-	4/-	Virtual Device: Banyan VINES 4.0
BLUEMAX	VX_	VXD	20270	35189	2/2	2/3	3/4	Virtual Device: Qualitas BlueMAX
BP1CP2	PC_	PCM	40218	77329	-/7	-/9	-/15	CG Brilliant I/Comp Pub II
CALC	EX_	EXE	27999	43072	3/5	5/7	7/12	Applet: Calculator
CALC	HL_	HLP	12989	18076	3/6	5/8	7/14	Help: Calculator
CALENDAR	EX_	EXE	37995	59824	3/-	4/-	6/-	Applet: Calendar
CALENDAR	HL_	HLP	13794	20656	3/-	5/-	7/-	Help Calendar
CAN_ADF	EX_	EXE	36591	69232	6/8	7/9	11/16	Soft Font Installer: LBPII, III.DRV
CANON10E	DR_	DRV	2652	6000	6/8	7/9	12/16	Printer Drv: Canon Bubble-Jet BJ-10e
CANON130	DR_	DRV	2931	7536	6/8	7/9	12/16	Printer Drv: Canon BJ-130e
CANON330	DR_	DRV	5694	20032	6/8	7/9	12/16	Printer Drv: Canon BJ-300/330
CANYON	MI_	MID	17632	33883	3/6	5/8	7/14	MIDI sound: Canyon

TABLE A.1   *(continued)*

Filename	Extension Comp.	Extension Exp.	File Size Comp.	File Size Exp.	Diskette 1.44	Diskette 1.2	Diskette 720	File Description
CARDFILE	EX_	EXE	48673	93184	3/5	4/6	5/11	Applet: Cardfile
CARDFILE	HL_	HLP	18523	24810	4/6	4/8	5/13	Help: Cardfile
CARDS	DL_	DLL	42646	148528	-/5	-/6	-/12	Library: Hearts game
CARS	BM_	BMP	332	630	4/7	3/8	6/14	Wallpaper: Cars
CASTLE	BM_	BMP	544	778	4/7	6/8	6/14	Wallpaper: Castle
CGA	2G_	2GR	1768	2106	2/3	2/3	3/5	Grabber: CGA standard mode
CGA40850	FO_	FON	3729	6352	2/3	2/3	3/5	DOS Window Font: code page 850
CGA40WOA	FO_	FON	3563	6336	2/3	2/3	3/5	DOS Window Font: code page 437
CGA80850	FO_	FON	3049	4320	2/3	2/3	3/5	DOS Window Font: code page 850
CGA80WOA	FO_	FON	3039	4304	2/3	2/3	3/5	DOS Window Font: code page 437
CGALOGO	LG_	LGO	902[†]	896	2/2	3/1	4/5	Logo Code: CGA startup
CGALOGO	RL_	RLE	3815	11878	2/-	3/-	4/-	Logo Screen: CGA display
			3842	13440	-/3	-/2	-/5	
CHARMAP	EX_	EXE	12015	22016	3/6	3/8	5/14	Applet: Character Map
CHARMAP	HL_	HLP	4689	10797	4/7	4/6	6/14	Help: Character Map
CHIMES	WA_	WAV	10591	15920	3/6	4/8	5/13	Sound: Exit
CHITZ	BM_	BMP	3294	19918	4/-	5/-	6/-	Wallpaper: Chitz
CHORD	WA_	WAV	11235	24982	3/-	3/-	5/-	Sound: Question
CIT24US	DR_	DRV	8493	30912	6/8	7/9	12/16	Printer Driver: Citizen 24-pin
CIT9US	DR_	DRV	6979	24800	6/8	7/9	12/16	Printer Driver: Citizen 9-pin
CITOH	DR_	DRV	2422	4720	6/8	7/9	12/16	Ptr Drv: C-Itoh 8510, AT&T 470/475
CLIPBRD	EX_	EXE	11384	18512	5/-	4/-	7/-	Applet: Clipboard Viewer
			39481	78848	-/5	-/7	-/11	Applet: Clipbook Viewer
			39205	78336				Same, on Add-On (upgrade) diskettes
CLIPBRD	HL_	HLP	7668	13071	4/-	6/-	5/-	Help: Clipboard Viewer
			23155	31090	-/6	-/7	-/12	
CLIPSRV	EX_	EXE	10967	19968	-/6	-/8	-/14	DDE Server: Clipbook
			10979	19968				Same, on Add-On (upgrade) diskettes
CLOCK	EX_	EXE	10140	16416	3/6	4/8	5/13	Applet: Clock
COMM	DR_	DRV	7157	9280	1/-	2/-	2/-	Communications Driver
			7362	9632	-/3	-/3	-/4	
COMMCTRL	DL_	DLL	33863	48112	-/5	-/7	-/11	Library: custom controls
COMMDLG	DL_	DLL	50924	89248	4/-	4/-	10/-	Library: common dialogs
			54579	97984	-/5	-/6	-/13	
CONTROL	EX_	EXE	10270	15872	5/6	4/8	7/13	Applet: Control Panel
CONTROL	HL_	HLP	95210	121672	2/-	3/-	4/-	Help: Control Panel
			116119	145067	-/1	-/2	-/3	
CONTROL	INF	INF	20993[‡]	20993	5/-	6/-	10/-	Info: Control Panel, printer
			21015[‡]	21015	-/6	/-8	-/12	

TABLE A.1 *(continued)*

Filename	Extension Comp.	Exp.	File Size Comp.	Exp.	Diskette 1.44	1.2	720	File Description
CONTROL	SR_	SRC	1278	3609	5/7	6/8	9/14	Source Template: CONTROL.INI
COUR	FO_	FOT	428	1318	5/7	6/8	9/9	TT Font Resource: COUR.TTF
COUR	TT_	TTF	53733	72356	5/7	6/6	9/9	TT Font: Courier New
COURB	FO_	FON	8118	21856	5/7	6/8	10/14	Screen font: Courier 10,12,15 (EGA)
COURBD	FO_	FOT	430	1320	5/7	6/8	10/13	TT Font Resource: COURBD.TTF
COURBD	TT_	TTF	56871	78564	5/7	6/6	9/9	TT Font: Courier New Bold
COURBI	FO_	FOT	437	1334	6/7	6/8	9/9	TT Font Resource: COURBI.TTF
COURBI	TT_	TTF	64330	84436	5/7	6/6	9/9	TT Font: Courier New Bold Italic
COURE	FO_	FON	8612	23408	5/6	6/8	10/13	Screen font: Courier 10,12,15 (VGA)
COURF	FO_	FON	11021	31712	5/6	6/8	10/14	Screen font: Courier 10,12,15 (8514/a)
COURI	FO_	FOT	435	1324	5/7	6/8	9/9	TT Font Resource: COURI.TTF
COURI	TT_	TTF	60757	80588	5/7	6/6	9/9	TT Font: Courier New Italic
CPWIN386	CP_	CPL	48841	104816	1/2	1/2	1/4	Control Panel extension, enh. mode
DD1CP1	PC_	PCM	76630	36225	-/7	-/9	-/15	CG Distinct Doc I/Comp Pub I PCM
DDEML	DL_	DLL	22366	36864	4/-	5/-	8/-	Library: DDE management
			23477	38400	-/6	-/7	-/12	
DEC1150	WP_	WPD	1875	6006	6/8	7/9	11/15	PS Desc.: Digital DEClaser 1150
DEC2150	WP_	WPD	1835	5900	6/8	7/9	11/15	PS Desc.: Digital DEClaser 2150
DEC2250	WP_	WPD	1972	6434	6/8	7/9	11/15	PS Desc.: Digital DEClaser 2250
DEC3250	WP_	WPD	2012	6580	6/8	7/9	11/15	PS Desc.: Digital DEClaser 3250
DECCOLOR	WP_	WPD	1308	4271	6/8	7/9	11/15	PS Desc.: Digital ColorMate PS
DECLPS20	WP_	WPD	1533	4944	6/8	7/9	11/15	PS Desc.: Digital LPS print server
DECNB	38_	386	4860	9375	2/-	2/-	4/-	VDD: DEC Pathworks NetBios
DECNET	38_	386	5817	14058	2/-	2/-	4/-	VDD: DEC Pathworks network
DEMILAYR	DL_	DLL	31890	48304	-/5	-/7	-/11	Library: WGA system services layer
DEPCA	DO_	DOS	11004	15593	-/8	-/10	-/17	NDIS Driver: DEC EtherWorks
DICONIX	DR_	DRV	2201	4256	6/8	7/9	12/16	Printer Driver: Kodak Diconix
DING	WA_	WAV	6011	11598	5/7	5/8	6/8	Sound: Beep
DM309	DR_	DRV	3225	6688	-/8	-/9	-/16	Printer Driver: Olivetti DM 309
DMCOLOR	DL_	DLL	14744	18480	6/7	7/9	12/15	Library: universal color printer driver
DOSAPP	FO_	FON	16721	36656	2/3	3/3	3/5	DOS Window Font: code page 437
DOSX	EX_	EXE	27426	32682	2/2	2/3	3/4	DOS extender, standard mode
DRIVERS	CP_	CPL	21385	41440	4/6	5/7	6/12	Control Panel: installable drivers
DRWATSON	EX_	EXE	18559	26864	4/6	4/8	7/14	Fault detection utility
DSWAP	EX_	EXE	18810	27474	4/6	5/8	8/14	Task Swapper, std mode DOS
E20NDIS	DO_	DOS	7471	16300	-/8	-/10	-/17	NDIS Driver: Cabletron E2010-X
E21NDIS	DO_	DOS	7888	16710	-/8	-/10	-/17	NDIS Driver: Cabletron E2112
EGA	3G_	3GR	9460	14336	1/3	1/3	2/5	Grabber: EGA enhanced mode
EGA	DR_	DRV	43319	71552	1/2	2/2	1/5	Display Driver: EGA

TABLE A.1   *(continued)*

Filename	Extension Comp.	Exp.	File Size Comp.	Exp.	1.44	1.2	720	File Description
EGA	SY_	SYS	4190	5039	2/-	2/-	3/-	Display Driver: EGA MS-DOS
			4180	5264	-/3	-/3	-/4	
EGA40850	FO_	FON	4058	8384	2/3	2/3	4/5	DOS Window Font: code page 850
EGA40WOA	FO_	FON	3933	8368	2/3	2/3	3/5	DOS Window Font: code page 437
EGA80850	FO_	FON	3243	5328	2/3	2/3	3/5	DOS Window Font: code page 850
EGA80WOA	FO_	FON	3259	5312	2/3	2/3	3/5	DOS Window Font: code page 437
EGACOLOR	2G_	2GR	2729	3260	1/3	2/3	2/5	Grabber: EGA standard mode
EGAFIX	FO_	FON	2534	4240	1/3	1/3	2/5	Sr ft: EGA (640×350), AT&T (640×400)
EGAHIBW	DR_	DRV	26886	45264	2/2	2/3	3/4	Display Driver: EGA black & white
EGALOGO	LG_	LGO	1105	1136	1/3	2/3	2/5	Logo code: EGA
EGALOGO	RL_	RLE	5125	17082	1/-	2/-	3/-	Logo screen: EGA
			5878	18946	-/3	-/3	-/4	
EGAMONO	2G_	2GR	2563	3030	2/3	2/3	4/5	Grabber: EGA monochrome std. mode
EGAMONO	DR_	DRV	26941	45328	2/2	2/3	3/4	Display Driver: EGA monochrome
EGAMONO	LG_	LGO	1073	1104	2/3	2/3	3/5	Logo code: EGA monochrome startup
EGAMONO	RL_	RLE	4619	15966	2/-	3/-	4/-	Logo screen: EGA monochrome
			4916	18946	-/3	-/3	-/4	
EGAOEM	FO_	FON	3027	4176	1/3	2/3	2/5	Terminal font: EGA (640×350), AT&T (640×400)
EGASYS	FO_	FON	2879	5264	1/3	2/3	2/5	Sys ft: EGA (640×350), AT&T (640×400)
EGYPT	BM_	BMP	225	630	3/7	5/8	6/14	Wallpaper: Egypt
ELNK16	DO_	DOS	7318	9792	-/8	-/10	-/17	NDIS Driver: 3Com EtherLink 16
ELNK3	DO_	DOS	9179	12466	-/8	-/8	-/17	NDIS Driver: 3Com EtherLink III
ELNKII	DO_	DOS	8172	11322	-/8	-/10	-/17	NDIS Driver: 3Com EtherLink II
ELNKMC	DO_	DOS	7454	9542	-/8	-/10	-/17	NDIS Driver: 3Com EtherLink/MC
ELNKPL	DO_	DOS	10308	17116	-/8	-/8	-/17	NDIS Driver: 3Com EtherLink Plus
EMM386	EX_	EXE	52996	110174	4/3	4/6	6/13	DOS Expanded-Memory Manager 386
EPL75523	WP_	WPD	1554	4714	6/8	7/9	11/15	Epson EPL-7500 PS description file
EPSON24	DR_	DRV	5158	14960	6/-	7/-	12/-	Printer Driver: Epson 24-pin
			5843	17072	-/8	-/9	-/16	
EPSON9	DR_	DRV	6872	22192	6/-	7/-	12/-	Printer Driver: Epson 9-pin
			7681	24960	-/8	-/9	-/16	
ESCP2	DR_	DRV	4488	7904	6/8	7/9	12/16	Printer Drv: Epson ESCP2 dot matrix
EVX16	DO_	DOS	5869	11299	-/8	-/10	-/17	NDIS Driver: Everex SpdLnk /PC16
EXECJET	DR_	DRV	5979	20240	6/8	7/9	12/16	Printer Driver: IBM ExecJet
EXP16	DO_	DOS	8064	11668	-/8	-/10	-/17	NDIS Driver: Intel EtherExpress 16
EXPAND	EXE	EXE	15285[‡]	15285	3/6	3/8	5/6	DOS-based file expansion utility
FINSTALL	DL_	DLL	110030	200368	6/7	7/9	11/15	Library: Soft Font Instlr: HPPCL5/A
FINSTALL	HL_	HLP	15386	19202	6/7	7/9	12/15	Help: soft font installer, HPPCL5/A

TABLE A.1 *(continued)*

Filename	Extension Comp.	Exp.	File Size Comp.	Exp.	1.44	Diskette 1.2	720	File Description
FLOCK	BM_	BMP	468	1630	3/-	3/-	6/-	Wallpaper: Flock
FRAMEWRK	DL_	DLL	135054	221232	-/4	-/5	-/8	Library: WGA application framework
FUJI24	DR_	DRV	5907	17088	6/-	7/-	12/-	Printer Driver: Fujitsu 24-pin
FUJI9	DR_	DRV	3478	8576	6/-	7/-	12/-	Printer Driver: Fujitsu 9-pin
GDI	EX_	EXE	167674	220800	1/-	1/-	3/-	Graphics Device Interface core
			167671	220800	-/1	-/1	-/2	component
GENDRV	DL_	DLL	49648	99328	6/7	7/9	11/15	Library: generic printer driver
GLOSSARY	HL_	HLP	37606	46570	3/-	3/-	6/-	Help: Glossary
			43462	54546	-/5	-/6	-/11	
HERC	3G_	3GR	5988	9216	2/3	2/3	3/4	Grabber: Hercules mono enh. mode
HERC850	FO_	FON	3524	8880	2/3	2/3	3/5	DOS Win Fnt: code page 850, Hercules
HERCLOGO	LG_	LGO	1019 [†]	1008	2/3	2/3	3/5	Logo Code: Hercules mono. startup
HERCLOGO	RL_	RLE	4690	15808	1/-	2/-	2/-	Logo Screen: Hercules display
			5086	19546	-/3	-/3	-/4	
HERCULES	2G_	2GR	1809	2155	1/3	2/2	2/5	Grabber: Hercules mono std. mode
HERCULES	DR_	DRV	27462	47296	3/2	2/3	3/5	Display Driver: Hercules
HERCWOA	FO_	FON	3509	8864	2/3	2/3	3/5	DOS Window Font: code page 437
HERMES_1	WP_	WPD	781	1937	6/8	6/9	11/14	PS description: Hermes H 606 PS (13)
HERMES_2	WP_	WPD	1424	4411	6/8	6/9	11/15	PS description: Hermes H 606 PS (35)
HIMEM	SY_	SYS	9384	13824	5/6	4/8	7/13	DOS Extended-Memory Manager
HONEY	BM_	BMP	345	854	4/7	4/8	6/14	Wallpaper: Honey
HP_3D522	WP_	WPD	1642	4988	6/8	6/9	11/15	PS description: LaserJet IIID PS
HP_3P522	WP_	WPD	1566	4784	6/8	7/9	11/15	PS description: LaserJet IIIP PS
HPDSKJET	DR_	DRV	23308	61856	6/-	7/-	12/-	Printer Driver: HP DeskJet Series
			28391	78688	-/8	-/8	-/16	
HPEBIOS	38_	386	2108	9348	1/3	3/3	4/5	VDD: EBIOS, HP machines enh. mode
HPELI523	WP_	WPD	1592	4899	6/8	6/9	11/15	PS description: HP LaserJet IIISi
HPIID522	WP_	WPD	1556	4799	6/8	6/9	11/15	PS description: HP LaserJet IID
HPIII522	WP_	WPD	1540	4725	6/8	6/9	11/15	PS description: HP LaserJet III
HPIIP522	WP_	WPD	1547	4762	6/8	6/9	11/15	PS description: HP LaserJet IIP
HPLANB	DO_	DOS	7893	11744	-/8	-/10	-/17	Hewlett-Packard LAN
HPMOUSE	DR_	DRV	2540	4896	2/3	2/3	4/5	Mouse Driver: HP HIL
HPPCL	DR_	DRV	54150	153120	6/-	7/-	12/-	Printer Driver: HP LaserJet II
			54030	152192	-/7	-/9	-/15	
HPPCL5A	DR_	DRV	185016	428672	6/-	7/-	12/-	Printer Driver: HP LaserJet III
HPPCL5A	HL_	HLP	17386	21805	6/-	7/-	12/-	Help: HP LaserJet III printer driver
HPPCL5MS	DR_	DRV	46127	114784	-/7	-/9	-/15	Printer Driver: HP LaserJet III
HPPCL5OP	HL_	HLP	8013	13195	6/-	7/-	12/-	Help: HP LaserJet III printer driver
HPPLOT	DR_	DRV	34950	66680	6/8	6/9	11/16	Printer Driver: HP Plotter

TABLE A.1 *(continued)*

Filename	Extension Comp.	Exp.	File Size Comp.	Exp.	Diskette 1.44	1.2	720	File Description
HPSYSTEM	DR_	DRV	2108	2832	2/3	2/3	3/5	System Driver: HP Vectra for Windows
I82593	DO_	DOS	5276	7427	-/8	-/10	-/17	NDIS Drv: Intel motherboard module
IBM17521	WP_	WPD	1034	2695	6/8	6/9	11/16	PS Description: IBM 4019 (17 fonts)
IBM39521	WP_	WPD	1675	5165	6/8	7/9	11/15	PS Description: IBM 4019 (39 fonts)
IBM4019	DR_	DRV	30069	68368	6/8	7/9	12/16	Printer Driver: IBM Laser Printer 4019
IBM5204	DR_	DRV	4797	16304	6/8	7/9	12/16	Printer Driver: IBM Quickwriter 5204
IBMCOLOR	DR_	DRV	12699	21424	6/8	7/9	12/16	Printer Driver: IBM Color
IBMTOK	DO_	DOS	7062	10064	-/8	-/10	-/17	NDIS Driver: IBM Token Ring
IMPEXP	DL_	DLL	34169	66448	-/5	-/7	-/11	Library: Mail message file import
IPX	OB_	OBJ	15111	20340	2/8	2/-	4/17	Comm Driver: Novell NetWare workstation. Not included on Add-On (upgrade) diskettes.
IPXODI	CO_	COM	13552	20903	2/8	3/-	4/17	Comm Driver: Novell NetWare workstation (ODI). Not included on Add-On (upgrade) diskettes.
KBDBE	DL_	DLL	2049	2449	2/3	2/3	4/5	Library: Belgian keyboard layout
KBDCA	DL_	DLL	2127	2673	2/3	2/3	4/5	Library: French-Canadian keyboard
KBDDA	DL_	DLL	2032	2364	2/3	2/3	4/5	Library: Danish keyboard layout
KBDDV	DL_	DLL	1000	1332	2/3	3/3	4/5	Library: US-Dvorak keyboard layout
KBDFC	DL_	DLL	2272	2769	2/3	2/3	4/5	Library: Canadian multilingual keybd.
KBDFI	DL_	DLL	2079	2404	2/3	2/3	4/5	Library: Finnish keyboard layout
KBDFR	DL_	DLL	1928	2353	2/3	2/3	4/5	Library: French keyboard layout
KBDGR	DL_	DLL	1976	2481	2/3	2/3	4/5	Library: German keyboard layout
KBDHP	DR_	DRV	6835	8480	1/3	1/3	3/2	Keyboard driver: H-P computers
KBDIC	DL_	DLL	1412	1724	2/3	2/3	4/5	Library: Icelandic keyboard layout
KBDIT	DL_	DLL	1806	2146	2/3	2/3	4/5	Library: Italian keyboard layout
KBDLA	DL_	DLL	2091	2465	2/3	2/3	4/5	Library: Latin American keyboard
KBDMOUSE	DR_	DRV	1078	1408	2/-	3/-	4/-	Mouse Drv: Olivetti/AT&T keyboard
KBDNE	DL_	DLL	2029	2358	2/3	2/3	4/5	Library: Dutch keyboard layout
KBDNO	DL_	DLL	2059	2402	2/3	2/3	4/5	Library: Norwegian keyboard layout
KBDPO	DL_	DLL	1982	2352	2/3	2/3	4/5	Library: Portuguese keyboard layout
KBDSF	DL_	DLL	2002	2489	2/3	2/3	4/5	Library: Swiss-French keyboard layout
KBDSG	DL_	DLL	1374	1653	2/3	2/3	4/5	Library: Swiss-German keyboard layout
KBDSP	DL_	DLL	2074	2401	2/3	3/3	5/5	Library: Spanish keyboard layout
KBDSW	DL_	DLL	2070	2374	2/3	3/3	4/5	Library: Swedish keyboard layout
KBDUK	DL_	DLL	1153	1428	2/3	2/3	4/5	Library: British keyboard layout
KBDUS	DL_	DLL	996	1300	2/3	3/3	4/5	Library: US keyboard layout
KBDUSX	DL_	DLL	1329	1641	2/3	2/3	4/5	Library: US-International keyboard
KEYBOARD	DR_	DRV	6115	7568	2/3	2/3	2/3	Keyboard Driver

TABLE A.1 *(continued)*

Filename	Extension Comp.	Exp.	File Size Comp.	Exp.	Diskette 1.44	1.2	720	File Description
KRNL286	EX_	EXE	55774	71730	2/2	2/2	3/3	Kernel core component, standard mode
KRNL386	EX_	EXE	59399	75490	2/2	2/2	4/3	Kernel core component, enhanced mode
L100_425	WP_	WPD	1620	4885	-/8	-/9	-/15	PS Description: Linotronic 100 v42.5
L200230&	WP_	WPD	749	1863	6/-	7/-	11/-	PS Description: Linotronic 200/230
			1712	5182	-/8	-/9	-/15	
L300_471	WP_	WPD	1851	5315	-/8	-/9	-/15	PS Description: Linotronic 300 v47.1
L300_493	WP_	WPD	1713	5182	-/8	-/9	-/15	PS Description: Linotronic 300 v49.3
L330_52&	WP_	WPD	859	2335	6/-	7/-	11/-	PS Description: Linotronic 330
			1707	5182	-/8	-/9	-/15	
L500_493	WP_	WPD	1806	5182	-/8	-/9	-/15	PS Description: Linotronic 500 v49.3
L530_52&	WP_	WPD	858	2335	6/-	7/-	11/-	PS Description: Linotronic 530
			1799	5486	-/8	-/9	-/15	
L630_52&	WP_	WPD	859	2335	6/-	7/-	12/-	PS Description: Linotronic 630
			1762	5384	-/8	-/9	-/15	
LANGDUT	DL_	DLL	1425	3072	2/3	2/3	4/5	Library: Dutch language
LANGENG	DL_	DLL	1430	3072	2/3	2/3	4/5	Library: general international language
LANGFRN	DL_	DLL	1457	3072	2/3	3/3	4/5	Library: French language
LANGGER	DL_	DLL	1425	3072	2/3	2/3	4/5	Library: German language
LANGSCA	DL_	DLL	1429	3072	2/3	2/3	4/5	Library: Finnish, Icelandic, Norwegian, Swedish language
LANGSPA	DL_	DLL	1494	3072	2/3	2/3	4/5	Library: Spanish language
LANMAN	DR_	DRV	26011	63488	2/-	2/-	4/-	Network Driver: LAN Manager 2.0
LANMAN	HL_	HLP	14000	31724	2/-	3/-	4/-	Help: LAN Manager 2.0 network driver
LANMAN10	38_	386	1550	8786	2/3	2/3	4/5	Virtual Device: LAN Manager
LBPII	DR_	DRV	26846	65968	6/8	7/9	11/16	Printer Driver: Canon LBP-8 II
LBPIII	DR_	DRV	36482	89504	6/8	7/9	11/16	Printer Driver: Canon LBPIII
LEAVES	BM_	BMP	4616	15118	4/7	6/8	6/14	Wallpaper: Leaves
LM21DRV	UP_	UPD	578	904	-/3	-/3	-/5	Upgrade List: LAN Manager drivers
LMOUSE	CO_	COM	22326	34658	2/2	2/3	3/4	Mouse Driver: MS-DOS level Logitech
LMOUSE	DR_	DRV	7898	12928	2/3	2/3	4/4	Mouse Driver: Logitech
LMSCRIPT	EX_	EXE	3568	4801	-/8	-/10	-/17	Workgroups LAN Mgr. script support
LMSCRIPT	PI_	PIF	220	545	-/8	-/10	-/17	PIF for above
LSL	CO_	COM	6278	7662	2/8	2/2	4/17	Novell NetWare workstation link support layer (ODI). Not included on Add-On (upgrade) diskettes.
LVMD	38_	386	4018	9688	2/3	2/3	4/5	Virtual Device: Logitech mouse
LZEXPAND	DL_	DLL	6551	9936	-/3	-/3	-/4	Library: Control Panel file expansion
MAC586	SY_	SYS	6253	8709	-/8	-/10	-/17	NDIS Driver: DCA 10Mb
MAILMGR	DL_	DLL	25935	51632	-/6	-/7	-/12	Library: Mail Mgr. API support

TABLE A.1 *(continued)*

Filename	Extension Comp.	Extension Exp.	File Size Comp.	File Size Exp.	Diskette 1.44	Diskette 1.2	Diskette 720	File Description
MAILSPL	EX_	EXE	28456	46912	-/5	-/7	-/13	Mail spooler
MAIN	CP_	CPL	89396	148560	4/-	5/-	10/-	Main Control Panel extension
			89416	148592	-/3	-/5	-/8	
MAPI	DL_	DLL	32829	53440	-/5	-/7	-/11	Library: messaging API
MARBLE	BM_	BMP	7666	27646	4/-	4/-	6/-	Wallpaper: Marble
MCICDA	DR_	DRV	8368	13824	4/6	5/8	10/14	MCI Driver: CD-ROM
MCISEQ	DR_	DRV	16359	25264	4/6	5/8	7/14	MCI Driver: MIDI sequencer
MCIWAVE	DR_	DRV	17133	28160	4/6	6/8	7/14	MCI Driver: Waveform audio
MIDIMAP	CF_	CFG	7333	34522	4/7	6/8	10/14	MIDI Mapper: configuration data
MIDIMAP	DR_	DRV	34150	52784	4/5	4/7	6/11	MIDI driver: MIDI Mapper
MMSOUND	DR_	DRV	2829	3440	1/3	2/3	2/5	Sound Driver: MultiMedia
MMSYSTEM	DL_	DLL	35478	61648	4/5	5/7	10/6	Library: MultiMedia System
MMTASK	TS_	TSK	777	1104	5/7	6/8	8/8	MultiMedia background task
MMTLHI	DR_	DRV	43941	82702	-/2	-/2	-/3	Display Driver: ET4000 large fonts
			60735 [‡]	56241 [§]				same, on Add-On (upgrade) diskette
MMTLLO	DR_	DRV	43557	79712	-/2	-/2	-/4	Display Driver: ET4000 small fonts
MODERN	FO_	FON	4376	8704	5/7	6/8	10/14	Vector Font: Modern (all resolutions)
MONOUMB2	38_	386	1017	4745	4/3	4/3	4/5	VDD: monochrome video (B000) area
MORICONS	DL_	DLL	40447	118864	3/5	4/7	5/11	Library: Icon file
MOUSE	CO_	COM	31328	56408	4/5	4/7	10/13	Mouse driver: Microsoft
MOUSE	DR_	DRV	8000	10672	2/3	2/3	3/4	Mouse Driver: Microsoft
MOUSE	SY_	SYS	30733	55160	4/5	5/7	10/12	Mouse Driver: Microsoft
MOUSEHP	CO_	COM	20729	34061	4/4	4/8	10/12	Mouse Driver: HP HIL for MS-DOS
MOUSEHP	SY_	SYS	20642	33909	4/6	5/8	7/12	Mouse Driver: HP HIL for MS-DOS
MPLAYER	EX_	EXE	21454	33312	3/6	5/7	7/12	Applet: Media Player
MPLAYER	HL_	HLP	7872	12896	3/7	3/8	5/14	Help: Media Player
MPU401	DR_	DRV	5265	7088	4/7	4/8	5/14	MIDI Driver: MPU401 compatibles
MSADLIB	DR_	DRV	10495	22064	3/5	3/8	5/6	MIDI Driver: Adlib compatibles
MSC3BC2	DR_	DRV	2823	4832	2/3	3/3	4/5	Mse Drv: Mouse Systems COM2/3 button
MSCDEX	EX_	EXE	16710	25431	-/6	-/8	-/14	CD-ROM Driver: MS Extensions 2.21
MSCMOUSE	DR_	DRV	2901	4960	2/3	2/3	4/5	Mouse Drv: Mouse Systems serial/bus
MSCVMD	38_	386	3257	9327	1/3	2/3	3/5	Virtual Device: Mouse Systems mouse
MSD	EXE	EXE	155538 [‡]	155538	4/-	5/-	8/-	Diagnostics utility
			158413 [‡]	158413	-/4	-/7	-/4	
MSD	IN_	INI	350	620	5/7	6/8	5/14	Diagnostics utility initialization
MSHEARTS	EX_	EXE	58302	111616	-/5	-/5	-/10	Applet: Hearts
MSHEARTS	HL_	HLP	8661	13048	-/6	-/8	-/13	Help: Hearts
MSIPX	CO_	COM	15538	27130	-/8	-/10	-/17	NDIS-compliant IPX protocol

TABLE A.1   *(continued)*

Filename	Extension Comp.	Extension Exp.	File Size Comp.	File Size Exp.	Diskette 1.44	Diskette 1.2	Diskette 720	File Description
MSIPX	SY_	SYS	1825	4301	-/8	-/10	-/17	NDIS shim for MSIPX.COM to use NDIS drivers
MSMAIL	EX_	EXE	170050	298576	-/3	-/3	-/10	Applet: Mail
MSMAIL	HL_	HLP	57896	72051	-/5	-/5	-/10	Help: Mail
MSNET	DR_	DRV	4619	7072	1/3	2/3	2/2	Network Driver: generic
MSREMIND	EX_	EXE	19392	28944	-/6	-/6	-/14	Schedule+ bkgnd. reminder notification
MSSCHED	DL_	DLL	134853	214848	-/4	-/5	-/13	Library: Schedule+
MSSFS	DL_	DLL	162891	260944	-/3	-/4	-/7	Library: shared file system transport
MT_TI101	WP_	WPD	1392	4383	6/8	7/9	11/16	PS Description: Microtek TrueLaser
N2090522	WP_	WPD	1465	4444	6/8	7/9	11/16	PS Description: NEC Silentwriter2 90
N2290520	WP_	WPD	1373	4328	6/8	7/9	11/16	PS Description: NEC Silentwriter2 290
N2990523	WP_	WPD	1499	4544	6/8	7/9	11/16	PS Description: NEC Silentwriter2 990
N890_470	WP_	WPD	1414	4462	6/8	7/9	11/16	PS Desc: NEC Silentwriter LC890
N890X505	WP_	WPD	1415	4462	6/8	7/9	11/16	PS Desc: NEC Silentwriter LC890XL
NCM40519	WP_	WPD	687	2069	6/8	7/9	11/14	PS Description: NEC Colormate PS/40
NCM80519	WP_	WPD	1248	4103	6/8	7/9	11/16	PS Description: NEC Colormate PS/80
NDDEAPI	DL_	DLL	9526 / 9470	15520 / 15392	-/6	-/8	-/13	Lbr: ntwk DDE—DDE shares API support same, on Add-On (upgrade) diskettes
NDDENB	DL_	DLL	9433	15152	-/3	-/3	-/5	Library: netw.DDE drv for NetBIOS
NDIS39XR	DO_	DOS	12375	34880	-/8	-/10	-/17	NDIS Driver: Proteon Token Ring
NE1000	DO_	DOS	9621	13944	-/8	-/10	-/17	NDIS Driver: Novell/Anthem NE1000
NE2000	DO_	DOS	9865	13766	-/8	-/10	-/17	NDIS Driver: Novell/Anthem NE2000
NEC24PIN	DR_	DRV	10791	29552	6/8	6/9	11/16	Printer Driver: NEC 24-pin
NET	EX_	EXE	250066	415252	-/8	-/10	-/16	Workgroups DOS network redirector
NET	MS_	MSG	35106	70629	-/8	-/9	-/17	Message file for above
NETAPI	DL_	DLL	65602	115712	-/2	-/1	-/3	Library: Workgroups API
NETAPI20	DL_	DLL	60347	113520	2/-	2/-	4/-	Library: LAN Manager API
NETDDE	EX_	EXE	45120	81920	-/2	-/2	-/3	Network DDE background application
NETH	MS_	MSG	44969	104570	-/8	-/9	-/17	Workgroups DOS netw. redir. help msgs.
NETWARE	DR_	DRV	59787	125712	2/8	2/10	4/17	Net Drv: Novell NetWare for Windows
NETWARE	HL_	HLP	18204	34348	2/8	3/10	5/17	Help: Novell NetWare network driver
NETWATCH	EX_	EXE	19230	40448	-/6	-/8	-/14	Applet: Net Watcher
NETWATCH	HL_	HLP	8224	13433	-/6	-/8	-/13	Help: Net Watcher
NETWORK	INF	INF	38606	38606	-/2	-/2	-/4	Network installation information
NETWORKS	WR_	WRI	26489	68096	3/-	3/-	6/-	Readme File: for networks
NETWORKS	WR_	WRI	10155	22528	-/3	-/3	-/6	
NETX	CO_	COM	38642	52443	2/8	3/10	4/17	Novell NetWare workstation shell
NI6510	DO_	DOS	5515	10040	-/8	-/10	-/17	NDIS Driver: Racal-Interlan NI6510
NOMOUSE	DR_	DRV	315	416	2/3	2/3	3/5	Mouse Driver: No Mouse

TABLE A.1   *(continued)*

Filename	Extension Comp.	Exp.	File Size Comp.	Exp.	1.44	1.2	720	File Description
NOTEPAD	EX_	EXE	20018	32736	3/6	3/8	6/12	Applet: Notepad
NOTEPAD	HL_	HLP	8334	13894	4/7	4/8	5/13	Help: Notepad
NWPOPUP	EX_	EXE	1577	2992	2/8	3/10	5/17	Novell NetWare message popup utility
O5241503	WP_	WPD	1496	4521	6/8	7/9	11/16	PS Description: OceColor G5241
O5242503	WP_	WPD	1476	4447	6/8	7/9	11/16	PS Description: OceColor G5242
OKI24	DR_	DRV	5720	20752	6/8	7/9	12/16	Printer Driver: Okidata 24-pin
OKI9	DR_	DRV	4129	11072	6/8	7/9	12/16	Printer Driver: Okidata 9-pin
OKI9IBM	DR_	DRV	3769	10736	6/8	7/9	12/16	Ptr. Driver: Okidata 9-Pin IBM Model
OL840518	WP_	WPD	1575	4759	6/8	7/9	11/15	PS Description: Oki OL840/PS
OLECLI	DL_	DLL	45422	83456	5/5	4/6	10/11	Library: OLE client
OLESVR	DL_	DLL	14552	24064	4/6	5/8	8/14	Library: OLE server
OLIBW	DR_	DRV	27824	47744	2/1	2/3	4/4	Display Driver: Olivetti/AT&T PVC
OLIGRAB	2G_	2GR	2618	3714	1/3	2/3	3/5	Grabber: Olivetti/AT&T PVC std. mode
OLITOK	DO_	DOS	46330	59554	-/8	-/10	-/17	NDIS Driver: Olivetti TokenExpr.16/4
OLIVETI1	WP_	WPD	784	1937	6/8	7/9	12/14	PS Desc: Olivetti PG 306 PS (13)
OLIVETI2	WP_	WPD	1428	4411	6/8	7/9	11/16	PS Desc: Olivetti PG 306 PS (35)
P4455514	WP_	WPD	1619	5134	6/8	7/9	11/15	PS Description: Panasonic KX-P4455
PABNSP	DL_	DLL	25396	44576	-/6	-/7	-/12	Library: Pers. Address Book name svc.
PACKAGER	EX_	EXE	40667	76480	3/5	4/7	7/11	Applet: Object Packager
PACKAGER	HL_	HLP	16647	21156	3/6	3/8	5/14	Help: Object Packager
PAINTJET	DR_	DRV	2903	5616	6/-	7/-	12/-	Printer Driver: HP PaintJet
			2960	5776	-/8	-/9	-/16	
PANSON9	DR_	DRV	4789	16352	6/8	7/9	12/16	Printer Driver: Panasonic 9-pin
PANSON24	DR_	DRV	4405	14592	6/8	7/9	12/16	Printer Driver: Panasonic 24-pin
PBRUSH	DL_	DLL	4904	6766	3/7	4/8	6/14	Library: Paintbrush
PBRUSH	EX_	EXE	102781	183376	3/3	5/5	7/8	Applet: Paintbrush
PBRUSH	HL_	HLP	31527	40269	3/5	4/7	5/12	Help: Paintbrush
PCSA	DR_	DRV	6177	9168	2/-	2/-	4/-	Network Driver: DEC Pathworks
PE2NDIS	EX_	EXE	26306	30721	-/8	-/10	-/17	Xircom Pocket Ethernet II
PENDIS	DO_	DOS	18041	22266	-/8	-/10	-/17	NDIS Driver: Xircom Pkt. Ethernet II
PG306	DR_	DRV	18336	43392	6/-	7/-	12/-	Printer Driver: PG 306
PHIIPX	WP_	WPD	1219	3984	6/8	7/9	11/16	PS Description: Phaser II PX PS
PIFEDIT	EX_	EXE	25970	55168	5/6	5/7	6/12	Applet: Program Info. File Editor
PIFEDIT	HL_	HLP	27098	33270	3/6	5/7	5/12	Help: Program Information File Editor
PLASMA	3G_	3GR	6405	9728	2/3	2/3	3/4	Grabber: Compaq Port. enh. plasma
PLASMA	DR_	DRV	27311	47216	2/3	2/3	4/4	Display Drv: Compaq Portable plasma
PMSPL	DL_	DLL	17012	31744	-/3	-/3	-/5	Library: LAN Manager spooler API
PMSPL20	DL_	DLL	22506	43328	1/-	2/-	4/-	Library: LAN Manager printer API
POWER	DR_	DRV	9461	15504	2/3	3/3	4/5	Device Driver: Adv. Power Mgmnt.

TABLE A.1 *(continued)*

Filename	Extension Comp.	Extension Exp.	File Size Comp.	File Size Exp.	Diskette 1.44	Diskette 1.2	Diskette 720	File Description
POWER	HL_	HLP	7763	13100	2/3	2/3	5/4	Help: Adv. Power Mgmnt. device driver
PRINTERS	WR_	WRI	15312	44928	3/-	3/-	6/-	Readme File: for printers
			14719	37760	-/3	-/7	-/6	
PRINTMAN	EX_	EXE	27709	43248	4/-	4/-	8/-	Applet: Print Manager
			41493	69504	-/5	-/7	-/11	
PRINTMAN	HL_	HLP	32765	40880	3/-	4/-	10/-	Help: Print Manager
			45782	60638	-/5	-/6	-/11	
PRO4	DO_	DOS	13718	29090	-/8	-/10	-/17	NDIS Driver: Proteon ISA Token Ring
PROGMAN	EX_	EXE	56919	115312	4/5	4/6	8/10	Applet: Program Manager
PROGMAN	HL_	HLP	23516	30911	5/6	5/7	6/12	Help: Program Manager
PROPRINT	DR_	DRV	3576	8288	6/8	7/9	12/16	Printer Driver: IBM Proprinter series
PROPRN24	DR_	DRV	3539	8208	6/8	7/9	12/16	Printer Driver: IBM Proprinter 24 pin
PRORAPM	DW_	DWN	30224	37022	-/8	-/10	-/17	Network Driver: Proteon Token Ring
PROTMAN	DO_	DOS	8944	21680	-/8	-/10	-/17	NDIS Driver: Wrkgrp protocol mgr.
PROTMAN	EX_	EXE	6010	13760	-/8	-/10	-/17	Workgroups protocol manager TSR
PRTUPD	INF	INF	15855 ‡	15855	6/7	6/8	11/14	Info. file for printer driver updates
PS1	DR_	DRV	3768	11872	6/8	7/9	12/16	Printer Driver: IBM PS/1
PSCRIPT	DR_	DRV	135968	312848	6/-	7/-	11/15	Printer Driver: Postscript
			138797	318112	-/7	-/9	-/15	
PSCRIPT	HL_	HLP	32727	43793	6/7	7/9	11/15	Help: Postscript printer driver
Q2200510	WP_	WPD	1621	5182	6/-	7/-	11/-	PS Description: QMS-PS 2200
			1624	5190	-/8	-/9	-/15	
Q820_517	WP_	WPD	1520	4942	6/8	7/9	11/16	PS Description: QMS-PS 820
QWIII	DR_	DRV	4709	14832	6/8	7/9	12/16	Printer Driver: IBM QuietWriter III
RAMDRIVE	SY_	SYS	3765	5873	4/7	5/8	7/14	MS-DOS RAMDrive utility
README	WR_	WRI	32717	99584	3/-	3/-	5/-	Readme file
			36279	97280	-/3	-/7	-/6	
RECORDER	DL_	DLL	7779	10414	3/7	3/8	5/14	Library: Recorder
RECORDER	EX_	EXE	24091	39152	3/6	3/7	6/12	Applet: Recorder
RECORDER	HL_	HLP	12440	18200	4/6	3/5	5/14	Help: Recorder
REDBRICK	BM_	BMP	459	630	4/7	3/8	6/14	Wallpaper: Redbrick
REGEDIT	EX_	EXE	20050	32336	4/6	3/8	7/12	Applet: Registration Editor
REGEDIT	HL_	HLP	16339	22681	4/6	6/8	5/14	Help: Registration Editor
REGEDITV	HL_	HLP	10677	15731	5/6	5/8	8/13	Help: Registration Editor adv. mode
RINGIN	WA_	WAV	10676	10026	-/6	-/8	-/14	Sound: Chat applet, incoming ring
RINGOUT	WA_	WAV	2870	5212	-/7	-/8	-/12	Sound: Chat applet, outgoing ring
RIVETS	BM_	BMP	159	630	4/7	4/8	6/14	Wallpaper: Rivets
ROMAN	FO_	FON	6356	13312	5/7	6/8	10/14	Vector Font: Roman (all resolutions)
ROUTE	CO_	COM	3414	4262	-/8	-/10	-/17	Token Ring IPX source routing support

TABLE A.1 *(continued)*

Filename	Extension Comp.	Exp.	File Size Comp.	Exp.	1.44	Diskette 1.2	720	File Description
SCHDPLUS	EX_	EXE	289451	489760	-/3	-/4	-/6	Applet: Schedule+
SCHDPLUS	HL_	HLP	83512	104115	-/4	-/5	-/6	Help: Schedule+
SCHEDMSG	DL_	DLL	39938	75920	-/5	-/7	-/11	Library: Schedule+ message forms
SCRIPT	FO_	FON	5502	12288	5/7	6/8	10/14	Vector font: Script (all resolutions)
SCRNSAVE	SC_	SCR	2626	5328	3/6	4/8	6/14	Screen-Saver: default
SEIKO_04	WP_	WPD	1385	4612	6/8	7/9	11/16	PS Desc: Seiko ColorPoint PS 04
SEIKO_14	WP_	WPD	1472	4789	6/8	7/9	11/16	PS Desc: Seiko ColorPoint PS 14
SENDFILE	DL_	DLL	3878	6064	-/7	-/8	-/14	Library Sendfile custom command
SERIFB	FO_	FON	18777	45536	5/6	6/8	10/14	Sr Fnt: MS Serif 8,10,12,14,18,24 (EGA)
SERIFE	FO_	FON	21454	57936	5/6	6/8	10/12	Sr Fnt: MS Serif 8,10,12,14,18,24 (VGA)
SERIFF	FO_	FON	27241	81728	5/6	5/7	7/12	Sr Fnt: MS Serif 8,10,12,14,18,24 (8514/a)
SETUP	EXE	EXE	422080 ‡	422080	1/-	1/-	1/-	Setup application file
			478256 ‡	478256	-/1	-/1	-/1	
SETUP	HL_	HLP	33683	41453	1/-	1/-	1/-	Help: Setup
			35700	44307	-/2	-/2	-/4	
SETUP	INF	INF	59118 ‡	59118	1/-	1/-	1/-	Info: Setup
			59552 ‡	59552	-/1	-/1	-/-	
			60100 ‡	69100	-/-	-/-	-/1	
			59551 ‡	59551	-/1	-/-	-/-	Same, on Add-On (upgrade version)
SETUP	INI	INI	92 ‡	92	3/1	3/4	5/5	Setup Initialization
SETUP	RE_	REG	1364	3508	5/-	6/-	6/-	Registration Database template
			1370	3466	-/7	-/8	-/14	
SETUP	SHH	SHH	6525 ‡	6525	1/-	1/-	1/-	Automated Setup template
			10303 ‡	10303	-/1	-/1	-/1	
SETUP	TXT	TXT	41724 ‡	41724	1/-	1/-	1/-	Readme File: for Setup
			42561 ‡	42561	-/1	-/1	-/1	
SF4019	EX_	EXE	33831	58800	6/8	7/9	11/16	Soft font installer: IBM Laser Ptr 4019
SFINST	EX_	EXE	35394	67360	6/-	7/-	11/-	Soft font installer for PG 306 Printer
SHELL	DL_	DLL	25821	41600	4/-	5/-	8/-	Library: Shell
			25820	41520	-/6	-/7	-/14	
SL	DL_	DLL	9547	16512	2/3	2/3	5/5	Library: Advanced Power Mgmnt. SL
SL	HL_	HLP	9094	15841	2/3	2/3	5/4	Help: Adv. Power Mgmnt. SL DLL
SMALLB	FO_	FON	10928	22016	5/6	6/8	10/14	Screen Font: Small fonts (EGA)
SMALLE	FO_	FON	12501	26112	5/6	6/8	10/14	Screen Font: Small fonts (VGA)
SMALLF	FO_	FON	10489	21504	5/6	6/8	10/14	Screen Font: Small fonts (8514/a)
SMARTDRV	EX_	EXE	17324	43609	4/6	5/8	7/14	SmartDrive disk-caching utility
SMC_ARC	DO_	DOS	12273	20327	-/8	-/10	-/17	NDIS Driver: SMC ArcNet
SMC3000	DO_	DOS	5908	12271	-/8	-/10	-/17	NDIS Driver: SMC 3000 series
SMCMAC	DO_	DOS	11706	17408	-/8	-/10	-/17	NDIS Drv: SMS EtherCard PLUS

TABLE A.1   *(continued)*

Filename	Extension Comp.	Exp.	File Size Comp.	Exp.	Diskette 1.44	1.2	720	File Description
SND	CP_	CPL	4986	8192	4/7	6/8	8/14	Sound Control Panel extension
SNDBLST	DR_	DRV	10122	13808	3/5	3/8	5/6	DSP Driver: SoundBlaster 1.0
SNDBLST2	DR_	DRV	10445	14464	3/5	3/8	5/6	DSP Driver: SoundBlaster 1.5
SOL	EX_	EXE	62451	180688	3/4	4/5	7/10	Applet: Solitaire
SOL	HL_	HLP	8208	13753	3/6	5/8	6/14	Help: Solitaire
SOUNDREC	EX_	EXE	31764	51305	3/5	4/8	5/11	Applet: Sound Recorder
SOUNDREC	HL_	HLP	10058	17686	3/6	3/8	5/11	Help: Sound Recorder
SQUARES	BM_	BMP	163	630	4/7	6/8	6/14	Wallpaper: Squares
SSERIFB	FO_	FON	18968	50608	5/6	6/8	6/14	Sr Fnt: MS S Serif 8,10,12,14,18,24 (EGA)
SSERIFE	FO_	FON	21643	64544	5/5	5/7	10/12	Sr Fnt: MS S Serif 8,10,12,14,18,24 (VGA)
SSERIFF	FO_	FON	27627	89680	5/6	5/7	10/12	Sr Fnt: MS S Serif 8,10,12,14,18,24 (8514/a)
SSFLYWIN	SC_	SCR	9705	16160	3/6	3/8	6/13	Screen-Saver: Flying Windows
SSMARQUE	SC_	SCR	9635	16896	3/6	4/8	6/13	Screen-Saver: Marquee
SSMYST	SC_	SCR	11282	19456	3/-	4/-	6/-	Screen-Saver: Mystify
SSSTARS	SC_	SCR	9444	17536	4/6	4/8	6/13	Screen-Saver: Stars
STORE	DL_	DLL	143146	247984	-/4	-/4	-/7	Library: message store support
STRN	DO_	DOS	30176	41946	-/8	-/10	-/17	NDIS Driver: NCR Token Ring
SUPERVGA	DR_	DRV	44303	73504	2/2	2/2	3/3	Display Drv: SVGA (800 × 600 × 16)
SYMBOL	FO_	FOT	428	1308	6/7	6/8	9/9	TT Font Resource: SYMBOL.TTF
SYMBOL	TT_	TTF	50450	64516	6/6	6/6	9/9	TT Font: Symbol
SYMBOLB	FO_	FON	19890	48352	5/6	6/8	10/14	Sr Fnt: Symbol 8,10,12,14,18,24 (EGA)
SYMBOLE	FO_	FON	21296	56336	5/6	6/8	10/12	Sr Fnt: Symbol 8,10,12,14,18,24 (VGA)
SYMBOLF	FO_	FON	27198	80912	5/6	3/7	10/12	Sr Fnt: Symbol 8,10,12,14,18,24 (8514/a)
SYSEDIT	EX_	EXE	10761	18896	5/6	5/8	8/14	Applet: System Editor
SYSINI	WR_	WRI	16616	53760	3/-	3/-	6/-	Readme File: for SYSTEM.INI
			20786	58496	-/3	-/8	-/6	
SYSTEM	DR_	DRV	1780	2304	1/3	2/3	2/4	System Driver
SYSTEM	SR_	SRC	642	1009	1/-	2/-	1/-	Source Template: SYSTEM.INI
			755	1196	-/3	-/3	-/5	
TADA	WA_	WAV	23658	27804	3/-	4/-	5/-	Sound: Start
TARTAN	BM_	BMP	4498	32886	4/-	4/-	6/-	Wallpaper: Tartan
TASKMAN	EX_	EXE	2230	3744	5/7	6/8	5/14	Applet: Task Manager
TBMI2	CO_	COM	6616	17999	2/3	3/3	5/4	Novell Net. wrkstation task-switching
TCCARC	DO_	DOS	7578	19972	-/8	-/10	-/17	NDIS Driver: Thomas Conrad TC6x4x
TERMINAL	EX_	EXE	84383	148160	4/4	4/5	7/8	Applet: Terminal
TERMINAL	HL_	HLP	25674	36279	3/6	4/7	7/12	Help: Terminal
TESTPS	TX_	TXT	1242	2640	6/7	7/9	12/15	Postscript test text file
THATCH	BM_	BMP	210	598	3/5	4/8	6/14	Wallpaper: Thatch
THINKJET	DR_	DRV	2305	4720	6/8	7/9	12/16	Printer Driver: HP ThinkJet (2225 C-D)

TABLE A.1 *(continued)*

Filename	Extension Comp.	Exp.	File Size Comp.	Exp.	Diskette 1.44	1.2	720	File Description
TI850	DR_	DRV	2156	4352	6/8	7/9	12/16	Printer Driver: TI 850/855
TIGA	DR_	DRV	38829	74352	1/2	2/2	2/4	Display Driver: TIGA
TIGAWIN	RL_	RLM	23493	42658	2/2	2/3	3/4	TIGA firmware code for Windows
TIM17521	WP_	WPD	1048	2686	6/8	7/9	11/16	PS Description: TI MicroLaser PS17
TIM35521	WP_	WPD	1577	4688	6/8	7/9	11/15	PS Description: TI MicroLaser PS35
TIMER	DR_	DRV	3166	4192	3/5	3/8	5/11	Timer Driver: MultiMedia
TIMES	FO_	FOT	436	1326	5/7	6/8	9/9	TT Font Resource: TIMES.TTF
TIMES	TT_	TTF	69074	83260	5/6	6/6	9/9	TT Font: Times New Roman
TIMESB	FO_	FON	10361	21088	5/6	6/8	10/13	Sr Fnt: Times New Roman 8,10 (EGA)
TIMESBD	FO_	FOT	437	1328	5/7	6/8	9/9	TT Font Resource: TIMESBD.TTF
TIMESBD	TT_	TTF	63489	79804	5/7	6/6	9/9	TT Font: Times New Roman Bold
TIMESBI	FO_	FOT	445	1342	5/7	6/8	10/13	TT Font Resource: TIMESBI.TTF
TIMESBI	TT_	TTF	60539	76452	5/7	6/6	9/9	TT Font: Times New Rmn. Bold Italic
TIMESI	FO_	FOT	439	1332	5/7	6/8	9/9	TT Font Resource: TIMESI.TTF
TIMESI	TT_	TTF	61880	78172	5/7	6/6	9/9	TT Font: Times New Roman Italic
TKPHZR21	WP_	WPD	1510	5175	6/8	7/9	11/16	PS Description: Phaser II PX I
TKPHZR31	WP_	WPD	1613	5422	6/8	7/9	11/15	PS Description: Phaser III PX I
TLNK	DO_	DOS	6659	12426	-/8	-/10	-/17	NDIS Library: 3Com TokenLink
TOOLHELP	DL_	DLL	10372	14128	5/6	5/8	8/13	Library: Tool Helper
TOSHIBA	DR_	DRV	3320	8000	6/8	7/9	12/16	Printer Driver: Toshiba p351/1351
TRIUMPH1	WP_	WPD	785	1937	6/8	7/9	11/14	PS Desc.: Tri. Adler SDR 7706 PS (13)
TRIUMPH2	WP_	WPD	1428	4411	6/8	7/9	11/16	PS Desc.: Tri. Adler SDR 7706 PS (35)
TRNSCHED	DL_	DLL	8847	12960	-/6	-/8	-/13	Library: Schedule+ shared file system
TTY	DR_	DRV	16675	30496	6/8	7/9	12/16	Printer Driver: Generic / Text only
TTY	HL_	HLP	8859	14666	6/8	7/9	11/16	Help: Generic / Text only printer driver
U9415470	WP_	WPD	1345	4320	6/8	7/9	11/16	PS Desc.: Unisys AP9415
UNIDRV	DL_	DLL	72378	119296	6/-	7/-	12/-	Library: Universal printer driver
			77841	128240	-/7	-/9	-/15	
UNIDRV	HL_	HLP	23219	31429	6/-	7/-	12/-	Help: Universal printer driver
			32380	42333	-/7	-/9	-/15	
USER	EX_	EXE	195465	264016	2/-	3/-	2/-	User-interface core component
			195464	264016	-/1	-/1	-/2	
V7VDD	38_	386	19315	40385	1/2	2/3	2/4	Virtual Device: Video Seven display
V7VGA	3G_	3GR	8960	13824	2/3	2/3	3/5	Grabber: Video Seven enhanced mode
V7VGA	DR_	DRV	47671	99296	2/2	2/2	3/3	Display Driver: Video 7 (256 colors)
VADLIBD	38_	386	1952	5542	3/6	3/8	5/11	Virtual Device: DMA for Adlib
VBROWSE	38_	386	10665	19860	-/3	-/3	-/5	Virtual Device: network browsing
VCD	38_	386	6362	8204	-/7	-/8	-/14	Virtual Device: communications
VDD8514	38_	386	27808	46161	1/2	2/3	2/3	Virtual Device: 8514/a display

TABLE A.1 *(continued)*

Filename	Extension Comp.	Exp.	File Size Comp.	Exp.	Diskette 1.44	1.2	720	File Description
VDDCGA	38_	386	8906	15227	2/3	2/3	5/5	Virtual Device: CGA display
VDDCT441	38_	386	18366	40007	1/-	1/-	2/-	Virtual Device: 82C441 VGA display
VDDEGA	38_	386	19421	40584	1/2	2/3	2/4	Virtual Device: EGA display
VDDHERC	38_	386	7023	10426	2/3	2/3	4/4	Virtual Device: Hercules mono. display
VDDTIGA	38_	386	27647	41997	1/2	1/3	2/4	Virtual Device: TIGA display
VDDTLI4	38_	386	19014	39996	-/2	-/3	-/4	Virtual Device: Tseng ET4000 SVGA
VDDVGA30	38_	386	19651	40945	1/2	1/3	1/4	Virtual Device: VGA display (ver. 3.0)
VDDXGA	38_	386	20367	40906	1/2	2/3	2/4	Virtual Device: XGA display
VDMAD	38_	386	8566	12246	-/6	-/8	-/14	Virtual Device: DMA
VER	DL_	DLL	6307	9008	2/3	2/3	4/4	Library: Ver. Resource & File Instal.
VFORMS	DL_	DLL	84293	142896	-/4	-/5	-/10	Library: Mail viewed forms
VGA	3G_	3GR	11256	16384	1/3	1/3	2/5	Grabber: VGA enhanced mode
VGA	DR_	DRV	43952	73200	2/2	3/2	4/5	Display Driver: VGA
VGA30	3G_	3GR	9803	14848	2/3	3/3	3/5	Grabber: VGA enh. mode (ver. 3.0)
VGA850	FO_	FON	3264	5232	2/3	2/3	4/5	DOS Window Font: code page 850
VGA860	FO_	FON	3237	5184	2/3	2/3	4/5	DOS Window Font: code page 860
VGA861	FO_	FON	3260	5184	2/3	2/3	4/5	DOS Window Font: code page 861
VGA863	FO_	FON	3266	5200	2/3	3/3	4/5	DOS Window Font: code page 863
VGA865	FO_	FON	3261	5184	2/3	3/3	4/5	DOS Window Font: code page 865
VGACOLOR	2G_	2GR	3658	4484	2/3	2/3	2/5	Grabber: standard mode
VGACOLRX	GR_	GR2	3499	4297	-/3	-/3	-/5	Grabber: with Tseng ET4000 drivers
VGADIB	3G_	3GR	10382	15360	2/3	2/3	3/5	Grabber: DIB (8514/a, VGA mono)
VGAFIX	FO_	FON	2715	5360	2/3	2/3	3/5	System Font: VGA fixed
VGALOGO	LG_	LGO	1245	1280	2/3	2/3	3/5	Logo Code: VGA startup
VGALOGO	RL_	RLE	9204	26778	2/-	3/-	3/-	Logo Screen: VGA display
			11472	35704	-/2	-/3	-/5	
VGAMONO	2G_	2GR	3644	4472	2/3	2/3	3/5	Grabber: VGA mono standard mode
VGAMONO	DR_	DRV	26679	45024	2/2	2/3	3/5	Display Driver: VGA monochrome
VGAOEM	FO_	FON	3219	5168	2/3	2/3	3/5	Terminal Font: VGA
VGASYS	FO_	FON	3111	7280	1/3	2/3	2/5	System Font: VGA
VIPX	38_	386	8864	19197	2/8	2/10	4/17	Virtual Device: Novell NetWare IXP
VNB	38_	386	26708	41201	-/8	-/10	-/17	Virtual Device: NetBEUI protocol
VNETBIOS	38_	386	18767	37320	-/2	-/3	-/5	Virtual Device: NetBIOS interface
VNETSUP	38_	386	7928	14592	-/3	-/3	-/4	Virtual Device: network support
VNETWARE	38_	386	3903	10102	2/8	2/10	4/17	Virtual Device: Novell NetWare API
VPD	38_	386	2768	9287	-/7	-/8	-/13	Virtual Device: printer
VPICD	38_	386	7460	11784	-/7	-/4	-/14	Virtual Device: programmable int. ctrlr.
VPOWERD	38_	386	2224	9426	2/3	3/3	5/5	Virtual Device: Adv. Power Mgmnt.
VREDIR	38_	386	64507	100614	-/2	-/2	-/3	Virtual Device: network redirector

TABLE A.1 *(continued)*

Filename	Extension Comp.	Extension Exp.	File Size Comp.	File Size Exp.	Diskette 1.44	Diskette 1.2	Diskette 720	File Description
VSBD	38_	386	2463	5650	3/6	3/8	5/11	Virtual Device: SoundBlaster
VSERVER	38_	386	35710	64058	-/2	-/2	-/4	Virtual Dev: network file/print server
VSHARE	38_	386	9765	26689	-/6	-/8	-/	Virtual Device: file sharing
VTDAPI	38_	386	1824	5245	3/6	3/8	5/11	Virtual Device: MultiMedia timer
VWC	38_	386	2812	9334	-/3	-/3	-/5	Virtual Device: client
WFWNET	DR_	DRV	165600	282736	-/1	-/1	-/2	Network Driver: Workgroups
			165511	282640	-/1			Same, on Add-On (upgrade) version
WFWNET	HL_	HLP	34193	42878	-/2	-/3	-/5	Help: Workgroups network driver
WFWSETUP	CP_	CPL	101625	200000	-/2	-/2	-/1	Control Panel network setup extension
WGPOMGR	DL_	DLL	46200	79408	-/5	-/6	-/13	Library: Post Office manager functions
WIN	CN_	CNF	10101	16112	1/3	1/3	1/1	Startup code
WIN	SR_	SRC	1666	2272	1/-	1/-	1/-	Source Template: WIN.INI
			1705	2341	-/3	-/3	-/5	
WIN386	EX_	EXE	284215	544789	4/4	5/4	8/8	Enhanced-mode core components
WIN386	PS_	PS2	418	852	5/7	6/8	6/14	PS/2 BIOS data for enhanced mode
WIN87EM	DL_	DLL	8973	12800	4/6	4/8	6/13	Library: 80x87 math co-proc. emulation
WINCHAT	EX_	EXE	18442	37888	-/6	-/7	-/14	Applet: Chat
WINCHAT	HL_	HLP	9578	13622	-/6	-/8	-/13	Help: Chat
WINDOWS	LO_	LOD	878	1988	2/3	3/3	4/5	Qualitas 386MAX/BMax module
WINFILE	EX_	EXE	89663	146864	3/-	4/-	7/-	Applet: File Manager
			104615	169168	-/4	-/5	-/7	
WINFILE	HL_	HLP	56961	76855	4/-	3/-	8/-	Help: File Manager
			65124	85793	-/5	-/5	-/10	
WINGDING	FO_	FOT	430	1314	6/7	6/8	9/9	TT Font Resource: WINGDING.TTF
WINGDING	TT_	TTF	52533	71052	6/7	6/6	10/11	TT Font: WingDings
WINHELP	EX_	EXE	163861	256192	1/1	1/2	2/2	Applet: Help Engine
WINHELP	HL_	HLP	20313	26960	3/6	3/8	5/12	Help: Help Engine
WININI	WR_	WRI	9556	31104	3/-	3/-	6/-	Readme File: for WIN.INI
			8559	23168	-/3	-/7	-/8	
WINLOGO	BM_	BMP	12211	38518	4/6	4/8	6/14	Wallpaper: Windows Logo
WINMETER	EX_	EXE	10545	18432	-/6	-/8	-/13	Applet: System Performance Meter
WINMINE	EX_	EXE	13634	27776	3/6	4/8	5/14	Applet: MineSweeper
WINMINE	HL_	HLP	7098	12754	4/7	4/8	6/14	Help: MineSweeper
WINOA386	MO_	MOD	30564	49248	4/5	4/7	7/12	DOS window component, enh. mode
WINOLDAP	MO_	MOD	16879	31232	5/6	5/8	10/14	DOS window component, std. mode
WINPOPUP	EX_	EXE	15453	27344	2/-	2/-	5/-	Applet: LAN Manager network popup
WINPOPUP	HL_	HLP	1289	2476	2/-	3/-	5/-	Help: LAN Manager network popup
WINTUTOR	DA_	DAT	51813	57356	3/5	4/6	5/13	Data File: Tutorial
WINTUTOR	EX_	EXE	66632	124416	3/5	3/5	5/10	Applet: Tutorial

TABLE A.1 *(continued)*

Filename	Extension Comp.	Exp.	File Size Comp.	Exp.	Diskette 1.44	1.2	720	File Description
WINVER	_	EXE	1820	3904	5/-	5/-	7/-	Windows-version utility
			1827	3904	-/7	-/8	-/6	(lacks extension on 1.44 Wrk. diskette)
WORKGRP	SY_	SYS	5538	7268	-/8	-/9	-/17	Wrkgrp real-mode stub, net. redir.
WRITE	EX_	EXE	154980	244976	3/4	3/4	6/7	Applet: Write
WRITE	HL_	HLP	29556	36971	3/5	4/3	6/13	Help: Write
WSWAP	EX_	EXE	11757	16302	5/6	5/8	10/14	Task Swapper: standard mode
XGA	DR_	DRV	55181	139776	1/2	1/2	2/3	Display Driver: XGA
XLAT850	BI_	BIN	440[†]	407	2/2	1/3	3/5	Translation Table: Intl. code page 850
XLAT860	BI_	BIN	412[†]	407	2/2	2/3	4/5	Trans. Tbl: Portuguese: code page 860
XLAT861	BI_	BIN	415[†]	407	2/1	2/3	5/5	Trans. Table: Icelandic: code page 861
XLAT863	BI_	BIN	415[†]	407	2/3	1/3	3/5	Trans. Tbl: French-Can: code page 863
XLAT865	BI_	BIN	410[†]	407	2/1	3/3	4/5	Trans. Tbl: Norwegian, Danish c.p. 865
XMSMMGR	EXE	EXE	14144[‡]	14144	1/1	1/1	1/1	Setup extended memory manager
ZIGZAG	BM_	BMP	210	630	4/7	3/8	6/14	Wallpaper: Zigzag

[*] Windows 3.1 information based on LAYOUTS.WRI file included with *Windows Resource Kit*. That file contains an erroneous column describing 360 Kb diskettes, which do not exist. Workgroups information collated from distribution diskettes. Versions listed separately if file size varies. Diskette number format:

    a/b   Windows/Workgroups diskette number.

    -/b   Not supplied with Windows 3.1

    a/-   Not supplied with Windows-for-Workgroups.

[†] Note that these file sizes decrease (see *File Size Comparisons* in Chapter 4).

[‡] These files are not compressed.

[§] Defective version of MMTLHI.DRV. See *Cannot Load MMTLHI.DRV* error message in Chapter 2.

Abbreviations:

    PCM   Printer Cartridge Metric (*not* Pulse Code Modulation)

    PS   PostScript

    TT   TrueType

    VDD   Virtual Device Driver

    (*xx*)   number of fonts supported

Windows Directory Listings

Table B.1 compares the contents of three Windows directories. The first example shows the contents of a typical version 3.0 Windows directory, and the second example shows the effect of a minimum upgrade to version 3.1. The final example is of a full Windows 3.1 installation.

Table B.2 shows the contents of the System directory in Windows versions 3.0 and 3.1.

Both tables are intended as guidelines only. Your own Windows and System directory listings will no doubt be different, based on installed video system, printer, network, etc.

TABLE B.1 Typical Listings in Windows Directory

Filename	Ext.	3.0 Installation		3.0-3.1 Upgrade		3.1 Full Installation		Notes
		Size	Date	Size	Date	Size	Date	
256COLOR	BMP					5078	03-10-92	1
3270	TXT	9058	10-31-90					2
ACCESSOR	GRP	7159	11-25-91	6459	06-10-92	9447	06-12-92	3, 4, 5
APPLICAT	GRP							5
APPS	HLP					15694	03-10-92	1
ARCADE	BMP					630	03-10-92	1
ARCHES	BMP					10358	03-10-92	1
ARGYLE	BMP					630	03-10-92	1
BOOTLOG	TXT			1181	06-10-92	1181	06-12-92	3, 4
BOXES	BMP	630	10-31-90	630	10-31-90			6
CALC	EXE	40480	10-31-90	40480	10-31-90	43072	03-10-92	7
CALC	HLP	22506	10-31-90	22506	10-31-90	18076	03-10-92	7
CALENDAR	EXE	64352	10-31-90	64352	10-31-90	59824	03-10-92	7
CALENDAR	HLP	33214	10-31-90	33214	10-31-90	20656	03-10-92	7
CANYON	MID					33883	03-10-92	1
CARDFILE	EXE	53952	10-31-90	53952	10-31-90	93184	03-10-92	7
CARDFILE	HLP	31569	10-31-90	31569	10-31-90	24810	03-10-92	7
CARS	BMP					630	03-10-92	1
CASTLE	BMP					778	03-10-92	1
CHARMAP	EXE					22016	03-10-92	1
CHARMAP	HLP					10797	03-10-92	1
CHESS	BMP	153718	10-31-90	153718	10-31-90			6
CHIMES	WAV					15920	03-10-92	1
CHITZ	BMP					19918	03-10-92	1
CHORD	WAV					24982	03-10-92	1
CLIPBRD	EXE	20512	10-31-90	18512	03-10-92	18512	03-10-92	3
CLIPBRD	HLP	15940	10-31-90	15940	10-31-90	13071	03-10-92	7
CLOCK	EXE	11136	10-31-90	11136	10-31-90	16416	03-10-92	7
CONTROL	EXE	161824	10-31-90	15872	03-10-92	15872	03-10-92	3
CONTROL	HLP	70459	10-31-90	121672	03-10-92	121672	03-10-92	3
CONTROL	INI	1578	10-31-90	3694	06-10-92	3609	03-10-92	3, 4
DEFAULT	PIF	545	11-25-91	545	06-10-92	545	06-12-92	3, 4, 8
DIGITAL	FON	1712	10-31-90	1712	10-31-90			6
DING	WAV					11598	03-10-92	1
DOSPRMPT	PIF			545	06-10-92	545	06-12-92	3, 4, 8
DRWATSON	EXE					26864	03-10-92	1
EGYPT	BMP					630	03-10-92	1
EMM386	EXE			110174	03-10-92	110174	03-10-92	3, 4

TABLE B.1 *(continued)*

Filename	Ext.	3.0 Installation		3.0-3.1 Upgrade		3.1 Full Installation		Notes
		Size	Date	Size	Date	Size	Date	
EMM386	SYS	60994	10-31-90	60994	10-31-90			6
EXPAND	EXE					15285	03-10-92	1
FLOCK	BMP					1630	03-10-92	1
GAMES	GRP	1482	11-25-91	1482	11-25-91	1480	06-12-92	3, 4, 5
GLOSSARY	HLP					46570	03-10-92	1
HIMEM	SYS			13824	03-10-92	13824	03-10-92	3, 4
HONEY	BMP					854	03-10-92	1
LEAVES	BMP					15118	03-10-92	1
MAIN	GRP	5064	11-25-91	5071	06-10-92	5822	06-12-92	3, 4, 5
MARBLE	BMP					27646	03-10-92	1
MORICONS	DLL			118864	03-10-92	118864	03-10-92	3
MOUSE	INI					28	06-12-92	1
MPLAYER	EXE					33312	03-10-92	1
MPLAYER	HLP					12896	03-10-92	1
MSD	EXE			155538	03-10-92	155538	03-10-92	3
MSD	INI			620	03-10-92	620	03-10-92	3
MSDOS	EXE	46640	10-31-90	46640	10-31-90			6
NETWORKS	TXT	30665	10-31-90					2
NETWORKS	WRI					68096	03-10-92	1
NOTEPAD	EXE	31936	10-31-90	31936	10-31-90	32736	03-10-92	7
NOTEPAD	HLP	26169	10-31-90	26169	10-31-90	13894	03-10-92	7
PACKAGER	EXE					76480	03-10-92	1
PACKAGER	HLP					21156	03-10-92	1
PAPER	BMP	9662	10-31-90	9662	10-31-90			6
PBRUSH	DLL	7724	10-31-90	7724	10-31-90	6766	03-10-92	7
PBRUSH	EXE	161200	10-31-90	161200	10-31-90	183376	03-10-92	7
PBRUSH	HLP	60122	10-31-90	60122	10-31-90	40269	03-10-92	7
PIFEDIT	EXE	40124	10-31-90	55168	03-10-92	55168	03-10-92	3
PIFEDIT	HLP	43039	10-31-90	43039	10-31-90	33270	03-10-92	7
PRINTERS	TXT	20558	10-31-90					2
PRINTERS	WRI					44928	03-10-92	1
PRINTMAN	EXE	33968	10-31-90	43248	03-10-92	43248	03-10-92	3
PRINTMAN	HLP	23857	10-31-90	23857	10-31-90	40880	03-10-92	7
PROGMAN	EXE	55200	10-31-90	115312	03-10-92	115312	03-10-92	3
PROGMAN	HLP	94692	10-31-90	94692	10-31-90	30911	03-10-92	7
PROGMAN	INI	184	11-25-91	252	06-10-92	205	06-12-92	3, 4
PYRAMID	BMP	630	10-31-90	630	10-31-90			6
RAMDRIVE	SYS	5719	10-31-90	5873	03-10-92	5873	03-10-92	3, 4

TABLE B.1 *(continued)*

Filename	Ext.	3.0 Installation		3.0-3.1 Upgrade		3.1 Full Installation		Notes
		Size	Date	Size	Date	Size	Date	
README	TXT	36320	10-31-90					2
README	WRI					99584	03-10-92	1
RECORDER	DLL	11774	10-31-90	11774	10-31-90	10414	03-10-92	7
RECORDER	EXE	40096	10-31-90	40096	10-31-90	39152	03-10-92	7
RECORDER	HLP	28075	10-31-90	28075	10-31-90	18200	03-10-92	7
REDBRICK	BMP					630	03-10-92	1
REG	DAT			2556	06-10-92	2556	06-12-92	3, 4
REGEDIT	EXE			32336	03-10-92	32336	03-10-92	3
REGEDIT	HLP					22681	03-10-92	1
REGEDITV	HLP					15731	03-10-92	1
REVERSI	EXE	16688	10-31-90	16688	10-31-90			6
REVERSI	HLP	11984	10-31-90	11984	10-31-90			6
RIVETS	BMP					630	03-10-92	1
SCRNSAV	SCR					5328	03-10-92	1
SETUP	EXE	207984	10-31-90	422080	03-10-92	422080	03-10-92	3
SETUP	HLP	71981	10-31-90	41453	03-10-92	41453	03-10-92	3
SETUP	TXT			41724	03-10-92	41724	03-10-92	3
SMARTDRV	EXE			43609	03-10-92	43609	03-10-92	3, 4
SMARTDRV	SYS	7746	10-31-90	7746	10-31-90			6
SOL	EXE	180880	10-31-90	180880	10-31-90	180688	03-10-92	7
SOL	HLP	15388	10-31-90	15388	10-31-90	13753	03-10-92	7
SOUNDREC	EXE					51305	03-10-92	1
SOUNDREC	HLP					17686	03-10-92	1
SPART	PAR			268	06-10-92	268	06-12-92	3, 4
SQUARES	BMP					630	03-10-92	1
SSFLYWIN	SCR					16160	03-10-92	1
SSMARQUE	SCR					16896	03-10-92	1
SSMYST	SCR					19456	03-10-92	1
SSSTARS	SCR					17536	03-10-92	1
STARTUP	GRP			44	06-10-92	44	06-12-92	3, 4, 5
SYSINI	TXT	21573	10-31-90					2
SYSINI	W31			1171	06-10-92			9
SYSINI	WRI					53760	03-10-92	1
SYSINI2	TXT	21991	10-31-90					2
SYSINI3	TXT	27602	10-31-90					2
SYSTEM	INI	1171	11-25-91	1533	06-10-92	1557	03-10-92	3, 4
TADA	WAV					27804	03-10-92	1
TARTAN	BMP					32886	03-10-92	1

TABLE B.1 *(continued)*

| Filename | Ext. | 3.0 Installation | | 3.0-3.1 Upgrade | | 3.1 Full Installation | | Notes |
		Size	Date	Size	Date	Size	Date	
TASKMAN	EXE	3296	10-31-90	3744	03-10-92	3744	03-10-92	3
TERMINAL	EXE	141696	10-31-90	141696	10-31-90	148160	03-10-92	7
TERMINAL	HLP	49954	10-31-90	49954	10-31-90	36279	03-10-92	7
THATCH	BMP					598	03-10-92	1
WEAVE	BMP	190	10-31-90	190	10-31-90			6
WIN	COM	19358	11-25-91	44170	06-10-92	44170	06-12-92	3, 4
WIN	INI	1236	11-25-91	2980	06-10-92	3294	06-12-92	3, 4
WINFILE	EXE	106288	10-31-90	146864	03-10-92	146864	03-10-92	3
WINFILE	HLP	64187	10-31-90	64187	10-31-90	76855	03-10-92	7
WINHELP	EXE	193552	10-31-90	256192	03-10-92	256192	03-10-92	3
WINHELP	HLP	48465	10-31-90	48465	10-31-90	26960	03-10-92	7
WININI	TXT	25099	10-31-90					2
WININI	W31			1236	06-10-92			9
WININI	WRI					31104	03-10-92	1
WININI2	TXT	18466	10-31-90					2
WINLOGO	BMP					38518	03-10-92	1
WINMINE	EXE					27776	03-10-92	1
WINMINE	HLP					12754	03-10-92	1
WINTUTOR	DAT					57356	03-10-92	1
WINTUTOR	EXE					124416	03-10-92	1
WINVER	EXE	8704	10-31-90	3904	03-10-92	3904	03-10-92	3, 4
WRITE	EXE	211168	10-31-90	244976	03-10-92	244976	03-10-92	3
WRITE	HLP	50885	10-31-90	36971	03-10-92	36971	03-10-92	3
ZIGZAG	BMP					630	03-10-92	1

	69 files	75 files	114 files
	3,103,770 bytes	3,734,714 bytes	4,601,185 bytes

1 3.1 file, not installed during minimum upgrade.

2 3.0 file discontinued in 3.1, deleted during upgrade or new installation.

3 3.1 file added during upgrade or new installation. Replaces 3.0 file (if present) during upgrade.

4 3.1 Windows directory on network client system.

5 APPLICAT.GRP presence and size depends on applications found on drive(s). All GRP filesizes vary according to installed color depth. 16-color depth in this Table.

6 3.0 file discontinued in 3.1, but not deleted during upgrade.

7 3.0 file not replaced by available 3.1 equivalent during minimum upgrade.

8 3.1 Additional PIF files depend on DOS applications found on drive(s).

9 3.1 INI file template created during upgrade only.

TABLE B.2 Typical Listings in System Directory*

Filename	Ext.	File Size 3.0	File Size 3.1	Filename	Ext.	File Size 3.0	File Size 3.1
APPS	INF		57475	SERIFE	FON		57936
CGA40WOA	FON	6704	6336	SETUP	INF	42809	59118
CGA80WOA	FON	4672	4304	SETUP	REG		3508
COMM	DRV	7088	9280	SHELL	DLL		41600
COMMDLG	DLL		89248	SMALLE	FON		26112
CONTROL	INF		20993	SND	CPL		8192
COURE	FON	21360	23408	SOUND	DRV	3622	3440
CPWIN386	CPL		104816	SSERIFE	FON		64544
DDEML	DLL		36864	SWAPFILE	EXE	38912	
DOSAPP	FON		36656	SYMBOLE	FON	56912	56336
DOSX	EXE	36496	32682	SYSEDIT	EXE	17344	18896
DRIVERS	CPL		41440	SYSTEM	DRV	2784	2304
DSWAP	EXE		27474	TIMER	DRV		4192
EGA40WOA	FON	8736	8368	TMSRE	FON	53520	
EGA80WOA	FON	5680	5312	TOOLHELP	DLL		14128
GDI	EXE	129691	220800	USER	EXE	231680	264016
HELVE	FON	59696		VER	DLL		9008
KERNEL	EXE	68928		VGA	3GR		16384
KEYBOARD	DRV	7041	7568	VGA	DRV	72144	73200
KRNL286	EXE	59600	71730	VGA	GR3	14848	
KRNL386	EXE	60368	75490	VGACOLOR	2GR		4484
LZEXPAND	DLL	6016	9936	VGACOLOR	GR2	4326	
MAIN	CPL		148560	VGAFIX	FON	5776	5360
MCISEQ	DRV		25264	VGALOGO	LGO	1120	26778
MCIWAVE	DRV		28160	VGALOGO	RLE	14782	1280
MIDIMAP	CFG		34522	VGAOEM	FON	5584	5168
MIDIMAP	DRV		52784	VGASYS	FON	6368	7280
MMSOUND	DRV		3440	VTDAPI	386		5245
MMSYSTEM	DLL		61648	WIN	CNF	3456	16112
MMTASK	TSK		1104	WIN386	EXE	504440	544789
MODERN	FON	9728	8704	WIN386	PS2	582	852
MOUSE	DRV	4896	10672	WIN87EM	DLL	12800	12800
OLECLI	DLL		83456	WINOA286	MOD	41520	
OLESVR	DLL		24064	WINOA386	MOD	29520	49248
ROMAN	FON	14336	13312	WINOLDAP	MOD	41904	31232
SCRIPT	FON	13312	12288	WSWAP	EXE		16302
				41 3.0 files		1,731,101	
				65 3.1 files			2,908,696

* TrueType fonts (TTF and FOT) not included in listing.

C

Error Message Finder

The context in which an error message appears is often a sufficient indicator of the general nature of the problem, and therefore of the chapter in this book where the error message may be found. However, if the message is ambiguous, or seems to have nothing to do with the actual problem, then it may not be immediately clear where to turn for help. In this case, try your luck right here. Find the error message (or a reasonable variation on it) in this list, then consult the chapter, or chapters, in which that message is described.

The messages listed here are often abbreviated, especially those that ramble on for several sentences. Nevertheless, the fragment seen here should be sufficient to track down the appropriate chapter. The general subject of each chapter is summarized here; this may be a help in deciding where to search first.

Chapter	Subject	Chapter	Subject
0	DOS 6.0	7	DOS Applications
1	Setup Procedures	8	Clipboard and Clipbook
2	Startup and Exit Troubleshooting	9	Printer and Port Configuration
3	Desktop	10	Fonts
4	General Troubleshooting	11	Control Panel
5	StartUp Group Window	12	Control Panel (Drivers, Multimedia)
6	File Manager	13	Memory

Error Message	Chapter
Access denied.	6
Access has been denied.	9
Action cannot be completed because . . .	8
Annotations damaged.	4
Anti-Virus warning.	0
Application . . .	
attempted to access device being used . . .	7
has insufficient memory for its display.	7
requested abnormal termination.	5
running in exclusive mode because of . . .	7
still active.	7
violated system integrity.	4
was communicating on the network.	6
was unable to access the video display.	7
(*Application name*) is already running.	12
Back Fill: Unable to start Enhanced Mode Windows.	13
Backup has not been configured.	0
Bad command or filename.	2
Bookmarks are damaged.	4
Call to undefined Dynalink.	2, 3, 4
Can run only one copy of Setup at a time.	1
Cannot . . .	
access this file.	0, 6
copy (*filename.ext*): Access denied.	6
delete (*filename.ext*): Access denied.	6
display. Data is in binary format.	8
execute *filename.ext*.	7
Cannot find . . .	
any icons in this file.	3
Database (*or anything else*).	12
Cannot find file . . .	
. . .messages.	2, 6

Error Message	Chapter
Cannot find file . . . *(continued)*	
Check to ensure path and filename are correct.	7
(*name or description*) file.	4
needed to run in 386 enhanced mode.	2
filename.ext.	1, 4
filename.ext (or one of its components).	4, 7
filename.ext needed to run in standard mode.	2
needed to run Windows in standard mode.	2
NETWORK.DRV.	11
(*path and name*) specified in (*location*).	11
UNIDRV.DLL.	9
WIN386.EXE needed to run in 386 enhanced mode.	2
WINOA386.MOD.	7
WINOLDAP.GRB, WINOLDAP.MOD.	7
Cannot load . . .	
COMMAND.COM, system halted.	2
(*driver description*) driver.	12
file *filename.ext.*	1
MMTLHI.DRV.	2
Cannot move (*filename.ext*).	6
Cannot open Help file.	4
Cannot open program-group file.	2
Cannot operate on file.	6
Cannot play the selected sound. Make sure . . .	12
Cannot print file.	6
Cannot print. Be sure that the printer is connected . . .	9
Cannot read . . .	
drive *x:*. Please verify the drive door is closed.	12
file SETUP.INF.	1
from drive *X*.	12
from drive *X*. (*Kodak Photo CD.*)	12
from drive *X* (*when attempting a Paste operation*).	8

Error Message	Chapter
Cannot reconnect *x* : to (*remote computer*) because . . .	11
Cannot run . . .	
in 386 enhanced mode.	2
non-Windows application from the second instance . . .	7
Program: File Manager cannot open or print file.	6
Program: There is no application associated with file.	6
Windows because of Video Device Conflict.	2
Windows in 386 enhanced mode with . . .	2
Windows in standard mode.	2
Cannot share drives.	12
Cannot start Windows in standard mode.	2
Cannot switch to a full screen.	7
Cannot unload. UNDELETE is not the last resident program.	0
Changes have been written to your MOUSE.INI file.	11
CHARMAP—An error has occurred in your application.	10
CHARMAP caused a General Protection Fault in module . . .	10
Check this box only if you have the following . . .	10
Clipboard information is not available in this format.	8
ClipBook Viewer cannot currently access the information.	8
Closing Print Manager will cancel all pending print jobs.	9
Closing the selected file may cause the user to lose data.	6
Closing this application may not allow MS-DOS TSRs to . . .	0
Compatibility test for floppy disks . . .	0
Compression header for catalog is corrupt.	0
Computer . . .	
does not have enough space to install programs.	0
name or share name is invalid.	9
name specified in network path cannot be located.	9
uses a disk-compression program.	0
uses SuperStor disk compression.	0
Configuration or hardware problem has occurred.	12
Connection could not be established to . . .	8

Error Message	Chapter
Connection has not been restored.	6
Contact Beta support.	2
Continuing (*log-off*) will cancel these operations.	6
Control caused General Protection Fault in MAIN.CPL.	11
Control Panel cannot . . .	
display International dialog box.	11
perform current operation.	9
Conventional memory in your system is fragmented.	13
Corrupt permanent swap file found on drive *x*.	13
Could not locate driver WORKGRP.SYS (MS-DOS error 2).	6
Current Sound Device cannot be used.	12
Currently installed (*filename.ext*) is newer.	1
Data is in binary format.	8
Device . . .	
cannot play.	12
Conflict on LPT*x*.	11
file specified in SYSTEM.INI file is corrupt.	2
specified in SYSTEM.INI conflicts with (*another*) device.	2
specified more than once in SYSTEM.INI.	2
Directory does not exist. Do you want to create it?	6
Disk error.	6
Display driver cannot display information . . .	8
Divide by 0 (*not zero*).	1
Divide by zero.	4
Do you want to quit printing the document?	9
Document is a copy of file that was being edited . . .	6
DOS Version is Incorrect or Unsupported.	2
Drive . . .	
cannot be updated.	9
I does not exist.	6
is not compressed.	6
was not logged.	0

Error Message	Chapter
Duplicated device:.	2
Dynalink call, undefined.	2, 3
Equation Editor (*any*).	10
Error . . .	
2: The specified file was not found.	2, 8
3: The specified file was not found.	11
#11.	7
#109.	0
3653: The protocol manager could not be found.	6
6101.	11
6111.	6
#10002: Error Soundex.IDX (*Compton Multimedia Ency.*).	12
#S020.	1
decompressing file.	4
has occurred in your application.	7, 8
has occurred. Clipbook Viewer cannot complete . . .	8
Error loading . . .	
filename (*no extension listed*).	2
GDI.EXE.	2
MMTLHI.DRV.	2
PROGMAN.EXE.	2
SYSTEM.DRV.	2
USER.EXE.	2
Error message of unknown origin.	4
Error occurred . . .	
reading drive *x:*.	6
while reconnecting.	6
while reconnecting LPT*x:*.	9
while reconnecting LPT*x*: to (*computer name*).	11
while trying to share . . .	6
while trying to unlock the password-file list.	2
Error printing on (*printer name*).	9

Error Message	**Chapter**
Error . . .	
reading (or writing to) drive *N*.	4
reading backup directory.	4
reading from Drive *X*.	7
Error. This is not the correct disk.	0
Exception Error #*nn* @ (*code segment:instruction pointer*).	2
Exception Error 12.	4
Executable not found.	2
Extremely low on memory.	7
Fault in MS-DOS Extender.	1
Fault outside of MS-DOS Extender.	2
File . . .	
is in use.	6
is not a Windows Help file.	4
is read-only. Use a different filename.	6
name is not valid.	6
progman.ini is write-protected.	3
server encountered a critical error and terminated.	11
File Manager cannot . . .	
[copy *or* move] (*path and directory name*).	6
find the specified path.	6
open or print the specified file.	6
print multiple files.	9
Filename was not found, is corrupt.	2
Filename.ext is write-protected.	2
Font and Style not available.	10
Font (*name*) is compressed and cannot be installed.	10
General hardware failure *xx* (*during Backup*).	4
General network error has occurred.	9
General Protection Fault . . .	
CLIPBOOK, CLIPBRD.	8
General Protection Fault (*any*).	4

Error Message	**Chapter**
General Protection Fault . . . *(continued)*	
paste operation.	8
WIN87EM.DLL.	11
Help. . .	
application corrupt.	4
not available.	4
Text file not found.	4
topic does not exist.	4
unavailable while printers are being set up, [*or*] . . .	4
HP LaserJet 4/4M is not set as default printer.	9
If you stop sharing (*directory*), the files will close.	6
Incorrect system version.	7
Information is in a binary format.	8
Input file already in expanded format.	4
Installed A20 handler number *xx.*	13
Insufficient . . .	
conventional memory to run . . .	13
extended memory available.	13
Insufficient disk space . . .	
for temporary file.	4
on drive *X.* Desired disk space: *xxx* K.	7
Insufficient memory . . .	
for application requested, for required space.	7
for application's required EMS [*or* XMS] memory.	7
for address space.	13
to perform this operation.	3
to run application.	7, 13
Intel 80286, 80386, 80486 processor.	1
Internal system error.	13
Interrupt setting does not match those on the card.	12
Invalid . . .	
COMMAND.COM.	2

Error Message	Chapter
Invalid . . . *(continued)*	
DMA channel specified.	4
HIMEM.SYS.	13
IRQ, I/O port address specified.	4
parameter specified.	13
Path: There is no association for *path\filename.ext.*	6
volume information block detected.	0
VxD dynamic link call.	2
Item (*applet description*) is using the same shortcut key.	3
Jobs waiting in this queue.	9
KB Required value is too large. Decrease PIF KB Required.	7
KRNL386: Unable to enter Protected Mode, to load . . .	2
LOADHI: An invalid region was specified.	13
LPT*x* (*any*).	9
Make sure your computer has an Intel 80286, 80386, . . .	1
MCI device does not support specified command.	12
Memory error message . . .	13
after installing Logitech mouse software.	11
during Clipboard operations.	8
during Setup.	1
Message number: If you are installing Windows, . . .	1
Microsoft Anti-Virus warning.	0
Microsoft Mouse not found.	11
MIDI Mapper (*any*).	12
Missing HIMEM.SYS.	13
Mouse, Mouse driver (*any*).	11
Movie is still playing!	12
MS-DOS Path has not been specified.	0
MSAVIRUS.LST not found.	0
Multimedia timers are being used by other applications.	12
Multimedia Viewer.	12
Music example could not be played (*Multimedia Beethoven*).	12

Error Message	**Chapter**
Network . . .	
drive is not available.	6
error has occurred.	9
functionality will not be available.	6
jobs waiting to print.	9
No . . .	
application associated with specified file.	7
deleted files found.	0
fonts found.	10
header in file (file might not be compressed).	4
MIDI devices installed on the system.	12
mixer device drivers are available.	12
network printers currently connected.	9
wave device that can play files in the current format . . .	12
Not able to open this file.	6
Not enough disk space to print.	9
Not enough memory . . .	
(*see* Table 13.7).	7, 13
available to perform this operation.	4
for this task.	11
to convert all the program icons.	3
to load *filename* high. Packed file is corrupt.	13
Not possible to send PRINT field data to the printer.	9
Not ready reading drive C.	4
Number you specified is too large.	13
One of the libraries needed to run this application . . .	7
Operation cannot be performed to your own computer.	6
Out of . . .	
environment space.	2
memory.	13
memory (*Microsoft Bookshelf*).	12
Packed file is corrupt.	4

Error Message	Chapter
Parity error.	13
Password: If you change the password, . . .	6
Path (*drive, path, and filename.ext*) is invalid.	3
Path specified in the *group name* group is invalid.	2
Permanent swap file . . .	
is corrupt.	0, 13
cannot be created.	13
has been found.	13
Please make sure the (*application name*) CD is in *X:*.	12
Port setting does not match those on the card.	12
Port settings may not match those required by your printer.	9
Port with jobs queued was removed.	9
Previously created swap file has been found.	13
Privileged operation exception.	13
Program cannot be swapped out to disk.	13
Print Manager (*any*).	9
Print queue does not exist.	9
Printer . . .	
is stalled.	9
(*name*) on LPT*x* is shared as . . .	9
on this port is not responding, out of paper, . . .	9
specified share name cannot be found.	9
Problem . . .	
drawing or printing object.	8
with disk drive *x*.	1
with media device.	12
with Object/Link.	6, 8
Program . . .	
cannot be swapped out to disk.	7
is needed to run files with extension '*EXT*.'	6
not found. Cannot find *filename*.exe.	6
or one of its components is compressed.	4

Error Message	Chapter
Program-group file is invalid, damaged, write-protected.	2
Protocol Manager could not be found.	6
Protocol Manager: Error 3653: The protocol manager . . .	6
Read-only file.	1
Real-mode error messages.	2
Root directory of your hard disk contains some . . .	0
Serious disk error occurred while writing to drive *x*.	0
Serious disk error on file *filename.ext*.	4
Setup error #S020.	1
Setup messages (*any*).	1
Shared directory cannot be found.	6
Smart Drive (*any*).	13
Sound Recorder cannot record or play back because . . .	12
Source and destination drives are incompatible.	6
Specified . . .	
device is not open or is not recognized by MCI.	12
drive letter is invalid.	6
file cannot be played on specified MCI device.	12
MIDI device is already in use.	12
path points to a file that may not be available later.	4
path points to a file that may not be available.	12
share name cannot be found. [SYS0067].	6
Stack fault.	4
Stack overflow.	1, 4
Standard Mode: Windows for Workgroups network . . .	6
Startup application error. Application requested abnormal . . .	5
Symbol font is not available on the default printer.	10
[SYS0067]. Specified share name cannot be found.	6
System does not have enough disk space . . .	1
System integrity violation.	4
SYSTEM.INI file is unusually large (above 32K).	1
Temporary file created by Print Manager corrupted.	9

Error Message	Chapter
There are . . .	
x file(s) open by users connected to (*directory*).	6
x user(s) connected to (*directory*).	6
x users connected to (*printer name*).	9
There does not exist a mixing device.	12
There is currently no printer connected to LPT*x*.	9
There is not enough free space on drive C to install DOS.	0
This (*driver name*) driver is required by the system.	12
To set orientation for your mouse properly, . . .	11
Track 0 bad.	4
Tried to show movie.	12
TrueType system was disabled.	10
Unable to . . .	
access Pointer options.	11
allocate extended memory.	13
copy disk.	6
enter protected mode.	2
load KRNL386.EXE.	2
show Help information.	4
Unable to start . . .	
enhanced mode Windows.	0
enhanced mode Windows due to base memory back fill.	13
Help, Windows help system.	4
Undefined Dynalink call.	2, 3, 4
Undetectable problem in loading specified device driver.	12
Unexpected MS-DOS error #11.	7
Unknown compression algorithm.	4
Unrecognized error #109.	0
Unrecoverable disk error on file *filename.ext*.	4
Unrecoverable error on *filename.ext*.	6
Version conflict.	1
Version of Help file not supported.	4

Error Message	Chapter
Video device conflict . . .	13
(with Qualitas *386MAX*).	2
VNETSUP: Network features are not available because . . .	11
VNETSUP: The following error occurred while loading . . .	11
Volume in drive C is HOST_FOR_C.	0
VSafe error message (*any*).	0
Waiting for system shutdown.	13
Warning: . . .	
Unable to use a disk cache on specified drive.	13
Use Terminate button only as a last resort.	7
Wassily Kandinsky was a great painter.	1
WINA20.386: You must have the file in the root . . .	4
WINA20.386: You must have WINA20.386 in the root . . .	2
Windows . . .	
3.1 could not be located on your computer.	1
cannot set up an upper memory block at segment *xxxx*.	13
does not run with this version of MS-DOS.	1
for Workgroups network driver was not loaded.	11
may not run correctly with the 80386 processor . . .	2
will not run in real mode.	2
will not use more than the virtual memory specified by . . .	13
WINOLDAP caused a page fault.	7
Working directory is invalid.	2
You are . . .	
already sharing the directory . . .	6
already using Control Panel, Print Manager.	9
attempting to run Setup from within Windows.	1
attempting to set up Windows 3.1 from OS/2 DOS session.	1
not logged on.	6
running the MS-DOS Shell.	0
sharing the directory . . .	6
still not logged on.	6

Error Message   **Chapter**

You are . . . *(continued)*

   using an expanded memory manager.   13

You attempted to install Windows with 8086, 88 . . .   1

You can . . .

   only share resources on your computer.   6, 9

   only upgrade from version 3.0.   1

   run this application only on a full screen.   7

You cannot . . .

   access any DoubleSpace compressed drives.   0

   connect the selected port to a shared printer.   9

   delete setup (*setup name*) because it is currently in use.   12

   run this application in a window or in the background.   7

   run this application while other high-resolution . . .   7

You have . . .

   a saved connection on *x:* to . . .   6

   inserted a *xxx* KB diskette.   0

You must have . . .

   431K of conventional memory free to install MS-DOS 6.   0

   WINA20.386 in the root directory.   2, 4, 13

You need an Intel 80386 processor to run Windows . . .   2

You started workgroup software for DOS before Windows.   6

You will not be able to change any settings because . . .   12

D ▼ ▼ ▼

Getting More Help

On the off-chance this little tome hasn't told you everything you ever wanted to know about everything, this Appendix offers some suggestions for getting extra help when you need it. Several help services are briefly described, beginning with the most obvious and often most frustrating one.

Call Tech Support

Sooner or later we all try calling the company to see if anyone there knows how to get their star product to actually work as advertised. Although details vary from one company to another, the general procedure is as follows:

Dial the Tech Support number (if you can find one) and listen to an interminable series of "press this/press that" announcements choreographed by someone who either doesn't like you, or is—to be politically correct—communicationally challenged. Eventually, you may work your way up (more likely, down) through the labyrinth to the right sub-basement. Here, the audio portion of your encounter begins with the cheery news that "to ensure quality service, your call may be monitored" (but never by anyone who knows what "ensure quality service" really means). Now it's time to settle back, relax, and listen to the audio equivalent of a wallpaper bitmap. After spending a significant part of your life expectancy and phone bill, a quasihuman voice picks up and, if you haven't forgotten why you called by now, does his/her/its best to make you very sorry you did.

So much for the good news. The bad news is that your problem couldn't possibly be caused by the manufacturer's software or hardware. No doubt there is something else in the computer that prevents the whatever-it-is from delivering the flawless performance that you and you alone seem incapable of realizing. Either that, or you're just not clever enough to understand the product.

Since this little essay appears in a Windows book, readers may suspect the above is a reasonable description of the Microsoft Technical Support Service. Fortunately, it is not. In fact, Microsoft phone support varies from good to excellent. The obligatory opening recording could be better organized, since the default assumption is that you called tech support when you really wanted somebody else, and you *must* listen to alternative routing instructions before you can get down to serious button pressing. After that, be prepared (in most cases) to punch in your product serial number, which is either printed on the inside back cover of the Windows *Getting Started* manual, or in the case of other applications, displayed on the application's About... screen. This brings up the usual musical interlude, but here we have programming with a difference. It's presided over by an actual human being, who lets you know how many people are waiting in each holding queue and how long you can expect to dangle there.

If you do decide to call, more often than not you'll reach a responsive support technician within a few minutes. However, Microsoft techies have their good days and their bad days, just like everyone else—except authors. If you reach someone who in your judgment isn't doing much to help, you can get nasty—or just be polite, hang up, and try again later. Microsoft employs more than 1000 people on its help lines, so the odds on getting the same person are remote. By the way, don't try any of this immediately after a new product is introduced, for at such times, the phone lines go into overload mode for several weeks. At other times, try one of the phone numbers listed in Table D.1.

Tech Support at other companies is sometimes better than at Microsoft, but often much worse, as was discovered again and again in preparing this opus. Conspicuous among the best were, in alphabetical order: Computer Associates, Dell, Grolier, Kodak, PC Connection, Truevision, and several others. Conspicuous among the less-than-best were some others who are not mentioned here, since most have attorneys looking for some means to justify their fees—or perhaps even to raise them.

Tech Support via Modem

An accumulating body of evidence suggests that a single area of the brain handles two basic functions: computer design and communication skill. According to theory, as more space is allocated to the former, less is available for the latter. It follows, therefore, that anyone capable of designing and implementing a sophisticated piece of computer hardware or software will be genetically incapable of mastering the telephone. Clearly, such people must be protected from contact with the rest of us, and voice mail was especially designed for this purpose. To verify that the system is configured according to design, just call anyone about anything. If the system works properly, you'll get a message saying that "I'm either on the phone or away from my desk." Thus, the theory is proved: The brain that designed the latest high-tech wonder isn't quite sure where it is at the moment. Record a message if you like, but you can be reasonably sure it won't be understood.

Fortunately, there is a workaround. Just have your modem call their modem and leave a message as an ASCII text file. Chances are, you'll get an answer—if not instantly, then at least within a day or two. For example, many otherwise phone-shy software and hardware manufacturers are well represented on CompuServe, either in a dedicated forum or within a section of a multivendor forum. In most cases, each such forum also supports a library of files containing often-requested information such as text files, updated drivers, or general utility programs. The following sections briefly review CompuServe itself, and the use of its forums and libraries as sources of technical support.

CompuServe

CompuServe describes itself as "the world's largest informational resource service." Among its many resources is an extensive electronic network of support services for the computer user in search of assistance with just about any aspect of computers and computing—including Windows, of course.

This section briefly reviews a few CompuServe services that may be helpful for general Windows configuration problems. It's assumed here that the reader has already heard of CompuServe, and may in fact be a subscriber. If you need additional information about CompuServe itself, it's available at:

```
CompuServe International    (800)848-8990
P. O. Box 20212            (614)457-8650
Columbus, OH 43220
```

The Forums

One of the advantages of subscribing to, and using, CompuServe for Tech Support is that you reach not one, but many experts—sometimes hundreds of them. Using Microsoft as one example, the company supports multiple forums, each presided over by several Microsoft employees, who do their best to answer the questions. But the real power of the forum is the large audience of forum regulars who are interested enough in the topic to log on regularly, perhaps several times a week or even daily. Their expertise ranges from beginning level to expert, and it's difficult to come up with a problem that one of them hasn't already encountered, or better yet, solved.

To improve your odds, be very specific. If you clearly describe your problem, and stifle your personal observation that the company is obviously staffed by Neanderthals, you'll probably get an answer shortly. In fact, you may get several if others on the forum have already been down the same street that you describe.

Tables D.2 – D.5 list some of the forums that may be of use to the Windows user in search of an answer to a configuration problem. To access any forum, just type GO *xxxxxx* at the CompuServe prompt, where *xxxxxx* is the first six letters of the forum name. Then join the forum and follow the on-screen prompts for reading and/or composing messages.

Libraries

Most forum sections maintain a library of files related to the forum subject. You can browse the libraries for a list and description of available files, or perhaps one of the forum regulars will suggest a specific file that will be of interest. In addition, there are a few special-purpose libraries, such as the two described here.

The Microsoft Windows Driver Library (GO MSL).   This is a database of device drivers for printers, displays, audio devices, and network card adapters. It also contains some other software, such as the *Access Pack* and a Novell *NetWare* upgrade.

The database is periodically updated, and its complete contents are cataloged in a WDL.TXT text file which may be downloaded for review. If you're not sure of the file you need, then download WDL.TXT and examine its contents. When you find the file you want, log back onto CompuServe, go to the Library, and download it as *filename*.EXE. Note that every filename is six characters or less, and must be expanded after downloading, to extract the file(s) contained within it.

TABLE D.1   Microsoft Technical Support Phone Numbers*

Product	Phone	Product	Phone	Product	Phone
Access	635-7050	Languages	637-7096	Project	635-7155
Ballpoint	635-7040	Macro Assembler	646-5109	Publisher	635-7140
BASIC PDS†	635-7053	Mail	637-9307	Quick	635-7010
Bookshelf	454-2030	Money	637-7131	Sound System	635-7040
C, C++	635-7007	Mouse	635-7040	Test	635-7052
Cobol	637-7096	Multimedia	635-7172	Video	635-7172
Entertainment	637-9308	Pascal	637-7096	Windows	635-7098
Excel	635-7070	PowerPoint	635-7145	Word	462-9673
FORTRAN	635-7015	Profiler	635-7015	Works	635-7130

Other	454-2030 (for products not listed above)		

Startup/Installation Support

BASIC PDS †	635-7053	Quick BASIC	646-5101
Entertainment Pack	637-9308	SDK	635-3329
LAN Manager	635-7020 (first 30 days)	SQL Server	637-7095 (first 30 days)
Mail Gateways	635-7242 (first 30 days)	Visual BASIC	646-5105
MS-DOS	646-5104 (first 90 days)		

Fast Tips (automated answers to frequently-asked questions)‡

Access	635-7051	Visual BASIC	646-5107
Excel	635-7071	Windows	635-7245
Fox products	635-7190	Word	635-7231
MS-DOS	646-5103	Workgroups	635-7245
Project	635-7156		

Fee-Based Support	$2/Minute	Credit Card	Cost per Call
BASIC (all)	(900)896-9999	(206)646-5106	$20.00
MS-DOS	(900)555-2000	(206)646-5108	$25.00
Network, SQL Server	— —	(206)635-7022	$175.00
Visual BASIC	(900)896-9876		

*Service available Monday-Friday, 6:00AM–6:00PM Pacific time. Unless otherwise noted, area code is 206.

†PDS: Professional Development System.

‡Available 24-hours, daily.

TABLE D.2   Microsoft Windows Forums on CompuServe*

Forum Name and Section	Forum Name and Section	Forum Name and Section	Forum Name and Section	Section Number
Windows	**Workgroups**	**Shareware**	**Fun**	
GO MSWIN	**GO MSWRKGRP**	**GO WINSHARE**	**GO WINFUN**	
Non-Technical Service	Non-Technical Serv.	General Interest	General Interest	1
Setup	Setup	File Utilities	Card Games	2
Mouse	Connectivity	Communication	Other Gms, Fun	3
Video/Display	Shared Resources	Memory	Screen-Savers	4
Std., Enhanced Modes	Workgroup Conn.	Networks	Sounds	5
Swapfile/32-bit Access	Accessories	General Utilities	—	6
Memory	File Manager	Font Utilities	Icons	7
Smart Drive	—	Disk Utilities	—	8
Program, File Manager	—	Program Managers	Btmps, Graph.	9
Accessories, OLE	—	Gen. Win Apps	—	10
DOS Applications	—	Business, Finance	AVI	11
Printing, Fonts	MS Mail for PC	PIM, Info. Utilities	—	12
Multimedia	—	—	—	13
Communications	MS Main for Mac	—	—	14
Networks	MS Schedule+	—	—	15
—	MS Eforms	—	—	16
—	MAPI	—	—	17

*Type GO *forum name* at the CIS prompt. Only the first six letters of the forum name are required.

Once you have downloaded the correct file, place it on a diskette, a RAM drive, or some other temporary location. Do *not* place the EXE file in your Windows directory. At the DOS prompt, type *filename*.EXE and press the Enter key. This will produce one or more additional files in the directory, including the driver you require, supplemental files (if any), and perhaps a README file. If the latter exists, it contains information that may help you make proper use of the other files. Once the expanded files are available, copy the ones you need into your Windows or System directory, as appropriate. You may want to store the original compressed file somewhere else for safekeeping, just in case you need the same data again later on.

A recent list of printer drivers in the Library is given as Table 9.5 in Chapter 9. If you already use one of these files, compare its date against that listed in the table. If your own file predates the Library file, you may want to download the newer version to take advantage of the latest upgrades.

TABLE D.3   Microsoft Windows Forums on CompuServe*

Forum Name and Section	Forum Name and Section	Forum Name and Section	Forum Name and Section	Section Number
DOS	**Applications**	**Excel**	**Word**	
GO MSDOS	**GO MSAPP**	**GO MSEXCEL**	**GO MSWORD**	
Non-Technical Serv.	General Info.	General Info.	Non-Tech. Serv.	1
Setup & Install	PowerPoint	Excel for the Mac	—	2
Hardware	Video for Windows	Excel for the PC	Suggestions	3
Compatibility	Win Sound System	Excel for PM	Windows Supp.	4
Networks	Works for the Mac	—	Mac Support	5
Commands, Utilities	—	—	DOS Support	6
DOS Shell	Windows Project	—	OS/2 Support	7
BASIC Conversions	Project for the Mac	—	—	8
Shareware	Works for the PC	—	—	9
Developer's Exchange	Works for Windows	—	—	10
DoubleSpace	Mouse, Paintbrush	—	—	11
Memory	—	—	Project Wktbl.	12
Unmonitored Chat	Publisher	Desktop III	Windows: Word	13
Stacker Conversion	Non-Technical Serv.	Non-Technical Serv.	Mac: Word	14
—	Flight Simulator	—	DOS: Word	15
—	MS Multimedia	—	OS/2: Word	16
—	Money	EIS Pak		17

*Type GO *forum name* at the CIS prompt. Only the first six letters of the forum name are required.

The IBM File Finder (GO IBMFF). There are so many CompuServe forums supporting IBM-compatible hardware and software, that sometimes it's difficult to find just the right one for the assistance you need. Consider the following scenario: Your usual quasi-reliable computer expert has told you of some "speaker software" that can be installed on a system that lacks a sound card, in order to play waveform audio over the PC speaker. Naturally, your expert doesn't recall the name of the file, the forum in

TABLE D.4 Third-Party Forums on CompuServe*

Forum Name and Section	Forum Name and Section	Forum Name and Section	Forum Name and Section	Section Number
CD-ROM	**MIDI Forum**	**Multimedia**	**WUGNET**	
GO CDROM	**GO MIDIFORUM**	**GO MULTIMEDIA**	**GO WUGNET**	
General Information	General Information	General Information	Windows Advisor	1
Titles	Synths/Samplers/FX	Video and Audio	New Products	2
Macinntosh	New to MIDI	Animation	Application Support	3
DOS/Windows/OS-2	Atari ST	Interface Design	System Configuration	4
Networking	Macintosh	Macintosh/Apple II	Connectivity	5
Stand-alone platforms	Amiga	Windows/DOS/OS-2	Programming Appls.	6
Drives/hardware	MS-DOS/IBM compat.	Amiga	System Development	7
CD-ROM production	Preowned equipment	Other platforms	Industry Trends	8
Industry news	Composing/Editing	Education/training	Electron Pub/Mmed.	9
Marketplace	Recording/Audio	Sales/marketing	Windows NT	10
TBA	Windows Media Sound	Hypertext/Documents	User Group Support	11
Nautilus	MIDI controllers	Science/Engineering	WinCIS	12
Standards	Music discussions	Entertainment	Third-Party Drivers	13
OPA	Guitar/Drum/Acoust	Legal issues	Client/Server	14
—	Sound Cards	Marketing your work	Vendor of the Month	15
—	Video Sound	Producer directory	Doc It	16
—	Jam Session	CD-Interactive	—	17

*Type GO *forum name* at the CIS prompt. Only the first six letters of the forum name are required.

which it is located, or any other scrap of useful information. This is not a farfetched account: There are regular postings on just about every CompuServe forum in which a participant describes a file (without giving its name, of course) and remarks that it's in "one of the libraries." Or if the filename is given, it's identified as say, SPEAKER.DRV, which could not possibly exist in a library, since such files *must* have a filename of six characters or less.

There is a very simple solution to such problems: Give up. Or, if you're persistent, log onto the IBM *File Finder* by typing **GO IBMFF** at the CompuServe prompt. The *File Finder* is a large file-description database of files stored at almost 100 different locations.

TABLE D.5 Third-Party Vendor Forums on CompuServe

Vendor	GO WINAP_†	Section	Vendor	GO WINAP_†	Section
3-D Visions	A	12	InfoAccess	B	4
Abacus	C	9	Jensen-Jones	A	8
Access Softek	A	2	Kidasa	B	9
Aristosoft	C	15	Knowledge Garden	B	15
Asymetrix	A	1	Matesys	C	1
Attitash	A	9	Metz Software	C	7
Bell Atlantic	C	2	Micrografx	A	10
Berkeley Systems	C	4	NBI	B	3
Campbell Services	C	6	Playroom	A	17
CaseWorks	B	1	Polaris	A	11
ChipSoft	B	5	Protoview	C	14
Comp Presentations	B	13	Pub tech	A	13
Future Soft	A	4	Saros	C	11
GeoGraphix	A	5	Softbridge	B	11
GFA	C	12	SoftCraft	B	10
Gilbert & Assoc.	C	17	Stirling Group	C	3
Gold Disk	C	16	Wall Data	C	10
Gold Hill	C	13	WilsonWare	A	15
hDC	A	6	WindowCraft	B	14
HI-Q Intl	A	7	Zenographics	B	12
ICOM	A	16			

† Type GO WINAP_, but replace the underlined character with indicated letter.
  Unassigned sections: A3, A14, B2, B6, B7, B8, B16, B17; C5, C8.

Search Procedure. You can search the database by any of the onscreen search criteria shown here:

SELECT SEARCH CRITERIA:

1 Keyword   6 File Name
2 Submission Date   7 File Submitter
3 Forum Name   8 Display Selected Titles
4 File Type   9 Begin a New Search
5 File Extension

Option 6 (File Name) is probably the best search criterion, but of course you have to know a name in order to search for it. Furthermore, the name as it appears in the database might not be the actual name under which the file will eventually be used. For example, the SPEAKER.DRV file discussed in Chapter 12 is part of a compressed SPEAK.ZIP (or was it SPEAK.EXE?)

file in the database. Or worse: the MPLAYER.EXE file (also Chapter 12) is buried in a massive VFWRUN.ZIP file. You might make a lucky guess and find SPEAKER.DRV by searching for SPEAK, with no extension if you're not sure what is is. However, it would take more than luck to guess that MPLAYER is in VFWRUN.

Table D.6 shows the results of a search for a SPEAK file. Here, the extension was omitted, as would be the case if you weren't sure what it is. The search turns up 15 files in which SPEAK is the beginning of the filename. With luck, the brief explanation of each file will provide a sufficient clue to determining which is the file of interest.

If you don't know the specific filename, then try a search based on a few keywords. For example, Table D.7 shows the results of four keyword searches, the first two of which are searches for the source of the SPEAKER.DRV file mentioned above. The first search (for *Speaker* and *Driver*) finds eight files; since this list is not overly large, it's easy enough to scan it for the most likely candidates. However, if your keyword search found too many files, you can narrow the search by selecting option 1 again and adding another keyword (in this case, *PC*). Or, you might have begun the search with the keywords *PC* and *Speaker* and *Driver*. In either case, the table shows that two files meet these search criteria.

TABLE D.6 GO IBMFF: Sample Results on Filename Search

Search for *SPEAK* (no extension given)	Search Results: 15 Files
1 Speak-EZ v1.2 English Lang. Query System CLIPPER/3rd Party Products SPEAK1.EXE	9 Amipro/Monolog4Win macro LOTUSWP/Ami Pro Macros SPEAK.ZIP
2 Speak-EZ English Lang. Query System Docs CLIPPER/3rd Party Products SPEAKD.EXE	10 Special info on MCS Stereo/Labtec Speaker MIDIAVEN/Animotion Files SPEAKR.TXT
3 Speaker's Resources Textbase Manager IBMAPP/Gen. Apps [A] SPEAK.ZIP	11 PC Speaker WAV driver for Windows 3.1 MIDIFORUM/Windows Media SPEAK.EXE
4 A 'speak your mind' door for Wildcat! 3.x IBMBBS/BBS Doors [B] SPEAK2.ZIP	12 'Speak Your Mind' program for Wildcat! 3.x PCVENA/Mustang Software SPEAK2.ZIP
5 how to attach a 1 amp external speaker to XT IBMHW/Gen. Hardware [H] SPEAKE.ARC	13 PC Speaker driver WINAPA/Asymetrix SPEAK.EXE
6 install speaker switch in PC/AT IBMHW/Gen. Hardware [H] SPEAKO.ARC	14 speakr.zip WINAPA/Future Soft Engr SPEAKR.ZIP
7 Speakeasy/External Speech Synthesizer IBMSPECIAL/Hardware SPEAKE.TXT	15 Play WAV files in WIN 3.1 through speaker ZENITH/Windows SPEAK.EXE
8 Talking Program IBMSPECIAL/Software SPEAK.COM	

TABLE D.7   GO IBMFF: Sample Results of Keyword Searches

Keywords and Files Found

Keywords: *Speaker* and *Driver*

1 SideKick Plus SERVMDTR.BIN turn off spkr.
   BORAPP/SK,Plus, TL, Eureka SPKOFF.ARC
2 Speaker device driver-music over internal spkr.
   IBMNEW/Music [4] SPKDD1.ARC
3 Music files for SPKDD1.ARC
   IBMNEW/Music [4] SPKDD2.ARC
4 Speaker device driver for buffered music play
   IBMSYS/General Utils [S] SPKDD1.ARC

5 Application illustrating use of sndPlaySound()
   MSBASIC/Visual Basic - Win SNDPLY.ZIP
6 PLAYSND.ZIP - Play sound without sound card
   WINAPA/Asymetrix PLYSND.ZIP [†]
7 PC Speaker driver
   WINAPA/Asymetrix SPEAK.EXE [‡]
8 Play WAV files in WIN 3.1 through speaker
   ZENITH/Windows SPEAK.EXE

Keywords: *PC* and *Speaker* and *Driver*

1 PLAYSND.ZIP-Play sound without sound card
   WINAPA/Asymetrix PLYSND.ZIP [†]

2 PC Speaker driver
   WINAPA/Asymetrix SPEAK.EXE [‡]

Keywords: *Media Player*

There were no articles found that match
your search criteria.

Keywords: *Media* and *Video*

1 WAV error messages, Lethal Enforcers game
   MIDIFORUM/Windows Media LETHAL.ZIP
2 Video for Windows Runtime Installation
   MSAPP/Video for Windows VFWRUN.ZIP

3 MEDIAscript Multimedia Support
   ULTIBTOOL/Net. Tech. MS0002.TXT
4 MEDIAscript OS/2 PE - V 1.1 - Fact Sheet
   ULTIBTOOL/Net. Tech. PE0001.TXT

[†] PLYSND.ZIP found in both Keyword searches, but not in filename search for SPEAK
 (see Table D.6).
[‡] SPEAK.EXE found in both Keyword searches, and in filename search for SPEAK
 (see 13 in Table D.6).

The last two examples in Table D.7 show that being specific does not always work. In a search for *Media Player,* nothing was found. To refine the search, remember that the desired file is included with *Video for Windows.* Since *Media Player* was not recognized, try *Media* and *Video.* As shown in the table, this brings up four possible choices. From the brief explanations, it appears that the desired file is item 2.

To verify that item 2 is what you're looking for, just type "2" at the prompt to display additional details, such as those shown here:

Forum Name: MSAPP	Library: Video for Windows (3)
Accesses: 123	Size: 478575
File: VFWRUN.ZIP	Submitted [76711,167] 08-Mar-93

Runtime files for Video for Windows. Includes SETUP program to install them into your Windows directory. It updates Media Player so that it can be used as an OLE server as well.

Use the same general procedure described here to find whatever it is you're looking for. And if the first search turns up too much, or not enough, try tweaking the search criteria as required.

File Download Procedure. Once you've located the file you want, you can download it directly from the *File Finder* if you have any of the following software packages:

DOSCIM 2.0 or greater
MacCIM 1.6 or greater
WinCIM

Otherwise, log onto the indicated forum, join it (if you haven't done so already), select the appropriate library, and begin the download. In many cases, the file will be one of several compressed into a single file with an EXE or ZIP extension. If so, expand it to retrieve the file of interest, which should now appear with the appropriate filename and extension. Occasionally you may find a single file whose name has been truncated to meet the CompuServe limitation of six characters, and which requires renaming before use.

Technical References

Microsoft publishes two comprehensive technical reference manuals with detailed technical information about Windows and Windows-for-Workgroups (see Table D.8). The complete titles and current (1993) prices are:

Microsoft Windows Resource Kit for Operating System Version 3.1	$19.95
Microsoft Windows for Workgroups Resource Kit	$29.95
for Operating System Version 3.1	

Both contain a wealth of information that the serious Windows-tweaker will find useful in optimizing system configuration. Needless to say, the Resource Kits were valuable references in preparing this little book. Many of the lines in the various INI files are described, and although descriptions run the gamut from great to Greek, a "casual" reading of these pages can turn up all sorts of interesting information, much of which is actually useful.

Either *Resource Kit* is available from the Microsoft Sales Department at (800) 426-9400.

TABLE D.8   Windows Resource Kit Contents

Windows 3.1	Windows-for-Workgroups 3.1

Windows 3.1

Installation and Setup
1 Windows 3.1 Installation
2 Windows Setup Information Files
3 Windows Files
4 Windows Initialization Files

Configuring Windows 3.1
5 Windows 3.1 and Memory Mgmt.
6 Tips for Configuring Windows 3.1

Non-Windows-Based Applications
7 Setting Up Non-Windows Apps
8 PIFs and PIF Editor

Using Windows 3.1
9 Fonts
10 Printing
11 Compound Documents in Win 3.1

Networks and Windows 3.1
12   Networks and Windows 3.1

Troubleshooting Windows 3.1
13 Troubleshooting Windows 3.1
14 The Windows Resource Kit Disk

References, Resources, and Appendixes
A   Windows Resource Directory
B   Hardware Compatibility List
C   Windows 3.1 Disks and Files
D   Articles

Technical Overview
1 Networking—A Technical Discussion
2 Windows-for-Workgroups Architecture

Windows-for-Workgroups 3.1

Installation and Setup
3 Windows-for-Workgroups Installation
4 Windows-for-Workgroups Files
5 Windows-for-Workgroups Setup Info Files
6 Windows-for-Workgroups Initialization Files

Special Topics
7 Additional Windows-for-Workgroups Info
8 Network Integration with Microsoft LAN
   Manager and Novell NetWare

Configuring Windows-for-Workgroups
9 Tips for Configuring Windows-for-Workgroups

Using Windows-for-Workgroups
10   New and Updated Accessories
11   Network DDE
12   Mail
13   Schedule+

Troubleshooting Windows-for-Workgroups
14   Troubleshooting Windows-for-Workgroups

References, Resources, and Appendixes
–   Glossary
A   Windows-for-Workgroups Resource Directory
B   Microsoft Mail Configuration Guide
C   Flow Charts for Troubleshooting
D   Accessibility for Individuals with Disabilities
E   Integrating Additional Protocols

WUGNET: The Windows User Group Network

WUGNET describes itself as an international technical organization for Microsoft Windows professionals. In addition to its CompuServe forum (see Table D.4, column 4), WUGNET publishes the bimonthly *WUGNET Windows Journal,* a 30-to-40-page newsletter of field reports, configuration, and development information. The *Journal* is usually accompanied by a diskette containing utilities or other Windows-related goodies. Notable among these is a diskette containing the contents of the *Windows Resource Kit Version 3.1.* Once installed, this electronic version adds a few bells-and-whistles not available in the printed version. For example, the flow charts

Figure D.1 The WUGNET *System Engineer* application window provides 15 access icons for convenient editing of SYSTEM.INI and WIN.INI files.

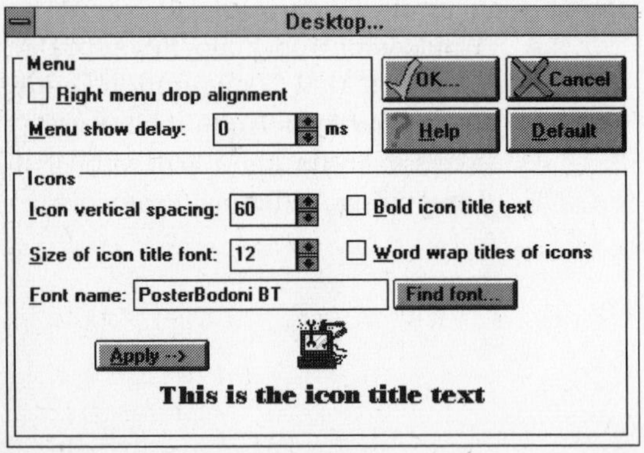

Figure D.2 The WUGNET *Desktop* icon (lower right-hand corner, Figure D.1) opens the Desktop... dialog box menu and icon configuration controls. As changes are made within the dialog box, the appropriate INI file lines are revised as required.

are available in an interactive format in which each step in the chart is displayed sequentially. Click on a Yes or No button, as appropriate to move to the next step.

Another helpful program is the WUGNET *System Engineer*, an extensive editing utility for the Windows WIN.INI and SYSTEM.INI files. Figure D.1 shows the *System Engineer* application window, in which 15 applet icons provide access to various sections of the INI files. As a typical example, double-click on the *Windows desktop* icon to open the Desktop dialog box shown in Figure D.2. The figure shows the effect of applying Bitstream's *Poster Bodoni* font to icon titles. The dialog box also provides the means to change vertical spacing between icons, an adjustment described here in the *Change Icon Spacing* section of Chapter 3.

For membership information, contact WUGNET at:

P. O. Box 1967
107 S. Monroe Street, 2nd Floor
Media, PA 19063
(215) 565-1861 (voice)
(215) 565-7106 (fax)

Or, leave a message on their CompuServe forum.

Local User Groups

Help may be available just around the corner, across town, or over in the next village where the local computer user group meets. If the group is typical of most, membership level ranges from beginner to expert, and most members are happy to share what they know. As a typical example, the *Long Island Computer Association* (Nassau County, New York; 516/293-8368) holds monthly general-interest meetings, plus others devoted to special interests, such as Windows and DOS at beginning, intermediate, and advanced levels.

If a monthly trip to Long Island is more than you had in mind, one of the following resources may be useful in tracking down the nearest user group:

- *Computer Shopper* magazine prints a list of user groups, sorted by state and zip code.
- Call Microsoft at (800) 426-9400. At the recorded announcement, press 2 and ask for the name and address of the user group nearest to your zip code.
- Your local library is another likely resource. Many user groups leave their publications at the reference desk, or the reference librarian may have details about meetings.

E

Time Out

Many Windows snoopers love nothing better than to burrow through the code looking for undocumented features that may or may not come to the surface in future versions. One favorite pastime is to go on an "Easter Egg" hunt—this technical term borrowed (or perhaps swiped) from the Apple side of the industry, where it describes a little screen that lists the developers of the application, often with a bit of animation thrown in.

The hidden egg (or *doodad, gang screen, credit list,* or whatever) can be made visible by anyone who knows the secret code, which is usually some obscure combination of key presses. Some industry observers who have perhaps lost their sense of humor feel that such nonsense has no place in serious programming. And certainly it has no place in a learned document such as the one you're reading now. Nevertheless, here it is anyway, for the benefit of those readers who have not yet lost the ability to smile every now and then. Besides, if you've read more than one chapter of this book you're probably more-than-ready for a chuckle or two.

Each of the following sections describes a key sequence that will bring up the credit screen hidden in that application. This Appendix does not include configuration information, a Troubleshooting section, nor are there any error messages to describe. If you're looking for such things, you're in the wrong place.

Access

1. Open the File Menu and open the NWIND.MDB file that is included with *Access*.
2. Create a new table with one field of any data type.
3. Save the table as "cirrus" in lowercase letters.
4. At the "Create a primary key?" prompt, click on the No button.
5. Click anywhere in the Database: NWIND window to make it active.
6. Highlight the "cirrus" entry.
7. Open the Help Menu and select the About Microsoft Access... option.
8. Place the mouse pointer over the key logo.
9. Press and hold down Ctrl+Shift keys and double-click on the secondary mouse button.

After the lightning blasts the ducks out of the water, a series of credit screens goes by. If you get impatient, press the Escape key to toggle forward to the next credit screen. Watch the last screen carefully ("Special Thanks To") and see if you recognize any of the names, especially the last one.

AfterDark

This one is easy. Just move the mouse pointer into the blue *After Dark* area in the After Dark Control dialog box. When the question mark appears, click on the mouse button to start the credit crawl.

AMI Pro

1. Open the Help Menu and select the About AMI Pro... option.
2. Hold down the Ctrl+Alt+Shift keys while performing step 3.
3. Press function key F7, then type the letters SPAM.
4. From the Memory: figure, type the last number, then the third-from-last number.
5. Release the Ctrl+Alt+Shift keys.
6. When photo images appear, click on each one to hide it.

When the images of the developers appear, you can kill them off by clicking on them one by one. All except for T. King. You just can't kill T. King. Press the Escape key when you've had enough.

Excel 3.0

1. Open *Excel* and make sure Sheet 1 is visible.
2. Open Formula Menu, select G̲oto... option, IV16384, and make that cell the only one visible.
3. Open the Format Menu and set Row Height and Column Width options to 0.
4. Double-click on the only visible button in the upper left-hand corner of the display.

Excel 4.0

5. Open the Options Menu, select the T̲oolbars... option and show the *Standard* Toolbar.
6. Place the mouse pointer on the Toolbar and click the *secondary* mouse button.
7. Select the Customize... option.
8. Select the Custom option.
9. Drag the *Solitaire* icon (pack of cards, top row) to any empty spot on the Toolbar.
10. In the Assign to Tool dialog box, click on the OK button, then on the Close button.
11. Hold down the Ctrl+Alt+Shift keys and click on the *Solitaire* icon.

One of the best reasons for not upgrading to *Excel* version 4.0a is that the version 4.0 credit screen (see Figure E.1) has been suppressed. Some authorities claim it was removed after certain unpleasant noises were heard coming from the direction of the competition. Other authorities say nothing at all.

hDC Microapps

1. Open Control Menu and select the A̲bout... option.
2. When the *hDC* logo appears, note the position between the "h" and the "C" at which a star periodically appears.
3. Place the mouse pointer at that position.
4. Hold down the Ctrl+Shift keys and press either mouse button (different credit lines for each).

Norton Desktop for Windows

1. Open the Help Menu and select the About... option.
2. Place the mouse pointer over the Norton icon.
3. Hold down the NDW keys and double-click on the icon.

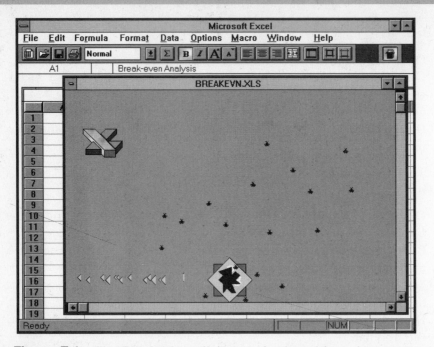

Figure E.1 The Excel 4.0 credit screen begins with an irreverent review of the competition. The *Excel* logo swoops in from upper stage left to clear the screen, after which the credits are seen.

Object Vision

1. Open the Help Menu and select the About... option.
2. Place the mouse pointer over the icon and double-click the secondary mouse button.

PC-Kwik WinMaster

1. Double-click on the *Toolbox* icon.
2. Open WinMaster Control Menu and select the About... option.
3. Hold down Ctrl+Alt+Shift keys and click on OK button.

Solitaire

They're not credit screens, but the four card decks shown in Figure E.2 have an animation mode. It's not exactly full-motion video, but it may have to do if you're not yet set up for *Video for Windows*.

1. Open the Game Menu, select Options..., and check the Timed Game box.

Figure E.2 No credits here, but these four *Solitaire* decks add a bit of animated fun to your game.

2. Reopen the Game Menu, select the De<u>c</u>k... option, and choose one of the following decks.

Robot	Once the game starts, the robot's meter and lights are activated.
Castle	The bats' wings flap. They're difficult to see, but that's the way it is with bats.
Palm Tree	Move the mouse pointer off any card that shows the palm tree. Twice every minute the sun turns into a face and sticks out its tongue.
Hand: 3 Aces	The fourth ace slips into view every 15 seconds.

3. Successfully conclude a game and all the cards go flying.

You can "freeze" the sun or the fourth ace by holding down the primary mouse button as soon as either appears.

Cheating at Cards. *Solitaire* deals three cards at a time if the Draw <u>T</u>hree radio button in the Options dialog box is enabled. If you can't play the top card, and your conscience won't keep you awake at night, open the Game Menu and select the <u>U</u>ndo option to put the last three-card deal back on the deck. Now hold down the Ctrl+Alt+Shift keys. *Solitaire* will redeal the cards one at a time for as long as you hold down the keys.

Windows 3.1, Windows-for-Workgroups 3.1

1. Open any Help Menu and select the <u>A</u>bout... option.
2. Hold down Ctrl+Shift keys.
3. Double-click on the Windows (or applet) logo.
4. Click on OK to clear the <u>A</u>bout screen.
5. Repeat Steps 2–4. A dedication and waving flag appear.
6. Click on OK to clear the <u>A</u>bout screen.
7. Repeat Steps 2–4. A figure appears and the credits scroll by.
8. Click on OK to quit.

Figure E.3 shows four variations on the opening credit screen. The Windows mascot shown in one of the screens makes several other cameo appearances, one of which is visible to the unaided eye. A BEAR.EXE file is seen in the Selected Font area of the Font Selection dialog box (see Figure 7.7) if the selected character box has a vertical dimension of 6 or 8 pixels. This bear lives in WINOA386.EXE, and six others hide out in the USER.EXE file.

Word-for-Windows

1. Open the Tools Menu and select the Macro... option.
2. In the Macro dialog box, type "Spiff" (without the quotes).
3. Click on the Global Macros radio button and then on the Edit button.
4. Delete everything from the macro, including the Sub Main and End Sub statements.
5. Open the File Menu and select the Save All option.
6. Open the Help Menu and select the About... option.
7. Click double-click on the Word logo.

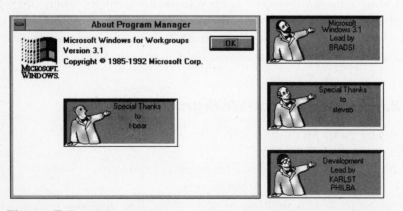

Figure E.3 Within Windows and Windows-for-Workgroups, the credit crawl appears in a small window presided over by Microsoft's (a) T. Bear, (b) Brad Silverberg, (c) Steve Ballmer, and (e) an unidentified Redmond employee. It couldn't be Bill Gates, who doesn't have a bow tie.

Index

32-bit access (FastDisk), 120, 970–971, 988
386 Enhanced applet, 741–745
   SYSTEM.INI record, 745
   troubleshooting, 821
386 Enhanced dialog box, 741–744
386MAX, *see* Qualitas Memory
    Manager (386MAX.SYS)
386MAX.PRO file, 940–942
386SPART.PAR file, 962
386UTIL.COM file, 942, 944

A

A20 Line Handler, troubleshooting, 313
About
   screen (Windows Help), 278–280
   File Size Information option
    (*Windows Resource Kit*), 373
   Help option (Windows Help), 280
   option (Control menu), 232
   Program Manager screen, 183
   Vsafe Manager option, 66
Access, see Microsoft *Access*
Accessories dialog box (Windows Setup), 130, 131
Accessories Group Window
   and Express Setup, 121
   list of applets installed, 102
   list of files, 132–133
   list of help files, 276
active window, 221
Add (Drivers) dialog box, 837–839
Add Fonts dialog box, 658, 660, 661–662
Add/Remove Windows Components
   option (Windows 3.1 Setup applet), 156
Advanced Options dialog box (PIF Editor), 443, 453–456
After Dark, 745–749
   audio vs. other WAV audio, 749
   AUTOEXEC.BAT modifications, 747
   configuration, 746–749
   configuring as Control Panel applet, 748–749
   configuring audio, 749
   configuring from Desktop applet, 746–748

Control menu, 746
conventional operation, 746
credit screen, 1100
hiding icon, 749
INI file modifications, 747
list of files, 747
loading as part of StartUp Group, 746
Runner, 771, 772
Agfa *Discovery TrueType Pack*, 662–665
Agfa *Type Director*, 680–681
Alert Always option (Print Manager), 572, 608
All File Details option (File Manager), 376
allocation units, DoubleSpace, 14
Alt+Enter keys, 431
Alt+Esc keys, 247–248
Alt+Spacebar keys, 431
Alt+Tab keys, 247, 431
Always On Top options
   Control menu, 232–233
   in StartUp Group Window, 341
   Windows Help, 280
AMI Pro, credit screen, 1100
Annotate option (Help), 288–289
Anti-Stealth option (Anti-Virus Options dialog box), 34
Anti-Virus, 7, 28–31
   Anti-Stealth option, 34
   Check All Files option, 34–35
   checklist file (CHKLIST.MS), 37
   CHKLIST.MS file, 37
   Clean option, 31
   configuration, 34–36
   configuration options file (MWAV.INI), 37
   Control menu, 31
   Create Backup option, 35
   Create Checksums on Floppies option, 35
   Delete CHKLIST Files option, 32
   Detect option, 32
   Disable Alarm Sound option, 35
   error messages, 87–90
   Exit Anti-Virus option, 32
   File Manager access to, 375
   Help menu, 33
   infected file (*filename*.VIR), 37
   installing Windows version, 162
   menus, 31–33
   Options dialog box, 34–35

Options menu, 32–33
Prompt While Detect option, 35
Save Settings on Exit option, 32
Scan menu, 31–32
Set Options option, 33
Statistics screen, 31
support files, 36–37
troubleshooting, 79–82
Verify Error dialog box, 30, 36
Verify Integrity option, 35–36
Virus Found dialog box, 30, 36
Virus List option, 32
Virus Signature Update Files, 37
Wipe Deleted Files option, 36
applets
   adding to Control Panel, 735–736
   in APPS.INF [dontfind] section, 141
   configuration in Control Panel, 740
   defined, 96
   font configuration, 702–704
   installed during Windows Setup, 102–103
   installing in Program Manager, 386
   installing screen savers as, 774–775
   removing from Control Panel, 739
   startup, loading via WIN.INI, 381–382
   in StartUp Group Window, 338–341, 344–345, 408
   unassigned during installation, 103
application swap file (WOA*xxxx*.TMP), 961
application window, defined, 220
applications
   applications-found list, 147–148
   compatibility checklist, 302–304
   compatibility help file, 277
   defined, 96
   failure to run, 319
   icons, 222
   list of those recognized by Windows Setup, 142–146
   problematic, 111–115
   running at startup, 163, 337
   selecting in Custom Windows Setup, 141, 147
   selecting in Express Windows Setup, 140
   see also DOS applications; Windows applications
APPS.HLP file, 277

APPS.INF file
[dontfind] section, 141
[pif] section, 141, 441, 444, 445,
446–447
Arrange Icons option (File Manager),
379
Arrange Icons option (Window
menu), 243
ASQ.EXE file (Qualitas), 926, 927
Associate option/dialog box (File
Manager), 365–367, 389–391
association, *see* file associations
ATTRIB command (DOS), 265, 271
attribute, typeface, 636
see also file attributes
audio systems
audio sources, 883, 884
checking, 882–883
signal paths, 879–882
and Sound Blaster, 881
Auto Arrange option (Program
Manager), 241
Auto Floppy Configure button
(Backup), 43–44
Auto option (Clipboard), 523
AUTOEXEC.BAT file
and 386MAX, 939
After Dark, modifications to, 747
basic, 115–117
disabling lines in, 290
and disk caching software, 114
editing with SYSEDIT, 290–292
modifications by third-party setups,
152–153
modifying in Custom Windows
Setup, 137–138
and MSCDEX, 843–845
and problem applications, 111–115
and QEMM386, 945
revising before
installing/upgrading
Windows, 111–115
and Smart Drive, 965–966, 967
troubleshooting at DOS bootup,
77–79, 977
and Windows for Workgroups, 396
AVI files, 848, 885

B

background/foreground priorities
DOS applications, 452, 453–454
Windows applications, 607, 742–745
Background Printing
dialog box (Print Manager), 607
option (Workgroups), 572
Priority, 607
Backup applet, 7, 37, 39
Auto Floppy Configure button,
43–44
Backup catalog (*filename*.FUL),
48–49
buttons, 38–40
Catalog menu, 41
Compatibility Test dialog box,
42–43
configuration, 42–45
configuration record
(MWBACKUP.INI), 49–50
data file (*filename*.00x), 49
DEFAULT.SET file, 46–48

Delete Setup option, 40
DOS Backup selection file
(*filename*.SLT), 50
error messages, 90–91
Exit option, 40
File menu, 40–41
File Manager access to, 375
Help menu, 41–42
installing Windows version, 162
launching setup files from Program
Manager, 45
master catalog (*filename*.CAT), 49
menus, 40–42
Open Setup option, 40
Print option, 40
Printer Setup option, 40
Save Setup As option, 41
Save Setup option, 40
saving configuration record, 44,
49–50
Setup File List option, 41
setup files (*filename*.SET), 46–48
setup reconfiguration, 45
support files, 46–50
temporary restore file
(WINBACK.TMP), 50
troubleshooting, 82
Backup Catalog (*filename*.FUL), 48–49
backup/restore procedures
backing up hard disk before
running Windows Setup,
118
backing up INI and GRP files, 151
backing up SYSEDIT files, 292
error messages, 327
troubleshooting, 317
where to put files, 297
see also Backup applet
BAK files, 110–111
BASIC programs
disabling lines in, 290
for printing symbol set, 708, 709
batch files
for DOS TSRs, 958–959
for dual Windows versions
(SWAP.BAT), 215
for enhanced mode operation
(WINSTART.BAT),
213–214, 958
for EXPAND utility, 296
for Font Installer font
downloading, 684, 725
for memory management, 958–959
for PIFs (Program Information
Files), 475
running Windows with, 209–215
for Windows mode checking
(WINMODE.BAT), 212–213
for Windows startup (WIN.BAT),
210–212
baud rate, greater than 19200, 815
Biff (Binary Interchange File Format),
503
binary INI files, 1006–1007
BIOS, 98–99
Bitmap file format, 503
bitmap files, 507–516, 534–535
color depth, 508–509, 534–535
comparing, 516
data section, 512–516
palette-based, 509, 510–512
RGB tables in, 509, 510–512

vs. TGA (Targa) files, 508, 509
TrueColor, 509, 512, 514–516
as wallpaper, 779–781
bitmap fonts, *see* raster fonts
Bitstream *FaceLift for Windows*, 672–673
configuration record
(FACELIFT.INI), 675, 680
display driver, 673
Dynamic Download option, 677,
680
extended character set, 675–677,
678–679
installing fonts, 672–673
list of fonts, 674
printer driver, 673, 675
troubleshooting, 710
using with new printer, 677, 680
Bitstream *TrueType Font Pack*, 665–667
Blank Screen screen saver, 771, 772
BMP files, *see* bitmap files
BNC connectors, 107–108, 822
Bookmark option (Help), 289
boot diskettes, 4, 974
boot sector
checking for viruses, 68
protecting, 69, 70
BOOTLOG.TXT file, 164, 179–181
bootup, *see* system bootup
Border Width box (Desktop dialog
box), 778
Browse button, 258–259
Browse dialog box, 230, 231, 258–259
buffers, and Smart Drive, 957, 969
Buffers= line (CONFIG.SYS), 957–958,
969
By File Type option (File Manager),
376

C

cables, 107–108, 822
Calendar applet
in StartUp Group Window, 338
troubleshooting printing, 619
CANYON.MID file, 857–858, 871, 872
Cardfile applet
Clipboard data formats for, 502
default font usage, 652
Cascade option (Window menu), 243,
244, 380
cascading
group windows, 243, 244
menus, 229
CAT files (Backup), 49
catalog, Backup (*filename*.FUL file),
48–49
Catalog menu (Backup), 41
CD audio, 841, 843, 855, 879–880
CD-ROM
audio configuration, 841, 843, 855,
879–880
audio problems, 889–890
and CONFIG.SYS file, 843
drive failures, 890
error messages, 901–904
and MSCDEX, 843–845
product-specific problems, 891–893
signal paths, 879–880, 884
software problems, 891
troubleshooting, 888–891
video problems, 891

Change
   Drive/Directory option
      (Undelete), 51
   Icon button, 255, 258
   Icon dialog box, 254, 258–259
   Password dialog box, 772–773, 774
   System Settings option (Windows
      3.1 Setup applet), 153–154
Character Map applet, 688–691
   Bitstream *FaceLift* fonts in, 710
   copying characters, 690
   custom font usage, 687
   default font usage, 652
   displaying italic and/or bold fonts,
      690–691
   enlarging characters, 689, 711
   error messages, 726
   selecting typeface, 689
   size of window, 709
   troubleshooting, 709–711
   as troubleshooting tool, 708
   viewing terminal font character set,
      439, 466
character sets
   code page configuration, 463–465
   viewing terminal font, 439, 466
Chat applet (Workgroups), 873
Check Executable Files option
   (VSafe), 68
checklist file (CHKLIST.MS), 37
CHKDSK /f
   running after exiting Windows,
      319–320
   running before running Windows
      Setup, 116
   when not to run, 117
CHKLIST.MS file (Anti-Virus), 37
Choose Drives for Delete Sentry dialog
   box, 59, 60
clean bootup, 4, 78, 974
Clean option (Anti-Virus), 31
client, defined, 393, 499
Clipboard, 497–498, 516–517
   application window, 516–517
   basic copying/pasting, 531–532
   in Clipbook, 519
   configuration, 531–546
   Control menu, 523
   copying/pasting fonts, 533–534
   defined, 497
   Display menu, 523–524
   displayed formats, 537–538
   Edit menu, 524–525
   error messages, 552–559
   File menu, 525–529
   Help menu, 523
   menus, 523–531
   object formats, 499–507
   overview, 497–498
   page separator, Clipboard file as,
      606
   transfer conditions, 497
   troubleshooting, 546–552
Clipboard files, *see* CLP files
Clipboard Object Format List option,
   523–524, 529
Clipboard Viewer applet, *see* Clipboard
Clipbook, 497, 517
   application window, 517–523
   basic copying/pasting, 531–532
   Clipboard in, 519
   configuration, 531–546

Control menu, 523
   copying/pasting fonts, 533–534
   defined, 497
   Edit menu, 524–525
   error messages, 552–559
   File menu, 525–529
   Help menu, 523
   icons, 522–523
   local, defined, 499
   local vs. remote windows in,
      519–522
   menu bar, 518
   menus, 523–531
   pages in, 520–522, 525
   password-protecting, 521, 535–537
   remote, defined, 499
   status bar, 520, 530
   Thumbnails in, 520–522
   title bar, 518
   Toolbar, 518–519, 531
   troubleshooting, 546–552
   View menu, 529–531
   Window menu, 531
Clipbook Preview file format, 503
Clipbook Viewer applet, *see* Clipbook
Clock applet, in StartUp Group
   Window, 338–339
Close option on Control Menu
   DOS Window, 432–433
   File Manager, 359
   Program Manager, 234
Close Window on Exit box (PIF
   Editor), 452–453, 458
CLP files
   characteristics of, 538–543
   creating, 527, 538
   as custom page separator files, 606
   loading automatically, 540–541
   restoring, 543–544
   and video drivers, 542–543
code page configuration, 463–465
Collapse Branch option (File
   Manager), 376
collapsible directory icon (File
   Manager), 354
Color applet, 749–751
   Color dialog box, 752–763
   Custom Color Selector, 759–763
   record in INI files, 763–765
   troubleshooting, 818
color depth
   defined, 508–509
   determining, 534–535
Color Palette button, 752
color purity, defined, 760
color schemes, *see* colors
colors
   changing, 752–759
   checking application compatibility,
      303
   CONTROL.INI record, 764–765
   customizing, 759–762
   dithered, 754–758
   in DOS Window mode, 429
   flicker check, 759
   icon text, 261
   reconfiguring matrix, 758–759
   saving color schemes, 762
   selecting color scheme, 763
   startup problems, 186, 188
   terminology, 759–760
   troubleshooting, 818

   use by Windows applications, 763
   Windows Desktop elements,
      750–751
   WIN.INI record, 764
   see also Color applet
COM port addresses, 816–817
Command Line box (Program Item
   Properties dialog box), 160,
      255
COMMDLG.DLL file, 818
company name (Windows Setup), 129
compatibility
   applications checklist, 302–304
   applications help file (APPS.HLP),
      277
   BIOS, 98–99
   hardware, 120, 124
   Compatibility Test dialog box
      (Backup), 42–43
components, Windows
   adding/removing after initial
      Setup, 156, 161–162
   list of files, 132–134
   selecting in Windows Setup,
      129–134
   see also hardware requirements
compressed drives (DoubleSpace),
   14–15, 70–71
compressed files, 295–296
compressed volume file (CVF)
   changing size, 74–75
   DBLSPACE.000, 13, 14, 76
   overview, 13
   size limitations, 75
compression ratios (DoubleSpace),
   14–15, 71–72
Compton Encyclopedia (CD-ROM),
   troubleshooting, 891–892
CompuServe, 1085
   forums, 1086, 1088–1091
   IBM File Finder, 1089–1094
   libraries, 1086, 1088–1094
   Microsoft Windows Driver Library,
      1086, 1088
computer name (on network),
   defined, 393
CONFIG.SYS file
   and 386MAX, 929, 939
   basic, 115–117
   buffers= line, 957–958, 969
   and CD-ROM driver, 843
   disabling lines in, 290
   dos= line, 930–931
   editing with SYSEDIT, 290–292
   files= line, 958
   and memory management, 955,
      957–958
   modifications by third-party setups,
      152–153
   modifying in Custom Windows
      Setup, 137
   and problem applications, 111–115
   and QEMM386, 929, 945
   revising before
      installing/upgrading
      Windows, 111–115
   and Smart Drive, 964–965
   stacks= line, 115, 958
   troubleshooting at DOS bootup,
      77–79, 975–977
   and Windows for Workgroups,
      394–396

Configure Delete Protection option (Undelete), 56
Configure Delete Sentry dialog box, 58–60
Configure Option (Media Player), 855
Confirmation option (File Manager), 373
Connect dialog box, 582–583, 600, 601, 602–603
Connect Network Drive option (Workgroups), 359–362
Connect Network Printer option/dialog box (Workgroups), 575, 584–585
Connect option (Clipbook), 526
CONNECT.DAT file, 823
connectors, 107–108, 822
Contents option (Windows Help), 280
context-sensitive help
    F1 key, 282
    Help button, 281
Control menu
    After Dark, 746
    Anti-Virus, 31
    Clipboard/Clipbook, 523
    within Control Panel applets, 734
    in DOS Window, 432–436
    File Manager, 357–359
    Help option on, 234, 281
    Program Manager, 232–237
    Video for Windows, 850–851
    VSafe, 65
Control-menu box, 223–224
Control Panel, 731–910
    accessing, 577, 587
    adding applets to, 735–736
    applet configuration, 740
    configuration, 734–745
    configuring *After Dark* as applet in, 748–749
    Control menu, 734
    CONTROL.INI record, 735, 741
    error messages, 828–833, 901
    Help menu, 734
    list of applets, 733
    list of icon files, 733
    menus, 732–734
    removing applets from, 739
    resequencing icons within, 736–739
    Settings menu, 734
    status bar, 731, 740
    title bar, 740
    troubleshooting, 818
    window size and position, 735
    see also names of applets
CONTROL.FIL file, 64
CONTROL.INF file
    [country] section, 781, 783, 784, 785, 787
    editing, 786
CONTROL.INI file
    [Color Schemes] section, 1011, 1012
    Control Panel record, 741
    [current] section, 1011, 1012
    [Custom Colors] section, 764–765, 1011, 1012
    default sections, 1010–1013
    [Don't Load] section, 739, 1013
    [drivers.desc] section, 1013
    [installed] section, 585, 1013–1014
    [MMCPL] section, 735, 736, 1014

[patterns] section, 770–771, 1011, 1013
reconstructing, 1010–1014
[related.desc] section, 1014
screen saver record, 777, 778, 1014
[userinstallable.drivers] section, 1014
CONTROL.SRC file, 1010–1013
conventional memory
    basic configuration, 953
    defined, 912–913
    and DOS 6.0, 954
    managing, 950, 951–954
    PIF configuration, 473
    and third-party memory managers, 954
    troubleshooting, 183
cookie boxes, 128
Copy Disk option (File Manager), 362
Copy Object option (Media Player), 855
Copy option
    Clipbook, 524–525
    File Manager, 367, 368
    File menu, 238
Copy Program Item dialog box, 238
copying
    directories (File Manager), 367, 387–388
    files (File Manager), 367, 387–388
    using Clipboard/Clipbook, 531–534
country (International applet), 781
COURE.FON file, 641–642
CPL files, resequencing, 736–737
CPSTOOLS.INI file, 65
Create Directory option (File Manager), 367
credit screens, 1099–1105
CSV (Comma-Separated Values) file format, 503
Ctrl+Alt+Del
    local reboot, 308–311
    when Windows not open, 193, 988
currency format (International applet), 785
current directory icons (File Manager), 355–356
cursor blink rate, 768
cursor visibility, 320
custom colors
    applying, 762
    CONTROL.INI record, 764, 765, 1011, 1012
    creating, 759–762
    saving, 762
Custom Windows Setup, 121
    applications-found list, 147–148
    AUTOEXEC.BAT file, modifying, 137–138
    component selection, 129–134
    CONFIG.SYS file, modifying, 137
    directory selection, 121–123
    exiting, 148–149
    file transfer, 128–129
    hardware compatability list, 124
    network driver installation, 139–140
    printer installation, 138–139
    selecting applications, 140–147
    system cookie, 128
    system information review, 123–128
    user's name and company, 129
    virtual memory configuration, 134–137

and Windows applications, 140–147
    and Windows tutorial, 148
Customize Toolbar option (Workgroups), 374, 391
CVF (compressed volume file), 13, 14, 74–75, 76

D

date
    display configuration, 766–767
    formatting (International applet), 785
Date/Time applet, 766–767
    Date & Time dialog box, 766
    troubleshooting, 818–819
DBLSPACE.000 file, 13, 14, 76
DBLSPACE.BIN file, 13, 76
DBLSPACE.INI file, 72–74, 76–77
DEBUG utility (DOS), 268–269
DebugLocalReboot= line (SYSTEM.INI), 310
DECOMP.EXE file, 294
decompression utilities, 293–296
Default Format option (Clipbook), 529
default printer, 578
_DEFAULT.PIF file, 441
DEFAULT.SET file, 46–48
Define Custom Colors button, 759
defragmenting hard disks
    before running Windows Setup, 118
    and swap files, 984
    and troubleshooting Sound Recorder, 900
    and Windows startup, 193
Delete CHKLIST Files option (Anti-Virus), 32
Delete Document option (Workgroups), 571, 612
Delete option
    Backup Catalog menu, 41
    Clipbook, 525
    File Manager, 367–368
    File menu, 238–239
Delete Sentry (Undelete)
    all files vs. specified files, 58
    and archived files, 58–59
    configuring Delete Sentry dialog box, 58–60
    control file (CONTROL.FIL), 64
    deleting saved files, 59, 60
    excluding files, 60
    and network drives, 60
    protected file, 64
Delete Setup option (Backup), 40
Delete Tracker (Undelete), 60, 64
Desktop, 217, 248
    colors, 749–765
    configuration, 248–265
    error messages, 273–274
    font location, 654
    group window configuration, 253–255
    group window troubleshooting, 265–269
    icon configuration, 255–263
    icon troubleshooting, 271–273
    menu configuration, 250–252
    menu troubleshooting, 270–271
    program item configuration, 253–255

Program Manager configuration, 249–250
properties configuration, 253–255
screen elements, 750–751
shortcut key configuration, 263–265
shortcut key troubleshooting, 269
startup problems, 185–188
SYSTEM.INI font specification, 654–656
title bar, 223, 235, 249
troubleshooting, 265–273
window configuration, 249–250
WIN.INI font specification, 656–658
Desktop applet, 767–781
configuring *After Dark* from, 746–748
troubleshooting, 819–821
Desktop dialog box, 767–781
Desktop-Edit Pattern dialog box, 769, 770
destination, defined, 499
Detect option (Anti-Virus), 32
device= line (WIN.INI), 1030
device=CHKSTATE.SYS line (CONFIG.SYS), 977
device?= line (CONFIG.SYS), 78
device contention, 741–742
device drivers
adding, 837–839
configuring from Drivers dialog box, 840
error messages, 904–905
general protection faults, 313–314
incompatible with Windows, 112–114
moving into UMB area, 953
MS-DOS, and Windows for Workgroups, 396
and MSCDEX configuration, 845
NDIS, 395
removing, 839–840
reviewing files, 841, 842
in startup files, 116–117
SYSTEM.INI record, 840–841
third-party, uninstalling, 109–110
troubleshooting, 164–165, 887, 888, 893, 894
virtual, 318, 840–841, 888, 898, 911
see also types of drivers
device font, defined, 633–634
Device menu (Media Player), 855
diagnostic aids, Windows, 304–307
DiagSoft *QAPlus/Win*, 1039, 1042
dialog boxes, 230–231
DIALOG.FON file, 644
DIB (Device Independent Bitmap) file format, 503
DIF (Data Interchange Format), 504
DIR /C report, 71–72
DIR /CH report, 72
directories
copying (File Manager), 367, 387–388
deleting (File Manager), 367–368
for icons, 259–260
installing fonts in, 661
moving (File Manager), 368, 388
printing contents of, 151
SYSTEM directory listing, 1066
WINDOWS directory listing, 1062–1065
see also shared directories

Directory Only option (File Manager), 376
directory windows, File Manager, 352–356
changing font, 374, 384, 701, 702, 703
Control menu, 359
icons, 354–355
listing, 380
multiple, configuring, 383–386
Disconnect Network Drive option (Workgroups), 362
Disconnect Network Printer option (Workgroups), 575
Disconnect option (Clipbook), 527
Discovery *TrueType Pack* (Agfa), 662–665
disk caching utilities
and Smart Drive, 968
when to disable, 17
disk drives, *see* drives
Disk menu (File Manager), 359–365
disks, mounting (DoubleSpace), 72
Display Bytes as KB option (*Windows Resource Kit*), 373
Display menu (Clipboard), 523–524
display problems, troubleshooting, 185–188, 981
Display Text file format, 504
distribution diskettes
defective, 166
defined, 96
list of files on, 1043–1060
Windows files not found on, 151
dithered colors, 754–758
DMA channels
assignments, 300–301, 302
error messages, 328
troubleshooting, 317
document files, 386
document icon (File Manager), 355
Document menu (Workgroups Print Manager), 571–572, 611, 612
document windows, 220
dos= line (CONFIG.SYS), 930–931
DOS, defined, 2–3
see also MS-DOS Editor
DOS 6.0, 3–6
ATTRIB command, 265, 271
bootup, 4, 77–79, 974–977
configuration, 27–28
considerations in installing Windows for Workgroups, 108
DEBUG utility, 268–269
list of files, 4, 5–6
MemMaker utility, 936–937, 954
memory management, 4, 78–79
minimum configuration, 27–28
supplemental program installation, 25–26
troubleshooting bootup, 77–79, 974–977
User's Guide, 4, 6
DOS 6.0 Setup, 3, 18–24
begin upgrade, 24
error messages, 85–87
first time, 18
minimum configuration, 18
old DOS files, 27
post-Windows-Setup modifications, 162

pre-Setup procedures, 17
supplemental program installation, 25–26
System Settings screen, 19–20
and Uninstall diskette, 18, 24
Welcome screen, 19
DOS applications
background/foreground priorities, 452, 453–454
and CPU time, 742–744
defined, 428
and device contention, 741–742
executing within Windows, 430–432
exiting, 433, 452
icons, 260
and local reboot (Ctrl+Alt+Del), 309–310
problems, 476–477
setting up in Program Manager, 159–161
toggling among, 431
toggling between video modes, 431–432
troubleshooting, 476–478
Windows incompatibilities, 112–114
DOS backup selection file (*filename*.SLT), 50
DOS communication settings, 816
DOS EDLIN utility, 293
DOS exclusive mode, 430, 452, 469
DOS full screen mode, 428, 430, 468
DOS Memory utility (MEM.EXE), 919–920, 950–952
DOS prompt
at application exit, PIF configuration, 474–475
inserting Windows reminder in, 472
modifying Windows Setup from, 161–162
DOS Prompt dialog box, 435–436
DOS screen savers, 115
DOS sessions
beginning, 430
closing, 430, 432–433, 452–453
configuration, 467–473
disabling full screen mode, 468
disabling window mode, 468
environment size, 469–470, 471
error messages, 486–496
exclusive-mode options, 430, 452, 468–469
font troubleshooting, 481–483
mouse troubleshooting, 483–484, 827
PIF troubleshooting, 484–486
PrintScreen key, 471–472
removing screen message, 472
shortcut key problems, 477–478
troubleshooting, 476–481
window problems, 478–481
DOS video modes
color values, 429
DOS Window mode, 428–429
exclusive mode, 430, 452, 468–469
full-screen mode, 428, 430, 468
toggling between, 431–432
in Windows enhanced mode, 428–429
in Windows standard mode, 429–430
DOS Window, 427
adjusting borders, 459

DOS Window (*cont'd*)
  batch files, 958–959
  changing display mode (screen
      lines), 460–463
  character set (code page)
      configuration, 463–465
  closing, 431, 432–433, 452–453
  configuration, 458–473
  Control menu, 432–436
  custom font usage, 687
  default font usage, 652
  disabling, 468
  error messages, 486–496
  fonts in, 436–440
  number of lines displayed,
      461–463
  size adjustments, 459–463
  troubleshooting, 478–481
  video modes, 428–430
DOSAPP.INI file, 480
double buffering, Smart Drive, 964–965
DoubleSpace
  allocation units, 14
  compressed volume file (CVF), 13,
      14, 74–75, 76
  compression ratios, 14–15, 71–72
  configuration, 70–77
  configuration file
      (DBLSPACE.INI), 72–74,
      76–77
  drive size estimation, 14–15
  error messages, 92–93
  File Fragmentation Index,
      changing, 74
  host drive, 14, 70–71
  mounting disks, 72
  overview, 11–16
  reliability, 15–16
  SmartDrive considerations, 75
  support files, 76–77
  and swap files, 964
  system file (DBLSPACE.BIN), 13, 76
  troubleshooting, 83–85
  uninstalling, 13
  viewing from File Manager, 71
Doublespace Info option (File
      Manager), 375
downloading files, 296
Dr. Watson, 304–307, 339
drag-and-drop feature
  copying directories/files with,
      387–388
  error messages, 414–415
  in File Manager, 386–388
  moving directories/files with, 388
  moving icons by, 262
drive caching, Smart Drive, 965–966
drivebar (File Manager), 351, 353, 374
Drivebar option (Workgroups), 374
driver files, 313–314, 841
drivers, *see* device drivers
Drivers applet, 836–851
  CD audio driver, 841, 843
  CD-ROM discs and MSCDEX,
      843–845
  configuration procedures, 841–851
  Drivers dialog box, 837–840
  MCI Sound, 847–848
  PC speaker driver, 845–847
  SYSTEM.INI record, 840–841
  troubleshooting, 893–894
  Video for Windows, 848–851

Drivers dialog box, 837–840
DRIVER.SYS file, troubleshooting, 407
drives
  compressed, 14–15, 70–71
  corrupt files following system
      crashes, 318
  diskette drive access problems, 318
  error messages, 328–329
  troubleshooting, 317–318
DRV files, 313–314
DRWATSON.EXE file, 163, 304–307
dynamic link libraries (DLLs), 915

E

Edit menu
  Clipbook, 524–525
  Help, 288–289
  Media Player, 855–857
Edit option (DOS Window Control
      menu), 433–434
Edit Pattern dialog box, 769, 770
editing utilities
  MS-DOS Editor, 292
  MS-DOS EDLIN utility, 292–293
  SYSEDIT, 290–292
  using for line-disabling, 290
EditLevel= line (PROGMAN.INI), 252
EDLIN utility, 292–293
/EISA switch (HIMEM.SYS), 932
embedding object packages, 387
EMM386.EXE file, 934–936
EMMExclude= line (SYSTEM.INI),
      930, 956
enhanced mode
  batch file (WINSTART.BAT), 213–214
  defined, 97
  and DOS applications, 428–429
  error messages, 203–209
  PIF Editor dialog box, 442, 444–453
  RAM drive considerations, 971
  troubleshooting, 182, 318
Enter Network Password dialog box,
      536
environment size, DOS sessions,
      469–470, 471
Equation Editor
  error messages, 727–729
  font troubleshooting, 724
  MTFONTS.INI support file, 672
  TrueType fonts, 669–672
error messages
  alphabetical list of, 1068–1081
  Anti-Virus, 87–90
  Backup, 90–91
  backup/restore, 327
  CD-ROM, 901–904
  Character Map, 726
  Clipboard/Clipbook, 552–559
  Control Panel, 828–833, 901
  Desktop, 273–274
  DMA channels, 328
  DOS 6.0 Setup, 85–87
  DOS sessions, 486–496
  DoubleSpace, 92–93
  drag-and-drop, 414–415
  drive-related, 328–329
  drivers, 904–905
  enhanced mode, 203–209
  Equation Editor fonts, 727–729
  exiting DOS sessions, 495–496

file expansion, 326–327
File Manager, 411–414
font installation, 726–727
help screens, 322–326
I/O ports, 328
IRQ lines, 328
Media Player, 905–908
memory-related, 990–1000
MIDI Mapper, 908–910
mouse-related, 829–831
Network applet, 831–833
network-related, 416–425
parity error, 989–990
in Print Manager status bar, 570
print-related, 414–416, 623–631
Qualitas Memory Manager,
      943–944
real mode, 201–202
Sound and Sound Recorder
      applets, 910
standard mode, 202–203
startup, 194–201
StartUp Group Window, 345
swap file, 1001–1003
Undelete, 91–92
virtual memory configuration, 137
VSafe, 87–90
Windows Setup, 167–175
Excel, see Microsoft *Excel*
exclusive mode, 430, 452, 468–469
executable files, protecting (VSafe), 69
Exit option
  Clipboard/Clipbook, 527
  File Manager, 368
  File menu, 239
  Print Manager, 575, 576
Exit Windows dialog box, 230, 231
Exit Windows option (File menu), 239
Expand
  All option (File Manager), 376
  Branch option (File Manager),
      376
  One Level option (File Manager),
      376
Expand utility, defined, 96
expandable directory icon (File
      Manager), 354
expanded memory
  defined, 913
  emulator (EMM386.EXE),
      934–936
  and RAM drives, 971–972
EXPAND.EXE file, 294, 295, 296
expanding files, 293–296
Express Windows Setup, 120–121
  and 32-bit disk access, 120
  Accessories Group Window, 121
  exiting, 148–149
  file transfer, 128–129
  hardware compatibility, 120
  network driver installation, 139–140
  and permanent swap file, 120
  printer installation, 120, 138–139
  selecting applications, 140
  selecting directory, 121–123
  user's name and company, 129
  and Windows applications, 121
  and Windows tutorial, 148
extended characters
  in *Bitstream FaceLift for Windows*,
      675–677, 678–679
  printing, 717

extended memory
  defined, 913, 914
  and HIMEM.SYS, 931–934
  troubleshooting, 184
extensions, *see* filename extensions

F

F1 key (Help), 282
F5 key (DOS 6.0 bootup), 4, 78, 974
F8 key (DOS 6.0 bootup), 4, 77–78,
  974–975, 976
FaceLift for Windows, see Bitstream
  FaceLift for Windows
FACELIFT.INI file, 675, 680
Fast Switching box (Desktop dialog
  box), 767–768
FastDisk (32-bit access), 970–971, 988
FAT (file allocation table), corruption
  of, 318
Fences font, 724
file associations
  changing, 390
  creating, 365–367, 390
  and [Extensions] section of
    WIN.INI, 389–391
  overriding, 485–486
  removing, 390–391
  troubleshooting, 409
file attributes, 265, 271
file expansion, 293–295
  error messages, 326–327
  troubleshooting, 316
file formats
  Clipboard, displayed, 537–538
  of Clipboard objects, 499–507
  of INI files, 1006–1007
File Fragmentation Index, changing
  (DoubleSpace), 74
file icon, other (File Manager), 355
File Info option (Undelete), 51–53
File Manager, 347–348
  application window, 349–352
  assigning as Windows shell,
    381–382
  assigning shortcut keys to, 383
  changing horizontal icon spacing,
    384–385
  checking video systems from, 885
  configuration, 381–392
  confirmation messages, disabling,
    388–389
  Control menu, 357–359
  custom font usage, 687
  default font usage, 652
  directory font, 701, 702, 703
  directory windows, 352–356, 374, 384
  Disk menu, 359–365
  drag-and-drop in, 386–388
  error messages, 411–414
  exiting, 368
  File menu, 365–372
  and file sharing, 359, 363–365, 389
  font selection, 701–702, 703
  icons, 223, 353–356
  Info menu (*Windows Resource Kit*),
    357, 373
  menus, 356–381
  Move option, when not to use, 694
  Options menu, 373–374
  reconfiguring access, 383

reconfiguring file associations,
    389–391
  and Registration Database,
    399–406
  selecting multiple files, 388
  setting menu restrictions, 357
  in StartUp Group Window, 339
  status bar, 351–352, 374
  Toolbar (Workgroups), 350–351,
    374, 391
  Tools menu (DOS 6.0), 374–375
  Tree menu, 375–376
  troubleshooting, 406–408
  Utility menu (*Workgroups Resource
    Kit*), 357, 377–379
  View menu, 376–377
  viewing DoubleSpace from, 71
  Window menu, 379–381
  windows in, 348–353
File menu
  Backup, 40–41
  File Manager, 365–372
  Help, 283
  Program Manager, 237–241
  Undelete, 51–55
file sharing
  disabling (File Manager), 389
  enabling (File Manager), 359,
    363–365
files
  associating, 365–367, 390
  comparing sizes, 295
  compressed, 295–296
  copying (File Manager), 367,
    387–388
  creation date, 149–151
  decompressing, 293–296
  deleting (File Manager), 367–368
  on distribution diskettes, 1043–1060
  DOS 6.0, lists of, 4, 5–6
  downloading, 296
  essential to Windows, 178–179
  executable, protecting (VSafe
    option), 69
  expanding, 293–296
  Microsoft Tools, lists of, 8–10
  moving (File Manager), 368, 388
  opening (File Manager), 369
  organizing, Windows help, 288
  selecting (File Manager), 388
  self-expanding, 296
  transferring during Windows
    Setup, 128–129
  Windows 3.0, 110–111
files= line (CONFIG.SYS), 958
FILESIZE.DLL file, 373
Find Deleted File option (Undelete),
    53–54
Find File option (*Workgroups Resource
    Kit*), 377–379
FINSTALL.DIR file, 685–686
First Apps applet, 339
fixed system fonts
  changing, 696–697
  list of, 638
fixedfon.fon= line (WIN.INI), 460,
    653, 655, 696–697
Flash if Inactive option (Print Manager),
    572, 608
flexframe UMB loading, 942–943, 944
floppy disks, protecting boot sector
    (VSafe option), 69

Flying Windows screen saver, 771, 772,
    773, 774
FON files, 642, 645
font box, defined, 634
Font dialog boxes, various, 702–704
Font Installer, 681–686
Font option (File Manager), 374
Font option (Print Manager), 573
Font Selection dialog box, 460
fonts, 633–639
  adding new, 658–662
  categories of, 639–650
  changing, File Manager directory
    window, 384
  changing screen fonts, 687–688
  Character Map applet, 688–691
  and Clipboard copy/paste
    functions, 533–534
  configuration, 687–707
  Control Panel usage, 739–740
  default location, 654
  default screen fonts, 651–653
  defined, 634
  deleted, troubleshooting, 650,
    711–712, 718–719
  deleting files from disk, 706–707
  deleting from WIN.INI, 706–707
  DOS Window, 436–440
  error messages, 726–729
  File Manager directory font, 701–702
  filename extensions, 651
  fixed system font, 638, 696–697
  for icon titles, 652, 687, 698–699
  HP Font Installer, 681–686
  INI file configuration, 696–702
  installation error messages, 726–727
  installing, 658–662
  installing with HP Font Installer,
    681–686, 725
  leading gauge, 691–693
  for menus, 251
  moving, 693–696
  names of, 639
  printer, 635, 715–720
  raster, 639–645
  relocating on hard disk, 693–696
  removing, 706–707
  screen, 636, 651–653, 687–688,
    711–715, 717–720
  searching for files, 660–661
  selecting
    for applets/applications,
      702–704
    in File Manager, 702, 703
    in Paintbrush, 702, 703
    in word processors, 702–704
    in Write, 702, 703
  sizes of, 640–642
  sources of, 662–680
  status bar text, 652, 688, 700
  SYSTEM.INI changes, 696–698
  terminal, *see* terminal fonts
  for title bars, 249, 740
  troubleshooting, 707–725
  TrueType, *see* TrueType fonts
  vs. typefaces, 634, 635
  variable-width system font, 638,
    639, 655, 697–698, 699–700
  vector, 645–647, 712, 718
  when-all-else-fails troubleshooting,
    708–709
  WIN.INI changes, 699–701

fonts (*cont'd*)
    Windows HP Font Installer, 681–686
    WINFILE.INI changes, 701–702
    wrong font, 713, 714, 715–716, 718, 722, 723
Fonts applet, *see* Fonts dialog box
Fonts dialog box, 658, 659, 662, 694–695, 696
Fonts option (DOS Window Control menu), 435
fonts.fon= line, 653, 655, 697–698
foreground/background priorities
    DOS applications, 452, 453–454
    Windows applications, 607, 742–745
Format Disk option (File Manager), 362
formatting, HD low level (VSafe), 69
FOT files, 647, 662, 694–696
frame= parameter (EMM386.EXE), 935
FUL files (Backup), 48–49
Full Page option (Clipbook), 530
full Windows Setup configuration, 103
function key (F1) help, 282

G

Games Group Window
    list of applets installed, 102
    list of files, 133
    list of help files, 276
GDI heap, 916
general protection faults
    specific conditions, 313–316
    troubleshooting, 312–316
General Write Protect option (VSafe), 68–69
Generic/Text Only dialog box, 581–582
Getting Started option (Windows Help), 280–281
grabber files, 481–482, 484
Granularity box (Desktop dialog box), 778
graphics device interface (GDI.EXE), 916
gray scale, defined, 760
group files, *see* group windows
group icons, 223, 260
group windows
    adding program items to, 159–160
    any one as StartUp Group Window, 341
    changing file attribute, 265, 271
    configuration, 253
    creating, 158–159
    damaged, 266–269
    icon capacity, 259, 260
    missing, 269
    Program Manager, 220–221
    troubleshooting, 265–269
    user-specified, 220
    Window menu list, 243
    write-protected, 271
GRP files, 257–258, 266, 268
Guinness *Multimedia Disc of Records* (CD-ROM), troubleshooting, 892

H

hard disks
    backing up before running Windows Setup, 118
    defragmenting, 118, 193, 900, 984

drivers for, 117
low level formatting (VSafe), 69
protecting boot sector (VSafe), 70
reformatting before running Windows Setup, 118
space requirements, 100, 101
hardware compatibility
    in Custom Windows Setup, 124, 125–127
    in Express Windows Setup, 120
    list, 124, 125–127, 128
hardware requirements, 98
    BIOS, 98–99
    hard disk space, 100, 101
    memory, 100
    microprocessor, 98
    and Windows upgrades, 101
hDC
    First Apps, in StartUp Group Window, 339
    memory viewer, 924–926
    Microapps, credit screen, 1101
header bar (Print Manager), 569
heaps, 915
Help button, 281
help files
    list of, 276–277
    opening, 283–284
    organizing, 288
Help key (F1), 282
help macros, 287
Help menu, 277–281
    Anti-Virus, 33
    Backup, 41–42
    Clipboard/Clipbook, 523
    Control Panel, 734
    Undelete, 56
    VSafe, 65
Help option (Control menu), 234, 281
help screens
    "+" pushbuttons, 283
    << or >> buttons, 283
    Back button, 282
    configuration, 285–289
    Contents button, 282
    default font usage, 652
    Edit menu, 288–289
    editing, 288–289
    elements of, 282–283
    error messages, 322–326
    Glossary button, 282
    History button, 282
    Index button, 282
    jump text, 285–286
    popup glossary, 286
    pushbutton bar, 282
    Search button, 282
    size/position of, 287
    troubleshooting, 311–312
    underlining on, 283
help system, 275–289
Hewlett-Packard LaserJet printers
    fonts for LaserJet 4, 667–669
    HP Font Installer for, 681–686
    setup for, 580, 589, 593, 594
Hewlett-Packard *TrueType Screen Font Pack*, 667–669
Hewlett-Packard *Type Director*, 680–681
High DOS Area, defined, 914
High Memory Area (HMA)
    and /hmamin= switch, 932
    defined, 914

managing, 956–957
moving DOS into, 953
High Priority option (Print Manager), 573, 607
HIMEM.SYS file, 931–934
HLP files, 276–277, 288
HMA, *see* High Memory Area (HMA)
/hmamin= switch (HIMEM.SYS), 932
host drives (DoubleSpace), 14
    changing letter, 74
    viewing information about, 70–71
hot keys, 229
How to Use Help option (Windows Help), 280–281
HP Font Installer, 681–686
    batch file for downloading, 684, 725
    FINSTALL.DIR file, 685–686
    permanent soft fonts, 683–684
    screen fonts, 684–685
    soft font reinstallation, 685, 686
    temporary soft fonts, 683
hue, defined, 760

I

I/O ports
    assignments, 300, 301
    error messages, 328
    troubleshooting, 317
i= parameter (EMM386.EXE), 935
IBM File Finder (CompuServe), 1089–1094
IBM Proprinter, setup for, 581
icons, 221–223
    application, 222
    application vs. program-item, 222
    arranging group icons, 243, 262
    auto-arranging, 241
    Browse button, 258–259
    capacity of group windows, 259, 260
    changing, 258
    changing spacing, 261
    changing titles, 254, 260–261
    Clipbook, 522–523
    configuration, 255–263
    creating directory for, 259–260
    for DOS applications, 260
    duplicate, 272
    File Manager directory windows, 353–356
    filenames, 259
    fonts for titles, 652, 687, 698–699
    generic, 272–273
    group, 223, 260
    installing new, 259
    in MORICONS.DLL, 256, 257
    moving by dragging and dropping, 262
    Print Manager, 570–571
    in PROGMAN.EXE, 256, 257, 259, 269
    program-item, 222, 254, 261
    resequencing within Control Panel, 736–739
    selecting, 257–259
    sources for, 256, 257
    spacing, 261, 768
    and system resources, 917
    for Task Manager, 245
    text colors, 261
    titles, 249, 254, 260–261

troubleshooting, 271–273
for Windows screen savers, 775, 776
wrapping titles, 768–769
ICONS subdirectory, 259–260
IFJumpColor= line (WIN.INI), 286, 312
IFPopupColor= line (WIN.INI), 286, 312
Ignore if Inactive option (Print Manager), 572, 609
Index option (Windows Help), 280
Indicate Expandable Branches option (File Manager), 376
infected files (*filename*.VIR), 37
Info menu (*Windows Resource Kit*), 373
INI files, 1005–1006
  After Dark modifications, 747
  binary, 1006–1007
  comparing, 1038–1039
  disabling lines in, 290
  file format, 1006–1007
  font configuration, 696–702
  font information in, 651–653
  housecleaning, 1039–1042
  reconstructing, 1007–1010, 1034–1038
  and rerunning Windows Setup, 1007–1009
  size limitations, 1006
  third-party editors for, 1038–1042
  see also names of INI files
Install Driver dialog box, 579
installing
  fonts, 658–672
  Microsoft Tools, 19, 20–23
  mouse drivers, 791–793
  multimedia, 106
  network cards, 107–108
  network drivers, 139–140
  new icons, 259
  printers, 120, 138–139
  Windows for Workgroups, 106–108
  see also DOS 6.0 Setup; Windows Setup
/int15= switch (HIMEM.SYS), 932
Intel i387 Coprocessor, troubleshooting, 314
interactive bootup, 4, 77–78, 974–975, 976
internal PC speaker, 845–847, 881
International applet, 781–787
  SYSTEM.INI record, 787
  WIN.INI record, 787
International dialog box, 781–786
International-Time Format dialog box, 785
interrupts, *see* IRQs
IRQs
  and COM port configuration, 816–817
  error messages, 328
  line assignments, 298–300
  and mouse configuration, 791, 792
  troubleshooting, 317

J

Joystick applet, 787–789
jump help
  troubleshooting, 311–312
  using, 285–286
JumpColor= line (WIN.INI), 286, 312

K

Kandinsky, Wassily, 175
Kbyte, defined, 914
kernel (KRNL*x*86.EXE), 916
keyboard
  accessing Task Manager with, 244–245
  layout (International applet), 782
  repeat rate, 789
Keyboard applet, 789–790
  record in INI files, 789–790
  troubleshooting, 821–822
Keyboard dialog box, 789, 790
Kodak Photo CD (CD-ROM), troubleshooting, 892
Kodak PhotoEdge (CD-ROM), troubleshooting, 892–893
KRNL*x*86.EXE file, 916

L

Label Disk option (File Manager), 362
LAN Manager, 812
language (International applet), 782, 784, 787
leading, screen vs. printer, 714
leading gauge, font, 691–693
LGO files, 186
line disabling, 290
Link file format, 504
LinkCpy file format, 504
load= line (WIN.INI), 191, 337, 382
LOADHI.OPT file, 947–948
local Clipbook, defined, 499
local computer, defined, 393
local reboot (Ctrl+Alt+Del), 308
  disabling, 311
  and DOS applications, 309–310
  troubleshooting, 310–311
  and Windows applications, 308–309
local user, defined, 565
LocalReboot= line (SYSTEM.INI), 311
Logitech MouseWare utilities, 795, 797
logo (Windows), troubleshooting, 185–186
Logon Settings dialog box, 813–814
Low Priority option (Print Manager), 573, 607
luminosity, defined, 760

M

/machine: switch (HIMEM.SYS), 932
MacroColor= line (WIN.INI), 287
Main Group Window
  Control Panel in, 577, 587, 731, 732
  list of applets installed, 102
  list of help files, 276–277
MAIN.CPL file, 562, 563
  resequence icons in, 737–739
Make System Disk option (File Manager), 363
MANIFEST.EXE file, 926, 927
Marquee screen saver, 771, 772, 773–774, 775
master catalog (*filename*.CAT) (Backup), 49
Maximize
  button, 224, 225, 236–237
  option (Control menu), 234–235
  utility (MAXIMIZE.EXE) (Qualitas), 938–939
Mbyte, defined, 914
MCI (Media Control Interface), defined, 835
MCI Sound, driver configuration, 847–848
MCI Waveform Driver Setup dialog box, 847–848, 855
measurement unit (International applet), 785
media file, defined, 836
Media Player applet, 851–858
  Device menu, 854–855
  Edit menu, 855–857
  error messages, 905–908
  Mark-In/Mark-Out buttons, 853–854
  menus, 854–857
  OLE example, 857–858
  playback control buttons, 853–854
  Scale menu, 857
  Step-Forward/Step-Reverse buttons, 854
  troubleshooting, 895–897
  versions of, 851–852
  waveform file problems, 897
Media Vision *Pocket Recorder*, 877, 878
Media Vision *Pro Audio Spectrum 16*, 878–879
Medium Priority option (Print Manager), 573, 607
MEM command (DOS), 470, 471
MEM utility (MEM.EXE)
  DOS 5.0 version, 919, 950, 951–952
  DOS 6.0 version, 919–920, 950, 951–952
MEMMAKER.EXE file, 936–937, 954
memory, 911–912
  batch files for managing, 958–959
  and CONFIG.SYS file, 957–958
  conventional, 912–913, 950, 951–954
  error messages, 990–1000
  extended, 913, 914, 931–934
  hardware requirement, 100
  high (HMA), 914, 953, 956–957
  software for managing, 918–949
  system, 949
  terminology, 912–915
  troubleshooting, 183–184
  troubleshooting at bootup, 959, 974–982
  troubleshooting management software, 972–982
  troubleshooting Windows, 982–984
  upper, 913, 928–930, 954–956, 981, 982
  virtual, 134–137, 960
  when to add, 983
memory management utilities, 918–927
  DOS memory utility (MEM.EXE), 919–920
  hDC memory viewer, 924–926
  Microsoft Diagnostics utility (MSD.EXE), 920–922
  PC-Kwik *WinMaster*, 924
  Qualitas ASQ utility (ASQ.EXE), 926, 927
  Quarterdeck Manifest utility (MANIFEST.EXE), 926

memory management utilities (*cont'd*)
  System Meter utility
    (SYSMETER.EXE),
    922–923
memory managers
  Microsoft, 928–938
  third-party, 938–949, 954
memory regions, defined, 914–915
menu bars
  Clipbook, 518
  File Manager application window, 350
  Print Manager, 567
  Program Manager, 226
menu heap, 916
menus
  alignment of, 250–251
  Anti-Virus, 31–33
  cascading, 229
  Clipboard/Clipbook, 523–531
  Control Panel, 732–734, 740
  dimmed menu options, 270
  disabled options, 230–231
  in DOS Window, 432–436
  File Manager, 356–381
  fonts for, 240, 251
  list of, 232–244
  Media Player, 854–857
  missing, 270
  missing options, 270
  Print Manager, 571–577
  setting restrictions, 232, 251–252
  shortcut keys for, 226–228
  troubleshooting, 270–271
  Windows, 226–244
message box (Print Manager), 568
message notification, 608–609
metafiles, 506, 606–607
MicroHelp *Uninstaller*, 1039–1042
microprocessors
  defined, 96
  hardware requirement, 98
Microsoft
  Library, printer drivers in, 596,
    597–599
  Mouse, 793–794, 795, 796
  MS Line Draw font, 646, 672
  technical support, 1084, 1087
  Windows, *see* Windows, *etc.*
  Windows Driver Library
    (CompuServe), 1086, 1088
Microsoft Applets, Applications,
    Utilities
  Access, credit screen, 1100
  diagnostics (MSD.EXE), 920–922,
    982–983
  Equation Editor, TrueType fonts,
    669–672
  Excel
    Clipboard data formats for, 502
    credit screens, 1101, 1102
    general protection faults, 314
  LAN Manager, 812
  memory managers, 928–930
    EMM386.EXE, 934–936
    HIMEM.SYS, 931–934
    MEMMAKER.EXE, 936–937
    summary, 937–938
  Multimedia Beethoven (CD-ROM),
    troubleshooting, 893
  Tools
    Anti-Virus, 7, 28–37, 79–82
    Backup, 7, 37–50, 82

Group Window, 162, 277
  installing after Windows
    installation, 162
  list of files, 8–10
  Setup, 19, 20–23
  troubleshooting, 79–85
  Undelete, 7–8, 51–65, 82–83
  VSafe, 11, 65–70, 79–82
TrueType Font Pack for Windows
  installing fonts, 662
  list of fonts, 649, 650
Video for Windows, 848–851
Windows and *Workgroups Resource
    Kits*, 1094–1095
MIDI (Musical Instrument Digital
    Interface), defined, 836
MIDI Mapper applet, 859–860
  adding new MIDI setup, 869–870
  audio, on CD-ROM disc, 879
  CANYON.MID file, 871–872
  channel assignments, 859
  configuration, 860–863
  configuration file
    (MIDIMAP.CFG), 859–860
  configuration tests, 871–872
  deleting MIDI Mapper setup, 870
  device problems, 898
  error messages, 908–910
  icon missing, 897–898
  installing new MIDI port, 869
  invalid MIDIMAP.CFG file,
    898–899
  Key Maps dialog box, 868–869, 870
  MIDI file format, 859
  Patch Maps dialog box, 865–868
  Setup dialog box, 863–865
  patch map test, 872
  revising configuration, 869–871
  SYSTEM.INI record, 872–873
  troubleshooting, 897–899
MIDI Mapper dialog box, 861–863
MIDIMAP.CFG file, 859–860, 862, 863,
    1008
Minimize button, 224, 225, 236–237
Minimize on Use option
  File Manager, 374
  Program Manager, 241–242
Minimize option (Control menu), 235
minimum Windows Setup
    configuration, 101–103
MODE command (DOS), 461, 816
modes, *see* DOS video modes;
    operating modes
Modify File Type dialog box, 399–402
Monitor utility (SMARTMON.EXE),
    968, 969
monospace fonts, 634, 638, 655
More Windows option (Window
    menu), 243
MORICONS.DLL file, 256, 257, 259
mounting disks, 72
mouse
  accessing Task Manager with, 245
  buttons, 797
  customizing configuration,
    805–808
  in DOS Window, 483–484, 827
  drivers
    for DOS, 791–792
    installing, 791–793
    SYSTEM.INI record, 809
    for Windows, 793

error messages, 829–831
  hardware installation, 791
  installing drivers, 791–793
  IRQ configuration, 791, 792
  MOUSE.INI record, 810
  pointers
    support for, 793
    troubleshooting, 827–828
  port configuration, 791, 792, 807,
    817
  serial port configuration, 817
  software configuration, 795–808
  software installation, 791–795
  SYSTEM.INI record, 809
  troubleshooting, 483–484, 824–828
  WIN.INI record, 809, 1030–1031
Mouse applet, 791–810
  configuration options, 798–805
  default mouse, 793, 794
  error messages, 829–831
  and mouse software, 791–795
  MOUSE.INI record, 810
  software configuration, 795–808
  SYSTEM.INI record, 809
  troubleshooting, 824–828
  WIN.INI record, 809
Mouse dialog boxes, 793–794
MOUSE.INI file, 792, 810
  editing, 805–806
  reconstructing, 1034
MOV files, 885
Move Document Down option
    (Workgroups), 571, 611
Move Document Up option
    (Workgroups), 571, 611
Move option
  Control menu, 235
  File Manager, 368
  File menu, 239
moving
  directories (File Manager), 368, 388
  files (File Manager), 368, 388
  files (Program Manager), 239
  fonts, 693–696
  icons by dragging and dropping,
    262
  windows, 235, 249
MPLAYER.EXE file, *see* Media Player
    applet
MS-DOS
  Editor, 292
  EDLIN utility, *see* EDLIN utility
  see DOS, *etc.*
MS Line Draw font, 646, 672
MS Sans Serif font, 573, 651, 653, 656
MSCDEX (Microsoft Compact Disc
    Extensions)
  and AUTOEXEC.BAT file, 843–845
  and CD-ROM discs, 843–845
  configuration, 845
  defined, 836
  SYSTEM.INI support, 845
MSD (Microsoft Diagnostics utility),
    920–922
  and 386MAX, 922
  file summary, 922
  and QEMM386, 922
  troubleshooting, 982–983
MT Extra Plain font, 724
MTFONTS.INI file, 672
Multimedia Beethoven (CD-ROM),
    troubleshooting, 893

multimedia systems
and application compatibility, 303
audio systems, 879–883
overview, 877–879
Pro Audio Spectrum 16, 878–879
terminology, 835–836
video systems, 883–885
and Windows installation, 106
MWAV.INI file, 37
MWBACKUP.INI file, 49–50
Mystify screen saver, 771, 772

N

Native file format, 504
NDIS drivers, 395
NetBEUI, defined, 393
NetBIOS, defined, 393
NetWare, 812
Network applet, 810–814
error messages, 831–833
Logon Settings dialog box, 813–814
Network Settings dialog box, 810–813
SYSTEM.INI record, 814
troubleshooting, 822–823
network cards, installing, 107–108
Network Connections option (Print Manager), 573
network drivers, installing, 139–140
network drives
connecting, 359–362
defined, 393
disconnecting, 362
icon (File Manager), 354
network printers
configuration, 583–585
connecting/disconnecting, 563–564, 575
defined, 565
selecting ports for, 599–600
troubleshooting, 617, 620–621
Network Properties dialog box (Workgroups), 398
Network Settings dialog box (Network applet), 810–813
Network Settings option (Print Manager), 573, 605, 608
networks
configuration, 392–398
defined, 393
error messages, 416–425
SYSTEM.INI record, 814
terminology, 393–394
troubleshooting, 408–411
see also Network applet; Windows for Workgroups
New option (Program Manager), 158, 160, 239
New Program Object dialog box, 158, 160
New Window option (File Manager), 380
Next option (Control menu), 235–236
NoClose= line (PROGMAN.INI), 252
noems parameter (EMM386.EXE), 935
NoFileMenu= line (PROGMAN.INI), 252
/nohi switch (EMM386.EXE), 935
NOMOUSE.DRV file, 808
non-Windows application, defined, 427–428

see also DOS applications
Norton *Desktop for Windows*, credit screen, 1101
NoRun= line (PROGMAN.INI), 252
NoSaveSettings= line (PROGMAN.INI), 242, 252
NoShareCommands= line (WIN.INI), 611
Notepad applet
Clipboard data formats for, 502
default font usage, 652
troubleshooting printing, 621
Novell NetWare, 812
number format (International applet), 786

O

object formats, Clipboard, 499–507
Object Vision, credit screen, 1102
ObjectLink file format, 504
ObjectLinkCpy file format, 504
object, defined, 499
OEM fonts, *see* terminal fonts
OEM Text file format, 504
OEM.INF file, 841
oemfonts.fon= line (SYSTEM.INI), 436, 439, 464, 655–656, 698
OEMSETUP.INF file, 594, 841, 842
OLE, Media Player example, 857–858
online help system, 275–289
Open dialog box (Help), 283, 284
Open dialog box (Sound Recorder), 240
Open Files dialog box (Workgroups), 397–398
Open New Window on Connect option (Workgroups), 374
Open option
Clipboard/Clipbook, 527
File Manager, 369
Help, 283
Program Manager, 239–240
Open Setup option (Backup), 40
operating modes
batch file for checking (WINMODE.BAT), 212–213
defined, 97
troubleshooting, 182, 318
see also enhanced mode; standard mode
Optimize utility (OPTIMIZE.EXE), 947
Options dialog box (Anti-Virus), 34–35
Options menu
Anti-Virus, 32–33
File Manager, 373–374
Print Manager, 572–575
Program Manager, 241–242
Undelete, 56
VSafe, 65–66
Windows 3.1 Setup applet, 153–156
Options option (Control menu), 236
Options option (Media Player), 855–856
Other Net Queue option (Print Manager), 576
Other Network Printer option (Workgroups), 576, 577
Owner Display file format, 504
OwnerLink file format, 504–505

P

pages, Clipbook, 520–522, 525
Paintbrush applet
Clipboard data formats for, 502
font selection, 702, 703
palette-based bitmap files, 509
data section, 512–514
RGB tables in, 510–512
Palette file format, 505–506
Paper Size box (Printer Setup dialog box), 581, 781–782
parallel ports, 601, 742
parity errors, 986, 989–990
Partial Details option (File Manager), 377
PAS-16 (Media Vision) audio card, 878–879
passwords
Clipbook, 535–537
network logon, 812–813
screen savers, 772–773, 775, 778
Paste dialog box (Clipbook), 525, 526, 532
pasting, using Clipboard/Clipbook, 525, 531–534
patterns, Desktop, 769–770
adding, 769
changing, 770
CONTROL.INI record, 770–771
removing, 770
Pause Printer option (Print Manager), 575
Pause Printing Document option (Workgroups), 572, 612
PC-Kwik *WinMaster*, 924, 1102
PC speaker, internal, 845–847, 881
PCTRACKR.DEL file, 64
peer-to-peer system, defined, 394
permanent swap file, 962, 983
in Express Windows Setup, 120
Windows 3.0, removing, 109
Picture file format, 506
PIF Editor applet, 442–458
Advanced Options dialog box (PIF Editor), 443, 453–456
help system, 444
PIF Editor dialog box (enhanced mode), 442, 444–453
PIF Editor dialog box (standard mode), 457–458
PIF Editor vs. Program Item Properties dialog box, 444
typical PIF settings, 444, 445, 446, 447
PIFs (Program Information Files), 441
batch file techniques, 475
configuration, 473–475
memory considerations, 450, 454–455, 473
and multitasking, 453–454
PIF search path, 442
setting screen mode, 473
shortcut keys, 456, 458, 473–474
troubleshooting, 484–486
and video memory, 450, 455, 457
pitch, defined, 635
"plain vanilla" Windows Setup configuration, 111
plotter font, defined, 635
see also vector fonts
Pocket Recorder applet, 877, 878

point sizes
    defined, 635
    do not display or print, 720
POINTER.DLL file, 793
POINTER.EXE file, 793
points box, defined, 635
popup help
    troubleshooting, 311–312
    using, 286
PopupColor= line (WIN.INI), 286, 312
ports
    changing list, 602
    configuration, 599–603
    and device contention, 741–742
    EPT, 601
    file, 601
    list of, 600–602
    mouse configuration, 791, 792,
        807, 817
    for network printers, 599–600
    parallel, 601, 742
    serial, 601, 602–603, 817
Ports applet, 603, 604, 814–817
    COM addresses, 816–817
    and DOS communication settings,
        816
    IRQ configuration, 816–817
    mouse serial port configuration,
        817
    Settings dialog box, 815–816
    vs. Terminal applet settings, 815,
        816
    troubleshooting, 823
Ports dialog box, 603, 604
Print File Size option (Print Manager),
    576, 604–605
print jobs
    deleting from queue, 612
    pausing queue, 612
    queue for, 611–612
    resequencing, 612
    take too long, 717
Print List option (Undelete), 54–55
Print Manager, 565–567
    background printing, 607
    bypassing local Print Manager, 609
    configuration, 603–614
    custom font usage, 688
    custom separator file preparation,
        606–607
    default font usage, 652
    Document menu (Workgroups),
        571–572
    enabling/disabling, 604
    exiting, 575, 576
    header bar (Workgroups), 569,
        604–605, 618–619
    icons, 570–571
    loading at startup, 604
    local Print Manager file, 614
    menu bar, 567
    menus, 571–577
    message bar configuration, 605
    message box, 568
    message notification, 608–609
    Options menu, 572–575
    print queue, 611–612
    Printer menu, 575–576
    printer sharing configuration,
        609–611
    remote Print Manager file, 614
    setting printing priority, 607

shared printer data file
    (SHARES.PWL), 614
SPL files, 613, 614
status bar (Workgroups), 570, 575,
    605
support files, 613–614
temporary directory use, 613
title bar, 567
Toolbar, 567–568, 569, 575
View menu, 576–577
window, 567–570
window configuration, 604–605
workspace, 569
Print option, disabled,
    troubleshooting, 621–622
Print option (Backup), 40
Print option (File Manager), 370
print queue
    defined, 565
    deleting jobs in, 612
    document icons, 571
    drag-and-drop resequencing, 612
    pausing jobs in, 612
    resequencing jobs in, 611–612
Print Setup dialog box, 614–616
printer drivers
    Generic/Text Only (TTY.DRV),
        581–582
    installing, 578, 579–580
    list of, 585–593
    in Microsoft Library, 596, 597–599
    reinstalling, 594–595
    supplied with Windows (list),
        595–596
    support files, 596–599
    in SYSTEM directory, 593–594
    uninstalling, 110
printer fonts
    defined, 635
    double-underlining problems, 717
    garbled characters at top of
        printed page, 717
    troubleshooting, 715–720
    wrong font printed, 715–716
printer installation
    in Custom Windows Setup, 138–139
    in Express Windows Setup, 120,
        138–139
Printer Management Group Window
    adding Print Manager applet, 563
    configuration, 561–565
    creating window, 562
    flow chart, 564–565
    installing applets, 562–563
    selecting applet font, 563
Printer menu (Print Manager),
    575–576
Printer Paper Size (International
    applet), 781
Printer Setup dialog box, 580–581
    for HP LaserJet printers, 580
    for IBM Proprinter, 581
    Options dialog boxes, 580, 581
    Paper Size box, 581, 781–782
Printer Setup option
    Backup, 40
    Print Manager, 574
    Undelete, 55
printer sharing
    configuration, 609–611
    enabling/disabling, 576
    troubleshooting, 617, 623

printers
    default, 578
    installed, list of, 578
    installed, removing, 593
    internal font check, 708, 709, 710
    see also network printers
Printers - Network Connection dialog
    box, 583–584
Printers applet, 565
    configuration, 577, 585–599
    see also Printers dialog box
Printers dialog box, 138–139, 577–585
printing
    background, 607
    contents of Windows directories, 151
    drag-and-drop, 387
    error messages, 414–416, 623–631
    from File Manager File menu, 370
    raster fonts, 645
    symbol sets, 708, 709
    troubleshooting, 616–623
    TrueType fonts, 648
    vector fonts, 646–647
PrintScreen key, 471–472
Pro Audio Spectrum 16 (Media Vision),
    878–879
PROGMAN.EXE file, 219, 256, 257,
    259, 269
PROGMAN.INI file
    and group windows
        troubleshooting, 266, 268
    reconstructing, 1035–1036
    restoring group windows,
        1035–1036
program files, 386
Program Group Properties dialog box,
    158–159, 253, 254
program icon (File Manager), 356
program item
    adding to group windows, 159–161
    configuration, 253–255
    creating, 159–161
    defined, 159
    icons, 222, 254, 261
Program Item Properties dialog box,
    158, 160–161, 254–255
Program Manager, 219–226
    active window, 221
    application windows, 220
    changing title bar text, 264–265
    document windows, 220
    File menu, 237–241
    group windows, 220–221
    installing applets via
        drag-and-drop, 386
    launching Backup setup files from, 45
    modifying Setup via, 156–161
    new group windows, 158–159
    new program items, 159
    new Windows applets, 159
    new Windows applications, 156–157
    non-Windows applets, 159
    Options menu, 241–242
    previously-installed Windows
        applications, 157–158
    replacing as shell, 219
    selecting group windows, 159–161
    shortcut key for, 264–265
    in StartUp Group Window, 340
    Window menu, 243–244
    Windows Tutorial option, 148,
        280–281

programs= line (WIN.INI), 1031
Properties dialog boxes, *see* Program
 Group Properties dialog box;
 Program Item Properties
 dialog box
Properties option (File Manager),
 369–370
Properties option (Program Manager),
 240, 253, 258, 340
PROTMAN.DOS file, 394
protocol manager, Windows for
 Workgroups, 394–395
PROTOCOL.INI file (Workgroups),
 395, 812, 1036–1037
PS/2 systems, troubleshooting exit
 from, 192, 193
Purge Delete Sentry File option
 (Undelete), 55
PWL files, 536, 537

Q

QAMatch utility, 1039, 1042
QAPlus/Win utilities, 1039, 1042
QEMM386.SYS file, 944–949
Qualitas ASQ utility, 926, 927
Qualitas Memory Manager
 (386MAX.SYS), 938
 386MAX.PRO file, 940–942
 adding drivers/TSRs after
  installing, 943
 and CONFIG.SYS file, 929, 939
 error messages, 943–944
 flexframe UMB loading, 942–943,
  944
 installing, 939–944
 Maximize utility
  (MAXIMIZE.EXE),
  938–939
 and MSD.EXE, 922
 troubleshooting boot failure,
  977–979
Quarterdeck Expanded Memory
 Manager (QEMM386.SYS),
 944–945
 and CONFIG.SYS file, 929, 945
 LOADHI.OPT file, 947–948
 operating parameters, 945–946
 Optimize utility (OPTIMIZE.EXE),
  947
 and Smart Drive, 948
 and SYSTEM.INI, 948–949
 troubleshooting boot failure, 979
Quarterdeck Manifest utility
 (MANIFEST.EXE), 926, 927
queue, *see* print queue

R

RAM drives, 971
 enhanced mode considerations, 971
 in expanded memory, 971–972
 and Smart Drive, 972, 973
 standard mode considerations, 971
 ram parameter (EMM386.EXE), 936
raster fonts, 639–640
 base vs. expanded, 640–642
 FON files, 642
 HPPCL printer note, 645
 list of, 643, 644

missing, 712
 naming, 642, 644
 printing, 645
 relocating on hard disk, 693–694
 Windows, 642–644
 Word-for-Windows, 644
read caching, Smart Drive, 966
README files, 132, 256
READTHIS file, 164, 182
real mode
 defined, 97
 error messages, 201–202
 troubleshooting, 313
rebooting, *see* system bootup
Rebuild option (Backup Catalog
 menu), 41
redirector, defined, 394
reformatting hard disks, before
 running Windows Setup, 118
Refresh option (File Manager), 380
Refresh option (Print Manager), 577
REG files, 406
REG.DAT file, 399, 405
REGEDIT.EXE file, 163, 399
regions, memory, 914–915
registration database
 editing, 402–404
 rebuilding, 405–406
 and WIN.INI, 404–405
Registration Editor (REGEDIT.EXE),
 163
Registration Info Editor applet,
 399–406
reinstalling Windows 3.1, 106
REM keyword, 290
remote Clipbook, defined, 499
remote computer, defined, 394
Remove (Fonts) dialog box, 706–707
Rename option (File Manager), 371
repeat rate, keyboard, 789
ReservedHighArea= line
 (SYSTEM.INI), 956
resident programs (VSafe), 70
restarting Windows, 148
Restore button, 225, 236–237
Restore option (Control menu), 236
Resume Printer option (Print
 Manager), 575
Resume Printing Document option
 (Workgroups), 572
Retrieve option (Backup Catalog
 menu), 41
REVERSI files, 150
Rich-Text format, 506
RIFF (Raster Image File Format), 506
RLE files, 186
RTF files, *see* Rich-Text Format
run= line (WIN.INI), 191, 337, 382
Run Minimized box (Program Item
 Properties dialog box), 160,
 255, 340
Run option (File Manager), 371
Run option (Program Manager), 156,
 240–241

S

sans serif, defined, 636
saturation, defined, 760
Save As option (Clipboard/Clipbook),
 527, 538, 541–542

Save Settings on Exit option
 Anti-Virus, 32
 File Manager, 374
 Program Manager, 242
Save Setup As option (Backup), 41
Save Setup option (Backup), 40
SaveSettings= line (PROGMAN.INI),
 242
saving Windows settings without
 exiting Windows, 242
Scale menu (Media Player), 857
Scan menu (Anti-Virus), 31–32
screen credits, 1099–1105
screen elements, *see* Windows Desktop
screen fonts
 changing, 687–688
 default, 651–653
 defined, 636
 sluggish screen display, 714
 troubleshooting, 711–715, 717–720
screen savers
 adding to StartUp Group, 775–776
 After Dark Runner, 771, 772
 assigning shortcut keys, 265
 configuration, 772–773
 CONTROL.INI record, 777–778,
  778
 creating other flying objects,
  776–777
 Desktop dialog box, 771–778
 DOS, disabling, 115
 file descriptions, 771, 772
 icons, 775, 776
 installing as applets, 774–775
 list of files, 133
 passwords for, 772–773, 775, 778
 record in INI files, 777–778
 SYSTEM.INI record, 777
 troubleshooting, 819–820
 WIN.INI record, 777
 see also After Dark
scroll bars, 225–226
Search dialog box example, 230, 231
Search dialog box (File Manager), 371
Search option (File Manager),
 371–372, 408
Search option (Windows Help), 281
Select Computer dialog box
 (Clipbook), 526
Select Drive option (File Manager), 363
Select Files option (File Manager), 372
Select or Unselect by Name option
 (Undelete), 56
Selected Net Queue option (Print
 Manager), 577
selecting files, 388
Selection option (Media Player), 857
selectors and system resources,
 917–918
separator pages, 574, 606–607, 621
Separator Pages option (Print
 Manager), 574, 606
serial ports, 601
 configuration, 602–603
 mouse configuration, 817
serif, defined, 636
server, defined, 394, 499
SERVER.EXE file, 293
Set Column Widths option (Print
 Manager), 575, 605
Set Default Printer option (Print
 Manager), 576

SET files (Backup)
  launching from Program Manager, 45
  overview, 46–48
  renaming, 45
Set Options option (Anti-Virus), 33
Set Up Applications option (Windows
    3.1 Setup applet), 155–156
Settings for COM*x* dialog box, 602–603
Settings menu (Control Panel), 734
Settings option (DOS Window Control
    menu), 435–436
Setup
  defined, 97
  files (*filename*.SET), 45, 46–48
  undocumented Windows applets,
    163–164
  see also DOS 6.0 Setup; Windows
    Setup
Setup Applications dialog boxes, 140,
    147, 155–156
Setup File List option (Backup), 41
SETUP.INF file, 266–267
  [keyboard.tables] section, 782, 784,
    787
  [language] section, 782, 784, 787
  and problem applications, 111, 113,
    114
  [progman.groups] section, 342–343
SETUP.TXT file, 113, 114
SFLPT*x*.BAT file, 725
/shadowram: switch (HIMEM.SYS),
    933–934
Share As option (Workgroups), 359,
    363–365
Share Clipbook Page dialog box
    (Clipbook), 527, 528
Share Directory dialog box
    (Workgroups), 363–365
Share option (Clipbook), 527–528
Share Printer As option (Workgroups),
    576, 609, 610, 611
Share Printer dialog box
    (Workgroups), 609–610
shared directories
  defined, 394
  icon (File Manager), 354–355
  listing, 361–362
SHARE.EXE file and Windows for
    Workgroups, 397
SHARES.PWL file, 611, 614
shell, assigning File Manager as,
    381–382
shell= line (SYSTEM.INI), 344, 345
shortcut keys
  assigning in Program Item Properties
    dialog box, 160, 255
  assigning to Program Manager,
    264–265
  assigning to screen savers, 265
  DOS session problems, 477–478
  duplicate key assignment, 263
  hot keys, 229
  menus, 226–228
  overrides, 263–264
  PIF configuration, 456–458,
    473–474
  Task Manager, 244–245, 248
  troubleshooting, 269, 320
Show File Size Information option
    (*Windows/Workgroups Resource
    Kit*),
    373, 379

Show Icon option (VSafe), 66
signal paths, audio, 879–880
Size option (Control menu), 236, 249,
    250
sizing grid, record in WIN.INI, 778
sizing of windows, 236, 249, 250
SLT files (Backup), 50
Smart Drive, 964
  /S switch, 968
  and AUTOEXEC.BAT, 965–966,
    967
  and buffers, 957, 969
  and CONFIG.SYS, 964–965
  configuration, 966–967
  controlling, 968–969
  device conflicts, 985–986
  double buffering, 964–965, 987
  DoubleSpace considerations, 75
  drive caching, 965–966
  enhanced mode problems, 986
  loading techniques, 967–968
  Monitor utility, 340, 968, 969
  and parity errors, 986
  and performance slowdown, 987
  and QEMM386, 948
  and RAM drive configuration, 972,
    973
  startup problems, 985
  and system crashes, 318
  and system lockup, 987
  and third-party disk caching
    utilities, 968
  troubleshooting, 985–987
Smart Drive monitor, 340, 968, 969
SMARTDRV.EXE file, 114, 964,
    966–967
SMARTDRV.SYS file, 964
Solitaire
  card deck animation, 1102–1103
  cheating at, 1103
Sort by option (File Manager), 377
Sort by option (Undelete), 56
Sound applet, 873–876
  driver requirements, 873
  error messages, 910
  event-checking utility
    (SOUNDEX.EXE), 875
  event usage in Windows, 875
  Sound dialog box, 873–875
  troubleshooting, 899
  waveform files supported, 875–876
  WIN.INI record, 875, 876
Sound Blaster, 881
Sound dialog box, 873–875
Sound Recorder applet, 876–877, 878
  error messages, 910
  file list example, 240
  troubleshooting, 899–901
  waveform files supported, 877
SOUNDEX.EXE file, 875
sounds, list of files, 133–134
source, defined, 499
source template files (*filename*.SRC),
    1009–1010
SPART.PAR file, 962
SPEAK.EXE file, on CompuServe,
    846–847
speaker, internal PC, 845–847, 881
SPL files, 613, 614
Split option (File Manager), 377
SRC files, 1009–1010
Stacker drives, 193

stacks= line (CONFIG.SYS), 115, 958
standard mode
  defined, 97
  and DOS applications, 429–430
  error messages, 202–203
  PIF Editor dialog box, 457–458
  RAM drive considerations, 971
  troubleshooting, 182, 318
  when to use, 97, 984
  and Windows for Workgroups, 396
Standard Protection (Undelete), 60–64
Starfield Simulation screen saver, 771,
    772
startup
  batch file for (WIN.BAT), 210–212
  display problems, 185–188
  enhanced mode troubleshooting,
    189–191
  error messages, 194–201
  group window troubleshooting, 188
  loading applets via WIN.INI,
    381–382
  onscreen message, 186–187
  printer connection problems, 617
  running applications at, 163, 337
  system locks up, 185
  system reboots, 184–185
  troubleshooting, 184–189, 982–983
  Windows does not run, 184–185
  and WIN.INI file, 188–189
  see also AUTOEXEC.BAT file;
    CONFIG.SYS file
StartUp Group Window, 163, 337
  After Dark in, 746
  any group window as, 341
  applet loading sequence, 340–341
  applet selection, 338–340
  Calendar in, 338
  Clock in, 338–339
  configuration, 340–343
  disabling, 341–342
  Dr. Watson in, 339
  error messages, 345
  File Manager in, 339
  hDC *First Apps* in, 339
  Print Manager in, 604
  Program Manager in, 340
  recreating, 342–343
  running applets minimized, 340
  system monitoring utilities in, 340
  troubleshooting, 188, 344–345, 408
  using Always-on-Top option, 341
startup= line (WIN.INI), 341
STARTUP.GRP file, 337
status bar
  Clipbook, 520, 530
  Control Panel, 731, 740
  File Manager, 351–352, 374
  fonts for, 652, 688, 700
  Print Manager, 570, 575, 605
Status Text option (Workgroups), 576,
    604–605
Stop Sharing Directory dialog box
    (Workgroups), 364, 365
Stop Sharing option (Workgroups),
    359, 365, 529
Stop Sharing Printer option
    (Workgroups), 576, 611
stroke fonts, *see* vector fonts
style, typeface
  defined, 636
  incorrectly displayed, 712–713

swap files, 960
application (WOA*xxxx*.TMP), 961
configuration, 962–963
and DOS 6.0 DoubleSpace, 964
error messages, 1001–1003
maximum size, 962
permanent (386SPART.PAR and
SPART.PAR), 962
recommended size, 963
space available for, 962
temporary (WIN386.SWP),
961–962
troubleshooting, 984–985
types of, 960–962
SWAP.BAT file, 215
Switch To option (Control menu), 236
switches, Setup, 115, 118–119
SYD files, 292
Sylk (SYmbolic LinK) file format, 507
Symbol fonts, 721, 724
symbol sets
defined, 636
IBM PC8, 708, 709
ID codes for, 710
printing, 708, 709
SYSEDIT utility, 290–292
backing up files, 292
custom font usage, 688
default font usage, 652
setting up as Windows applet, 291
SYSEDIT.EXE file, 163, 290–292
SYSMETER utility, 307, 340, 922–923
system bootup
Ctrl+Alt+Del reboot, 193, 988
memory-related error messages,
990–993
rebooting after Windows Setup, 148
troubleshooting, 973–982
unwanted reboot, 184–185, 192
see also local reboot (Ctrl+Alt+Del)
system bootup, DOS 6.0
AUTOEXEC.BAT troubleshooting,
77–79, 977
clean vs. interactive, 4, 78, 974
CONFIG.SYS troubleshooting,
77–79, 975–977
disabling function key options, 977
F5 function key, 4, 78, 974
F8 function key, 4, 77–78, 974–975,
976
troubleshooting, 974–977
see also system bootup
system clock, off-speed, 320–321
system cookie, 128
SYSTEM directory
essential files in, 178
file listing, 1066
font files in, 654
installing fonts in, 661
system fonts
changing, 697–698
defined, 636–637
list of, 638
monospaced, 638, 655
non-default, 699–700
in SYSTEM.INI, 654, 655–656,
697–698, 699
variable-width, 638, 639, 655,
697–698, 699–700
system information review
in Custom Windows Setup,
123–124, 128

and system cookie, 128
system memory, managing, 949
System Meter Utility
(SYSMETER.EXE), 307, 340,
922–923
system requirements, 98–100
system resources, 915
GDI heap, 916
graphics device interface
(GDI.EXE), 916
the heap, 915
and icons, 917
kernel (KRNL*x*86.EXE), 916
leakage of, 917
menu heap, 916
monitoring of, 307, 916–917
and selectors, 917–918
text string heap, 916
user heap, 916
user interface (USER.EXE), 916
SYSTEM.INI file
[386Enh] section, 745, 1016–1019
backing up, 1024
[boot] section, 1015, 1019–1021
[boot.description] section, 1015,
1019–1020
changing font information in,
687–688, 696–698
[ClipShares] section, 541
current screen saver record, 777
[DDE Shares] section, 1016, 1021
default font information in, 651–653
default sections, 1015–1022
driver installation record, 840–841
[drivers] section, 1016, 1022
editing with SYSEDIT, 290–292
joystick record, 789
keyboard record, 787, 789–790
[keyboard] section, 1015, 1019–1020
language record, 787
[mci] section, 1016, 1022
MIDI Mapper record, 872–873
mouse record, 809, 1022–1023
MSCDEX support, 845, 1017–1018
multimedia sections, 1023
network record, 814, 1023
[NonWindowsApp] section, 1016,
1022
printing of, 104
and QEMM386, 948–949
reconstructing, 1015–1024
restoring custom configuration,
1023–1024
speaker driver record, 847
specifying system font in, 654,
655–656, 697–698, 699
[standard] section, 1016, 1022
and swap files, 961, 962
SYSTEM.SRC file, 1015–1022

T

Table of Contents option (Clipbook),
530
Targa (TGA) vs. bitmap (BMP) files,
508, 509
Task List dialog box, 246–247
Task Manager, 244
icon for, 245
keyboard access, 244–245
list of dialog box buttons, 246–247

mouse access, 245
shortcut keys, 227, 244–245, 248
Task List dialog box, 246–247
task switching using Alt+Tab, 247
viewing open applications using
Alt+Esc, 247–248
TASKMAN.EXE file, 244
TDF files, 665, 666–667
technical support
calling, 1083–1084
Microsoft, 1084, 1087
via modem, 1085–1086
see also CompuServe
TEMP directory, 111, 613
temporary files, 110–111
temporary swap file, 193, 961–962
Terminal applet vs. Ports applet
settings, 815, 816
terminal fonts
changing, 459–460, 698
defined, 436, 637
list of matrixes, 639
sources of, 436–438
in SYSTEM.INI, 655–656, 698
in Windows applicatons, 465–467
Text file format, 507
text for icon titles, 260–261, 652, 687,
698–699
text string heap, 916
third-party drivers, uninstalling, 109–110
third-party memory managers
and conventional memory, 954
Qualitas Memory Manager
(386MAX.SYS), 938–944
Quarterdeck Expanded Memory
Manager (QEMM386.SYS),
944–949
third-party setups, file modifications
by, 152–153
three-finger salute, 308
Thumbnails option (Clipbook), 531
TIFF (Tagged Image File Format), 507
Tile option
File Manager, 380, 381, 382
Program Manager, 243–244, 245
time
display configuration, 766–767
formatting (International applet),
785
Time/Date Sent option (Print
Manager), 576, 604–605
title bars
changing, 249
clicking on, 223
Clipbook, 518
Control Panel, 740
defined, 223
Desktop, 223, 235, 249
dragging, 235, 249
File Manager windows, 349–350, 352
Print Manager, 567
Program Manager, 264–265
TMP files, 614
Toolbar option
Clipbook, 531
Print Manager, 575
Workgroups, 374
Toolbars
Clipbook, 518–519, 531
File Manager (Workgroups),
350–351, 374, 391
Print Manager, 567–568, 569, 575

Tools menu (File Manager), 374–375
Tracks option (Media Player), 857
Tree and Directory option (File Manager), 377
Tree menu (File Manager), 375–376
Tree Only option (File Manager), 377
troubleshooting
    32-bit access, 988
    386 Enhanced applet, 821
    Anti-Virus, 79–82
    AUTOEXEC.BAT, 977
    Backup, 82
    backup/restore utilities, 317
    bootup problems, 972–982
    Calendar file printing, 619
    CD-ROM, 888–893
    Character Map applet, 709–711
    Clipboard/Clipbook, 546–552
    Color applet, 818
    CONFIG.SYS, 975–977
    Control Panel, 818
    conventional memory, 183
    Ctrl+Alt+Del reboot, 193, 988
    Date/Time applet, 818–819
    defective Windows distribution
        diskettes, 166
    deleted fonts, 650, 711–712,
        718–719
    Desktop, 186–188, 265–269, 819–821
    device drivers, 164–165, 887, 888,
        893–894
    display problems, 185–188
    DMA channels, 317
    DOS 6.0 bootup, 77–79, 974–977
    DOS fonts, 481–483
    DOS sessions, 476–481
    DoubleSpace, 83–85
    drive-related, 317–318
    DRIVER.SYS file, 407
    enhanced mode, 189–191, 318
    Equation Editor fonts, 724
    error messages, 620
    exiting Windows, 191–209
    extended memory, 184
    file expansion, 316
    File Manager, 406–408
    fonts, general, 707–709
    fonts, when-all-else-fails, 708–709
    general protection faults, 312–316
    group windows, 265–269
    help screens, 311–312
    I/O ports, 317
    icons, 271–273
    IRQs, 317
    Keyboard applet, 821–822
    local reboot (Ctrl+Alt+Del), 310–311
    logo problems, 185–186
    Media Player applet, 895–897
    memory managers, 972–982
    memory-related problems,
        183–184, 972–988
    menus, 270–271
    MIDI device problems, 898–899
    MIDI Mapper applet, 897–899
    missing text in applets, 321
    mode testing, 182
    mouse, DOS sessions, 483–484, 827
    mouse-pointer, 827–828
    mouse-related, 824–828
    MSD utility, 982–983
    Network applet, 822–823
    network operations, 408–411

network printer problems, 617,
    620–621
new Windows Setup procedures,
    166–167
Notepad file printing, 621
permanent swap file setup, 984
PIFs (Program Information Files),
    484–486
Ports applet, 823
printer connections, 617
printer fonts, 715–720
printing problems, 616–623
PS/2 systems, 192, 193
Qualitas 386MAX boot failure,
    977–979
Quarterdeck QEMM386 boot
    failure, 979
real mode, 313
screen fonts, 711–715, 717–720
screen savers, 819–820, 821
shared printers, 617, 623
shortcut keys, 269, 320
Smart Drive, 985–987
Sound applet, 899
Sound Recorder, 899–901
Stacker drives, 193
standard mode, 318
startup, 184–189, 617
startup/exit overview, 178–184
StartUp Group Window, 188,
    344–345, 408
swap files, 984–985
system bootup, 973–982
TrueType fonts, 720–723
Undelete, 82–83
upgrade Windows Setup
    procedures, 164–166
upper memory, 981, 982
vector fonts, 712, 718
video problems, 981
virtual device drivers, 888, 898
VSafe, 79–82
waveform files, 886–887, 899–901
when-all-else-fails, 321–322
WIN command, 189–191
Windows, 301–302, 319–321
Windows does not run, 184–185
Windows for Workgroups, 408–411
Windows memory-related
    problems, 982–984
WIN.INI file, 188–189
TrueColor bitmap files
    data section, 514–516
    defined, 509
    and RGB tables, 512
TrueType dialog box, 704–705
TrueType fonts, 647
    Agfa *Discovery TrueType Pack*,
        662–665
    and application compatibility, 304
    Bitstream *TrueType Font Pack for
        Windows 3.1*, 665–667
    configuration, 704–706
    deleting, 706–707
    FOT files, 647, 662, 694–696
    Hewlett-Packard *TrueType Screen
        Font Pack*, 667–669
    installing, 658–672
    lists of, 648, 649, 650
    for Microsoft *Equation Editor*, 669–672
    Microsoft *TrueType Font Pack for
        Windows*, 662

vs. non-TrueType fonts, 705
    printing, 648
    printing as graphics, 706, 708–709,
        714, 722
    relocating on hard disk, 694–696
    simulated typeface styles, 648
    sources of, 662–672
    troubleshooting, 720–723
    TTF files, 647, 662, 694–696
    Windows, 648–650
TSRs
    batch files for, 958–959
    defined, 915
    incompatible with Windows,
        112–114
    loading before running DOS
        applications, 475
    moving into UMB area, 953, 954
TTF files, 647, 662, 694–696
TTFONTS.INI file, 669
TTINFO.INI file, 669
TTSUBS.INI file, 669
TTY.DRV file, 581
Type Director, 680–681
typeface family, defined, 637, 639
typefaces
    defined, 637
    vs. fonts, 634, 635
    names of, 639
    style, 636, 712–713

U

UMB area
    and 386MAX flexframe loading,
        942–943, 944
    and CONFIG.SYS file, 929, 930
    enabling, 953
    moving AUTOEXEC.BAT TSRs
        into, 954
    moving CONFIG.SYS device drivers
        and TSRs into, 953
    and SYSTEM.INI, 930, 956
undocumented Windows applets,
    setup of, 163–164
Undelete, 7–8, 51
    buttons and menus, 51–55
    Change Drive/Directory option, 51
    configuration, 56–64
    configuration record
        (UNDELETE.INI), 64
    CONTROL.FIL file, 64
    custom search record
        (CPSTOOLS.INI), 65
    Delete Sentry, 58–60
    Delete Tracker, 60
    error messages, 91–92
    Exit option, 51
    File Info option, 51–53
    File menu, 51–55
    Find Deleted File option, 53–54
    Help menu, 56
    installing Windows version, 162
    Print List option, 54–55
    Printer Setup option, 55
    Purge Delete Sentry File option, 55
    Standard Protection, 60–64
    support files, 64
    troubleshooting, 82–83
    Undelete option, 55
    Undelete To option, 55

Undelete option (File Manager), 372
Undelete option (Undelete), 55
Undelete To option (Undelete), 55
UNDELETE.INI file (Undelete), 64
undocumented features, 1099–1105
UNIDRV.DLL file, 585, 593, 621–622
Uninstall diskette, 17, 24
Uninstaller utility, 1039–1042
uninstalling
    printer drivers, 110
    third-party drivers, 109–110
    video drivers, 110
    Windows applications, 1039–1042
upgrading Windows, 104–106
upper memory
    defined, 915
    managing, 954–956
    and SYSTEM.INI, 930, 956
    troubleshooting, 981, 982
    utilization in DOS Window, 930
    and Windows 3.1, 928–930, 956
upper memory block (UMB), defined, 915
user heap, 916
user interface (USER.EXE), 916
User's Guide (DOS 6.0), 4, 6
user's name (Windows Setup), 129
Utilities option (*After Dark*), 746
Utility menu (*Workgroups Resource Kit*), 377–379

V

variable-width fonts, 638, 639, 655, 697–698, 699–700
vector fonts, 645
    on dot-matrix printers, 646–647
    FON files, 645
    list of, 646
    MS Line Draw font, 646, 672
    printing, 646–647
    relocating on hard disk, 693–694
    troubleshooting, 712, 718
    Windows, 646
    Word-for-Windows, 646, 672
Verify Error dialog box (Anti-Virus), 30, 36
VFWRUN.ZIP file, on CompuServe, 848
VGALOGO.LGO file, 186
video drivers
    and CLP files, 542–543
    installing, 545–546
    uninstalling, 110
Video for Windows
    Control menu in AVI Window, 850–851
    driver configuration, 849–851
    video modes, 849
    WIN.INI record, 851
video memory, 450, 455, 457
video modes
    for DOS applications, 428–430
    for Video for Windows, 849
Video Options Playback dialog box, 849–851, 855
video systems
    checking, 884–885
    checking from File Manager, 885
    signal path, 884
    video sources, 885
View menu

Clipbook, 529–531
    File Manager, 376–377
    Print Manager, 576–577
VIR files (Anti-Virus), 37
virtual device drivers, 318, 840–841, 888, 898, 911
virtual memory, 134–137, 960
    see also swap files
Virtual Memory button (386 Enhanced dialog box), 745
Virtual Memory dialog box (Windows Setup), 134–135
Virus Found dialog box (Anti-Virus), 30, 36
Virus List option (Anti-Virus), 32
Virus Signature Update files (Anti-Virus), 37
VPD.386 file, on CompuServe, 742
VSafe, 11
    About VSafe Manager option, 66
    configuration, 66–70
    Control menu, 65
    error messages, 87–90
    Exit option, 66
    Help menu, 65
    installing, 24–25
    loading as an option, 25
    loading VSafe automatically, 25
    menus, 65–66
    Options menu, 65–66
    overview, 11, 65
    Show Icon option, 66
    troubleshooting, 79–82
    VSafe Manager for Windows, 11, 24–25, 67–70
    VSafe Options dialog box, 67–70
VSAFE.COM, disabling, 17

W

wallpaper
    centering vs. tiling, 780, 781
    list of files, 133–134
    selecting, 779
    sources of, 779–781
    WIN.INI record, 781
WAV files, *see* waveform audio
Wave Audio file format, 507
waveform audio
    and *After Dark*, 749
    defined, 836
    signal path, 879
    Sound applet, 875–876
    Sound Recorder applet, 877
    troubleshooting, 886–887, 899–901
win= parameter (EMM386.EXE), 936
WIN command, troubleshooting, 189–191
WIN.BAT file, 210–212
WIN.CNF file, 186
WIN.COM file, 186
WIN.INI file
    changing font information in, 687–688, 698–701
    [colors] section, 764, 1031–1032
    [Compatibility] section, 1024, 1025, 1026–1027
    country-specific record, 787
    default font information in, 651–653
    default sections, 1024–1031

deleting fonts from, 706–707
    [Desktop] section, 1025, 1027
    editing with SYSEDIT, 290–292
    [embedding] section, 1032
    [extensions] section, 365–367, 389–391, 1025, 1027–1028
    [fonts] section, 642–644, 647, 657, 1032–1033
    [FontSubstitutes] section, 657–658, 700–701, 1025, 1028
    [HPPCL] section, 1033
    [intl] section, 787, 788, 1025, 1029
    keyboard default configuration, 790
    loading applets at startup via, 382
    [mci extensions] section, 1025, 1029
    [Microsoft Word 2.0] section, 1026, 1029
    mouse record, 809, 1030–1031
    multimedia sections, 1033
    [ports] section, 600, 602, 815, 1026, 1030
    printer sections, 585, 594–597, 1033–1034
    printing of, 104
    and registration database, 404–405
    screen saver record, 777
    sizing grid record, 778
    [sounds] section, 875, 876, 1026, 1030
    specifying fonts in, 654, 656–658
    troubleshooting of, 188–189
    [TrueType] section, 1026, 1030
    video record, 851
    wallpaper record, 781
    [windows] section, 1025, 1030
    word processor settings, 1034
WIN.SRC file, 1024–1031
WIN386.SWP file, 961–962
WINBACK.TMP file, 50
WINCHECK.COM file, 212–213
window background, defined, 223
Window menu
    Clipbook, 531
    File Manager, 379–381
    Program Manager, 243–244
Windows
    batch files for, 209–215
    Control menu, 232–237
    credit screen (version 3.1), 1103–1104
    defined, 1–2
    diagnostic aids, 304–307
    dual versions, batch file for, 215
    essential files, 178–179
    executing DOS applications within, 430–432
    exit procedure, 234
    exit troubleshooting, 191–209
    INI files, 1005–1042
    local reboot, 308–311
    Maximize button, 224
    Maximize/Minimize/Restore button summary, 236–237
    menu structure, 226–244
    Minimize button, 224
    restarting, 148
    Restore button, 225
    saving settings without exiting, 242
    setting up applets in Program Manager, 159

starting without executing StartUp Group applets, 342
startup troubleshooting, 184–189, 982–983
and system clock, 320–321
troubleshooting, 301–302, 319–321
undocumented applets, 163–164
without Minimize or Maximize buttons, 225
see also Windows for Workgroups; Windows Setup
windows
application workspaces, 223
components of, 221–226
Control menu box, 223–224
icons, 221–222
menu bar, 226
moving, 235, 249
overview, 217–219
scroll bars, 225–226
sizing, 236, 249, 250
sizing buttons, 224–225
title bars, 223, 235, 249
within Windows, 218–219
Windows 3.0, 109, 110–111
Windows 3.1 Setup applet, 153–161
Windows applications
background/foreground priorities, 607, 742–745
in Express Windows Setup, 121
finding during Setup, 140–148
installing with Run option, 156–158
and local reboot (Ctrl+Alt+Del), 308–309
previously installed, 157–158
selecting in Custom Windows Setup, 147
uninstalling, 1039–1042
and Windows 3.1 Setup applet, 155–156
WOA terminal fonts in, 465–467
windows bug fix= line (WIN.INI), 713
WINDOWS directory
essential files in, 178
file creation date check, 149–151
file listing, 1062–1065
for new installation, 122
new installation in existing, 122–123
printing contents of, 151
re-installation after incomplete Setup, 123
selecting, 121–123
and Windows Setup, 121–123
Windows-exclusive foreground mode, 430, 469
Windows for Workgroups
and AUTOEXEC.BAT file, 396
and CONFIG.SYS file, 394–396
configuration, 394–399
credit screen, 1103–1104
DOS 6.0 considerations, 108
hardware for, 107–108
help file, 277
installing, 106–108
and MS-DOS device driver, 396

and NDIS drivers, 395
and protocol manager, 394–395
shared file report, 397–398
and SHARE.EXE, 397
and standard mode, 396
support for network software, 812
troubleshooting, 408–411
Windows for Workgroups Resource Kit, 350, 357, 377–379, 1094–1095
Windows help system, 275–289
Windows HP Font Installer, 681–686
Windows Resource Kit, 350, 357, 373, 786, 922–923, 1094–1095
Windows Setup
and 32-bit disk access, 120
applications-found list, 147–148
BOOTLOG.TXT file, 164
Custom, *see* Custom Windows Setup
defined, 97
distribution diskettes, 166
error messages, 167–175
examples, 162–164
exiting, 148–149
Express, *see* Express Windows Setup
file transfer, 128–129
files created during, 151
hardware compatibility, 120, 124, 125–127
methods, Custom vs. Express, 120–121
modifying AUTOEXEC.BAT file during, 137–138
modifying CONFIG.SYS file during, 137–138
modifying from DOS prompt, 161–162
and multimedia installation, 106
network drivers, 139–140
new installation, 106, 166–167
and permanent swap file, 120
post-Setup modifications, 152–162
pre-Setup procedures, 104–108
printer installation, 120, 138–139
READTHIS file, 164
reinstallation of Version 3.1, 106
rerunning to restore INI files, 1007–1009
review of, 149–151
running, 118–148
selecting applications, 140–147
selecting components, 129–134
selecting directory, 121–123
switches, 115, 118–119
system cookie, 128
system information review, 123–124, 128
troubleshooting, 164–167
upgrading from earlier versions, 105–106
user's name and company, 129
virtual memory configuration, 134–137
Windows for Workgroups, 106–108
Windows Setup dialog boxes, 130–131, 153

Windows tutorial, 148, 280–281
Windows User Group Network (WUGNET), 1096–1097
WINFILE.INI file
changing font information in, 701–702
reconstructing, 1037–1038
[Settings] section, 391
Wingdings font, 721
WINHELP applet, 283–285
WINHELP.EXE file, 163
WININI.WRI file, 786
WINLD.FON file, 646, 672
WinMaster utility, 924, 1102
WINMODE.BAT file, 212–213
WINOA286.MOD file, 151
WINOLDAP.MOD file, 150–151
WINSTART.BAT file, 192, 213–214, 958
Wk1 file format, 507
WMF files, 606–607
WOA fonts
in DOS Window, 436, 438
required location, 694
in Windows applicatons, 465–467
see also terminal fonts
WOA*xxxx*.TMP file, 961
Word for Windows
Clipboard data formats for, 502
credit screen, 1104–1105
default font usage, 652
Line Draw font, 646, 672
missing italic cursor, 715
raster fonts, 644
troubleshooting, 314–315
Word-Formatted Text file format, 507
word processors
font selection, 702–704
workgroup, defined, 394
Workgroups, *see* Windows for Workgroups
Workgroups Resource Kit, see Windows for Workgroups Resource Kit
Working Directory box (Program Item Properties dialog box), 160, 255
workstation, defined, 394
WRI files, 256
Write applet
Clipboard data formats for, 502
credit screen, 1105
font selection, 702, 703
write caching, Smart Drive, 966
write-protected files, 271
WUGNET (Windows User Group Network), 1096–1097

X

x= parameter (EMM386.EXE), 936

Z

ZIP files, 296